OPERATIONS MANAGEMENT

ABOUT THE AUTHORS

Sang M. Lee is University Eminent Scholar, Regents Distinguished Professor, and Chairman of the Department of Management at The University of Nebraska, Lincoln. He received his Ph.D. in management science from the University of Georgia in 1968, and has taught production and operations management courses in undergraduate, graduate, and executive programs. Dr. Lee has authored over 20 textbooks and 130 journal articles, and has served in a wide variety of editorial positions. He has consulted extensively in both service and manufacturing organizations—for multinational firms as well as U.S. organizations such as the Dorsey Laboratories and the U.S. Agricultural Extension Service. Dr. Lee is President of the Pan-Pacific Business Association and the Society of Franchising, and a Fellow in the Academy of Management and the National Decision Sciences Institute.

Marc J. Schniederjans is a Professor of Management at The University of Nebraska, Lincoln. He received his Ph.D. in management science from Saint Louis University in 1978, and has taught production and operations management courses to undergraduate and graduate students since 1977. Dr. Schniederjans has authored several textbooks and over 70 journal articles, and has acted as editor and advisor to journals such as *Production and Operations Management, Computers and Operations Research,* and *Journal of Operations Management,* as well as the newsletters *POM Spectrum* and *POMS Chronicle.* Dr. Schniederjans, whose experience includes working as lead person in a warehouse and operating his own trucking firm, has served as a consultant to major manufacturers, including Ralston Purina Corporation and the American Tool Company. He is a member of APICS and POMS.

OPERATIONS MANAGEMENT

Sang M. Lee
University of Nebraska — Lincoln

Marc J. Schniederjans
University of Nebraska — Lincoln

HOUGHTON MIFFLIN COMPANY **Boston** **Toronto**
Geneva, Illinois Palo Alto Princeton, New Jersey

This book is dedicated to the memory of Sang M. Lee's mother and Marc J. Schniederjans' father.

Sponsoring Editor: Diane L. McOscar
Basic Book Editor: Elizabeth Morgan
Senior Project Editor: Paula Kmetz
Associate Production/Design Coordinator: Caroline Ryan
Senior Manufacturing Coordinator: Priscilla Bailey
Marketing Manager: Robert D. Wolcott

Cover designer: Len Massiglia
Cover image: Michel Tcherevkoff

Printed in the U.S.A.

Library of Congress Catalog Card Number: 93-78633

Student Edition ISBN: 0-395-56084-5
Exam Copy ISBN: 0-395-69235-0

123456789-DH-97 96 95 94 93

CONTENTS IN BRIEF

CONTENTS

PREFACE

Working in operations management has never been so challenging as it is in the 1990s. We have tried to meet that challenge by creating a textbook that will answer both today's and tomorrow's needs. *Operations Management* offers faculty: (1) flexibility in customizing the content of the book to the OM course, (2) a focus on current trends in OM, (3) a chapter structure and pedagogical aids based on well-established learning principles, and (4) a complete package of high-quality ancillaries.

FLEXIBILITY OF COVERAGE

Flexibility is a competitive advantage of this textbook. Many of the traditional quantitative methods and techniques of operations management have been shifted from the body of the text to chapter-end supplements and book-end appendixes. This restructuring provides many benefits, as outlined below.

- *The instructor controls the depth of coverage.* A common complaint about OM textbooks is that they are narrowly focused at either the sophomore or graduate level. To accommodate a range of needs, we have placed some of the more involved methods in chapter-end supplements. Special or advanced content that is common to graduate or certification-level courses is located in these supplements, including rough-cut capacity planning, capacity requirements planning, and simulation and queuing analysis. We feel this approach gives the instructor greater flexibility to customize the course to students' needs and to the time constraints of a semester or quarter term.
- *The instructor can cover all the subjects in the book.* Instructors and students often complain that books are too long to be covered in their entirety in a single semester or quarter. By excluding some of the optional supplements and appendixes, instructors will find they can easily complete all fifteen chapters without sacrificing quality of coverage.
- *The instructor controls the depth of quantitative coverage.* Few instructors have expressed complete contentment with the balance between the quantitative and qualitative content of OM textbooks. Because we have placed many of the quantitative methods in chapter-end supplements and book-end appendixes, instructors can easily include or exclude topics like linear programming, the transportation method, and decision analysis. We provide a range of

applications for these methods, from conceptual material (found primarily in the text of the chapters) to model formulations (found primarily in chapter-end supplements) to algorithmic computations (found primarily in the book-end appendixes). The result is unparalleled flexibility for instructors at all levels.

UP-TO-DATE CONTENT

Operations Management contains a number of unique features that stress current concepts, applications, and issues in the field. They include:

- *The central theme: Integrating Management Resources* The highly competitive business environment of the 1990s requires operations managers to grapple with new quality-management ideas, Japanese and European methods of production, and the integration of advanced computer-based systems. For this reason, the American Production and Inventory Control Society (APICS) has declared the 1990s the decade for integrating human, technological, and system management resources. This textbook recognizes the importance of the successful integration of management resources. Every chapter includes a special section that describes how real organizations have increased their efficiency, productivity, and competitiveness by integrating their management resources.
- *Total Quality Management (TQM)* One of the most current OM topics is the implementation and use of TQM principles and methods. Every chapter in this textbook contains some coverage of quality management, and Chapter 2 is devoted entirely to this critical topic. Extensive coverage of the more traditional quality assurance subjects is found in Chapter 12.
- *Computer-integrated systems* Computer-integrated systems are discussed and illustrated throughout this textbook. We provide a more extensive presentation of IBM, Hewlett-Packard, and other computer-integrated software systems that any other textbook published to date. We fell strongly that an introduction to these real-world systems and their components will give students, who will probably use such systems at some time in the future, a tangible head start in their careers. Though little has been written on computer-integrated service systems (CISS), we describe several that were placed into operation in the early 1990s.
- *International production methods* Coverage of international production and service system strategies, philosophies, and methods is not limited to a single chapter. Instead, we have presented them in comparative fashion throughout

the text, together with alternative U.S. methods. We feel this approach is more logical, and gives the instructor greater opportunity to compare foreign and domestic methods, than an approach that presents international topics separately.

- *Global management and technology* The need for global strategic planning as a means of coping with international competition is stressed in almost every chapter. In addition, we devote an entire chapter (Chapter 15) to this subject.
- *American Production and Inventory Control Society (APICS) educational standards* We have made a special effort to conform to those subjects that APICS deems basic to an education in OM, while at the same time including the traditional content instructors expect to find in an OM textbook. A variety of APICS definitions, articles, and educational materials will be found throughout the book.

SUPERIOR ORGANIZATION AND PEDAGOGY

This textbook is comprised of fifteen chapters divided into three parts. Part I, Concepts and Prerequisite Methodology, includes three chapters that cover preliminary concepts, Total Quality Management, and forecasting. These chapters provide the foundation on which the rest of the textbook builds. Part II, Planning and Controlling Operations, includes a series of seven chapters that focus on some basic operations management activities. Aggregate and capacity planning, materials management, inventory management, scheduling, and project management are among the typical planning and controlling topics covered in this part. In Part III, Improving Products and Systems, the five remaining chapters suggest ways that operations managers can improve existing products and processes, to meet the ever-increasing challenges in today's business environment.

Each chapter includes some special pedagogical features to help students master the content. They include:

- *Chapter outline* Each chapter begins with an outline that includes the major headings, cases, articles, and supplements in the chapter.
- *List of chapter objectives* Each chapter begins with topical objectives designed to orient students to important information contained in the chapter.
- *Highlighted terms* Terms and technologies that are unique to operations management are printed in boldface at first mention.
- *Question and Answer boxes* These short boxed displays are used both to test immediate knowledge of a subject and to extend readers' knowledge with additional information on unique or special applications.

- *Icons to highlight coverage of services and quality* The management of services and of quality is currently receiving a great deal of emphasis in operations management courses. To help students identify these discussions, we have placed icons in the margins:

  S identifies coverage of services

  Q identifies coverage of quality
- *Integrating Management Resources sections* Each chapter ends with a section that illustrates how human, technological, and system resources are being integrated into modern operations management practices.
- *Summary sections* Each chapter is summarized in a special section that reviews and reinforces important concepts presented in the chapter.
- *Discussion and Review Questions* Each chapter includes a series of questions that can be used by students as a review of the chapter content, or by instructors as the basis for class discussion.
- *Problems* Chapters that present OM methodologies include a series of problems, almost 300 in all. The icon **C** identifies computer-based problems. Answers to selected problems are given in Appendix J.
- *Cases* Most chapters include two case studies that test students' knowledge of both concepts and methodology.
- *Articles* Selected chapters include short articles on current OM issues, written by industry professionals. They are meant to help students see the material presented in the chapter from a practitioner's point of view.
- *Chapter-end supplements* A variety of optional supplements are presented at the end of selected chapters. They can easily be excluded by those instructors who do not wish to cover certain methods in depth.
- *Book-end appendixes* A variety of optional appendixes are presented at the end of the book. Appendix A presents a discussion of the normal probability distribution and basic statistics, for those who have not yet completed a basic course in statistics or who need a review of the subject. Appendix B contains instructions for playing the in-class Forecasting Simulation Game. Appendix C presents a series of decision-making methods, including expected value analysis and decision trees. Appendix D presents linear programming formation procedure and a graphic solution method for solving LP problems. Appendix E presents the simplex solution method for LP problems. Appendix F contains a random number table used in simulation analysis, and Appendix G offers an exponential probability distribution used in probability estimation. Appendix H presents instructions for using the *Micro Production* software system available with this book. Appendix I covers the formulation and solution of transportation method problems. Appendix J presents the solutions to selected problems in the textbook, so students can check their own answers. Finally, Appendix K presents a cumulative Poisson probability distribution, for use in estimating quality assurance probabilities.

A COMPLETE PACKAGE OF ANCILLARY MATERIALS

A number of ancillary materials have been developed to support the instructor's use of the textbook and the student's understanding of the content.

- *Video package* A series of video programs covers the latest in international technology, computer-based systems, and human resource utilization. This collection of professionally prepared videos is unlike any other on the market.
- *Instructor's Resource Manual* Prepared by the authors, the *Instructor's Resource Manual* includes lecture outlines, solutions to problems and cases, and suggestions on how best to use selected questions. This manual also includes a detailed explanation of the Forecasting Simulation Game located in Appendix B of the text. The data and game guidelines included will help make this exercise an enjoyable learning experience. A software source is listed for those who want to check their game results by computer.
- *Lecture Bank* This interactive, IBM PC-based software allows instructors to customize the lecture outlines printed in the *Instructor's Resource Manual.*
- *Test Bank* Prepared by the authors, the *Test Bank* is a compilation of over 1,300 multiple-choice, true/false, and problem questions for use with this textbook. The questions are organized by chapter, coded for complexity, and referenced to specific pages in the textbook.
- *Computerized Test Bank* An IBM PC-compatible disk allows instructors to select, edit, and scramble questions and to convert multiple-choice problems to short-answer format.
- *Study Guide* Prepared by the authors, the *Study Guide* is designed to provide additional educational materials for students who need them. The *Study Guide* includes key points of inquiry; a list of acronyms; true/false, multiple-choice, and problem questions; a set of computer-based completion questions; and a complete answer guide for all questions. The completion questions are designed to be used with the *Micro Production* software available with this book.
- *Computerized Study Guide* The *Study Guide* is also available in an interactive, IBM PC-based computerized version.
- *Micro Production software* Prepared by the authors, *Micro Production* is a complete IBM PC-based, menu-driven software system. This software is designed to support the methods presented in the textbook, as well as more complex applications required by faculty who teach on a more advanced quantitative level.
- *Transparency package* A complete package of acetate transparencies is available to instructors who adopt the book.

ACKNOWLEDGMENTS

We would like to acknowledge the many colleagues and students who have contributed to this book. The helpful suggestions of the following content reviewers are especially appreciated:

Jayanta Bandyopadhyay
Central Michigan University

Charles F. Bimmerle
University of North Texas

Charles W. Dane
Oregon State University

Norbert E. Enrick
Late of Kent State University

P. K. Eswaran
Ohio University

Alfred L. Guiffrida
Canisius College

Marilyn Jones
Winthrop College

Joel Knowles
California State University, Sacramento

Matthew J. Liberatore
Villanova University

Michel Mallenby
Creighton University

David M. Miller
University of Alabama

Joseph R. Munn
Baylor University

Jon Ozmun
Northern Arizona University

C. Carl Pegels
SUNY, Buffalo

Michael J. Pesch
St. Cloud State University

Peter A. Pinto
Bowling Green State University

Ranga Ramasesh
Texas Christian University

James W. Rice
University of Wisconsin, Oshkosh

Leonard E. Ross
California Polytechnic University

Roberta Russell
Virginia Polytechnic Institute and State University

Brooke A. Saladin
Wake Forest University

Samia Siha
University of Northern Iowa

Ramesh G. Soni
Indiana University of Pennsylvania

R. Stansbury Stockton
Indiana University

Shahram Taj
University of Detroit Mercy

Richard Tellier
California State University, Fresno

Emre A. Veral
Baruch College, CUNY

Barry L. Wisdom
Southwest Missouri State University

Bruce Woodworth
University of Texas, El Paso

Five reviewers painstakingly combed the manuscript and proofs of the text and solutions for errors and inaccuracies. We would like to acknowledge their considerable contribution to the project.

Jeff Burbick, *University of Cincinnati*

Hemant Kher, *University of South Carolina*

Richard Metters, *University of North Carolina*

Vincent Vargas, *University of North Carolina*

Joe Wert, *University of Cincinnati*

Finally, we would like to thank a key staff person at the University of Nebraska, Cathy Jensen, who assisted in the many drafts of this book. We would also like to thank the many Houghton Mifflin people, especially Diane McOscar, Elizabeth Morgan, and Paula Kmetz, whose creative talents are an important part of this book.

S.M.L.
M.J.S.

CHAPTER 1
Preliminary Concepts in Operations Management

CHAPTER 2
Total Quality Management

CHAPTER 3
Forecasting

CHAPTER 4
Strategic, Tactical, and Operational Planning

CHAPTER 5
Aggregate and Capacity Planning

CHAPTER 6
Materials Management

CHAPTER 7
Inventory Management: Dependent Demand Inventory

CHAPTER 8
Inventory Management: Independent Demand Inventory

CHAPTER 9
Scheduling in Manufacturing and Service Operations

CHAPTER 10
Project Management

CHAPTER 11
Product and Service Design

CHAPTER 12
Quality Assurance

CHAPTER 13
Facility Location Analysis and Layout Design

CHAPTER 14
Job Design and Work Measurement

CHAPTER 15
Improving Technology and International Integration of Operating Management Systems

P A R T I

CONCEPTS AND PREREQUISITE METHODOLOGY

1

Preliminary Concepts in Operations Management

CHAPTER OUTLINE

CHAPTER OBJECTIVES

The material in this chapter should prepare you to do the following:

1. Define *operations management*
2. Explain why operations management is a necessary subject in the business curriculum
3. Describe what an operations management system is and give examples
4. Differentiate between various types of operations
5. Describe the functions of operations management
6. Discuss the importance of productivity, flexibility, and competitive advantage.
7. Describe operations management activities
8. Explain the interface between operations and other departmental areas in an organization
9. Describe the importance of the external environment to the operations manager
10. Explain the history of operations management and cite examples of important contributions to this field

As you begin reading this chapter, you may be contemplating a career in operations management. If that is the case—or if you are an accounting, finance, marketing, or management information systems major—you need to understand the essential role the operations manager plays in the modern, technology-based organizations of the 1990s.[1]

We begin our exploration of operations management with a simple definition. **Operations management (OM)** is the study of concepts, procedures, and technologies used by managers, administrators, and employees in the operation of all organizations. This definition of OM is intentionally broad to reflect the extensive demands of those who currently function as operations personnel.

Operations management has evolved over the last twenty years from its subset field of study called production and inventory management. **Production and inventory management,** also referred to as **manufacturing management** or **industrial management,** traditionally was concerned with managing the production of tangible products. (Examples of tangible products include automobiles, canned food, and television sets.) The growth of service industries in the United States during the last three decades, however, created a need for a more general term to also encompass the management of service operations, whose output is a nonphysical or intangible service product. (Examples of intangible products include health care, transportation, information, and hotel lodging.) The term *operations management* has filled that need.

The purposes of this chapter are to provide prerequisite management basics and to introduce the subject of operations management. We present the terms, concepts, and classifications of OM systems and describe the functions of the operations manager in typical business organizations. The *business* organization setting is used here only as a point of departure. Operations management concepts can be applied in all types of organizations, including non-business organizations such as educational institutions, hospitals, and government agencies. We will not only define *what* operations managers do, we will explain *why* OM is a necessary subject in business management. We will also present some of the current trends facing organizations and the need for operations managers to adjust to meet the challenges posed by these new trends. We next examine the types of environments in which OM personnel operate. The functional relationship of OM with accounting, finance, marketing, and information systems will then be presented to enhance the understanding of the role operations managers play within an organization. The demands of the external environment (the industry within which the organization operates) will also be discussed. This chapter concludes with a brief history of the development of operations management.

• • •

[1] A. Satir and G. S. Goyal, "Undergraduate Curriculum for Production and Operations Management," *Production and Inventory Management,* 28, No. 2 (1987), 10–14.

WHY OPERATIONS MANAGEMENT IS NECESSARY

Operations management is a necessary subject in the business curriculum because this subject provides knowledge that is crucial in maintaining and improving a high quality of life. As many of the 1990s-era presidents and chief executive officers know, for a nation to live well, a nation must produce well. The well-being of the citizens of a nation is based on how well the OM function is handled in that nation. If a nation produces quality products and services better than others, it is guaranteed a secure and comfortable future.

The importance of operations management can be seen in light of several significant current trends. First, the era of the domestic economic system has given way to the age of the global economic system. A nation's economic system no longer functions in an isolated environment. We are witnessing the emergence of an interlinked borderless global economic system. The European Economic Community becoming a reality in the 1990s is an example of this phenomenon. In such a global economy, the most powerful element is the customer. Customers have the power and right to choose the best product or service that their money can buy, from anywhere in the world. Organizations that produce high-quality goods and services will succeed and those who fail to do so will disappear. Thus, meeting customer needs through effective OM functions is becoming the most important concern of organizations. Increased global competition will force organizations to identify and develop unique competitive advantages that OM can help them provide. Effective operations management is essential for prosperity in the global economic system.

Another important trend is the transition from the industrial age to the intelligence age. The economic system in the United States is no longer dominated by manufacturing of industrial and consumer goods. Eighty to ninety percent of our work force is composed of workers who bring specialized knowledge to their jobs rather than just physical labor. Also, worker creativity and innovative effort are extended through the use of computers. The integration in organizations of human creativity and artificial intelligence is expanding the horizons of possibility. Organizations need flexibility in their human, technological, and system resources to adapt to these changes.

The third important trend is the declining rate of increase in productivity in the United States. As we can observe in Figure 1-1, the United States lags behind other industrialized nations in this important area. The impact of this lag in productivity is profound. The United States, although still the biggest producer of goods and services in the world, ranks eighth in per capita income. The U.S. share of world gross national product (GNP) is currently around 34 percent, down from 52 percent in 1950. The United States, while still a prominent economic force in the industrialized world, is no longer dominant, nor does it set the economic rules for the world.

A fourth important trend is the dramatic shift in the U.S. economy from the goods-producing manufacturing sector to the service-producing sector (see Figure 1-2). Today, service industries employ more than 77 percent of U.S. workers, whereas manufacturing represents 18 percent of total employment. Moreover, approximately 90 percent of all new jobs created today are in the service sector. Thus, it may appear that the appropriate

FIGURE 1-1 U.S. AND FOREIGN GROWTH IN PRODUCTIVITY

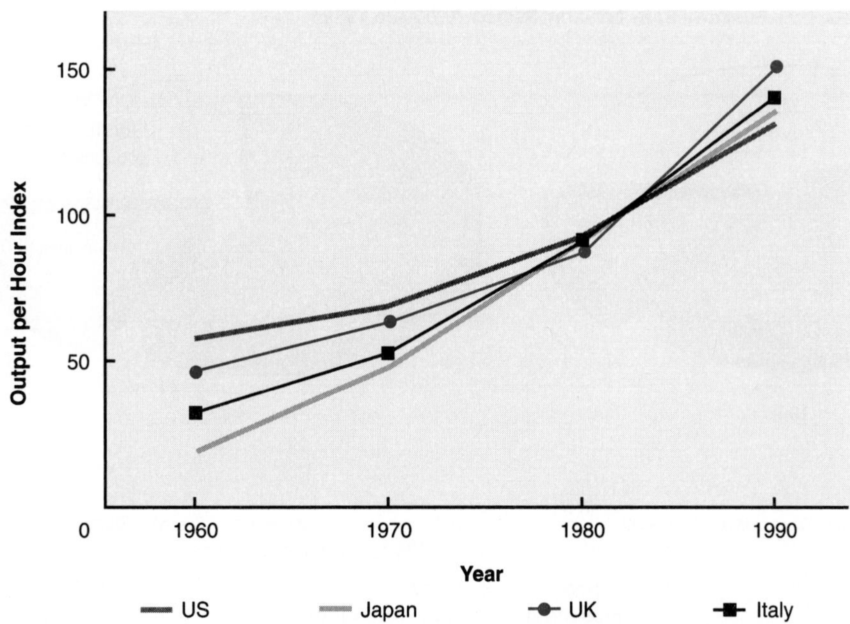

Source: "Annual Indexes of Manufacturing Productivity and Related Measures, 12 Countries," *Monthly Labor Review,* 115 (January 1992), 120. (The output index is based on a ratio of manufacturing output per hour of labor with the base year of 1982 = 100.)

strategy would be to focus resources on the service sector, and perhaps neglect manufacturing, for the good of the U.S. economy as a whole. We must remember, however, that a healthy service sector requires a healthy manufacturing sector. If the manufacturing sector suffers from low productivity, poor product quality, and slow technological innovations, the service sector will also suffer. A good example of this is the U.S. banking service industry. In 1960, when the U.S. manufacturing sector was healthy and prospering, seven of the top ten banks in the world were U.S. banks. In 1991, Citicorp ranked eighth, and the other nine top banks were all foreign owned. The point of this example is that excellence in both manufacturing and service is necessary to maintain world economic leadership. We must also have the flexibility to be able to shift from manufacturing to service operations (or from service to manufacturing) as customer markets shift.

The increasing importance of operations management can also be viewed from the perspective of the individual corporation. The changing environment faced by each corporation operating within the global economic system will give rise to a variety of new corporate needs. Based on the previously stated trends, these needs can be generalized for all corporations to include (1) the need for improved productivity, (2) the need for improved flexibility, and (3) the need to develop competitive advantages.

FIGURE 1-2 EMPLOYMENT SHIFTS IN SERVICE- AND GOODS-PRODUCING INDUSTRY SECTORS

(A) DISTRIBUTION OF PAYROLL EMPLOYMENT BY INDUSTRY SECTOR, 1950 AND 1989

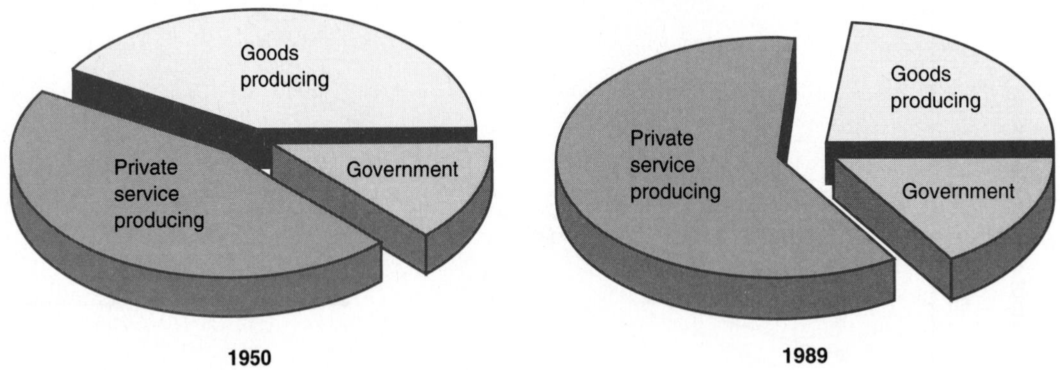

(B) PAYROLL EMPLOYMENT, SEASONALLY ADJUSTED, 1969-1989

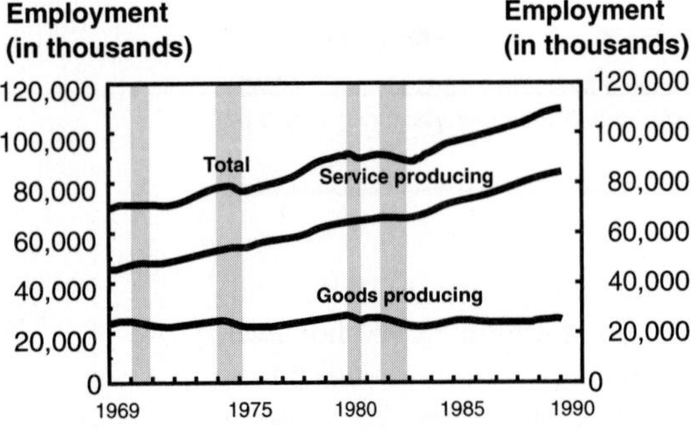

(C) INDEXES OF EMPLOYMENT CHANGE DURING THE 1980s, BY INDUSTRY SECTOR

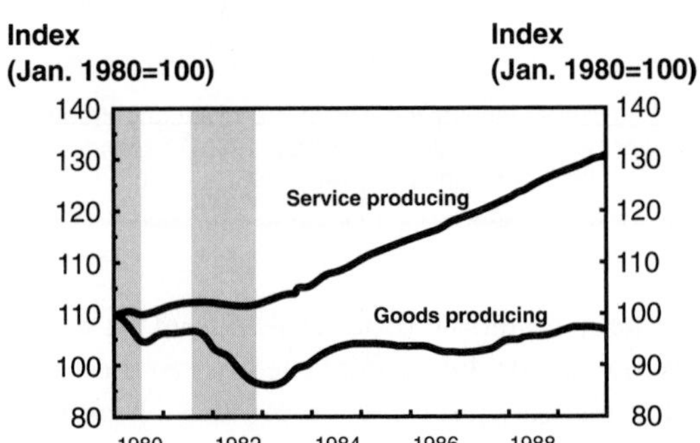

Note: In (B) and (C), shaded areas are recessionary periods, as designated by the National Bureau of Economic Research.
Source: "Job Growth and Industry Shifts in the 1980's," *Monthly Labor Review,* 113 (September 1990), 5–6.

Corporations need to continually improve product or service productivity to reduce the cost (or increase the value) of their products to their customers to remain competitive in the marketplace. Corporations must also improve their production flexibility to be able to adapt quickly to the rapidly changing environment. They must be flexible enough to change the products and services they offer to retain old markets and seize new ones. Corporations must identify and develop competitive advantages that give them an edge on their competition and ensure their successful survival. A **competitive advantage** is a unique capability, such as being able to provide the highest-quality products in an industry or having the best delivery record in the industry for on-time shipments.

Uniquely positioned within the organization, operations managers control and manage a major portion of the means by which these needs can be satisfied. These means include the following management resources:

1. Human resources (workers, managers, staff experts)
2. Technology resources (production equipment, robots)
3. System resources (computer information systems, production methods)

Operations managers must be able to take these management resources and effectively integrate them to satisfy the needs of the organization. OM organizations, such as the American Production and Inventory Control Society (APICS), recognize that global pressures are continually and increasingly demanding innovations within organizations. To help operations managers in the 1990s deal with what APICS called "the integrated management revolution," new education courses and a new APICS certification program have been developed.[2] The new program is based on the APICS definition of **resource management:** "The effective management and integration of an organization's resources to produce and deliver competitive products or services."[3]

The authors of this textbook have chosen "integrating management resources" for its central theme; it is essential that operations managers be knowledgeable about this strategy to ensure their organizations' success in the 1990s. To highlight this central theme, each chapter will contain a section called "Integrating Management Resources." Within these sections we will discuss how operations managers are using human, technology, and system resources to improve productivity, flexibility, and competitive advantage.

STRATEGIES IN OPERATIONS MANAGEMENT

Successful U.S. corporations in the 1990s will adapt and take advantage of the trends in the global economic system. Top management in many U.S. organizations believe that their organization's future success in accomplishing corporate mission or goals depends on how well they achieve their operations management goals.

Corporate Strategy

To achieve their corporate mission or goals, top or executive-level managers of corporations establish their **corporate strategies,** or long-term plans for the organization as a whole. Corporate strategies usually answer a number of questions that define what

---

[2] B. Russell, "The Integrated Management Revolution," *P&IM Review with APICS News* (February 1991), 9.

[3] Ibid.

the corporation will be doing over an extended period of time, such as five or ten years. Among other things, corporate strategies try to answer questions such as what types of businesses the corporation should continue in or enter into and who the organization's customers are or should be. These questions are answered by analyzing customer needs, opportunities, and threats in the organization's environment and the organization's competitive strengths in being able to meet new challenges. The corporate strategies are derived from the corporate mission and its strategic goals. A corporate mission or goal for a service operation, such as an airline, might be to provide the best on-time service to customers in the industry. A corporate mission or goal for a manufacturer might be to become technology or product quality leader in an industry.

Once a corporate mission or goals are set, then corporate strategy can be established with policies and criteria to enable the organization to meet its goals. The criteria are usually in the form of performance objectives, such as a target level of profit, to measure goal accomplishment. We will be discussing the development of corporate strategies in detail in Chapter 4.

The corporate strategy establishes long-term goals and a means to evaluate the organization's progress in achieving them. Once the corporate strategy is set, it must be translated into individual strategies for each functional area—like operations management—within the organization.

Operations Management Strategy

An operations management strategy specifies how operations managers will achieve the organization's overall goals within the framework of the corporate strategy. The OM strategy is developed by top-level operations managers to be implemented by all managers throughout the OM functional area. The following steps are required to develop and implement an OM strategy. They are the detailed subjects of future chapters.

1. Interpret the implications of the corporate strategy for the OM area (discussed in Chapter 4).
2. Develop an OM strategy that defines specific OM goals and evaluates measures of success (discussed in Chapters 2, 4, and 5).
3. Determine the necessary OM resource requirements to accomplish OM goals (discussed in Chapters 4 through 10).
4. Determine the OM resource capacities to meet the OM goal requirements (discussed in Chapter 5).
5. Design OM systems to accomplish OM goals (discussed in Chapters 11 through 15).
6. Devise detailed implementation plans to schedule and specifically achieve OM goals (discussed in Chapters 4, 9, and 10).
7. Control and follow up the progress of goal accomplishment by reviewing evaluation measures of success (discussed in Chapters 4 through 10).

How operations management strategies are developed is logically related to the organization's mission. Research has shown that some organizations link their corporate mission and OM strategy.[4] For example, organizations with a mission of technological innovation are usually driven by their own product research and development to constantly introduce new technologically advanced products. Research has shown that the goals of such organizations include improved flexibility to accommodate the rapid changes in new products that they introduce to the market. For such organizations, operations management is essential for accomplishing the corporate mission. Their OM strategy might focus on improving flexibility in human resources (perhaps by increasing worker job skills), improving flexibility in technology (such as by acquiring highly flexible robots to accommodate a wide range of product designs), and improving flexibility in systems (perhaps by acquiring information systems that can be reconfigured to accommodate new production requirements). Other organizations whose corporate mission could be characterized as exploiters of technology would be more interested in taking leading-edge technology developed by others and improving the value (quality or cost/benefit) of the product to their customers. Exploiters of technology focus OM strategy development on improving product quality or lowering the costs of the product to their customers to give themselves a quality or cost competitive advantage over the technology leaders. Again, the OM area is essential to these organizations' achieving improved product quality or lower production costs and giving them their competitive advantage.

QUESTION: Do organizations really benefit by establishing long-term corporate and operations management strategic goals?

ANSWER: In almost every situation the answer is yes. For example, Motorola Corporation's corporate strategy during the 1980s was to have the highest-quality products in the electronics industry. To implement its corporate strategy, its OM strategic goals included having the best-educated work force on quality control methodology. Based on factual cost and quality savings data, Motorola's investment in improving quality was highly beneficial. It was estimated that for every dollar invested in training its work force, Motorola received a $33 return.[5]

Although we will be discussing corporate and operations management strategic planning throughout the rest of this book, and particularly in Chapter 4, a popular example of a 1990s corporate and OM strategic plan for world-class competitive

[4] P. R. Richardson, A. J. Taylor, and J. R. M. Gordon, "A Strategic Approach to Evaluating Manufacturing Performance," *Interfaces,* 15, No. 5 (1985), 15–27.

[5] L. Dobyns and C. C. Mason, *Quality or Else* (Boston: Houghton Mifflin, 1991), p. 134.

advantage is presented in Chapter 2, Total Quality Management. In this chapter we want to establish an essential link between corporate and OM strategy. This link must be developed if the organization is to be successful. To better understand how OM strategies can be developed and implemented, we must begin with a basic understanding of the composition of OM systems.

THE SYSTEM OF OPERATIONS MANAGEMENT

Most industries in the United States comprise numerous competing business organizations. The businesses in turn are made up of systems that function to perpetuate the organization. These systems are sometimes referred to as **functional areas** within an organization and include accounting, finance, marketing, personnel, and operations. Regardless of the functional area in which a manager works, it is important to recognize the operations management function in a system.

The Operations Management System Itself

The system in which operations managers operate is not limited to just manufacturing industries but includes service industries as well. For operations managers that system is referred to as the operations management system. As can be seen in Figure 1-3, the operations management system consists of five basic elements: input, transformation subsystem, output, control subsystem, and feedback.

INPUT The input of the operations management system includes all physical and nonphysical resources coming into an organization. These resources include the human resources (labor), materials, and equipment typically used in manufacturing. The input also includes human knowledge such as information, experience, intelligence, and skills typically used in many production and service organizations.

TRANSFORMATION SUBSYSTEMS Transformation subsystems are the active processes that change physical goods or restructure human resource activities to provide the desired goods or service output. They include concepts, procedures, and nonequipment technologies as well as rules, guidelines, and steps used to convert input into desired output.

OUTPUT The output of the operations management system is the net result of the transformation subsystems. The output of an OM system can be either a tangible object such as an automobile or a intangible service such as a doctor's diagnosis.

FIGURE 1-3 OPERATIONS MANAGEMENT SYSTEM

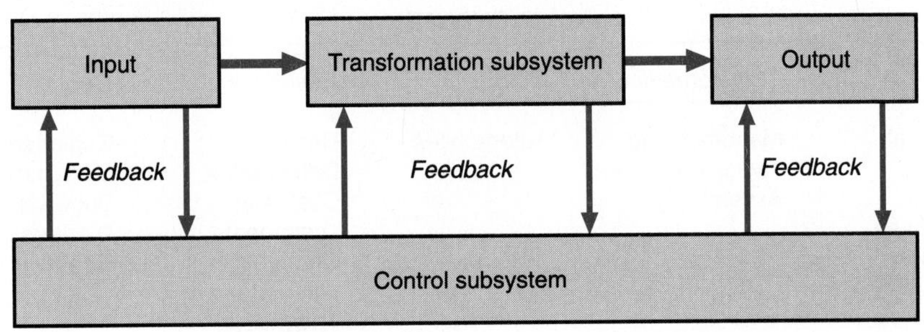

CONTROL SUBSYSTEMS Control subsystems are integrated into the input, transformation subsystems, and output elements to monitor and correct system behavior that is deviating from desired operations management objectives. A typical example is the quality control systems used to ensure that products have zero defects. This subsystem is usually made up of one or more operations managers who monitor system performance and take corrective actions when necessary. Electronic monitoring sensors and electronic robots have taken over much of the routine and corrective actions in both manufacturing and service OM systems from the workers in recent years.

FEEDBACK Feedback is any verbal, written, or electronic information describing the physical structure and behavioral use of the goods and services that are incoming, outgoing, and being transformed in the OM system. The feedback element of the operations management system represents a communication link between the input, transformation subsystems, and output elements and the control subsystems.

To understand how an operations management system functions, we must identify its elements. Several manufacturing and service systems are shown in Table 1-1, and some of the elements specific to each one are identified. It is interesting to note in Table 1-1 that the input for one type of service system can be the output of one type of manufacturing system. For example, the input for the automobile retailing industry—automobiles—is the output of the automobile manufacturing industry. Understanding the relationships among different OM systems and how they are integrated has been a central focus of OM research in recent years. Many of the benefits of the Japanese methods of production are derived from utilizing the relationships among various business systems. We will be discussing foreign and domestic methods of production and their impact on interbusiness and intrabusiness system relationships throughout the text.

TABLE 1-1 EXAMPLES OF OPERATIONS MANAGEMENT SYSTEMS

Type of System	ELEMENTS				
	Input	Transformation	Output	Feedback	Control
Automobile manufacturing	Equipment Labor Supplies Engineering Facilities Parts	Manufacturing small parts Assembling	Automobiles	Recalls Defect rates Customer comments Changes in market share Technology	Engineers Managers Supervisors Workers Robots
Automobile retailing	Automobiles Salespeople Facilities	Ordering and preparing automobiles Providing garage service	Automobiles sold Automobiles mechanically serviced	Unit jobs Customer comments Inventory	Owner Sales manager Service personnel
Bakery	Dry goods Seasoning Ovens and utensils Chefs and cooks Recipes	Mixing and pouring Baking Preparing food Packaging food	Pies Cakes Pastries Bread	Unit sales Expenses Customer comments	Chef Owner Workers
Farm	Labor Land Equipment Seed Fertilizer Animals	Planting Watering Harvesting	Crops Herds	Per acre yield Profitability	Owner Farmer
Hospital	Doctors Nurses Patients Facilities Equipment	Performing surgery Imparting knowledge Administering drugs and therapy	Extending life Restoration of physical and mental well being	Operation success rate Expenses Facility utilizations	Hospital administrators Doctors Nurses Sensors
Post office	Equipment Labor Facilities	Sorting mail Transporting mail	Mail delivery	Unit delivery rates Expenses Consumer comments	Postmaster Postmistress Workers
Restaurant	Food Hungry customers Equipment Labor	Cooking Serving	Service Prepared food Content customers	Customer complaints Food leftovers	Owner Head waiter Manager Workers
Steel plant	Crude ore Labor Processing equipment	Heating Pouring Mixing	Steel ingots Steel sheeting Steel plates	Production rates Expenses	Plant managers Supervisors Accountants Workers

TABLE 1-1 (CONTINUED)

Type of System	ELEMENTS				
	Input	*Transformation*	*Output*	*Feedback*	*Control*
Truck delivery service	Trucks Facilities Labor	Picking up goods Transporting goods	Delivered goods	Cost per mile Truck utilization rates Miles traveled	Terminal manager Distribution manager Supervisors Drivers
University	Educators Students Equipment	Imparting and acquiring knowledge	Educated people Research Service	Alumni donations External grant funding Student evaluations	Administrators Professors

Types of Operations

The operations management system just described is generally applicable to all types of business systems. There exists, however, a good deal of variety in OM systems. To help sort out this diversity, researchers find it useful to classify the various types of operating systems. One obvious way that we can classify OM systems is to refer to them as either a service or manufacturing system. *Service systems* usually offer intangible products to their customers such as travel advice from the American Automobile Association (AAA), a doctor's diagnosis, or an advertisement on a radio. *Manufacturing systems* offer tangible products to their customers such as a textbook from Houghton Mifflin or a microcomputer from Apple Computer. S

Some organizations offer their customers both a service and manufactured product. For example, many of the major oil refineries in the United States own the majority of their retail gas station outlets. The refinery operation is manufacturing or processing S

QUESTION: When a drugstore sells a package of chewing gum to a customer, is it providing a tangible or intangible product? S

ANSWER: The customer is receiving an intangible product from the drugstore. The chewing gum is tangible, but it is the output of the manufacturer that produced it. Drugstores are retail outlets and are principally service organizations—they do not produce chewing gum. The output of the drugstore is the intangible service of delivering the chewing gum to the customer.

salable oil, and the retail outlets provide a delivery service for the final customer. In such cases, it is more accurate to divide the organization into separate service and manufacturing operations. In organizations in which either service or manufacturing activities dominate, the organization can be classified as one or the other. For example, General Motors (GM) is chiefly considered an automobile manufacturer. Yet GM provides many customer services such as financial services, computer systems, and car rentals that are intangible products.

Another way of classifying operations management systems is to characterize them by various criteria such as product size, type of human resource or equipment used, or the number of units produced at one time. In accordance with this type of classification system there are five basic types of operations: job, repetitive or continuous process, job-lot, project, and limited-lot, as shown in Figure 1.4.

JOB A job operation tends to produce a single item or order, usually requiring small-scale, custom work. The job operation is also characterized by equipment that has general applicability and by multiskilled personnel. Figure 1-4 lists several examples of job operations, which encompass both manufacturing and service operations. Custom jewelry crafted by a skilled goldsmith or silversmith is a small-scale, specialized product manufactured to an individual's unique tastes and desires. A department store's retail sales activity, which is a service, is also a custom effort focused toward each individual customer.

S

REPETITIVE OR CONTINUOUS PROCESS A repetitive or continuous process operation tends to be a high-volume, mass production operation generating a homogeneous product. A repetitive operation is also characterized by its specialized equipment, such as conveyor systems for a particular product, and by its use of typically semiskilled labor. A brewery that produces a single type of beer is an example of a repetitive or continuous process manufacturing operation. Its output is a homogeneous beer product manufactured by specialized equipment (vats, cooling systems). Each type of beer the brewery produces has its own specialized equipment. A state drivers licensing office where applications are processed is an example of a repetitive service operation. As with the manufacturing operation, the service operation can offer more than one product. A state drivers licensing office may process operator licenses for both automobiles and trucks, and each is a high-volume, homogeneous product generated using a repetitive processing procedure.

S

JOB-LOT A job-lot operation is a combination of both job and repetitive type operations. A job-lot operation tends to produce a small lot of a limited-edition product. A jeweler designing a special-edition, limited-quantity diamond ring is a manufacturing example of a job-lot operation in that it represents both custom and repetitive work. A car pool transportation service involving the pickup and delivery of a limited number of passengers to a single location is an example of a service job-lot operation.

PROJECT A project operation tends to produce large-scale, customized, single-item products. In project manufacturing operations, human resources and equipment are

FIGURE 1-4 TYPES OF OPERATIONS

S

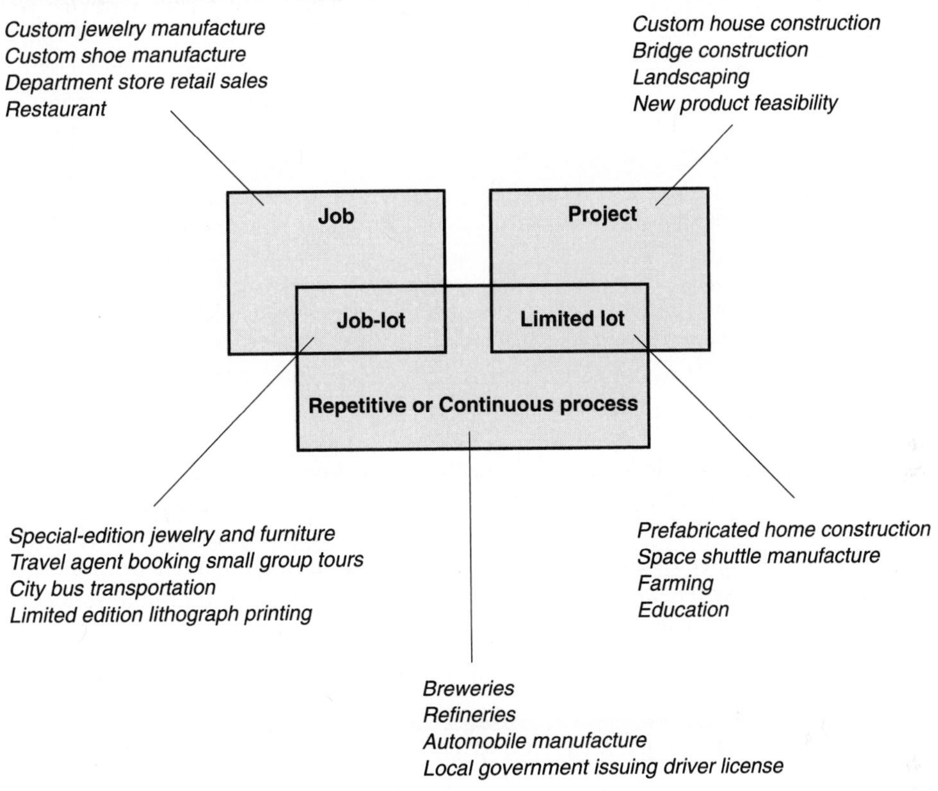

usually brought together to produce the product such as a dam or a bridge. Clearly, a dam is a large-scale project that is unique and custom made for its particular location. Because of the large scale of project operations, both skilled and unskilled human resources are used. The type of equipment also ranges from highly specialized, such as cranes used in constructing high-rise office buildings, to general purpose, such as hammers used in home construction. The size of the equipment also varies considerably to fit the diversity of tasks required in project operations. For example, in a project service operation such as landscaping, the equipment may include a small hand shovel for planting flowers as well as a bulldozer. S

LIMITED-LOT A limited lot operation is a combination of both repetitive and project operations. A limited-lot operation tends to produce limited lots of medium- to large-scale products. The manufacture of NASA space shuttles is an example of a limited-lot operation, as only a limited number of shuttles are produced for NASA. Because each shuttle is basically a duplicate of the other, their manufacture is characteristic of repetitive operations. Also, the manufacture of each shuttle is a large-scale activity, which is

S

characteristic of the project operation. An example of a limited-lot service operation is an instructor teaching a classroom of students. The number of students (customers) is limited to the size of the classroom, and satisfying the educational needs of a group of students is clearly a large-scale project, which lasts several months.

S

QUESTION: What operation classifications can we use to describe a medical doctor diagnosing a patient's illness?

ANSWER: A doctor diagnosing a patient represents a service operation. This work can also be characterized as a job operation because it is a small-scale, custom service provided to the patient.

Although it is possible for a single organization to have more than one of these five classifications of operations, organizations are usually classified by the dominant product or service they offer their customers. Our interest in classifying operations is that it helps us understand the operating system and the diversity that distinguishes one from another. This classification system also provides an efficient reference point for the introduction of other operation management terminology.

FUNCTIONS OF OPERATIONS MANAGEMENT

Basic Management Functions

Operations management involves the management of human, technology, and system resources. To manage these resources, operations managers must perform the same basic functions that all managers are expected to perform. The operations management functions include planning, directing, organizing, staffing, motivating, and controlling.

PLANNING Planning is a management function that involves the establishment of goals and objectives toward which employees direct a course of action. There are many different types of planning activities. **Strategic planning** involves the establishment of long-term goals for the entire organization or system. An example of an OM strategic plan is to achieve a goal of growth by building and locating a new production facility. Planning that involves a more specific effort to establish a means by which to achieve the desired goals and objectives in the medium term is sometimes referred to as **tactical planning.** An example of an OM tactical plan is the stepwise implementation procedures for locating a new plant. **Operational planning** is shorter-term planning that implements the tactical objectives. If the first step of an OM tactical plan to locate a new plant is to determine which state the plant is to be located in, an operational plan might establish a team of researchers and detailed methodology to be used by the team to facilitate their state selection decision. The importance of planning in OM is critical, and we devote an entire chapter (Chapter 4) to strategic, tactical, and operational planning. Some types of planning are unique to OM. We will focus on these OM-related planning functions in Chapter 5.

DIRECTING The directing function of management involves supervising, ordering, and commanding. Examples of directing in operations management include making daily job assignments, giving directions to employees on job-related procedures, and ordering people to perform specific tasks.

ORGANIZING The organizing function involves structuring the organization's systems to achieve planned objectives. Examples of organizing in operations management include structuring the tasks that make up an employee's job, defining the procedures that are required to produce a product, and coordinating individual and group activities.

STAFFING The staffing function of management includes recruiting employees, screening job applicants, and selecting and training personnel. Staffing can also include writing **job specifications,** which are the job requirements that each worker is expected to perform for a specific job (for example, learning to use microcomputers), and **job descriptions,** which define the type of tasks involved (such as keeping inventories in the stock room).

MOTIVATING The motivating function of management involves guiding, coaching, and inspiring employees to achieve planned objectives. In operations management, motivating employees involves understanding psychological and sociological factors that affect employee behavior in the workplace. In recent years, the motivating function of management has shifted from the study of the psychology of the individual working in the OM system to how the individual interacts with the OM system. Management is learning how the OM system can be structured to motivate the employee to achieve planned objectives.

CONTROLLING The controlling management function involves setting standards, monitoring, measuring, observing, and when necessary, taking appropriate actions to adjust the system to keep it on track to achieve planned objectives. Both human and physical resources require some type of control. Examples of operations management controlling include using computerized lasers to spot defects in paint jobs and auditing freight bills to determine the accuracy of vendor delivery times and charges.

In the last decade, innovations in the way these management functions are performed have changed organization behavior. Although operations managers are still performing all of the basic OM functions, many are being assigned to *cross-functional teams,* sometimes called *critical process teams.* The purpose of these teams is to define or study critical process problems and identify solutions for their resolution. A cross-functional team is usually made up of individuals who work in different departments (operations, accounting, engineering, marketing) and perform different functions within an organization. By using individuals who collectively share a broad picture of the organization's entire operating system, the team can more easily locate problems or unnecessary processing or business activities. For example, a marketing manager knowledgeable about customer product desires could be teamed with a product design engineer and an operations manager to change a product design to minimize product flow difficulties in an automated material handling system. Cross-functional teams are often used to identify and eliminate waste or non-value–added processing activities in the OM system.[6] They also support management activities such as quality control by improving processes (and therefore the quality of products that come from the processes). Cross-functional teams illustrate the need for and benefits of integrating human resources in an organization: they are an example of how organizations are using integration as a strategy to improve resource utilization.

Promoting Productivity, Efficiency, and Effectiveness

Operations managers use these six functions to achieve their organizational objectives. Typical OM concepts used to measure or describe a manager's success in accomplishing OM objectives include productivity, efficiency, and effectiveness.

Productivity is the relative measure of output per labor hour or machine hour, often expressed as a ratio of output to input. The greater the productivity ratio, the more efficient the operating system. **Efficiency** is a measure that shows the relationship between the use of resources (input) and the resulting output. Operations managers are always seeking ways to increase output while keeping input constant or decreasing input while keeping output constant. As productivity is increased, so is the OM system's efficiency. An OM system, for example, that generates greater output this week than last week, while keeping the input at the same level in both weeks, has increased efficiency.

Increasing efficiency by itself may not increase an OM system's productivity. To understand how an increase in efficiency may not increase productivity, we must define another term that is always combined with efficiency: effectiveness. **Effectiveness** is a measure of how well an organization (or system or functional area) accomplishes its goals. If an OM system accomplishes its objectives, it is effective.

Operations managers must be both efficient and effective in performing their jobs. When only one of these objectives is achieved the operations manager risks being unproductive. Unfortunately, efficiency and effectiveness are often at odds with one another. For example, an organization producing high-quality automobiles has the OM system objective of being defect-free. If the manufacturing plant can produce 100 defect-free automobiles in 100 hours of operation, the plant productivity ratio for the current operation is as shown at the top of page 19.

---

[6] D. J. Talley, *Total Quality Management* (Milwaukee, Wis.: ASQC Quality Press, 1991), p. 55.

$$\text{Current plant productivity ratio} = \frac{\text{Output}}{\text{Input}} = \frac{\text{Number of automobiles}}{\text{Hours of operation}} = \frac{100}{100} = 1$$

A new procedure in the production of automobiles can improve efficiency by saving 20 percent of the labor hours required to produce the automobiles. The new procedure is implemented to save the input of labor, and the plant's new productivity ratio is

$$\text{New plant productivity ratio} = \frac{100}{80} = 1.25$$

The new productivity ratio reflects the increase in productivity (and efficiency) caused by the decrease in required input for desired output. After using this new efficient procedure for some time, however, the operations manager observes that it causes defects in the automobiles. Because the organization is no longer accomplishing its objective of producing defect-free automobiles, it is no longer performing its job effectively. To correct the defects in the automobiles, the current 80 hours of operation must be increased to 120 hours. The productivity ratio is then revised to

$$\text{Revised plant productivity ratio} = \frac{100}{120} = .833$$

By producing defect-free automobiles, the organization is again effectively performing its job. Unfortunately, as the last ratio indicates, it is not performing its job as efficiently or productively as it was before it changed the manufacturing procedures.

Ideally, this automobile manufacturer should try to continue to be effective and at the same time improve efficiency, such as by decreasing labor input, to truly increase its productivity. Typically, an organization must improve quality to improve overall productivity because by doing so, costs of reworking and scrap caused by poor quality are reduced.

Maximizing the Productivity Cycle

The impact on an organization of increasing productivity is characterized by the concept of productivity cycling. The productivity cycle, shown in Figure 1-5, represents a logical sequence of events by which an organization can reap benefits because of an increase in productivity. The sequence of events can occur in any order but includes the following:

1. Improvements in productivity or flexibility (or both) are incurred by improved product quality, increased skills of human resources, improved work systems or procedures, or the introduction of new technology (or a combination).
2. The improvements permit an organization to reduce its input relative to its output, which can reduce operating costs. Improved product or service quality, for example, can reduce rework and scrap costs; improved flexibility can reduce setup costs during changeovers for different products.

FIGURE 1-5 THE PRODUCTIVITY CYCLE

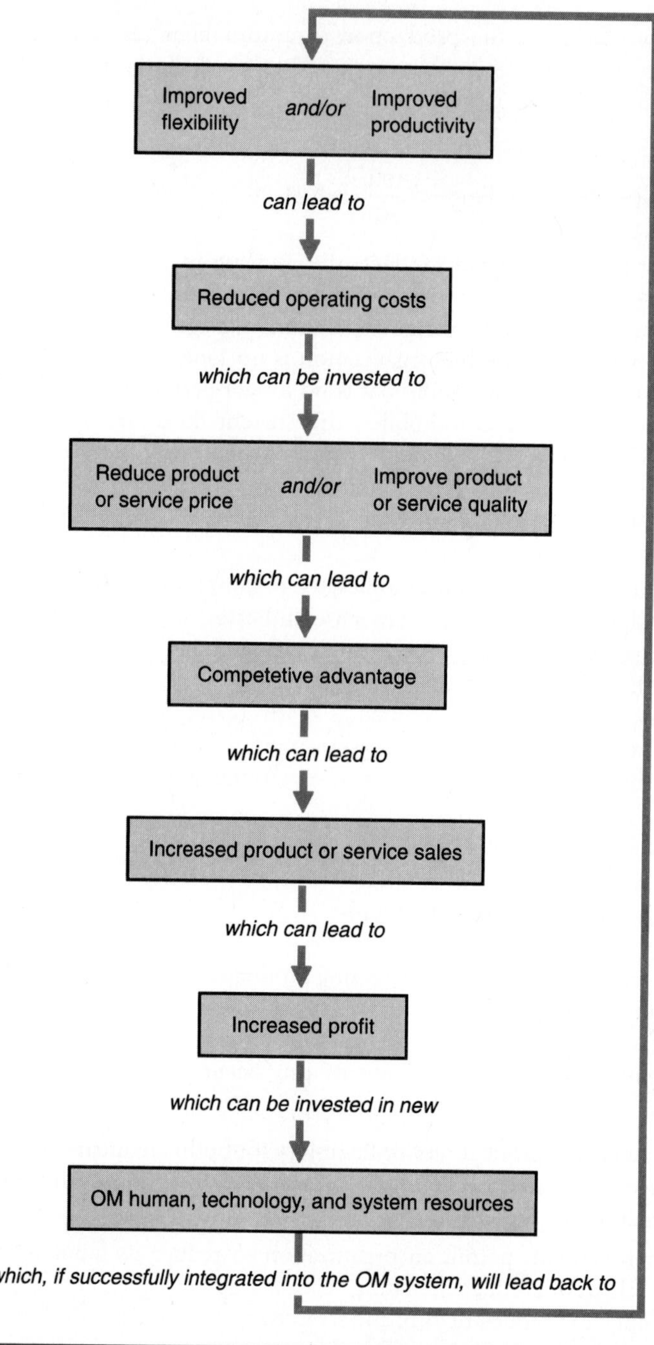

3. Reducing operating costs permits the organization to lower the prices of its products or services or invest in resources to further improve product quality.
4. The relative improvement in product price or quality gives the organization a competitive advantage in the marketplace.
5. The relative advantage increases customer satisfaction for the organization's product or service, and the market responds by consuming a greater quantity of the product or service.
6. The increase in sales increases the organization's profits.
7. The increased profits permit new investment in operations management resources. A greater investment in human resources attracts the most productive workers in the industry. A greater investment in technology and systems can improve quality and responsiveness to change (flexibility). If operations managers can successfully integrate these management resources, the results of the new investment will further increase productivity and these seven steps will repeat.

QUESTION: Does the productivity cycle have to start with an improvement in flexibility or productivity to work?

ANSWER: No. Any event listed in any box in Figure 1-5 can trigger the productivity cycle working. Actually, we can skip through some of the sequence of events as connected in Figure 1-5 to more accurately model the events that take place in any type of organization. For example, an improvement in product quality can lead to reduced operating costs (skipping through an entire cycle), which in turn can reduce the product or service price, leading to a competitive advantage, and so on. The productivity cycle should be viewed as an engine that can be started from any point in the sequence of events that make it up.

The productivity cycle represents a dynamic change element in an organization. Like the ripples of water caused by a stone dropped in a pond, once the cycle begins, it can continue for a long time or until operations managers put an end to it. Although the productivity cycle can have a dramatic effect in some organizations, in other organizations it may never achieve a full cycle because of ineffective management. For example, an organization that does not lower its product's price after incurring a cost reduction from a productivity increase will probably not attain the increase in sales required to continue the productivity cycle.

The relationship of the productivity cycle to operations management strategy and corporate strategy is quite dramatic. Maximizing the productivity cycle should be viewed as a strategic OM mission or goal because it is directly related to integrating OM resources. Maximizing the productivity cycle does not equal maximizing productivity.

Maximizing the productivity cycle means passing the maximum benefits of each step to the next. The eventual outcome of maximizing the productivity cycle is market dominance. This outcome supports common corporate strategies of seeking growth in market share, developing a competitive advantage, improving quality, increasing sales, and increasing profits. The application of productivity cycling also supports OM strategies by reducing operating expenses, improving production flexibility and productivity, improving product quality, and increasing human, technology, and system resources.

Q

QUESTION: Would maximizing productivity alone have the same impact on an organization as maximizing the productivity cycle?

ANSWER: Many total quality management experts, such as W. Edwards Deming, would say no (see further references to Deming in Chapters 2 and 12). According to Deming, improvements in quality will lead to improvements in productivity in the longer term.[7] On the other hand, just stressing improvements in productivity can lead to poor quality in the short term (because quality-enhancing activities take time away from producing). Poor quality in turn can lead to a longer-term subsequent reduction in productivity (because defective products that customers return have to be reworked). Indeed, sacrificing quality can actually cause the productivity cycle to work against the company by increasing operating costs, which in turn reduce productivity. (Note in Figure 1-5 how a decrease in quality might reverse the flow of the productivity cycle against a company.)

One of the most important keys in making the productivity cycle work is being able to integrate the management resources to achieve desired operations management strategies. To help accomplish the integration task, operations managers must perform a number of management activities that help make up the operations manager's job.

ACTIVITIES IN OPERATIONS MANAGEMENT

In addition to the management functions, operations managers perform many other activities. These operations management activities are what make up an operations manager's job and are often included in OM job descriptions and job specifications. The OM activities listed in Figure 1-6 can be organized into three categories of activities: planning for the future, planning and controlling operations, and improving products and systems.

---

[7] For an excellent review of this internationally known expert on quality and productivity, see M. Walton, *Deming Management at Work* (New York: Putnam, 1990).

FIGURE 1-6 ACTIVITIES IN OPERATIONS MANAGEMENT

ACTIVITY	CHAPTER LOCATION	
Total Quality Management	Chapter 2	PLANNING FOR THE FUTURE
Forecasting	Chapter 3	
Improving technology and international integration of OM systems	Chapter 15	
Production planning	Chapters 4 and 5	PLANNING AND CONTROLLING OPERATIONS
Materials management	Chapter 6	
Inventory management	Chapters 7 and 8	
Scheduling	Chapters 9 and 10	
Product and service design	Chapter 11	IMPROVING PRODUCTS AND SYSTEMS
Quality assurance	Chapter 12	
Facility location and layout design	Chapter 13	
Job design and work measurement	Chapter 14	

Planning for the Future

Operations managers must anticipate the future and plan for it today. Three activities that are focused on planning for the future are total quality management, forecasting, and improving technology and international integration of OM systems.

TOTAL QUALITY MANAGEMENT Total quality management (TQM) is primarily concerned with the principles and overall philosophy that drive an organization to seek quality in the products and services that it provides to customers. TQM is a corporate-level strategy that becomes an operations management strategy for manufacturing and service excellence. TQM is so prerequisite to OM success that it is presented in detail in Chapter 2.

FORECASTING Operations managers must be able to accurately forecast demand for timely production of their products. They must be able to forecast human resource needs to acquire necessary worker inputs into their transformation process. Managers must be acquainted with different types of forecasting that affect the OM system. We will examine various types of quantitative and nonquantitative forecasting techniques in Chapter 3.

IMPROVING TECHNOLOGY AND INTERNATIONAL INTEGRATION OF OM SYSTEMS International competition is forcing operations managers to develop global planning strategies. Adapting and integrating international strategies require operations managers to understand the various restrictive roles the integration of management resources can play, and the strategic opportunities offered by advanced OM technology. For example, manufacturing firms during the 1980s that chose a strategy of cost reduction to be competitive with international manufacturers found their strategy to be successful in the 1990s when coupled with the mid-1980s devaluation of the U.S. dollar. Indeed, exports in electrical machinery and small manufactured goods increased more than 130 percent from 1986 to 1990, and some U.S. manufacturing organizations were actually increasing their U.S. manufacturing operations rather than building new operations in foreign countries because it was less expensive to operate in the United States.[8] We discuss the internationalization of operations management in Chapter 15.

We also examine in Chapter 15 the operations manager and the role that technological change plays in the evolution and revolution of OM system dynamics. We culminate our discussion in that chapter with a review of the most recent technological advances introduced (and some not introduced) in previous chapters and outline strategies on how organizations can change rapidly to improve productivity, flexibility, and competitive advantages.

Planning and Controlling Operations

Another category of operations management activities involves basic planning and controlling activities. These activities include production planning, materials management, inventory management, and scheduling.

PRODUCTION PLANNING As previously stated, production planning activities involve setting and achieving goals. We will discuss the basics of strategic, tactical, and operational planning in Chapter 4. In Chapter 5, we will focus on planning activities that are specifically related to operations management planning of management resources.

MATERIALS MANAGEMENT The materials management activity involves the grouping of management functions supporting material flow. Materials management includes activities such as the purchase and internal control of production materials; the planning and control of work-in-process (unfinished products in various stages of production);

---

[8] S. Nasar, "Boom in Manufacturing Exports Provides Hope for U.S. Economy," *New York Times,* April 12, 1991, pp. 1, 22.

and the warehousing, shipping, and distribution of the finished product. We will examine the materials management activity in Chapter 6.

INVENTORY MANAGEMENT The inventory management activity is concerned with the planning and control of inventories. There are two general types of inventory: dependent demand inventory and independent demand inventory. Dependent demand inventory is made up of inventory items that are consumed within an organization to produce a finished product. For example, rubber—the raw material used by the Goodyear Company to produce automobile tires for consumers—is an example of a dependent demand inventory item. Dependent demand inventory items depend on consumer demand of finished products. Independent demand inventory comprises inventory items consumed by customers external to the organization. For example, a grocery store's inventory of flashlight batteries is an independent demand inventory item. Because of the importance inventory management plays in the operations management system, separate chapters are devoted to dependent (Chapter 7) and independent (Chapter 8) inventory management.

S

SCHEDULING Scheduling involves assigning specific tasks, jobs, and work for equipment, facilities, and human resources in accordance with a timed planning horizon. In Chapter 9, we will discuss scheduling activities in manufacturing and service operations. Because of the importance of project activities in operations management, Chapter 10 is devoted to this subject.

Improving Products and Systems

Operations management activities in the 1990s must also support continuous improvement of products and systems. These activities include product and service design, quality assurance, facility location analysis and layout design, and job design and work measurement.

PRODUCT AND SERVICE DESIGN Product and service design includes all the activities that are required to create and structure a product or service. Although the design stage largely involves design engineers and marketing personnel, operations managers are often included as well, to ensure that the end result is producible. Examples of activities in product design include performing cost analyses to determine if new product designs are economically feasible, linking activities between computer-aided design systems and actual production facilities, and sequencing activities to ensure an ordered sequence of production tasks to complete the product. We will examine product design for both manufacturing and service products in Chapter 11.

QUALITY ASSURANCE The quality assurance activity involves the rules and methodological and technological aspects of manufacturing and service product quality. It includes a comprehensive analysis of the entire operations management system from input to output on any attribute that can be used to define quality. Quality assurance seeks to implement TQM as an OM strategy. Examples of quality assurance include reducing product defects, maintaining a customer service department, and monitoring the quality of incoming raw materials. We will be examining quality assurance in Chapter 12.

FACILITY LOCATION AND LAYOUT DESIGN The facility location activity involves determining where to establish a manufacturing plant or a service facility. The layout design activity involves determining how the internal facility (departments, equipment, and service or work stations) will be arranged. In Chapter 13 we discuss typical location and design problems such as determining the best location of a retail outlet store, determining the best layout for a manufacturing company's various production departments, and determining the investment in workstation equipment necessary for an assembly operation.

S

JOB DESIGN AND WORK MEASUREMENT The job design activity involves the structuring of work tasks assigned to an employee. Job design is the study of the tasks that make up a job. The work measurement activity involves the timing of the tasks that comprise a job. In Chapter 14 we examine job design and work measurement activities such as determining employee performance measures, determining a fair day's work, and estimating the impact of fatigue on work performance.

Not all operations managers perform all of these activities. Many managers make a productive career out of performing just one of the activities listed in Figure 1-6. To be a successful operations manager, however, you must have some knowledge of all of these activities and the role they play in an organization.

COMMUNICATION IN OPERATIONS MANAGEMENT

In this age of information, operations managers must be able to communicate and interact with the people with whom they work and with those for whom the work is performed. We refer to communication or interaction within the organization as **cross-functional relations.** Communication or interaction with individuals outside the organization is referred to as **external relations.**

Cross-functional Relations

Operations managers perform their management functions and activities within the framework or structure of their organizations. The framework or structure that makes up an organization is often referred to as the internal environment of the organization. All managers in the organization can be grouped into either a line or staff position.

Line managers work to achieve the organization's objectives by supervising, delegating authority, and making work assignments. **Staff managers** work to achieve the organization's objectives indirectly by providing line managers with advice, suggestions, and research support. The relationship between line and staff managers can be simply expressed as "line commands" and "staff advises."

Operations managers are usually line managers. Some OM personnel, however, perform staff functions. For example, an industrial engineer who provides a line manager with technical advice concerning an OM system is performing a staff function. The organization chart for a small grain storage business is presented in Figure 1-7. The lawyer and accountant represent staff positions because they provide counsel and advice to line management. The staff positions are not part of the line that defines the flow of commands from the president down to the employees through the organization.

Organizations are also characterized as being flat or tall. A **flat organization** tends to have few layers of management, a structure that is characteristic of small firms such as the business depicted in Figure 1-7. A **tall organization** tends to have many levels of management, which is characteristic of large organizations such as the manufacturing business in Figure 1-8.

Organizations can also be structured by the primary product they offer their customers or by departmental areas within the organization. For example, the grain storage business in Figure 1-7 is structured under the president into three divisions, by the three S

FIGURE 1-7 ORGANIZATION CHART FOR A SMALL GRAIN STORAGE BUSINESS

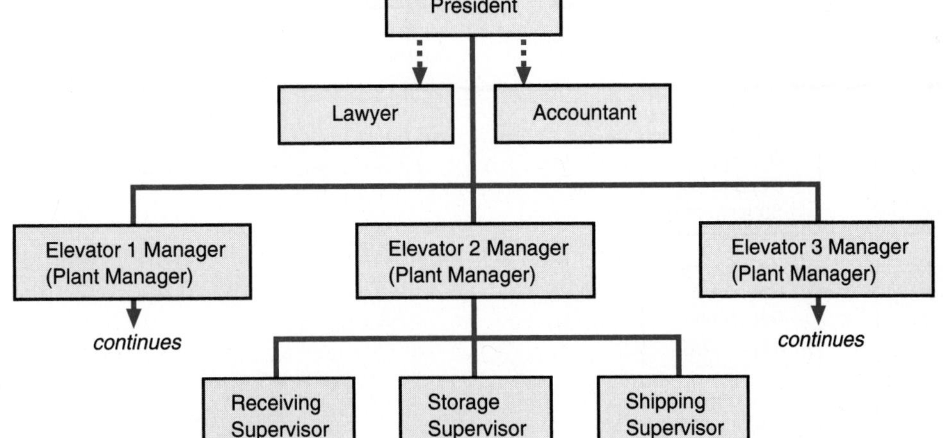

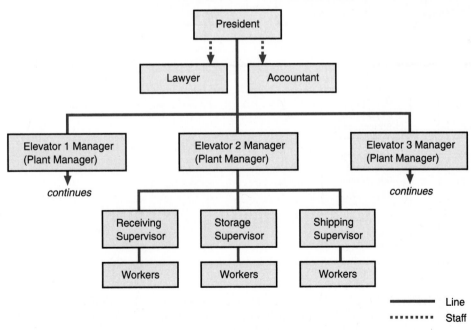

FIGURE 1-8 ORGANIZATION CHART FOR A LARGE MANUFACTURING BUSINESS

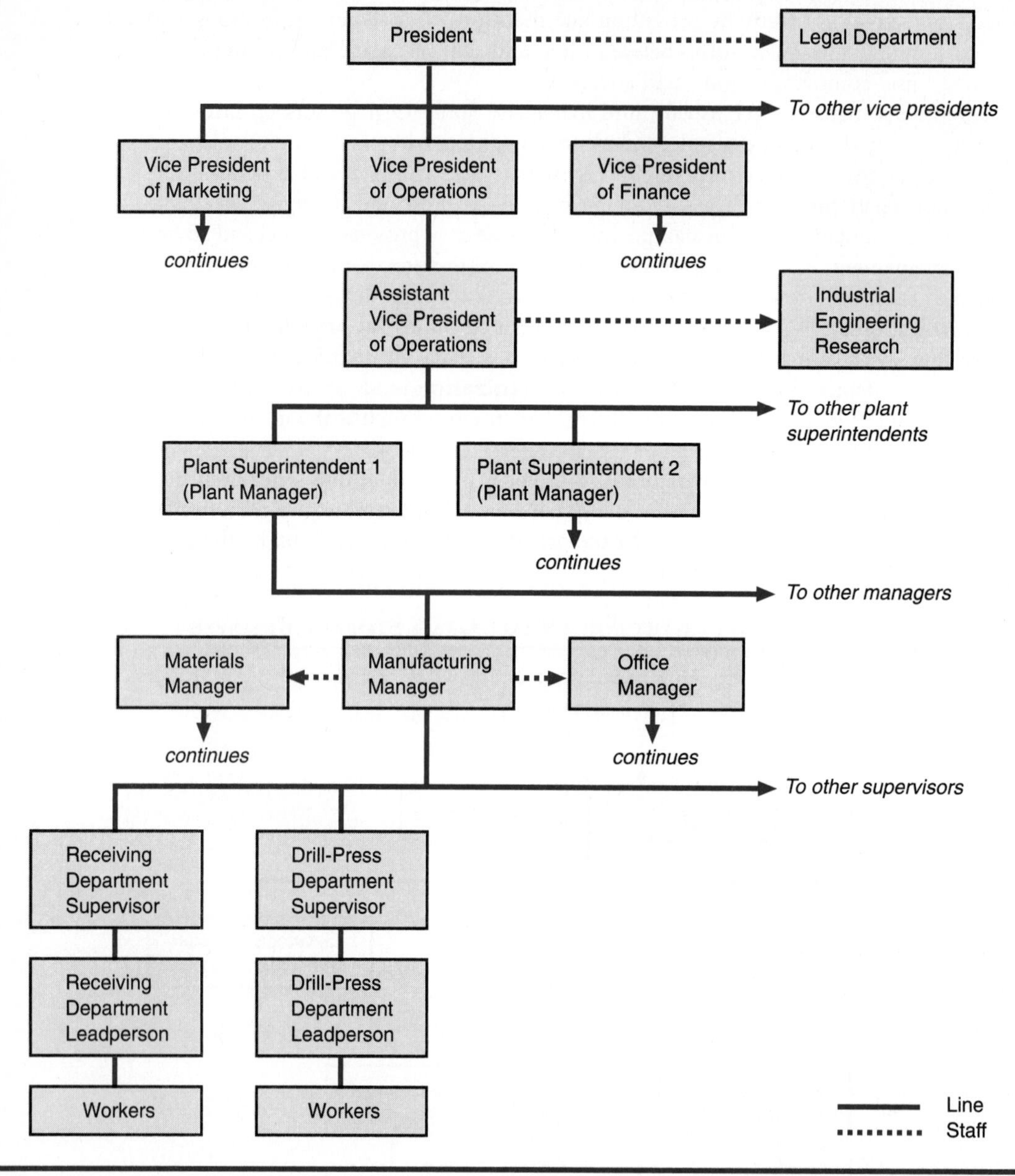

storage elevators it offers its customers. (Storage service is the company's product.) Other organizations, such as the one shown in Figure 1-8, are organized by the departmental areas of marketing, operations, finance, and others not shown such as personnel, accounting, and information systems.

Regardless of how the organization is structured, the operations manager must be able to successfully work and interact with the various departmental areas within the internal environment of the organization. To accomplish this interaction, the operations manager must understand what each of the departmental areas does for him or her and what he or she is expected to do for each department. Typical departmental areas within an organization's internal environment are presented in Figure 1-9 and include accounting, marketing, finance, information systems, personnel, technical specialists, and operations management. The two-way arrows in Figure 1-9 illustrate the interactive exchanges that take place between these seven departmental entities in the organization.

ACCOUNTING The accounting department in an organization performs financial reporting duties. The operations manager receives cost information and budgets from the accounting department relating to human resources, materials, and other inputs. This information is used in the OM control subsystem (see Figure 1-3). Accounting also provides many useful auditing functions necessary for controlling inventory and monitoring purchasing. The operations manager is usually expected to provide the accounting department with transaction data (such as receipts, bills, and shipping reports) describing all aspects of OM system activity. Because of recent advances in information technology, accounting functions have changed a great deal. We will be discussing new cost accounting methods and other accounting practice issues in later chapters.

FIGURE 1-9 DEPARTMENTAL AREAS WITHIN THE INTERNAL ENVIRONMENT OF THE ORGANIZATION

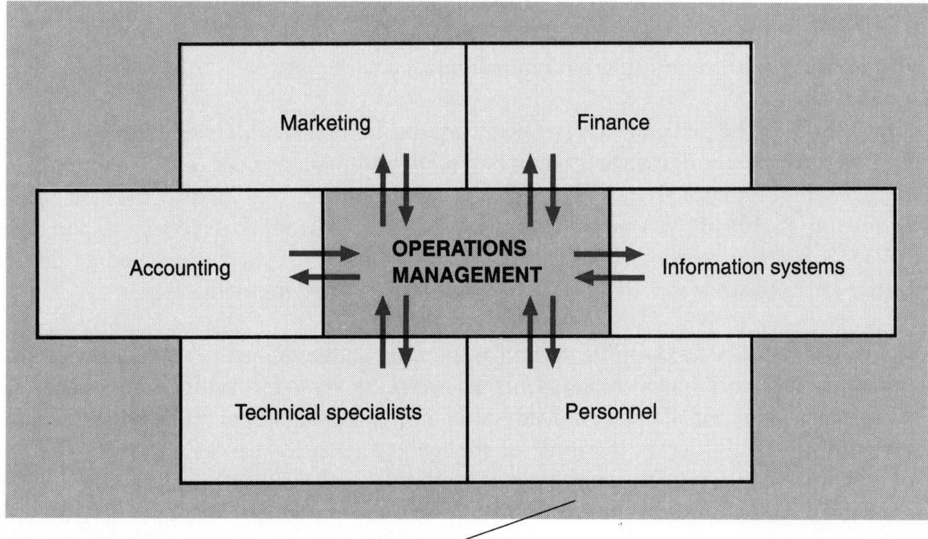

MARKETING The marketing department in an organization monitors customer needs and sells the output of the operations management system. The operations manager receives information from the marketing area that includes the number, quantity, and quality of products the OM system should provide. The marketing area also provides the OM control subsystem with information on how customers are responding to the OM system's output. The operations manager is usually expected to provide the desired output defined by the marketing department (that is, the product or service) in a timely manner. The operations manager is also expected to provide information on the capabilities of the OM system to meet customer product demands and expectations. Advances in design and order entry technology are changing the role of OM. We will discuss some of these changes in later chapters.

FINANCE The finance department in an organization obtains the maximum return on the company's investments and minimizes the company's cost of capital. The operations manager receives cost information, approval, and necessary funds for equipment and facility investment from the financial area. The operations manager is expected to provide the finance department with information, both technical and financial, on investment alternatives for evaluation purposes. As we will see in later chapters, the speed of technological change is altering the way financial benefits derived from technology are evaluated.

INFORMATION SYSTEMS The information systems department provides timely information to support decision making throughout an organization. The operations manager receives a wide variety of information and reports, including general information such as organizational objectives and detailed information such as an individual manufacturing department's work assignment for a particular day. The operations manager is expected to provide the information systems department with daily activities data on the OM system, information on the usefulness of the reports provided daily, and design change suggestions for future information report improvements.

PERSONNEL The personnel department acquires human resource input for the organization. The operations manager receives worker and management resource input from the personnel functional area. The operations manager is expected to provide information on the quantity, timing, and type of human resources necessary. Operations managers and the personnel department share the responsibility of screening and selecting job applicants as well as necessary training and development.

TECHNICAL SPECIALISTS The technical specialist department in many organizations represents specialized staff departments that can be included within the operations management functional area or outside of it. For example, a department that provides operations research (that is, the study of applied mathematics) can be a staff department for an entire organization providing mathematical modeling and analysis support for managers throughout the organization. Many operations managers are also using outside consultants who possess special expertise not available within the organization. Both specialists and consultants provide the operations manager with useful information on the present and future operation of manufacturing and service systems. The operations manager is expected to provide these specialists and consultants with the necessary information to allow them to analyze the OM system.

The operations manager is expected to provide some type of information to each of these functional areas. To provide such information, an operations manager must also be knowledgeable about each departmental area. We will examine OM concepts, procedures, and technologies throughout this text that are commonly used in all of these departments. By understanding these commonly used processes, operations managers can do a better job of interacting, communicating, and integrating management resources within the internal environment of the organization.

External Relations

We just discussed how the operations manager works within the internal environment of the organization. The organization's external environment (any entity outside of the organization) also affects the operations manager. The external environment shown in Figure 1-10 consists of entities such as customers, public interest groups, competitors, stockholders and owners, suppliers, and the government. Although the environment external to the organization can consist of many things, these six entities are of particular

FIGURE 1-10 THE ORGANIZATION AND THE EXTERNAL ENVIRONMENT

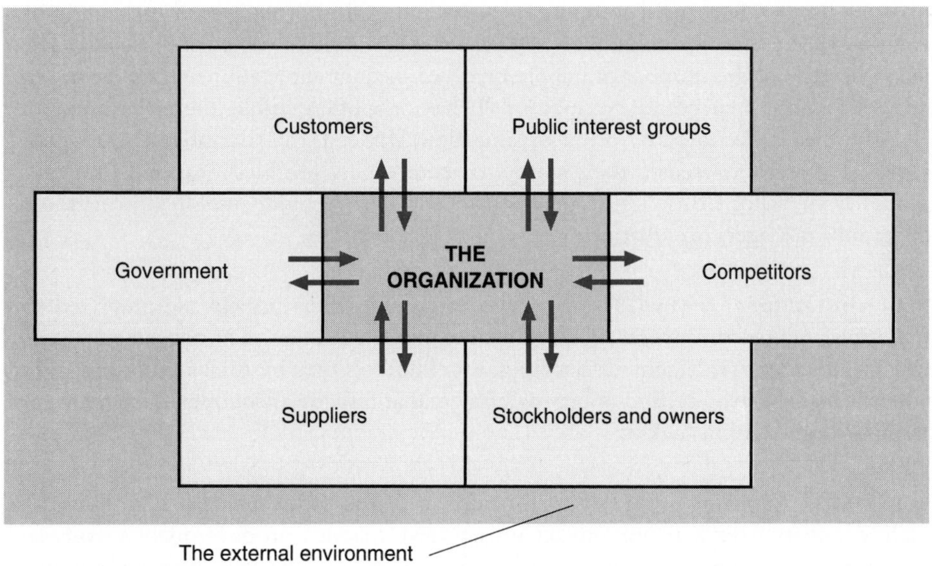

importance because of their influence on OM. The impact of the external environment often pressures the organization to make changes in the way it does business. The two-way arrows in Figure 1-10 illustrate the interactive exchange (or external relations) that takes place between these six entities and the organization. The operations manager must be able to cope with changes in the organization that are caused by the external environment. To cope with change, an operations manager must understand the role these entities play in the external environment.

CUSTOMERS Customers are the primary reason for any organization to exist. The old adage is "the customer is the king." Japanese organizations have gone one step further by saying, "The customer is not our king. The customer is our god." Customers do more than just consume the organization's output. Customers also provide useful information for operations managers on product improvements, quality, and distribution. They are the major motivators for OM flexibility and productivity. Customers also provide ideas on new products, technologies, and even competitive advantages.

PUBLIC INTEREST GROUPS Public interest groups, made up of public-spirited individuals, attempt to change what they perceive as injustices. They pressure or influence organizations and whole industries by activities such as product boycotts, which cause poor publicity and possibly lead to changes in the laws governing the operation of the organization. Public interest groups clearly help identify which of an organization's activities are unacceptable to consumers. For example, in one of operations management's areas of concern—water, air, and noise pollution—public interest groups have pressured organizations to improve technology that will reduce such pollution.

COMPETITORS Successful competitors provide useful information on improving operations. OM concepts, techniques, and practices are some of the most difficult to keep secret because of the number of people involved in their application and the actual size of OM systems. A successful competitor's behavior is often visible, therefore, and tends to be studied and copied by other organizations. Indeed, the success of some organizations is directly related to their ability to acquire new product ideas and OM techniques from other firms. Unsuccessful firms can also provide useful information to operations managers on what not to do in their operations.

STOCKHOLDERS AND OWNERS Stockholders and owners usually monitor, and can sometimes define, the overall goals of an organization. They may also take an active role in operations management activities. Stockholders can, by their ownership rights, vote to change personnel and operating policies that directly affect operations managers' planning and decision making.

SUPPLIERS Suppliers provide a major portion of the input into an OM system. As such, suppliers have a major impact on an OM system's product quality, cost, and distribution. Suppliers also provide useful information on new procedures, technologies, and products.

GOVERNMENT The entity *government* includes federal, state, and local governments. Collectively, these governments provide guidelines, laws, and restrictions on how managers perform their OM activities. The government also defines acceptable product quality for some products. For example, the U.S. Department of Agriculture grades meats.

Adapting to the changes that these six entities require of an operations management system is part of the challenge of integrating management resources. By being able to integrate the human, technology, and system resources within the OM functional area to serve and satisfy the needs of the external environment, the organization will be better able to achieve its organization mission and goals.

A BRIEF HISTORY OF OPERATIONS MANAGEMENT

The history of operations management can be viewed as a process of integrating evolving operations management concepts and technology over time. Because of the rapid change in OM concepts and technologies, we present the history of OM in three time periods: the Industrial Revolution, the development of managerial theory, and the development of managerial science and systems.

The Industrial Revolution

When the first settlers came to the Americas, operations management could be characterized by small job operations such as silversmiths and blacksmiths. The majority of OM activities took place on farms in typical limited-lot operations. This period lasted until about the 1770s.

Starting with the technological developments of the 1760s, factories began developing in the northeastern region of the United States. One of the first large-scale factories in the United States was started in 1790 near Providence, Rhode Island, by an experienced English textile mill manufacturer, Samuel Slater. It generated the first automatically produced cotton yarn in the United States. From the late 1770s through the 1850s, writers and researchers developed new and revolutionary concepts and management procedures. Adam Smith, an economist and philosopher, wrote the book *Wealth of Nations,* which provided the foundation for the United States' *laissez faire* economy and stressed the importance of the division of labor. Eli Whitney, who developed the cotton gin for separating seeds from cotton, introduced the concept of interchangeable parts in 1798. Other researchers, listed in Table 1-2, made many conceptual and procedural contributions to the advancement of management. The development of these concepts and procedures continued until about 1890.

TABLE 1-2 HISTORICAL CONTRIBUTIONS TO OPERATIONS MANAGEMENT

Approximate Date	*Contribution*	*Contributor*
1769	Steam engine used in industry	J. Watt
1770	Spinning jenny (textile machine)	J Hargreaves
1776	Economic justification of the division of labor	J. Perronet and A. Smith
1780	Job design and work standards	J. Watt and M. Boulton
1798	Use of interchangeable parts	E. Whitney
1832	Concepts in time study and wage differentials by skill grade	C. Babbage
1893	First alternating current generator and the first radio-controlled robot	N. Tesla
1911	Principles of scientific management and formalized time study methods	F. W. Taylor and M. L. Cooke
1911	Concepts in industrial psychology and applied motion studies in industry	F. Gilbreth and L. Gilbreth
1913	Moving assembly line	H. Ford
1913	Production planning charting systems and morale studies	H. Gantt
1915	Economic order quantity inventory system	F. W. Harris
1916	Waiting line theory	A. K. Erlang
1927	Hawthorne studies on worker motivation	E. Mayo
1931	Statistical sampling tables for inspection and quality control	W. Shewhart, H. F. Dodge, H. G. Romig, and R. Fisher
1934	Work sampling	L. H. C. Tippett
1941	Transportation methodologies	F. L. Hitchcock
1947	Simplex algorithm for linear programming	G. B. Dantzig
1950	Equipment replacement theory	G. Terborgh and J. Dean
1957	Program evaluation and review technique (PERT) project evaluation procedure	U.S. Navy
1957	Critical path method (CPM) project evaluation procedure	J. E. Kelly and M. R. Walker
1958	Group technology principles first proposed	S. P. Mitrofanov
1960	Mainframe transistorized computers	IBM (U.S.)
1962	First industrial robot	H. A. Ernst Unimation (U.S.)
1962	Quality control circles and just-in-time (JIT) concepts	T. Ohno
1963	Computer-aided design (CAD)	I. Sutherland
1964	Material requirements planning (MRP) inventory system	J. Orlicky

TABLE 1-2 (CONTINUED)

Approximate Date	*Contribution*	*Contributor*
1965	Flexible manufacturing systems (FMS)	Molin Ltd. (U.K.)
1977	Microcomputers for home and industry use	S. Wozniak and S. Jobs
1982	Japanese JIT and TQC concepts introduced in U.S.	W. E. Deming, Y. Monden, and J. M. Juran
1985	CIM protocol computer software	General Motors (U.S.)
Present	Computer-integrated manufacturing (CIM) and computer-integrated service systems (CISS)	IBM, Hewlett-Packard, Arthur Andersen

The Development of Managerial Theory

The development of managerial theory spanned about fifty years, and includes the management movement and the human relations period.

THE MANAGEMENT MOVEMENT From about 1890 to 1927 the concepts and procedures of management underwent a formalization process. The practice of management was evolving into a science. Professional operations management societies emerged during this period: The American Society of Mechanical Engineers (1910), The Society to Promote the Science of Management (1910), The Industrial Relations Association of America (1914), and The Society of Industrial Engineers (1917). Developments in the concepts and procedures of management also underwent important changes by researchers whose contributions are still included in basic OM texts. Frederick W. Taylor, for example, wrote *Principles of Scientific Management* in 1911, which proposed that scientific laws govern human resource productivity and therefore managers could use these laws to increase work effort. Other researchers at the same time, such as Frank and Lillian Gilbreth, reinforced Taylor's concepts and included a more complete psychological analysis of the impact of the concepts on worker behavior.

This period in the history of operations management was also marked by technological improvements. In 1913 Henry Ford started the first moving assembly line that typified the classical repetitive operation in the United States.

THE HUMAN RELATIONS PERIOD The period from about 1927 through the 1940s brought major changes in operations management concepts. The concepts of the management movement, particularly those put forward by Taylor, were changed radically by the Hawthorne Studies conducted by Elton Mayo and others from 1927 to 1932 at the Western Electric Plant in Hawthorne, Illinois. These studies sought to confirm Taylor's principle that less light in a workplace would generate less productivity by the workers. Surprisingly, as researchers reduced the light in the work area, workers actually increased their productivity. The results of the study showed that just being chosen for the study motivated workers to continually improve production regardless of environmental conditions. This apparent rebuff of Taylor's concepts motivated many organizations in the 1930s and 1940s to establish a human relations or personnel department to foster more motivated and productive workers.

The Development of Managerial Science and Systems

The development of managerial science and systems has spanned the last fifty years, and includes the management science period and the integrated systems period.

THE MANAGEMENT SCIENCE PERIOD The management science period covers the history of operations management from about 1940 through the 1970s. Management science and operations management are separate fields, but many of the technologies and procedures currently used in OM were developed by management science researchers. The development of complex model solution procedures, such as George Dantzig's simplex method in 1947, permitted the typical OM multivariable problem to be systemically solved. This period also saw the development of mainframe computers in the early 1950s that researchers used to solve large-scale OM problems.

During this period the field of operations management emerged in colleges of industrial engineering and business administration. Numerous societies were created to help professionalize the field of OM. One of the more notable societies is the American Production and Inventory Control Society (APICS). In recognition of the importance of OM in U.S. business, the primary business college accreditation organization, the American Assembly of Collegiate Schools of Business (AACSB), started requiring production and operations management content in business curriculum.

THE INTEGRATED SYSTEMS PERIOD Several changes in operations management concepts, procedures, and technologies have been taking place since the late 1970s that represent a change in direction for research and practice of OM. These changes include an increased shift in the emphasis of OM management practices toward integrated computerized systems and new Japanese and European OM concepts.

Advances in computer technology and the development of microcomputers in the late 1970s have motivated organizations of all sizes to integrate internal organization subsystems such as purchasing with inventory management. This integration has usually been achieved by the adoption of a computer-based, large-scale management information system (MIS system) or, in the operations management area, a computer-integrated manufacturing system (CIM system). While the concept of large-scale MIS or CIM systems has existed since the 1960s, commercial OM software systems for mainframe computers integrating most or all of the OM subsystems have only been available since the 1970s. The development in the 1980s of universal or protocol software, which permits a common computer language to integrate OM technology, has enabled U.S. organizations to more quickly integrate all areas of their operations.

Another characteristic of this period in operations management history is the emergence of Japanese and European production and operations management techniques. In Japan, pioneers such as Taiichi Ohno helped develop and implement for Toyota the quality improvement ideas now being implemented by U.S. manufacturing. Researchers such as W. Edwards Deming and Yasuhiro Monden and corporations such as General Motors and Molin (U.K.) have helped bring European and Japanese product quality concepts, procedures, and techniques to the United States. Integrating these foreign methods into U.S. operations management manufacturing and service systems is a major challenge facing managers now and into the twenty-first century.

INTEGRATING MANAGEMENT RESOURCES: USING COMPUTER-INTEGRATED SYSTEMS FOR COMPETITIVE ADVANTAGE

As previously stated, this section of each chapter will be devoted to explaining how integrating one or more of the management resources—human, technological or system resources—can achieve operations management objectives or strategies for improved productivity, flexibility, and competitive advantage. Because of the important contribution to the OM system that computer-integrated systems (CIS) are making, we devote this section in Chapter 1 to an overview and introduction of CIS as a means of achieving a competitive advantage.

It is generally accepted by both operations management practitioners and scholars that much of the future of OM is one of computer-integrated systems (CIS).[9] Both manufacturing and service systems are becoming increasingly computer integrated. Examples of this integration are "islands of automation," where computer-controlled manufacturing is limited to small areas (such as a line of computer-controlled robots painting objects), and computer systems contained within a single departmental area such as accounting. The term *computer-aided manufacturing* (CAM) originated from these limited computer applications. A fully integrated computer system, on the other hand, integrates all the departments within an organization. This might be achieved with a management information system (MIS) used to integrate information systems between departments, or a computer-integrated manufacturing system used to integrate the OM department activities.

[9] See R. E. Ducharme and D. A. Lewis, "The Academic/Practitioner Gap in Production and Inventory Management," *Production and Inventory Management,* 28, No. 1 (1987), 88–95; A. Satir and S. Goyal, "Undergraduate Curriculum for Production and Operations Management," *Production and Inventory Management,* 28, No. 2 (1987), 12–14; T. Baer, "Justifying CIM: The Numbers Really Are There," *Managing Automation* (March 1988), 30–35; and R. Miller, "Where CIM Is Just Business as Usual," *Managing Automation* (August 1988), 62–67.

Computer-integrated Manufacturing Systems

To introduce CIMs, let's examine the operation presented in Figure 1-11. Currently, manufacturing organizations are moving in the direction depicted in Figure 1-11, but few are competely computer integrated.

In CIM, a computer, rather than a human being, is used to direct the flow of product through a manufacturing organization. As we can see in Figure 1-11, customer orders are taken and entered into the computer system by the marketing department who use a computer terminal or a microcomputer networked (wired) to the main computer. The main computer acts as a leader to direct all of the computerized production activities (product design, manufacturing, inventory storage). For orders requiring the development of new products, product design engineers take the marketing department's product description and, with the help of *computer-aided design* (CAD) software, develop, test, and design a new product completely within the computer system. The resulting new product designs are channeled by the main computer back to the marketing department and possibly to the customer for acceptance of design specifications. The main computer also directs the CAD system to send the new product designs to a minicomputer that is on or near the site of the manufacturing facility. (In some facilities, the main computer does not use minicomputers, but performs all of the activities itself.) The main computer might also send the orders for existing parts or products to the minicomputer, whose job it is to direct the manufacturing and delivery of the finished product. During the interactive sessions with the minicomputer, delivery time estimates are made using operations management methodology-based software and sent to the marketing department for customer service information.

The minicomputer, using a *data base* (an extensive file of information), defines the specific work requirements for each product on each order and conveys them to the individual workstations in the manufacturing facility. The network of workstations is usually linked with the minicomputer or, in some cases, has individual microcomputer-processing capability to perform independent computer operations. The minicomputers, as well as the main computer, use many of the operations management methodologies and techniques we will describe in later chapters to plan, schedule, and direct the activities of the computer systems and human resources at their command.

Once a work order is received at a workstation by a human being or robot, the work order is processed by entering it in the computer system for control and order-tracking purposes. For finished manufactured products (or unfinished products within the manufacturing department), the minicomputer directs an *automated guided vehicle* (AGV) to move the products from and to the appropriate locations for additional processing or storage.

The minicomputer is also in control of the *automated storage and automated retrieval* (AS/AR) facility. The AS/AR facility can be a humanless operation that stores, retrieves, and prepares product orders for shipping. The minicomputer directs the automated systems, including robots and AGVs, to specific product storage locations so that customer orders can be picked, packed, and shipped according to

Figure 1-11 A Computer-integrated Manufacturing (CIM) System

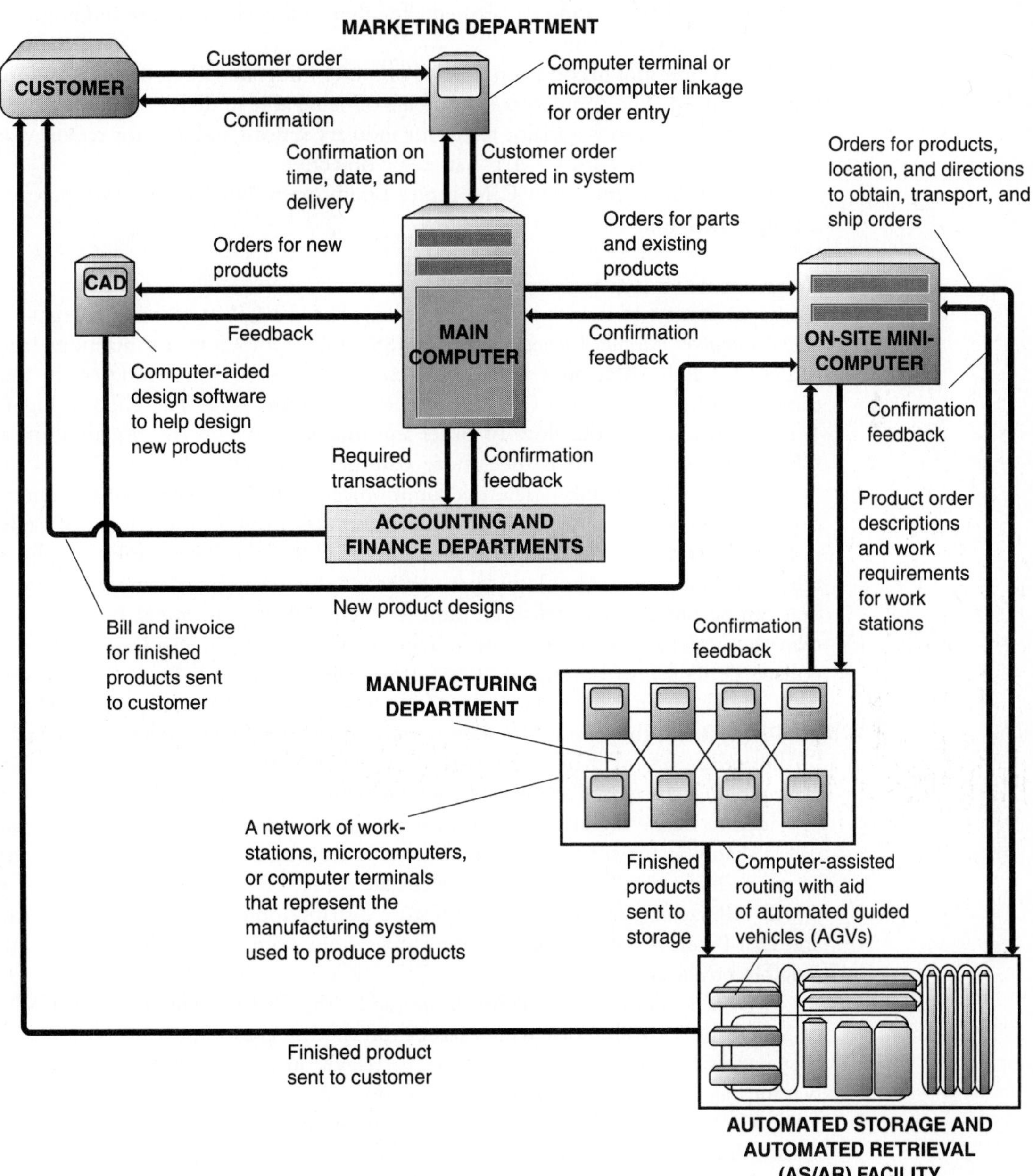

customers' unique specifications. At the same time that ordered units are being shipped, the main computer processes the customer's bill and channels it through the finance and accounting departments for their information before sending it to the customer for payment.

As organizations become more fully computer integrated, their order processing time is reduced. The competitive advantage of being able to deliver a product faster than competitors can is a major factor for industry success and a major reason why firms are moving toward CIM as a strategic objective.

We will be refining the CIM topics briefly mentioned here as we progress through the book.

Computer-integrated Service Systems

Computerization of service organizations has created a CIM version of integration called *computer-integrated service systems* (CISS). Like CIM, few organizations have achieved a fully integrated CISS, but many have made some progress in that direction. One version of a CISS is presented in Figure 1-12. The CISS in Figure 1-12 has the same basic flow of order information through the organization as CIM. One element that is seen more commonly in CISS than in CIM is the "telecommunication link." The telecommunication link between the customer's order and the service organization's main computer may be in the form of cable, radio, telegraph, telefax, telephone, or television system. The breakthroughs in telecommunications technologies have provided the means by which service products can be ordered and delivered more conveniently to customers. For example, telecommunication systems are now being used by state universities to broadcast college courses into remote locations of a state where schools cannot be cost-justified. Although it is certainly true that telecommunications can be and are used in CIM systems, they are more often associated with modern CISS.

S

Providing any service may involve both tangible and intangible products. For example, a lecture in a college cannot be delivered unless a physical facility is provided to house the class, and you cannot get your hair washed by a beautician unless shampoo is available. The need to consider tangible items with the delivery of intangible service products may necessitate some CIM system elements such as an AS/AR facility. In fact, department store distribution centers like those of Sears and J.C. Penneys are considered service operations even though they handle only tangible products.

S

A typical example of a CISS is illustrated by the Cable Value Network (CVN) of Minneapolis, Minnesota, which has begun the integration of its television mass merchandising sales operations. Most of its television customers call in orders to a waiting sales staff for products promoted on a 24-hour merchandising show. In 1988, CVN integrated the customer-ordering function directly into its computer system; human sales staff now deals only with the occasional problem. Customers now place orders directly into the CVN computer system by following a set of interactive instructions. The customers' telephone actually becomes a computer terminal link between the customer and CVN's main order-processing computer.

S

FIGURE 1-12 A COMPUTER-INTEGRATED SERVICE SYSTEM (CISS)

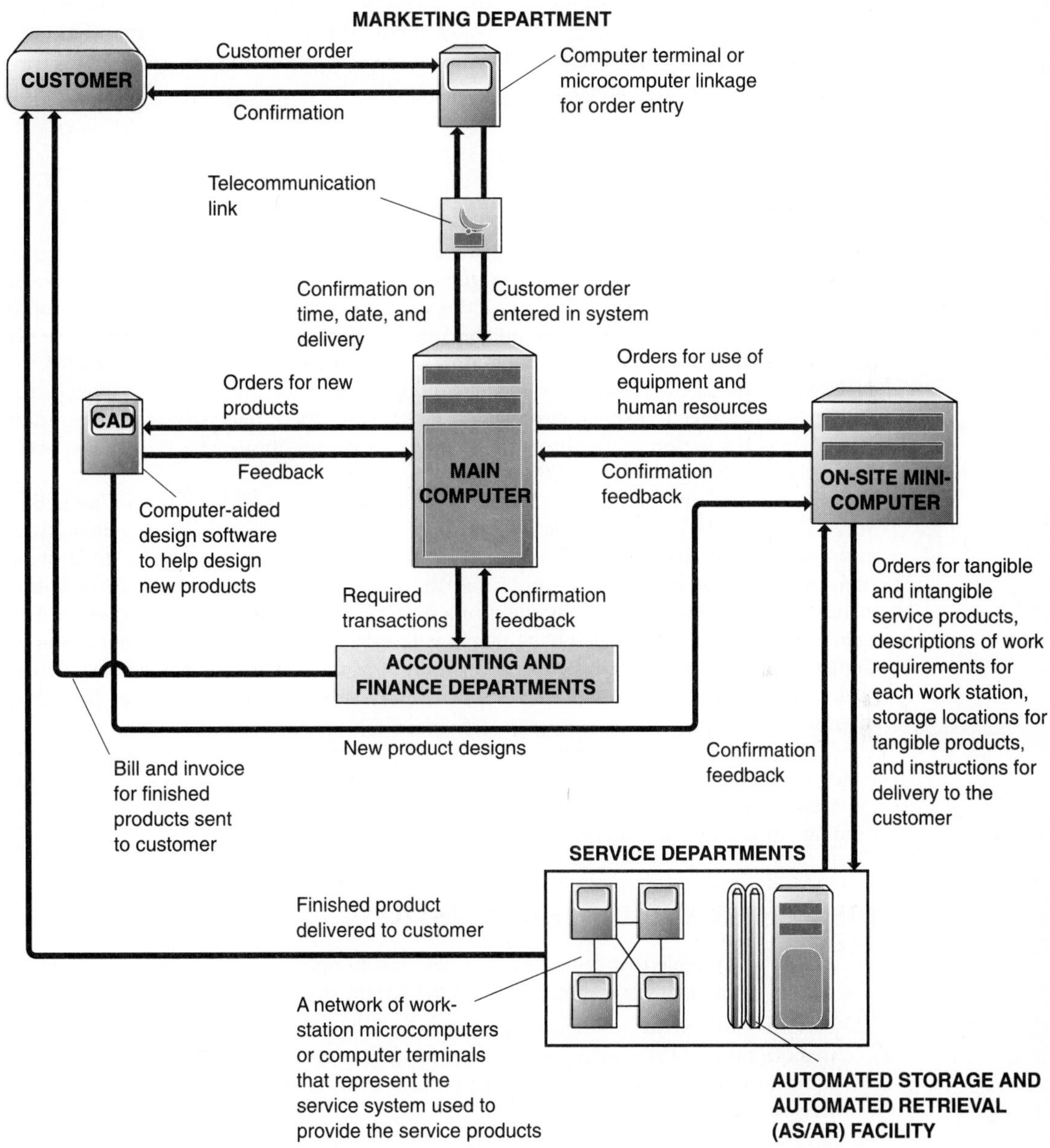

Although no research has been published on this CISS, it is obvious that the customers benefit from the system because linking directly to the order entry computer reduces order-entry time. Customers are given a code number that accesses their address file, which saves them additional ordering time. This time savings, particularly for the high-volume, repeat customer, can represent an important competitive advantage. It also benefits the company by reducing the need for sales staff.

SUMMARY

The purpose of this chapter has been to provide an overview of what operations management is about and of the basic prerequisite management concepts. We have introduced the concept of the OM system, its functional relationships within an organization, and the impact of the internal and external environment on the operations manager. In this chapter, we also presented numerous definitions of commonly used OM terms, a brief history of OM, and an introduction to the contents of the remaining chapters of the text. This introductory chapter was designed to explain what OM is about, why OM is necessary as a field of study, and where OM personnel perform their jobs in an organization. The rest of this text is devoted to the *how* and *when* of OM.

We end this introductory chapter with an article entitled "The Key to Competitive Success in the 1990's." The article reemphasizes the importance of the management topics introduced in this chapter as well as touches on most of the topics we will be discussing in later chapters. It is interesting to note that the article views future success in operations management requiring the development of a strategic plan around the integration of management resources. This article's basic theme will surface many times throughout this book. (In reading the article you should not worry about OM terms that have not yet been defined in the text. Everything discussed in this article will be mentioned several times throughout the rest of the book.)

The photo insert that presents a tour of the General Motors Saturn plant provides a pictorial overview of a 1990s state-of-the-art integrated management resource manufacturing facility. The Saturn plant typifies the general direction in which all businesses are heading—toward a fully integrated operation.

DISCUSSION AND REVIEW QUESTIONS

1. Create an example that can be used to describe an operations management system. Be sure to define the five elements of the OM system as they apply to your example.
2. Identify each of the following operations by whether it is a service OM system or manufacturing OM system: (1) a college football team winning a game, (2) a discount food store retailing food, (3) a college professor conducting a class, and (4) a meal at a five-star restaurant.
3. Identify each of the operations in question **2** by type (job, job-lot, repetitive or continuous process, limited-lot, or project).
4. Explain the difference between a corporate strategy and an OM strategy. Give an example to illustrate this difference.
5. What does *cross-functional* mean?

6. Discuss how the OM concepts of productivity, efficiency, effectiveness, and the productivity cycle are related.
7. What is the difference between productivity and the productivity cycle?
8. Explain how integrating management resources will help satisfy OM needs in the 1990s and beyond.
9. Describe in your own words OM's relationship to the internal environment of the organization.
10. Describe in your own words OM's relationship to the external environment of the organization.
11. Of the historical contributions listed on Table 1-2, which do you think is the most important and why?
12. If you had to choose as the most serious one of the current problems facing operations managers, which would you choose and why?
13. What is CIM? Give an example.
14. Define CISS and give an example.

ARTICLE 1-1

THE KEY TO COMPETITIVE SUCCESS IN THE 1990s

by Frank W. Hazeltine and Ross J. Baragallo

In the past, the American manufacturer has set the rules for the manufacturing game. He has viewed himself as not only the key player, but also the referee. However, there are new players, and the rules of the manufacturing game have dramatically changed. The American manufacturer is no longer guaranteed winning, and therefore must understand these new rules, as well as how to play the game, in order to successfully compete in the future.

Today's field of play for manufacturing is global in nature, which implies intense competition from foreign manufacturers. This competition does not solely come from Japanese manufacturers, but also from market entry by the Koreans, the Chinese, and other developing countries. In addition, this competition will surely be intensified by recent developments such as the European Single Market Act and legislation on the Canadian Free Trade Agreement. These developments will aid in breaking down barriers to trade which, in the past, helped keep American manufacturers on top.

American management can no longer be content in competing on financial strategies alone, but must now learn how to compete on a price and quality basis. Today's consumer is much more sophisticated, and will no longer accept delays in shipment, substandard quality, and poor service. Based on these recent events, how can the American manufacturer once again be a winner in the new game of global manufacturing? The key to competitive success is to develop, implement, and adhere to a *manufacturing strategy*. This strategy should provide the basis for continuous, incremental improvement, by which organizations can regain their competitive advantage.

STRATEGY DEVELOPMENT TODAY

Strategy development for most organizations has a heavy financial emphasis dealing in short-term profit objectives, overreliance on mergers and acquisitions to gain competitive stature, and a misdirected em-

---

Source: Reprinted with permission from *P&IM Review*, February 1990 issue, copyright 1990 TDA Publications Inc.

phasis on labor cost reductions. Top management constantly feels the pressure of U.S. financial markets, and thereby misses the real issue of building for *long term competitiveness.* Many times, mergers and acquisitions fail to add value to the corporation, and therefore miss the intended goal of increasing competitive stature. In today's manufacturing environment, labor cost accounts for roughly 10 percent of total product cost. Efforts focused on reducing labor costs only mis-allocate scarce resources that could more appropriately be used in reducing material and overhead costs. These areas are where the real opportunities exist for cost reduction.

In addition, the strategic planning process fails to consider the critical element of human resources and its continued development. In today's rapidly changing technological environment, acquired skills of manufacturing personnel become obsolete faster than ever before. This fact makes corporate education critical to the continued success of organizations, and must therefore be a key pillar in any future strategic plans.

The critical weakness of current strategy development is the failure to provide plans for the changing environment. Manufacturing organizations tend to be reactive, rather than *pro-active* in dealing with factors that impact day-to-day operations. This leads to extremely inefficient allocation of scarce resources, and hinders the ability to constantly improve operations and remain competitive.

STRATEGY DEVELOPMENT IN THE 1990s

Corporate strategy development in the future must have an enhanced focus on manufacturing. Those companies that are successfully competing today are doing so by emphasizing cost and quality in manufacturing.

These organizations have learned the strategic elements necessary to compete in the global marketplace. The key strategic elements can be grouped into three distinct categories: (1) Flexibility; (2) Integrated Technology; and (3) Human Factor.

A thorough understanding of the above principles can mean the difference between success or extinction in the 1990s.

If there is one overriding element needed to successfully compete in the future, it is flexibility. Flexible manufacturing organizations can respond more quickly to changing customer tastes and values. Manufacturing flexibility is the ability to change production of one product type to another with minimal down-time and disruption. Flexibility is achieved through reduced set-up times, cross-training of employees, the use of group technology work centers, efficient layout of equipment, improved supply-chain management, and simultaneous engineering.

One of the major challenges facing manufacturers is to fully adapt to today's shorter product life cycles. Those organizations that can satisfy today's sophisticated consumer will reap the benefits of increased market share. In addition, flexible organizations have the ability to more fully utilize available capacity, thereby reducing cost to manufacture and achieving greater output per capital dollar invested.

The second key element to consider when developing manufacturing strategy is integrated technology. Few people would dispute the importance of utilizing technology as a mechanism to achieve strategic goals. However, with the vast array of technological solutions available today, the problem becomes choosing the correct solution. Many companies have implemented a series of projects utilizing advanced technologies, but have not been able to achieve their intended strategic objectives. The result is what is referred to as "islands of automation," or specific areas of implemented technology, not linked with other areas in the organization. This creates a situation where the optimal benefits of these new technologies are not realized.

Integrated technology requires the effective implementation of advanced systems and techniques that facilitate the management decision making process. This is accomplished by the process of networking information and providing access to data throughout the organization. A typical benefit of integrated technology is the reduction in product cost and the R&D life cycle. By linking design engineering with manufacturing engineering ("simultaneous engineering"), many of the costs associated with new product introductions are avoided because the product is designed to accommodate the manufacturing process. In addition, the life cycle is reduced through the elimination of time-consuming product re-designs.

The use of integrated technology has obvious implications on product quality. Products can be improved through faster communication of defects from the field directly to the plant floor for necessary corrective action. Product design changes are easily communicated to other areas within the organization, as well as to suppliers. Problems in the production process can be communicated to manufacturing engineering for quicker resolution. The integration of advanced production methodologies with inspection techniques can also aid in the improvement of product quality by locating defects and allowing for their correction before a significant volume of finished product is produced.

One major weakness exhibited in today's strategy development is the lack of adequate consideration of the human factor and its impact on an organization's competitive ability. An organization's employees must be viewed as its most significant resource, and therefore the area of greatest potential. Employees, in this context, refers to *all* members within the organization—from the "executive suite" to the "shop floor." The shop floor workers represent a major, untapped asset in most organizations. Who would know better about product improvement and work place design than the person responsible for actually building the product?

In order to optimally utilize an organization's employees, it is necessary that a corporate culture for improvement be in place. This means that employee involvement and development must be both encouraged and nurtured by management, and not merely be given "lip service." How many times have organizations failed in their attempts to implement state-of-the-art systems by not having the active participation and commitment of the employees? Such commitment can only be gained through the continuous enhancement of employees' technical skills, so that they are prepared to work with tomorrow's new technologies. In addition, multi-functional employees, who are versed in these new technologies, will provide the added benefits of enhanced flexibility and quality.

A major component of management's role in the next decade will be to develop and motivate employees. The current "adversarial" relationship that exists between management and line employees must give way to a relationship based on mutual trust and respect. As much as 50 percent of a line manager's time should be spent in these efforts. Future performance measures of line managers must be based on this key principle.

Effective manufacturing strategy requires that all three key elements be integrated. This integration increases the probability of successful implementation.

In order to implement the three strategic elements of flexibility, integrated technology, and the human factor, the manufacturing strategy must incorporate the necessary tools. Manufacturing management approaches are one example of tools required to assist in the achievement of these strategic elements. Just-In-Time manufacturing principles, Total Quality Control, and Supply Chain Management are representative of the types of proven management approaches that will help American manufacturers to become world class competitors again.

Any strategy that calls for the use of manufacturing tools must include a thorough understanding of technology and its impact on an organization's effectiveness. The use of technology in manufacturing has changed dramatically over the past few decades, and there is every reason to expect that this trend will continue through the 1990's. Manufacturing management must therefore allocate resources to stay abreast of these changes. Though there is plenty of technology currently available, the challenge becomes what technologies are appropriate for the specific manufacturing environment. Therefore, strategy development must appraise an organization's current situation, as well as its ability to adapt to future improvements. Some of the proven technological tools available for evaluation and incorporation in strategy development are: (1) Computer-Integrated Manufacturing; (2) Manufacturing Resource Planning; (3) Computer Aided Design/Manufacturing; (4) Robotics; and (5) Flexible Manufacturing Systems.

The above is not meant to be all-inclusive, but to merely serve as a sampling of the types of proven technologies that can be used in improving manufacturing competitiveness. The key point, however, is to select the appropriate solutions based on the manufacturing environment and organization's needs.

Technology, in and of itself, will not lead to significant competitive advantage. In order to fully exploit the benefits of technology, it must be combined with the involvement and commitment of all levels of employees in an organization. People, therefore, must be viewed as a tool by which an organization enhances its competitive stature when developing manufacturing strategy. How can management change its practices to fully utilize its people?

The manager's major role in the 1990s will be to facilitate this process. His/her responsibilities will include:

- Planning
- Motivating
- Educating
- Training

The intended objective of this is to create a culture and environment that encourages participation of all levels of employees. Managers should not be measured on short term objectives as in the past, but rather based on their ability to foster this cultural change. Examples of these measurements could include percent of cross-trained employees in a department, number of new cost-saving ideas generated and implemented, and percent of corporate education objectives met or exceeded.

The benefits that can be realized by fully utilizing people are significant and long term. They include enhanced flexibility to enable quicker response to market changes, improved product quality, reduced production cycle times, reduced waste, and increased productivity.

CONCLUSION

Staying competitive in the next decade will require the development of, and commitment to, a strategy focused on improving manufacturing cost and quality. Manufacturing's role in the next decade will be to provide a sustainable competitive advantage for the entire organization. Strategies driven by marketing or finance alone will not be sufficient to effectively compete in the changing global market place. The process of developing a manufacturing strategy must consider the key strategic elements of flexibility, integration of technology, and the human factor. The effective utilization of the human asset, more than any other strategic element, must not be overlooked, since this represents the greatest untapped resource in any organization.

Many tools are available to manufacturing management that can facilitate the implementation of these strategic elements. It is the responsibility of today's manufacturing managers to be familiar with these tools and how they are used. It is also their obligation to communicate potential benefits to top management.

Development of an effective manufacturing strategy is a complex and time-consuming task. It requires commitment and involvement from all levels of manufacturing management. It is an evolving, long-term process that lays the foundation, and creates the direction necessary, for future improvement. Without this direction, the efforts of the entire organization will not be focused. Adherence and dedication to this concept will enable American manufacturers to once again be the winner in the game of global manufacturing.

2 Total Quality Management

CHAPTER OUTLINE

CHAPTER OBJECTIVES

The material in this chapter should prepare you to do the following:

1. Describe several different approaches to defining quality
2. Explain why total quality management (TQM) is necessary
3. Describe several TQM principles and explain the role of the human resources function in their implementation
4. Describe several TQM tactics
5. Describe concurrent engineering and explain how it is related to TQM
6. Explain how empowerment of personnel is a technique of TQM
7. Describe a strategy for implementing TQM
8. Describe the Malcolm Baldrige National Quality Award
9. Cite examples of how TQM has helped organizations achieve manufacturing or service excellence
10. Explain how integrating TQM in an organization can result in a competitive advantage.

We live today in a global economic system: A borderless economic system is gradually becoming reality. Emergence of the European Economic Community has the potential to change greatly the economic map of the world. The United States has been working with Canada and Mexico toward a free trade agreement. In borderless global economic systems, the consumer has greater freedom in product choice. The consumer becomes king and determines the success or failure of any business organization.

In a consumer-dominated economic system, meeting or exceeding the customer's requirements is a prerequisite for survival. In the marketplace of the 1990s and beyond, one of the most prerequisite concepts to success in operations management (OM) is product or service quality. *Quality* can be defined in a number of different ways—according to transcendent, product-based, user-based, manufacturing-based, or value-based approaches.

According to the **transcendent** view, quality is synonymous with "innate excellence." This approach claims that quality cannot be defined precisely: It is a simple, unanalyzable property we learn to recognize only through experience. Cadillac, Mercedes-Benz, and Rolls-Royce are products of the automobile industry that have achieved this level of excellence.

Product-based definitions view quality as a precise and measurable variable. Differences in quality reflect differences in the quantity of some ingredient or attribute possessed by a product. High-quality ice cream has a high butterfat content; fine rugs have a large number of knots per square inch. This approach lends a vertical or hierarchical dimension to quality because goods can be ranked according to the amount of the desired attribute they possess. This approach, however, has limitations as well. A one-to-one correspondence between product attribute and quality does not always exist. For example, it is difficult for a non-expert to explain in detail the differences in quality between a master artist's work and that of an undergraduate student. When quality is a matter of aesthetics, the product-based approach is lacking, for it fails to accommodate differences in tastes.

In the **user-based** approach, the goods or services that best satisfy individual consumers' different wants or needs are regarded as having the highest quality. This view of quality is idiosyncratic and personal. It is also highly subjective and focuses on issues of "fitness for use" by the individual consumer. For example, a student using a microcomputer for the first time might evaluate the quality of the computer substantially differently than would an experienced user who better understands user friendliness.

While user-based definitions of quality are rooted in consumer preferences, **manufacturing-based** definitions focus on producers of goods and services and are primarily concerned with engineering and manufacturing practices. Virtually all manufacturing-based definitions identify quality as conformance to requirements. Once design or specifications have been established, any deviation implies a reduction in quality. So the quality of a twelve-ounce can of beer will be determined by whether the can actually contains twelve ounces. Any deviation from the stated twelve-ounce manufacturing specifications is viewed as a deviation from the desired quality level.

A **value-based** approach defines quality in terms of costs and prices. A quality product is therefore one that provides performance or conformance at an acceptable price or cost. An inexpensive product is expected to be of lower quality than a similar, more expensive product.

However quality is to be defined, its management is a primary factor in the survival and success of all organizations. Whether public or private,[1] manufacturing[2] or service,[3] all organizations must successfully manage the quality of their products in the highly competitive, global markets of the 1990s.

During the early 1980s the subject area of managing quality in operations management had evolved into what is called *total quality control* (*TQC*).[4] TQC is an effective philosophy or approach for integrating the quality development, quality maintenance, and quality improvement efforts of the various groups in an organization to enable marketing, engineering, production, and service to perform at the most economical levels to fully satisfy customers. (We will discuss TQC and its methodology in Chapter 12.) Because TQC has a major impact on all management and engineering practices, it has provided the foundation for the evolution of total quality management.

Total quality management (TQM) is a management concept that focuses the collective efforts of all managers and employees on satisfying customer expectations by continually improving operations management processes and products.[5] TQM is a philosophical strategy for manufacturing and service excellence that includes, but goes beyond, the concepts and methods of total quality control.

The purpose of this chapter is to explain the basic principles, tactics, and techniques that embody the total quality management philosophy. We will also explain how TQM can be used as a management strategy for achieving manufacturing and service excellence and describe how TQM can be implemented.

• • •

---

[1] L. Reynolds, "Promoting Quality in the Public and Private Sectors," *Management Review* (May 1989), 16–17.

[2] J. R. Johnson, "Hallmark's Formula for Quality," *Datamation* (February 15, 1990), 119–122; J. Oberle, "Quality Gurus," *Training* (January 1990), 47–52; B. T. Raffield and F. B. Bingham, "Balancing Product Quality, Costs, and Profits," *Industrial Marketing Management,* 18 (1989), 293–299.

[3] L. L. Berry, V. A. Veithaml, and A. Parasuraman, "Five Imperatives for Improving Service Quality," *Sloan Management Review* (Summer 1990), 29–38; G. DeSouza, "Now Service Businesses Must Manage Quality," *Journal of Business Strategy* (May/June 1989), 21–25.

[4] K. Ishikawa, *What Is Total Quality Control?* (Englewood Cliffs: Prentice-Hall, 1985).

[5] See T. H. Berry, *Managing the Total Quality Transformation* (New York: McGraw Hill, 1991); J. R. Jablonski, *Implementing Total Quality Management* (Albuquerque, N.M.: Technical Management Consortium, 1991); C. N. Weaver, *Total Quality Management* (Milwaukee, Wis.: ASQC Quality Press,1991); D. J. Talley, *Total Quality Management* (Milwaukee, Wis.: ASQC Quality Press, 1991).

WHY TOTAL QUALITY MANAGEMENT IS NECESSARY

At the height of the Cold War in the 1950s, there were two military superpowers (the United States and the Soviet Union) and one economic superpower (the United States).[6] After the collapse of communism and communist governments in the former Soviet Union and Central and Eastern Europe, there is now only one military superpower, the United States. There are now, however, three economic superpowers: Europe, Japan, and the United States. The only basic weapon for economic superiority today and in the twenty-first century is product or service quality. World-class quality provides an organization with the only insurance that it can compete successfully—whether it is American, European, or Japanese.

Total quality management can be viewed as a necessary means to achieve increased sales, reduce costs, develop a competitive advantage through enhanced product quality, or all three. TQM can also be seen as the key strategy for an organization's survival. In Chapter 1, we introduced the productivity cycle as an integrated system that possessed a product quality element. As we can see in Figure 2-1, an improvement in product quality can lead to development of a competitive advantage, increased sales, and eventually reduced operating costs. The result of putting the productivity cycle in motion is usually the positive benefits of increased profit and market share. Manufacturing and service organizations that have embraced the principles and ideas of TQM have found them to be quite rewarding.

Q Manufacturing organizations in the United States have been using some of the principles of total quality management for a number of years. In 1985, Velcro USA of Manchester, New Hampshire, a manufacturer of tapes and binding fabrics for automobile interiors, was on the verge of losing its major customer, General Motors.[7] Velcro had begun to install a total quality control program of statistical process control but had assigned responsibility for the program exclusively to quality control personnel, rather than making the program a company-wide project for all managers and employees. The result was that General Motors ended up with scrap rates as high as 8 percent using the Velcro tape products. Velcro was focusing on improving its own processes rather than seeking information from its customers on their perceptions of quality and what was important to them. Velcro responded to this survival-threatening situation by (1) redefining higher levels of quality for the materials it obtained from its suppliers, (2) meeting and exceeding General Motors's finished product requirements; (3) fully implementing its TQC program to identify and solve quality control problems within its own production systems, and (4) making quality a responsibility of all managers and employees. As a result, Velcro not only retained General Motors's business, but reduced

---

[6] Lester C. Thuron, "Who Owns the Twenty-First Century?" *Sloan Management Review* (Spring 1992), 5–17.

[7] K. T. Krantz, "How Velcro Got Hooked on Quality," *Harvard Business Review* (September–October 1989), 34–40.

FIGURE 2-1 QUALITY AND THE PRODUCTIVITY CYCLE

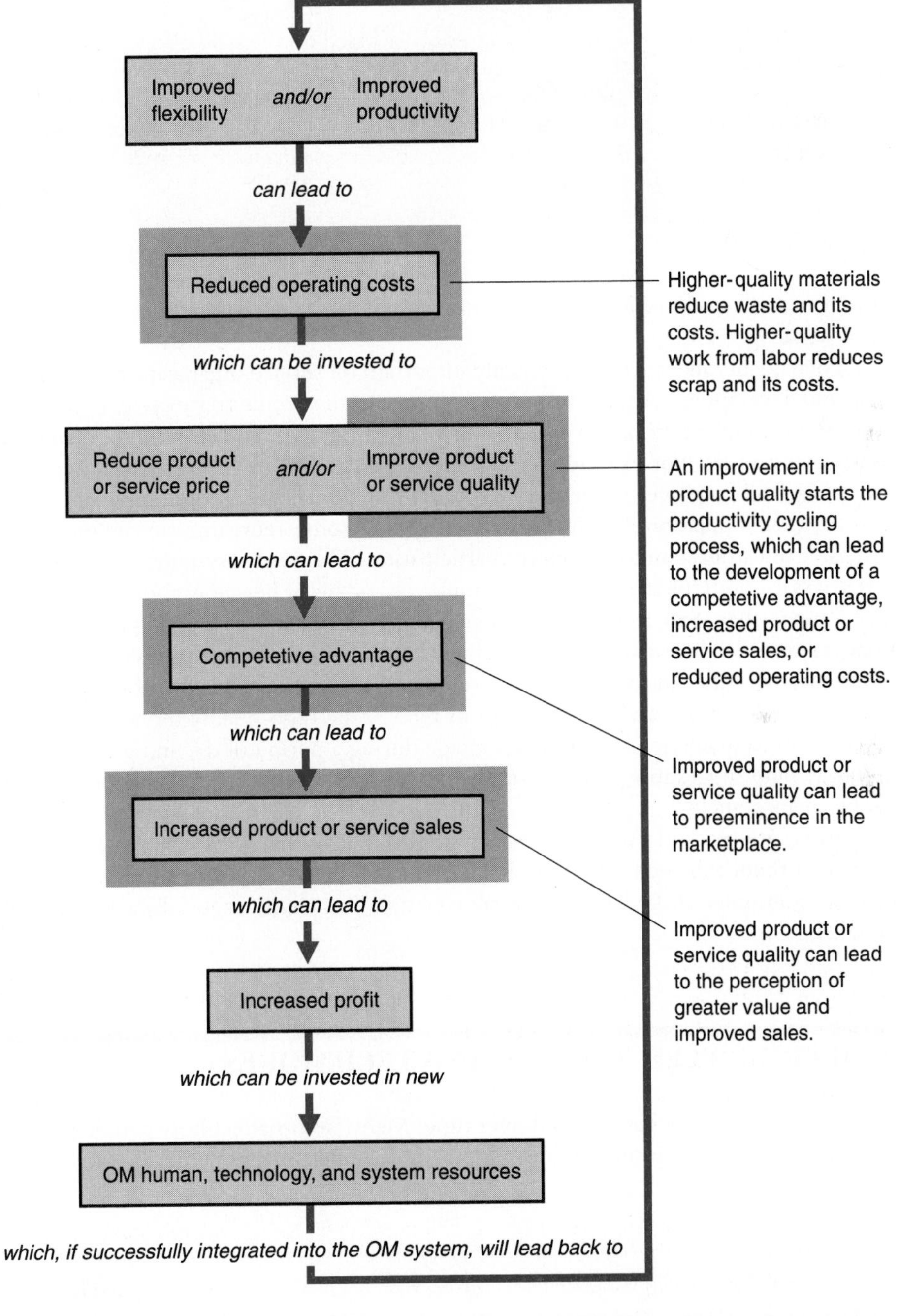

QUESTION: What is the cost of poor quality?

ANSWER: There are many different estimates based on the type of operation and who is making the estimate. Some quality experts estimate that the cost of poor quality can range from 20 to 25 percent of sales.[8] Other experts believe that the range is closer to 5 to 15 percent of sales.[9] Based on these estimates, a firm with a profit margin of 10 percent of sales can increase its profits from 50 to 250 percent if it can eliminate poor quality.

its own waste by 45 to 50 percent per year. Velcro was moving in the direction of total quality management.

Total quality management is equally important for service organizations in reducing costs and developing a competitive advantage to start the productivity cycle. By reducing costs, service organizations can pass greater value (a value-based definition of quality) on to their customers. For example, in the late 1980s American Airlines introduced "Innovations," an employee suggestion program to help management identify cost-cutting areas in their operations.[10] The program required some reorganization effort and an extensive reward system to encourage participation. The reward system included awards and prizes for both the idea-generating employee and his or her supervisor. The program saved more than $50 million in twelve weeks of operation and demonstrated the importance to both management and labor of teamwork in problem solving. At a time when most airlines had to cut costs and service, American Airlines was able to cut costs to remain competitive and still maintain its recognized high-quality service. It was able to maintain its quality competitive advantage during a period of declining quality in its industry. The suggestion program moved American Airlines in the direction of total quality management.

While Velcro and American Airlines moved toward total quality management, neither of them achieved what we characterize as TQM today. Organizations have to embrace a number of the TQM principles, tactics, or techniques to fully achieve TQM benefits.

TQM PRINCIPLES, TACTICS, AND TECHNIQUES

The concept of quality has changed over time. Many factors affect how people perceive "quality," such as economic conditions, social values, personal preferences, and financial

[8] T. H. Berry, *Managing the Total Quality Transformation* (New York: McGraw-Hill, 1991), p. xv.

[9] D. J. Talley, *Total Quality Management* (Milwaukee, Wis.: ASQC Quality Press, 1991), p. 57.

[10] D. K. Denton, "The Service Imperative," *Personnel Journal* (March 1990), 66–74.

status. In general, however, the concept of quality is profoundly influenced by the degree of balance between supply and demand. For example, Russians waiting in a line for hours to buy a loaf of bread would not argue about the bread's quality. On the other hand, a shopper at the Neiman Marcus store in Houston would be very picky about the quality of a product or service.

The principles, tactics, and techniques of TQM are constantly undergoing change. Some of the characteristics of TQM principles, tactics, and techniques are presented in this section.

TQM Principles

Today's TQM should be a part of, if not the heart of, a business strategy. TQM is also a vehicle for managing change, which is a critical challenge facing every organization in today's dynamic business environment. It recognizes that a strategic goal of quality requires an integrated approach that helps an organization develop and produce products and services that not only meet or exceed customer expectations but also can be produced in a cost-effective and timely manner.[11]

The following principles and concepts of today's total quality management differ from past approaches to quality improvement.

SYSTEMATIC IMPROVEMENT TQM is a systematic, rather than a piecemeal, approach to quality. Many past programs were focused on specific, limited problems driven by statistics; delegated to subordinates; or characterized by the slogan of the moment. Instead, today's TQM is a broader organizational improvement strategy that is essentially a commitment to change the entire organization's way of thinking.

FOCUS ON THE CUSTOMER In total quality management, the focus is on the customer, not the process. TQM takes the definition of quality beyond the past narrow view of technical product specifications, service requirements, or strict productivity measures. It is a more holistic approach that includes conforming to customer requirements by making the customer the focal point of all business processes.

LONG-TERM COMMITMENT In total quality management, the quality race is a marathon, not a 100-meter dash. For many organizations, real quality will not occur without fundamental changes in organizational culture and ways of doing business. TQM recognizes that to see payoffs on the bottom line, companies must invest a good deal of time systematically overhauling the way employees are managed and inspiring them to make every product the best possible and every customer's experience a positive one.

---

[11] T. E. Benson, "The Gestalt of Total Quality Management," *Industry Week* (July 1, 1991), 30–32; B. T. Raffield and F. G. Bingham, "Balancing Product Quality, Costs, and Profits," *Industrial Marketing Management,* 18, No. 4 (1989), 293–299; W. D. Reitsperger and S. J. Daniel, "Japan vs. Silicon Valley: Quality-Cost Trade-off Philosophy," *Journal of Business Studies,* 21, No. 2 (1990), 289–300.

Follow-up feedback, constant reinforcement, and renewal of TQM values and processes are also critical to its success.

PROBLEM PREVENTION Because the best defense is a good offense, total quality management is strategic and prevention-oriented, not defensive and concerned only with correcting quality defects. It encourages the identification of problems and potential problem areas to reduce product and service deficiencies. TQM also requires tailoring human resources policies and programs to motivate employees to identify problem areas and bring them to management's attention. It is important to provide rewards, not criticism or punishment, for those who uncover problems or mistakes.

QUALITY AS EVERYONE'S JOB In total quality management, quality is everyone's job, not the preserve of a staff specialist. Every area of a business contributes to quality and to customers' perceptions of products or services. TQM involves the total organization, from the executive office to the shop floor. Clearly demonstrated commitment from top management is essential to the success of TQM, as is participation by employees at all levels. Teamwork is also important to reinforce mutual support and cooperation in meeting the challenge of providing top-quality products and services.

TQM Tactics

As we discuss in Chapter 4, organizations can use total quality management as a strategy to achieve world-class service or manufacturing quality. To implement a TQM strategy, an organization must use TQM tactics. There are fundamental total quality management tactics that apply to all organizations, whether they are businesses in the manufacturing or service sectors, nonprofit organizations, government agencies, or academic institutions. Several of these tactics are explained below.[12]

THE TQM CULTURE There are two aspects to total quality management: an analytical side that focuses on product improvement and a behavioral side that focuses on human resource improvement. In many respects, it is the latter that is the more critical and the more difficult to achieve. While U.S. culture prizes rugged individualism, the adoption of TQM requires teamwork and a focus on collective common goals. TQM is effective only when every member of an organization understands the objectives and is empowered to assume additional responsibilities to solve quality-related problems.

LEADERSHIP FROM THE TOP Improving quality can begin anywhere, at the bottom, middle, or the top of an organization. For total quality management to endure, however,

[12] D. J. Talley, *Total Quality Management* (Milwaukee, Wis.: ASQC Quality Press, 1991), pp. 31–40; R. Sparks and J. M. Dorris, "Organizational Transformation," *Advanced Management Journal* (Summer 1990), 13–18; S. A. Marash, "Blueprint for Quality Improvement," *Personnel Journal* (March 1989), 120–123.

it must have the commitment and personal involvement of the chief executive or members of the senior management team. They must be driven by the goal of customer satisfaction, and quality must be the fundamental business principle. Each leader must set the tone to create the right environment for change, and the most powerful signal is his or her personal behavior. Leaders must act as role models and use quality as a management strategy in all areas of the organization.

CUSTOMER SATISFACTION Fundamental to quality is the concept of satisfying the customer, both the external and the internal next-in-line customer. Thus, the design and delivery of products and services begin with understanding stated and unstated customer needs. Similarly, measurements of performance and improvement efforts should take into account the customer's perspective.

CONTINUOUS IMPROVEMENT OF PROCESSES Total quality management emphasizes continuous improvement in the way work is done, including traditional white-collar and staff activities. Organizations that practice continuous improvement typically enjoy a greater improvement rate than their non-TQM competitors. Crucial to the success of continuous improvement is the use of analytical methods, such as basic statistical tools and control charts to monitor and reduce deviation from quality goals. (We discuss these analytical methods in Chapter 12.)

BENCHMARKING **Benchmarking** is an organization's comparison of its own performance and practices with those of the industry leaders. Benchmarking is helpful in closing the gap between the current and desired states. Many leading organizations such as Baldrige Award winners IBM, Federal Express, Motorola, Milliken, and Wallace use as many as 200 different benchmarking firms in their self-evaluations.

TEAMWORK With total quality management, individuals must begin to work as members of teams, as members of functions, and as parts of processes, all pulling toward common organizational goals. Therefore, the policies and practices of hiring, performance appraisals, career progression, reward and recognition, as well as education and training, must be revised to support teamwork.

COOPERATIVE PARTNERSHIPS Total quality management replaces traditionally antagonistic or adversarial relationships with cooperative ones. This spirit of cooperation is often manifested in the form of partnership relations that form between a manager and the work group, the union and management, or different departments in an organization. It also extends beyond the enterprise to include suppliers, customers, competitors, and other associations. This winning tactic can be developed by respecting the goals of each party and seeking solutions that satisfy common needs.

These individual tactics can be combined to achieve a global or general business strategy used to express an organization's TQM program. For example, the Boeing

Q S

FIGURE 2-2 BOEING'S TQM STRATEGY

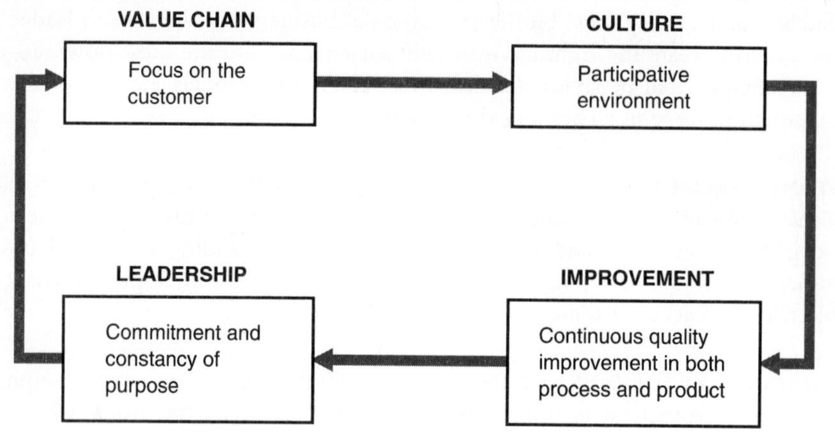

Source: Adapted from D. J. Talley, *Total Quality Management* (Milwaukee, Wis.: ASQC Quality Press, 1991), p. 18.

Commercial Airplane Company's total quality management strategy, presented in Figure 2-2, is a continuous quality model.[13]

TQM Techniques

A wide range of techniques can be used to help implement total quality management principles and carry out TQM tactics. Many of the statistical and analytical methods used in a TQM program will be discussed in Chapter 12. We will focus here on three behavioral techniques related to TQM. These techniques include concurrent engineering/interfunctional teams, empowerment of personnel, and performance-based reward systems.

CONCURRENT ENGINEERING/INTERFUNCTIONAL TEAMS Traditionally, the creation of a product starts with a program development effort to identify the idea for a product. This phase of developing a product is then followed sequentially by a series of additional activities, as presented in Figure 2-3(a). Engineers begin their efforts to develop the product, and when the product design is fairly complete (i.e., there is always continuous engineering effort), materials acquisition personnel begin their efforts to locate and acquire materials for the product. Once the sources of materials are chiefly acquired,

[13] D. J. Talley, *Total Quality Management* (Milwaukee, Wis.: ASQC Quality Press, 1991), p. 18.

operations personnel determine the producibility of the product given their OM resource capabilities and production processes. Once the processes of production are determined, actual production can begin and the distribution personnel can begin to develop logistic systems.

Alternatively, in **concurrent engineering,** as presented in Figure 2-3(b), sequential development and production activities are undertaken almost simultaneously by all participants. This permits information on materials, capacity, and distribution limitations early in the development of the product to save development time of creating a product that cannot be produced. For example, if the materials acquisition personnel cannot afford to obtain a material for a new product, the engineering design effort that would

FIGURE 2-3 CONCURRENT ENGINEERING

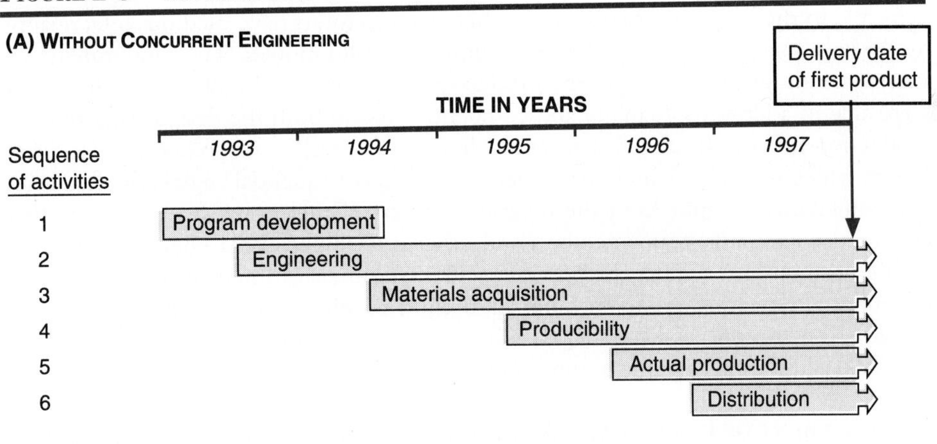

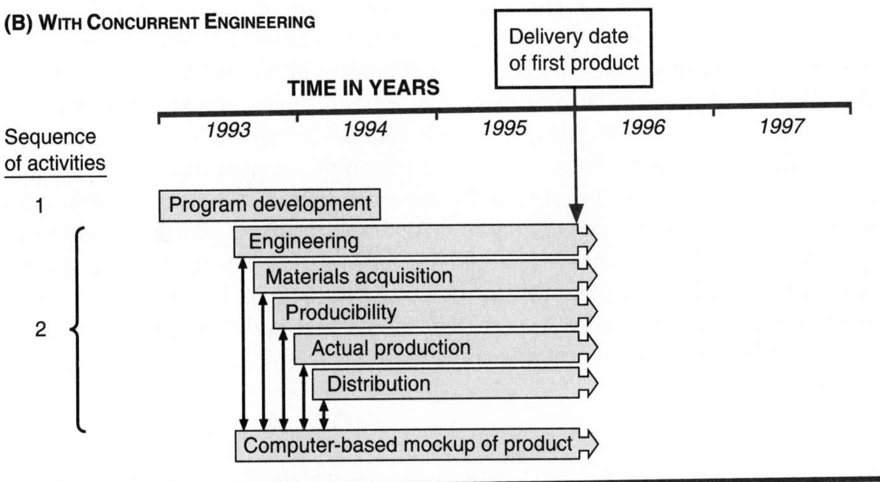

have been wasted in the assumed use of that material is saved when the reality of cost limitation is communicated early in the product design. The use of a computer-based mockup of the product during its creation helps all participants quickly conceptualize and address problems in their respective areas. To help achieve early integration of information from all participants, many organizations use cross-functional or **inter-functional teams** composed of one or more individuals from engineering, operations, distribution, and other areas of the organization. These teams expedite communication by directly and personally discussing mutual problems and minimizing formal written communications between departments.

In summary, this approach has two major benefits: (1) it helps organizations expedite the development of products or services and hasten their introduction to the market by shortening the product or service development cycle time; and (2) it helps organizations quickly pinpoint problem areas and resolve them before the product or service is delivered to the customer. Major automobile manufacturers have used this total quality management technique to develop their more successful models. Their interfunctional teams include designers, engineers, production specialists, and customers. The teams were able to address profitability and competitiveness in both the design stage and the production process. In an effort to rationalize a car's mechanical components and the way in which it would be built, team members replaced sequential engineering activities with simultaneous input from the diverse members of the group. So before the first clay model was built, team members and other related personnel knew how the car would be assembled. Under the previous systems, manufacturing managers did not see the models they were going to build until eight or nine months before production started. The success of these TQM efforts is cited as a major factor in some U.S. automakers' renewal as premier automobile producers.

EMPOWERMENT OF PERSONNEL Another important total quality management technique is the empowerment of individuals and groups to come up with ideas and make the necessary decisions to carry them out. **Empowerment of personnel** means allocating responsibility and authority to management and workers to complete any problem-solving task they might face. This particularly means giving workers the authority to make decisions (usually reserved for management) within the domain of their duties and to act on their decisions. This technique can be implemented by altering job descriptions for employees to define their participation in activities that will contribute to product quality. The major benefits of this approach include (1) quick identification of problems, which reduces waste and its costs; (2) an increased number of solutions to quality problems; and (3) improved employee motivation to participate in quality enhancement efforts. For example, Kodak increased productivity by grouping workers into teams, teaching them how to inspect their own work, and then listening to their suggestions.[14] Now assembly workers who make x-ray cassettes and spools, canisters,

[14] W. J. Prezzano, "Kodak Sharpens Its Focus on Quality," *Management Review,* 78 (May 1989), 39–41.

and cartons for Kodak film arrange their own hours, keep track of their productivity, and fix their machines.

PERFORMANCE-BASED REWARD SYSTEM An important principle of total quality management is that the rewards for quality improvement must be shared with the participants responsible for the improvement, which is accomplished through performance-based reward systems. As the quality improves, bonuses, salary increases, and gain-sharing plans go into effect for those responsible. Other rewards that can be used include increased training, promotions, and the opportunity for people to use their creative abilities and skills. Performance-based reward systems are a key to the difference between talking about quality through advertising slogans and actually delivering quality through the employees to the customers.

Total quality management principles, tactics, and techniques are often refined to suit the particular organization's needs. They are then mixed together to form a TQM program. To help install the program, a TQM implementation strategy can be used.

TQM IMPLEMENTATION STRATEGY

A variety of approaches can be used to implement total quality management. The five-step procedure presented in Figure 2-4 is a composite of several TQM implementation strategies.[15] These steps include the following:

First: Determine What Quality Is. One of the best definitions of quality in total quality management is meeting or exceeding customer expectations. Although it is important to recognize that quality is customer driven, putting quality into operation in TQM requires the setting of specific goals. Motorola's famous "Six Sigma" quality goal is an example.[16] This means that Motorola feels it can meet its customers' expectations with only 3.4 defects per million opportunities or with production that is 99.99966 percent defect-free. For comparison, airlines have a 6.5-sigma performance in air safety (although their baggage handling performance is only between 3.5 and 4 sigma); and pharmacists strive for an accuracy of 5 sigma in filling prescriptions.

[15] C. N. Weaver, *Total Quality Control: A Step-by-Step Guide to Implementation* (Milwaukee, Wis.: ASQC Quality Press, 1991); J. Oberle, "Quality Gurus," *Training* (January 1990), 47–52; F. Price, "Out of the Bedlam: Management by Quality Leadership," *Management Decision,* 27, No. 3 (1989), 15–21; J. E. Cornell and S. M. Herman, "The Quality Difference," *Training and Development Journal* (August 1989), 55–57; L. E. Coate, "TQM on Campus," *NACUBO Business Officer* (November 1990), 26–35; C. Hammons and G. A. Maddux, "An Obligation to Improve," *Management Decision,* 27, No. 6 (1989), 5–8.

[16] B. M. Cook, "In Search of Six Sigma: 99.9997 Defect-free," *Industry Week,* 239 (October 1, 1990), 60–62+.

FIGURE 2-4 A TQM IMPLEMENTATION STRATEGY

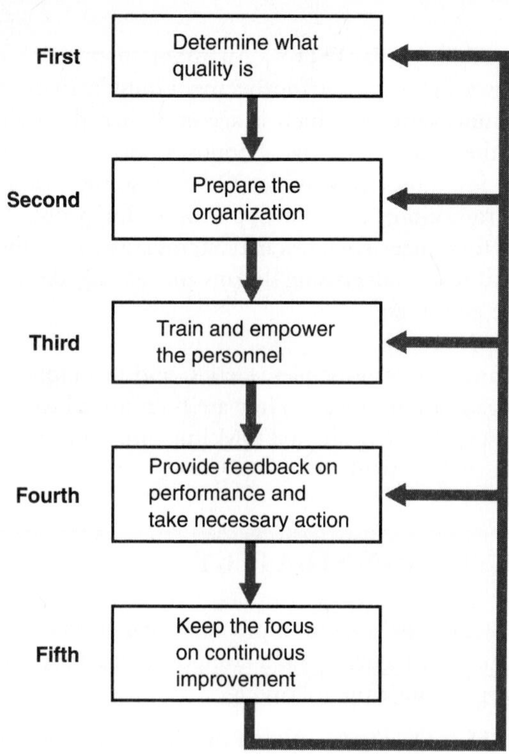

Second: Prepare the Organization. This step involves communicating top management's strategy of TQM and encouraging teamwork among employees to support it. Some of the primary ideas that are communicated during this phase include (1) getting everyone to realize that quality is the responsibility of the entire organization and not the exclusive domain of the quality control department; (2) determining the readiness of personnel to accept a TQM strategy; and (3) identifying key "movers and shakers" who can help communicate and sell TQM ideas to others and then motivating these people to accomplish TQM goals. One of the biggest challenges is closing the gap between what management is saying and what the employees perceive is happening.

Third: Train and Empower the Personnel. Two types of total quality management training are typically provided. One type is statistical training that can be used in measuring performance, identifying problem areas, and eliminating the causes of problems. The second type is problem-solving training that is designed to address issues that are best handled with a nonquantitative approach.

Fourth: Provide Feedback on Performance and Take Necessary Action. Problems in quality must first be identified before their causes can be determined or solutions can be proposed. Feedback systems must be installed for every aspect of the product- or service-generation process. From suppliers, through work-in-process (WIP), to the final customers, feedback on quality must be continuously received and acted on. It is common for total quality management manufacturers to actually audit and help organize the quality systems used by potential suppliers as a means of qualifying them for the manufacturers' business.[17] Monitoring WIP quality involves installing total quality control systems (both computer and human controlled) that can check for quality conformance at each stage in the production process. Because the focus of TQM is on satisfying the customer, substantial customer feedback systems must be installed to permit the customer to easily report both good and bad quality. The GE Answer Center is an 800-number telephone customer information service that not only provides customers with information on how to use General Electric products, but also acts to collect information on problems customers are having when using the products. GE uses the information to correct and resolve customer problems, improve customer satisfaction, identify and resolve manufacturing problems in the design of its future products, improve production-processing methods that may be causing poor quality, and identify and correct quality problems with external suppliers' parts. In most service operations such as restaurants, customer comment cards are placed on tables or near places of service delivery to permit customers to comment on various aspects of service quality.[18] The mail-in comment card shown in Figure 2-5 for the photocopying company Kinko's illustrates the types of information that can be obtained on the quality of service being delivered at a particular store.

Fifth: Keep the Focus on Continuous Improvement. This step ensures that total quality management is not abandoned because the organization either has trouble with implementation or believes that no further changes are needed. This step has proven critical to the success of many organizations including Toyota, which uses *kaizen* (continuous improvement) to lead the way in producing high-quality cars.[19] Toyota employs what has been called "rapid inch-up," which is continuous, small improvements that eventually result in its outdistancing the competition. In fact, *kaizen* has been attributed with helping Toyota produce a greater variety of models at lower prices than its

---

[17] E. Raia, "1990 Medal of Professional Excellence," *Purchasing,* 109 (September 27, 1990), 41–43+; S. Cayer, "Welcome to Caterpillar Quality Institute," *Purchasing,* 109 (August 16, 1990), 80–81+; J. Dreyfuss, "Shaping Up Your Suppliers," *Fortune,* 119 (April 10, 1989), 116+.

[18] G. DeSouza, "Now Service Businesses Must Manage Quality," *The Journal of Business Strategy* (May/June 1989), 21–25.

[19] K. Imai, *Kaizen: The Key to Japan's Competitive Success* (New York: Random House, 1986).

Q

S

FIGURE 2-5 COMMENT CARD FOR COLLECTING QUALITY INFORMATION

You are Kinko's valued customer.

What you have to say is important to us. Please take a moment to let us know how we are doing by filling out this form or calling our Customer Service Hotline at 1-800-933-2679.

SERVICE	Excellent	Satisfactory	Needs Improvement	Unacceptable
Co-Worker Helpfulness	❒	❒	❒	❒
Efficiency	❒	❒	❒	❒
QUALITY	❒	❒	❒	❒
STORE APPEARANCE	❒	❒	❒	❒

Additional Comments/Suggestions: ______

What other services or products would you like Kinko's to offer?

For your convenience, what other businesses would you like to see Kinko's located near? ______

How do you know about Kinko's? Newspaper ❒ Yellow Pages ❒ School ❒ Radio ❒ Television ❒ Referral ❒

Date: / / Time of Day: ______

Store Visited: ______

(Optional Information)

Name: ______

Address: ______

City/State/Zip: ______

(______) ______ ______

Area Code Telephone Occupation

Source: Reprinted with permission of Kinko's Service Corporation, © 1992 by Kinko's Service Corporation.

Q

competitors. Toyota is not the only firm using such an approach. Ford, for instance, implemented a continuous improvement program in its automobile division to increase the quality of its products. Within only a couple of years, Ford's Taurus model, in 1991, finally cracked the J. D. Power top-ten list of quality automobiles.

The five steps in this implementation strategy can procedurally help an organization install a total quality management program. To help motivate the organization to want to implement TQM, top management must establish a strategic goal of manufacturing or service excellence.

Clearly, human resources professionals are positioned to play a major role in helping their organizations develop and implement today's total quality management program.[20] The successful implementation of the principles of TQM rely heavily on effective management of human resources. Implementing TQM requires continuous adjustment of every facet of the work environment/corporate culture, organizational structure, policies, reward systems, and more. The human resources function can play an important role in the TQM assessment, planning, and implementation process as well as in annual monitoring and review. Some of the principal ways in which human resources management can be involved in TQM include those listed on pages 63 and 64.

1. *Diagnosing organizational readiness* Quality programs cannot be dictated by managerial authority. The human resource professional recognizes that an organization is not just authority lines and boxes but a complex combination of structures, processes, resources, and staffing. Implementing TQM often imposes the need for new structural and work environment alterations. Thus, a careful analysis of organizational readiness for TQM must be made before launching the program.
2. *Conducting value chain analyses* Because all functions contribute to customers' perceptions of quality, it is important to understand and document how everyone's work fits together to meet customer expectations. The resulting document is called a **value chain.** An example of a value chain for a travel agent serving a customer is presented in Figure 2-6.
3. *Restructuring performance measurement and reward systems* Human resources personnel should proactively encourage managers to set and maintain high standards to stimulate continuous improvement in performance and quality. The human resources function is in the best position to ensure that nontraditional reward systems supporting total quality management, such as profit sharing or employee stock ownership, exist to provide incentives.
4. *Planning a long-term, customer-oriented culture change* Essential to principles of total quality management is a fundamental change in corporate culture. The vision of all employees sharing responsibility for customer satisfaction must be presented and reinforced at all levels. Because of the human resources department's vantage point in the organization, it can help senior management "feel the pulse" of the organization and prepare a blueprint for change.
5. *Developing total quality management communications aand training programs* Based on assessing what it will take to change an organization's culture, human resources personnel can help tailor a program to instill a customer-oriented culture by assisting senior managers in an organization-wide communications effort. Development of a customer-oriented culture should include substantial communication between headquarters staff and employees who directly contact customers daily. Managers and employees must also develop the skills required

[20] W. R. Roth, "Quality Through People: A Hit for HR," *Personnel* (November 1989), 50–52; F. Luthans, "Quality Is an HR Function," *Personnel* (May 1990), 72.

FIGURE 2-6 VALUE CHAIN FOR A TRAVEL AGENT PROCESSING A CUSTOMER'S AIRLINE TICKET

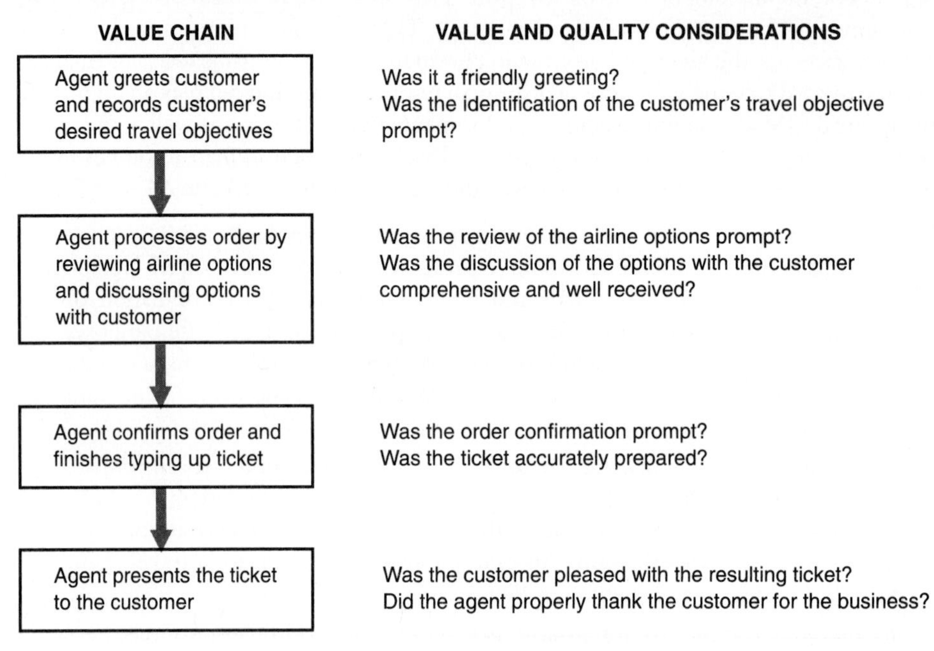

to implement the organization's quality concepts. Continued training, job rotation, and job enlargement programs are important as well.

VALUE CHAIN
VALUE AND QUALITY CONSIDERATIONS
Agent greets customer and records customer's desired travel objectives
Was it a friendly greeting?
Was the identification of the customer's travel objective prompt?
Agent processes order by reviewing airline options and discussing options with customer
Was the review of the airline options prompt?
Was the discussion of the options with the customer comprehensive and well received?
Agent confirms order and finishes typing up ticket
Was the order confirmation prompt?
Was the ticket accurately prepared?
Agent presents the ticket to the customer
Was the customer pleased with the resulting ticket?
Did the agent properly thank the customer for the business?

TQM AS A STRATEGY FOR ACHIEVING MANUFACTURING AND SERVICE EXCELLENCE

What is manufacturing and service excellence? To answer this question, many organizations have used the Malcolm Baldrige National Quality Award criteria.[21]

The Malcolm Baldrige National Quality Award

The Malcolm Baldrige National Quality Improvement Act of 1987 (Public Law 100-107, signed by President Reagan on August 20, 1987) established an annual United States National Quality Award. The purposes of the award are to promote quality

[21] M. G. Brown, *Baldrige Award Winning Quality* (Milwaukee, Wis.: ASQC Quality Press, 1991); *Profiles of Malcolm Baldrige Award Winners* (Boston: Allyn and Bacon, 1992).

awareness, recognize quality achievements of U.S. companies, and publicize successful quality strategies. The Baldrige Award is administered by the National Institute of Standards and Technology (NIST), which is a branch of the Department of Commerce.

The award formally recognizes companies that attain preeminent leadership in the area of quality and permits these companies to publicize and advertise their awards. It encourages other companies to improve their quality management practices, and thereby to compete more effectively. NIST develops and publishes award criteria that also serve as quality improvement guidelines for use by U.S. companies. Furthermore, NIST widely disseminates nonproprietary information about the quality strategies of the award recipients. It gets the word out that quality is achievable.

Up to two awards may be given each year in each of three categories: (1) manufacturing companies or subsidiaries, (2) service companies or subsidiaries, and (3) small businesses. Fewer than two awards may be given in a category if no organization meets the high standards of the award program. Businesses incorporated and located in the United States may apply for the award. Subsidiaries, or divisions or business units of larger companies, are eligible if they primarily serve either the public or businesses other than the parent company. For companies engaged in both services and manufacturing, the larger percentage of sales determines the classification. For purposes of the award, small businesses are defined as independently owned businesses with not more than five hundred full-time employees.

The Baldrige criteria apply to manufacturing and service businesses of any size. The criteria permit evaluation of the strengths and areas for improvement in the applicant's quality systems and the results. It addresses all aspects of quality improvement results using the following seven evaluation categories: (1) leadership, (2) information and analysis, (3) strategic quality planning, (4) human resource utilization, (5) quality assurance of products and services, (6) quality results, and (7) customer satisfaction.

1. *The Leadership category* examines how senior executives created and sustain a clear and visible quality system, along with a supporting management system, to guide all activities of the company toward quality and excellence. Examiners also consider senior executives' and the company's quality leadership and support of quality developments, both inside and outside the company.

2. *The Information and Analysis category* examines the scope, validity, use, and management of data and information that underlie the company's total quality system. This category also examines the adequacy of the data and information to support quality-based decision making.

3. *The Strategic Quality Planning category* examines the company's planning process for retaining or achieving quality leadership and the company's integration of quality improvement planning into the overall business plan. It includes the company's priorities to achieve or sustain (or both) a quality leadership position.

4. *The Human Resource Utilization category* examines the effectiveness of the company's efforts to develop and utilize the full potential for quality of its work force—including management—and to maintain an environment conducive to full participation, continuous improvement, and personal and organizational growth.

5. *The Quality Assurance of Products and Services category* evaluates the company's systematic approaches for total quality control of goods and services, based primarily on process design and control, including control of procured materials, parts, and services. In addition, this category includes consideration of how effectively an organization integrates quality control with continuous quality improvement.
6. *The Quality Results category* examines quality levels and quality improvement, using objective measures derived from analysis of customer requirements and expectations and from analysis of business operations. This category also considers current quality levels in relation to those of competing firms.
7. *The Customer Satisfaction category* evaluates the company's knowledge of the customer, customer service systems, responsiveness, and ability to meet requirements and expectations. This category also examines current levels and trends in customer satisfaction.

Receiving the Baldrige Award is viewed as a sign of manufacturing and service excellence. The similarity of the Baldrige Award criteria and total quality management principles and tactics is a fortunate coexistence. Interestingly, TQM began to blossom at about the same time as the Baldrige Award was instituted. Clearly, TQM is a very efficient implementation strategy for improving an organization's performance in each of the seven award quality evaluation categories. TQM has become the primary strategy for achieving the recognition of the Baldrige Award through world-class manufacturing and service excellence.

Some Baldrige Award Winners

Since 1988, many world-class firms have won the Baldrige Award, including Motorola, IBM, Xerox, Wallace, and Milliken. We will look at two well-known winners, the Cadillac division of General Motors and Federal Express, as well as some lesser-known winners.

CADILLAC (MANUFACTURING) During the early 1980s the Cadillac division of GeneralMotors lost a sizable portion of its 1970s market share to foreign and domestic competitors. In the late 1980s Cadillac was able to reverse the decline in market share and boast the highest percentage of repeat buyers in the automobile industry. Cadillac accomplished this reversal by embracing total quality management principles, tactics, and techniques. In the mid-1980s Cadillac initiated a form of concurrent engineering that helped implement design changes for its products and services. These design changes were guided by meeting or exceeding customer-driven product expectations. Cadillac management combined workers, customers, and suppliers into interfunctional teams called *simultaneous engineering teams* and made them responsible for defining, engineering, marketing, and continuously improving all Cadillac products. The company also renegotiated a new partnership with the United Auto Workers union to permit greater participation of workers in the production and quality of products. Cadillac also required its external suppliers to demonstrate continuous improvement in meeting "targets of excellence."[22]

FEDERAL EXPRESS (SERVICES) In the early 1970s Federal Express started the air-express industry. Its philosophy of "People-Service-Profit" encourages employees to be innovative and motivates them to make decisions that advance the organization's quality goals. The Federal Express quality improvement program focuses on twelve service quality indicators (such as timeliness of delivery) that are tied to customer expectations. Although customer satisfaction has always been high, Federal Express continuously sets higher standards for service and customer satisfaction. The company has established two corporate-wide interfunctional teams of 1,000 employees each, which work on quality improvements. As a tangible demonstration of its partnership for quality with its workers, Federal Express management has installed a no layoff philosophy and has a guaranteed fair treatment procedure for handling employee grievances. Despite substantial competitive pressure during the 1980s, the Federal Express total quality management approach to service gave the company almost three-fourths of the market for domestic U.S. overnight and second-day deliveries in 1990.[23]

Q S

OTHER RECENT WINNERS The 1991 Baldrige Award Winners include the following firms:

Q

Small business category: Marlow Industries, Dallas, Texas

Manufacturing Category: Solectron Corporation, San Jose, California; and Zytec Corporation, Eden Prairie, Minnesota

Although these firms are relatively obscure when compared with the previous winners of the award, they are also quality innovators. Although these firms are different from each other, their quality programs share several common characteristics.

Top-down commitment to quality

Emphasis on human resources

Use of data as a basis for quality strategies

Management focus on the customer

Use of the Baldrige Award criteria as a basis for the quality improvement process

INTEGRATING MANAGEMENT RESOURCES: USING TQM FOR COMPETITIVE ADVANTAGE

In the service industry it has been observed that (1) it costs five times as much to obtain a new customer as to keep an old one, (2) it takes twelve positive service

[22] *Profiles of Malcolm Baldrige Award Winners* (Boston: Allyn and Bacon, 1992), pp. 61–64.

[23] *Profiles of Malcolm Baldrige Award Winners* (Boston: Allyn and Bacon, 1992), pp. 65–67.

transactions to overcome one negative one, and (3) 25 to 50 percent of a company's operating expense is attributable to poor service quality.[24] It is no wonder that many organizations and researchers in the field of operations management view total quality management as an integration strategy for achieving competitive advantage.[25] For TQM to be successful, management must integrate all of the organization's resources (i.e., human, technology, and systems) to focus on satisfying customer needs for quality. In addition, management must integrate the internal environment of the organization (described in Chapter 1) with the external environment.

The Wallace Company of Houston, Texas, is a service operation that distributes pipes, valves, and fittings to chemical and petrochemical industries. In 1985, Wallace adopted a long-term strategy of continuous quality improvement that involved building new partnerships with customers and suppliers, installing communication technology to facilitate learning more about customers' requirements, and improving the monitoring of the quality of suppliers' goods. It also instilled one primary objective in its work force: total customer satisfaction. To fully integrate the idea of TQM in its organization, Wallace trained all of its employees in quality improvement concepts and methods. Its efforts helped establish a new level of quality service in its industry. For example, its creation of the Total Customer Response Network system established a standard of quality in being able to respond to customer inquiries and complaints within sixty minutes. The competitive advantage of such service quality did not go unrewarded in the market. From 1987 to 1990, Wallace's sales volume grew 69 percent and its market share increased from 10.4 to 18 percent. The improved quality resulted in greater efficiency by minimizing wasted time, cost, and materials. The improved efficiency benefitted its profitability by increasing operating profits in 1990 by 7.4 times their 1987 level. Wallace received the 1990 Malcolm Baldrige Award for Quality.[26]

SUMMARY

TQM is a philosophy that can strategically lead an organization to excellence in product quality. This chapter has been positioned in Part I, Concepts and Prerequisite Methodology, because of the prerequisite nature of quality management for operations management in the 1990s and TQM's theme of integration. Of all the OM subjects we will discuss in this textbook, TQM is one of the most fundamental and far-reaching. No single principle, tactic, or technique of TQM will help an organization achieve total customer satisfaction. It takes a combination of TQM principles, tactics, and techniques to formulate a winning TQM strategy. It also takes the integration and focusing of human resources, technology resources, and system resources to satisfy the quality needs of the customer.

---

[24] L. A. Liswood, "A New System for Rating Service Quality," *Journal of Business Strategy* (July/August 1989), 42–45.

[25] H. L. Gilmore, "Continuous Incremental Improvement: An Operations Strategy for Higher Quality, Lower Costs, and Global Competitiveness," *Advanced Management Journal,* 55 (Winter 1990), 21–25.

[26] M. G. Brown, *Baldrige Award Winning Quality* (Milwaukee, Wis.: ASQC Quality Press, 1991), p. 41.

In this chapter, we began our discussion of TQM with several definitions of quality. We described several of the most common TQM principles and tactics. We briefly described TQM techniques, including concurrent engineering/interfunctional teams, empowerment of personnel, and performance-based reward systems. A TQM implementation strategy was also presented as a means of installing a TQM program. The Malcolm Baldrige National Quality Award was described as a means of defining manufacturing and service excellence.

This chapter concludes with two articles on TQM. Students are encouraged to read these articles because they reinforce some of the ideas presented in the chapter and because they represent the opinions of practitioners who know and can speak from experience about TQM as an essential strategy for business success.

DISCUSSION AND REVIEW QUESTIONS

1. What is the transcendent view of quality? Give an example.
2. Describe the product-based definition of quality. Give an example.
3. What is the user-based approach to quality? Give an example.
4. Explain how the manufacturing-based approach to quality differs from the user-based approach.
5. What is the value-based view of quality? Give an example.
6. How is the productivity cycle related to TQM?
7. Explain why total quality management (TQM) is necessary for a manufacturing business.
8. Explain why TQM is necessary for a service operation.
9. What are the TQM principles?
10. What important role does the human resources function of an organization play in a TQM program? Explain and give examples.
11. How is a business culture related to TQM?
12. What is a value chain? How is it used in TQM?
13. Why must improvements in quality be continuous?
14. What are TQM tactics? How are they used?
15. What are TQM techniques? How are they used?
16. What is concurrent engineering? What is an interfunctional team? How are they related to TQM?
17. What are the TQM benefits of using the technique of empowerment?
18. What are the general steps of TQM implementation strategy?
19. What is the Malcolm Baldrige National Quality Award? What criteria are used to determine the winners?
20. Why is the Malcolm Baldrige National Quality Award important? How is it related to TQM?
21. How is TQM a strategy for manufacturing excellence? Explain and give an example.
22. How is TQM a strategy for service excellence? Explain and give an example.
23. How can integrating TQM into an operation achieve a competitive advantage? Explain and give an example.
24. Is quality worth the price of a TQM program? Explain and give an example.

CASE 2-1

TOTAL QUALITY MANAGEMENT, TOTALED!

President Jones runs an accounting service operation, providing accounts receivable and accounts payable (AR/AP) services for small and medium-sized businesses. The Jones operation used a staff of accounting personnel who were paid based on the volume of AR/AP transactions they processed. The more AR/AP transactions the staff processed in a day, the more income they received. For more than a decade, the Jones Accounting Service organization prospered under this system. During this decade, there was also little competition in the area it served. A few years ago, though, competition on the service products Jones offered started increasing. The entry of new competitors had not only stopped the growth in the Jones business, but was actually causing the loss of some of its long-term customers. This competitive problem needed to be solved and President Jones was just the person to do it.

President Jones talked with twenty of the company's long-term customers that had recently withdrawn their business and asked them why they had left. The reasons they gave and the percentage of those who responded are presented in Exhibit 2C-1. Based on these responses, President Jones decided that total quality management was called for to correct the customer service problem.

President Jones met with all of the AR and AP department managers and laid out the following step-wise plan to correct the problem.

- *Step 1. Install a new bonus plan.* All accounting personnel would be given the incentive of a 5 percent bonus on their salary to do a better job of handling customer problems. The bonus would be paid with the last paycheck of the year—to all accounting personnel except those who had more than ten customer complaints that had not been resolved by year's end.
- *Step 2. Let department managers know that they are responsible for quality.* President Jones made it clear that the department heads were free to fire anyone who did not comply with improved quality directives. President Jones also let the managers know their jobs were on the line.

EXHIBIT 2C-1 REASONS THAT CUSTOMERS LEFT JONES ACCOUNTING SERVICE

Percentage of Customers	*Reason*
45	Inaccurate accounting (errors in accounting)
35	Poor response time to customer complaints and delay in corrective action
30	Poor attitude of Jones's customer service representative
10	Cost of services

- *Step 3. Reduce cost of services to customers.* A new cost rate, lowering the cost of services, was prepared by President Jones. This new cost rate was to be sent out to all the customers they had lost.
- *Step 4. Invite the customers to offer their comments on service quality.* A customer service card was to be placed in each AR/AP report given to customers. The card would permit the customer to comment on the quality of the service Jones was providing.

President Jones felt these steps would just be the beginning of the firm's TQM program. More would be needed to put Jones back on top of the AR/AP business.

CASE QUESTIONS

1. Does the plan offered by President Jones embrace any of the TQM principles discussed in this chapter? Identify which ones it does embrace and how. Identify which ones it does not embrace and what might be done to include them.
2. Does the plan offered by President Jones use any of the TQM tactics discussed in this chapter? Which ones? Which ones are not used?

A Tour of the General Motors Saturn Plant

1. **The Saturn Facility.** The Saturn production facility located in Springhill, Tennessee is comprised of manufacturing and service facilities. While there are numerous service buildings, including those for education and administration, the manufacturing buildings are divided into three groups: Body Systems, Vehicle Systems, and Power Train. The Body Systems group is responsible for manufacturing all the polymer and steel panels, assembling the spaceframe and cockpit, and painting the completed assemblies. When finished, these component parts and subassemblies are sent to the Vehicle Systems group. The Vehicle Systems group is the final assembly area. The Power Train group contains a foundry where engine blocks are cast and the engines and transmissions are assembled. Let's go on a minitour of the Saturn facility.

Photos courtesy of Saturn Corporation.

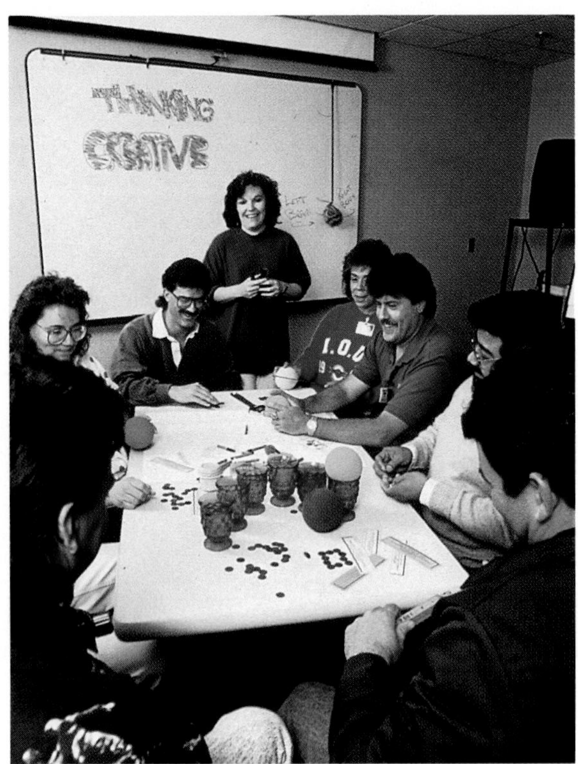

2. **Saturn Planning Session.** To understand the way the Saturn facility operates, you must understand the way the people at Saturn (called team members) do their jobs. The Saturn facility and the automobiles produced there are the result of a cooperative planning effort between General Motors (GM) Corporation and the United Automobile Workers (UAW) international labor organization. All employees (management and labor) work in teams to study problems and plan their resolution.

3. **Saturn Education and Training.** No one does a job before they know how to do it right. The Saturn facility includes an educational complex where university-level and advanced-technology courses are taught to employees.

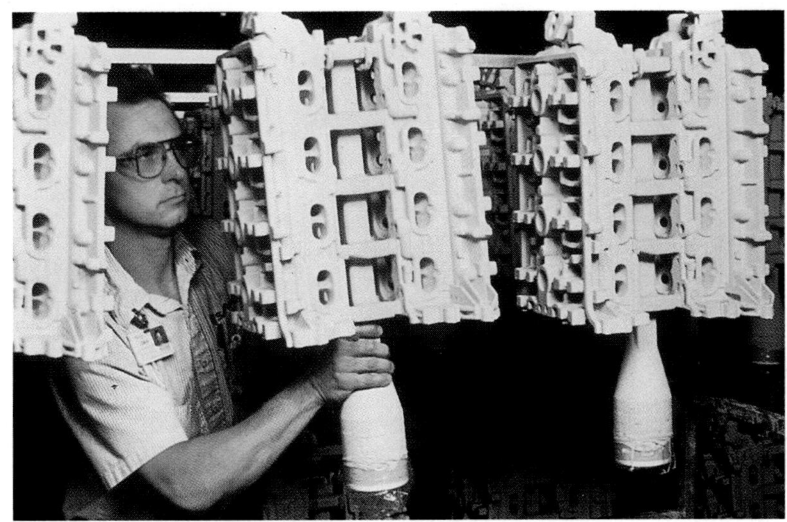

4. **Foam Patterns for Use in Casting Engine Blocks.** A Saturn automobile is made up of component parts. In the Power Train area of the facility, foam patterns are used to help cast the engine blocks. This technologically advanced system results in higher-quality engine casting than that produced by more conventional methods currently used by competitors.

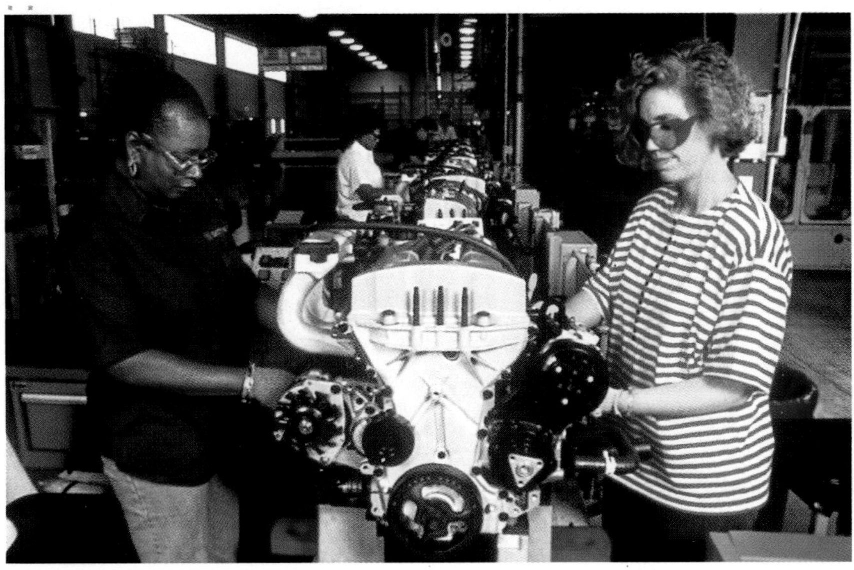

5. **Engine Assembly.** Once the block is cast, other component parts arrive "just-in-time" for their assembly into a complete power train system made up of the engine and transmission subassembly.

6. **Body Panel Fabrication.** While the power train is being finished, the body panels are fabricated and hand finished for their eventual assembly. These are the body parts that make up the outside of the car. One of the unique features of the Saturn automobile is the use of dent-resistant linear body panels made of polymers, rather than conventional metals. Metal panels are used on the hoods and top of the automobile.

7. **Door Assembly.** Making sure the doors and door components work correctly is an important criterion for automobile quality. While robots play a role in the manufacture of Saturn automobiles, important areas of quality are personally controlled by team members.

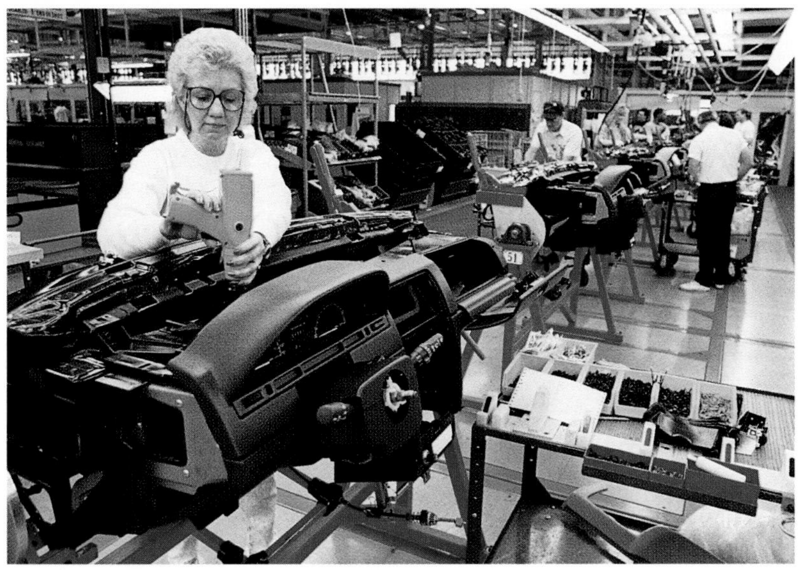

8. Dash Assembly. Subassemblies, such as the dash (or cockpit, as Saturn calls it) in this photo, are assembled and conveyed to the automobiles being assembled in the Vehicle Systems area using cranes mounted in the ceiling of the Saturn facility.

9. Robotic Welding. The steel spaceframes fabricated in the Body Systems area are brought to the Vehicle Systems area to begin the final assembly. GM-manufactured robots are used to weld together the steel framework for each automobile. Afterwards, the steel framework is bathed in a corrosion-resistant chemical solution.

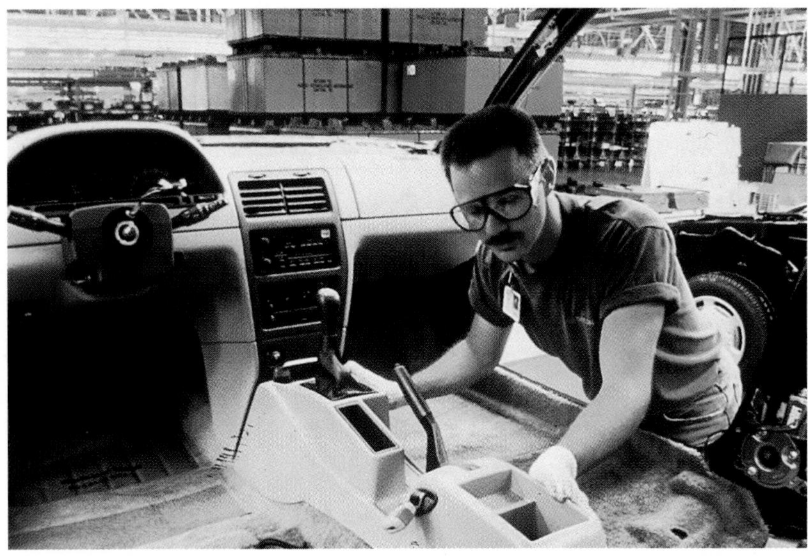

10. Interior Assembly and Quality Control. Saturn uses human resources to perform many of the final assembly activities. Saturn does this because it feels that humans are more likely than robots to catch quality defects. It is this type of personal touch that is characteristic of Saturn and that makes it "a different type of car company."

11. Preparation for Final Assembly. Continuing in the Vehicle Systems area, the automobiles are ready for seats, which can be brought into the interior of the car easily since the paneling and doors are the last items to go on the automobile. Another advantage of waiting to incorporate the panels and doors in the final assembly is that there is less damage to their finish and less resulting scrap is generated.

12. Power Train Quality Checks. Final quality control checks are made on the engine and the computer-based systems to ensure world-class performance for Saturn cars.

13. Final Detail Quality Checks. Throughout each phase of manufacturing and in this final visual check of the finished automobile, the Saturn organization feels that its team members represent the best quality control system in the company.

14. Temporary Storage of Automobiles. The Saturn facility operates under a "just-in-time" inventory management system that minimizes on-hand inventory stock. The picture above shows finished Saturns ready for shipment.

15. Saturn's World-Class Products. As of 1993, the Saturn Corporation offers three basic automobile models: sedans, station wagons, and coupes. Each model is made in the United States, with the best skills and technology the world has to offer.

3. Does the plan offered by President Jones use any of the TQM techniques discussed in this chapter? Which ones?
4. Do you think Jones's plan will achieve TQM in the Jones Accounting Service organization? Explain.

ARTICLE 2-1

BACK TO THE BASICS
To regain greatness, U.S. manufacturing must retool its thinking.

by Edward L. Hennessy Jr.
Mr. Hennessy is chairman/CEO of Allied-Signal Inc.

CEOs seldom have all the answers. Over the years our collective failure to properly manage this nation's once-mighty manufacturing sector left the door wide open for the Japanese and other foreign producers to shoulder U. S. companies aside in a growing number of core industries.

What happened? Simply put, the success of America's manufacturing establishment during and after World War II went to our heads. Our domination of world markets in the 1950s and '60s led to complacency, arrogance, even sloppiness.

About this time a new breed of executives began taking over at many companies. Tightly focused on finance, marketing, legal, and administrative concerns, these executives often showed little interest in or appreciation for manufacturing. Consequently, they failed to properly manage their investment in worker skills, plant, and equipment.

The Japanese rushed in to fill the void, spending precisely where their money could do the most good—in improvements in manufacturing. Japanese products also began reflecting economy of design and ease of operation.

It's time for America to seize the manufacturing high ground once again. Some have suggested that we do this by thinking and acting more like the Japanese, that we change our culture. Nonsense. America's real strength *is* its culture—free-thinking individuals with creativity and enterprise. The Japanese learned many of their manufacturing techniques from us.

What we must now change, if we are to restore this country to greatness, is not our culture, but our technique. We must retool our thinking about quality, design, productivity, participative management, and more. We must never think of product quality as a manufacturing problem . . . but as the solution. By managing for quality, we build low cost and high productivity into manufacturing. In addition, we must stop thinking in terms of the most sophisticated product or process design, and start thinking about simplified style and ease of assembly. We must get back to basics.

That is exactly what a growing number of American manufacturers are starting to do. Hewlett-Packard, for example, sent its people around the world looking for better ways to run its business. It then embarked in a number of new directions, including a total-quality management approach. Motorola also launched common-sense improvements. By uniting design and production engineers from day one, it designs products that are easier to manufacture. It also teaches employees to inspect their own work and to maintain their own machines.

Allied-Signal's automotive products group has undertaken sweeping changes in managing. Teamwork is now rampant; functions formerly separate are tied together. Our brake plant in Sumter, S. C., for example, has adopted the "just-in-time" approach to control inventories. We've also opened new lines of communication between upper management and first-line supervisors, and factory workers have much greater responsibility for product quality.

Source: Reprinted with permission from *Industry Week*, November 20, 1989. Copyright Penton Publishing, Inc., Cleveland, Ohio.

In the rebirth of manufacturing, few firms have been a bigger inspiration than Ford Motor Co. When U. S. automakers were rocked in the early '80s by the import explosion, Ford responded with a no-holds-barred drive to improve quality. Among the vital lessons Ford learned: simpler is better. For example, it redesigned an instrument console for the 1987 Escort with only six parts, compared with 22 in the '84 model. The results were dramatically reduced material and labor costs—and vastly improved quality. Allied-Signal's jet engine design for the new LHX Army helicopter includes 80 major parts that can be replaced or maintained in the field with only six basic hand tools.

Which brings us back to the role of CEOs. The impetus for change must come from the top. We must steadfastly work toward an environment where change is recognized and rewarded, where teamwork across all factory operations is actively encouraged, where continual improvement is a way of manufacturing life. We must, in sum, get back to the basics.

ARTICLE 2-2

QUALITY'S UP, BUT NOT ENOUGH
To compete effectively, U.S. must make 'perfect' products.

by Armand V. Feigenbaum
Dr. Feigenbaum is president/CEO of General Systems Co. Inc., Pittsfield, Mass., and the originator of Total Quality Control (TQC).

What good is a warranty to a mother of three on a Monday morning with four loads of laundry and a broken washing machine? How can a small telemarketing company remain in business when its state-of-the-art telephone system breaks down every other day?

Sales and market share are influenced by the quality of product performance. Warranty or no warranty, an unreliable product breeds an unsatisfied customer.

While American industry has made substantial quality gains, international quality leadership is still a long way ahead. With import vulnerability increasing, American manufacturers must make essentially perfect products to compete effectively.

There are some very concrete realities American industry must deal with, and urgently:

- Eight out of ten consumer and industrial buyers regard quality as equal to, or more important than, price in purchase decisions.
- The prevailing judgment is that a strong foreign manufacturer with a quality strategy can't help but succeed in the U. S. today, whether the dollar goes up or down.
- Nearly all American nondefense manufactured products will have import vulnerability by the early 1990s.

A manufacturer once was considered honorable for having a "we'll always fix it for you" policy. Today, there is little tolerance for any failures. One-third of all resolved customer complaints requiring product service leave a dissatisfied customer.

The pressure on manufacturers to produce essentially perfect products comes from abroad as well as at home. Many foreign manufacturers do not believe that the majority of U. S. companies take quality seriously. Therefore, the single most important competitive task facing all U. S. businesses is accelerating quality improvement.

Certain basic benchmarks of total-quality management must be adopted by a company intent on improving quality:

Source: Reprinted with permission from *Industry Week,* December 4, 1989. Copyright Penton Publishing, Inc., Cleveland, Ohio.

- Quality must be structured to support both the quality work of individuals as well as the quality teamwork among departments.
- Quality must be perceived to be what the buyer says it is—not what an engineer, marketer, or general manager says it is.
- Modern quality improvement requires the application of new technology; it is not a matter of dusting off a few traditional quality-control techniques.

The greatly increased speed of new-product development significantly increases the need for front-end quality emphasis. Although TV took 20 years to mature as a product, the personal computer required only four years, and many new integrated-circuit devices now need no more than 12 months. In more and more innovative companies the old series approach to development, in which quality is examined at the end of each stage of a step-by-step process, has been replaced by a parallel approach in which both product development and quality development systematically proceed together. To introduce quality control at the beginning of product development, manufacturers must:

- Make quality a full, equal partner with innovation from the onset of product development.
- Emphasize getting high-quality product design and process matches upstream—before design freezes the quality alternatives.
- Make the acceleration of new-product introduction a primary measure of the effectiveness of a quality program.

When this is done effectively, not only is new-product quality more likely to be very high, but product-development cycles will also be cut by one-third or more because of the reduction of continual engineering changes for quality reasons.

Such American industries as consumer household durables, electrical equipment, diesel engines, aircraft, and agricultural equipment set the world-leadership example in quality. It is time for this list to grow longer.

3 Forecasting

CHAPTER OUTLINE

CHAPTER OBJECTIVES

The material in this chapter should prepare you to do the following:

1. Explain why forecasting is necessary
2. Describe the different types of forecasts
3. Describe the types of variation that may exist in forecasting data
4. Explain what judgmental forecasting methods are and how they are used
5. Explain what secondary source information is and how it can be used in forecasting
6. Explain what the Delphi method is and how it can be used in forecasting
7. Describe how correlation analysis is used to select variables for forecasting models
8. Explain what simple and multiple regression methods are and how they are used in forecasting
9. Describe the differences and similarities among the three smoothing models: centered moving averages, weighted moving averages, and exponential smoothing
10. Explain how to select the best forecasting method and minimize forecasting error

What is forecasting? In simple terms, it is an attempt to look into the future. A **forecast** is sometimes called a prediction, estimate, guess, opinion, or extrapolation. One thing is certain: No forecast is "for sure." A perfect forecast is clearly the exception.

Despite the uncertainty of forecasts, forecasting is continuously gaining widespread acceptance as an integral part of business planning. Most service and manufacturing organizations use forecasting in areas such as corporate strategic planning, sales planning, marketing research, pricing, production planning and scheduling, financial planning, and program planning. To meet the forecasting needs of these widely varied functions, a number of forecasting methods have been developed.

In this chapter several nonquantitative and quantitative forecasting methods will be discussed. (Note that the general use of the term *method* in this chapter and throughout the rest of this textbook is interchangeable with other terms such as *technique, procedure,* or *model.*) Although the specific set of forecasting methods included in this chapter does not represent a comprehensive treatment of the subject, it does provide a basic understanding of forecasting methodology expected of all operations managers. Although most sales and economic forecasting is performed by other specialists, operations managers are expected to understand the forecasts provided by these specialists. For this reason, operations managers must be familiar with forecasting model terminology and technology. This chapter also presents a discussion of types of forecasting and procedures that can be used to select the best forecasting model.

• • •

WHY FORECASTING IS NECESSARY

In business, managers develop strategic, tactical, or operational objectives, and then set out to achieve them. Forecasting helps define and clarify those objectives. Forecasting is an essential activity for planning the input and output of the operations management system and affects many of the management activities required of operations managers. Without a forecast as a guide, planners would not know, for example,

1. How to schedule work effort to satisfy customer demand
2. What and how many units of supplies and materials to acquire
3. What type and how much personnel to hire
4. What and how large a facility to acquire

Alternatively, with an accurate forecast the organization can

1. Save inventory expenses by not overstocking (interest on capital tied up in inventory) or understocking (lost sales)
2. Save labor costs by not overhiring (costs of layoffs) or underhiring (overtime expenses)

3. Save needless investment expenses in equipment and facilities when future product demand declines
4. Gain competitive advantage by meeting customer needs more quickly

The need for forecasting is pivotal because of its initiating role in strategic operations management planning and decision making. Let's illustrate the importance of forecasting and its role in providing answers to questions necessary for OM planning. Suppose a company establishes a corporate strategy of growth. The OM area of the company then has to establish its OM strategic, tactical, and operational objectives to support achievement of the corporate strategy. The company might establish an OM strategic objective of acquiring additional buildings and facilities for long-term use. How will the company know whether it can achieve a strategic OM objective of manufacturing or service facility growth of 5 percent, 10 percent, or more if managers don't know whether future sales will support such growth? To pursue the OM strategic objective, the company might establish an OM tactical objective of acquiring some equipment with a useful life of two to five years. How will the company know if the types of equipment it plans on buying will have a useful medium-term life if it does not have a forecast on the demand for products the equipment will be producing? To implement the OM tactical objective, the company might establish a short-term OM operational objective of a specific configuration of plant layout (a temporary layout of the equipment and personnel within the plant to satisfy a short-term production goal). It will be extremely difficult to know what the best short-term configuration and integration of management resources are if the company does not know how many units of the product it is planning to produce. The answers to these questions permit managers to decide how

Q

QUESTION: Total quality management (TQM) was described in Chapter 2 as one of the most important strategies of the 1990s to meet world-class competition. How does forecasting help implement this strategy?

ANSWER: Accurate forecasting can help a TQM program in many ways. For example, TQM manufacturers need to establish long-term contracts with their suppliers. Accurate forecasting gives manufacturers the information they need on their customer demand to better estimate their supplier needs in the long-term. Accuracy in forecasting reduces costly changes in the renegotiation of long-term contracts. For service organizations, which usually require an initial outlay of capital for service facilities, long-term forecasting allows the service personnel to accurately estimate the size of facility requirements (such as the size of a retail store to meet demand for customer products). The more accurately the size of the service facility matches the customer demand, the better the service quality of timely delivery (that is, there will be no waiting lines due to the facility being over its capacity) and the better the value quality (that is, costs will be lower because the facility is not operating under its capacity).

S

best to accomplish their OM strategic, tactical, and operational plans. Forecasting provides the necessary information with which to initiate most types of OM planning and decision making.

In this chapter, the procedural and computational aspects of forecasting are presented in the hope that they will help provide the necessary understanding of how forecasting methods can aid managers in accomplishing their desired goals and objectives. The better we understand the methodology, the better we will be prepared to understand its informational value and limitations.

Before we can understand how to forecast, however, we must first master some fundamentals, including the different types of forecasts operations managers must make and the types of variation found in forecasting data.

FORECASTING FUNDAMENTALS

Types of Forecasts

Three basic types of forecasts are long-range, medium-range, and short-range. Each type of forecast can differ in timing, purpose of use, and methodology.

LONG-RANGE FORECASTS Long-range forecasts usually have a planning horizon (time period of use) of five years or more and are generally used in strategic long-range planning. Examples of long-range planning in which long-range forecasting is required include plant expansion or location and long-term research and development projects for new services or products. Long-range forecasting is characterized by its general and broad nature. Most long-range forecasting is qualitative and subjective because an accurate prediction far into the future is almost impossible. Long-range forecasting methods include judgmental forecasts from experts on such changes as technology, economic trends, and lifestyles that may affect product demand or judgmental information from the sales force, executives, or other knowledgeable employees on factors that in the long-term may affect product demand. Other long-range forecasting methods we will be discussing in this chapter include secondary source forecasts on industry and product demand patterns from research conducted by public or private forecasting institutes.

MEDIUM-RANGE FORECASTS Medium-range forecasts usually have a planning horizon of one to two years. This type of forecast is typically used for intermediate planning. Examples of intermediate-range planning in which medium-range forecasting is required include aggregate planning (the next one or two years' aggregate or total unit production), analyzing operations systems for possible change, and yearly budgeting. Medium-range forecasting is different from long-range forecasting in that numerical computation in some fashion is almost always required or feasible. For yearly budgeting, for example, it is necessary to forecast specific dollar values for anticipated expenses, although the resulting budget figures may not be so specific that each individual expense

QUESTION: How is long-term forecasting used in international or global markets?

Q

ANSWER: Europe's Airbus Industrie consortium provides one example. A manufacturer of aviation equipment, Airbus is planning its productivity cycling (see Chapter 1) concerning the commercial jet industry market.[1] In 1990, about 85 percent of the world's airline jets were made in the United States. Long-term forecasts have indicated that worldwide sales of commercial jet airliners between 1990 and 2008 will total 11,500 units (which is worth about $600 billion in 1991 dollars). In 1970, recognizing the long-term value of this market, European countries started to subsidize Airbus so that it could improve its product quality and manufacturing process productivity. Improvements in its product quality (over a longer-term period since 1970) have been recognized by customers, and Airbus has started to gain more market share. Airbus is now capturing one-third of new worldwide contracts for commercial jets and is the world's second largest jet supplier after Boeing (a U.S. manufacturer of aviation equipment).

item is clearly defined. In other words, medium-range forecasting requires greater specificity and accuracy than long-range forecasting but does not need to be completely detailed.

Medium-range forecasting methodology can include formation from the sales force, executives, and other knowledgeable employees. Because such information is often based on personal opinion, it usually needs to be refined to improve its specificity and accuracy. One method used to generate and improve subjective forecast information is called the Delphi method. We will discuss this forecasting technique and other medium-range forecasting methods including the mathematical modeling procedures of correlation analysis, regression analysis, and classical decomposition later in this chapter.

SHORT-RANGE FORECASTS Short-range forecasts usually have a planning horizon of less than one year. An example of short-range planning in which short-range forecasting is required is the monthly, weekly, or day-by-day scheduling of production. Short-range forecasting differs from medium-range forecasting in that a relatively accurate computation is required and more frequent forecasting is needed.

Types of Variation in Forecasting Data

The purpose of forecasting is to predict the future, usually based on some type of historic information. Because forecasts are set in the future and we usually express the future in terms of time, most forecasts are based on time series data. A **time series** is any set of

[1] R. J. Samuelson, "The Assault from Airbus," *Newsweek*, July 8, 1991, p. 46.

numbers that measures the status of some ongoing process over time. This includes most business and economic activity. Table 3-1 presents examples of the functional area activities that have been tracked historically as time series data.

Unfortunately, the type of data used in developing a forecast can be complex. The complexity arises from the different types of variation that can exist in the data. One of the unique features of time series data is its variation. Figure 3-1 presents four types of variation that can occur in a time series (product demand). They include

Trend. The short- or medium-range increase or decrease in product or service demand. A trend can either be linear or nonlinear.

Seasonal. The short-range cycling behavior of the rise and fall of product or service demand during a season or a year.

Cyclical. The long-range cyclical behavior of the rise and fall of product or service demand. A business cycle is divided into four phases (depression, recovery, prosperity, and recession) that can reveal the current position of product or service demand.

Irregular. The remaining variation in the data that cannot be explained by the other types of variation. The greater the amount of irregular variation in the data, the more difficult it is to use for forecasting.

Identifying these variations in time series data helps in understanding and forecasting product demand. Many different types of forecasting procedures can be used to identify

TABLE 3-1 FUNCTIONAL AREA ACTIVITIES THAT CAN BE EXPRESSED AS TIME SERIES DATA

Functional Area	*Activities*
Production	Product demand Material costs Material requirements Inventory levels Labor costs Labor requirements Plant utilization Capital investment
Marketing	Market share Product sales Pricing (consumer products) Consumer trends
Finance	Cash flow Budgeting Expenses Pricing (supplies and materials) Interest rates)

FIGURE 3-1 TYPES OF VARIATION THAT CAN EXIST IN TIME SERIES DATA

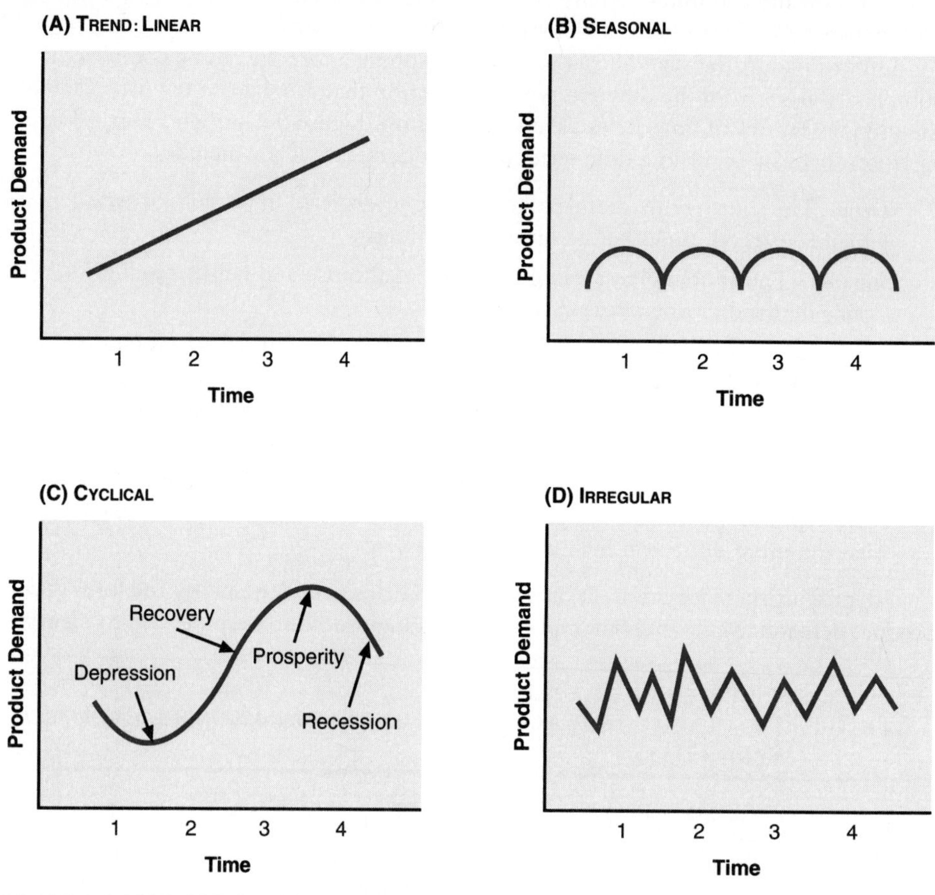

and understand the variation in time series data. We will examine several of these in this chapter.

FORECASTING METHODS

Virtually all forecasting involves the use and manipulation of numbers. The output of forecasting efforts is a set of numbers. There are both nonquantitative and quantitative forecasting methods. Nonquantitative forecasting methods are means by which operations managers can obtain forecasts and information with little or no computation. We will discuss three nonquantitative forecasting methods: judgmental, secondary sources, and the Delphi method.

Judgmental Forecasting Methods

Judgmental forecasting methods are based on a process of collecting educated opinions from individuals who could include members of the sales force, executives, managers, and staff within the organization. Information can also be collected from other individuals outside the organization. These individuals might include consultants, panels of experts, and consumers.

The judgmental forecasts generated within the organization about an item like product demand are typically collected using a bottom-up approach. A **bottom-up approach** requires individuals who are closest to the consumer—that is, at the bottom level of an organization—to estimate what they think product demand will be and transmit this information up to the next level of management. The information is then summarized and adjusted by that manager to reflect the greater source of information the manager has available from all of the subordinates' forecasts. These revised forecasts are then repeatedly passed from lower- to upper-level managers, up through the organizational hierarchy until they reach a point where they cannot or need not be further revised. Managers hope that the result is a fairly accurate forecast based on the best judgment throughout the organization. Such an approach avoids complicated and expensive forecast modeling.

Organizations can also collect judgmental information from individuals outside their organizations. Most firms commonly use consultants and panels of experts to forecast for specific organizational needs such as information about whether a new service facility is needed to satisfy consumer demand. Some organizations are large enough to maintain in-house staff specialists who exclusively perform forecasts for facility acquisition justification. Many organizations, however, experience only infrequent need for such specialized forecasts. In dealing with these infrequent or specialized forecasting jobs, consultants or panels of experts can be a most efficient and effective vehicle for obtaining a forecast. Survey methods are also used to obtain forecasting information directly. Although conducting a survey is less expensive than hiring experts, survey results do not always yield useful information because of biases inherent in survey methods.

Judgmental forecasting has been successfully employed in industry.[2] It is particularly useful when a forecast must be prepared quickly and where extensive historic data are not available for quantitative projection methods.

Secondary Source Information

Some of the best sources of forecast information are secondary sources. **Secondary sources** of information are outside organizations that perform forecasting studies or research. These sources include public organizations such as federal, state, and local

---

[2] See A. H. Ashton, "An Empirical Study of Budget Related Predictions of Corporate Executives," *Journal of Accounting Research,* 20 (1982), 440–449; and H. J. Einhorn, "Quality of Group Judgment," *Psychological Bulletin,* 84 (1977), 158–172.

government agencies and public institutions such as state universities. Secondary sources of information can also include private organizations such as research institutes or commercial organizations like the Standard & Poor's division of McGraw-Hill. Secondary sources can provide almost any type of industry and related companies' forecasts. Secondary sources are also particularly useful in providing information that is used to identify **predictive variables,** variables used in forecast models to predict or forecast product demand.

Virtually thousands of publications provide forecast information. Operations managers can actually save the time and effort of developing a forecasting model if they know how to locate from secondary sources the forecast information they need. One commonly used private source of forecast information on industries is the *Standard & Poor's Industry Surveys*. This publication provides trend analysis on hundreds of industries and discusses major problems in these industries that may affect industry and company product demand. This publication also provides information on sales and earnings so that individual companies can compare their profit margins over a period of time. A similar secondary source publication is *U.S. Industrial Outlook*. This publication provides extensive information from government sources and is published by the U.S. Department of Commerce's International Trade Administration.

One of the most useful secondary source publications is *Predicast's Forecasts*. This private publication provides industry and product forecasts. It also identifies the research publications from which the forecasts originate and can thereby help forecasters locate models and procedures for their individual companies. This forecasting publication provides users with product consumption, production, and exports by industry, as well as annual growth rate projections. Forecasts on individual items are sufficiently detailed to provide users with very valuable forecast information. For example, under the category tobacco production, the products are first divided by major product lines like chewing tobacco, smoking tobacco, and snuff, and then, within each product line, different products are categorized (for example, snuff products are categorized into dry snuff and moist snuff).

Secondary sources of industry information can be converted easily into company forecasting information if we know a given company's position in the industry. By combining the company's market share of the industry with the overall industry forecast of product demand, we can forecast the company's product demand using the following expression:

$$\begin{array}{c}\text{Our company's}\\ \text{product demand}\\ \text{forecast}\end{array} = \left[\begin{array}{c}\text{Our company's market}\\ \text{share of the industry's}\\ \text{product demand}\end{array}\right] \times \left[\begin{array}{c}\text{Secondary source forecast}\\ \text{of the industry's}\\ \text{product demand}\end{array}\right]$$

The market share percentage is easily computed by taking last year's company product demand and dividing it by last year's industry product demand, with some subjective adjustments for the next year.

In this expression, we are relying on the accuracy of the market share percentage and the forecast demand. Because we rely on forecasts developed by others, secondary source forecasts should be obtained from a reputable research organization.

One type of predictive variable used in many forecasting models of time series data is called leading indicator or lagging variable. A **leading indicator** (which is used as a **lagging variable** in a model) is any type of information or data that can be used to explain a time-lagged response in other data we are trying to forecast. Basically some time series data lag behind other variables. In other words, one variable we would like to forecast might be related to another variable that we can predict, but lags a month or two behind in time. This delayed time relationship can permit the predictive variable to be a useful forecaster because changes in the predictor precede the variable we are trying to predict. A practical example of this lagged effect can be seen in measurements in retail product prices. For example, a downward shift in retail gasoline prices can lag behind a downward shift in wholesale gasoline prices by several weeks. Thus, wholesale gasoline prices can be a useful leading indicator or predictive variable in a model that will forecast retail gasoline prices several weeks ahead of time. Numerous public and private secondary sources of information on lagged variables are published every month. One of the most commonly used secondary sources of lagged variables is the *Index of Leading Indicators* published by the U.S. Department of Commerce.

For operations managers who cannot afford the time or money to develop their own forecasts, the use of secondary source forecasting may be a very efficient source of information. The effectiveness of this type of forecasting method can be determined with research. We will discuss the procedure for evaluating forecasting methods later in this chapter.

The Delphi Method

Another nonquantitative forecasting technique is the Delphi method. The **Delphi method** uses a group of individuals to arrive at a consensus on a forecast. The Delphi method is based on the logic that a group of experts can arrive at a better solution than a single individual. The Delphi method can be used in any type of situation, but is ideally used in forecasting situations that involve subjective or judgmental forecasting. Examples of operations management decision situations in which the Delphi method might be particularly useful in long-range and medium-range forecasting might include determining next year's inventory levels, predicting yearly aggregate staff needs, forecasting technological improvements, and forecasting long-term aggregate product demand. One of the advantages of this forecasting method is that it uses the expertise of an organization's operations managers, their staff, and technical experts whose understanding of a problem is unique to their organization.

The person who needs the forecast is the person who must use the Delphi method and conduct the procedure. This could be the president of the firm, a vice president of operations management, or a department head. The procedure for the Delphi method consists of the following steps:

Step 1. Select a group of people (experts) to make a forecast. These experts should have some practical knowledge or expertise about the item that is the subject of the forecast. They should also be kept anonymous from one another to prevent bias.

Step 2. Send each of the experts in the group a questionnaire requesting a forecast. The questionnaire should clearly state all necessary forecast parameters such as the time period over which the forecast is to be made.

Step 3. The responses from each of the experts should be collectively summarized in a statistical presentation. Providing an average or measure of central tendency (mean, medium, or mode values) along with its range and variance values is necessary to motivate a consensus forecast. The experts who are distant from the average forecast should be asked to justify their deviation.

Step 4. Each of the experts is sent a new summarized report on the newly forecast values and asked if they want to revise their prior forecast. The effect of the average forecast statistics usually will motivate the individual experts to shift their forecasts toward the group average value.

Step 5. Step 4 is repeated until the group of experts agrees on a specific forecast or until the experts' forecasts remain constant. If the experts cannot all agree on a single forecast, the outliers (that is, the forecasts most distant from the average) can be ignored and a new average can be computed to generate a useable forecast.

This nonquantitative method of forecasting was first developed by N. C. Dalkey in 1950 at the Rand Corporation's Think Tank. The Delphi method, named after the ancient Greek oracle at Delphi, has been successfully used by major manufacturing organizations for forecasting. The Goodyear Tire and Rubber Company has used the Delphi method in planning future tire research.[3] A more recent application involved forecasting economic development in Alaska.[4]

Quantitative Methodology Concepts

The three nonquantitative forecasting methods—judgmental methods, secondary source information, and the Delphi method—have one thing in common: The user must rely on someone else for the forecast. While some operations managers choose to use these nonquantitative forecasting methods, others prefer to do their own forecasting using their own quantitative forecasting methodology.

There are many different types of quantitative forecasting methods. While most of these quantitative forecasting methods have been developed to examine time series data, they can also be applied to other forecasting situations. The time series forecasting

---

[3] A. R. Fusfold and R. N. Foster, "The Delphi Technique: Survey and Comment," *Business Horizons,* 14 (1971), 63–74.

[4] T. G. Eschenbach and G. A. Geistauts, "A Delphi Forecast for Alaska," *Interfaces,* 15 (November–December 1985), 100–109.

methods vary in quantitative sophistication and application. All of them, however, use one of two basic approaches to forecasting time series: the self-projecting approach or the cause-and-effect approach.

Self-projecting approaches, often referred to as **univariate methods,** derive forecasts solely from the historic behavior of the series of data itself. They are self-projecting because only historic information is used for forecasting the future period. They include naive mathematical procedures such as moving averages, weighted moving averages, and exponential smoothing. As we will see, the advantages of such methods include the following: (1) they are quickly and easily applied, (2) they require a minimum amount of data, and (3) they are reasonably accurate for medium- and short-term forecasting.

Cause-and-effect methods, often referred to as **multivariate methods,** establish a mathematical relationship between the time series (or any type of data) to be forecast and one or more influencing factors (other predictive variables). These methods recognize that in some forecasting situations the activity or process to be forecast is affected by a variety of factors. For example, a company's product demand can be affected by the company's advertising effort and the competitor's pricing. Cause-and-effect methods of time series forecasting try to take these influences into account. These other predictive variables are viewed as related series of data that can explain or cause the behavior of the time series variable we are trying to predict. Multivariate methods include correlation analysis and regression analysis. As we will see, the advantages of these methods include the following: (1) they take into account the interrelationships among predictive variables used in forecasting models, (2) they can provide accurate forecasts for medium-range and long-range forecasting, and (3) they permit relevant information to be included in the forecasting model.

Correlation Analysis

Some forecasting models rely on predictive variables to help generate forecast values. These types of forecasting models are based on a cause-and-effect method. A predictive variable, usually referred to as an **independent variable,** is used to relate or explain the behavior of another variable such as a company's product demand. Examples of predictive variables include time, economic indexes, and competitors' prices. What we seek to predict or forecast is called the **dependent variable** and might include, for example, a company's sales, unit product demand, or human resource needs. The value of the dependent variable is "dependent" on that of the independent variables. **Correlation analysis** is used in forecasting as a screening process to identify dependent variables that can be used in forecasting models. Correlation does not ensure a cause-and-effect relationship between the dependent and independent variables. Correlation analysis uses statistics that help identify the predictive variables that have the strongest relationship with, and therefore are the best predictors of, the dependent variable. We will examine three correlation statistics: the correlation coefficient, the coefficient of determination, and the coefficient of nondetermination.

The simple correlation model received its name from the use of the correlation coefficient, denoted as r, as follows:

$$r = \frac{n(\Sigma XY) - (\Sigma X)(\Sigma Y)}{\sqrt{[n(\Sigma X^2) - (\Sigma X)^2]\,[n(\Sigma Y^2) - (\Sigma Y)^2]}}$$

where

r = the correlation coefficient
Y = the dependent variable
X = the independent variable
n = the number of paired comparisons between X and Y

The value of r always falls between -1 and 1. The **correlation coefficient** is a statistic that provides information on the degree of relationship or association between the dependent and independent variables. The interpretation of the correlation coefficient is quite simple. The closer the value of r is to either -1 or 1 the stronger is the degree of relationship between the dependent and independent variables. Similarly, the closer the value of r is to zero, the weaker is the degree of relationship. The coefficient sign determines the direction of the relationship. A positive r is interpreted as indicating that as the X increases, Y will also increase. A negative r is interpreted as an inverse relationship and indicates that as X increases, Y decreases.

When the dependent and independent variables are expressed on a graph as X and Y coordinate data points, they form a **scatter diagram.** The correlation coefficient expresses the linear relationship between the dependent and independent variables in the same way that we might draw a straight line through a scatter diagram. In Figure 3-2, four scatter diagrams are shown with their correlation coefficients. In Figure 3-2(a) and (b) there is a strong degree of relationship between the dependent and independent variables; the direction of the relationship is positive in (a) and negative in (b). In Figure 3-2(c), there is no relationship between X and Y, and in (d) there is a very poor relationship between the two variables.

QUESTION: If you have a choice between a strong negative correlation coefficient and a weaker positive correlation, which would you choose if the choice is to be based on the degree of relationship between the variables?

ANSWER: Select the stronger negative correlation coefficient. The direction of relationship, either positive or negative, has nothing to do with the degree of relationship between the dependent and independent variables. We always want to select the independent variable that has the strongest degree of relationship with the dependent variable for forecasting purposes.

FIGURE 3-2 SCATTER DIAGRAMS WITH CORRELATION COEFFICIENTS

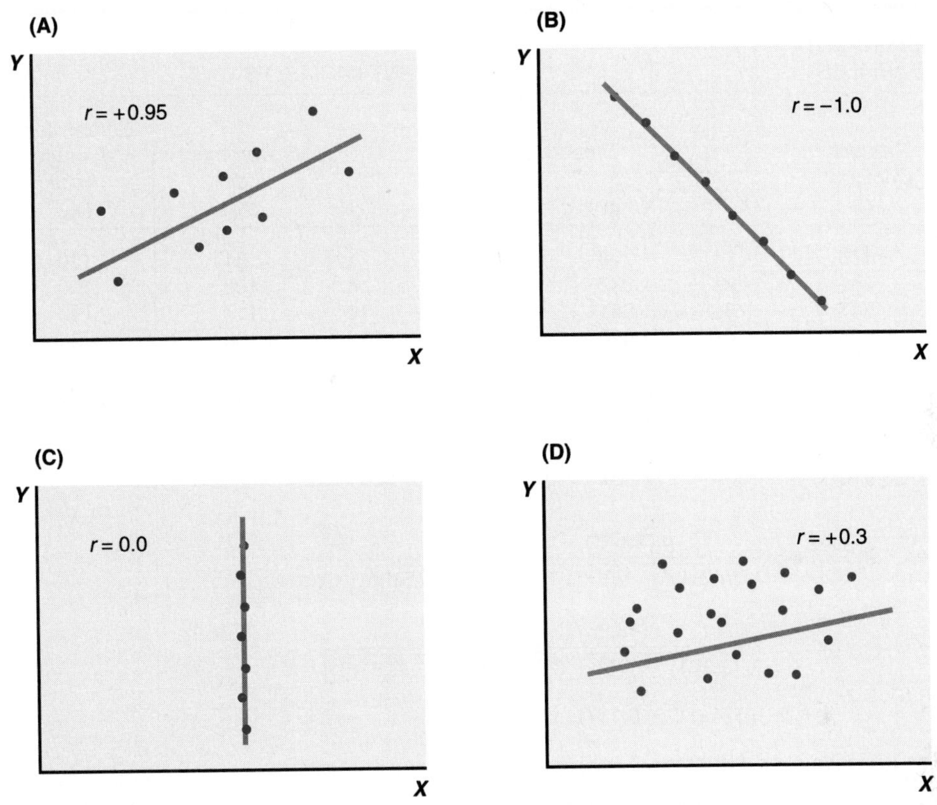

To illustrate the use, computation, and interpretation of the correlation coefficient, let's look at the following problem. Suppose we wanted to predict a company's product demand by selecting the best predictive variable from a set of three variables: time expressed in years, government index values, and a competitor's average yearly product prices. Our objective is to develop a forecasting model for product demand using one of these three predictive or independent variables. To select the best independent variable, we can compute their correlation coefficients with the dependent variable and choose the one that has the greatest degree of relationship. In Table 3-2 the data for the variables, the summed computations for the correlation formulas, and the computed correlation coefficients are presented for the time in years variable. The independent variables are labeled with subscripted X variables (time in years is X_1, government index is X_2, and competitor's average price is X_3). Based on the results, we can see that the independent variable X_1 (time in years) has the weakest degree of relationship, but is positively related to the dependent variable product demand (that is, as time in years increases, so does product demand). The independent variable government index (X_2)

TABLE 3-2 CORRELATION COEFFICIENTS FOR THE THREE INDEPENDENT VARIABLES

DEPENDENT VARIABLE	*INDEPENDENT VARIABLES*					
Product Demand	*Time in Years*				*Government Index*	*Competitor's Average Price*
(Y)	(X_1)	(X_1Y)	(Y^2)	(X_1^2)	(X_2)	(X_3)
378	1	378	142,884	1	81	130
491	2	982	241,081	4	100	100
547	3	1,641	299,209	9	117	90
524	4	2,096	274,576	16	105	95
485	5	2,425	235,225	25	98	110
391	6	2,346	152,881	36	83	120
417	7	2,919	173,889	49	90	110
685	8	5,480	469,225	64	151	80
Σ3,918	Σ36	Σ18,267	Σ1,988,970	Σ204		

For Y and X_1: $r = \dfrac{n(\Sigma X_1Y) - (\Sigma X_1)(\Sigma Y)}{\sqrt{[n(\Sigma X^2) - (\Sigma X_1)^2][n(\Sigma Y^2) - (\Sigma Y)^2]}}$

$= \dfrac{8(18{,}267) - (36)(3{,}918)}{\sqrt{[8(204) - (36)^2][8(1{,}988{,}970) - (3{,}918)^2]}}$

$= 0.371\ (r^2 = 0.137)$

For Y and X_2: $r = 0.986\ (r^2 = 0.971)$

For Y and X_3: $r = -0.938\ (r^2 = 0.881)$

is positively related to product demand (the dependent variable) and has the strongest degree of relationship of the three independent variables. Competitor's average price is also very strongly related to product demand but is negatively related (as our product demand goes up, competitor average yearly prices go down). (The computation for these two variables are left to the student to confirm.) Based solely on the correlation coefficients we would select the government index variable to be included in our forecasting model.

The correlation coefficient does not provide researchers with a precise statistical degree of relationship between the X and Y variables. To obtain this information another statistic, the coefficient of determination, is commonly used. The **coefficient of determination,** found by squaring the correlation coefficient (r^2), presents the precise degree of linear relationship between the dependent and independent variables. It defines the proportion of variation in Y that is explained by X. Conversely, the **coefficient of nondetermination** $(1 - r^2)$ defines the degree of relationship between the dependent and independent variables that cannot be explained by using X to predict Y. The value of r^2 will always be between 0 and 1. The closer r^2 is to 1, the greater the proportion of variation in the dependent variable explained by independent variables and the more desirable the independent variable is for use in the forecasting model. The closer r^2 is to 0, the weaker the degree of relationship. This degree of relationship is expressed as a percentage of change in Y for each unit change in X. If, for example, we had a coefficient of determination of $r^2 = 1.00$, it would mean that 100 percent of variation in Y is explained by the variation in X. Alternatively, if we had a coefficient of determination of $r^2 = 0.00$, it would mean that 0 percent of variation in Y is explained by the variation in X.

QUESTION: What are the coefficients of determination and nondetermination for the time in years and government index independent variables presented in Table 3-2? How would you interpret each of these coefficients?

ANSWER: For the independent variable time in years or X_1, the coefficient of determination is $r^2 = (0.371)^2 = 0.137$. Its interpretation is that only 13.7 percent of the variation in product demand (Y) is explained by the variation in the number of years (X_1). The coefficient of nondetermination is $1 - r^2 = 1 - 0.137 = 0.863$. Its interpretation is that 86.3 percent of the variation in product demand is not explained by the variation in time in years. For the independent variable government index or X_2, the coefficient of determination is $r^2 = (0.985)^2 = 0.971$. Its interpretation is that 97.1 percent of the variation in actual demand (Y) is explained by the same variation in the government index values (X_2). The coefficient of nondetermination is $1 - r^2 = 1 - 0.971 = 0.029$. Its interpretation is that 2.9 percent of the variation in product demand is not explained by the government index values.

Correlation analysis can help find predictive variables but does not generate forecast values. To obtain forecast values we need to develop a forecasting model that will use the predictive variables.

Regression Analysis

Regression analysis is used to depict a linear trend in sales or product demand data over a period of time.[5] It involves the development of an equation that can be used to

---

[5] For additional information on the mathematical procedures of simple linear regression, see R. D. Mason and D. A. Lind, *Statistical Techniques in Business and Economics*, 8th ed. (Homewood, Ill.: Irwin, 1993), Chapters 13 and 14; L. L. Lapin, *Statistics for Modern Business Decisions*, 5th ed. (San Diego: Harcourt Brace Jovanovich, 1990), Chapter 10; and A. Webster, *Applied Statistics for Business and Economics* (Homewood, Ill.: Irwin, 1992), Chapters 12 and 13.

generate forecast values. There are several types of regression models.[6] We will examine the simple linear regression and multiple regression models.

SIMPLE LINEAR REGRESSION A **simple linear regression** model expresses the linear relationship between the dependent variable and one independent variable. The functional relationship can be expressed as follows:

$$\overline{Y}_p = a + bX$$

where

$\overline{Y}_p$ = the average predicted (or forecast) value of the dependent variable

a = the constant value (the Y-axis intercept value)

b = the per unit change value representing the change in Y for each unit change in X (the slope of the line)

X = the predictive or independent variable

The value of b is particularly important to forecasters in that the sign of the slope of the line defines the trend of the dependent variable. If the slope is positive, the trend line increases positively as in Figure 3-2(a). If the slope is negative, the trend line decreases negatively as in Figure 3-2(b).

One of the most widely used mathematical procedures to generate the simple regression model is the least-squares method. The **least-squares method** mathematically fits data into a single line. In Figure 3-3 we have a scatter diagram of data that have been regressed to a single line. In Figure 3-3 historic product demand data over a period of time have been used to generate the linear model by regressing all of the data points to a single line. Once the historic data have been expressed as a linear equation, an operations manager can use the equation to predict future demand by substituting values of a predictive variable (X) into the model and deriving averaged product demand values ($\overline{Y}_p$). The difference between the actual product demand and the predicted values on the regession line represent forecast **error.** Deriving the values of a and b in the regression model requires the following formulas:

$$b = \frac{n(\Sigma XY) - (\Sigma X)(\Sigma Y)}{n(\Sigma X^2) - (\Sigma X)^2}$$

$$a = \frac{\Sigma Y}{n} - b\frac{\Sigma X}{n}$$

[6] For additional information on the application of simple regression in forecasting, see L. L. Lapin, *Statistics for Modern Business Decisions*, 5th ed. (San Diego: Harcourt Brace Jovanovich, 1990), Chapter 18; and A. Webster, *Applied Statistics for Business and Economics* (Homewood, Ill.: Irwin, 1992), Chapter 16.

FIGURE 3-3 SCATTER DIAGRAM AND REGRESSION LINE

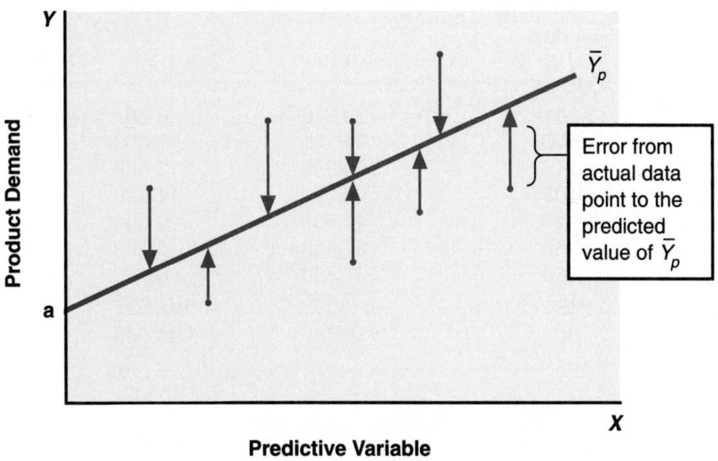

where

n = the sample size
X = the independent variable
Y = the dependent variable

To illustrate the use of the least-squares method to generate the regression model, let's look at a problem. Suppose we want to predict product demand (the dependent variable) for a company using a simple regression model. Let's suppose that we decided to use government index values of the company's industrial product demand as the independent variable in the model. In Table 3-3, eight government index and product demand paired values, which are used as data in the model, are presented. Based on these data the regression model parameters of *a* and *b* are computed to develop a simple linear regression model. (A **parameter** is a constant value in a model.)

$$\overline{Y}_p = 40.555 + 4.356X$$

This equation indicates that the slope is positive, so the trend for this company's product demand is positive. That is, as government index values increase, so will the company's product demand. We can also use this model to forecast or predict product demand in future years. For example, if the next period's government index value is 101, then the forecast value of the company's product demand is estimated as

$$\overline{Y}_p = 40.555 + 4.356(101)$$
$$= 480.51$$

TABLE 3-3 SIMPLE REGRESSION MODEL USING LEAST-SQUARES METHOD

Product Demand (Y)	*Government Index (X)*	*(XY)*	X^2	Y^2
378	81	30,618	6,561	142,884
491	100	49,100	10,000	241,081
547	117	63,999	13,689	299,209
524	105	55,020	11,025	274,576
485	98	47,530	9,604	235,225
391	83	32,453	6,889	152,881
417	90	37,530	8,100	173,889
685	151	103,435	22,801	469,225
3,918	825	419,685	88,669	1,988,970

PARAMETERS

$$b = \frac{n(\Sigma XY) - (\Sigma X)(\Sigma Y)}{n(\Sigma X^2) - (\Sigma X)^2} = \frac{8(419{,}685) - (825)(3{,}918)}{8(88{,}669) - (825)^2} = 4.356$$

$$a = \frac{\Sigma Y}{n} - b\frac{\Sigma X}{n} = \frac{3918}{8} - 4.356\frac{825}{8} = 40.555$$

REGRESSION MODEL

$$\overline{Y}_p = a + bX = 40.555 + 4.356X$$

MULTIPLE REGRESSION A **multiple regression** model expresses the linear relationship between the dependent variable and a set of independent variables. The functional relationship can be expressed as follows:

$$\overline{Y}_p = a + b_1X_1 + b_2X_2 + \ldots + b_nX_n$$

where

$\overline{Y}_p$ = the average predicted (or forecast) value of the dependent variable

a = the constant value (the Y-axis intercept value)

b = the partial per unit change values representing the change in Y for each unit of X

X = the set of predictive or independent variables

n = the number of predictive or independent variables that make up the set of variables in the model

The b parameters are referred to as **net regression coefficients** because they measure the change in $\overline{Y}_p$ for each change in one unit of an independent variable while holding all of the other independent variables constant.

The computational process used to derive a multiple regression model is quite tedious and will not be presented here.[7] Operations managers and forecasters do not calculate simple or multiple regression models manually. Instead they use computer packages that contain multiple regression models. Computer packages such as *SPSS (Statistical Package for the Social Sciences)* for mainframe computers and *Micro Production* for microcomputers can be used to derive multiple regression models. The convenience of computers has placed increased emphasis on the use and understanding of both simple and multiple regression in forecasting.[8]

Smoothing Models

One of the disadvantages in using simple linear regression analysis is that it converts historic raw data into a simple linear expression. Yet we know that some types of data can follow a cyclical or nonlinear behavior pattern. A group of forecasting models used to examine the nonlinear behavior of data are called **smoothing models.** Smoothing models seek to smooth out the variations in data to reveal the true nonlinear behavior patterns of the data. Figure 3-4 presents an example of how product demand data might look if we were to smooth out some of the variation that exists in the actual demand data. We will examine three types of smoothing models: centered moving averages, weighted moving averages, and exponential smoothing.

CENTERED MOVING AVERAGE A **centered moving average (CMA)** is an averaging technique used to smooth raw data in order to reveal nonlinear variation, such as cyclical variation. A centered moving average is not typically used to forecast specific values, but instead is used to help us understand nonlinear variation trends in cyclical variation (long-term trends). If sufficient nonlinear behavior is observed in the product demand data, then centered moving average statistics can also be used to support the use of nonlinear forecasting models in place of linear forecasting models.

Before we can compute centered moving averages, we must decide on the number of values to use in the average. Such a decision is usually based on the nature and degree of the variation in the demand data being examined. The greater the variation, the greater the number of values required to smooth out the variation. The exact number can be defined by research or arbitrary selection. We discuss how the exact number can be determined by research later in this chapter. The objective is to smooth out the random variation to reveal the nonlinear trend or cyclical variation. The greater the number of values used in the centered moving average, the greater the total reduction

---

[7] For additional information on the mathematical procedures of multiple regression see L. L. Lapin, *Statistics for Modern Business Decisions,* 5th ed. (San Diego: Harcourt Brace Jovanovich, 1990), Chapter 11; and W. E. Becker and D. L. Harnett, *Business and Economics Statistics with Computer Applications* (Reading, Mass.: Addison-Wesley, 1987), Chapter 10.

[8] For an interesting comparative application see E. S. Gardner, "Box-Jenkins vs. Multiple Regression: Some Adventures in Forecasting for Blood Tests," *Interfaces,* 9, No. 4 (1979), 49–54.

FIGURE 3-4 SMOOTHED DATA

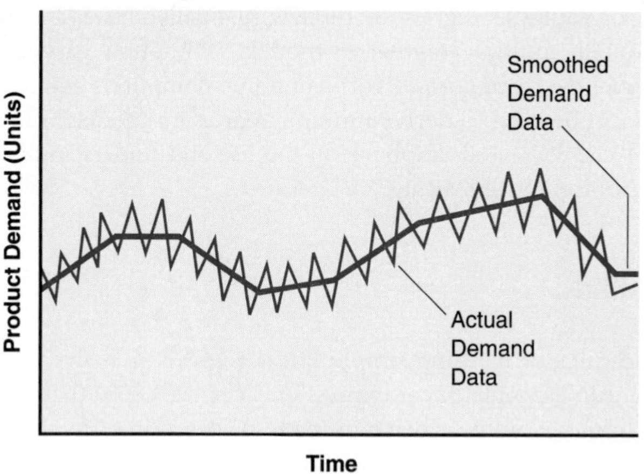

in variation. Unfortunately, the greater the number of values used, the fewer number of data points available for plotting.

Once we know the number of values to use in the average, the centered moving averages can be computed. To illustrate the computational procedure, let's look at an example. Suppose a company experienced a yearly product demand in units as presented in Table 3-4. As we can see in Table 3-4, the product demand during the ten-year period has a range of 562 units—a considerable demand variation. To smooth out some of the variation and attempt to identify the nonlinear trend in cyclical variation, we might choose to use a two-value CMA. The two-value CMAs are presented in Table 3-4. To obtain the two-value CMA of 350 we averaged 367 and 333. The 350 is "centered" in time between the first and second years. This centering process is why we call the value generated a *centered* moving average. The second CMA of 414 was obtained by averaging 333 and 495. By moving down the list of product demand values by year, we are generating moving average values. This yearly movement is why we call the value a centered moving average.

Having completed all of the two-value CMAs we can see that the variation has been reduced from 562 to 450, as measured by the two-value CMA range. Table 3-4 also presents CMA values for three-value and five-value models. As expected, the variation in the centered product demand data is reduced as the number of values are increased in computing the CMA. We can also see that the number of CMA values calculated decreases as the number of data in the average are increased. In Figure 3-5 each of the three CMAs are graphically presented with the actual product demand data. As we move from Figure 3-5(a) to Figure 3-5(c) and increase the number of values used in our average, the actual product demand data are reduced to a simpler curve with a single low demand point (in year 3) and a single high demand point (in year 6).

TABLE 3-4 CENTERED MOVING AVERAGE VALUES

Year	Actual Product Demand (unit)	Two-Value Centered Moving Average	Three-Value Centered Moving Average	Five-Value Centered Moving Average
1	367			
		350		
2	333		398.3	
		414		
3	495		477.7	475.0
		550		
4	605		558.3	486.6
		590		
5	575		535.0	599.0
		500		
6	425		631.7	641.0
		660		
7	895		675.0	633.0
		800		
8	705		721.7	605.0
		635		
9	565		568.3	
		500		
10	435			
Range*	562	450	323.4	166.0

* The range is found by subtracting the smallest value from the largest value.

The cyclical nature of product demand for this company is clearly revealed in this CMA-generated graph. We can interpret the direction of the curve, particularly in Figure 3-5(c), as indicating that this company's product demand is beginning to experience a downturn in demand (a recessionary period). Such information is particularly useful in making long-term investment decisions.

WEIGHTED MOVING AVERAGE Some of the oldest and simplest smoothing techniques used in forecasting are weighted moving averages.[9] A **weighted moving average (WMA)** is an extension of a centered moving average and is achieved by mathematically weighting the values used to compute the moving average. The weighted moving average technique can be used as a forecasting technique as well as a smoothing technique to help reveal cyclical variation in raw data. The mathematical expression for a weighted moving average can be expressed as follows:

$$f_t = a_{t-1}(w_1) + a_{t-2}(w_2) + \ldots + a_{t-n}(w_n)$$

[9] See P. R. Winters, "Forecasting Sales by Exponentially Weighted Moving Averages," *Journal of the Royal Statistical Society,* Series A, Vol. 146, Part 2 (1960), 150–157; E. Adam, "Individual Item Forecasting Model Evaluation," *Decision Science,* 4, No. 4 (1973), 458–470; and E. J. Elton and M. J. Gruber, "Earnings Estimates and the Accuracy of Expectational Data," *Management Science,* 18, No. 8 (1972), B409–B424.

FIGURE 3-5 CENTERED MOVING AVERAGES

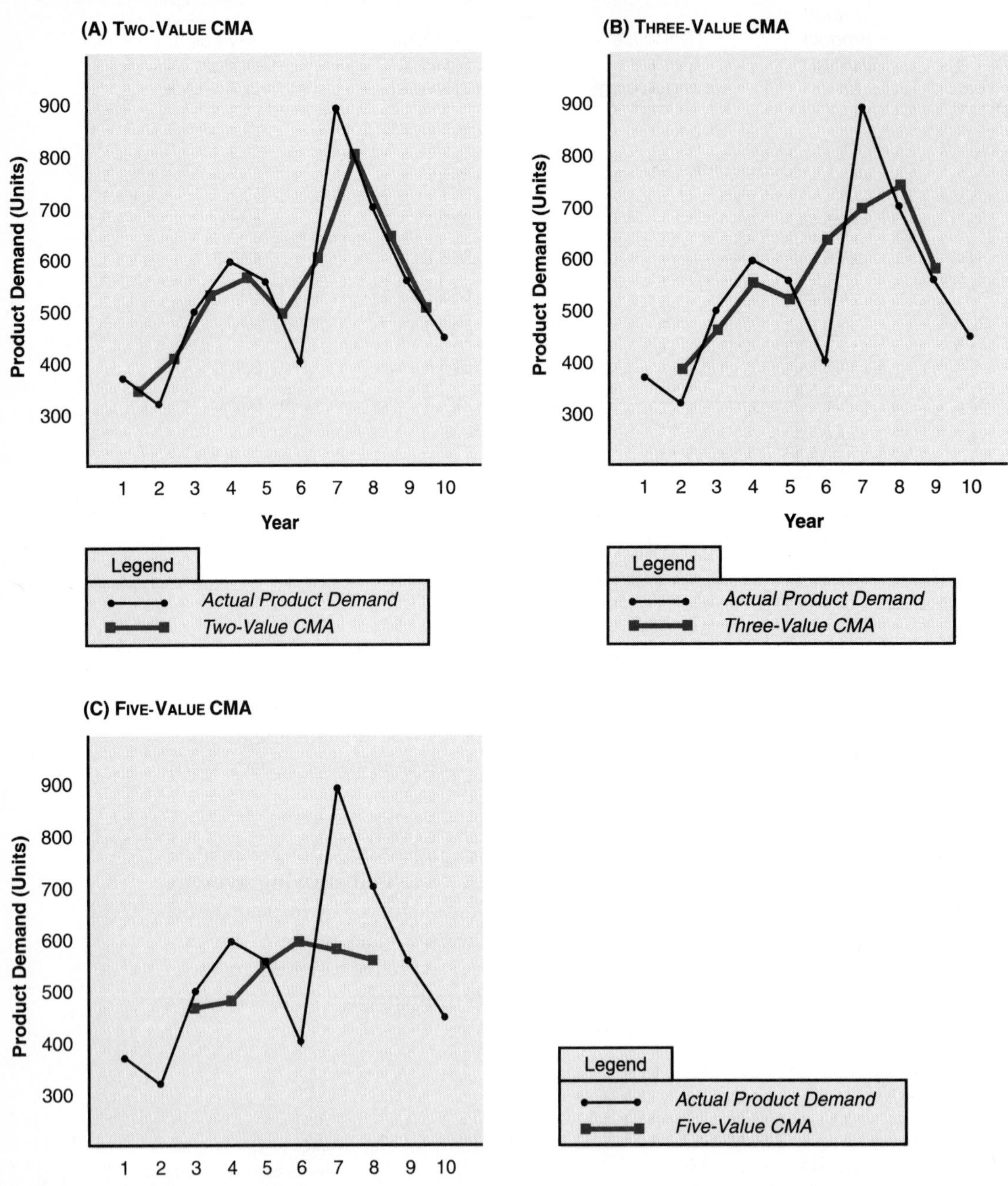

where

f_t = the forecast value for the current time period t

a_{t-i} = the actual value that occurred in the ith time period

w_i = the mathematical weight attached to the ith time period's value

n = some number of past time periods chosen for averaging purposes

The summation of the mathematical weights in this expression must equal one. The selection of the n number of values to use in the average and the selection of the mathematical weights are critically important in determining the accuracy of the weighted moving average forecasting model. The actual selection of the number of values to average and the weights are usually determined by research. The procedure for selecting these model parameters is discussed later in this chapter.

Let's examine how the weighted moving average is computed and used in forecasting. In Table 3-5, eight years of actual product demand data are presented. If we decide to use a three-value WMA with weights of 0.60, 0.20, and 0.20, respectively, we will develop the six forecast values presented in Table 3-5. The forecast value for year 4 is computed using the formula above as follows:

$$f_4 = 735(0.60) + 814(0.20) + 673(0.20)$$
$$= 738.4 \text{ units}$$

In this formula, we are using the weighted actual product demand data during the last three years to forecast the next year's demand. The process is repeated until we finally use the last three years of actual demand to forecast the ninth year's demand.

TABLE 3-5 FORECAST VALUES USING A WEIGHTED MOVING AVERAGE MODEL

Year *(t)*	*Actual Demand* *(a_t)*	*Forecast* Demand* *(f_t)*
1	673	—
2	814	—
3	735	—
4	542	738.4
5	584	635.0
6	625	605.8
7	704	600.2
8	787	664.2
9	—	738.0

* Forecast is based on weighted moving average of three values with weights of 0.20, 0.20, and 0.60, respectively.

EXPONENTIAL SMOOTHING One of the most commonly used quantitative models in forecasting is exponential smoothing.[10] **Exponential smoothing** is a type of weighted average forecasting technique that, depending on the formulation, uses a single time period to forecast into the future. The forecasting formula for the single time period exponential smoothing model is

$$f_t = f_{t-1} + \alpha\,(a_{t-1} - f_{t-1})$$

where

f_t = the value to be forecast in the current time period t
f_{t-1} = the last time period's forecast value
α (alpha) = a mathematical weight or smoothing constant
a_{t-1} = the actual product demand data that occurred in the last time period

The difference between a_{t-1} and f_{t-1} is the forecasting error in the last forecast time period. The mathematical weight of α must be a value between 0 and 1, which represents the means by which we can weigh the importance of past forecasting inaccuracies in the forecast for the next time period. The smaller the α (values closer to zero), the slower the response rate to rapid changes in actual product demand data. The larger the α, the more the forecast values of f_t will be smoothed. For this reason, α is referred to as a *smoothing constant.*

To illustrate the use of the exponential smoothing model in forecasting, let's look at a simple forecasting situation. Suppose we want to forecast the demand of a product by using a simple exponential smoothing model with an $\alpha = 0.4$. Because the simple exponential smoothing model requires a single prior forecast time period, we will start from year 0 in Table 3-6. We can use the actual demand of 350 in year 0 to compute the forecast of the first year's demand, f_1. We must also make an assumption concerning the initial forecast to be used in calculating f_1. We will assume for this example that f_{t-1} will equal a_{t-1} for the initial forecast of f_1.

To obtain this initial forecast value, we can choose to average several prior actual demand values. The selection of the initial forecast value becomes less important as we use more values prior to the year that we intend to forecast.

Averaging the prior values for an initial forecast represents the assumption that each of the data used are of equal importance in the estimate of f_t. Yet in many situations older data are not as relevant and therefore should be weighted less than more current data. One approach to allow the model to exponentially weight the prior data (and also useful where we are limited to only a few prior actual a_t values) is to restructure the

[10] See E. S. Gardner, "Evolutionary Operation of the Exponential Smoothing Parameter: Revisited," *OMEGA,* 11, No. 6 (1983), 612–623; E. S. Gardner, "Exponential Smoothing: The State of the Art," *Journal of Forecasting,* 3 (1984), 23–27; E. S. Gardner and D. G. Dannenbring, "Forecasting with Exponential Smoothing: Some Guidelines for Model Selection," *Decision Sciences,* 11, No. 2 (1980), 370–383.

TABLE 3-6 FORECAST VALUES USING AN EXPONENTIAL SMOOTHING MODEL

Year* (t)	Actual Demand (a_t)	MODEL PARAMETERS† (α)	(a_{t-1})	(f_{t-1})	Forecast Demand‡ (f_t)
0	—	.4	350	350.0	350.0
1	400	.4	350	350.0	350.0
2	450	.4	400	350.0	370.0
3	550	.4	450	370.0	402.0
4	600	.4	550	402.0	461.2
5	500	.4	600	461.2	516.72
6	400	.4	500	516.72	510.032
7	300	.4	400	510.032	466.0192
8	400	.4	300	466.0192	399.6115
9	—	.4	400	399.6115	399.7669

* Actual demand of year 0 is used as a_{t-1} and f_{t-1} for the initial f_t.

† Assume initial forecast is equal to actual demand of 350 in prior period of year 0.

‡ Forecast is based on model: $f_t = f_{t-1} + \alpha(a_{t-1} - f_{t-1})$.

exponential smoothing model to include as many prior values as available. This restructuring can be illustrated for the situation in which we will use two prior values of a_t. Given the original exponential smoothing equation,

$$f_t = f_{t-1} + \alpha(a_{t-1} - f_{t-1})$$

we know that the following must also be true for a prior t-1 time period:

$$f_{t-1} = f_{t-2} + \alpha(a_{t-2} - f_{t-2})$$

We can also restructure the right-hand side of the original exponential smoothing equation in terms of f_{t-1}:

$$f_t = \alpha(a_{t-1}) + (1 - \alpha)(f_{t-1})$$

Finally, we can substitute the equation for f_{t-1} into the restructured original exponential smoothing equation to give us the exponentially weighted model containing the two prior values of a_t:

$$f_t = \alpha(a_{t-1}) + (1 - \alpha)(f_{t-1})[\alpha(a_{t-2}) + (1 - \alpha)(f_{t-2})]$$

This model can be expanded for any number of prior actual values as follows:

$$f_t = \alpha(a_{t-1}) + \alpha(1 - \alpha)(a_{t-2}) + \alpha(1 - \alpha)^2(a_{t-3}) + \alpha(1 - \alpha)^3(a_{t-4}) + \ldots$$

Notice how the exponential weighting pattern of the model is revealed in this equation. If we let $\alpha = 0.5$, it is easy to see how the model establishes the higher weights (that is, 0.5) for the more recent data (that is, a_{t-1}) and, likewise, the lesser weights to less recent data:

$$f_t = 0.5(a_{t-1}) + 0.25(a_{t-2}) + 0.125(a_{t-3}) + 0.0625(a_{t-4}) + \ldots$$

The model parameters and computations for the forecast values using the simple exponential smoothing model are presented in Table 3.6. In this example we smoothed eight years (years 1 to 8) of demand data and are only able to forecast one year, year 9. The forecast value for demand in year 9 is 399.7669. It is interesting to note in this example that the forecast demand or smoothed data for years 1 to 8 have a smaller range (166.72 = 516.72 − 350.00) than the actual demand data (300 = 600 − 300). This is quite in keeping with the objective of smoothing the data by reducing variation in the data set. As with the other quantitative forecasting models, we may need to reexamine the selection of what we should use for the value for α (the model parameters) to improve the forecasting ability of the model. This selection is derived from researching the models' accuracy and will be discussed later in this chapter.

Classical Decomposition

Classical decomposition is a process by which we can identify the four basic types of variation (trend, seasonal, cyclical, and irregular) in time series data. One of the many decomposition models assumes that product demand data are a function of the four types of variation. This can be expressed as

$$Y = T \times S \times C \times I$$

where

Y = product demand
T = trend variation
S = seasonal variation
C = cyclical variation
I = irregular variation

In this decomposition model the variation values are computed using a variety of forecasting methods. Classical decomposition uses such forecasting methods as regression and moving averages. In this text, we will not present the computational procedures for the classical decomposition model. Computerization of the classical decomposition procedures permit easy access to and use of this forecasting method. Operations managers, however, should understand the meaning of decomposition model output to effectively use this method.

Although many different computer packages are available for computing the classical decomposition variation values, we will examine the output of the Micro Production package. Understanding the basic presentation of any one computer software system's output of classical decomposition can help you understand many other computerized decomposition model outputs. In this computer package, trend is computed by using simple linear regression, and the trend values are presented in the same units of measure as the data (units or dollars). The values for seasonal and irregular variation are expressed as index values. The interpretation of the index values is based on an index average of

100. Specifically, if the index is less than 100, below-average seasonal activity is indicated, and if the index is more than 100, above-average seasonal activity is indicated.

Because seasonal variation is an element in the decomposition model, we must have data that divide the year into equal time periods to reveal seasonal fluctuations. We also need to have two or more years of data to satisfy seasonal and cyclical behavior requirements of the model used in the computer program. In Table 3-7 the sample data for a time series problem are presented. The individual quarters are numbered for identification purposes.

In Figure 3-6 the computer printout of the decomposition statistics is presented. To obtain this solution, we choose to use a four-value (that is, four quarters in a year) moving average. The selection of the number of values for smoothing is required as an input (number of moving periods) for this and most other computer programs.

We can interpret the printout in Figure 3-6 as follows:

Moving average. This is a moving average of cyclical variation. The cyclical variation obtained from a four-value moving average of the data [for example, $(34 + 37 + 39 + 45)/4 = 38.75$] shows a constant increase in demand indicating a period of growth in product demand.

Trend forecast. The trend forecast of the product demand is estimated by using simple regression on the moving average values. By regressing the cyclical variation to a line indicating the trend, we remove the cyclical variation. The resulting trend forecast indicates that demand is increasing in each quarter. For short-term or intermediate-term planning, we have a favorable increase in product demand that might signal the need for increases in human resources and inventory.

Seasonal-irregular component. The seasonal-irregular component is an index of what is left over after trend and cyclical variations are removed from the actual demand data. The basic logic used to derive the index values is simply expressed in the equation shown on page 102.

TABLE 3-7 SAMPLE DATA FOR TIME SERIES DECOMPOSITION PROBLEM

Year	*Quarter (no.)*	*Product Demand*
1988	1 (1)	34
	2 (2)	37
	3 (3)	39
	4 (4)	45
1989	1 (5)	52
	2 (6)	61
	3 (7)	65
	4 (8)	68
1990	1 (9)	76
	2(10)	80

FIGURE 3-6 COMPUTER PRINTOUT OF TIME SERIES DECOMPOSITION PROBLEM RESULTS

Program: Demand Forecasting / Decomposition Multiplicative Model

Problem Title: Sample Problem

***** Input Data *****

Number of Moving Periods : 4
Number of Observations : 10

Data values entered are shown below

***** Program Output *****

Period	Data	Moving Average	Seasonal-Irregular Component	Deseasonalized Data
1	34.000		1.275	26.670
2	37.000		1.141	32.429
3	39.000	38.750	1.021	38.187
4	45.000	43.250	1.024	43.946
5	52.000	49.250	1.046	49.705
6	61.000	55.750	1.100	55.464
7	65.000	61.500	1.062	61.223
8	68.000	67.500	1.015	66.982
9	76.000	72.250	1.045	72.741
10	80.000		1.019	78.500

<< Short Range Forecast >>

Period	Trend Forecast	Seasonal Factor	Forecast
11	84.259	0.976	82.212
12	90.018	0.955	85.985
13	95.777	1.051	100.670
14	101.536	1.018	103.364

***** End of Output *****

$$\text{Seasonal irregular variation } (S \times I) = \frac{\text{Variation in actual data}}{\text{Trend} \times \text{cyclical variation}} \text{ or } \frac{T \times S \times C \times I}{T \times C}$$

Having determined the trend and cyclical variation components, they are used to algebraically isolate the remaining seasonal and irregular variation components. The chief forecasting value of the seasonal-irregular component is the computation of seasonal data and seasonal variation.

Deseasonalized data. Deseasonalized data are the adjusted demand data with the seasonal variation removed. This is an additional source of information not always included in the time series analysis. It is particularly important in forecasting when seasonal variation is a dominant source of variation in the actual data. We can see that the deseasonalized data have the effect of reducing demand in each quarter. Deseasonalized data are very useful in medium-term planning (for one or two years) when operations managers are determining average demand requirements for aggregate human resouces, inventory, and production and are not as concerned about short seasonal variation.

Seasonal factor. The seasonal factor is the adjusted seasonal-irregular component with the irregular variation removed. It represents an index value used to describe seasonal variation from an average level of demand. As we can see, seasonal variation is responsible for the below-average demand (below an index of 1.00) in quarters 11 and 12 as well as the above-average demand in quarters 13 and 14. This permits operations managers to conduct short-term planning. The seasonal factor also represents a percentage adjustment factor to adjust the trend forecast value (a regressed average value) for the effects of seasonal variation. By multiplying the seasonal factor by the trend forecast, we obtain the seasonally adjusted forecast values that can be used in short-term—quarterly in this example—planning of needs such as human resource requirements.

Forecast. The forecast values are average values that have been adjusted for trend, cyclical, seasonal, and irregular variation. Operations managers use them to provide a forecast of demand that is an average value of demand per quarter but considers the unique variations that exist in the actual demand data.

The presentation of the decomposition method in this section is only an introduction to this subject. The underlying assumptions required in using decomposition models are numerous, and the brief discussion presented here hardly does justice to this very powerful forecasting tool. The application does illustrate some of the different types of forecasting information provided by the classical decomposition model and how an operations manager might use that information in forecasting and operations planning.

Other Quantitative Forecasting Methods

There are many quantitative forecasting methods other than those mentioned in this chapter. Although it is not possible to discuss in detail all of the forecasting methods currently used in industry, two of the more popular methods worth noting include the Box-Jenkins method and the Census Method II.

The **Box-Jenkins method** is used to analyze time series data in a way similar to that of classical decomposition; it is chiefly used for short- and medium-range forecasting. The Box-Jenkins method of forecasting uses several forecasting methods including regression and moving averages, and it can provide very accurate time series forecasts.[11]

---

[11] For detailed information on the Box-Jenkins procedures see J. C. Hoff, *A Practical Guide to Box-Jenkins Forecasting* (Belmont, Calif.: Lifetime Learning Publications, 1983).

The **Census Method II** forecasting process is a decomposition forecasting model that was developed by the U.S. Bureau of the Census. This forecasting model is different from the classical decomposition method in that it smooths out irregular fluctuations by removing values that are abnormally high or low and provides test statistics that can be used to show how well the decomposition process has been achieved. The Census Method II model can be applied to medium-term forecasting, but unfortunately it requires a major amount of data for model-building purposes.

SELECTING THE BEST FORECASTING METHOD

An individual or an organization might select a particular forecasting method and consider it the best for many reasons.[12] Some of these reasons are qualitative (for example, timeliness of forecast) and some are quantitative (for example, cost of forecast).

Qualitative Factors in Method Selection

Three qualitative factors that help determine the type of forecasting method to select include time, input characteristics, and output characteristics.

TIME The forecasting method's ability to forecast over time (forecasting into long-, medium-, or short-range time periods) must match the appropriate time span of the nature of the demand the method is to model. A short-range forecast of daily demand for a service product, like tow truck demand, is best estimated by using short-range methods, like the weighted moving average, rather than long-term methods, like time series analysis. The time-related urgency of receiving a forecast and updating it also helps determine which method is to be selected. Forecasting methods that take longer to use than operations managers can afford to wait can be qualitatively screened out during the selection process.

INPUT CHARACTERISTICS The amount of input data required for a forecasting model to generate an effective forecast can be used to screen prospective forecasting methods. If no data exist on a subject such as technology trends, then judgmental forecasting methods may be the only methods available. Some models, like the weighted moving average, may take only a couple of data points to provide a forecast, whereas other

[12] For a review of the basics see J. C. Chambers, S. K. Mullick, and D. C. Smith, "Selecting the Best Forecasting Technique," *Harvard Business Review* (July–August 1971), 10–15; D. W. McLeavey, et al., "An Empirical Evaluation of Individual Item Forecasting Models," *Decision Sciences,* 12, No. 4 (1983), 708–714; R. Winkler and S. Makridakis, "The Combination of Forecasts: Some Empirical Results," *Journal of the Royal Statistical Society,* 146 (1983), 150–157; E. Mahmoud, "Accuracy in Forecasting: A Survey," *Journal of Forecasting,* 3 (1984), 139–159; and A. E. Bopp, "On Combining Forecasts: Some Extensions and Results," *Management Science,* 31, No. 12 (December 1985), 1492–1498.

methods like time series analysis need considerably more data. Also, the variability in the data can limit the types of forecasting methods used. If data behave cyclically, then linear models like the regression models presented in this chapter may not be as applicable as the nonlinear models.

OUTPUT CHARACTERISTICS The amount of detail-reporting requirements necessary for users should be customized to users' needs. If forecasts are required, daily, then forecasting methods that provide short-range forecasts of daily fluctuations of demand should be selected.

Operations managers should take these qualitative factors and subjectively weigh and decide which forecasting method provides the best fit with the unique nature of their operation. One qualitative method that can be used to determine the best forecasting method from a collection of methods is to qualitatively rank each method and add up the ranks as a score. A group of individuals or a single manager can rank each forecasting method by specific selection criteria. The ranks are then added to form a score of desirability for the method used in that operation. This selection process is called a scoring method of selection.

QUESTION: Suppose that a company had to choose one of three forecasting methods (models A, B, or C) based on the operations manager's qualitative ranking of their fitness to provide timely information, require the least input, and maximize forecasting output. The operations manager's ranking of the forecasting models are as follows:

	FORECASTING MODEL		
Selection Criteria	*A*	*B*	*C*
Timeliness	3	1	2
Input	2	1	3
Output	3	2	1
Total	8	4	6

If a rank of 1 represents the best fit and a rank of 3 is the worst fit, which of the three models should be selected based on a scoring method?

ANSWER: From the summation of the ranks, the best-fitting model is model B.

Quantitative Factors in Method Selection

Two quantitative factors that help determine the selection of forecasting method include cost and accuracy.

COST The cost of forecasting can be quite an operating expense. The cost of computers, software systems, system maintenance personnel, and forecasting staff (in larger organizations) can all be quite expensive. If the cost of a forecasting method is greater than the cost-saving information it will provide, it will not be selected.

ACCURACY The more accurate the forecast provided by a forecasting method, the more desirable the method's selection. Likewise, the more inaccurate or error ridden the forecasting, the less desirable the method's selection.

The importance of a relatively error-free forecasting method is considered by many to be the key issue in method selection.[13] To help forecasters assess error, a number of statistics that indicate the degree of forecasting error have been specially devised.

Minimizing Forecasting Error

By minimizing the forecast error, we can determine which forecasting model will be the best for our use. To determine the forecasting error we can use several statistical procedures including the mean absolute deviation (MAD), mean of the squared error (MSE), and tracking signals. The **mean absolute deviation** or **MAD** statistic is the average of the absolute differences between forecasted and actual values. The MAD statistic is given by the equation

$$\text{MAD} = \frac{\sum_{t=1}^{n} |a_t - f_t|}{n}$$

where

n = the number of time periods used
a = an actual value that occurred in a tth time period
f = the forecast value for the tth time period

The **mean of the squared errors** or **MSE** statistic is the sum of squared differences between actual and forecast behavior divided by n. The formula for the MSE statistic is quite similar to the MAD statistic:

$$\text{MSE} = \frac{\sum_{t=1}^{n} (a_t - f_t)^2}{n}$$

[13] J. S. Armstrong, "Forecasting by Extrapolation: Conclusions from 25 Years of Research," *Interfaces*, 14, No. 6 (November–December 1984), 52–66.

PROCEDURE FOR COMPARING METHODS Regardless of which of these two statistics are chosen to measure forecasting error, the criterion for selecting the best forecasting model is fairly simple. The ideal forecasting model will have a MAD or a MSE equal to zero. Unfortunately, the possibility of these statistics equaling zero is almost nonexistent. The next best selection criterion is to choose a model that gives the smallest MAD or MSE. A MAD or MSE value close to zero indicates a low error rate when using that forecasting model.

In actual practice, the selection of a forecasting model is a very important decision. Operations managers usually allow their organization's specialists or researchers to determine the best model (or models) from a performance comparison of many forecasting models. The procedure for this research is simple but tedious. The procedure of selecting the best forecasting model usually consists of the following steps:

1. Determine which types of models are possible candidates for the forecasting activity.
2. Select typical historic forecasting data for comparative purposes.
3. Develop a separate forecasting model based on each type of model selected in step 1.
4. Generate forecast values for the same period of time as the historic data period determined in step 2.
5. Compute comparative statistics (MAD, MSE) on each model's forecasting performance in predicting the actual historic data.
6. Select the model whose comparative statistics minimize the forecasting error.

To illustrate the use of the MAD and MSE statistics and the model selection steps, let's look at a model selection problem. Suppose we want to determine which of two models, a least-squares model or an exponential smoothing model, is the more accurate forecasting model of a service organization's customer demand. The selection of these two particular forecasting models was determined by the availability of computer software for the forecasting methods. Having determined the forecasting methods to use in the comparison, we collect historic data for projection purposes.

In Table 3-8, eight time periods of actual service demand data have been collected to compare the effectiveness of the two models. The forecast of the demand data in Table 3-8 was made by first developing a least-squares model ($\overline{Y}_p = 862.4 + 20.7X$) and then substituting the time period (the independent variable X) numbers into the model to derive the forecast demand values. Based on the differences between the actual and forecast demand, we can compute the MAD and MSE statistics for comparative purposes. The MAD statistic of 71.03 and the MSE statistic of 6,761.03 reflect the existence of forecasting error when the least-squares model is used to forecast service demand in this problem. By themselves, these statistics will not tell us whether we should use the least-squares method or not. It is only when compared with the MAD and MSE statistics of other models, using the same data, that a decision can be made on which model would be the best selection for forecasting demand.

TABLE 3-8 CALCULATION OF MAD AND MSE STATISTICS FOR LEAST-SQUARES FORECASTING MODEL

Time Period (t)	*Actual Demand (a)*	*Forecast Demand (f)**	$a - f$	$\lvert a - f\rvert$	$(a - f)^2$
1	750	883.1	−133.1	133.1	17,715.61
2	886	903.8	−17.8	17.8	316.84
3	999	924.5	74.5	74.5	5,550.25
4	1,043	945.2	97.8	97.8	9,564.84
5	1,077	965.9	111.1	111.1	12,343.21
6	978	986.6	−8.6	8.6	73.96
7	963	1,007.3	−44.3	44.3	1,962.49
8	947	1,028.0	−81.0	81.0	6,561.00
Total				568.2	54,088.20

$$\text{MAD} = \frac{\sum_{t=1}^{n} |a_t - f_t|}{n} = \frac{568.2}{8} = 71.03$$

$$\text{MSE} = \frac{\sum_{t=1}^{n} (a_t - f_t)^2}{n} = \frac{54{,}088.20}{8} = 6{,}761.03$$

* Based on least-squares model, $\overline{Y}_p = a + bX$, where X = actual demand and the resulting model is $\overline{Y}_p$.

In Table 3-9 an exponential smoothing model is used to forecast the same actual demand that was forecast in the least-squares model. For purposes of this example we arbitrarily let $\alpha = 0.3$ and let the initial forecast be equal to the first period's actual demand of 750. As can be seen in Table 3-9, the application of the exponential smoothing model resulted in a MAD statistic of 92.36 and a MSE of 15,788.96. Comparing both the MAD and MSE statistics of the least-squares model with those of the exponential smoothing model, it is clear that the least-squares model's forecast error is smaller and, as such, provides a more accurate forecast. If we were to base the selection decision of forecasting models solely on accuracy, we would choose the least-squares model in this example.

SELECTING THE BEST PARAMETER In the model selection problem we arbitrarily selected an α of 0.3 for the exponential smoothing model. The selection of such an important parameter for this type of model can have a dramatic effect on its accuracy and use. In Figure 3-7 the relationship between forecasting error and the parameter α selection is presented. As can be seen in Figure 3-7, an α exists that will minimize the forecasting error. Accuracy statistics such as MAD can be used to research and select the best parameters for use in forecasting models. Similar to the model selection process, the parameter selection is a matter of substitution.

TABLE 3-9 CALCULATION OF MAD AND MSE STATISTICS FOR EXPONENTIAL SMOOTHING FORECASTING MODEL

Time Period (t)	*Actual Demand (a)*	*Forecasted Demand (f)**	*a − f*	*|a − f|*	*(a − f)²*
1	750	750	0	0	0
2	886	750	136.0	136.0	18,496.00
3	999	790.8	208.2	208.2	43,347.24
4	1,043	853.3	189.7	189.7	36,001.26
5	1,077	910.2	166.8	166.8	27,828.24
6	978	960.2	17.8	17.8	315.87
7	963	965.6	−2.6	2.6	6.55
8	947	964.8	−17.8	17.8	316.53
Total				738.9	126,311.70

$$\text{MAD} = \frac{\sum_{t=1}^{n} |a_t - f_t|}{n} = \frac{738.9}{8} = 92.36$$

$$\text{MSE} = \frac{\sum_{t=1}^{n} (a_t - f_t)^2}{n} = \frac{126,311.70}{8} = 15788.96$$

* Based on exponential smoothing model, $f_t = f_{t-1} + \alpha\,(a_{t-1} - f_{t-1})$ when $\alpha = .3$ and initial forecast $f_1 = 750$.

FIGURE 3-7 RELATIONSHIP BETWEEN FORECASTING ERROR AND α PARAMETER SELECTION

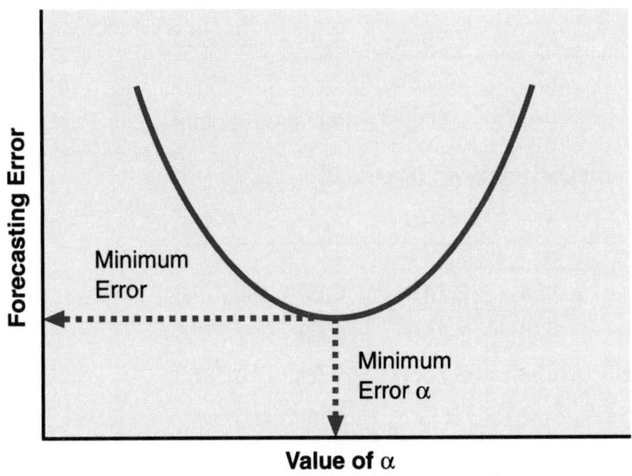

To illustrate how we determine the best parameter, let's look at the following parameter selection problem. Suppose we want to determine the α parameter for an exponential smoothing model that will minimize forecasting error. In Table 3-10(a) a service organization's actual demand is presented over a historic forecast horizon of ten time periods. As a first phase in our analysis, we must arbitrarily decide on a value of α to incorporate into our exponential smoothing model. With the availability of computers to remove the tedious burden of computation, we might choose to run fractional

TABLE 3-10 EXPONENTIAL SMOOTHING VALUES AND RESULTING MAD STATISTICS

(A) STATISTICS FOR DIFFERING αS (PHASE 1)

Time Period (t)	Actual Demand (a)	Forecasted Demand (f)*	a − f	|a − f|
1	200	200	0	0
2	205	200	5	5
3	210	200	10	10
4	204	200	4	4
5	207	200	7	7
6	209	200	9	9
7	212	200	12	12
8	210	200	10	10
9	207	200	7	7
10	209	200	9	9
				73

$$\text{MAD} = \frac{\sum_{t=1}^{n} |a_t - f_t|}{n} = \frac{73}{10} = 7.3 \text{ (for } \alpha = 0.0)$$

α	MAD	α	MAD	α	MAD
0.0	7.3000	0.4	2.8838	0.8	2.9642
0.1	5.1247	0.5	2.7707	0.9	3.0404
0.2	3.7177	0.6	2.7942	1.0	3.1000
0.3	3.1000	0.7	2.8786		

Minimum points (α = 0.5 and 0.6)

(B) STATISTICS FOR DIFFERING αS (PHASE 2)

α	MAD	α	MAD	α	MAD
0.51	2.7634	0.54	2.7494	0.57	2.7710
0.52	2.7566	0.55	2.7564	0.58	2.7786
0.53	2.7505	0.56	2.7636	0.59	2.7863

Minimum point (α = 0.54)

* Based on exponential smoothing model, $f_t = f_{t-1} + \alpha(a_{t-1} - f_{t-1})$, where $\alpha = 0.0$.

numbers from zero to one (0.1, 0.2, 0.3, etc.). The α value must be positive and in most situations will probably be a small number close to zero. We simply substitute the differing αs into the exponential smoothing model, generate the forecasts, and determine the MAD statistics for each α.

We can see in Table 3-10 the MAD computations for α. The first phase of our α search consists of selecting the αs between zero and one and computing the MAD statistics based on the forecasted results. These MAD statistics are presented in Table 3-10(a). The minimum MAD value occurs when an α between 0.5 and 0.6 is selected. A second phase of selection involves substituting αs between 0.51 and 0.59 into the exponential smoothing model, which is presented in Table 3-10(b). The α that minimizes forecast error at the end of this second phase of the search is 0.54. We might continue to a third or fourth phase to refine our α if such precision is necessary or desired.

Using Tracking Signals To Monitor Forecasting Error

Once the model and parameters are selected, based on past historic information, the forecasting process begins. Unfortunately, past history does not continuously repeat itself. Our earlier discussion of factors that influence product and service demand attest to the potential for change in the future. For this reason managers must continuously review the accuracy performance of their forecasting models. One of the ways operations managers can build a control mechanism into their forecasting information system is through a tracking signal. **Tracking signals (TS)** are statistical techniques used to signal when the accuracy of a forecasting model is in doubt. Several tracking techniques have been developed for use in forecasting. The most commonly used tracking signal, and the one described in the *Dictionary of the American Production and Inventory Control Society*, can be expressed as follows:

$$TS_t = \frac{\sum_{t=1}^{n} (a_t - f_t)}{\text{MAD}} \quad \text{or} \quad \frac{\text{RSFE}}{\text{MAD}}$$

where

TS_t = tracking signal in the tth time period
n = the number of time periods used
a = an actual value that occurred in the tth time period
f = the forecast value for the tth time period
MAD = mean absolute deviation
RSFE = running sum of the forecast error

The difference between the actual demand values, a, and their respective forecast values, f, are summed for each t of the n time periods. The difference of $a_t - f_t$ is the forecast error. As we sum the forecast error, the accumulation is called the *running sum of the forecast error (RSFE).* We compute the ratio of the RSFE with a given MAD statistic. The MAD statistic remains constant over the n time periods. The assumption in using this tracking signal is that the sum of the positive forecasting error and the negative forecasting error should equal zero. This means that the sum of TS for each t time period should average to zero.

As variation in the future behavior of an organization's product or service demand changes the expected variation in demand data, the tracking signal eventually will be violated or "tripped." A tracking signal is tripped when the value of TS exceeds a predetermined boundary. The boundary values are sometimes determined by a manager's experience, historic use of the technique (for example, standard operating policy), or by various statistical techniques. One statistical approach to establishing the boundaries is based on the concepts of the normal distribution and the standard deviation. (Students unfamiliar with these concepts should review the material in Appendix A: The Normal Probability Distribution.) The square root of the MSE statistic gives us an estimate of the standard deviation of forecasting error. If we assume that the forecast errors are normally distributed, we can also assume that the distribution can be divided into standardized boundaries using the MSE statistic. The formula for upper and lower control limits or boundaries based on this concept is presented in Table 3-11. The tracking signal boundaries in Table 3-11 are usually used on an absolute basis (once the tracking signal exceeds the boundary, the signal is considered tripped). In practice, managers usually do not wait until the boundary is tripped. If a pattern of TSs falls consistently above or below the zero line, an investigation of the forecasting model is warranted.

In Figure 3-8, a graphic illustration of a tracking signal, boundaries, and the tripping signal are presented. In Figure 3-8, historic data are used to develop the forecasting model and MAD statistics. When using TS_t for some number of time periods, the graph of the TS (the jagged line on the graph) stays quite close to the expected value of zero. As the forecasting model is then used in future time periods, the variation from the expected value of zero becomes sufficiently great to exceed the upper boundary. The implication of this trip signal suggests that sufficient variation exists between the forecast values and the actual data to reexamine the accuracy of the forecasting model. In this way a tracking signal can help forecasters identify the need for corrective behavior.

TABLE 3-11 FORMULA FOR TRACKING SIGNAL BOUNDARIES

	*PERCENTAGE OF TS_t FALLING WITHIN THE BOUNDARIES**		
Boundary	*68.27%*	*95.45%*	*99.81%*
Upper	$1\sqrt{MSE}$	$2\sqrt{MSE}$	$3\sqrt{MSE}$
Lower	$-1\sqrt{MSE}$	$-2\sqrt{MSE}$	$-3\sqrt{MSE}$

* The percentage for the formulas above are not statistically exact and may in some applications possess some estimation error.

FIGURE 3-8 ILLUSTRATIVE TRACKING SIGNAL

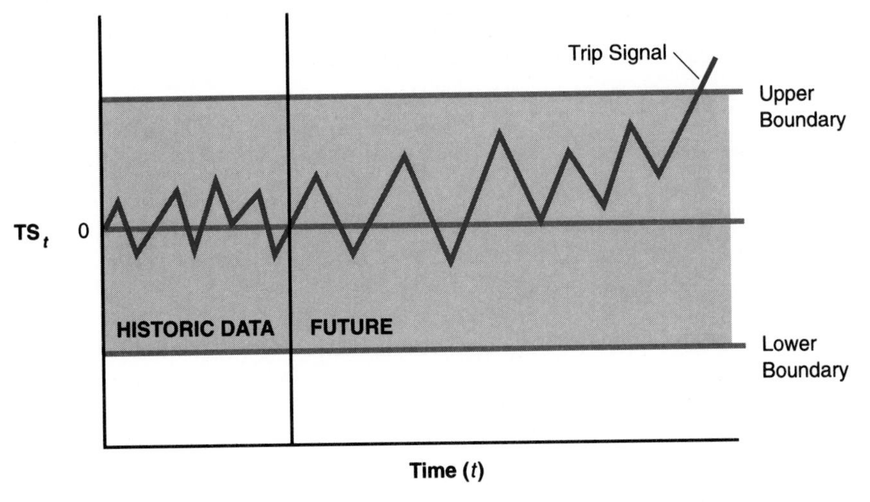

To illustrate how the tracking signal is used as a management control device in forecasting, let's examine the following tracking signal problem. Suppose we were to install a simple exponential forecasting model and a tracking signal system. Letting α = 0.4 and with an initial forecast value of 1,850, we will use the actual data shown in the program output of the Micro Production software in Figure 3-9. As we can see in Figure 3-9, the exponential smoothing forecasts for the eight periods of actual data are presented along with the forecast error, RSFE, MAD, and tracking signal. The tracking signal in the computer output represents the number of MADs that exists in the RSFE (TS = RSFE/MAD). Because we want to develop a tracking signal for future forecasting purposes, the TSs for the first eight periods in the computer printout are not of any real value for the future use of the system. The MSE (3,261.8397), however, for all eight periods is useful in that it is used to develop tracking signal boundaries at the bottom of the output. We can interpret the first boundary in Figure 3-9 as indicating that 68.27 percent of the future forecast error should fall within $\pm$57.113 ($\sqrt{3{,}261.8397}$). If we set the tracking signal system at the level of 68.27 percent and more than 68.27 of the forecast error values fall beyond $\pm$57.113, then we need to reconsider the accuracy of the simple exponential forecasting model in this example.

INTEGRATING MANAGEMENT RESOURCES: USING FORECASTING SYSTEMS TO INCREASE PRODUCTIVITY AND FLEXIBILITY

Increasing the Productivity of Human and Physical Resources

Forecasting models represent a systems resource. They can be used to forecast and plan human resource needs in operations management to achieve improved productivity by means of reduced costs. One example of such a systems application is

FIGURE 3-9 MICRO PRODUCTION SOFTWARE OUTPUT OF TRACKING SIGNAL PROBLEM

Program: Demand Forecasting / Exponential Smoothing

Problem Title: Sample Problem

***** Input Data *****

Alpha	:	0.400
Initial Estimated Forecast	:	1850.000
Number of Periods	:	8

Data values entered are shown below

***** Program Output *****

Period	Actual Data	Forecast	Forecast Error	RSFE	MAD	Tracking Signal
1	1850.000	1850.000	0.000	0.000	0.000	0.000
2	1920.000	1850.000	70.000	70.000	35.000	2.000
3	1800.000	1875.000	−78.000	−8.000	49.333	−0.162
4	1875.000	1846.800	28.200	20.200	44.050	0.459
5	1960.000	1858.080	101.920	122.120	55.624	2.195
6	2040.000	1898.849	141.152	263.272	69.879	3.768
7	1980.000	1955.309	24.691	287.963	63.423	4.540
8	2100.000	1965.185	134.815	422.778	72.347	5.844
9		2019.111				

MAD	:	72.3472
MSE	:	3261.8397

<< Tracking Signal Boundaries >>

		lower	upper
68.27%	:	−57.113	57.113
95.45%	:	−114.225	114.225
99.81%	:	−171.338	171.338

***** End of Output *****

U.S.-based West Atlantic Corporation's use of an exponential smoothing model to forecast the size of maintenance crews and plan work schedules for its maintenance workers.[14]

[14] C. A. Ntuen, "Forecasting Maintenance Crew Size Requirements Based on Periodic Maintenance Records," *Production and Inventory Management,* 30, No. 2 (1989), 41–43.

Q

A special group of maintenance workers at West Atlantic Corporation provided emergency maintenance service in various regions for its manufacturing facilities throughout the country. Manufacturing equipment in the plants would occasionally break down and require service. West wanted to effectively match the needs for maintenance personnel with actual demand for the maintenance work. A good match would minimize idle time of personnel crews (and the associated costs) while avoiding a shortage of maintenance personnel for emergency situations. West felt that if it could determine an ideal maintenance crew size using a forecasting model, its personnel costs might be reduced and it could still provide adequate maintenance support services. To deal with this crew sizing problem, an exponential smoothing model was developed using two mathematical weights. The model was expressed as

$$M_t = M_{t-1} + \alpha(NU_t - NU_{t-1}) + \beta(NE_t - NE_{t-1})$$

where

$$\begin{aligned}
t &= \text{the maintenance planning period} \\
M_t &= \text{the forecasted crew size required during period } t \\
M_{t-1} &= \text{the crew size available in the last maintenance period} \\
U_t &= \text{the number of unplanned repairs during } t \\
E_t &= \text{the emergency crew size during } t \\
NU_t - NU_{t-1} &= \text{the net maintenance requirements level during } t \\
NE_t - NE_{t-1} &= \text{the net emergency crew size available during } t \\
\alpha &= \text{the maintenance severity index (based on past records)} \\
\beta &= \text{the emergency failure severity index (based on past records)}
\end{aligned}$$

Both of the mathematical weights (α and β) ranged from 0 to 1. The value of β in the model represented the probability of an emergency failure's occurring and α represented the level of maintenance to be designed into the operations management system.

The results of using this forecasting model helped West Atlantic Corporation reduce its idle maintenance crew work. The forecasts provided by the model permitted the firm to better match its human resources requirements to meet service demand requirements. The results reported by the company amounted to more than a 25 percent savings in maintenance costs over the previous year's costs.

Q S

Red Lobster Restaurants uses computer technology to forecast customer demand.[15] Each night a store manager must determine what the estimated demand for menu items will be for the next day to accurately order and start the food preparation activities. Each restaurant uses a computer software system that estimates the next day's customer demand based on the same day of the previous week and the same day of the previous year. Based on this historic information, the computer

[15] J. Harris, "Dinnerhouse Technology," *Forbes,* July 8, 1991, 98–99.

program forecasts the number of customers that will require service and the individual items that will be demanded. This forecast allows the store manager to pull from inventory and order an exact number of pounds of shrimp, crab, pollack, and other items necessary to cover the forecast customer demand. Although no historic-based forecasting system is entirely accurate, the president of Red Lobster has estimated that its computer system has cut food waste for the chain of stores by $5 million per year. The accuracy of the system in forecasting has also improved scheduling, which resulted in a cut in labor costs of 16 percent of revenues or $10 million. In the low-margin restaurant industry, such reductions in costs represent an improvement in efficiency and an improvement in operation productivity.

Increasing Flexibility

The forecasting methods presented in this chapter are usually embedded in software systems as either stand-alone applications (like the Micro Production package that accompanies this book) or as an integrated system that shares the forecast information with an organization's larger management information system.

One example of a forecasting application used within a computer-integrated manufacturing system is IBM's Forecasting System Technology (FCST) module. FCST is an integrated part of the larger *Manufacturing Accounting and Production Information Control System,* Version 2 (MAPICS II). MAPICS II is a collection of nineteen interrelated computer applications (software modules) that permit a manufacturing operation to integrate business activities of accounting, marketing, finance, and operations into one management information system. (The MAPICS II system is quite extensive and, although its description here will be brief, it will be discussed more fully in other chapters in this book.) Because forecast information plays such an important role in guiding the daily transactions in all areas of a business, an integrated system like MAPICS II is designed to share changes in forecast demand on an interactive basis as changes are reported by users.

A brief overview of the FCST application is presented in Figure 3-10, with numbers indicating the interactive steps taken by MAPICS II and its forecasting applications. As actual orders are entered into the MAPICS system (step 1) they are used by the FCST application to provide management with a number of planning reports (step 2). These periodic reports include the following:

Forecast Detail Report. This report shows forecast performance data (such as expected versus actual demand) and one-year forecasts in units for individual items. The report permits managers to see how the short-term actual business activity compares with expected forecast values, so that short-term changes in production (for example, shifting work effort from one product to another) can be implemented if needed.

Forecast Summary Report. This report shows aggregate forecasts in units and the standard cost for each product line or class of items. This report allows

FIGURE 3-10 AN OVERVIEW OF THE IBM FORECASTING APPLICATION USED IN THEIR MANUFACTURING ACCOUNTING AND PRODUCTION INFORMATION CONTROL SYSTEM (MAPICS II)

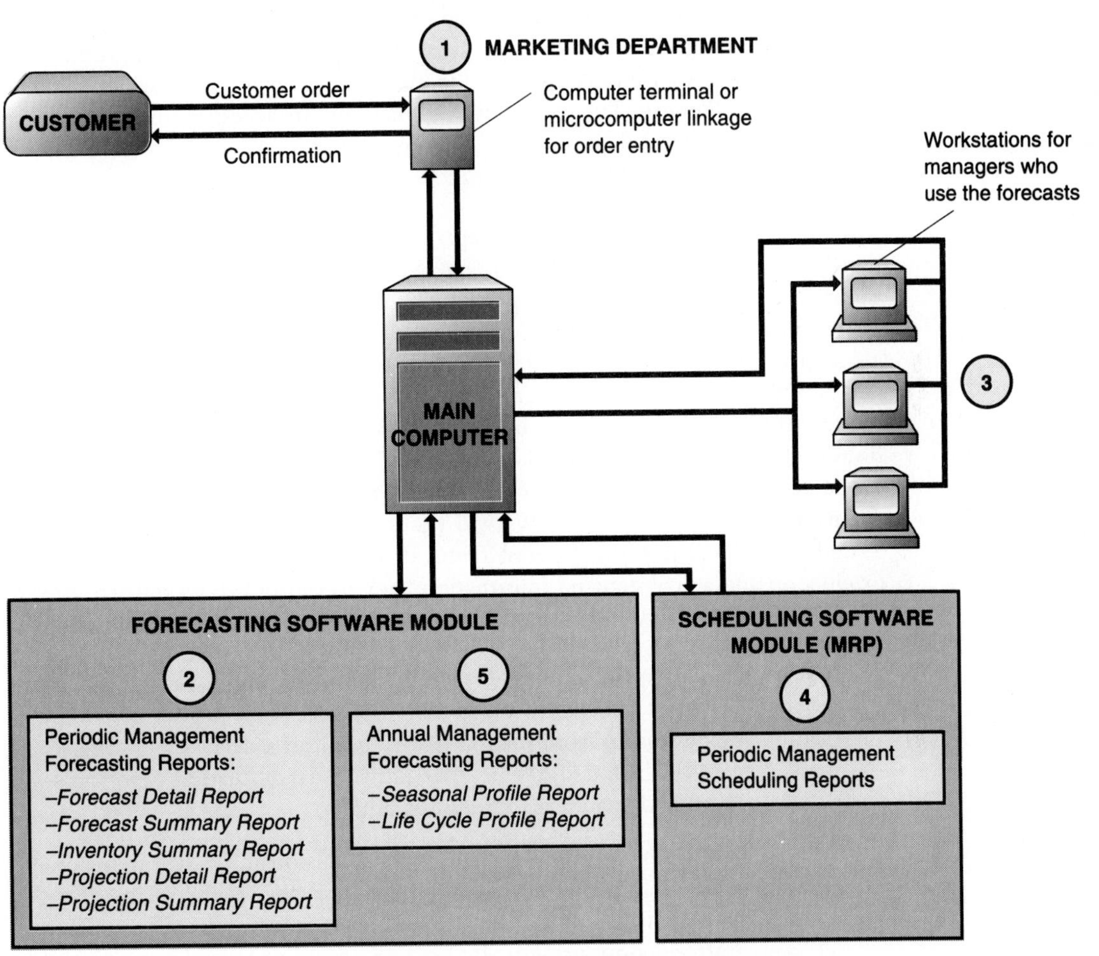

managers to better judge the distribution of demand by product line and permits them to make adjustments in production (for example, instituting layoffs or allowing overtime) if needed.

Inventory Summary Report. This report shows a summary of the cost associated with existing inventory policies on carrying stock and ordering inventory. This report allows managers to access cost aspects of forecasting inaccuracies and helps them identify possible inventory policies that need to be changed in light of changes in demand.

Projection Detail Report. This report shows projections for individual items for more than two or three years. It is a medium-range version of the Forecast Detail Report.

Projection Summary Report. This report shows projections for aggregate items for more than two or three years and standard cost for each product line or class of products. It is a medium-range version of the Forecast Summary Report. The report allows managers to access medium-range adjustments in production (that is, adding or discontinuing a shift of workers) as they relate to forecasting inaccuracies.

These five reports are periodically prepared and can be reviewed by managers at their computer workstations (step 3). The MAPICS system allows these reports to be prepared up to thirteen times per year. If the forecast values generated by the system are not acceptable (perhaps because the system's tracking signals suggest they are suspect), the user can override the forecasts and enter his or her own forecast values. Once the forecast values are judged acceptable, the user interactively sends the forecast back through the main computer to other MAPICS software applications such as the scheduling module (step 4). The MAPICS scheduling module is called materials requirements planning (MRP) and is used to schedule production and plan inventory transactions. (We will discuss MRP in Chapter 7). As production is undertaken to meet the forecast demand, the MAPICS system channels the production and actual demand information back to the FCST module to prepare annual forecasting reports (step 5). These annual reports include the following:

Seasonal Profile Report. This report shows details on individual items or grouped product line values on a seasonal basis. This report provides medium-range seasonal information that is based on a data base of several years. The report includes graphics that allow visual evaluation of seasonal patterns of actual demand and forecast parameters.

Life Cycle Profile Report. This report shows details on individual items or grouped product line values on a quarterly basis for several years. This report allows managers to graphically see the stage of an item's product life cycle (introduction, growth, etc.) over a period of several years. Such information can guide long-term production decisions in plant and equipment.

While functioning on an interactive and real-time basis, the FCST module of MAPICS can be used to quickly generate new forecasts, make changes in current forecasts, and implement these changes throughout the entire business organization. This real-time flexibility of adjustment to planning reports in accounting, marketing, finance, and operations departments is one of the major advantages of all computer-integrated systems. It will permit organizations to adapt quickly and hence take advantage of opportunities in the shifting markets they face.

SUMMARY

Forecasting is the science of minimizing error in predicting the future. In operations management, the chief purpose of forecasting is to provide information that will help identify and predict the future behavior of the organization's external environment (changes in customer demand, changes in industry demand, changes in OM technology, and so on).

In this chapter we have discussed a number of qualitative forecasting methods that are based on human resources input. These methods include judgmental methods, secondary source information, and the Delphi method.

The models requiring computer support that we discussed in this chapter include regression analysis, smoothing models, classical decomposition, and other quantitative forecasting methods. These methods are chiefly incorporated in decision support systems (DSS) or some type of management information system (MIS), where they are applied to generate forecast information. The other computer-based quantitative methods we discussed in this chapter, including correlation analysis and forecasting error statistics (MAD, MSE, RSFE, and TS), are basically used to improve forecasting models. Tracking signals are used to control error in a variety of computer-based systems including monitoring variation in product quality during the production process and software systems that generate exception reports when vendor deliveries fail to be met. We will discuss these applications in later chapters.

Collectively, all of the forecasting techniques and approaches presented in this chapter can help operations managers achieve objectives placed on the internal environment of the organization to meet the changes in the external environment. To determine objectives and implement these changes, an operations manager must plan for them. In the next chapter, we will discuss the subject of strategic, tactical, and operational production planning.

DISCUSSION AND REVIEW QUESTIONS

1. Why is forecasting necessary in operations management?
2. Explain the four types of variation that can exist in time series data.
3. Explain the similarity between the Delphi method and the judgmental forecasting methods.
4. Why do we use correlation and regression analysis in forecasting?
5. In what areas of OM do we use a centered moving average (CMA)?
6. Why do we want to smooth data using methods like the weighted moving average?
7. Explain how we can use MAD and MSE statistics in forecasting.
8. Explain how the α value for an exponential forecasting model should be determined.
9. Explain why upper and lower boundaries are beneficial in forecast tracking signals. How would this information help an operations manager?
10. How can the integration of forecasting systems improve flexibility in a service operation?
11. How can the integration of forecasting systems improve flexibility in a manufacturing operation?
12. How does the forecasting module of MAPICS II help integrate management resources?

PROBLEMS

The following data are used in Problems 1, 2, and 3.

Year	*Product Demand*
1	345
2	276
3	189
4	400
5	256
6	323

*1. Compute a three-value and a five-value centered moving average. Using a range statistic to reflect variation, determine whether variation is reduced from the three-value to the five-value moving average.

*2. Forecast the seventh year's product demand using a four-value weighted moving method, where $w_1 = .50$, $w_2 = .20$, $w_3 = .20$, and $w_4 = .10$. Can you calculate the eighth year's product demand?

*3. a. Forecast the seventh year's product demand using a simple exponential smoothing model with an α of 0.2, and assume the initial forecast is equal to the actual product demand. Can you forecast the eighth year's product demand? Compute the MAD statistic for this model.

b. Forecast the seventh year's product demand using a simple exponential smoothing model with an α of 0.5, and assume the initial forecast is equal to the actual product demand. Can you forecast the eighth year's product demand? Compute the MAD statistic for this model.

c. Based on the MAD statistics computed in (a) and (b), which α provides the better forecast?

The following data are used in Problems 4, 5, and 6.

Year	*U.S. Raw Steel Output* (000s tons)*
1982	73,570
1983	43,309
1984	51,904
1985	50,446
1986	43,952

* *Source:* American Iron and Steel Institute.

4. Compute a two-value and a four-value centered moving average. Using a range statistic to reflect variation, has variation been reduced from the two- to four-value moving average?

---

* The solutions to the problems marked with an asterisk can be found in Appendix J.

5. Forecast the output for 1987 using a three-value weighted moving method, where $w_1 = .30$, $w_2 = .50$, and $w_3 = .20$. Can you forecast output for 1988?

6. a. Forecast the output for 1987 using a simple exponential smoothing model with an α of 0.1, and assume the initial forecast is equal to the actual 1982 output. Compute the MAD statistic for this model.
   b. Forecast the output for 1987 using a simple exponential smoothing model with an α of 0.3. Assume the initial forecast is equal to the actual 1982 output. Compute the MAD statistic for this model.
   c. Forecast the output for 1987 using an exponential smoothing model with an α of 0.5, and assume the initial forecast is equal to the actual 1982 output. Compute the MAD statistic for this model.
   d. Based on the MAD statistics computed in (a), (b), and (c), which α does a better job of forecasting?

The following data are used in Problems 7, 8, and 9.

Product Demand (Y)	*Advertising Expenditures* (X_1)	*Quality Control Expenditures* (X_2)
7	4	1
12	7	2
17	9	5
20	12	8

7. a. Derive the simple regression model for Y and X_1.
   b. Derive the correlation coefficient and the coefficient of determination for Y and X_1. Interpret the meaning of r^2 for this specific problem.
   c. Compute the MAD and MSE statistics for the Y and X_1 model. Establish a 95.45 percent boundary for forecast error as a tracking signal and explain what this boundary means.

8. a. Derive the simple regression model for Y and X_2.
   b. Compute the correlation coefficient and the coefficient of determination for Y and X_2. Interpret the meaning of r^2 for this specific problem.
   c. Compute the MAD and MSE statistics for the Y and X_2 model. Establish a 95.45 percent boundary for forecast error as a tracking signal and explain what this boundary means.

9. Of the two independent variables in problems 7 and 8, which will make a better predictive variable? How do the variation statistics of MAD and MSE reinforce your decision?

The following data are used in Problems 10, 11, and 12.

Year	*Average Weekly Haircuts (Y)*	*Average Weekly Earnings* (X_1)*	*Average Hours Worked Per Week* (X_2)*
1985	430	\$386	9.54
1986	340	396	9.73
1987	270	403	9.84

* *Source:* Bureau of Statistics, U.S. Labor Department.

*10. a. Derive the simple regression model for Y and X_1.
b. Compute the correlation coefficient and the coefficient of determination for Y and X_1. Interpret the meaning of r^2 for this specific problem.
c. Compute the MAD and MSE statistics for the Y and X_1 model. Establish a 66.27 percent boundary for forecast error as a tracking signal.

11. a. Develop the simple regression model for Y and X_2.
b. Derive the correlation coefficient and the coefficient of determination for Y and X_2. Interpret the meaning of r^2 for this specific problem.
c. Compute the MAD and MSE statistics for the Y and X_2 model. Establish a 66.27 percent boundary for forecast error as a tracking signal.

12. Which of the two models developed in problems 10 and 11 would be the "best" to forecast average weekly haircuts? Justify your answer.

*13. Suppose you have been given the following tracking signal computer printout from a forecasting model used by your organization.

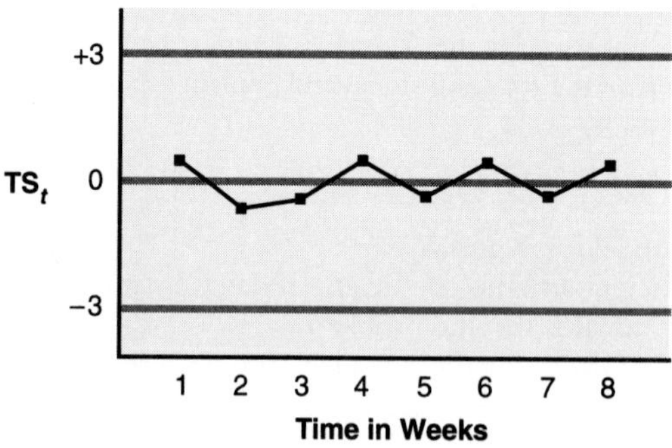

What is your interpretation of this forecasting model's accuracy given the stated tracking signal boundaries of ± 3?

14. A tracking signal computer printout from a forecasting model (shown at the top of the next page) has been handed to you.

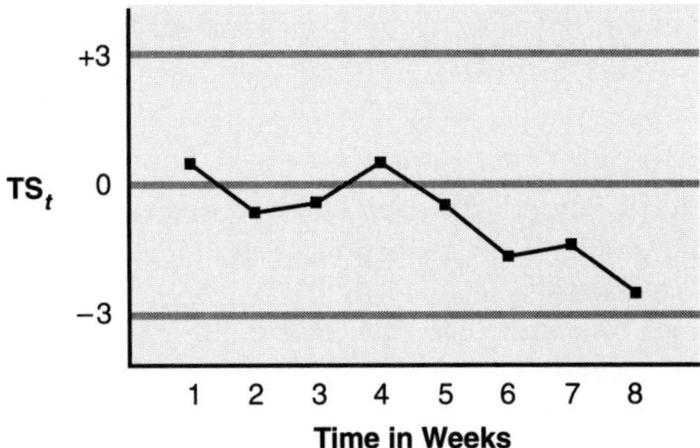

Interpret this forecasting model's accuracy given the stated tracking signal boundaries of ±3.

15. Suppose the following tracking signal computer printout from a forecasting model has been observed.

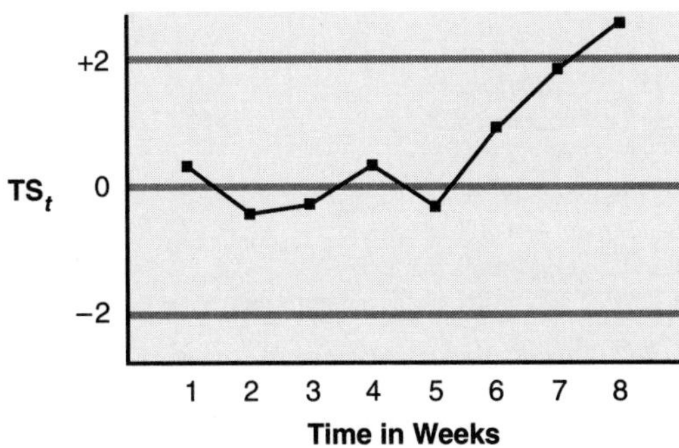

What is your interpretation of this forecasting model's accuracy given the stated tracking signal boundaries of ±2?

*16. Suppose we want to forecast our company's product demand from secondary sources. Based on our research, we find that the industry's forecast market demand of our product next year will be 20 million units. From last year's record, we know that we maintained a 23.5 percent market share of the entire industry's product demand of 17.8 million units or $345 million dollars. The marketing people in our organization believe that our market share for the next year will be the same as this year's market share. Based on this information, what is next year's forecast product demand in units?

*17. Given the following monthly sales information:

1992: 13, 12, 10, 10, 11, 14, 17, 18, 19, 24, 25, 20
1993: 11, 10, 9, 8, 10, 12, 14, 15, 16, 18, 19, 18

a. Use a two-value moving average to smooth the data. Plot the original data and plot the smoothed data using a line graph. What reduction in the range of the actual data from the smoothed data occurred?
b. Use a five-value moving average to smooth the data. Plot the original data and all three smoothed data using a line graph. Comment on the smoothing effect of the larger five-value over the two-value moving average.

18. The following are quarterly sales in units of sailboats by a small manufacturer:

    1991: 19, 10, 8, 10
    1992: 13, 18, 8, 20
    1993: 11, 12, 16, 18

    a. Use a two-value moving average to smooth the data. Plot the original data and plot the smoothed data using a line graph. What reduction in the range of the actual data from the smoothed data occurred?
    b. Use a four-value moving average to smooth the data. Plot the original data and all three smoothed data using a line graph. What reduction in the range of the actual data from the smoothed data occurred? Comment on the smoothing effect of the larger four-value compared with the two-value moving average.

19. A construction company wants to determine a model for forecasting its company's home construction. Following is the construction company's home construction contracts (what they want to forecast) and housing affordability information (by year) from the National Association of Realtors.

Year	*Contracts*	*Median-Priced* Existing Home*	*Average Mortgage* Rate (%)*
1988	1,300	$90,600	9.31
1989	1,370	93,100	10.11
1990	1,490	97,500	10.04
1991	1,678	99,700	9.51

* *The World Almanac and Book of Facts, 1992* (New York: Scripps Howard Company, 1991), p. 720.

    a. Using a regression model and correlation analysis, which one of the variables in the table is the best forecasting or predictive variable? Explain and show your work.
    b. Compare the regression model using the best predictive variable with an exponential smoothing model with an α of 0.5 (assume that the initial forecast is equal to actual contracts for 1988). Which of the models is best using the MAD statistic as the criterion?

*20. Given the following sales information:

Sales	*Time in Years*
10	1
12	2
14	3
16	4
18	5
20	6
24	7
30	8

    a. What are the two-value moving average values of sales?
    b. What are the four-value moving average values of sales?
    c. What are the weighted values of sales if we use $n = 3$, $w_1 = .2$, $w_2 = .3$, and $w_3 = .5$?

21. Given the following sales data:

Sales	*Time in Years*
105	1
162	2
184	3
196	4
208	5
250	6
294	7
320	8

a. What are the four-value moving average values of sales?
b. What are the weighted average values of sales if we use $n = 3$, $w_1 = .5$, $w_2 = .3$, and $w_3 = .2$?
c. Comment on the reduction of variation in the two resulting smoothed sets of sales data.

22. Following are the productivity index values for one worker during a ten-day period in a factory: 120, 127, 115, 112, 104, 106, 98, 80, 94, 90.
a. What are the weighted average values of the index values if we use $n = 3$, $w_1 = .8$, $w_2 = .1$, and $w_3 = .1$?
b. What are the weighted average values of the index values if we use $n = 3$, $w_1 = .1$, $w_2 = .1$, and $w_3 = .8$?
c. Comment on the differences in the two resulting smoothed sets of index data.

*23. Given the following sales information:

Years	*Sales*
1	80
2	40
3	30
4	20
5	20
6	11

Using the MAD statistic, determine the best forecast model parameter of n for a centered moving average of the sales data, where n is limited to $n = 2$ or $n = 3$.

24. Given the following sales information:

Years	*Sales*
1	436
2	345
3	388
4	370
5	355
6	341
7	339
8	311

Using the MAD statistic, determine the best forecast model parameter of n for a centered moving average of the sales data, where n is limited to $n = 2$ or $n = 3$.

25. Given the following sales information:

Years	*Sales*
1	176
2	165
3	128
4	160
5	130
6	111
7	129
8	151
9	123
10	141

Using the MAD statistic, determine the best forecast model parameter of n for a centered moving average of the sales data, where n is limited to $n = 2$, $n = 3$, or $n = 4$.

*26. Given the following manufacturing division productivity index values:

	DIVISION PRODUCTIVITY INDEX	
Years	Y_1	Y_2
1	75	111
2	74	115
3	53	123
4	42	111
5	32	127
6	81	90
7	42	171
8	92	157

Which of the two division productivity measures is best predicted by the passage of time? Explain and show your work.

27. Given the following manufacturing division productivity index values:

	DIVISION PRODUCTIVITY INDEX				
Years	Y_1	Y_2	Y_3	Y_4	Y_5
1	125	122	115	126	189
2	124	105	125	145	137
3	153	103	135	114	179
4	142	101	145	114	138
5	132	107	155	115	108
6	121	100	165	126	189
7	142	101	145	117	133
8	112	107	145	118	102
9	111	117	165	129	182
10	121	115	105	109	102

Which of the five division productivity measures is best predicted by the passage of time? Explain and show your work.

28. You have just reviewed a computer printout that provides tracking signal boundaries on five products that are being forecast using five different regression models. The resulting TS_t for the five forecasting regression models are $TS_1 = 0.04$, $TS_2 = 1.44$, $TS_3 = 2.54$, $TS_4 = 0.78$, and $TS_5 = 0.98$.
   (a) Without any specific criteria to guide your decision, which of the five forecasting models might you want to re-evaluate as a forecasting method? Explain your answer.
   (b) If you were given a 60 percent confidence level (that is, about 60 percent of the TSs should fall between the upper and lower boundary), which of the forecasting models would you have to re-evaluate as a forecasting method? Explain your answer.

*29. Suppose we have the following decomposition model computer printout:

Period	*Trend Forecast*	*Seasonal Factor*	*Forecast*
1	78	1.20	93.6
2	82	1.50	82.0
3	86	.95	81.7
4	90	.90	81.0

If time period is in quarters, what is the interpretation of the two types of variation illustrated in these data?

30. Suppose we have the following decomposition model computer printout:

Time	*Trend Forecast*	*Irregular Component*	*Seasonal Factor*
1	65	1.01	1.00
2	63	.89	.90
3	62	1.12	.75
4	60	1.22	1.10
5	58	1.05	1.20
6	56	.90	1.00
7	54	.80	.85
8	52	.80	1.20

If time is in quarters, what is the interpretation of the three types of variation illustrated in these data?

CASE 3-1

A QUESTION OF ACCURACY IN FORECASTING

The Video-Connection Tape Rental Company (VCTRC) has been operating for seven years and currently offers customers their choice of more than 5,000 prerecorded videotapes for rent. VCTRC is owned and managed by its president. VCTRC is located in the southwestern region of the United States, in a city of approximately 250,000 persons.

In the first few years of operation VCTRC had a virtual monopoly on the videotape rental business in the city in which it was located. The company had very substantial profits during these early years, which the president wisely reinvested in videotape rental stock. During the fourth year of the company's successful operation a competitor opened a store directly across the street from VCTRC. The competitor was a franchise operation of a national chain of video rental stores. Rental sales of VCTRC dropped rapidly at first as curiosity about the new video rental offerings of the competitor drew a notable number of VCTRC's customers. A price war ensued and eventually VCTRC recovered most of its customers because of its extensive inventory of rental tapes. The competitor's bureaucracy simply did not permit individual stores to have the capital to build as varied a stock of tapes as VCTRC.

The president of VCTRC decided to develop a standard operating procedure for handling its tape-rental pricing. A rental price was chosen that was as feasibly low as VCTRC could stand, was easy to manage, satisfied most of the customers, and permitted profitable operation by avoiding price wars with the competitor. During the eight quarters of 1991 and 1992, VCTRC maintained a fixed price of $2.50 for the basic one-day rental of a videotape. During the same time VCTRC's competitor used various rental prices for its one-day tape rental service. The competitor's prices were not determined by the local store's manager, but by the national franchisor. VCTRC's competitor's average quarterly per tape rental prices during the 1991 and 1992 period are presented in Exhibit 3C-1. Because the national franchisor sets prices on a national level, the next quarter's (the future quarter) average rental price per tape could fairly easily and accurately be obtained from the national franchisor's national advertising director.

The availability of this pricing information, and the possibility of a relationship (note Exhibit 3C-1) between VCTRC's unit sales and the competitor's average rental price, caused the president to consider developing a forecasting model that could be used for planning operations. The president of VCTRC did not remember enough from his college courses to develop a forecasting model. Instead he hired a consultant to develop a forecasting model to predict VCTRC's quarterly rentals at least one quarter into the future. The president believed that such information would help VCTRC reduce human resource costs, which represented more than 60 percent of the operating budget of VCTRC. By forecasting the approximate quarterly rental demand, the necessary human resource needs for the next quarter could be more easily and accurately predicted. The president believed that improved labor scheduling would eliminate employee idle time during slack periods of consumer demand and save the company personnel costs.

The president's knowledge of forecasting methods was limited to simple exponential smoothing and simple regression analysis. Because the president himself would use the model to calculate the forecasts long after the consultant had completed the model, the president requested that the consultant develop both a simple exponential smoothing model and a simple regression model. The consultant was further directed to provide some comparative statistics that would enable the president to decide which of the two models would be the most accurate in

EXHIBIT 3C-1 TIME SERIES DATA FOR VCTRC 1991–1992 OPERATION

TIME		*Competitor's Average Price Per Rental*	*VCTRC's Quarterly Rentals (000)*
Year	*Quarter (no.)*		
1991	1 (1)	$2.05	79.6
	2 (2)	2.50	108.3
	3 (3)	3.15	160.0
	4 (4)	2.75	135.2
1992	1 (5)	2.75	137.6
	2 (6)	3.20	178.0
	3 (7)	2.85	142.2
	4 (8)	2.55	115.1

forecasting VCTRC's rentals. With these directives in mind the consultant proceeded to develop the desired forecasting models and statistics.

CASE QUESTIONS

1. Using the competitor's average price per rental data to predict quarterly rentals, develop a simple regression model.
2. If we use the simple exponential smoothing model, how do we determine what value of α we should use? What is the best α value in this model (rounded to only two places behind the decimal point)? State the exponential smoothing model.
3. Using the simple regression model, what is the forecast for the first quarter of 1993 (the ninth time period)?
4. Using the simple exponential smoothing model, what is the forecast for the first quarter of 1993? Assume that the initial forecast period is equal to its actual quarterly rentals.
5. What are the MAD statistics for both models? Which model should be recommended to the president as more effective?

CASE 3-2

THE ACME BURGLAR ALARM COMPANY

The Acme Burglar Alarm Company (ABAC) has locations in several cities in the New England region of the United States. ABAC manufactures household protection devices for home owners and has yearly sales of $30 million. ABAC offers customers about a dozen different household protection products. The company's products range from small battery-operated door theft alarms with a retail price of $20 to household security alarm systems that can cost as much as $5,000. Twelve years ago, when the company was starting up, the battery-operated alarms represented as much as 75 percent of the company's total sales. Based on the 1988 sales, the battery-operated alarms represented only 18 percent of total sales. ABAC management wanted to determine if the downward trend in battery systems might continue and what the impact on sales would be.

ABAC had in the past used fairly simple forecasting procedures to estimate the next year's sales for each of its products. The forecast values were primarily used as information to convince the company's banks to loan it the necessary operating capital for the year's operation. Indeed, in the early years of operation, ABAC sold every unit of product it produced. As the market for protection devices matured in the New England area, the importance of accurate forecasting in minimizing excess production became obviously clear to ABAC management. Finished goods inventory of battery-operated systems began piling up and even the bank officers were encouraging ABAC to unload some of its inventory.

The general manager in charge of the manufacturing operations called in the staff planner whose job was to provide product forecasts. The staff planner was directed to determine if the trend for the battery-operated protection systems would continue downward or if it would reverse next year. If the forecast trend continued further downward, the battery-operated system would be discontinued and existing inventory would be used to fill all future orders. If the forecast trend indicated an increase in sales in the next year, then the general manager would continue to manufacture the product in accordance with the forecast value.

To make this determination, the staff planner went to a local university library to review the secondary sources on protection device forecasts. Unfortunately, no recent forecasts were available in the literature. The staff planner did learn that researchers had clearly established a three-year lag relationship between the actual occurrence of crime in the United States and the purchase of protection devices. So the staff planner decided that predictive variables would have to be located that might be useful in forecasting the sales of the battery system.

The staff planner reasoned that the motivation for purchasing protection devices, regardless of the lagged relationship, is to protect households from theft and burglaries. Logically then, there must be a cause-effect relationship between the number of thefts and burglaries and consumers' purchasing household protection systems. So the staff planner researched government sources of U.S. crime statistics. From the Bureau of Justice Statistics the staff planner gathered crime statistics on violent crimes, personal theft, household theft, and burglaries in the United States for the years 1976 to 1986. These statistics for U.S. households touched by crime are presented in Exhibit 3C-2. The staff planner also

EXHIBIT 3C-2 ABAC BATTERY ALARM SALES AND U.S. CRIME STATISTICS

			PERCENTAGE OF U.S. HOUSEHOLDS TOUCHED BY CRIME				
Actual Year	*ABAC Lag Year*	*ABAC Battery Alarm Sales (millions)*	*Violent Crime*	*Personal Theft*	*Household Theft*	*Burglary*	*Households in U.S. (millions)*
1976	1979	10.1	5.6	16.2	10.3	7.4	74.528
1977	1980	10.0	5.7	16.3	10.2	7.2	75.908
1978	1981	9.5	5.7	16.2	9.9	7.2	77.578
1979	1982	9.3	5.9	15.4	10.8	7.1	78.964
1980	1983	8.7	5.5	14.2	10.4	7.0	80.622
1981	1984	7.7	5.9	13.9	10.2	7.4	82.797
1982	1985	6.5	5.6	13.9	9.6	6.9	85.178
1983	1986	6.0	5.1	13.0	8.9	6.1	86.146
1984	1987	5.4	5.0	12.3	8.5	5.5	87.791
1985	1988	5.2	4.8	11.5	8.1	5.3	88.852
1986	1989	—	4.7	11.2	8.0	5.3	90.014

Source: Data excerpted from *The World Almanac* (New York: Scripps Howard Company, 1988), p. 822.

obtained ABAC's yearly sales, appropriately lagged in Exhibit 3C-2. So in Exhibit 3C-2, we can see that 1976 crime statistics are best related to ABAC's 1979 sales, assuming that the three-year lag relationship reported in the forecasting literature holds true.

CASE QUESTIONS

1. Give one reason why simple regression might be a good instrument for forecasting trends in ABAC sales.
2. Which one of the four U.S. crime statistics is the best related variable to predict ABAC's sales?
3. Using simple regression analysis, what is the 1989 predicted sales value? Is the trend of the ABAC battery-operated protection device up or down in 1989?
4. Using an exponential smoothing model, determine the 1989 predicted sales value. Is the trend of the ABAC battery-operated protection device up or down in 1989? In developing your forecast, use all of the data in Exhibit 3C-2 and assume t_0 is the 1979 ABAC sales year to start the model's computations.
5. Which forecast method is better: regression or exponential smoothing? Why?

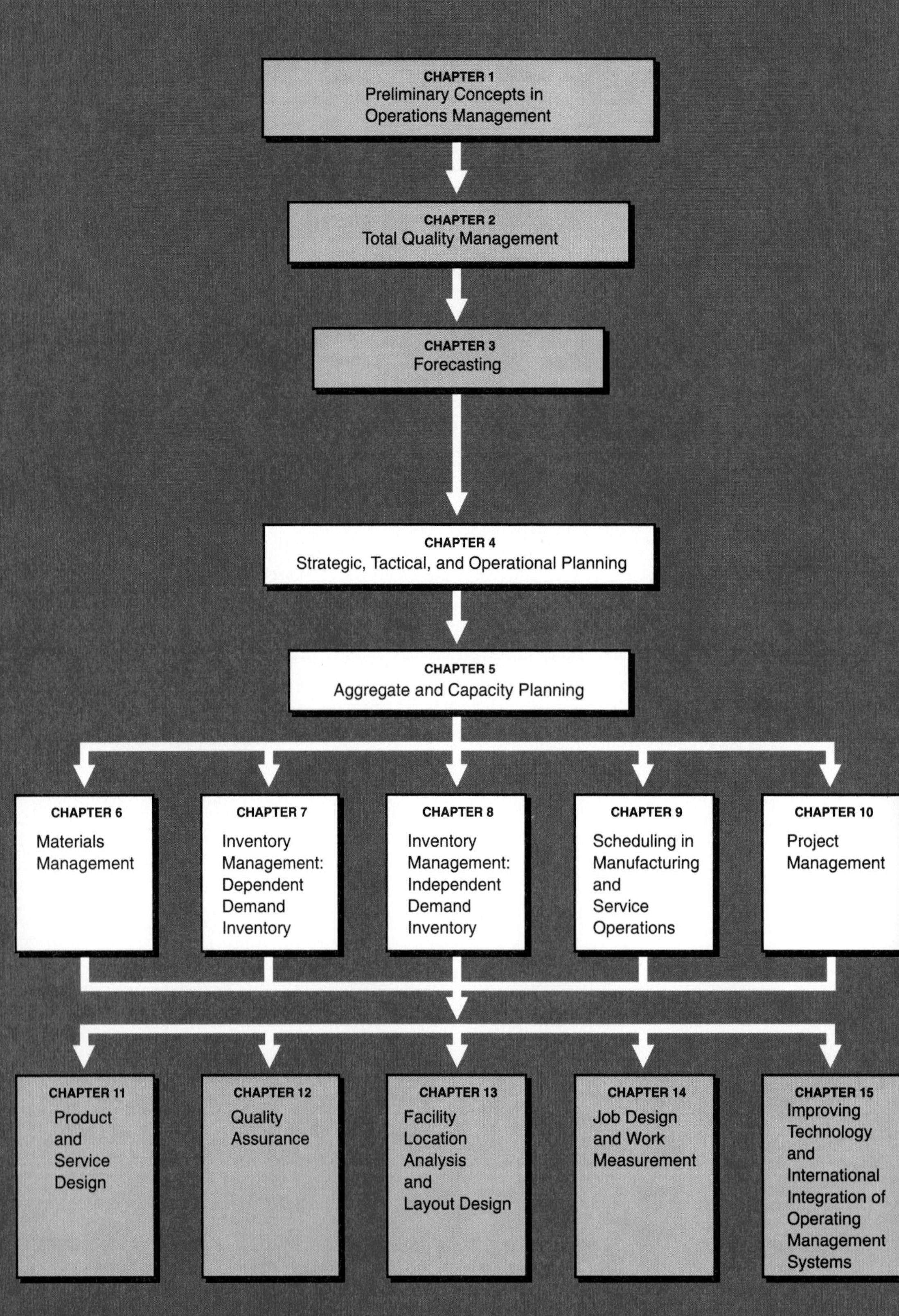
CHAPTER 1
Preliminary Concepts in Operations Management
CHAPTER 2
Total Quality Management
CHAPTER 3
Forecasting
CHAPTER 4
Strategic, Tactical, and Operational Planning
CHAPTER 5
Aggregate and Capacity Planning
CHAPTER 6
Materials Management
CHAPTER 7
Inventory Management: Dependent Demand Inventory
CHAPTER 8
Inventory Management: Independent Demand Inventory
CHAPTER 9
Scheduling in Manufacturing and Service Operations
CHAPTER 10
Project Management
CHAPTER 11
Product and Service Design
CHAPTER 12
Quality Assurance
CHAPTER 13
Facility Location Analysis and Layout Design
CHAPTER 14
Job Design and Work Measurement
CHAPTER 15
Improving Technology and International Integration of Operating Management Systems

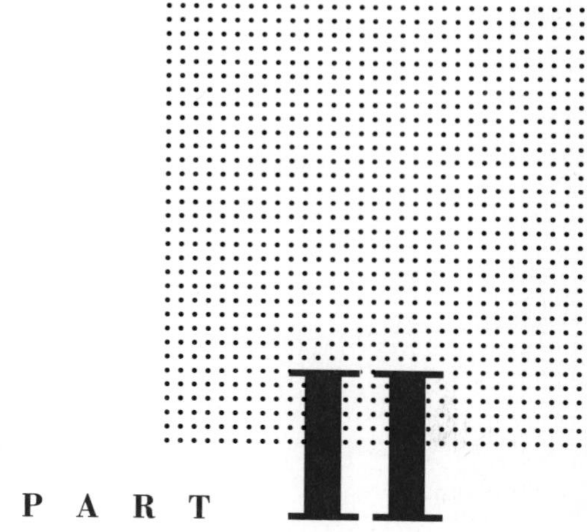

PART II

PLANNING AND CONTROLLING OPERATIONS

4

Strategic, Tactical, and Operational Planning

CHAPTER OUTLINE

CHAPTER OBJECTIVES

The material in this chapter should prepare you to do the following:

1. Explain the organizational planning process.
2. Understand why strategic, tactical, and operational planning are necessary.
3. Describe the components of strategic planning and their link to operations management.
4. Discern the difference between corporate strategic planning and OM strategic planning.
5. Describe tactical planning and its link to operations management.
6. Describe operational planning and its link to operations management.
7. Explain the output of strategic, tactical, and operational planning and give examples.
8. Describe how the TOWS analysis is used in strategic planning.
9. Explain how to use critical success factors in strategic planning.
10. Describe the components of a strategic information system (SIS).

As described in Chapter 1, planning is one of the most important functions performed by any manager in any operation. All managers devote some time to planning, and some people devote their entire careers solely to planning activities. Organizations employ consultants and staff specialists experienced in planning new factories or products. Line managers, like vice presidents and general managers, also plan new factories or products but approach planning in a much different way than staff specialists. Just as different types of people perform different planning functions, there are different types of planning.

We can group planning functions in a manufacturing or service organization into three broad types as listed in Table 4-1: strategic, tactical, and operational. Managers at all levels must be able to perform each of these types of planning to some degree, although the major focus of planning varies according to management level.[1] Strategic planning is predominantly undertaken by upper-level management to achieve long-term (two or more years) corporate or organizational objectives. Tactical planning is primarily assumed by middle-level management to achieve medium-range (one to two years) departmental objectives that support corporate objectives. Operational planning is usually performed by lower-level management to achieve short-range (less than one year) objectives at the first level or shop-floor level of a department. Typical examples of these types of planning as they relate to management resources are presented in Table 4-2.

These three types of planning occur in a hierarchy from the strategic to the operational level and represent what is known as the organizational planning process. The **organizational planning process** is the collective planning effort that moves an organization from a statement of general objectives (strategic plans) to a specific production or service schedule (operational plans) that defines exactly how many units of each product will be produced or services delivered each day, hour, or minute. All planning functions, whether in finance, marketing, personnel, or—most importantly—operations management, fall within the organizational planning process overviewed in

TABLE 4-1 LINKAGE OF TYPES OF PLANNING, MANAGEMENT LEVELS, AND PLANNING TIME HORIZONS

Types of Planning	*Management Levels*	*Planning Time Horizons*
Strategic	Upper	Long-range (2 or more years)
Tactical	Middle	Medium-range (1 to 2 years)
Operational	Lower	Short-range (less than 1 year)

[1] L. A. Digman, *Strategic Management,* 2nd ed. (Homewood, Ill.: Irwin, 1990), p. 54.

TABLE 4-2 LINKAGE OF PLANNING TIME HORIZONS AND MANAGEMENT RESOURCE PLANNING

Time Horizon in Planning	*MANAGEMENT RESOURCES*		
	Human	*Technology*	*System*
Long-range	Planning the development of a research group Planning education programs	Planning the design and building of a new robotic factory	Planning a new management information system (MIS)
Medium-range	Planning the restructuring of departments Defining skill requirements for newly developed products	Planning the installation and start-up of robotic equipment in a newly built robotic factory	Planning the installation and debugging of software in a new MIS
Short-range	Planning seasonal hiring and layoffs	Scheduling robots for production runs	Scheduling computer time to handle daily MIS requirements of various departments

Figure 4-1. The purpose of this chapter is to explain how the organizational planning process presented in Figure 4-1 is accomplished and the critical role OM plays in each step of the planning process.

• • •

WHY STRATEGIC, TACTICAL, AND OPERATIONAL PLANNING ARE NECESSARY

Strategic, tactical, and operational planning each contributes to an organization's success by focusing management's attention on the need to improve productivity, improve flexibility, and develop a competitive advantage. All three types of planning must be collectively applied to achieve the best results.

Strategic planning helps organizations recognize the need to meet changes in the external environment (see Chapter 1) that might pose a threat or create opportunities for new products or services. In doing so, strategic planning is a cognitive exercise that forces managers to identify and explore organizational opportunities that can foster competitive advantages within their industry. It is a necessary mental learning activity that focuses managers' attention on the need to adapt to external changes and improve flexibility.

FIGURE 4-1 OVERVIEW OF ORGANIZATIONAL PLANNING PROCESS

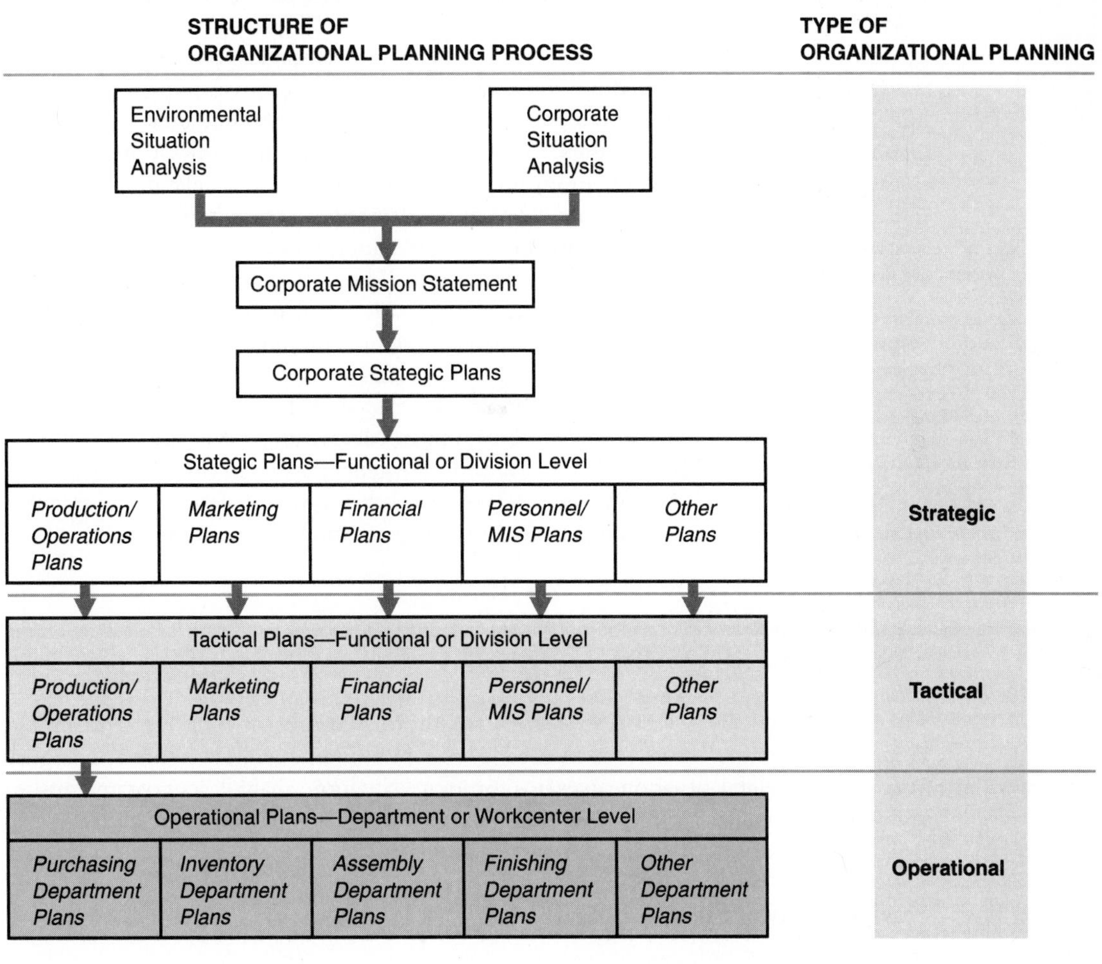

Tactical planning helps functional or division areas, like operations management, convert the generally stated organization-wide strategic plans into more narrowly focused division objectives. It may also entail the development of a general "road map" to achieve an OM strategy. Through tactical planning, operations managers are forced to examine and re-examine new production methods or new service delivery methods as a means of achieving yearly or quarterly objectives required to achieve a broader strategic objective. It is a process of matching aggregate OM demand requirements (for products or services) with the organization's aggregate capacity to meet demand. This planning requires operations managers to constantly re-examine the constraints imposed on aggregate production capacity and find new ways to increase capacity. In doing so, tactical planning focuses managers' attention on the need to improve productivity in OM and other divisions.

Operational planning helps department heads and workcenter employees convert the tactical plans into detailed monthly, weekly, or daily objectives. Operational planning converts tactical ideas into a detailed schedule of daily resource uses. This type of planning is the final step necessary to convert tactical plans into time-related, feasible substeps achievable by the organization's employees. Operational planning is chiefly directed toward implementing tactical resource decisions necessary to achieve broader strategic plans. This stage in the organizational planning process focuses management's attention on issues of capacity limitations at the shop floor level of the operations management functional area. In doing so, operational planning forces managers to improve productivity in OM workcenters, equipment, and individuals to meet detailed capacity requirements.

In summary, all three types of planning are necessary for every organization. Although organizations may approach the planning process differently from one another, the structure presented in Figure 4-1 represents the general stages in the planning process practiced by all. In the next three sections of this chapter, we will describe the strategic, tactical, and operational planning stages of the organizational planning process.

STRATEGIC PLANNING

Although known by a variety of terms, **strategic planning** is long-range planning. Strategic planning is usually composed of the five components presented in Figure 4-2: environmental situation analysis, corporate situation analysis, corporate mission statement, corporate strategic plans, and operations management strategic plans.

Environmental Situation Analysis

The external environment of an organization usually includes customers, public interest groups, competitors, the government, suppliers, stockholders, and owners. In the strategic planning process, the organization attempts to assess opportunities and threats that these entities pose over a long-range planning horizon of two or more years. An **environmental situation analysis** is an assessment of the external environment made by an organization to determine product expectations of customers, the potential threats of public interest groups, the threatening positions of industry competitors, the threats and opportunities of newly enacted governmental regulations and laws, suppliers' ability to satisfy long-range material requirements, and the needs of stockholders and owners. The firm is also vitally interested in knowing whether the economic situation of the industry is in a "boom" or "bust" condition; if customer expectations on product factors of price, quality, and appearance are changing; if unfilled customer needs in the

FIGURE 4-2 TYPICAL STRATEGIC PLANNING CONSIDERATIONS

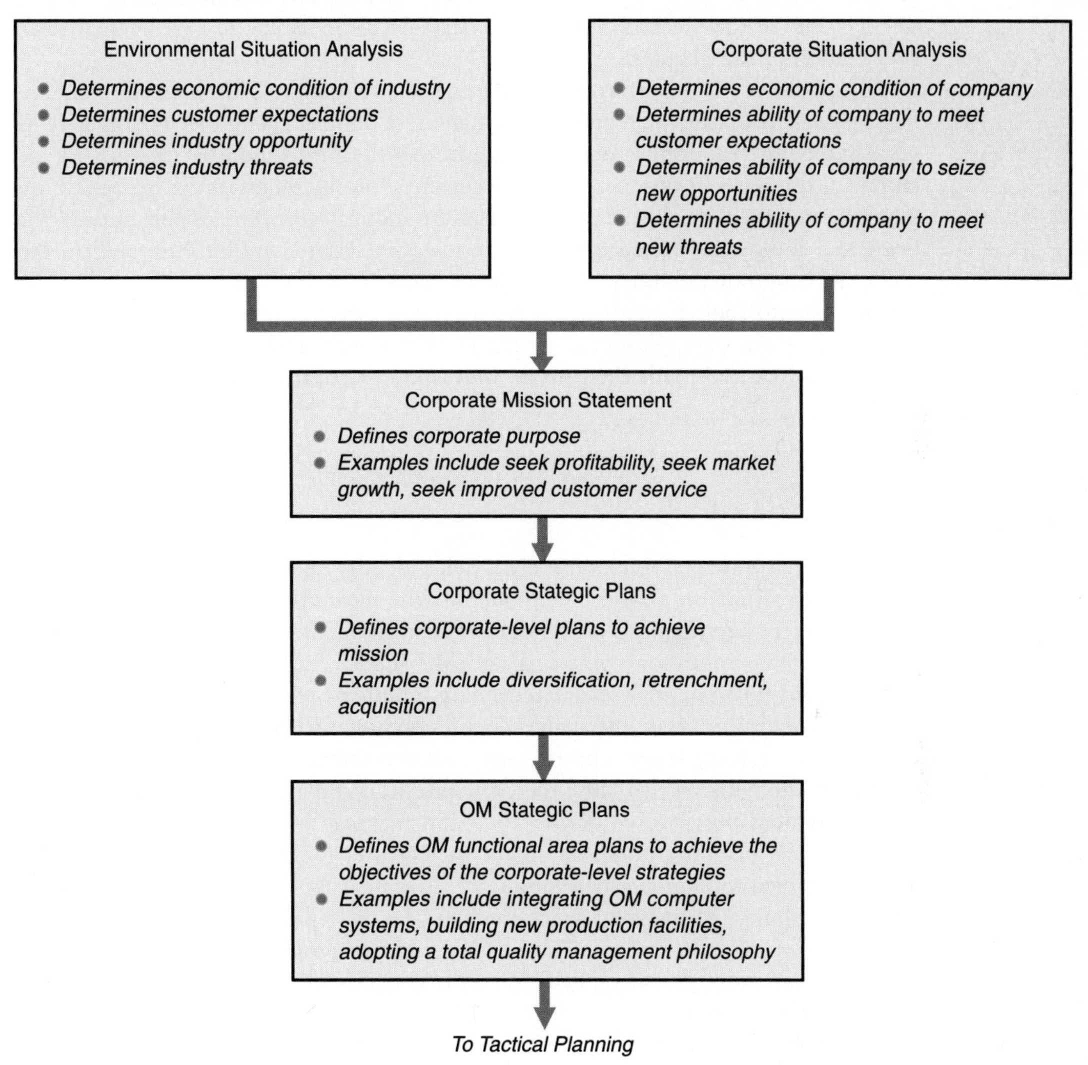

industry might represent an opportunity for the firm; and if competitors will be challenging the firm on any of its products or services.

An environmental situation analysis focuses on a firm's industry or principal markets (which may be international). The data for this type of analysis can be quite substantial. Many firms use consultants or experts whose knowledge of a particular industry is current and who are able to project long-range behavior in critical areas of industry activity. Other firms, because of secrecy or out of necessity, use their own top executives or staff analysts to prepare environmental situation reports on the industry. We will discuss some of the methods used to aid strategic planners in this type of analysis in a later section of this chapter.

Regardless of who performs the environmental situation analysis, its outcome must be a general condition statement. This statement should cover the next two to five years and define economic trends taking place in the firm's industry, customer expectations of the types of products the firm currently produces, customer expectations on new types of products that might appear in the industry (product opportunities for the firm), and competitor threats to the firm. This general statement informs the firm about the broad economic, industry, and product directions of the future. It provides the basis for the firm to look to its internal environment (see Chapter 1) to see how it can successfully participate within the external environment. The analysis that provides the information that can guide the firm in this planning activity is called a *corporate situation analysis*.

Corporate Situation Analysis

Just as an environmental situation analysis helps identify needs or industry requirements, a **corporate situation analysis** helps identify the means or company capacity to meet the industry requirements. The corporate situation analysis begins by determining a firm's economic condition compared with the industry as a whole, using typical accounting and financial analyses. Determining whether the economic condition of the company is strong or weak, the analysis focuses on how well the firm can meet customer expectations, industry opportunities, and industry threats discovered in the environmental situation analysis. Because the corporate situation analysis is strategic, the planning effort does not involve detailed decision making. Instead, it deals with general issues. Typical planning questions might include the following: Does the firm have sufficient capital to launch a new product in the next two years? Does the firm have sufficient cash flow to finance a growth rate in sales of 10 percent? Will growth in profit for the next five years support a new quality service program? The answers to these long-range questions should be based on fairly general estimates of the firm's economic and financial condition.

The information for this analysis is usually obtained internally. Information for strategic planning is not very precise but is expected to be generally accurate. A judgmentally estimated percentage increase or decrease in resources from a prior planning period provided by an executive or staff specialist is often used for planning information at this stage of the analysis. Such percentages are derived by extrapolating long-range trends and analyzing an industry's potential directions. These long-range trends are usually obtained by the same long-range forecasting methods discussed in Chapter 3. The forecasts are not just of product demand but of human resource availability trends, technology trends, and system development trends. An organization must always consider human, technology, and system resources in any type of planning. Some of the forecasting methods used at this stage of the planning process include judgmental forecasting methods to predict technology and system development trends and secondary source information from the federal and state governments that can be used to forecast human resource availability for the firm. Because long-range implications of the trends or availability of these management resources involve some risks, the decision-making methods dealing with risk decision environments can also be applied. **Decision theory,** the decision-making method used for selecting strategies, can be used to minimize the risk of adopting attractive new product opportunities in the industry. (For a review of decision theory methods see Appendix C.)

The outcome of the corporate situation analysis is a general statement on the firm's abilities to cope with the changes in the external environment. Specifically, the corporate situation analysis will state how well the firm is equipped to compete in the industry in the next two to five years, new areas of business opportunities to explore, and old areas of business activity that should be strengthened or discontinued.

Corporate Mission Statement

A **corporate mission statement** is a company statement of purpose; it defines why the corporation conducts business. Most corporate mission statements tend to be a statement about what the firm does. American Telephone & Telegraph's (AT&T) corporate mission statement helps define its role in the information age: "AT&T's business is the electronic movement and management of information—in the United States and around the world."[2] Although AT&T does not revise its mission statement each year, or even every five years, changes in mission statements are periodically necessary to keep current with the changes observed through the environmental situation analysis and the corporate situation analysis. S

Effective mission statements should be market oriented, feasible, motivating, and specific.[3] They should clearly state the market or markets in which the firm is doing business. The market orientation gives the firm a clear domain in which to focus its business activity. The mission statement that is defined too narrowly may limit a firm's ability to operate successfully. Alternatively, the mission statement that is defined too broadly may propose an infeasibly large area of activity. A mission statement should take a middle-ground orientation that permits healthy growth within the firm's capacity. A successful mission statement motivates everyone in the firm and challenges them to strive for success in its activities. A mission statement should also be specific enough to express major policies and guidelines while allowing management the discretion to establish its own strategies and courses of action. Research has shown that productive and high-performing organizations have effectively developed mission statements embodying these characteristics.[4]

---

[2] American Telephone & Telegraph, *Annual Report,* 1984, p. 5.

[3] L. A. Digman, *Strategic Management,* 2nd ed. (Homewood, Ill.: Irwin, 1990), pp. 73–74.

[4] J. A. Pearce and F. David, "Corporate Mission Statements: The Bottom Line," *Academy of Management Executive,* 1, No. 2 (1987), 112.

QUESTION: Do organizations really risk everything for a corporate mission or do they simply change the mission statement if the "going gets rough"?

ANSWER: Although mission statements are meant to be modified to take environmental changes into consideration, many organizations have and continue to risk their survival in an effort to pursue their corporate mission. For example, Michelin Tire Company has maintained a primary corporate mission of growth. After World War II, it risked its future by transferring the firm's entire resources to producing a single type of new experimentally designed "radial" tire.[5] This brash move proved to be a major success: Michelin was able to capture a large portion of the market by having its product available when customers demanded radial tires.

The outcome of a mission statement should be general, long-range strategic objectives that the firm can seek. (For certain industries, such as paper products and mining, strategic plans may cover ten to fifty years.) The strategic objectives can include economic objectives such as improved profitability or improved market growth. They can also include objectives concerning improved product quality, technology, or customer service.

Corporate Strategic Planning

Corporate strategic planning involves establishing strategies to achieve the objectives expressed in the mission statement. Corporate strategic planning usually begins with the determination of a number of alternative plans to achieve each strategic objective. Then alternative strategic plans are evaluated in light of the information provided by the corporate situation analysis. The best set of strategies to achieve the objectives are then accepted by upper management and passed on to middle-level management to implement the tactical planning stage of the organization planning process.

The way in which a firm formulates its corporate strategic alternatives and chooses the best ones depends on a number of variables, including the organization's size. Smaller firms usually conduct their corporate strategic planning in-house using their own expertise or by hiring consultants to advise them. A number of medium- and large-sized organizations have turned to computer data base subscription systems to support corporate strategic planning efforts. One such system is the **Profit Impact of Market Strategy (PIMS)** data base, which is a research data base that contains information on the corporate strategic planning behavior of more than 3,000 businesses.[6] Subscriber

[5] E. S. Browning, "On a Roll," *Wall Street Journal,* January 5, 1990, pp. 1–8.

[6] R. D. Buzzell and B. T. Gale, *The PIMS Principle: Linking Strategy to Performance* (New York: The Free Press, 1987).

QUESTION: Suppose a company has a corporate strategic objective of having the highest-quality products in the industry. What could be in its corporate strategic plan?

ANSWER: The corporate strategic plan might be to institute a total quality management (TQM) program throughout the corporation, like those discussed in Chapter 2. TQM involves not just operations management, but the entire organization. How the TQM program would be structured to support specific product quality goals related to the OM functional area (such as improving supplier relations and improving material quality) would involve a more OM-specific level of planning called OM strategic planning.

Q

organizations provide the data base information on their own corporate strategic planning decisions. The system then provides feedback to the subscribers on how the results of their strategic decisions compare with those of other companies. The system also provides suggestions on corporate strategic changes that hold promise for improving the firm's return on investment.

The outcome of the corporate strategic planning stage is a set of corporate strategic plans that can be used by functional or division heads as guidelines in structuring their own areas of responsibility. As presented in Figure 4-2, typical corporate strategic plans might include diversification, retrenchment, acquisition, or a combination of all three.

QUESTION: Corporate strategic goals seem to sometimes be very generally stated and distant from the day-to-day activities of a corporation. Does changing a generally stated corporate strategic goal really affect the bottom-line of an organization?

ANSWER: Yes, it can! One of the classic examples occurred when, in the early 1980s, Florida Power & Light (FP&L) set out to be "the best-managed electric utility in the U.S." It wanted to be the utility known for setting the industry standards for quality service performance, so it set its corporate strategic goal as having the highest quality of service of the U.S. utility industry. Implementing a TQM program developed by Japanese consultants rapidly improved its organization's customer service. For example, the unscheduled downtime of FP&L's fossil fuel power plants fell from a level of more than 14 percent in 1986 to only 4 percent in 1989. Customer complaints during the same period dropped by 60 percent, and the yearly lost time from injuries fell from 1.28 per 100 employees to only 0.39.[7]

Q

S

[7] R. C. Wood, "A Hero Without a Company," *Forbes,* March 18, 1991, pp. 112–114.

If a corporate strategic objective is to reduce the risk of operation, a diversification corporate strategic plan to increase product line can reduce the risk in producing a limited set of vulnerable products. If a corporate strategic objective is to reduce operating costs, a retrenchment corporate strategic plan that eliminates less-productive resources can guide the organization into a less costly operation. If a corporate strategic objective is for growth, then an acquisition corporate strategic plan can help motivate and guide the organization to expand through acquisition.

In summary, the corporate strategic planning stage in the organization planning process can be viewed as a corporatewide planning activity. The results of the planning effort are a set of corporate strategic objectives and corporate strategic plans to achieve the objectives. These plans begin the process by which the objectives are converted into individual functional- or division-level plans. These plans begin the narrowing process by which a corporatewide strategy is divided into functional- or division-level strategic plans.

Strategic Planning in Operations Management

Although corporate strategic planning is performed at the upper levels of management, operations management has an important functional planning role in the development of competitive advantages. Operations managers are taking an ever-increasing role in choosing strategic plan alternatives to achieve corporate strategic objectives. Some of the strategic opportunities identified by research as related to OM include reducing product cost; increasing product line breadth; developing product innovation; enhancing product value; improving operation flexibility, production technology, quality, and service; determining geographic location; and scheduling.[8] The same research has shown that the OM area could account for almost 30 percent of the categories of strategic opportunities for competitive advantages. No other functional area (marketing, finance, accounting, MIS, and so on) offers a greater percentage of opportunity than OM in seeking a sustainable or long-range competitive advantage.

In addition to the operations management's contribution in selecting the corporate strategic plans, operations managers must convert the corporate strategic plans into more specific OM-related strategies. This type of planning narrows the corporate strategies to OM considerations. Performed by both upper- and middle-level management, this type of planning bridges both levels of management as the planning effort moves toward the tactical planning stage of the organizational planning process. If a corporation, for example, established a strategic objective of improved product quality, then typical OM strategies might include the long-range adoption of quality control systems or the development of technologies that would improve product quality. If the corporation establishes a corporate strategic objective to improve the organization's ability to adapt to changes in the marketplace, then a typical OM strategy might include seeking a long-range change in product facilities to be highly flexible to changes in products or services.

---

[8] D. A. Aaker, "Creating a Sustainable Competitive Advantage," *California Management Review* (Winter 1989), 91–106.

QUESTION: Can long-range strategic planning be applied to a product whose entire product life cycle may be one year or less?

ANSWER: Yes, strategic planning is useful in all types of product planning. Because knowing the time horizon of a new product's life cycle is difficult, strategic planning is conducted in the same manner for all types of new products even if their life span ends up being short.

To illustrate how an operations management strategy might be developed and its relationship to time, let's look at a classic product life cycle planning problem. The **product life cycle** is a four-phased sequential process that all products and services undergo in the marketplace. As we can see in the top of Figure 4-3, the sales level for any product (or product line) starts out at a fluctuating low level in the introduction stage, increases in the growth stage, becomes fairly stable in the maturity stage, and finally decreases or is completely eliminated in the decline stage. Some products' life cycles are short lived. The Coleco Corporation's original Cabbage Patch Doll lasted only about a year, yet other products like typewriters have lasted decades.

The life cycle of a product that will last about ten years is presented in Figure 4-3. Let's assume that the results of the initial environmental and corporate situation analyses result in a strategic planning mission statement that will seek market growth. This growth mission would be a logical consideration in the introductory and growth stages of the product. The mission statement, corporate strategy, and operations management strategy each share the same time frame of the first five years of the product's life. Because competition increases as a product matures (rendering the market growth mission less applicable), the strategic planning concerning the product must also shift. The organization's mission statement shifts as the product proceeds toward the maturity and decline stages of its life. The growth mission changes to a profit mission. The shift does not alter the time horizon for the strategic planning. Again the mission statement, corporate strategy, and OM strategy all share the five-year planning horizon.

In summary, operations management strategic planning involves a general view of the allocation of OM resources (human, technology, or system) to achieve a competitive advantage. To perform this planning, OM planners must be able to convert broad, corporate strategic objectives into OM-related considerations necessary to achieve a competitive advantage.

TACTICAL PLANNING

Strategic planning defines a firm's corporate objectives and provides a framework to develop strategic operations management plans for achieving those objectives. The firm then must develop a set of more specific objectives for each functional area within the

FIGURE 4-3 CORPORATE STRATEGY AND THE PRODUCT LIFE CYCLE

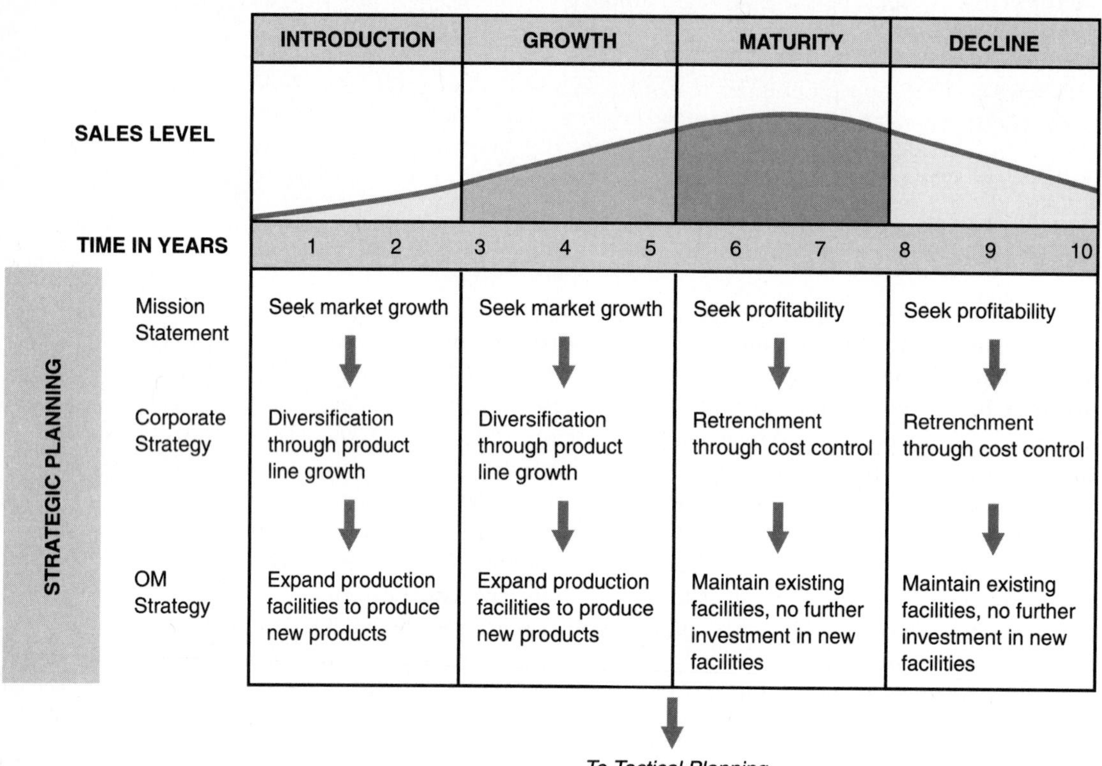

firm. **Tactical planning** is the planning effort that moves broad, strategic objectives into separate functional or division levels within the business organization. It moves the long-range OM strategic plans into medium-range tactical planning considerations. The outcome of the tactical planning stage in the organizational planning process (in Figure 4-1) is a set of specific, medium-range plans covering one to two years that detail aggregate resource requirements and resource capacities.

Tactical planning, often referred to as the **business plan** when it appears in final form, focuses on matching and balancing the aggregate resource demand requirements for the next year or two with the firm's aggregate capacity. The aggregation of a firm's resources (that is, total human resource requirements, total production capacity) at this stage of planning is more specific than at the strategic stage of planning, but it is not as detailed as the next stage (that is, operational planning) in the organizational planning process.

As presented in Figure 4-4, tactical planning in each of the functional areas or levels of an organization has a sequence of activity. First, the marketing area within the firm establishes yearly, quarterly, or monthly aggregate demand requirements. The detail of

QUESTION: If a corporate strategic objective is "improved profitability," what would a related operations management tactical objective be?

ANSWER: A large number of OM tactical objectives can support a strategic objective of improved profitability. One tactical objective might be to acquire a new inventory system that, after taking two years to install, could reduce costs and improve the corporation's long-range profitability.

the estimates is usually not in terms of individual product types or sizes, but in terms of total unitary production for the time period involved. This provides a basis for aggregate operations management demand requirements. Each functional area also has its own unique resource requirements that are estimated as a part of the organization's overall tactical planning process. Because this book's focus is on OM we will use the OM area to illustrate the type of planning effort that takes place in a functional area during the tactical planning stage.

The planning process used in operations management to determine aggregate demand requirements for personnel, inventory, and production rates in most organizations is called aggregate planning. **Aggregate planning** focuses on the total collection or aggregation of OM resources including the total number of workers that make up the work force size, the total inventory size, and the production capacity/rates used to meet the demand requirements in the next one or two years. In the process of determining production rates of personnel and equipment, the OM area also determines its aggregate production capacity. The planning process used to determine the firm's aggregate production capacity is called *capacity planning*. (We will be discussing aggregate planning and capacity planning concepts and methods in Chapter 5 and other chapters throughout this book.) Tactical planning incorporates both aggregate planning and capacity planning to ensure that aggregate capacity resources can meet the aggregate demand requirements.

QUESTION: If a corporate strategic objective is to increase the rate of new product introduction, what would a related operations management strategy and OM tactical objective be?

ANSWER: An OM strategy that would support the corporate strategy might be to use computer-integrated manufacturing (CIM) systems to permit rapid computer-aided changeovers from one product to another. An OM tactical objective that would support the OM strategy (and therefore the corporate strategy) might be to implement a computer-aided design (CAD) system to support the broader CIM system.

FIGURE 4-4 TYPICAL TACTICAL PLANNING CONSIDERATIONS

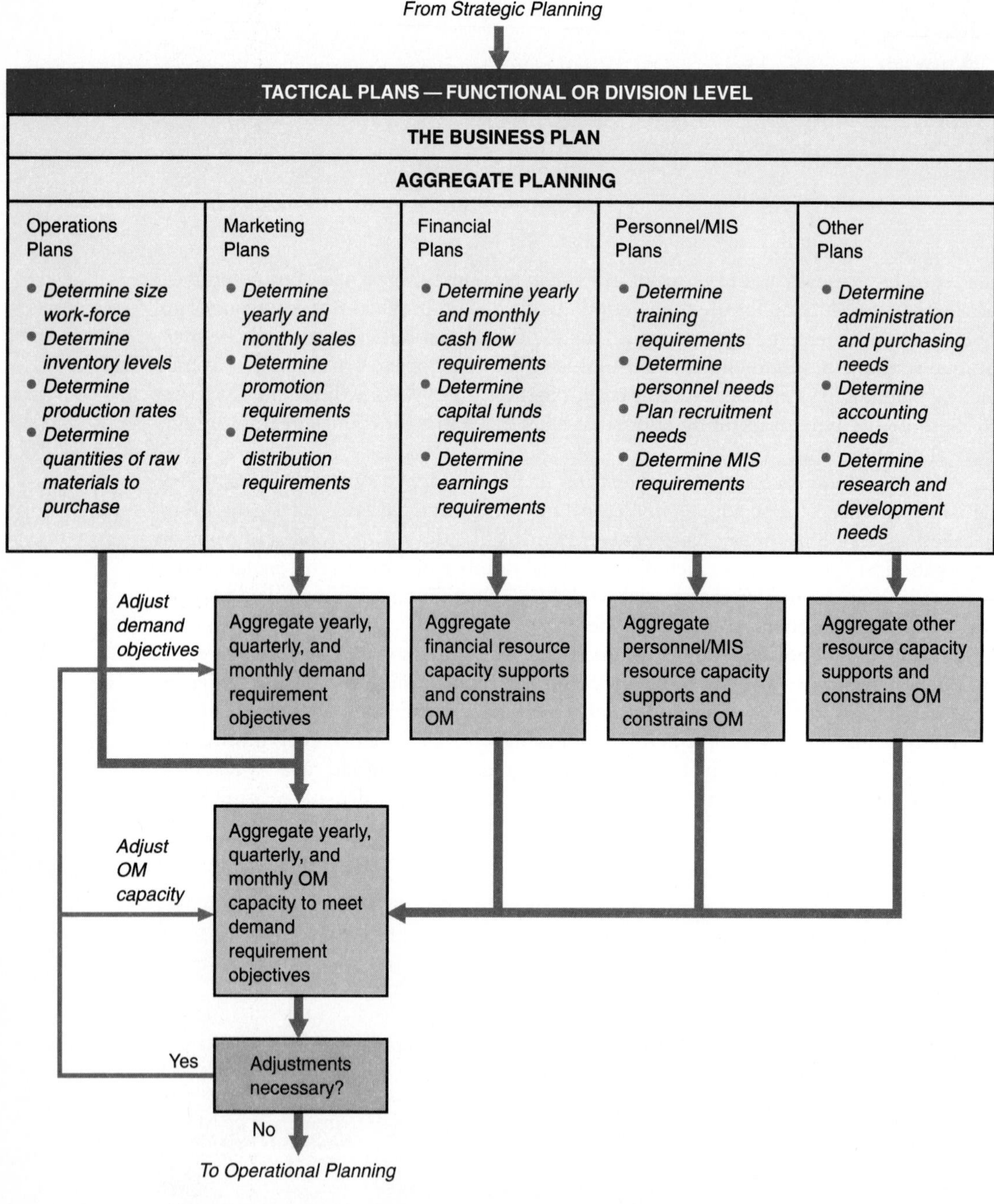

Although a great deal of tactical planning activity is performed by functional areas other than operations management, most of this activity is centered and directed toward supporting the OM function requirements. This is usually the case whether the organization is a manufacturer or a service company. The reason that OM is the center of attention lies in the sequence of tactical planning in the organizational planning process. The sequence is simply that marketing defines the aggregate needs and OM defines the aggregate means to satisfy the needs. Finance, human resources, and other functional areas provide support roles to assist the OM area. Although each functional area plays a critical role in the organization's survival, at the tactical stage of planning only OM-area decisions actually define what human, technology, or system resources will be needed to meet aggregate demand requirements. Unfortunately, limitations within the functional areas of OM, finance, and personnel/MIS as well as other areas can constrain the OM activities. A lack of production facilities, insufficient cash flow to support the acquisition of OM equipment, or a shortage of skilled work force to staff a new OM plant can all lead to OM's failure to achieve its desired aggregate demand requirements. As presented in Figure 4-4, an adjustment might be needed either to change the OM capacity to fulfill the desired demand requirements or to revise the demand requirements provided in the aggregate marketing plan. Eventually, the planned aggregate demand requirements and the planned aggregate capacity resources must be brought into equilibrium with each other.

This equilibrium is only achieved when specific tactical decisions are made to achieve the tactical objectives. These decisions are at the heart of tactical planning. They usually concern the aggregate planning of personnel, inventory, and production rates. For example, Procter & Gamble's inventory level of its Crest toothpaste is tactically set at a level above the highest peak of forecast sales.[9] This permits the firm to avoid stocking out, and it supports the strategic objective of excellent customer service. Some examples of tactical decisions in operations management are presented in Table 4-3. The outcome of this tactical planning stage of the organizational planning process is a set of tactical decisions that plan the use of the firm's resources. These tactical decision plans will eventually have to be implemented in the OM departments and at the shop-floor level of the organization. Planning this implementation at these lower levels in the organization is called operational planning.

In Figure 4-5, the product life cycle from Figure 4-3 is shown, with related operations management tactical planning included. Notice that unlike the five-year strategies of strategic planning, the OM tactics differ for each of the medium-range, two-and-a-half year quarters of the product life cycle. In other words, the tactics used in each quarter of the product's life are different to deal with the unique nature of the demand levels occurring in that period. Note also that there is more detail and a greater number of tactics per strategy as the planning moves from the more general strategic planning to the more specific tactical planning.

---

[9] D. H. Holt, *Management: Principles and Practices,* 2nd ed. (Englewood Cliffs, N.J.: Prentice-Hall, 1990), p. 224.

TABLE 4-3 TYPICAL TACTICAL DECISIONS IN OPERATIONS MANAGEMENT

OM Area	*Types of Decisions*
Technology	Upgrade equipment to improve flexibility or productivity. Move from labor-intensive to technology-intensive systems to improve product quality.
Facilities	Increase or decrease buildings and materials management systems to avoid excess capacity costs. Acquire or close down facilities to match medium-range forecast for product demand. Relocate plants to maintain nearness to customers and keep transportation costs low.
Energy	Change energy systems to use a variety of energy sources (coal, electricity, fuel oil, etc.) to permit greater flexibility and enable operation to shift to least expensive source.
Human resources	Renegotiate union agreements to permit workers to perform a variety of work tasks to permit them to perform quality control activities in accordance with product quality–oriented just-in-time methods.
Distribution systems	Revise shipping policies to permit a greater use of a variety of transport organizations to broaden and enhance customer delivery service.

OPERATIONAL PLANNING

Operational planning is the detailed planning activities that bring the tactical plans down to the individual department or workcenter levels of the organization. This planning is considered to be short-range, spanning from one day to less than a year. Although each of the organization's functional areas performs its own version of operational planning, we will focus here on the operations management functional area. The plans for the OM area are detailed and specific in terms of type of product, timing of production, and number of units produced per hour, day, or week. The planning effort at this stage of the organizational planning process is usually performed by OM department heads, first-line supervisors, and even workers.

A considerable number of decision support systems are available to support operational planning. Computer-based inventory systems such as material requirements planning (MRP) systems can be used to plan inventory usage. More complex computer-integrated manufacturing (CIM) systems not only support material planning activities but also provide a current or real-time level of human, technology, and system resources.

From the tactical planning stages depicted in Figure 4-4, the adjusted aggregate operations management plans are directed down to the department or workcenter levels. As shown in Figure 4-6, the departmental areas develop their own set of plans to

FIGURE 4-5 CORPORATE STRATEGY, OM TACTICAL PLANNING, AND THE PRODUCT LIFE CYCLE

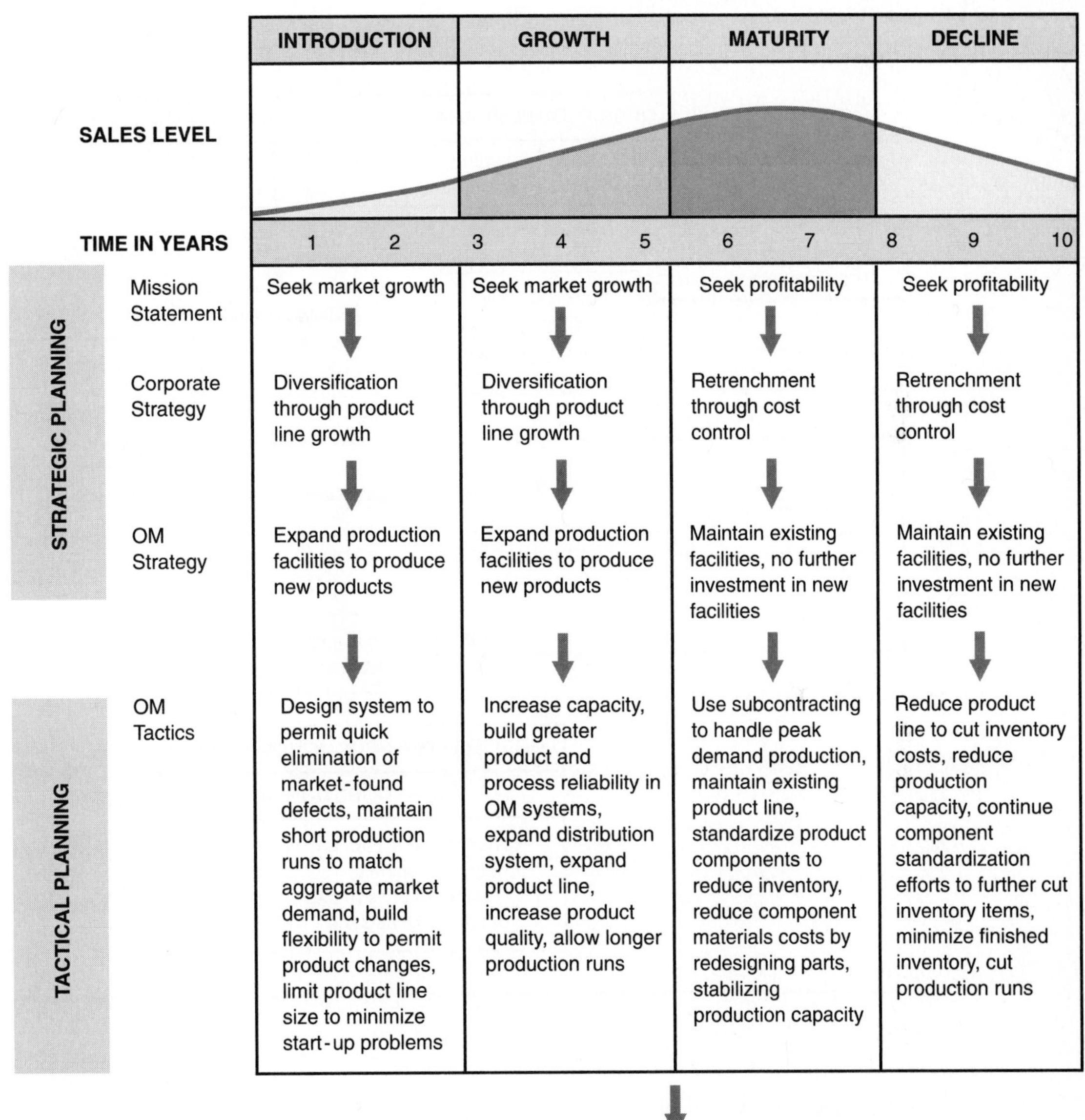
INTRODUCTION
GROWTH
MATURITY
DECLINE
SALES LEVEL
TIME IN YEARS
1 2 3 4 5 6 7 8 9 10
STRATEGIC PLANNING
TACTICAL PLANNING
Mission Statement
Corporate Strategy
OM Strategy
OM Tactics
Seek market growth
Seek market growth
Seek profitability
Seek profitability
Diversification through product line growth
Diversification through product line growth
Retrenchment through cost control
Retrenchment through cost control
Expand production facilities to produce new products
Expand production facilities to produce new products
Maintain existing facilities, no further investment in new facilities
Maintain existing facilities, no further investment in new facilities
Design system to permit quick elimination of market-found defects, maintain short production runs to match aggregate market demand, build flexibility to permit product changes, limit product line size to minimize start-up problems
Increase capacity, build greater product and process reliability in OM systems, expand distribution system, expand product line, increase product quality, allow longer production runs
Use subcontracting to handle peak demand production, maintain existing product line, standardize product components to reduce inventory, reduce component materials costs by redesigning parts, stabilizing production capacity
Reduce product line to cut inventory costs, reduce production capacity, continue component standardization efforts to further cut inventory items, minimize finished inventory, cut production runs
To Operational Planning

FIGURE 4-6 TYPICAL OPERATIONAL PLANNING CONSIDERATIONS

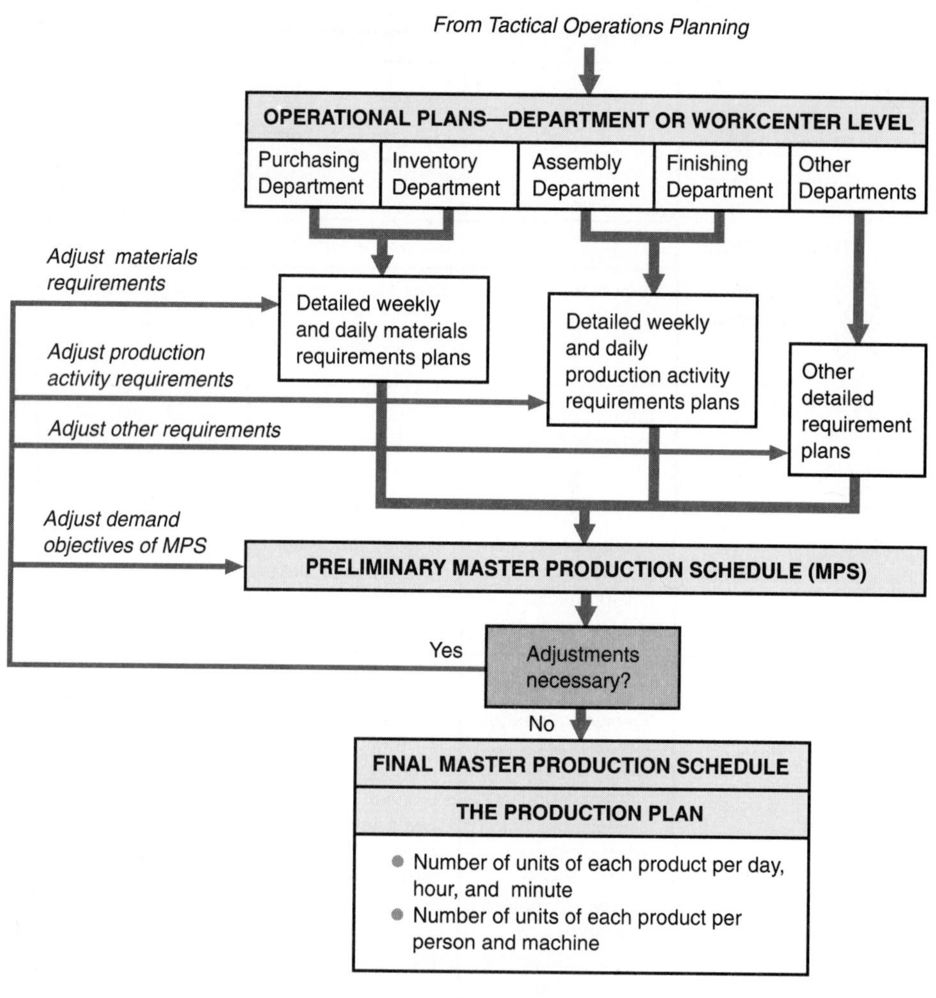

implement the tactical plans. The focus of planning at this level is narrowly directed at what each department should do. For example, let's examine operational planning in a department such as purchasing. A relatively long-range operational planning consideration might include how many buyers the department will need to support next season's or next quarter's purchasing activity. A more short-range plan—such as that for a day—might include changing daily lot-sizes for incoming orders of purchased goods, changing distributors to reduce material costs, and changing transporters to improve delivery service. Each of these planning considerations requires an operational planning decision dealing with human, technology, or system resources.

Once resource decisions are made on the operational requirements for implementing the aggregate tactical demand requirements, a preliminary master production schedule is prepared. A **master production schedule (MPS)** or **production plan** is a formal schedule that defines exactly how many units of each product are to be produced in a medium-range planning horizon of a month, quarter, or year. Some MPSs are so specific in scheduling that they plan production by the hour or even by the minute. Before the MPS is formalized (that is, accepted by all levels of management), the demand requirements within each department (or workstation) are compared with the capacity for the given planning horizon. If demand requirement objectives and capacity resources are not balanced, then adjustments must be made to bring them in line with one another. (We discuss adjustment and capacity planning methods for operational planning throughout all the chapters in Part II.) The outcome of the adjustment planning is a final MPS, which is used to guide production activities at the shop-floor level of the organization.

Relating operational planning to the product life cycle in Figure 4-7, we can see that the planning horizons are substantially reduced to "time-buckets" of weeks or even days. Within these time-buckets the same set of basic scheduling decisions have to be made: unit production, personnel usage, inventory usage, product distribution, and so on. What differs between operational planning and tactical planning is the repetitive nature of decisions and the short-range nature of change. As we see in Figure 4-7, OM tactics can be varied. For example, tactics of short production runs may exist in one two-and-a-half year period and then change to long production runs in the next period.

QUESTION: Why change from short production runs in the introduction life cycle stage to long production runs in the growth stage of the life cycle?

ANSWER: Short runs during the introduction stage, which is characterized by a period of low demand, allow companies to switch between runs of several newly introduced products. As a new product becomes successful over time, which happens in the growth stage, a greater commitment of resources (longer production runs) is necessary to again tactically match customer demand requirements.

Operational planning decisions would focus on short-range, incremental changes from day-to-day that would move the production system from the short runs in the introductory stage to the long runs in the growth stage of the product life cycle.

FIGURE 4-7 OM TACTICAL PLANNING, OM OPERATIONAL PLANNING, AND THE PRODUCT LIFE CYCLE

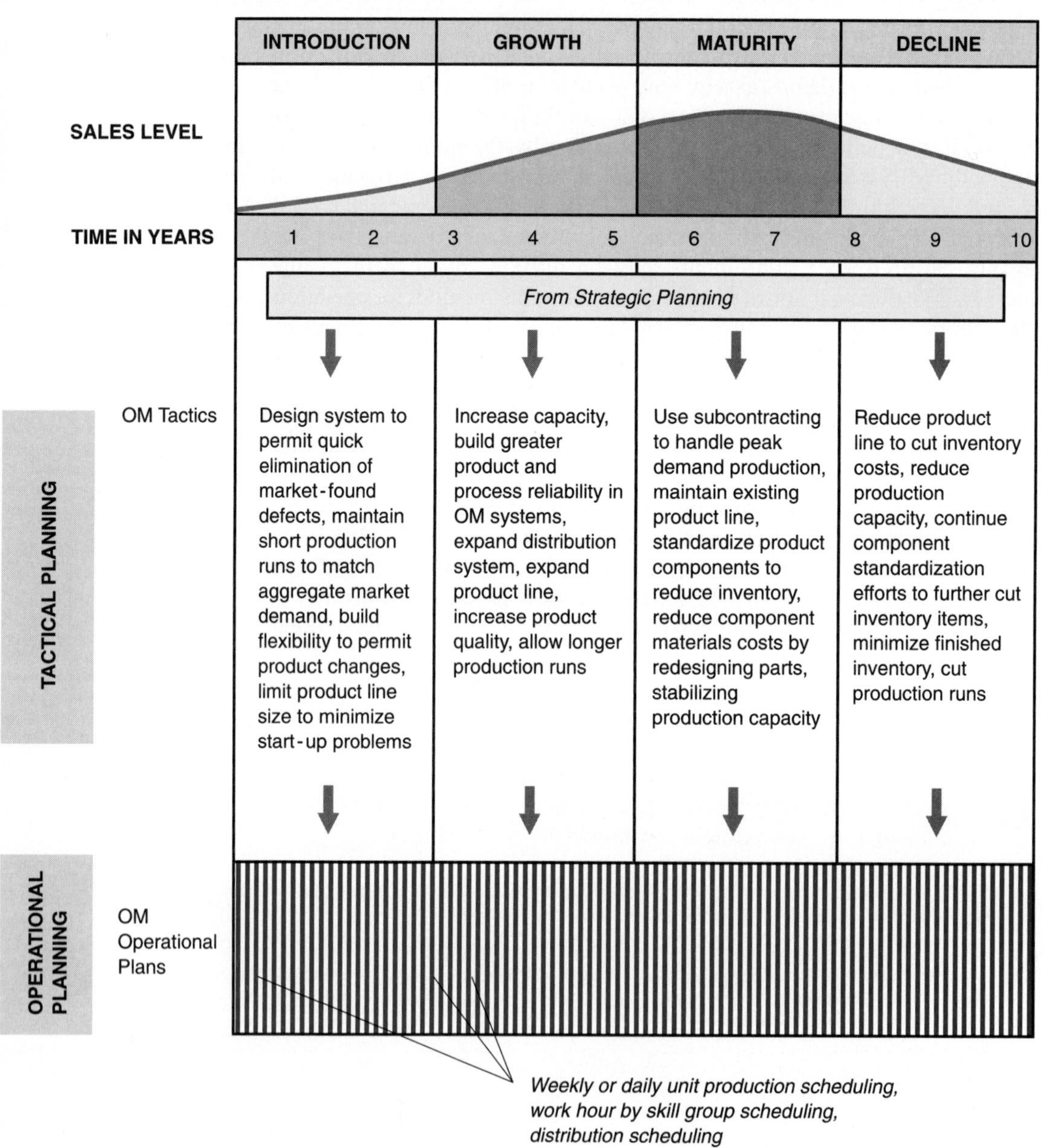
INTRODUCTION
GROWTH
MATURITY
DECLINE
SALES LEVEL
TIME IN YEARS
1 2 3 4 5 6 7 8 9 10
From Strategic Planning
TACTICAL PLANNING
OM Tactics
Design system to permit quick elimination of market-found defects, maintain short production runs to match aggregate market demand, build flexibility to permit product changes, limit product line size to minimize start-up problems
Increase capacity, build greater product and process reliability in OM systems, expand distribution system, expand product line, increase product quality, allow longer production runs
Use subcontracting to handle peak demand production, maintain existing product line, standardize product components to reduce inventory, reduce component materials costs by redesigning parts, stabilizing production capacity
Reduce product line to cut inventory costs, reduce production capacity, continue component standardization efforts to further cut inventory items, minimize finished inventory, cut production runs
OPERATIONAL PLANNING
OM Operational Plans
Weekly or daily unit production scheduling, work hour by skill group scheduling, distribution scheduling

QUESTION: What would some of the operational planning decisions be during the short production runs in the introduction life cycle stage and the long production runs in the growth life stage of the life cycle?

ANSWER: For a short production run during the introduction stage, operational planning decisions might concern the number of units to produce during a single day to achieve the small lot size of the new product's production run. Particularly important for short runs are to make sure that labor and production capacity are adequate for daily production setup requirements (labor, tools, and so on)—that is, to complete the run. For a long production run during the growth stage, operational planning decisions might be concerned with how many units to produce each day to achieve a weekly or monthly total unit production. To meet shifting market demand requirements, the decision to change a fixed daily production quantity will usually take place during the long production runs (that is, minor shifts up or down from the fixed daily production quantity). Planning daily production setup requirements becomes less important because there are fewer setups with longer production runs. The daily operational impact of changes in labor capacity (such as those caused by absentees) becomes more important as they are more likely during the longer period of extended production runs. Hence, there are similarities and differences in the day-to-day operational planning activities during each stage of the product life cycle.

Some additional typical operational decisions in operations management are presented in Table 4-4.

By conducting strategic, tactical, and operational planning, organizations can better plan for change to meet the changing needs of the market. To help them conduct planning, a variety of methods exist. While most of the methods in this book can be applied to tactical and operational planning, some methods are uniquely applied in strategic planning.

STRATEGIC PLANNING METHODS

Many organizational planning methods are available to aid in strategic, tactical, and operational planning. Because we will be discussing many tactical and operational planning methods in the next five chapters, we will discuss in this section two methods devoted exclusively to strategic planning.

TABLE 4-4 TYPICAL OM OPERATIONAL DECISIONS

OM Area	*Types of Decisions*
Product	Number of units to produce per size, shape, or style per day Order in which products will be completed during a day
Human resources	Number of employees to call into work or lay off each day Daily work assignments for each workstation
Facilities	Which piece of equipment will be used each day to satisfy the day's orders How production cells along an assembly line should be set up for the day's production
Inventory	Weekly target levels for each inventory item
Maintenance	Allocation of preventive maintenance resources
Distribution	Which carriers to use to ship goods

TOWS Analysis

One strategic planning method is called the **Threats, Opportunities, Weaknesses, and Strengths (TOWS) analysis.** One of the more well-known organizations that is generally credited with developing TOWS analysis is the Boston Consulting Group. The TOWS strategy matrix presented in Figure 4-8 is a conceptual diagram that helps organizations develop strategies for competitive advantages. The organization uses the strategy matrix to focus its analysis effort on first identifying opportunities and threats in the external environment and then identifying its own strengths and weaknesses. The purpose of the focused research is to help the firm to find matches between its strengths and the opportunities that exist in the external environment. TOWS can also be used to uncover areas of business activity where the organization is not only weak but could be seriously threatened.

As a conceptual model, the TOWS strategic matrix serves as a guide to organizing the information that is collected. Where does the information come from to fill the cells in the TOWS strategy matrix? It can be obtained from consultants, experts, or top management within the organization whose job it is to perform strategic planning. In fact, TOWS analysis actually combines information obtained from the environmental situation analysis with that from the corporate situation analysis. Many business organizations seek outside consulting firms to perform the analysis.

Critical Success Factor Scoring Methods

A strategic planning method that is useful for evaluating competitors' threats combines critical success factors and a rating-scoring method. A **critical success factor (CSF)**

FIGURE 4-8 STRATEGY MATRIX FOR TOWS ANALYSIS

		THE EXTERNAL ENVIRONMENT	
		OPPORTUNITIES	THREATS
THE FIRM	STRENGTHS	Seek to match strengths with opportunities	Avoid threats
	WEAKNESSES	Avoid weaknesses	Avoid completely

Source: Adapted from J. Heizer and B. Render, *Production and Operations Management,* 2nd ed., (Boston: Allyn & Bacon, 1991), p. 34.

can be defined as criteria that a firm views as critical for survival.[10] They are often based on economic factors such as sales, product price, cost factors, and profitability. They can also be based on social aspects (management-union relations, supplier relationships), political aspects (new federal laws, city or state regulations), and operations management–related aspects such as a technological advantage a firm has that poses a threat to another firm. Indeed, CSFs are the competitive advantages of a firm that competitors to some degree view as a threat.

Once an organization's CSFs are determined, they are evaluated in light of how they can withstand a threat by a competitor in an industry or marketplace. The evaluation, which is usually performed by experts, consultants, or experienced top management, consists of assessing the degree of threat that each competitor poses toward the firm's CSFs. One method of assessing a competitor's threat involves using a rating score. A **rating score** is usually a number on a continuous scale between 1 and 5, where 1 represents a rating in which the competitor poses a high degree of threat for the firm's CSF, and a 5 represents a low or no-threat rating. (Rating scores can be any type of numbers over any kind of scale.) The rating scores are assessed for each competitor's potential threat toward the firm's CSFs, and the sum of the rating scores are used to determine which competitors pose the biggest threat. The rating scores can also be modified by a mathematical weight. The purpose of the mathematical weight is to adjust the values of the multiple CSFs' rating scores to reflect each one's relative importance in the final assessment of the rival firms' competitive threat to the firm. The

---

[10] J. R. Leidecker and A. V. Bruno, "Identifying and Using Critical Success Factors," *Long-Range Planning,* 17, No. 1 (1984), 23–32.

mathematical weight is usually a number between 0 and 1, and the sum of the weights for all CSFs equals 1.

The competitor analysis can be conducted using a tabular form similar to that presented in Figure 4-9 and can consist of the following steps:

1. Select the qualified personnel to do the scoring. It might be one person or several. If several are used, the rating scores will have to be added or averaged for each company and each CSF.
2. Select the *n* number of CSFs based on company strengths or competitive advantages found in the corporate situation analysis.
3. If desired, determine the relative importance of each CSF by establishing a *w* CSF weighting for each CSF.

FIGURE 4-9 COMPETITOR ANALYSIS FORM

CRITICAL SUCCESS FACTOR	CSF WEIGHT (w_i*)	COMPETITOR RATING SCORE (s_i†) A	B →
Price advantage	w_1	$(w_1)\ S_{1A}$	$(w_1)\ S_{1B}$
Cost advantage	w_2	$(w_2)\ S_{2A}$	$(w_2)\ S_{2B}$
Quality advantage	w_3	$(w_3)\ S_{3A}$	$(w_3)\ S_{3B}$
Sales advantage	w_4	$(w_4)\ S_{4A}$	$(w_4)\ S_{4B}$
Technology advantage	w_5	$(w_5)\ S_{5A}$	$(w_5)\ S_{5B}$
Sales force advantage	w_6	$(w_6)\ S_{6A}$	$(w_6)\ S_{6B}$
↓	↓	↓	↓
Distribution advantage	w_n	$(w_n)\ S_{nA}$	$(w_n)\ S_{nB}$
	$\sum_{i=1}^{n} w_i$	$\sum_{i=1}^{n} (w_i)\ S_{iA}$	$\sum_{i=1}^{n} (w_i)\ S_{iB}$
		Weighted CSF scores for each competitor	

**The sum of w_i is usually set at 1.*

†The scores of s_i are usually set on a continuous basis. For example, we can set a score of 1 = greatest or highest threat, 2 = above-average threat, 3 = average threat, 4 = below average threat, and 5 = lowest or no threat.

4. Let the personnel selected in step 1 establish their *S* rating scores for the CSF and each competitor. If CSF weighting is used, the mathematical rating score should be multiplied by the rating scores to produce a weighted rating score value.
5. Add the values from step 4 for each competitor to determine the total competitor rating score.
6. Interpret the total competitor rating score from step 5. If the 1-to-5 scale proposed in Figure 4-9 is used, the competitors with the smallest total competitor rating scores should be interpreted as posing the greatest threat to the firm.

QUESTION: Suppose a firm wants to determine which of two competitors (A or B) poses the greatest competitive threat. The firm feels that its CSFs include price, cost, quality, technology, and distribution advantages. These CSFs' relative importance to the firm is assessed by upper management as being 0.10, 0.20, 0.60, 0.05, and 0.05, respectively. Assume that a rating score of 1 represents the greatest CSF threat and a 5 represents the lowest or no threat. Given that Competitor A's rating scores for each of the CSFs are 3, 4, 1, 3, and 5, respectively, and Competitor B's rating scores for each of the CSFs are 1, 1, 4, 1, and 1, respectively, which of the two competitors appears to pose the greater threat?

ANSWER: The calculations for each competitor's total rating scores are presented in Figure 4-10. If we go strictly by the weighted score, Competitor A has the smaller ($2.10 < 2.80$) and more threatening score. *Note:* This example illustrates the importance that mathematical weighting can play in the final decision. Although Competitor B has greater threats on four of the five CSFs with ratings of 1, the relative weight of 0.60 on the quality advantage CSF tips the weighted summation in favor of Competitor A. Indeed, had we not included the mathematical weighting and only added the rating scores, Competitor B, with a total of 8 ($1 + 1 + 4 + 1 + 1$), would have been more threatening than Competitor A, with a total of 16 ($3 + 4 + 1 + 3 + 5$).

This procedure is limited by the accuracy of the rating scores and the mathematical weighting. Rating and scoring methods used as they have been presented should be used only as an approximate method for discrimination, rather than a descriptive index of a competitor's threat. In other words, the total competitor rating scores are best used to discriminate between competitors when their values differ greatly. A difference of, say, 0.10 and 0.11 should not be viewed as an index or a precise measurement of a discriminant competitive threat. In situations in which the resulting total competitor rating scores are very close, the interpretation that one competitor is definitely more threatening than another or ranked as a higher threat may be inappropriate.

FIGURE 4-10 COMPETITOR ANALYSIS EXAMPLE

CRITICAL SUCCESS FACTOR	CSF WEIGHT	COMPETITOR RATING SCORE*	
		A	B
Price advantage	0.10	(0.10) 3 = 0.30	(0.10) 1 = 0.10
Cost advantage	0.20	(0.20) 4 = 0.80	(0.20) 1 = 0.20
Quality advantage	0.60	(0.60) 1 = 0.60	(0.60) 4 = 2.40
Technology advantage	0.05	(0.05) 3 = 0.15	(0.05) 1 = 0.05
Distribution advantage	0.05	(0.05) 5 = 0.25	(0.05) 1 = 0.05
Total	1.00	2.10	2.80
		Competitor A's Weighted Score	Competitor B's Weighted Score

The scores are set at 1 = greatest or highest threat, 2 = above-average threat, 3 = average threat, 4 = below average threat, and 5 = lowest or no threat.

INTEGRATING MANAGEMENT RESOURCES: USING COMPUTER-ASSISTED DESIGN AND STRATEGIC INFORMATION SYSTEMS FOR COMPETITIVE ADVANTAGE

As previously mentioned, many different types of methods exist to support tactical and operational planning. Software and mathematical methods abound chiefly because, at the tactical and operational levels of planning, much of the data are quantifiable. Whether the issue is aggregate demand and capacity requirements at the tactical level or detailed individual demand and capacity requirements at the operational level of planning, the primary data under consideration to support the planning effort are quantitative. We have already seen an example in Chapter 3 of computer-integrated technology used at the operational level of planning. In Chapter 3 we discussed IBM's MAPICS II computer-integrated forecasting system, which can be used to update detailed scheduling at the operational level of planning. Throughout the rest of this book we will continue to discuss a variety of technologies and methods that support tactical and operational planning.

Computer-Assisted Design Systems

One of the most important management resource systems for operations management tactical planning decision making is a software application called *computer-*

aided design (CAD). CAD systems are specialized computer software used in product design and related engineering analysis. Sometimes called electronic drafting boards, CAD systems allow product or service design changes to be modeled within a computer and visually displayed so the designer can see and implement design changes electronically. What word processing has done for typing, CAD has done for drafting.

CAD systems in service operations are only just starting to evolve beyond stand-alone computer applications (that is, as aids to service product design but not integrated with other computer applications necessary to deliver the service product). Typically, service CAD systems are dedicated computer hardware, software, and data bases for use in service product design. A CAD system that has recently appeared in the service industry is a system used by doctors and pharmacists to keep track of prescription drug interactions. When patients take multiple prescription drugs, drug interaction can sometimes result in serious side-effects. A data base on known side-effects, maintained by the doctor or the pharmacist, can be consulted each time an additional drug is prescribed for a patient. When possible negative drug interactions are reported by the computer system for the collection of drugs the patient is consuming, the report can be used by the doctor to prepare an alternative prescription avoiding such interactions. The data base can actually be used by the doctor to search for (or design) a combination of drugs that will satisfy the patient's medical needs and minimize the drug's negative side-effects. Most major prescription drugstores in the United States maintain such computer systems as an added service for their customers. Other service CAD systems that have recently appeared include a U.S.–developed plastic surgery system that pictorially presents possible plastic surgery adjustments (such as a new nose) on a patient's actual face so the patient can see the effect of the adjustment and select the desired magnitude of change, and a French-developed CAD that aids customers in selecting an appropriate perfume based on income and social behavior.

CAD systems in manufacturing environments have evolved to more fully integrate the entire operation. A CAD system in a manufacturing environment usually consists of six components: (1) a computer (a stand-alone microcomputer, a minicomputer tied to other computer-integrated manufacturing (CIM) systems, or an interactive mainframe terminal tied into a fully operational CIM); (2) a user interface such as a keyboard, a mouse, or some kind of touch-screen system to permit user interaction; (3) graphics software for pictorial representations; (4) engineering software for design analyses; (5) a communications interface with the rest of the CIM system; and (6) a data base. The computer hardware involves a cathode ray tube (CRT) for displaying pictorially or graphically the image of the product to be designed. The designer, using a keyboard or some type of user interface, creates, transforms, and displays his or her ideas about the design of the product. In effect, the CAD replaces traditional drafting boards and drawings by electronically converting the designer's ideas into pictorial or symbolic data by way of the graphics software. The product image provided by the graphics software can range from simple two-dimensional pictures to multicolor representations in three dimensions. These representations can be structured to feature sculptured surfaces (shading used to create the illusion of depth) and moving parts that can be rotated like a three-dimensional object in space.

The data base in a CAD stores existing product specifications. If a customer needs an existing product, the CAD can quickly generate the blueprints or specifications for manufacturing. If a customer needs a slight modification in an existing product, CAD saves time by allowing the designer to quickly call the specifications of the existing product as a beginning point for a new design. Even if a customer needs a new product, the designer can easily experiment with applications of possible components of existing products.

Once a prototype of a product is designed, it is usually tested within the computer system in a variety of ways to ensure that it will meet the customers' expectations. This saves the usual prototype development time required when tangible models of the design are prepared and tested for structural problems. The engineering software permits some of these structural tests to be made on the computer-generated design so that necessary design changes can be electronically implemented if necessary. The engineering software consists of sophisticated mathematics that allow patterns of stress and the effects of loading to be simulated and analyzed. These tests permit the designer to evaluate material strength used in the product and make decisions on thickness, clearances, tolerances, volume, and weight.

Q During the late 1980s a new form of CAD called *stereolithography* emerged as a major technological breakthrough. Stereolithography combines laser and x-ray technologies with a CAD system to permit designers not only to design products but to actually create physical representations of the product out of plastic during the design phase. Unlike current CAD systems that require designers to physically prepare a tangible prototype of a new product or component part, the stereolithographic CAD integrates the laser and x-ray technologies in such a way as to actually transform the electronic image of the CAD into a tangible plastic prototype model of the image suitable for testing purposes. Still undergoing experimentation in the early 1990s, stereolithography CAD systems have shown that they are capable of preparing small component parts for products, like automobile transmission parts, with greater precision than possible with human beings and with a greater than 95 percent design time savings.

CAD is an important tactical planning technology of CIM and computer-integrated service systems (CISS) operations. CAD systems can help improve product decision making and save time, which permits users to provide better service to their customers. CAD is a basic element in computer-integrated systems. Researchers believe that the development of CAD and its early integration with computer-aided manufacturing (CAM) systems, like robots, formed the basis of what is today called CIM. The integrated CAD/CAM system allows the computer to convert design specifications directly into detailed manufacturing machine instructions so CAM-controlled robots or NC machines can perform their tasks without the need for human involvement. Products can go from design to manufacture in less time, with less human resource requirements, and in what some call a "paperless" environment. The result is reduced lead time in providing the customer a product (improved service) and improved productivity. This technology supports the productivity cycle (described in Chapter 1) and can eventually lead to a competitive advantage for users.

Strategic Information Systems

Researchers have suggested that both the qualitative and quantitative data used at the strategic level of the organizational planning process could be integrated into a single computer-based system called a *strategic information system (SIS).*[11] An SIS differs from a management information system (MIS) in the type of information it provides. An MIS provides formal, structured, and objective information such as MIS-generated scrap rate reports for operations management. An SIS, on the other hand, would permit a high degree of flexibility in information reporting and access. An SIS would also be able to process information on a subjective basis in the same way that human planners subjectively weight and assess information.

In Figure 4-11, we present a structure of a strategic information system. The SIS would consist of computer data bases and software modules. The SIS would begin with the same basic steps in the strategic planning process that have been discussed in this chapter: an environmental and corporate situation analysis. Computer-based assistance in developing these data bases might be accomplished by networking the SIS with the previously discussed PIMS program, a computer-based TOWS software module, or both. The difference that SIS makes in planning is that the data for these analyses could be in "real time," which would permit management to respond quickly at the strategic planning level. Being able to quickly respond to changes in the environment is one of the ways organizations can develop competitive advantages.

From the environmental and corporate data bases, the engine of the SIS would be based on the same set of logic rules, subjective weightings, and priorities that are found in strategic planning activities at the organization's upper level of management. Mimicking the expert judgment of corporate upper management, the software module would possess a rule-based artificial intelligence (AI) incorporated into an expert system.[12] Collectively, these rules, weightings, and priorities could be programmed into software to form an AI to guide the program in identifying corporate mission statements. Depending on the sophistication of the SIS and the desired specificity, the corporate mission statements might also be a predetermined input for the system. Given the mission statement and drawing on forecast economic information, the subjective AI-driven SIS would match company strengths with environmental opportunities (perhaps with TOWS) to define strategic objectives

---

[11] L. A. Digman, *Strategic Management,* 2nd ed. (Homewood, Ill.: Irwin, 1990), pp. 284–286; and C. H. Chung, J. R. Lang, and R. N. Shaw, "An Approach for Developing Support Systems for Strategic Decision Making," *OMEGA,* 17, No. 2 (1989), 135–146.

[12] Rule-based systems for analysis are capable of incremental knowledge growth, can cope with unplanned but useful information, and can perform deductive reasoning. For a review of the capabilities of rule-based systems see J. P. Ignizio, *Introduction to Expert Systems* (New York: McGraw-Hill, 1991), pp. 74–104; and P. H. Winston, *Artificial Intelligence,* 2nd ed. (Reading, Mass.: Addison-Wesley, 1984), pp. 166–202.

FIGURE 4-11 STRUCTURE OF STRATEGIC INFORMATION SYSTEM (SIS)

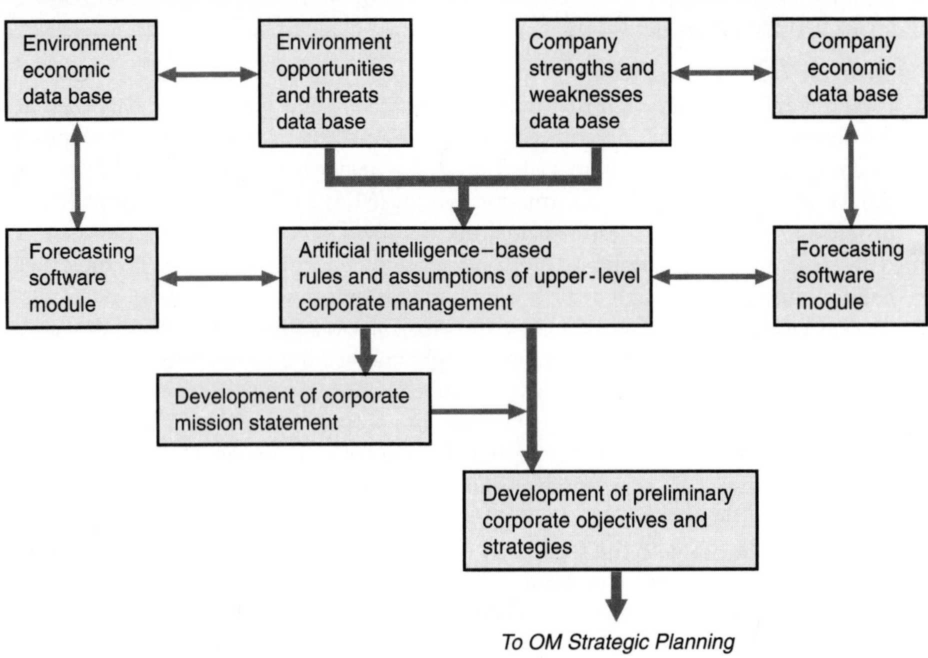

to support the generally expressed mission statements. In doing so, the SIS would be revealing possible areas of competitive advantage far more rapidly than a non-computer-based strategic planning process. Once the corporate-level strategic plans are defined, they could conceivably be downloaded to other tactical and eventually operational planning computer-based systems for a detailed division of information at each level in the organization. The integrating software to accomplish such a purposeful downloading has yet to be reported in the literature.

In summary, the advantages of an SIS are chiefly the speed with which the organization can

1. Recognize possible environmental threats and opportunities
2. Recognize possible company strengths and weaknesses
3. Identify possible competitive advantages for the corporation by matching environmental opportunities with company strengths
4. Develop mission statements, corporate objectives, and strategies

Despite these advantages, an SIS has disadvantages. Disadvantages include the costs of constantly updating data bases and management rules and the inflexibility in changing rules (or minds) during the planning period, which could result in missed competitive advantages. An additional disadvantage is that the ability of the human mind in cognitive exercises (like strategic planning) unfortunately cannot always be matched by expert systems with AI.[13]

SUMMARY

Planning is a major activity for all operations managers. This chapter is the first in Part II, Planning and Controlling Operations, which focuses on the broad aspects of what is called the organizational planning process. In this chapter, we have seen how organizational planning is divided into the three stages of strategic, tactical, and operational planning. We have discussed how planning efforts move from general considerations at the strategic level to detailed considerations at the operational level. The planning methods discussed in this chapter dealt with conceptual aspects (such as TOWS), and methods like critical success factors and rating methods were discussed as a way of bringing some objectivity to an otherwise subjective process.

Although this chapter provides a framework for organizationwide planning, it has left out considerable detail on how the mechanics of planning are conducted at the tactical and operational levels. In the next chapter, we start elaborating on some of the detailed planning activity by discussing tactical aggregate planning and capacity planning.

DISCUSSION AND REVIEW QUESTIONS

1. What is the organizational planning process?
2. Why are strategic, tactical, and operational planning necessary?
3. What is strategic planning? How is it linked to operations management?
4. What is an environmental situation analysis? How is it linked to strategic planning?
5. What is a corporate situation analysis? How is it linked to strategic planning?
6. What is a corporate mission statement? How is it linked to strategic planning?
7. Does a mission statement need to be rewritten each time a corporate situation analysis is performed?
8. What is a corporate strategic plan? Explain and give an example.
9. Can quality be a strategic goal? Explain and give an example.
10. What is an OM strategic plan? Explain and give an example.
11. What is tactical planning? How is it linked to OM?
12. What is a business plan? How is it linked to tactical planning?
13. What is operational planning? How is it linked to OM?
14. How are strategic, tactical, and operational planning related?
15. What is a TOWS analysis? How is it used in the organizational planning process?
16. What are critical success factors? How are they used in the organizational planning process?

---

[13] J. P. Ignizio, *Introduction to Expert Systems* (New York: McGraw-Hill, 1991), pp. 41–43.

17. What is an SIS? What are its advantages and disadvantages?
18. How can artificial intelligence and expert systems be used for strategic planning?

PROBLEMS

*1. Suppose a firm attempts to determine which of three competitors (A, B, or C) poses the greatest competitive threat. The firm has identified three CSFs—price, cost, and quality—that represent competitive advantages that could be threatened. Assume a rating score of 1 represents the greatest CSF threat and a 5 represents the lowest or no threat. Suppose Competitor A's rating scores for each of the CSFs are 4, 1, and 5, respectively; Competitor B's rating scores for each of the CSFs are 1, 4, and 2, respectively; and Competitor C's rating scores for each of the CSFs are 2, 3, and 1, respectively. Which of the three competitors appears to pose the greatest threat? Show your work.

2. Suppose a firm wanted to determine which of five competitors (A, B, C, D, or E) poses the greatest competitive threat. The firm believes that four CSFs—technology, price, cost, and quality—represent its competitive advantages. Assume a rating score of 1 represents the greatest CSF threat and a 5 represents the lowest or no threat. Competitor A's rating scores for each of the CSFs are 2, 2, 1, and 1, respectively; Competitor B's rating scores for each of the CSFs are 1, 3, 3, and 2, respectively; Competitor C's rating scores for each of the CSFs are 2, 3, 4, and 1, respectively; Competitor D's rating scores for each of the CSFs are 2, 5, 2, and 3, respectively; and Competitor E's rating scores for each of the CSFs are 1, 5, 5, and 4, respectively. Determine which of the five competitors appears to pose the greatest threat. Show your work. What are you assuming in your decision? Explain.

3. During a strategic planning session a firm wanted to determine which of three competitors (A, B, or C) posed the greatest competitive threat. The firm has identified four CSFs—sales, price, cost, and quality—as its competitive advantages that could be threatened. The firm also felt that a weight should be attached in the analysis to each of the CSFs in accordance with the following distribution: 0.20 for sales, 0.20 for price, 0.40 for cost, and 0.20 for quality. Assume that a rating score of 1 represents the greatest CSF threat and a 5 represents the lowest or no threat. Based on environmental analysis, Competitor A's rating scores for each of the CSFs are 2, 1, 2, and 5, respectively; Competitor B's rating scores for each of the CSFs are 4, 1, 3, and 5, respectively; and Competitor C's rating scores for each of the CSFs are 3, 1, 3, and 2, respectively. Which of the three competitors appears to pose the greatest threat? Show your work.

4. During a strategic planning process, a firm attempts to determine which of six competitors (A, B, C, D, E, or F) poses the greatest competitive threat. The firm has determined that five CSFs—sales, distribution, price, cost, and quality—represent its competitive advantages that could be threatened. The firm has established that the weight that should be attached to each of the CSFs should be distributed as follows: 0.10 for sales, 0.10 for distribution, 0.15 for price, 0.20 for cost, and 0.45 for quality. Assume that a rating score of 1 represents the greatest CSF threat and 5 represents the lowest or no threat. Based on environmental analysis, Competitor A's rating scores for

* The solution to the problem marked with an asterisk can be found in Appendix J.

each of the CSFs are 5, 2, 1, 3, and 3, respectively; Competitor B's rating scores for each of the CSFs are 3, 3, 1, 3, and 5, respectively; Competitor C's rating scores for each of the CSFs are 4, 4, 1, 3, and 2, respectively; Competitor D's rating scores for each of the CSFs are 3, 2, 1, 3, and 4, respectively; Competitor E's rating scores for each of the CSFs are 1, 5, 1, 3, and 5, respectively; and Competitor F's rating scores for each of the CSFs are 2, 1, 1, 1, and 2, respectively. Determine which of the six competitors appears to pose the greatest threat. Show your work. What are you assuming in your decision? Explain. What competitor poses the least threat? What are you assuming in this decision?

5. In the process of its strategic planning, a firm wanted to determine which of six competitors (A, B, C, D, E, or F) poses the greatest competitive threat. The firm has determined eight CSFs as their competitive advantages. The weights assigned to each of the CSFs are as follows: 0.10, 0.04, 0.12, 0.21, 0.05, 0.05, 0.18, and 0.25. Assume that a rating score of 1 represents the greatest CSF threat and 5 represents the lowest or no threat. Competitor rating scores for each of the CSFs are shown in the following table:

	CSF RATINGS							
Firm	*1*	*2*	*3*	*4*	*5*	*6*	*7*	*8*
A	5	5	2	1	3	1	3	3
B	2	3	3	4	4	3	3	5
C	2	4	5	3	4	1	3	2
D	1	1	1	3	2	4	4	3
E	1	1	2	3	3	1	3	5
F	1	2	1	1	4	4	5	2

Determine the competitor that appears to pose the greatest threat based solely on the rating scores (i.e., no mathematical weight used). Show your work. Determine the competitor that appears to pose the greatest threat based on the weighted rating scores. Show your work. Is there a difference in the results? Explain. Which choice would you use as a final recommendation on posing a threat? Explain your answer. What are you assuming in your decision?

6. Company X has the industry-leading quality product. The quality of its product is judged by five criteria: durability, appearance, ease of use, service, and value. Three companies (Companies A, B, and C) in Company X's industry are going to market new products next year that will compete directly with Company X's leading quality product. Based on advanced product testing results with consumers the products of each of the three companies were examined in light of the five quality criteria. Using a CSF rating score in which 1 is highest quality and 5 is lowest quality, the three competitive company's products rating scores are presented in the following table:

	RATING SCORES ON QUALITY OF EACH COMPANY'S NEW PRODUCT				
Company	*Durability*	*Appearance*	*Ease of Use*	*Service*	*Value*
A	1	3	5	1	1
B	2	2	2	4	4
C	3	3	1	2	1

Which of the companies will pose the greatest competitive threat to Company X? If Company X felt that the quality characteristic of durability should be weighted equal in importance to all of the other four combined, what would the weights be? Does the weighting change the unweighted decision? Show your work.

CASE 4-1

WHO'S THE GREATEST THREAT?

The Paxton Hospital operates a medium-sized full-service hospital in a major metropolitan area. The hospital has successfully operated its facility for twenty years in the same area. During this time, it has expanded its operation from a one hundred–bed facility to a five hundred–bed facility. The management of Paxton attributes its successful growth to several competitive advantages that the hospital possesses over the five other competitors. These competitive advantages include its substantial investment in advanced medical equipment in cancer detection, advanced burn-treatment facilities, advanced laboratory equipment for running accurate and rapid diagnostic tests, advanced x-ray equipment, and expert pulmonary specialists.

The administrative officers of the hospital, who are charged with administering the affairs of the organization (that is, upper management), conduct a strategic planning board meeting once a year. The purpose of the meeting is to examine how the hospital is progressing toward its long-range strategic objectives and to make revisions in its strategic plans if changes in the external environment warrant it. Regional consultants specializing in hospital management are hired to prepare the environmental situation analysis report. Paxton's accountants and financial officers are assigned the task of preparing the corporate situation analysis report. Based on these two reports, the board re-examines the hospital's mission statement and strategies to see whether they are still appropriate.

One of the basic hospital mission statements that has never changed is that of growth. Paxton wants to grow into the largest hospital in the metropolitan area it serves. Unfortunately, two items emerged from the analysis to threaten its plans for growth. From the environmental situation analysis Paxton found that some of its competitors are making large investments in the same types of equipment in which Paxton felt it had a competitive advantage. This recent investment activity is viewed as a serious threat because the other hospitals have other competitive advantages that Paxton cannot afford to threaten in the foreseeable future. So the competitors might cause Paxton to be perceived as a second-rate institution in all areas of health care. From the corporate situation analysis the board found that Paxton is prohibited from acquiring any substantial additions to its equipment and facilities because of zoning laws and county regulations.

Facing the environmental threat from competitors and its own organizational weakness to do anything about it, Paxton explored changing its existing strategic plans to continue the mission of growth. One new strategic plan that surfaced at the board meeting was that of acquisition. Board members suggested acquiring a competitor because all of the area hospitals are publicly owned and could be acquired. Paxton found from the corporate situation analysis that it had an abundance of cash with which to acquire another hospital. In the process, it would also be able to circumvent the restrictive zoning laws and county regulations by acquiring and operating more equipment through the acquired hospital.

Logically, the best hospital to acquire should be the one most threatening to Paxton. To determine which hospital represents the greatest threat to Paxton, one of the outside consultants who performed the environmental situation analysis was asked to rate the other competitors' abilities to threaten Paxton's competitive advantages. These ratings are presented in Exhibit 4C-1.

EXHIBIT 4C-1 RATINGS OF COMPETITOR'S THREAT TO PAXTON'S COMPETITIVE ADVANTAGES

	*COMPETITIVE HOSPITAL RATING SCORES**				
Competitive Advantages	*1*	*2*	*3*	*4*	*5*
Advanced medical equipment in cancer detection	1	2	5	4	1
Advanced burn-treatment facilities	4	1	5	2	1
Advanced laboratory equipment diagnostic tests	5	2	4	4	1
Advanced x-ray equipment	3	2	5	3	1
Expert pulmonary specialists	2	1	4	1	3

* Based on a rating where 1 = high competitive threat and 5 = no competitive threat.

CASE QUESTIONS

1. Based on the ratings of the competitors by the consultant, which of the five hospitals should Paxton acquire? Show your work. What are you assuming about the mathematical weight of the ratings when they are just summed?
2. Assume the five competitive advantages are given a mathematical weight to reflect their importance to Paxton of 0.10, 0.10, 0.10, 0.30, and 0.40, respectively. Which of the five hospitals now should be selected for acquisition? Show your work.

CASE 4-2

ORGANIZING THE PLAN

The Acme Speciality Company is a medium-sized electronics firm specializing in home appliances. Acme started ten years ago making a single type of toaster for a single retail chain located in Texas. Word of its high product quality and competitive prices quickly spread to other retailers, and Acme's sales doubled in its first year of operation. In the second year, sales quadrupled and continued to quadruple for each of the next five years.

The owner of Acme, who likes to tinker with product ideas and make them into realities, came up with a new knife sharpener at the end of the sixth year of operation. (This was just at the time that the toaster's sales started leveling off.) The knife sharpener was a big success, and sales began the same spiraling course of growth as the toaster.

At the end of the first ten years, Acme's products were selling in retail stores all over the United States and in Canada. The organization added personnel as it recruited entry-level or shop floor employees and promoted strictly from within. Acme's current organizational chart is presented in Exhibit 4C-2. With the exception of the vice president of personnel, all of the employees worked their way up from entry-level positions. No one had completed a college education or taken business planning courses. Up until this time, the lack of education had not kept the company from making a great deal

EXHIBIT 4C-2 ORGANIZATION CHART OF ACME SPECIALTY COMPANY

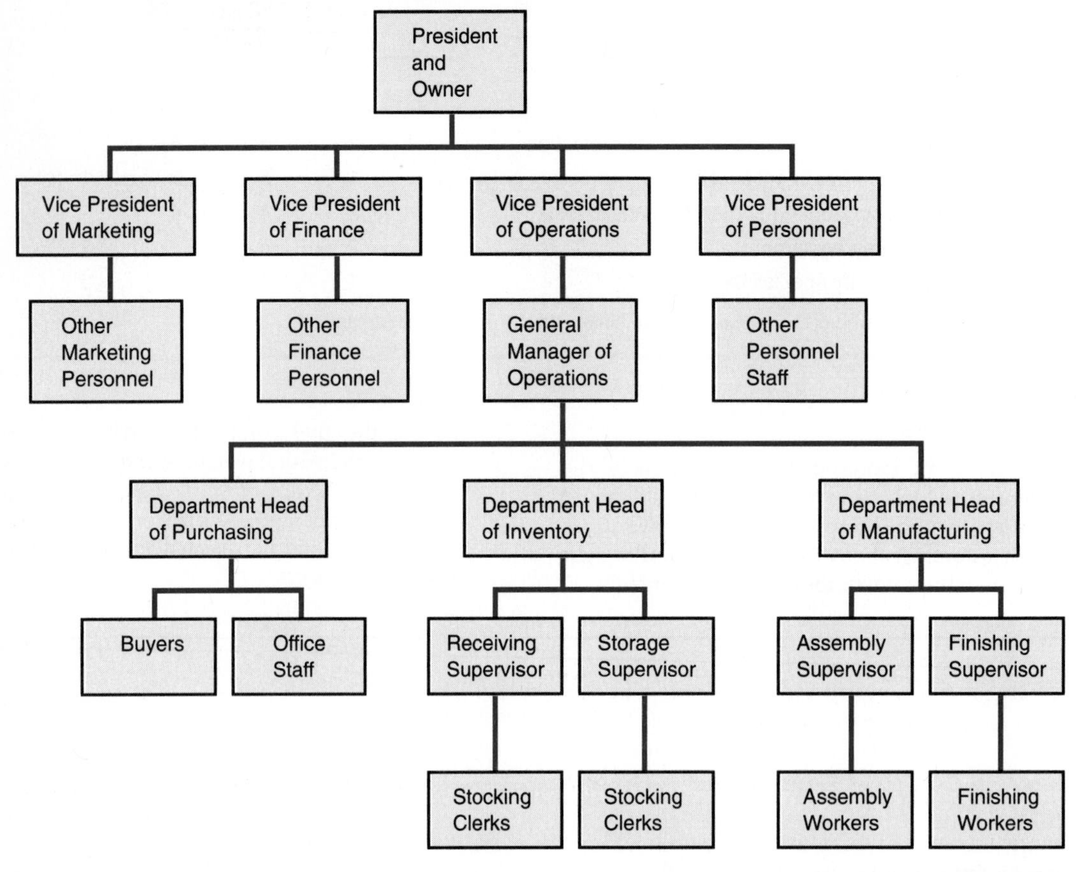

of money. Everybody, particularly the owner, was quite content to continue as they had in the past. The focus of business activity was on meeting production goals that were driven strictly by sales demand. Acme purchased production capacity as needed to meet upward shifts in demand.

Acme's current gross sales reached $100 million but was starting to decline. The sales of its toaster product had been declining for the last few years, and the sales of the knife sharpener started leveling off in the last year. The owner planned on marketing a new product in the fall, but was hesitant because of the fear that the company might go under, and a great deal of money would be wasted in developing a new product that might not make it to market. The marketing vice president was uncertain why Acme's product sales were behaving in this manner and a marketing consultant was called in to advise the company.

The consultant spotted the problem quickly as being related to the product life cycle of Acme's products. The toaster had reached the decline stage, and the knife sharpener was in the maturity stage of the product life cycle. The marketing consultant suggested a number of marketing tactics to alter the two products' positioning in their life cycles, and the owner was encouraged to go ahead with the new product. In addition, a management consultant was called in to educate and advise the management of Acme on the need for longer-range planning, which the firm obviously had never performed.

CASE QUESTIONS

1. Suppose you were the management consultant who was to advise Acme. How would you organize the planning activities of this firm? Be specific and outline the basic stages of the organizational planning process for this firm. Give one example of each type of planning activity at each stage of the planning process for the Acme toaster.
2. Given the organization chart in Exhibit 4C-2, what personnel should perform the strategic planning stage of the organizational planning process you outlined in Question 1? Who should do the tactical planning? Who should do the operational planning?

ARTICLE 4-1

WHAT'S HAPPENED TO STRATEGIC PLANNING?

by Bill McIlvaine

Since the 1950s, when corporate managers realized that old methods of planning were no longer adequate in rapidly changing economic and market conditions, strategic planning has been both a valuable business practice and something of a passing fancy. The need to "be strategic" has sometimes been overstated as an end in itself, with the whole idea being questioned as soon as the strategy doesn't produce the desired results.

"Strategic planning is the managerial process of developing and maintaining a strategic fit between the organization and its changing market opportunities," according to Philip Kotler in *Strategic Planning,* a 1986 publication by University Associates (San Diego, Calif.), a strategic planning consulting firm. This process takes into consideration, among other things, decisions on how to manufacture strategically, or deploy capital for automation. But listen to the head of one large industrial automation supplier today: "Strategic planning is a waste of time. Nobody knows what's going to happen in five years."

At its best, strategic planning is the process a company uses to lay the groundwork for the decisions that will allow it to move successfully into the future. But that idea worked better in the 1950s and 1960s, before Japanese imports, energy crises, tax reform, merger mania, and global competition began to make five-year plans look like wishful thinking. The pace of technological change and the heat of competition have caused too many U.S. companies' plans to be "blind-sided," in the words of one manufacturing planning consultant.

This is partly because many companies still confuse planning with forecasting. Charles Jones, a partner in the Strategic Consulting Group at Price Waterhouse & Co. in St. Louis, Mo., says many corporate planners still make "extrapolated budgets—a one-year plan that's copied four times." Even with good planning, "it's unrealistic to look beyond three years," says Helene Mawyer, vice president of corporate planning and business strategy at GE Fanuc Automation North America Inc. (Charlottesville, Va.).

What value does strategic planning still have, especially to manufacturers, who have to make long-range decisions about the use of capital, equipment, and labor? Have the concepts of the 1950s and 1960s fallen out of favor? Or has strategic planning become

---

Source: Reprinted with permission of the Managing Editor. From *Managing Automation,* July 1988, pp. 42–43.

business as usual? Several planning consultants believe it is evolving to adapt to some 1980s realities.

"There hasn't been as much of a change in planning as in the environment in which it's done," says William Lehman, a management consultant at Price Waterhouse in New York, N.Y. "There's been a fundamental change in who does it."

Strategic planning was once considered the domain of the company's top brass—often with a sizable support staff in tow. The result frequently was a comprehensive document, neatly printed and bound, that was soon filed away and forgotten until next year. Now, says Lehman, "the big staffs or corporate departments on strategic planning have been cut back and become a formal part of the manufacturing or engineering managers' jobs. Strategic planning has evolved to involve more people in the process."

And the plans themselves are changing their shape. Says Michael O'Guin, a consultant with A. T. Kearney (Los Angeles, Calif.), "By and large, planning is less rigorous than it used to be. There's more strategic thinking, but less documentation. The plans are getting thinner, but there are more strategic insights."

That's because, in O'Guin's view, the question being asked more frequently in a planning session is, "What do we have to do to be competitive?" Increasingly, he says, that is not a financial question but a strategic one. O'Guin points to a client of his, a major hardware manufacturer that invested millions of dollars in automation to be No. 1 in its business, not just to save costs. "In the 1960s, the financial people would have looked at that as purely a dollar decision, not a strategic opportunity," he says.

"Cost is definitely not the main issue," echoes Victor Bellott, corporate director of management information systems and computer-integrated manufacturing at Gleason Corp. (Rochester, N.Y.), a maker of gears for the auto industry. Bellott, who sits on his company's planning committee, says strategic planning has to address immediate, middle, and long-range goals simultaneously. "Saving money or making money—that can fund your interim or long-term strategies," he reasons.

Another thing that has affected the image of "classic" strategic planning is an emphasis on the planning process itself. "In the '70s, certain consulting firms popularized the notion that tools were the essence," says Jones of Price Waterhouse. Those tools went by such arcane names as the commodity-premium scale, vulnerability analysis, and experience curves. Many a plan formulated on one or more of these concepts was incomprehensible to all but the professional planners.

"The staffs were young pups and they ran amok with these tools," says Jones. "The tools were overpromised. There was frustration, they fell into disfavor, and companies disbanded their corporate planning. The notion that a planning exericse and tools will supplement judgment and risk-taking is crazy."

What kinds of decisions are corporate planners making now? Those who remember the planning issues of the 1960s and early 1970s, for instance, are facing situations that weren't particularly critical back then—for instance, the wave of international mergers.

In the automation market itself, these factors have affected GE Fanuc. Not only is GE Fanuc the product of an international joint venture, but, increasingly, its competition is also. According to Mawyer, two recent developments that have had an effect on the company's strategy were the sale of Gould Inc.'s programmable controller operations to AEG of West Germany, and Siemens' recent moves in the American PLC market.

"I can't say that we planned for AEG to buy Gould, but we took a look at our competition," says Mawyer. Faced with that competition, the most strategic of GE Fanuc's changes is the decision to manufacture more in the U.S. "We're doing more manufacturing in the U.S. than we planned to do a year and a half ago," says Mawyer.

For Gleason, major enhancements to its computer-aided design and manufacturing systems, connected with just-in-time and manufacturing resource planning, were part of a strategy to cut lead times in producing parts and prototypes, thus getting a competitive edge. Zeroing in on an immediate need, he explains, produced long-term results.

Consultants and planners agree that strategic manufacturing plans—for higher volumes, lower cost, reduced lead times, or other goals—must fit with the company's business plan. "Lots of key manufacturing or engineering people couldn't tell you what the business plan is," says Bellott.

And business plans are moving targets because they are based on market opportunities, which change quickly and sometimes unforgivingly. Because of that, he continues, it is important that everyone involved in planning understand what the company's goals and market opportunities are. "That avoids the problem of vice presidents coming back and saying that while you're working on that grand plan we're going out of business," Bellott says.

"Occasionally, flexible automation and technology are adopted by manufacturers as a strategy to deal with uncertainties of marketing or engineering development," explains Lehman. "That gives them comfort that they have a strategy."

But a manufacturing strategy alone cannot compensate for lack of planning in marketing or engineering, or even that "blindside" attack from an unexpected competitor or a new technology. An outward-looking, almost abstract, strategic plan is the best defense in volatile businesses, says Jones of Price Waterhouse.

Adds GE Fanuc's Mawyer: "You have to have the flexibility to change. A technological lead won't last long. We are making decisions for three years down the road. We have no choice."

5

Aggregate and Capacity Planning

CHAPTER OUTLINE

CHAPTER OBJECTIVES

The material in this chapter should prepare you to do the following:

1. Explain why aggregate and capacity planning are necessary operations management activities.
2. Explain what type of aggregate planning decisions an operations manager is likely to face.
3. Describe the different aggregate planning variables as well as strategies for their manipulation.

4. Explain how aggregate planning is performed.
5. Describe master production scheduling and the role it plays in production planning.
6. Explain how to use capacity planning in production planning.
7. Explain and illustrate how to use production worksheet methods as a production planning aid.
8. Describe the types of planning information a computer-integrated management information system generates.
9. Explain and illustrate how to use linear programming as a production planning aid.
10. Explain and illustrate how to use the transportation method as a production planning aid.

Production planning is a comprehensive term used to describe all manufacturing or service operations planning. This includes all operations management planning activities, from the creation or sale of a product or service to its delivery. Production planning is unique to the OM function and sets operations management apart from the organization's other functional areas by its focus on the use of OM resources. In this chapter we will discuss two different types of production planning: aggregate planning and capacity planning. We also discuss production scheduling and a variety of planning methods. In the last section of the chapter we decribe how production planning is integrated with a state-of-the-art computer information system.

• • •

WHY AGGREGATE AND CAPACITY PLANNING ARE NECESSARY

The purpose of production planning is to provide an organization with a feasible production plan that will satisfy market demand and minimize costs. A production plan is essential to identify and correct imbalances between product demand and production capacity. Without production planning, it is difficult for an organization to determine the following:

1. Adequate production capacity to meet forecast demand levels
2. Whether to use subcontracting or overtime to achieve production goals
3. Whether to change company policies on such items as inventory levels or **backordering** (that is, accepting an order but not producing it until a later date)
4. The number of new employees to hire (or fire) for the next year's, month's, or week's production

Alternatively, with a production plan the organization can

1. Minimize the inventory cost of providing goods and services to its customers
2. Avoid underutilization or overutilization (or both) of human resources and plant facilities
3. Establish a master production schedule that details required work activities

In Chapter 4 we discussed how strategic production plans are established to allow the operations management functional area to assist in accomplishing an organization's corporate mission. Strategic planning, either at the corporate or OM functional level, is long-range in nature, covering a time period of two or more years. As we can see in Figure 5-1, aggregate production plans are derived from strategic plans as a tactical means of implementation. Aggregate production plans are medium-range plans covering a time period of about one season to two years. An aggregate plan seeks a general allocation of OM resources—labor, inventory, and production capacity—rather than a detailed plan of individual product items. To determine the available amounts of these resources, operations managers conduct an additional planning activity, called capacity planning. Capacity planning determines what the aggregate existing and required capacity will be over a specific planning period. Capacity planning helps establish a workable aggregate production plan by ensuring that production goals are within resource capacity limitations. We discuss several different types of capacity planning later in this chapter.

The aggregate production plan provides the basis on which a more detailed plan of production can be developed. This detailed tactical plan is called a master production schedule (MPS), which is a detailed plan for individual item production. It is a medium-range plan designed to cover a period of about one year. It specifies the types of products, the number of units, and the timing of production during a week or month. To help ensure that existing operations management resources can achieve their individual item production goals in the MPS, a number of special types of capacity planning can be conducted.

Aggregate and capacity planning are necessary operations management activities because they help generate a workable MPS. The MPS, which is an output of aggregate

FIGURE 5-1 RELATIONSHIP BETWEEN THE TYPE AND NATURE OF PRODUCTION PLANS

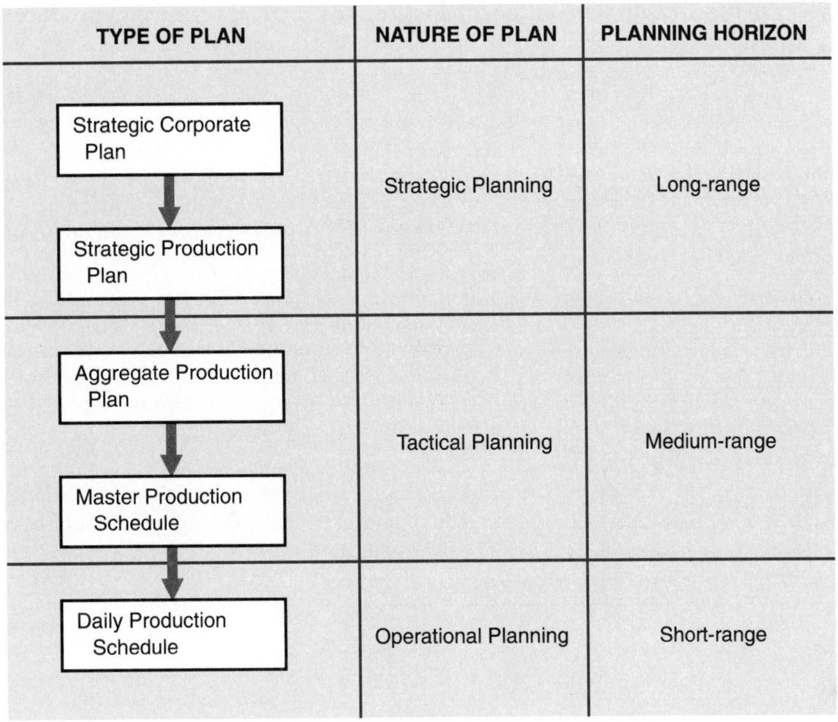

TYPE OF PLAN	NATURE OF PLAN	PLANNING HORIZON
Strategic Corporate Plan ↓ Strategic Production Plan	Strategic Planning	Long-range
↓ Aggregate Production Plan ↓ Master Production Schedule	Tactical Planning	Medium-range
↓ Daily Production Schedule	Operational Planning	Short-range

and capacity planning, is a necessary step in operationalizing the tactical and strategic plans of the corporation.

AGGREGATE PLANNING

Aggregate planning is the process of planning an operation's total production effort to satisfy market demand. The planning horizon for aggregate planning is medium-range, covering a time period from one season to two years.[1] In this type of planning,

[1] F. L. DuBois and M. D. Oliff, "Aggregate Production Planning in Practice," *Production and Inventory Management Journal,* 32, No. 3 (1991), 26–30; and J. R. Freeland and R. D. Landel, *Aggregate Production Planning* (Reston, Va.: Reston Publishing Company, 1984).

the manager does not plan the production of individual products, but instead aggregates all of the organization's products into a single group or groups of composite products that share resources. By grouping products that share common resources, an operations manager can more easily plan for the total aggregate resources required to produce those products.

QUESTION: What is an example of aggregating a resource in a manufacturing operation?

ANSWER: Equipment is a production resource that is often used in manufacturing. Let's say that a company uses five pieces of equipment to produce its products. The total number of hours of possible production usage for each of the machines per month can be added (that is, aggregated). We might therefore have a total of 1,200 hours of machine time available for all product production in January, 1,200 hours in February, and so on, for all the months in the entire planning period of one or two years. Factors that might change the hourly availability of machines each month such as routine maintenance and expected downtime of equipment can also be included.

Not all firms aggregate product demand for production planning. Some firms only have a single product and thus have no need to aggregate demand or resources. These firms still determine production requirements and plan their application, but they do not need aggregation. Other firms, particularly those in service industries, have such volatile market demand that a meaningful aggregate demand forecast is impossible. Instead of focusing on aggregate demand, these firms focus their planning efforts on allocating production resources to satisfy some preset level or quality of service demand.

Why should an organization aggregate its demand and resources? Aggregation provides planners with a general overview of the organization's total production requirements and the organization's capacity to satisfy these requirements. (We discuss capacity planning in a later section.) In addition, aggregate capacity planning activities enable operations managers to identify costly plant or facility capacity underutilization and overutilization in future time periods. In Figure 5-2, the imbalance between forecast market demand and an organization's output capacity is presented. As you can see, the aggregate production rate or capacity of this plant is constant, whereas the market demand varies by month. When market demand exceeds production capacity, inventory from previous production periods must be used to satisfy the excess demand. If sufficient inventory is unavailable during a certain time period, then more production is necessary.

Unfortunately, a production increase may increase production costs because of the need to hire more employees, subcontract work to other manufacturers, or pay overtime to existing employees. When the production rate exceeds market demand, inventory builds up. Inventory buildup can also be expensive because of the cost of capital tied up in the inventory, costs associated with holding the inventory, price cuts to unload the inventory, or temporary layoffs of employees (sometimes at full or partial pay).

In aggregate planning, a basic objective is to smooth out the imbalance between demand and production output. By balancing the aggregate market demand and the output rate of an organization, the firm reduces its costs and is generally more efficient in resource utilization.

QUESTION: What is an example of aggregating a resource in a service operation?

ANSWER: Labor hours are a production resource used in a service operation. Let's say a service company has a staff of twelve full-time employees to provide customer service. Suppose each staffer can provide 8 hours of customer service per day. If January has 23 working days, then the total number of possible hours of service production for each worker in January is 184 hours (23 × 8). Aggregating the labor hours for the entire staff, the service operation can offer 2,208 (12 × 184) total (that is, aggregated) service hours in the month of January. The hours for the 20 working days in February can be aggregated at 3,680 hours, and so on, for all the months in the entire planning period of one or two years. Factors such as absenteeism and vacations that might change the hourly availability of staffers each month can be included to generate more accurate monthly estimates of aggregate labor hours.

There are three primary aggregate planning variables that operations managers work with to balance output with market demand.

1. *Work force size* refers to the aggregate number of production or service employees working in an organization, including staff in service organizations who perform service product activities.
2. *Production rates or capacities* refer to the aggregate number of product units that can be produced over a fixed period of time. Such unit production is often dictated by the capacity of production equipment, availability of overtime, idle time of resources, company policy, labor contract agreements, or the resources available during the fixed period of time.

FIGURE 5-2 IMBALANCE BETWEEN AGGREGATE MARKET DEMAND AND AGGREGATE UNIT PRODUCTION OUTPUT

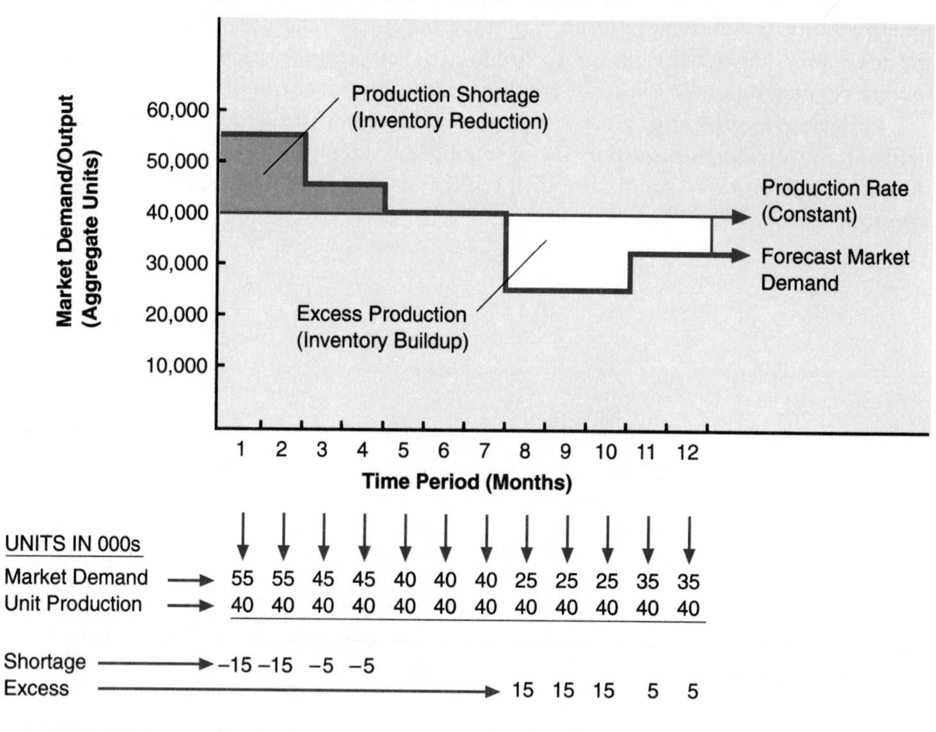

3. *Inventory levels* refer to the total inventory (in units) permitted over a fixed period of time.

Although additional variables such as product pricing and promotion can affect aggregate planning, these variables are usually controlled by other functional departments within the organization. The three variables outlined in the preceding list are chiefly controlled by the operations manager and are of primary importance in all operations management planning.

As mentioned previously, some organizations do not need to aggregate their activities. Many small or medium-sized organizations have few human, technology, or system resources to aggregate for planning purposes. In small service organizations, such as a single travel agency, aggregating the human resources provided by three or four staff members who make up a single agency's personnel pool might represent a waste of planning time. Alternatively, if the travel agency consisted of dozens of other agencies, and the personnel were combined with other agencies' human resources in an effort to plan their combined capacity to meet travel demands over a two-year period, the planning effort might be worth the investment of time.

The Aggregate Planning Process

The steps required for aggregate production planning can differ for each organization based on the products and services the organization provides. The basic steps in the aggregate planning process are presented in Figure 5-3. To begin, an organization determines the new products and services that it plans to offer in the next year or two, as well as the existing products and services that it plans to continue offering. This information is based in part on strategic planning efforts. Once the products and services are determined, forecasts are generated using forecasting methods such as those presented in Chapter 3. The forecasts of individual products and **open orders** (orders unfinished from a previous period) currently being processed by an organization are combined to generate aggregate product demand. The information provided by forecasts for the new and existing products and services may indicate the need to adjust the product mix offered by the organization. A **product mix** is the variety of individual products that make up the total production and sales volume.

If the product mix is acceptable to management, then the operations manager must determine how to provide the product mix in the desired time and quantity dictated by aggregate product demand. The answer to how the aggregate demand is to be met depends in part on the selection of an aggregate planning strategy. An **aggregate planning strategy** is simply a production policy that guides the general course of production activity. The selection of an aggregate planning strategy is based upon the comparative advantages to an organization in the manipulation of the three primary aggregate planning variables within their capacity limitations. (We discuss several aggregate planning strategies and their advantages and disadvantages for selection purposes in the next section.) Once an initial aggregate production plan is selected, it must be checked for feasibility against aggregate capacity requirements necessary for its implementation. The operations manager is basically concerned with whether a sufficient production capacity exists to meet the aggregate demand requirements and must determine the aggregate capacity of the current work force size, production rates, and inventory levels.

The operations manager then determines what adjustments must be made to the aggregate planning variables to satisfy the market demand requirements. Once the values for the variables are determined, the operations manager is in a position to finalize the aggregate planning strategy to act as a guide for future production. There are as many different types of aggregate planning strategies as there are business operations.

Aggregate Planning Strategies

If the market demand for a product were constant, production or aggregate planning would be fairly simple. The plan would establish a constant production output rate,

FIGURE 5-3 THE AGGREGATE PLANNING PROCESS

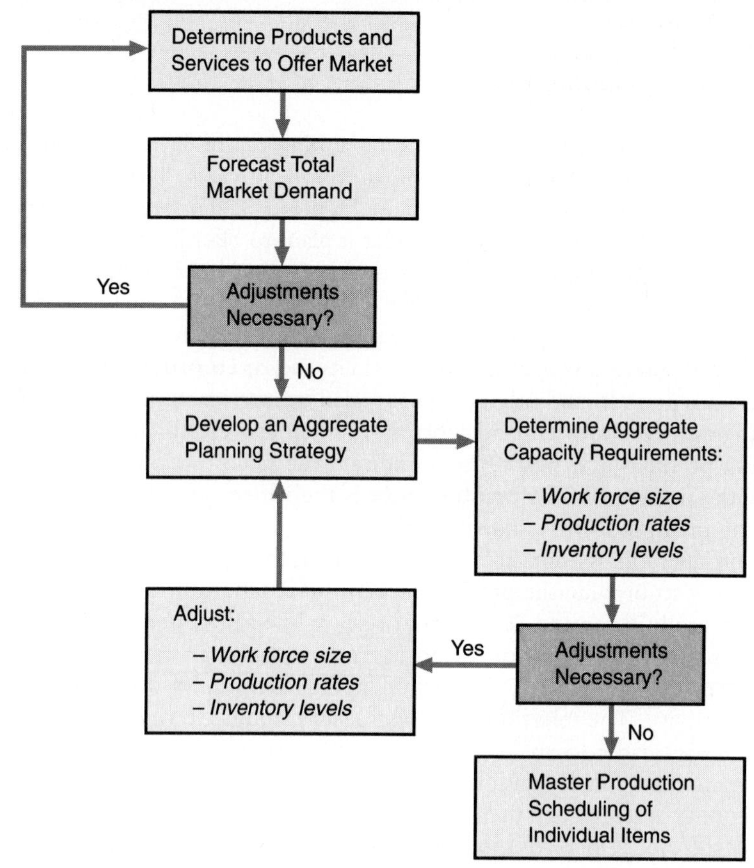

constant work force size, and constant inventory level (that is, the three aggregate planning variables). Unfortunately, as we mentioned in Chapter 3 on forecasting, market demand can vary considerably. Factors such as competitive pricing behavior, seasonal variation, and an organization's own promotion effort can cause market demand to fluctuate a great deal over a medium-range planning horizon. The result of such variation in market demand is nonuniform demand. Operations managers cope with nonuniform demand by developing a strategy that best suits the unique market demand they face. Many different strategies can be developed by altering the three aggregate planning variables. Some of these strategies are listed on the next two pages.

1. *Allow inventory levels to change in response to market demand behavior.* Under this strategy, production in units is constant over the planning horizon and inventory levels are allowed to fluctuate to absorb the shifts in market demand. The advantages of such a strategy include
   a. Minimized production scheduling effort because unit demand is constant
   b. Mimized scheduling and hiring of production personnel (no overtime work or unexpected hiring is necessary)
   c. Simplified ordering systems for raw materials and supplies because production usage is constant

   Some of the disadvantages of such a strategy include
   a. An inability to function if sudden shifts increase demand beyond inventory levels
   b. The requirement of an extensive and possibly costly supply of finished goods inventory
   c. The possible creation of an excessive amount of inventory if market demand decreases for an extended time
   d. The requirement of a backordering system (which could represent a decline in customer service) or the use of subcontractors if demand differs from expected production

   This type of strategy is common when a plant or service organization operates at full capacity.

2. *Change the work force size to balance production with the shifts in market demand.* Under this strategy, weekly and sometimes daily shifts are made in the number of production personnel to increase or decrease unit production. The shifts are based on actual market demand figures or very short-term forecasts of market demand. The advantages of such a strategy include
   a. Minimized use of subcontractors
   b. Minimized finished goods inventory
   c. Improved service because the organization is more responsive to market demand

   Some of the disadvantages of such a strategy include
   a. Increased scheduling effort for production and inventory because unit demand is variable
   b. Increased scheduling and hiring effort for production personnel (people may quit these jobs because they cannot afford the uncertainty of recurring layoffs)
   c. Poor worker morale because of the uncertainty of employment

   This strategy is commonly used in industries in which the investment in finished inventory is far greater than the costs of layoffs.

3. *Change the production rate to balance it with shifts in demand.* Under this strategy, weekly and sometimes daily shifts are made in production rates to increase or

decrease unit production. The work force size and inventory levels are held relatively constant. The changes in the production rate are based on actual market demand or very short-term forecasts of market demand. The advantages of such a strategy include the following:

a. It is usually easier to implement an arbitrary change in a production level than changes in the work force or inventory levels because such a change is made at management's discretion
b. It minimizes costly finished goods inventory
c. It minimizes work force hiring and scheduling

Some of the disadvantages of such a strategy include the following:

a. It increases scheduling effort of production and inventory because unit demand is variable
b. It inefficiently uses the work force when market demand decreases and production rates are set below capacity
c. It tends to create poor worker morale because of the uncertainty of work effort expected (that is, some days the workers are rushed and other days they may have almost nothing to do)

This strategy is commonly used in industries in which the capital costs of investment in finished inventory are major and organizations want to minimize or keep their inventory at a constant low level. This strategy is useful in other industries such as oil refining in which the work force is highly skilled and the complexity of jobs requires a fairly constant number of workers on station regardless of the oil-flow production rates.

In each of these three strategies, at least one of the three aggregate planning variables is allowed to vary or change while the remaining are basically held constant. In actual practice, many combinations or mixtures of the three aggregate planning strategies are possible. Determining which strategy might best achieve an organization's aggregate planning objectives requires balancing the advantages and disadvantages with the strategic production goals of the organization.

Disaggregating to the Master Production Schedule

After the aggregate strategy is determined and the aggregate capacity requirements are adjusted to meet aggregate demand requirements, managers using an aggregate plan must disaggregate the demand back to individual product items. These individual items are then scheduled for production over the next planning horizon. The formal document that defines unit production over time is called a master production schedule (MPS). The **master production schedule** defines the type and volume of each item to be produced over the planning horizon. It is a detailed plan specifying a more exact timing of unit production of each individual product than the aggregate plan. The detail of the MPS can, and usually does, include a month-by-month or week-by-week plan of production activity.

Disaggregating the aggregate plan to the master production schedule is usually performed by reversing the process of aggregation. For example, Figure 5-4 shows an aggregate plan listing the total monthly demand for all four of a company's microcomputer products. Referring to the forecasts and open orders for this company, we could develop a master production schedule for the individual microcomputer products. As can be seen in Figure 5-4, the aggregate demand of two hundred microcomputers in January is broken down in unit demand for each of the four microcomputer products A, B, C, and D.

MASTER PRODUCTION SCHEDULING

The master production scheduling process presented in Figure 5-5 involves the planning activities necessary to determine whether an operation can achieve its production in units as stated in the MPS. We start with a preliminary MPS and end with a final MPS that will be used to guide daily production activities in units of product. Two supplementary planning activities that can be a part of the MPS process include material requirements planning (MRP) and capacity requirements planning (CRP). **Materials requirements planning** involves determining the timed flow of materials and inventory to achieve a preliminary MPS. **Capacity requirements planning** involves determining whether adequate production capacity exists to achieve the preliminary MPS.

QUESTION: Do service organizations have to perform both MRP and CRP?

ANSWER: Material requirements planning is usually used in manufacturing because the availability and timeliness of dependent demand inventory are critical factors that determine the MPS. Most service organizations do not carry much dependent demand inventory and will in fact not use MRP. For these service organizations, MRP is not a part of their MPS process. Most service organizations will perform capacity requirements planning to assess whether they will be able to meet a given level of expected market demand. Manufacturing organizations, on the other hand, do not have to use MRP, but usually use it in combination with CRP to see whether a preliminary MPS is capable of being achieved.

Because we devote Chapter 7 to these two planning activities, here we simply list the steps for carrying them out within a manufacturing operation.

FIGURE 5-4 DISAGGREGATING TO THE MASTER PRODUCTION SCHEDULE

AGGREGATE PLAN FOR MICROCOMPUTERS

MONTH	JAN	FEB	MAR	APR	MAY	JUN ...
Total Number of Microcomputers per Month	200	200	200	200	200	200 ...

MASTER PRODUCTION SCHEDULE FOR MICROCOMPUTERS

MONTH	JAN	FEB	MAR	APR	MAY	JUN ...
Units To Produce:						
Microcomputer A	50	50	50	40	60	50 ...
Microcomputer B	30	50	50	50	50	50 ...
Microcomputer C	70	50	50	60	40	20 ...
Microcomputer D	50	50	50	50	50	80 ...
Total	200	200	200	200	200	200 ...

1. Use MRP and preliminary MPS to determine the **gross requirements** (total unit demand in units of finished product) for each product. Use MRP to determine the gross requirements for each unit of material, components, subcomponents, and so on per time period.
2. Subtract any on-hand inventory (units from on-hand inventory or those expected during the time period from a vendor or subcontractor) from gross requirements. The difference between gross requirements and on-hand inventory is referred to as **net requirements.** If any type of inventory (that is, finished goods, components) is inadequate to meet the preliminary MPS, then it may be necessary to revise or adjust the MPS to consider this limitation.
3. Transform the adjusted net requirements into planned order releases. A **planned order release** is an order amount for a specific time period (a day, a week, etc.). The goal of this step is to establish a time-phased schedule that will define unit or lot-sized production during the planning time period.
4. Convert the planned order releases into capacity requirements using CRP. These capacity requirements are usually stated as load reports. A **load report** defines the amount of work activities for machines, employees, and workstations for a specific time period. If the capacity of the machines, employees, or

FIGURE 5-5 THE MASTER PRODUCTION SCHEDULING PROCESS

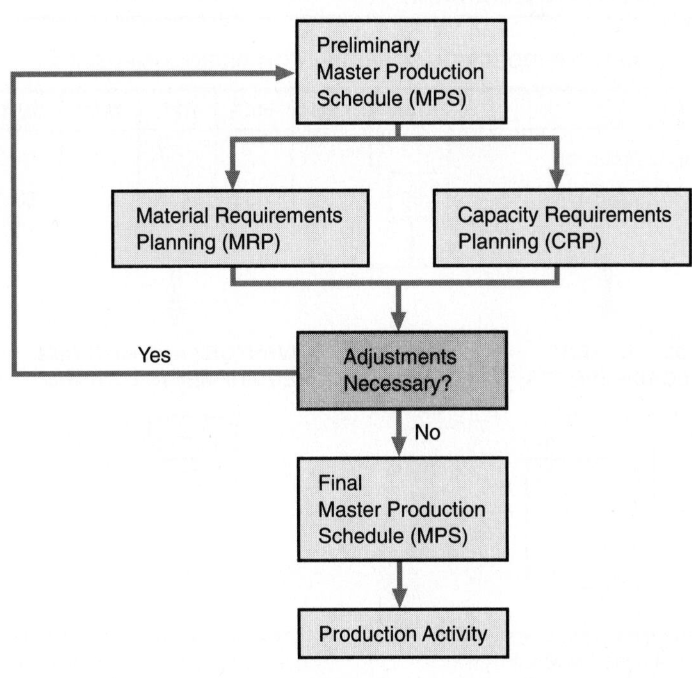

workstations is inadequate to meet the master production schedule, then it might be necessary to revise or adjust the existing production capacity, the MPS, or the inventory, as indicated in Figure 5-5.

In developing load reports, the MPS process begins defining the individual product resource requirements to meet production requirements. To actually manufacture a product, management and shop floor–level personnel must procure the parts and materials necessary for the product. The purchasing department usually performs this procurement function. Management must also know the amount of human resources required for each product. MRP and CRP can be used together to disaggregate the material and component requirements for planning production activity. We can continue, for example, to disaggregate each of the individual microcomputer products in our example into human resource and inventory part requirements as presented in Figure 5-6. As we continue to disaggregate, we move from medium-range planning to short-range planning of daily production scheduling. What we are left with is a final MPS that can actually guide daily production in units. (We discuss short-range scheduling in Chapter 9.)

Because the MPS is usually based on a forecast, the actual production output and actual market demand may not always remain perfectly balanced. To correct any imbalance, operations managers may need to modify the MPS by altering tactics.

FIGURE 5-6 MASTER PRODUCTION SCHEDULE DISAGGREGATED TO MATERIAL REQUIREMENTS

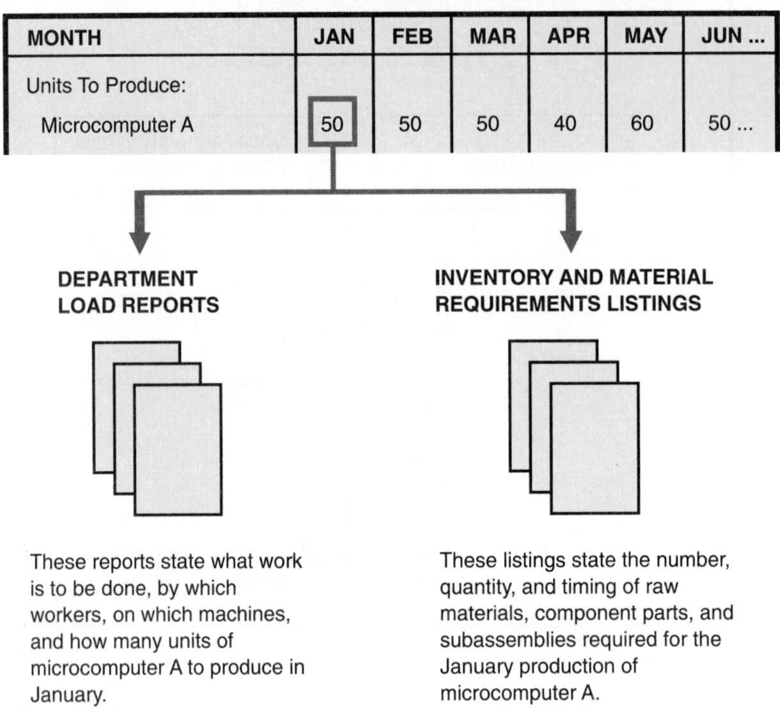

MASTER PRODUCTION SCHEDULE FOR MICROCOMPUTERS
MONTH
JAN
FEB
MAR
APR
MAY
JUN ...
Units To Produce:
Microcomputer A
50
50
50
40
60
50 ...
DEPARTMENT LOAD REPORTS
INVENTORY AND MATERIAL REQUIREMENTS LISTINGS
These reports state what work is to be done, by which workers, on which machines, and how many units of microcomputer A to produce in January.
These listings state the number, quantity, and timing of raw materials, component parts, and subassemblies required for the January production of microcomputer A.

Operations managers can modify production or aggregate plans once they are in use by adopting one or more of the following tactical methods:

Modify the product or service. Management can temporarily modify the size or proportion of the product or service that is being delivered. For example, restaurants may alter food proportions (less of one vegetable and more of another) when they start running out of some food items toward the end of the day.

Change inventory levels. Allowing inventory levels to decrease during periods of high demand and to increase during periods of low demand can alleviate short-term demand shifts without changing production rates. Some organizations build up inventories purposely to cushion them during periods of high product demand.

Change the work force. Allowing changes in the size, hours, or number of shifts of the work force can easily alter production rates. Among the many options are hiring and laying off workers; using overtime, short-time (that is, less than a full eight-hour day's work), and part-time workers; and moving vacation times for employees.

Change backordering policy. Allowing the number of backorders to shift with demand (for example, high backorder loads when demand is high) will often adjust any aggregate plan.

Change product pricing. If demand is above forecast levels, increasing the product's price may decrease demand. If demand is below forecast levels, decreasing the product's price usually increases demand.

Allow subcontracting. If demand is greater than the aggregate plan provides, allow a subcontractor to produce the excess units demanded.

Defer maintenance. If demand is greater than the aggregate plan provides, one source of short-term increase in the production work force might be achieved by deferring routine maintenance and using the saved labor for production purposes.

QUESTION: How do service organizations perform the MPS process?

ANSWER: Most service organizations start with a forecast of market demand of their services and perform the CRP step (step 4) of the manufacturing MPS process to see if they can achieve a preliminary customer-based MPS. In other words, they convert service planned-order releases into capacity requirements using CRP. Service organizations must schedule to have service capacity available to meet expected demand requirements. Therefore, management must be aware of the service organization's capacity to provide service for specific periods of time. For example, more buses and airplanes are scheduled to provide transportation services during the day when people want to travel instead of at night when people want to sleep. The capacity planning might focus on determining the number of passengers that can be served, the number of arrivals that can be handled in and out of a transportation hub, and the total number of personnel required at each transportation hub to maintain a given level of quality service. As with the manufacturing MPS process, the service organization's preliminary MPS might have to be adjusted if capacity is unavailable to meet demand requirements. The final MPS in a service organization would be a scheduling document that would define an hourly, daily, or weekly service resource allocation of service personnel, equipment, and so on. S

Some of these tactics can be costly to the organization if used improperly. Deferring maintenance can be disastrous if continued for long. Implementing these tactics, therefore, must be carefully considered in light of the unique business setting in which they are applied.

In summary, the MPS process brings detail to the aggregate planning strategy and moves scheduling from the medium term to the short term to allow management at the shop floor level to start to plan production activity of individual items. Both the master production scheduling and aggregate planning processes require information about capacity to determine production capabilities to meet the forecast demand. We examine several types of capacity planning in the next section.

CAPACITY PLANNING

Capacity is the output rate at which work is completed or withdrawn from a system, given an existing level of production resources. The capacity of an operations management system can be controlled by either its input or output rate. In Figure 5-7, we compare capacity to a tub of water to illustrate this point. If the rate of water flowing into the tub is greater than the rate of water flowing out of the tub, a buildup of water occurs. Similarly, if the input into an operations management system is greater than its output, a buildup—called a queue of work, **load** (or the volume of work in the system), or work-in-process (WIP)—occurs. In this situation—when input rate exceeds output rate—capacity is controlled by the output rate. Alternatively, if the input rate is less than the output rate, then the input rate determines the system's capacity because no buildup will occur.

Measuring and Calculating Capacity

It is important to understand the difference between measuring capacity and calculating capacity. Measuring capacity in an operations management system involves collecting historical output data (for example, units produced in a day or week) and either determining the maximum output of the system over a period of time or averaging output over a period of time. If an OM system is usually operating at a maximum output level, then a maximum output measure might be appropriate. Alternatively, if an OM system's output fluctuates greatly, the average capacity measure might more accurately capture the output capacity of that system.

QUESTION: What is the weekly measured capacity of a department whose production during the last three weeks generated 250, 267, and 260 **standard hours of work force** (that is, a predetermined amount of time allowed for labor or work force setup of equipment and producing one unit of a product)?

ANSWER: The weekly measured capacity can be the maximum output of 267 hours or the average of the three weeks, 259 hours [(250 + 267 + 260)/3].

FIGURE 5-7 CAPACITY PRESENTED AS A RATE OF OUTPUT

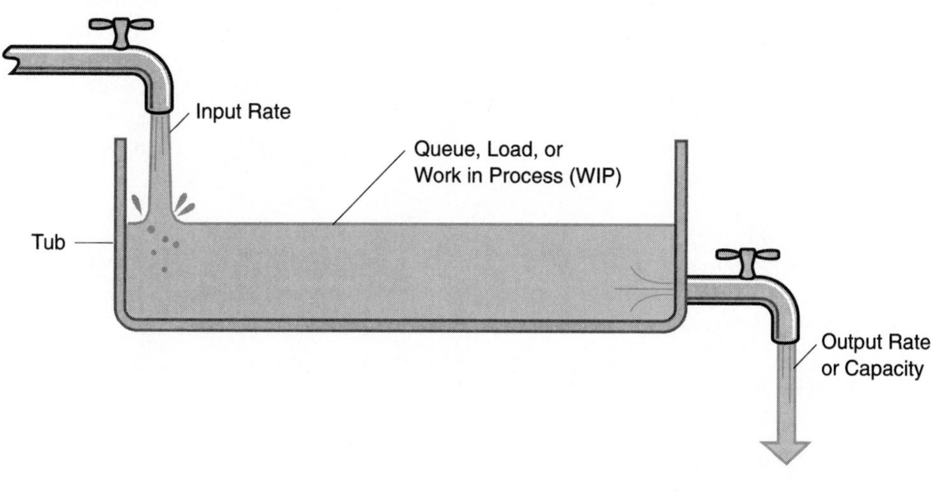

Calculating capacity in an operations management system usually involves the following relationship:

$$\text{Capacity} = \text{Available time} \times \text{Utilization} \times \text{Efficiency}$$

where

Available time is the total production time available for production purposes

Utilization is a proportion that measures how intensively a resource is being used (for example, the proportion of time a piece of equipment is being used)

Efficiency is a proportion that measures how closely predetermined standards such as a productivity index are achieved

Although capacity and the elements that make it up can be computed in different ways, the formulas for utilization and efficiency indexes or rating values can be expressed in percentage as

$$\text{Utilization index} = \frac{(\text{Hours available} - \text{Hours not used}) \times 100}{\text{Hours available}}$$

$$\text{Efficiency index} = \frac{\text{Standard hours allowed} \times 100}{\text{Hours used}}$$

When the utilization and efficiency index values are used to determine the calculated capacity as stated in the formula for capacity, they are converted to decimal values by dividing the index by 100.

QUESTION: Suppose that a department consisted of two machines staffed for one 8-hour shift for five days a week. (A total of 80 hours are available, derived from 8 hours × 5 days × 2 machines.) During the last month, records revealed that a weekly average of 8 hours of downtime occurred, reducing the total hours available for production. Records also revealed that during the last month the department produced a weekly average of 90 standard hours of output. What are this department's utilization and efficiency index values?

ANSWER: The department had a total of 80 hours available for production purposes but experienced a weekly average of 8 hours of downtime. The machine downtime causes the utilization index or rate for the department to be 10 percent below average (average is 100 percent), or

$$\text{Utilization index} = \frac{(\text{Hours available} - \text{Hours not used}) \times 100}{\text{Hours available}}$$

$$= \frac{(80 \text{ hours} - 8 \text{ hours}) \times 100}{80 \text{ hours}}$$

$$= \frac{72 \text{ hours} \times 100}{80 \text{ hours}}$$

$$= 90 \text{ percent}$$

The department produced the equivalence in output of 90 hours of standard production while only taking 72 hours. This results in an efficiency index or rating of 25 percent above average, or

$$\text{Efficiency index} = \frac{\text{Standard hours allowed} \times 100}{\text{Hours used}}$$

$$= \frac{90 \text{ hours} \times 100}{72 \text{ hours}}$$

$$= 125 \text{ percent}$$

Note: The relationship of calculated capacity to utilization and efficiency indexes in this problem can be confirmed by simply plugging the values into the calculated capacity formula as follows:

$$\text{Capacity} = \text{Available time} \times \text{Utilization (decimal)} \times \text{Efficiency (decimal)}$$

$$= 80 \text{ hours} \times 0.90 \times 1.25$$

$$= 90 \text{ hours of standard output}$$

The descriptive statistics used in the calculation of measured or calculated capacity, utilization, and efficiency are routinely generated in computer-based capacity reports. These statistics are used to help identify areas within an operation (such as a department or workcenter) in which capacity demand and supply need adjustment. They are prerequisite concepts to what is called capacity planning.

Capacity Planning Techniques

Capacity planning includes the management activities of establishing, measuring, and adjusting limits and levels of human and physical production capacity. To accomplish these activities a collection of planning techniques can be applied in long-range, medium-range, and short-range planning to determine and allocate an organization's capacity resources. As we can see in Figure 5-8, capacity planning techniques include resource requirements planning, rough-cut capacity planning, capacity requirements planning, input/output control, and operation sequencing.

RESOURCE REQUIREMENTS PLANNING **Resource requirements planning** involves a set of capacity planning techniques that are useful in guiding the major resource allocations of the organization from a strategic plan to the aggregate production plan. An example of the output of resource requirements planning is a manufacturing firm's planning the acquisition of a trucking firm to achieve the strategic goal of an improved distribution system. Other examples include a hospital's planning for building additions to meet long-range illness projections ten years in the future or a utility company's planning for new power stations to meet anticipated electrical usage ten or twenty years into the future. S

ROUGH-CUT CAPACITY PLANNING **Rough-cut capacity planning** is "the process of converting the production plan or the master production schedule into capacity needs for key resources: manpower, machinery, warehouse space, vendor's capabilities, and in some cases, money."[2] Rough-cut capacity planning is usually performed by examining the load reports of the aggregate production resources. By aggregating the load report capacities, an operations manager can estimate the capacity of the operations management system to meet the product demands stated in the master production schedule. The focus of planning at this stage is on meeting expected demand by matching departmental available capacity with departmental required capacity. A rough-cut capacity planning method is presented in Supplement 5-1.

CAPACITY REQUIREMENTS PLANNING **Capacity requirements planning (CRP)** is the planning process by which an organization determines how much work force and machine resources are needed to process the materials used to satisfy product demand requirements. CRP is more detailed and specific than rough-cut planning. Its focus is at the workstation or workcenter level of operations rather than at the organization or department level, as is the rough-cut planning effort. CRP can be used in service

---

[2] Reprinted with permission of the American Production and Inventory Control Society, Inc., *APICS Dictionary,* 7th edition, 1992.

FIGURE 5-8 OVERVIEW OF CAPACITY PLANNING TECHNIQUES

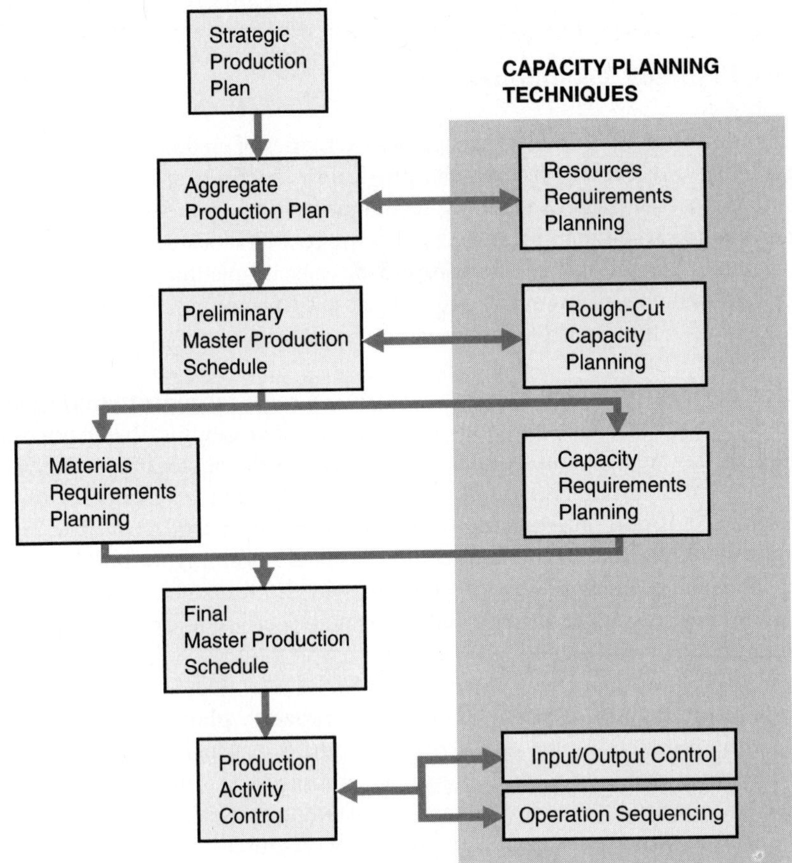

Source: Reprinted with permission, American Production and Inventory Control Society (APICS), 1987, CPIM Study Guide.

organizations to identify personnel load problems in providing service products. CRP can also be applied in the area of material requirements planning (MRP) in manufacturing organizations. We discuss CRP and MRP in Chapter 7.

INPUT/OUTPUT CONTROL **Input/output control** is actually a capacity control process used to control the input and output at a workstation. Production activity control, as shown in Figure 5-8, is usually the last stage of planning conducted at the shop floor level. The planned workstation input and output is defined in the capacity requirements plan. The monitoring techniques used to perform this control process may be computer-based or manual. We discuss input/output control in Chapter 9.

OPERATION SEQUENCING **Operation sequencing techniques** are techniques used for planning job orders through operations management workstations. The techniques

QUESTION: How important is capacity planning for organizations seeking world-class quality service for their customers?

ANSWER: Capacity planning is critical for both service and manufacturing organizations seeking world-class quality, when quality is measured by an organization's ability to provide timely response to customers' needs. Capacity planning allows management to determine their organization's capacity to meet customers' needs. (Remember from Chapter 2 that being customer focused is a total quality management tactic for world-class service.) As such, capacity planning helps measure timeliness of response to customers and assess improvement ideas (that is, alterations in capacity) implemented by the organization to enhance speed of response. Capacity planning can also help identify bottlenecks or problems areas in service load that need reallocation to improve customer response time. For example, by using capacity planning, universities can identify registration lines where student demand (that is, service load) will exceed registration processing capacity. Reallocating processing capacity resources from identified areas of underutilization to identified areas of overutilization, a university can reduce student registration processing time (that is, improve customer response time).

Q

can consider the capacity requirements planning and existing human and machine resources to devise a job sequencing plan. We discuss job sequencing in Chapter 9.

In summary, capacity planning involves the determination of need for and allocation of an organization's production resources. It is an evolutionary process that is used to interpret the production demand requirements of the strategic production plan through production activity control.

OTHER PRODUCTION PLANNING METHODS

There are many types of commonly used production planning methods. Some of these methods are used in conjunction with computer information systems, and others emerged from industry practice before the introduction of computer systems. Two types of production planning methods are graphic methods and work sheet methods.

Graphic Methods

Graphic production planning methods involve the use of graphs to clearly depict the differences between the forecast market demand behavior and the effect of various production planning strategies on an organization's future operation. Such graphs are usually structured to fit an organization's unique information needs. For example, some organizations might be financially concerned about maintaining high levels of inventory (because of investment tied up in finished goods inventory) and thus need an information system to alert them to excessive inventory levels.

In Figure 5-9 two aggregate planning graphs are presented. In the top graph a constant production rate strategy is compared with forecast demand. From just looking at the top graph it would appear that an inventory shortage will occur during the beginning of the first four months of the planning horizon. Most businesses do not begin a new year without some inventory. The inventory that is carried over from a previous time period is called the **beginning inventory.** If, as presented in the bottom graph in Figure 5-9, we start in period 0 with a beginning inventory of 30,000 units,

FIGURE 5-9 AGGREGATE PLANNING GRAPHS

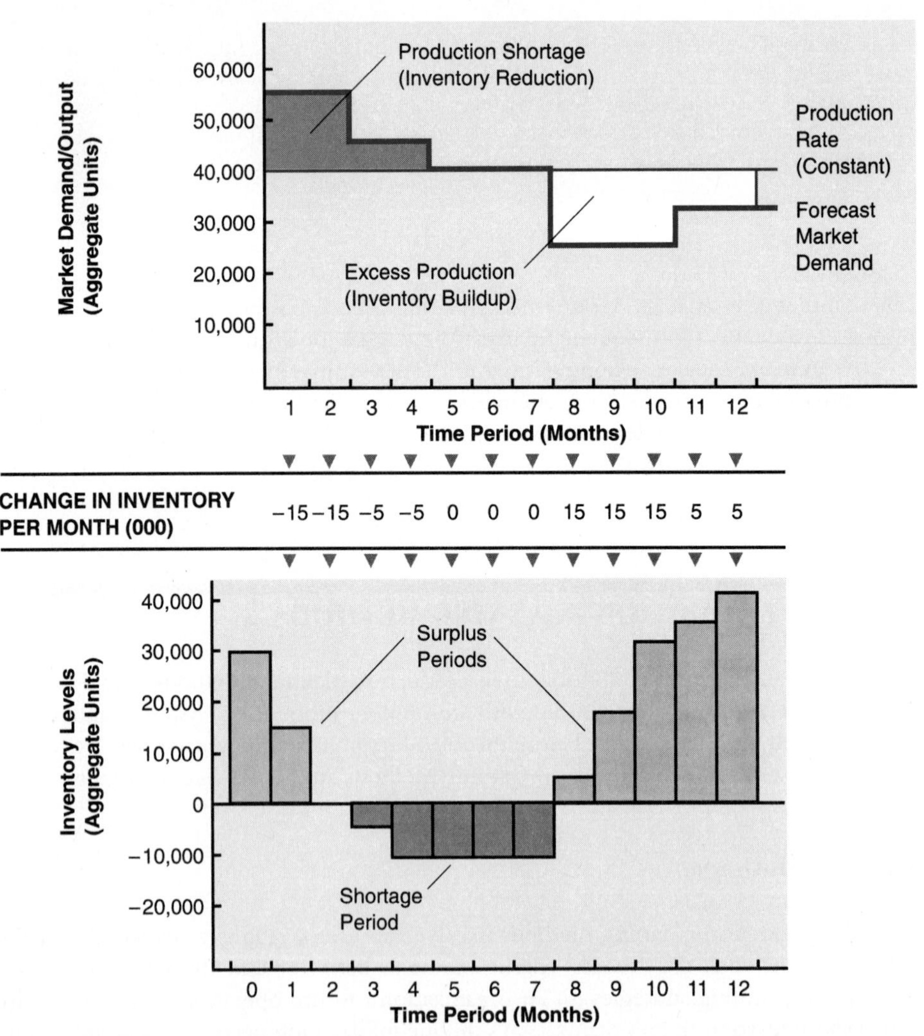

the inventory shortage period does not begin until period 4. By developing the graph for the aggregate planning variable of inventory levels, we can easily identify inventory shortage and surplus periods. Many computerized aggregate planning systems automatically provide graphs of the principal aggregate planning variables to aid in the identification of problems. Most of the computerized systems use graphic information obtained from worksheet aggregate planning methods.

Worksheet Methods

Worksheet methods are tabular planning methods that can be used in most areas of production planning. They do not require a computer system but are often incorporated into spreadsheet software systems.

In Table 5-1, a basic production planning worksheet is presented. Most worksheets tend to be divided into two parts. One part of the worksheet deals with unit production and the other deals with the unit production cost determination. The elements of the worksheet in Table 5-1 can be defined as shown on page 198.

TABLE 5-1 PRODUCTION PLANNING WORKSHEET

	TIME PERIOD				
	1	*2*	*3*	*. . . n*	*Total*
UNIT PRODUCTION WORKSHEET					
Forecast demand					
Prior backorder					
(Beginning inventory)					
Required production					
Type of production					
(Regular time production)					
(Overtime production)					
(Subcontract production)					
Units for backorder or ending inventory					
Backorder					
Ending inventory					
COST WORKSHEET					
Total output costs					
Regular time production					
Overtime production					
Subcontract production					
Backorder costs					
Inventory costs					
Total costs per period					
Total costs for all periods					

Forecast demand The forecast demand in units per time period for *n* time periods

Prior backorder The backorders from the previous time period

Beginning inventory The inventory from the previous time period

Required production The net difference of forecast demand + prior backorder − beginning inventory

Regular time production The number of units of product produced using the regular or normal production workforce (that is, using no overtime production)

Overtime production The number of units of product produced using overtime workforce

Subcontract production The number of units of product produced using subcontracts

Units for backorder or inventory The difference of required production − (regular time production + overtime production + subcontract production)

Backorder The number of units that were not satisfied by this month's production and were carried over and added to next month's demand (satisfied by next month's prior backorder)

Ending inventory The number of units that were not absorbed by this month's demand and will have to be subtracted from next month's required production (that is, via next month's beginning inventory)

Total output costs The cost per unit times the number of units produced per time period for each of the three types of production costs

Backordering costs The cost per unit (cost of lost sales because the customer did not want to have the order backordered) times the number of units backordered during the time period

Inventory costs The inventory carrying cost per unit times the number of units carried from one period to the next.[3]

Total costs per period The sum of total output costs + backordering costs + inventory costs for only the period in which they occur

Total costs for all periods The running sum of total costs per period for all periods

To illustrate how the worksheet method for production planning operates, let's look at a sample problem. An organization faces nonuniform market demand. Suppose that the firm wants to determine which of the following two production planning strategies is less costly to operate over four time periods of the planning horizon:

Strategy 1 The operation will produce at a constant rate of 260 units per period and will not permit overtime production. It will permit backordering, and its inventory levels may vary to absorb the variations in market demand.

[3] Another approach to determine the number of units to multiply for this cost factor is to use the period's average inventory. We will use ending inventory in this chapter for reasons of simplicity.

Strategy 2 The operation will produce at a constant rate of 260 units per period and will not permit backordering. It will permit overtime production, and its inventory levels may vary to absorb the variations in market demand.

Let's assume that the organization has no beginning inventory. To make a comparison of the two production strategies, the worksheets require cost information. The cost per unit for regular time production is $12; overtime production, $14; backordering cost per period, $2; and inventory cost per period per unit, $5. Based on these data, we can now develop the production planning worksheets for operating under each strategy.

In Table 5-2, the resulting costs for operating under strategy 1 are presented. In Table 5-2, we can see in period 1 that regular time production of 260 units results in an ending inventory of 20 units. These 20 units are then subtracted in the calculation of the next period's required production. Note that no overtime was used to avoid the backordering costs in periods 2 and 3. The cost for period 1 is found by adding the

TABLE 5-2 WORKSHEET EXAMPLE OF CONSTANT PRODUCTION STRATEGY WITH VARIABLE BACKORDERING AND INVENTORY LEVELS: NO OVERTIME PRODUCTION PERMITTED

	TIME PERIOD				
	1	*2*	*3*	*4*	*Total*
UNIT PRODUCTION WORKSHEET					
Forecast demand	240	320	280	200	1,040
Prior backorder	0	0	40	60	100
(Beginning inventory)*	0	20	0	0	20
Required production	240	300	320	260	1,120
Type of production					
(Regular time production)*	260	260	260	260	1,040
(Overtime production)*	0	0	0	0	0
Units for backorder or ending inventory	20	40	60	0	80
Backorder	0	40	60	0	100
Ending inventory	20	0	0	0	20
COST WORKSHEET					
Total out put costs					
Regular time production ($12 per unit)	$3,120	$3,120	$3,120	$3,120	
Overtime production ($14 per unit)	0	0	0	0	
Backorder costs ($2 per unit)	0	80	120	0	
Inventory costs ($5 per unit)	100	0	0	0	
Total costs per period	$3,220	$3,200	$3,240	$3,120	
Total costs for all periods	$3,220	$6,420	$9,660	$12,780	

* These values are subtracted from the other positive values in each column.

regular time production costs of \$3,120 (\$12 × 260) and the inventory costs of \$100 (\$5 × 20). The total costs per period are then accumulated over the four periods to generate a total cost for this production planning strategy of \$12,780.

In Table 5-3, the cost of operation for strategy 2 is presented. Because any back-ordering was not permitted under this strategy, we did incur some overtime production in periods 2 and 3 to meet market demand. The total resulting cost using this strategy over the four time periods is \$13,720. Because the total cost for strategy 2 is greater than that for strategy 1, the firm should choose strategy 1 if minimizing cost is the primary objective.

Management Science–Based Production Planning Methods

There are many different types of computer-based planning methods that are used in production planning. Most of these methods are from the field of management science. Because of their mathematical complexity and the introductory nature of this textbook, we will only briefly discuss several of the more commonly used models in manufacturing and service applications, including linear programming, the transportation method, linear decision rule, heuristic search methods, expert systems, and goal programming.

LINEAR PROGRAMMING **Linear programming (LP)** is an optimization technique, ideal for handling the multiple variables that exist in aggregate planning. As an optimization method, an LP solution cannot be improved upon given the resource limitations of the manufacturing or service operation it is used to model. The LP technique uses a series of mathematical expressions to model constrained resources such as resource limitation on labor hours, machine hours, and raw materials inherent in most manufacturing or service planning problems. It was used as early as the 1960s to help schedule textile mill manufacturing and continues in the 1990s to help organizations such as AMOCO accomplish their strategic product distribution plans.[4] LP has also been used as a planning aid in materials procurement to help a furniture manufacturing organization minimize the cost of the acquisition of raw materials.[5] Special versions of LP have also been used or can be applied in service industries. Nonlinear programming (a mathematical programming method permitting nonlinear functions) has been used to help select the best mix of tenants in a shopping mall to maximize the present worth of all the lease agreements for the entire mall.[6] Zero-one linear programming (an LP method requiring the decision variables to be equal to only zero or one) has been demonstrated

S

[4] See K. Eisemann and W. M. Young, "Study of a Textile Mill and the Aid of Linear Programming," *Management Technology,* 1 (January 1960), 52–63; J. S. Mehring and M. M. Gutterman, "Supply and Distribution Planning Support for AMOCO (U.K.) Limited," *Interfaces,* 20, No. 4 (1990), 95–107; and S. M. Shafer, "A Spreadsheet Approach to Aggregate Scheduling," *Production and Inventory Management Journal,* 32, No. 4 (1991), 4–10.

[5] H. F. Carino and C. H. LeNoir, "Optimizing Wood Procurement in Cabinet Manufacturing," *Interfaces,* 18, No. 2 (1988), 10–19.

[6] J. C. Bean et al., "Selecting Tenants in a Shopping Mall," *Interfaces,* 18, No. 2 (1988), 1–9.

TABLE 5-3 WORKSHEET EXAMPLE OF CONSTANT PRODUCTION STRATEGY WITH VARIABLE OVERTIME PRODUCTION AND INVENTORY LEVELS: NO BACKORDERING PERMITTED

	TIME PERIOD				
	1	*2*	*3*	*4*	*Total*
UNIT PRODUCTION WORKSHEET					
Forecast demand	240	320	280	200	1,040
Prior backorder	0	0	0	0	0
(Beginning inventory)*	0	20	0	0	20
Required production	240	300	280	200	1,120
Type of production					
(Regular time production)*	260	260	260	260	1,040
(Overtime production)*	0	40	20	0	60
Units for backorder or ending inventory	20	0	0	60	80
Backorder	0	0	0	0	0
Ending inventory	20	0	0	60	80
COST WORKSHEET					
Total output costs					
Regular time production ($12 per unit)	$3,120	$3,120	$3,120	$3,120	
Overtime production ($14 per unit)	0	560	280	0	
Backorder costs ($2 per unit)	0	0	0	0	
Inventory costs ($5 per unit)	100	0	0	300	
Total costs per period	$3,220	$3,680	$3,400	$3,420	
Total costs for all periods	$3,220	$6,900	$10,300	$13,720	

* These values are subtracted from the other positive values in each column.

as a project planning tool in information system project planning.[7] In Supplement 5-2, LP models are formulated to demonstrate how they can be used in production planning and to demonstrate some of their limitations when applied to production planning. (Students unfamiliar with LP formulation methods should read Appendix D at the end of this book.)

THE TRANSPORTATION METHOD The transportation method is a special type of linear programming. It is used chiefly as a modeling technique for deriving an optimal allocation of goods or services from multiple sources of supply to multiple demand destinations. Transportation models have been applied in the trucking industry to help

S

[7] K. Muralidhar et al., "A 0-1 Linear Programming Model for Information System Project Selection," *Journal of Management Science and Policy Analysis,* 3, No. 1 (1989), 34–44.

determine optimal truck rental needs for firms that rent trucks throughout a network of trucking terminals.[8] It has also been used in aggregate planning to help determine backordering and plan production.[9] In Supplement 5-3, the transportation method is presented as a planning aid to help determine a master schedule and perform capacity planning activities.

THE LINEAR DECISION RULE The linear decision rule is a mathematical procedure that was first proposed in the 1950s.[10] In this procedure, the three basic aggregate planning variables are combined to form a nonlinear equation that defines the production costs for a given time period. Using calculus, two linear expressions are then derived from the equation. These two linear equations are then used to determine optimal production rates and plan appropriate work force levels. Although this model has been popular for research purposes in the past, it is fairly limited in real-world applications.

COMPUTER SEARCH (HEURISTIC) METHODS As an alternative to an optimization model, computer search or heuristic methods for aggregate planning started appearing in the literature in the late 1960s.[11] A heuristic method is a set of decision rules that search, by trial and error, for the best combination of values for the aggregate planning variables. The decision rules are used to guide a computer program through a network of simple linear expressions representing the aggregate planning situation. The computer program simulates change in one aggregate planning variable and examines the cost-minimizing effect on other variables. The search procedure can be adaptive and heuristic. That is, once the computer program finds a significant cost-reducing path through the network of mathematical expressions, it will intensify its search efforts along that particular path.

There has been considerable applied research on computer search and heuristic production planning methods in recent years.[12] Indeed, research comparing search

---

[8] M. J. Schniederjans and N. K. Kwak, "A Simulated Transportation Problem for Improved Operational Planning: An Application in the Trucking Industry," *Computers and Operations Research,* 5, No. 2 (1979), 149–155.

[9] M. E. Posner and W. Szwarc, "A Transportation Type Aggregate Production Model with Backordering," *Management Science,* 29, No. 2 (February 1983), 188–199; and K. Singhal and V. Adlakha, "Cost and Shortage Trade-offs in Aggregate Production Planning," *Decision Sciences,* 20, No. 1 (1989), 158–165.

[10] C. C. Holt, F. Modigliani, J. F. Muth, and H. A. Simon, "A Linear Decision Rule for Production and Employment Scheduling," *Management Sciences,* 1 (October 1955), 1–10.

[11] See W. H. Taubert, "A Search Decision Rule for the Aggregate Scheduling Problem," *Management Science,* 14 (February 1968), B343–B359; and M. D. Oliff and G. K. Leong, "A Discrete Production Switching Rule for Aggregate Planning," *Decision Sciences,* 18, No. 4 (1987), 582–597.

[12] F. J. Vasko et al., "An Efficient Heuristic for Planning Mother Plate Requirements at Bethlehem Steel," *Interfaces,* 21, No. 2 (1991), 1–7; and J. P. Moily, "Optimal and Heuristic Procedures for Component Lot-Splitting in Multi-Stage Manufacturing Systems," *Management Science,* 32, No. 1 (January 1986), 113–125.

methods' performance as an aid in aggregate planning with other methods, such as linear programming and the linear decision rule, has clearly demonstrated the search methods' superiority.[13]

EXPERT SYSTEMS Closely related to rule-based heuristic methods are expert systems. Expert systems are computer-based systems that are designed to mimic human or expert decision-making efforts. They are sometimes embedded with decision support methodology including artificial intelligence systems, rule-based logic systems, management science methodology, and substantial data bases of limited or focused knowledge domains.[14] The expert system software orchestrates the various decision support systems to support operations managers' decision making. Research on expert systems used in OM has shown a substantial growth in their use in production planning. New expert systems developed for OM planning include the PEP 38 system used in capacity planning, ISIS system used in master production scheduling, and the PATRIARCH system used in aggregate planning.[15] One of the more recent applications of an expert system in a service industry involved planning auditing activities for health insurance claims.[16] The expert system helped users identify errors in claims and saved needless payments and overpayments to subscriber companies.

S

GOAL PROGRAMMING Goal programming (GP) is a mathematical programming procedure that is similar to linear programming.[17] The primary advantages of GP over LP are that the GP model permits multiple conflicting objectives (LP only permits one objective at a time) and allows the objectives to be prioritized. GP provides an important modeling feature for planners in that the three differing variables in aggregate planning models inherently conflict with one another. By being able to prioritize the production rate and work force size, for example, operations managers can obtain solutions that are logically consistent with real-world ranking requirements that might favor production rate over work force size. Although GP suffers from some of the same limitations as

---

[13] See W. B. Lee and B. M. Khumawala, "Simulation Testing of Aggregate Production Models in an Implementation Methodology," *Management Science,* 20 (February 1974), 903–911.

[14] G. Plenert, "What Does a Decision Support System (DSS) Do for Manufacturing?" *Production and Inventory Management Journal,* 33, No. 1 (1992), 17–19; M. M. Helme, P. Dileepan, and L. P. Ettkin, "Expert Systems for Managing Operations," *Production and Inventory Management Journal,* 31, No. 1 (1990), 24–28.

[15] H. R. Rao and B. P. Lingaraj, "Expert Systems in Production and Operations Management: Classification and Prospects," *Interfaces,* 18, No. 6 (1988), 80–91.

[16] J. L. Martin and R. F. Eckerle, "A Knowledge-Based System for Auditing Health Insurance Claims," *Interfaces,* 21, No. 2 (1991), 39–47.

[17] For a review of the basics of GP, see S. M. Lee, *Goal Programming for Decision Analysis* (Philadelphia: Auerback, 1972); and M. J. Schniederjans, *Linear Goal Programming* (Princeton, N.J.: Petrocelli Books, 1984).

LP, it has been one of the most popular production planning models used since the 1960s.[18]

INTEGRATING MANAGEMENT RESOURCES: USING MANAGEMENT INFORMATION SYSTEMS TO INTEGRATE PRODUCTION PLANNING AND CONTROL

The tactics suggested in this chapter to change a master production schedule are one approach to adjusting to changes in market demand requirements. The rapid changes expected in the global marketplace and cost of materials in the 1990s are creating an ever-greater need for production planning flexibility to permit a quick response to those changes.[19] To enhance flexibility in production planning, many organizations are developing strategies to improve their production planning information systems. Production planning is based on information. As improvements in the timeliness of information are implemented, they will permit a more resilient response to needed changes. To improve the timeliness of production information, many organizations are moving toward a highly integrated production management information system (MIS).

One MIS used to integrate production planning and production control activities is Arthur Andersen and Company's MAC-PAC software system. Designed in the 1990s, it is used for integrating robotic systems, capacity planning, order processing, and accounting with the production activities taking place on the shop floor. The MAC-PAC system consists of ten fully integrated computer applications in manufacturing planning and control activities. The focus of this computer system is to integrate the planning and control activities required for implementing production activities from the master schedule to the completion of the product. A brief description of some of the MAC-PAC computer applications and the information they provide operations managers are presented in Figure 5-10. As with most integrated systems, the planning information provided by the system is used in a variety of management activities. This system provides an overview of the other types of production management activities (materials management, inventory management, and scheduling) that we will be exploring in the next five chapters.

---

[18] See D. A. Goodman, "A New Approach to Scheduling Aggregate Production and Work Force," *AIIE Transactions,* 5 (June 1973), 135–141; S. M. Lee and L. J. Moore, "A Practical Approach to Production Scheduling," *Production and Inventory Management,* 15 (1st Quarter, 1974), 79–92; T. Rakes, L. Franz, and J. Wynn, "Aggregate Production Planning Using Chance-Constrained Goal Programming," *International Journal of Production Research,* 22 (1984), 673–684; and B. Dean et al., "A Goal Programming Approach to Production Planning for Flexible Manufacturing Systems," *Journal of Engineering and Technology Management,* 1, No. 6 (1990), 207–220.

[19] M. W. Pelphrey, "Flexibility Is the Key to Survival for Manufacturing," *APICS: The Performance Advantage,* 2, No. 4 (1992), 37–41; and J. T. Vesey, "The New Competitors: They Think in Terms of Speed to Market," *Production and Inventory Management Journal,* 33, No. 1 (1992), 71–77.

FIGURE 5-10 SELECTED MAC-PAC INTEGRATED MANAGEMENT INFORMATION SYSTEM COMPUTER APPLICATIONS

Item Definition
The framework established and maintained in this application is critical to accurate planning. MAC-PAC maintains complete definitions of item structure and tracks changes to those definitions. Through inquiries and reports by item revision level, you can control the proliferation of unnecessary modifications. You can even track product changes by type and sequence and automatically generate exception reports. Item Definition also lets you associate free-form comments with any item on the system to document special characteristics or considerations.

Process Definition
With this application you can define, organize, and maintain data for routings and production centers. This information is tightly integrated with other MAC-PAC applications and serves as the foundation for planning, costing, and simulation. Process Definition helps you monitor costs, build product quality into the manufacturing process, and increase your productivity through manpower and facilities planning.

Master Scheduling
The Master Scheduling application lets you quickly develop a comprehensive production schedule that accounts for inventory balances, capacity constraints, planning policy rules, and customer demand factors reported by other applications. Should any of these factors change, production is rescheduled to balance and maintain customer service. Key facility capacities determined by the application in rough-cut capacity planning help you produce and deliver your goods on time. "What if" simulations even allow you to see the impact of proposed master schedule changes—without affecting your current schedule.

Forecasting
The key to realistic production planning is accurate prediction of market demand. MAC-PAC supports this function by providing an interface that extracts sales history information captured by the Order Processing module and downloads it to a microcomputer. Once downloaded, the data can be used with a microcomputer-based forecasting package. The interface can then upload forecast demand for use in generating your master production schedule.

Material Requirements Planning
Material Requirements Planning determines what you need and when you need it so you can manage inventory and plan production schedules. This application gives you information that helps you respond to changes in demand and project future material requirements.

CONBON
CONBON—Card Order Notice, Bring Out Notice—is Andersen Consulting's adaptation of the Japanese *Kanban* production technique. This application suggests and prints CON cards, which authorize production, and BON cards, which authorize transfer to the next production center. CONBON cards, either bar-coded or conventionally printed, are the shop floor production schedule in a JIT environment. They facilitate smooth production of material based on consumption. They also help you control inventory surplus and reduce lead time. Plus, you can determine bottlenecks and work to eliminate them. Overall, CONBON cards keep your personnel in touch with activities on the floor and facilitate "management by eye" rather than "management by number".

Just-In-Time—Repetitive Manufacturing
The Just-In-Time—Repetitive Manufacturing application brings together the best of JIT and MRPII into a single manufacturing environment. You can plan production by orders or, for JIT-planned parts, by flow schedules. What you get is a practical schedule that can be used to run your operations. Or use it as a guide for our CONBON application, which supports dual-card, single-card, or cardless/container methods of production and transfer.
Use this application to facilitate a paperless factory, where reporting time and effort is minimal and is performed by part rather than order.

Purchasing
The Purchasing application covers the full scope of the purchasing process, from planning and the identification of part requirements through receiving and the final disposition of items. You'll know which company should get your business because MAC-PAC rates suppliers by on-time delivery, quality, and price. Once material is delivered, you have the flexibility to define it's unique receiving instructions, from a simple receipt to more complex quality control requirements.

Order Processing
Order processing helps you achieve excellence in customer service through on-line, up-to-the-minute maintenance of customer orders, from order entry to invoice creation. With this application, you can create quote orders and then convert them to sales orders. You can check inventory availability, manage customer credit, and look at shipping schedules and orders. MAC-PAC allows several types of orders, including standard ship orders, blanket orders, and back orders. Order Processing will automatically check inventory levels, delivery dates, and credit information, and will

FIGURE 5-10 (CONTINUED)

release orders that have been held or backordered. All these capabilities give you greater control over pricing, sourcing, and cash flow.

MAC-PAC's Electronic Data Interchange (EDI) functionality can help you reduce the time and effort involved in entering customer orders. This interface allows you to receive sales orders and to send order acknowledgments and invoices electonically. Using standard transactions and regular telephone lines, MAC-PAC can communicate directly with your customers. The electronic transmission increases accuracy at the same time it reduces paperwork.

Inventory Control

Inventory Control helps you manage the levels, locations, and movement of your inventory. In addition, MAC-PAC offers lot control and lot trace funtions if you require full lot traceability—from supplier to customer and from customer to supplier—and allows quality control specifications for lot inventory. Plus, MAC-PAC offers the flexibility of many business funtions by warehouse, such as pricing, costing, sourcing, and cycle counting.

The on-line maintenance of production, order release dates, and inventory enables you to meet precise delivery specifications, issue timely status reports, minimize paperwork, and discover shortages immediately. With such information, you can be flexible and responsive to shifts in demand.

Shop Floor Control

In an MRPII manufacturing environment, Shop Floor Control schedules the work required to complete each order and measures labor and machine efficiency by comparing actual hours spent in an operation to established standards. With MAC-PAC you can increase the productivity of your work force, keep items and products moving smoothly through production, reduce scrap, and set production priorities.

Capacity Planning

By identifying resource demand by workcenter, this application helps you detect bottlenecks, streamline operations, use equipment and workers more productively, and develop up-to-date and accurate capacity projections. Capacity information can be presented in an easy-to-use graphic format, allowing you to pinpoint capacity problems quickly, then eliminate them.

Product Costing

Product Costing lets you develop item costs based on materials and operations specified in the Item Definition and Process Definition applications. You can define an unlimited number of cost categories, which can be rolled up to the total product cost. Product Costing helps you evaluate profit margins, simulate costs, and perform "what if" analyses, providing the flexibility you need to react quickly to cost changes.

Inventory Accounting

This application lets you record changes in your inventory value from one period to the next. These changes are recorded at the level of detail you desire. From the company level down to the item level, you can reconcile period beginning and ending values by item number, company, and warehouse. Inventory Accounting lets you see the value of work-in-process inventory at any time, warehouse-wide or company-wide, with variances highlighted. Inventory Accounting is also integrated with the General Ledger application. Inventory Accounting tracks all inventory movement transactions—distribution and manufacturing— and automatically transfers this data to the General Ledger. You can control the cost of your inventory and be assured that your accounts are up to date.

General Ledger

This comprehensive application gives you a flexible and clear presentation of critical financial information. Here, information from all the other pieces of the system comes together to give you the bottom line. Accounting structures are flexible to correspond to your company's organization, and user-defined reports present detailed information in the format you choose. Application features enable you to measure planned-versus-actual performance for each unit in your organization, control many budgets and fiscal years simultaneously, post daily or weekly, and make different types of journal entries, such as recurring or standing. Intercompany and multicurrency processing are also supported.

International Processing

MAC-PAC provides the flexibility you need to stay on top of today's global marketplace. Financial transactions can be processed in any currency; MAC-PAC will convert them to the base currency for your location and maintain the foreign currency detail. Intercompany transactions are supported between different base currencies, and financial data may be translated from multiple locations for consolidation on one single-currency financial statement. When exchange rates change, MAC-PAC can fully revalue accounts and generate realized and unrealized exchange gains and losses to help you keep pace with constantly shifting international markets. MAC-PAC also provides flexible value added tax (VAT) processing. You specify which locations use VAT processing—and how VAT calculations are performed at each. At a customer level you can specify additional VAT options.

Source: Used with permission from *MAC-PAC for IBM AS/400,* 1991, pp. 3–8.

SUMMARY

The purpose of this chapter has been to introduce the production planning activities of aggregate planning, master production scheduling, and capacity planning. This chapter also presented several methods that can be used in these production planning activities. Some additional production planning methods are presented in the supplements at the end of this chapter.

The feasibility of an aggregate production plan becomes clear only when the MPS is converted into detailed requirements. To produce the products dictated by the MPS requires a combination of work force, equipment, and materials. To help us understand how the materials necessary to complete the scheduled output must flow into and out of an operations management system, we will examine the subject of mateials management in the next chapter.

MRP systems can play a part in the successful implementation of computer-integrated manufacturing systems (CIM). Since CIM systems are for some organizations a means of achieving operations management strategies, the role MRP systems play in production planning can be critical. The article at the end of this chapter provides some insight on the important relationship between CIM and MRP in production planning.

DISCUSSION AND REVIEW QUESTIONS

1. For what reasons is aggregate production planning such an important operations management activity?
2. What is the aggregate production plan?
3. What are the aggregate planning variables?
4. Discuss the logical steps necessary for planning production from strategic planning to the shop floor product activity planning.
5. What is a master production schedule (MPS)? How is it related to aggregate planning?
6. Briefly describe net requirements and how they fit into production planning.
7. Is there any difference in the way an MPS is prepared for a service or manufacturing organization?
8. What type of tactical changes can be made to bring an MPS into balance with actual demand?
9. What is capacity planning? How is it related to aggregate planning?
10. What is the difference between measured and calculated capacity? Explain.
11. Discuss the different capacity planning techniques.
12. Discuss the advantages and disadvantages of using work sheet methods in production planning.

PROBLEMS

* 1. Suppose that we would like to determine the total cost of production, backordering, and inventory for a small manufacturing operation over a four-month planning horizon. Based on our research of the firm, we find the following demand and allowable unit production during the planning horizon:

	TIME PERIOD			
	1	*2*	*3*	*4*
Forecast demand (units)	150	240	300	200
Regular time production (units)	220	220	220	220

We also find that there is no beginning inventory and that the company will use overtime production to meet demand requirements if necessary. There is a $10 per unit regular time production cost rate, a $15 per unit overtime production cost rate, a $1 per unit backordering cost rate, and a $3 per unit inventory carrying cost rate.

a. Develop a unit production worksheet for this production planning problem.
b. Develop a cost worksheet for this production planning problem.
c. What is the total cost of production, inventory, and backordering during the four-month period planning horizon?

2. Assume that we change the production planning strategy in Problem 1 to permit regular time production to vary as follows:

	TIME PERIOD			
	1	*2*	*3*	*4*
Regular time production (units)	200	220	280	220

a. Develop a unit production worksheet for this production planning problem.
b. Develop a cost worksheet for this production planning problem.
c. What is the total cost of production, inventory, and backordering during the four-period planning horizon?

3. Suppose that we have been asked to determine the total cost of production, backordering, and inventory for a manufacturing firm over a four-quarter planning horizon. Based on our initial research about the firm, we have determined the following demand and allowable unit production during the planning horizon:

	TIME PERIOD			
	1	*2*	*3*	*4*
Forecast demand (units)	870	650	900	1,000
Regular time production (units)	800	800	800	800

Beginning inventory is 100 units, and the company is willing to use overtime production to meet demand requirements if necessary. There is an $8 per unit regular time production cost rate, a $12 per unit overtime production cost rate, a $2 per unit backordering cost rate, and a $4 per unit inventory carrying cost rate.

* The solutions to the problems marked with an asterisk can be found in Appendix J.

a. Develop a unit production worksheet for this production planning problem.
b. Develop a cost worksheet for this aggregate planning problem.
c. What is the total cost of production, inventory, and backordering during the four-quarter planning horizon?

4. Assume that we change the production planning strategy in Problem 3 to permit regular time production to vary as follows:

	TIME PERIOD			
	1	*2*	*3*	*4*
Regular time production (units)	700	900	800	600

a. Develop a unit production worksheet for this production planning problem.
b. Develop a cost worksheet for this production planning problem.
c. What is the total cost of production, inventory, and backordering during the four-period planning horizon?

5. A manufacturing firm attempts to determine the total cost of production, backordering, and inventory over a six-month planning horizon. Based on the research of the engineering staff, the following demand and allowable unit production during the planning horizon have been determined:

	TIME PERIOD					
	1	*2*	*3*	*4*	*5*	*6*
Forecast demand (units)	370	450	400	500	450	500
Regular time production (units)	400	400	400	400	400	400

Beginning inventory is 150 units, and the company will use overtime production to meet demand requirements. There is a $3 per unit regular time production cost rate, a $5 per unit overtime production cost rate, a $2 per unit backordering cost rate, and a $4 per unit inventory carrying cost rate.

a. Develop a unit production worksheet for this production planning problem.
b. Develop a cost worksheet for this production planning problem.
c. What is the total cost of production, inventory, and backordering during the four-period planning horizon?

6. Assume that we change the production planning strategy in Problem 5 to permit regular time production to vary as follows:

	TIME PERIOD					
	1	*2*	*3*	*4*	*5*	*6*
Regular time production (units)	300	450	500	450	450	600

a. Develop a unit production worksheet for this production planning problem.
b. Develop a cost worksheet for this production planning problem.
c. What is the total cost of production, inventory, and backordering during the four-period planning horizon?

* 7. (This problem requires the contents of Supplement 5-2.) Suppose that we want to model a company's production system to develop a production plan that will determine total unit production. The firm uses a constant production strategy in such a way that

it produces four products on a monthly basis: Products A, B, C, and D. Each product uses three types of resources as defined in the following table:

	UNIT USAGE BY PRODUCT				*UNIT SUPPLY OF RESOURCE*	
Resource	*A*	*B*	*C*	*D*	*Maximum*	*Minimum*
Work force	1	3	2	1	2,400	1,100
Material	1	1	1	1	1,350	450
Supplies	2	1	4	2	4,200	800

Production costs are as follows: Product A, \$6; B, \$8; C, \$9; and D, \$7. Because of storage restrictions, a maximum capacity of production for all products is limited to 5,000 units per month. The company can sell every unit of the products it produces. Formulate this production problem as a linear programming model. Clearly define the decision variables.

C

8. Solve the LP model formulated in Problem 7. What is the optimal production schedule? Which resources, if any, are in excess?

9. (This problem requires the contents of Supplement 5-2.) Assume that the model in Problem 7 must be structured for a second month because the unit supply of resources will shift in the second month as follows:

	UNIT USAGE BY PRODUCT				*UNIT SUPPLY OF RESOURCE*	
Resource	*A*	*B*	*C*	*D*	*Maximum*	*Minimum*
Work force	4	5	3	1	2,000	1,000
Material	1	3	5	7	1,200	300
Supplies	3	5	7	8	4,000	600

Formulate this problem as an LP model. Clearly define the decision variables.

10. (This problem requires the contents of Supplement 5-2.) A manufacturer wants to model its production system to develop a production plan. The firm is currently using a constant production strategy and produces four products on a monthly basis: Products A, B, C, and D. Each product requires three types of resources in the units defined below:

	UNIT USAGE BY PRODUCT				*UNIT SUPPLY OF RESOURCE*	
Resource	*A*	*B*	*C*	*D*	*Maximum*	*Minimum*
Work force	4	5	3	1	400	100
Material	1	3	5	7	350	250
Supplies	3	5	7	8	1,200	800

Production costs are as follows: Product A, \$56; B, \$78; C, \$89; and D, \$99. Because of storage restrictions, a maximum capacity of production for all products is limited to 2,500 units per month. Contractual requirements specify that the company must produce at least 100 units of Product A and at least 100 units of D. Also, an inventory limitation prohibits Product C from exceeding 500 units. The company can sell every unit of the products it produces. Formulate this production problem as an LP model. Clearly define the decision variables.

11. Solve the LP model formulated in Problem 10. What is the optimal production schedule? Which resources, if any, are in excess? C

12. (This problem requires the contents of Supplement 5-2.) Assume that the model in Problem 10 must be structured for a second month because the unit supply of resources will shift in the second month as follows:

	UNIT USAGE BY PRODUCT				*UNIT SUPPLY OF RESOURCE*	
Resource	*A*	*B*	*C*	*D*	*Maximum*	*Minimum*
Work force	4	5	3	1	500	200
Material	1	3	5	7	600	300
Supplies	3	5	7	8	1,300	900

Formulate this production planning problem as an LP model. Clearly define the decision variables.

13. (This problem requires the contents of Supplement 5-3.) Suppose that we have the following transportation problem formulation of a production plan. Note that no backordering is permitted. (The darkened cells should be assigned a very large cost value to ensure that backordering is not permitted.) Solve this problem for the optimal production schedule. Clearly define how many units should be produced in each month, using regular or overtime labor. C

		FORECAST DEMAND TIME PERIODS Jan.	Feb.	Mar.	Ending Inventory	Unused Capacity	Available Capacity
Beginning Inventory		0	2	4	6	0	50
JAN. Capacity	Regular time	5	7	9	11	0	200
	Overtime	7.5	9.5	11.5	13.5	0	45
FEB. Capacity	Regular time		5	7	9	0	300
	Overtime		7.5	9.5	11.5	0	50
MAR. Capacity	Regular time			5	7	0	300
	Overtime			7.5	9.5	0	50
Total		200	300	200	50		

*14. (This problem requires the contents of Supplement 5-3.) Suppose that we want to determine the cost of a manufacturing operation for the next three months using the transportation method of production planning. From our analysis of the problem, the operation can be described as follows:

a. Only regular time and overtime production are permitted.
b. Cost per unit of regular time production is \$2, and cost per unit of overtime production is \$3.
c. No beginning inventory exists.
d. Backordering is not permitted.
e. Ending inventory of 100 units is required.
f. The planning horizon will cover the months of January, February, and March.

g. The regular time production capacity in January is 500 units; in February, 250 units; and in March, 150 units.
h. The forecast demand in January is 300 units; in February, 300 units; and in March, 200 units.
i. The inventory carrying cost (the cost to carry a unit in inventory) per unit per month is $1.
j. Overtime production cannot exceed 20 percent of regular time production.
k. No subcontracting is permitted.
l. There is no cost for unused capacity.

Formulate this problem using the transportation method of production planning.

C 15. Solve the problem formulated in Problem 14. **Hint:** When backordering is not permitted, the backordering cost cells should be a very large cost value that will prohibit the computer from making assignments to them. What is the optimal production schedule?

16. (This problem requires the contents of Supplement 5-3.) Suppose that we wanted to determine for a manufacturing operation the cost of using the transportation method of production planning over the next three months. The operation has the following features:

a. Only regular time and overtime production are permitted.
b. Cost per unit of regular time production is $5, and cost per unit of overtime production is $7.
c. Beginning inventory is 100 units.
d. Backordering is permitted at a cost of $1 per unit per month.
e. Ending inventory of 100 units is required.
f. The planning horizon will cover the months of January, February, and March.
g. The regular time production capacity in January is 250 units; in February, 350 units; and in March, 450 units.
h. The forecast demand in January is 400 units; in February, 300 units; and in March, 200 units.
i. The inventory carrying cost (the cost to carry a unit in inventory) per unit per month is $2.
j. Overtime production cannot exceed 100 units.
k. No subcontracting is permitted.
l. There is no cost for unused capacity.

Formulate this problem using the transportation method of production planning.

C 17. Solve the problem formulated in Problem 16. What is the optimal production schedule?

18. (This problem requires the contents of Supplement 5-3.) Suppose that a company wants to determine the cost of the next four months of a manufacturing operation using the transportation method of production planning. From our research, we find that the operation can be described as follows:

a. Regular time, overtime, and subcontract production are permitted.
b. Cost per unit of regular time production is $3, cost per unit of overtime production is $4, and cost per unit of subcontract production is $5.
c. Beginning inventory is 200 units.
d. Backordering is permitted at a cost of $1 per unit per month.
e. Ending inventory of 100 units is required.
f. The planning horizon will cover the months of January, February, March, and April.

g. The regular time production capacity is a constant 600 units per month.
h. The forecast demand in January is 850 units; in February, 700 units; in March, 500 units; and in April, 300 units.
i. The inventory carrying cost (the cost to carry a unit in inventory) per unit per month is $2.
j. Overtime production cannot exceed 10 percent of regular time production.
k. Subcontract production cannot exceed 20 percent of regular production.
l. There is no cost for unused capacity.

Formulate this problem using the transportation method of production planning.

19. Solve the problem formulated in Problem 17. What is the optimal production schedule? C

20. (This problem requires the contents of Supplement 5-3.) An operations manager has used a simple transportation problem formulation to determine the least expensive transportation schedule for a manufacturing organization. The transportation problem formulation is given below:

FROM \ TO	St. Louis	Omaha	New York	Dallas	Supply
Chicago	2	4	3	5	4,500
Richmond	5	7	4	4	7,800
Atlanta	5	4	6	5	10,500
Demand					

The weekly supply of units available for shipping are obtained from capacity planning reports, and the weekly demand is dictated by contract customer demand. The supply remains constant from week to week. A simple microcomputer program was used by the operations manager to determine the schedule that minimizes costs. Unfortunately, the customer demand contract expired and the organization had to start forecasting its weekly demand. The forecast of the next week's demand was computed using a regression model, and the forecast is expressed as an interval estimate. The minimum and maximum interval forecasts generated for the next week's demand are as follows:

	MARKET			
Type of Demand	*St. Louis*	*Omaha*	*New York*	*Dallas*
Minimum demand	4,500	2,000	8,900	3,700
Maximum demand	7,500	3,000	9,800	4,500

In addition to including the interval forecast values, the next week's model should reflect that shipments between Chicago and St. Louis are prohibited by a union contractual agreement. Formulate this transportation method problem as a linear programming model.

★21. A manufacturing operation has an assembly line plant that produces units of a single product. The last five days the daily output was 123, 125, 130, 132, and 134 units, respectively. What is the measured capacity of this system? Explain your answer.

22. A video rental chain has decided to measure the output capacity of its two stores based on the number of videotapes rented per day as an output measure. Store A had the

following ten days of rentals: 225, 252, 281, 235, 198, 102, 274, 273, 233, and 331. Store B had the following ten days of rentals: 305, 311, 311, 325, 318, 302, 324, 313, 313, and 311. What is the measured capacity of each store using maximum output for a capacity measure? Which store's measured capacity is the greatest? If you rewarded the management of each store based on measured capacity, which store would receive the greatest rewards? Is such a system of rewards fair? Explain your answer.

23. In Supplement 5-1 a rough-cut capacity example was used to determine a bill of work force and compute the required capacity using the bill of work force method for a manufacturing company. What are the revised capacity values when you substitute the data in the following table for the data in the example in Supplement 5-1? These data are the standard times for chair product items, and all other data are to be the same.

Department	*Item*	*Run Time per Item*	*Setup Time per Lot*	*Lot Size*
Woodwork	Leg	12 min	180 min	80 units
Woodwork	Brace	9 min	110 min	40 units
Seat Assembly	Seat	5 min	90 min	20 units

24. Again, in Supplement 5-1, substitute the data in the following table for the data in the example. (The data are the standard times for chair product items.) Compute the utilization index (and rate) in the Woodwork Department assuming the minutes not used are 12,000. Compute the utilization index (and rate) in the Seat Assembly Department assuming the minutes not used are 8,000. If the Woodwork Department on average uses 57,600 minutes per week and generates 61,000 standard minutes of output, what is its efficiency index (and rate)? If the Seat Assembly Department on average uses 7,200 minutes per week and generates 7,000 standard minutes of output, what is its efficiency index (and rate)? Use these utilization and efficiency rates in combination with the following data to determine the new bill of labor and required capacity information for the manufacturing company in Supplement 5-1.

Department	*Item*	*Run Time per Item*	*Setup Time per Lot*	*Lot Size*
Woodwork	Leg	17 min	210 min	80 units
Woodwork	Brace	11 min	140 min	40 units
Seat Assembly	Seat	6 min	120 min	20 units

CASE 5-1

WHO DOES WHAT NEXT YEAR?

The Ace Manufacturing Company produces electronic appliances for and under the brand name of major retail organizations. In any given year, its product line consists of twenty different toasters. Its products, even when manufactured for competing retailing organizations, are basically the same except for cosmetic or external changes. That is, all of the internal working parts of Ace's toasters are the same and only the outside shells differ per retailer specifications. Such product consistency reduces the need for sophisticated production planning systems (Ace currently uses graphic and worksheet methods) and has helped the firm become a profitable enterprise.

Ace Manufacturing has successfully operated for more than fifteen years. Part of the success story of Ace is its management's planning efforts. As a part of their yearly management activities, the president and vice presidents of marketing, finance, and production develop an aggregate plan in November for the following six months' operations. In recent years, the popularity of Ace's high-quality products and their low unit cost to retailers increased product demand beyond the company's manufacturing capability. The management of Ace decided that if the company were to continue to experience the success it had in the past, it would have to start systematizing its production planning procedure. The management wanted a production planning method that could facilitate the following:

1. *Capacity planning,* to quickly identify and adjust (that is, with overtime or subcontract production) any capacity restrictions or overloads in its production operation
2. *Master scheduling,* to easily prepare and transmit its plans to operating personnel before the beginning of the production planning period
3. *Production cost reduction,* so the company's prices will remain competitive

Ace's top management decided to hire a consultant to develop and install the new production planning system. After a brief review of management's information objectives and the manufacturing operation, the consultant believed that the transportation method of production planning might be appropriate. To illustrate the transportation method's usefulness to planning production, the consultant decided to model the first six months of Ace's next year's operation. The consultant obtained forecast demand information from the marketing department, cost information from the production and accounting departments, and production capacity information from the production department. From the consultant's research, the following information was obtained:

1. Regular time, overtime, and subcontract production are permitted.
2. Cost per unit of regular time production is \$14.50, cost per unit of overtime production is \$20, and cost per unit of subcontract production is \$28.
3. Beginning inventory is 2,500 units.
4. Backordering is permitted at a cost of \$0.50 per unit per month.
5. Ending inventory of 1,000 units is required.
6. The planning horizon will cover the months of January, February, March, April, May, and June.
7. The regular time production capacity is a constant 1,000 units per month.
8. The forecast demand in January is 1,500 units; in February, 2,000 units; in March, 2,500 units; in April, 1,000 units; in May, 500 units; and in June, 500 units.
9. The inventory carrying cost per unit per month is \$1.
10. Overtime production cannot exceed 10 percent of regular time production.
11. Subcontract production cannot exceed 20 percent of regular time production.
12. There is no cost for unused capacity.

CASE QUESTIONS

1. What is the transportation method formulation for this production planning problem? Prepare

the transportation table framework and enter cost, supply, and demand information.
2. What is the linear programming formulation for this production planning problem?
3. (This question requires computer software.) What is the optimal production schedule?
4. Why is the transportation method superior to graphic or worksheet methods?
5. Compared with the transportation method, what additional information would the LP model solution provide management?

CASE 5-2

THE STEVENSON MANUFACTURING COMPANY

Stevenson Manufacturing Company is located in Cincinnati, Ohio. Stevenson produces personal stereo headphone radios. The particular headphone model it manufactures has to be both durable and sensitive. The manufacture of such devices requires unique production resources: High-precision electronic equipment, cleanliness in the workplace, and above all, highly skilled workers.

Despite the levels of skilled work force required, the Stevenson Company is a nonunion operation. In the past, management-labor relations were marked by understanding and cooperation. In recent months, however, relations had become strained. Both sides had begun to talk of unionization and increased wage demands and to present numerous complaints. At the same time, the cost of production seemed to be increasing to levels that did not permit profitable operations. The company appeared to be out of control, with customer sales dropping and orders not being filled from lack of finished goods inventory. Management realized that something had to be done to save the company.

To see if a solution to these problems could be found, a management consulting firm was invited to send a team of specialists to investigate Stevenson's situation. The consulting team comprised four specialists in the areas of labor-relations, operations management, systems analysis, and organization development. After a week of intensely studying the company, the consultants' research revealed the primary reason for the crisis at Stevenson: It was directly traceable to the company's production planning and scheduling system. Basically, the company hired and laid off personnel to fit the demand requirements of their customers. During most of the company's existence, the demand had always increased. This meant that few people ever were laid off and, in fact, the company was hiring workers, offering overtime, and even subcontracting its products to other manufacturers to satisfy the demand. In recent months, however, as the consultants' research uncovered, demand was fluctuating and quite a number of the regular workers were laid off. Then in subsequent months, the demand increased and the company was forced not only to rehire the workers it had laid off but also to offer overtime and subcontract work. This monthly contradiction of repeated layoffs followed by overtime work appeared to the workers as mismanagement that occasionally cost them their wages. The dissatisfaction of the workers took many direct routes (such as complaints to management) and indirect routes (such as demands for higher wages and the threat of unionization).

The production cost problems were also related to the poor planning and scheduling system. In the months that employees were laid off, they were still paid partial wages according to company policy. This policy added to labor cost without production and increased production costs. In the months that employees were brought back to work, the overtime and subcontracting increased total production costs beyond normal cost control limits. The consultants found that the regular time (no overtime) radio production cost per unit, for a unit that would be shipped the same month, was $12. For each month the radio was held in inventory at the plant, the resulting holding cost was $1 per unit. The cost for permitting unit production by overtime averaged $1.50 per radio beyond the regular time production costs. The added cost for permitting unit production by subcontracting averaged $3.50 per radio. Just before the labor problems started, Stevenson's management was considering whether to permit backordering, but the idea was cancelled because the estimated backordering costs would have added $0.50 per unit to regular time production costs.

The team of consultants suggested that Stevenson adopt a scheduling plan that could help control the cost of production. Such a plan would solve most of the labor problems and permit production planning that would minimize total production costs, including holding costs. The scheduling plan incorporated the following guidelines:

1. Permit a beginning inventory.
2. Permit an ending inventory.
3. Require at least a four-month horizon to allow workers to know what their future employment outlook will be.
4. Reflect all available production resources (that is, regular time, overtime, and subcontracting).
5. Include estimates of all available capacities from production resources.
6. Include estimates of all demand requirements from customers.
7. Reflect appropriate regular time production costs, overtime production costs, subcontracting production costs, holding costs, and if permitted, backordering costs.

Stevenson's management agreed with the findings of the consulting team and asked them to develop the suggested production scheduling plan. To make the scheduling plan easy for management to use, the information on the next four months of actual production was suggested as a test case for the scheduling system. This test case of the production scheduling plan included the following information:

1. The available supply of unit production by month and by production resource that can be used to produce the radios during the four-month planning horizon (presented in Exhibit 5C-1).

EXHIBIT 5C-1 AVAILABLE PRODUCTION CAPACITY

Production Resource	*UNIT PRODUCTION CAPACITY BY MONTH* 1	2	3	4
Regular time	1,000	1,200	1,200	1,400
Overtime	100	120	120	140
Subcontracting	500	600	600	700

2. Beginning inventory is 300 units, the production cost of which will not be reflected in the current planning horizon.
3. Ending inventory should be 100 units.
4. Costs per unit for holding, regular time, overtime, and subcontracting that had been determined by previous research were still applicable.
5. Any unused capacity of the production resources does not cost anything.
6. The forecast unit demand in month 1 = 1,500 units, month 2 = 1,500, month 3 = 1,200, and month 4 = 1,000.
7. No backordering will be permitted on this first test case.

Because controlling costs was a major objective for Stevenson's management, a second test case situation was requested of the consultants. Management wanted the consultants to include the possibility of allowing backordering in a second test case situation. Although the rest of the information just given remained true, the possibility of reducing total production costs by allowing backordering was considered an important outcome of the consultants' research.

CASE QUESTIONS

1. What type of quantitative method can be used to determine the cost-minimizing production schedule? Why?
2. What is the structure for the first-case scheduling situation when the problem is formulated using the quantitative method selected in Question 1?

3. What is the structure for the second-case scheduling situation when the problem is formulated using the quantitative method selected in Question 1?
4. What is the cost-minimizing production schedule for the first-case situation? What is total production cost?
5. What is the cost-minimizing production schedule for the second-case situation? What is total production cost?
6. Should backordering be permitted if cost minimization is the primary determining factor?

ARTICLE 5-1

COMPETITIVE GLOBAL STRATEGIES
The Role of Information in CIM

by Joe Trino
Vice President and General Manager, MSA Advanced Manufacturing, Inc., New York, New York

Leading manufacturers are changing the way they operate along a host of fronts, from the way they make products to the way they distribute them. One element common to nearly all those successful in the "remaking" of American manufacturing is the redistribution of decision-making.

In the simplest of terms, it has meant moving decision making to the source: workers on the line make decisions about quality in production; shift foremen make decisions about production priorities; and plant managers make decisions about product mix.

INFORMATION: A COMMON THREAD

In all this, information is the common thread, and the trend is to keep short the thread between the source and the point of decision-making. This trend is being fostered in large part by the changing nature of the market. Manufacturers are beginning to appreciate the importance of being responsive to the market. To be responsive–valid, timely, accurate information is critical.

Source: Reprinted with permission from *P&IM Review with APICS News,* June 1988 issue, copyright 1988 TDA Publications.

At the same time, they are beginning to appreciate the changing nature of information in a world market being remade by Computer-Integrated Manufacturing (CIM). Three things are vital:

(1) Information is valid for shorter periods of time; (2) Old information can have devastating consequences; and (3) If you don't use information, most likely it will be used against you.

CHANGE IN "COMPUTER CULTURE"

Partly as a result of this change, as well as supporting and hastening this change, has been a major change in what we might call the corporate computing culture.

Perhaps the most significant change in computer technology has been that smaller systems are becoming more powerful at the same time they are becoming less expensive.

This has permitted moving more computing power, more function, out of the corporate computer room, closer to the source. In the most graphic sense, it has put desktop PCs within reach of the workforce. Again, at the same time more applications have been made available, or "moved" closer to the source.

As a consequence, all this has led to greater end-user sophistication. This has fueled a growing desire to "do more" with information in the system, to be more creative, more productive, and ultimately for the company, more successful, more profitable in the market.

WORLD-CLASS SOFTWARE TO SUPPORT CIM

In designing distributed processing strategies to support CIM, leading manufacturers have discovered the critical importance of "commonality" of applications between systems. A survey of *Fortune* 1000 companies reveals that what manufacturers are looking for in assessing distributed processing strategies, in moving applications out of the corporate information center into decentralized plant facilities, are systems that have a commonality of logic, look and feel, and function—whether the application is done on the micro, mini, or mainframe computer. In the most basic sense, the issue is connectivity: that one system can "talk" to another. Not only talk, but understand—precisely.

For example, both the mid-range system at the remote manufacturing plant and the mainframe system at corporate should logically treat the field in the system for "quantity on hand" in exactly the same manner. If one system meant "gross quantity on hand" and the other "net," the confusion is obvious. (To us, in understanding here the significance of the difference, it is obvious, but in an actual computing environment, it would not be obvious: and therefore, the problem.)

Another critical issue is the importance of a greater scope, or world-view, within applications. In this I mean the "globalizing" of software. Financial software must be able to handle the realities, for example, of a global manufacturer. Multi-language, multi-currency conversion, and multi-national legal reporting requirements are all critical issues the software must address.

DISTRIBUTED STRATEGIES FOR MANAGING CIM

How would distributed processing support the complete integration of a global manufacturing strategy?

In working with leading manufacturers who are designing and implementing distributed computer informations systems strategies, one thing is clear: there is no one, perfect model to follow. Each company does it a little different. In truth, this is the beauty—and the power—of distributed processing's flexibility. A manufacturer can design it to fit their unique needs, reflecting the particular production and competitive market dynamics of its environment.

With that said, however, it is still possible to delineate some broad-brush trends within the distributed processing scenario. At a very high level, we can state that planning will remain a centralized function performed on the corporate mainframe computer. Execution will become more of a decentralized function, in keeping with the idea of moving the decision-making closer to the end-user level. This will be performed and managed on the mid-range computer. Obviously, there will be some areas of overlap. But to help graphically illustrate how a distributed processing strategy might be implemented, we will construct a hypothetical manufacturing enterprise and highlight how the major planning and execution functions might be relegated in an integrated environment.

Sales forecasting, order processing, purchasing, and Material Requirements Planning (MRP), coupled with master scheduling, most likely will all be done on the corporate mainframe, along with financial reporting and cash management for the entire business enterprise.

Companies either work from a forecast or firm orders, or a combination of the two. Once you have your "game plan," as reflected by the forecast, or once you know what your firm commitments are, based on firm orders, the corporate planning function can massage requirements and capacity for the entire global distributed manufacturing enterprise and delegate which plant is going to satisfy what demand.

Because of the economy of the scale of the entire corporation, it makes sense to have purchasing a centralized function as well. Centralized purchasing can consolidate material requirements from all plants and negotiate the best price. Further, centralized purchasing can track and manage supplier performance on price, quality, and on-time shipment, and manage accounts payable most efficiently on an enterprise basis.

MRP and master scheduling is necessary at the corporate level in order to determine what is needed, and when, on a global basis to satisfy the forecast or the demand represented by firm orders. MRP and master scheduling are also required to aid in determining the most effective, efficient balance of output among all plants or facilities.

At the local plant level, MRP and master scheduling are also necessary from a planned production execution standpoint. The local plant is in the best position to know how to manage, or balance its own production to satisfy the demand delegated to it from corporate. In essence, this is what a distributed stategy is all about: moving the decision making to the level in the organization where it makes the most sense from a tactical standpoint. The local plant management can review what's currently on hand or already in production to satisfy the demand, as well as how to schedule production to meet the global enterprise commitment. In addition, the local plant needs an order management capability to report the status of goods shipped to the corporate system so that the centralized system can maintain accurate and timely information on satisfying demand.

At the local level there is also need for purchasing receipt capability as well as financial information control and reporting capability. In the context of Just-In-Time (JIT), it makes sense to have purchasing receipt capability in order that the local plant can manage local suppliers. At minimum, the local plant needs to be able to keep and report data on goods received, with regards to what was actually received, price, and quality, so that it can pass summary information to the corporate system—with a particular eye to variances.

The local plant also needs a financial information management capability in order to prepare summary reporting information to the centralized corporate general ledger system. Trial balances need to be developed at the local level before they are posted as line items in the corporate general ledger. The financial reporting capability at the local level also supports detailed audit trails on all ledger items as well.

CONCLUSION

A distributed information processing strategy directly supports the strategic goal of enabling manufacturers to be more flexible and responsive to the competitive dynamics of the market. In this, information is key and a decentralized information processing system provides the management tools needed at the level they are needed, making it possible to move decision-making closer to the source. What is critical in designing and implementing your distributed strategy is to remember to "close the loop" on the flow of all information. To be successful, the left hand always needs to know what the right hand is doing.

SUPPLEMENT 5-1
A Rough-Cut Capacity Planning Method

(This is an optional supplement for those interested in capacity planning.)

As presented in Figure 5-8, rough-cut capacity planning is a medium-range planning aid. It is used to verify that enough available capacity exists to accomplish a projected master production schedule (MPS). Rough-cut capacity planning is not as accurate (because it uses estimated values like averages) or as specifically detailed (because it focuses on capacity at the department level rather than at a specific workstation) as other capacity planning techniques such as capacity requirements planning. Rough-cut capacity planning provides aggregate information to top management far enough in advance to permit management to make changes in capacity (that is, hire more people, buy more equipment) to accomplish a given MPS.

There are several rough-cut capacity planning methods including the bill of labor approach, capacity planning using overall factors, and the resource profile approach.[20] We will limit our discussion to the more commonly used bill of labor approach of rough-cut capacity planning.[21]

The **bill of labor** is a listing by component item of the amount of work force required to produce each item. It lists the amount of time required per item that makes up a finished product, by each department in which the item is manufactured. A bill of labor can be made up for an entire product or just selected component items used in the manufacture of an entire finished product. The bill of labor approach involves combining the bill of labor with the MPS to calculate capacity of labor and production resources on a quarterly or yearly basis. To illustrate this capacity planning approach, let's look at an example.

Suppose that a furniture company manufactures wooden furniture. Its manufacturing facility has a number of departments that are used to produce the single wooden chair. Other departments—even some that work on the chair—in which capacity is not limited will not be considered in the analysis.

The **bill of materials** (a listing of the parts, materials, and inventory items that go into a single unit of a finished product) for the chair product is presented in Exhibit 5S-1. As we can see in Exhibit 5S-1, it takes four legs, two braces, one seat, and one chairback to make up a single unit of the chair product. The four legs and two braces are produced in the Woodwork Department and the seat item is assembled in the Seat Assembly Department. Let's say that the chairback and wooden blocks are acquired from a vendor. Because these items are external to the furniture manufacturing company they will not be considered in this capacity planning problem. Let's also assume that no capacity problem exists in the Chair Assembly Department and therefore it will not be a part of capacity analysis. The manufacturing company does want to prepare a rough-

[20] T. Vollmann, W. L. Berry, and D. C. Whybark, *Manufacturing Planning and Control Systems* (Homewood, Ill.: Irwin, 1988).

[21] J. H. Blackstone, *Capacity Management* (Cincinnati: South-Western Publishing Company, 1989).

EXHIBIT 5S-1 BILL OF MATERIALS FOR CHAIR PRODUCT

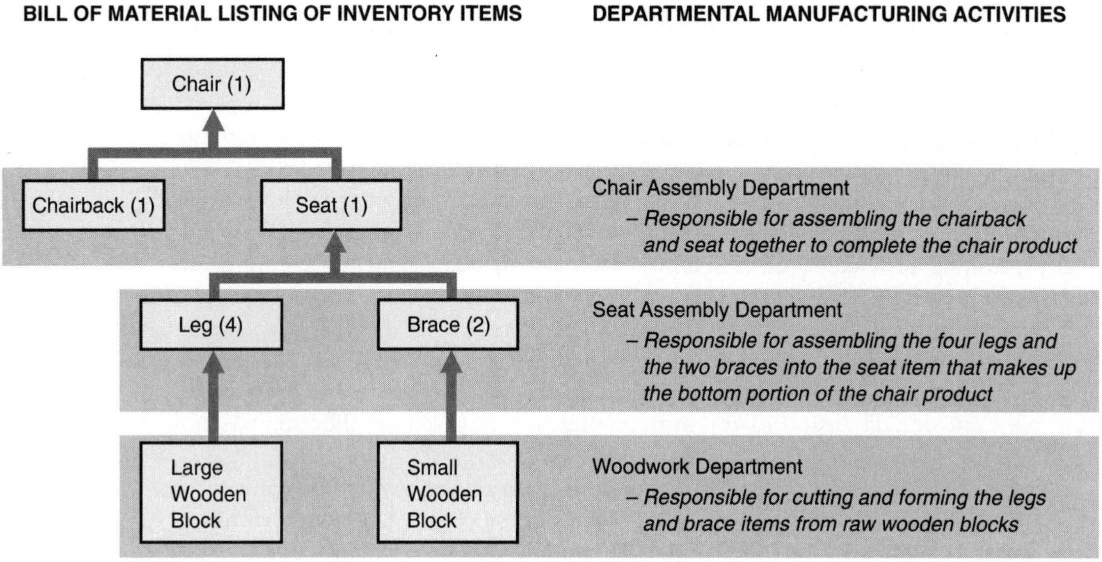

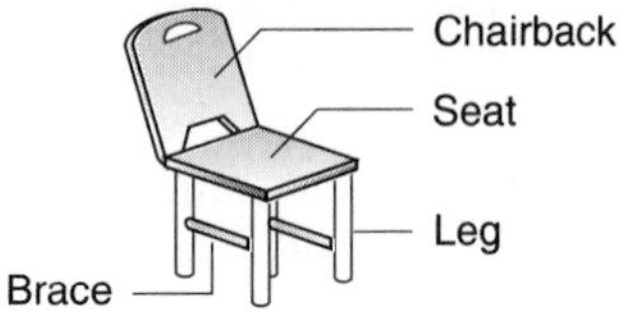

Inventory Item	Number Required Per Chair
Chairback	1
Seat	1
Leg	4
Brace	2

cut capacity plan to determine whether the available capacity in the Woodwork and Seat Assembly departments is adequate to meet the capacity requirements to complete its scheduled production of the chair product.

To begin the rough-cut analysis we need to compute available capacity in the Woodwork and Seat Assembly departments. Using the formula presented in Chapter 5, available capacity in standard time in minutes per quarter (thirteen weeks) can be found as

$$\text{Available capacity} = \text{Available time} \times \text{Utilization} \times \text{Efficiency}$$

To determine available time the number of workers in each department must be known along with the number of minutes of work per week. Let's say there are twenty-four workers in the Woodwork Department and three workers in the Seat Assembly Department. If we allow 2,400 minutes per week per worker and if there are thirteen weeks in a quarter, then there are 748,800 minutes (24 workers × 2,400 min per week

× 13 weeks per quarter) of total time available per quarter. With three workers in the Seat Assembly Department the total available time is 93,600 minutes (3 workers × 2,400 min per week × 13 weeks per quarter). To compute available capacity using this formula, information on utilization and efficiency rates needs to be determined in the manner described in Chapter 5.

Let's assume that the utilization and efficiency rates given in Exhibit 5S-2 are representative of the furniture company. Combining the available time information with given utilization and efficiency information, the available capacity per department can be calculated as presented in Exhibit 5S-2. The available capacity for the Woodwork Department is 741,162.24 standard minutes; for the Seat Assembly Department, 96,314.40 standard minutes. Management hopes that the required capacity for the manufacture of chairs scheduled for production will be less than or equal to the available capacity in each department. To determine this, we will continue with the bill of labor approach to capacity planning by preparing the bill of labor for the two departments.

To prepare the bill of labor some standard time information must be given. In Exhibit 5S-3, the standard time in minutes for each inventory item produced in the two departments is presented. As stated in Exhibit 5S-3, each inventory item leg takes 10 standard minutes to produce. When it is produced it is run in lot-sized batches of forty each, and the setup time allowed to position the equipment for the run is 150 standard minutes. This timing information is converted into an operation time per piece as a means of estimating the total time per item. The formula to compute the operation time per piece is

$$\text{Operation time per piece} = \text{Run time per piece} + \frac{\text{Setup time per lot}}{\text{Lot size}}$$

The operation times for each inventory item by department can be computed as follows:

$$\text{Operation time for legs} = 10 + 150/40 = 13.75 \text{ standard minutes}$$

$$\text{Operation time for braces} = 7 + 90/20 = 11.50 \text{ standard minutes}$$

$$\text{Operation time for seats} = 3 + 60/10 = 9.00 \text{ standard minutes}$$

Using these values we can prepare the bill of labor as presented in Exhibit 5S-4. The operation times in the bill of labor provide planners with the per item time requirements in each department. Although the bill of labor allows for all items to be produced in all departments, no seats are produced in the Woodwork Department and no legs or braces are produced in the Seat Assembly Department. These items are therefore given a zero time value.

EXHIBIT 5S-2 CALCULATION OF AVAILABLE CAPACITY

Department	*Available Time*	×	*Utilization*	×	*Efficiency*	=	*Available Capacity*
Woodwork	748,800 (std. min)		.98		1.01	=	741,162.24 (std. min)
Seat Assembly	93,600 (std. min)		.98		1.05	=	96,314.40 (std. min)

EXHIBIT 5S-3 STANDARD TIMES FOR CHAIR PRODUCT ITEMS

Department	*Item*	*Run Time per Item*	*Setup Time per Lot*	*Lot Size*
Woodwork	Leg	10 min	150 min	40 units
Woodwork	Brace	7 min	90 min	20 units
Seat Assembly	Seat	3 min	60 min	10 units

To compute the rough-cut required capacity in each of the departments we must be given the master production schedule (MPS) of each of the items. To compute the rough-cut required capacity we can use the following formula:

$$\text{Required capacity (rough-cut)} = \text{Total units per item required} \times \text{Operation time per item}$$

Although many MPSs are weekly, rough-cut capacity planning is usually on a longer-term basis of a quarter or even a year. In this example we have an MPS requirement of 10,000 chairs to be completed during the first quarter of the year. Breaking this 10,000 units of finished chair items into component items (using the bill of materials) of legs (40,000 units), braces (20,000 units), and seats (10,000 units) and multiplying the units by the appropriate operation times, we can determine the rough-cut required capacity as presented in Exhibit 5S-5. The required capacity in the Woodwork Department is 780,000 standard minutes; in the Seat Assembly Department, 90,000 standard minutes.

A graphic comparison, much like those generated in computer-based systems, of the required and available capacity (computed in Exhibit 5S-2) is presented in Exhibit 5S-6. As we can see in Exhibit 5S-6 there is a capacity shortage in the Woodwork Department and a surplus in the Seat Assembly Department. Management can use this information to acquire additional capacity in areas of shortage, shift production resources from departments with surpluses, or revise the MPS to eliminate the capacity shortages. In this way management can use rough-cut capacity planning to validate a given MPS and plan to ensure they have the necessary available capacity to meet the required capacity of a given MPS.

Once the available capacity and rough-cut required capacity are adjusted into some level of equilibrium, the MPS plan may be considered to be approved and ready for actual scheduling. Some organizations load their MPS plan into scheduling software

EXHIBIT 5S-4 BILL OF LABOR FOR CHAIR PRODUCT ITEMS

	TIME REQUIRED PER ITEM (STD. MIN)		
Department	*Leg*	*Brace*	*Seat*
Woodwork	13.75	11.50	0
Seat Assembly	0	0	9.00

EXHIBIT 5S-5 ROUGH-CUT COMPUTATION OF REQUIRED CAPACITY

Department	*Item*	*MPS Requirement (units)*	×	*Operation Times*	×	*Required Capacity*
Woodwork	Leg	40,000		13.75		550,000 (std. min)
Woodwork	Brace	20,000		11.50		230,000 (std. min)
Total Woodwork						780,000 (std. min)
Seat Assembly	Seat	10,000		9.00		90,000 (std. min)

like a material requirements planning (MRP) system (we discuss this system in Chapter 7). The output of such scheduling software provides a specific and detailed guide to actual production within each department. While some organizations do not need to break down the capacity any further (to the workstation or workcenter shop floor level),

QUESTION: How many additional workers would it take in the Woodwork Department to achieve the given MPS?

ANSWER: There are currently twenty-four workers in the Woodwork Department. If we increase the number of workers to twenty-five, with 2,400 minutes per week per worker and if there are thirteen weeks in a quarter, then there are 780,000 minutes (25 workers × 2,400 min per week × 13 weeks per quarter) of total time available per quarter. To compute the capacity we use the formula again:

$$\begin{aligned}\text{Capacity} &= \text{Available time} \times \text{Utilization} \times \text{Efficiency}\\ &= 780{,}000 \times .96 \times 1.01\\ &= 756{,}288 \text{ standard min}\end{aligned}$$

Because this is still less than the 780,000 standard minutes required, we must add additional workers. If we increase the number of workers to twenty-six, then there will be 811,200 minutes (26 workers × 2,400 min per week × 13 weeks per quarter) of total time available per quarter. To compute the capacity we use the formula again:

$$\begin{aligned}\text{Capacity} &= \text{Available time} \times \text{Utilization} \times \text{Efficiency}\\ &= 811{,}200 \times .98 \times 1.01\\ &= 802{,}925.76 \text{ standard min}\end{aligned}$$

Because 802,925.76 exceeds the required capacity of 780,000 standard minutes, we know that we need to plan to hire an additional two workers in the Woodwork Department to meet the given MPS demand on chairs.

many need to check the capacity at the shop floor. For these firms, the completion of rough-cut capacity planning means that the next phase of capacity planning can begin. As presented in Figure 5-8, the next phase of capacity planning at the workstation level can be accomplished by using capacity requirements planning (CRP). Because CRP is often associated with MRP, the CRP method is presented in Supplement 7-1.

EXHIBIT 5S-6 GRAPHIC COMPARISON OF REQUIRED AND AVAILABLE CAPACITY

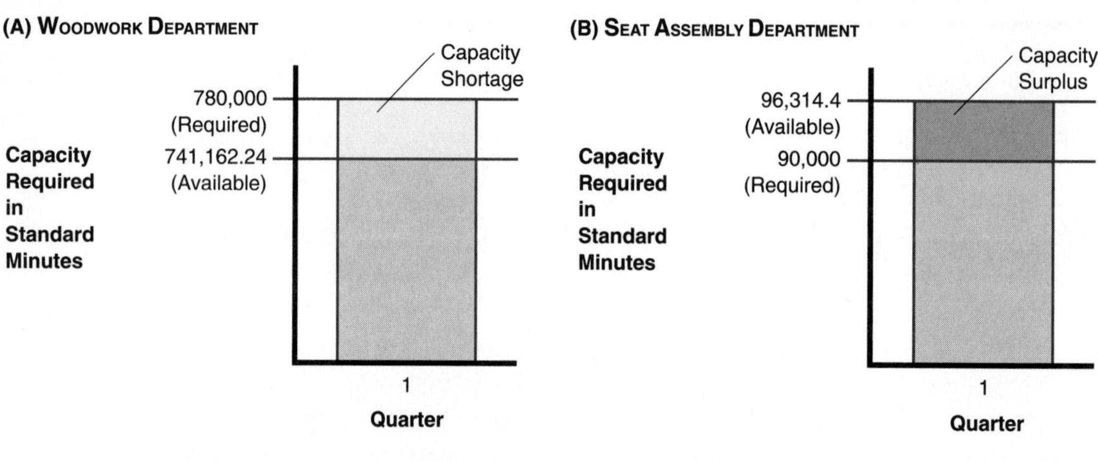

SUPPLEMENT 5-2
Linear Programming and Production Planning

Linear programming (LP) is a general-purpose modeling technique. It provides operations managers with a modeling system that can incorporate as many or as few of the aggregate planning variables as desired. LP can also be used for master scheduling. (Students are encouraged to review the formulation procedure of linear programming in Appendix D at the end of this book. Although we will be using Micro Production software to obtain our answers, students who are interested in the mechanics of the LP solution procedure should also review Appendix E at the end of this book.)

To illustrate the use of LP in production planning, let us formulate an LP model for a production planning situation. Suppose that a manufacturer operates two manufacturing plants: Plant 1 and Plant 2. Both plants produce the same three products: Product A, Product B, and Product C. Assume that the plants are limited to regular time production (no overtime or subcontracting is allowed). A normal day's production rates of Plant 1 are such that it can produce 100 units of Product A, 80 units of Product B, and 50 units of Product C. A normal day's production rates of Plant 2 are 200 units of Product A, 60 units of Product B, and 60 units of Product C. Because of existing customer orders, the plants must produce a given minimum number of units each month during the next year. Both plants combined must produce 7,000 units or more of Product A, 3,000 units or more of Product B, and 2,500 units or more of Product C. The daily cost is \$5,000 to operate Plant 1 and \$7,000 for Plant 2. What is the optimal number of days to operate these two plants to meet product demand and minimize operation costs?

The LP formulation for this problem is as follows:

$$\text{Minimize } Z = 5{,}000x_1 + 7{,}000x_2$$

$$\begin{aligned} \text{subject to: } 100x_1 + 200x_2 &\geq 7{,}000 \text{ (Product A demand)} \\ 80x_1 + 60x_2 &\geq 3{,}000 \text{ (Product B demand)} \\ 50x_1 + 60x_2 &\geq 2{,}500 \text{ (Product C demand)} \\ x_1, x_2 &\geq 0 \end{aligned}$$

where

x_1 is the number of days Plant 1 should be operated per month
x_2 is the number of days Plant 2 should be operated per month
Z is total costs

We obtained the solution to this LP problem using the Micro Production software system. (Instructions on how to use the Micro Production software system are presented in Appendix H at the end of this book.) The LP solution is presented in Exhibit 5S-7. The optimal LP problem solution is $x_1 = 20$ days and $x_2 = 25$ days. By substituting these solution values for the decision variables into each of the three constraints, we obtain production of 7,000 [(100 × 20) + (200 × 25)] units of Product A, 3,100 [(80 × 20) + (60 × 25)] units of Product B, and 2,500 [(50 × 20) + (60 × 25)] units of Product C. So, to optimize our daily production, Products A and C will be produced at their minimum demand levels and Product B will be produced at a daily rate 100 units greater than its minimum demand level. This type of daily, detailed information could be used in a master schedule of production for this organization.

EXHIBIT 5S-7 MICRO PRODUCTION SOFTWARE SOLUTION OUTPUT OF PRODUCTION PLANNING PROBLEM

```
Program: Linear Programming

Problem Title : Aggregate Planning - LP Formulation

***** Input Data *****

Min Z = 5000X1 + 7000X2

Subject to

C1  100X1 + 200X2 >= 7000
C2  80X1 + 60X2 >= 3000
C3  50X1 + 60X2 >= 2500

***** Program Output *****

Final Optimal Solution

Z = 275000.000

------------------------------------------
Variable              Value    Reduced Cost
------------------------------------------
 X 1                 20.000           0.000
 X 2                 25.000           0.000
------------------------------------------

------------------------------------------
Constraint  Stack/Surplus      Shadow Price
------------------------------------------
 C 1                  0.000         -12.500
 C 2                100.000           0.000
 C 3                  0.000         -75.000
------------------------------------------

***** End of Output *****
```

The major drawbacks of linear programming for production planning are centered around the model size and parameter accuracy. LP models can become very large and tediously complex when the decision variables are defined in multiple dimensions. For

QUESTION: Suppose that we have a similar production planning problem as just expressed in the LP model. The only difference is that minimum demand fluctuates monthly and, because of inventory restrictions, the total production of Product A for both months cannot exceed 16,000 units. The minimum demand for the next two months is as follows:

	MINIMUM DEMAND PER MONTH	
Product	*1*	*2*
A	7,000	8,700
B	3,000	4,500
C	2,500	3,700

Formulate an LP model to determine the number of days the plants should remain open during these two months.

ANSWER: For this problem we need to add additional decision variables to the model to reflect the time aspect of the problem. The LP model formulation for this production planning situation is as follows:

$$\text{Maximize } Z = 2{,}500x_1 + 3{,}500x_2 + 2{,}500x_3 + 3{,}500x_4$$

subject to:

$$100x_1 + 200x_2 \geq 7{,}000 \text{ (Product A demand in Month 1)}$$
$$80x_1 + 60x_2 \geq 3{,}000 \text{ (Product B demand in Month 1)}$$
$$50x_1 + 60x_2 \geq 2{,}500 \text{ (Product C demand in Month 1)}$$
$$100x_3 + 200x_4 \geq 8{,}700 \text{ (Product A demand in Month 2)}$$
$$80x_3 + 60x_4 \geq 4{,}500 \text{ (Product B demand in Month 2)}$$
$$50x_3 + 60x_4 \geq 3{,}700 \text{ (Product C demand in Month 2)}$$
$$100x_1 + 200x_2 + 100x_3 + 200x_4 \leq 16{,}000 \text{ (Maximum product of Product A)}$$
$$x_1, x_2, x_3, x_4 \geq 0$$

where

x_1 is the number of days Plant 1 should be operated in Month 1
x_2 is the number of days Plant 2 should be operated in Month 1
x_3 is the number of days Plant 1 should be operated in Month 2
x_4 is the number of days Plant 2 should be operated in Month 2
Z is total costs

example, a simple decision variable can be defined in terms of resources (that is, work force hours). We can also define it in terms of two dimensions: work force and time (number of work force hours in each time period). This multidimensional aspect of LP production planning models notably increases the size of the model (both in decision variables and constraints), the formulation effort, and computational time. The static parameter requirement (parameters used in the model must be assumed as constant) of LP is also unrealistic in actual production planning because parameters frequently change over time. In addition, the linearity requirement of the model may also be unrealistic because many production functions are nonlinear. For example, a worker's productivity is usually nonlinear over time because of such factors as physical exhaustion in the short term and morale or learning experience in the long term. Despite the disadvantages of LP, the current research and applications continue to demonstrate its use for production planning. The advances in microcomputer technology now permit the largest of problems to be efficiently and inexpensively solved. Even complex nonlinear cost structures common in production planning can easily be dealt with using existing microcomputer technology.

SUPPLEMENT 5-3
The Transportation Method and Production Planning

Operations managers may find that understanding how to formulate the transportation problem as a production planning aid is useful. The general framework of the aggregate planning problem formulated as a transportation problem is presented in Exhibit 5S-8. The basic transportation problem allocates supply to meet demand. The supply in production planning is the available production capacity in units for each time period (usually a month). The demand is the forecast unit of customer demand. The framework of a production planning problem allocates the rows as sources of supply (available production capacity) and the columns as demand destination (forecast demand). In using this method, our objective is to minimize total production costs, inventory costs, and if permitted, backordering costs. The model permits unused capacity (or the excess capacity left over after forecast demand is fully satisfied) to be assigned a cost. For the purpose of simplicity, we will always assume that there is no cost for unused capacity, although in real-world situations there often is a cost. The model also permits beginning inventory and ending inventory levels to be established. Consistent with the usual transportation problem, the intersection of the rows and columns represent cost cells. The cost cells can contain any one or all of the three costs (production, inventory, or backordering) that the production planning problem seeks to minimize.

To illustrate how the transportation method can be used for production planning, let's examine a sample problem. Suppose we wanted to determine the minimized cost of the next three months of operation for a small company. The company's operations are described in the list at the top of page 232.

EXHIBIT 5S-8 GENERAL FRAMEWORK OF THE PRODUCTION PLANNING PROBLEM FORMULATED USING THE TRANSPORTATION METHOD

	FORECAST DEMAND TIME PERIODS 1 2 3 . . . n	Ending Inventory	Unused Capacity	Available Capacity
Beginning Inventory	Inventory Carrying Costs per Unit		Unused Capacity Costs per Unit	Beginning Inventory in Units
Production Capacity Time Periods 1 2 3 . . . n	Production Costs, Inventory Carrying Costs, and Backorder Costs per Unit			Product Supply in Units
	Total Forecast Demands in Units	Total Ending Inventory in Units	Total Unused Capacity in Units	Total Available Capacity in Units

1. The production schedule allows both regular time and overtime.
2. The cost per unit of regular time production is $5 and the cost per unit of overtime production is $7.50.
3. Beginning inventory is 30 units.
4. Backordering is permitted at a cost of $1 per unit per month.
5. Ending inventory of 50 units is required.
6. The planning horizon will cover the months of January, February, and March.
7. The regular time production capacity in January is 150 units; in February, 150 units; and in March, 550 units.
8. The forecast demand in January is 200 units; in February, 300 units; and in March, 220 units.
9. The inventory carrying cost per unit per month is $2.
10. Overtime production can equal only 10 percent of regular time production.
11. There is no cost for unused capacity.

The formulation of this problem using the transportation method is presented in Exhibit 5S-9. The formulation was done using the following steps:

1. *Determine available capacity.* In this sample problem, we need to calculate the overtime, which is 10 percent of the regular time production, and sum the values to determine total available capacity. The other values, including beginning inventory, were given.
2. *Determine unused capacity.* This value is found by adding the forecast demand values together with ending inventory and subtracting the sum from total available capacity found in step 1.
3. *Determine cost values for all cells.*
   a. The beginning inventory first row value is usually assigned a zero cost unless there is a carrying cost from another planning period. Each subsequent cell in the row is found by adding the inventory carrying cost collectively across the row. In our sample problem, this reflects the fact that if a unit is carried in inventory from January to February, that unit will cost the organization $2 more because of the inventory carrying costs to store it. (We have denoted carrying cost with a C in each cell.)
   b. The regular time and overtime production units used in the same month they are produced will only incur the production costs. (We have denoted the production cost with a P in each cell.) In our example, January's regular time capacity used to satisfy demand in January will cost $5 per unit. Likewise, overtime capacity in February used for demand in the same month will cost only $7.50 per unit. These cost values (that is, all of the $5 and $7.50 cells) represent just the production costs of the units in the model.
   c. The inventory carrying costs are added to the production costs on a monthly basis. These are the cost cells to the right of each of the production cost cells. (We have denoted these cells as P + C costs.) In Exhibit 5S-9, we

EXHIBIT 5S-9 TRANSPORTATION METHOD FORMULATION FOR SAMPLE PROBLEM

		FORECAST DEMAND TIME PERIODS			Ending Inventory	Unused Capacity	Available Capacity
		Jan.	Feb.	Mar.			
Beginning Inventory		0	2 C	4 C	6 C	0	30
JAN. Capacity	Regular time	5 P	7 P + C	9 P + C	11 P + C	0	150
	Overtime	7.5 P	9.5 P + C	11.5 P + C	13.5 P + C	0	15
FEB. Capacity	Regular time	6 P + B	5 P	7 P + C	9 P + C	0	150
	Overtime	8.5 P + B	7.5 P	9.5 P + C	11.5 P + C	0	15
MAR. Capacity	Regular time	7 P + B	6 P + B	5 P	7 P + C	0	550
	Overtime	9.5 P + B	8.5 P + B	7.5 P	9.5 P + C	0	55
Total		200	300	200	50	215	965

can see that if we use January's regular time capacity to produce a unit and intend to keep it in inventory until February it will cost \$7 (that is, \$5 for production and \$2 for one month's inventory carrying costs).

d. The backordering costs are also added to the production costs on a monthly basis. These are the cost cells to the left of each of the P production cost cells. (We have denoted these cells as P + B costs.) In Exhibit 5S-9 we can see that if we use February's regular time capacity to produce a unit that was ordered in January, it will cost \$6 (that is, \$5 for production and \$1 for one month's backordering costs).

Having formulated the aggregate planning problem as a transportation problem, we are now ready to solve it using the transportation method solution procedures. A variety of transportation problem solution methods are available. One of the more common computer-based methods is called the **modified distribution method (MODI),** which is an algebraic process of allocating the supply and demand requirements based on an index calculated from the cost values in each cell of the transportation problem. Fortunately, this rather tedious process can be avoided by using computer software. (Students interested in understanding the transportation method solution procedure should review Appendix I.)[22]

[22] For additional information about the MODI method and other transportation method solution procedures see S. M. Lee, L. J. Moore, and B. W. Taylor, *Management Science,* 4th ed. (Boston: Allyn & Bacon, 1993), Chapter 5.

The objective of our transportation problem is to allocate the beginning inventory and available capacity in each row of the transportation table in Exhibit 5S-9 to satisfy the forecast demand, ending inventory, and unused capacity in each column to the least-cost cells. When we arrive at a solution, the allocation of units of production in each row and each column should add up to the supply and demand requirements in those rows and columns. Whatever available capacity that is left over is placed in the unused capacity column. If there is a capacity shortage, some of the demand requirements will not be satisfied. Capacity shortages, once identified, are usually satisfied by procuring additional capacity and repeating the transportation problem formulation and solution.

The allocation of the units of beginning inventory and available capacity to forecast demand, ending inventory, and unusual capacity is presented in Exhibit 5S-10. The new values in each cell of Exhibit 5S-10 represent the allocation of units (that is, the solution values) in each row and each column. These values were obtained using the Micro Production software whose printout is presented in Exhibit 5S-11. (Instructions for using the Micro Production software system are presented in Appendix H. Notice that the upper table in Exhibit 5S-11 represents the cost, supply, and demand requirements of the problem from Exhibit 5S-10, and the lower table in Exhibit 5S-11 represents the allocation of units from Exhibit 5S-10). The rows and columns of the transportation problem are converted in the computer output to numbers (for example, beginning inventory row is 1; January regular time production is row 2). Because the column for unused capacity has all zero values as costs, the software did not require them as input, but automatically output them in the solution to make the problem's supply and demand requirements balance.

EXHIBIT 5S-10 TRANSPORTATION METHOD SOLUTION FOR SAMPLE PROBLEM

		FORECAST DEMAND TIME PERIODS			Ending Inventory	Unused Capacity	Available Capacity
		Jan.	Feb.	Mar.			
Beginning Inventory		[0] 30	[2]	[4]	[6]	[0]	30
JAN. Capacity	Regular time	[5] 150	[7]	[9]	[11]	[0]	150
	Overtime	[7.5]	[9.5]	[11.5]	[13.5]	[0] 15	15
FEB. Capacity	Regular time	[6]	[5] 150	[7]	[9]	[0]	150
	Overtime	[8.5]	[7.5]	[9.5]	[11.5]	[0] 15	15
MAR. Capacity	Regular time	[7] 20	[6] 150	[5] 200	[7] 50	[0] 130	550
	Overtime	[9.5]	[8.5]	[7.5]	[9.5]	[0] 55	55
Total		200	300	200	50	215	965

EXHIBIT 5S-11 MICRO PRODUCTION SOFTWARE SOLUTION OUTPUT OF SAMPLE PRODUCTION PROBLEM

Program: Transportation

Problem Title : Sample Problem - Transportation Method

***** Input Data *****

Minimization Problem :

	1	2	3	4	Supply
1	0.0	2.0	4.0	6.0	30.0
2	5.0	7.0	9.0	11.0	150.0
3	7.50	9.50	11.50	13.50	15.0
4	6.0	5.0	7.0	9.0	150.0
5	8.50	7.50	9.50	11.50	15.0
6	7.0	6.0	5.0	7.0	550.0
7	9.50	8.50	7.50	9.50	55.0
Demand	200.0	300.0	200.0	50.0	965.0

***** Program Output *****

Optimal Solution by MODI

	1	2	3	4	5	Supply
1	30.0	0.0	0.0	0.0	0.0	30.0
2	150.0	0.0	0.0	0.0	0.0	150.0
3	0.0	0.0	0.0	0.0	15.0	15.0
4	0.0	150.0	0.0	0.0	0.0	150.0
5	0.0	0.0	0.0	0.0	15.0	15.0
6	20.0	150.0	200.0	50.0	130.00	550.0
7	0.0	0.0	0.0	0.0	55.00	55.0
Demand	200.0	300.0	200.0	50.0	215.0	965.0

Optimal Solution : 3890.0
<Multiple optimal solutions>

***** End of Output *****

The interpretation of the solution in a tabular form, with cost information, is presented in Exhibit 5S-12. As we can see in Exhibit 5S-12, the transportation method solution provides very specific production planning information. The schedule presented in Exhibit 5S-12 details the unit production assignments per month. This type of information can be used to prepare a master schedule. The output also defines when backordering must take place and where excess capacity (unused capacity) exists. This type of information is useful in capacity planning by allowing managers to identify specific surpluses of capacity in a future planning horizon. By making changes in policies (such as not permitting backordering) and reworking the same transportation problem, the transportation method also provides cost information that can be used to compare alternative production planning policies. We can see in Exhibit 5S-12 that the total cost-minimizing solution for the current sample problem is $3,890. By reworking the same problem, but not permitting backordering, we might be able to use overtime, which would change the production allocation schedule (the solution) and maybe its cost.

The transportation method, like LP, is dependent on the accuracy of the parameters used in the model. It is also limited to an analysis of only a few aggregate planning factors (that is, unit production, backordering, and inventory). When other factors or aggregate planning variables must be added, another method must be used.

EXHIBIT 5S-12 EXPLANATION OF THE COMPUTER PRINTOUT FOR THE TRANSPORTATION METHOD SOLUTION OF THE SAMPLE PROBLEM

From Capacity Time Period	*To Demand Time Period*	*Type of Labor*	*Backordered from Time Period*	*Unused Capacity*	*Number of Units*	*Cost per Unit*	*Total Cost*
Beginning Inventory	1				30	0	$ 0
1	1	Regular			150	5	750
1	1	Overtime		15		0	0
2	2	Regular			150	5	750
2	2	Overtime		15		0	0
3	1	Regular	1		20	7	140
3	2	Regular	2		150	6	900
3	3	Regular			200	5	1,000
3	Ending Inventory	Regular			50	7	350
3	3	Regular		130		0	0
3	3	Overtime		55		0	0
				215	750		$3,890

6

Materials Management

CHAPTER OUTLINE

CHAPTER OBJECTIVES

The material in this chapter should prepare you to do the following:

1. Define the purpose of materials management in an operations management system.
2. Understand how the materials flow process functions in an organization.
3. Explain the function of production control in materials management.
4. Explain the function of inventory control in materials management.
5. Explain the function of materials handling in materials management.
6. Understand what an automatic storage and automatic retrieval system does.
7. Explain how a just-in-time purchasing system works.
8. Explain how a kanban system is used in a materials flow system.
9. Explain the differences between the traditional and state-of-the-art warehousing systems.
10. Illustrate how the transportation method can be used to minimize shipping department costs.

The U.S. Bureau of the Census has consistently reported that the cost of materials used in the manufacture of goods exceeds 50 percent of the total value of the goods produced.[1] Such an enormous investment requires a special type of management, referred to as materials management. **Materials management** is defined as "the grouping of management functions supporting the complete cycle of material flow, from the purchase and internal control of production materials to the planning and control of work-in-process to the warehousing, shipping and distribution of finished product."[2] Materials management is a broad term that encompasses much of the operations management function (inputs, transformation process, outputs, and so on). It involves the entire flow of materials in and out of the organization. In some organizations the materials manager may have the title of vice president; in other organizations the role of materials manager may be decentralized to departmental specialists, such as a purchasing or inventory manager performing materials management functions. Regardless of who is responsible for materials management, the objectives are to provide an adequate supply of materials for use in and out of the organization in the most efficient and effective manner.

In many organizations, efficiency and effectiveness of materials management are measured on a basis of cost minimization. These objectives are often difficult to achieve because they conflict. For example, should a purchasing manager acquire a large number of component parts even though the inventory costs of storing the parts may be greater than the price discount that motivated the purchase? Should an inventory manager maintain a large raw materials inventory to prevent a materials shortage in production if the cost of storing the inventory may be greater than the cost of a shortage in production? Such questions cannot be easily answered without understanding how materials flow affects the cost, efficiency, and effectiveness of the whole organization in meeting goals. Specifically, efficiency in the form of reduced costs in one department may decrease efficiency in another department. When a purchasing manager acquires a large supply of parts at a significantly reduced price, the inventory manager may have to increase parts storage capacity and therefore the cost of storage capacity to accommodate the additional parts. Materials management has evolved to deal with such conflicting departmental objectives by integrating the departments into a single system that controls all of the materials flow in an organization.

Materials management can be divided into three overlapping functions: production control, inventory control, and materials handling. **Production control** is the function of directing or regulating the movement of goods through the entire manufacturing cycle from purchasing through finished product. **Inventory control** is the function of maintaining a stock of raw materials, work-in-process, or finished products at desired levels. **Materials handling** is concerned with the management of the resources used to move physical goods into, through, and out of the organization. It is a broad term sometimes narrowly referred to as traffic, distribution, or logistic functions.

---

[1] *Statistical Abstract of the United States,* 111th ed. (Washington, D.C.: U.S. Department of Commerce, 1991), p. 739.

[2] Reprinted with permission of the American Production and Inventory Control Society, Inc., *APICS Dictionary,* 7th edition, 1992.

The relationship of the three functions of materials management is best understood by tracing the flow of materials through an organization—beginning with a supplier and ending with the delivery of the finished product to a customer. In Figure 6-1 we present the materials flow process. The **materials flow process** is a stepwise process (that is, each step is usually represented as a department in the organization) through which materials must flow to be transformed and delivered to the customer. Later in the chapter we discuss the purpose and activities of each of these departments as they relate to the three functions of materials management,

The materials flow process presented in Figure 6-1 is typical of manufacturing organizations. Although materials management is concerned with physical materials, it can also apply to some service industry organizations. Many service organizations, such as airlines and automotive repair shops, must maintain adequate parts and supply inventories. Indeed, all retailing service operations require materials managers. The three materials management functions presented in Figure 6-1 are applicable to various types of service industry situations as well as to manufacturing. S

• • •

WHY MATERIALS MANAGEMENT IS NECESSARY

Not all organizations have a materials manager, but all organizations need to manage their materials. If a service organization such as a hospital runs out of a single item like syringes, most of its operations could conceivably come to a standstill. Not only would nurses be unable to give patients routine injections of medicine, but doctors might not be able to perform surgery because preoperation procedures cannot be performed without syringes. Of course, a hospital could contact a vendor and place a rush order for syringes. But how much more expensive would this rush order for syringes be compared with a planned order the price of which a purchasing manager would have the time to negotiate? S

If an organization's materials are correctly managed, there will be no shortages and the materials will be obtained at the right time and place, and will be of the quality and quantity necessary to meet prescribed production or service objectives. Without some type of materials management, however, the organization will most likely experience costly shortages or surpluses of materials. By carefully coordinating the flow of materials, the organization can reduce shortages or excessive materials as well as their costly consequences. A materials manager not only coordinates the flow of materials but also manages the flow to avoid the cost of inefficiencies and save resources within the organization. For example, acquiring a conveyance system to move parts to the assembly operation may save assembly line workers' replenishment time (the time it takes to obtain items from inventory), time that can be used to increase production.

Another reason why materials management is necessary for operations management involves its role in helping integrate management resources. A smooth flow of materials

FIGURE 6-1 THE MATERIALS FLOW PROCESS

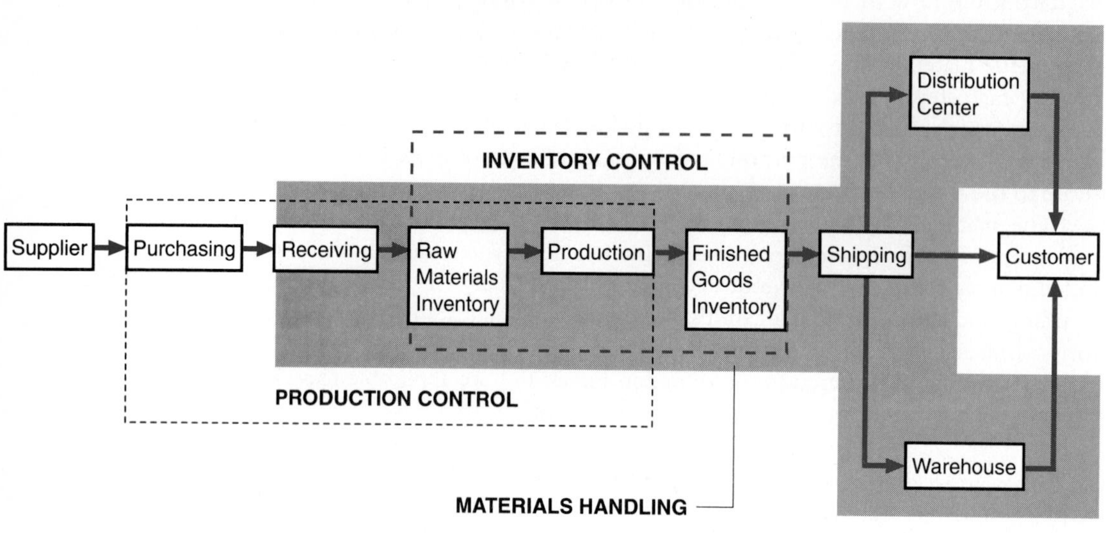

into and out of an organization improves productivity by avoiding the wasted human resource time caused by material delays. A smooth flow of materials also helps avoid wasted costs of capital tied up in idle inventory and speeds the delivery of product or service to customers, thereby improving customer service. These improvements in operation can result in a possible competitive advantage to help the organization achieve its strategic goals. It takes more than the coordination of materials to permit a smooth flow. It also takes the management of human, technology, and system resources to receive and process the materials efficiently and effectively.

Another reason why materials management is necessary concerns its support of organization and operations management strategic goals. If an organization has an OM strategy of expanding its production facilities to support a strategic goal of growth, tactical changes to the materials management system to handle the growth in materials flow will be a critical part of the OM goal-achievement process. Because materials management involves the flow of materials, it will affect the implementation of many OM tactics as well as goals. It is well documented that the successful tactical implementation of just-in-time (JIT) inventory systems (we introduce JIT later in this chapter) and time-based competition (where the major competitive advantage is the speed of response time from a customer's placement of an order to a customer's receipt of a product or service) are dependent on materials management.[3]

[3] E. H. Frazelle, "Materials Handling Systems Support Materials Management Strategies in the 90s," *APICS—The Performance Advantage,* 2, No. 3 (March 1992), 20–23.

QUESTION: How can organizations really use materials management to achieve operations management strategic goals such as improved flexibility and improved service quality?

Q

ANSWER: Materials management provides a supportive but critical role in OM strategic goal achievement, as illustrated at the Quaker Furniture Company of Hickory, North Carolina, a manufacturer of office furniture.[4] Quaker management decided in late 1990 to implement a **synchronous manufacturing system** (synchronizing manufacturing activity directly to customer demand requirements) as a tactical approach to being more customer responsive. Synchronous manufacturing systems are driven by customer orders and therefore are customer focused (a principle of total quality management discussed in Chapter 2). To support a new manufacturing layout, materials handling systems were revised at Quaker to be activated by customer orders. This helped Quaker management identify idle inventory on its shop floors and cut costs by eliminating it. By cutting lot sizes to exact customer demand requirements, materials handling systems had to be modified to avoid waste in handling a reduced amount of inventory. The reduction had the effect of freeing up materials handling capacity, which, in turn, permitted more flexibility in delivery amounts and more frequent deliveries to workcenters on the shop floors. The total impact of these changes in a little more than one year were a cut in work-in-process (WIP) of 39 percent and an improvement in delivery performance to its customers of 25 percent. Quaker was also able to improve its flexibility in meeting customers' orders by increasing its furniture model options to customers, while at the same time reducing its labor force by 16 percent. In summary, the move to a synchronous layout, supported by the necessary and critical changes in materials management systems, allowed Quaker to improve the flexibility and quality of its customer service delivery.

By integrating and coordinating the flow of materials in an organization, a materials manager can help the organization achieve its production objectives efficiently and effectively. To better understand the role of the materials manager, let's look at the production control function of materials management.

PRODUCTION CONTROL

In Figure 6-2 we show that the function of production control consists of purchasing, receiving, raw materials inventory, and production (that is, the transformation process). In many organizations these four areas are departmentalized and each is assigned a manager who in turn works for a general manager. Production control is limited to

[4] E. F. Libby, "Quaker Furniture Manages Materials Using Synchronous Manufacturing," *APICS—The Performance Advantage,* 2, No. 3 (March 1992), 24–26.

FIGURE 6-2 THE PRODUCTION CONTROL FUNCTION OF MATERIALS MANAGEMENT

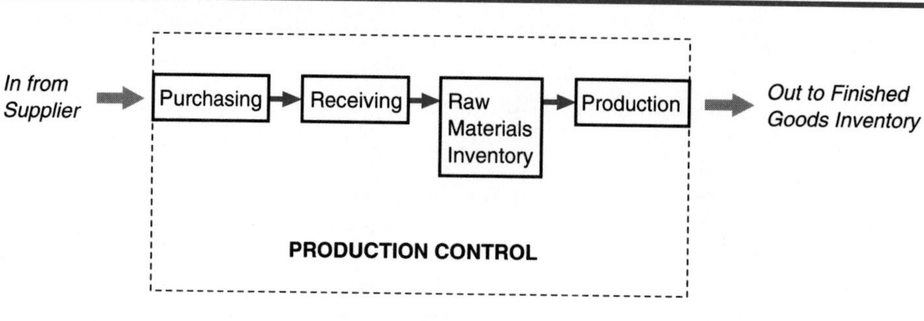

materials flow aspects. The materials management function of production control is not concerned with how or when products are manufactured. It is concerned with ensuring that an adequate supply of materials is available for production and that the supply is obtained in the most efficient and effective manner possible. Let's examine each of the four departments that usually comprise the production control function of materials management.

Purchasing

The main task of a purchasing department is to acquire the raw materials and to handle inventory and supplies that the organization needs in the time, quantity, and quality desired at the least possible cost. Some organizations do not have a formal purchasing department, but instead let individual department heads purchase their respective materials and supplies—a decentralized strategy. This can sometimes be a successful strategy when purchasing quantities are small and timeliness of supplies is critical. Many small service organizations adopt this type of strategy because of the crucial nature of a materials shortage to their operation. As an organization grows and its needs for materials and supplies increase, a centralized purchasing department may be more effective in reducing the cost of goods. With centralized purchasing, an organization can more readily obtain purchase discounts through acquiring materials in large quantities by grouping orders from many departments and thus significantly reduce the cost of goods for the entire organization. The U.S. General Services Organization (GSO) is the largest purchasing agent in the United States. This department within the U.S. government acquires most of the supplies and materials used by U.S. federal government agencies.

The tasks a purchasing department performs for an organization can include the following:

1. Processing requisitions for materials and supplies from other departments in the organization
2. Locating suppliers or vendors to obtain necessary materials and supplies

3. Negotiating purchasing contracts and quantity discounts
4. Conducting bidding procedures to acquire certain inventory items
5. Evaluating supplies and vendors in terms of their promised price, quality, and punctuality

These tasks can be assigned to a single purchasing manager or, in larger purchasing departments, distributed to various specialists. A purchasing specialist typically is called a **buyer.** Some buyers are so specialized that they purchase only a particular type of material. Many organizations also hire outside specialists, such as contract consultants or contract lawyers, to negotiate purchasing terms. A purchasing department, which performs a staff function (i.e., a management support function) in the organization, usually has a relatively small number of employees, rarely representing more than one-half of one percent of an organization's total work force.[5] The increasing importance of this function in business, however, has helped make purchasing a career opportunity for many in operations management. Indeed, the National Association of Purchasing Managers (NAPM) currently offers certification to people interested in pursuing a career in purchasing management.

Receiving

One function that is closely related to purchasing is receiving. **Receiving** is responsible for processing incoming shipments of materials and supplies. In many organizations, receiving is included in the purchasing function because of the information it provides purchasing management. In other organizations, receiving is a separate department with a separate manager or supervisor. The tasks a receiving department performs for an organization can include the following:

1. Unpacking incoming orders of supplies and materials
2. Physically inspecting quantity and quality of incoming orders of supplies and materials to ensure that they are consistent with what was ordered
3. Breaking down incoming orders of supplies and materials for use in inventory or production
4. Preparing receiving reports

A receiving report contains quantity, price, and descriptive information on incoming items. This type of information is necessary for the accounting department to arrange payments, for the inventory department to arrange storage space, and for the production department to prepare to use the item in the transformation process. Receiving reports also provide the receiving clerk with an opportunity to comment on the item's arrival condition and other delivery information that the purchasing department needs to evaluate the vendors on their promised service performance.

---

[5] T. E. Hendrick and F. G. Moore, *Production/Operations Management,* 9th ed. (Homewood, Ill.: Irwin, 1985), p. 337.

Raw Materials Inventory

Raw materials inventory represents the input materials that will be transformed or manufactured into finished products. In the manufacture of steel, for example, raw materials inventory might include coal, which is used to power furnaces to produce the steel. The raw materials inventory function involves storing inventory items for later use in the transformation process.

Many organizations do not distinguish raw materials inventory from finished goods inventory when both require the same type of storage space. If an organization's raw materials storage is drastically different from its finished goods inventory storage, then separate inventory departments might be needed. For example, yard goods (cloth rolled by the yard) are a very different type of inventory than the clothing (the finished goods) that the yard goods are made into. Each requires a different type of inventory management system. In organizations in which raw materials inventory and finished goods inventory are separated into two departments, the raw materials inventory department's tasks can include the following:

1. Repackaging and labeling incoming stock for use in production
2. Storing and protecting raw materials from pilferage and damage
3. Auditing existing raw materials inventory
4. Locating and retrieving raw materials from stock
5. Replenishing stock

The inventory of raw materials can represent the single greatest investment of resources in an organization. As such, it represents the greatest opportunity to reduce costs. Many U.S. organizations use computer systems, such as a materials requirement planning (MRP) system, to manage their raw materials. We discuss how MRP is used in inventory management in Chapter 7.

Production

The materials management function referred to as **production** is used here in a general sense to describe the transformation process in all types of manufacturing organizations. In materials management we are concerned with the availability of materials and supplies required during the transformation process. As work-in-process is transformed into a finished product, necessary supplies and materials are needed at the right time and place, and in the right quantity, to complete the product. The materials management tasks the production department performs for an organization can include the following:

1. Monitoring the flow of raw materials (work-in-process) through the transformation process
2. Determining and adjusting inventory storage capacity restrictions at workstations that restrict a smooth flow of work
3. Identifying materials flow bottlenecks that delay production operations

In some organizations the production function of materials management might include the entire system from purchasing to shipping. In other organizations the production function of materials management may just be limited to the transformation process.

Collectively, these four materials management functions of purchasing, receiving, raw materials inventory, and production describe how some organizations acquire, receive, store, and conduct the flow of materials into finished products. In the production control segment of the materials management flow presented in Figure 6-1, the critical location of the production function defines the objectives for all four departments. The production control function is primarily concerned with the materials management objective of providing a sufficient supply of materials for production purposes. As mentioned earlier, the availability of materials must be balanced with the costliness of providing those materials. Inventory control is primarily concerned with cost minimization.

INVENTORY CONTROL

The tasks of an inventory control manager in raw materials inventory and production departments are basically the same as those in production control. The primary objective, however, shifts from supply to cost minimization. Specifically, the primary objective of inventory control is to minimize the cost of the materials inventory. The inventory control function of materials management is presented in Figure 6-3 as consisting of three departments: raw materials inventory, production, and finished goods inventory.

The overlapping departments of raw materials inventory and production with the production control function (see Figure 6-1) can cause conflicts with the inventory control function. Miminizing the cost of inventory chiefly requires reducing its size, and possibly its availability, in all of the departments under inventory control's jurisdiction. While reduction efforts of finished goods inventory tend not to overlap with the production control function, reductions in raw materials inventory can. Materials management positions are created to resolve this type of conflict. In organizations in which

FIGURE 6-3 THE INVENTORY CONTROL FUNCTION OF MATERIALS MANAGEMENT

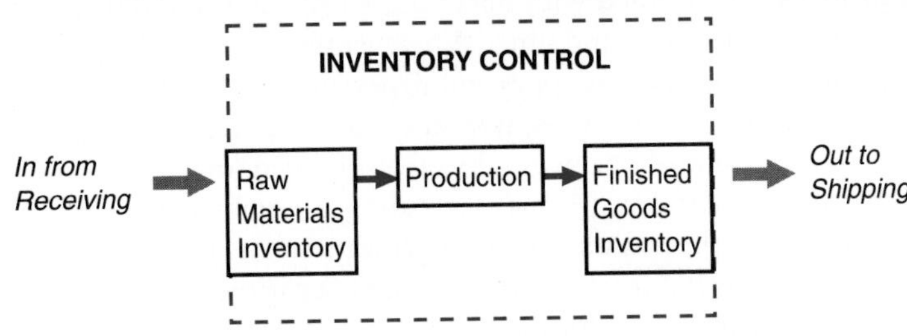

materials managers are organizationally positioned over production and inventory managers, the materials manager can act as an arbitrator to balance the production control manager's needs for greater materials supplies with the inventory manager's cost minimizing (and materials reducing) needs.

The tasks a finished goods inventory department performs for an organization can include the following:

1. Physically inspecting product quality
2. Storing and protecting finished goods from pilferage and damage
3. Auditing finished goods inventory
4. Locating and retrieving finished goods from stock
5. Replenishing stock in order-picking areas

Because the size of a finished goods inventory is solely determined by management, the opportunity to minimize its cost is under the control of management. Many U.S. organizations plan their finished goods inventory requirements on market demand strategies. One such planning strategy is called just-in-time (JIT) inventory management. We discuss how JIT is used in inventory management in Chapter 7.

MATERIALS HANDLING

Materials handling refers to the physical movement of materials through an organization. Specifically this means the use of all convenience equipment, facilities, and personnel to physically move the materials from the receiving dock in a plant to the customer's doorstep. Equipment such as that shown in Figure 6-4, including pallet trucks and forklift trucks, convenience facilities such as assembly lines and pneumatic tubes, and personnel to operate and service the equipment and facilities are the responsibility of materials handling managers. Materials handling is sometimes narrowly referred to as traffic, physical distribution, or logistics. **Traffic** is a function of arranging the most economic method of shipment for both incoming and outgoing materials and products. **Physical distribution,** on the other hand, is the activities associated with the movement of materials, usually finished products or parts, from the manufacturer to the customer. **Logistics** is concerned with obtaining, producing, and distributing materials and products at the proper place and time. Whatever term is used, the primary objective of materials handling is to move supplies and materials to a desired location in a timely and cost-effective manner. This objective does not conflict with either production control's or inventory control's primary objectives. Indeed, materials handling exists to support the other two functions. Materials handling is simply a convenience service to move goods into, through, and out of the organization. As we can see in Figure 6-5, materials handling covers the previously mentioned departments of receiving, raw materials inventory, production, and finished goods inventory. It also includes the shipping department, warehouse, distribution centers, and the customer.

FIGURE 6-4 MATERIALS HANDLING EQUIPMENT

(A) MANUALLY OPERATED EQUIPMENT

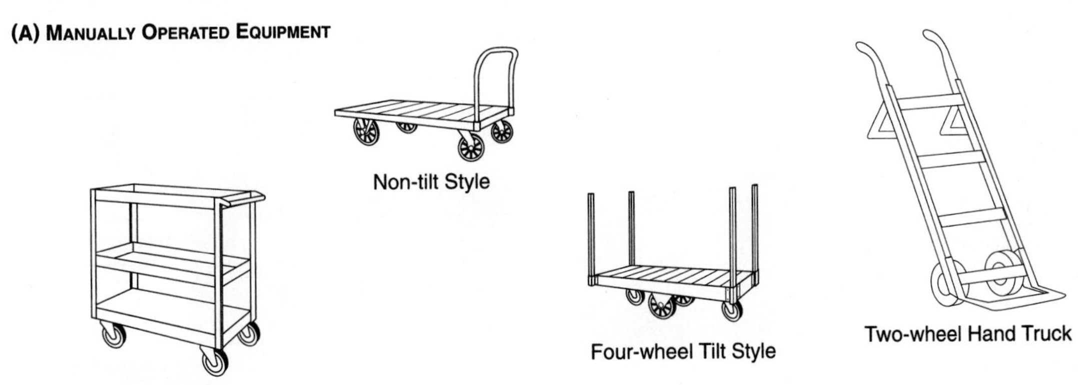

(B) HYDRAULICALLY, ELECTRICALLY, OR MECHANICALLY OPERATED FORK-LIFT EQUIPMENT

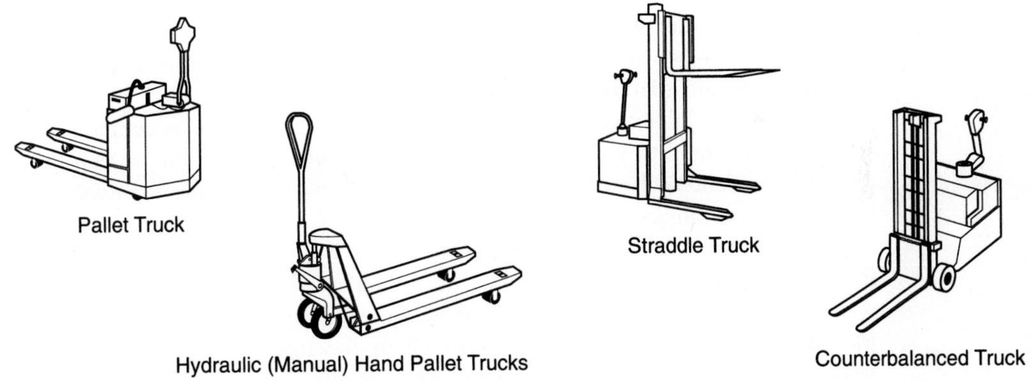

The **shipping** function in an organization delivers goods from finished goods inventory to the organization's customers. The tasks a shipping department performs for an organization can include the following:

1. Staging or organizing orders to be shipped
2. Physically checking orders to make sure their contents are consistent with their packing list
3. Weighing, labeling, and packing orders to be shipped
4. Arranging transportation for orders
5. Loading orders onto trucks

FIGURE 6-5 THE MATERIALS HANDLING FUNCTION OF MATERIALS MANAGEMENT

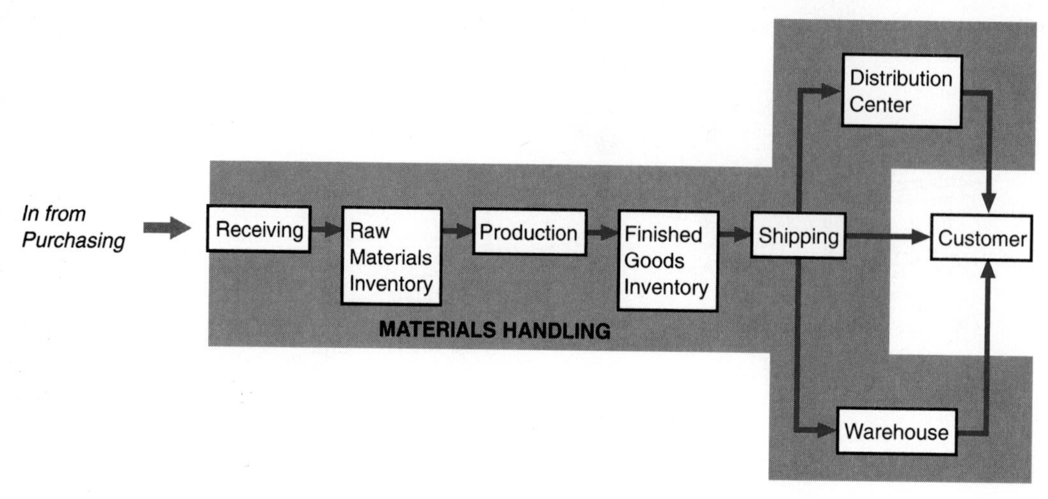

When an order is shipped from a manufacturing plant, it may go directly to a customer or it may be sent to a warehouse or distribution center for temporary storage. **Warehouses** and **distribution centers** are physical facilities used to store and ship inventory. One difference between a warehouse and a distribution center is that distribution centers tend to be placed closer to the markets (that is, customers) they serve. Distribution centers also tend to have greater shipping capabilities than warehouses, to better serve customers.

Distribution centers, for example, may have *will-call* customer facilities (that is, a service that permits customers to pick up merchandise at the distribution center), and warehouses generally do not. Warehouses can serve customers but are commonly used to store raw materials that will be shipped to the manufacturing organization or as finished goods inventory storage for retailing organizations.

Production control, inventory control, and materials handling, when broken down to their departmentalized functions, describe some of the steps materials take in their flow through the organization. To effectively manage the materials as they pass through the department, various types of technologies and methods are required.

MATERIALS MANAGEMENT TECHNOLOGY

Recent advances in technology have caused revolutionary changes in materials management. In this section, we discuss the use of materials management technologies, including robots and automated storage and automated retrieval (AS/AR) systems.

Robots

TYPES The Japanese divide robots into six categories.[6]

1. *Physical or manually operated manipulator* This type of robot is a manipulator (such as a mechanical arm and hand) that is worked by an operator. Workers are able to pick items up with the manipulator. The manipulator is used to protect human beings from an unsafe environment. It may be used, for example, to move radioactive elements.
2. *Fixed-sequence robot* This robot is a manipulator that performs a sequence of operations according to a predetermined set of procedures. It usually is designed to do a specific number of sequential tasks. These robots are generally less flexible because they are designed to do a limited or fixed number of activities. That is, they do not have the versatility of task or sequence change that more expensive robots do. These robots were some of the first to appear in assembly-line operations where work specialization reduces the sequence of job tasks to a small and fixed number. This robot's sequence of actions is usually triggered by electronic sensors (photoelectrical or physical devices separate from the robot) that detect when a unit of product is in position for work.
3. *Variable-sequence robot* This type of robot is a manipulator similar to the fixed-sequence except that it is designed to have its sequence of tasks easily changed.
4. *Playback robot* A playback robot is a manipulator that can produce a sequence of operations from memory. This type of robot can perform a much more involved sequence of operations than the variable-sequence robot and different types of sequences with minor changes to its computer memory. To program this type of robot, a human being would first use it to perform the job tasks required to produce a unit of product. Then the robot "plays back" the work task performance of the human being (which was stored in its memory) to produce the subsequent units.
5. *Numerical control (NC) robot* An NC robot is a manipulator that can perform a set of job task operations based on numerical data. The data are usually fed into the robot via some form of electronic media, punched tapes, data cards, or digital switches. This type of robot is ideal when high precision is required in manufacturing such as in tooling or machinery parts manufacture. Using this type of robot usually requires human support to position the materials (such as sheets of metal) that the robot will work on. Once the materials are in position, the robot is fed data electronically for a particular type of product, and the robot performs those particular program instructions. Some NC robots actually retrieve equipment and help in their own setup requirements for differing products.

---

[6] K. Swinehart, W. R. Boulton, and J. H. Blackstone, "The Current State of Robotics in Japan: Some Implications," *Production and Inventory Management Journal,* 28, No. 3 (1987), 44–49; and J. A. Rehg, *Introduction to Robotics: A Systems Approach* (Englewood Cliffs, N.J.: Prentice-Hall, 1985).

6. *Intelligent robots* This type of robot is a manipulator that uses visual or tactile perception (or both) to perceive the environmental conditions of the workplace. It is usually equipped with its own on-board computer that can make decisions about the environmental situation it faces and proceed according to those decisions. These are the most advanced and expensive robots currently in existence. Unlike the other robots, intelligent robots do not have to be in a fixed position where materials and products are required to be moved to them. Instead, this type of robot can move to where the work is to be performed or it may take the work to where it can be performed by others.

PHYSICAL CAPABILITIES Robots are also described by their physical capabilities. The **work envelope** of a robot is the physical movement capabilities of the robot's arms and hands. In Figure 6-6 we can see the four primary types of fixed-position robot categorized by work envelopes: polar, cylindrical, cartesian, and revolute. The work envelopes in Figure 6-6 are the geometric figures next to each robot. Knowing a robot's work envelope is essential for layout design considerations. Many robots pass component parts or materials to one another in the process of manufacturing a product along an assembly line. When the component parts are moved, they must fall within the work envelope of the fixed-position robots. The more intelligent robots, which have the capability of movement, are usually used to move the product through the transformation process. This robot mobility allows management to easily change the behavior of the robots to complete different types of products using the same production facility. Robots allow management flexibility in layout design. In Chapter 13 we refer to this flexibility in changing the operating system as a *flexible manufacturing system*.

The design of robot hands or its **grippers** is also an important part of classifying robots for usage purposes. In Figure 6-7 several types of robot hand diagrams are presented. The jaw hand is usually used to pick boxes up, turn them, or move them to a nearby conveyor or location within their work envelope. Jaw hands are not used for detailed work and, like most robot hands, are operated pneumatically (which is the cheapest method), hydraulically (for heavy-duty work with large payloads), or electri-

FIGURE 6-6 INDUSTRIAL ROBOT WORK ENVELOPES

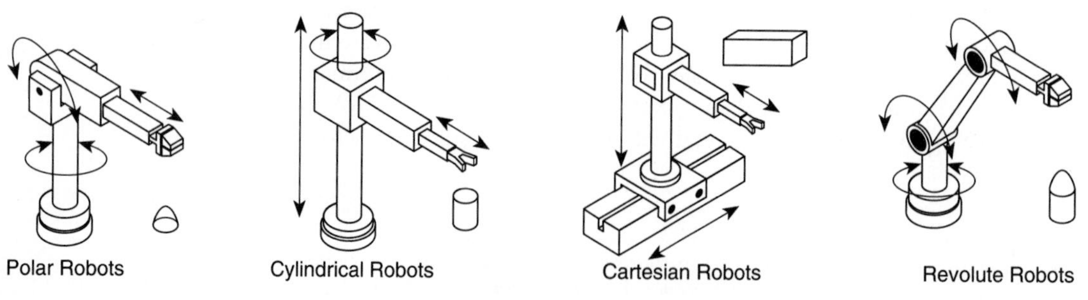

FIGURE 6-7 ROBOT HANDS

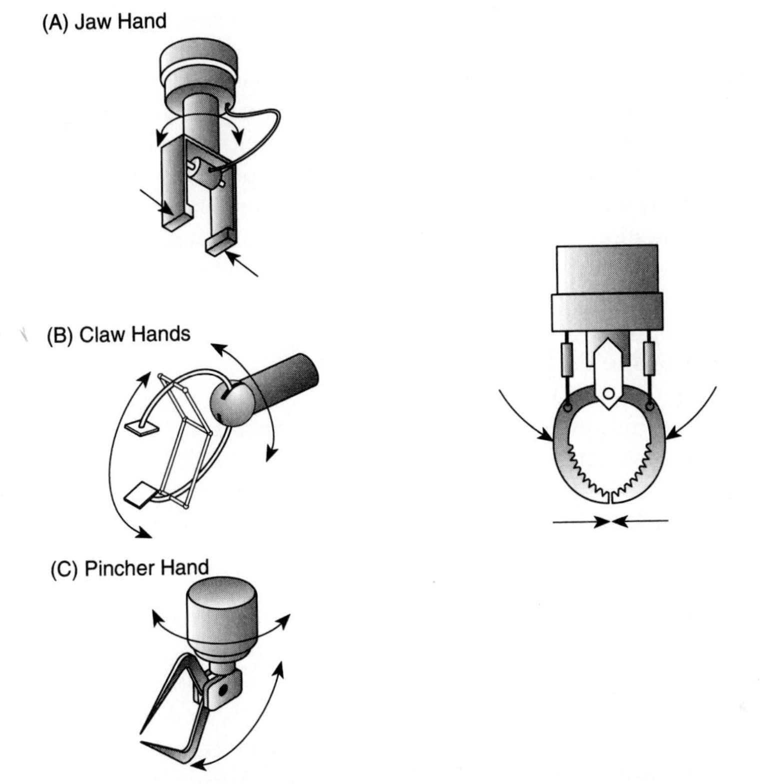

cally (for light-weight work). A claw hand can be used in both heavy-duty and light-weight or detailed work. Some claw hands have teeth to better grasp inventory items. Pincher hands are usually used for detailed work with very small items (such as nuts and bolts). Some robots have tools in place of hands. The tools can include spray guns, sanders, drills, screwdrivers, and welding equipment. It is interesting to note that robots' use of tools is superior to that of human beings, not just because of the consistency of application, but also in the physical movement of the hand-tool interface. For example, in the operation of spraying paint, a human being's normal hand movement limitation is 210 degrees; robots, however, can move 360 degrees.[7]

[7] G. T. Wilson, "Industrial Robots for Smaller Firms," *Production and Inventory Management Journal,* 32, No. 1 (1991), 25–27; K. Swinehart, W. R. Boulton, and J. H. Blackstone, "The Current State of Robotics in Japan: Some Implications," *Production and Inventory Management Journal,* 28, No. 3 (1987), 44–49; and J. Bergant, "Achieving a Successful First Robot Installation," *Robotics Today,* 4, No. 1 (February 1982), 63–66.

USES Robots are also classified by their application in industry. Robots are generally used in repetitive operations, although some job-lot operations can also economically use robots. Two basic types of robot applications are processing and pick-and-place. In a **processing application,** the robot is a tool that performs a job on a product that is moved to the robot. A **pick-and-place application** usually involves the robot's moving the product, such as in loading and unloading parts from pallets, and transferring parts from one assembly point to another. The pick-and-place application is the materials management–type function. In the 1990s robots are expected to find more plantwide use while becoming less "human like." The armlike manipulators now in use will give way to more application-specific robots with more sophisticated sensors and easier-to-use controls.[8]

Automated Storage and Retrieval Systems

Automated storage and automated retrieval (AS/AR) systems are mechanically operated materials handling systems that are usually computer controlled. Some systems are as simple as a single robot that retrieves inventory items in a small section of a plant. Larger AS/AR systems include whole warehouses with dozens of computer-controlled pallet movers loading incoming and outgoing inventory.

AUTOMATED GUIDED VEHICLES In the past, storage and retrieval activities were usually centered around shelving or specific storing functions of inventory items and order-picking activities. The type of materials handling equipment that was used in the past (and is still used in many organizations today) includes those depicted in Figure 6-4. Today, AS/AR refers to computer-integrated aspects of inventory stocking and picking functions and automated materials handling functions.[9] **Automated guided vehicles (AGVs)** can be used to store and retrieve inventory items from stock. Sometimes referred to as a "rolling robot" when it has an on-board intelligent computer system, the AGV typifies the automatic or nonhuman aspect of the AS/AR system.

The General Motor's Buick automobile plant in Flint, Michigan, uses a type of computerized materials handling called Portec automated guided vehicles.[10] Portec AGVs move car engines from workstation to workstation for assembly. Portec AGVs are like small electronic cars that are self-powered and directionally guided by on-board computers that follow wire guides on the floor. The AGVs replaced a fixed assembly line–type of operation at the GM plant. The observed benefits of using this type of materials handling system instead of the previous fixed assembly line system at GM are listed at the top of the next page.

---

[8] R. E. Morley, "Sneak Preview of the 1990s," *Manufacturing Systems,* 8, No. 4 (April 1990), 19–24.

[9] T. Slattery, "New Trends in Material Handling," *Managing Automation* (June 1989), 38–43; and for an excellent application of more current automated materials handling in the steel industry, see T. P. Pare, "The Big Threat to Big Steel's Future," *Fortune,* July 15, 1991, pp. 106–108.

[10] 1986 Reference Guide and Directory Issue, *Production and Inventory Review,* 5, No. 11 (1986), 51.

1. Greater flexibility in production operations (that is, the AGVs can be programmed to go in any order to the workstations. In the assembly line operation, on the other hand, the materials had to flow through all of the workstations as they existed on the assembly line)
2. Greater materials flow control by the worker (that is, the AGVs usually have to be dismissed by the worker before they are allowed to go to their next workstation, which permits the worker to remove a particular product on the assembly line if he or she identifies a problem needing correction)
3. Greater product quality and productivity
4. A quieter and cleaner work environment

Some AGVs use a combination of computer and human control. These semiautomatic AGVs operate autonomously on their guide paths (strips of magnetic tape on the floor that the AGV's sensor directs the vehicle to follow) to a specific position, such as a workstation, and then they signal a human operator with built-in horns, bippers, or lights. The human operator then can perform a job on the material that the AGV carries and simply flip a switch that tells the AGV to continue along the path to the next workstation. Some AGVs are actually designed in a similar fashion to the straddle truck pallet mover in Figure 6-4. Unlike the mechanized pallet mover, the AGV can move independently and travel the guide paths without the aid of human beings. The operator simply performs the more difficult maneuvering tasks of positioning the pallet-moving forks of the AGV to secure the desired inventory item and then replaces the AGV on the guide path to continue its trip to its next location.

CONVEYANCE SYSTEMS In addition to handling equipment like AGVs, AS/AR makes use of conveyor-type systems. In many cases, the conveyor actually becomes an extension of the inventory shelving. The shelving used in AS/AR systems is often mechanized to move inventory itself. In Figure 6-8(a) we can see how shelving can be structured or angled to permit inventory items to move either on a gravity or vibratory basis (that is, motors are used to vibrate angled shelves, which moves boxes toward the front of the shelf). Each of the shelves are replenished from the back of the bin as the inventory item moves toward the front of the shelf.

To make this system work, the inventory items must be stored in fairly standardized boxes and on a unitary or single-usage basis. This is quite acceptable in inventory reduction methods such as JIT and *kanban* systems that require unit usage standardization of inventory items. (We discuss JIT and *kanban* systems later in this chapter.) In the front of each shelf, a trip control device keeps boxes of the inventory items from advancing or spilling out of the shelf onto the conveyor. Each of these devices is controlled by the main computer system of the computer-integrated manufacturing (CIM) system or computer-integrated service system (CISS). When a particular inventory item is picked for a customer order, the computer releases the control device at the location of the particular inventory item and the box falls onto the conveyor line located at the front of the bin.

Two types of conveyor systems are shown in Figure 6-8(b). The conveyors send the boxed items to an order-processing area for robots or human beings to collect and

FIGURE 6-8 SHELVING USED IN AS/AR SYSTEMS

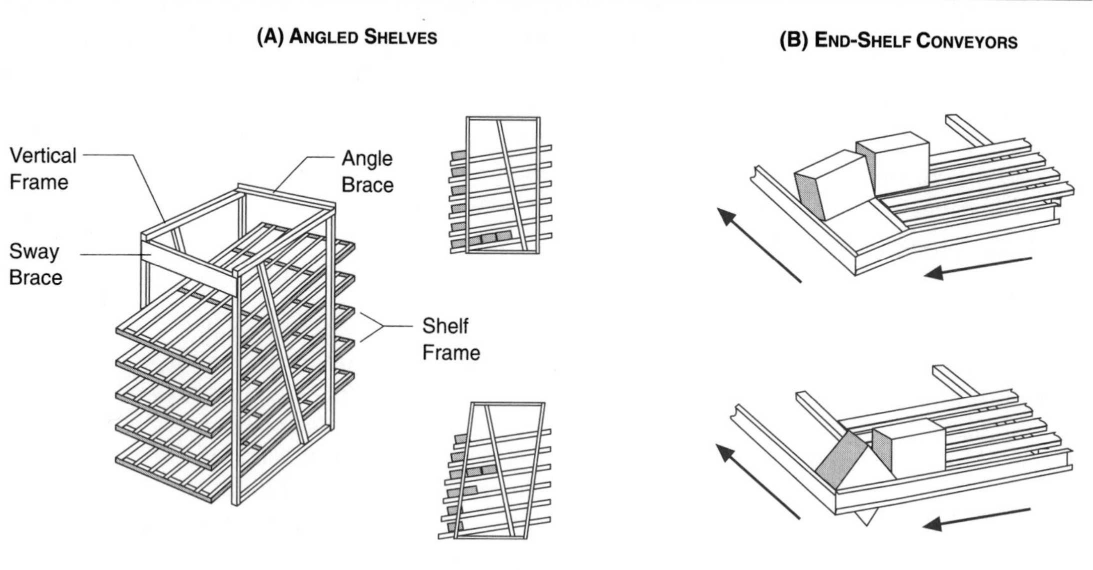

match up the computer-generated list of inventory-ordered items with those sent by the automatic retrieval system. Storage can be accomplished by using AGVs in the same way that the computer picks an order. That is, the AGVs are directed by computer to locate and replenish boxes of inventory (which the AGV carries from the receiving areas) in desired locations. The AGV follows along its guide path until a sensor indicates the location of the bin, and then either its on-board computer or the warehouse facility's main computer activates its lifting forks to position the inventory item on the appropriate shelf.

To further illustrate the use of AS/AR systems we compare a traditional warehousing operation with a state-of-the-art fully integrated computer-controlled warehousing facility later in this chapter.

MATERIALS MANAGEMENT METHODS

There are many different types of materials management methods. Whereas some are capable of being incorporated in an organization's computer-based management information system (like the transportation method presented in Supplement 6-1), others are philosophical or simple card systems that do not require any sophisticated computer support. We will examine several materials management methods including just-in-time (JIT) purchasing, *kanban* card systems, and the ABC classification system.

Just-in-Time Purchasing

Just-in-time (JIT) purchasing is a Japanese approach to timing the acquisition process, the basic idea of which is to reduce the size of delivery quantities and to try to time them as closely to their use in production as possible.[11] The objective of this system is to reduce the purchase quantities to a very small quantity or even a single unit and have that unit arrive exactly in time for its use in production. Because incoming materials go directly into production, JIT purchasing eliminates raw materials inventory and the various costs of storing and moving that are associated with that inventory.

Some traditional purchasing management practices (often labeled as the just-in-case approach) differ from this Japanese purchasing philosophy. As we can see in Table 6-1, the purchasing activities differ in procedure and in the objectives of the purchasing activities. The benefits of the JIT purchasing system over a more traditional system include[12]

1. Reduced inventory carrying costs because of the reduced size of inventory
2. Reduced scrap by minimizing rework
3. Increased product quality because parts and materials are supplied from a reduced number of vendors who might have each generated differing levels of product quality
4. Increased productivity because of the reduction in parts-related delays
5. Increased administration productivity because of fewer vendors and less paperwork to process

JIT purchasing is a part of the broader JIT production philosophy that we discuss in Chapter 7.

Kanban Systems

A ***kanban*** (pronounced kahn-bahn) **system** is a Japanese production and inventory control system that was originated by the Toyota Motor Company. The Japanese term *kanban* can be interpreted as meaning "sign post" or "card." A *kanban* system embodies most areas of materials management. To use *kanbans,* an organization must have supplies,

---

[11] P. A. Nelson and A. B. Jambekor, "A Dynamic View of Vendor Relations Under JIT," *Production and Inventory Management,* 31, No. 4 (1990), 65–70; A. Ansari and B. Modaress, "Just-in-time Purchasing as a Quality and Productivity Centre," *International Journal of Production Research,* 26, No. 1 (1988), 19–26; R. G. Newman, "The Buyer-Supplier Relationship Under Just-in-time," *Production and Inventory Management Journal,* 29, No. 3 (1988), 45–49; and M. J. Schniederjans, *Topics in Just-In-Time Management* (Boston: Allyn & Bacon, 1993), Chapter 3.

[12] R. J. Schonberger, *Japanese Manufacturing Techniques* (New York: The Free Press, 1982), pp. 160–161; R. A. Esparrago, "Kanban," *Production and Inventory Management Journal,* 29, No. 1 (1988), 6–10; and A. Ansari and B. Modaress, "The Potential Benefits of Just-In-Time Purchasing for U.S. Manufacturing," *Production and Inventory Management Journal,* 28, No. 2 (1987), 30–36.

TABLE 6-1 COMPARISON OF TRADITIONAL AND JIT PURCHASING PRACTICES

Purchasing Activity	*JIT Purchasing*	*Traditional Purchasing*
Determining purchase lot size	Purchase in small lots with frequent deliveries.	Purchase in large quantities with infrequent deliveries.
Selecting vendor	Single source of supply for a given part in close geographical area with a long-term contract.	Reliance on multiple sources of supply for a given part and short-term contracts.
Evaluating vendor	Emphasis is placed on product quality, delivery performance, and price. *No* percentage of rejects from vendors are acceptable.	Emphasis is placed on a certain acceptable level of product quality, delivery performance, and price.
Negotiating and bidding process	Primary objective is to achieve the best product quality through a long-term contract.	Primary objective is to obtain the lowest possible price.
Paperwork	Less formal paperwork. Delivery time and quantity level can be changed by telephone calls.	Requires a great deal of time and formal paperwork. Changes in delivery date and quantity require new purchase orders.
Packaging	Small standardized containers used to hold individual items or exact quantity.	Standardized packaging for all part types.

materials, and inventory items stored in single-use containers (such as trays or boxes). Single-use containers hold all of one type of component part or material used in the manufacture of a product. *Kanban* systems also require some initial inventory to begin the operation.

In a *kanban* system, cards are used to initiate transactions. The production, conveyance, and purchase of items are the transactions. There are several types of *kanbans*.

1. *Production authorization card* is used to signal that production of a part can begin. This *kanban* usually lists the product's name, identification number, description, and the materials required in its production.
2. *Vendor authorization card* is used to signal that a vendor is authorized to send the organization a certain specified number of units of supplies and materials. This *kanban* usually lists the product's name, purchasing company's identification number, vendor's identification number and name, and an order quantity.
3. *Conveyance authorization card* is used to signal that a materials handling agent is authorized to move supplies, materials, or inventory items to a specified destination. This *kanban* usually lists the product's name, identifying number, and the location the item is to be delivered to.

Not all of these *kanbans* need to be used in an operation. Some organizations use a single-card system and others use a dual-card system.[13] Regardless of which system is used, *kanbans* can serve the purpose of authorizing the production, purchase, and movement of materials and inventory throughout the organization.

SINGLE-CARD SYSTEM In a single-card system only the conveyance card is used. More organizations use the single-card system than the dual-card system. Once a single-card system is in place, it is an easy step to convert to a dual-card system by adding a production *kanban* or vendor *kanban*.

To illustrate the single-card system let's look at the assembly line depicted in Figure 6-9. Suppose an assembly line worker needs inventory to complete a product. A conveyance *kanban* is issued from the assembly line area defining the inventory required. The *kanban* is then placed in an empty tray at point A in Figure 6-9. This *kanban* notifies the materials handlers that inventory is required and they are authorized to obtain it from the inventory department. A materials handler moves the empty tray to the inventory department and drops it off at point B keeping the *kanban*. The materials handler then picks up the desired inventory from the tote trays at point C. Note that some initial inventory must be waiting for pickup, otherwise the materials handler will not be able to use that particular conveyance *kanban*. From point C the materials handler moves the tray to point D in the assembly area where it can be processed by assembly workers. The materials handler then goes back to point A to begin the cycle again.

The single-card system works fine as long as some initial inventory is available for pickup at the inventory station. Because the *kanban* represents a continuous flow materials system, the initial excess inventory can be reduced by eliminating some of the *kanbans* once the system is underway. The number of cards in the system defines the amount of inventory to be moved or produced. In the single-card system, for example, if we had required three trays of inventory, we would have had to issue three *kanbans*. Likewise, if we had an ongoing *kanban* system and wanted to eliminate some of the excess inventory in the system, we might issue only two *kanbans* when in fact we need and will use three trays of materials for the particular order. The effect on the operating system will be a reduction of one tray of inventory. We generally would not underissue *kanbans* unless excess inventory exists in the system and we want to eliminate it. The single-card system is most appropriate in repetitive-type operations. Only standardized containers or trays can be used in this type of system. They are standardized to lot-size production. If we produce, for example, one radio at a time, then a container might include only the parts to manufacture one radio. If, on the other hand, an organization produces five radios at a time, then the tray must contain parts for five radios.

---

[13] R. J. Schonberger, "Applications of Single-Card and Dual-Card Kanban," *Interfaces,* 13, No. 4 (August 1983), 56–67; R. A. Esparragos, "Kanban," *Production and Inventory Management Journal,* 29, No. 1 (1988), 6–10.

FIGURE 6-9 SINGLE-CARD KANBAN SYSTEM

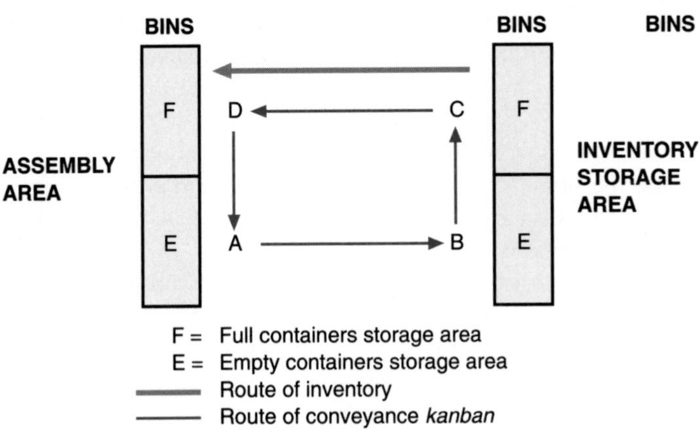

DUAL-CARD SYSTEM In a dual-card *kanban* system we use two separate cards. To illustrate the dual-card system let's look at the assembly line depicted in Figure 6-10. In this situation, the organization obtains its materials from a vendor. The conveyance *kanban* is used in the same manner as in the single-card system (that is, the conveyance *kanban* travels from A to B to C to D and back to A). A vendor *kanban* is introduced at point X in Figure 6-10. The card authorizes a vendor, point Y, to obtain and deliver specified materials. Once the materials are delivered they may have to be broken down into a prescribed container unit at point Z. Many vendors who service organizations

FIGURE 6-10 DUAL-CARD KANBAN SYSTEM

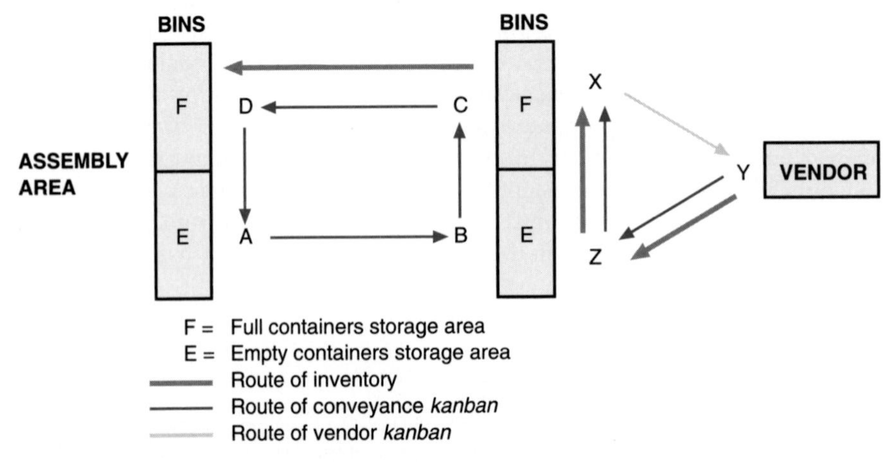

that use a *kanban* system provide this materials-sorting activity as a part of their service. An empty container is obtained at point Z by the vendor for materials storage. The filled container is then placed in the bins at point X where it will stay until a materials handler brings a conveyance card from point B to point C to authorize its movement. Once the container is authorized to be moved, its vendor *kanban* is removed and sent to the vendor where the system repeats itself.

We can see in Figure 6-10 that the two separate *kanbans* are in closed loops and continue to circulate until they are withdrawn by management. As market demand for a product increases, the number of *kanbans* can be increased to meet the greater demand. As the market demand decreases, the number of *kanbans* can be decreased to meet the lesser demand. This provides both production control and inventory control in materials management.

A *kanban* system has been used very successfully by many organizations.[14] One of its chief limitations, however, is its heavy dependence on the people that make up the operations management system. If a vendor fails to make a delivery or a worker loses a *kanban,* the organization runs the risk of the entire OM system's being shut down. A *kanban* system is best used when it is combined with a just-in-time (JIT) inventory system. We discuss the JIT inventory system in Chapter 7.

ABC Classification System

In organizations that have thousands of different types of materials to manage, it is easy to lose sight of the efficiency objective of materials management. One of the major reasons that materials management objectives are not always efficiently achieved is because human and physical resources can be periodically misallocated. For example, an inventory control person may spend as much time and effort managing an inventory item that has a value of $10,000 as he or she spends on an item that costs only $10.

To keep an organization from misallocating its material management resources, control systems need to be installed that will direct control efforts efficiently throughout the organization. One type of control system that has been used in the inventory control function of materials management is called the ABC classification system. The **ABC classification system** classifies inventory items by their total dollar volume so inventory control resources can be allocated on that basis. In other words, the greater the total dollar value represented by the weighted total dollar volume of an inventory item, the greater the control effort that should be allocated to that item. There are many different

[14] A. S. Sohol and D. Naylor, "Implementation of JIT in a Small Manufacturing Firm," *Production and Inventory Management Journal,* 33, No. 1 (1992), 20–26; B. Wilkinson and N. Oliver, "Power, Control, and the Kanban," *Journal of Management Studies,* 26, No. 1 (1989), 47–58; M. Gravel and W. L. Price, "Using the Kanban in a Job Shop Environment," *International Journal of Production Research,* 26, No. 6 (1988), 1105–1118; R. J. Schonberger, "Applications of Single-Card and Dual-Card Kanban," *Interfaces,* 13, No. 4 (1983), 56–67; and Y. Monden, "Adaptable Kanban Helps Toyota Maintain Just-in-production," *Industrial Engineering,* 13, No. 5 (May 1981), 29–46.

types of ABC systems. One procedure for instituting an ABC classification system is as follows:

1. List all of the inventory items that the organization carries during the year.
2. List the unit cost of the inventory items.
3. List the annual unit demand of the inventory items.
4. Multiply the cost in step 2 by the unit demand in step 3 to derive the annual dollar volume of the inventory items.
5. Assign the items using one of three classifications judgmentally to differentiate their relative dollar volume: The classification A indicates a high-dollar volume inventory item, B indicates a moderate-dollar volume inventory item, and C indicates a low-dollar volume inventory item.
6. Group the inventory items by their classification in step 5 and determine their total dollar volume percentage by classification.
7. Multiply the total available materials management resources (for example, budgeted dollars for inventory control) by the proportions in step 6 to determine the allocation of resources by item classification.

The goal of step 6 is to determine the proportion of materials management resources that should be allocated to the inventory items by classification—that is, to determine the percentage of resources that should be allocated to all the inventory items with the A classification, the B classification, and finally the C classification. The three proportions will sum to one, and are usually distributed with the greatest proportion of resources going to the A items. As a general rule, the approximate proportions of dollar volume items falling into each of the three inventory classifications range in accordance with the following values:

Classification	*Approximate Dollar Volume as a Percentage of Total Dollar Volume*
A (high-dollar volume)	60 to 85%
B (moderate-dollar volume)	10 to 40
C (low-dollar volume)	5 to 20

The percentages are listed only as general guidelines, and will vary from organization to organization. Indeed, the actual divisions between the classifications are subjective and judgmental in nature. The idea is to group the most valued inventory items into a group representing the majority of the dollar volume of inventory. The A group is rightfully considered, based on inventory dollar volume, the most important group of inventory items and should be allocated the greatest share of inventory control resources. Likewise, the lesser-dollar volume inventory items, classified as C items, should be allocated proportionally fewer inventory control resources.

It usually turns out that the relationship between the percentage of the dollar volume of inventory and the percentage of volume of the inventory items are inversely related.

This inverse relationship means that a smaller allocation of resources should be made on the more voluminous quantities of inventory. This permits a greater allocation of inventory control resources to be devoted to the more valuable and less voluminous inventory with an A classification. Periodic checks on the actual expenditure of inventory control resources and their allocation consistent with their percentage of total dollar volume can be an effective way of monitoring and controlling inventory resource allocation within an organization. In many of today's computer-based CIM or CISS environments, such checks can be accomplished quickly for corrective control action.

QUESTION: How would you judgmentally classify the following inventory items to differentiate their relative dollar volume?

Item	*Item Cost ($)*	*Annual Demand (units)*	*Total Annual Dollar Volume ($)*
222	400	50	(400 × 50) = 20,000
212	510	40	(510 × 40) = 20,400
202	10	600	(10 × 600) = 6,000
192	11	500	(11 × 500) = 5,500
182	0.50	1,000	(0.50 × 1,000) = 500
172	0.25	1,500	(0.25 × 1,500) = 375

ANSWER: Because the idea of the ABC classification is to differentiate the inventory items by dollar volume, we should judgmentally view each item's percentage of total volume as a means of classifying the item. We can see that inventory items 222 and 212 have a significantly greater percentage of total dollar volume than the other four items, so they should be assigned an A classification. Likewise, inventory items 202 and 192 have a significantly greater percentage of total dollar volume than the remaining two items, so we should assign 202 and 192 a B classification. The remaining two items can then be classified as C items.

Item	*Item Cost ($)*	*Annual Demand (units)*	*Total Annual Dollar Volume ($)*	*Percent of Total Dollar Volume*	*ABC Classification*
222	400	50	$20,000	37.9%	A
212	510	40	20,400	38.7	A
202	10	600	6,000	11.4	B
192	11	500	5,500	10.4	B
182	0.50	1,000	500	0.9	C
172	0.25	1,500	375	0.7	C
			$52,775		

QUESTION: Suppose that we have the following inventory items, their unit cost, and annual demand rates:

Inventory Item	*Unit Cost ($)*	*Annual Demand (units)*
1001	1,250	10
1002	2	2,500
1003	200	60
1004	300	45
1005	12	500
1006	60	100
1007	150	70
1008	300	40
1009	300	40
1010	50	140

Structure these items into an ABC classification system.

ANSWER: On a subjective basis, the ten items can be structured into an ABC classification as follows:

Inventory Item	*Unit Cost ($)*	*Annual Demand (units)*	*Total Annual Dollar Volume ($)*	*Classification*
1001	1,250	10	$12,500	A
1002	2	2,500	5,000	C
1003	200	60	12,000	A
1004	300	45	13,500	A
1005	12	500	6,000	B
1006	60	100	6,000	B
1007	150	70	10,500	A
1008	300	40	12,000	A
1009	300	40	12,000	A
1010	50	140	7,000	B
		3,505	$96,500	

Based on this allocation, a total of 75.1 percent [that is, (12,500 + 12,000 + 13,500 + 10,500 + 12,000 + 12,000) ÷ 96,500] of the total annual materials management resources should be allocated to managing class A inventory items, and only 5.2 percent (that is, 5,000 ÷ 96,500) of the total annual materials management resources should be allocated to manage class C inventory items. If we were allocating materials management resources based on unit volume, the allocation to class A would be 7.6 percent [that is, (10 + 60 + 45 + 70 + 40 + 40) ÷ 3,505] and the allocation to class C would be 71.3 percent (that is, 2,500 ÷ 3,505). Note the inverse relationship between the allocation based on inventory value and inventory volume.

QUESTION: Can the ABC system be based on other criteria than cost-column information?

ANSWER: Yes, any criteria can be used in the ABC system just presented to allocate or rank the importance of select inventory items for differentiation purposes. For example, the ABC system can be used to designate the increased importance of the higher perishability of some food items in retail grocery stores over other food items that have a long shelf-life. Other product or inventory item criteria that can be used in conjunction with the ABC system include the cost of the product, the positioning of a product in its product life cycle (the older the item, the higher the classification), the ease with which a product is susceptible to engineering changes (the easier the item is to change, the higher the classification of its importance), and the physical size of a product (the larger the item, the more important it is to move through the system to save space). S

The discussions of the materials management methods in this section are meant only as a brief introduction to the subject. Many of the materials management methods focus on monitoring and scheduling the flow of materials into, through, and out of a production facility. We examine many other applicable methods throughout this book, particularly when we discuss scheduling methods in Chapter 9.

INTEGRATING MANAGEMENT RESOURCES: USING AUTOMATED STORAGE AND AUTOMATIC RETRIEVAL FOR COMPETITIVE ADVANTAGE

The purpose of this section is to illustrate the differences between a traditional nonintegrated storage and retrieval system and a state-of-the-art fully integrated computer-controlled system. We have chosen a warehouse facility to illustrate the technology differences because warehousing facilities are used by both manufacturing and service organizations. We will first present a traditional warehouse facility and then present a comparable state-of-the-art fully computer-integrated warehouse facility. We will end this section by reviewing the contrasting differences that exist in these technologically different systems and discussing how they satisfy an organization's need for improved productivity, flexibility, and competitive advantage.

A Traditional Nonintegrated Warehouse Facility

In Figure 6-11 a facility layout for a traditional furniture warehouse facility is presented. We will assume that this warehouse facility is owned by a furniture manufacturing organization. In this facility, incoming stock from the company's manufacturing plants or outside vendors and suppliers arrive on the loading docks in pallets or in boxes. The inventory stock is unloaded by the truck drivers using the company's materials handling equipment.

QUESTION: Is the competitive globalization or internationalization of operations management changing materials management methods?

ANSWER: Yes, materials management methods are changing in many ways because of the demands of international competition. Materials management is now viewed as playing a critical role in measuring and improving the performance of firms in international or global markets. It is often difficult for some international operations to find common measures of performance to determine the success of their international operations. For example, high finished goods inventory levels might be a sign of high levels of productivity in one operation and poor inventory planning in another operation. Likewise, high profits for a firm in one country might be viewed favorably whereas high profits for another firm in another country might be viewed as culturally unacceptable profiteering. To help firms that operate in the global environment of the 1990s measure their international operations, common measures of performance measurement are being suggested that directly relate to the materials management function.[15] International performance measurements and the ways that materials management supports them include (1) increasing **throughput** (that is, the rate at which a manufacturing system generates money through sales), which is directly aided by a highly efficient materials handling system that can quickly move the product to customer delivery; (2) decreasing inventory, which is accomplished by a reliable materials handling system that does not require buffer inventory for contingency shortages; and (3) reducing operating expenses, which can be accomplished by minimizing waste and spoilage in a well-managed materials handling system. So it appears that international measurement methods now favor many of the activities performed in the materials management function. As such, the materials management function will be increasingly important to the measured success of an operation.

The receiving department's staff of three compares its company-generated invoices for incoming goods with the invoices the delivery drivers bring with the goods. The receiving department obtained its invoices from the manufacturing facility's computer system. The invoices were sent by pneumatic tubes (if the manufacturing plant is located nearby) or by mail (if the manufacturing plant is located some distance from the warehouse). If everything matches, the goods are inspected for quality and quantity. If any shortages are observed they are recorded by the staff on the driver's invoice for credit and adjustment by the supplier. The goods are then moved, using some materials handling equipment, to appropriate locations in the order-picking areas. These picking areas are used both for storing inventory and for order picking. The large items such as sofas, tables, and chairs are stored on their pallets and placed on the shelves in specific locations.

[15] M. E. Kane, "Companies Must Integrate Global Measurements," *APICS—The Performance Advantage,* 2, No. 3 (March 1992), 32–34.

FIGURE 6-11 TRADITIONAL WAREHOUSE FACILITY LAYOUT

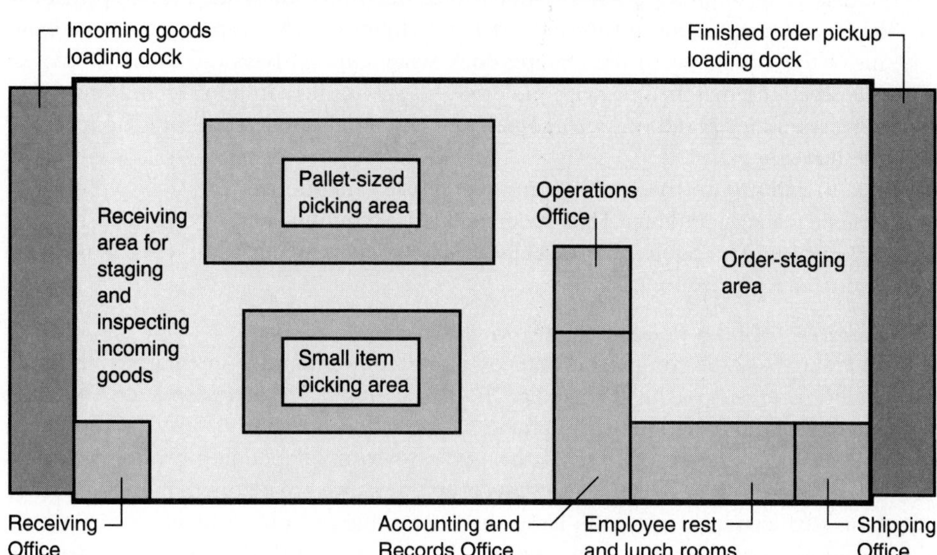

Shelf locations in warehouses are usually identified by a combination of numbers and letters that are used to label each of the rows and shelves that make up the picking area. The locations of the furniture, the contents of the pallet (for example, the type of furniture, its color), and other information such as manufacturing date and who stored it are recorded on paper inventory cards. These inventory cards are then filed and held in the accounting and records office for use in filling future orders. Computer printout orders for goods (furniture) are received in the operations office from the organization's customers (the retail outlets that the warehouse serves). After the accounting functions necessary for processing the orders are performed by the accounting staff, the records staff pulls the necessary inventory cards to fill the orders. If insufficient furniture is available, the orders are corrected by the records personnel and forms initiating backorders are sent to the manufacturing operation or suppliers for the additional furniture. The order-picking staff takes the orders and the inventory cards pulled by the records staff and pulls the furniture for the orders using its own materials handling equipment. As the orders are pulled, they are staged close to the shipping area. The results of the order-picking staff's efforts (that is, items picked, items short, etc.) are recorded on the orders; one copy of the order is left with the goods in the order-staging area and one copy of the order is returned to the records office for further processing. Records personnel manually record the changes in the inventory and update their computer records.

The accounting staff also uses the order information to begin the collection process from the customer (outside customers who are not part of the manufacturing organization) or the inventory documentation process for company-owned retail outlets. The shipping office personnel box (for small items such as lamp shades), label, and prepare the inventory orders for shipping. The shipping personnel also move the goods out to the loading dock when truck drivers call them. Copies of the orders are matched up with the driver's copy of the computer-generated order, corrections are noted on both copies, and the goods are loaded into the truck by the driver.

In addition to the warehousing staff already mentioned, the facility requires a general manager and receiving, order-picking, accounting and records, and shipping supervisors. The facility also usually employs several security officers and several maintenance personnel.

A State-of-the-Art Computer-integrated Warehouse Facility

In Figure 6-12 the comparable state-of-the-art fully computer-integrated warehouse facility is presented. In this facility the truck drivers are provided with the same type of materials handling equipment as presented in Figure 6-4(b) but they must unload the materials on one of the two conveyors, depending on the material's size. In this type of operation the inventory items are boxed on an individual usage basis (for example, only one lamp shade per box and only one chair per pallet). Each box is also labeled with a universal product code (UPC) label that identifies its own individual data file.[16] The data file consists of manufacturing information (such as the product's number and name, its color, unique features, the date of manufacture, federally controlled substance contents, and production run numbers).

After loading the shipment on the conveyors, the driver then inserts the invoice into an *automatic reading port* (something like a dollar bill changer machine). Computerized optical scanners review the invoice and compare it with the manufacturing invoice electronically sent to the main computer system in the operations office. Once matched, the individual boxes and pallet loads are checked against the invoice. Just inside the incoming goods loading dock doors, jaw-handed polar robots correct the position of the unloaded boxes on the conveyor so a UPC scanner can identify the contents of the boxes by their individual UPC labels. To further enhance the input data collected by the automatic reading port, **speech recognition technology** (technology that translates human speech into text) can be used to allow the driver to note exceptions in the order verbally at the time of delivery.[17]

The operations office computer, which controls the entire AS/AR system, is in continuous contact with the manufacturing organization's computer as part of the organization's computer-integrated network. Once the computer has identified all of the incoming shipment items, which may only take a few minutes, the truck driver's copy of the invoice is automatically processed by the computer port. The copy still inserted in the automatic reading port makes any corrections for shortages

---

[16] "Bar Code System Integrates Production Distribution, Inventory," *Production and Inventory Management Review,* 10, No. 1 (1990), 45–47; and W. Munroe, "Shop Floor Bar Code Can Bring Technological Advances and Avoid Chaos," *Production and Inventory Management Review,* 11, No. 5 (1991), 42–45.

[17] R. Byford, "Time to Talk?" *Production and Inventory Management Review,* 11, No. 5 (1991), 34–36.

FIGURE 6-12 STATE-OF-THE-ART COMPUTER-INTEGRATED WAREHOUSE FACILITY LAYOUT

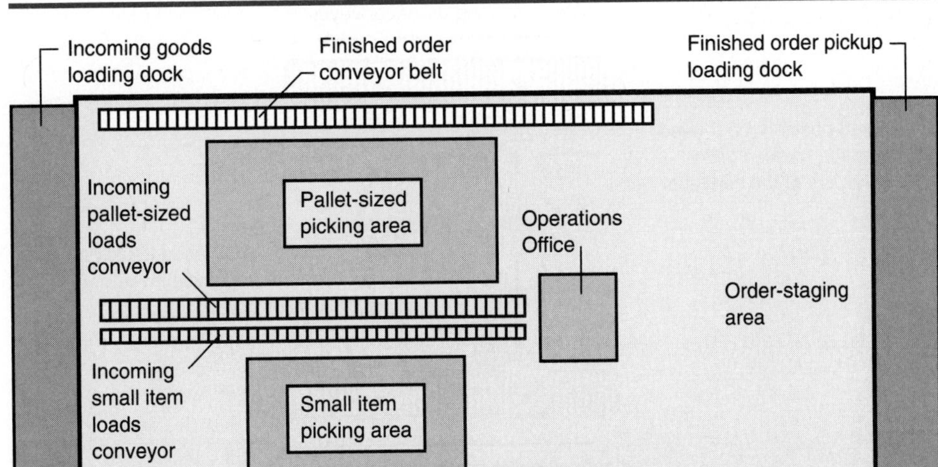

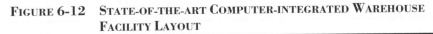

or incorrectly shipped items and authorizes the invoice for the driver. The corrected invoice is returned through the reading port to the driver, and the driver departs. The equipment on the loading docks and the facility's equipment is monitored by one security officer (in the operations office) with video cameras located throughout the facility and on the loading docks.

As the incoming inventory items pass down the conveyors to the picking areas, additional fixed-position robots take the boxes off the conveyor and hand them to AGV robots that can move up and down the aisles of the picking areas. As we can see in the detailed view of the layout for the pallet-sized picking area in Figure 6-13, the robots are given forks instead of hands with which to move the goods. The AGV robots for pallet-sized loads not only automatically store the items on shelves, but also communicate their locations to the main computer in the operations office. These computer-stored locations will be used to locate and pick the item when the AGV is used to fill an order.

The shelves in the small-item picking area are designed for specific items (that is, a shelf is reserved for each specific inventory item). The shelves are designed like those shown in Figure 6-8 with end-shelf conveyors. The end-shelf conveyors are positioned to feed from the individual item shelves to the finished order conveyor. We can see the positioning of the robots for the small-item picking area in Figure 6-14. Each of the inventory shelves is controlled by the main computer.

When an order requires a specific item, the computer activates a trip switch that releases a single box (a single inventory item) from its appropriate location.

FIGURE 6-13 DETAILED VIEW OF PALLET-SIZED PICKING AREA LAYOUT

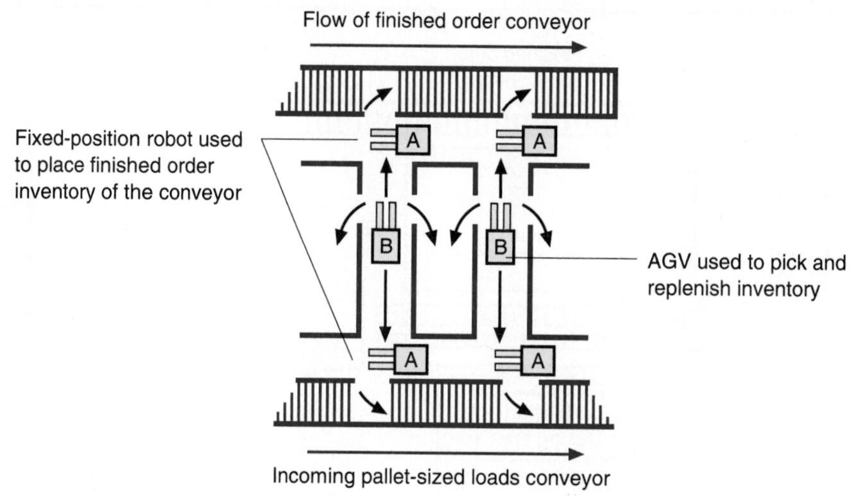

The items for a single order can all be released at a single time and will eventually meet on the finished order conveyor. As the boxes pass down the finished order conveyor, each has its UPC label scanned again by a series of sensors located along the conveyor. Each box or pallet order is taken off the conveyor and placed on an AGV to travel to a staging area. This screening also serves to check the order-picking activity of the system because it matches the order requirements with the goods actually picked. The detailed position of the robots, the AGVs, and their guide paths are shown in Figure 6-15.

Because the boxes coming off the finished order conveyor are not grouped by a customer's order, each of the boxes or pallets that make up a customer's order must be put in a specific place or staged in the order-staging area. The AGVs pass the inventory items from the conveyors as in Figure 6-15 and then travel to an open area in the order-staging area. Once a box or pallet is placed in a specific area, the AGV records its location and sends that information to the main computer.

When a truck driver arrives to pick up goods, the main computer contacts the AGVs and directs them to the locations of the boxes and pallets for the particular customer's order. Truck drivers arriving for loads submit their order invoices through the same kind of automatic reading port as used by the incoming goods' drivers and also indicate the specific docking bay they are located at. The main computer then reads the order and locates the positions of the boxes that make up the order in the order-staging area. The AGVs are then directed by the main computer to pick up the order loads and to carry them to the appropriate finished-order pick up loading dock bay. When the AGVs arrive at the truck driver's designated bay, they stop. They then can be manually controlled by the truck driver to direct the shipments into the truck. The driver then places the empty AGV on

FIGURE 6-14 DETAILED VIEW OF SMALL-ITEM PICKING AREA LAYOUT

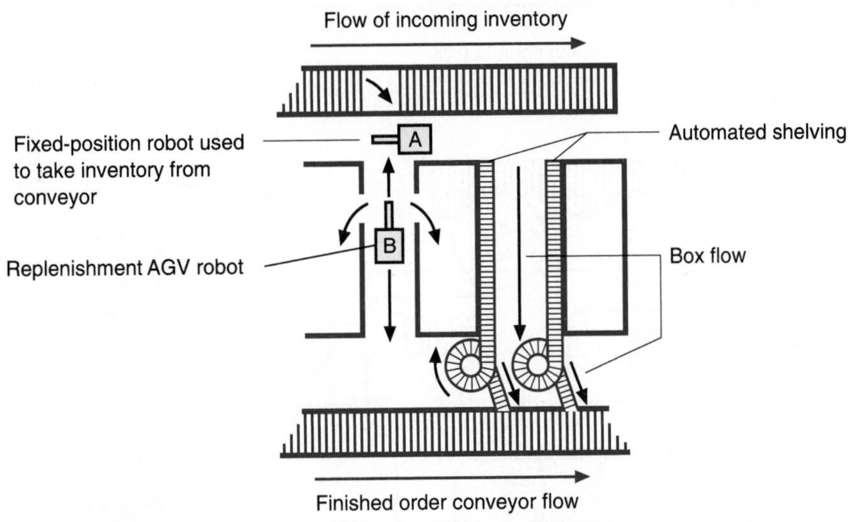

the guide path and flips a manual switch that turns the control of the AGV back to the main computer. The AGV then proceeds back into the facility to retrieve the next load, either off the conveyor line or from a staging location.

When the shipment is completed, the automatic reading port adjusts the order invoice and returns the paper order form back to the driver. The main computer also simultaneously carries out the accounting transactions, inventory transactions, and backordering (if needed) and provides this information to the manufacturing company's computer network for additional processing. In this system, only one general-purpose supervisor is necessary to manage the operation of the plant. The operations supervisor occasionally might be needed if goods are incorrectly sent to the warehouse facility, if a box accidentally falls off a shelf or is replenished incorrectly, or if truck drivers need some instruction on facility operations. This operation also requires a few part-time, specialized maintenance personnel to perform preventive and routine maintenance on the robots and materials handling equipment. Because the robots and AGVs are state-of-the-art equipment, most of them have built-in sensors to detect overheating or irregular behavior. In total, about five or six persons can run this entire facility.

Advantages of Automatic Storage and Automatic Retrieval

The differences between the traditional and state-of-the-art warehouses focus on all three management resources: human, technology, and systems. The workers in an AS/AR operation must be well trained in the technology that they must use. Also, there is a notable reduction in personnel and some reduction in the size of

FIGURE 6-15 AGV GUIDE PATH IN ORDER-STAGING AREA AND LOADING DOCKS

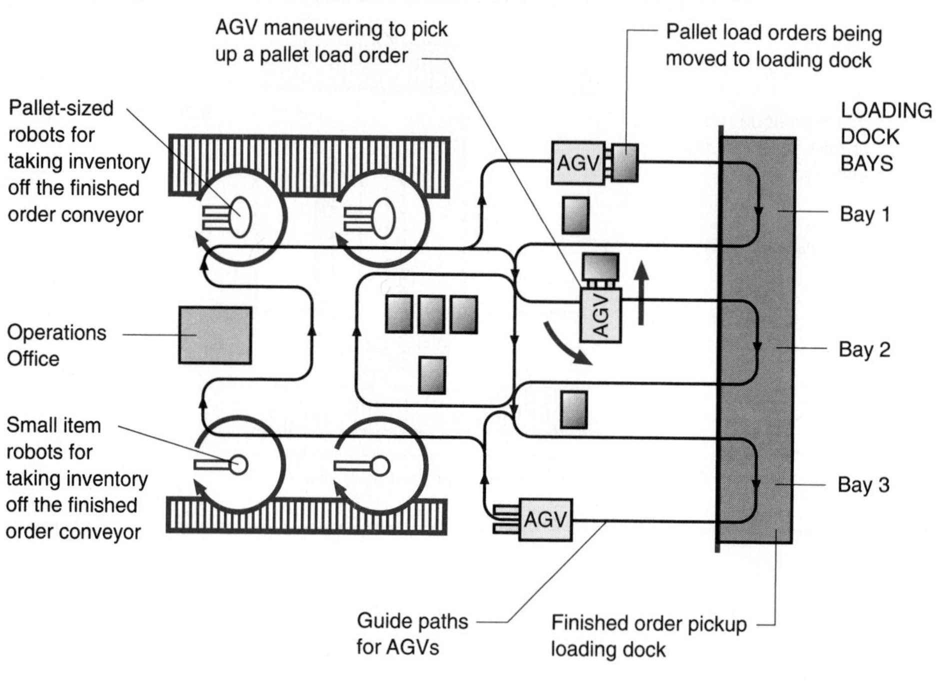

the facility. The required use of single-item boxing in the state-of-the-art operation does require a little extra shelving space. But the robots use less space than their human counterparts; the operation needs only a small lunch room or none at all (the few support personnel can eat in the operations office), does not need a receiving area or office, does not need an accounting and records office, and does not need a shipping office (the boxes are prepackaged with UPC labels); and employees need little space for parking outside the facility. These reductions in personnel and facilities help reduce operation costs and support the costs of the automated equipment.

The automated equipment improves the operation's productivity by eliminating rework caused by human error and by being able to process orders more quickly. For example, the AS/AR system reacts electronically more quickly to an order with a wide variety of instructions than a worker who must physically locate and pick order items that may be spread all over a warehouse facility. The automated equipment's use of UPC labeling improves flexibility for implementing changes in product names, prices, or production codes because physical relabeling in the traditional warehouse is replaced with quick and simple changes in computer memory.

The state-of-the-art facility can also be a paperless operation. While the truck drivers use paper documentation (either for governmental or legal requirements), no paper is used within the facility itself. At every stage in the state-of-the-art operation, time is saved over its traditional counterpart. The difference in materials processing time between the two systems for activities such as inspection, accounting, and paperwork is comparable to the difference between human and computer-processing speeds. The timing differences become evident when correspondence must be sent in the traditional system by mail; in the state-of-the-art system, correspondence is sent by electronic interface through the computer network. This type of timing difference converts days into seconds and greatly improves the organization's efficiency and service in all aspects of its operation (accounting, marketing, manufacturing, and so on). Because one of the major competitive advantages a warehousing facility can offer an organization is timeliness of order processing, the implementation of an AS/AR can be viewed as a tactical plan for achieving strategic organization goals in customer service.

The state-of-the-art system does have its disadvantages, and operations managers should be aware of them to minimize their possible impact. The state-of-the-art warehouse is very dependent on people (that is, truck drivers, maintenance personnel, and vendors). The truck drivers have to be knowledgeable about the operations procedures for both incoming and outgoing loads. This may require special training or self-explanatory instructions outside the facility. Maintenance personnel must be competent and reliable to do their job because the entire automated system is very vulnerable to a single subsystem failure. Vendors and suppliers should also be reliable because the goods coming into the facility are not inspected; only the UPC label is checked against the order invoice. If the item inside the box or pallet is not what the UPC label indicates it should be, there will be no human observation or inspection to detect it until it is delivered to the customer.

The state-of-the-art system is also dependent on the reliability of the system elements. If a single robot sensor goes out in a strategic area of a plant, it could

QUESTION: How do these automated materials handling systems support strategic goals dealing with product or service quality?

ANSWER: Automation is usually used as a tactic to achieve an operations management strategic goal such as improved product quality. In many ways, automated materials handling systems like AS/AR speed customer order processing and reduce transaction time. This improves the quality of the service by reducing customer order-processing time. Automated robots and AGVs can also reduce damage to items that human beings cause by accidentally dropping inventory items during processing. Reducing damage to components and finished goods improves quality in the resulting product the customer receives.

shut the entire facility down. Indeed, a breakdown can represent a considerable cost of time because of the complexity of the equipment. Some operations managers actually use human beings as backups for robots when robots break down. Current state-of-the-art technology in warehousing and in most manufacturing or service applications does little to protect automated systems from these types of outside dependencies. It is left up to operations managers to ensure that the technology performs its stated objectives while overcoming system dependencies.

SUMMARY

This chapter has presented a discussion of the materials management system of operations management. The interrelated roles of production control, inventory control, and materials handling were also discussed as they together define the various functions that comprise materials management. Materials management technology and methods were also illustrated as aids in this field of management.

A major function of materials management is inventory control. The presentation of inventory management in this chapter was brief and provided only an introduction. Managing inventory is one of the most important roles an operations manager can perform. No subject in the operations management area has attracted more interest or been the subject of more research than inventory management. We devote the next two chapters to this subject.

DISCUSSION AND REVIEW QUESTIONS

1. What is materials management?
2. What are the three basic functions of materials management?
3. How does materials management support strategic planning?
4. How is production control related to inventory control? How are they not related?
5. What are the six Japanese categories of robots? Which robots would be more likely to be employed in materials management?
6. What are robot work envelopes and can we use them in OM?
7. Describe what an AS/AR system is and how it is used.
8. How is an AGV different from the fork-lift trucks in Figure 6-4(b)?
9. What is the JIT purchasing philosophy of management?
10. How is JIT purchasing different from more traditional purchasing?
11. What is a *kanban* and how is it used in production control?
12. What is the difference between single-card and dual-card *kanban* systems?
13. What will happen in a *kanban*-based system if the system has no initial inventory?
14. What happens in a *kanban*-based system if *kanban* conveyance cards are added to the system?
15. What happens in a *kanban*-based system if *kanban* production cards are added to the system?
16. What happens in a *kanban*-based system if *kanban* vendor cards are added to the system?

17. Is it possible to take *kanban* cards out of an OM system that uses a *kanban* system? What will happen if you remove conveyance *kanbans,* for example?
18. How is the ABC classification system used in materials management?
19. Why is the ABC classification system based on dollar volume?
20. What is the difference between an A and a C classified inventory item?
21. Describe ways that an operations manager can monitor materials management departments to see if they are operating efficiently.
22. What is the difference between the traditional storage and retrieval system and the state-of-the-art AS/AR system discussed in this chapter?
23. How are UPC labels used in AS/AR systems?
24. How is computer-integrated software used in AS/AR? What contribution does it make to the operating system?
25. How is the transportation method used in materials management (see Supplement 6-1)?

PROBLEMS

* 1. Suppose that we have the following inventory items, their units costs, annual demand rates, and ABC inventory classifications:

Inventory Item	*Unit Cost ($)*	*Annual Demand (units)*	*Classification*
1	100	13	A
2	69	20	B
3	59	30	B
4	1	700	C
5	3	800	C

What proportion of our total materials management resources should be allocated to each of the three classifications?

2. Suppose that a firm has the following inventory items, their unit costs, annual demand rates, and ABC inventory classifications:

Inventory Item	*Unit Cost ($)*	*Annual Demand (units)*	*Classification*
1	140	10	A
2	45	50	B
3	80	20	B
4	3	480	C
5	2	500	C

What proportion of the firm's total materials management resources should be allocated to each of the three classifications?

* The solutions to the problems marked with an asterisk can be found in Appendix J.

3. Following is a list of inventory items, their unit costs, annual demand rates, and ABC inventory classifications:

Inventory Item	*Unit Cost ($)*	*Annual Demand (units)*	*Classification*
1	240	10	A
2	45	50	B
3	80	20	B
4	3	480	C
5	2	500	C
6	240	8	A
7	245	4	A
8	180	12	A
9	1	600	C

What proportion of total materials management resources should be allocated to the three classifications? If you had a budget of $10,000 for materials management resource control, how many dollars should be allocated for each of the three classified inventory items? How do the proportions compare with the general guidelines present in the chapter?

C * 4. (This problem requires the contents of Supplement 6-1). A manufacturer operates four plants and four warehouses. The four plants, A, B, C, and D, produce one item, a custom table. Next week's production capacity in units at each of the four plants is fixed at 800 units per plant. Next week's demand in units at each of the four warehouses the company owns is as follows: Warehouse 1 needs 1,000 tables to satisfy market demand, Warehouse 2 requires 600 tables, Warehouse 3 requires 500 tables, and Warehouse 4 requires 1,100 tables. The cost per unit to ship the tables from each plant to each warehouse is given in the following table:

	WAREHOUSE			
Plant	*1*	*2*	*3*	*4*
A	$12	$13	$ 8	$10
B	10	11	9	17
C	16	19	10	10
D	12	13	8	10

Formulate this problem using the transportation method. What is the least-cost shipping schedule for this problem?

C 5. (This problem requires the contents of Supplement 6-1.) A manufacturer operates three plants and four warehouses. The three plants, A, B, and C, produce portable radios called "boom boxes." Next week's production capacity in units at each of the plants is as follows: Plant A can generate 500 radios, Plant B can generate 400 radios, and Plant C can generate 300 radios. Next week's demand in units at each of the four warehouses the company owns is as follows: Warehouse 1 will require 400 radios to satisfy market demand, Warehouse 2 will require 400 radios, Warehouse 3 will require 200 radios, and Warehouse 4 will require 200 radios. The cost per unit to ship a radio from Plant A to Warehouse 1 is $10, to Warehouse 2 is $12, to Warehouse 3 is $13, and to Warehouse 4 is $15. The cost per unit to ship a radio from Plant B to Warehouse

1 is $6, to Warehouse 2 is $7, to Warehouse 3 is $5, and to Warehouse 4 is $4. The cost per unit to ship a radio from Plant C to Warehouse 1 is $8, to Warehouse 2 is $4, to Warehouse 3 is $6, and to Warehouse 4 is $2. Formulate this problem using the transportation method. What is the least-cost shipping schedule for this transportation problem?

6. (This problem requires the contents of Supplement 6-1.) A manufacturer operates three plants and three warehouses. The three plants, A, B, and C, produce barbecue pits. Next week's production capacity in units at each of the plants is as follows: Plant A can generate 1,000 pits; Plant B, 600 pits; and Plant C, 300 pits. Next week's demand in units at each of the company's three warehouses is as follows: Warehouse 1 will need 350 pits to satisfy market demand, Warehouse 2 will need 450 pits, and Warehouse 3 will need 1,100 pits. The cost per unit to ship a barbecue pit from Plant A to Warehouse 1 is $5, to Warehouse 2 is $5, and to Warehouse 3 is $6. The unit transportation cost from Plant B to Warehouse 1 is $6, to Warehouse 2 is $3, and to Warehouse 3 is $5. The cost per unit to ship a barbecue pit from Plant C to Warehouse 1 is $8, to Warehouse 2 is $4, and to Warehouse 3 is $6. Formulate this problem using the transportation method. What is the least-cost shipping schedule for this transportation problem? C

7. (This problem requires the contents of Supplement 6-1.) A manufacturer operates four plants and five warehouses. The four plants, A, B, C, and D, produce a single unit product. Next month's production capacity in units at each of the plants is as follows: Plant A can produce 800 units; Plant B, 200 units; Plant C, 400 units; and Plant D, 100 units. Next week's demand in units at each of the manufacturer's five warehouses is as follows: Warehouse 1 will require 240 units to satisfy market demand, Warehouse 2 will require 360 units, Warehouse 3 will require 600 units, Warehouse 4 will require 250 units, and Warehouse 5 will require 50 units. The cost to ship a unit from Plant A to Warehouse 1 is $2, to Warehouse 2 is $3, to Warehouse 3 is $6, to Warehouse 4 is $8, and to Warehouse 5 is $3. The unit shipping cost from Plant B to Warehouse 1 is $4, to Warehouse 2 is $1, to Warehouse 3 is $3, to Warehouse 4 is $4, and to Warehouse 5 is $1. The cost to ship a unit from Plant C to Warehouse 1 is $4, to Warehouse 2 is $4, to Warehouse 3 is $5, to Warehouse 4 is $7, and to Warehouse 5 is $3. The unit shipping cost from Plant D to Warehouse 1 is $4, to Warehouse 2 is $2, to Warehouse 3 is $4, to Warehouse 4 is $5, and to Warehouse 5 is $4. Formulate this problem using the transportation method. What is the least-cost shipping schedule for this transportation problem? C

8. (This problem requires the contents of Supplement 6-1.) A manufacturer operates four plants and five warehouses. The four plants, A, B, C, and D, produce a uniform product. Next month's production capacity in units at each of the plants is as follows: Plant A can produce 500 units; Plant B, 200 units; Plant C, 300 units; and Plant D, 100 units. Next week's demand in units at each of the five warehouses the manufacturer owns is as follows: Warehouse 1 will require 700 units to satisfy market demand, Warehouse 2 will require 400 units, Warehouse 3 will require 300 units, Warehouse 4 will require 360 units, and Warehouse 5 will require 100 units. C

The cost to ship a unit from Plant A to Warehouse 1 is $6, to Warehouse 2 is $5, to Warehouse 3 is $4, to Warehouse 4 is $3, and to Warehouse 5 is $1. The unit shipping cost from Plant B to Warehouse 1 is $4, to Warehouse 2 is $1, to Warehouse 3 is $3, to Warehouse 4 is $4, and to Warehouse 5 is $3. The cost to ship a unit from Plant C to Warehouse 1 is $2, to Warehouse 2 is $4, to Warehouse 3 is $5, to Warehouse

4 is $7, and to Warehouse 5 is $7. The unit shipping cost from Plant D to Warehouse 1 is $4, to Warehouse 2 is $7, to Warehouse 3 is $4, to Warehouse 4 is $3, and to Warehouse 5 is $4. Formulate this problem using the transportation method. What is the least-cost shipping schedule for this transportation problem?

9. Suppose that a firm has the following inventory items, their unit costs, and annual demand rates information:

Inventory Item	*Unit Cost ($)*	*Annual Demand (units)*
1001	400	10
1002	46	500
1003	20	80
1004	40	50
1005	3	800
1006	100	100
1007	70	150
1008	35	50
1009	5	400
1010	35	140

Structure these items into an ABC classification system. Are the resulting proportions for this problem consistent with the general guidelines presented in the chapter?

10. Suppose that we have the following inventory items, their unit costs, and annual demand rates:

Inventory Item	*Unit Cost ($)*	*Annual Demand (units)*
1001	4	1,000
1002	6	1,200
1003	40	80
1004	70	50
1005	3	800
1006	100	10
1007	70	40
1008	35	100
1009	5	1,400
1010	35	120

Structure these items into an ABC classification system. Are the resulting proportions for this problem consistent with the general guidelines presented in the chapter?

ARTICLE 6-1

PHYSICAL INVENTORY IN AN AUTOMATED WAREHOUSE

by Joseph P. Becker and Arthur R. McPherson

In late 1980 Texas Instruments in Lubbock, Texas began operating the first Mid-Rise Automated Storage/Automated Retrieval (AS/AR) warehouse, using intelligent lift trucks (without operators) in the United States.

In mid-1983 it became critical that the Consumer Products Group verify what material it had in its AS/AR warehouse. In April of that year a new management team was put into place. Their main tasks were to completely update the hardware, software and inventory accuracy of this three-year old system.

THE TASK

The warehouse management team was asked to physically inventory this warehouse's 8300 skids of material valued at almost 50 million dollars. At the same time all nonessential inventory such as obsolete, warranty repair and finished goods was to be moved to another location. In addition a six million dollar (34 trucks) backlog of inventory waiting at the receiving dock was to be received, inventoried, and stored. The time allocated was just seven days.

This AS/AR warehouse (Exhibit 6A-1) was designed to handle 512 skids in an eight-hour shift. At that rate, working two shifts it would still take us eight days just to do the inventory.

THE APPROACH

We began by categorizing the inventory into two groups. The first was bulk material carriers, defined as one skid containing only one part number in unopened vendor packaging. The second group was multipart carriers—skids containing several part numbers. Bulk material would be verified in the storage racks using teams operating the AS/AR cars in a manual model. The multipart carriers would be inventoried by aisle rather than prioritizing by inventory value as in the past.

The management team then divided the warehouse personnel into teams. Team A would handle the physical inventory. Team B would process the dock backlog of material. Team C would pull the nonessential inventory, count it, ship it and receive it into an offsite manual warehouse. Each team would have sufficient personnel to operate two 10-hour shifts (Exhibit 6A-2). Only Repair and Maintenance (R&M) support people worked three shifts.

Each team consisted of an area supervisor, team captain, counters, verifiers and control auditors. The control auditors audited the inventory as we counted—rather than at the end as had been done in previous years. The physical inventory teams were assigned to 30 work/count stations serviced by the AS/AR system, with each team being responsible for two stations. Team A had the additional function of manually verifying (before starting the inventory) that all carriers were indeed in the storage rack locations that the system thought they were.

To control the inventory process two count coordinators were assigned to:

1. Identify bulk carriers to be inventoried manually;
2. Identify multipart carriers to be recalled through the AS/AR system; and
3. Insure no duplicity of inventory effort.

To determine what to inventory, a part location report was used that indicated: part number by location and quantity, carrier identification number, and inventory value. Physical inventory cards were not used. Instead all corrections were made *real time* via the computer terminals located by the work stations.

THE COUNT SEQUENCE

On day one the carrier location audit was accomplished.

Source: Reprinted with permission from *P&IM Review with APICS News,* January 1985 issue, copyright 1984 TDA Publications Inc.

EXHIBIT 6A-1

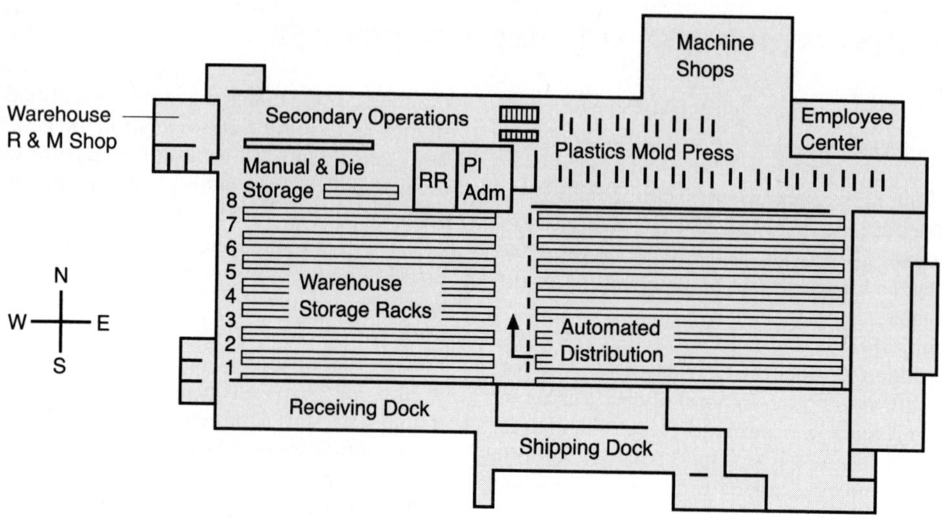

- Sequence for manual bulk inventory is as follows: Aisles 1-8-7-2-3-4-5-6
- We'll inventory levels 1 through 5 starting with level 1 going first East on level 1, West on level 2, etc.

On day two we started receiving and shipping. In addition, we started the physical counts using the following concurrent actions:

- Multipart carriers were recalled via the automated systems from aisles 1, 7 and 8—completing the inventory of material in each aisle before proceeding to the next.
- Aisles 2 through 6 were manually entered with count teams and supervisors to inventory all bulk material carriers in those aisles.
- Upon completing the manual bulk material counts in aisles 2 through 6 *and* after completing the system recalls from aisles 1, 7 and 8, the bulk material in aisles 1, 7 and 8 were manually inventoried.
- The inventory continued by recalling multipart carriers in aisles 2 through 6 via the AS/AR system.

THE RESULTS

1. We had received all 34 trucks on our dock by day five (1520 skids).
2. We had pulled and shipped 1435 skids to the offsite warehouse location also by day five.
3. We finished the physical counts by the end of the first shift on the sixth day (6272 skids). *ONE DAY AHEAD OF SCHEDULE!!*
4. We demonstrated that it was not the number of people needed to inventory, but how efficiently they were used.
5. In total a system that was designed to handle 512 skids per shift was proved to be able to handle 736 skids per eight hour shift.

CONCLUSION

As in all raw material warehouses, we are not responsible for how much inventory there is, but instead how accurate is the inventory. We are a service and support group for the manufacturing site. We must always be ready to react to the needs of the manufacturing line to enable them to produce.

EXHIBIT 6A-2

DAILY SCHEDULE

	Start	*Break*	*Lunch*	*Break*	*Stop*
1st Shift	6:00 AM	8:30–8:50 AM	11:00–11:40 AM	2:00– 2:20 PM	4:00 PM
2nd Shift	3:30 PM	5:40–6:00 PM	8:20– 9:00 PM	11:10–11:30 PM	1:30 AM

Exception: The count control coordinator, team captains, correction support personnel on both 1st and 2nd shift will come to work one hour early.

In this case we had ten days to formulate and present two plans of action to the Operations staff, and execute the inventory. The first plan (at the staff's request) called for the inventory to be completely done manually. That plan entailed using almost four hundred people plus the expense of safety shoes, hard hats, pencils, razor, etc. It was prohibitive. The second plan, and the plan we used, called for less than 200 people. The warehouse had 100 people so only 100 volunteers would be needed from other plant areas.

As always *motivation is the key*. You would be surprised what FREE donuts and Cokes at break times and a FREE party at the end did for the morale of the people asked to work six straight days through a weekend and a holiday.

SUPPLEMENT 6-1
The Transportation Method and Distribution of Materials

The transportation method can be used by the shipping department to minimize the cost of transporting goods from multiple manufacturing plants to multiple warehouses or distribution centers. (Students unfamiliar with the transportation method should see Appendix I at the end of this book.) In organizations in which incoming materials are stored in warehouses until required for production, the transportation method can reduce incoming materials transportation costs. In Supplement 5-3, we were introduced to the transportation method as an aid in aggregate planning that could be used to minimize the cost of scheduling production. We will use it in this supplement as a cost-minimizing aid in transportation scheduling.

The basic framework for a transportation problem formulation is presented in Exhibit 6S-1. In the transportation problem we have m number of supply sources. The supply sources are usually production plants generating s amounts of supply. Production at each plant can differ, but the value of s must be determined for some specific time horizon such as a day, week, or month. In the transportation problem we also have n number of demand destinations. The demand destinations are usually warehouses requiring d amounts of product demand. Demand at each demand destination can differ, but the value of d must be forecast for some specific time horizon to coincide with the supply time horizon. Units of materials are shipped from the supply sources to the demand destinations.

The objective of the transportation model is to develop a shipping schedule that will minimize total transportation costs. The intersection of the rows and columns represent cost cells. Each cost cell contains the cost to ship one unit of supply from a supply source to a demand destination. In practice the estimation of these cost values is usually a combination of variable and fixed transportation cost estimates.[18]

The formulation of a transportation problem is fairly simple. The formulation involves little more than loading the supply, demand, and cost information into a transportation problem table as presented in Exhibit 6S-1. To illustrate, let's look at a sample problem.

Suppose that a printing press manufacturer operates three plants and four warehouses. The three plants, A, B, and C, produce printing presses. Next week's production capacity in units at each of the plants is as follows: Plant A can generate 250 presses, Plant B can generate 300 presses, and Plant C can generate 150 presses. Next week's demand in units at each of the four warehouses the company owns is as follows: Warehouse 1 will require 200 presses to satisfy market demand, Warehouse 2 will require 200 presses, Warehouse 3 will require 150 presses, and Warehouse 4 will require 150 presses. The cost per unit to ship a press from Plant A to Warehouse 1 is \$100, to Warehouse 2 is \$120, to Warehouse 3 is \$40, and to Warehouse 4 is \$90. The cost per unit to ship a press from Plant B to Warehouse 1 is \$50, to Warehouse 2 is \$75, to

[18] D. L. Eldredge, "A Cost Minimizing Model for Warehouse Distribution Systems," *Interfaces,* 12, No. 4 (1982), 113–119.

EXHIBIT 6S-1 TRANSPORTATION PROBLEM FORMULATION

FROM \ TO		NUMBER OF DEMAND DESTINATIONS 1 2 3 . . . n	TOTAL AVAILABLE SUPPLY AT EACH SUPPLY SOURCE
NUMBER OF SUPPLY SOURCES	1		s_1
	2		s_2
	3		s_3
	.	COST OR MILEAGE MATRIX	.
	.		.
	.		.
	m		s_m
TOTAL DEMAND AT EACH DEMAND DESTINATION		d_1 d_2 d_3 . . . d_n	

Warehouse 3 is $210, and to Warehouse 4 is $130. The cost per unit to ship a press from Plant C to Warehouse 1 is $150, to Warehouse 2 is $35, to Warehouse 3 is $85, and to Warehouse 4 is $180. What is the least-cost shipping schedule that will minimize costs while satisfying demand requirements?

The procedure to formulate this transportation problem is as follows:

1. Draw the transportation framework, allowing a separate row for each of the supply sources and a column for each of the demand destinations.
2. Enter the total available supply at the end of each row and the total demand at the bottom of each column. The sum of the supply must equal the sum of the demand or there will be a surplus of one or the other. If a surplus exists, create a dummy row (if the surplus is in demand) or a dummy column (if the surplus is in supply) to absorb the surplus.
3. Enter the cost values in the appropriate cells. If a dummy row or column is necessary, assign a zero cost value in all of the cells. This represents the fact that nonexistent or dummy units will not incur a transportation cost because they will not be shipped.

The formulation for this sample problem is presented in Exhibit 6S-2. (Students interested in understanding the transportation method solution procedure should review Appendix I in the back of this text.) The Micro Production computer solution for this

EXHIBIT 6S-2 SAMPLE TRANSPORTATION PROBLEM FORMULATION

FROM \ TO		DEMAND DESTINATIONS 1	2	3	4	TOTAL AVAILABLE SUPPLY AT EACH SUPPLY SOURCE
SUPPLY SOURCES	A	100	120	40	90	250
	B	50	75	210	130	300
	C	150	35	85	180	150
TOTAL DEMAND AT EACH DEMAND DESTINATION		200	200	150	150	700

problem is presented in Exhibit 6S-3. (Instructions for using the Micro Production software are presented in Appendix H at the end of this book.) As we can see in Exhibit 6S-3, the optimal transportation schedule results in a minimized total cost of $40,500. This cost figure is the total cost to ship all 700 units from each of the three plants to each of the four warehouses. The schedule not only uses all of the supply to satisfy forecast demand but does so with an optimal cost-minimizing allocation.

As with most quantitative methods, the major limitation of the use of the transportation method in materials management is the model's dependency on estimated parameters. The unit supply values are usually obtained from plant capacity reports, which can contain considerable error. The demand values are usually obtained from forecast estimates, which can also contain error. The cost values are usually obtained from average cost estimates (that is, averaged over the number of units to be shipped) from accounting records that may possess considerable cost variation from the "true" cost value. In fully integrated CIM environments, such cost information is becoming more readily available and accurate. The transportation method is best used in production settings where a manufacturer produces a single item. Otherwise separate transportation problems have to be worked out for each of the different products.

EXHIBIT 6S-3 MICRO PRODUCTION SOFTWARE SOLUTION OF THE SAMPLE TRANSPORTATION PROBLEM

Program: Transportation

Problem Title : SAMPLE TRANSPORTATION PROBLEM

***** Input Data *****

Minimization Problem :

	1	2	3	4	Supply
1	100.0	120.0	40.0	90.0	250.0
2	50.0	75.0	210.0	130.0	300.0
3	150.0	35.0	85.0	180.0	150.0
Demand	200.0	200.0	150.0	150.0	700.0

***** Program Output *****

Initial Solution by Minimum-Cell-Cost Method

	1	2	3	4	Supply
1	0.0	0.0	150.0	100.0	250.0
2	200.0	50.0	0.0	50.0	300.0
3	0.0	150.0	0.0	0.0	150.0
Demand	200.0	200.0	150.0	150.0	700.0

Initial Solution : 40500.0

Optimal Solution by MODI

	1	2	3	4	Supply
1	0.0	0.0	150.0	100.0	250.0
2	200.0	50.0	0.0	50.0	300.0
3	0.0	150.0	0.0	0.0	150.0
Demand	200.0	200.0	150.0	150.0	700.0

Optimal Solution : 40500.0

< Initial solution is the Optimal solution >

***** End of Output *****

7 Inventory Management: Dependent Demand Inventory

CHAPTER OUTLINE

CHAPTER OBJECTIVES

The material in this chapter should prepare you to do the following:

1. Explain what dependent demand inventory is and how it is used in the operations management system.
2. Explain what a material requirements planning (MRP) system is and how it is used in inventory management.
3. Describe the information inputs necessary for an MRP system.
4. Explain how a bill of materials file is used in an MRP system.
5. Describe and illustrate a product structure.
6. Illustrate how MRP processing programs work.
7. Describe the information outputs of an MRP system.

8. Explain what low-level coding is and why it is used.
9. Explain what an MRP II system is and how it is used in an OM system.
10. Describe the Japanese philosophy of just-in-time inventory management.

Inventory can be any physical item used in the operations management system. A manufacturing organization may store only a single inventory item, or it may store hundreds of thousands. Even service organizations, which may not have an inventory of tangible finished products, must maintain an inventory of supplies to provide service. For example, a gasoline station whose product is the service of distributing gas must maintain an inventory of gas to supply customer demand. All manufacturing and service organizations require some type of inventory management. S

Inventory can be classified into two groups: independent demand inventory and dependent demand inventory. **Independent demand inventory** is the final demand goods—the goods that will be consumed or used up by the customer as finished goods. Independent demand inventory items can also include replacement or component parts that the manufacturer considers a finished product. For example, a tire is an independent demand inventory item for Goodyear Tire Company, but a dependent demand inventory item for General Motors. Independent demand inventory is determined only by customer demand. **Dependent demand inventory** is items that are used in the manufacture of a finished product. In manufacturing a telephone, for example, the dependent demand inventory items usually include raw materials (such as steel, iron, plastic, copper, and aluminum) and component parts (such as plastic-coated wire, a telephone housing, a dial, and a phone handle). The use of these items is determined within the operations management system. In other words, these inventory items' demand is determined by the independent demand of finished telephones.

The difference in the usage behavior of independent and dependent demand inventory can be shown graphically. Suppose that a finished product is produced by assembling some component parts. We will further assume in this example that the manufacturer is a job-lot operation (discussed in Chapter 1) that produces a fixed lot-size quantity of finished goods at one time. This inventory situation is presented in Figure 7-1. In the top graph the usage (or demand) of the finished product is depicted. This demand follows a five-week usage/replenishment cycle. That is, a quantity, Q, of finished goods is assembled and made available at the beginning of the five-week period. In the fourth week, finished goods inventory is so depleted that a new batch or lot of finished goods is ordered. We call this level an **order point (OP).** In this example, it takes one week to assemble the complete batch or lot-size of Q of finished goods so they can be made available at the end of the fifth week. We call the period of time when an order is placed to when it is delivered (or in this case produced), the **lead time.**

In the graph at the bottom of Figure 7-1 the demand for the component parts is presented. In this example, the order for the finished goods inventory in the fourth week triggers the call for the component parts in the fourth week. The entire inventory of component parts for the batch or lot-size of finished goods is pulled for production in the fourth week. Because the order point for the dependent demand inventory is tripped, a new order of component parts is placed with a vendor to allow lead time for the next order to arrive. This order arrives two weeks later and replenishes the inventory for the next job-lot run in the ninth week.

Comparing the demand curves of the independent and dependent demand inventory items, we can see that the usage of these two different types of inventory varies considerably. Independent demand inventory depends on customer demand, which is usually not controlled by the operations manager. As we saw in Chapter 3 on forecasting, this type of inventory usage may be unpredictable, and its demand curve may be far more irregular than the one depicted in the top of Figure 7-1. As we will see in this and the next few chapters, control over the lot-size quantity and lead time permits managers some planning discretion in managing this type of inventory. The demand curve for dependent demand inventory, on the other hand, is to a much larger extent under the control of the operations manager. In addition to controlling lot-size quantity and lead times, management is better able to control order point values because they are determined by how many units of finished product management wants to produce at one time (that is, product lot-size).

In summary, we can see in this example that there are comparative differences in the demand, quantity, and timing of inventory usage between independent and dependent demand inventory items. These differences in types of inventory have caused differences in their management. In previous years, separate inventory systems were developed to manage independent and dependent demand inventories. Recently, however, new approaches to inventory management have been devised to permit the integration of both types of inventory into a single management system. This evolution of inventory systems is a logical reflection of the computer-integrated systems period of operations management history discussed in Chapter 1.

In this chapter we will examine several dependent demand inventory systems. We will also discuss how computer technology is integrating these systems. Because of the importance of inventory management in operations management, we devote this entire chapter to dependent demand inventory management; we devote the next chapter to independent demand inventory management.

• • •

FIGURE 7-1 A COMPARISON OF INDEPENDENT AND DEPENDENT DEMAND INVENTORY USAGE

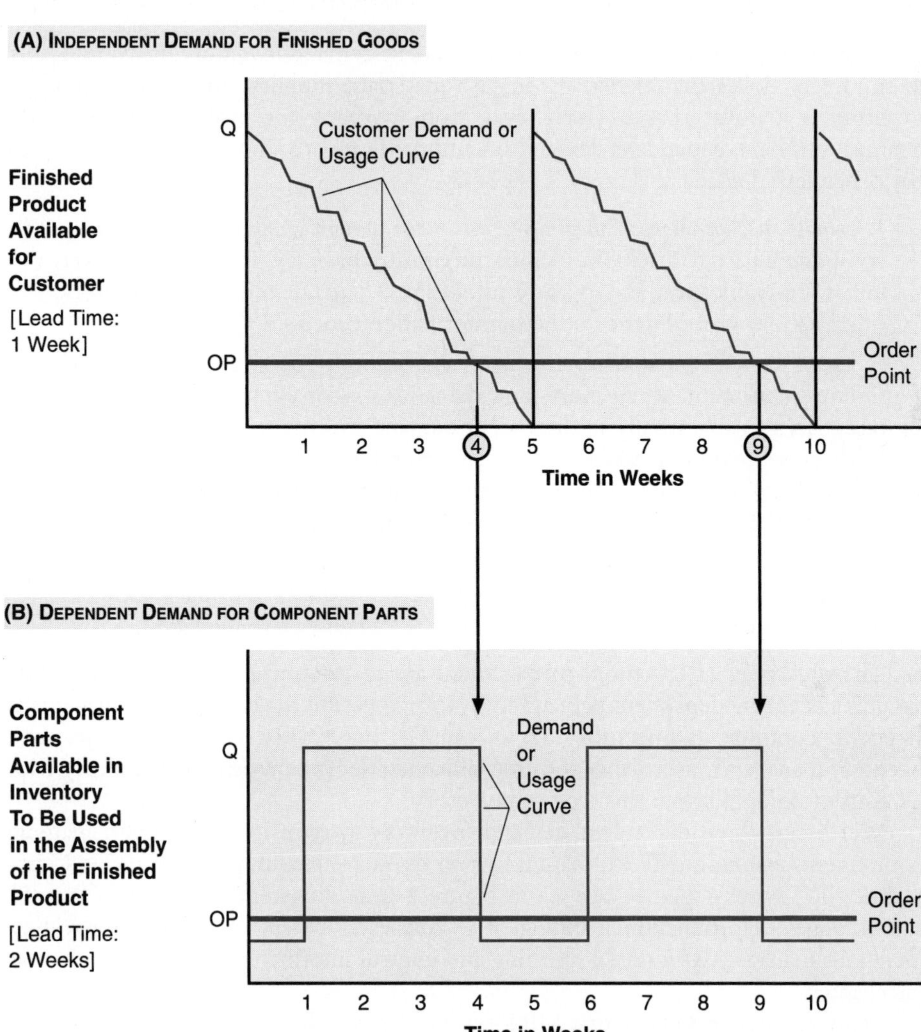

WHY DEPENDENT DEMAND INVENTORY MANAGEMENT IS NECESSARY

If an organization could operate without dependent demand inventory, it would gladly do so. Every dollar that is tied up in raw materials, supplies, and work-in-process inventory is a dollar that is taken away from working for profits. Why then do organizations have dependent demand inventory? Here are some of the basic reasons that dependent demand inventory is necessary.

1. *It permits the operations management system to function.* Assemblers must have component parts to assemble, manufacturers must have raw materials to convert into component parts, and so on. Without some dependent demand inventory, organizations cannot perform the transformation process.
2. *It permits continuous operations.* Inventory can smooth operations to allow continuous production when short-term demand is inconsistent with production rates. An available supply of dependent demand inventory located within the OM system permits workers to keep working during delays caused by bottlenecks in assembly line systems. Inventory can also protect the organization from shortages caused by delayed deliveries from vendors.
3. *It permits acquisition cost reductions.* Inventory allows an organization to reduce its unit price by taking advantage of quantity discounts. During inflationary periods, large purchases can also act as a hedge against price increases.

The objectives of inventory management are to minimize inventory costs while providing adequate dependent demand inventory to permit the operations management system to continue its operation. To accomplish these often conflicting objectives, inventory managers must balance the costs of having dependent demand inventory with the costs of doing without this type of inventory.

We discuss three dependent demand inventory systems in this chapter: material requirements planning (MRP), manufacturing resources planning (MRP II), and just-in-time (JIT) systems. As we can see in Figure 7-2, each system is applied to assist in various stages of production planning. The role each system can play in providing operations managers with useful planning and control information will be described in this chapter.

Many researchers believe that MRP systems historically have made a fundamental software development contribution that has helped cause computer-based systems to integrate and therefore aid in the development of computer-integrated manufacturing (CIM) systems.[1] In this context, an MRP system can be viewed as a production implementation strategy that can move an organization from a noncomputer-based to a fully computer-based CIM operation. Others believe that MRP's extended version, MRP II, is the vital link in completing a CIM system.[2] In addition, MRP systems

---

[1] T. F. Wallace, "MRP and MRP II: The First 25 Years," *Manufacturing Systems* (July 1989), 14–16.

[2] L. Mannis, "Extending the Reach Toward CIM," *Manufacturing Systems* (November 1986), 32–36.

FIGURE 7-2 DEPENDENT DEMAND INVENTORY SYSTEMS AND PRODUCTION PLANNING

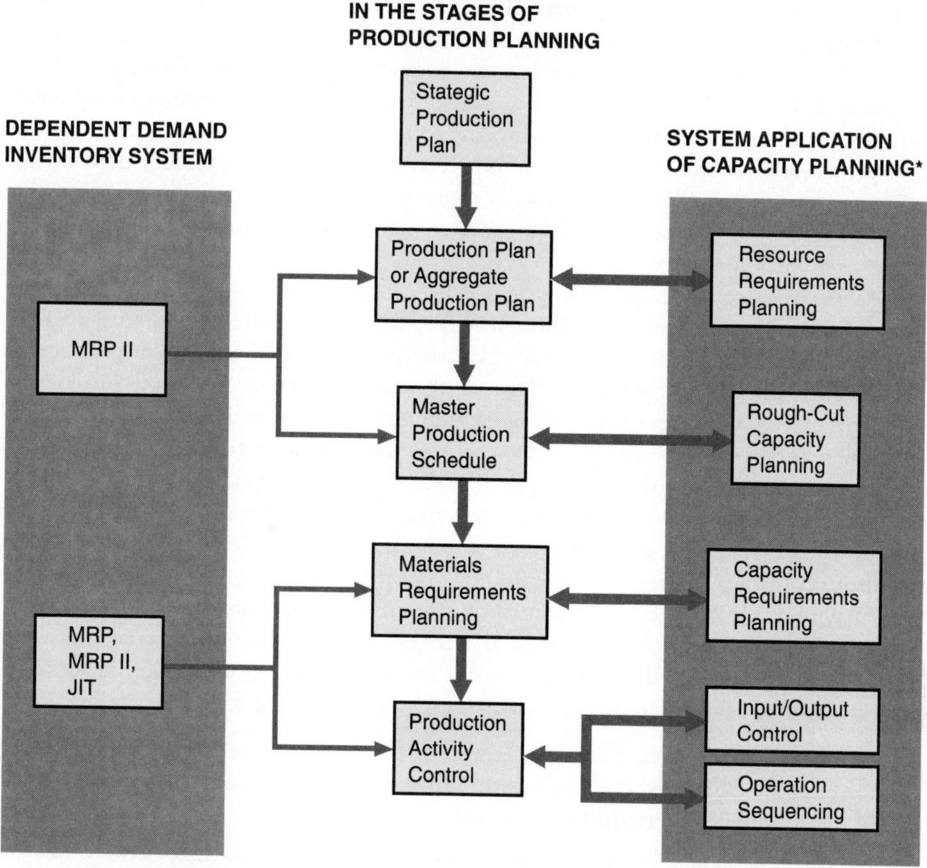

* This section of the figure is adapted and reprinted with permission, American Production and Inventory Control Society (APICS), 1987, CPIM Study Guide.

support the planning and control of dependent demand inventory and are most popular in U.S. organizations that have substantial dependent demand inventory to manage. JIT, on the other hand, is by origin a Japanese production management concept or philosophy that can be used to reduce dependent demand inventory. As we will see later in this chapter, JIT's impact on reducing dependent demand inventory helps improve materials flow and has been integrated into the CIM software as an effective production control system.

MATERIAL REQUIREMENTS PLANNING SYSTEM

One of the most common dependent demand inventory systems used in the United States is the **material requirements planning (MRP)** system.[3] MRP is a computer-based management information system designed to manage dependent demand inventory items in the transformation process of operations management. This includes any products that are made from dependent demand inventory items such as components or raw materials. This computerized inventory system was developed in the 1960s to deal primarily with the timing and tedious record keeping of dependent demand inventory transactions. MRP, however, is more than just a computerized system that tabulates inventory transactions. MRP processes information for production scheduling and capacity planning as well.

As an inventory management system, MRP can be used to plan inventory needs over a fixed planning horizon. Although MRP can plan inventory requirements for a period of from a single day to several years, the information the program generates is usually based on weekly intervals. That is, the planning of specific unit production inventory needs will be defined on a weekly inventory usage basis. In MRP terminology, the weeks (or other time period chosen) are referred to as **time buckets.**

One of the primary objectives of an MRP system is to provide an adequate supply of dependent demand inventory when required for production. MRP also seeks to provide useful inventory, production scheduling, and capacity planning information for inventory control purposes.

As with any computerized information system, there are information inputs, processing, and outputs. An overview of the MRP information system is presented in Figure 7-3. Before an MRP system can be installed, certain prerequisite information must be defined. This prerequisite information can include the following items:

1. *Existing customer orders* These are customer orders that have been contracted for future delivery and open orders (unfinished orders) that must be completed in the production period being planned.
2. *Forecast of demand* This is a detailed forecast of each product that defines the number of units needed and when they will be required over the planning horizon.
3. *Rough-cut capacity plan* This optional plan provides general capacity information that can be used to anticipate and correct resource shortages as well as provide the general guidelines necessary to complete the master production schedule. (We discussed rough-cut capacity planning in Chapter 5.)
4. *Product structure* This information provides a detailed file of the dependent demand inventory items in the various stages or levels of the transformation

[3] See J. Olicky, *Material Requirements Planning* (New York: McGraw-Hill, 1975); T. F. Wallace, "MRP and MRP II: The First 25 Years," *Manufacturing Systems* (July 1989), 14–16.

FIGURE 7-3 OVERVIEW OF THE MRP SYSTEM

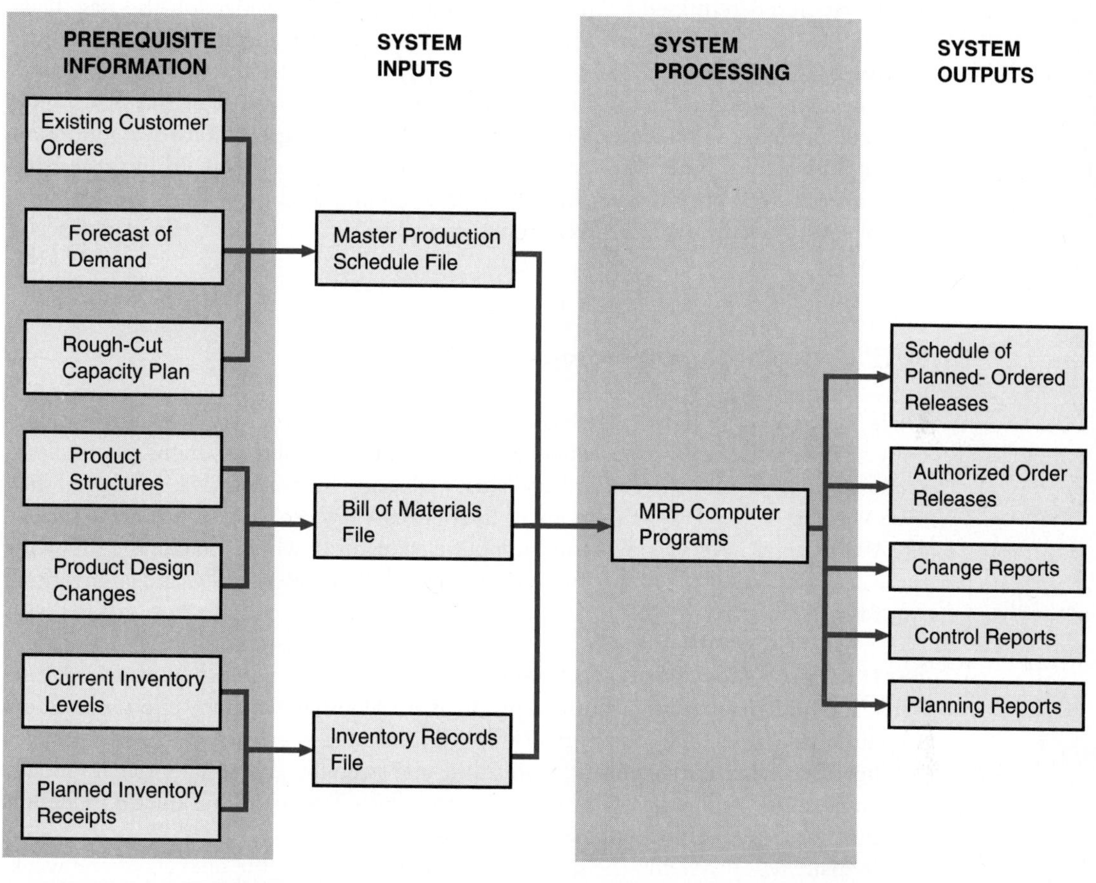

process. This file of information defines the steps by which dependent demand inventory items come together to create a finished product.

5. *Product design changes* This information defines possible changes in inventory requirements caused by product design changes expected during the planning horizon.
6. *Current inventory levels* This information defines the existing or available inventory levels at the beginning of the planning horizon.
7. *Planned inventory receipts* This information defines the amounts of ordered, purchased, or contracted inventory items that an organization expects to receive during the planning horizon.

This prerequisite information is not only required to install an MRP system, but it may also have to be maintained daily or weekly. The frequency of data input into the MRP system is determined by the type of MRP system an organization chooses. There are two types of MRP systems: regenerative systems and net-change systems. A **regenerative MRP system** is a periodic data input system. Under this system, changes in input data are saved until a specific time, such as the end of a week or end of a month. Changes are then run on a group or batch basis. A **net-change system** is a continuous data input system. Under this system, changes are immediately entered into the computer. New MRP planning information is then recomputed for all of the elements in the inventory system that are affected by the changes.

MRP System Information Inputs

Once we have collected the prerequisite information for the MRP system, we must convert it into data that are acceptable to the MRP computer programs. Many commercial software MRP systems are available, and many businesses have developed their own versions of MRP systems to meet their specific needs. Despite this great variety, all MRP systems have several common input data features, which include the following three data files: a master production schedule file, a bill of materials file, and an inventory records file.

MASTER PRODUCTION SCHEDULE FILE A master production schedule file defines when and how many units of finished products are required. The schedule also includes the cumulative lead-time requirements for activities such as procurement, internal processing in receiving and inventory, fabrication, and assembly. These activities are usually sequential, and each has its own timing requirements. The master production schedule file must contain these time-phased requirements by activity.

In many MRP systems, the time horizon is divided into time buckets of one week. Finished goods requirements are defined in units per week in the master schedule file based on the prerequisite information. This means that the MRP system is based on uncertain information such as forecasts. Because of the uncertainty, the master production schedule file requirements may not even be feasible. One of the underlying assumptions in using an MRP system for planning is that production capacity is sufficient to produce everything required in the master production schedule. Unfortunately, production variables are unstable: For example, lead time may not be long enough to permit everything to be accomplished by predesignated dates according to the master production schedule. To avoid an infeasible schedule, the MRP program is usually run repeatedly until a feasible solution is obtained by making some changes in the master production schedule, lead times, or inventory requirements. For example, the use of a subcontractor could reduce some material requirements in the next planning horizon and permit a feasible master production schedule. The MRP program is thus used as a simulation procedure to check an organization's production capacity to satisfy a given master production schedule of product demand requirements.

BILL OF MATERIALS FILE The finished product is referred to as the **parent** of the individual components that make it up. A **bill of materials (BOM)** is a listing of all the subassemblies, intermediates, parts, and raw materials that go into a parent assembly showing the quantity of each required to make an assembly.[4] A BOM file is a structure that defines how all of the dependent demand inventory items are combined to generate a unit of finished product. The BOM file also shows the hierarchical levels or phases of production that a product goes through on its way to being completed. This information is combined into a product structure. A product structure is often a graphic presentation of dependent demand inventory items used in each phase of production.

In Figure 7-4 a product structure chart is presented. In this chart one unit of a finished product (the parent) and its nine different component parts (A through I) are presented by level or phase of production.

QUESTION: Is the parent product always an end product ready for the customer's use or consumption?

ANSWER: No, the parent product can actually be a component part, a subassembly, or a part in any state of completion that the manufacturing operation considers as a finished product. The parent is simply a finished product as far as that manufacturing facility is concerned because it has finished its work on the part's production.

To understand how the chart is structured let's begin with the finished product at level 0. This chart is prepared for only one unit of finished product. Because this product is finished, it is assigned a 0 to indicate that no further levels of production are necessary. The more distant the completion of the finished product, the greater the level number. These levels can be used to group activities by production phase, such as the movement of work-in-process from department to department. The levels can also be used to identify the work-in-process as it moves from workstation to workstation on an assembly line. Generally the levels of completion simply represent the grouping of work activities in the hierarchical phases of the production process.

Continuing with the example in Figure 7-4, the finished product is assembled from three component parts A, B, and C. The "(2)" next to part A means that two units of A are required for each unit of its parent. In the hierarchy of the product tree, the component parts at lower levels are parented by the inventory item at the next higher level. In level 2 the components are used in the assembly of their respective parents in level 1. We can see that the parent of component parts D and three units of E is A, the parent of four units of F is B, and the parent of four units of G and A is C. At the third

[4] Reprinted with permission of the American Production and Inventory Control Society, Inc., *APICS Dictionary,* 7th edition, 1992.

FIGURE 7-4 A PRODUCT STRUCTURE CHART

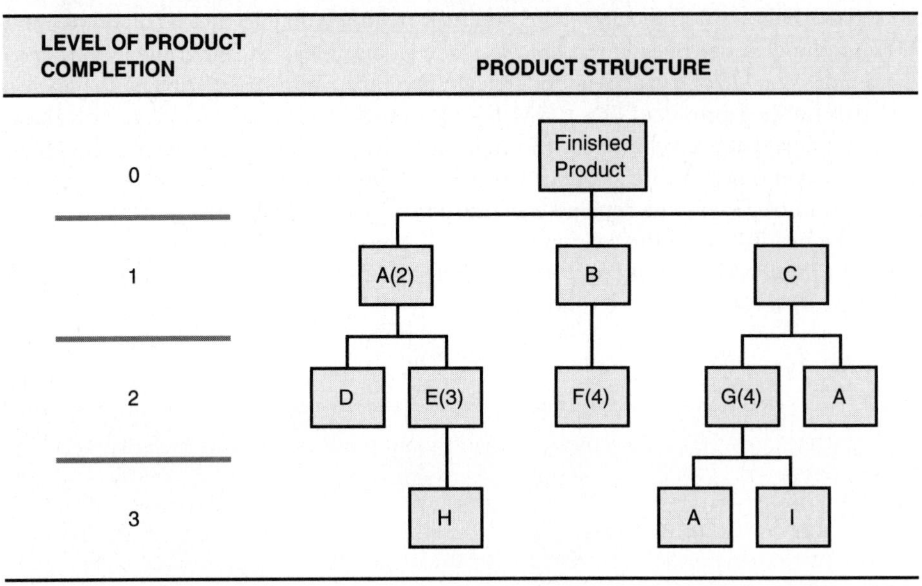

level of product completion, component part H is parented by E and parts A and I are parented by G. Note that each unit of A at level 1 requires three units of E. So if the finished product requires two units of A at level 1 then it will require six units (2 × 3) of E.

As shown in Figure 7-4, component part A is used in more than one level of production. This situation can cause some inefficiency in computer processing because more than one level of processing will have to be considered by the MRP program in processing the material requirements. A restructuring of the product tree structure, performed by the computer, can remedy this situation. This restructuring is called low-level coding and simply involves lowering all of the same component items to the same level in the hierarchy. We discuss this procedure in the section of this chapter called Other Features of an MRP System.

INVENTORY RECORDS FILE The inventory records file contains information on inventory levels—specifically, what the current levels of inventory will be at the beginning of the planning horizon and the scheduled receipts of inventory during the period. Additional information such as inventory item numbers and descriptions are stored in this file.

Inventory records files also include supplementary information for planning purposes. This information includes vendor names, vendor addresses, lead times, and purchase quantities.

QUESTION: How many units of each of the nine different parts in Figure 7-4 are required to complete one unit of the finished product?

ANSWER: Keeping in mind the unitary usage by level of product completion, the units required for each component part are as follows:

A = 7 (2 As at level 1 + 1 A at level 2 + 1 A required for each of the four Gs at level 2)

B = 1

C = 1

D = 2 (1 D for each of the two As at level 1)

E = 6 (3 Es for each of the two As at level 1)

F = 4

G = 4

H = 6 (1 H for each of the six Es required at level 2)

I = 4 (1 I for each of the four Gs required at level 2)

MRP System Information Processing

Once the data are collected and entered into the MRP processing programs, operations managers can use the computer programs in a descriptive or prescriptive mode. In a descriptive mode the data are entered, the programs are run, and the output is used to schedule the operations for the next planning horizon. The programs simply process the data and descriptively generate the appropriate production and inventory requirements for this planning period. Alternatively, operations managers can use the MRP programs in a prescriptive mode and run a series of alternative inventory requirement situations. Specifically, changes in the master production schedule or inventory requirements are simulated and their effect on the change is observed by running the MRP programs to prescribe the best course of action. Whichever mode is used, the MRP programs process the input data to generate a plan of production and inventory transactions.

We refer to MRP programs in the plural because the entire MRP processing system consists of a collection of computer programs. There are two basic MRP systems that are made up of these collections of programs: a net-change system and a regenerative system. In the net-change MRP system, the programs generate new information on only those products that are affected by a change. So if a change in a component part affects inventory planning of only a few products out of hundreds, in a net-change MRP system revised inventory planning information is generated only about the impact on the few products. The regenerative MRP system actually regenerates a whole new basic plan of operation each time that system is rerun.

TIME-PHASED REQUIREMENTS SCHEDULE The internal processing of an MRP system is fairly simple. The MRP system "explodes" the finished product requirements into a time-phased requirements schedule. The **time-phased requirements schedule** charts the lead time requirements for the completion of a lot-size run of a product. For example, suppose the finished product in Figure 7-4 required the lead times for procurement and assembly as presented in Table 7-1. Based on those lead times, the product explosion in Figure 7-5 was determined by an MRP program by starting with the lead time of the finished product and exploding the other lead times backward to complete all of the procurement and assembly activities that make up the product.

In addition to time-phased requirements scheduling, the MRP processing programs determine the quantities of dependent demand inventory needed for production in each time bucket during the planning horizon. To understand the MRP processing system behavior and some of the management planning information provided by the system, we must understand the following MRP terms:

1. ***Gross requirements*** This is the total demand for the inventory item per time bucket. For a finished product the gross requirements come from the master schedule. For all other dependent demand inventory items, the gross requirements are dictated by the parent products' planned-order releases.
2. ***Scheduled receipts*** This is the incoming supply of inventory from vendors or other sources. This serves as an accounting function to notate the arrival of inventory.

TABLE 7-1 LEAD TIMES FOR TIME-PHASED REQUIREMENTS CHART

(A) PROCUREMENT TIME

Item	*Lead Time for Procurement (weeks)*
A	1
D	1
F	2
H	1
I	1

(B) ASSEMBLY TIME

Parent Item	*Component Parts for Parent Item*	*Lead Time for Assembly (weeks)*
Finished product	A(2), B, and C	2
A (level 1)	D and E(3)	1
B (level 1)	F(4)	1
C (level 1)	G(4) and A	1
E (level 2)	H	1
G (level 2)	A and I	1

FIGURE 7-5 MRP TIME-PHASED REQUIREMENTS CHART

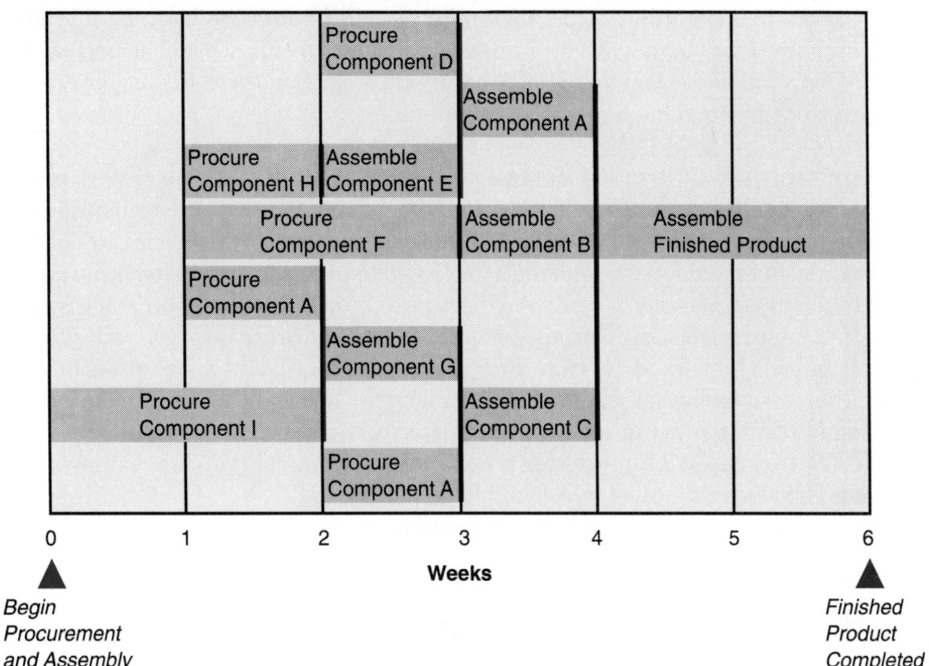

3. ***Available inventory*** This is the total inventory available that can be used to satisfy gross requirements. This inventory includes available inventory carried over from a prior period and the addition of scheduled receipts less gross requirements.
4. ***Net requirements*** This is the total amount of inventory that must be obtained in the time period in which it is listed. It is the difference between gross requirements and available inventory.
5. ***Planned-ordered receipts*** The amount of net requirements inventory we want to satisfy in the time period. The exact amount of net requirements we choose to satisfy depends on inventory ordering policy.
6. ***Planned-ordered releases*** The amount of net requirements inventory we want to satisfy adjusted for lead time requirements. This usually involves pushing the planned-ordered receipts backward in time equal to the lead time for that type of inventory.

The MRP processing programs determine the net requirements for inventory items and then time-phase those requirements so inventory planners know how much inventory is required and when it is required for production. A time-phased requirements processing chart is presented in Figure 7-6. At the top is the master schedule for the finished item. The time buckets are usually dated for some *n* number of periods (in this case, weeks). In the bottom of the figure the six MRP terms are listed by inventory item. Each inventory item will have its own gross requirements, scheduled receipts, and so on. There will be as many of these inventory item boxes as there are inventory items required to complete the lot-size production order.

LOT-FOR-LOT ORDERING VERSUS FIXED LOT-SIZE ORDERING As mentioned, inventory ordering policy determines how much of the net requirements an organization will satisfy in a particular time bucket. Two commonly used ordering policies are lot-for-lot ordering and fixed lot-size ordering. In a **lot-for-lot ordering system,** inventory equal to the net requirements is ordered or manufactured. That is, the order lot is equal to the net requirements lot. This may require a different order quantity each time an order is placed. In a **fixed lot-size ordering system** a fixed lot-size is established, which is ordered each time some net requirements are needed. Thus, in a fixed lot-size ordering system the order quantity stays the same each time an order is placed.

To illustrate the MRP processing programs at work under two different inventory ordering policies, let's look at two examples.

Suppose that we have the following situation:

1. The planning horizon is ten weeks.
2. Finished product demand of 800 units each is needed in the fifth and tenth weeks (a total of 1,600 units).
3. Initial finished product available inventory is 70 units, and the component part guts available inventory is 1,000 units.
4. Scheduled receipts of 50 units of finished product are expected in week 2 and week 7 because of a contract with an outside vendor.
5. The finished product has the following product structure:

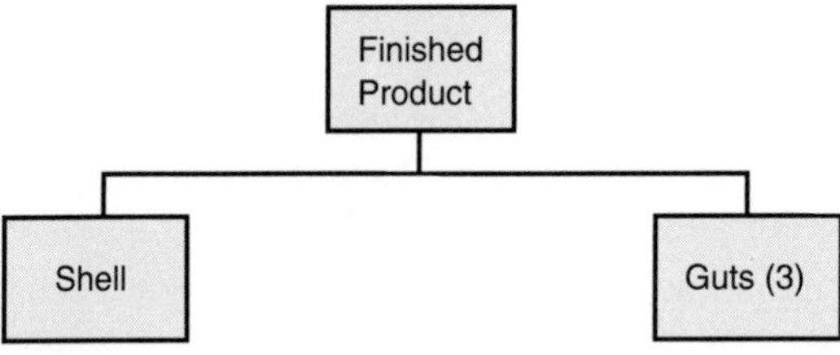

6. Inventory items have the following lead time requirements:

Inventory Item	*Lead Time (weeks)*
Finished product	1
Shell	3
Guts	2

7. A lot-for-lot inventory ordering system is used.

FIGURE 7-6 TIME-PHASED REQUIREMENTS PROCESSING CHART

MASTER SCHEDULE FOR FINISHED ITEM	Week Number	1	2	3	...	*n*
	Quantity					

INVENTORY ITEM • Name: • Number per Parent: • Lead Time:					...	
	Gross Requirements					
	Scheduled Receipts					
	Available Inventory					
	Net Requirements					
	Planned-ordered Receipts					
	Planned-ordered Releases					

Given the inventory requirements just described, the MRP processing programs would generate the time-phased quantity requirements for dependent demand inventory items. These requirements are presented in Figure 7-7.

The master schedule defines the 800-unit requirement for the finished products in weeks 5 and 10. This same amount is entered in the finished product inventory item chart as gross requirements (below the master schedule). The available inventory as stated is 70 units in week 1. Fifty more units are obtained in week 2 from a subcontractor and are added to the available inventory to bring it up to 120 units. This amount is carried over to week 5 where it is subtracted from gross requirements to result in a shortage of 680 units (that is, −680). The 680 units become the net requirements that the company will need to produce or obtain from some source of supply.

In a lot-for-lot ordering system the amount of net requirements is equal to the planned-ordered receipts. Using this policy the company obtains just the quantity of inventory it needs. Because the lead time for the finished product is one week, the planned-ordered releases are required one week ahead of the planned-ordered receipts. The arrows in the finished product requirements chart shown in Figure 7-7 mark the adjustment for the one week of lead time.

Consistent with the product structure, the finished product item is the parent to the shell and guts components of the product. The gross requirements for these two components are defined by their parent's planned-ordered releases. Only 1 unit of the shell component is required for each unit of the finished product, and 3 units of the guts component are required for each unit of the finished product. The gross requirements for guts is therefore 2,040 parts (680 × 3) in week 5. The net requirements for both components are computed in the same way as the finished product. The lead time for the shell is shifted backward three weeks and the lead time for the guts is shifted only two weeks to determine their planned-ordered releases. As we can see in Figure 7-7, 680 shells need to be ordered in week 1 and 1,040 guts in week 2, which will be used to produce 680 finished products in week 4 to have the 800 units of finished

FIGURE 7-7 TIME-PHASED REQUIREMENTS PROCESSING CHART: LOT-FOR-LOT ORDERING POLICY

MASTER SCHEDULE FOR FINISHED ITEM	Week Number	1	2	3	4	5	6	7	8	9	10
	Quantity					800					800

INVENTORY ITEM		1	2	3	4	5	6	7	8	9	10
• Name: Finished Product	Gross Requirements					800					800
• Number per Parent: 1	Scheduled Receipts		50					50			
	Available Inventory	70	120	120	120	−680		50	50	50	−750
	Net Requirements					680					750
	Planned-ordered Receipts					680					750
• Lead Time: 1 week	Planned-ordered Releases				680					750	

INVENTORY ITEM		1	2	3	4	5	6	7	8	9	10
• Name: Shell	Gross Requirements				680					750	
• Number per Parent: 1	Scheduled Receipts										
	Available Inventory										
	Net Requirements				680					750	
	Planned-ordered Receipts				680					750	
• Lead Time: 3 weeks	Planned-ordered Releases	680					750				

680 x 3 = 2040 750 x 3 = 2250

INVENTORY ITEM		1	2	3	4	5	6	7	8	9	10
• Name: Guts	Gross Requirements				2040					2250	
• Number per Parent: 3	Scheduled Receipts										
	Available Inventory	1000	1000	1000	−1040					−2250	
	Net Requirements				1040					2250	
	Planned-ordered Receipts				1040					2250	
• Lead Time: 2 weeks	Planned-ordered Releases		1040					2250			

product available in week 5. A similar process is used to determine the time-phased inventory requirements for the 800 units of finished product in week 10.

Suppose that we have the same inventory requirements as just described for the lot-for-lot example, except that we have a fixed lot-size ordering policy on all component parts. This fixed lot-size ordering policy sets the planned-ordered releases for the shells to be exactly 900 units and the guts to be exactly 2,000 units.

Given these inventory requirements, the MRP processing programs would generate the time-phased quantity requirements for dependent demand inventory items. These requirements are presented in Figure 7-8. As shown, the fixed lot-size requirements have changed the available inventory levels for both component parts relative to the lot-for-lot ordering policy. Under the fixed lot-size ordering policy an excess of components inventory can build up. We can see in Figure 7-8 that both component parts'

FIGURE 7-8 TIME-PHASED REQUIREMENTS PROCESSING CHART: FIXED LOT-SIZE ORDERING POLICY

MASTER SCHEDULE FOR FINISHED ITEM	Week Number	1	2	3	4	5	6	7	8	9	10
	Quantity					800					800

INVENTORY ITEM		1	2	3	4	5	6	7	8	9	10
• Name: Finished Product	Gross Requirements					800					800
	Scheduled Receipts		50					50			
• Number per Parent: 1	Available Inventory	70	120	120	120	−680		50	50	50	−750
	Net Requirements					680					750
	Planned-ordered Receipts					680					750
• Lead Time: 1 week	Planned-ordered Releases				680					750	

INVENTORY ITEM		1	2	3	4	5	6	7	8	9	10
• Name: Shell	Gross Requirements				680					750	
	Scheduled Receipts										
• Number per Parent: 1	Available Inventory				−680	220	220	220	220	−530	370
	Net Requirements				680					530	
	Planned-ordered Receipts				900					900	
• Lead Time: 3 weeks	Planned-ordered Releases	900					900				

680 x 3 = 2040　　750 x 3 = 2250

INVENTORY ITEM		1	2	3	4	5	6	7	8	9	10
• Name: Guts	Gross Requirements				2040					2250	
	Scheduled Receipts										
• Number per Parent: 3	Available Inventory	1000	1000	1000	−1040	960	960	960	960	−1290	710
	Net Requirements				1040					1290	
	Planned-ordered Receipts				2000					2000	
• Lead Time: 2 weeks	Planned-ordered Releases		2000					2000			

Note: Component part shell is produced in fixed lot sizes of 900, and component part guts is produced in fixed lot sizes of 2,000.

excess inventory is starting to build. The shell component, for example, only had net requirements of 680 units in week 4, but the inventory ordering policy required 900 units. The inventory buildup difference of 220 units (900 − 680) is automatically placed in the fifth week's available inventory by the MRP program. This amount is carried each week until it is used in week 9. Managers can use the information on these time-phased requirement charts to schedule production, observe inventory buildup or shortages, and plan inventory transactions with vendors.

From the time-phased requirements illustrated by these two inventory policy examples, the MRP processing programs combine the master production schedule file (that is, what products the firm wants to make and when) with the inventory file information (that is, what the firm has to make the products with) and the production requirements from the BOM file (that is, how and what it takes to make the products) to see if the organization can accomplish its production goals. When exploding the lead time requirements, it sometimes takes more than a year to accomplish a year's production. As previously mentioned, MRP programs unfortunately assume an unlimited production capacity to accomplish its master production schedule. In such a case, inventory managers must change inputs and production plans to accomplish the master production schedule goals.[5] Some of the more advanced commercially available MRP systems permit the software to conduct rough-cut resource capacity planning to identify resource bottlenecks (for example, vendor delivery problems). By simulating the effects of resource bottlenecks and possible corrective action, inventory managers can use MRP as a capacity planning tool to accomplish production goals. We discuss MRP capacity requirements planning later in this chapter.

MRP System Information Outputs

In Figure 7-3 the output of an MRP system includes five types of information: schedule of planned-ordered releases, authorized order releases, change reports, control reports, and planning reports. These are presented here as broad categories of informational outputs of the MRP system. Actually, many additional types of reports and planning information are generated by MRP systems, and most permit users to customize their own reports.

1. *A schedule of planned-ordered releases* is a detailed printout defining the amount of inventory required in a specific time bucket. This printout includes information for all orders and inventory requirements over the designated planning horizon. The information is usually presented in a fairly simple report or reports that list the inventory item by name and number and define the time-phased quantities by time bucket over the planning horizon.
2. *Authorized order releases* are short-term order releases. They authorize a department such as purchasing to acquire a specific amount of inventory for use in a specific period.
3. *Change reports* are initiated by an MRP system if and when planned orders cannot be achieved in the time and quantity originally stated in the master schedule. The change reports can include revisions to order due dates, order quantities, orders that need to be delayed or suspended, orders that will be expedited, and orders that must be cancelled.
4. *Control reports* are generated by the MRP system in the form of statistics on inventory levels status. The reports include information such as averages and

[5] For a complete review of MRP processing see T. E. Vollman, W. E. Berry, and D. C. Whybark, *Manufacturing Planning and Control Systems,* 2nd ed. (Homewood, Ill.: Irwin, 1988).

tallies of orders that will not arrive on due dates, stockouts, and inventory cost information. A special type of control report is called an **exception report,** a report used to signal discrepancies in items such as excessive scrap rates and order delivery dates and to convey other reporting errors. For example, the MRP system will generate an exception report when data are entered that do not make sense to the computer (such as entering data on a nonexistent part or a vendor's not making a scheduled delivery date).

5. *Planning reports* can include many different types of information on inventory requirements. Planning reports might examine the cost of inventory purchase trends, capacity planning, or safety stock levels.

In Figure 7-9, an actual finished goods stock status report is presented. This report was generated by an MRP system for a nationwide electronics manufacturer. This information includes the inventory item's number, description, fixed order quantity (FOQ; under a fixed lot-size policy the FOQ is the planned-order quantity) of 125 units, a unit price to the manufacturer, units on-hand at the beginning of the planning period, the company's demand forecast in units for this product per week (the time bucket in this case), and the weekly sales in units that are used by the MRP program to decrease the available quantity (AVL QTY). The MRP program rounds the weekly sales figure in this application from a 3.9 unit level to a 4.0 weekly demand rate.

The manufacturing quantity (MFG QTY) is the quantity in units that the organization will manufacture. In the example in Figure 7-9, all MFG QTY are zero because the organization does not need to manufacture any units, as the available quantity is sufficient to meet demand. The ordered quantity (ORD QTY) is the units that are already ordered for that week. The planned quantity (PLN QTY) is the amount of inventory required after available inventory is subtracted, or the same as the planned-ordered receipts we discussed previously. The available quantity (AVL QTY) for the first week is derived by adding the planned quantity and the on-hand units and subtracting them from the ordered quantity and the weekly sales. This results in an available quantity at the end of the week dated 1/17 of 108 units (125 + 5 − 18 − 4). For the subsequent weeks, until a new planned quantity arrives in week 4/25, the available quantity is just decreased by the weekly sales level of four units. The cycle then repeats itself in week 4/25. This type of report is useful in planning inventory levels. We can see in Figure 7-9 that anticipated inventory levels do not go below 56 units. An inventory manager may believe that this safety stock is too much and should be decreased. On the other hand, this additional stock may be considered as being too low to meet expected demand surges that are not completely reflected in the average weekly sales figure.

Other Features of an MRP System

In this section we will address some of the additional features of an MRP system in an organization.

FIGURE 7-9 FINISHED GOODS STOCK STATUS REPORT

ITEM	DESCRIPTION	FOQ	PRICE	ON-HAND	FORECAST	WKLY SALES
00193S	MULTIBAND BASE	125	20.970	5	6	3.9

	1/17	1/24	1/31	2/07	2/14	2/21	2/28	3/07	3/14	3/21	3/28	4/04	4/11	4/18	4/25
MFG QTY															
ORD QTY	18														
PLN QTY	125														125
AVL QTY	108	104	100	96	92	88	84	80	76	72	68	64	60	56	177

CAPACITY REQUIREMENTS PLANNING **Capacity requirements planning (CRP)** tries to establish a match between the objectives of the master production schedule and the realities of the production capacity of an organization. Production capacity is the maximum output rate of the whole operation, department, or workstation. An organization may have idle excess capacity and as a result operate inefficiently. An organization may also have too little capacity to complete its master schedule objectives and may lose sales. Operations managers' objective in capacity requirements planning is to ensure that sufficient capacity is available where and when it is needed to accomplish planned production. (Students are encouraged to read Supplement 7-1 to understand some of the methodological aspects of performing a CRP analysis.)

Without materials, productive capacity is idle, and without productive capacity, materials are idle. To plan capacity, an operations manager needs to coordinate capacity requirements planning with materials requirements planning. The lead times that are used in input files include capacity requirements in the production area. If, for example, we say that fifty units of a product can be assembled in ten hours, we are defining production capacity. Production capacity is usually allocated to departments or workstations in an MRP system. To monitor usage and to act as a planning aid, MRP systems generate load reports. A **load report** is a comparative analysis of the expected versus actual capacity usage in a department or at a work station. Load reports can be very detailed and prescribe units of output required and labor hours by skill level or even by employee required.

In capacity planning, we need to determine the capacity of a department or workstation. Once we have this information, we can compare the given capacity with the requirements placed on it by the MRP program in meeting the master production schedule. A graph of a department's capacity requirements is presented in Figure 7-10(a) to illustrate the information contained in a load report. The graph in Figure 7-10(a) consists of units of the product that will still be incomplete (work-in-process) in the next planning horizon and new units that are being planned for production (planned-ordered releases). This department's capacity is exceeded in weeks 3, 5, 7, and 10. In Figure 7-10(b) a typical computer-generated detailed load report is presented. The Hewlett-Packard MRP System load reports detail the percentages by which the planned production capacity is outside existing capacity capabilities.

These load reports clearly identify overload time buckets in the planning horizon. Operations managers must then decide to obtain additional capacity (by overtime or

FIGURE 7-10 MRP LOAD REPORTS

(A) A GRAPHIC LOAD REPORT OF A DEPARTMENT'S CAPACITY REQUIREMENTS

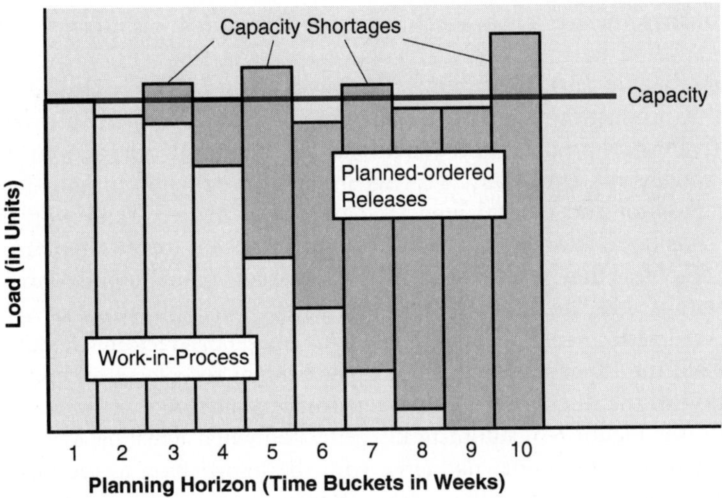

(B) A HEWLETT-PACKARD LOAD PROFILE REPORT

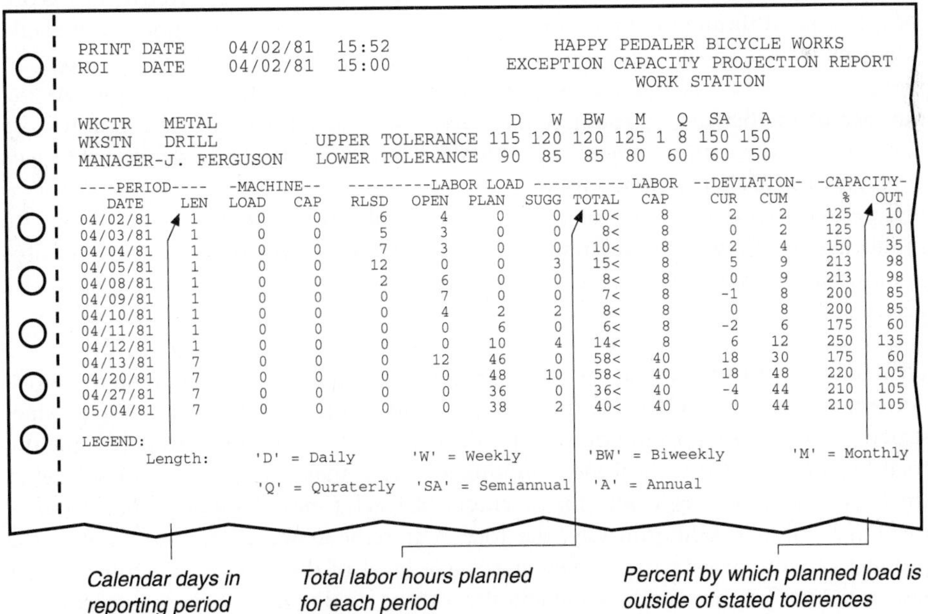

PRINT DATE 04/02/81 15:52
ROI DATE 04/02/81 15:00

HAPPY PEDALER BICYCLE WORKS
EXCEPTION CAPACITY PROJECTION REPORT
WORK STATION

WKCTR METAL
WKSTN DRILL
MANAGER-J. FERGUSON

	D	W	BW	M	Q	SA	A
UPPER TOLERANCE	115	120	120	125	1 8	150	150
LOWER TOLERANCE	90	85	85	80	60	60	50

----PERIOD----		-MACHINE--		---------LABOR LOAD				----------	LABOR	--DEVIATION-		-CAPACITY-	
DATE	LEN	LOAD	CAP	RLSD	OPEN	PLAN	SUGG	TOTAL	CAP	CUR	CUM	%	OUT
04/02/81	1	0	0	6	4	0	0	10<	8	2	2	125	10
04/03/81	1	0	0	5	3	0	0	8<	8	0	2	125	10
04/04/81	1	0	0	7	3	0	0	10<	8	2	4	150	35
04/05/81	1	0	0	12	0	0	3	15<	8	5	9	213	98
04/08/81	1	0	0	2	6	0	0	8<	8	0	9	213	98
04/09/81	1	0	0	0	7	0	0	7<	8	-1	8	200	85
04/10/81	1	0	0	0	4	2	2	8<	8	0	8	200	85
04/11/81	1	0	0	0	0	6	0	6<	8	-2	6	175	60
04/12/81	1	0	0	0	0	10	4	14<	8	6	12	250	135
04/13/81	7	0	0	0	12	46	0	58<	40	18	30	175	60
04/20/81	7	0	0	0	0	48	10	58<	40	18	48	220	105
04/27/81	7	0	0	0	0	36	0	36<	40	-4	44	210	105
05/04/81	7	0	0	0	0	38	2	40<	40	0	44	210	105

LEGEND:
Length: 'D' = Daily 'W' = Weekly 'BW' = Biweekly 'M' = Monthly
'Q' = Qurarterly 'SA' = Semiannual 'A' = Annual

Source: Part (B) of figure copyright 1986 Hewlett-Packard Company. Reproduced with permission.

subcontracting work) to achieve the given master production schedule or they must decide which orders will not be completed. To allocate production capacity to those orders that will be completed, operations managers can use a priority system that most MRP systems are equipped with. This priority system expedites orders according to a ranking dictated by management or established by the MRP system to maximize work flow.

MRP systems also help in capacity planning at the production activity control level or shop floor level of production planning (see Figure 7-2). MRP systems provide detailed work reports for unit production requirements for individual workstations or individual workers weekly and even daily. This type of unit production information allows managers to monitor and control input and output of materials and worker performance on the shop floor. Workers in a CIM-based MRP system are often required to log on and log off jobs as they complete them. This current input/output control provides managers with up-to-date information on the status of materials usage as well as the workers' expected performance as determined by the master production schedule. If a worker falls behind the expected schedule a manager might receive an exception report to call attention to the discrepancy. An **exception report** is one of the many MRP control reports (see Figure 7-3) automatically generated when actual behavior of the operations management system does not agree with the information in the input files of the system. We will discuss exception reports later in this chapter.

Sometimes the discrepancy between the master production schedule and actual work is not due to worker performance but rather the sequence of operations (or the routing of jobs through the transformation process) defined in the BOM file. Work must be routed through the transformation process to its final completion as efficiently as possible. Occasionally, the routing of one job may delay another job, creating an inefficient sequence of operations or routing for the completion of the job. As the number of inefficient job routings increases, the total number of jobs that will be completed by the entire production system decreases. The MRP program lets managers experiment with alternative job routings to see if a more efficient sequence of operations will permit a greater amount of work to be completed by the overall operation. By simulating the effects of the different routings and helping managers choose the capacity-minimized routes for jobs, MRP programs become an operation sequencing capacity planning technique.

LOW-LEVEL CODING When the MRP processing programs start processing the product structures in the BOM file, the programs start at the highest level of the product structure and work up to the finished product at level 0. The programs determine the total requirements for each of the component parts as they proceed from each level to the next. Checks are made with the inventory file each time a component part requirement is identified. Unfortunately, the total requirements for a component part of a product cannot always be identified at a single level of the product structure. As we saw in Figure 7-4, the same component part can be used at more than one level in the completion of a finished product. For example, the same sized bolt can be used in different stages of the manufacture of a car. This multilevel use of the same component part can make the MRP computer program operate very inefficiently: The MRP program has to scan the entire product structure and reorganize the data into a useful format rather than processing just the information sequentially by level of product completion. This reformatting is often referred to as *low-level coding* because it can involve the creation of lower levels of operations for various component parts. What the computer does in low-level coding is to bring all of the same component parts to a single level of product completion. Because MRP processing programs scan a single level at one time, the total requirements for a part can be much more easily determined if all of the same parts are on a single level.

To illustrate low-level coding reformatting, let's revise the product structure in Figure 7-4 so the component part A is on a single level of the tree. This reformatted product structure is presented in Figure 7-11. As we can see, all of the A component parts are at the third level of product completion. We can also see that there are now two additional levels (4 and 5). Although the addition of these lower levels will add some extra processing time for this product structure, it can still be processed much faster than the structure presented in Figure 7-4 since the program will not have to skip back and forth to various levels for the same component part.

BUFFER STOCK, SAFETY STOCK, AND SCRAP ALLOWANCES The lead time estimates used in MRP programs may be inaccurate because few people can precisely anticipate future events such as materials deliveries. Shortages of materials do not only occur because an operations management system fails to receive a timely delivery of materials. Sometimes an OM system can create its own shortages. Absenteeism or machine breakdown can delay work-in-process between workstations. Workers may also accidentally waste or destroy component parts. These wasted parts become scrap that must be reworked (which can delay other parts) or eliminated from the system. Parts and other inventory items can also be eliminated from the system when they are stolen or damaged. How does the MRP system, which is so dependent on every part being in the right place at the right time, survive these types of shortages?

One way to keep the operation going even with delays in materials is with buffer stocks and safety stocks. The buffer stocks or extra inventory is usually positioned at workstations to keep workstation activity constant during temporary inventory shortages. This extra inventory buffers the workstations against shortages at various workstations. Safety stocks are extra inventory items that buffer the entire operations management system from shortages external to the organization. A safety stock can be either the raw materials, component parts, or supplies entering the OM system, or it can be finished goods inventory. The exact amount of buffer or safety stock necessary is usually determined by researching the unique requirements of the manufacturing system. We discuss estimating buffer and safety stock in Chapter 8. Once the amount of buffer or safety stock is determined, it is added to the materials requirements in the MRP program. The extra stock is then allocated automatically with the expected amount to fit inventory requirements.

LOT SIZING As we saw in the section MRP System Information Processing, an inventory ordering policy on lot sizing is a necessary prerequisite to install the MRP

FIGURE 7-11 LOW-LEVEL CODING OF A PRODUCT STRUCTURE FOR COMPONENT A

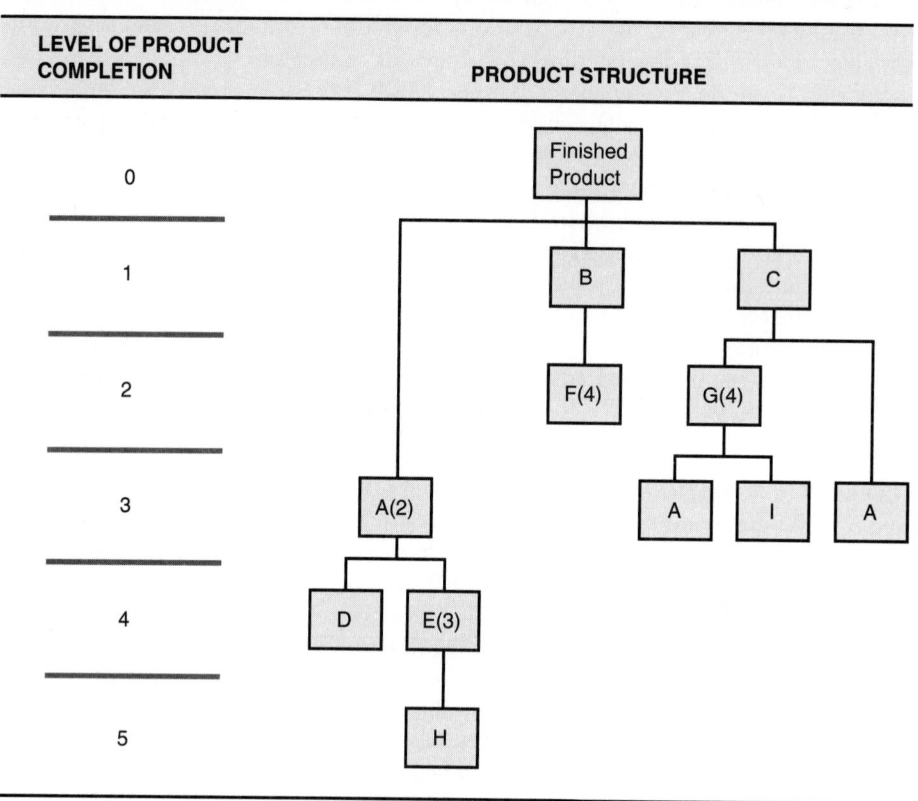

system. Several ordering policies can be used including lot-for-lot and fixed order quantity. These policies and other lot sizing plans are determined by combining inventory cost information with production scheduling productivity considerations to select the least costly or most productive policy to follow. For this reason, we will expand our discussion of lot sizing in the next few chapters, which deal with inventory and production scheduling.

A lot-for-lot ordering policy is usually used by organizations that schedule their production on a **produce-to-order** basis. A firm that produces to order produces for known demand (that is, existing orders and backorders) and may not use uncertain forecasts to plan production. The lot-for-lot ordering system entails inventory requirements equaling the demand requirements that were not satisfied by existing inventory levels. This type of system minimizes inventory because it orders only the net requirements (demand requirements minus existing stock); it does not permit the organization much opportunity to take advantage of quantity discounts, however, because large planned order quantities are not possible.

A fixed order quantity policy is usually practiced by organizations that schedule their production to permit the buildup of finished goods inventory. These organizations are called **produce-to-stock** firms. These firms use existing orders, backorders, and forecasts of future demand to plan and schedule their production. Under a fixed order quantity policy, a fixed quantity is ordered each time an order is placed as long as costs (such as the cost of ordering and carrying costs) remain the same. One of the most common fixed order quantity methods is called the economic order quantity (EOQ) model. (We discuss the EOQ model in Chapter 8.)

Advantages and Disadvantages of an MRP System

The cost of the software for an MRP system for a manufacturing concern can range from $150 (for a microcomputer system) to $500,000 (for a mainframe system). This is only a small part of the true cost of the system. The computer system has to be installed and people must be trained to use it. In addition, the software must be modified to serve the acquiring firm's reporting and control needs, validated and tested for any possible errors, and, most importantly, maintained. The most costly aspect of the MRP system, however, is the amount of data that must be continuously collected and entered into the MRP system because of the time and care involved. Nevertheless, for many organizations the advantages of using the MRP system outweigh the disadvantages. Advantages of using an MRP system include the following:

1. It is a detailed means of controlling inventory items on a current (with a net-change system) or almost current (with a regenerative system) basis.
2. It improves production scheduling because the system sets deadlines on material arrivals and production activities.
3. It reduces all types of inventory levels because the timing of materials minimizes the need for safety and buffer stocks.
4. It aids in capacity planning.
5. It provides a way to examine different inventory ordering policies by simulating their possible impact on the operations management system.

Some of the disadvantages include the following:

1. Planning and implementation time for MRP systems can and usually does take years.
2. Data entry requirements and file maintenance are very time consuming and require substantial personnel training and education.
3. Dependence of the entire system on forecasts and estimated lead times can make the informational value of the MRP output questionable and can even mislead managers on the actual capability of the operations management system.

4. Although microcomputer systems exist to support small OM operations, in practice an MRP system requires the costly computer time of a large-scale or mainframe computer system.[6]

MRP systems' popularity has continued to increase as they are combined with other technologies. The use of bar codes (universal product codes or UPC labels) on inventory items and optical scanning equipment for input into the computer system has been shown to be a very successful method of information input when speed of information input is of critical importance or personnel are not trained.[7] Despite the disadvantages of MRP systems, they have been a successful management planning tool for many organizations.[8]

MANUFACTURING RESOURCE PLANNING SYSTEM (MRP II)

Like most management information systems, MRP systems used for inventory planning can be expanded to support other operations management functions like production scheduling and purchasing. This expansion can continue beyond the boundaries of the OM department and include sharing information with the engineering, accounting, marketing, and finance departments. Integrating some or all of these departmental areas within the organization redefines the nature of the computer-based MRP system into a full-scale management information system for manufacturing organizations. Inventory managers call this type of multidepartmental information-sharing integrated system a **manufacturing resource planning** or **MRP II** system. The purpose of MRP II systems is to integrate and share timely information with managers throughout an organization. This timely and increased information permits respective department managers to make better planning decisions; control operations more closely; and make quick changes in materials, methods, and products to respond to changes in the organization's external environment.

A number of commercially developed MRP II systems are available to support the information needs of most manufacturing organizations. Arthur Andersen Company's MAC-PAC system (described in Chapter 5), IBM's Manufacturing Accounting and Production Information Control System or MAPICS (which we discuss in Chapter 9), and Hewlett-Packard's HP Manufacturing Management II System are all different versions of the MRP II system. To provide some idea of the depth of information and

[6] Developments in microcomputers and MRP software have allowed some application of microcomputer MRP systems. See D. L. Turnipseed, O. M. Burns, and W. E. Riggs, "An Implementation Analysis of MRP Systems: A Focus on the Human Variable," *Production and Inventory Management Journal,* 33, No. 1 (1992), 1–6; and A. H. Greene, "Micro Systems Still Have My Vote," *Production and Inventory Management Review,* 9, No. 1 (1989), 30–31.

[7] H. A. Bailey, "Bar Coding: The Universal Language," *Production and Inventory Management Review,* 9, No. 12 (December 1989), 45–47.

[8] T. F. Wallace, "MRP and MRP II: The First 25 Years," *Manufacturing Systems* (July 1989), 14–16.

integration of these systems, we describe Hewlett-Packard's Manufacturing Management II System in this section.

The major characteristic of all MRP II systems is that they integrate information from different departments within an organization. As we can see in the overview of Hewlett-Packard's MRP II system in Figure 7-12, select department activities of operations management, marketing, and accounting are integrated to form the system. Hewlett-Packard's MRP II system basically consists of eight fully integrated modules. Each module is a separate software system that users can choose to integrate or not integrate into the complete system. This permits potential users to exclude the marketing or accounting-related modules if they choose to do so. Because the real strength of an MRP II system is increased by the sharing of information, users are encouraged to include as many software modules as possible.

Each of the eight basic software modules have a number of management planning and control features. The features for the three operations management–related modules on materials management, production management, and purchasing are presented in Figures 7-13, 7-14, and 7-15, respectively. The HP Materials Management module in Figure 7-13 is basically an MRP program that is integrated into the other modules. The HP Production Management module in Figure 7-14 extends the MRP system into

FIGURE 7-12 HEWLETT-PACKARD (HP) MANUFACTURING MANAGEMENT II SYSTEM MODULES

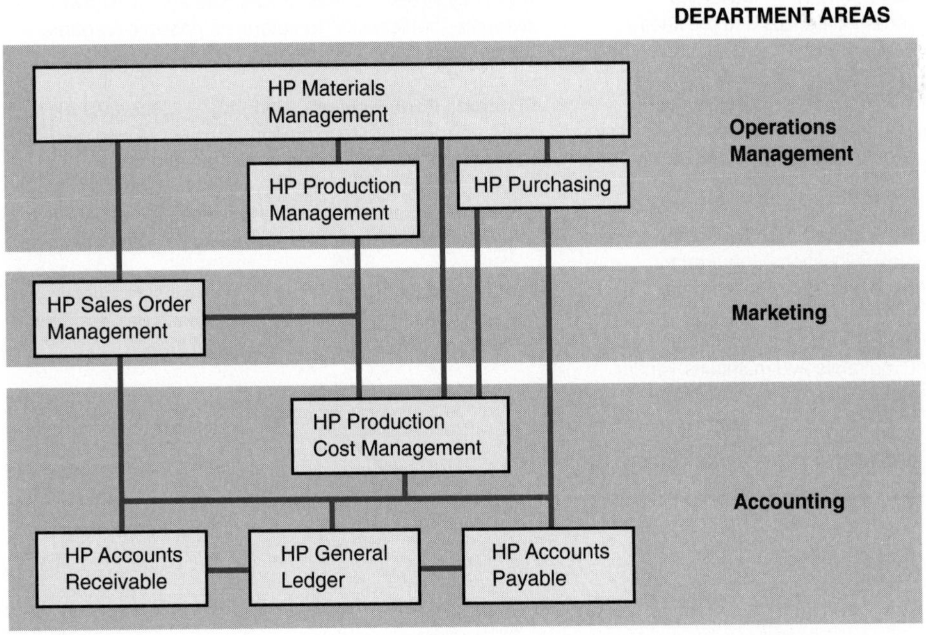

FIGURE 7-13 HP MATERIALS MANAGEMENT MODULE OVERVIEW AND FEATURES

(A) MODULE OVERVIEW

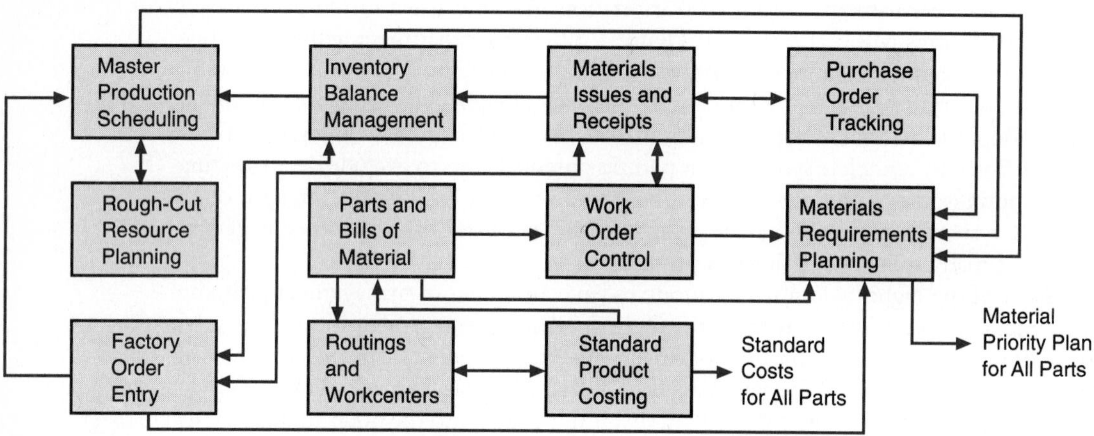

(B) MANAGEMENT PLANNING AND CONTROL FEATURES

Master Production Scheduling — Provides the capability for on-line production schedule development and on-line "What If" simulation.

Inventory Balance Management — Maintains information about inventory balances and provides control of cycle counting and management of inventory locations.

Material Issues and Receipts — Provides the facility for issues and receipts of materials and also maintains the audit trail.

Work Order Control — Tracks scheduled receipts and monitors planned issues (allocations) required for assembly. Also maintains and tracks backorders.

Purchase Order Tracking — Monitors scheduled receipts of purchased materials and maintains vendor information. Provides purchase order commitment information.

Factory Order Entry — Provides a flexible method to enter, maintain, and initiate shipment of factory orders.

Rough-Cut Resource Planning — Provides the capability to test the master schedule against known resource "bottlenecks" to determine possible resource constraints.

Materials Requirements Planning — Generates the materials plan with recommendations about what and how much material to order and when to order it.

Standard Product Costing — Provides the capability to roll-up current costs and to accurately set standard costs.

Parts and Bills of Materials — Maintains descriptive, cost, and planning information about each part and how it relates to other parts in product structures.

Source: Copyright 1986 Hewlett-Packard Company. Reproduced with permission.

FIGURE 7-14 HP PRODUCTION MANAGEMENT MODULE OVERVIEW AND FEATURES

(A) MODULE OVERVIEW

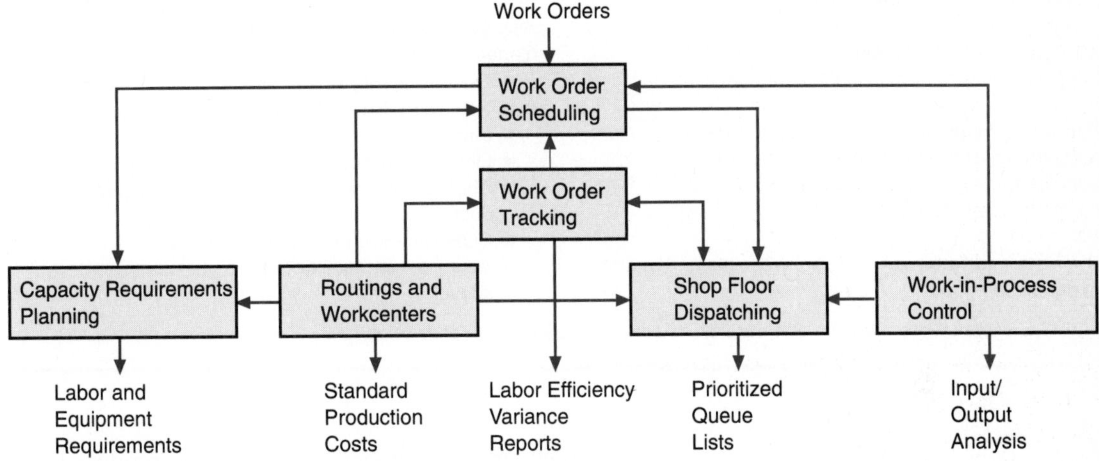

(B) MODULE MANAGEMENT PLANNING AND CONTROL FEATURES

Routings and Workcenters — Maintains descriptive, cost, and planning information about each workcenter in a manufacturer's production facility and the routing sequence necessary to build each assembled or fabricated part.

Work-in-Process Control — Provides a variety of tools to analyze the progress of the manufacturing plan and allows production managers to fine-tune the shop floor control process.

Work Order Scheduling — Calculates start and completion dates for each sequence of every production work order under the control of HP Production Management.

Shop Floor Dispatching — Maintains production priorities to ensure that manufacturing resources are devoted to the right tasks at all times.

Work Order Tracking — Records the progress of each work order as well as related labor charges and exception information.

Capacity Requirements Planning — Develops labor and other manufacturing resource requirements on the basis of in-process production work orders and/or planned work orders from a Materials Requirements Planning system.

Source: Copyright 1986 Hewlett-Packard Company. Reproduced with permission.

production scheduling (the subject of Chapter 9). The HP Purchasing module in Figure 7-15 is fully integrated into accounting functions to record purchasing transactions and provide information that links it to financial planning aspects.

The marketing department interface in this system is through the HP Sales Order Management module in Figure 7-16. One of the most attractive features of MRP II systems is their ability to provide information on available to promise production. **Available to promise** represents units of finished goods inventory that are available to be promised to a customer in the future. MRP II systems provide sales personnel

FIGURE 7-15 HP PURCHASING MODULE MANAGEMENT PLANNING AND CONTROL FEATURES

Purchase Order Requests (PORs) — Links the material planning function and the purchasing function.

Purchase Order Management — Converts the purchase order request into a vendor commitment.

Vendor Management — Provides the capability to store and retrieve all the information necessary to select the appropriate vendor and negotiate the best possible terms for a purchase order.

Receipts and Returns — Controls receipts and returns of purchased goods.

Link to Financials — Provides for the matching of receipts to the appropriate invoice and purchase order. Also posts appropriate financial information to HP General Ledger and HP Accounts Payable.

- On-line visibility of MRP-suggested PORs
- Review PORs by POR number or part number
- Multiple line items per POR number
- Line item consolidation by due dates
- Ability to add requirements to meet independent demand
- POR remarks in multiple languages
- Approval step for PORs to provide controller level security

Source: Copyright 1986 Hewlett-Packard Company. Reproduced with permission.

with information as to when certain units of finished goods will be produced and available for sale to customers. Before MRP II systems, this type of information was only available from operations managers based on tabular estimation at best, and sometimes on judgmental guessing. With an MRP II system, unit production per time bucket in the future is a fairly exact science based on predetermined production scheduling. Sales representatives can actually access the production scheduling module through their own computer facilities and obtain the necessary product availability information without the need for judgmental decision making by operations management. This timely information can give salespeople a competitive advantage because they are more reliably able to confirm the timing of delivery dates while closing the sale with customers.

The accounting department interface in this system is through four HP modules: HP Production Cost Management, HP Accounts Payable, HP Accounts Receivable, and HP General Ledger (shown in Figures 7-17, 7-18, 7-19, and 7-20, respectively). As we can see in these figures, an enormous amount of accounting and operations management information is provided by these modules. The MRP II system helps the accounting department accomplish its OM information role, which we outlined in Chapter 1. The MRP II system provides timely on-line reports that allow operations managers to keep track of costs and to control their variation from expected levels.

The HP MRP II system can also be expanded with additional modules to interface other financial, marketing, operations management, and accounting functions. As the modules are added, the MRP II system becomes a broader-based management information system to support planning and control in all areas of the business organization. Some people believe that MRP II systems are actually the foundation of computer-integrated manufacturing (CIM).[9]

---

[9] T. Lippolt, "MRP II: The Foundation of CIM," *Production and Inventory Management Review* (November 1986), 35–37.

FIGURE 7-16 HP SALES ORDER MANAGEMENT MODULE PLANNING AND CONTROL FEATURES

Marketing Link to Manufacturing — Provides the ability to pass order demand information automatically to manufacturing, receive shipping instructions from manufacturing, and determine Available to Promise.

Sales Order Tracking — Provides on-line entry of sales orders, change orders, and delivery schedules.

Shipping — Generates picking and shipping documents if the order passes the appropriate system checks. Triggers relief of finished goods inventory upon shipment confirmation.

Billing — Generates invoices with both product and miscellaneous charges. Also provides the ability to issue debit and credit memos.

Credit Checking — Provides on-line customer credit checking when the order is placed and/or when the order is to be shipped. Access into the customer's A/R balance as well as age of oldest invoice is provided.

Sales Analysis — Provides sales information by customer, product, order type, sales territory, product classification, and/or user-defined criteria.

- On-line update for new and changed order information in HP Materials Management
- Real time "available to promise" and inquiry to master scheduled parts
- Cross-reference between marketing part number and manufacturing part number

Source: Copyright 1986 Hewlett-Packard Company. Reproduced with permission.

QUESTION: How does MRP II help organizations achieve their product quality goals?

ANSWER: MRP II systems can substantially help organizations achieve product quality goals by providing information on which quality-related decisions can be made quickly and efficiently.[10] In inventory management a computer-based MRP II system can avoid non-value–added materials handling when changes in order priorities or inventory locations occur or orders are cancelled. Customer service is also enhanced by quick access to computer-based records on product specifications. In an MRP II system, component part and finished product specifications can be quickly checked against unique customer requirements. This improves the quality of customer service because timely information on the manufacturer's ability to provide unique products is available. Information on product quality is also shared in an MRP II system with managers, engineers, and workers. The sharing of information on-line allows workers to communicate quality problems to managers quickly and managers to share information with engineers for their resolution. The quicker the quality problems are identified and resolved, the less scrap and waste is generated and the further along the organization will be in achieving its product quality goals.

[10] J. Cingari, "What Is the Role of MRP II in Quality?" *APICS—The Performance Advantage,* 2, No. 2 (February 1992), 24–25.

FIGURE 7-17 HP PRODUCTION COST MANAGEMENT MODULE PLANNING AND CONTROL FEATURES

GENERAL FEATURES

- Support single or multiple manufacturing systems
- Provides work-in-process inventory valuation and reporting
- Provides labor and material variancing and reporting
- Variances actual to standard costs and actual to current costs
- Offers simulation and exception reporting with user-selected criteria
- Uses on-line, user-maintained account tables
- Creates vouchers for automated general ledger input with support audit trail
- Standard cost based — job order cost accumulation
- Automatic journal voucher creation and general ledger posting

COST ACCOUNTING SYSTEM

Inventory Cost Control — Accumulates and reports on work orders and manufacturing orders opened on the manufacturing floor.

FEATURES

- Provides work-in-process inventory valuation through reports and on-line reviews
- Offers a data entry feature for on-line add, change, and delete activities. Provides capability to enter non-order related transactions. Posting reports supply the audit trail.
- Maintains work order and manufacturing order information
- Vouchers material issues and receipts
- Vouchers labor hours
- Sends vouchers for automated general ledger input
- Offers a complete range of clear, concise reports and review screens

Variance Cost Control — Calculates financial and operational variances for closed orders and provides a formal standard revision process for work-in-process inventory.

FEATURES

- Compares actual to standard costs to calculate financial variances
- Compares actual to current costs to calculate operational variances
- Reports and posts many variances — for example:

Material Variances	Labor Variances
Usage	Efficiency
Yield	Yield
Substitution	Substitution
Scrap	Scrap
Discrepancy	Discrepancy

- Standard revision — reporting and simulation

Source: Copyright 1986 Hewlett-Packard Company. Reproduced with permission.

A JUST-IN-TIME (JIT) INVENTORY MANAGEMENT SYSTEM

The just-in-time (JIT) system is a Japanese philosophy that is used to manage all types of inventory, purchasing, and production functions in an organization. Our presentation in this chapter will concentrate on the JIT inventory function.[11] Unlike an MRP system, many Japanese inventory systems are not dependent on computer support.

[11] For a comprehensive review of JIT inventory principles see M. J. Schniederjans, *Topics in Just-In-Time Management* (Boston: Allyn & Bacon, 1993), Chapter 2.

FIGURE 7-18 HP ACCOUNTS PAYABLE MODULE FEATURES AND MANAGEMENT REPORTS

(A) MODULE FEATURES

- On-line vendor review and analysis with quick access to vendors by a short name
- Automatic voucher numbering
- Corporate vendor turnover information for better visibility of total turnover with several vendors from the same corporation
- Effective discount analysis for better cash control
- Automatic payment proposals with on-line maintenance, review, and approval for the proposals
- Cash or accrual methods
- Recurring payments automatically booked in each period
- Automatic Use Tax, Value Added Tax, discount, and due date calculations
- Flexible accounting distribution with system controlled balances
- Multiple banks and multiple currencies with automatic reconciliations
- Automatic booking of any currency gain or loss

(B) MODULE MANAGEMENT REPORTS AND REVIEW STATEMENTS

- Corporate Review
- Summary Aged Trial Balance
- Vendor Review
- Detail Aged Trial Balance
- Single Open Item Review
- Reconciliation Report
- Cash Requirements Forecast
- Recurring Payments
- Discounts Taken/Lost
- Payment Proposal
- Open Item Register
- Open Items by Vendor
- Open Item Ranking
- Open Item Detail
- Trial Balance
- Audit Report
- Bank Reconciliation
- Vendor Listing
- Tax Reports
- Payment Register

Source: Copyright 1986 Hewlett-Packard Company. Reproduced with permission.

The goal of a JIT inventory system is to eliminate or reduce all types of inventory (raw materials, work-in-process, and finished goods). Why do organizations want to eliminate inventory? By eliminating inventory, the costs of maintaining that inventory are eliminated as well. This is accomplished by using the following logic:

1. Acquire raw materials just in time to have them manufactured into component parts.
2. Manufacture component parts just in time to have them assembled into finished products.
3. Assemble finished products just in time for their consumption in the marketplace.

Waiting until the inventory items (raw materials, components, and finished products) are required in production minimizes their time as inventory items. In the ideal JIT system, inventory items—not just raw material inventory, but all inventory throughout the entire operation—are continuously moving through the operations management system and are not stored at any point. This includes raw materials, buffer stocks, and finished goods inventory at the manufacturing plant, warehouse, and retail outlets. To illustrate the JIT approach, let's compare a typical lot-size non-JIT assembly operation (that is, an organization that orders, produces, and distributes in lot-size quantities) with a comparatively sized JIT assembly operation.

FIGURE 7-19 HP ACCOUNTS RECEIVABLE MODULE FEATURES AND MANAGEMENT REPORTS

(A) MODULE FEATURES

- On-line customer review and analysis with quick access to customers by a short name
- Corporate turnover information for better control of accumulated credit limits
- Automatic discount calculation and write-offs
- Flexible aging by due date, invoice date, or estimated payment date, based on customer's actual payment history
- Flexible automatic or manual cash application features
- Recurring invoices booked in any future period
- Delinquency notices automatically printed in any language
- Direct debiting
- Multiple payment methods with automatic bank reconciliation
- Multiple currencies with automatic booking of currency gain or loss

(B) MODULE MANAGEMENT REPORTS AND REVIEW STATEMENTS

- Corporate Review
- Summary Aged Trial Balance
- Customer Review
- Detail Aged Trial Balance
- Open Items by Customer
- Open Item Register
- Open Item Review
- Open Item Ranking
- Open Item History
- Trial Balance
- Credit Limit Listing
- Payment History Analysis
- Audit Report
- Bank Reconciliation
- Customer and Corporate Listing
- Recurring Entries
- Customer Statements
- Delinquency Notices
- Unearned Discount

Source: Copyright 1986 Hewlett-Packard Company. Reproduced with permission.

Typical Lot-Size Inventory System

A typical lot-size inventory/manufacturing system is presented in Figure 7-21. In a lot-size system, which is typically used by produce-to-stock firms, orders or unit use of inventory is characterized by a "push" system. That is, demand is forecast, and finished goods production is pushed through the system to satisfy the anticipated demand. The dependent demand inventory used to satisfy the production schedule is pushed through the operations management system to meet market demand. In a lot-size system, a manufacturer tends to acquire raw materials or incoming inventory items in large lot-size quantities. The inventory is acquired from a large number of vendors so the purchaser can keep vendors' prices competitive. These acquisitions require a large receiving department to receive and process the incoming order of goods. An inspection is usually performed to check for quality and quantity of the incoming inventory items. In the lot-size system, most companies will accept a lot of incoming inventory even if it has a small percentage of defective items. The cost to reject an entire lot for a few defects is prohibitive with such large lot sizes. The defective items, if found, are usually sent back to the vendor to be reworked or credited to the purchaser's account.

A large raw materials inventory department and a substantial materials handling staff are also required to move and store the large shipments of incoming inventory. In the lot-size system, the assembly area (or manufacturing area) must be large enough to store buffer stock. This buffer stock is used by workers when a shortage of an item occurs between workstations. Shortages can occur when defects are found in materials or parts, when feeder assembly lines (auxiliary lines used to transport component parts to assembly line workers) break down, or when materials handlers cannot keep up with demand.

FIGURE 7-20 HP GENERAL LEDGER MODULE FEATURES AND MANAGEMENT REPORTS

(A) MODULE FEATURES

- On-line or batch data entry, validation, and posting
- Multiple companies with unique charts of accounts, cost center organizations, security, fiscal year, and accounting policies
- Total flexibility in defining charts of accounts and cost centers
- Three separate budgets kept by accounts, cost center, or account within cost centers
- Responsibility reporting and on-line analysis of expenses
- Accruals provide automatic reversal bookings
- Standard vouchers automatically posted each period
- Ability to post future or past periods
- Automatic period and year-end closing procedures

(B) MODULE MANAGEMENT REPORTS AND REVIEW STATEMENTS

- Voucher Review
- Balance Sheet
- Subsidiary Journal Review
- Profit and Loss Statement
- Account Summary Review
- Account Detail Review
- Maintenance Reports
- Trial Balance Review
- Trial Balance
- Management Information
- Responsibility Reports
- Audit Reports
- Batch Status

Source: Copyright 1986 Hewlett-Packard Company. Reproduced with permission.

When the products are finished, they go through a finished product quality control inspection to make sure that the product meets the company's production standards. If the quality is not satisfactory, the product is either scrapped or reworked. If the quality is satisfactory, the product is temporarily placed in finished goods inventory. A substantial finished goods inventory is needed in a lot-size operation because the large lot size of production runs is necessary to satisfy customer demands, which are also in large lot-size orders. Eventually, the finished goods are sent to customers whose customers themselves place large orders. The orders necessitate a large shipping department for order-staging purposes. Most lot-size manufacturers store finished goods inventory for distribution in a warehouse. The warehouses eventually send the finished goods to customers or retail outlets where they are stored until the market requires them. Because the retail outlets receive lot-size orders, they must also maintain a substantial inventory.

Typical JIT Inventory System

In Figure 7-22, we present a typical JIT operations management system. The JIT system, typically used by a produce-to-order firm, is referred to as a "pull" system because inventory is pulled through the system by market demand. In other words, the demand for the product must exist before the product is ordered into production and the actual "in-hand" or known demand for the finished product begins the inventory acquisition process. In the JIT inventory system, firms place very small and frequent orders for inventory items. Japanese firms using the JIT inventory approach tend to acquire their raw materials (incoming) inventory from a few, fairly small vendors located close to the manufacturing facility.

FIGURE 7-21 TYPICAL LOT-SIZE INVENTORY AND MANUFACTURING SYSTEM

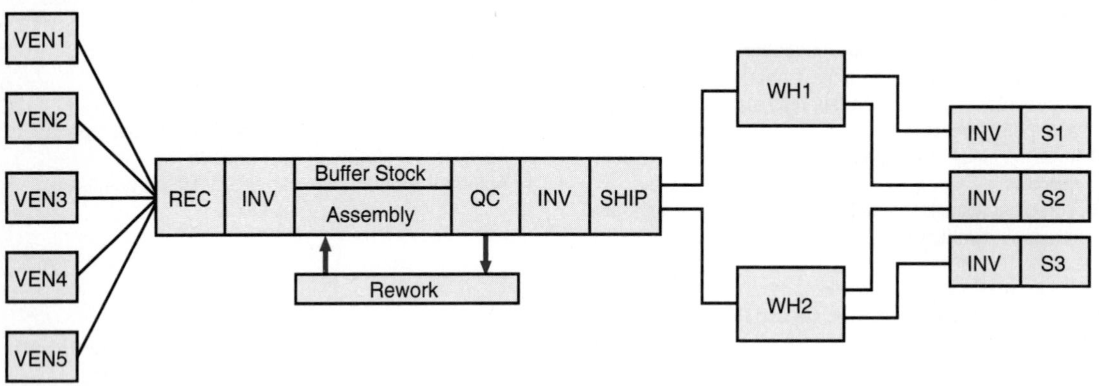

KEY
VEN = vendor
WH = warehouse facility
INV = inventory facility
S = retail store facility
REC = receiving department facility
QC = quality control department facility
SHIP = shipping department facility

Although the JIT approach might appear to open the manufacturer to possible price increases by the vendor, the Japanese usually negotiate the price on a long-term contracted basis far in advance of demand. Some companies use contracts that allow the price to "float" within a predescribed interval based on market conditions. This type of arrangement permits a competitive environment to exist and provides some protection to the purchaser. Because the vendors are usually very small, the total percentage of business the purchaser provides is usually very large. The result is better service for the purchasers because of their importance to the vendor's survival. The vendors also tend to be located geographically close to the purchaser. This helps ensure reliable delivery of goods and a quick response if defective goods are detected.

Because the incoming orders are small, the receiving area in a JIT firm can also be small. A JIT receiving department performs little quality control inspection before the inventory is moved directly to the assembly area. As we mentioned in Chapter 6 in our discussion of JIT purchasing, Japanese firms do not accept any defects in incoming inventory. They expect the incoming small lots of materials to be 100 percent free of all defects. Many JIT firms, both in the United States and Japan, will send an entire lot back to a vendor if a single inventory item is defective.

Once in the assembly area, the inventory items undergo the transformation process. The JIT approach to production differs from the traditional approach in many ways, which we will discuss throughout the rest of the text. One of these differences that

FIGURE 7-22 TYPICAL JIT INVENTORY AND MANUFACTURING SYSTEM

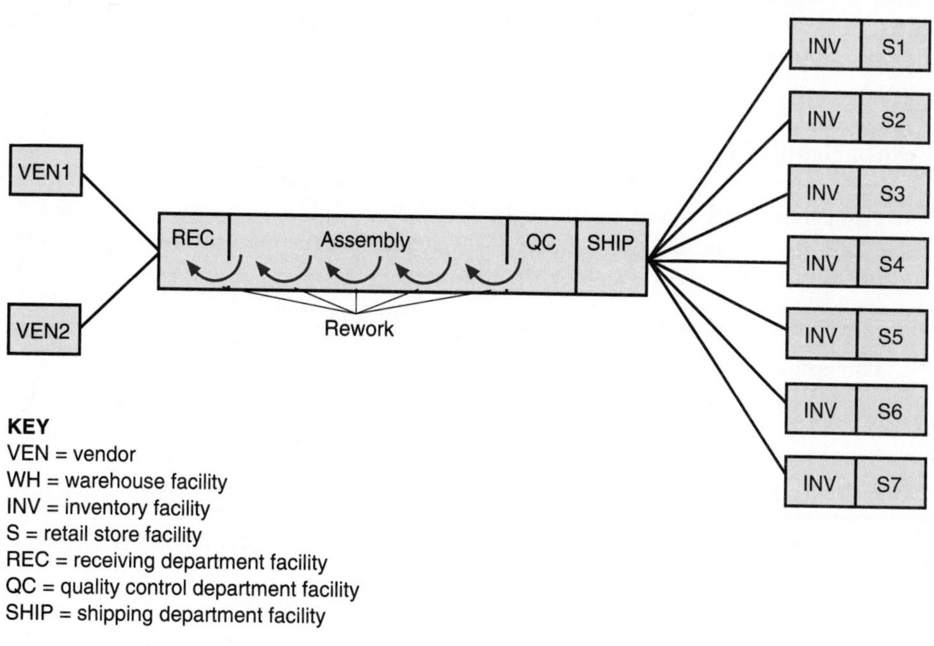

affects inventory is the procedure used in handling defective work. Defective items, whether caused by defective incoming inventory or by workers along the line, are immediately sent back to the source from which they came. Each worker along the assembly line is responsible for performing quality control checks on the inventory as it passes through the operations management system. If the receiving department sends defective items to the assembly line, the first workstation on the assembly line will call the defects to the attention of management and the defective items will be sent back to the receiving department and returned to the vendor. If the second workstation on the assembly line finds a defect in the work performed at the first workstation, the work is sent back to the first workstation, and so on. In this way the workers on the assembly line check and recheck the quality of the work being performed at each step of the assembly process. The result is that rework and scrap is greatly reduced because a finished item does not have to be completely broken down to correct a minor defect. The inspections performed by assembly line workers also reduce the need for a finished goods quality inspection department.

The orders sent to other JIT companies also tend to be small and frequent, which permits the shipping department to be smaller than its comparable lot-size operation. Because demand is known, warehouses have little need to store finished goods waiting for a customer. Consistent with the pull nature of the JIT system, the retail stores can also be small. Indeed, some stores mainly carry samples for display purposes only and operate like catalog stores. Additionally, by having a greater number of retail outlets, each JIT store does not need to carry as much inventory as their counterpart lot-size stores. A greater number of outlets allows the company to be closer to the customer market and therefore provides more convenient service.

Comparison of the Two Systems

The comparative differences between the lot-size and JIT systems are summarized in Table 7-2. As we can see, the Japanese JIT systems virtually eliminate inventory. The benefits of the JIT approach include the following:

1. The amount and therefore the investment in all types of inventory is reduced.
2. The cost of scrapped inventory is reduced.
3. Labor costs of reworking defective items are saved.

TABLE 7-2 COMPARISON OF LOT-SIZE AND JIT INVENTORY SYSTEMS

		INVENTORY SYSTEM	
Department	*Criteria*	*Lot-size*	*JIT*
Vendor	Number	Many	Few
	Size (volume of sales)	Large	Small
	Percentage of vendor's total business	Small	Large
	Size of purchase order	Large	Small
Receiving department	Number of personnel	Many	Few
	Size (area of plant)	5 to 10%	Little or none
Raw materials inventory department (incoming)	Number of personnel	Many	Few or none
	Size (area of plant)	10 to 30%	Little or none
Assembly department	Number of personnel	Many	Same or more
	Size (area of plant)	50 to 70%	Same or more
	Buffer stock required	Much	None
Quality control department	Number of personnel	Many	Little or none
	Size (area of plant)	5 to 10%	Little or none
Finished goods department (categorizing)	Number of personnel	Many	Little or none
	Size (area of plant)	10 to 30%	Little or none
Shipping department	Number of personnel	Many	Same
	Size (area of plant)	5 to 10%	Less than 5%
Warehousing	Number of personnel	Many	Little or none
	Size (storage area)	Large	Little or none
Retail store	Number	Few	Many
	Size (area of facility)	Large	Small
	Size of inventory (area of facility)	30 to 70%	Less than 30%

4. Quality control defects are quickly detected.
5. The size of plant and the amount of materials handling equipment are reduced.
6. Product quality is improved.

These benefits are not assumptions but the observed facts of many organizations throughout the world. JIT is fast becoming a dominant inventory strategy for U.S. organizations. There are many JIT success stories.[12] For example, in Cupertino, California, Hewlett-Packard maintains a computer manufacturing plant. After instituting a JIT system for their minicomputer product, the printed-circuit work-in-process inventory value was cut from $670,000 to just $20,000.[13] Another computer company, IBM of Owego, New York, was able to reduce its work-in-process inventory by 70 percent using a JIT system.[14] Implementing JIT has also reduced an operation's size. In West Mifflin, Pennsylvania, the Westinghouse organization operates a plant that manufactures (among other things) subway controlling devices. This plant instituted a JIT system and found that it was able to cut production floor space from 125,000 square feet to only 52,000 square feet and reduce materials storage area, which represented 66 percent of the plant's storage space, to only 15 percent of available space.[15]

JIT Implementation Strategy

To help the philosophy of JIT become a reality, an organization needs a strategy for implementing the inventory planning system. Implementing a new inventory system takes more than a commitment from the inventory manager. It takes a commitment from the entire organization, from purchasing to shipping and from top management to the workers at the shop floor level of the organization. It may also require a commitment from vendors and customers. Vendors must be willing to ship the manufacturer's smaller-sized orders, to perhaps relocate near the manufacturing facility they supply, and to provide defect-free products. Having a long-term contract is often a great motivator for vendors to participate in JIT programs. Customers may have to be willing to accept more frequent and small-sized orders. The record of improved quality and speed of service provided under a JIT system has made selling this idea to customers a relatively easy task.

Some managers make radical changes and others are more conservative, preferring to ease into the JIT system. The implementation strategy outlined on the next two pages is structured to accommodate both types of managers:

---

[12] For a good review of many of the JIT success stories see K. A. Wantuck, *Just-In-Time for America* (Milwaukee, Wis.: The Forum, 1989); E. J. Hay, *The Just-In-Time Breakthrough* (New York: John Wiley & Sons, 1988); and R. J. Schonberger, *World Class Manufacturing* (New York: The Free Press, 1986), pp. 229–236.

[13] R. J. Schonberger, *World Class Manufacturing* (New York: The Free Press, 1986), p. 229.

[14] *OWEGO FOCUS*, IBM Federal Systems Division Newsletter, February 1, 1985, p. 7.

[15] "Assembling a World-Class Shop," *Pittsburgh Engineer* (Summer 1985), 16–17.

1. Before implementing JIT, arrange with vendors to have more frequent and reduced inventory order quantities. Alternatively, locate new, smaller-sized vendors. A radical strategy would be to reduce inventory order quantities by 90 percent and a conservative strategy would be to reduce inventory order quantities by 10 percent.)

2. Before implementing JIT, arrange with members of the distribution system (such as warehouse managers and retail store managers) and customers to receive more frequent and reduced inventory order quantities.This step may not be necessary if the organization uses a warehouse facility to stage the desired larger orders some customers may require.

3. Before implementing JIT, explain to operations management personnel their new roles and responsibilities. This may require in-house education programs, worker training programs, and even renegotiated union contracts. The workers need to be trained to accept greater responsibility for inspecting product quality and calling attention to defects in inventory. We explain this role more fully in Chapters 8 and 9. All operations managers must understand the JIT process and make a total commitment to successfully implementing the JIT system.

4. Begin implementing JIT by scheduling smaller lot-sized orders. In a lot-size operations management system, the lots might be cut to match incoming inventory from Step 1. If the operation is not disrupted by the reduction in inventory, start reducing buffer stock at all of the workstations. As the buffer inventory cushion is gradually decreased, stress increases in the operating system because there is less of a cushion to hide inventory shortage problems. This gradual inventory reduction process is called **inventory stressing.** Care must be taken to ensure that the implementation of reduced inventory is paced so as not to overstress or totally disrupt the operating system. The idea is to reveal inventory problems, not cause them.

5. Eventually, as raw materials inventory and buffer stock are reduced, a shortage of inventory will occur. In a JIT system, when an inventory shortage occurs, the entire operations management system can come to a standstill. This places pressure on workers and management to resolve the inventory problem as quickly as possible so work can resume. When an inventory shortage occurs, managers should ask the question: Why didn't the inventory item arrive just in time? If everybody is doing his or her job, just enough inventory should always be available to keep the operation going. Identifying the reasons why inventory is not where it should be is one of the ways JIT helps locate inventory problems that might have been hidden by buffer or safety stock inventory in the system. These problems can include defects in materials, poor product design, variations in vendor delivery service, and materials handling failures. Also, shortages to a firm's customers or retailing organizations can help it identify its own shipping and transportation problems.

6. As the problems identified in Step 5 are addressed by management and resolved, the inventory/production system will stabilize with a fairly continuous production rate between orders. At this point the best strategy is to make further reductions in all inventory levels and repeat Step 5 until the system treats each inventory item as a separate order. This is called **unitary production** and is viewed as a goal for JIT systems to achieve.

Step 6 embodies the very important JIT principle of continuous improvement. As presented in Chapter 2, Total Quality Management, continuous improvement is a guiding principle or tactic for achieving world-class manufacturing and service operations. In inventory management, continuous improvement involves the continual identification and elimination of all problems that inhibit the movement of inventory to, through, and out of the production system. Continuous improvement efforts help motivate the productivity cycle (discussed in Chapter 1) to lead to improved productivity, flexibility, and eventually a competitive advantage.

Research on JIT has shown that the more frequent orders required in a JIT system place pressure on workers to develop new and more efficient equipment and facility setup procedures.[16] Indeed, inventory managers are also pressured to keep the operations management system going by solving problems as they surface, and this in turn will reduce lead time. **Order lead time** is the time from when an order is accepted by an organization to when the order is finished for delivery to the customer. Problems that add to order lead time include order-entry delays and errors, long setup times, high defect levels in parts or materials, poor order scheduling, and undependable vendors. Any inventory or production problem that slows an order increases order lead time. Examples of JIT implementation and its beneficial effects on order lead time abound. Omark Industries implemented in its Guelph, Ontario plant a JIT system that reduced order lead time from twenty-one days to one day for its chain saw production process. In its Onalaska, Wisconsin plant, order lead time for a gun cleaning kit product was reduced from two weeks to only one day with an inventory reduction of 94 percent.[17]

MONITORING PERFORMANCE WITH DEPENDENT DEMAND INVENTORY SYSTEMS

The particular approach chosen by an organization to monitor the use of dependent demand inventory items depends on the type of system it uses to plan its inventory

[16] A. S. Sohal and D. Naylor, "Implementation of JIT in a Small Manufacturing Firm," *Production and Inventory Management Journal,* 33, No. 1 (1992), 20–26; S. K. Johnston, "JIT—Maximizing Its Success Potential," *Production and Inventory Management Journal,* 30, No. 1 (1988), 82–86; and K. M. Crawford et al., "A Study of JIT Implementation and Operating Problems," *International Journal of Production Research,* 26, No. 9 (1988), 1561–1568.

[17] R. J. Schonberger, *World Class Manufacturing* (New York: The Free Press, 1986), p. 230.

requirements. In an MRP environment, the computer system greatly helps monitor the operations management system's performance by generating control reports. An exception report is an example of how the system monitors and informs management that there is an inconsistency between what is actually happening in the OM system and the previously defined input data files. The following are typical examples of criteria used for measuring MRP system performance:

1. Missed deliveries per time bucket by vendors
2. Delayed orders between workstations per time bucket
3. Missed deliveries of customer orders from MRP-prescribed delivery dates
4. Average dependent demand unit inventory carried per planning horizon
5. Rush orders placed with vendors for additional dependent demand inventory

Any of these criteria can cause an exception report to be generated. In the Hewlett-Packard MRP II system, one set of control reports that originate from the HP Production Cost Management module are called variance cost control reports, which were briefly listed in Figure 7-17. As we can see from the description of these reports in Figure 7-23, they provide detailed control information on which to monitor operations management systems. Notice in the screen printout of a standard material variance report in Figure 7-23 that the actual yield quantity per unit (Act Qty Per) for order nos. 0220100 and 0320100 were some units above the expected or standard yield quantity per unit (Std. Yld Qty Per), resulting in a positive total standard material variance (Tot Std Matl Var) of 120 and 40 percent of standard material variance. This type of detailed information clearly identifies areas of the operation that management needs to investigate to determine the factors that have contributed to such a deviation from expected materials usage.

In a JIT environment, a simple control criterion measures the product lead time.[18] For some manufacturing operations or even service organizations, lead time can be fairly easy to measure. This measure can be taken by stamping the hour and date on the product or service order when it arrives at a plant and again when it is considered a finished product ready for delivery. The difference in the time and dates is the product lead time. The Village Inn Pancake House chain, for example, uses time-stamping machines to determine product lead time in processing customer orders. Once a number of the product lead times are collected, the average lead time can be computed as a quantitative criterion to compare one time period's performance with another. The smaller the product lead time, the better management is improving product and inventory flow.

---

[18] K. A. Wantuck, *Just-In-Time for America* (Milwaukee, Wis.: The Forum, 1989), p. 372; and R. J. Schonberger, *World Class Manufacturing* (New York: The Free Press, 1986), pp. 13–14.

FIGURE 7-23 HP VARIANCE COST CONTROL REPORTS

MATERIAL VARIANCE REPORTS

These reports give the material variance, lower-level labor and lower-level overhead variance by part and work order number. The reports also present key factors that affect production performance such as standard and actual material costs, quantity ordered, quantity started into production, and quantity completed in production. Also included are dates of work order opening and closing, variancing information, and labor information.

LABOR VARIANCE REPORTS

The labor variance reports provide a wide range of labor-related information in addition to the dollar variances. Presented by cost center, this information includes workcenter and workstation date, order quantities, orders opened and closed, varianced dates, and setup and run variance hours.
The summary reports highlight, by part number and cost center, the hour and dollar variances related to the period's labor activity.

LABOR OPERATION VARIANCE REPORTS

Many manufacturers organize production capacity by labor operations. The labor operations reports enhance the information provided in the labor variance reports by providing the information by operation.

CLOSED ORDER STANDARD VARIANCE REPORT

This report provides a comprehensive review of financial variances. It identifies the variance information by variance category. It separates the labor variance into efficiency, yield, substitution, scrap, and discrepancy categories. The material variances are separated into usage, yield, substitution, scrap, and discrepancy. This level of detail complements the information found on the labor and material variances analysis and problem resolution cycle.

```
PCM      Review Standard Material Variance
Company  EYES     Company Name   Eagle Eyes, Inc.
Selection Criteria: Order No ______ for Part No ______
                    Component Part ____________

Order No   Comp/Par   Std Qty Per   Act Per   Tot Std Var
--------   --------   -----------   -------   -----------
0120100    20100           4.0000      4.00         .0000
0220100    20100           4.0000      5.50      120.0000
0320100    20100           4.0000      4.50       40.0000
0420100    20100           4.0000      4.00         .0000

Rev Std    print   Rev Pln    Rev Pln            browse
Labr Var           Labr Var   Matl Var           backward
```

STANDARD REVISION REPORTS

A well-designed standard cost based system should provide a tool to formally revise inventory values as well as simulate proposed changes. The standard revision reports provide information required to

- Assess the dollar impact on work-in-process inventory
- Simulate a standard revision to evaluate the financial impact of proposed changes to standard costs. This is useful for "what-if" types of analysis.
- Estimate the impact by specific part or work order in addition to your company total
- Create the audit trail and supporting data for a standard revision variance, which is entered into the general ledger
- Indicate the original standard, new standard, and incremental "delta" amounts

Source: Copyright 1986 Hewlett-Packard Company. Reproduced with permission.

INTEGRATING MANAGEMENT RESOURCES: USING MRP II AND JIT TO IMPROVE PRODUCTIVITY

Research has shown that in batch or large job-lot production environments MRP planning and control systems operate better than JIT systems.[19] In other studies, a JIT system has been favored over an MRP system in highly repetitive unitary or

[19] L. P. Rees et al., "Comparative Analysis of an MRP Lot-for-lot System and a Kanban System for a Multistage Production Operation," *International Journal of Production Research,* 27, No. 8 (1989), 1427–1443; and R. Westbrook, "Time to Forget 'Just-in-Time'? Observations on a Visit to Japan," *International Journal of Production Management,* 8, No. 4 (1987), 5–21.

small lot-size production environments.[20] Unfortunately, many manufacturers can be characterized as a combination of both large lot-size and small lot-size batch operations. This is particularly true of organizations that are in the process of converting from a large lot-size MRP operation to a small lot-size JIT operation. As a result, some researchers have recommended combining MRP II software systems with JIT as a means of improving productivity and allowing for the implementation of JIT systems in MRP II environments.[21]

One operations management software system that integrates MRP II and JIT is the Hewlett-Packard (HP) Manufacturing Management II System that we described earlier in this chapter. As an additional module to the HP MRP II system, the HP JIT module permits users to have a computer-based JIT system. The HP JIT system is a stand-alone software module that can be used in place of the HP Materials Management module (the MRP system) or in combination with it to provide the informational benefits of both systems.

A unique feature of the HP JIT module is its ability to operate in a "mixed-mode" environment in which both MRP and JIT production elements are present. The HP JIT module allows management to decide which products should be produced in the MRP environment and which should be produced in the JIT environment. Management can then use the HP Materials Management module to plan and control MRP production and the HP JIT module to plan and control JIT production while sharing the same data base. This shared information permits management to capitalize on the strengths of both systems. Unlike the typical noncomputerized application of JIT, the HP JIT system enables management to efficiently monitor the progress of production or work-in-process on-line with the same types of MRP reports that management used under an MRP system. (In JIT, only environmental monitoring work-in-process requires a time-consuming physical audit.) Yet, management and particularly the workers are allowed to base production on a demand pull concept of a "rate-based" production. A **rate-based** production schedule is based on actual demand rather than the MRP forecast demand push system. The result of rate-based production is that the amount of

---

[20] J. L. Funk, "A Comparison of Inventory Cost Reduction Strategies in a JIT Manufacturing System," *International Journal of Production Research,* 27, No. 7 (1989), 1065–1080; R. C. Walleigh, "What's Your Excuse for Not Using JIT?" *Harvard Business Review* (March–April 1986), 38–54; and D. Y. Golhor et al., "JIT Implementation in Small Manufacturing Firms," *Production and Inventory Management,* 30, No. 1 (1989), 44–48.

[21] R. Discenza and F. R. McFadden, "The Integration of MRPII and JIT Through Software Unification," *Production and Inventory Management Journal,* 29, No. 4 (1988), 49–53; B. Belt, "MRP and Kanban—A Possible Synergy?" *Production and Inventory Management Journal,* 28, No. 1 (1987), 71–80; G. J. Miltenburg, "Changing MRP's Costing Procedures to Suit JIT," *Production and Inventory Management,* 30, No. 1 (1989), 77–83; and R. R. Boccard, "Push vs. Pull: Is One Better Than the Other?" *Production and Inventory Management Review,* 10, No. 2 (1990), 39–40. (See the article at the end of this chapter, "JIT versus MRP," for a more applied explanation of companies that have experienced some of the benefits of a joint JIT-MRP system.)

Q

QUESTION: What is an example of how the combination of MRP II and JIT systems can benefit product quality?

ANSWER: Information on **order tracking** (or the process of determining the stage of manufacturing or location in a shop of an order currently being produced) can be an important part of quality service for some customers. Unlike JIT, MRP II systems are computer based and can keep accurate track of individual orders as they go through various stages of production. When customers require status reports on their order processing, the MRP II system can provide that type of customer service quickly and efficiently. Unlike most MRP II systems, a JIT operation seeks smaller but more frequent orders being processed. This results in shorter lead times between deliveries to customers. By combining the two systems, the quality of customer service (in delivery and information on delivery) can be improved.

dependent demand inventory, work-in-process, and finished goods inventory is reduced in the OM system. Workers also have time to participate in many of the other JIT activities (such as quality control and preventive maintenance) that result in improved productivity.

SUMMARY

In this chapter we have examined two types of dependent demand inventory systems: MRP and JIT. The MRP system was presented as an order push system based on meeting forecast market demand. This computer-based system was defined in terms of its input, processing, and output system requirements. The MRP system's adaptations, as well as its advantages and disadvantages, were also discussed.

An MRP II system was also described in this chapter. Some of the reporting features of the MRP II were presented as a means of monitoring and controlling dependent demand inventory.

The Japanese JIT inventory philosophy was presented as an order pull system. In a JIT system, finished products are produced on demand, so the orders pull the materials through the operations management system. The logic by which JIT processes dependent demand inventory items was also discussed. A comparison was used to illustrate the basic JIT process and how it differs from non-JIT lot-size inventory systems. A JIT inventory system implementation strategy was also briefly discussed.

As discussed earlier, the JIT philosophy is much more than a dependent demand inventory system; it also involves finished goods inventory. As such, the JIT system presented in this chapter can also be considered in part an independent demand inventory system, as we will see in the next chapter. (Indeed, because of the importance of the JIT philosophy, we will be exploring its use in most of the operations management topical areas throughout the rest of this book.)

DISCUSSION AND REVIEW QUESTIONS

1. What is the difference between dependent and independent demand inventory? Give an example of each type of inventory.
2. What are the informational prerequisites of an MRP system?
3. What is the difference between a regenerative and a net-change MRP system?
4. How is a master production schedule (MPS) used in an MRP system?
5. What is a BOM? How is it used in an MRP system? What role does a product structure play in the BOM?
6. What are time-phased requirements?
7. How is exploding a product related to a planned-ordered release?
8. How does an inventory ordering system affect MRP processing?
9. What are the system outputs of an MRP system? Give three examples.
10. What is low-level coding?
11. What are some of the advantages and disadvantages of an MRP system?
12. How is an MRP II system different from an MRP system?
13. How does an MRP system support production planning? How does an MRP II system support production planning?
14. What role can MRP II systems play in producing a quality product?
15. What role can an MRP II system play in a CIM system?
16. What is the basic philosophy of JIT in inventory management? Explain with an example.
17. What is the difference between a pull and a push inventory system? Give an example of each.
18. How does a JIT manufacturing system differ from a typical lot-size manufacturing system?
19. What is a major risk factor with JIT systems? How might inventory managers try to overcome this risk in their implementation of the JIT system?
20. How does an MRP system help management monitor the performance of the inventory system? Give a specific example of what the system does to direct management's attention to problem areas.

PROBLEMS

* 1. Suppose that we have the product structure shown at the top of page 331.

Prepare a list that defines the total number of component parts required to produce one unit of finished product.

---

* The solutions to the problems marked with an asterisk can be found in Appendix J.

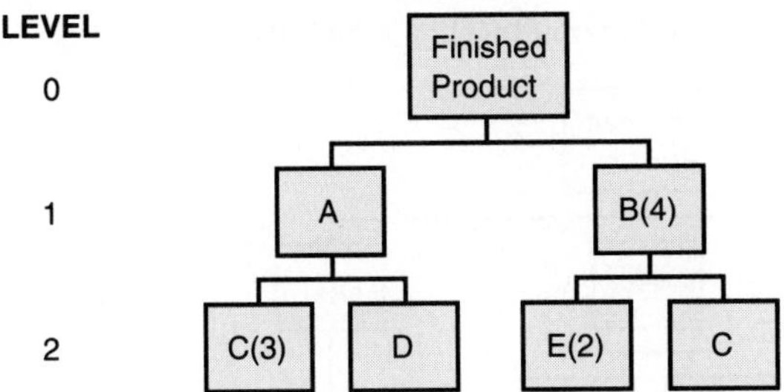

2. If each inventory item in the product structure in Problem 1 requires one week lead time, what is its time-phased requirements chart? Draw the chart.

3. Suppose that we have the following product structure:

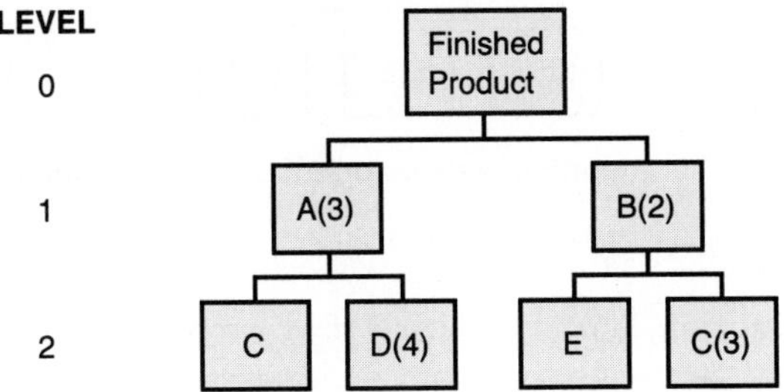

Prepare a list that defines the total number of component parts required to produce one unit of finished product.

4. If the finished product in Problem 3 requires three weeks lead time; components A, B, and C require two weeks lead time; and D and E require one week lead time, what is its time-phased requirements chart? Draw the chart.

5. Suppose that we have the following product structure:

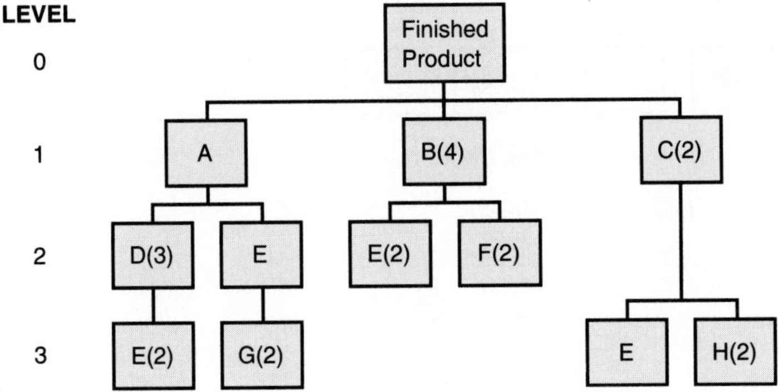

Prepare a list of the total number of component parts required to complete one unit of finished product.

6. How would the new product structure look in Problem 5 if we reformatted it for low-level coding? Draw the chart.

7. Suppose that a manufacturer has the following product structure:

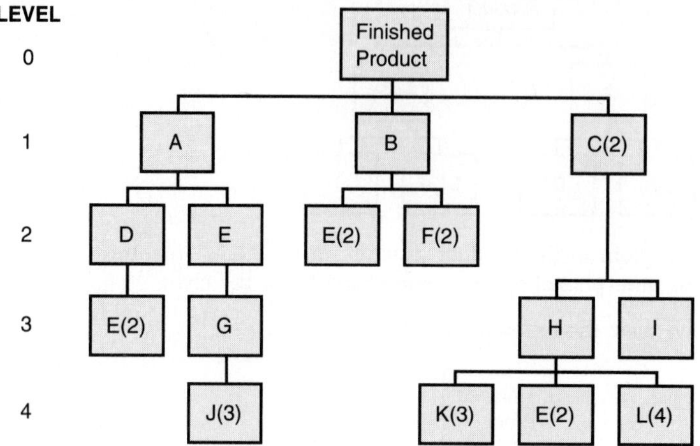

Prepare a list of the total number of component parts required to complete one unit of finished product.

8. How would the new product structure look in Problem 7 if we reformatted it for low-level coding? Draw the chart.

C

9. A manufacturer has the following product structure:

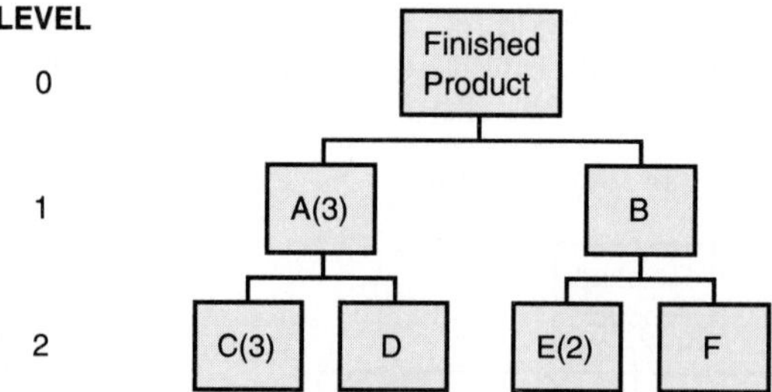

Suppose also that the lead times for these inventory items are as follows:

Inventory Item	*Lead Time for Procurement and Assembly (weeks)*
Finished product	3
A	1
B	2
C	3
D	1
E	1
F	2

What is the time-phased requirements processing chart for these items? Based on the lead times, what is the total time from when the first item is procured to when the finished product is ready for delivery?

C

10. Suppose that we have the following product structure:

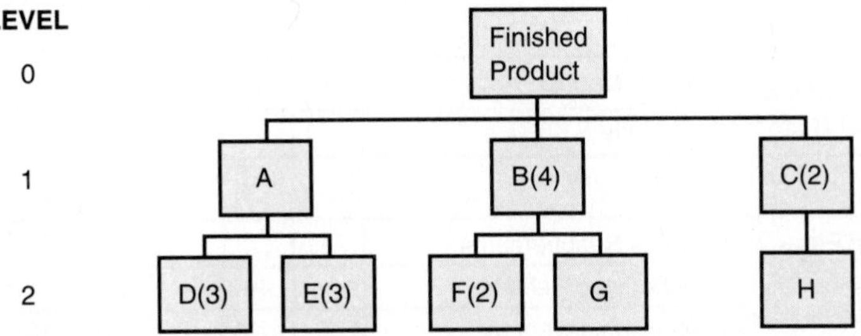

Suppose also that the lead times for these inventory items are as follows:

Inventory Item	*Lead Time for Procurement and Assembly (weeks)*
Finished product	1
A	2
B	1
C	1
D	2
E	2
F	2
G	1
H	3

What is the time-phased requirements processing chart for these items? Based on the lead times, what is the total time from when the first item is procured to when the finished product is ready for delivery?

11. Following is a time-phased requirements processing chart. Redraw the chart and correct any processing errors.

MASTER SCHEDULE FOR FINISHED ITEM	**Week Number**	**1**	**2**	**3**	**4**	**5**
	Quantity					100

INVENTORY ITEM • Name: Finished Product • Number per Parent: 1 • Lead Time: 2 weeks		1	2	3	4	5
	Gross Requirements					200
	Scheduled Receipts	30	10	10		
	Available Inventory	30	10	10	10	10
	Net Requirements					180
	Planned-ordered Receipts					180
	Planned-ordered Releases				180	

INVENTORY ITEM • Name: A • Number per Parent: 1 • Lead Time: 2 weeks		1	2	3	4	5
	Gross Requirements				180	
	Scheduled Receipts		40			
	Available Inventory					
	Net Requirements				180	
	Planned-ordered Receipts				180	
	Planned-ordered Releases	180				

12. Following is a time-phased requirements processing chart. Redraw the chart and correct any processing errors.

MASTER SCHEDULE FOR FINISHED ITEM	Week Number	1	2	3	4	5
	Quantity					1000

INVENTORY ITEM		1	2	3	4	5
• Name: Finished Product	Gross Requirements					800
• Number per Parent: 1	Scheduled Receipts		40			
	Available Inventory	30	10	10	10	10
	Net Requirements					790
	Planned-ordered Receipts					790
• Lead Time: 1 week	Planned-ordered Releases				790	

INVENTORY ITEM		1	2	3	4	5
• Name: A	Gross Requirements				790	
	Scheduled Receipts					
• Number per Parent: 1	Available Inventory					
	Net Requirements				790	
	Planned-ordered Receipts				790	
• Lead Time: 3 weeks	Planned-ordered Releases	790				

790 x 3 = 2370

INVENTORY ITEM		1	2	3	4	5
• Name: B	Gross Requirements				2370	
	Scheduled Receipts					
• Number per Parent: 3	Available Inventory	1000	1000	1000	1000	
	Net Requirements				1370	
	Planned-ordered Receipts				1370	
• Lead Time: 2 weeks	Planned-ordered Releases		1370			

13. Suppose that we have the following inventory requirements situation:
    a. The planning horizon is 10 weeks.
    b. Finished product demand of 300 units each is needed in weeks 5 and 10 (a total of 600 units).
    c. Initial finished product available inventory is 100 units, and the component part A available inventory is 60 units.
    d. Scheduled receipts of 10 units of finished product is expected in weeks 3 and 8.
    e. The finished product has the following product structure:

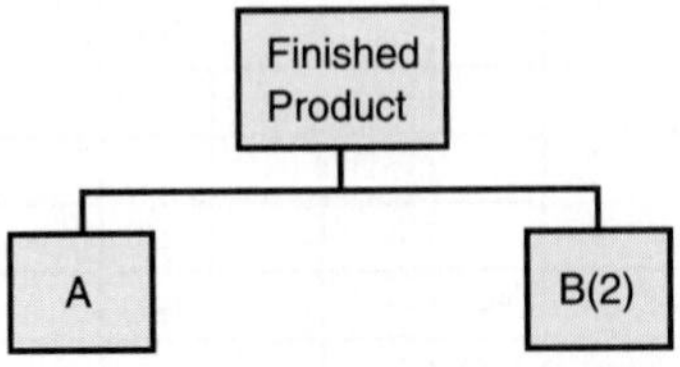

f. The lead time requirements are as follows:

Inventory Item	*Lead Time (weeks)*
Finished product	1
A	2
B	2

g. A lot-for-lot inventory ordering system is used.

Given the inventory requirements, generate the time-phased quantity requirements for the inventory items.

14. Suppose that we have the same inventory situation as in Problem 13 except that we must use a fixed lot-size inventory ordering system. Part A's fixed lot-size is 280 units and part B's fixed lot-size is 580 units. Given these inventory requirements, generate the time-phased quantity requirements for the inventory items.

15. Suppose that a firm has the following inventory requirements situation:
    a. The planning horizon is 5 weeks.
    b. Finished demand of 1,200 units each is needed in week 5.
    c. Initial finished product available inventory is 1,000 units, component part A's available inventory is 900 units, component part B's available inventory is 700 units, and component part C's available inventory is 2,000 units.
    d. Scheduled receipts of 250 units of finished product is expected in week 2.
    e. The finished product has the following product structure:

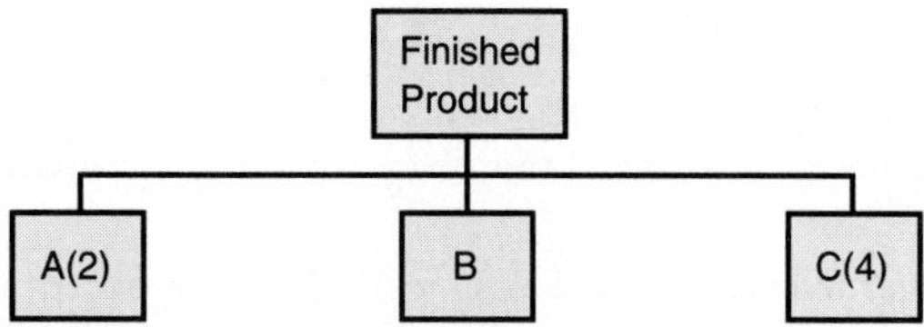

f. The lead time requirements are as follows:

Inventory Item	*Lead Time (weeks)*
Finished product	1
A	1
B	1
C	2

g. A lot-for-lot inventory ordering system is used.

Given the inventory requirements, generate the time-phased quantity requirements for the inventory items.

16. Suppose that we have the same inventory situation as in Problem 15 except that we must use a fixed lot-size inventory ordering system. Part A's fixed lot-size is 1,800 units, part B's lot-size is 1,000 units, and part C's fixed lot-size is 3,800. Given these inventory requirements, generate the time-phased quantity requirements for the inventory items.

17. Suppose that we have the following inventory requirements situation:
    a. The planning horizon is 10 weeks.
    b. Finished product demand of 400 units each is needed in week 5 and week 10 (a total of 800 units for the 10 weeks).

c. Initial finished product available inventory is 100 units, component part A's available inventory is 80 units, component part B's available inventory is 200 units, component part C's available inventory is 200 units, and component part D's available inventory is 100 units.

d. The finished product has the following structure:

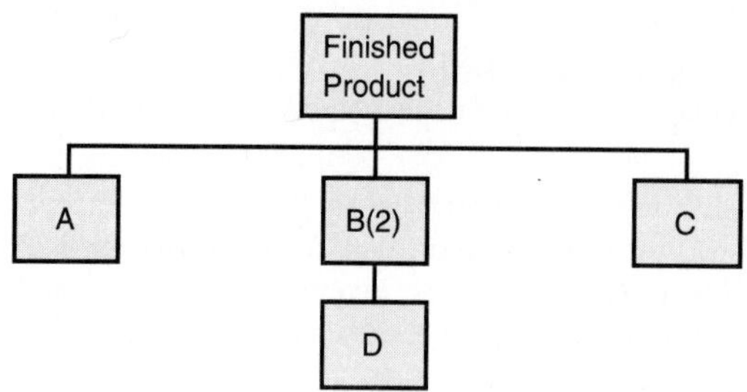

e. The lead time requirements are as follows:

Inventory Item	*Lead Time (weeks)*
Finished product	1
A	2
B	1
C	2
D	2

f. A lot-for-lot inventory ordering system is used.

Given the inventory requirements, generate the time-phased quantity requirements for the inventory items.

18. Suppose that we have the same inventory situation as in Problem 17 except that we must use a fixed lot-size inventory ordering system. Part A's fixed lot-size is 400 units, part B's fixed lot-size is 790 units, part C's fixed lot-size is 400 units, and part D's fixed lot-size is 800 units. Given these inventory requirements, generate the time-phased quantity requirements for the inventory items.

*19. (This problem requires the contents of Supplement 7-1.) Rework the available capacity in Exhibit 7S-1 in the example problem presented in Supplement 7-1, using a utilization rate of 60 percent and an efficiency rate of 70 percent. Substitute the following new planned-ordered releases in place of the values in Supplement 7-1:

	UNITS OF PARTS PER WEEK			
Part No.	*1*	*2*	*3*	*4*
1	100	100	100	100
2	75	75	75	75

Answer the following questions:

a. What are the revised available capacity values?
b. What are the revised required capacity values for the planned-ordered releases?
c. What are the revised total capacity requirements for this problem?
d. Comment on the CRP information. How can it be used to help plan capacity in this problem?

20. (This problem requires the contents of Supplement 7-1.) Rework the available capacity in Exhibit 7S-1 in the example problem presented in Supplement 7-1, using a utilization rate of 95 percent and an efficiency rate of 85 percent. Use the other data required for the analysis from the tables in the supplement. Substitute the following new planned-ordered releases for the one in the supplement:

	UNITS OF PARTS PER WEEK			
Part No.	*1*	*2*	*3*	*4*
1	50	200	50	200
2	100	130	120	0
3	0	120	90	300

Complete the entire CRP four-step procedure presented in Supplement 7-1 using the additional data from that example. In what workcenters do we have surplus capacity? In what workcenters do we have a shortage of capacity?

21. (This problem requires the contents of Supplement 7-1.) Rework the available capacity in Exhibit 7S-1 in the example problem presented in Supplement 7-1, using a utilization rate of 80 percent and an efficiency rate of 90 percent. Substitute the following new planned-ordered releases in place of the values in Supplement 7-1:

	UNITS OF PARTS PER WEEK			
Part No.	*1*	*2*	*3*	*4*
1	110	100	110	110
2	85	85	85	95
3	100	100	100	100

Answer the following questions:
a. What are the revised available capacity values?
b. What are the revised required capacity values for the planned-ordered releases?
c. What are the revised total capacity requirements for this problem?
d. Comment on the CRP information. How can it be used to help plan capacity in this problem?

22. (This problem requires the contents of Supplement 7-1.) Rework the available capacity in Exhibit 7S-1 in the example problem presented in Supplement 7-1, using a utilization rate of 90 percent and an efficiency rate of 95 percent. Use the other data required for the analysis from the tables in the supplement. Substitute the following new planned-ordered releases for the one in the supplement:

	UNITS OF PARTS PER WEEK			
Part No.	*1*	*2*	*3*	*4*
1	150	200	150	200
2	200	230	220	200
3	100	120	190	300

Complete the entire CRP four-step procedure presented in Supplement 7-1 using the additional data from that example. In what workcenters do we have surplus capacity? In what workcenters do we have a shortage of capacity?

CASE 7-1

TO MRP OR NOT TO MRP

Ashlyn's House of Toys Manufacturing Company (AHTM) is an old, established toy company located on the U.S. west coast. Its current product line consists of more than one hundred different toy products, which it markets through its own retail stores located throughout the country. As AHTM's product line grew, so did its inventory of parts. Although some product parts were interchangeable, some could not be used on more than one toy. As the company's inventory grew, so did the cost of the inventory it was carrying each month. By the end of the last year, AHTM's cost of inventory had finally plunged the company into an unprofitable operation for the first time in more than a century of business. The president of AHTM decided that an inventory consultant should be called in to help solve the company's dependent demand inventory problems.

The consultant quickly identified the fact that the parts inventory was virtually out of control and required a new inventory control system. Although the company operated on a lot-for-lot inventory ordering system to minimize inventory, it did not operate very efficiently. For example, inventory orders were being placed when the inventory was actually required for production, and not before. Employees jokingly called this a "last-minute ordering system." This meant that work-in-process would sit around for two or three weeks until component part orders were filled by either the company's own production department or by a vendor. The current inventory manager of AHTM had read an article on JIT and created the last-minute ordering system as a basis on which to make the transition to a JIT system.

Despite the attempt of the inventory manager to move toward a JIT system, the consultant recommended an MRP system to help the company better manage its dependent demand inventory items. The president had heard of MRP at business luncheons of the American Production and Inventory Control Society, but really did not understand what it was about and how it would help AHTM. The consultant decided to illustrate how MRP operates by demonstrating the MRP processing of a single product the firm manufactures. The product selected for the illustration typified the overstock problem characteristics of the entire line of the organization. The toy is called a Mellon Patch Doll and consists of eight different component parts: right leg, left leg, right arm, left arm, torso, head, hair patches, and eyes. When a doll is assembled, it requires five units of hair patches and two units of eyes. AHTM manufactured all of the component parts except the torso of the body, which they obtained from a vendor. The consultant collected some of the Mellon Patch Doll product data, which are shown in Exhibits 7C-1, 7C-2, and 7C-3. The available head inventory for the week of 7/1 is estimated at 120 units. The consultant decided to illustrate how the AHTM operation could operate using a lot-for-lot inventory ordering system.

CASE QUESTIONS

1. What is the MRP time-phased processing requirement chart for the finished product Mellon Patch Doll?
2. Prepare a time-phased processing requirements chart for the component part head. Include the time-phased processing requirements charts for the master schedule, the finished product, and the component part head. In what weeks do the planned-ordered releases for this component part occur?
3. Suppose that the organization incurs a cost of $0.25 per unit on average weekly available inventory. Now suppose that the organization could obtain a cost reduction if it adopted a fixed lot-size inventory order policy on the head component part only. Assume a fixed lot-size order of 100 units. Using this new policy, the cost per unit of head is only $0.20 per unit on average weekly available inventory. Determine the available inventory under a fixed lot-size policy for the component part head. Which inventory ordering policy is the least costly for this component part? Show your work.

EXHIBIT 7C-1 LEAD TIME FOR MELLON PATCH DOLL INVENTORY

Item	*Lead Time for Procurement or Assembly*
Mellon Patch Doll (MPD)	2
Right leg (RL)	1
Left leg (LL)	1
Right arm (RA)	1
Left arm (LA)	1
Trunk (T)	2
Head (H)	1
Hair patches (HP)	3
Eyes (E)	1

EXHIBIT 7C-2 DEMAND REQUIREMENTS AND SUBCONTRACTED SUPPLY SOURCES OF THE FINISHED PRODUCT MELLON PATCH DOLL

Date (weeks)	*Forecast Demand (units)*	*Subcontracted Supply*
7/1		
7/8		50
7/15	100	
7/22		
7/29		100
8/5	200	
8/12		
8/19		50
8/26	100	
9/2		

EXHIBIT 7C-3 PRODUCT STRUCTURE FOR THE MELLON PATCH DOLL

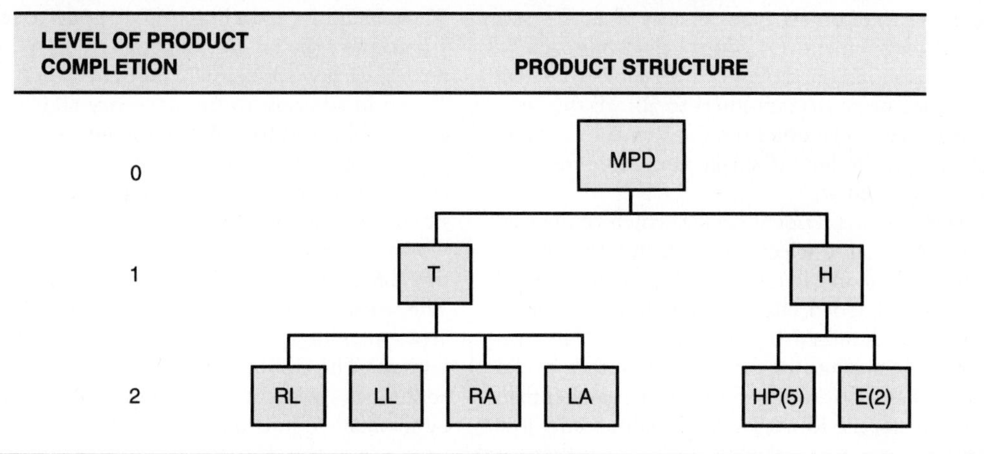

CASE 7-2

TO JIT OR NOT TO JIT

The Kendall Manufacturing Company assembles small electrical appliances for major distributors throughout the United States and Canada. Its product line ranges from citizen's band (CB) radios to electric toasters. Many of Kendall's customers are located in North America. Kendall is classified as a make-to-stock operation that produces large fixed lot-sizes of several electrical appliances it specializes in manufacturing. Kendall operates a single manufacturing plant located in Eastern Canada. It usually devotes its entire operation to producing one item at a time in a single production run of that item. When it finishes producing the desired production run quantity, it starts on a different product. Its usual fixed lot-size for products exceeds 50,000 units in a single production run of a small appliance. Once completed, the entire fixed lot-size order is usually sent directly to its customer's central warehouse for disbursement to individual retail stores.

During the 1980s, many of the distributors selling their products to U.S. department stores started requesting smaller fixed lot-sizes and more frequent orders. Their customers were interested in converting from the large lot-size ordering policies to a smaller fixed lot-size JIT philosophy in hopes of achieving some of the inventory reduction benefits reported in the business literature. The president of Kendall felt that two courses of action could be used to satisfy its customers' new smaller fixed lot-size demand requirement: (1) adopt a JIT approach to its manufacturing operations or (2) establish Kendall warehouses nearer to customers to absorb the large fixed lot-size production from the Kendall plant and distribute the products in smaller and more frequent orders to customers.

To help the president decide which of the two courses of action to select, a manufacturing consultant was called in. Because of international legal problems and added cost, the warehousing choice was quickly dismissed by the consultant. The cost to buy and maintain the foreign warehouses would make the cost of Kendall products much higher than U.S. competitors. Kendall would undoubtedly lose its U.S. customers to U.S. manufacturers. The president of Kendall, though, was not very enthusiastic about changing its existing manufacturing plant to accommodate and embrace the JIT philosophy. The president had heard of JIT operations in the United States that had experienced inventory shortages causing entire plants to be shut down for lack of inventory. It was up to the consultant to convince the president that the merits of JIT outweighed the risks. The consultant would also have to develop a strategy for implementing JIT.

To convince the president of the merits of JIT, the consultant decided to compare Kendall's typical policy of 50,000 unit lot-size production runs with a JIT policy. The consultant felt that comparing the current manufacturing layout with the reductions for buffer stock and inventory areas that might be possible under a JIT policy would permit the president to more easily see the merits of using a JIT system.

To make the comparison, the consultant had to collect some data on the current manufacturing operation and describe the product to be manufactured. The product to be manufactured in this comparative study was an electric toaster. Each toaster is assembled by combining six different component parts—one different part at each of the six different workstations in the Kendall plant layout in Exhibit 7C-4. Kendall used a buffer stock policy of allowing 1 percent of the lot-size in components to be stored next to each workstation. This buffer stock was purchased in addition to the necessary 50,000 units of each component to make up for any defective components workers found or any scrap caused by its efforts. The company also had a component part storage area where, under current policy, a week's worth of component parts were stored for each of the different electrical products it manufactured. The week's worth of component parts stored in this area represent an additional 10 percent of the fixed lot-size. The finished goods inventory required an additional 4 percent of finished goods inventory to be maintained beyond the 50,000 unit lot-size cus-

EXHIBIT 7C-4 PLANT LAYOUT OF KENDALL MANUFACTURING COMPANY

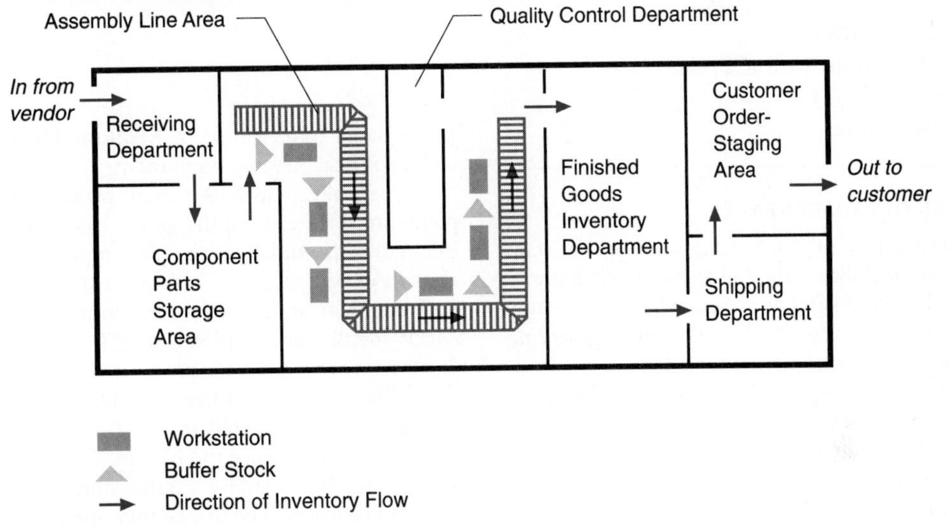

tomer order requirements. The consultant also found that the component parts were ordered in large fixed lot-sizes to accommodate all of the order and inventory requirements at one time. The amount of time the inventory stayed in the components parts storage area ranged from one to three weeks before its use.

CASE QUESTIONS

1. Compare the current non-JIT operation with a comparable JIT operation as presented in this chapter. In making the comparison, answer the following questions: What happens to the relative size of the necessary receiving department, component parts department, assembly line area, quality control department, finished goods inventory department, shipping department, and customer order-staging area? What happens to buffer stocks and component parts inventory? What assumptions are you making in this comparison?
2. What additional information would be useful to compare these two types of operations?
3. Provide a JIT implementation plan for Kendall. How should it start the changeover? At what levels should the buffer stocks be set to make a radical or conservative change?

ARTICLE 7-1

JIT VERSUS MRP:
The Push-Pullers Call a Truce

by Douglas Williams

POINTING OUT DIFFERENCES

Misunderstanding of the concepts led to belief in their incompatibility. "By and large there's a pretty high level of confusion as to just what just-in-time means," says University of Michigan engineering professor David Cole.

"Some suppliers see JIT as the OEM's [Original Equipment Manufacturer's] having them do the warehousing of inventory," he says. "In general though, it means a very short inventory—trying to get as close back to the ore pile as possible. The motivation is more from a quality standpoint than inventory reduction."

Ideally JIT and MRP should fit together. "MRP has to do with the collection of materials, JIT is the implementation of that planning," Cole explains. But though they may fit together, MRP and JIT are not similar systems.

"They are two entirely different concepts," says John Kinsey, associate director of the AIAG [Automotive Industries Association Group]. "The classic MRP system started out as a planning document. Basically it takes that plan and says, 'All you guys, go do this, pass that work on to the next station.' It's a 'push' kind of planning system.

"The JIT philosophy, on the other hand, says the only time you really need something is when the customer demands it, or the next work station needs it," continues Kinsey. "So it's a 'pull' kind of system. JIT says ultimately you want a lot-size of one. Inventory covers up all the imbalances you've got, so JIT ultimately solves problems."

DEERE'S THREE STUDIES

When talking to the MRP and JIT experts, three names repeatedly turn up: Holley Carburetor; John Deere; and Inductoheat, a Madison Heights, MI maker of heat treating equipment.

Deere now has MRP in all plants, and is implementing JIT around the globe. "We see MRP as the master scheduling of the planning and JIT as the execution of that plan," says Sean Battles, a senior staff engineer at Deere. Deere completed its first MRP installation in 1979 and JIT came along in 1981.

"We said we understood the concepts well enough, but we wanted to put JIT in one of our factories to understand the benefits," says Battles.

Deere then made a careful study using three different factories. The first factory operated business as usual. The second was what Battles calls KTI, for Known Technology Improvemnt, which involved smaller lot sizes and reduced inventories, plus expected added technology and an MRP "push" system.

Third was KTI with JIT—"a streamlined, focused, minimum setup 'pull' type system," Battles says. "JIT was the significant winner. After that we started going to all our plants," he says.

At the Ottumwa Works in Iowa where Deere makes hay and forage equipment, JIT worked wonders. Welders in different booths on different shifts used to produce eight subassemblies in batches up to 200 pieces. Those were collected and trucked outside for storage. Elaborate paperwork kept track of them. They were trucked back inside when needed for assembly; some were rusted, some damaged.

Now, using JIT, one welder and two assemblers work together to produce the parts in the exact quantities needed each day. The paperwork is gone. Inventories have been reduced 58%, the system saves \$130,000 a year in this one operation.

At Holley Carburetor, Mike Hecker says the current MRP-JIT work dates to late 1980, when the need to replace the existing computers with state-of-the-art equipment forced a re-evaluation of their MRP work and a need for SPC (statistical process control) training.

Source: Reprinted with permission. From *Automotive Industries* (July 1986), pp. 30–31.

JUST A PART ON TOUR

Part of their study took senior management on a plant tour—not a wide aisle tour in electric carts to glance at different operations. Instead, in a truly inspired approach, Holley honchos were told to take the tour as though they were a specific part running through the plant.

They literally came in the receiving docks, wound their way through the machining operations and ended up on the shipping dock. One Holley executive saw that simply by moving a machine from one side of a sub-assembly line to the other completely eliminated an entire storage bank.

"We found that technique to be just an outstanding way of doing it," says Hecker. "Our overall plan says MRP is a computer-based tool that assists us in overall planning. We recognize that the plan will never be static; for instance, when a customer comes in and asks for a change.

"JIT is what we call an operational philosophy, not a computer-based system. They compliment each other," Hecker says. MRP at Holley is fully in place. "With respect to JIT, we are constantly looking for ways to use it."

Hecker likens JIT to "the frog that jumps halfway to the pond every time it leaps. In theory you never get there, there are always some areas we should be able to improve," he says.

In 1980 Holley turned inventory four times a year; they now turn it 14 times. At its Water Valley, MS plant, where Holley makes fuel injection systems, they turned inventory five times in 1980; it's now 25 times with 50 expected by year's end.

At another Holley plant, the workers brought in a video camera to time and tape a machine setup. By spending $150 for a couple of hand tools, cut setup time from 90 to 38 minutes.

JIT AND THE JOB SHOP

So much for production, automotive style. But what about the less than cookie-stamper type operation? "The assumption is too frequently made that a nonrepetitive manufacturer cannot do much with just-in-time manufacturing," says Robert W. Hall of Indiana University.

In a persuasive paper titled, "Workplace Organization Comes to Inductoheat—JIT in the Job Shop," Hall documents striking efficiency and productivity gains in what he terms, "the quintessential job shop."

Inductoheat management attended an Oliver Wight MRP II seminar in 1980, shopped for an MRP package and bought one for $15,500. They installed it in four months and started running the system in mid-1981. It helped, "but operations were still amiss," according to Hall.

So in 1982 Inductoheat began a shop floor workplace organization that entailed five points: First, removing everything unnecessary, not just inventory; second, creating a place for everything. Cleanliness, discipline and participation were points three, four and five.

Out went five semi-trailer dumpsters of excess material, equipment, tooling and trash, Hall reports. In came some new rules:

- All material for a specific job was to be delivered within the two weeks established as the staging time for a job. Each new job was assigned a clear location and roped off.
- Delivery times were enforced by either shipping back material arriving early, or refusing to pay for it.
- Simplifying and clarifying operating practices led to eliminating backup equipment, extra workpieces, gages, and personal effects.

LOCATING LOGJAMS

According to Hall, building visibility is one of the major objectives. The point is to "create a situation in which non-performance is an obvious disturbance in a normal pattern of work."

So how has it worked out? Inductoheat is private, but VP of operations Steve Stoll says sales for 1986 will be 3.6 times those of 1981; return on owner's equity about 28% compared to 13.3% in '81, -2% in '82, and 24.2% in '85. Inventory is about half what it was five years ago, with workturns increased about four times. Employment is about 130, compared to 150 at the much lower sales rate. And floor space was halved.

"MRP is a tool, a system," explains Stoll. "We use MRP as a planning tool, period. JIT is a philosophy—the philosophy of the elimination of waste."

SUPPLEMENT 7-1
Capacity Requirements Planning (CRP) Methodology

In Supplement 5-1 we presented a procedure called rough-cut capacity planning as a means of determining if the available departmental capacity requirements of an operation were adequate to satisfy the required departmental capacity and accomplish a given master production schedule (MPS). Rough-cut capacity planning is a long-range capacity planning method that focuses on planning on a quarterly or even yearly basis. (Students are encouraged to review the material in Chapter 5 on capacity planning.) **Capacity requirements planning (CRP),** on the other hand, is a medium-range capacity planning method used to examine daily or weekly capacity requirements. CRP is used to determine if available capacity exists to satisfy required capacity within a department area. A department usually consists of work areas called workcenters. A **workcenter** is a production facility consisting of one or more persons, machines, or both. The CRP method presented here is designed to provide a breakdown of capacity requirements at the workcenter level of an operation. In doing so it provides greater detail at the shop floor level of planning. CRP is also considered the final step in the approval process of a given MPS.

The purpose of this supplement is to introduce students to one CRP method.[22] This presentation seeks to provide some understanding of what computer-based systems such as IBM's MAPICS or Hewlett-Packard's Production Management Module generate in their capacity planning reports (see Figure 7-14). Although more efficient CRP methods may exist, the multistep procedure presented in this supplement provides a basic understanding of the mathematics used in generating CRP reports.

CRP is a natural continuation of material requirements planning (MRP), though we do not have to use an MRP system to perform CRP. When we use MRP, we assume that we have infinite capacity to achieve the MPS. We load the MPS into MRP software, and the planned-ordered releases are generated daily or weekly whether we have the capacity to complete them or not. CRP allows us to take the required capacity to accomplish the planned-ordered releases and compare it with available capacity at each workcenter, workstation, or machine used within a department. Our presentation here will require understanding of what planned-ordered releases are in the MRP system presented in Chapter 7.

The basic CRP procedure presented here involves the following four steps:

1. Calculation of available capacity for each workcenter.
2. Calculation of required capacity of planned-ordered releases.
3. Calculation of required capacity of released orders.
4. Generation of CRP comparative capacity requirements.

The output of the four steps is a comparative capacity report, load report, or simply a CRP plan that defines how well the expected load of work at each workcenter is

---

[22] J. F. Cox, *Capacity Management* (Cincinnati: South-Western Publishing, 1989), Chapter 4.

EXHIBIT 7S-1 WORKCENTER MASTER FILE AND AVAILABLE CAPACITY

Workcenter	*Minutes Available per Week*	×	*Utilization Rate*	×	*Efficiency Rate*	=	*Available Capacity in Minutes*
WC1	2,400		1.00		1.00		2,400
WC2	2,400		1.00		1.00		2,400
WC3	2,400		1.00		1.00		2,400

matched by its capacity to process the load. To explain each of these steps, let's work through an example.

Suppose that we have a department that consists of three workcenters (WC1, WC2, and WC3) in which three parts (part 1, part 2, and part 3) are produced. We want to generate the CRP plan that compares available capacity with required capacity on a weekly basis, over a four-week planning period. Let's approach this problem using the steps previously listed.

1. *Calculation of available capacity for each workcenter* To calculate a workcenter's available capacity we can use the formula given in Chapter 5:

   Available capacity = Time available × Utilization × Efficiency

   While data in this formula require some effort to determine (see Chapter 5), let's assume that the information given in Exhibit 7S-1 applies to the company in question. The total available capacity in each of the three work centers is 2,400 minutes (the number of minutes in a forty-hour week).

2. *Calculation of required capacity of planned-ordered releases* The planned-ordered releases are those that are being planned through the master production schedule. Let's assume that we have run the MPS in an MRP and obtained the listing of part production as presented in Exhibit 7S-2. As we can see in Exhibit 7S-2, 250 units of part 1 are required in week 1 and another 250 in week 3. In addition to the planned-ordered releases, we need to have information on the production routing, setup time, run time, and lead time for the production of each part within each workcenter. This information is presented in Exhibit 7S-3. As we can see in Exhibit 7S-3, part 1 is routed only through WC1, with

EXHIBIT 7S-2 PLANNED-ORDERED RELEASES FROM MRP PROGRAM

	UNITS OF PARTS PER WEEK			
Part No.	*1*	*2*	*3*	*4*
1	250	0	250	0
2	75	50	75	50
3	0	200	0	200

EXHIBIT 7S-3 ROUTING FILE FOR EACH PART THROUGH EACH WORKCENTER

Part No.	Workcenter	Workcenter Routing	Setup Time in Minutes per Lot	Run Time in Minutes per Piece	Lead Time in Weeks per Lot per Piece
1	WC1	—	100	1.50	1
2	WC2	1	60	15.50	1
	WC3	2	80	1.25	1
3	WC2	1	40	1.00	1
	WC3	2	120	2.25	1
	WC1	3	20	1.50	1

a setup time of 100 minutes per lot, a run time per piece of 1.50 minutes, and a lead time of one week. Part 2 is routed first through WC2, which takes one week of lead time, and then it must go through WC3, which takes an additional week for production. Part 3 is routed through WC2, then WC3, and finally WC1. Because each workcenter takes one week of lead time we would have to have begun part 3 three weeks ago to have it complete in the present week.

With the information in Exhibits 7S-2 and 7S-3, we can determine the setup time requirements for each workcenter, by each part. This information is presented in Exhibit 7S-4. To determine these values let's start with part 1

EXHIBIT 7S-4 SETUP TIME MATRICES FOR EACH WORKCENTER

		SETUP TIME IN MINUTES PER WEEK					
Workcenter	Part No.	1	2	3	4	5	6
WC1	1	(250)100	0	(250)100	0		
	2	0	0	0	0		
	3	0	0	0	(200)20		(200)20
	Total	100	0	100	20		
	Part No.	1	2	3	4	5	6
WC2	1	0	0	0	0		
	2	(75)60	(50)60	(75)60	(50)60		
	3	0	(200)40	0	(200)40		
	Total	60	100	60	100		
	Part No.	1	2	3	4	5	6
WC3	1	0	0	0	0		
	2	0	80(75)	80(50)	80(75)	80(50)	
	3	0	0	120(200)	0	120(200)	
	Total	0	80	200	80		

Note: Values in parentheses are the unit production from the planned-ordered releases from Exhibit 7S-2.

EXHIBIT 7S-5 RUN TIME MATRICES FOR EACH WORKCENTER

		RUN TIME IN MINUTES PER WEEK					
Workcenter	*Part No.*	*1*	*2*	*3*	*4*	*5*	*6*
WC1	1	375	0	375	0		
	2	0	0	0	0		
	3	0	0	0	300		300
	Total	375	0	375	300		
	Part No.	*1*	*2*	*3*	*4*	*5*	*6*
WC2	1	0	0	0	0		
	2	1,162.5	775	1,162.5	775		
	3	0	200	0	200		
	Total	1,162.5	975	1,162.5	975		
	Part No.	*1*	*2*	*3*	*4*	*5*	*6*
WC3	1	0	0	0	0		
	2	0	93.75	62.5	93.75	62.5	
	3	0	0	450	0	450	
	Total	0	93.75	512.5	93.75		

on Exhibit 7S-2. We can see that we are required to produce 250 units of part 1 in weeks 1 and 3. So a setup of a lot-size of 250 units is required on the WC1, part 1 row in Exhibit 7S-4. (Note the bracketed 250-unit production values by the 100-minute setup times.) The setup time of 100 minutes is given in Exhibit 7S-3. As parts travel in and out of departments with lead times, the setup times have to be lagged by the lead time requirements in the same way that the MRP program time-phases materials requirements. The difference is that we are now exploding the materials forward instead of backwards, as is usual with MRP. For example, part 2 requires processing in WC2 and WC3. The processing in WC3 has to be lagged by one week (from Exhibit 7S-3). As we can see in the boxed areas that are joined together in Exhibit 7S-4, the setup time for part 2 in WC2 is lagged at WC3 by one week, for each week's production. (Note that the requirements are being pushed out of the four-week planning period.) The total setup time for each workcenter can then be determined by summing the values in each matrix.

Once the setup time requirements are determined, the run time requirements can be calculated. These values are presented in Exhibit 7S-5. These values were computed by taking the run time per piece values in Exhibit 7S-3 and multiplying them times the unit production values located in the bracketed values in Exhibit 7S-4. For example, in WC1, part 1 requires 375 minutes (250 units $\times$ 1.50 minutes). The total run time for each workcenter can then be determined by summing the values in each matrix.

EXHIBIT 7S-6 REQUIRED CAPACITY OF PLANNED-ORDERED RELEASES

	TOTAL REQUIRED CAPACITY IN MINUTES PER WEEK			
Workcenter	*1*	*2*	*3*	*4*
WC1	475	0	475	320
WC2	1,222.5	1,075	1,222.5	1,075
WC3	0	173.75	712.5	173.75

Summing the totals from Exhibits 7S-4 and 7S-5 gives the capacity requirements for all planned-ordered releases. These values are presented in Exhibit 7S-6. As we can see in Exhibit 7S-6, WC1 requires a total of 475 minutes (100 minutes + 375 minutes) of capacity in week 1.

3. *Calculation of required capacity of released orders* In addition to the planned-ordered releases, some orders already will undoubtedly be in the production system. We call these work-in-process orders released orders. The capacity that will be used by these released orders needs to be included in the calculation of capacity in the four-week planning period. An MRP system usually gives current information on released orders. Let's assume that we are given the number of released orders as presented in Exhibit 7S-7(a). As we can see in Exhibit

EXHIBIT 7S-7 PLANNED-ORDERED RELEASES CURRENTLY IN PROCESS

(A) RELEASED ORDERS

Part No.	*Number of Parts on Order*	*Due Date (week no.)*
1	200	1
2	100	1
3	100	1

(B) ROUTING TO THE WORKCENTERS FOR RELEASED ORDERS

	WEEK NO.		
Part No.	*−1*	*0*	*1*
1	—	—	WC1
2	—	WC2	WC3
3	WC2	WC3	WC1
	Released order work that has been completed in the prior planning period ←		→ *Released order work remaining and should be added to the planned order releases during week no. 1*

EXHIBIT 7S-8 REQUIRED CAPACITY OF RELEASED ORDERS

(A) CALCULATIONS

Part No.	*Workcenter*	*Setup Time in MInutes*	*Run Time Calculation*	*Run Time*	*Total Time*
1	WC1	100	200 (units) × 1.5 (min) =	300	400
2	WC3	80	100 (units) × 1.25 (min) =	125	205
3	WC1	100	100 (units) × 1.5 (min) =	150	250

(B) RELEASED ORDER REQUIRED CAPACITY IN MINUTES

Workcenter	*Week No. 1*
WC1	650
WC2	0
WC3	205

7S-7(a) a total of 200 units of part 1, 100 units of part 2, and 100 units of part 3 are expected in one week. As presented in Exhibit 7S-7(b), we can see that the routing of these three parts requires some capacity to produce them in the period prior (weeks −1 and 0) to the four-week period we are examining. As such, we will only include in the capacity requirements those requirements remaining to finish the product during week 1. The computations of the remaining released order capacity requirements are presented in Exhibit 7S-8(a). Adding the requirements together the resulting released orders requirements are determined as presented in Exhibit 7S-8(b).

4. *Generation of CRP comparative capacity requirements* Combining the planned-ordered releases and released orders requirements from Exhibits 7S-6 and 7S-8, the total CRP required capacity can be determined. The CRP capacity requirements are presented in Exhibit 7S-9. As we can see in Exhibit 7S-9, the total required capacity for WC1 in week 1 is 1,125 minutes (475 minutes + 650 minutes). Most computer-based systems present the CRP available and required capacity information in the form of bar graphs, like those in Exhibit 7S-10. It is obvious in Exhibit 7S-10 that there is more than enough capacity

EXHIBIT 7S-9 TOTAL REQUIRED CAPACITY

	TOTAL REQUIRED CAPACITY IN MINUTES PER WEEK			
Workcenter	*1*	*2*	*3*	*4*
WC1	1,125	0	475	320
WC2	1,222.5	1,075	1,222.5	1,075
WC3	205	173.75	712.5	173.75

in each workcenter to accomplish the given MPS-driven MRP planned-ordered releases and released orders. Had, in this example, one or more of the workcenters lacked sufficient capacity to accomplish the order requirements, management would have to shift or acquire additional capacity to accomplish the MPS.

The graphic presentation of the available capacity and required capacity allows managers to identify capacity surpluses or shortages in workcenters on a weekly basis. Unlike rough-cut capacity planning, which focuses on the department level and on a quarterly basis, CRP allows managers to bring the MPS on a weekly basis down to the shop floor level of production to identify production resource capabilities in very specific areas (such as a single machine or an individual worker) of an operations management system.

EXHIBIT 7S-10 CAPACITY REQUIREMENTS PLAN (CRP) FOR MRP SCHEDULED PRODUCTION

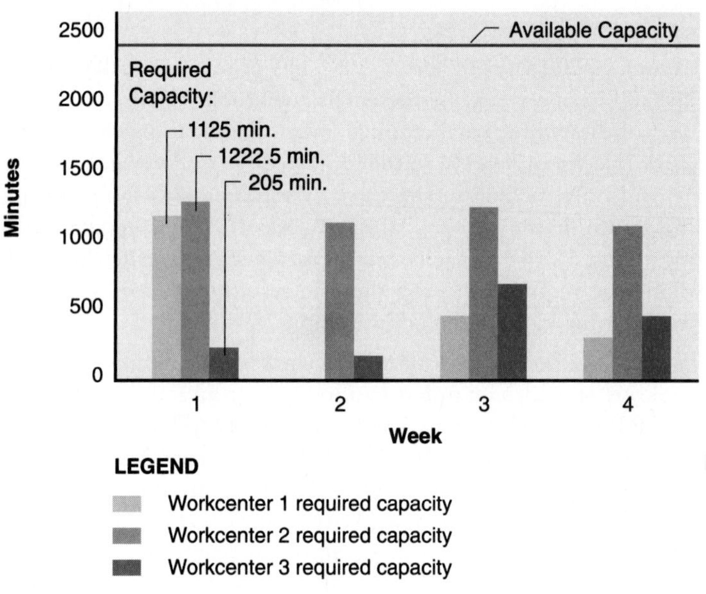

CHAPTER OUTLINE

8 Inventory Management: Independent Demand Inventory

CHAPTER OBJECTIVES

The material in this chapter should prepare you to do the following:

1. Explain why independent demand inventory is necessary.
2. Describe how fixed order quantity systems are different than fixed order period systems.
3. Explain the development of economic order quantity models: their assumptions, mathematical development, and application.
4. Explain how inventory models can be used to determine lot-sized production quantities.
5. Explain why customer service level is an important consideration in the development of all inventory models.
6. Determine inventory ordering quantities and timing.
7. Explain the development of an economic order period model: its assumptions, mathematical modeling, and application.

8. Explain how order quantity modeling can help in the implementation of a just-in-time inventory system.
9. Explain how computer-integrated inventory systems are using electronic data interchange to improve inventory ordering.
10. Describe how the Monte Carlo simulation method can be used in inventory planning.

A manufacturer may produce an end item or end product (such as tires) that it will sell to another manufacturer (such as an automobile producer) to use as component parts of its finished product (such as an automobile). Although the automobile manufacturer that will use these tires considers them dependent demand inventory, the supplier of the tires considers them finished products—products that mark the end of the transformation process. The demand for end items from suppliers is subject to customer demand, and therefore considered as independent demand inventory.

S

In service operations, most tangible inventory items are component parts that are used in the completion or delivery of the service product. McDonald's Restaurants, Inc., needs napkins for each customer's food order, a newspaper delivery service needs rubber bands to wrap its papers for delivery, and a drugstore needs bottles to fill prescriptions. Because the tangible inventory items are closely related to delivery of the finished service product, they are treated as independent demand inventory items.

Each manufacturer or service provider offers one or more end items, end products, or finished products. When these products are placed into inventory for sale to customers we call them **independent demand inventory.** In this chapter, we will examine **independent demand inventory systems,** which are the policies, methods, and procedures used to manage inventory items that have independent demand.[1] Some of these policies, methods, and procedures are based on mathematics such as calculus, statistical assumptions such as the normal distribution, and philosophies like the zero-inventory goal of just-in-time (JIT) ordering. All, however, are designed to help managers accomplish their organization's inventory objectives.

One objective of an independent demand inventory system is to maximize the level of customer service by providing a manufactured or service product when and where it is needed. All businesses want to have the right quantity of inventory in the right

---

[1] Reprinted with permission of the American Production and Inventory Control Society, Inc., *APICS Dictionary,* 7th edition, 1992.

place and at the right time to help them sell their finished products. To accomplish their maximum level of customer service, they must establish a quantity of units that they can produce or order from suppliers, vendors, or subcontractors that will satisfy customer demand. We call this quantity of inventory an **order quantity** or **lot-size**—that is, the quantity of a particular item that is ordered for a single delivery from a plant or vendor. A firm must also establish a timing plan for placing the order to meet the customer demand requirements. If the timing of the order does not match the customer demand requirements, the firm might run out of inventory and dissatisfy customers.

A second objective of an independent demand inventory system is to minimize the cost of inventory. Inventory costs are interrelated and directly affect the objective of maximizing customer service. For example, we might choose to decrease the order quantity and thereby reduce all costs of carrying a reduced lot-size inventory. Unfortunately, an organization that reduces inventory risks incurring stocking out costs and must place a greater number of orders in a year to meet a fixed level of customer demand (which increases fixed order costs). Likewise, an organization that reduces order costs as well as minimizes the risk and costs of stocking out must increase carrying costs.

Ideally, every organization wants to establish the inventory policy that facilitates right decisions on order quantity and timing of the arrival of the order quantity to maximize customer service while minimizing costs. In this chapter, we will examine a number of independent demand inventory systems that can help an organization establish policy to realize these objectives.

• • •

WHY INDEPENDENT DEMAND INVENTORY IS NECESSARY

Independent demand inventory is necessary for a variety of reasons that depend on the type of inventory item and the two objectives of maximizing customer service levels and minimizing costs.

Types of Inventory

Three basic types of inventory items are finished goods, work-in-process (WIP), and raw materials. **Finished goods** are the end items, end products, or finished products that are outputs of the production process. **Work-in-process** and **raw materials,** as we saw in Chapter 7, are used as input into the production process to complete the finished goods. Although WIP and raw materials are usually considered dependent demand inventory items, they are considered independent demand inventory when they are the end product or finished product for a company. For example, the separate parts divisions of General Motors (GM) Automotive Division manufacture component parts (engines, radios) and raw materials (copper wire, lead). These inventory items represent the output of the separate parts divisions; that is, they are the independent demand inventory of the separate parts divisions. These same parts, however, can still be considered dependent demand inventory for GM's Automotive Division, which manufactures completed automobiles. The automobiles are GM's independent demand inventory. Planning and controlling the independent demand inventory items in the separate parts divisions and the finished cars for the automotive division necessitate different inventory systems than the typical MRP system used to manage the GM Automotive Division's dependent demand inventory.

Reasons Related to Maximizing Customer Service

Meeting the customer's requirements is the primary objective of all organizations. Most recent management approaches, such as total quality management or customer-focused management, are oriented toward meeting this objective. Proper management of independent demand inventory also intends to maximize the level of customer service, as discussed in the following sections.

Q **MEET FORECAST DEMAND** Organizations forecast customer use of independent demand inventory items and then plan production to meet those forecast demand levels. If an organization has an adequate supply of inventory available when and where it is demanded, it will maximize customer service by satisfying customer needs. Some products require considerable production and delivery lead time and if a supply of inventory is not on hand when demanded by customers, customers are dissatisfied.

AID MARKETING OF PRODUCT Most customers of end-time products want to examine the product they are buying. To help marketing agents complete the sale of a product, available end-item inventory can help customers become more familiar with a company's product and remove any of their doubts. The end result is, again, a better satisfied customer.

Reasons Related to Minimizing Cost

In addition to maximizing customer service, independent demand inventory can minimize cost, as outlined in the following sections.

REDUCE PURCHASE COSTS When a firm plans for the existence of independent demand inventory, other organizations' purchasing agents can place large orders that will reduce their cost per unit. Purchasing agents occasionally observe **order cycles** (or seasonal periods when demand increases or decreases and then returns to a normal level). Purchasing agents periodically group inventory orders during these cycles to place large order quantities, and they can often obtain price discounts from vendors that will lower the cost per unit of the item. Also, in times of inflation when costs are increasing, a large acquisition today saves the cost of purchasing higher-priced inventory in the future. Large purchase quantities can also save fixed ordering costs because fewer smaller orders will be needed in the future.

REDUCE COSTLY PRODUCTION INEFFICIENCIES By having a finished goods inventory to act as a cushion against surges in demand or seasonal fluctuations, the organization can maintain smooth production year round. This smoothed production rate will reduce the need for costly overtime in periods of demand surges. The organization can also avoid the equally costly paid layoffs in periods of demand decline by simply placing the surplus production in finished goods inventory.

REDUCE SHORTAGE COSTS Stocking out of independent demand inventory is not always caused by surges in customer demand. Production and vendor lead times may be inaccurate and thus interrupt a scheduled delivery of finished product from being made in time for its sale or delivery to a final customer. By having an adequate finished product inventory, stockouts can be minimized or avoided. This will protect the organization from incurring the different types of shortage costs associated with stocking out.

Q

QUESTION: What is the relationship between quality and the two objectives (maximize customer service and minimize costs) of independent demand inventory management?

ANSWER: Quality can be defined in terms of customer service and product value to the customer. Ideally, independent demand inventory managers will avoid having too little or too much inventory. Managers can maximize customer service by making the finished product available to the customer when demanded and in the quantity desired. Likewise, managers can minimize the cost of inventory by minimizing the amount not required to satisfy customer demand. By minimizing excess inventory (and its costs), the cost savings can be passed on to the customer (by way of the productivity cycle in Figure 1-5 in Chapter 1) to increase the value of the product to the customer.

HOW INVENTORY ORDERING SYSTEMS WORK

Order Period Versus Order Quantity

We can generally categorize inventory ordering systems as either fixed order period systems or fixed order quantity systems. A **fixed order period system** is an inventory ordering system in which the timing of the order is fixed but the order quantity is variable. Under this system, a set period of days, weeks, or months is fixed until the next order should be placed. The amount of order quantity is flexible to meet the shifts in demand that occur over the fixed time period. The amount that is to be ordered is based on demand (either actual or forecast) and is set to bring the inventory up to some targeted level that is expected to satisfy demand for the future fixed time period.

One simple way of determining the inventory target level is by taking total forecast demand and dividing it by the number of planned order periods per year. This type of inventory system is ideal when it is easy to determine on-hand inventory stocks (such as in a computer-based on-line inventory monitoring system) or when there is a small amount of expensive inventory items. Expensive and limited quantities of prescription medicine in drugstores and mid-season reordering of automobiles by dealerships are examples of products for which a monthly or a seasonal time period (or order cycle) can be used to determine the fixed time to place an order. The relatively small on-hand inventory stock of medicine and automobiles can easily be counted in a physical audit by inventory management. The order quantity of medicine and automobiles is dependent on the actual demand that occurs in the fixed time period from when the last order was received. A fixed order period system is also used by organizations that seek to minimize their purchasing costs. As previously mentioned, the period grouping of inventory orders into order cycles permits purchase prices for several items to be lowered through negotiation with vendors.

A fixed order period system is presented in Figure 8-1(a). The small steplike line in order period 1 represents the typical movement of actual independent demand inventory. For illustration purposes (and for modeling purposes discussed later in this chapter), we will assume that the darker linear line drawn through the smaller steplike line represents the consumption or demand of inventory by customers. Each of the order time periods in Figure 8-1(a) are fixed at ten days. Note that the number of units ordered in each period varies.

One advantage of this system is that ordering inventory can be timed to meet order cycles of customers; thus the time the items spend as inventory waiting for the customer is minimized. Another advantage is that the arrival, materials handling, and production processing of the inventory can be timed to fit the available resources and capacities of the organization. A disadvantage of having to wait to place an order is that a shortage of inventory can occur if demand exceeds forecast expectations. An organization might have to turn customers away while waiting for the next order period to begin. Another disadvantage, as we can see in Figure 8-1(a), is that the order quantity may need to fluctuate considerably. This necessitates maintaining excessive storage capacity levels (for example, for units ordered in period 3) even during the low order periods (for example, period 4). A costly purchasing agreement may need to be maintained with suppliers to permit this flexibility in order quantities.

A **fixed order quantity system** is an inventory ordering system in which the order quantity is fixed for each order placed but the timing of the order varies to meet shifts in demand. Under this system, we assume that the on-hand inventory stock is monitored continuously and when additional inventory is needed a fixed order quantity of the same size is placed with suppliers or vendors. The size of the fixed order quantity is based on a combination of demand and cost considerations. This type of inventory system is ideal for managing a large number of different inventory items. WIP and raw materials inventory whose usage is based on actual customer orders or forecasts are frequently ordered using fixed order quantity systems.

A fixed order quantity system is presented in Figure 8-1(b). The variability caused by shifts in demand is absorbed by altering the timing of the order rather than the order

FIGURE 8-1 COMPARISON OF FIXED ORDER PERIOD AND FIXED ORDER QUANTITY SYSTEMS

(A) FIXED ORDER PERIOD SYSTEM

ORDER PERIODS

1 2 3 4

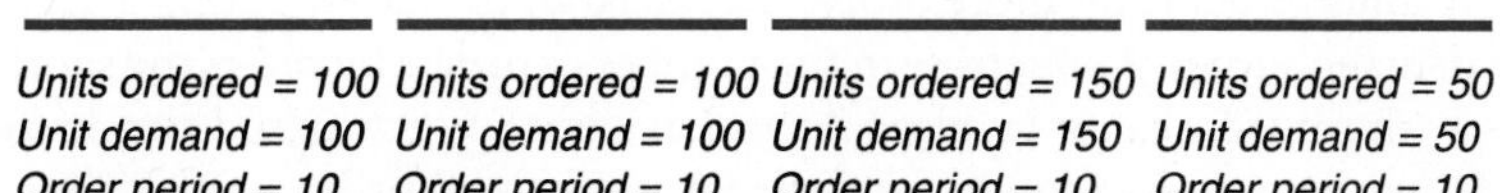

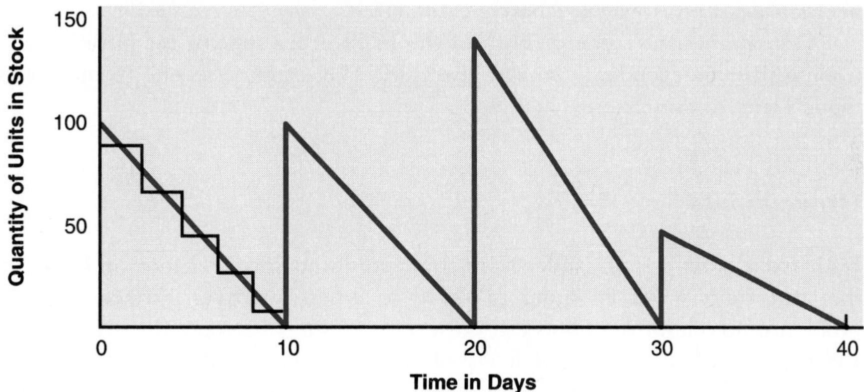

(B) FIXED ORDER QUANTITY SYSTEM

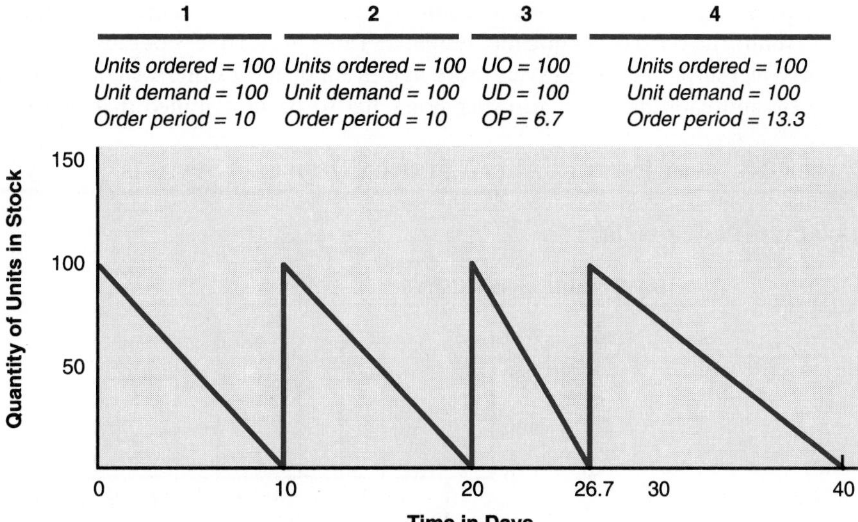

quantity. One of the advantages of this ordering system is that storage capacity requirements are level. As we can see in Figure 8-1(b), an organization needs only to maintain storage capacity for 100 units, as opposed to the fixed order system requiring a maximum storage capacity of 150 units. Another advantage is that order quantity sizes do not have to be estimated each time the order is placed, which saves time. One of the disadvantages of the fixed order quantity system is that because order quantity does not change to meet shifts in demand, more orders may need to be placed during a year to compensate for demand surges. An increase in the number of orders increases the short-term ordering costs (the fixed charge to place an order with a vendor) and can increase long-term ordering costs (for example, an increase in planned order units from a vendor might necessitate a more costly purchasing contract).

Organizations use one or both of the fixed order systems for planning and controlling their independent demand inventory. We examine several fixed order system models later in this chapter.

Order Points

Both fixed order systems suffer from the same limitation—reliance on **lead time,** or the time from when an order is placed to when it arrives. Strikes, transportation problems, or vendor stockouts can cause a discrepancy between the planned lead time and the actual lead time of a delivery of inventory. The result of a discrepancy can be an inventory shortage or a surplus that must be carried over to the next period. In either case, planned shortage costs or carrying costs will be increased.

We can see a simple example of the effect of lead time on ordering systems in Table 8-1. Ideally, we would operate with a zero-week lead time: demand and units ordered are equal, as in Table 8-1(b). If we permit a lead time of only one week under a fixed order period system, we can see in Table 8-1(c) that both shortages and surpluses will exist. While the fixed order quantity system in Table 8-1(d) does not cause any shortages, its carryover surpluses are relatively more significant than the other systems. To minimize shortage and carrying costs, an order point has to be determined that will minimize

TABLE 8-1 THE EFFECT OF LEAD TIME ON ORDERING SYSTEMS

(A) ACTUAL DEMAND IN UNITS

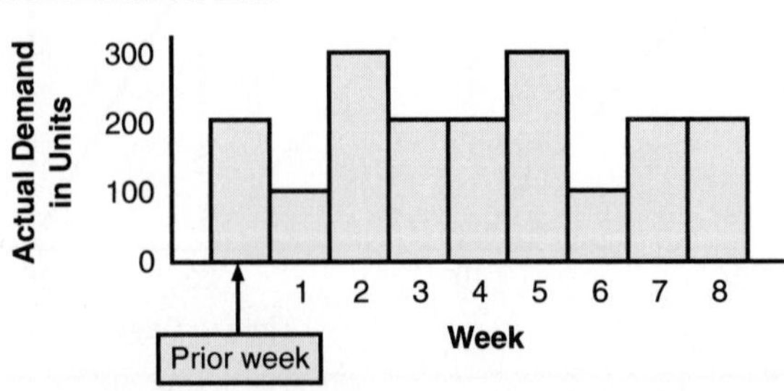

TABLE 8-1 (CONTINUED)

(B) A ZERO-WEEK LEAD TIME, FIXED ORDER PERIOD SYSTEM

	WEEK							
	1	*2*	*3*	*4*	*5*	*6*	*7*	*8*
Carryover from last week	0	0	0	0	0	0	0	0
Units ordered	100	300	200	200	300	100	200	200
Total units	100	300	200	200	300	100	200	200
Actual demand	(100)	(300)	(200)	(200)	(300)	(100)	(200)	(200)
Resulting carryover to next week	0	0	0	0	0	0	0	0

(C) A ONE-WEEK LEAD TIME, FIXED ORDER PERIOD SYSTEM*

	WEEK							
	1	*2*	*3*	*4*	*5*	*6*	*7*	*8*
Carryover from last week	0	100	(100)	0	0	(100)	100	0
Units ordered	200**	100	300	200	200	300	100	200
Total units	200	200	200	200	200	200	200	200
Actual demand	(100)	(300)	(200)	(200)	(300)	(100)	(200)	(200)
Resulting carryover to next week	100	(100)	0	0	(100)	100	0	0

(D) A ONE-WEEK LEAD TIME, FIXED ORDER QUANTITY SYSTEM*

	WEEK							
	1	*2*	*3*	*4*	*5*	*6*	*7*	*8*
Carryover from last week	0	700	400	200	0	500	400	200
Units ordered	800	0	0	0	800	0	0	0
Total units	800	700	400	200	800	500	400	200
Actual demand	(100)	(300)	(200)	(200)	(300)	(100)	(200)	(200)
Resulting carryover to next week	700	400	200	0	500	400	200	0

* A positive carryover from last week is a surplus and a negative carryover (in parentheses) is a shortage. All units ordered in (A) are delayed one week.

** Based on "prior week" of 200 units in Table 8-1(A) to allow for the lead time of one week.

both shortage and carrying costs while maximizing the service objective of inventory management.

An **order point** (also called a **reorder quantity**) is a fixed quantity of inventory that triggers when an order should be placed so the inventory will arrive in a timely manner to the purchaser. When inventory levels drop to the order point, an order should be placed with vendors and suppliers. We discuss methods of determining order points later in this chapter.

Accounting for Inventory

To ascertain how many units to order in a fixed order quantity system or to know when to place an order in a fixed order period system, a manager must first find out how many units of inventory are currently on hand. To support the basic accounting functions of auditing and cost control, inventory accounting systems have been developed. Two types of inventory accounting systems that can provide on-hand inventory information are a periodic system and a continuous system. A **periodic inventory system** involves a periodic audit of available stock. For companies operating under manual systems, a physical audit usually involves human beings counting inventory stock to determine on-hand stock levels. In a computer-integrated organization, electronic audits are conducted using electronic sensors to determine available stock. Some automated storage and automated retrieval (AS/AR) systems have electronic sensors built into the automated shelving. These sensors are designed to automatically count the remaining boxes in each shelf location and pass the information to the appropriate inventory accounting module in the computer-integrated manufacturing (CIM) or computer-integrated service system (CISS) software. The timely nature of periodic inventory systems complements fixed order period ordering systems. The exact timing of the periodic inventory determination is based on the informational needs of the organization.

A **continuous inventory system** (or **perpetual system**) involves keeping track of additions and removal of inventory on a continuous basis. Under ths accounting system inventory is monitored continuously so when order points are reached, new orders for new inventory can be placed. For companies operating manual systems, one continuous inventory system that can be used is the two-bin system. The **two-bin system** is an inventory system in which the total inventory for each item is stored in two bins. Under this system, inventory is consumed out of one bin until it is empty. The empty bin is the triggering signal used to inform management that inventory needs to be ordered equivalent to two bins. The inventory in the second bin provides the necessary lead time between the placement of the order and its arrival to replenish both bins. Companies that are operating computer-based systems often keep track of additions and removals by using optical scanning equipment. The packaging of inventory for AS/AR systems allows the placement of a universal products code (UPC) label or bar code label that optical scanners can read, recognize, and transmit to a computer system inventory accounting software module. The positioning of such scanning equipment to monitor incoming and outgoing inventory allows inventory transactions to be continuously recorded and summarized by software modules. The continuous inventory system is ideally suited to support a fixed order quantity ordering system.

Regardless of the type of inventory accounting system used, CIM or CISS software seeks to convert accounting transactions into useful planning and control reports. The information obtained from manual or computer-based systems can be used as input into

Q

QUESTION: What is an example of how bar coding has helped inventory planning in the real world?

ANSWER: Chicago-based Williams Electronics Games Inc. is an internationally known leader in the production of coin-operated pinball and video games.[2] Its manufacturing facilities in Chicago are set up to produce production runs of a single product (a single model of game) for several months at a time. When all the orders are filled for that game, the firm discontinues that game permanently and works on the next game. This could easily lead to excessive inventory levels if accurate records on inventory are not maintained to check demand requirements with available inventory production. Williams reported that three years before it implemented a bar code system, inventory errors were so common that production lines were frequently stopped. The stoppages were caused by inventory shortages, and excess stock on-hand at the end of production runs resulted in costly waste. By implementing a bar code system, Williams reported a 95 percent or better inventory accuracy score on its inventory records. Computer-read bar codes eliminated handwritten and keypunch errors and improved the accuracy and timeliness of the inventory information. This represented a substantial improvement in inventory accuracy and also permitted the organization to implement a just-in-time (JIT) system. Because JIT operations (discussed in Chapters 6 and 7) hold little inventory, the accuracy of inventory records becomes critical. The bar coding system helped provide that necessary accuracy to make JIT a success for Williams during a period when the demand for its products increased by 100 percent. It reported a substantial lowering of WIP inventory and was able to avoid unplanned shutdowns caused by inventory shortages. Williams credits much of the success of its operation to the tight control over inventory that resulted from using bar coding.

CIM or CISS software for processing into inventory information. As we can see in Figure 8-2, the output of periodic and continuous accounting systems can include a number of different planning and control reports. The Arthur Andersen MAC-PAC Integrated Management Information System (outlined in Chapter 5) generates several reports, including

Inventory control reports, which facilitate a continuous comparison of on-hand and on-order inventory levels to help management identify shortages and surpluses in current and near-future inventory usage periods.

Inventory accounting reports, which allow a periodic comparison between beginning and ending inventory levels for finished goods, WIP, and materials. They also help management identify differences between expected and actual materials and labor usage.

[2] E. M. Fleischaker, "Bar Coding Helps Game Company Score in Emerging Markets," *APICS—The Performance Advantage,* 2, No. 11 (November 1992), 43–44.

FIGURE 8-2 INPUT/OUTPUT OF PERIODIC AND CONTINUOUS INVENTORY ACCOUNTING SYSTEMS

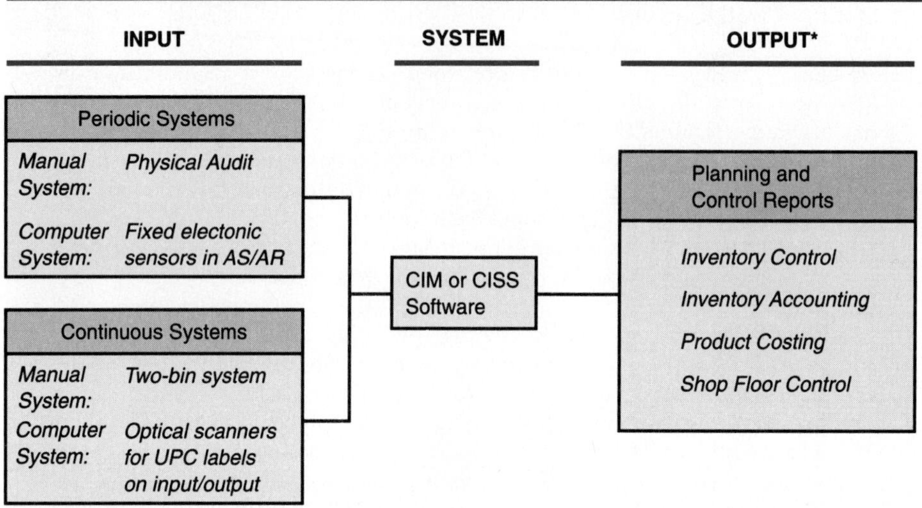

* This collection of planning and control reports are based on the MAC-PAC Integrated Management Information System outlined in Figure 5-10, in Chapter 5.

Product costing reports, which facilitate a periodic summary of work force, materials, and overhead costs for planning budgets and profit margins.

Shop floor control reports, which allow a continuous status report on WIP inventory flow as well as compare expected and actual labor usage to monitor productivity. They also help identify and reduce scrap at the shop floor level where it is generated.

These reports provide quantity and cost information in both periodic and on-line continuous inventory systems. Both quantity and cost information, as well as actual and forecast demand information, are necessary to establish inventory ordering systems.

FIXED ORDER QUANTITY SYSTEMS

When F. W. Harris proposed the use of calculus to derive the first economic order quantity (EOQ) model, it was meant as an approach to inventory management and not just a mathematical formula.[3] The **EOQ approach** is the application of mathematical

[3] F. W. Harris, *Operations and Cost*—Factory Management Series (Chicago: A. W. Shaw Co., 1915), Chapter 4.

modeling to inventory planning. This approach can involve the derivation of inventory planning models, or where models already exist, the identification and adoption of the appropriate model. While it was first applied (during the Scientific Management era) to the development of fixed order quantity systems, the EOQ approach was also expanded to include fixed order period systems and other inventory concepts. It was later improved by R. H. Wilson, who combined EOQ analysis with the concept of buffer stocks.[4]

In this section we will examine how the modeling approach is used to develop fixed order quantity EOQ models. For each of the three EOQ models we will examine, we will present model assumptions, variable and parameter definitions, model formulation, and an example of the use of the model.

Many inventory managers research existing EOQ models to find one that best fits their own inventory situation. Models are researched by reviewing their assumptions and comparing them with the inventory requirements of a particular item and the unique cost structure of an organization. Because a large number of EOQ models are available, such a search may be inefficient. The EOQ approach to inventory management was not, however, meant to be an inefficient search for models. Rather, the EOQ approach to inventory management requires the development of a mathematical model that will define the least-cost inventory order quantity for a particular inventory item. The model is developed to custom-fit the particular inventory environment of the item and organization. The models developed in this chapter are intended as an introduction and require only algebra and a few differential calculus rules. They illustrate what the modeling process should be when applied in a real-world situation.

We will examine models that have only one variable: order quantity. All other parameters in the model are assumed to be constant.

As previously stated, the EOQ approach to inventory management involves the development of mathematical models. The procedure to develop these models consists of the following steps:

1. *Collect all relevant inventory cost and unit demand information.* Depending on the type of inventory item and the organization's cost structure, the cost information typically includes carrying costs, ordering costs, setup costs, and shortage costs. Unit demand of the inventory item under consideration also must be forecast.

2. *Develop a total annual cost (TAC) function.* This TAC expression defines total annual cost as a function of a single variable: order quantity (we will denote quantity as Q):

$$TAC = f(Q)$$

In this model we are stating that TAC is a function of Q. Our objective is to find a Q that will minimize TAC.

---

[4] R. H. Wilson, "A Scientific Routine for Stock Control," *Harvard Business Review,* 13, No. 1 (October 1934), 116–128.

QUESTION: Once an EOQ model is developed, do we need to know calculus to use it?

ANSWER: No, the models formulated in this chapter can be applied as long as the situation fits the assumptions of the model. Many operations managers simply identify existing EOQ models to fit their organizations' unique cost situation. Others who know calculus can derive their own EOQ models. The presentation in this chapter includes the step of using calculus because it is a formal part of the EOQ modeling process.

3. *Use differential calculus to find the derivative of the TAC function.* The derivative of a function defines its slope.
4. *Set the derivative equal to zero and derive the EOQ formula.* The *TAC* function is usually a U-shaped cost curve like the one shown in Figure 8-3. *TAC* is a function of the order quantity Q. If we can find the **zero-slope value** (or the value of Q where the slope of $f(Q)$ equals zero), then we can determine the cost-minimizing EOQ value or Q^*. (The asterisk is to signify that Q^* is the optimal Q of all possible Qs.) We accomplish this by simply setting the derivative found in step 3 equal to zero and solving algebraically for Q. The result is an EOQ formula that can be used to determine the optimal order quantity or Q^*, given specific cost data such as carrying and ordering costs. Q^* is an optimal value along the *TAC* function.

These four steps represent the classic EOQ approach to inventory management. Let's use them to derive three EOQ formulas that can be used in different inventory situations.

Basic EOQ Model

ASSUMPTIONS The basic EOQ model, like all fixed order quantity models, is based on a number of assumptions. If an organization's inventory situation matches the model's assumptions, the model's results will be valid. The assumptions for the basic EOQ model include the following:

1. Annual carrying costs per unit and costs per order can be accurately estimated and are the only relevant costs. This assumption really requires that all cost information must be known with certainty, which is rarely possible.
2. Annual demand can be estimated and is linearly consumed by customers. This assumption requires the annual demand estimate to be known with certainty. From Chapter 3 on forecasting, we know that annual demand estimates can

FIGURE 8-3 ZERO-SLOPE VALUE FOR A *TAC* FUNCTION

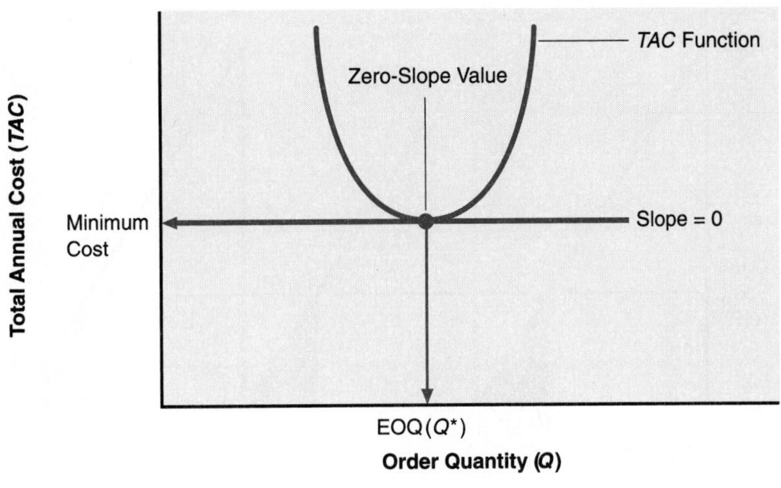

rarely be known with certainty. In addition, this assumption also requires the linear consumption of inventory, as presented in Figure 8-1(b), and not the steplike progression shown in Figure 8-1(a) for period 1. In reality, independent demand inventory is usually ordered by customers in finite lot sizes or order quantities producing a steplike consumption function.

3. Average inventory level is the order quantity Q divided by 2. This assumption requires that only an amount of Q inventory can be available. If a safety stock is left over from a previous period, then average inventory would be greater than $Q/2$.
4. With demand linear and certain, there need be no stockout costs. This assumption basically prohibits the stocking out of inventory, as costs are almost always associated with being unable to meet a customer's demand requirements. If stockout is not possible, there will be no stockout costs.
5. There are no quantity discounts on large orders.
6. Lead time is known and fixed.

INFORMATION REQUIREMENTS In the basic EOQ model, we want to determine the EOQ value (that is, Q^*). We also need to determine an order point (*OP*) in units to know when to place the next Q^* size order. As presented in Figure 8-4, inventory order of Q^* arrives and is used linearly until it reaches the order point. A second inventory order of Q^* is then placed at the beginning of the lead time (*LT*) period. As time passes, the units of inventory are consumed until another order of Q^* arrives. This same sequence of events continues to repeat over time. If an inventory manager can determine Q^* and *OP*, the entire fixed quantity inventory ordering system for that

FIGURE 8-4 BASIC EOQ MODEL BEHAVIOR

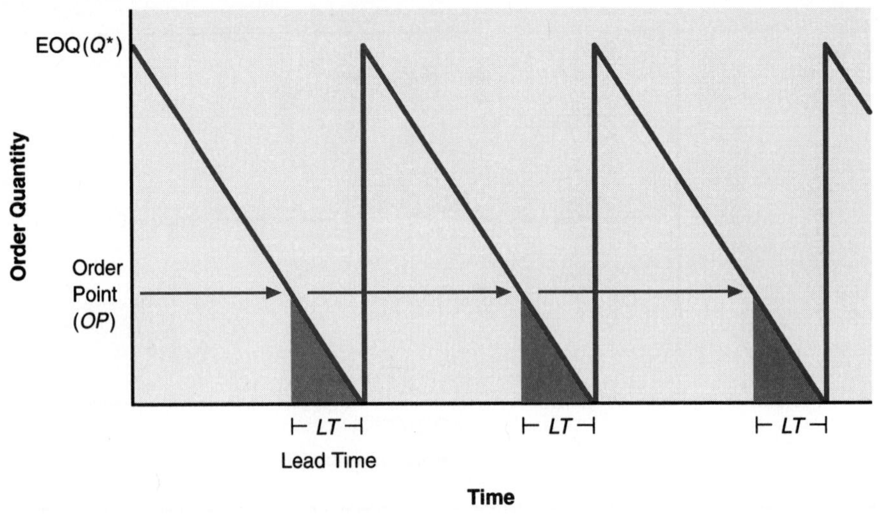

item is defined. The information requirements of this type of system then are Q^* and *OP*. We will discuss procedures for determining *OP* in the next section.

MODEL FORMULATION To formulate the basic EOQ model we will use the four-step EOQ modeling approach.

1. *Collect cost data.* Two types of cost data are relevant for this model: carrying costs and ordering costs. **Carrying costs** include insurance, inventory taxes, handling, shrinkage (pilfering), obsolescence, and the cost of capital. **Ordering costs** include any fixed charges to place an order with a vendor (for example, many vendors pass on the cost of processing an order to their customers by setting a fixed charge per order) and the purchasing firm's human resource cost for placing the order. Together they create the *TAC* function as follows:

$$TAC = \text{Annual carrying costs} + \text{Annual ordering costs}$$

2. *Develop the TAC function.* Because there are two types of costs, we will develop these costs separately and then add them together to arrive at the *TAC* function. To obtain annual carrying costs, let's define the following model elements:

I = annual inventory carrying cost rate (that is, the proportion of total costs that are related to carrying inventory), or the following ratio:

$$I = \frac{\text{Carrying costs per year}}{\text{Total of all costs of inventory per year}}$$

C = cost of the inventory item

Q = order quantity (unknown at this point in the model formulation process)

$\frac{Q}{2}$ = average inventory

If we multiply I by C, we obtain the cost to carry one unit for one year in inventory. So the resulting expression for carrying costs is the product of the cost per unit of inventory and the average inventory held in stock:

$$\text{Annual carrying costs} = IC\left(\frac{Q}{2}\right)$$

To obtain the annual ordering cost function we denote the following elements:

S = cost in dollars to place one order (that is, the average ordering costs per order)

D = annual demand in units of inventory

If we divide D by Q we obtain the number of orders placed per year. So the resulting expression for ordering costs is the product of the cost to place one order and the number of orders placed per year:

$$\text{Annual ordering costs} = S\left(\frac{D}{Q}\right)$$

We can now add annual carrying costs together with annual ordering costs to obtain the TAC curve.

$$TAC = \text{Annual carrying costs} + \text{Annual ordering costs}$$

$$TAC = IC\left(\frac{Q}{2}\right) + S\left(\frac{D}{Q}\right)$$

As presented in Figure 8.5, the combination of the two cost functions results in a U-shaped TAC curve. This curve has a minimum cost value of Q^*, which is the economic order quantity. To obtain that EOQ point we must use the rules of differential calculus to find the slope of the TAC function.

3. *Use calculus to find the slope.* The TAC function has only one variable, Q. The other values are constants.

   The derivative of the TAC function denoted as $d(TAC)$ with respect to Q is

$$\frac{d(TAC)}{d(Q)} = \left(\frac{IC}{2}\right) - [(SD)Q^{-2}]$$

4. *Set the derivative equal to zero and solve for Q.* Putting the expression in terms of Q is strictly an algebraic exercise. By letting

$$\left(\frac{IC}{2}\right) - [(SD)Q^{-2}] = 0$$

FIGURE 8-5 BASIC EOQ MODEL TOTAL ANNUAL COST CURVE DEVELOPMENT

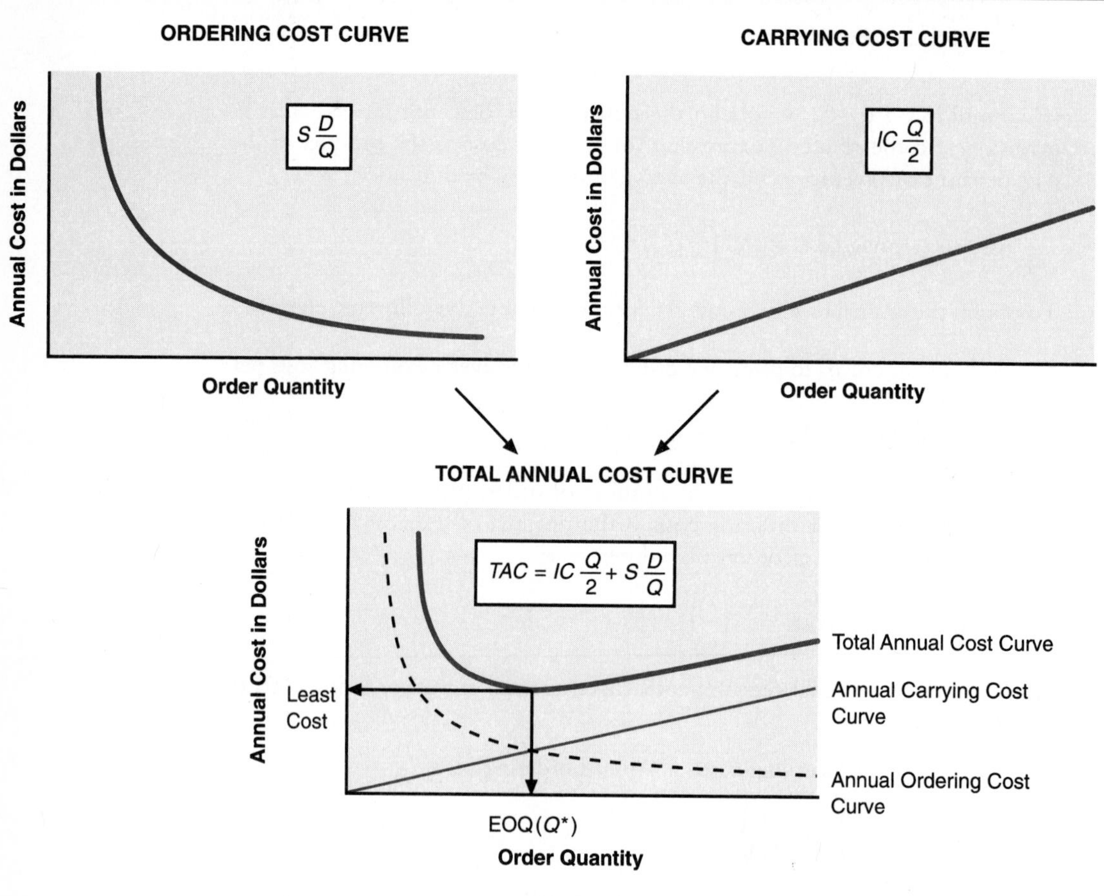

we can now simplify as follows:

$$\frac{IC}{2} = (SD)Q^{-2}$$

$$\frac{IC}{2SD} = Q^{-2}$$

$$\frac{IC}{2SD} = \frac{1}{Q^2}$$

$$Q^2IC = 2SD$$

$$Q^2 = \frac{2SD}{IC}$$

and finally taking the square roots on both sides we obtain

$$Q^* = \sqrt{\frac{2SD}{IC}}$$

The value of Q in this formula is denoted as $Q^\star$ because it is the cost-minimized value of all possible Qs. This formula is the EOQ formula F. W. Harris first proposed in 1913. If an inventory situation fits the model's assumptions, this formula will generate a cost-minimized order quantity. The summary of the steps to derive the basic EOQ model is presented in Table 8-2.

AN EXAMPLE To illustrate the use of the EOQ model as an aid in independent demand inventory management, let's apply the model to a simple inventory problem. Suppose that an organization must acquire an inventory item and the inventory environment fits the basic EOQ model's assumptions. Suppose further that the cost per unit of inventory C is \$20, the annual demand D for the inventory is 1,000 units, the holding cost rate I is 10 percent of the cost per unit, and the cost to place an order S is \$9. The EOQ for this inventory situation is as follows:

$$Q^* = \sqrt{\frac{2SD}{IC}} = \sqrt{\frac{2(9)\ (1000)}{(0.10)\ (20)}} = 94.868 \simeq 95 \text{ units}$$

Based on the model's results this firm's fixed order quantity is 95 units. The EOQ of 95 units is an optimal order quantity. That is, this EOQ will generate the smallest total annual cost, and any other EOQ value will result in a larger *TAC*. (Students are encouraged to confirm this by selecting values above and below the EOQ and determining their respective *TAC*s.) As the stock is used and the desired order point (unknown at this point) is reached, the next order of 95 units is placed. If all of the assumptions and cost values hold, this company can continue to use the Q^* indefinitely. If the cost values change, then the company needs only to plug the new cost values into the EOQ formula and derive a revised Q^* value. The four steps used to derive the EOQ formula need not be repeated unless the assumptions to the model are violated in some way.

Quantity Discount EOQ Model

A **quantity discount model** (also called the **all-units discount model**) recognizes that many vendors give quantity discounts that can lower the unit cost of the product. The price breaks for the purchaser are usually stated in a quantity discount schedule. A quantity discount schedule is presented in Figure 8-6. In this example we have three price break intervals of which the purchaser can take advantage to reduce the cost per unit. The larger the quantity purchased, the lower the unit cost to the purchaser. Unfortunately, the price breaks make product cost a variable (it was assumed a constant value in the basic EOQ model), and this complicates the inventory modeling situation.

TABLE 8-2 BASIC EOQ MODEL

ASSUMPTIONS

1. Annual carrying costs and ordering costs can be accurately estimated and are the only relevant costs.
2. Annual demand can be estimated and is linearly consumed by customers (i.e., not steplike as presented in Figure 8-1(a), period 1).
3. Average inventory level is the order quantity Q divided by 2, which implies that there is no safety stock and inventory is used up when next order arrives.
4. There are no stockout costs.
5. There are no quantity discounts on large orders.
6. Lead time is known and fixed.

MODEL ELEMENT DEFINITIONS

D = annual demand in units
Q = order quantity in units
I = carrying cost rate (percentage of total cost of unit)
C = cost of the inventory item
S = cost in dollars to place an order
TAC = total annual costs of stocking inventory item in dollars

COST FORMULAS

Annual carrying costs = Cost to carry a unit × Average inventory = $IC(Q/2)$
Annual ordering costs = Cost per order × Orders per year = $S(D/Q)$
Total annual costs (TAC) = Annual carrying costs + Annual ordering costs
= $IC(Q/2) + S(D/Q)$

DERIVATION OF EOQ MODEL

1. TAC function: $TAC = IC(Q/2) + S(D/Q)$
2. Take derivative with respect to Q: $d(TAC)/d(Q) = (IC/2) - [(SD)Q^{-2}]$
3. Set derivative equal to zero and solve for Q: $(IC/2) - [(SD)Q^{-2}] = 0$
4. The resulting Q^* is: $Q^* = \sqrt{2SD/IC}$

ASSUMPTIONS For this model we make the following assumptions:

1. Annual carrying costs and ordering costs can be accurately estimated.
2. Annual demand can be estimated and is linearly consumed by customers.
3. Average inventory level is the order quantity Q divided by 2.
4. As a consequence of (2), there are no stockouts.

INFORMATION REQUIREMENTS The information requirements of this type of model are the same as the basic EOQ model: Q^* and OP.

FIGURE 8-6 QUANTITY DISCOUNT SCHEDULE AND COST FUNCTION

DISCOUNT PRICE (COST) SCHEDULE

Quantity Purchased	Price
Q_1 to Q_2	P_1
more than Q_2 to Q_3	P_2
more than Q_3	P_3

where $P_1 > P_2 > P_3$

DISCOUNTED PRODUCT PRICES (COSTS)

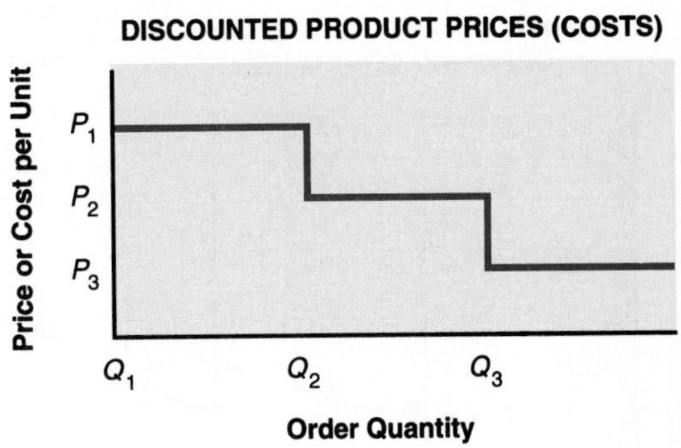

MODEL FORMULATION To formulate this model we will again use the four-step EOQ modeling approach.

1. *Collect cost data.* Three types of cost data are relevant for this model: carrying costs, ordering costs, and product unit costs. Product unit costs are the per unit costs the organization must pay for the inventory item. This means that the *TAC* function consists of the following:

$$TAC = \text{Annual carrying costs} + \text{Annual ordering costs} + \text{Annual product costs}$$

   Unfortunately, the unit cost discount causes the *TAC* curve to be discontinuous. That is, as we change the level of Q, the product unit costs also change. The quantity discount model's *TAC* curve development is presented in Figure 8-7. The discount product price graph is created by a quantity discount schedule. When we add the *TAC* costs (carrying and ordering costs) together with a quantity discount unit price, the result is a discontinuous discount *TAC* curve. As we can see in Figure 8-7, the *TAC* curve for a quantity discount has breaks in it at Q_2 and Q_3.

   This discontinuous *TAC* curve violates the mathematical requirements of the calculus procedure used to find its slope. The only way to treat this type of situation is to break the *TAC* into separate continuous segments of the curve and determine the EOQ for each of these separate segments. In the discount total annual cost curve in Figure 8-7, there is an EOQ candidate in each of the three segments of the curve. The problem is to determine which EOQ candidate is the least costly and therefore the optimal Q^* for the entire *TAC* curve. We will discuss this supplemental procedure in step 4.

2. *Develop the TAC function.* By breaking the *TAC* curve into several continuous segments, the cost per unit is not a variable within each segment. The quantity discount model then consists of three types of costs added together: carrying

FIGURE 8-7 QUANTITY DISCOUNT EOQ AND *TAC* CURVE DEVELOPMENT

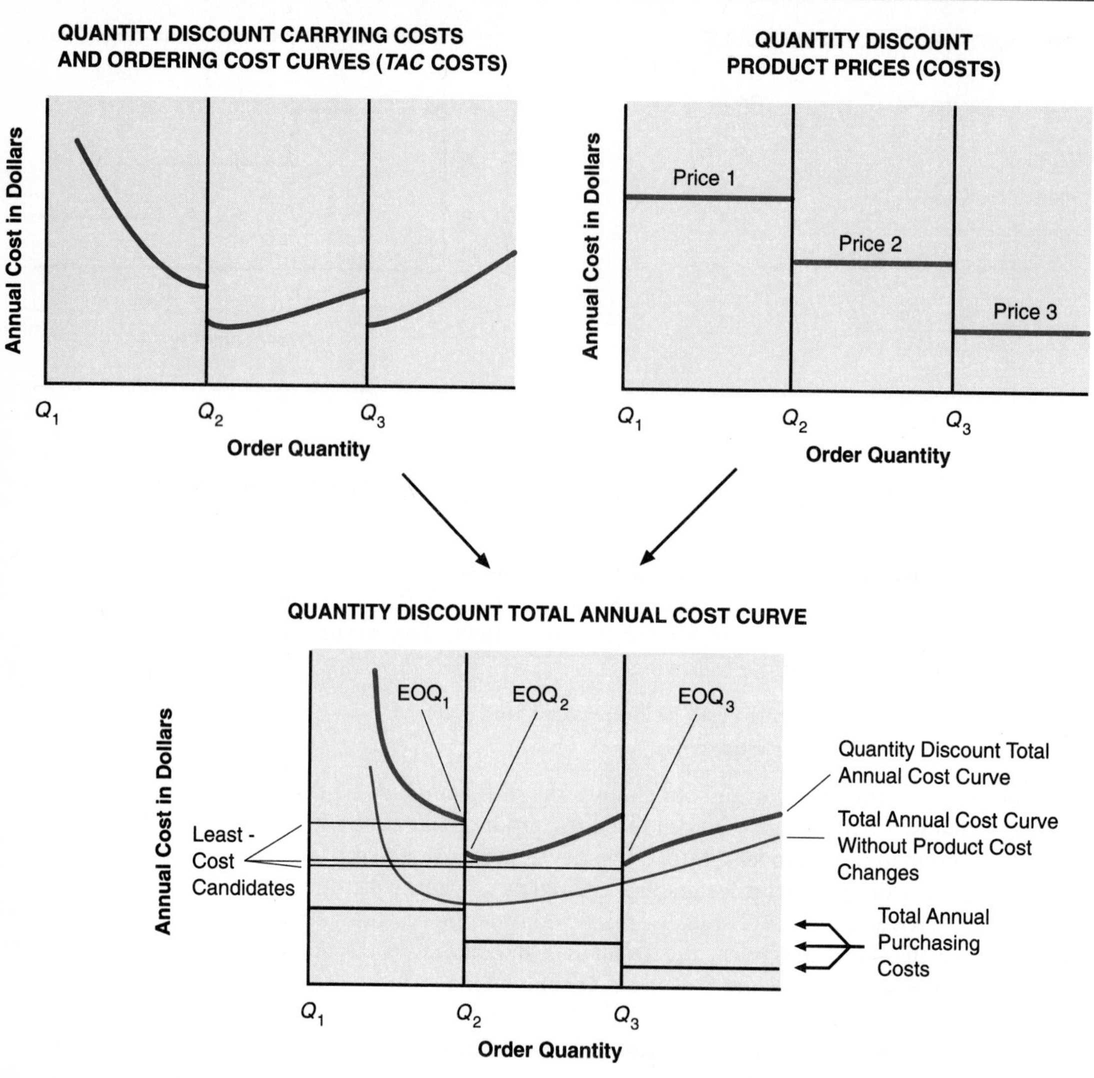

costs, ordering costs, and product costs. Using the same notation as the basic EOQ model, we can express annual product costs per segment as the product of the cost per unit in a particular segment C and the number of units demanded per year D. The resulting three cost functions are

$$\text{Annual carrying costs} = IC\left(\frac{Q}{2}\right)$$

$$\text{Annual ordering costs} = S\left(\frac{D}{Q}\right)$$

$$\text{Annual product costs} = CD$$

We can add the three costs together to obtain the *TAC* curve:

$$TAC = \text{Annual carrying costs} + \text{Annual ordering costs} + \text{Annual product costs}$$

$$TAC = IC\left(\frac{Q}{2}\right) + S\left(\frac{D}{Q}\right) + CD$$

3. *Use calculus to find the slope.* The derivative of the *TAC* function above is

$$\frac{d(TAC)}{d(Q)} = \left(\frac{IC}{2}\right) - [(SD)Q^{-2}]$$

4. *Set the derivative equal to zero and solve for Q.* This results in the same expression as the basic EOQ model. By letting

$$\left(\frac{IC}{2}\right) - [(SD)Q^{-2}] = 0$$

we can simplify to

$$Q^* = \sqrt{\frac{2SD}{IC}}$$

Because the cost per unit C in the formula changes per segment of the cost function, the formula is only valid in the segment of the function that contains the bottom of the U-shaped segment. This leads to some complication in the application of the EOQ formula that is overcome by following the supplemental steps described in the next paragraph.

To use this model to find Q^* over the entire discounted *TAC* curve, we must perform the following supplemental steps:

a. Use the EOQ formula to derive a Q^* for each price break interval. The value of C will change for each Q^*, resulting in different EOQ values.
b. Check the resulting Q^* values to see if they are actually in the prescribed price break interval. If Q^* is within the boundary of the price break interval, then we can assume that it is the EOQ for that interval. If the resulting Q^* is greater than the last value of the price break interval boundary, then we can assume that the EOQ for that interval occurs at the last value of the interval. If the resulting Q^* is less than the first value of the price break interval boundary, then we can assume that the EOQ for that interval occurs at the first value of the interval. The resulting EOQs are candidates for the overall least-cost Q^*. In Figure 8-7, the least-cost candidates occur at the lowest points on the *TAC* curve segments. When the EOQ values are

FIGURE 8-8 LOCATING EOQ VALUES ON DISCOUNT TOTAL ANNUAL COST CURVES

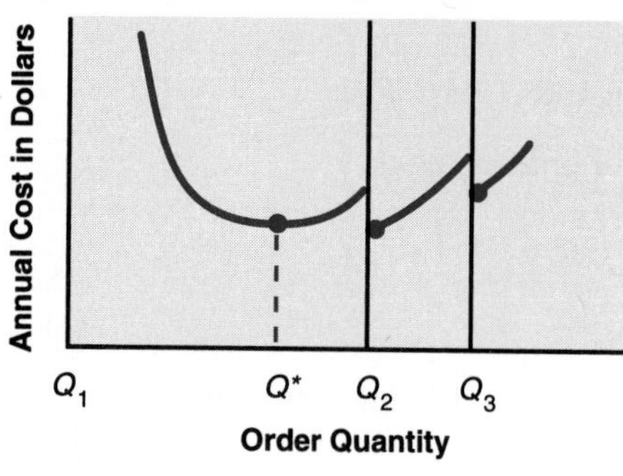

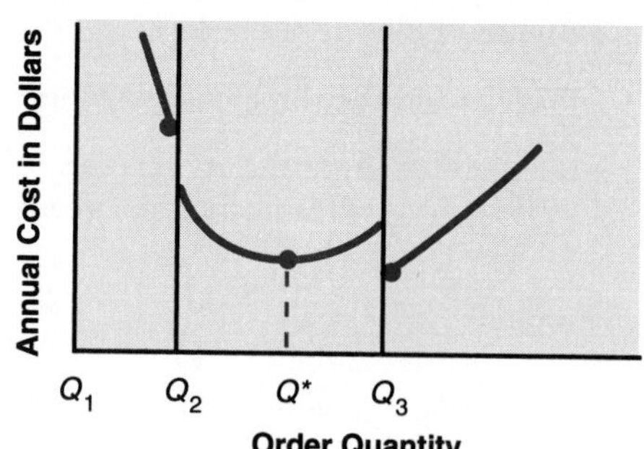

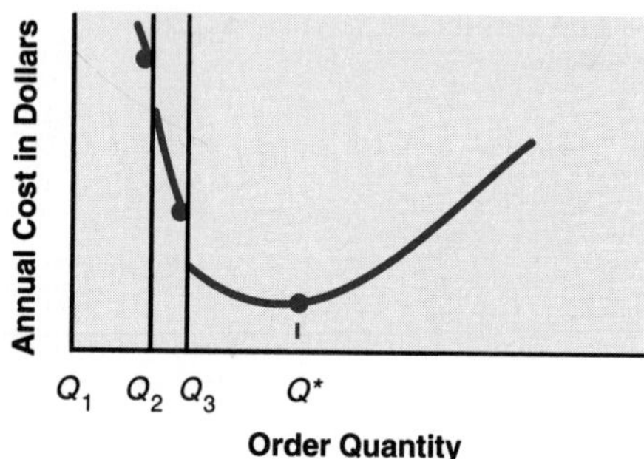

● *Denotes location of EOQ candidate on each segment of the* TAC *curve*

outside the boundaries of the price break intervals, they signal that the U-shaped curve occurs in another segment of the *TAC* function.[5] Examples of locating EOQ candidates are presented in Figure 8-8. As we can see, one segment of each of the three curves in Figure 8-8 has the U shape and the EOQ candidates will be on the segment of the other curves closest to the U-shaped section.

c. Take the EOQ candidates and plug them into the *TAC* function to derive the total annual cost (which includes product costs).

d. Select the EOQ that generates the smallest total annual cost as Q^*. The summary of the steps to derive the quantity discount EOQ model is presented in Table 8-3.

[5] It is mathematically possible to construct *TAC* curves that violate the logic presented in this step. Fortunately, such *TAC* curves do not usually occur.

TABLE 8-3 QUANTITY DISCOUNT EOQ MODEL

ASSUMPTIONS

1. Annual carrying costs and ordering costs can be accurately estimated.
2. Annual demand can be estimated and is linearly consumed by customers.
3. Average inventory level is the order quantity Q divided by 2.
4. There are no stockouts.

MODEL ELEMENT DEFINITIONS

D = annual demand in units
Q = order quantity in units
I = carrying cost rate (percentage of total cost of unit)
C = cost of the inventory item
S = cost in dollars to place an order
TAC = total annual costs of stocking inventory item in dollars

COST FORMULAS

Annual carrying costs = Cost to carry a unit × Average inventory = $IC(Q/2)$
Annual ordering costs = Costs per order × Orders per year = $S(D/Q)$
Annual product costs = Cost per unit × Annual demand = CD
Total annual costs (TAC) = Annual carrying costs + Annual ordering costs + Annual product costs
= $IC(Q/2) + S(D/Q) + CD$

DERIVATION OF EOQ MODEL

1. TAC function: $TAC = IC(Q/2) + S(D/Q) + CD$
2. Take derivative with respect to Q: $d(TAC)/d(Q) = (IC/2) - [(SD)Q^{-2}]$
3. Set derivative equal to zero and solve for Q: $(IC/2) - [(SD)Q^{-2}] = 0$
4. The resulting optimal Q^* is: $Q^* = \sqrt{2SD/IC}$

AN EXAMPLE To illustrate the use of the quantity discount EOQ model as an aid in independent demand inventory management, let's apply the model to a simple inventory problem. Suppose that a firm must acquire an inventory item and the inventory environment fits the quantity discount EOQ model's assumptions. Suppose further that the per unit cost of inventory C is defined by the following quantity discount schedule:

Order Quantity or Price Break Intervals	*Unit Price to Purchaser*
0 to 2,499 units	\$1.20
2,500 to 3,999 units	\$1.00
4,000 and more units	\$0.98

The annual demand D for the inventory is 10,000 units, the carrying cost rate I is 2 percent of the cost per unit, and the cost to place an order S is \$4. The EOQ for this inventory situation requires the use of the four supplemental steps just presented.

1. *Determine the EOQ for each price break interval.*

   For 0 to 2,499:

$$Q_1 = \sqrt{\frac{2[SD]}{[IC]}} = \sqrt{\frac{2[(4)\ (10{,}000)]}{[(0.02)(1.20)]}} = 1{,}825.7 \simeq 1{,}826$$

   For 2,500 to 3,999:

$$Q_2 = \sqrt{\frac{2[(4)(10{,}000)]}{[(0.02)(1.00)]}} = 2{,}000$$

   For 4,000 and more:

$$Q_3 = \sqrt{\frac{2[(4)(10{,}000)]}{[(0.02)(0.98)]}} = 2{,}020$$

2. *Determine the actual EOQ values for each segment of the TAC function.* Because 1,826 falls within its interval of 0 to 2,499, it is assumed to be the EOQ for that segment of the TAC function. Both of the other two EOQ candidates fall outside (that is, before the first value in their price break interval) and so their actual EOQ is assumed to be the first value in their respective intervals (2,500 and 4,000, respectively). We can see the shape of this TAC function in Figure 8-9. Note that the lowest point on each of the last two segments of the TAC curve is at the beginning of those segments. We now have the three EOQ candidates of 1,826, 2,500, and 4,000.

3. *Determine the least-cost EOQ value.* To determine the least-cost Q^* we substitute the EOQ values into the TAC function for the quantity discount inventory model. The TAC function as stated earlier is

$$TAC = IC\left(\frac{Q}{2}\right) + S\left(\frac{D}{Q}\right) + CD$$

   The TACs for each price break are as follows:

   For price break interval 0 to 2,499: EOQ = 1,826, $C = 1.20$

$$\begin{aligned} TAC &= (0.02)(1.20)\left(\frac{1{,}826}{2}\right) + (4)\left(\frac{10{,}000}{1{,}826}\right) + (1.20)(10{,}000) \\ &= \$12{,}043.82 \end{aligned}$$

FIGURE 8-9 DISCOUNT *TAC* CURVE FOR EXAMPLE PROBLEM

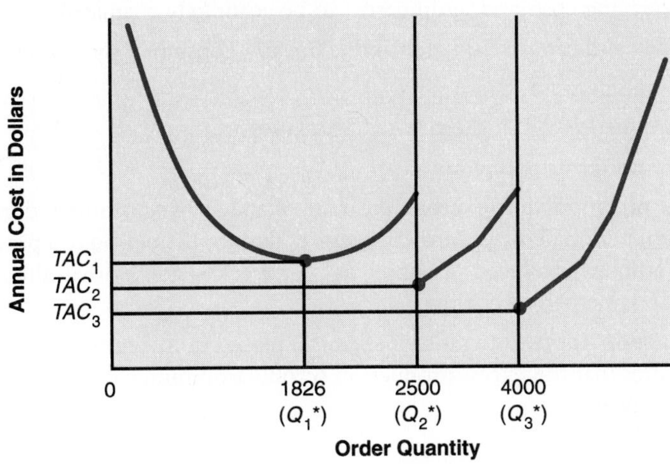

For price break interval 2,500 to 3,999: EOQ $=$ 2,500, $C = 1.00$

$$TAC = (0.02)(1.00)\left(\frac{2{,}500}{2}\right) + (4)\left(\frac{10{,}000}{2{,}500}\right) + (1.00)(10{,}000)$$
$$= \$10{,}041.00$$

For price break interval 4,000 and more: EOQ $=$ 4,000, $C = 0.98$

$$TAC = (0.02)(0.98)\left(\frac{4{,}000}{2}\right) + (4)\left(\frac{10{,}000}{4{,}000}\right) + (0.98)(10{,}000)$$
$$= \$9{,}849.20$$

4. *Select the least-cost EOQ.* Based on the three *TAC*s, the least-cost *TAC* of \$9,849.20 is possible when the EOQ is 4,000. So the Q* for the entire discount *TAC* curve (that is, all three segments) is 4,000.

   Based on the model's results this firm should place an order for 4,000 units of inventory. When the stock reaches a desired order point (unknown at this time), the next order of 4,000 units should be placed.

Economic Manufacturing Quantity (EMQ) Model

The **economic manufacturing quantity (EMQ) model** can be used by a firm manufacturing units for demand or inventory, not ordering units from a vendor. This model is also called an economic production run (EPR) model or economic lot-size (ELS) model.

ASSUMPTIONS For this model, we make the following assumptions:

1. Annual carrying costs and setup costs can be accurately estimated.
2. Annual demand can be estimated and is linearly consumed by customers.
3. There is no safety stock.
4. As a consequence of (2), there are no stockouts.
5. There are no quantity discounts.
6. The rate of production exceeds the rate of usage by customers during the production period. This assumption requires that for the period of a production run, the amount produced per hour, day, or week is greater than the demand during the same period of time.
7. All production not used to satisfy demand is placed in inventory. This assumption requires that the excess production (production minus demand) has to be placed in inventory.

INFORMATION REQUIREMENTS The information requirements of a production run or EMQ model are different than the basic EOQ model because the EMQ value (Q^*) is being determined for lot production not order quantity. As such, this type of model can be applied in determining lot sizes for production runs in manufacturing facilities. What we want to determine is the cost-minimizing lot size for a production run of an item that we will place in inventory. In this sense, the EMQ generates information that can also be used in planning dependent demand inventory systems such as MRP.

In addition to determining the EMQ value that indicates how many units to produce at one time, we can also determine the timing requirements between production runs. To do this we will derive the optimal number of production runs per year and the time period between those production runs.

MODEL FORMULATION To formulate this model we will again use the four-step EOQ modeling approach.

1. *Collect cost data.* Two types of cost data are relevant for this model: carrying costs and setup costs. Setup costs are all of the costs that are incurred to prepare the production facility for the production run. These costs include the work force to adjust equipment for the production run, materials handling costs associated with the run, and any other costs such as supplies that can uniquely be attributed to a specific production run. For the EMQ model the TAC function will consist of the following:

$$TAC = \text{Carrying costs} + \text{Setup costs}$$

2. *Develop the TAC function.* Let's define the following model elements:

Q = manufacturing quantity

Q^* = economic manufacturing quantity

t_p = time period in days, weeks, or months of a production run (the time that production is continuously performed)

t_s = time period between production run starts
u = a constant usage rate over a specific time period (the number of units used from inventory in a day, week, etc.)
p = a constant production rate over a specific time period (the number of units to produce per day, week, etc.)
q = maximum buildup of inventory during the t_p period
I = annual carrying cost rate
C = cost per unit of inventory (production cost)

An EMQ model's behavior is presented in Figure 8-10. In this model inventory is continually being used, even while it is being produced. To have an inventory the production rate must exceed the usage rate. In accordance with the EMQ model we plan to produce Q^* units during the t_p period, and at a rate p that is greater than our usage rate u. This results in a total inventory buildup of only q units. Because units are being used during the t_p period, the Q^* lot-size level in inventory is never achieved.

We can model these relationships in a *TAC* curve by determining the two costs items (carrying costs and setup costs) separately and adding them to create the function. The carrying cost function is slightly different than the basic EOQ model's. If we let $p - u$ be inventory buildup per time period (such as a day or a week), and if we multiply it by t_p, then $[(p - u)(t_p)]$ is unit inventory buildup q during a production run. This also means the average inventory is

$$\frac{(p - u)(t_p)}{2}$$

Unfortunately, this expression for average inventory does not contain Q as it did with the basic EOQ model. The value Q must be present in a cost expression or its derivative will force it to drop out of the *TAC* curve. The value Q can be included in the average inventory expression by deriving t_p. If we multiply the number of items we produce, say per day, by the number of days we produce items we obtain Q:

$$Q = (p)(t_p)$$

By simplifying this expression in terms of t_p we obtain

$$t_p = \frac{Q}{p}$$

We can now substitute this ratio into the previous average inventory expression.

$$\frac{(p - u)(t_p)}{2}$$

This gives us

$$\frac{(p - u)(Q)}{2p}$$

FIGURE 8-10 ECONOMIC MANUFACTURING QUANTITY MODEL BEHAVIOR

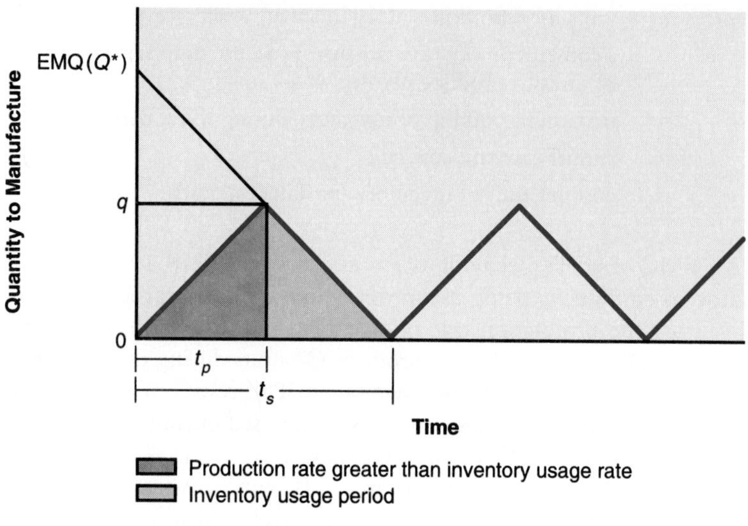

Multiplying this revised average inventory ratio, we obtain the annual carrying cost function for the EMQ model:

$$\text{Annual carrying costs} = IC\frac{(p - u)(Q)}{2p}$$

Setup costs are incurred when a production facility is restructured to handle a new production run. Let's define the following model elements:

S = setup costs for a production run (an average per run)
D = annual demand in units of inventory

So the ratio of D/Q still represents the number of setups required per year. By multiplying this ratio by S, we obtain the annual setup cost function for the EMQ model:

$$\text{Annual setup costs} = S(D/Q)$$

We can add annual carrying costs together with annual setup costs to obtain the TAC curve:

$$TAC = \text{Annual carrying costs} + \text{Annual setup costs}$$

$$= IC\frac{(p - u)(Q)}{2p} + S(D/Q)$$

3. *Use calculus to find the slope.* The derivative of the revised *TAC* function is

$$\frac{d(TAC)}{d(Q)} = IC\frac{(p - u)}{2p} - SD(Q^{-2})$$

4. *Set the derivative equal to zero and solve for the EMQ formula for Q.* By letting

$$IC\frac{(p - u)}{2p} - SD(Q^{-2}) = 0$$

we can restructure it in terms of Q as follows:

$$IC\frac{(p - u)}{2p} = SD(Q^{-2})$$

$$IC(p - u) = \frac{SD}{Q^2}(2p)$$

$$Q^2 = \frac{SD(2p)}{IC(p - u)}$$

By taking the square roots on both sides of the expression we arrive at the EMQ formula:

$$Q^* = \sqrt{\frac{SD(2p)}{IC(p - u)}}$$

The optimal number of production runs per year can then be found by dividing annual demand *D* by Q*. To determine the time periods between production runs we would use the following ratio:

$$\frac{\text{Time periods in a year (365 days, 52 weeks, 12 months)}}{\text{Optimal number of production runs } (D/Q^*)}$$

A summary of the steps to derive the EMQ model is presented in Table 8-4.

AN EXAMPLE To illustrate the use of the production run EMQ model, let's apply the model to a simple inventory problem. Suppose that a firm must manufacture an inventory item and the inventory environment fits the production run EMQ model's assumptions. Suppose further that the production rate *p* is 10 units per day, the inventory usage rate *u* is 6 units per day, the annual demand *D* for the inventory is 2,190 units, the setup costs *S* are $80 per production run, the carrying cost rate is 25 percent of the cost of the unit, and the production costs per unit are $100. What is the EMQ? How many production runs will be required per year? How much time will there be between the start of each of the production runs? The EMQ for this example is shown at the top of page 383.

TABLE 8-4 EMQ MODEL

ASSUMPTIONS

1. Annual carrying costs and setup costs can be accurately estimated.
2. Annual demand can be estimated and is linearly consumed by customers.
3. There is no safety stock.
4. As a consequence of (2), there are no stockouts.
5. There are no quantity discounts.
6. The rate of production (p) exceeds the rate of usage (u) by customers during the production period (t_p).
7. All production not used to satisfy demand is placed in inventory.

MODEL ELEMENT DEFINITIONS

D = annual demand in units

Q = quantity in units to produce in a single production run

I = carrying cost rate (percentage of total cost of unit)

C = cost of the inventory item

t_p = time period of a production run (the time period that production is continuously performed)

t_s = time period between production run starts

u = a constant usage rate of inventory over a specific time period (usually a day)

p = constant production rate of inventory over a specified time period (usually a day)

q = maximum buildup of inventory in units during the t_p production run

TAC = total annual costs of manufacturing the inventory item in dollars

S = setup cost in dollars per production run

COST FORMULAS

Annual carrying costs = Cost to carry a unit × Average inventory = $IC\{[(p - u)(Q)]/(2p)\}$

Annual setup costs = Cost per setup × Number of setups per year = $S(D/Q)$

Total annual costs (TAC) = Annual carrying costs + Annual setup costs

$$IC\{[(p - u)(Q)]/(2p)\} + S(D/Q)$$

DERIVATION OF EMQ MODEL

1. TAC function: $TAC = IC\{[(p - u)(Q)]/(2p)\} + S(D/Q)$
2. Take derivative with respect to Q: $d(TAC)/d(Q) = IC[(p - u)/(2p)] - SD(Q^{-2})$
3. Set derivative equal to zero and solve for Q: $IC[(p - u)/(2p)] - SD(Q^{-2}) = 0$
4. The resulting optimal Q^* is: $Q^* = \sqrt{SD(2p)/IC(p - u)}$

$$Q^* = \sqrt{\frac{(S)(D)[2(p)]}{(I)(C)(p - u)}} = \sqrt{\frac{(80)(2{,}190)[2(10)]}{(0.25)(100)(10 - 6)}} = 187.190 \simeq 188$$

$$\text{Optimal number of production runs per year} = \frac{D}{Q^*} = \frac{2{,}190}{188} = 11.65$$

$$\text{Number of days between production runs} = \frac{365}{(D/Q^*)} = \frac{365}{11.65} = 31.33$$

Based on the model's results, this firm should plan to produce a lot-size of 188 units on each production run. (Note that we generally round up the EMQ values to avoid the possibility of stockouts). We can expect to have 11.65 production runs per year with a production run beginning every 31.33 days.

ORDER POINT SYSTEMS

In addition to determining EOQ values, we must also determine the order point (*OP*), or when to place the next order. The order point has to be set to provide enough units of inventory to last during the lead time (*LT*) from when the order is placed to when it arrives. The order point is determined by the **demand during lead time (*DDLT*).** For example, if a company knew with certainty that it would use 100 units of inventory per day and its lead time would be exactly 10 days, then it would use an order point of 1,000 units (100 units × 10 days). Unfortunately, a company's demand during lead time and lead time can both vary considerably owing to market demand surges, supplier stockouts, purchase order processing problems, or truck delivery strikes. The expected demand during lead time is a function of the variation in both demand and lead time.

If inventory is not available when demanded by a customer, a stockout occurs. Stockouts incur shortage costs (for example, missed sales) and are chiefly avoided by operations managers by establishing a safety stock. A **safety stock (*SS*)** is an additional amount of inventory that is purchased to protect against the variations in demand and lead time. It is a one-time purchase of extra inventory that will hopefully cushion the inventory supply against surges in demand or a longer-than-expected lead time. Determining the right amount of safety stock involves balancing the costs of having too little (and incurring excessive shortage costs) with the costs of having too much (and incurring excessive carrying costs). In summary, to determine an order point we must first determine the expected demand during lead time and safety stock.

To maximize customer service, an organization must provide inventory when it is demanded. One of the more common measurements used to judge customer service performance levels in providing inventory is called the stockout percentage. The **stockout percentage** is the proportion of orders or items that were not filled from inventory during a fixed period of time. The stockout percentage can be computed using either of the ratios shown at the top of page 384 for a fixed period of time (day, week, month, or year).

$$\frac{\text{Total stockout orders}}{\text{Total orders processed}}$$

or

$$\frac{\text{Number of stockout line items}}{\text{Total number of line items processed}}$$

(A "line" is usually an individual item on an order.) The ideal stockout percentage from a customer service level point of view is zero. Establishing an order point that will provide an adequate supply of inventory will minimize the stockout percentage and help maximize customer service levels. Unfortunately, variability in demand during lead time might prevent a zero stockout percentage from occurring. To compensate for this variability, marketing managers often define customer service as a probability. For example, an adequate customer service level measured by the stockout percentages might be to fully complete all customer orders 95 percent of the time or to have a 95 percent probability of fully completing a customer order. To be able to establish an order point that will accomplish this type of service level goal, we must understand the probabilistic behavior of demand during lead time (*DDLT*).

Demand During Lead Time

The variation in *DDLT* can be characterized by either a discrete or continuous distribution. When the demand in units is in whole (or integer) values, the *DDLT* distribution is discrete. A discrete *DDLT* distribution is presented in Figure 8-11(a). The discrete *DDLT* distribution is a frequency distribution in which the demand in units was tallied from a sample of 100 lead times. Note that the range in demand is limited to integer values from a low of 3 units to a high of 10 units. A discrete *DDLT* distribution is common in component inventory, small appliances, and service product demand such as tow-truck or fast-food services. When the demand in units is sufficiently large that the shape of the curve appears like a continuous line looking like a bell-shaped curve, the *DDLT* distribution is continuous. A continuous *DDLT* distribution is presented in Figure 8-11(b). In reality, the demand of a continuous *DDLT* consists of a very large number (that is, a wide range of demand) of discrete integer values such as component parts or noninteger units of raw materials (half barrels of oil, fertilizer, or lawn chemicals).

The type of *DDLT* distribution determines the method necessary to estimate the demand during lead time. In addition to variation caused by *DDLT*, variation can also be caused by lead time. The lead time (*LT*) in days for order arrivals may also be characterized by its own unique distribution. To assess the total variation caused by *DDLT* and *LT*, we usually combine the distributions (or their mean values) into an expected *DDLT* value or *EDDLT*. Although *EDDLT* is the mean of the *DDLT* distribution, its computation takes the *LT* distribution into consideration as well. As we will see in several of the examples presented in this section, the exact value of *EDDLT* and *SS* are also determined by the desired service level that the organization seeks to

FIGURE 8-11 *DDLT* DISTRIBUTIONS

(A) A DISCRETE *DDLT* DISTRIBUTION

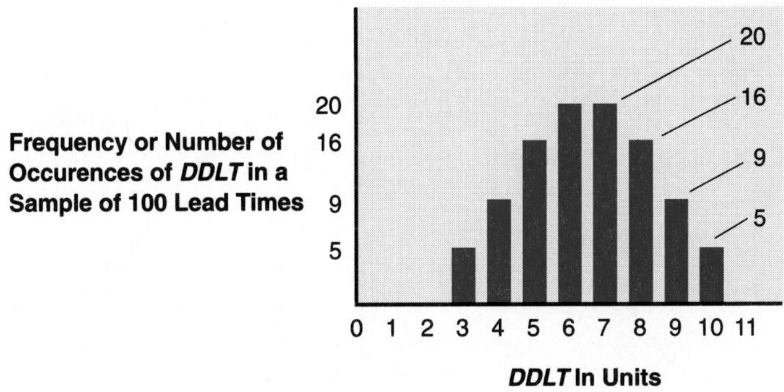

(B) A CONTINUOUS *DDLT* DISTRIBUTION

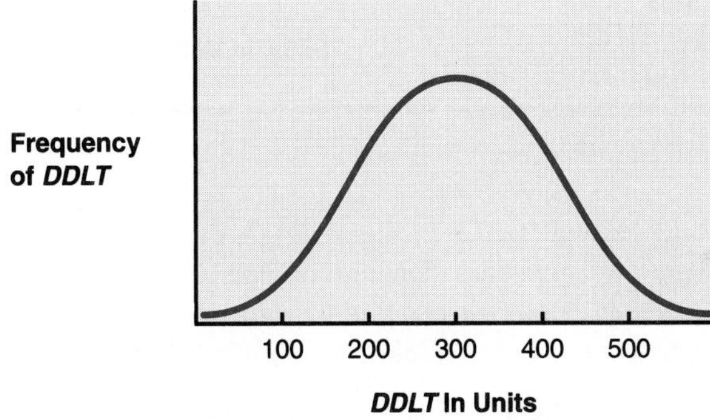

maximize. The simple relationship between *OP*, *EDDLT*, and *SS* can be expressed as follows:

$$OP = EDDLT + SS$$

Let's assume that all possible variation in *DDLT* can be expressed as the continuous distribution presented in Figure 8-12. An order point is determined by first establishing *EDDLT* and then adding to that value a value representing an additional amount of safety stock inventory. Despite this *OP* value, the probability of a stockout, as expressed in Figure 8-12, may still exist. While this probability can be minimized by increasing safety stock, we do so at the expense of increased inventory carrying costs. Safety stock does provide for greater flexibility to absorb the fluctuations in demand. We can see this flexibility by relating the distribution in Figure 8-12 to the demand curves presented

FIGURE 8-12 RELATIONSHIP BETWEEN *DDLT*, *EDDLT*, *SS*, *OP*, AND THE PROBABILITY OF A STOCKOUT

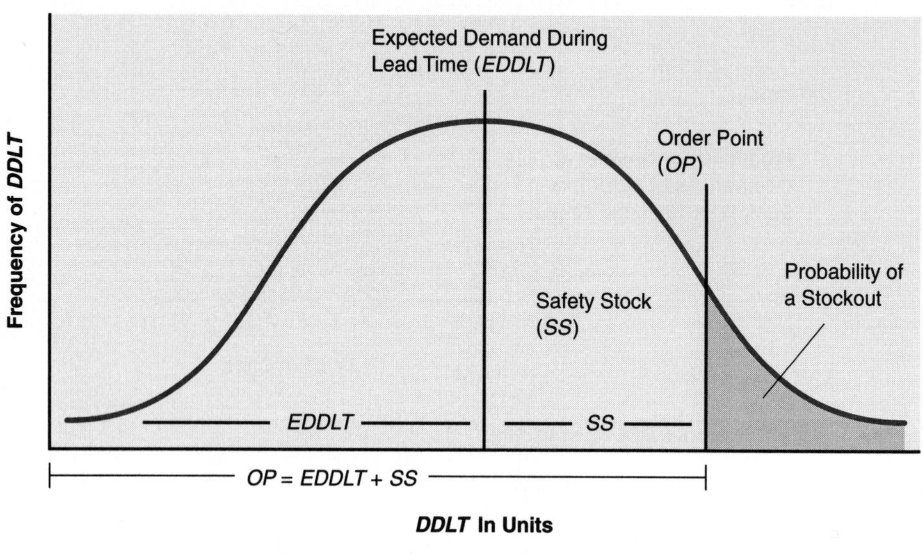

in Figure 8-13. As we can see in Figure 8-13, the safety stock permits the demand rate to range from the expected demand of line Q^* (*A*) to the more accelerated rate represented by the steeper sloped line Q^* (*B*). One of the ways that we can determine an appropriate level of safety stock is to express *OP*, *EDDLT*, and *SS* as follows:

$$SS = OP - EDDLT$$

Determining the Estimated Demand During Lead Time, Safety Stock, and Order Point

How operations managers determine expected demand during lead times, safety stocks, and order points is a function of the inventory situation and the desired service levels. Many different formulas are available to model inventory systems. We will examine several of the more commonly used formulas.

SQUARE ROOT OF *EDDLT* METHOD In inventory situations in which stockouts are not particularly costly, organizations can use a simple method to determine the order point that adjusts for variation in *EDDLT*. The square root of *EDDLT* method increases *OP* as *DDLT* and *LT* increase and conversely decrease *OP* when *DDLT* and *LT* decrease. The formula for this method is as follows:

FIGURE 8-13 RELATIONSHIP BETWEEN *EDDLT*, *SS*, *OP*, AND *Q**

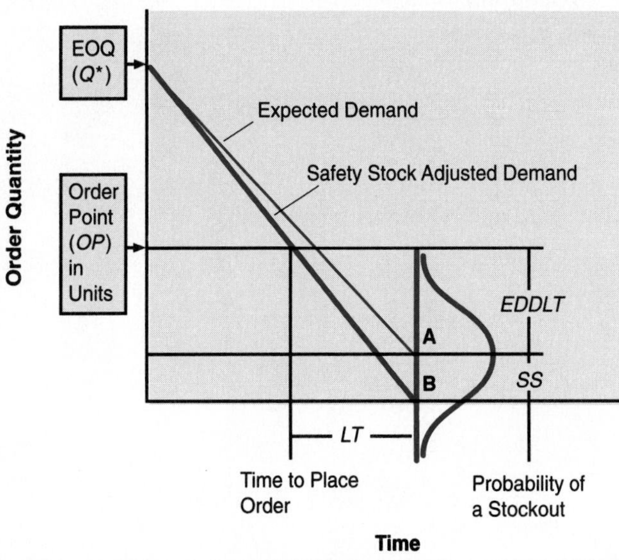

$$OP = EDDLT + \sqrt{EDDLT}$$

where

$$EDDLT = \bar{d} \times \overline{LT}$$

$\bar{d}$ = mean demand in units per day

$\overline{LT}$ = mean lead time in days

In this formula, the square root of *EDDLT* is used as a safety stock value. Large variations in mean daily demand and lead times are converted to fairly small safety stock values. Indeed, the square root of 100 is 10 and the square root of one tenth of 100 is 3.1 or more than 31 percent of 10. This tends to limit this method to inventory items that have a small daily unit demand value or a short lead time.

QUESTION: A company has an inventory item that is consumed at a mean or average daily rate of 5 units. Experience with the current vendor for the inventory item shows a mean lead time of 10 days for the delivery of the inventory item. Using the square root of *EDDLT* method, what are *SS* and *OP* for this inventory item?

(*continued*)

ANSWER: Given that $\bar{d} = 5$ units per day and $\overline{LT} = 10$ days, we can find *SS* by first computing the *EDDLT*:

$$EDDLT = \bar{d} \times \overline{LT}$$
$$= 5 \times 10$$
$$= 50 \text{ units}$$

The value *SS* is the square root of *EDDLT*:

$$SS = \sqrt{EDDLT}$$
$$= \sqrt{50}$$
$$= 7.07 \text{ units}$$

Finally, *OP* can be found:

$$OP = EDDLT + \sqrt{EDDLT}$$
$$= 50 + 7.07$$
$$= 57.07 \text{ units}$$

Based on the above information, the company's order point is 57.07 units, which includes a safety stock of 7.07 units.

DISCRETE *DDLT* DISTRIBUTION METHODS In an inventory situation in which the mean demand per day and the mean lead time in days can be determined, demand during lead time can be expressed as a discrete probability distribution, and service level can be designated as a percentage (or probability), we can determine *OP* and *SS* using the following steps:

1. Convert the discrete *DDLT* frequency distribution into a cumulative probability distribution of service level in which the probability of *DDLT* or less occurs (that is, cumulative from smaller to larger).
2. Plot the *DDLT* distribution as a graph. The vertical axis of the graph is the service level (or the probability of *DDLT* or less) and the horizontal axis is *DDLT*.
3. Determine *OP* by taking the given service level percentage (or probability) and finding the horizontal intercept value for the cumulative probability distribution in the graph from step 2. For discrete *DDLT* distributions that consist of finite intervals, approximate the intercept values by assuming a continuous line through the midpoints of each interval.
4. Determine *EDDLT*, where $EDDLT = \bar{d} \times \overline{LT}$.
5. Determine *SS* by substitution, where $SS = OP - EDDLT$.

S

QUESTION: Suppose that a car dealership needs to establish its order point and safety stock for a supply of automobiles it will be ordering from a manufacturer. The dealership obviously needs to order a discrete number of cars. Based on past demand behavior, the mean demand for the car model being ordered is 6 units per day with a mean lead time of 10 days. The actual demand during lead time historically follows the frequency distribution of the unit demand intervals presented in Figure 8-14(a). If the dealership wants to provide a 90 percent service level (that is, the probability that 90 percent of all demand during lead time will be satisfied), what is the appropriate order point and level of safety stock?

ANSWER: We will follow the steps just outlined.

Step 1. Convert the actual *DDLT* frequency distribution into a service level distribution by adding the frequencies presented in Figure 8-14(a).
Step 2. The service level can then be related to the actual *DDLT* as presented in the graph in Figure 8-14(b). The stepwise function of the actual *DDLT* is approximated by drawing a continuous line through the midpoints of each step in the graph.
Step 3. Locate the intercept value of the continuous line and the given service level of 90 percent (that is, draw a horizontal line over from the 90 percent service level to the continuous line), and locate the *OP* of 75 units on the horizontal axis.
Step 4. Find the *EDDLT* of 60 units by multiplying the given mean demand daily rate of 6 units by the mean *LT* of 10 days.
Step 5. We can finally determine *SS* by substituting *OP* and *EDDLT* into the following expression:

$$\begin{aligned} SS &= OP - EDDLT \\ &= 75 - 60 \\ &= 15 \text{ units} \end{aligned}$$

With an order point of 75 units and its built-in safety stock of 15 units, this car dealership should be able to handle 90 percent of all the demand during the car's lead time.

When an organization wants to balance shortage costs with overage costs and when the *DDLT* behavior can be expressed as a discrete probability distribution, an expected value approach can be used to determine *OP* and *SS*. In this approach, we seek an *OP* that will balance the expected value of shortage costs with the expected value of overage costs. (Overage costs can include carrying costs for unwanted inventory and return order costs for units that customers can send back for credit.) The procedure to determine *OP* and *SS* involves the steps listed on pages 390–391.

FIGURE 8-14 DISCRETE *DDLT* DISTRIBUTION SAMPLE PROBLEM DATA

(A) ACTUAL *DDLT* DISTRIBUTION AND CUMULATIVE *DDLT* DISTRIBUTION

Actual *DDLT*	Frequency	Service Level (Cumulative Probability of *DDLT* or Less)
40 – 49	.10	.10
50 – 59	.25	.35
60 – 69	.30	.65
70 – 79	.25	.90
80 – 89	.10	1.00

(B) GRAPH OF SERVICE LEVEL AND CUMULATIVE *DDLT* DISTRIBUTION

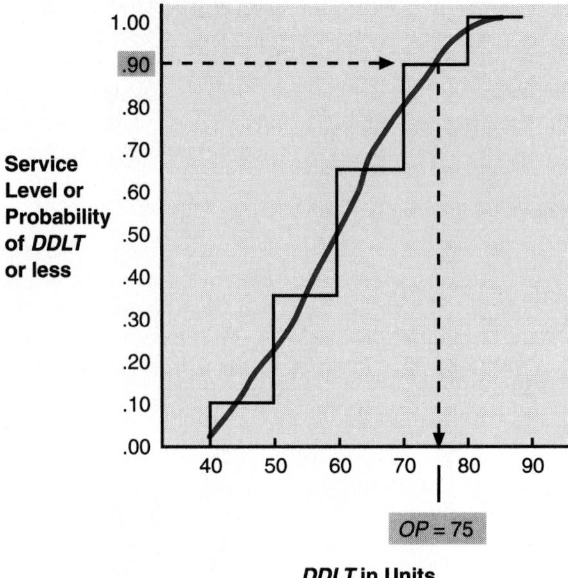

1. Determine the discrete *DDLT* probability distribution [the $P(DDLT_j)$ in Figure 8-15] by converting frequency *DDLT* behavior into percentages.
2. Determine the shortage costs per unit of inventory and the overage costs per unit of inventory.
3. Construct the cost payoff tables where the *i*th vertical columns are headed by actual $DDLT_j$ that have been observed and the *i*th rows are possible OP_i alternatives that are being considered. There are as many as *n* vertical columns and *m* rows in the payoff table. When *OP* is matched exactly with *DDLT* the equality of these two values will always result in total shortage and overage costs of zero. The cost payoff table elements should be positioned in the table as presented in Figure 8-15. The shortage costs elements are always placed in the upper right-hand-side of the table and are additive from the right of the diagonal of zero cost values in the center of the table. The overage costs elements are always placed in the lower left-hand-side of the table and are also additive from the left of the diagonal of zero values.
4. Take the *DDLT* probability values from step 1 and multiply them by the cost values in the payoff table from step 3 to determine the expected cost values for each combination of *DDLT* and *OP*.

FIGURE 8-15 CONSTRUCTION OF *OP* PAYOFF TABLES

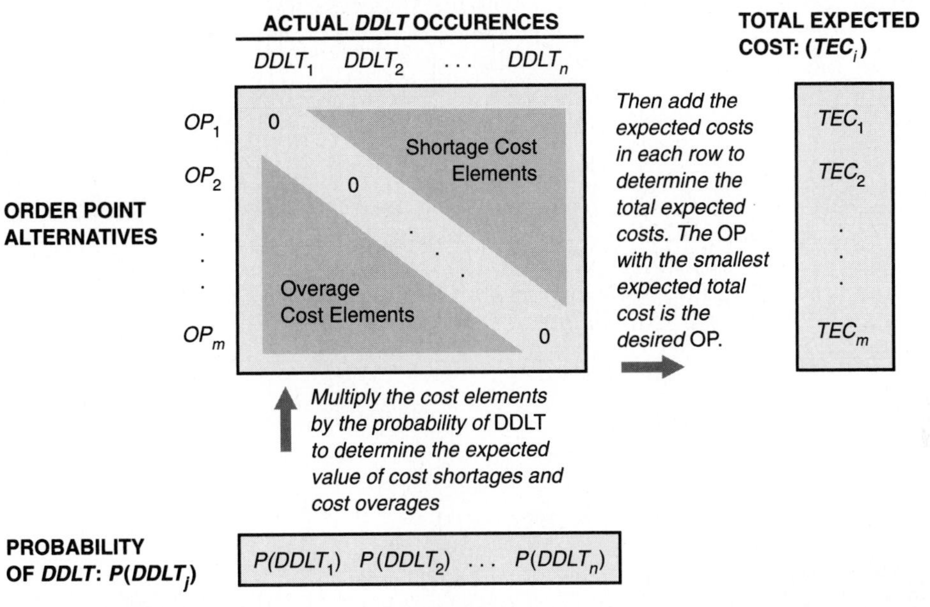

5. Take the expected cost values from step 4 and add them together by row to determine the total expected cost (TEC_i) for each OP_i.
6. Select the OP_i that minimizes TEC_i.
7. Determine *EDDLT*, where $EDDLT = P(DDLT) \times DDLT$.
8. Determine *SS* by substitution, where $SS = OP - EDDLT$.

This approach is commonly referred to as a single-period inventory model because the decision on *OP* and *SS* may be applicable for a period of a day, week, month, or year. This payoff table model is used for short-lived inventory such as published items (magazines, textbooks, newspapers), seasonal fashions (swimwear), and perishable food. This approach is chiefly limited to inventory situations in which the discrete *DDLT* is fairly small and the shortage and overage cost values are easily determined. The prob-

QUESTION: A company's inventory item's *DDLT* has the following percentage chances of occurring: 5 units at 10 percent, 6 units at 40 percent, 7 units at 30 percent, and 8 units at 20 percent. The shortage costs per unit are estimated at \$25, and overage costs per unit are estimated at \$10 per unit. If the company wants to balance the shortage and overage costs in its selection of *OP* and *SS*, what should these values be?

(continued)

ANSWER: Because there are only four *DDLT*s, we would only look at the four *OP* alternatives of 5, 6, 7, and 8. The payoff table cost values are presented in Table 8-5(a). Note that the equality of *DDLT* and *OP* results in a diagonal of $0s because inventory demand and availability are equal. Alternatively, we can see that a *DDLT* of 6 and an *OP* of 5 will result in a single unit shortage cost of $25. These costs are doubled as we go across the first row in Table 8-5(a) to reflect the additive per unit shortage costs. As we can also see, the cost structure is reversed for the overage costs. The expected costs for each combination of *OP* and *DDLT* are presented in Table 8-5(b). They were calculated by multiplying the actual cost values in Table 8-5(a) by the *DDLT* probabilities [$P(DDLT_j)$]. The total expected costs (TEC_i) are determined by totaling the expected cost in each row. The minimum *TEC* of $11 ($2 + $4 + $0 + $5) occurs for the *OP* alternative of 7 units. Therefore, the cost-balanced *OP* is 7 units. The *EDDLT* is found by

$$EDDLT = P(DDLT) \times DDLT$$

$$= (.10 \times 5) + (.40 \times 6) + (.30 \times 7) + (.20 \times 8)$$

$$= 6.6 \text{ units}$$

The value for the safety stock becomes

$$SS = OP - EDDLT$$

$$= 7 - 6.6$$

$$= .4$$

Because the value is less than one, it is rounded up to the next whole value of $SS = 1$.

ability distribution of *DDLT* also has to be fairly accurate for purposes of making future *OP* and *SS* decisions.

CONTINUOUS *DDLT* DISTRIBUTION METHODS In inventory situations in which variation in *DDLT* can be expressed as a continuous distribution, the standard normal distribution (also called z distribution) is used to estimate the variation in demand. (A review of Appendix A, The Normal Probability Distribution, may be helpful to understand the logic behind the formulas presented in this section.) The normal distribution allows the desired level of service (expressed as a percentage or probability) to be converted into units of deviation called z units. The greater the number of z units, the greater the level of service and the larger the *OP*.

In an inventory situation in which the *DDLT* is normally distributed and the service level can be expressed as a percentage or probability, we can determine *OP* using the following formula:

$$OP = EDDLT + z(\sigma_{DDLT})$$

TABLE 8-5 PAYOFF TABLE FOR SAMPLE PROBLEM

(A) PAYOFF TABLE COST VALUES

Order Point Alternatives (OP_i)	DDLT *OCCURRENCES* 5	6	7	8
5	$0	$25	$50	$75
6	10	0	25	50
7	20	10	0	25
8	30	20	10	0

(B) PAYOFF TABLE EXPECTED COST VALUES

	Order Point Alternatives (OP_i)	DDLT *OCCURRENCES* 5	6	7	8	*Total Expected Costs* (TEC_i)
	5	$0	$10	$15	$15	$40.00
	6	1	0	7.5	10	18.50
	7	2	4	0	5	11.00 [Min. *TEC*]
	8	3	8	3	0	14.00
$P(DDLT_j)$		.10	.40	.30	.20	

where

$$EDDLT = \text{mean } DDLT = \frac{\Sigma DDLT}{n}$$

n = number of sample $DDLT$ values used in determining the mean $DDLT$

$$\sigma_{DDLT} = \text{standard deviation of } DDLT = \sqrt{\frac{\Sigma(DDLT - EDDLT)^2}{n}}$$

z = units of standard deviation that relate service level to percentage or probability of completion. This value is found in Appendix A, Table A, for a one-tail value (that is, we are only looking at the probability at one end of the distribution; see the shaded area of Figure 8-12).

$$OP = EDDLT + z(\sigma_{DDLT})$$

$$SS = OP - EDDLT$$

In this formula, $EDDLT$ is simply the mean $DDLT$, and variation is measured by the standard deviation of the $DDLT$ distribution. The z value is found by using Table A in Appendix A. For example, a 90 percent service level (also known as confidence level) requires a z of 1.28, 95 percent requires a z of 1.645, and a 99 percent requires a z of 2.33.

QUESTION: An inventory item has past *DDLT* of 200, 210, 220, and 230, respectively. If the behavior of the past *DDLT* tends to follow a normal distribution and if a 95 percent service level is desired, what should *OP* and *SS* be?

ANSWER: The *EDDLT* and the standard deviation of *DDLT* are computed for the sample of four values of *DDLT*:

$$EDDLT = \frac{\Sigma\, DDLT}{n} = \frac{200 + 210 + 220 + 230}{4} = 215 \text{ units}$$

$$\sigma_{DDLT} = \sqrt{\frac{(200-215)^2 + (210-215)^2 + (220-215)^2 + (230-215)^2}{4}}$$

$$= 11.18 \text{ units}$$

The appropriate z value for a service level of 95 percent can be found in Appendix A, Table A, at 1.645. Given a $z = 1.645$ the calculation of *OP* and *SS* then becomes

$$OP = EDDLT + z(\sigma_{DDLT})$$

$$= 215 + 1.645(11.18)$$

$$= 233.4 \text{ or } 234 \text{ units}$$

$$SS = OP - EDDLT$$

$$= 234 - 215$$

$$= 19 \text{ units}$$

In an inventory situation in which unit demand per day is available and has a normal distribution, and the lead time can be assumed constant, *OP* can be determined using the following alternative continuous distribution formula:

$$OP = LT(\bar{d}) + z\sqrt{LT(\sigma_d)^2}$$

where

LT = constant lead time in days

$\bar{d}$ = mean demand per day

$EDDLT$ = constant $LT \times$ mean demand per day $= LT(\bar{d})$

z = units of standard deviation that relate service level to percentage of probability of completion. This one-tail value is found in Appendix A.

$$\sigma_d = \text{standard deviation of demand per day} = \sqrt{\frac{\Sigma(d_i - \bar{d})^2}{n}}$$

$$\sigma_{DDLT} = \sqrt{LT(\sigma_d)^2}$$

$$SS = OP - EDDLT$$

In this formula *EDDLT* is the product of the constant *LT* and the mean demand per day. The variation is again measured by the standard deviation of the *DDLT* distribution, but estimated using only the variance in the demand per day (that is, *LT* is constant). The z value is found by using Table A in Appendix A and determined for a given service level percentage as previously stated.

QUESTION: An inventory item has a past demand per day of 300, 310, 320, and 330 units, respectively. The behavior of the past daily demand in units tends to follow a normal distribution and the lead time is a constant rate of 10 days. If a 95 percent service level is desired, what should *OP* and *SS* be?

ANSWER: The *EDDLT* and the standard deviation of *DDLT* are computed for the sample of four values of *DDLT*:

$$\bar{d} = \text{mean demand per day}$$

$$= \frac{300 + 310 + 320 + 330}{4}$$

$$= 315 \text{ units}$$

$$EDDLT = \text{constant } LT \times \text{mean demand per day}$$

$$= LT(\bar{d})$$

$$= 10(315)$$

$$= 3{,}150 \text{ units}$$

$$\sigma_d^2 = \text{standard deviation of demand per day}$$

$$= \sqrt{\frac{\Sigma(d_i - \bar{d})^2}{n}}$$

$$= \sqrt{\frac{(300-315)^2 + (310-315)^2 + (320-315)^2 + (330-315)^2}{4}}$$

$$= 11.18 \text{ units}$$

(continued)

$$\sigma_{DDLT} = \sqrt{LT(\sigma_d)^2}$$
$$= \sqrt{10(11.18)^2}$$
$$= 35.35 \text{ units}$$

The appropriate z value for a service level of 95 percent can be found in Appendix A, Table A, at 1.645. Given that $z = 1.645$, the calculation of OP and SS then becomes

$$OP = EDDLT + z(\sigma_{DDLT})$$
$$= 3{,}150 + 1.645(35.35)$$
$$= 3{,}208.1 \text{ or } 3{,}208 \text{ units}$$

$$SS = OP - EDDLT$$
$$= 3{,}208 - 3{,}150$$
$$= 58 \text{ units}$$

Determining the Best Order Point

There are many other methods for selecting the order point than those just presented. Selecting the "best" method can only be determined by measuring how well it satisfies the objectives of the inventory system. Some organizations believe that maximizing customer service level is more important than minimizing inventory costs. Most organizations try to achieve a balance between these two conflicting objectives.

One of the ways to determine if a given order point has a desirable effect on helping the organization accomplish its inventory objectives is to simulate its impact using past, present, and future data. Many computer-based systems maintain substantial historic demand, production, and inventory usage information in an easy-to-access format. The IBM Communications-Oriented Production Information and Control System (COPICS) introduced in Chapter 9 permits users to experiment with changes in order point and EOQ values. Through a series of "what-if" questions, users can incorporate different values of *OP* and see what would happen to customer service in meeting demand and inventory costs if the various values of *OP* were to be used. This software permits inventory managers to measure the positive or negative effect of a change in *OP* without actually risking the operation. Most of these software systems' ability to simulate inventory decision making are based on mathematical methods such as the Monte Carlo simulation method. (The mathematical procedure that comprises the Monte Carlo simulation method is presented in Supplement 8-1.)

FIXED ORDER PERIOD SYSTEM

In a fixed order period system, an organization needs to determine an order time period, or the period of time between placing orders for inventory. One fixed order period model is called the **economic order period (EOP) model.** In the EOP model, the variable an organization seeks to optimize is time and not order quantity, as in the EOQ models. Order quantity in the EOP model is determined each time an order is placed using the following formula:

$$\text{Order quantity} = \text{Upper inventory target} - \text{Current inventory level} + EDDLT$$

where

Upper inventory target = a targeted maximum inventory level (including safety stock) constrained by storage space or limitations imposed by management

Current inventory level = current inventory in stock in units

$EDDLT$ = expected demand during lead time, calculated using the square root, discrete, or continuous distribution methods previously presented

Although the order quantity is allowed to vary for each order, the optimal time period, represented by T, remains constant until a change in one or more of its parameters necessitates a revision in T. The value of the variable T is expressed as a percentage of a year. It can be converted into days, weeks, or months as needed by multiplying T times the number of days, weeks, or months in a year. Similar to the development of EOQ systems, the EOP model involves assumptions, model element definitions, cost formulas, and a derivation. The development of the EOP model is summarized in Table 8-6.

QUESTION: A company wants to determine the optimal order period for an inventory item it stocks. The annual demand of the product D is 10,000 units, the costs to place each order S is \$50, the costs per unit C is \$15, and the carrying cost rate I is estimated at 20 percent. The last five values of $DDLT$ were collected from past records and found to be 245, 267, 231, 274, and 233 units. Because of environmental concerns, the company does not want to store more than 2,000 units at a time. The firm currently has 425 units on hand. What are the optimal order period and the next order quantity, assuming the EOP model applies in this situation?

(continued)

ANSWER: Given that $D = 10{,}000$, $S = \$50$, $C = \$15$, and $I = 0.20$, then T is

$$T = \sqrt{\frac{2S}{DIC}}$$

$$= \sqrt{\frac{2(50)}{(10{,}000)(0.20)(15)}}$$

$$= 0.0577 \text{ years or 21 days } (0.0577 \times 365 \text{ days})$$

Assuming that we can determine the *EDDLT* in this situation by taking its average, we find

$$EDDLT = \frac{\Sigma DDLT}{n}$$

$$= \frac{[245 + 267 + 231 + 274 + 233]}{5}$$

$$= 250 \text{ units}$$

Then given the upper inventory target of 2,000 units and the current inventory level of 425 units, the next order quantity will be

$$\text{Order quantity} = \text{Upper inventory target} - \text{Current inventory level} + EDDLT$$

$$= 2{,}000 - 425 + 250$$

$$= 1{,}825 \text{ units}$$

So every 21 days the company should place an order, starting with the next order quantity at 1,825 units.

JUST-IN-TIME ORDER SYSTEMS

From a JIT point-of-view, independent demand inventory should not exist. In a JIT system a unit of finished goods is not produced until it is ordered. As soon as a unit of finished goods is completed, it does not go into inventory but is shipped to the customer. Whereas a goal of JIT is to eliminate all inventory (that is, zero inventory), most organizations continue to maintain inventory for all of the many reasons previously stated in this chapter. JIT ordering systems can be structured to recognize and allow for compromise between the ideal zero inventory goal and the real-world avoidance of stockout costs.

TABLE 8-6 ECONOMIC ORDER PERIOD (EOP) MODEL

ASSUMPTIONS

1. Annual carrying costs and ordering costs can be accurately estimated and are the only relevant costs.
2. Annual demand can be estimated and is linearly consumed by customers.
3. Average inventory level is the order quantity Q divided by 2, which implies that there is no safety stock and inventory is used up when next order arrives.
4. As a consequence of (2), there are no stockouts.
5. There are no quantity discounts on large orders.
6. The variable time will always be equal to or less than one year.

MODEL ELEMENT DEFINITIONS

D = annual demand in units
Q = order quantity in units
I = carrying cost rate (percentage of total cost of unit)
C = cost of the inventory item
S = cost in dollars to place an order
TAC = total annual costs of stocking inventory item in dollars
T = time, expressed as a proportion of a year

COST FORMULAS

Annual carrying costs = Cost to carry a unit × Average inventory = $IC(DT/2)$
Annual ordering costs = Cost per order × Orders per year = $S(D/DT)$ or S/T
Total annual costs (TAC) = Annual carrying costs + Annual ordering costs
= $IC(DT/2) + ST$

DERIVATION OF EOP MODEL

1. TAC function: $TAC = IC(DT/2) + (S/T)$
2. Take derivative with respect to T: $d(TAC)/d(T) = IC(D/2) - (S/T^2)$
3. Set derivative equal to zero and solve for T: $IC(D/2) - (S/T^2) = 0$
4. The resulting optimal T^* is: $T^* = \sqrt{2S/DIC}$

A JIT ordering system combines elements of both fixed order quantity and fixed order period systems. Ideally, a JIT system seeks a variable EOQ for a fixed EOP of a day, hour, or minute. In other words, a JIT ordering system seeks to equate an order quantity with the actual demand during the time period it is ordered. Because we use actual demand, the JIT system seeks to minimize inventory by waiting until the actual demand for inventory is known. Where inventory environments exist that permit actual demand to be known ahead of time (such as for contracted components or products), the JIT system can permit a fixed order quantity for a fixed time period (usually a day). This inventory situation can be expressed as shown at the top of page 400.

$$\text{Order quantity} = D/W$$

where

Order quantity = daily order quantity
D = annual demand
W = work days per year

In using this formula, we assume that inventory will be delivered each day and at the same time each day. When demand changes, a new order quantity is computed and implemented. In countries such as Japan where JIT ordering is the norm, this order quantity system works well. Unfortunately, few organizations have a completely implemented JIT inventory environment. In the United States and Europe, many companies still place large orders, which cause demand surges and necessitate substantial changes in daily order quantities. To compensate for this variation in customer order quantities, firms usually negotiate some allowable variation into the fixed order quantity with the vendors. (We discussed flexible ordering policies in the section on JIT purchasing in Chapter 6.) The order quantity formula for this type of JIT operation can be expressed as follows:

$$\text{Order quantity} = \text{Actual daily demand} \pm \text{Allowable variation}$$

The allowable variation element in this formula is used as a safety stock to cushion inventory stocks against an unexpected demand when added to actual daily demand or to reduce inventory stock when it is subtracted. For organizations that require little or no lead time in obtaining inventory from vendors and little or no lead time in providing the inventory item to customers, daily observation of actual unit demand permits order quantity to be easily determined and the need for an allowable variation to be minimized. As lead times increase, the potential amount of variation in demand also increases. That is, as we observe variation in daily demand over a greater number of days, we will observe a greater range of variation than we would observe in a single day. As we saw earlier in Table 8-1, a single period of time can greatly increase the amount of inventory expenses. The greater the variation, the greater the need for an estimation method to determine order quantities.

If we can assume that daily demand follows a continuous probability distribution, we can use the normal probability distribution to estimate a daily order quantity. The daily order quantity can be estimated using the following formula:

$$\text{Order quantity} = \text{Mean demand per day} + \text{Allowable variation} - \text{Carryover}$$

$$\text{Order quantity} = \bar{d} + (z)(\sigma_d) - c_o$$

where

$\bar{d}$ = mean demand per day. This mean value may be computed once and applied for a predetermined number of days (a month, quarter, year, etc.) or it may be recomputed each day as a moving average.

z = units of standard deviation that relate service level to percentage or probability of completion. This one-tail value is found in Appendix A, Table A.

σ_d = standard deviation of daily demand. This standard deviation value must be recomputed each time the mean demand per day is recomputed.

c_o = carryover in units from prior day. Currently stock is subtracted from the order quantity amount for the next day to keep inventory levels at a minimum.

In this formula, order quantity is the mean daily demand, plus an additional amount of inventory to cover the possible variation, minus the carryover from the prior day. Allowable variation in daily demand is measured by the standard deviation of the demand distribution multiplied by a desired service level value of z. The z value is found by using Table A in Appendix A. For example, a 90 percent service level requires a z of 1.28, 95 percent requires a z of 1.645, and a 99 percent requires a z of 2.33. By subtracting the carryover of inventory each day, the model will prohibit a substantial buildup of inventory.

QUESTION: A company has an inventory item whose average daily demand is 15 units with a standard deviation of 3 units. If the behavior of the past demand tends to follow a normal distribution and if a 95 percent service level is desired, what should JIT order quantities be for each of the five days of actual demand in units of 17, 14, 18, 13, and 15?

ANSWER: The appropriate z value for a service level of 95 percent can be found in Appendix A, Table A, at 1.645. Given that $z = 1.645$ and assuming zero carryover for the first day, the calculation of order quantities are as follows:

$$\text{Order quantity} = \bar{d} + (z)(\sigma_d) - c_o$$

$$\text{First-day order quantity} = 15 + (1.645)(3) - 0$$
$$= 19.93 \text{ or } 20 \text{ units}$$

Because actual demand is 17 units, the carryover to the second day is 3 units (20 − 17).

$$\text{Second-day order quantity} = 15 + (1.645)(3) - 3$$
$$= 16.93 \text{ or } 17 \text{ units}$$

We have a carryover of 3 units, which are added to the order quantity of 17 units for the second day, maintaining a stock of 20 units. With the demand of 14 units in the second day, the carryover to the third day is 6 units.

$$\text{Third-day order quantity} = 15 + (1.645)(3) - 6$$
$$= 13.93 \text{ or } 14 \text{ units}$$

(*continued*)

We have a carryover of 6 units, which are added to the order quantity of 14 units for the third day, maintaining a stock of 20 units. With the demand of 18 units in the third day, the carryover to the fourth day is 2 units.

$$\text{Fourth-day order quantity} = 15 + (1.645)(3) - 2$$
$$= 17.93 \text{ or } 18 \text{ units}$$

We have a carryover of 2 units, which are added to the order quantity of 18 units for the fourth day, maintaining a stock of 20 units. With the demand of 13 units in the fourth day, the carryover to the fifth day is 7 units.

$$\text{Fifth-day order quantity} = 15 + (1.645)(3) - 7$$
$$= 12.93 \text{ or } 13 \text{ units}$$

We have a carryover of 7 units, which are added to the order quantity of 13 units for the fifth day, maintaining a stock of 20 units. With the demand of 15 units in the fifth day, the carryover to the sixth day is 5 units.

INTEGRATING MANAGEMENT RESOURCES: USING ELECTRONIC DATA INTERCHANGE TO IMPROVE PRODUCTIVITY

Integrating inventory ordering systems with other elements of an organization's information system is important for improving productivity. One such computer-integrated system is called **electronic data interchange** (EDI).[6] EDI is a computer-to-computer exchange of business documents between two or more companies. It is a computer-integrated inventory ordering system that is designed to function in CIM, CISS, and even JIT environments.

The three main elements of EDI are a message standard, translation software, and communication network. The **message standard** is a predefined standardized format for the various types of messages (such as inventory orders) that companies plan on sending each other. In case of inventory orders, the purchasing company that wants to send an order will have its own order form and the supplier that takes the order will also have its own invoice form on which to record the order. Both forms contain basically the same information with the exception of some unique information used only for internally processing the order (for example, a purchase order number for the purchasing company or bin numbers for the supplier to locate the inventory items). For an EDI system both the purchasing company and the supplier will need to agree to a basic message standard of minimum information that can be shared in a format that each understands once it is received.

EDI's **translation software** is used to interpret the purchasing company's order message into the supplier's order form. The translation software converts the

[6] B. J. Elliott, "EDI: A New Method of Sending Your Orders," *Production and Operations Management Review with APICS News,* 10, No. 4 (April 1990), 50–52.

standard purchasing company's inventory order into the supplier's order form, despite the fact that both forms may contain unique information and be in different formats. The software also performs security functions by screening information that may appear on order forms that should not be shared (such as a purchaser's evaluation rating of a supplier's past performance or a supplier's special discount schedule unavailable to the purchaser). The translation software can also take advantage of the state of a firm's computer integration. The software can reach into an organization's computer-based system data base and retrieve order information that is then placed on the inventory orders each time they are received. The greater the computer integration of shared information, the greater the degree of access the software can achieve to obtain on-line information, such as credit ratings of purchasing companies and vendor delivery performance history.

The **communication network** is used to transmit the inventory orders. The most common communication network that supports the EDI system are public-access electronic mailboxes. An **electronic mailbox** is a computer terminal or computer at a workstation that can receive and send messages to other terminals or computers over telephone lines. Mail or inventory orders are electronically entered at a terminal at the purchaser's facility and sent to another terminal at the supplier's facility by way of the supplier's telephone number. The supplier's terminal or computer stores the message or order until the vendor accesses it. The vendor may need only to press a single return key to authorize an order to be picked. In fully computer-integrated systems, the vendor may be able to receive an immediate confirmation of the status of the order when it is entered via the terminal. In turn, the supplier may be able to communicate the status of the order—including any stockouts—back to the purchaser via the electronic mailbox in a matter of minutes rather than days.

How is the computer-based EDI method different from the usual manual method of mailing orders to suppliers? The answer is in the efficiencies that have been observed in its implementation. Some of the efficiencies reported by operations managers include the following:

1. Purchase order delivery time (the time that it takes for the purchasing company to send an order) to the supplier is reduced because the order is not carried through the mail but delivered at the speed of electricity to the supplier by telephone lines.
2. Invoice preparation time by the supplier is reduced or eliminated because the translation software converts the purchase order from the purchasing company into an invoice order for the supplier.
3. Order accuracy is improved because the order is not rewritten by human beings.
4. Two-way communication on order status is facilitated because the time from when an order is sent, received by the supplier, and checked by the supplier's computer is reduced. The current status of stock information can be electronically transmitted to the purchaser so stockout issues can be

resolved before they cause work stoppages for the purchasing company. This also improves the service provided by suppliers because stockouts can be detected quickly, avoiding costly problems for purchasing companies.

5. EDI takes advantage of and supports computer-based CIM and CISS operations. Even JIT inventory systems can be supported by EDI where electronic mailboxes are present. EDI provides an easy means of placing the daily or weekly orders that are characteristic of JIT operations.
6. Paper flow, document storage, and filing costs are reduced or eliminated because EDI messages can be entirely electronic in computer-integrated systems like CIM and CISS.

EDI typifies the many new developing technologies of the 1990s in that it supports the computer-integrated environments of CIM and CISS, while also having application in less computer-integrated environments like JIT. EDI, as an inventory ordering system, helps improve customer service in purchasing inventory and consequently minimizes the costs of placing orders. By improving service and minimizing costs, EDI helps managers accomplish their two primary independent demand inventory objectives as well as improve the productivity of the operations management system as a whole.

SUMMARY

In this chapter, we have examined the subject of independent demand inventory planning. A number of fixed order quantity systems were presented including the basic economic order quantity (EOQ) model, quantity discount EOQ model, and the economic manufacturing quantity (EMQ) model. In addition, a series of order point models were presented to aid the inventory planner in knowing when to place an order for inventory. Other inventory methods presented in this chapter include an economic order period (EOP) model and just-in-time models. We have also included the Monte Carlo simulation method in Supplement 8-1.

All of these methods seek to accomplish one or both of the often conflicting inventory management goals of minimizing costs and maximizing customer service levels. Understanding how these methods approach the two conflicting goals is an important step in their implementation. Equally important is the need to understand the basic assumptions necessary to apply each of the models. In some industries, JIT ordering systems and computer-based inventory monitoring in AS/AR systems are substituting daily or even hourly inventory ordering for the infrequent monthly EOQs of the past.

There has been criticism leveled at the EOQ approach to inventory modeling,[7] much of which can be traced to the user's lack of understanding the model's required assumptions and parameter accuracy. EOQ is a modeling approach to decision making and not just a formula. When timely, accurate, and relevant cost and demand information are combined in an EOQ model that is correctly formulated for a particular organization's inventory

---

[7] See J. M. Burnham and B. B. Mohanty, "Requiem for EOQ—But Unified Order Quantity is Alive and Well," *Production and Inventory Management,* 31, No. 1 (1990), 80–83; and R. E. D. Woolsey, "A Requiem for the EOQ: An Editorial," *Production and Inventory Management,* 29, No. 3 (1988), 68–72.

environment, it will provide the best cost-minimizing and service level–maximizing order quantities. As an inventory manager put it, "EOQ is alive and well and living everywhere that rational people are buying and making things."[8] Computer-integrated systems are contributing to the revival of inventory modeling. As computer-based systems more fully integrate organizations, cost and demand information can more accurately and quickly be made available. This data can be incorporated on a timely basis into models such as the EOQ, OP, and EOP to provide a more useful source of inventory planning information than previously experienced.

The JIT order system was designed for chiefly a noncomputer or manual environment. In more recent years, it is more frequently being incorporated into CIM software systems that control JIT production.[9] The daily tracking and ordering requirements of inventory in JIT as well as the occasional variation caused by EOQ ordering makes the use of computer-based CIM systems for monitoring inventory helpful for organizations with a substantially diverse inventory. Electronic data interchange (EDI) is a more recent development that, although requiring a fairly high stage of computer integration, supports and takes maximum advantage of any state of integration to improve the timeliness of inventory ordering.

In this chapter, we have examined the use of the economic manufacturing quantity (EMQ) model as a method for determining lot sizes for production runs. Determining a lot size and when the lot size should be produced in a production facility is the same as scheduling production. The act of scheduling is an important operations management planning and control function. In the next chapter, we will discuss scheduling in manufacturing and in service operations.

DISCUSSION AND REVIEW QUESTIONS

1. What is independent demand inventory?
2. Why is independent demand inventory necessary to operations management?
3. Why do we balance the conflicting objectives of minimizing costs and maximizing service levels in inventory models?
4. What is the difference between a fixed order quantity system and a fixed order period system?
5. Is lead time in inventory really important? How can mismanaging lead time cost a company money?
6. Why do we need order points? How are they related to fixed order quantity models? How can we determine what is the best order point?
7. What is the difference between a periodic and continuous accounting inventory system?
8. Under what assumptions do the EOQ models operate?
9. What is a single-period inventory model?
10. What are JIT order systems?
11. What is electronic data interchange?
12. What is simulation analysis?

---

[8] R. E. D. Woolsey, "Readers' Responses on EOQ," *Production and Inventory Management,* 30, No. 4 (1988), 75.

[9] See M. J. Schniederjans, *Topics in Just-in-Time Management* (Boston: Allyn & Bacon, 1993), Chapter 5.

PROBLEMS

* 1. Suppose that an organization must acquire an inventory item and the inventory environment fits the basic EOQ model's assumptions. Suppose further that
   - The per unit cost of inventory C is $10.
   - The annual demand D for the inventory is 1,500 units.
   - The carrying cost rate I is 15 percent of the cost per unit.
   - The cost to place an order S is $25.

   What is the optimal EOQ value? What does this value mean?

2. Suppose that an organization needs to purchase an inventory item and the inventory environment fits the basic EOQ model's assumptions. Some of the relevant information is as follows:
   - The per unit cost of inventory C is $15.
   - The annual demand D for the inventory is 10,000 units.
   - The carrying cost rate I is 10 percent of the cost per unit.
   - The cost to place an order S is $50.

   What is the optimal EOQ value? What does this value mean?

3. Suppose that an organization must acquire an inventory item and the simple EOQ model's assumptions apply, with the following information given:
   - The per unit cost of inventory C is $1.
   - The annual demand D for the inventory is 1,380 units.
   - The carrying cost rate I is 10 percent of the cost per unit.
   - The cost to place an order S is $2.

   What is the optimal EOQ value? What does this value mean?

* 4. A company has been using the simple EOQ model to compute its order quantity of 1,000 units for the last two months. In the next month, its per unit inventory cost C of $5 is going to increase to $6. Will the EOQ value of 1,000 units increase or decrease? Is this change logical in light of the increase in per unit costs? Explain.

5. A company has been using the simple EOQ model to compute its order quantity of 1,000 units for the last two months. In the next month, its per unit inventory cost C of $5 is going to decrease to $4. Will the EOQ value of 1,000 units increase or decrease? Is this change logical in light of the decrease in per unit costs? Explain.

6. A company has been using the simple EOQ model to compute its order quantity of 500 units for the last year. In the next year, its annual demand D of 7,600 units is going to increase to 8,000 units. Will the EOQ value of 500 units increase or decrease? Is this change logical in light of the increase in annual demand? Explain.

7. A company has been using the simple EOQ model to compute its order quantity of 500 units for the last year. In the next year, its annual demand D of 7,600 units is going to decrease to 7,000 units. Will its EOQ value of 500 units increase or decrease? Is this change logical in light of the decrease in annual demand? Explain.

8. A company has been using the simple EOQ model to compute its order quantity of 1,000 units for the last few months. In the next month, its annual carrying cost rate I of 12 percent is going to increase to 14 percent. Will the EOQ value of 1,000 units

---

* The solutions to the problems marked with an asterisk can be found in Appendix J.

increase or decrease? Is this change logical in light of the increase in annual carrying cost rate? Explain.

9. A company has been using the simple EOQ model to compute its order quantity of 1,000 units for the last few months. In the next month, its annual carrying cost rate I of 12 percent is going to decrease to 10 percent. Will the EOQ value of 1,000 units increase or decrease? Is this change logical in light of the decrease in annual carrying cost rate? Explain.

10. A company has been using the simple EOQ model to compute its order quantity of 5,000 units for the last two months. In the next month, its per order cost S of $25 is going to increase to $30. Will the EOQ value of 5,000 increase or decrease? Is this change logical in light of the increase in per order cost? Explain.

11. A company has been using the simple EOQ model to compute its order quantity of 5,000 units for the last two months. In the next month, its per order cost S of $25 is going to decrease to $20. Will the EOQ value of 5,000 increase or decrease? Is this change logical in light of the decrease in per order cost? Explain.

*12. Suppose that an organization plans to purchase an inventory item and the inventory environment fits the quantity discount EOQ model's assumptions. Suppose further that
   - The per unit cost of inventory C is defined by the following quantity discount schedule:

Order Quantity or Price Break Intervals	*Unit Price to Purchaser*
0 to 1499 units	$1.25
1500 to 2999 units	$1.15
3000 and more units	$1.14

   - The annual demand D for the inventory is 10,000 units.
   - The carrying cost rate I is 2 percent of the cost per unit.
   - The costs to place an order S are $5.

   What is the optimal EOQ and unit purchase price?

13. An organization plans to purchase an inventory item under the quantity discount EOQ model's assumptions. Suppose further that the following information is available:
   - The per unit cost of inventory C is defined by the following quantity discount schedule:

Order Quantity or Price Break Intervals	*Unit Price to Purchaser*
0 to 999 units	$0.45
1000 to 1999 units	$0.40
2000 and more units	$0.30

   - The annual demand D for the inventory is 500 units.
   - The carrying cost rate I is 25 percent of the cost per unit.
   - The costs to place an order S are $50.

   What is the optimal EOQ and unit purchase price?

14. An organization plans to acquire an inventory item under a quantity discount arrangement. The company has the following information:
   - The per unit cost of inventory C is defined by the quantity discount schedule shown at the top of page 408.

Order Quantity or Price Break Intervals	*Unit Price to Purchaser*
0 to 999 units	\$2.50
1000 to 2999 units	\$2.40
3000 to 5999 units	\$2.35
6000 or more units	\$2.25

- The annual demand D for the inventory is 20,000 units.
- The carrying cost rate I is 15 percent of the cost per unit.
- The costs to place an order S are \$30.

Determine the optimal EOQ and unit purchase price.

*15. An organization plans to manufacture an inventory item and the environment fits the production run EMQ model's assumptions. Suppose further that
- The production rate P is 100 units per day.
- The inventory usage rate U is 40 units per day.
- The annual demand D for the inventory is 14,600 units.
- The setup costs S are \$500 per production run.
- The carrying cost rate is 20 percent of the cost of the unit.
- The production costs per unit are \$12.

What is the EMQ? What is the optimal number of production runs per year having 365 days, and how many days will there be between each of the production runs?

16. Suppose that an organization plans to manufacture an inventory item and the environment fits the production run EMQ model's assumptions. Suppose further that
- The production rate P is 8 units per day.
- The inventory usage rate U is 4 units per day.
- The annual demand D for the inventory is 1,460 units.
- The setup costs S are \$250 per production run.
- The carrying cost rate is 18 percent of the cost of the unit.
- The production costs per unit are \$500.

What is the EMQ? What is the optimal number of production runs per year having 52 weeks, and how many weeks will there be between each of the production runs?

17. Suppose that an organization must manufacture an inventory item and the environment fits the production run EMQ model's assumptions. Suppose further that
- The production rate P is 25 units per day.
- The inventory usage rate U is 10 units per day.
- The annual demand D for the inventory is 3,650 units.
- The setup costs S are \$100 per production run.
- The carrying cost rate is 20 percent of the cost of the unit.
- The production costs per unit are \$45.

What is the EMQ? What is the optimal number of production runs per year having 12 months, and how many months will there be between the starts?

18. A company wants to assess a stockout percentage as one means of measuring its customer service level. Of 1,200 orders processed, 200 orders had stockouts. Of 130,000 line items on all of the orders the firm processed, 1,200 line items were stocked out. What two stockout percentages can be computed? What are the stockout percentages and how can they be used to measure the company's performance?

*19. A company has an inventory item, the demand for which is a mean or average rate of 10 units per day. The mean lead time for the delivery of the item from the vendor is

12 days. Using the square root of *EDDLT* method, what are the safety stock (*SS*) and order point (*OP*) for this inventory item?

20. A company has an inventory item that is purchased by customers at a mean or average rate of 7 units per day. The mean lead time for the delivery of the item from the vendor is 24 days. Using the square root of *EDDLT* method, what are the safety stock (*SS*) and order point (*OP*) for this inventory item?

*21. A company purchases automobile radios for installation into custom vans. Based on past records, the usage of radios is 8 units per day with a mean lead time of 12 days. The past demand during lead time follows a discrete distribution as follows:

Actual DDLT	*Frequency*
90 to 99	.12
100 to 109	.68
110 to 119	.20

If the installation company wants to provide an 80 percent service level, what are the appropriate order point (*OP*) and safety stock (*SS*)? Explain how you will use your answer for inventory planning and control.

22. A food company buys boxes of fruit for sale at a local market. Based on past records, the market for the fruit consists of consumers buying 20 boxes per day with a mean lead time of 4 days from the growers' warehouse to the food company. The past demand during lead time follows a discrete distribution as follows:

Actual DDLT	*Frequency*
70 to 79	.20
80 to 89	.30
90 to 99	.30
100 to 109	.20

If the food company wants to provide a 95 percent service level, what is the appropriate order point (*OP*) and safety stock (*SS*)? Explain how you will use your answer for inventory planning and control.

23. A company wants to develop a single-period inventory model for an item it currently stocks. The probability of a *DDLT* of 2 units has a 25 percent chance of occurring, a *DDLT* of 3 units has a 45 percent chance of occurring, and a *DDLT* of 4 units has a 30 percent chance of occurring. The shortage cost per unit is exactly $15, and the overage cost per unit is $10. Given the following payoff cost values, what should the order point (*OP*) and safety stock (*SS*) be?

Order Point Alternatives	DDLT *OCCURRENCES* 2	3	4
2	$ 0	$15	$30
3	10	0	15
4	20	10	0

24. A company has an inventory item whose shortage costs of $40 per unit are four times as great as its overage costs. Based on past records, the company's management has found that the probability of a *DDLT* of 4 units is 15 percent, a *DDLT* of 5 units is 32 percent, a *DDLT* of 6 units is 28 percent, and a *DDLT* of 7 units is 25 percent.

Given the following payoff cost values, what should the order point (*OP*) and safety stock (*SS*) for the inventory item be?

Order Point Alternatives	DDLT *OCCURRENCES* 4	5	6	7
4	$ 0	$40	$80	$120
5	10	0	40	80
6	20	10	0	40
7	30	20	10	0

*25. A company has an inventory item whose past daily *DDLT* values were observed to be 300, 318, 326, 378, and 389 units. If the past *DDLT* follows a normal distribution and if we want to achieve a 90 percent service level, what should the order point (*OP*) and safety stock (*SS*) be?

26. A company's inventory item has past daily *DDLT* values of 45, 67, 89, 94, 92, 96, 91, 95, 97, and 110 units. If the past *DDLT* approximates a normal distribution and if the company wants to achieve a 95 percent service level, what should the order point (*OP*) and safety stock (*SS*) be?

27. An organization has an inventory item whose past daily *DDLT* values were observed to be 50, 58, 56, 58, and 59 units. Assume a constant lead time of 14 days. If the past *DDLT* follows a normal distribution and if we want to achieve a 90 percent service level, what should the order point (*OP*) and safety stock (*SS*) be?

*28. If the annual demand of an inventory item is 5,000 units; the cost to place an order is $50; the cost per unit is $17; the carrying cost rate is 15 percent; the current inventory is 250 units; the maximum storage is 1,000 units; and the last four *DDLT* are 123, 130, 110, and 134, what are the EOP and next order quantity?

29. If the annual demand of an inventory item is 10,000 units; the cost to place an order is $60; the cost per unit is $5; the carrying cost rate is 20 percent; the current inventory is 170 units; the maximum storage is 3,000 units; and last five *DDLT* are 240, 220, 290, 340, and 222, what are the EOP and next order quantity?

*30. A company has a JIT inventory ordering system in place. Managers know that the annual demand will be 30,000 units because of fixed contractual arrangements for that amount for one year. If there are only 285 working days in the year, what should the order quantity for this operation be?

31. A company has implemented a JIT inventory ordering system. Under the terms of the vendor contract it has with a local supplier, order quantities can have an allowable variation of ± 3 units from the fixed daily order quantity of 10 units. The company places its order for next-day delivery over its EDI system. Suppose that the company experiences the following five days of unit demand: 12, 13, 9, 10, and 14. Assume that carryover is added to the next day's order quantity, stockouts are treated as lost sales (stockout demand is not carried over), and the first day's order quantity (related to the demand of 12 units) is set at 10 units. Using a carryover work sheet similar to that presented in Table 8-1, what are the total number of units that will have to be carried over and stocked out over the five days?

*32. A company has an inventory item whose average daily demand is 30 units with a standard deviation of 2. If the demand behavior of the past follows a normal distribution and if the company wants to maintain a 90 percent service level, what should the JIT order quantities be for each of the four days of actual demand of 32, 29, 35, and 28?

33. A company has an inventory item with an average daily demand of 40 units with a standard deviation of 10. If the demand behavior of the past approximates a normal distribution and if the company wishes to maintain a 95 percent service level, what should the JIT order quantities be for each of the five days of actual unit demand of 56, 48, 35, 30, and 50?

*34. (This problem requires the contents of Supplement 8-1.) Using the Monte Carlo simulation method, simulate 10 days of demand based on the following distribution and the random numbers from the first row in Appendix F.

Demand	*Frequency*
60	.14
61	.18
62	.28
63	.25
64	.15

35. (This problem requires the contents of Supplement 8-1.) A company would like to determine the average cost of using a fixed order inventory policy of 40 units per day. Assume that it costs $5 for each unit stocked out and $1 for each unit carried over to the next day. Using the Monte Carlo simulation method, simulate 10 days of demand based on the following distribution and the random numbers from the second row in Appendix F. What is the total average cost per day of this policy?

Demand	*Frequency*
38	.10
39	.30
40	.30
41	.15
42	.15

36. (This problem requires the contents of Supplement 8-1.) A company wants to determine which of two inventory policies it should select to minimize its total stockout and carryover costs. The demand on the inventory item varies from 3 units to 8 units daily. The company recorded 100 days of inventory demand transactions, which are expressed below as a frequency distribution: C

Demand	*Observed Frequency*
3	6
4	14
5	30
6	30
7	15
8	5

The two mutually exclusive inventory policies are as follows: (1) Using the *fixed order quantity policy,* the company will order exactly 6 units of the inventory item each day, regardless of demand. (2) Using the *variable order quantity policy,* the company will order a number of units equal to yesterday's observed demand. If the company will incur a stockout cost of $8 per unit per day and a carryover cost of $3 per unit per day, which of the two policies will best minimize costs over a 100-day period?

CASE 8-1

THE SAFETY STOCK THAT WASN'T SAFE

The Ashlyn Distributing Company (ADC) is located in New York City. ADC handles a complete line of plumbing equipment that it sells retail to do-it-yourselfers and wholesale to professional plumbers. Last year sales amounted to more than $45 million. ADC at last count was carrying more than 30,000 different independent demand inventory items. In the 1980s, the company's management decided to computerize its records, accounting, and inventory systems to keep track of its expanding number of inventory items. As a crucial part of its inventory system it decided to use EOQ models.

The EOQ models were used for only the inventory items that, during the year, needed to be ordered frequently, were ordered in large amounts, or both. The EOQ model used for all inventory items was a version of the simple EOQ model. The cost estimates for the model's parameters were calculated at the end of each year to determine the next year's EOQs and *OP*s. The annual demands for the products were forecast and then assumed to follow a linear pattern as required by the basic EOQ model. The lead times were obtained from vendor sales representatives. (ADC obtained all of its inventory from outside suppliers).

Once the inventory system was installed and debugged of computer misinformation, it appeared to greatly improve the operation of the company. For more than a decade the inventory system, with yearly updates on cost information, generated all the necessary EOQ and *OP* values. Over this time the marketing manager received an ever-increasing number of complaints about stock shortages from customers. A number of ADC's customers were not receiving their goods from ADC on time. The inventory manager responded by making a simple change in order quantities that would allow a 5 percent increase in inventory to act as a safety stock. This seemed to resolve some of the customer complaints for a while, but the marketing manager was continually pressured by the inventory manager to increase the safety stock to further reduce the stockouts.

Further percentage increases in the safety stock did not seem warranted in that some inventory items were starting to exceed normal or comfortable stock levels while a lesser number of other items experienced a stockout. If a system were to be installed that would individualize inventory items' safety stock levels, it would require a major overhaul or reprogramming effort of the entire inventory computer system. The inventory manager resisted changing the entire system to increase the supply of inventory because it would result in operating the company for several months without the benefit of a computer system. That is, the computer system would have to incur some downtime until it could be programmed to estimate safety stock. The usual course of action by the inventory manager when shortages were reported was to wire for rush orders to vendors. Sometimes taxicabs were used to deliver inventory to customers at ADC's expense. This cost of expediting the order did not show up in the accounting control system until the accounting system was revised to give that type of detailed information. When the cost of expediting orders came to the notice of the owner and president of ADC, the inventory manager and marketing manager were asked to come up with an approach to reduce this type of customer service/inventory cost and provide better service to customers.

It was about this time that ADC upper management started noticing the withdrawal of customer accounts. A large segment of the professional plumber customers of ADC tend to be the type of consumer who would wait until an inventory item is needed before they ordered it from ADC. Stockouts in this type of situation could cost the plumber a contract or costly delay in a plumber's construction project. Many of these customers temporarily went to ADC's competitors to obtain required inventory items. After repeated stockouts were incurred at ADC, these customers started permanently trading at the competitor's establishments.

The inventory and marketing managers tried to identify the problems involving stockouts by going over the computer records of inventory transactions. The cost and demand information used in the EOQ models seem to be reasonably accurate. They did find that no records on vendor delivery dates were kept. The computer only kept and used the prestated lead times for delivery that the vendor claimed they would provide ADC. The two managers decided to keep track of actual demand during lead times for several inventory items. One of these items is called the flush stopper and the promised delivery lead time was supposed to be a constant two weeks or 14 days. The actual demand during lead time for the last eight deliveries are presented in Exhibit 8C-1.

EXHIBIT 8C-1 ACTUAL DEMAND DURING LEAD TIME FOR THE INVENTORY ITEM FLUSH STOPPER

Delivery Number	*Actual Demand During Lead Time*
1	12
2	18
3	18
4	14
5	16
6	16
7	10
8	8

CASE QUESTIONS

1. If we assume that *DDLT* behaves like a normal distribution for the flush stopper item and management wants to achieve a 90 percent service level, what should the *SS* and *OP* be?
2. How do the *SS* and *OP* change if management wants a 99 percent level?

CASE 8-2

BONINI'S HOT PRETZEL COMPANY

Bonini's Hot Pretzel Company is a fast-food business lcoated in Portland, Maine. Bonini's produces, promotes, and sells its own products. Bonini's provides a mobile convenience food service throughout the tourist areas of the city of Portland. It currently markets a single product: hot pretzels.

The basic operation of the business is as follows: The hot pretzels are prepared in the food plant located in Westbrook, Maine. Once prepared, the pretzels remain fresh for only about eight hours. They are quickly transported to Bonini's downtown Portland distribution center. From the distribution center the pretzels are sold by peddlers who transport them in bicycle-driven pretzel stands. Each stand has a small battery-operated heater to keep the pretzels warm.

The peddlers each have their own routes through the tourist sections of the city. The peddlers hired by Bonini's are usually students from high schools or colleges. This permits Bonini's to keep labor costs at a minimum. In fact, the majority of the earnings that the peddlers make are from a small commission based on sales. Under the current marketing policies, peddlers load their mobile stands with the maximum number of pretzels (99) and try to sell as many as they can during their normal selling hours from 11:00 AM to 7:00 PM. Each pretzel is sold for \$1.50, a price it can command because of the company's reputation in the city. If peddlers run out of stock, they go home early. When the peddlers are out of stock they also are required to offer customers who stop them a \$0.10 coupon off the cost of their next purchase. If they have stock left over, it is turned in for credit against their sales for the day. The leftover stock is destroyed at the end of the day because it is unusable for resale. The cost of destroyed stock, including delivery and processing, is \$0.50 per pretzel.

The peddlers' sales vary considerably because of the volatile nature of the tourist business in Portland. The results of sales variations have created a cost crisis at Bonini's. The company has been losing money for the last two months, and Bonini's management realized that something has to be done fast. The problem of leftover stock was easily identified as the cost problem. The difficulty was in deciding what to do about it. To help management arrive at a solution a consultant was retained.

Because controlling costs was directly related to forecasting daily sales, the consultant suggested that a new policy on the number of units the peddlers should carry or be issued for sales is necessary. The management of Bonini's agreed and offered two alternative forecasting policies:

- *Policy 1* The number of pretzels issued to a peddler tomorrow will equal the sales that the peddler had today. To begin this system, the consultant let the pretzels issued on day 1 equal 91 units (the average for the last two months).
- *Policy 2* The number of pretzels issued each day will be the expected value of that particular peddler.

To determine which of these policies is the best at controlling costs and generating profits, the consultant wanted to obtain some unit sales data on a single peddler. The consultant reasoned that the results from the single peddler could be expanded to cover the other peddlers. A survey of the last two months' sales for a single peddler was conducted and is presented in Exhibit 8C-2. As can be seen in Exhibit 8C-2, for example, 1.2 percent of the time sampled the unit sales were 85 pretzels.

EXHIBIT 8C-2 DAILY PRETZEL SALES

Pretzel Sales	*Percentage*
85	1.2
86	2.1
87	3.3
88	3.7
89	4.9
90	8.3
91	10.3
92	12.4
93	14.6
94	12.4
95	9.1
96	5.8
97	4.1
98	4.1
99	3.7

While the cost of a destroyed pretzel is $0.50 (including the cost of goods sold), the cost of the goods sold for each pretzel is only $0.45. The consultant felt that this cost information could be incorporated with the frequency information in Exhibit 8C-2 to generate the expected demand

EXHIBIT 8C-3 RANDOM NUMBER TABLE

Day	*Random Number*	*Day*	*Random Number*	*Day*	*Random Number*
1	247	11	742	21	494
2	706	12	188	22	929
3	937	13	302	23	776
4	422	14	268	24	867
5	802	15	000	25	110
6	871	16	085	26	901
7	682	17	382	27	055
8	105	18	454	28	526
9	547	19	754	29	788
10	469	20	967	30	457

information desired. In addition, the consultant felt the randomly selected sample of 30 days of operations would be adequate to test the two forecasting policies. The consultant prepared a random number table, which is presented in Exhibit 8C-3.

CASE QUESTIONS

(These questions require the contents of Supplement 8-1.)

1. What type of quantitative method should be used to compare the two policies over a 30-day test period? Why?
2. What is the expected profit generated under the policy 1 forecasting system?
3. What is the expected profit generated under the policy 2 forecasting system?
4. Which policy should be recommended based on expected profit?

SUPPLEMENT 8-1
Simulation and Inventory Systems: The Monte Carlo Method

One of the major flaws in all of the inventory models we have discussed in this chapter is the way they deal with the variable nature of the model parameters. We have described models that assume discrete probability distributions and others that have continuous probability distributions (*DDLT*). Others assumed that constant parameters in EOQ and EOP models, like annual demand (*D*) or cost per unit (*C*), may also vary according to some probability distribution. Indeed, there may be multiple variables, each following its own unique probability distribution. Although there are many different types of inventory models to choose from, there are an even greater number of inventory situations, and no existing model will ideally fit. To handle these types of unique inventory problem situations, we can use the Monte Carlo simulation method.

The Monte Carlo simulation method can be used to simulate the probability behavior of inventory and other operations management systems. It is a general-purpose simulation procedure. It is also the basis for most of the probability computer-based simulation systems. This method randomly selects inventory parameter values in the same proportions or probabilities that are observed in actual behavior of the parameter. The selected parameter is then used as a discrete value in the computation of inventory values such as *TAC* and *Q*. Then, based on some number of simulated values of *TAC* and *Q* statistics, an inventory planner can determine the best model, order point, and so on. To use this method, one or more of the parameters in the inventory situation must behave probabilistically. While this method converts variable values to discrete values, we can use this method to model both discrete and continuous probabilistic parameter behavior.

One of the reasons that the Monte Carlo method is used in inventory planning and decision making is its ability to model short-term behavior. When we used expected values like *EDDLT* in the other inventory models, they represent the conversion of the variable parameters into long-term expected value. These long-term expected values are averaged values for demand or lead time that will occur over a long period of time of repeated usage. Their calculation takes into consideration the entire probability distribution of the parameter. Unfortunately, many inventory ordering situations require placement of only a few orders before the cost values change enough to necessitate altering order quantities. In other words, a short-term simulation of only a few of the most probable values of demand or lead time may more accurately capture the useful behavior in some inventory decision environments than the long-term expected value methods that include an entire range of variability.

The Monte Carlo simulation method for inventory planning consists of the following steps:

1. *Identify the inventory policies that are to be simulated and the rules used to judge the results of the simulation.* In any inventory modeling situation, we usually face a choice of selecting various values for EOQ, EOP, or *OP*. A typical inventory policy planning decision for which we might use simulation is whether to adopt a fixed order quantity system (like an EOQ) or to use a variable order

quantity system (like a JIT system). In this situation, we need to establish what fixed EOQ values would be simulated and what criteria (cost minimization or service maximization) would be used to judge the best inventory policy.

2. *Collect data for simulation.* The same means by which we obtained observed frequencies of the probabilistic behavior and cost or profit information for the other inventory models in this chapter can be used for this step. If more than one parameter behaves probabilistically, then separate data on each parameter's distribution are needed. The Monte Carlo method can handle any number of probabilistic parameters.

3. *Convert the probabilistic data into random number sampling distributions.* In this step we convert the observed frequencies into probabilities. Next, the probabilities are added to form a cumulative probability distribution. We then convert the cumulative probability distribution into a series of random numbers. The random numbers are assigned in equal number to their probable occurrence using the cumulative probability numbers. The random numbers allow for the random selection of parameter values that will simulate the actual behavior of the parameter. The parameter values that are being observed may be either integer (as in a discrete distribution) or real numbers (as in a continuous distribution). Regardless of the type of parameter value, they must be expressed in a cumulative probability distribution in order of smallest to largest number.

4. *Determine the number of samplings to be simulated.* In the Monte Carlo simulation method, we select a single parameter from a distribution of parameters. The idea in this step is to determine the best number of samplings of single parameters to represent the actual behavior of the parameter. A number of statistical techniques can be employed to determine the best number of samplings to take.[10] As a rule of thumb, the greater the number of samplings, the more accurate the simulation in representing the probability distribution.

5. *Determine a random-number generator system.* A random number is used to model the random behavior of the probabilistic parameter. To capture the random nature of a parameter we use a series of numbers that are randomly sorted. The assortment of random numbers has a uniform distribution (that is, each random-number digit has an equal probability of being selected). Most software systems have built-in random number generators (that is, a formula that generates random numbers) to allow programmers to obtain random numbers for simulation progams. A random number table like the one in Appendix F at the end of the book can also be used by selecting the digits in any row or column. Any row or column of random numbers in Appendix F may be chosen for the simulation.

---

[10] H. J. Watson and J. H. Blackstone, *Computer Simulation,* 2nd ed. (New York: John Wiley & Sons, 1989), Chapter 17.

QUESTION: Determine the random number sampling distribution for the following observed demand behavior:

Demand (units)	*Observed Frequency*
5	12
6	23
7	34
8	21
9	10

ANSWER: The demand values are set in order from a low of 5 to a high of 9 units. In the following table, we convert the observed frequencies in column (2) into probabilities in column (3). We then add the probabilities together to form the cumulative probability distribution in column (4). Next we want to assign a number of random number digits equal to the probability value for each unit demand level. The random number digits will be assigned as integer values in numerical order, and ranging from 0 to 9, 00 to 99 or 000 to 999, depending on the precision of the probablities. In this example the probabilities are two-digit values so the random number assignment will run from 00 to 99. By starting with double zero, the upper range for each demand level will equal one less than the cumulative probability value. As we can see for the demand level of 5 in column (5) below, the random number of sampling distribution assignment runs from 00 to 11. This interval permits twelve digits of one hundred to represent the demand level of 5 units. Likewise, twenty-three digits of one hundred represent a demand level of 6. These random number digits, presented in column (6), represent the probabilities of the demand levels occurring.

(1) Demand (Units)	*(2) Observed Frequency*	*(3) Probability*	*(4) Cumulative Probability*	*(5) Random Number Sampling Distribution*	*(6) Digits in Sampling Distribution*
5	12	.12	.12	00 to 11	12
6	23	.23	.35	12 to 34	23
7	34	.34	.69	35 to 68	34
8	21	.21	.90	69 to 89	21
9	10	.10	1.00	90 to 99	10
	100	1.00			

6. *Conduct the simulation and generate the desired inventory statistics.* A Monte Carlo simulation involves the following substeps:
   a. Select a random number.
   b. Determine where the random number occurs on the random number sampling distribution.
   c. Record the parameter's behavior from the random number sampling distribution.

d. Compute the inventory simulation statistics based on the parameters.
e. Repeat these substeps until the desired number of samplings have been simulated.

The Monte Carlo simulation method makes a number of assumptions that limit its use. Some of the more important to remember include

1. The probability distributions of variable parameters from past observations must represent the future.
2. The behavior of the variable parameter is random and doesn't follow any known sequence of behavior.
3. The number of randomly sampled values for a parameter will provide an adequate sampling from the existing probability distribution and will reflect the most probable future behavior of the parameter being simulated.
4. The number of replications of simulation runs accurately captures the randomness of all simulated behavior.

QUESTION: A company wants to determine which of two independent demand inventory system policies it should select to minimize its total stockout and carryover costs (costs of carrying units over from a previous period). The demand on the item under consideration varies from 8 units to 12 units daily. The company recorded 100 days of inventory demand transactions, which are expressed in the following table as a frequency distribution:

Demand in Units per Day	*Observed Frequency*
8	10
9	20
10	30
11	25
12	15

The two mutually exclusive inventory policies are as follows:

Fixed order quantity policy The company will order exactly 10 units of the inventory item each day, regardless of demand. This policy is based on the fact that the most frequent daily demand was observed to be 10 units.
Variable order quantity policy The company will order a number of units equal to yesterday's observed demand. This policy allows for adjustments of increases or decreases to the order quantity to reflect changes in observed demand.

If the company will incur a stockout cost of $5 per unit per day for lost sales and a carryover cost of $2 per day, which of the two policies will best minimize costs over a 15-day period?

(continued)

ANSWER: Other inventory models in this chapter could handle the variability observed in demand by computing an expected value like *EDDLT*. Because the problem states that the company is interested in seeing the simulated results of only fifteen days, the Monte Carlo simulation method is more appropriate to use than other long-term expected value methods previously presented in this chapter.

1. *Identify the inventory policies that are to be simulated and the rules used to judge the results of the simulation.* Two policies will be examined: a fixed order quantity policy and a variable order quantity policy. The rule for simulated success will be the policy that generates the least total cost in fifteen days of simulated behavior, where total cost is

   Total cost = Stockout cost + Carryover cost

   Because two policies are to be simulated, there will need to be two separate simulations.
2. *Collect data for simulation.* This information is given in the observed frequency table for inventory demand.
3. *Convert the probabilistic data into random number sampling distributions.*

Demand (units)	*Observed Frequency*	*Probability*	*Cumulative Probability*	*Random Number Sampling Distribution*
8	10	.10	.10	00 to 09
9	20	.20	.30	10 to 29
10	30	.30	.60	30 to 59
11	25	.25	.85	60 to 84
12	15	.15	1.00	85 to 99
	100	1.00		

4. *Determine the number of samplings to be simulated.* The number of samplings is stated in the problem to be fifteen days.
5. *Determine a random number generator system.* We will use the random number table in Appendix F. Specifically, we will use the first fifteen double-digit random numbers in the first column of the table. We will use the same numbers for each of the two simulations.
6. *Conduct the simulation and generate the desired inventory statistics.* To conduct a Monte Carlo simulation, we will start with the fixed order quantity policy situation. In Exhibit 8S-1, the simulated values for the fixed order quantity simulation are presented. The random numbers were taken from Appendix F. As we can see in Exhibit 8S-1, the first random number is 63. Because 63 falls in the random number sampling distribution between 60 and 84, it simulates a daily demand of 11 units. Under the fixed order quantity policy, though, the order quantity will always equal 10 units. The difference between the simulated demand of 11 units and an order quantity of 10 units is a one-unit stockout cost of $5 for day 1. This assumes no carryover from a previous day. Repeating the simulation process again for day 2 results in no stockout or carryover costs. Continuing to repeat the process for the desired fifteen days results in a total cost of $39 (stockout cost of $25 + a carryover cost of $14).

(continued)

EXHIBIT 8S-1 MONTE CARLO SIMULATION RESULTS FOR FIXED ORDER QUANTITY POLICY

Day	*Random Number*	*Simulated Demand (units)*	*Order Quantity (units)*	*Available Inventory* (units)*	*Stockout units*	*Carryover units*	*Stockout costs*	*Carryover costs*
1	63	11	10	10	1	0	$ 5	$ 0
2	51	10	10	10	0	0	0	0
3	23	9	10	10	0	1	0	2
4	19	9	10	11	0	2	0	4
5	84	11	10	12	0	1	0	2
6	98	12	10	11	1	0	5	0
7	27	9	10	10	0	1	0	2
8	46	10	10	11	0	1	0	2
9	37	10	10	11	0	1	0	2
10	72	11	10	11	0	0	0	0
11	65	11	10	10	1	0	5	0
12	59	10	10	10	0	0	0	0
13	81	11	10	10	1	0	5	0
14	45	10	10	10	0	0	0	0
15	72	11	10	10	1	0	5	0
					5	7	$25	$14

* Available Inventory = Order quantity + Carryover (from prior day)

EXHIBIT 8S-2 MONTE CARLO SIMULATION RESULTS FOR VARIABLE ORDER QUANTITY POLICY

Day	*Random Number*	*Simulated Demand (units)*	*Order Quantity (units)*	*Available Inventory* (units)*	*Stockout units*	*Carryover units*	*Stockout costs*	*Carryover costs*
1	63	11	10	10	1	0	$ 5	$ 0
2	51	10	11	11	0	1	0	2
3	23	9	10	11	0	2	0	4
4	19	9	9	11	0	2	0	4
5	84	11	9	11	0	0	0	0
6	98	12	11	11	1	0	5	0
7	27	9	12	12	0	3	0	6
8	46	10	9	12	0	2	0	4
9	37	10	10	12	0	2	0	4
10	72	11	10	12	0	1	0	2
11	65	11	11	12	0	1	0	2
12	59	10	11	12	0	2	0	4
13	81	11	10	12	0	1	0	2
14	45	10	11	12	0	2	0	4
15	72	11	10	12	0	1	0	2
					2	20	$10	$40

* Available Inventory = Order quantity + Carryover (from prior day)

For the variable order quantity policy we must assume an initial order quantity. Because 10 units is the most probable demand quantity, let's assume an initial order quantity of 10 units. As can be seen in Exhibit 8S-2, this assumption results in the same stockout cost as incurred in the fixed order quantity policy for day 1. As we move to day 2, we use the 11-unit demand from day 1 for the order quantity for day 2. Based on the simulated demand in day 2 we incur a carryover cost of one unit. This unit is carried over to the next day and added to the order quantity of 10 units for day 3, bringing available inventory for day 3 up to 11 units. The repeated application of the Monte Carlo method results in a fifteen-day total cost of the variable inventory policy of $50 (stockout cost of $10 + a total carryover cost of $40). Because the cost of $50 for the variable order policy is greater than the $39 fixed order policy, the rule of the simulation requires the selection of the fixed order policy as the cost-minimizing inventory order policy for this company.

9 Scheduling in Manufacturing and Service Operations

CHAPTER OUTLINE

CHAPTER OBJECTIVES

The material in this chapter should prepare you to do the following:

1. Explain why scheduling is a necessary operations management activity.
2. Describe several scheduling tactics for altering demand in service operations.
3. Describe several personnel scheduling approaches.
4. Explain job sequencing using Johnson's rules.
5. Describe lot-sizing rules and how they are used in scheduling.
6. Describe JIT principles and how they are used in scheduling.
7. Explain how to use the critical ratio method to determine if a schedule is on time.
8. Describe optimized production technology and its rules of operation.
9. Explain how input-output control is used to support scheduling efforts.
10. Explain queuing and simulation methods as aids in developing schedules.

Scheduling is a basic operations management activity that deals with the timing of production activity; it is performed in both manufacturing and service operations. As we can see in Table 9-1, **scheduling** focuses on the timed allocation of production resources including human resources, inventory, and facilities. Although the same basic types of resources are scheduled in both manufacturing and service operations, the type of operation does affect scheduling activities. In this chapter, we will discuss scheduling as it relates to job operations (that is, job and job-lot types discussed in Chapter 1), repetitive operations (that is, repetitive and limited-lot types also discussed in Chapter 1), and service operations. In the next chapter, we will focus on project scheduling.

Scheduling can be either a medium-range or a short-range planning activity that supports both strategic and tactical decision making in an organization. However, it is considered chiefly as an operational level production planning activity. As presented in Figure 9-1, operations management scheduling begins with aggregate planning after the goals of the strategic production plan are stated (discussed in Chapter 5). The aggregate production plan provides a medium-range aggregate resource utilization schedule that must be narrowed to short-range time horizons. Capacity planning examines the ability of the organization to service the demand requirements as the time horizons are narrowed and the detailed production requirements are revealed in the process of disaggregation to the master production schedule (MPS). The detailed demand requirements defined in the MPS or the production requirements defined by the material requirements planning (MRP) explosion are still further narrowed or disaggregated to a short-range planning horizon of a day, hour, or single customer job order. Once the detail and time-related production requirements are defined in the MPS they must be scheduled for completion at the shop floor level of production activity. The focus of this chapter is on this short-range planning called scheduling.

Related to scheduling is production activity control (listed in Figure 9-1). **Production activity control** involves any system or methods used to maintain and communicate the status of production activity on the shop floor. Keeping track of unit production or customer jobs during work-in-process (WIP) requires the use of methods that affect and alter scheduling requirements. In this chapter, we examine scheduling methods used in input-output control and operation sequencing.

• • •

WHY SCHEDULING IS NECESSARY

Scheduling operationalizes tactical plans by defining at the shop-floor level of production activity exactly what each worker has to do to complete the operations management transformation process. Scheduling provides the detailed instructions necessary to convert the production objectives of the MPS into day-to-day directives for workers who must perform different tasks.

Scheduling is a necessary operations management activity that helps the organization minimize inefficiency and maximize customer service. In scheduling, an organization

TABLE 9-1 EXAMPLES OF SCHEDULES IN MANUFACTURING AND SERVICE ORGANIZATIONS

Type of Organization	*Type of Schedule*
Automobile—manufacturing	Hourly schedule of robotic equipment Hourly work schedule for employees Inventory delivery schedule for vendor Schedule of daily production of finished automobiles
Paper—manufacturing	Hourly schedule of cutting machines Hourly work schedule of employees Daily production in board feet
University—service	Hourly schedule of classrooms Faculty office hours schedule for student advising Research assistant assignments Computer room daily schedule of use by students
Newspaper—service	Daily deadline schedule for reporters' news inserts for paper Advertising deadline schedules for daily papers Daily printing deadlines for delivery to customers

S

S

allocates its production capacity to meet timely customer demand requirements. If too much capacity is scheduled, idle workers and idle facilities will result in costly waste of productive resources. If too little capacity is scheduled, jobs will not be completed on time causing poor service to customers and possibly a loss of business to the organization. An organization that schedules the exact amount of capacity at the right time to meet customer demand will optimize its resources.

Scheduling is also a tactical means of achieving a competitive advantage. Some organizations have built flexibility into their scheduling systems to accommodate rapid changes in customer demand. By designing operations management production scheduling systems to be highly flexible, companies are better able to shift production activity to more profitable or sales-generating new markets as external demand shifts.

BASICS OF SCHEDULING

Schedules should be easy to use, easy to understand, easy to carry out, and flexible enough to accommodate necessary demand requirement changes. The primary objectives of short-range scheduling in any type of production operation include

1. Minimizing waste and inefficiency of human, technology, and system resources
2. Maximizing customer service

These objectives are universal to any type of operation.

FIGURE 9-1 RELATIONSHIP OF PRODUCTION PLANNING AND SCHEDULING

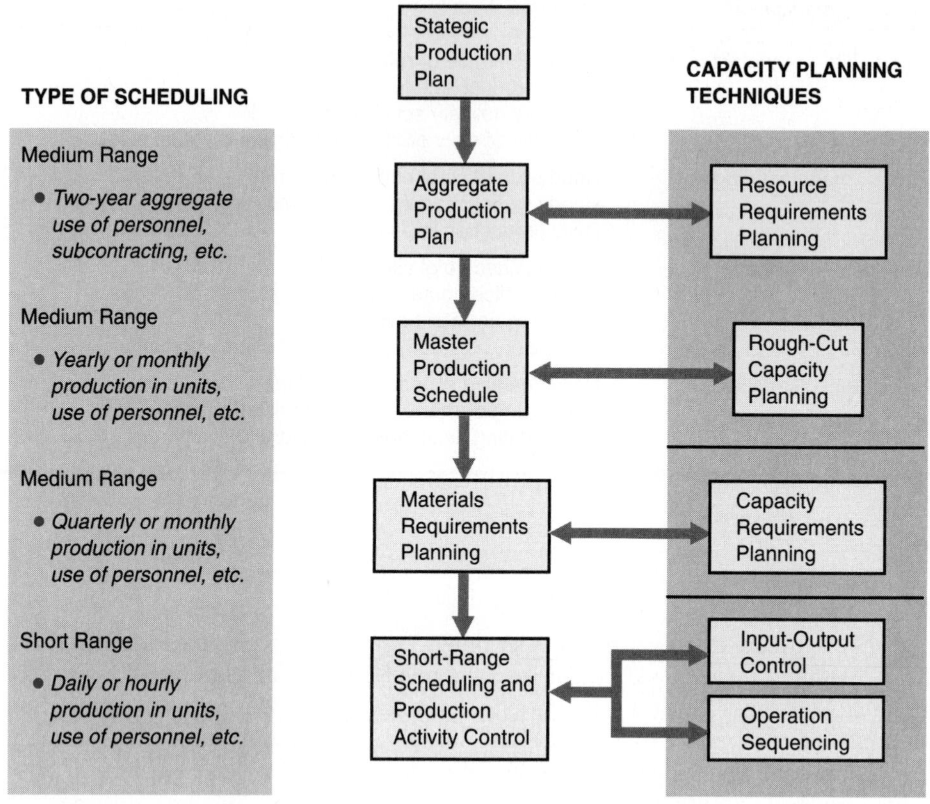

Source: Reprinted with permission, American Production and Inventory Control Society (APICS), 1987 CPIM Study Guide.

Scheduling Methods

Many different methods are used to develop a schedule in a job operation. The selection of method depends on the volume of orders and the nature of the operation. Most of the scheduling methods can be categorized as being forward scheduling, backward scheduling, or some combination of both. In **forward scheduling,** actual production activities begin when a job order is received. Materials and production capacity are immediately allocated to satisfy the job order on its arrival. Forward scheduling is used in fabrication operations in which custom products are the norm and product demand is unknown until announced by the customer. Scheduling operating rooms, doctors, nurses, and equipment for surgery in hospitals is one example of forward scheduling in a service operation. In **backward scheduling,** production activities are scheduled by their due dates; that is, starting in reverse order with the due dates for job orders, production activity is scheduled backward from the finished product to the procurement of materials. Backward scheduling is ideal for manufacturing organizations that use MRP systems and in service operations in which demand for services is known ahead of time. When a customer special orders an automobile from a manufacturer or a motion picture service organization produces a film, backward scheduling is necessary to complete these products.

Scheduling Activities

Regardless of the method, scheduling requires the use of routing information, job loading, job sequencing, and dispatching. To help management prepare a schedule, routing sheets or routing files must exist on each product. **Routing sheets** (hard copy) or **routing files** (electronic copy for computer-based operations) are a set of detailed information that explains how a product is to be produced in manufacturing or prepared in service operations. Routing information can include a list of operations that must be performed by workstation or employee, the sequence of operations necessary to complete a product, information on tooling, operator skill requirements, standard setup times for machines and runs, and even testing requirements. Routing is based on a product's production requirements and largely dictated by plant layout considerations.

Once the jobs are routed, management must load them into the operation. **Loading** is the scheduling process by which the jobs are assigned to individual workcenters or workstations. The loading process can be based on capacity restrictions—that is, managers simply load jobs into a workcenter up to its standard capacity. In operations in which capacity limitations are not critical, loading is based on assigning jobs to minimize costs by reducing idle time, inventory, and so on. Loading also involves the **sequencing** of jobs (that is, an initial ordering of jobs to achieve a specific objective for the production facility as a whole). We will be discussing job sequencing methods as a means of operation sequencing later in this chapter.

Closely related to job sequencing is the dispatching of job orders. **Dispatching** is the final act of releasing job orders to workers for completion. A job order is dispatched in accordance with a planned sequence, or the act of dispatching determines a job's sequence in the production process. In both manufacturing and service operations, **dispatching rules** or **priority rules** are used to schedule production activity. Common dispatching or priority rules include the following:

1. *First-come, first-served* Jobs arriving at a workstation or service center are processed as soon as they arrive in the order of their arrival. This rule is used in operations in which fairness may be a factor in customer service, such as waiting for service in a post office or for an amusement park ride.
2. *Earliest due date* The job arriving at a workstation or service center with the earliest due date is dispatched first, the next earliest second, and so on. This rule is used in job-type operations in which substantial backlogs can be justified by the customer service being provided, such as in military weapon component manufacturing, where failure to meet a due date will keep an entire weapon system from being completed.

3. *Longest processing time* The job arriving at a workstation or service center that requires the longest amount of processing time is dispatched first, the job requiring second longest amount of time second, and so on. This rule is based on the logic that jobs that take longer will be of more value to the organization and therefore should be completed first to maximize sales, profit, and service to important customers. A tool manufacturer, for example, can make more profit by processing a $1,000 tool order than a single tool order from a customer.
4. *Shortest processing time* The job arriving at a workstation or service center requiring the least amount of time is dispatched first, the job requiring the next larger amount of time second, and so on. This rule is based on the concept that maximizing the flow of completed jobs will reduce costs (such as those associated with inventory and idle capacity) and thereby maximize profits. For companies whose profit is chiefly in the handling charges they place on orders, the processing of a greater number of orders will maximize profit.

Dispatching operationalizes all production schedules including the master production schedule (MPS). It is the final step in planning the production activity. Once job orders are dispatched, management must then control the production activity to see that the schedule is implemented successfully and is achieving MPS objectives. To help control production activity once it is scheduled, a variety of capacity management techniques exist. We examine two of these capacity management techniques—input/output control and a sequencing control method called the critical ratio method—later in the chapter.

SCHEDULING BY TYPE OF OPERATION

Scheduling in manufacturing operations differs in many ways from scheduling in service operations. The greater material requirements necessary to complete manufactured products as well as product complexity are sources of some of these differences. For example, the substantial material requirements of a product such as an automobile necessitates a great degree of inventory scheduling effort to efficiently bring together vendors' deliveries and workers' use of material on the assembly line in a way to minimize waste and idle time. The greater complexity of multiple production stages required in manufactured products such as VCRs and television sets necessitates considerable scheduling effort to permit the efficient movement of the product through a production operation. On the other hand, demand requirements in service operations for immediate delivery of products focuses scheduling effort toward planning demand requirements rather than inventory requirements. A doctor's care of an ill person, for example, requires that a substantial amount of health care capacity (such as x-ray equipment and specialists) be available to meet the variety of possible demand requirements. Scheduling demand requirements of patients and medical personnel as a means to accomplish production effort becomes the critical factor in delivering a service product on time. Because of these differences the objectives and methodology of scheduling varies by type of operation.

Job Operations

Job operations (also called job shop, intermittent, or job-lot) are characterized by low-volume and sometimes custom products or services. The manufacture of products or delivery of services is usually made-to-order and scheduled on an individual or limited-lot basis. The custom and low-volume nature of job orders results in considerable variation in materials used, order processing, WIP, capacity planning, and setup time requirements. Much of management's tactical objectives in scheduling focus on efficiently eliminating variation in production factors. Scheduling methods used in these types of operations include Gantt charts, job sequencing methods, critical ratio, and input-output control methods. We discuss all of these methods in the next section of this chapter.

Repetitive Operations

Repetitive operations (also called continuous process) are characterized by the high-volume, mass production of a homogeneous product or delivery of service. The high volume and continuous nature of repetitive operations results in the need to closely control the flow of materials and application of labor resources to maximize flow of inventory and minimize idleness of workers. Much of management's scheduling efforts focus on achieving objectives of synchronizing customer demand with production activity, as well as avoiding queuing problems in the flow of materials that cause worker idleness (we discuss queuing problems later in this chapter). To aid managers in tactically achieving these objectives, scheduling methods similar to those of job operations can be used. In addition to discussing these methods we will also examine JIT scheduling principles, simulation methods, and queuing analysis, which are particularly applicable to repetitive operations.

Service Operations

In many service operations, production resources are constrained by human, technology, or system resources limitations. A typical doctor's office, for example, can only accommodate a fixed number of patients calling at one time. To deal with these limitations, tactical scheduling of demand may be a necessity. These scheduling tactics include appointment systems, reservation systems, and strategic product pricing.

APPOINTMENT SYSTEMS **Appointment systems** are commonly used to schedule an organization's resources, usually to meet an individual's demand requirements. Medical doctors and dentists providing routine service to patients, as well as counselors in schools S and the service department of automobile dealers, use appointment systems to schedule the demand on their services. Appointment systems are intended to control or alter the timing of customer arrivals (that is, customer demand). The purpose of an appointment system is to maximize the utilization of the limited time a service facility (or person) can be used and minimize the time a customer spends waiting at the scheduled appointment time. An appointment system does not guarantee that a customer will not have to wait. Indeed, an appointment system can be fully booked for months in advance.

Appointment systems are ideal in nonemergency service situations; in periods of emergency, however, the appointment system usually breaks down. For example, a doctor who is called away from an office to deal with an emergency will undoubtedly fail to meet scheduled appointments because of the emergency. For organizations that use an appointment system and face an occasional emergency, slack time or unscheduled time is usually built into the appointment schedule. Service operation slack time is the equivalent of buffer or safety stock in a manufacturing operation. If the slack time is not used in emergency situations, it can be used for rest or maintenance activities.

A schedule that is generated by an appointment system is usually just a list of the names of customers requiring service. Appointment systems vary in complexity from a Rolodex card system on a manager's desk to a computerized information system that defines a manager's activities for the day.

RESERVATION SYSTEMS Whereas appointment systems tend to be used to schedule an organization's resources to meet an individual's demand requirements, **reservation systems** are concerned with scheduling facilities and multiple resources together to meet customer demand requirements. For example, a hotel represents the multiple resources (the room, the beds, the television set, and so on) that must be scheduled when a person reserves a room in the hotel. In airline reservation systems, we do not make an appointment with the captain of the airplane; we make a reservation to use the services provided by the airline. These services, each requiring scheduling, include the other flight crew staff members, the airplane and the maintenance crews to keep it operational, the airline's administration to ensure that the flight services are acceptable, and the other multitudes of people and facilities that provide the airline service product.

A reservation system works like an appointment system in that customer demand is altered to improve the efficiency of providing the resources to meet that demand. Reservation systems also allow businesses to discontinue unprofitable business operations. For example, many travel tours have disclaimers in their contractual agreements that permit them to be cancelled if an insufficient number of customers sign up for the tour. Indeed, some businesses such as restaurants, where customer demand exceeds the business's ability or desire to provide the service, use a "reservations only" system to schedule their offerings. This selective approach minimizes floor space congestion and improves the general atmosphere in restaurant settings.

STRATEGIC PRODUCT PRICING Scheduling does not only occur day to day. Scheduling is sometimes necessary for an organization to meet seasonal shifts in the market demand. For example, city governments must plan snow removal for winter months.

An approach to smoothing out demand requirements on service facilities is **strategic product pricing.** Normally, a business wants to satisfy all of the demand for its services. But if the cost to satisfy short-term demand surges is greater than the profits received from the increased business, it makes little economic sense to provide the service. When a known increase in demand is expected, an organization might try to decrease its share of that increase by developing a pricing strategy that will reduce, but not eliminate, product demand.

S

For example, most electric companies must maintain a substantial investment in electricity-generating facilities. Most of these companies can satisfy most of their customers' yearly electricity needs. During the hotter months of the year, demand for electricity, because of air conditioners, can exceed an electric company's ability to generate it. Short-term shortages of electricity are usually made up by purchasing, at great expense, electric power from other utility companies. In the long run the electric companies must build additional power facilities. Unfortunately, in the winter months when demand for power is low, these additional electricity-generating facilities may be underutilized and inefficient to operate. Many U.S. electric companies therefore adopt a summer pricing strategy (a peak demand pricing system) that increases the cost of electricity to consumers, based on an increasing rate. That is, the more electric power a customer uses, the greater the price rate. The increase in the cost of electricity helps encourage customers to conserve the more expensive externally purchased electricity and thus reduces the peak demand of electricity during the months of the year that the demand might exceed existing capacity. Many telephone companies use a reduced pricing strategy to increase business during nonbusiness hours (after 5:00 PM and before 8:00 AM) to help smooth demand.

By smoothing customer demand, operational efficiency can be achieved by better utilizing equipment. Businesses that experience regular demand can more accurately judge their equipment needs and run the equipment more efficiently at a full capacity level. More importantly, in labor-intensive service organizations, regular and predictable demand permits easier scheduling and more consistent labor use and work assignments, which provides job security and can lead to improved employee morale.

Labor-intensive Operations

Scheduling personnel in labor-intensive operations is as difficult as scheduling production activity. The 1990s offer a number of challenges for planners because of the diversity of approaches currently used in scheduling personnel. So much scheduling diversity exists that managers may find it advantageous to ask employees' help in scheduling their own work times based on personal preferences. These personnel-aided scheduling approaches include those listed at the top of page 432.[1]

[1] J. Bailey and J. Field, "Personnel Scheduling with Flexshift Models," *Journal of Operations Management,* 5, No. 3 (1985), 327–338.

1. *Flextime* Employees are allowed some freedom to choose their start times and work hours as long as they accumulate forty hours per week.
2. *Flextour* Employees are allowed some freedom to choose their start times but must work 5 eight-hour days.
3. *Compressed workweek* Employees work 4 ten-hour days per week.
4. *Staggered times* Employees are assigned or select start times and work hours from a list of available shifts.
5. *Job splitting* Two employees share a job and work fewer than thirty hours per week.
6. *Part time* Employees work twenty hours or fewer per week.

Employers are increasingly using part-time workers to fill in schedules. For service organizations that have erratic demand during the day (such as a fast-food restaurant around lunch time) or during a season (for example, a department store during the Christmas season), scheduling part-time help is essential for the business's success. Many service organizations are now using what is called **permanent part-time employees,** or employees who work less than a forty-hour week but work during the whole year. In many states, such as Nebraska, the public primary and secondary school systems hire permanent part-time teachers because of the many advantages of using part-time employees. The John Deere Company (Dallas Parts Division) uses students as permanent part-time employees. Advantages of using part-time labor include the following:

1. The organization saves money because part-time employees do not usually receive retirement and fringe benefits.
2. Part-time workers may not experience job monotony (and may therefore be more productive) because they do not spend as much time on the job as full-time employees.
3. The organization saves money on wages and salaries because part-time employees usually start at the bottom of the wage scale and are not always covered by union or company merit increases.
4. Part-time employees tend to be more willing to take on undesirable or less-challenging jobs that full-time workers try to avoid or would not perform efficiently.

Part-time work also has advantages for workers. A worker can keep his or her regular job and also take a part-time job to

1. Gain job education, information, or new job skills
2. Earn extra money to increase standard of living
3. Shop around for a new job
4. Break into another career

SCHEDULING METHODS

In this section we will discuss a variety of principles, technologies, rule-based techniques, and analytical methods used in scheduling production activity. Scheduling methods include Gantt charts, job sequencing rules, lot-sizing rules, JIT scheduling principles, queuing analysis, simulation analysis, critical ratio method, optimized production technology, input-output control, and expert systems.

Gantt Charts

During the scientific period of operations management history, circa 1913, a U.S. scheduling expert developed a graphic approach to display production activity. Named after its originator, Henry L. Gantt, **Gantt charts** are simple bar graphs that can be used to schedule any type of operation.

Two basic types of Gantt charts are work-load charts and scheduling charts. A **workload chart** is usually used to depict workload levels for equipment, workstations, or departments. In these charts, the vertical axis usually lists different facilities used to manufacture or process job orders. The horizontal axis usually represents time. A Gantt workload chart is presented in Figure 9-2. As we can see, a series of machines (production equipment) is listed on the vertical axis and the jobs to which they need to be assigned are listed in rows.

FIGURE 9-2 GANTT CHART OF MACHINE WORK ALLOCATION

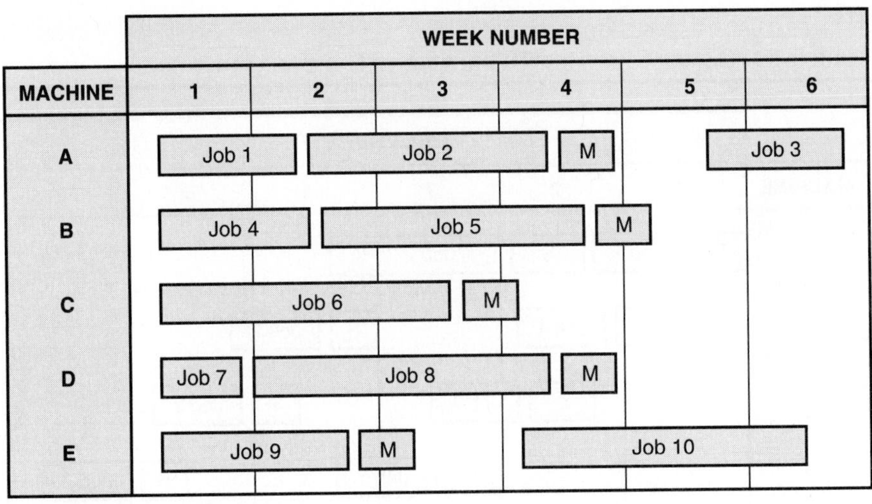

The chart clearly depicts the timing requirements for each job. The time estimates used in Gantt charts are usually obtained from standard time estimates based on the job. (We will discuss time-study estimation methods in Chapter 14). We can also see in Figure 9-2 how routine maintenance can be expected and planned by using this type of scheduling chart. This visual allocation of jobs provides managers with a quick and easy way of determining the total workload assigned to each machine. The space between jobs is idle time.

Gantt charts can dynamically adapt to scheduling requirement changes as they occur in the operations management system. For example, in Figure 9-2, we can see that most of the machines' assignable time in the first two weeks is completely scheduled. After the second week, machines are idle for periods of time. These idle periods can be filled with other unplanned jobs while managers and workers plan their schedules around the known job requirements.

A **Gantt scheduling chart** is used to track the progress of jobs as they pass through various departments in an organization. The vertical axis of these charts usually lists the departments in the sequence that jobs generally flow through them. The horizontal axis represents time. A Gantt scheduling chart is presented in Figure 9-3. As we can see, a job cannot be started in the next department until it is finished in the previous department. The chart makes it quite easy to see the time required for and the current status of each job.

We can also see in Figure 9-3 that departments B, C, and D have some periods of time between jobs that are not currently scheduled for work. These periods of idleness exist in most job operations. Managers should always try to minimize these unassigned periods to make the best use of existing capacity and improve efficiency in general. One way to minimize these departmental idle periods is by improving the sequencing of the jobs through the departments.

FIGURE 9-3 GANTT CHART OF DEPARTMENT JOB SCHEDULING

	WEEK NUMBER					
MACHINE	1	2	3	4	5	6
A	S, Job 1	S	Job 2			
B	S	Job 1		S, Job 2		
C		S	Job 1	S	Job 2	
D			S, Job 1		S	Job 2

S = Setup time for each department's job

Job Sequencing Rules

In all types of operations, the sequencing of jobs is a critical scheduling activity. **Operation sequencing** is a scheduling activity that is necessary to minimize the total time it takes to process a batch of job orders, improve the efficiency of an operation, and minimize the processing costs of a fixed number of jobs over a given period of time. When jobs go through only a single stage of production, they are scheduled one after another. If jobs go through two or more stages of production (for example, two or more departments), we run the risk of idle time occurring in some of the later stages or departments, as shown in Figure 9-3.

Johnson's job sequencing rules can be used when we have a set of known jobs (and timing requirements for each job) that must each go through a two-stage production process.[2] Scheduling beyond two stages can be accomplished by using other types of sequencing rules or heuristic procedures.[3]

In sequencing jobs we determine the order in which they will enter the production system. Once a job enters the first stage of the production process it can only go on to the second stage when the second stage is free to accept it. In scheduling orders we therefore structure only a single sequence of jobs to enter the first stage of production. Our objective in job sequencing is to minimize idle time; in doing so, we minimize the total time it takes to process a set of jobs. The total time to process a set of jobs represents the time from when the first job enters the first stage of the system for processing to the time when the last job leaves the second stage of the system. We call this time period **job flow time** or **makespan.**

The following job sequencing steps incorporate sequencing rules:

1. *Determine the number of jobs to be sequenced in a schedule and their respective time requirements in both stages of production.* The time requirements, including setup time if necessary, for service or manufacturing jobs must be determinable or else we cannot use this or any other scheduling procedure. In this first step a job sequence framework is prepared called the "unfilled" sequence of jobs. This framework is presented in Figure 9-4.

2. *Choose the job with the shortest time estimate in either stage of production.* For example, for three jobs there are a total of six time estimates (that is, 3 jobs × 2 stages of production) to choose from. The job with the shortest stage is selected, whether that stage is the first or the second.

---

[2] S. M. Johnson, "Optimal Two- and Three-stage Production Schedules with Setup Times Included," *Naval Research Logistics Quarterly,* 1 (March 1954), 61–68.

[3] See R. S. Russell and B. T. Taylor, "An Evaluation of Sequencing Rules for an Assembly Shop," *Decision Sciences,* 16, No. 2 (Spring 1985), 196–212; S. S. Panwalker and W. A. Iskandar, "A Survey of Scheduling Rules," *Operations Research,* 25, No. 1 (January–February 1977), 45–61; and E. M. Dar-El and R. A. Wysk, "Job Shop Scheduling—A Systematic Approach," *Journal of Manufacturing Systems,* 1, No. 1 (1962), 77–88.

FIGURE 9-4 FRAMEWORK FOR "UNFILLED" JOB SEQUENCE

Job to Enter First Stage of Production	First Job	Second Job	. . .	*n*th Job
Job Number or Letter	☐	☐	. . .	☐

3. *Schedule the job selected in step 2 according to the following rules:*
   a. If the shortest time is in the first stage, assign the job as early as possible in the unfilled job sequence.
   b. If the shortest time is in the second stage, assign the job as late as possible in the unfilled job sequence.
   c. If the shortest time is tied in two separate stages, assign the job with the shortest time in the first stage as early as possible in the unfilled job sequence, and assign the job with the shortest time in the second stage as late as possible in the unfilled job sequence.
   d. If the shortest time is tied in the same stage, the assignment is arbitrary.
4. *Delete the job assigned in step 3 and repeat step 2 until all of the jobs are sequenced.*

We will illustrate the use of this procedure through an example. Suppose that we must assign the following five jobs:

TIME REQUIRED FOR PRODUCTION PER STAGE

Job	*Stage 1 (hours)*	*Stage 2 (hours)*
A	4.00	2.50
B	3.00	2.00
C	2.00	3.50
D	1.50	1.50
E	0.50	4.00

Each job must pass through both stages of production to be completed. The time includes setup time and production time. How should we schedule these jobs to minimize job flow time?

We could use a simple first-come, first-served rule for processing orders. If we use this rule we will have a job sequence of A, B, C, D, and E. In Figure 9-5 we can see that this sequence results in a total job flow time of eighteen hours. The first-come, first-served rule does not, however, seek to minimize job flow time.

Let's apply the job sequencing procedure and see if it improves the eighteen-hour job flow time. Step 1 is given in the problem information. In step 2, we select the smallest time value from the ten given in the problem. The smallest time value is 0.50 in stage 1 for job E. Because the smallest value occurs in the first stage of production, this job should be assigned to the earliest slot of the unfilled portion of the job sequence

FIGURE 9-5 SCHEDULING PROBLEM SOLUTION USING FIRST-COME, FIRST-SERVED RULE

Time (in Hours)

Production Stage	1	2	3	4	5	6	7	8	9	10	11	12	13	14	15	16	17	18
1	A				B			C		D	E							
2					A			B		C			D		E			

Start Finish

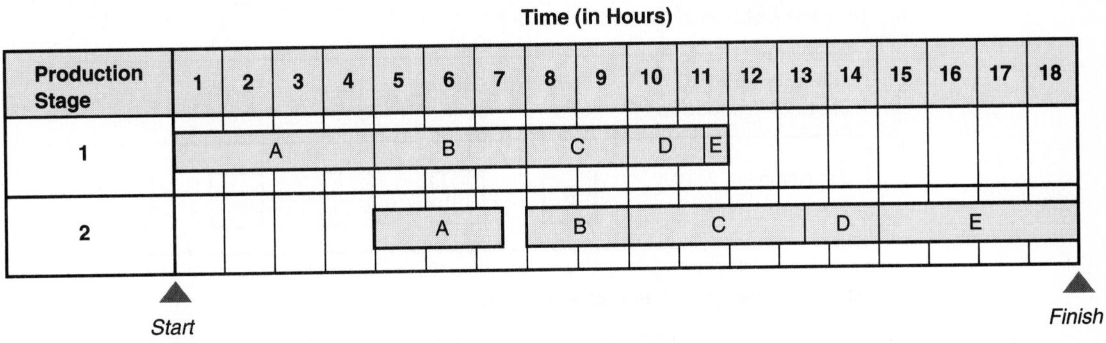

(see step 3(a) in the sequencing procedure). Consistent with step 4, we delete this job and its times from further consideration and repeat step 2.

The step-by-step sequencing for this sample problem is presented in Figure 9-6. The resulting job sequence is presented in Figure 9-7. As we can see in Figure 9-7, the total flow time for all of the jobs is only fourteen hours. The sequencing procedure improved the job schedule by reducing the job flow time by four hours (18 − 14) from the first-come, first-served rule–generated job sequence. Johnson's sequencing rules do not always generate an optimal assignment, but they do provide a systematic sequencing procedure that improves scheduling more than random chance assignments or first-come, first-served systems do.

Johnson's sequencing rules can also be applied to service industry scheduling in two-stage operations in which the job activities can be estimated. A two-stage automobile repair service job might consist of a first stage of performing the repair work and a second stage of testing the repaired automotive system to see that it has been repaired correctly. For example, a car tune-up (the first stage of production) may require an hour for repair or service time, and a test drive by the service manager (the second stage of production) may take 20 minutes. A particular automotive repair shop may have dozens of different types of two-stage jobs to complete (and schedule) for a given day (for example, brake repair, transmission work). Time estimates for many service industry jobs, such as automotive repair jobs, are determined by company or industry standards and are well established for application with the type of job sequencing rules discussed in this section.

Lot-Sizing Rules

Computer-based scheduling systems and all batch or lot production operations require rules to define the size of a production run. Lot-sizing rules are simple heuristics that are usually applied to ordering inventory items. Because such inventory orders trigger

FIGURE 9-6 JOB SEQUENCING STEPS USING JOHNSON'S RULES

(A) FIRST ASSIGNMENT BASED ON STEP 3-A

Job to Enter First Stage of Production	First Job	Second Job	Third Job	Fourth Job	Fifth Job
Job Number or Letter	E				

(B) SECOND ASSIGNMENT BASED ON STEP 3-D

Job to Enter First Stage of Production	First Job	Second Job	Third Job	Fourth Job	Fifth Job
Job Number or Letter	E	D			

(C) THIRD AND FOURTH ASSIGNMENTS BASED ON STEP 3-C

Job to Enter First Stage of Production	First Job	Second Job	Third Job	Fourth Job	Fifth Job
Job Number or Letter	E	D	C		B

(D) FIFTH ASSIGNMENT BASED ON STEP 3-B

Job to Enter First Stage of Production	First Job	Second Job	Third Job	Fourth Job	Fifth Job
Job Number or Letter	E	D	C	A	B

planned order releases in MRP systems, they determine scheduling of production activity. We can categorize these rules as either static or dynamic.

Static lot-sizing rules are used to schedule production (or order inventory) of a fixed quantity. The fixed order quantity (FOQ) rule is an example of a static lot-sizing rule. Under the FOQ rule, production scheduling might be dictated by the upper capacity of a piece of equipment or some minimized cost (e.g., carrying costs and production setup costs). One method that can be used to determine the cost-minimized

FIGURE 9-7 SCHEDULING PROBLEM SOLUTION USING JOHNSON'S SEQUENCING RULES

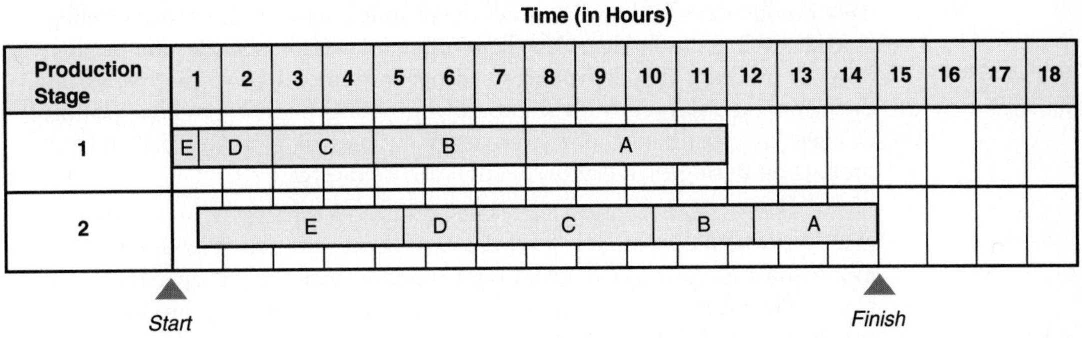

Time (in Hours)

Production Stage | 1 | 2 | 3 | 4 | 5 | 6 | 7 | 8 | 9 | 10 | 11 | 12 | 13 | 14 | 15 | 16 | 17 | 18

1: E D C B A

2: E D C B A

Start

Finish

FOQ is the economic lot-size (ELS) or economic manufacturing quantity (EMQ) model that we discussed in Chapter 8. It should be noted that the dynamic nature of cost and demand requirements organizations face in the 1990s requires a continuous process of reviewing static lot-sizes. For this reason, most organizations today use dynamic lot-sizing rules.

Dynamic lot-sizing rules are used to allow the amount of inventory scheduled (or ordered) to vary from production run to production run. The periodic order quantity (POQ) rule is an example of a dynamic lot-sizing rule. Under the POQ rule, order scheduling in an MRP environment would be equal to gross requirements plus any ending inventory or safety stock minus the projected on-hand inventory. For a job operation in which a few custom products are produced, a more common lot-sizing rule is lot-for-lot (L4L). The L4L rule sets lot-size production equal to lot-size demand requirements. Under the L4L rule more frequent and smaller lot-sizes are scheduled to permit costly ending inventory or safety stock to be eliminated.

Just-in-Time Principles

In a JIT operation customer demand determines the master production schedule (MPS). A JIT operation simply must be able to shift its production rate weekly or daily to match the shifting demand of the operation's customers. Production planners must design and equip their operations to be able to shift production rates within those stated boundaries so that the waste of labor, materials, and equipment is minimized. A JIT operation not only must be able to shift production rates, but it also must be able to shift production activity from one model of a product to another model quickly with a minimum of setup costs.

To help JIT managers accomplish production scheduling, a number of principles have been developed, as listed on pages 440 and 441.[4]

[4] M. J. Schniederjans, *Topics in Just-in-Time Management* (Boston: Allyn and Bacon, 1993), Ch. 3.

1. *Establish uniform daily production scheduling.* Uniform daily production scheduling allows little or no variation in production quantities between days. Uniform daily production scheduling requires the planning activity called load leveling. A load-leveling production plan allows unitary levels (i.e., single-unit production of a product) of each product to change from month to month but remain the same each day during the monthly planning period. Product quantity changes are permitted monthly to meet changes in customer demand but production during each day of the month is held level.
2. *Seek production scheduling flexibility.* The production capacity by which the demand is to be met is set at a level that will permit needed flexibility to meet minor shifts in customer demand on a monthly basis. A JIT operation must have sufficient flexibility to make monthly shifts in scheduled production to match the actual shifts in market demand.
3. *Establish a synchronized pull system.* A pull system operates only in a production environment where known customer orders drive the production effort. The schedule of production is pulled by, and hopefully synchronized to, the actual customer demand. The customer's placing an order acts to pull the inventory through and out of the production operation. Under this JIT principle an operation seeks a scheduling system that will synchronize production activity to the demand pulled through the operation by known customer orders. One of the most common pull system scheduling methods used to support a JIT operation is a kanban card system (presented in Chapter 6). Managers use kanban cards to control production scheduling and achieve a synchronized system.
4. *Improve worker flexibility.* A JIT operation needs highly qualified, multiskilled workers. The more highly qualified and skilled the workers are, the more flexible the organization is to handle any type of job. Two tactics to ensure a highly qualified and multiskilled work force are cross-training employees and using part-time workers who bring with them desired skills.
5. *Schedule ever smaller production lot-sizes and seek reduced setup costs.* The JIT principle of cutting inventory ordering lot-sizes and increasing the frequency of orders can create major production scheduling problems. As smaller orders of inventory are brought into a JIT operation, they force smaller but more frequent production runs to use the incoming inventory. How can setup costs be reduced in a JIT operation? Several tactics can be used, and all focus on eliminating waste. The so-called five S's of JIT—proper arrangement (the Japanese term *seiri*), orderliness (*seiton*), cleanliness (*seiso*), cleanup (*seiketsu*), and discipline (*shitsuke*)—can all help reduce setup times at workcenters.[5] Setup time can be reduced by having the right tool to do a job easily obtainable. If

[5] H. Hirano, *JIT Factory Revolution: A Pictorial Guide to Factory Design of the Future* (Cambridge, Mass.: Productivity Press, 1989), Chapter 2.

a workcenter is clean and the tools are properly arranged, they can be efficiently called into action when required.

6. *Allow workers to determine production flow and schedule.* Each workcenter along a production cell or assembly line should be designed to permit the worker to decide the flow of production. The workers should decide if they have completed their work assignment before the item is sent to the next workcenter. In turn, workers are in a better position to decide on what the production schedule should be. Many JIT operations design their production lines to stop work-in-process items at workcenters until the worker approves sending it along. When the workers believe that they have successfully completed the work assignment, a worker activates a brake release on the item to permit it to continue to the next workcenter. How can an organization achieve its MPS goals by allowing workers to determine production flow and schedule? The answer is by using production quotas as short-term production goals. Workcenter personnel are asked to establish reasonable daily unit production quotas as a means of achieving management MPS-set goals for the entire operation. But by letting workers control production flow, managers can better observe where production line work load imbalances or production problems exist that may affect the production schedule. Once identified, managers and workers can together solve the problems and improve the product flow. This production scheduling and problem-solving effort results in many of the benefits of the productivity cycling process discussed in Chapter 1.

QUESTION: How can JIT benefit scheduling and improve product quality?

ANSWER: In 1987, Texas Instruments' Antenna Department was challenged to manufacture a low-cost, defect-free, highly reliable spiral antenna.[6] It chose to use a JIT system that involved a fairly uniform daily scheduling system. It wanted to establish a link between demand requirements and daily production (that is, a demand-pull, synchronized system). To support this system, it improved flexibility by cross-training workers. It also reduced lot-sizes to reveal problem areas and worked with suppliers to resolve supply problems. The move to a JIT scheduling system forced workers to change the way they performed their jobs and helped identify quality control problems (such as excessive scrap from a 20 percent defect rate). To make the scheduling system work, all types of problems, including quality problems, had to be identified and solved. In just two years, this JIT program was credited with reducing cost per unit by 27 percent, reducing lead time to produce the product by 58 percent, and reducing defects per unit by 90 percent.

Q

[6] S. Ellis and B. Conlon, "JIT Points the Way to Gains in Quality, Cost, and Lead Time," *APICS—The Performance Advantage*, 2, No. 8 (August 1992), 16–19.

These six JIT production scheduling principles are in no way a complete set. They provide only a brief introduction to the basics of JIT production management. We hope that they illustrate the simplicity and beneficial logic of JIT production scheduling.

Queuing Analysis

Queuing analysis is the study of waiting lines and queuing systems. A queuing system consists of a **calling population** of people or equipment requiring some type of service and a **service facility** to provide the service that the calling population is seeking. If the arrival rate is greater than the service facility rate, a **queue** will result. Eventually the calling population is served and leaves the service facility. If the population service rate of the service facility is always greater than or equal to the rate at which the calling population is arriving at the service facility, usually no queue will form. A queuing system is presented in Figure 9-8.

QUESTION: How can a queue form if the service facility processing rate is greater than or equal to the calling population using the service?

ANSWER: Service rates are usually expressed as averages that possess some uncertainty. This uncertainty can be substantial in human resource–intensive service operations because of the natural variability of workers' performance. Because of the uncertainty in service facilities, the actual service time can occasionally fall below the requirements of the calling population, thus causing a queue to temporarily form.

S Many service operations are characterized by customers waiting in lines or queues to be served. People waiting at bank teller stations, trucks waiting in line to be washed at truck-washing facilities, and cars backed up in a fast-food drive-through are all examples of queues. Manufacturing organizations can also have queues. For example, automated materials handling equipment units (such as the AVGs discussed in Chap-

FIGURE 9-8 A QUEUING SYSTEM

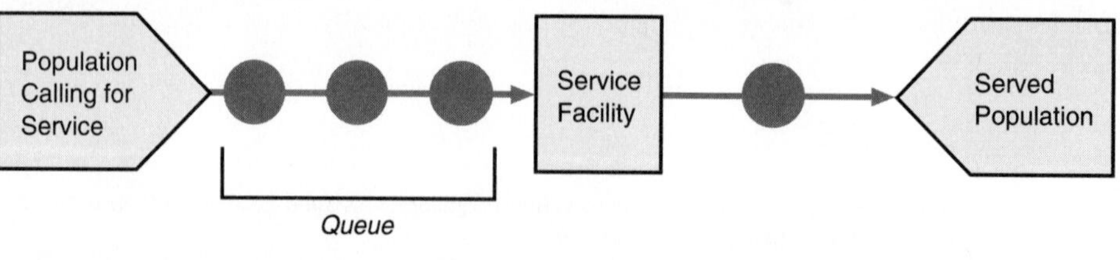

ter 6) waiting in line for processing by a worker in an automated manufacturing system can form a queue.

When a queue forms, it generally means that the units (people or equipment) in the queue are temporarily idle and waiting for service. This waiting or idle time is costly and can be avoided by properly scheduling production resources. One way to eliminate the queue is to schedule a sufficient amount of service facilities available to receive the calling population. Unfortunately, service facilities can become idle and very costly if there is not enough calling population to justify their existence. The objective of queuing analysis then is to provide information on which to balance the costs of waiting time with the costs of providing service facilities to process the calling population. The cost relationships of waiting time and providing service are presented in Figure 9-9. The costs of waiting or idle time (the upper left-hand graph in Figure 9-9) decrease as service facilities are increased. The costs of providing the service (the upper right-hand

FIGURE 9-9 QUEUE SYSTEM TOTAL EXPECTED COST CURVE

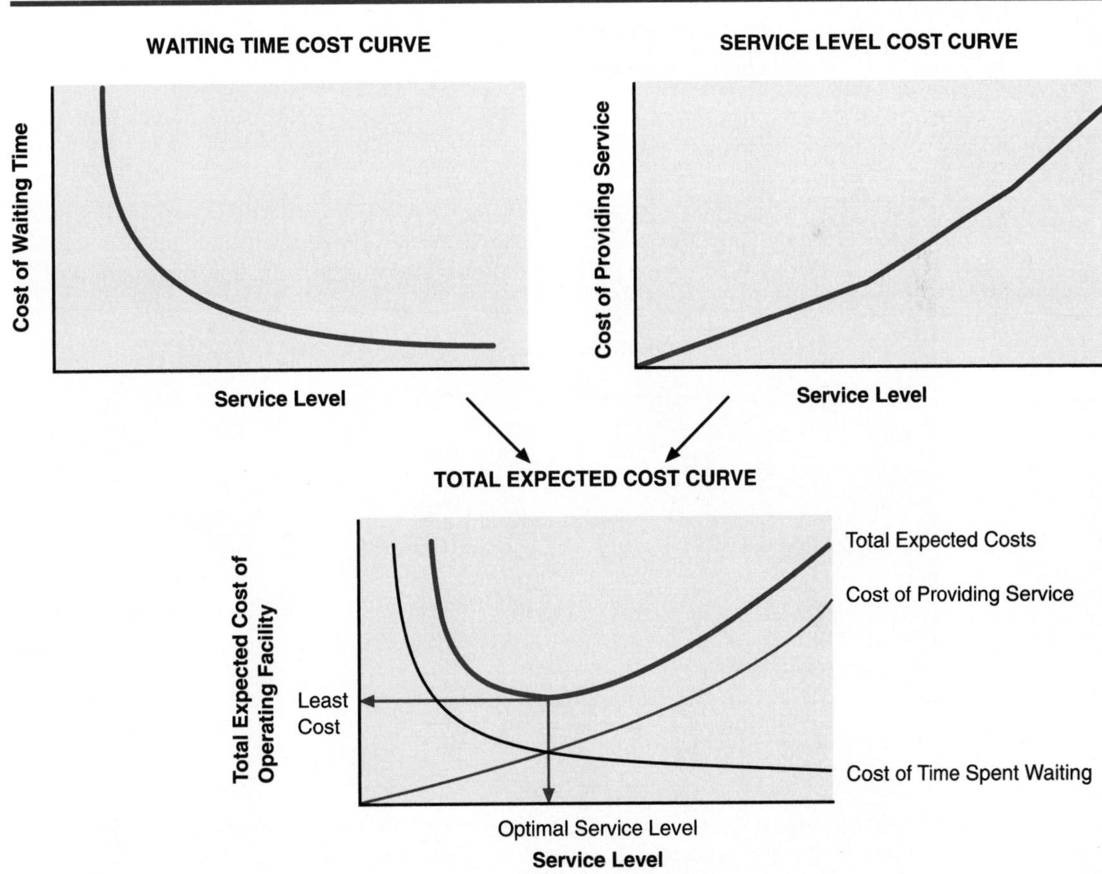

graph in Figure 9-9) increase as service is increased. By adding the two cost curves together (as we did for the EOQ model in Chapter 8), we obtain the total expected cost curve. The minimum cost point on this curve defines the optimal service level objective to guide tactical scheduling efforts. (To understand how queuing analysis and simulation methods are applied to scheduling, students are encouraged to read Supplement 9-1).

Critical Ratio Method

A sequencing rule that is used in job operations is called the critical ratio (CR). The **critical ratio** is a signaling method that is used to let schedulers know if a job is on schedule. The critical ratio is based on the following index number formula:

$$CR = \frac{\text{Due date} - \text{Today's date}}{\text{Production lead time remaining}}$$

or

$$CR = \frac{\text{Actual time remaining}}{\text{Scheduled time remaining}}$$

QUESTION: Suppose that today is day 20 for a job operation that currently has three jobs in WIP. The due dates and scheduled time remaining for each job are as follows:

Job	*Due Date*	*Work Days Remaining (lead time)*
1	25	7
2	32	14
3	27	5

What are the critical ratios for each job and what would the priority be for sequencing the jobs for the next day's production?

ANSWER: The critical ratios and priorities (where 1 = first job in sequence) are as follows:

Job	*Critical Ratio*	*Priority Order*
1	(25 − 20)/ 7 = 0.714	1
2	(32 − 20)/14 = 0.857	2
3	(27 − 20)/ 5 = 1.400	3

The lower the critical ratio, the higher the priority need in sequencing the job in the next day's production activities.

The dates and lead times are usually expressed in days. A critical ratio value of less than 1.0 means that the job is behind schedule, and a critical ratio value of more than 1.0 means that the job is ahead of schedule. The critical ratio is a dynamic index that lets managers know the daily status of a job and can help establish priorities for jobs that are behind schedule.

Optimized Production Technology (OPT)

Optimized production technology (OPT) originally appeared in the early 1980s as a planning and control software system for scheduling production.[7] This system can be used in conjunction with any other production system such as JIT, MRP, and CIM. The scheduling algorithms in the OPT software are based on optimization methods, simulation methods, and heuristics. The objective of the OPT system is to maximize throughput by focusing management's energies on bottlenecks in the production system. By maximizing throughput, the profit-making goal can be more readily achieved.

OPT has been used as a means of overcoming some of the limitations of other scheduling systems such as MRP and JIT. In an MRP operation, for example, a forecast of demand or production in units for a specific period of time such as a year is loaded into an MRP program, which determines the production schedule for that period of time. This is called **infinite backward scheduling** because we assume that infinite capacity is available and the schedule is determined by starting with future demand and working backward to schedule each stage of the production. If the MRP schedule is unacceptable because of limitations on production capacity, we can then estimate the production capacity needed to achieve the demand. We then acquire some estimated amount of additional capacity, and then load the new information into the MRP program to see if the next schedule will be an improvement on the last in terms of delivery dates, planned order releases, and so on. In a JIT operation, we simply adjust the work force and machine requirements to fit the demand as it occurs on a just-in-time basis. JIT operations work with a short-term planning horizon, and many JIT operations require a great deal of capacity flexibility to reduce personnel, idle equipment, or both. In a JIT system we also seek a unitary job order quantity of one. Yet there may be some jobs where specialization of work effort on a group of units may be far more efficient than repeated setups under a JIT system.

An OPT system differs from MRP in that it plans for **finite forward scheduling** and does not assume fixed lead times as do fixed order period MRP systems. The OPT system recognizes the real-world limitations on production resources and incorporates them as production constraints to schedules in the future. An OPT system differs from JIT in that some job order sizes can be increased if desirable. Yet the OPT system, like JIT, seeks to eliminate waste by efficiently using the most critical production resources—

---

[7] R. Fox, "MRP, Kanban, or OPT?" *Inventories and Production Magazine,* 2, No. 4 (1982), 21–25; and T. W. Vollman, "OPT as an Enhancement to MRP II," *Production and Inventory Management,* 27, No. 2 (1986), 38–45. For a classic review of the basics of OPT see E. M. Goldratt and J. Cox, *The Goal: Excellence in Manufacturing* (Croton-on-Hudson, N.Y.: North River Press, 1984).

specifically, those critical resources that control throughput. The OPT system, like MRP, is also a computer-based simulation system that allows managers to simulate improvements in scheduling. Once the simulations are run they are used to develop a final acceptable MPS. Like the MRP computer system reports described in Chapter 7, the OPT system provides detailed schedules at the floor level. Some of these reports include the following:[8]

1. *Stockperson report* The stockperson report specifies quantities of parts to be delivered to each particular resource at a specific time (like JIT). Unlike the cumbersome MRP II system, work order routings defining creation, release, printing, picking, starting, and closing of work orders are not necessary.
2. *Dispatch report* Scheduled by resource, this report shows time, quantity, and setups for both bottleneck and nonbottleneck resources. The OPT rule used here attempts to beat the schedule for the bottleneck resources but only to meet (not beat) the schedule for the nonbottleneck resources. Unlike a JIT system, which would seek improvement in all areas, the OPT system seeks to balance the bottleneck schedules with the nonbottleneck schedules. In other words, an OPT system would rather apply maximum resources to eliminate a specific bottleneck than spread the resources over the entire system.
3. *Daily supervisor report* This is a daily monitoring tool to ensure that jobs are started and finished according to the MPS.
4. *Raw material requirements report* This report shows the amounts of surplus and shortages of raw materials over a multimonth planning horizon. Production planners use this report to generate and adjust vendor orders to keep inventory under control while at the same time supporting the maximum throughput schedule with material.

OPT systems are currently available for microcomputer-based scheduling systems.[9] Whether a firm uses an OPT software package or not, OPT rules are changing the way we think about production planning and scheduling. Like JIT scheduling principles, these nine rules embrace the basic idea of the OPT system. Some of the OPT rules include the following:[10]

1. *Balance the flow of production, not its capacity.* Production should be scheduled to improve flow, not just minimize idle capacity. It is unacceptable to "make work for work's sake" by converting a great deal of inventory into unmarketed finished goods inventory. A Japanese rule that we should remember is, "If you don't need it, don't make it."

---

[8] R. Lundrigan, "What Is This Thing Called OPT?" *Production and Inventory Management,* 27, No. 2 (1986), 2–12.

[9] G. Briggs, "STC Unveils Just-In-Time Manufacturing Systems," *Management Information Systems Week,* April 10, 1989, p. 53.

[10] R. Lundrigan, "What Is This Thing Called OPT?" *Production and Inventory Management,* 27, No. 2 (1986), 2–12.

2. *Constraints determine nonbottleneck utilization.* Bottlenecks show us where critical resources such as human resources, machines, and inventory are needed. Bottlenecks determine the production rate of a line and are critical determiners of production schedules.
3. *Activation is not always equal to utilization.* If workstation A is bottlenecked by workstation B, then making A put out more units that will stand idle on the line in front of B increases WIP and wastes work force and machine resources.
4. *An hour lost at a bottleneck is an hour lost for the entire system.* An hour lost at a bottleneck station that is working at 100 percent can never be made up.
5. *An hour saved at a nonbottleneck is a mirage.* A project is usually made up of a series of activities. The timing of some of the activities may be critical if the project or job is to be completed in a specific period of time. Other activities may be noncritical and could be delayed quite some time before they would delay the completion of the entire project. If the time of a noncritical activity is decreased, it will not decrease the time of the project. If a word processor is purchased for a secretary to save time that is spent on longer coffee breaks, the word processor will not save time and its expense will be wasted. If an hour is saved in a nonbottleneck resource, it may only increase the bottleneck in some other area of the production system.
6. *Bottlenecks govern throughput and inventory.* It is impossible to use parts on an assembly line at stations below a bottleneck any faster than the bottleneck will allow. Thus, it does not make sense to make parts before they are needed.
7. *A transfer batch should not always equal a process batch.* A **process batch** is a production run for a finished item (for example, finished cars, refrigerators). A **transfer batch** is the items (chiefly inventory) that are used in completing the process batch. The size of a process batch, like cars, may be infinite, but the size of the transfer batch to the assembly line may only be one item. In a JIT environment, we seek unitary process and transfer batches. In OPT we allow flexibility to permit the system to take advantage of realistic constraints, like materials handling limitations on workstation delivery, to guide decisions on batch size.
8. *Process batches should be variable, not fixed.* In MRP II systems no relationship exists between lot-size and what is required to balance the flow of production. Specifically, the MRP II system usually has a fixed lot-size rule that defines production in units for a given time bucket or time period of a week. Like the Japanese pull system, OPT avoids constraining the system by letting the production flow determine the size of the batch.
9. *Set the schedule by examining all the constraints simultaneously.* In an MRP II system we predetermine the batch size, give the system fixed lead times, and set schedules according to lead times. Only when we run the schedule do we recognize the reality of capacity constraints. OPT considers all of the constraints of a complex network simultaneously. Such constraints include management policies, complex routings, setups, quantities, times to run, tooling, schedule

delays, maintenance, spoilage, changes in personnel, and changes in customer demands.

Evolving from a software application for manufacturing, OPT has more recently become the basis for an approach (called constraint management because it focuses on bottlenecks) that embraces every aspect of managing an organization.[11]

Input-Output Control

It is often difficult to achieve the flow objectives of OPT or other scheduling systems because individual workcenters or production cells become overloaded or underloaded. If workcenters are overloaded with work the facility can become crowded and backlogged with orders, which in turn can lead to inefficiencies and poor quality. Underloading workcenters can result in idle production capacity and wasted resources. Effective scheduling requires balancing production capacity and production performance.

One capacity planning technique that helps control the flow of production activity at the shop floor level of operation is called input-output control. **Input-output control** is a reporting system that allows managers to monitor work flow through workcenters. The reporting system generates time-based information to allow managers to see how planned work force or unit production goals are being accomplished. Virtually all computer-based operations management production planning systems incorporate input-output control reporting. An example of a workcenter's input-output report chart is presented in Figure 9-10. The charts that make up the input-output reports are not complex but are quite helpful in keeping a running total of the input of such resources as standard human resource hours allocated for production and the output of finished product (also expressed as standard work force hours). In the input chart in Figure 9-10, the planned input for the workcenter was 300 standard hours of work force whereas only 290 standard hours of production were actually input into the workcenter for week 1. The cumulative input deviation allows management to quickly see in this case that the workcenter is consistently being scheduled for input in excess of actual requirements. Similarly, the output chart reveals a consistent and growing excess of planned versus actual output from the workcenter. Typically, input-output charts also provide cumulative backlog information to let management see the progress being made in reducing (in this case) backlogged orders.

Expert Systems

Expert systems based on artificial intelligence methods have been used extensively for scheduling in operations management. Expert systems are becoming critically important for computer-based scheduling systems because of the speed with which they can

[11] S. E. Fawcett and J. N. Pearson, "Understanding and Applying Constraint Management in Today's Manufacturing Environments," *Production and Inventory Management Journal,* 32, No. 3 (1991), 46–55.

FIGURE 9-10 INPUT-OUTPUT CHART FOR A WORKCENTER (IN STANDARD HOURS)

INPUT CHART	WEEK			
	1	2	3	4
Planned Input	300	300	300	300
Actual Input	290	285	310	295
Cumulative Input Deviation*	−10	−25	−15	−20

OUTPUT CHART	WEEK			
	1	2	3	4
Planned Output	310	310	310	310
Actual Output	300	300	305	300
Cumulative Output Deviation†	−10	−20	−25	−35

SUMMARY CHART‡	WEEK			
	1	2	3	4
Cumulative Change in Backlog§	10	25	20	25

* Cumulative Input Deviation = Running sum of (planned input – actual input)
† Cumulative Output Deviation = Running sum of (planned output – actual output)
‡ Assume current backlog is zero.
§ Cumulative Change in Backlog = Running sum of (current backlog – actual input + actual output)

respond to changes. As the need to respond to rapid changes in customer demand increases in the future, more computer-based scheduling systems will require expert system modules to reduce human decision making (which can take considerable time and slow an organization's responsiveness).

Some of the scheduling expert systems that have appeared in the literature are listed on the top of page 450.

1. *Intelligent Scheduling and Information System (ISIS)* This system is designed to support job scheduling in which multiple constrained objectives exist.[12]
2. *Management Analysis Resource Scheduler (MARS)* This system is designed to schedule resources (such as human resources, computer systems, and simulators) for the space transportation system.[13]
3. *Knowledge-based Expert System (KEBS)* This system is designed to establish vehicle routings using a variety of optimization and heuristic procedures while taking into consideration traffic, truck size, and store requirements.[14]

A variety of other scheduling expert systems are constantly being developed and reviewed for use in industry.[15]

Mathematical Programming Methods

Several mathematical programming methods have been extensively used in scheduling. Two of the most commonly used are linear programming and goal programming.[16]

1. *Linear programming (LP)* LP is a multivariable, single objective, constrained optimization technique that has been used to schedule all types of production activity for more than forty years.[17] LP is currently used as a component in integrated computer-based scheduling systems such as OPT and other scheduling decision support systems.[18] It has also been used as a primary element in simulated optimization scheduling systems.[19] To illustrate how practical LP is in scheduling, an LP scheduling problem is formulated and solved in Supplement 9-2.

---

[12] M. S. Fox and S. F. Smith, "ISIS: A Knowledge-based System for Factory Scheduling," *Expert Systems,* 1, No. 1 (1984), 25–49.

[13] C. A. March, "MARS: An Expert System Using the Automated Reasoning Tool to Schedule Resources," *Robotics and Expert Systems—Proceedings of Robex's 85,* Instrument Society of America (1985), 123–125.

[14] P. Duchessi, S. Belardo, and J. P. Seagle, "Artificial Intelligence and the Management Science Practitioner: Knowledge Enhancements to a Decision Support System for Vehicle Routing," *Interfaces,* 18, No. 2 (1988), 85–93.

[15] E. Turban, "Review of Expert Systems Technology," *IEEE Transactions on Engineering Management,* 35, No. 2 (1988), 71–73; and Expert Systems in Production and Operations Management: Classification and Prospects," *Interfaces,* 18, No. 6 (1988), 80–91.

[16] F. N. Ford et al., "Use of Operations Research in Production Management," *Production and Inventory Management,* 28, No. 3 (1987), 59–63.

[17] C. E. Bodington and T. E. Baker, "A History of Mathematical Programming in the Petroleum Industry," *Interfaces,* 20, No. 4 (1990), 117–127.

[18] J. Blais, J. Lamont, and J. Rousseau, "The HASTUS Vehicle and Manpower Scheduling System at the Societe de Transport de la Communaute Urbaine de Montreal," *Interfaces,* 20, No. 1 (1990), 26–42.

[19] E. W. Moore, J. M. Warmke, and L. R. Gorban, "The Indispensable Role of Management Science in Centralizing Freight Operations at Reynolds Metals Company," *Interfaces,* 21, No. 1 (1991), 107–129.

2. *Goal programming (GP)* GP is a multivariable, constrained optimization technique that extends LP by considering the multiple and often conflicting objectives observed in scheduling problems. GP was first proposed as a production scheduling method by S. M. Lee and others in the early 1970s.[20] It continues to be applied as a scheduling method to deal with more current operations management topics and environments such as scheduling equipment usage in flexible manufacturing systems (FMS).[21] (We discuss FMS in Chapter 13.)

One question that is often asked concerning scheduling methods is how to determine the "best" method for a particular operation. That question is usually answered by comparing the time it takes, using different scheduling methods, for a fixed number of jobs to move through an operation. The method that does the best job of scheduling will move the jobs through the operation with the least amount of total job order flow time. This approach was illustrated earlier in this section by comparing the first-come, first-served rule of scheduling with Johnson's sequencing rules. In that illustration, Johnson's rules minimized total flow time for a particular set of jobs. Before making a final decision on a scheduling method, we might want to simulate a variety of these sets of jobs to more accurately capture the behavior of job flow in a particular operation. We could then compute an average total job order flow time for each method to make a final decision on a scheduling method.

Other criteria, such as the average number of jobs processed in a fixed period of time or the number of defect-free jobs completed, can also be used to compare and select the best scheduling methods.

Although we have examined a number of scheduling methods in this section, those listed here are only a brief introduction to many that are currently being used. We discuss other scheduling methods in the remaining chapters of this book.

QUESTION: Suppose that we want to determine which of two scheduling methods—the first-come, first-served rule, or Johnson's job sequencing rules—will minimize the average total job order flow time of an operation. We apply the first-come, first-served rule to a representative sample of five sets of ten job orders, and the total time in minutes to complete each set of jobs is 100, 110, 102, 111, and 123. We then apply Johnson's job sequencing rules to the same five sets of ten job orders, and the total time in minutes to complete each set of jobs is 100, 100, 104, 110, and 117. Based on the results of these data, which of the two scheduling methods should be selected to minimize total job order flow time in the operation?

(continued)

[20] S. M. Lee and L. J. Moore, "A Practical Approach to Production Scheduling," *Production and Inventory Management,* 15, No. 2 (1974), 79–92.

[21] B. Dean, Y. Yu, and M. J. Schniederjans, "A Goal Programming Approach to Production Planning For Flexible Manufacturing Systems," *Journal of Engineering and Technology Management,* 6 (1990), 207–220.

ANSWER: The average (which we assume is representative of all jobs in this operation) total job order flow time for the first-come, first-served rule is 109.2 minutes (100 + 110 + 102 + 111 + 123/5), and the average total job order flow time for Johnson's rules is 106.2 minutes (100 + 100 + 104 + 110 + 117/5). Based solely on average total job order flow time, Johnson's rules should be selected for the scheduling method in this operation.

INTEGRATING MANAGEMENT RESOURCES: USING SCHEDULING SYSTEMS TO IMPROVE CUSTOMER SERVICE AND INCREASE FLEXIBILITY

All aspects of production in computer-integrated manufacturing (CIM) systems and computer-integrated service systems (CISS) are scheduled by software-driven systems and methods. By understanding the logic of scheduling methods, you can understand how programmed versions of those methods create schedules in computer-integrated environments. All of the scheduling methods we have discussed in this chapter are currently available in CIM and CISS software systems. Most CIM systems and CISS integrate scheduling software to schedule production activity, personnel assignments, and inventory transactions. Integrating scheduling activities can help organizations achieve competitive advantages in service performance.

What is unique about scheduling in computer-integrated operations is the speed with which scheduling is performed. Customer orders can be directly entered into a manufacturer's computer system by electronic data interchange (EDI; discussed in Chapter 8). The customer order can also enter a CIM system through a marketing terminal and show up on the shop floor of the manufacturing facility in a matter of minutes (see Figure 1-11). This incredibly short order entry process can only be achieved by scheduling software within the main computer, which allocates and schedules human, technology, and system resources to complete the required customer order.

One of the more advanced and comprehensive CIM systems available today is IBM's Communications-Oriented Production Information and Control System (COPICS).[22] COPICS contains a Demand Management module that consists of a number of software subsystems, including the following:

1. *Customer Orders Service—Data and Order Management* This program controls order processing by permitting an order to be tracked on-line while it is in WIP. Most importantly, this program helps expedite entry of customer orders, permits workers to know available options or alterations allowed by customers in case changes need to be made during WIP, displays up-to-date information on customer questions, and allows changes in orders quickly.

[22] *COPICS Demand Management* (White Plains, N.Y.: IBM Corp., 1989).

2. *Customer Order Serving—Shipping* This program helps expedite orders to customers by organizing the most efficient picking order; making information on packing and shipping instructions easily available; and preprinting packing lists, delivery notices, and invoices.
3. *Inventory Planning and Forecasting* This program helps update forecast planning factors to avoid delays in satisfying customers' demands and to keep scheduling expectations up-to-date.
4. *Master Production Scheduling Planning* This program helps maintain and validate the production plan, convert the production plan into the MPS item requirements, make adjustments to changes in the production environment, provide production simulation answers to what-if scheduling questions, and provide available-to-promise information to customers.

These programs permit the IBM COPICS CIM to plan, control, and move customers' orders through manufacturing operations efficiently and with increased certainty on lead time requirements. The MPS program integrates the scheduling requirements in the overall CIM information system to automatically consider and adjust for all changes in the external environment (for example, a customer changing an order or a vendor failing to meet a delivery) or the internal environment (for example, equipment downtime). The result of using this system is to improve an operation's service (that is, reduce production lead time from order entry to delivery) and flexibility (that is, enhance the operation's ability to adapt to changes quickly). Software developers (like Arthur Andersen & Company, which developed the MAC-PAC CIM system introduced in Chapter 5) report as much as a 90 percent reduction in processing and scheduling lead times when a CIM system is adopted.[23] Some manufacturers believe that the competitive advantage CIM systems offer in scheduling and controlling operations is the only choice to maintain their markets.[24] Even small, custom job manufacturing operations are finding the scheduling and planning benefits of CIM are affordable.[25]

CISSs also benefit from the competitive advantage of speed of customer order and transaction processing. Indeed, the speed of order processing has become an important part of the service product that customers demand. A typical CISS is illustrated by an automated teller machine (ATM). In Figure 9-11 we present an overview of an ATM. The system demonstrates the quality of service to customers and the efficiency of transaction processing that banks receive from using CISS. CISS provides convenience and flexibility to customers who can use services at convenient locations, often twenty-four hours a day. These systems also reduce personnel scheduling activities (and therefore improve efficiency) because tellers are automated and fewer human tellers are needed at the banking facilities.

[23] *Trends in Information Technology,* 3rd ed. (Chicago: Arthur Andersen & Co., 1989), p. 84.

[24] "Mold Maker Moves to CIM," *Machine and Tool Blue Book* (January 1990), 51–54.

[25] J. Wright, "World-Class CIM on a Small Scale," *Manufacturing Systems* (November 1989), 42–48.

Q

QUESTION: What is an example of how CIM can help an organization compete successfully against competition and improve product quality?

ANSWER: Avondale Industries' Shipyard Division in New Orleans is one of the largest ship-building and refurbishing operations in the United States. During the 1970s, it got much of its business from the U.S. Navy because of global competition and a declining U.S. commercial market.[26] To comply with the information requirements of government specifications, Avondale decided to install COPICS as a foundation for its company-wide CIM system during the 1980s and fully integrate the system with all elements of ship building and refurbishing during the 1990s. The COPICS system has provided substantial improvement in materials handling and scheduling. The accuracy rate of its materials tracking and ordering reportedly went from 50 percent to 98 percent under the COPICS system. Accuracy in inventory availability and ordering saves inventory waste and management planning time. It has been estimated that COPICS saves Avondale's customers $1 million a ship in reduced waste alone. COPICS also allowed Avondale to redefine its production-scheduling process in building new ships. Insead of starting from the hull up approach, which permits a sequence of activities to be scheduled, COPICS could support a more complex sequence scheduling of production activities. This permitted Avondale to build ships in sections, which allows for a more efficient use of production resources and improved productivity. For example, it no longer had to work around weather conditions that could delay some types of work, and it could keep track of all sequenced activities. Ultimately, Avondale is expecting the COPICS system to provide the benefit of increasing productivity by 200 percent.

The COPICS system also supports quality control activities by ensuring that the right part is sent by the supplier. Using a bar code on parts, a part can be checked to ensure that it is the correct one that was ordered before it is installed. Also, grade of steel can be quickly checked against building plans incorporated in the on-line COPICS master production schedule. The quality performance of suppliers is also effectively considered by the COPICS system. Up-to-date records on what suppliers say they send and what actually comes in is easily monitored with COPICS to avoid shortages that idle labor. Using the COPICS system, Avondale reported being only twenty items short in one week compared with being three hundred items short before COPICS. All of these changes under the COPICS system have given Avondale a streamlined operation that is more than meeting its competition in productivity and quality.

[26] B. White, "Avondale Challenges the Competition," *APICS—The Performance Advantage,* 2, No. 2 (February 1992), 19–23.

FIGURE 9-11 A COMPUTER-INTEGRATED SERVICE SYSTEM (CISS): AN AUTOMATED TELLER

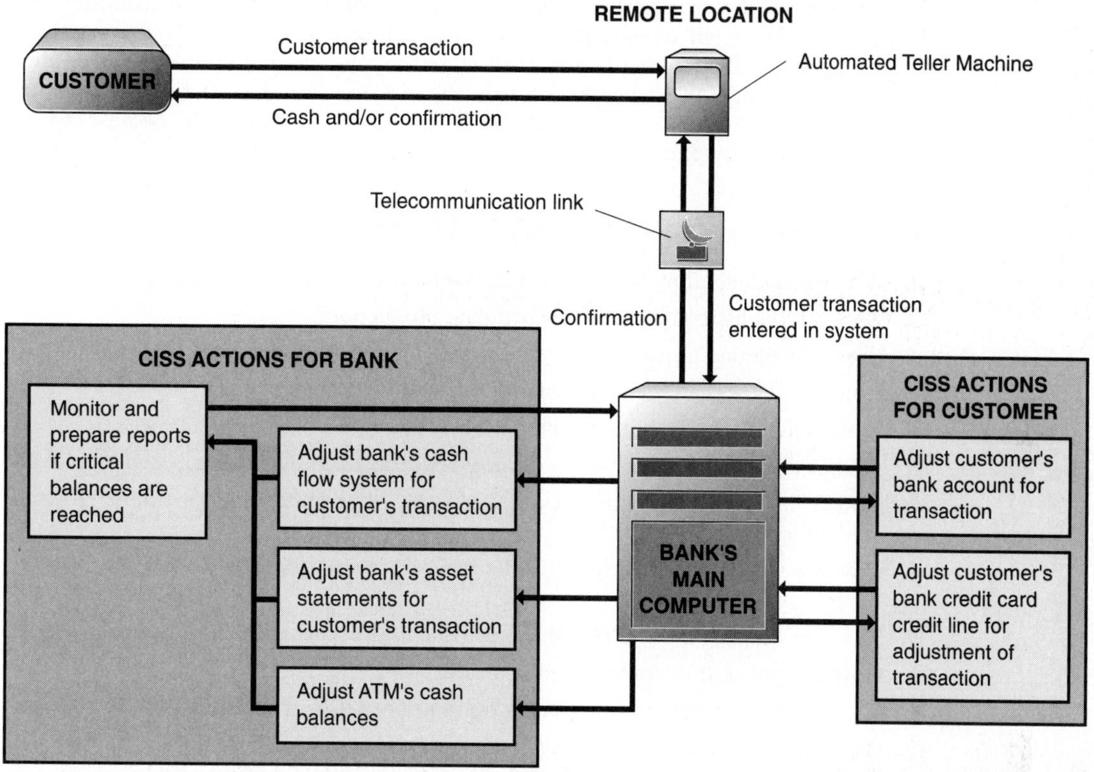

SUMMARY

In this chapter we examined some of the basic types of scheduling and activities that help create the management of scheduling in manufacturing and service operations. In addition, we described a number of scheduling principles, technologies, and methods that, while chiefly used in job and repetitive operations, can have limited application in any type of operation. Scheduling approaches used in many service organizations include appointment systems, reservation systems, and strategic product pricing designed to schedule demand. Scheduling approaches used to make decisions on scheduling and loading personnel resources include flextime, flextour, compressed workweek, staggered times, job splitting, and use of part-time workers. We also presented a variety of principles and technologies used in scheduling production activity including Gantt charts, job sequencing rules, lot-sizing rules, JIT principles, queuing analysis, simulation analysis, critical ratio method, OPT, input-output control, and expert systems. Collectively, all of these scheduling methods are used to make scheduling decisions on some type of production activity.

Meeting or beating a scheduled deadline for a product or service is advantageous if the product or service is of sufficient quality to satisfy the customer. If a product does not meet the customer's quality expectations, it may be returned for reprocessing. The company may then have to devote an unexpected amount of additional work satisfying the customer, which may disrupt the timing of other production activities and destroy the best scheduling efforts. Quality work, or "doing the job right the first time," in manufacturing and service companies is one of the most important goals for all organizations today. In the next chapter we discuss quality assurance in manufacturing and service organizations.

DISCUSSION AND REVIEW QUESTIONS

1. Why is scheduling important in manufacturing and service operations?
2. What are the basic objectives in scheduling production?
3. How will altering dispatching rules change the flow of work in a production system?
4. How does an appointment system differ from a reservation system?
5. What is the difference between flextime and flextour?
6. What is the difference between a Gantt work-load chart and a Gantt scheduling chart?
7. How is job sequencing different in purpose from the critical ratio method? How are they the same?
8. How are the JIT scheduling principles different from OPT rules? How are they the same?
9. How can queuing analysis be used to provide useful scheduling information?
10. How is input-output control used as a capacity planning method?
11. What is the contribution of expert systems in scheduling? Explain.
12. How does integrating scheduling systems improve customer service and production flexibility? Explain.

PROBLEMS

* 1. Several jobs arrive for processing in a department that uses dispatching rules to schedule work. Job A is estimated to take 3 hours and is due to be completed on the tenth day of the month, job B is estimated to take 2.5 hours and is due to be completed on the fifth day of the month, job C is estimated to take 4 hours and is due to be completed on the ninth day of the month, job D is estimated to take 5 hours and is due to be completed on the twentieth day of the month, and job E is estimated to take 1.5 hours and is due to be completed on the thirtieth day of the month. The jobs were received in the department in A, B, C, D, and E order.
   a. What is the job sequence schedule for these five jobs using the first-come, first-served rules of dispatching? What is the total flow time for these jobs?
   b. What is the job sequence for these five jobs using the earliest due date rule of dispatching? What is the total flow time for these jobs?
   c. Does it make any difference which rule is used regarding total flow time? Explain.

---

* The solutions to the problems marked with an asterisk can be found in Appendix J.

2. Several jobs arrive for processing in a department that uses dispatching rules to schedule work. Job A is estimated to take 3 hours and is due to be completed on the tenth day of the month, job B is estimated to take 2.5 hours and is due to be completed on the fifth day of the month, job C is estimated to take 4 hours and is due to be completed on the ninth day of the month, job D is estimated to take 5 hours and is due to be completed on the twentieth day of the month, and job E is estimated to take 1.5 hours and is due to be completed on the thirtieth day of the month. The jobs were received in the department in A, B, C, D, and E order.
   a. What is the job sequence schedule for these five jobs using the longest processing time rule of dispatching? What is the total flow time for these jobs?
   b. What is the job sequence for these five jobs using the shortest processing time rule of dispatching? What is the total flow time for these jobs?
   c. Does it make any difference which rule is used regarding total flow time? Explain.

3. Several jobs arrive for processing in a department that uses dispatching rules to schedule work. Job A is estimated to take 7 hours and is due to be completed on the first day of the month, job B is estimated to take 9.5 hours and is due to be completed on the seventh day of the month, job C is estimated to take 6 hours and is due to be completed on the fourth day of the month, job D is estimated to take 6.5 hours and is due to be completed on the twenty-third day of the month, job E is estimated to take 2.5 hours and is due to be completed on the fifteenth day of the month, and job F is estimated to take 1.5 hours and is due to be completed on the twentieth day of the month. The jobs were received in the department in A, B, D, C, E, and F order.
   a. What is the job sequence schedule for these six jobs using the longest processing time rule of dispatching? What is the total flow time for these jobs?
   b. What is the job sequence schedule for these six jobs using the shortest processing time rule of dispatching? What is the total flow time for these jobs?
   c. Does it make any difference which rule is used regarding total flow time? Explain.

★ 4. Suppose that we must schedule the following five jobs:

	TIME REQUIRED FOR PRODUCTION PER STAGE	
Job	*Stage 1 (hours)*	*Stage 2 (hours)*
A	7.00	2.00
B	4.00	2.00
C	2.00	3.00
D	3.50	6.50
E	9.50	4.00

Each job must pass through both stages of production to be completed. The time shown includes setup time and production time. How should we schedule or sequence these jobs to mimimize job flow time? What is the total flow time for all five jobs?

5. Refer to the data in Problem 4. Assume that the jobs arrive for processing in the order of A, B, C, D, and then E.
   a. What is the total job flow time if we use the first-come, first-served rule? What is the job sequence?
   b. Assuming that the total time in both stages of production represents the total time of the job, what is the total job flow time if we use the longest processing time rule? What is the job sequence?

c. Assuming that the total time in both stages of production represents the total time of the job, what is the total job flow time if we use the shortest processing time rule? What is the job sequence?
d. Of the three methods, what is the "best" method of scheduling if minimizing total job flow time is used as the selection criterion?

6. A company has the following six jobs to complete:

	TIME REQUIRED FOR PRODUCTION PER STAGE	
Job	*Stage 1 (hours)*	*Stage 2 (hours)*
A	6.00	3.00
B	3.00	3.50
C	1.00	4.00
D	3.50	8.50
E	2.50	4.00
F	2.75	5.00

Suppose that each job must pass through both stages of production. The time shown includes both setup time and production time. Determine the schedule or sequence for these jobs to minimize the total job flow time. What is the total flow time for all six jobs?

7. Refer to the data in Problem 6. Assume that the jobs arrive for processing in the order of A, B, C, D, E, and then F.
a. What is the total job flow time if we use the first-come, first-served rule? What is the job sequence?
b. Assuming that the total time in both stages of production represents the total time of the job, what is the total job flow time if we use the longest processing time rule? What is the job sequence?
c. Assuming that the total time in both stages of production represents the total time of the job, what is the total job flow time if we use the shortest processing time rule? What is the job sequence?
d. Of the three methods, what is the "best" method of scheduling if minimizing total job flow time is used as the selection criterion?

8. Consider the following seven jobs that must be scheduled:

	TIME REQUIRED FOR PRODUCTION PER STAGE	
Job	*Stage 1 (hours)*	*Stage 2 (hours)*
A	1.00	3.00
B	2.00	1.50
C	1.25	4.00
D	3.50	8.50
E	2.50	4.00
F	2.75	5.00
G	4.75	2.25

Assume that each job must pass through both stages of production. The time given includes both setup time and production time. Determine the best schedule for these jobs to minimize job flow time. What is the total flow time for all seven jobs?

9. Refer to the data in Problem 8. Assume that the jobs arrive for processing in the order of A, B, C, D, E, F, and then G.
   a. What is the total job flow time if we use the first-come, first-served rule? What is the job sequence?
   b. Assuming that the total time in both stages of production represents the total time of the job, what is the total job flow time if we use the longest processing time rule? What is the job sequence?
   c. Assuming that the total time in both stages of production represents the total time of the job, what is the total job flow time if we use the shortest processing time rule? What is the job sequence?
   d. Of the three methods, what is the "best" method of scheduling if minimizing total job flow time is used as the selection criterion?

*10. Suppose that today is day 10 for a job operation that currently has three jobs in WIP. The due date and scheduled time remaining for each job are as follows:

Job	*Due Date*	*Work Days Remaining*
1	16	2
2	22	8
3	18	1

What are the critical ratios for each job? What are priorities for sequencing the jobs for the next day's production?

11. Suppose that today is day 17 for a job operation that currently has five jobs in WIP. The due dates and scheduled time remaining for each job are as follows:

Job	*Due Date*	*Work Days Remaining*
1	34	12
2	25	10
3	19	20
4	23	10
5	40	17

What are the critical ratios for each job? What are priorities for sequencing the jobs for the next day's production?

12. A custom equipment cleaning company wants to establish a priority for sequencing the order in which to complete each of ten jobs it is currently working on. Each of the cleaning jobs takes a different amount of time to complete because the type of equipment is different for each job. The company has only a limited staff and it cannot complete all of the jobs as expected and promised. The company hopes that a priority system will help minimize customer dissatisfaction. Today is day 7 in its production scheduling of the ten jobs. The promised due dates and scheduled time remaining for each cleaning job are shown in the chart on the top of page 460.

Job	*Due Date*	*Work Days Remaining*
1	10	2
2	20	1
3	15	3
4	18	4
5	25	5
6	14	3
7	25	8
8	10	10
9	12	10
10	14	9

What are the priorities for sequencing the jobs for the next day's production? Show your work.

*13. Assume that the same input-output procedure used in Figure 9-10 is applicable in this question. What are the input-output values that fall in the boxes with question marks in the following figure? Assume a zero backlog.

INPUT CHART	WEEK			
	1	2	3	4
Planned Input	300	300	300	300
Actual Input	280	310	300	300
Cumulative Input Deviation	?	?	?	?

OUTPUT CHART	WEEK			
	1	2	3	4
Planned Output	310	310	310	310
Actual Output	340	289	310	315
Cumulative Output Deviation	?	?	?	?

14. Assume that the same input-output procedure used in Figure 9-10 is applicable in this question. Determine the input-output values that fall in the boxes with question marks in the figure on the top of the next page. Assume a zero backlog.

INPUT CHART	WEEK			
	1	2	3	4
Planned Input	100	120	130	140
Actual Input	120	110	100	100
Cumulative Input Deviation	?	?	?	?

OUTPUT CHART	WEEK			
	1	2	3	4
Planned Output	140	150	160	170
Actual Output	160	160	160	160
Cumulative Output Deviation	?	?	?	?

SUMMARY CHART	WEEK			
	1	2	3	4
Cumulative Change in Backlog	?	?	?	?

15. Assume that the same input-output procedure used in Figure 9-10 is applicable in this question. Determine the input-output values that fall in the boxes with question marks in the following figure (note that the output chart and the summary chart are on the top of page 462). Assume a zero backlog.

INPUT CHART	WEEK			
	1	2	3	4
Planned Input	200	230	230	230
Actual Input	210	210	210	210
Cumulative Input Deviation	?	?	?	?

OUTPUT CHART	WEEK			
	1	2	3	4
Planned Output	250	250	260	260
Actual Output	200	200	200	200
Cumulative Output Deviation	?	?	?	?

SUMMARY CHART	WEEK			
	1	2	3	4
Cumulative Change in Backlog	?	?	?	?

*16. (This problem requires the contents of Supplement 9-1.) Suppose that we have a queuing situation that can be analyzed by the single-channel model. Suppose further that $A = 10$ and $S = 12$. What are the values of L_s, L_q, T_s, T_q, and P?

17. (This problem requires the contents of Supplement 9-1.) Suppose that we have a queuing situation that can be analyzed by the single-channel model. Assume that $A = 4$ and $S = 5$. Determine the values of L_s, L_q, T_s, T_q, and P.

18. (This problem requires the contents of Supplement 9-1.) A small, one-chair beauty parlor has a mean arrival rate of two customers per hour and a service rate of five customers per hour. The store owner has observed that the cost of keeping customers waiting drastically diminishes tipping. It is estimated that the cost of keeping a customer waiting for an hour is \$2 in tips. The cost of hiring an extra hair care assistant is \$4 per hour and would allow the owner to increase the service rate to ten customers per hour. Let's assume that this queuing situation fits the single-channel queue model.
    a. During an eight-hour day, what is the mean number of customers expected to be waiting for service?
    b. What is the probability that the beautician performing the work will be busy?
    c. Should the extra hair care assistant be acquired to minimize the costs of lost tips and labor expenses? Show your work.

19. (This problem requires the contents of Supplement 9-1.) An ice cream store operates eight hours a day. The demand and general characteristics of the operation fit the single-channel queuing model. The store manager is considering adding an extra one or two workers to the current staff of one salesperson. A staff of one employee can handle an average of twenty customers per hour, a staff of two employees can handle forty customers per hour, and a staff of three employees can handle sixty customers per hour. The current demand rate is approximately fifteen customers per hour. The hourly cost of an employee is \$5, and the hourly cost of keeping customers waiting is \$40.
    a. What assumptions are we making in this problem?
    b. What are the values of L_s, L_q, T_s, T_q, and P for the one-person crew?
    c. What does a one-person crew cost for an 8-hour day?
    d. What are the values of L_s, L_q, T_s, T_q, and P for the two-person crew?
    e. What does a two-person crew cost for an 8-hour day?

f. What are the values of L_s, L_q, T_s, T_q, and P for the three-person crew?
g. What does a three-person crew cost for an 8-hour day?
h. How many persons should be on the crew to minimize total costs?

20. (This problem requires the contents of Supplement 9-1.) A local health food store operates eight hours a day. The general characteristics of the operation fit the single-channel queuing model. The store manager is considering adding an extra one or two workers to the current staff of one salesperson. A staff of one employee can handle an average of five customers an hour. A staff of two employees can handle ten customers per hour, and a staff of three employees can handle fifteen customers per hour. The current demand rate is approximately four customers per hour. The hourly cost of an employee is $7.50, and the hourly cost of keeping customers waiting is $65.
    a. What assumptions are we making in this problem?
    b. What are the values of L_s, L_q, T_s, T_q, and P for the one-person crew?
    c. What does a one-person crew cost for an eight-hour day?
    d. What are the values of L_s, L_q, T_s, T_q, and P for the two-person crew?
    e. What does a two-person crew cost for an eight-hour day?
    f. What are the values of L_s, L_q, T_s, T_q, and P for the three-person crew?
    g. What does a three-person crew cost for an eight-hour day?
    h. How many persons should be on the crew to minimize total costs?

21. (This problem requires the contents of Supplement 9-1.) A lawn-care company's customer demand is a function of the weather. The probable occurrence of weather and its impact on the number of lawn mowing jobs per summer is given by the following frequency distribution:

Resulting Lawn Jobs	*Weather Frequency*	*Weather*
550	25	Bad
680	20	Good
780	30	Better
900	25	Best

Using the Monte Carlo method and ten random numbers from the last column in Appendix F, simulate the average number of lawn mowing jobs this organization can expect to obtain given the weather frequency distribution. What are we assuming about the weather?

22. (This problem requires the contents of Supplement 9-1.) A company operates a five-person crew to handle all types of construction projects. The true demand for crew members for last season's jobs follows the following frequency distribution:

Required Crew Members	*Frequency*
3	35
4	45
5	65
6	30
7	25

The company would like to simulate twenty project applications to determine if its fixed scheduling strategy of a crew of five members is less costly than a variable schedule of rotating four members on one project and then six members on the next (that is, four then six then four then six). The cost of a crew member who ends up being idle averages $1,200 per project. The cost of the shortage of a crew member on a project is $2,000. Which scheduling strategy is the least costly? Use the first row of Appendix F to obtain your random numbers.

23. (This problem requires the contents of Supplement 9-1.) A consulting company operates a four-person team to handle all types of research and consulting projects. The true demand in team members for last season's jobs follows the following frequency distribution:

Required Team Members	*Frequency*
2	10
3	15
4	20
5	24
6	18
7	13

The company would like to simulate twenty-five project assignments to determine if its fixed scheduling strategy of a team of four members is less costly than a variable schedule of rotating four members on one project and then five members on the next (that is, four then five then four then five). The cost of a team member who ends up being idle averages $3,500 per project. The cost of the shortage of a team member on a project is $4,600. Which scheduling strategy is the least costly? Use the first column of numbers in Appendix F for your random numbers. Show your work.

C 24. (This problem requires the contents of Supplement 9-2.) Suppose that a company produces two products: A and B. The company wants to plan the unit production of each product for the next three months of January, February, and March. The company can sell all of the units it produces at a profit of $105 per unit for A and $15 per unit for B. Total unit production (both A and B) cannot exceed the capacity of 1,000 units in January, 2,000 units in February, and 3,000 units in March. Total production of all units of A for all three months must be at least 500 units, and total production of all B units for all three months must be at least 500 units. The company must also produce at least 200 units of each product each month. The company wants to determine the profit-maximizing schedule for products A and B.

CASE 9-1

WHY DO WE NEED TO SCHEDULE A SECOND CREW?

The XANCO Company of St. Louis, Missouri provides aircraft cleaning crews for private airplane owners and small commuter airline companies at the St. Louis International Airport. The service product it offers is custom cleaning of the interior aircraft compartments and washing the exterior of all sizes of aircraft. In the St. Louis area, the aircraft cleaning business is highly competitive with more than a dozen companies actively providing the same basic service. There is little customer loyalty by aircraft owners because many of them do not operate in the St. Louis area, but only pass through on their way to other destinations. Because of the large number of competitors, most commuter airlines did not contract XANCO's services. Some of the small commuter airlines operate on a fixed schedule for aircraft cleaning and maintenance that helps XANCO plan its services. Unfortunately, this competitive environment has resulted in a great deal of business going to XANCO's competitors when the demand for XANCO's services outstripped its ability to provide the service.

XANCO operated from 6:00 AM to 6:00 PM every day of the year. This was the same time schedule that virtually all of the other competitors used because air traffic (and the cleaning business) was the greatest during this time period. Because of the diversity of aircraft, the cleaning crew of fifteen persons had to be highly trained maintenance personnel who could handle any type of aircraft cleaning problem. The crew worked as a single unit when an aircraft was brought in for cleaning. When the crew finished with one aircraft, the next was brought in.

Despite the skill and self-motivation of XANCO's cleaning crew, the number of aircraft waiting for cleaning appeared to be increasing and so did the number of customers that went to XANCO's competitors. XANCO's owner felt the loss in business reflected the inability of the single crew to handle the company's current volume of business. The owner decided that some research was necessary to determine if a second crew could be used to handle the increasing demand and if the second crew could be cost justified. The cost of a crew sitting idle was estimated by the owner to be $1,100 per aircraft that they could have cleaned. In other words, if the crew could have cleaned four aircraft in an hour and only one was available for cleaning, the company would have incurred an idleness cost of $3,300 (3 × $1,100). The owner did not want to have two crews costing a total of $2,200 an aircraft sitting idle. At the same time the owner did not want to lose $1,300 an aircraft when the single crew operation was fully utilized.

A consultant was hired to perform the desired cost analysis research. The consultant initially thought that the company's problem was a simple queuing application. Unfortunately, the aircraft arrival rates did not follow any known type of probability distribution. The frequency distribution for the hourly arrival rates is presented in Exhibit 9C-1. (Clearly it does not match the Poisson probability distribution configuration present in Exhibit 9S-1 in Supplement 9-1.) The cleaning rate also had an unidentifiable frequency or probability distribution. The aircraft cleaning rate distribution is presented in Exhibit 9C-2. Because the arrival and service distributions did not fit any known probability distributions, the consultant decided that simulation analysis might be used to model this queuing situation. By simulating both the arrivals and service rates of the aircraft, crew shortages or surpluses could be determined and so could their resulting costs.

The consultant decided to conduct the simulation using the following rules:

1. A total of twenty-four hours of operation (two days) will be simulated.
2. Costs will be based solely on the simulated shortages or surpluses of aircraft cleaning requirements.

EXHIBIT 9C-1 AIRCRAFT ARRIVAL RATE DISTRIBUTION

Hourly Arrival of Aircraft	*Frequency*
1	10
2	14
3	22
4	32
5	22

EXHIBIT 9C-2 AIRCRAFT CLEANING RATE DISTRIBUTION

Number of Aircraft Cleaned per Hour	*Frequency (single crew of 15 employees)*
1	5
2	10
3	15
4	30
5	40

3. For purposes of this study, the same random number that is used to determine the arrivals in an hour will be used to determine the number of aircraft cleaned in the same hour.
4. Both a single-crew operation and double-crew operation will be simulated.
5. The aircraft cleaning rates for the double-crew operation will be twice that presented for the single crew in Exhibit 9C-2 (that is, the numbers in the first column of Exhibit 9C-2 will be doubled).
6. The costs for the double-crew operation will be twice those for a single-crew operation because there are twice as many crew members.

CASE QUESTIONS

1. Using the first column of random numbers in Appendix F, simulate the single-crew cleaning operation of XANCO using the Monte Carlo method. What are the total costs of lost business and crew idleness?
2. Using the first column of random numbers in Appendix F, simulate the double-crew cleaning operation of XANCO using the Monte Carlo method. What are the total costs of lost business and crew idleness?
3. How many crews should the consultant recommend that XANCO's owner employ?

CASE 9-2

AN ISSUE OF JOB SEQUENCING

The Job-Done-Right Company (JDRC) of San Diego, California is a very successful tee-shirt printing company. The company uses silk-screen and spray-painting methods to produce custom and special edition tee-shirts for company promotions, political events, and band concerts. The company started its business with a staff of two workers last year and currently employs ten workers. A backlog of work started on the first day JDRC was open for business and presently is at four months. The owner has seen some of JDRC's best customers cancel orders because of the backlog and realized that something needed to be done.

Unfortunately, the owner of JDRC has some capacity restrictions. Because of state regulations, personnel capacity cannot be increased. State employee regulations governing the number of workers and equipment per square feet of building space do not permit more than ten workers to be housed in JDRC's current building. JDRC felt that its location is critical to its long-range success (and it does not have the money to move). Even though JDRC has the latest and most technologically advanced (and therefore most efficient) equipment, it cannot acquire any additional equipment because of the space limitation by the state government.

Another capacity limitation concerns the company's current production methods. Production at JDRC can be viewed as a two-stage operation: procurement and painting. The procurement (or materials ordering) stage of production can take a matter of days or weeks to complete, depending on customer desires. Some of the tee-shirts come from foreign manufacturers and others from domestic sources so order lead times vary. The painting stage of production likewise varies from one day to several weeks depending on the number of colors and lot-size (number of tee-shirts) of the production run. The painting personnel are skilled workers and by union agreement cannot be asked to perform procurement work activities, despite the occasional bottlenecks in procurements that idle some of the painters. The production process for every order must first start with procurement and then go on to painting. No alteration of the sequence or the amount of time (given the fixed personnel and equipment resources) to complete customer orders is currently possible.

The owner of JDRC, realizing that neither the production resources nor the production methods can be changed, wants to know if scheduling methods can be changed to help reduce the backlog of orders. Currently, the scheduling system is based on a first come, first served priority. A customer order is dated when it comes in and is placed in the backlog queue. The job orders are then processed one at a time in the order that they are dated. As the backlog grows, the oldest orders are those that are placed into production first. In Exhibit 9C-3, the next ten customer job orders are listed in the order that they will be processed under the current scheduling method. For example, the September 1 (9/1) job will be first dispatched for production.

EXHIBIT 9C-3 UNFILLED JDRC JOB ORDERS AND ESTIMATED TIME REQUIREMENTS

Job Date	*Procurement Time (days)*	*Painting Time (days)*
9/1	18	50
9/3	10	8
9/4	34	10
9/5	27	38
9/10	50	12
9/12	61	11
9/26	12	46
10/2	15	76
10/7	20	10
10/14	45	12

CASE QUESTIONS

1. Under the current first-come, first-served dispatching rule for scheduling production, how long (in days) will it take to complete all of the ten jobs in Exhibit 9C-3?
2. Redo the order in which the jobs will be dispatched for production by using the longest processing time dispatching rule. How long (in days) will it take to complete all ten jobs under this scheduling system? (Add total processing times together to determine total processing time for all ten days.)
3. Redo the order in which the jobs will be dispatched for production by using the shortest processing time dispatching rule. How long (in days) will it take to complete all ten jobs under this scheduling system? (Add total processing times together to determine total processing time for all ten days.)
4. Redo the order in which the jobs will be dispatched for production by using Johnson's sequencing dispatching rules. How long (in days) will it take to complete all ten jobs under this scheduling system?
5. Which of the scheduling methods used in Questions 1 through 4 would you recommend for JDRC? Why?

SUPPLEMENT 9-1
Queuing Analysis and Simulation

The procedure by which we approach queuing analysis is basically the same as the EOQ modeling approach discussed in Chapter 8. We identify and model the relevant cost parameters of the queuing situation and plug the necessary data into the model to derive scheduling information with which to achieve a desired service level. Alternatively, we could find a queuing model that has already been derived that fits our queuing situation. That is, we could use existing queuing models that we find through research to fit a particular queuing situation. Identifying an existing queuing model's applicability to fit an organization's queuing situation requires a thorough understanding of queuing model characteristics.

QUEUING MODEL CHARACTERISTICS

The characteristics of a queuing model can be broken down into characteristics of its calling population, its queue, and its service facility.

Calling Population

The characteristics of a calling population are as follows:

1. *Arrival pattern* Do members of the calling population arrive all at one time at the service facility or do they arrive randomly? Many business calling populations arrive randomly and follow a Poisson probability distribution. A **Poisson probability distribution,** as seen in Exhibit 9S-1, is a discrete probability distribution similar in shape to the continuous normal probability distribution. The arrival pattern of customers at a telephone booth is an example of a Poisson distribution.
2. *Behavior pattern* Are customers stuck once they enter a queue or does the system permit balking? **Balking** is the ability of a customer to move out of a queue or to a different service facility, for example, to switch to a less busy checkout counter at a grocery store. Many queuing models assume that customers cannot balk and therefore must be used with great caution whenever the calling population involves people.
3. *Size of calling population* Is the calling population infinite or finite? People at a food market might be an example of infinite calling population because any number of people can go into the store. A doctor who limits practice to patients with heart disease has a finite calling population.

EXHIBIT 9S-1 POISSON PROBABILITY DISTRIBUTION FOR ARRIVAL OF CUSTOMERS AT A PHONE BOOTH

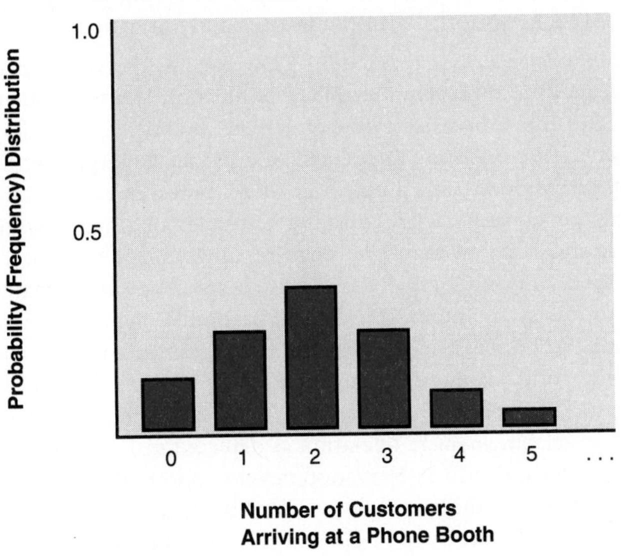

Queue

The primary characteristic of a queue is its maximum length. A queue is classified as either limited or unlimited. The waiting room of a hospital is limited by the floor space and can be considered a limited queue. The drive-through at a McDonald's restaurant may appear to be a limited queue if we restrict the queue to the restaurant's property. But if a large number of people want to use the drive-in windows, the cars waiting can spill out into the streets; the drive-through can therefore be considered virtually infinite.

Service Facility

1. *Service behavior pattern* The way that service facilities give service to those waiting in the queue is called service behavior pattern or **queue discipline.** The behavior pattern might be first-come, first-served, such as teller windows in a bank, or a priority pattern, in which the order of processing of the calling population is ranked. The service facility can have either a preemptive or a nonpreemptive discipline. A **preemptive discipline** permits the calling population to interrupt members already being served. In the military, for example, higher-ranking officers can often "bump" lower-ranking officers out of better

S

housing facilities on military bases. In a **nonpreemptive discipline** the person in the queue with the highest priority gets served first. Medical doctors' appointment scheduling systems are often based on giving patients with greater medical need higher priority than the less-seriously ill patients.

2. *Physical layout of queue and service facility* This refers to the way that the service facility is structured to receive the calling population from the queue. Exhibit 9S-2 illustrates the four basic types of service facility layouts. Some service facility layouts have only one queue and one service facility, as in Exhibit 9S-2(a). A hot-dog vendor using a push cart or a business operation using a single cash register for customer checkouts are examples of single-channel, single-stage operations. If more than one stage of operation is used to complete a service product and only one channel is used, we have single-channel, multi-stage operations, as in Exhibit 9S-2(b). The double window drive-through system at fast-food restaurants (that is, window 1 takes the money and window 2 delivers the food products) is an example of a single-channel, multistage operation. If several service facilities of the same type are used, we refer to this as a multichannel, single-stage operation as depicted in Exhibit 9S-2(c). Many U.S. postal offices and airline reservation ticket windows use this type of system to permit customers in the queue fast service on a first-come, first-served basis. A logical extension of this type of operation is to add more stages of operation as presented in Exhibit 9S-2(d) to form the multichannel, multistage operation. A student going through registration, where several stations are required to complete the registration process, is an example of a multichannel, multistage service operation.

3. *Service time processing behavior* Does the service facility take exactly the same amount of time to process each customer or is the time requirement behavior random? Many service facilities' service processing time behaves randomly and follows an exponential probability distribution. An exponential probability distribution is a negatively (to the left) skewed distribution, as shown by the pattern of phone customer calling times in Exhibit 9S-3. Many queuing models assume an exponential probability distribution of service facility time.

QUEUING ANALYSIS

Once we have identified the characteristics of the queue, we next search for the appropriate model from the many that have been previously developed and published. We could examine the current queuing model literature in journals such as *Management Science* or *Operations Research* or in textbooks or queuing handbooks. These published sources of queuing models save operations managers from having to develop their own models, and they provide detailed explanations of model characteristics and assumptions to ensure that an appropriate model will be selected.

Once a model is selected it is used to generate queuing statistics. Queuing statistics usually include the following: the mean number of customers in the queue and service

EXHIBIT 9S-2 PHYSICAL LAYOUT OF QUEUE SYSTEMS

(A) SINGLE-CHANNEL, SINGLE-STAGE OPERATION

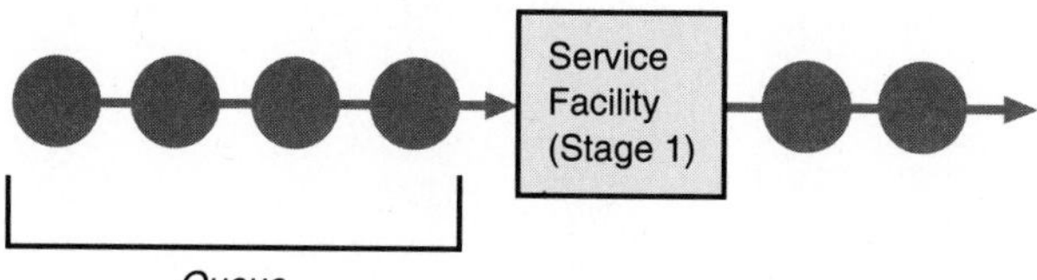

(B) SINGLE-CHANNEL, MULTISTAGE OPERATION

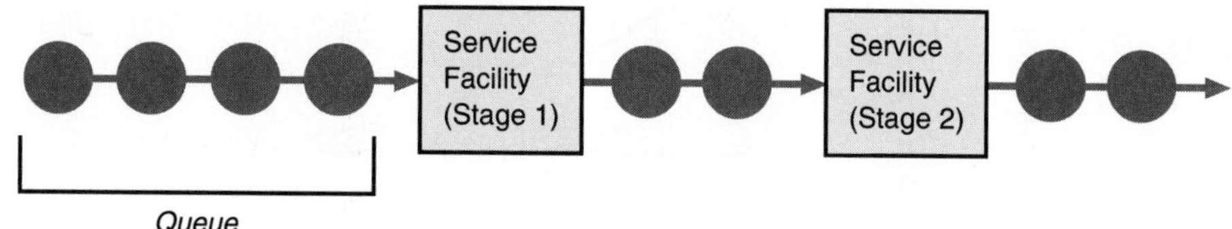

(C) MULTICHANNEL, SINGLE-STAGE OPERATION

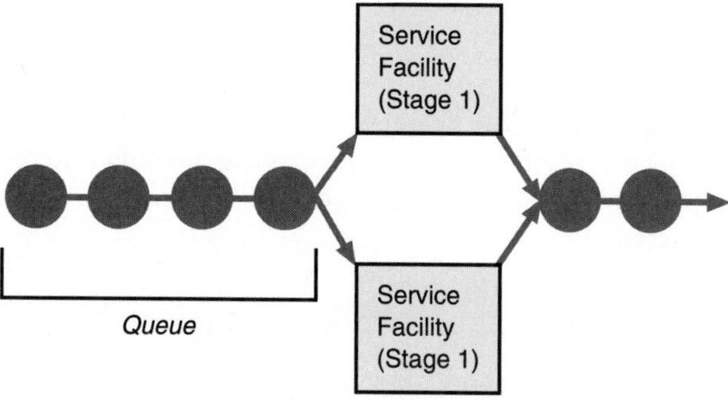

(D) MULTICHANNEL, MULTISTAGE OPERATION

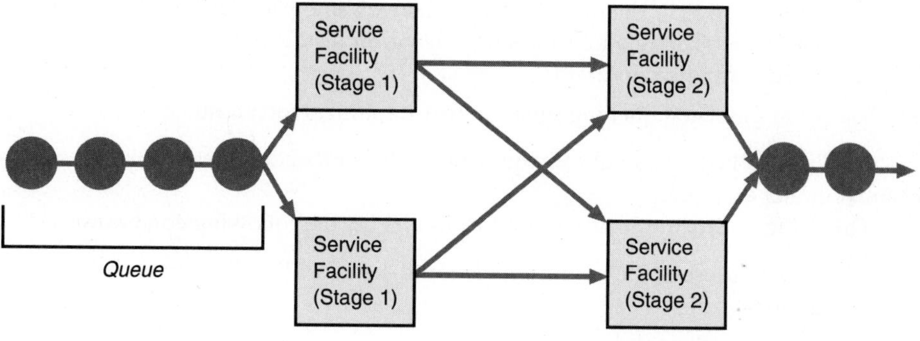

EXHIBIT 9S-3 EXPONENTIAL PROBABILITY DISTRIBUTION FOR CUSTOMER CALLING TIME IN MINUTES

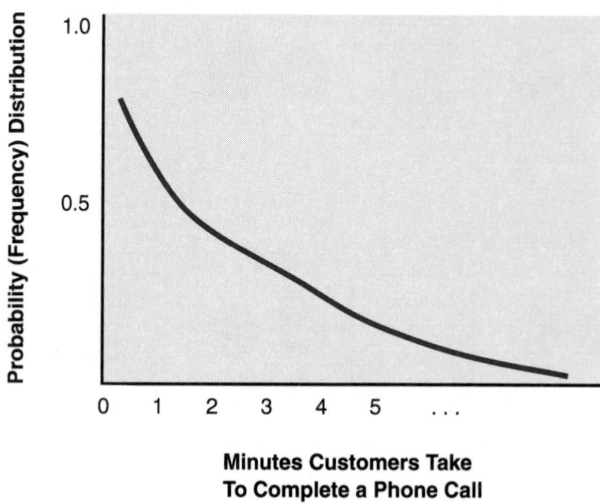

facility and the mean time spent in a queue or service facility. Some models also provide probability information that is used to assess the idleness of the service facility. We usually use these statistics to compare simulated changes in the existing queuing systems. By using a queuing model's statistics we can compare the costs of better service with the costs of providing that better service.

The queuing analysis procedure consists of the following steps:

1. Collect the queuing situation's necessary time and cost information.
2. Develop or select the appropriate queuing model based on fitting the queuing situation with the model's characteristics and assumptions.
3. Compute the queuing model's statistics.
4. Simulate a change in the queue (that is, change some parameter in the model and repeat step 3 until all changes have been simulated and queuing statistics have been computed on each).
5. Select the simulated queuing situation that minimizes total costs.

To illustrate how we might use queuing analysis procedure, let's look at a single-channel model example.

The queuing situation that we want to model fits the following conditions:

1. The arrival pattern of the calling population is described by a Poisson probability distribution.
2. Balking is not allowed.
3. The size of the service population is infinite.

4. The queue is considered to be unlimited.
5. The service behavior pattern is first-come, first-served.
6. There is only one channel and only one stage of service operations.
7. The service time is described by an exponential probability distribution.
8. The mean arrival rate is less than the mean service rate (that is, the variance of the two averages permits the arrivals to exceed the mean service rate occasionally, resulting in a queue).

We will use the following mathematical queuing formulas to derive queuing statistics for analysis.[27] First, let's define the following:

A = mean calling population arrival rate per unit of time (a minute, hour, day, and so on)

S = mean service facility processing rate (the number of customers served per unit of time)

L_s = mean length of the system (the number of customers in the queue plus the number being served), or

$$L_s = \frac{A}{S - A}$$

L_q = mean length of the queue (the number of customers in just the queue), or

$$L_q = \frac{A^2}{S(S - A)}$$

T_s = mean time spent waiting in the system (the queue time plus the service time), or

$$T_s = \frac{1}{S - A}$$

T_q = mean time spent waiting in the queue (the queue time only), or

$$T_q = \frac{A}{S(S - A)}$$

P = probability that a customer will have to wait for service because the service facility is busy, or

$$P = \frac{A}{S}$$

The queue statistics of L_s, L_q, T_s, T_q, and P are the information that we will use to guide us in scheduling production resources.

---

[27] From R. D. Cooper, *Introduction to Queuing Theory* (New York: Macmillan, 1972). See also S. M. Lee and J. P. Shim, *Micro Management Science,* 2nd ed. (Boston: Allyn & Bacon, 1990), Chapter 15.

Suppose that a business has one unloading dock for its trucks. The company currently has one crew of workers (the service facility) unloading the trucks. The trucks' mean arrival rate is two trucks per hour, and the crew's mean unloading rate is three trucks per hour. The crew works an eight-hour shift. The company is considering adding a second and third crew at the unloading dock. Based on research, the work effort of each additional crew is proportional to each other. So the addition of one more crew (a total of two crews) will result in a total mean service rate of six trucks per hour (2 crews × 3 trucks per hour). The addition of two more crews (a total of three crews) will result in a total mean service rate of nine trucks per hour (3 crews × 3 trucks per hour). The cost of one crew is $15 per hour. The company also owns the trucks, and their hourly cost is $45. The company wants to balance the costs of providing additional loading dock service in the form of additional crews, with the cost of idle trucks waiting for that service in such a way that they will minimize total costs.

Consistent with the five-step procedure for queuing analysis above we do the following:

1. *Collect the necessary time and cost information.* For this problem, $A = 2$, $S = 3$, the cost per hour for the trucks is $45, and the cost per hour for a dock crew is $15.
2. *Select the appropriate queuing model.* We are assuming that the queuing situation fits the selected single-channel model's characteristics and assumptions.
3. *Compute the queuing model's statistics.* The L_s value for one crew on the loading dock is computed as follows:

$$L_s = \frac{A}{S - A} = \frac{2}{3 - 2} = 2$$

The other four queuing statistics for the one-crew operation (that is, $S = 3$) are shown in Exhibit 9S-4.

4. *Simulate a change in the queue and repeat step 3.* We simply change S to 6 and 9 and generate the queuing statistics for the other two queuing situations of adding a second and third crew, respectively. These queuing statistics are also

EXHIBIT 9S-4 SAMPLE SINGLE-CHANNEL QUEUING PROBLEM STATISTICS

	NUMBER OF CREWS		
Queuing Model Statistic	*1 (S = 3)*	*2 (S = 6)*	*3 (S = 9)*
Mean number of trucks in the system (L_s)	2	0.500	0.286
Mean number of trucks in the queue (L_q)	1.333	0.167	0.063
Mean time spent by truck in system (T_s)	1	0.250	0.143
Mean time spent by truck in queue (T_q)	0.667	0.083	0.032
Probability that the loading dock is busy (P)	0.667	0.333	0.222

presented in Exhibit 9S-4. We can see from the statistics that more crews reduce the number of trucks in the system and reduce queue waiting time for service. We can use the mean number of trucks in the system, L_s, to indicate the expected costs of idle trucks (that is, the waiting time costs) in this queuing system. In Exhibit 9S-5 the truck cost and crew costs per number of crews are simulated. As we can see in Exhibit 9S-5, the L_s for one crew working an eight-hour shift is 2. With eight hours in a shift and a cost of $45 per hour, the total truck costs are $720 (2 × 8 × $45). The cost of the one-crew shift is only $120 (1 × 8 × 15). This gives us a total queuing cost of $840 ($720 + $120). Repeating the same computations for the two- and three-crew dock service facility arrangement, we see that the total costs vary from a low of $420 to a high of $840.

5. *Select the simulated queuing situation that minimizes total costs.* In this example, the least-cost service facility arrangement is to have two crews working on the loading docks. Note that the three cost values form a U-shaped cost curve as expected in Figure 9-9.

While in this application we did not use all of the queuing statistics in the cost computation, they can be used in many different ways and generally provide useful planning information. Most importantly, we have seen in this example that queuing analysis has helped define the scheduling needs.

SIMULATION ANALYSIS

In queuing analysis, we simulated changes in parameters and recomputed multiple queuing statistics. We referred to this type of simulation in Chapter 8 as a deterministic simulation because probability distributions concerning some of the parameters were unknown. In many queuing situations we must not only know the arrival behavior pattern and service facility probability distributions, but we must also know the type of distribution (that is, Poisson or exponential probability distribution) of model parame-

EXHIBIT 9S-5 TOTAL COST OF SINGLE-CHANNEL QUEUING SYSTEM PROBLEM

	TRUCK COSTS (WAITING COSTS)			*CREW COSTS (SERVICE FACILITY COSTS)*				
L_s	*Hours per Shift*	*Cost per Hour*	*Total*	*Number of Crews*	*Hours per Shift*	*Cost per Hour*	*Total*	*Total Queuing Costs*
2	8	$45	$720	1	8	$15	$120	$840
0.500	8	45	180	2	8	15	240	420
0.286	8	45	103	3	8	15	360	463

ters. In some queuing situations, however, we cannot assume that a Poisson or exponential probability distribution applies to arrival or service facility rates. In these situations simulation analysis can be used to derive useful planning information.

One of the most commonly used simulation procedures is the Monte Carlo method. The Monte Carlo method permits us to include probability distributions in a model without the distributions having to be classified as a particular type, such as a Poisson probability distribution. It can be used to model almost any type of random probability-based system, including queuing systems, inventory systems, or materials handling systems. We introduced the Monte Carlo simulation method as a six-step procedure in Supplement 8-1 as a planning method for inventory management. In this section, let's apply it as a scheduling aid.

S

Suppose that a company wanted to compare the costs of two alternative personnel scheduling strategies. The company operates a delivery service to numerous customers throughout a city. The company has a small fleet of vans but must schedule van drivers for the delivery service it offers to its customers. The company is considering a fixed scheduling strategy that will schedule seven truck drivers every day. The company's variable scheduling strategy is to use the number of drivers demanded today as the number of drivers to schedule for tomorrow's operation.

The cost of a van truck's being demanded and no driver's being available has been estimated by the company's cost accounting staff at $200 per truck per day. This cost represents the lost revenue that could have been obtained if a driver had been available to handle the customer demand and the cost of the idle truck. The cost of having a driver scheduled and available but not being used is $100 per truck per day. Based on fifty days of observations, the driver demand frequency distribution is presented in Exhibit 9S-6. As we can see in Exhibit 9S-6, the number of truck drivers demanded ranges from five to nine per day. The company would like a month's operation (twenty days) simulated to determine what it should expect in the way of total costs for both the fixed and variable driver scheduling strategies.

We can simulate this problem by using the six-step Monte Carlo procedure discussed in Supplement 8-1 as follows:

1. *Identify the simulation rules, policies, or strategies.* We have two strategies to simulate. The fixed strategy calls for scheduling seven drivers for each of the twenty days of operation. The variable strategy will use today's driver demand to equal the next day's scheduled number of drivers. We will let this strategy have the first day's schedule of seven drivers. The desired statistics for this simulation are the total costs for both operations for the twenty days of simulation period.
2. *Collect probability and relevant cost data.* The frequency data in Exhibit 9S-6 presents the probability information for this simulation study. The relevant costs are the costs of not having a driver when there is a demand (that is, a shortage of drivers), which is $200 per day per driver and the costs of having an idle driver (a surplus of drivers), which is $100 per day per driver.
3. *Convert the observed frequency distribution to a random number sampling distribution.* This is accomplished in Exhibit 9S-7 for the fixed schedule strategy. Note

EXHIBIT 9S-6 SAMPLE SIMULATION PROBLEM PROBABILITY DISTRIBUTIONS

Daily Number of Drivers Demanded	*Observed Frequency (number)*	*Probability (%)*	*Cumulative Probability (%)*	*Random Number Assignment*
5	10	20	20	00–19
6	4	8	28	20–27
7	18	36	64	28–63
8	10	20	84	64–83
9	8	16	100	84–99
	50	100		

that the random number assignment is related by frequency to the probability distribution and by number to the cumulative probability distribution.

4. *Select a random number generator system.* For this simulation study we will use random numbers from Appendix F. The random numbers selected from the appendix are listed in the second column of Exhibits 9S-7 and 9S-8.
5. *Determine how many time periods to simulate.* The company wanted to simulate a month's operation, or twenty days of operation.
6. *Conduct the simulation process to generate the desired statistics.* The fixed schedule service strategy is simulated in Exhibit 9S-7. In the case of simulation 1, a random number of 06 is used from the random number table in Appendix F. This gives us a simulated demand of truck drivers for the first day of five drivers. Under the company's fixed schedule strategy the company has seven drivers available to meet this demand, which results in a surplus of two drivers and incurs a total cost of being idle of $200 (2 drivers × costs of $100 per day). Having simulated the first day's cost of the fixed schedule strategy, we now continue using the same procedure to determine the other nineteen days of costs as presented in Exhibit 9S-7. The total simulated cost of twenty days using the fixed schedule strategy is $2,600 for the shortage and surplus costs. The variable schedule strategy is similarly simulated as presented in Exhibit 9S-8. With the exception of the first day's assumed scheduled value of seven drivers, the number of van truck drivers scheduled for one day is the same as the simulated demand of the prior day. We again determine the cost of the shortages and surpluses to determine the total simulated cost under the variable schedule strategy of $4,100. Based on the two strategies' total costs, it is obvious that we should choose the fixed schedule strategy to minimize costs.

This example illustrates the analytic ease by which the Monte Carlo method is performed and some of its advantages as a scheduling aid. For example, in the problem we were able to test the two scheduling strategies without actually risking the truck operation. The procedure did not require a great deal of model development or research.

EXHIBIT 9S-7 FIXED SCHEDULE SERVICE STRATEGY

Simulation Number (days)	*Random Number*	*Resulting Demand of Van Drivers*	*Number of Van Drivers Scheduled*	*Shortage of Van Drivers*	*Surplus of Van Drivers*	*Total Cost of Shortage*	*Total Cost of Surplus*	*Total Costs*
1	06	5	7		2		$200	$200
2	91	9	7	2		$400		400
3	69	8	7	1		200		200
4	34	7	7					
5	50	7	7					
6	23	6	7		1		100	100
7	41	7	7					
8	27	6	7		1		100	100
9	60	7	7					
10	61	7	7					
11	39	7	7					
12	19	5	7		2		200	200
13	74	8	7	1		200		200
14	38	7	7					
15	02	5	7		2		200	200
16	60	7	7					
17	74	8	7	1		200		200
18	92	9	7	2		400		400
19	13	5	7		2		200	200
20	09	5	7		2		200	200
								$2,600

It generated a statistic that clearly helped make the choice between the two strategies an objective choice. On the other hand, it should be mentioned that the randomization process may not be truly random if too few simulations are used in the study. While stimulation model validation is beyond the scope of this textbok, the validation of simulation models requires a large enough number of simulated behaviors to capture the real behavior of the system that is being modeled and thereby avoid nonrandom behavior.[28] The results of a nonrandom simulation could provide misleading information. In practice, a great deal of effort is usually devoted to validating simulation studies to ensure the usefulness of the information they generate.

The Monte Carlo method is a particularly useful approach for scheduling resources when we have multiple behaviors that follow probability distributions. For example, in a hospital, operating rooms are staffed with doctors, nurses, and trained specialists. We also use recovery rooms, instruments, and special equipment facilities. Each of these

[28] For a good review of simulation model development and validation, see H. J. Watson and J. H. Blackstone, *Computer Simulation* (New York: Wiley, 1989), pp. 544–560.

EXHIBIT 9S-8 VARIABLE SCHEDULE SERVICE STRATEGY

Simulation Number (days)	*Random Number*	*Resulting Demand of Van Drivers*	*Number of Van Drivers Scheduled*	*Shortage of Van Drivers*	*Surplus of Van Drivers*	*Total Cost of Shortage*	*Total Cost of Surplus*	*Total Costs*
1	06	5	7*		2		$200	$200
2	91	9	5	4		$800		800
3	69	8	9		1		100	100
4	34	7	8		1		100	100
5	50	7	7					
6	23	6	7		1		100	100
7	41	7	6	1		200		200
8	27	6	7		1		100	100
9	60	7	6	1		200		200
10	61	7	7					
11	39	7	7					
12	19	5	7		2		200	200
13	74	8	5	3		600		600
14	38	7	8		1		100	100
15	02	5	7		2		200	200
16	60	7	5	2		400		400
17	74	8	7	1		200		200
18	92	9	8	1		200		200
19	13	5	9		4		400	400
20	09	5	5					
								$4,100

* For simulation 1, an expected demand of seven drivers is scheduled to begin the process.

types of personnel and facilities have their own frequency or probability distribution of behavior. We can examine the possibility of scheduling these types of multiple resources when they are brought together for an operation. Our objective in this type of multiple scheduling problem is to optimize the use of operating rooms by modeling the use of the service resources in an operation using the Monte Carlo simulation method. Instead of just simulating one probability distribution, we would use a separate probability distribution for each type of resource that behaved probabilistically. This type of multiple scheduling problem in hospital operating rooms has been modeled using the Monte Carlo method and other simulation procedures.[29] Other simulation procedures that have been used to model service operations include specialized computer languages such as those listed at the top of page 480.

[29] See N. K. Kwak, H. H. Schnitz, and P. J. Kuzdrall, "Operating Room and Recovery Room Usage: Two Simulation Applications," in N. K. Kwak and M. J. Schniederjans (Eds.), *Managerial Application of Operations Research* (Washington, D.C.: University Press of America, 1982), pp. 367–384.

1. *General purpose simulation systems (GPSS) computer language* This type of simulation language is ideally structured to examine queuing situations and is capable of modeling almost any type of service or manufacturing operation.[30]
2. *Interactive financial planning systems (IFPS) computer language.* This type of simulation language is used to model financial reports and accounting statements. It uses the Monte Carlo simulation method to simulate and project pro-forma income statements.[31]
3. *Simscript computer language.* This is a general-purpose simulation language that can be applied to model manufacturing, communications, logistics, transportation, and gaming situations. Its special-purpose simulation nature has made it one of the easiest and most popular of the modeling languages to use for simulation.[32]

[30] T. J. Schriber, *Simulation Using GPSS* (New York: John Wiley & Sons, 1974). The microcomputer version of this language is GPSS/X; *GPSS/X User Manual* (White Plains, N.Y.: IBM, 1990).

[31] *EXECUCOM User's Manual* (Austin, Tex.: Execucom Systems Corporation, 1989).

[32] *SIMSCRIPT User Manual* (La Jolla, Calif.: CACI, Inc., 1990).

SUPPLEMENT 9-2
Linear Programming and Scheduling

In this supplement, we present an example problem to show how linear programming (LP) can be used as a scheduling method. (Students are encouraged to review the LP formulation procedure in Appendix D at the end of this book.) Although LP can be used to model any type of scheduling problem (scheduling human, technology, or system resources), the example presented here is meant only as a limited illustration of the scheduling capabilities of a powerful and far more versatile mathematical programming method than can be shown in a single problem.

Suppose that a company produces two products: product A and product B. This company wants to plan the unit production of each product for the next three months of January, February, and March. That is, it wants to know how many units of both products A and B should be produced in January, how many in February, and how many in March (that is, decision variables). The company can sell all of the units it produces at a profit of $25 per unit for product A and $27 per unit for product B. Production scheduling in this situation has to consider several capacity and marketing requirements (that is, constraints). Total unit production (both A and B) cannot exceed the capacity of 900 units in January, 775 units in February, and 1,000 units in March. Total production of all units during the three-month period must not exceed the capacity of 2,400 units. For marketing purposes, total production of all product A units for all three months must be at least 1,200 units and total production of all product B units for all three months must be at least 785 units. Also for marketing purposes, the company must produce at least 100 units of each product each month. The company wants to determine the profit-maximizing schedule for product A and product B.

In formulating this scheduling problem, it is necessary to define decision variables (such as x_j) as having two dimensions: units to produce per month and the month the units should be produced in. For this problem we have two products being produced in three months or a total of six unknowns. The resulting decision variables for this problem are

x_1 = number of units of product A to produce in January
x_2 = number of units of product B to produce in January
x_3 = number of units of product A to produce in February
x_4 = number of units of product B to produce in February
x_5 = number of units of product A to produce in March
x_6 = number of units of product B to produce in March

Because the profit per unit will not change by month, the contribution coefficients (that is, c_j) will be repeated in the object function as

$$\text{Maximize: } Z = 25x_1 + 27x_2 + 25x_3 + 27x_4 + 25x_5 + 27x_6$$

The capacity constraints all have total maximum right-hand-side values (that is, b_i) that represent resource limitations. Thus, these constraints will all be less-than or equal-to constraints. Because x_1 plus x_2 represents total production in January, the first constraint in the LP model representing the capacity limitation of 900 total units of production can be expressed as

$$x_1 + x_2 \leq 900 \text{ (January capacity limitation)}$$

Similarly, the February and March capacity constraints are

$$x_3 + x_4 \leq 775 \text{ (February capacity limitation)}$$

$$x_5 + x_6 \leq 1{,}000 \text{ (March capacity limitation)}$$

The total capacity constraint for all products in all months is

$$x_1 + x_2 + x_3 + x_4 + x_5 + x_6 \leq 2{,}400 \text{ (total capacity limitation)}$$

The marketing constraints set minimum production requirements and so they must all be greater-than or equal-to constraints. The constraint for the total minimum production of product A is

$$x_1 + x_3 + x_5 \geq 1{,}200 \text{ (total minimum of product A)}$$

The constraint for the total minimum production of product B is

$$x_2 + x_4 + x_6 \geq 785 \text{ (total minimum of product B)}$$

The individual production of each product per month requires a total of six constraints to express the minimum production level of 100 units each:

$$x_1 \geq 100 \text{ (total minimum of product A in January)}$$
$$x_2 \geq 100 \text{ (total minimum of product B in January)}$$
$$x_3 \geq 100 \text{ (total minimum of product A in February)}$$
$$x_4 \geq 100 \text{ (total minimum of product B in February)}$$
$$x_5 \geq 100 \text{ (total minimum of product A in March)}$$
$$x_6 \geq 100 \text{ (total minimum of product B in March)}$$

To complete the LP formulation we must also add the non-negativity requirements of

$$x_1, x_2, x_3, x_4, x_5, x_6 \geq 0$$

Having formulated the LP model of this scheduling model we now need to use the LP solution method to generate the model's optimized production schedule. To obtain our solution we will use the MICRO PRODUCTION software system. The printout of the LP model solution is presented in Exhibit 9S-9. As we can see in the program output section of the printout in Exhibit 9S-9, the resulting optimized profit is $62,400. This profit can be achieved by producing 100 units of product A in January, 800 units of product B in January, 475 units of product A in February, 300 units of product B in February, 625 units of product A in March, and 100 units of product B in March. The resulting solution for this problem illustrates how LP can be used to generate a master production schedule for the two products on a monthly basis while taking into consideration the capacity and marketing limitations of production activity.

EXHIBIT 9S-9 MICRO PRODUCTION SOFTWARE SOLUTION FOR THE SCHEDULING PROBLEM

Program: Linear Programming

Problem Title: PRODUCT SCHEDULING EXAMPLE

***** Input Data *****

Max. Z = 25x1 + 27x2 + 25x3 + 27x4 + 25x5 + 27x6

Subject to

```
C1  1x1 + 1x2 < = 900
C2  1x3 + 1x4 < = 775
C3  1x5 + 1x6 < = 1000
C4  1x1 + 1x2 + 1x3 + 1x4 + 1x5 + 1x6 < = 2400
C5  1x1 + 1x3 + 1x5 > = 1200
C6  1x2 + 1x4 + 1x6 > = 785
C7  1x1 > = 100
C8  1x2 > = 100
C9  1x3 > = 100
C10 1x4 > = 100
C11 1x5 > = 100
C12 1x6 > = 100
```

***** Program Output *****

Final Optimal Solution

Z = 62400.000

Variable	Value	Reduced Cost
x 1	100.000	0.000
x 2	800.000	0.000
x 3	475.000	0.000
x 4	300.000	0.000
x 5	625.000	0.000
x 6	100.000	0.000

Constraint	Slack/Surplus	Shadow Price
C 1	0.000	0.000
C 2	0.000	0.000
C 3	275.000	0.000
C 4	0.000	27.000
C 5	0.000	–2.000
C 6	415.000	0.000
C 7	0.000	0.000
C 8	700.000	0.000
C 9	375.000	0.000
C10	200.000	0.000
C11	525.000	0.000
C12	0.000	0.000

10

Project Management

CHAPTER OUTLINE

Why Project Management Is Necessary
Basics of Project Management
Project Management Methods
Integrating Management Resources: Using PERT To Increase Productivity
CASE 10-1 A Schedule of Insufficient Time
CASE 10-2 A Critical Path Nobody Would Follow

CHAPTER OBJECTIVES

The material in this chapter should prepare you to do the following:

1. Describe what project management involves.
2. Explain why project management is necessary in operations management.
3. Explain how Gantt charts can be used for controlling projects.
4. Describe PERT project planning.
5. Use PERT analysis to plan projects.
6. Describe the critical path method (CPM) of project planning.
7. Use CPM analysis to minimize project costs.
8. Explain the usefulness of PERT and CPM.
9. Describe some of the more recent extensions of PERT-based methods and technology currently being used in project planning.
10. Describe how PERT can be used to implement the integration of production systems.

A **project** is a one-time or single-use plan consisting of a set of tasks or activities with a specific objective.[1] To conduct a project, an organization must plan the schedule of tasks that make up the project. In the last chapter we discussed scheduling in repetitive and job operations. Scheduling production activity is also required in project operations. In Chapter 1 we introduced project operations (that is, limited lot operations) as producers of large-scale, single, or limited-edition products such as bridges or homes. Project operations include both manufacturing (building a space shuttle) and service (test-marketing a new product) organizations. **Project management** involves the management functions of organizing, planning, scheduling, and controlling in project operations and in operations of all types that conduct projects. S

• • •

WHY PROJECT MANAGEMENT IS NECESSARY

Project management is important and necessary for project planning because it helps managers define important product characteristics such as the timing of delivery for a product or a project completion date. Some project-oriented organizations take years to deliver their products. The production resource allocations of work force, materials, and equipment for a project over many years add substantial complexity to project planning. Because of the long-term and complex nature of some projects, the timing of delivery or project completion dates becomes an integral part of the product. Indeed, construction contracts are often awarded on the basis of when a construction firm can complete a structure rather than just on cost considerations alone. In organizations that undertake projects that take long periods of time, project planning can provide a competitive advantage in customer service by defining product delivery periods well ahead of actual production activity. Many project planning methods, which we discuss later in this chapter, can be used to determine accurate product delivery or completion dates. This type of project planning information is necessary to allow managers to define their product's timing characteristics. Q

Project management is also necessary for improved production scheduling flexibility. Many project planning methods can establish schedules that define completion times for all of the varied tasks that make up the project. In the process of defining a production schedule, these project scheduling methods define which tasks can be delayed without delaying the entire project if problems are encountered in production (that is, which tasks have **slack time**). Management can use this flexibility when scheduling individual production task activities to avoid idleness in production resources.

Project management is also necessary for controlling project production activity. In all projects, there is a series of tasks or activities that must be completed exactly on

[1] D. H. Holt, *Management,* 2nd ed. (Englewood Cliffs, N.J.: Prentice-Hall, 1990), p. 152.

schedule in order to avoid delaying the entire project. These are known as **critical tasks** or **critical activities.** In the complex and multiple-activity environment of projects such as building a jet engine, it is difficult to identify the particular set of tasks or activities that are critical from those that are noncritical. Project planning methods are necessary to identify these critical activities so management can efficiently and effectively focus its attention on their timely completion.

BASICS OF PROJECT MANAGEMENT

As previously stated, project management involves the management functions of organizing, planning, scheduling, and controlling. How these functions are applied in organizations depends on the basic characteristics of all project production activity.

Although each project is unique, all projects share a set of basic characteristics that include the following:

1. A number of sequential activities make up the project.
2. Some of the activities that make up the project can be performed concurrently.
3. The project has a start date and a completion date.
4. Each activity in the project has a start and completion date.
5. Some activities are critical and some (those that possess slack time) are noncritical.

QUESTION: Does an organization have to be a project operation to use project management ideas and methods?

ANSWER: No. Most organizations are not project operations, but they do conduct project activities that can benefit from project management ideas and methods.

Organizing

There is more than one way to structure project-oriented organizations. Some project-oriented organizations that pursue multiple projects have found it highly efficient to adopt a **matrix organization** structure. As we can see in Figure 10-1, each of the functional areas in a matrix organization are divided into separate units, each serving a different project for as many projects as the organization chooses to undertake. This type of organization structure is ideal in project operations that provide a single or only a few products. Airline jet manufacturers that make one or only a few jet airliners are

FIGURE 10-1 A MATRIX ORGANIZATION STRUCTURE

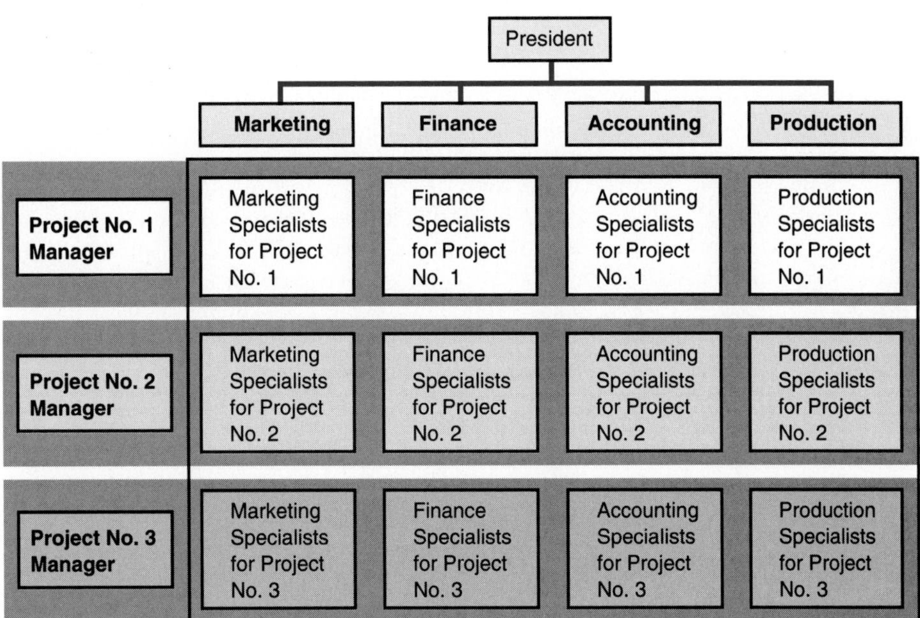

able to use this organization structure quite effectively. By organizing a smaller group of personnel and dedicating resources to specific products (or projects), the matrix organization can more efficiently concentrate production efforts to achieve its more singularly project-oriented production objectives.

In a small business project operation that focuses its production activity on only one or two projects at a time, the grouping of human, technology, and system resources is less formal than in the matrix organization in that substantial differences exist in the resources needed for various projects (that is, not all departments are represented in each project). These less-formal operations are called **project organizations.**

Organizations can also temporarily reorganize to handle infrequent project activities with an approach called "team management." **Team management** (or **team planning**) is a form of participative management in which a small group of managers and planning specialists are temporarily assigned responsibilities for initiating plans and objectives for specific activities or projects. The teams are organized at each level of management (upper-level, middle-level, and lower-level management) throughout the organization. Each team, at each level of management, passes its team's plans and objectives down to the next team at the next lower level of management. By dedicating a smaller number of individuals to handle a project and empowering them as a team to set plans and objectives for the project, organizations have benefitted by improved communication between management and staff specialists, improved communication between levels of management, and better planning, scheduling, and control in project planning.

Q

QUESTION: Can team management be used to support total quality management (TQM) in project planning?

ANSWER: Yes. A project is a product and TQM (discussed in Chapter 2) is an approach to improving product quality. Team management involves improving communication (a TQM implementation rule), which in turn helps identify project quality problems and aid in their resolution. Team management also supports the idea of teamwork (a TQM tactic), which helps motivate participants to work toward common product-quality goals. Team management also helps cooperative partnerships (a TQM tactic) between managers and staff specialists, and between managers at different levels in the organization.

Planning, Scheduling, and Controlling

In addition to altering their structure to accommodate project activity, all types of operations must undertake strategic, tactical, and operational planning efforts to define and achieve production objectives. At the strategic level of planning, project planners are concerned with selecting projects that will support long-range strategic objectives. Project planners use the output of strategic planning, such as the corporate mission statement, or a strategic objective like growth as criteria for choosing projects that will help the organization achieve its strategic objectives. Tactical planning of projects usually involves establishing the initial project planning schedule for the next year or two. This would consist of arranging items such as vendor supply contracts, equipment rental contracts, and transportation contracts to bring supplies and workers to the site location where the work will take place. A general plan for the project—called a **project plan**—is developed from tactical planning efforts. A project plan is similar to a master production schedule in repetitive manufacturing. The project plan provides estimated start and completion dates for all of the tasks or activities that make up a project as well as the project completion date. It is the master plan for achieving the project in a specific period of time. Operational planning in project management usually involves daily monitoring of project activity completions. It also involves controlling the project by making the necessary revisions of the project plan to keep it on schedule with the project completion date.

To accomplish the tactical and operational planning activities in project management, a number of project planning methods can be used to support scheduling and controlling at these planning stages. One of these methods is the Gantt chart. In Chapter 9 we discussed how Gantt charts are used in repetitive production scheduling. These charts are also commonly applied to scheduling project operations. As we can see in the example of the house-building project in Figure 10-2, a Gantt chart allows the timing of each of the activities that make up the project to be quickly conceptualized. The length of the horizontal bars in the chart clearly depicts the length of time allowed for each of the project activities and defines their planned start and completion periods (for example, the "locate site" activity takes three weeks). Note also that some of the activities in this project overlap (for example, activities a and c). One of the basic characteristics of project planning is that project activities can be performed concurrently. This concurrent or simultaneous production activity keeps project planning from becoming a simple matter of operation sequencing (discussed in Chapter 9).

The Gantt chart can also be structured to require a periodic status report. The status report may consist of a manager's confirming that an activity and all of its immediate sequential prior activities have been completed. As we can see in Figure 10-2, the status report required at the end of June should confirm that activity f (and all prior activities a through e) are complete if the project is to be finished by the project completion date in November. If the status reports show that activity f is behind its project plan completion date, the activity delay might cause a delay in the entire project. The delay will depend on whether f is a critical or noncritical activity. Although all activities must eventually be completed and are therefore important to the project's completion, the timing of completion of some activities makes them noncritical for a specific period of time. For example, the activity of designing the house's layout (activity c) in Figure

FIGURE 10-2 GANTT CHART OF HOUSE-BUILDING PROJECT

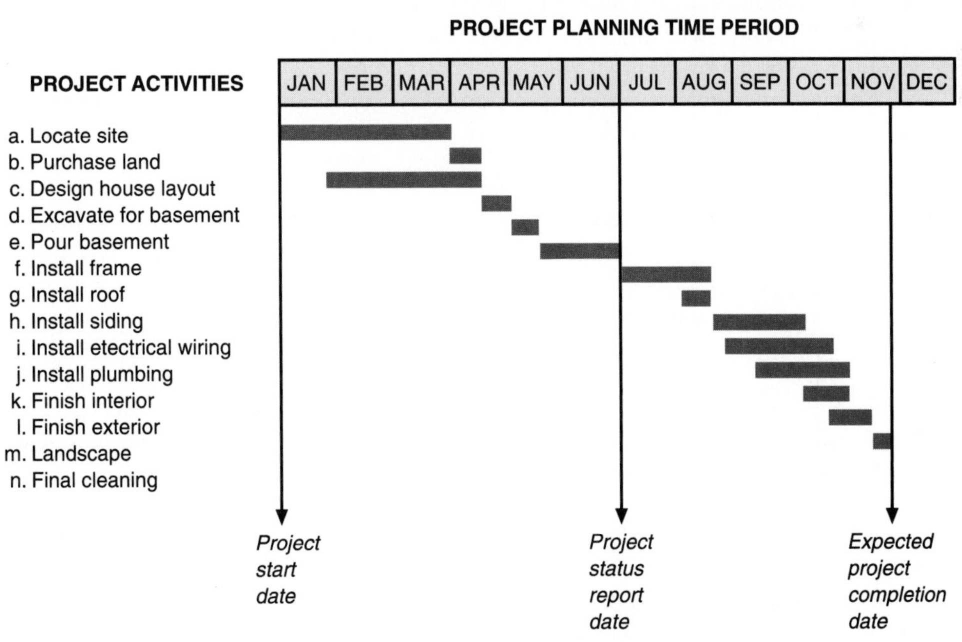

10-2 must be completed before the builder will know how to excavate (activity d) for the basement. Yet the design could have started early in the beginning of January, permitting some slack time and flexibility in scheduling. Identifying such areas of flexibility and using them to control the flow of production activity is an important part of project management.

To help managers with all aspects of project planning, a number of methods have been developed.

PROJECT MANAGEMENT METHODS

In this section we will discuss two of the most commonly used project planning methods: the program evaluation and review technique (PERT) and the critical path method (CPM). We will also discuss the usefulness and recent technology and methodology extensions of these planning methods.

Program Evaluation and Review Technique (PERT)

The **program evaluation and review technique,** or **PERT,** is principally used as a planning procedure for any project operation in service or manufacturing operations. It can also be used for scheduling any type of job requiring a sequence of multiple, concurrent activities. PERT was developed in the 1950s by the Special Projects Office of the U.S. Navy, working with representatives of Lockheed and Booz, Allen & Hamilton (a consulting group), to plan and control the manufacturing of Polaris missiles.

Among other project planning information, PERT analysis seeks to answer the following time-related scheduling questions:

1. What is the expected project completion date?
2. What are the expected start and finish dates for each activity that makes up the entire project?
3. Which activities are critical and must be completed exactly on schedule to keep the entire project on schedule?
4. How long can the noncritical activities be delayed before they cause a delay in the project?

PERT can also be used to examine the probability of completing a project in a given or desired amount of time.

PERT NETWORK Because PERT is as much a graphic scheduling method as it is a mathematical procedure, it is necessary to understand how to develop a PERT network. A **PERT network** is a graph of the activities that make up a project. An activity is usually represented by a circle called a **node** and an arrow coming from the node. These elements of a PERT network are shown in Figure 10-3(a). The activities in a

FIGURE 10-3 PERT NETWORK ELEMENTS

(A) NODES AND ARROW

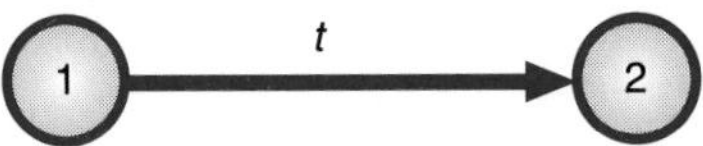

(B) A PERT NETWORK

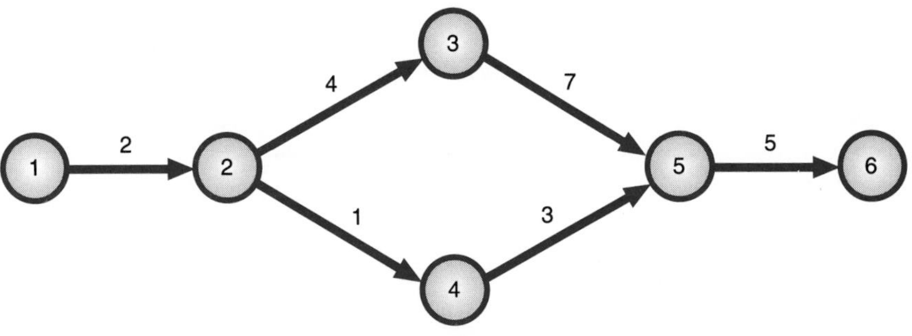

PERT network are usually assigned numbers. Node 1 in Figure 10-3(a) begins the activity that can be labeled 1–2. We verbally express this activity as "the activity of going from node 1 to node 2." The arrow indicates the direction of movement from one node to another and also helps define the sequence of activities that must be performed to complete the project. Thus, numbering the activities defines the subsequent activities and provides the sequential ordering of the activities. The *t* represents the estimated time it takes to complete each activity. Such activity time estimates are usually obtained from time studies on past worker performance or from subjective judgment of managers, supervisors, and employees.

A series of activities are combined to form a PERT network in Figure 10-3(b). The network in Figure 10-3(b) consists of six activities. Before activity 2–3 can be started, activity 1–2 must be complete. Likewise, before activity 5–6 can be started, activities 3–5 and 4–5 must be complete. The lengths of the arrows do not represent the length of time to complete each activity. In Figure 10-3(b) we can see that the total time required for activities 2–4 and 4–5 is only 4 (1 + 3), but in the same distance above them activities 2–3 and 3–5 require a total of 11 (4 + 7).

A PERT network begins with a single node and ends with a single node, and all activities must be on at least one continuous path through the network. The constraints can often cause problems when drawing the PERT network. Occasionally two activities leave one node and then travel to and enter the same node. This situation, which is presented in Figure 10-4(a), is not permitted in a PERT network. We can correct this situation by creating a dummy activity. A **dummy activity,** as shown by activity 2–3

FIGURE 10-4 THE CREATION OF A DUMMY ACTIVITY

(A) AN INCORRECT PERT NETWORK

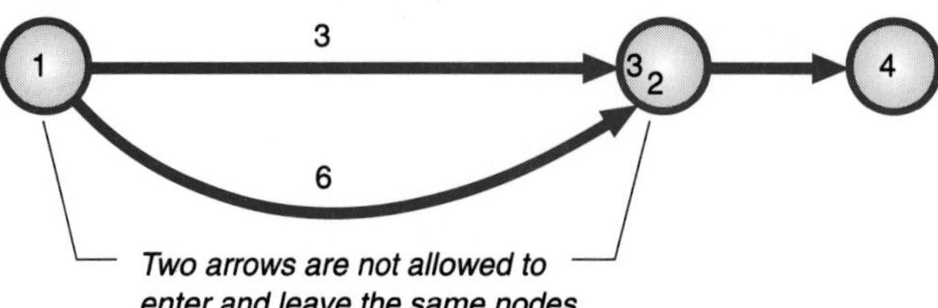

(B) A CORRECTED PERT NETWORK WITH DUMMY ACTIVITY

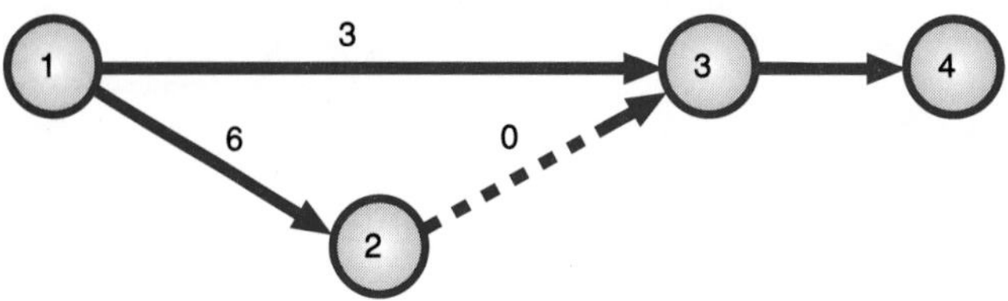

(C) APPLICATION OF DUMMY ACTIVITIES IN MEDICAL CARE EXAMPLE

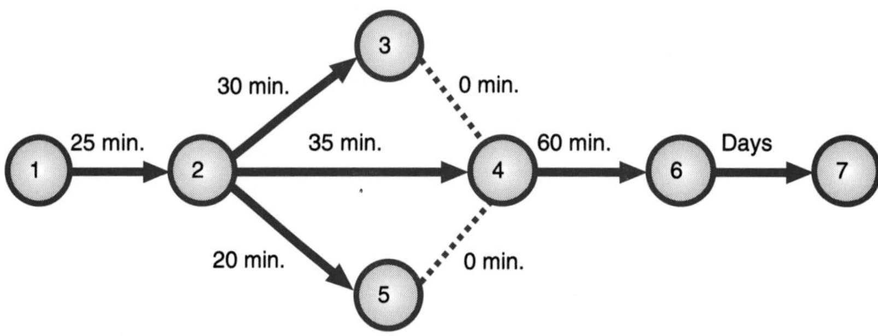

ACTIVITY	DESCRIPTION
1 – 2	Initial visit with doctor
2 – 3	Lab test 1
2 – 4	Lab test 2
2 – 5	Lab test 3
4 – 6	Doctor diagnosis
6 – 7	Treatment

S

QUESTION: What is a "real-world" example of a service product for which precedence relationships might require the use of dummy activities?

ANSWER: One example is the doctor-hospital diagnostic testing services offered in the medical industry.[2] When a patient visits a doctor in a hospital emergency room, the doctor usually needs the results of laboratory tests to help diagnose the patient's illness. As presented in Figure 10-4(c), these numerous lab tests may take different amounts of time, yet all must be completed before the doctor can diagnose the patient's illness and begin treatment. Dummy activities can clearly show that, regardless of the individual time requirements, all of the lab tests must be completed before the doctor can diagnose the patient's illness and begin treatment.

in Figure 10-4(b), does not exist except for notational purposes and is assigned zero time. A dummy activity is also used to correctly represent logical activity precedence relationships. In Figure 10-4(b), activity 1–2 might not have a direct relationship with activity 3–4 except that activity 1–2 must be complete before activity 3–4 can be started. Because activity 1–3 takes only 3 units of time and activity 1–2 takes 6 units of time, one might incorrectly assume that activity 3–4 could begin as soon as activity 1–3 is complete. The dummy makes clear that activity 3–4 cannot be started until both activities 1–3 and 1–3 are complete. Without the dummy in Figure 10-4(b), activity 1–2 would be a dead-end activity, which is not permitted.

Another graphing problem can occur when there appears to be a need to overlap arrows. This situation is presented in Figure 10-5(a). Overlapping arrows is not permitted and is actually unnecessary. No PERT network ever needs to overlap activity arrows. As shown in Figure 10-5(b), by unfolding node 1, we can bring it out and away from the other nodes and avoid overlapping arrows. In real-world applications, PERT networks can consist of thousands of activities. We will limit our discussion to networks consisting of ten or fewer activities. The PERT technique presented in the next section can handle project planning problems of any size.

PERT TECHNIQUE The PERT technique consists of five steps. To aid in understanding each step we will illustrate it with an example.

1. *Prepare a list of the project activities and their sequential order. Estimate each expected activity time (t) and its respective variance.* The following formula and the one on the next page are based on a six-value weighted average and variance statistics, and are used to determine these time estimates:

$$\text{Expected activity time} = \frac{a + 4(m) + b}{6}$$

[2] N. K. Kwak, J. J. Vargo, and M. J. Schniederjans, "The Value of Battery Testing in Clinical Laboratory: A PERT Network Case Study," *Journal of Medical Systems,* 8, No. 4 (1984), 239–247.

FIGURE 10-5 OVERLAPPING NETWORK ACTIVITIES

(A) AN INCORRECT PERT NETWORK

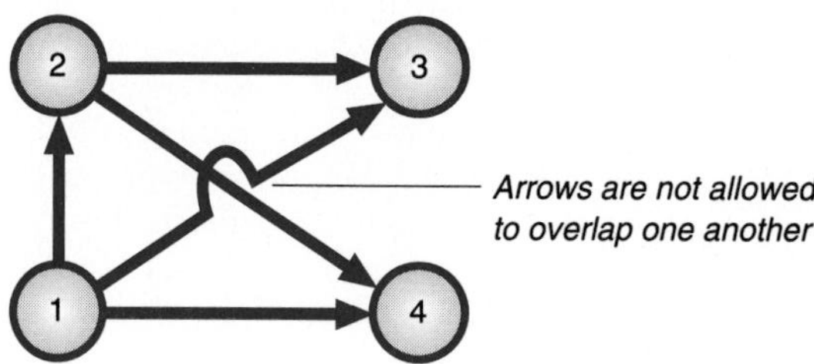

(B) A CORRECTED PERT NETWORK

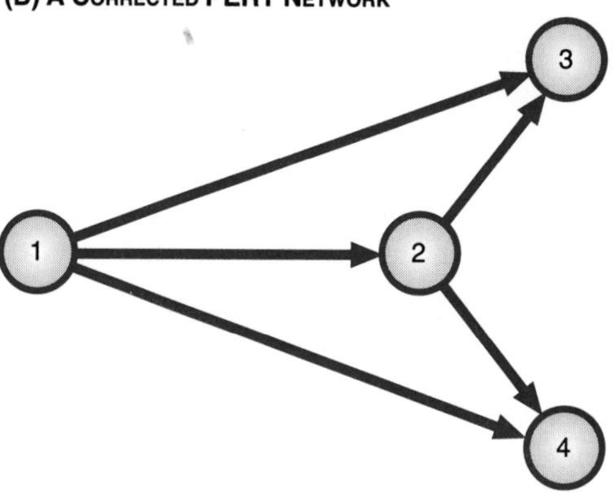

$$\text{Activity time variance} = \sigma_t^2 = \left(\frac{b - a}{6}\right)^2$$

where

a = an optimistic time estimate
m = a most probable time estimate
b = a pessimistic time estimate

The activity time variance statistic σ_t^2 serves the same purpose as a variance statistic about a mean value, and is used in the computation of a standard deviation statistic. (Students who are unfamiliar with standard deviation should review Appendix A at the end of this textbook.)

For our sample problem, the list of activities is presented in Table 10-1. The activities are numbered so as to provide a sequential ordering of the activities. The time estimates were calculated using the formula just given. For example, the expected time of five weeks for activity 1–2 was determined by

$$t = \frac{a + 4(m) + b}{6} = \frac{3 + 4(4) + 11}{6} = 5$$

and its variance was determined by

$$\sigma_t^2 = \left(\frac{b - a}{6}\right)^2 = \left(\frac{11 - 3}{6}\right)^2 = 1.778$$

2. *Develop the PERT network based on the data in Step 1.* The PERT network is presented in Figure 10-6. In developing networks, remember that we must always begin with node 1. From that node draw the necessary arrows to represent the number of activities that start from node 1. If it is necessary to violate networking rules temporarily, do not worry. Just go back and correct the network as shown in Figures 10-4 and 10-5.
3. *Determine the earliest start times and the earliest finish times for all of the activities in the PERT network.* **Earliest start time** is the earliest time we can start a given activity and still keep the entire project on time. **Earliest finish time** is the earliest time we can finish an activity and still keep the entire project on time. Let's define the following:

   ES = earliest start time
   EF = earliest finish time
   t = expected activity time

   Then

   $$EF = ES + t$$

   for each of the activities as we move from the beginning of time in the network.

TABLE 10-1 PERT EXAMPLE PROBLEM TIME ESTIMATES

	TIME ESTIMATES (WEEKS)				
Activity	*Optimistic* (a)	*Most Probable* (m)	*Pessimistic* (b)	*Expected Activity Time* (t)	*Activity Time Variance* σ_t^2
1–2	3	4	11	5	1.778
1–3	1	2	3	2	0.111
2–3	2.5	3.5	7.5	4	0.694
2–4	0.5	1	1.5	1	0.278
2–5	1	2	9	3	1.778
3–6	1	1.5	5	2	0.444
4–7	0.5	1	1.5	1	0.278
5–7	2	3	4	3	0.111
6–7	4	5	12	6	1.778
7–8	0.5	1	1.5	1	0.278

FIGURE 10-6 PERT NETWORK FOR EXAMPLE PROBLEM

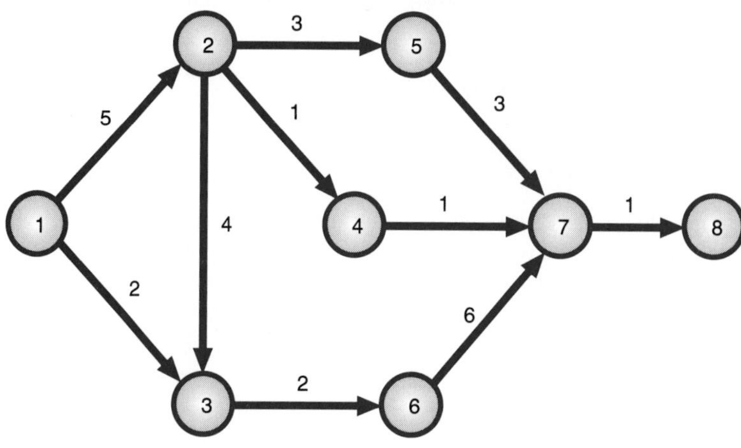

Time in a PERT network always begins with $ES = 0$. For example, activity 1–2 is the first activity in the sample problem network. It has $t = 5$, so activity 1–2 has an $ES = 0$ and an $EF = 5$. As we move forward through the network, we may need to use the earliest start time rule to complete all of the *ES* values. The earliest start time rule is as follows: The earliest start time for an activity leaving a node is equal to the largest value for the latest finish times for all activities entering the node.

The earliest start times and the earliest finish times for the problem are presented in Figure 10-7. The earliest start times are the darkened numbers at the beginning of each arrow, and the earliest finish times are the darkened numbers at the end of each arrow. Let's trace the paths as we proceed through the network. We start with $ES = 0$ for both activities 1–2 and 1–3. By adding their activity time of *t* to *ES* we obtain $EF = 5$ for activity 1–2 and $EF = 2$ for activity 1–3. The progression forward through the network then is a simple matter of addition. Note that all *ES*s for activities 2–3, 2–4, and 2–5 are the same as $EF = 5$ of the preceding activity 1–2. This situation reflects the fact that we cannot begin the next activity in a project until the previous activity is completed.

The addition rule of $EF = ES + t$ is continually applied throughout the network. The only use of the earliest start time rule in this network occurs in determining the *ES* for activities 3–6 and 7–8. For activity 3–6, the *ES* is nine weeks and for activity 7–8, the *ES* is seventeen weeks. These assignments were accomplished by using the earliest start time rule. The activity times selected were the largest activity times entering the node. Some networks are so simple that they may not even require the use of this rule.

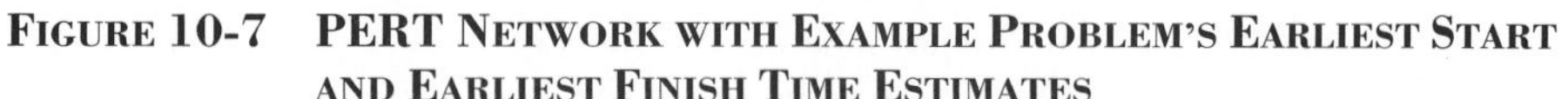

FIGURE 10-7 PERT NETWORK WITH EXAMPLE PROBLEM'S EARLIEST START AND EARLIEST FINISH TIME ESTIMATES

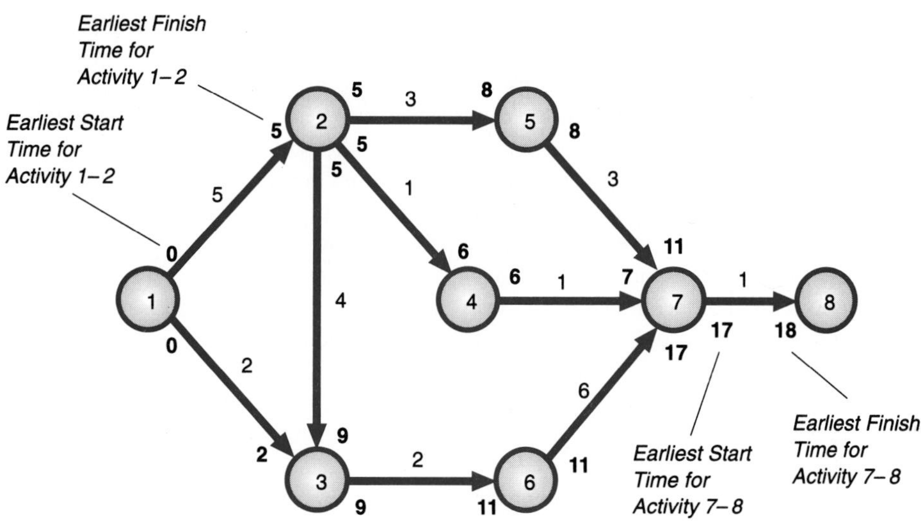

The earliest finish time for the last activity is the expected project completion date. In the example, the project will take an average of eighteen weeks to complete. The eighteen weeks is an estimate or average value that may or may not be accurate. Each of the *ES* and *EF* refer to this eighteen-week estimate as the scheduled on-time part of their definition. That is, the earliest start time for activity 7–8 that will still keep the entire project on schedule for its eighteen-week completion period is an *ES* of seventeen weeks.

4. *Determine the latest start times and the latest finish times for all of the activities in the PERT network.* **Latest start time** is the latest time we can start an activity and still keep the entire project on time. **Latest finish time** is the latest time we can finish an activity and still keep the entire project on time. Let's define the following:

LS = latest start time

LF = latest finish time

t = expected activity time

Then

$$LS = LF - t$$

for each of the activities as we move from the latest finish time for the last activity in the network. The earliest finish time in a PERT network is equal to the latest finish time for the last activity and for the entire project (that is, the earliest finish time for the last activity in the network). As we move backward through the network, we may need to use the latest finish time rule to determine all of the *LF* values. The latest finish time rule is as follows: the latest finish time for an activity entering a node is equal to the smallest value for the latest start times for all activities leaving the node.

The latest start times and the latest finish times for the example are presented in Figure 10-8. The latest start times are the darkened numbers at the beginning of each arrow, and the latest finish times are the darkened numbers at the end of each arrow. Let's trace the paths as we proceed backward through the network. We start with $LS = 18$, which is the completion time for the entire project. By subtracting the activity time of t we obtain $LS = 17$ for activity 7–8. The progression backward through the network then is simply a matter of subtraction. Note that all of the *LF*s for activities 4–7, 5–7, and 6–7 are the same as $ES = 17$ of the prior activity 7–8. The expression $LS = LF - t$ is continually applied throughout the network to obtain the *LS* and *LF* values. In the case of activity 1–2, we need to apply the latest finish time rule. The activity time we selected ($LF = 5$) was the smallest activity time leaving the node that activity 1–2 was entering.

5. *Determine the slack activity time and the critical path activities.* To determine the slack activity time (or the time each activity can be delayed without delaying the entire project), we can use either of the expressions given at the top of the next page.

FIGURE 10-8 PERT NETWORK WITH EXAMPLE PROBLEM'S LATEST START AND LATEST FINISH TIME ESTIMATES

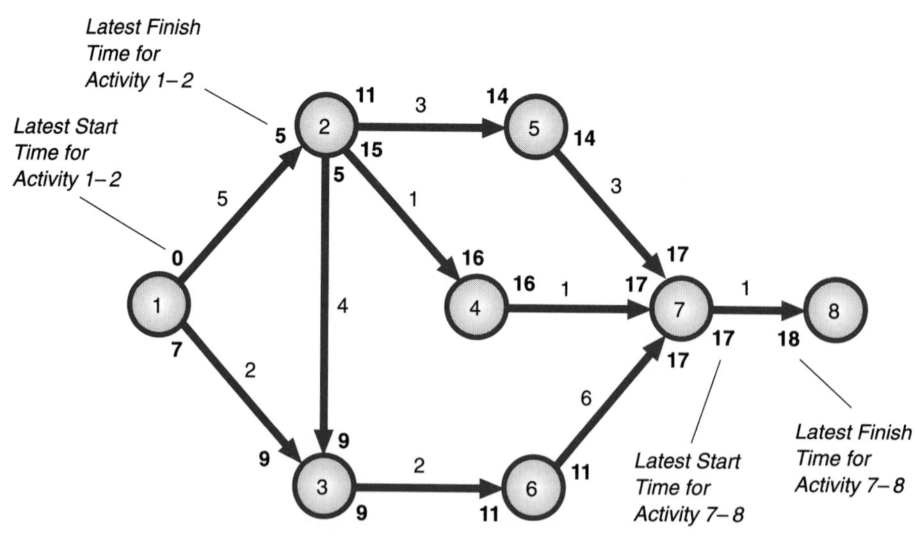

Slack = $LS - ES$

or

Slack = $LF - EF$

For our sample problem, the slack time is computed for each activity in Table 10-2. The slack of 7 for activity 1–3 indicates that this activity can be delayed by as much as seven weeks without delaying the entire project. This type of information is useful to identify idle periods where resources can be reallocated to other projects. The zero slack in activity 1–2 indicates that this activity is critical and must be completed exactly on time to keep the entire project on time. Collectively, all of the critical activities make up the **critical path** through the network. The critical path for this sample problem is presented in Figure 10-9 as a darkened line. If any activity along this path takes less or more time, it will change the completion date of the project. This path is always a continuous line from the first activity to the last. It will always be the longest path through the network.

Having found the *ES, EF, LS,* and *LF* values we now have the information that the PERT technique provides concerning the timing of the project. We now know how long the project will take (eighteen weeks), the start and finish dates for each activity (*ES, EF, LS,* and *LF*), which activities are critical (1–2, 2–3, 3–6, 6–7, and 7–8), and the remaining noncritical activities.

6. *Determine the probability of achieving a desired completion date.* (This step is optional.) PERT information can be used to obtain additional scheduling information based on the critical path completion date. We know that it will take on average eighteen weeks to complete this project. The *t* values that make up the eighteen-week project completion date are average values. So the eighteen-week value is an average time estimate for the project completion date. As we can see in Figure 10-10(a), the probability of completing a project based on an average is 50 percent.

TABLE 10-2 DETERMINE SLACK IN PERT EXAMPLE PROBLEM ACTIVITIES

Activity	*Latest Start*	*Earliest Start*	*Latest Finish*	*Earliest Finish*	*Weeks of Slack*
1–2	0	0	5	5	0
1–3	7	0	9	2	7
2–3	5	5	9	9	0
2–4	15	5	16	6	10
2–5	11	5	14	8	6
3–6	9	9	11	11	0
4–7	16	6	17	7	10
5–7	14	8	17	11	6
6–7	11	11	17	17	0
7–8	17	17	18	18	0

FIGURE 10-9 EXAMPLE PROBLEM'S CRITICAL PATH

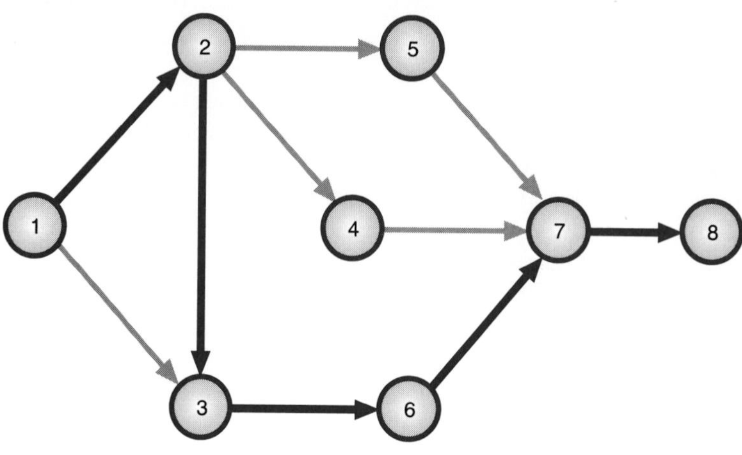

Suppose that we want to determine the probability of completing this project in twenty-two weeks. To determine this probability we need to convert the project time distribution shown in Figure 10-10(a) into z values based on a desired completion time. (Students unfamiliar with z values should review the material in Appendix A at the end of this textbook.) To do this we will use the following formula:

$$z = \frac{\text{Desired project time period} - \text{Expected project time period}}{\text{Standard deviation of the critical path activities}}$$

where

Desired project time = a subjectively derived date.

Expected project time period = the sum of the critical path activity times

Standard deviation of the critical path activities = square root of the sum of the critical path activity variances or $\sqrt{\Sigma\sigma_t^2}$

In our sample PERT problem, let's set the desired project time period at twenty-two weeks, even though on average we expect to complete it in eighteen weeks. What is the probability of completing the project in the desired twenty-two weeks?

FIGURE 10-10 PROBABILITY DISTRIBUTIONS FOR PROJECT COMPLETION DATES

(A) PROBABILITY DISTRIBUTION AND AVERAGE COMPLETION DATE

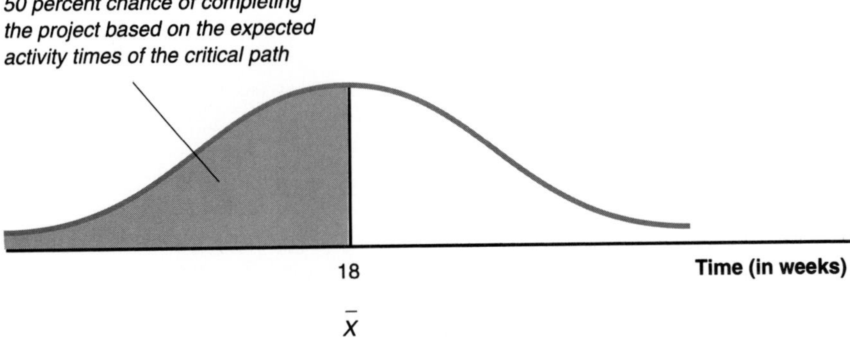

(B) PROBABILITY DISTRIBUTION FOR DESIRED COMPLETION DATE

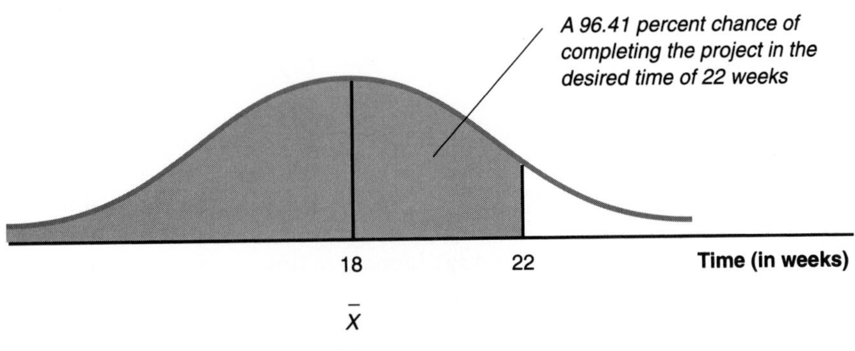

The standard deviation of the critical path activities is the square root of the sum of the variances for just the critical path activities. These variance values were computed in step 1 of the PERT technique and are listed with the resulting z value computations in Table 10-3. As shown in Table 10-3, the z value for the desired twenty-two-week completion period is 1.80. We look up this value's appropriate probability value in Appendix A, Table A. The resulting probability for a z value of 1.80 is 0.9641; that is, we have a 96.41 percent chance of completing this project in twenty-two weeks. This probability is also presented in Figure 10-10(b). For completion values less than the average critical time estimates, the probabilities decrease accordingly.

TABLE 10-3 PERT EXAMPLE PROBLEM PROBABILITY ESTIMATION

Critical Path Activity Number	*Critical Path Activity Time* (t)	Critical Path Activity Time Variance (σ_t^2)
1–2	5	1.778
2–3	4	0.694
3–6	2	0.444
6–7	6	1.778
7–8	1	0.278
	18	4.972

Critical path variance $= \Sigma\, \sigma_t^2 = 4.972$

Critical path standard deviation $= \sqrt{\Sigma\, \sigma_t^2} = \sqrt{4.972} = 2.23$

$$z = \frac{\text{Desired time} - \text{Critical path activity time}}{\text{Critical path standard deviation}} = \frac{22 - 18}{2.23} = 1.80$$

Critical Path Method

Suppose, by using PERT, we find that the expected time to complete a project is greater than what we desire. If it is possible to reduce the time it takes to perform some of the activities in the PERT network, we may choose to reduce the total time of the project by reducing some of the activity times in the PERT network. The process of reducing activity time is called **crashing.** Using overtime production, subcontracting production, and adding an extra shift are common approaches used to crash activity time. Unfortunately, reducing the time it would normally take to complete an activity or project is usually costly. Operations managers need some means of systematically planning and scheduling the reduction of activity times at least cost.

Just prior to PERT's development to plan and control the Polaris missile program for the U.S. Navy, another network planning method called the **critical path method (CPM)** was independently developed. In 1957, J. E. Kelly of Remington Rand and M. R. Walker of Du Pont developed CPM as an aid to the service planning for building maintenance of chemical plants for the Du Pont Corporation. Whereas PERT focuses on project timing considerations under uncertainty (that is, expected values are used for *t*), CPM is used to consider tradeoffs between time and cost in project planning.[3] In CPM analysis we are actually able to reduce critical activity times rather than just

[3] A version of PERT that is used to examine time-cost tradeoffs is called PERT/Cost. Our discussion in this section is applicable to this method as well as CPM analysis of time-cost tradeoffs.

measure individual activity variances and compute the probability of project completion as we do in PERT analysis.

In addition to providing the same activity timing information provided by PERT, CPM analysis provides answers to the following questions:

1. Which activities should be crashed to minimize the cost of reducing the entire project's completion time?
2. Which activities should not be crashed to minimize the cost of reducing the entire project's completion time?
3. How much of a reduction in the total time of the project is possible at a certain cost?

To illustrate the steps of CPM analysis we will work through an example. The steps of CPM analysis are as follows:

1. *Determine the normal and crash times and collect relevant cost information for each activity.* The **normal time** of CPM activities are the same as the expected activity times in PERT (t). The **crash time** of an activity is the amount of time the activity can, if needed, be reduced by using some method like overtime production. In Table 10-4 we have a project consisting of five activities. As we can see in column (2) in Table 10-4, the normal time is the expected t time it would normally take to complete each activity. The crash time in column (3) is the time to which each activity can be reduced. For example, activity 1–2 has a normal time of six days but can be reduced to only four days.

   Timing information is usually obtained from time studies or from the judgment of experienced employees and supervisors. Cost information can sometimes be obtained from previous projects, cost accounting experts, and bids provided by subcontractors. Five different types of cost information are necessary for a CPM analysis: total normal cost, total crash cost, crash cost per day, normal total project cost, and crash total project cost.

   The **total normal cost** in column (4) is the total cost of normal production. The **total crash cost** in column (5) is the total cost of crashed or expedited

TABLE 10-4 TIME AND COST DATA FOR CPM EXAMPLE PROBLEM

(1) Activity	(2) Normal Time (days)	(3) Crash Time (days)	(4) Total Normal Cost ($)	(5) Total Crash Cost ($)	(6) Maximum Crash Days	(7) Crash Cost per Day ($)
1–2	6	4	1,000	1,200	2	100
1–3	3	1	800	1,500	2	350
2–4	4	2	600	900	2	150
3–4	6	4	1,800	2,200	2	200
4–5	4	3	775	1,000	1	225
			4,975	6,800		

production effort. To determine maximum crash days we subtract column (2) from column (3) to determine the maximum number of days that can be reduced from normal time.

For example, activity 1–2 can be crashed two days from the normal time of six days (that is, 6 − 4). The maximum crash days are used to compute the crash cost per day in column (7). We simply divide the maximum crash days shown in column (6) into the difference between column (5) and column (4). For example, activity 1–2 normally costs $1,000, but if we reduce it by two days it will cost $1,200. This means that the additional cost per day (crash cost per day) is $100 [(1,200 − 1,000)/2]. The **normal total project cost** is the sum of the total normal cost for all of the activities [i.e., summation of column (4)], which for this problem is $4,975.

The **crash total project cost** is the sum of the total crash costs for all of the activities [summation of column (5)], which for this problem is $6,800. Completing this project using normal time will cost $4,975. Using as much overtime production or subcontracting as much overtime production as is possible will reduce the time of the project but increase the cost to $6,800.

2. *Based on the normal activity times, use PERT to determine the critical path activities.* This is the same process as we discussed in the previous section of this chapter. The PERT network for this five-activity project is presented in Figure 10-11(a). Because of the simplicity of this network, we can use a shortcut to determine the critical path activities. The only two paths through the network are presented in Figure 10-11(b). Because the critical path is always the longest path through the network, activities 1–2, 2–4, and 4–5 represent the critical path. (This can be confirmed by performing the entire PERT analysis).
3. *Determine the possible critical path activities that can be crashed and their respective costs.* As shown in Figure 10-12(a), the only possible activities that can be crashed and reduce the total time of the project are three critical path activities. Checking the crash cost per day in Table 10-4, column (7), we can see that the least-cost activity to crash or reduce is activity 1–2.
4. *Crash the least-cost activity (or activities) and use PERT to determine the new critical path activities.* In Figure 10-12(b) activity 1–2 is crashed and PERT (not shown) generates two separate critical paths through the network. The total cost of the project is now $5,075 ($4,975 + $100), and the total time of the project has been reduced to thirteen days (14 − 1).

   We will continue to repeat Steps 3 and 4 until one of the following happens:

   a. We run out of crash days.
   b. Further crashing will not reduce the total time of the project.
   c. We have crashed down to a predetermined or desired number of days.

   Let's assume that we have no predetermined or desired number of days to which we want to crash. In Figure 10-12(b) we can see that we still have one or more days for each activity to crash. Unfortunately, because both paths through the network are critical, both paths must be crashed simultaneously.

FIGURE 10-11 PERT NETWORK FOR CPM EXAMPLE PROBLEM

(A) PERT NETWORK

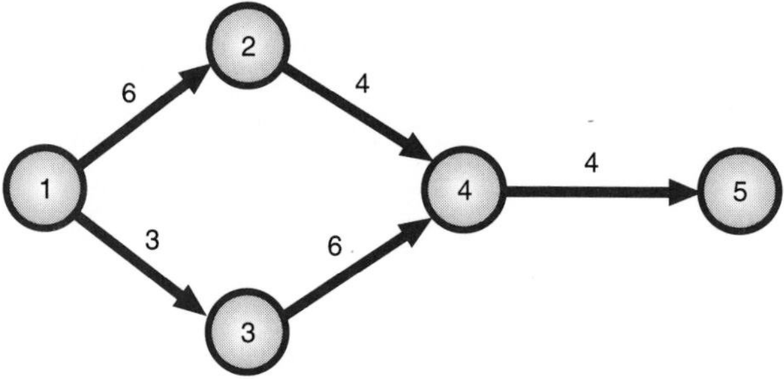

(B) POSSIBLE PATHS THROUGH THE PERT NETWORK

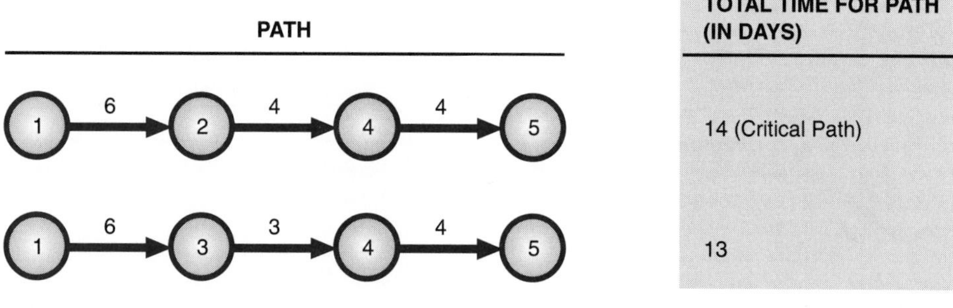

That is, if we only crashed one path, the other path would still be the longest, and we would not reduce the total time of the project.

There are four possible combinations of activities on the two paths that can be crashed simultaneously as well as the single activity 4–5. Of these five possibilities, the least cost is activity 4–5 at $225. We crash activity 4–5 in Figure 10-12(c), which reduces project time to twelve days but increases total cost to $5,300. We continue to repeat these steps in Figures 10-12(d), (e), and (f) until we reach a point that further reduction in activity time does not reduce the total time of the project. In Figure 10-12(f) we still have one crash day left (activity 1–3). If we reduce this one activity, however, it will not reduce the total time of nine days in the path containing activities 1–2, 2–4, and 4–5. Hence the total time of the project would remain nine days. The total cost of the nine-day project is $6,450, which is $350 less than the $6,800 total crash cost of the project. The difference reflects the savings of not performing the needless final crash of activity 1–3.

FIGURE 10-12 PERT NETWORKS FOR CPM EXAMPLE PROBLEM

(A) INITIAL PERT NETWORK

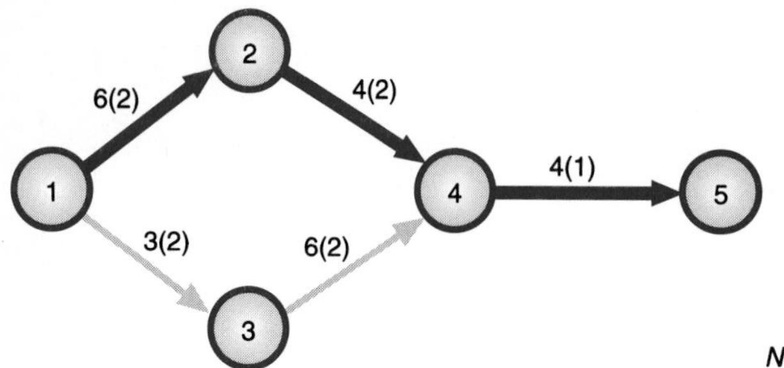

Total Cost of Project: $4,975
Total Time for Project: 14 days

Possible Activities to Crash

Activities	Total Cost
1 – 2 ◀	$100 ◀
2 – 4	150
4 – 5	225

Note: ◀ *denotes least cost activity that will be crashed*

(B) FIRST CRASHED NETWORK OF CPM EXAMPLE PROBLEM

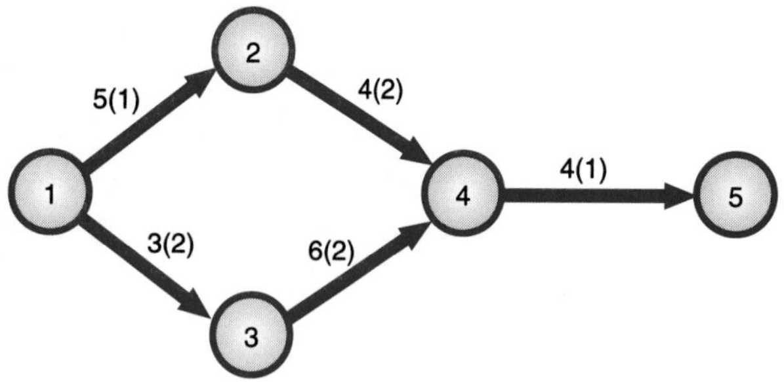

Total Cost of Project: $5,075
Total Time for Project: 13 days

Possible Activities to Crash

Activities	Total Cost
1 – 2, 1 – 3	$450
1 – 2, 3 – 4	300
1 – 3, 2 – 4	500
2 – 4, 3 – 4	350
4 – 5 ◀	225 ◀

(C) SECOND CRASHED NETWORK OF CPM EXAMPLE PROBLEM

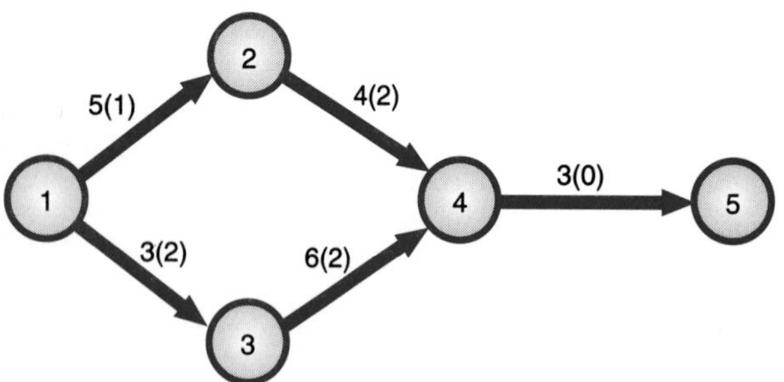

Total Cost of Project: $5,300
Total Time for Project: 12 days

Possible Activities to Crash

Activities	Total Cost
1 – 2, 1 – 3	$450
1 – 2, 3 – 4 ◀	300 ◀
1 – 3, 2 – 4	500
2 – 4, 3 – 4	350

FIGURE 10-12 (CONTINUED)

(D) THIRD CRASHED NETWORK OF CPM EXAMPLE PROBLEM

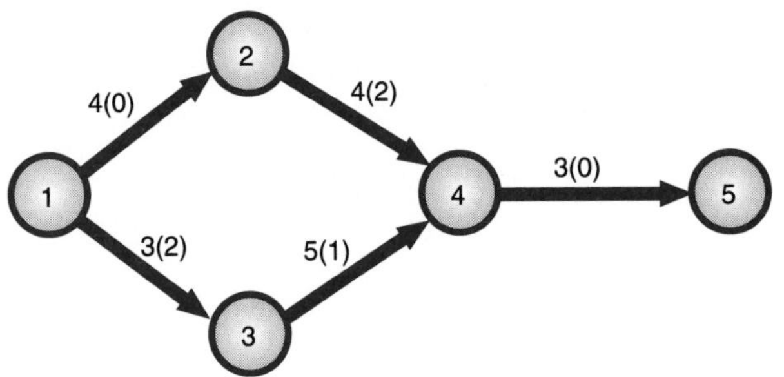

Total Cost of Project: $5,600
Total Time for Project: 11 days

Possible Activities to Crash

Activities	Total Cost
1 – 3, 2 – 4	$500
2 – 4, 3 – 4 ◀	350 ◀

(E) FOURTH CRASHED NETWORK OF CPM EXAMPLE PROBLEM

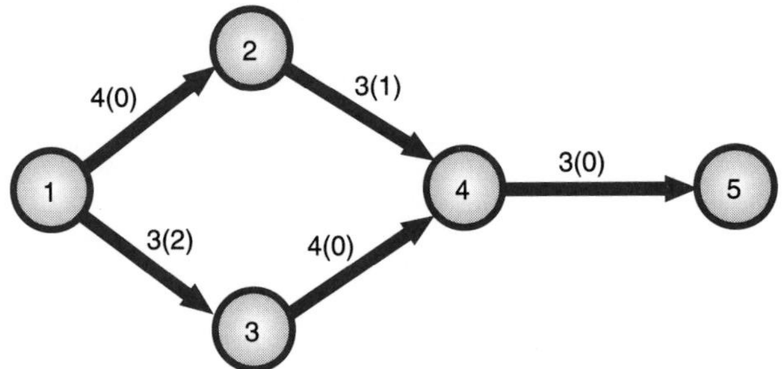

Total Cost of Project: $5,950
Total Time for Project: 10 days

Possible Activities to Crash

Activities	Total Cost
1 – 3, 2 – 4 ◀	$500 ◀

(F) FIFTH AND FINAL CRASHED NETWORK OF CPM EXAMPLE PROBLEM

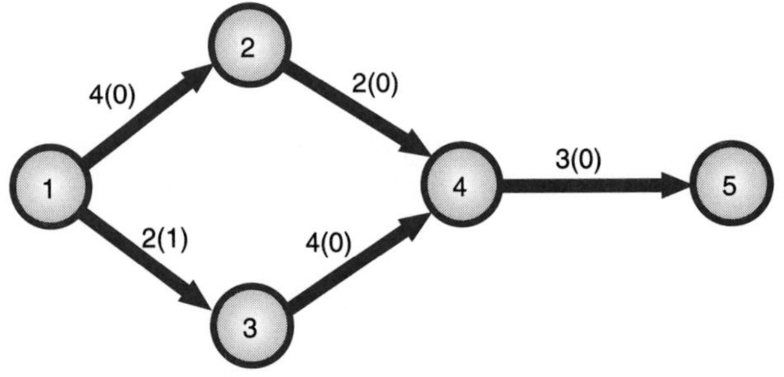

Total Cost of Project: $6,450
Total Time for Project: 9 days

Possible Activities to Crash

Activities	Total Cost
—	—

CPM analysis provides the least-cost order of crashing activities. Because the crashing of activities is planned, the needless crashing (and cost) of an activity (that is, activity 1–3) is also prevented. Finally, through CPM analysis, the total number of crash days possible (that is, nine days) is also determined. Such information is very valuable in many project planning activities. For example, in contract bidding on construction projects, the ability to complete a project quickly can be more important in obtaining a contract than the total cost bid for the project. CPM analysis gives an excellent breakdown of the costs that can aid in bidding.

Usefulness of PERT and CPM

PERT and CPM methods possess a number of advantages for project planners. These advantages include the following:

1. PERT and CPM are ideal for the tactical-level planning of projects in developing the project plan.
2. PERT and CPM are ideal for the operational-level controlling of projects by detailing start and completion dates of each project activity.
3. PERT and CPM provide a graphical display that aids users in understanding relationships among project activities. The simplicity of the mathematics involved aids in users' acceptance of results and permits small problems to be computed manually while large problems are easily programmed on microcomputer systems.
4. PERT and CPM are easily applied to any type of single project planning activity in any type of industry.
5. PERT and CPM are ideal for project planning activities in which known or certain activity times can be determined (such as automated environments in which robotic times have little or no variation).

PERT and CPM also have a number of disadvantages that limit their use in project planning. These disadvantages include the following:

1. Both methods are limited to single project planning operations. These methods cannot handle situations in which two or more projects must be planned together to share resources.
2. Their application is limited to projects in which sequential and precedence relationships are known with certainty. The use of resources based on chance availability (such as a piece of rental equipment being available when required) is not permitted with these methods.
3. PERT and CPM time and variance estimates are based on a six-value weighted average that does not always apply to every project. Research is showing, however, that although the weighted average is not universally applicable to

all planning situations, it can be modified to more accurately capture the behavior of activity times.[4]

4. Difficulty in estimating cost information can make the results of the CPM analysis questionable.

Despite the disadvantages of PERT and CPM, these methods have made contributions to project planning since their origins in the 1950s. From that time to the present, PERT and CPM have been supported by changes in technology and new ideas in network methodology.

The introduction of microcomputers in the late 1970s made the use of PERT and CPM affordable to even small businesses requiring project planning. The development of dedicated microcomputer PERT and CPM software in the 1980s helped make these methods the most common network systems applied to project planning. Microcomputer systems of the 1990s are efficient and powerful, and today microcomputer PERT and CPM software is highly efficient in generating project planning information. For example, how long would it take you to work through the two example problems in this section by hand? It only takes a minute to enter the data for these problems and a couple of seconds to generate the solutions using the Micro Production software system that accompanies this textbook. In Figure 10-13, the Micro Production software–generated input and output for the PERT example problem is presented, and in Figure 10-14, the Micro Production software–generated input and output for the CPM example problem is presented. One of the more powerful PERT- and CPM-based software systems is the Harvard Total Project Manager (HTPM) system. This system provides the usual PERT and CPM information as well as hourly cost summaries by functional area, department, and task. The HTPM system also considers raw material expenditure forecasts, cash flow analysis, vendor lead time information, and payment schedules for materials. HTPM extends project control analysis to include variance reports on planned versus actual costs and valuations of work-in-process.

In an effort to overcome some of PERT's limitations, an extension of the networking method was devised called **graphical evaluation and review technique (GERT).** GERT includes all the features of PERT but also permits users to establish probabilities for activities. In PERT, each activity has a 100 percent chance of being used. In GERT we can structure activities whose probable occurrence ranges from less than 100 percent to 0 percent (that is, the activity may not even be done at all). With PERT we move from the beginning activity in the network to the last activity in a forward motion. In a GERT network we can loop back and redo any activity if desired. GERT software was originally devised as a simulation approach to study network structures. The subsequent development of **Q-GERT** (the Q stands for queues) further improved the network capabilities of the software system to permit the simulation of servers and queues into network models.

---

[4] M. D. Troutt, "On the Generality of PERT Average Time Formula," *Decision Sciences,* 20, No. 2 (1989), 410–412.

FIGURE 10-13 MICRO PRODUCTION SOFTWARE PRINTOUT OF PERT EXAMPLE PROBLEM

Program: CPM/PERT / PERT

Problem Title : EXAMPLE PROBLEM

***** Input Data *****

Activity	Start	End	Optimistic	Likely	Pessimistic
1	1	2	3.000	4.000	11.000
2	1	3	1.000	2.000	3.000
3	2	3	2.500	3.500	7.500
4	2	4	0.500	1.000	1.500
5	2	5	1.000	2.000	9.000
6	3	6	1.000	1.500	5.000
7	4	7	0.500	1.000	1.500
8	5	7	2.000	3.000	4.000
9	6	7	4.000	5.000	12.000
10	7	8	0.500	1.000	1.500

***** Program Output *****

Activity	Activity Nodes		Mean	S.D.	Variance
1 *	1 -->	2	5.000	1.333	1.778
2	1 -->	3	2.000	0.333	0.111
3 *	2 -->	3	4.000	0.833	0.694
4	2 -->	4	1.000	0.167	0.028
5	2 -->	5	3.000	1.333	1.778
6 *	3 -->	6	2.000	0.667	0.444
7	4 -->	7	1.000	0.167	0.028
8	5 -->	7	3.000	0.333	0.111
9 *	6 -->	7	6.000	1.333	1.778
10 *	7 -->	8	1.000	0.167	0.028

(*: Critical Path Activities)

Expected Completion Time: 18.000

***** End of Output *****

INTEGRATING MANAGEMENT RESOURCES: USING PERT TO INCREASE PRODUCTIVITY

Project planning methods such as PERT are used to plan, schedule, and control project management resources, including the tactical and operational levels of planning, scheduling, and controlling human, technology, and system resources to achieve desired project objectives. PERT helps bring these resources together in the right quantity and at the right time to minimize idleness and waste, which in turn maximizes productivity.

FIGURE 10-14 MICRO PRODUCTION SOFTWARE PRINTOUT OF CPM EXAMPLE PROBLEM

Program: CPM/PERT / CPM With Crashing

Problem Title : CPM EXAMPLE PROBLEM

***** Input Data *****

Activity	Start	End	TIME Normal	TIME Crash	COST Normal	COST Crash
1	1	2	6.000	4.000	1000.000	1200.000
2	1	3	3.000	1.000	800.000	1500.000
3	2	4	4.000	2.000	600.000	900.000
4	3	4	6.000	4.000	1800.000	2200.000
5	4	5	4.000	3.000	775.000	1000.000

***** Program Output *****

Activity	Activity	Nodes	Crash by	Crashing Cost	Activity Time	Activity Cost
1 *	1 -->	2	2.000	200.000	4.000	1200.000
2 *	1 -->	3	1.000	350.000	2.000	1150.000
3 *	2 -->	4	2.000	300.000	2.000	900.000
4 *	3 -->	4	2.000	400.000	4.000	2200.000
5 *	4 -->	5	1.000	225.000	3.000	1000.000
(* : Critical Path Activities)				1475.000		6450.000

Expected Normal Completion Time : 14.000
Expected Crashed Completion Time : 9.000

***** End of Output *****

Project planning networks can be used as an integrated plan for implementing production system projects. Installing or implementing production systems such as the just-in-time (JIT) system discussed in several previous chapters can be viewed as a project for any type of organization. It has been suggested that a JIT system might best be implemented using PERT.[5] The guidelines for implementing and integrating JIT systems are presented as PERT networks (that is, activities lettered *P*, *A* through *I*, and *W*) in Figure 10-15. The eleven major activities that make up the implementation and integration phases are listed on pages 515 and 516.

[5] I. Nisanci and A. D. Nicoll, "Project Planning Network Is Integrated Plan for Implementing Just-In-Time," *Industrial Engineering*, 19 (October 1987), 50–55.

FIGURE 10-15 PERT NETWORK AND ACTIVITIES OF INTEGRATED PLAN FOR JIT IMPLEMENTATION PROJECT

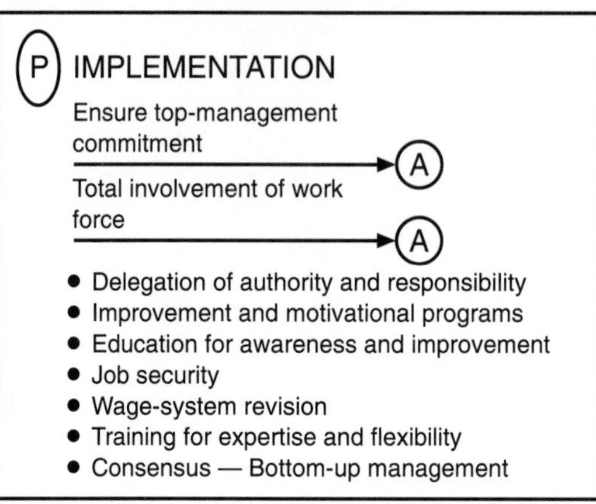

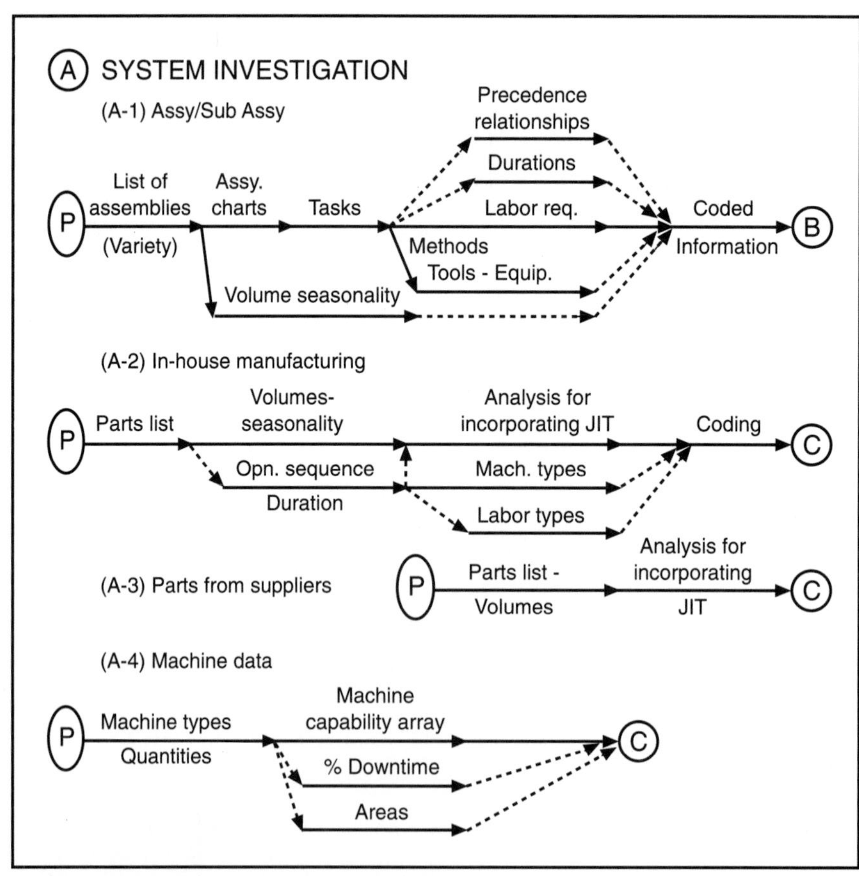

FIGURE 10-15 (CONTINUED)

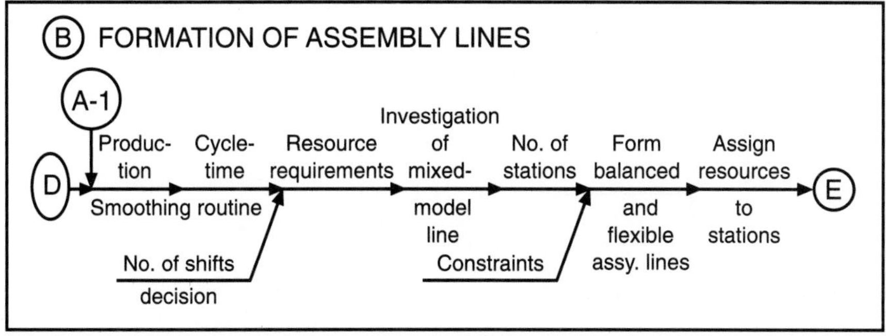

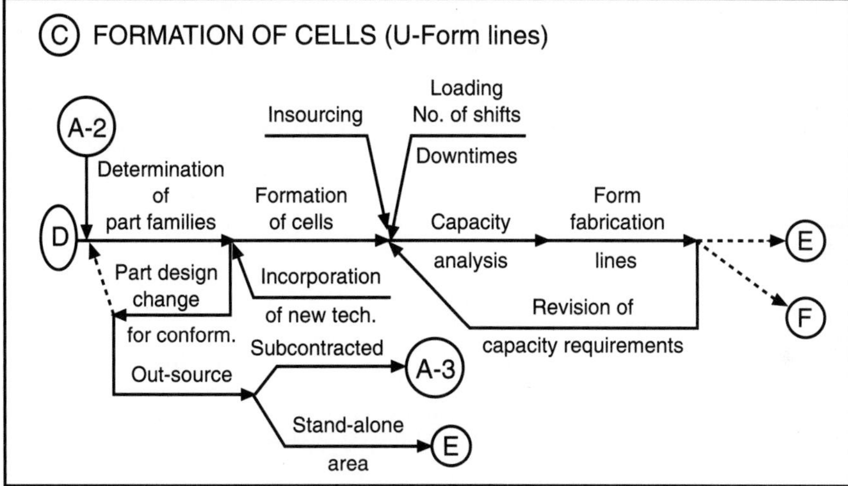

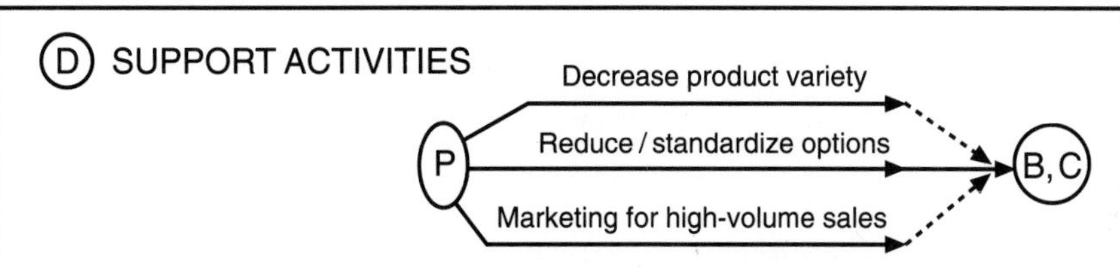

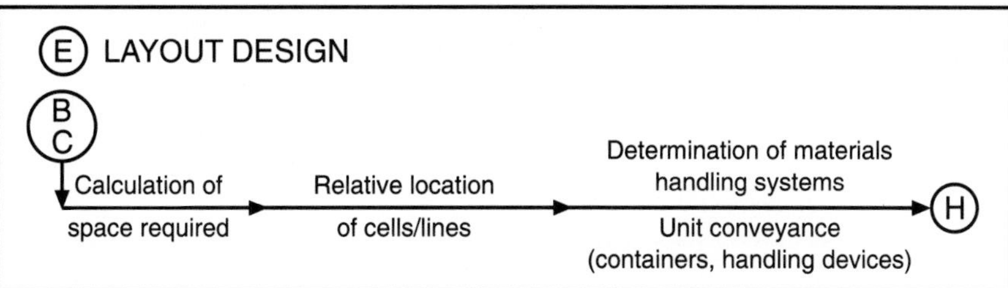

FIGURE 10-15 (CONTINUED)

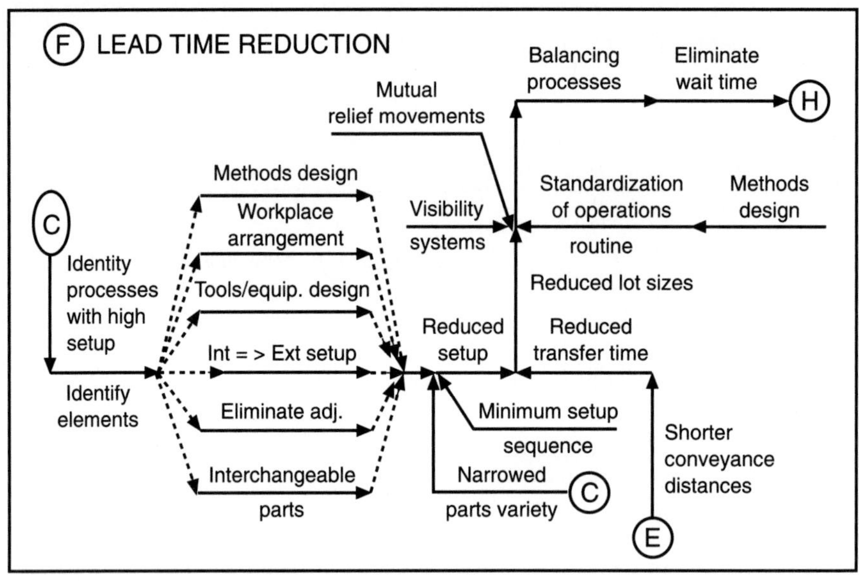

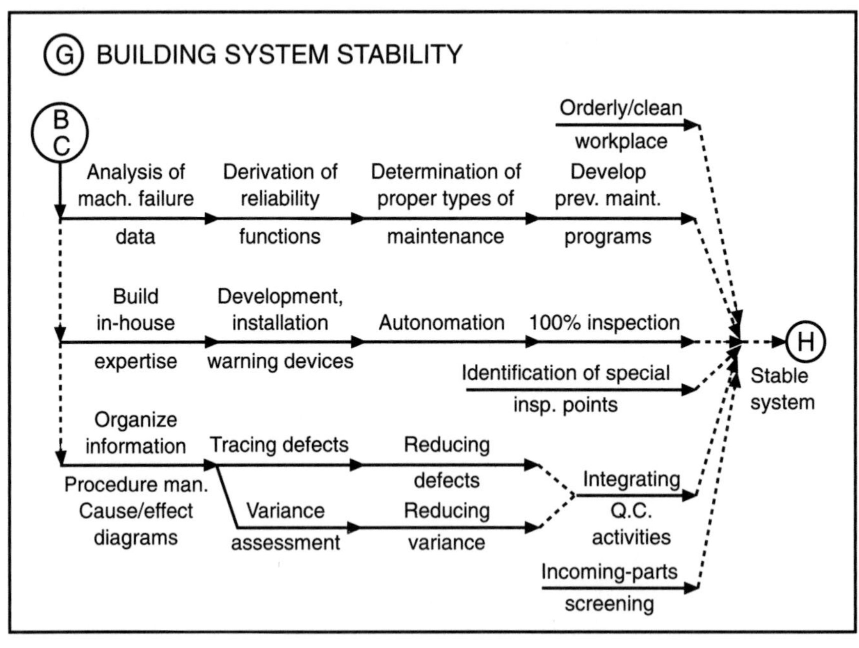

FIGURE 10-15 (CONTINUED)

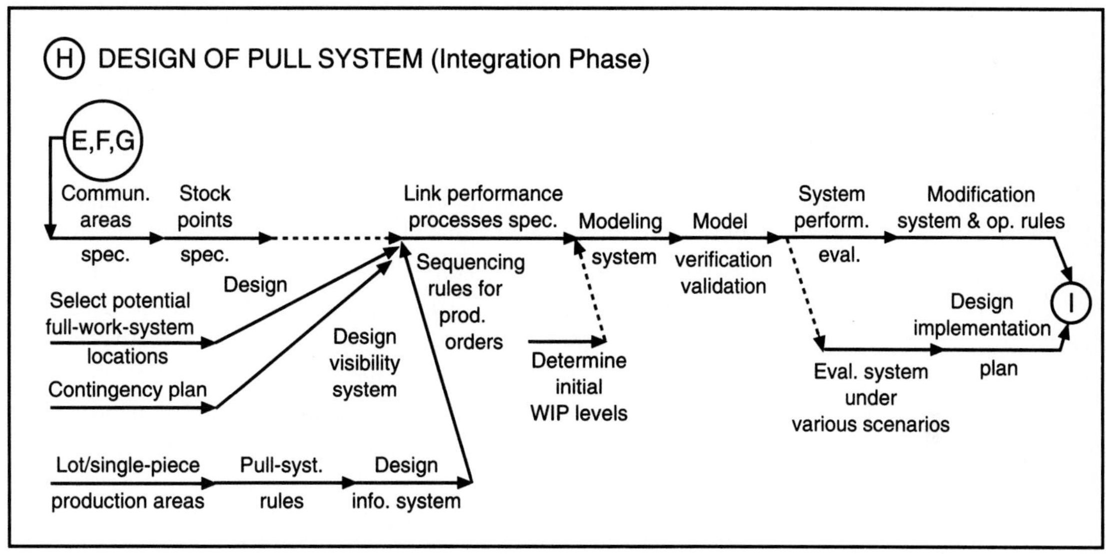

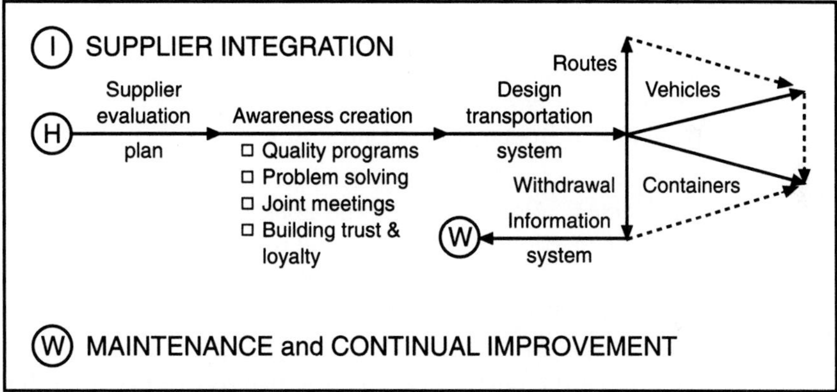

Source: Reprinted from *Industrial Engineering* magazine, October 1987, copyright 1987 Institute of Industrial Engineers, 25 Technology Park, Norcross, GA 30092.

1. *Activity P: Implementation* This initial preparation phase focuses on teaching workers to understand JIT and obtain commitment to make the process successful. This phase might include identifying and changing organizational philosophy to embrace JIT concepts.
2. *Activity A: System investigation* This is a study phase in which materials, equipment, and operating methods are examined in light of JIT's need for simplicity and avoidance of wasteful production activity.

3. *Activity B: Formation of assembly lines* Assembly lines are restructured to emphasize flexibility and continuous flow of a JIT production system.
4. *Activity C: Formation of cells* Assembly lines are divided into small, self-contained, and highly flexible production cells that can quickly change to produce a variety of products sharing a similar group of standardized part family components.
5. *Activity D: Support activities* During the same time as activity A, study effort is necessary to support the standardization of components for part families. Examining the marketing considerations of decreasing the number of products and standardizing components should be a part of study effort in this phase.
6. *Activity E: Layout design* This phase takes the formation efforts and transforms the conceptual manufacturing and assembly ideas into physical descriptions for layout designations and equipment acquisitions.
7. *Activity F: Lead time reduction* In this phase, setup times and their lead time requirements are determined. Ideas for new manufacturing methods are devised to help reduce lead time activities.
8. *Activity G: Building system stability* To ensure some control in the JIT process after it is in operation, this phase seeks to identify and install necessary information and monitoring systems. Once installed, these systems will help control variation from JIT quality and production goals. In this phase of the plan, management must recognize sources of variation in the production process and design systems during implementation to eliminate these sources in an effort to stabilize the production system.
9. *Activity H: Design of pull system* The heart of any JIT production operation is a pull system. At this phase of the implementation plan, management must define the operating plans, sequencing rules, and lead time objectives to integrate the entire production operation. A *kanban* system or any demand pull system must be installed to achieve a true JIT operation.
10. *Activity I: Supplier integration* As described in earlier chapters, integrating suppliers into a JIT operation is a critical step in expanding the JIT philosophy outside to the external environment of a business's operation. This phase involves screening suppliers to see if they have the resources and willingness to perform the JIT functions necessary to support the organization's JIT program. It may also involve studying and revising transportation systems to accommodate the JIT system.
11. *Activity W: Maintenance and continual improvement* Consistent with JIT principles, this activity may never be completed. Management and workers must have the JIT principles continually reinforced by an ongoing program of education. They must also continually seek improvement in all areas of the JIT system. This phase is usually performed by developing education programs to convey information to employees on new JIT methods and concepts.

This PERT approach to implementing the JIT system is not valuable just because it graphically helps detail and organize the planning effort. The PERT approach can also be used to identify critical activities in the planning project. As we can see in Figure 10-15, quite a number of subactivities make up each of the eleven major activities of the JIT implementation project. Project planners can assess the amount of time (optimistic, most probable, and pessimistic times) they expect each subactivity to take for completion. PERT analysis can then identify the critical activities where additional resources can be allocated to reduce or ensure accurate completion timing. PERT analysis is also useful to identify the slack activity time of implementation personnel that could be reallocated to other production activity. In doing so, PERT analysis helps management minimize waste during the implementation of a JIT system and therefore improve operating efficiency and productivity.

SUMMARY

In this chapter we have discussed some of the basic concepts and methods of project management. We have described how the project planning methods of PERT and CPM are used to help perform the planning, scheduling, and controlling functions in project management. Example problems were presented to illustrate the types of information that PERT and CPM provide project planners.

This chapter completes Part II, Planning and Controlling Operations. Once the planning function is completed, operations managers must begin producing their products and delivering their services. In Part III, Improving Products and Systems, we focus on product and system design activities and topics that operations managers face in the process of producing their products and services.

DISCUSSION AND REVIEW QUESTIONS

1. Why is project management necessary?
2. Can project planning be used in repetitive operations? Explain.
3. What is a matrix organization?
4. What is team management?
5. How can a Gantt chart be used in project management?
6. What type of information does PERT analysis generate for project planning purposes?
7. What are dummy activities and how are they used in PERT analysis?
8. Why is it so important to identify critical activities?
9. How are z values used in PERT analysis? Explain.
10. What type of information does CPM analysis generate for project planning purposes?
11. What are crash times and crash costs? How are they used in CPM analysis?
12. How does GERT differ from PERT? Explain.

PROBLEMS

* 1. Draw the PERT network for the following activities: 1–2, 2–3, 2–4, 2–5, 3–6, and 6–7. Are any dummy activities needed to allow all of the activities to be on a continuous path in the network?

2. Draw the PERT network for the following activities: 1–2, 1–3, 1–4, 2–5, 3–5, 4–5, 5–6, 4–6, 6–7, 5–7, and 7–8. Are dummy activities needed?

3. Draw the PERT network for the following activities: 1–2, 1–3, 1–4, 3–5, 5–6, 5–7, 5–8, 5–9, 7–8, 7–9, 7–10, and 10–11. Are any dummy activities needed?

4. Draw the PERT network for the following activities: 1–2, 2–3, 2–4, 2–5, 3–5, 5–6, 5–7, 6–8, 7–8, 7–9, 7–10, 8–9, 8–10, 9–11, 9–12, 10–11, 10–12, and 12–13. Are any dummy activities needed?

* 5. Suppose that a PERT network's five critical path activities had the following variances: 1.3, 1.0, 2.4, 2.1, and 3.4. What is the probability that the project will be completed in twenty days if the expected completion time for the project is fifteen days?

6. Suppose that a PERT network's six critical path activities had the following variances: 2.2, 2.0, 3.1, 1.0, 2.0, and 1.7. What is the probability that the project will be completed in thirty days if the expected completion time for the project is twenty days?

7. Suppose that a PERT network has ten activities with the following variances: 4.2, 2.3, 2.6, 3.7, 1.1, 2.2, 2.0, 2.0, 2.0, and 3.3. Assume that the five variances 2.3, 3.7, 2.2, 2.0, and 3.3 are on the critical path. What is the probability that the project will be completed in twenty-seven days if the expected completion time for the project is twenty-two days?

8. Suppose that a PERT network has twenty activities with the following variances: 4.1, 1.6, 6.5, 2.3, 4.7, 1.2, 3.9, 8.7, 6.5, 3.5, 4.2, 5.3, 2.6, 5.7, 1.1, 2.2, 6.0, 5.0, 2.0, and 9.3. Assume that the following twelve variances are on the critical path: 4.1, 1.6, 4.7, 1.2, 8.7, 6.5, 3.5, 5.3, 5.7, 2.2, 5.0, and 9.3. What is the probability that the project will be completed in 120 days if the expected completion time for the project is 100 days?

9. Suppose that we have the following PERT network with activity times. What is its critical path? Clearly define *ES, EF, LS, LF,* and slack time.

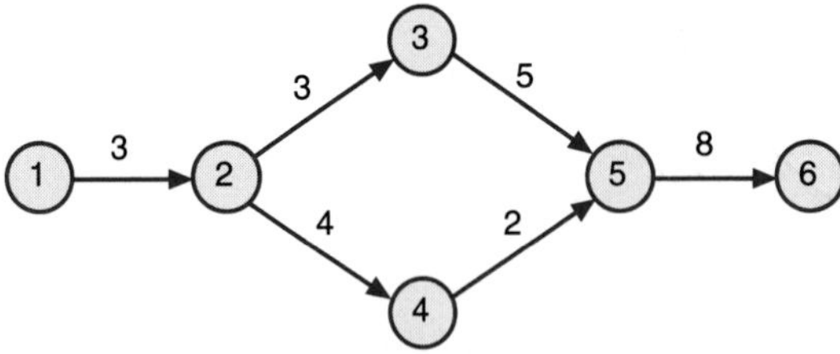

10. Given the PERT network with activity times shown at the top of the next page, determine its critical path. Define *ES, EF, LS, LF,* and slack time.

---

* The solutions to the problems marked with an asterisk can be found in Appendix J.

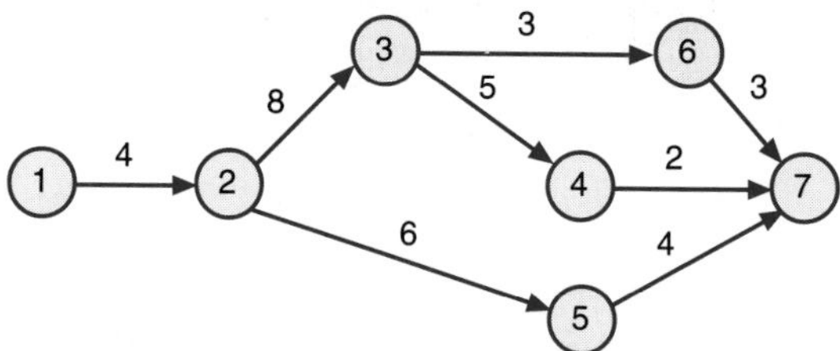

11. Given the following PERT network, determine the critical path. Identify *ES, EF, LS, LF,* and slack time.

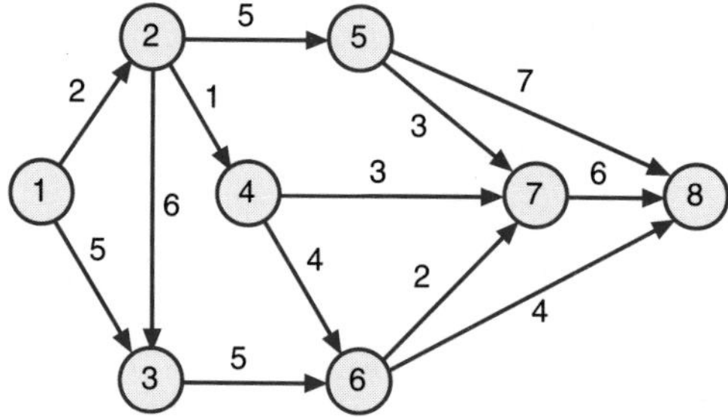

12. Suppose that we have the following PERT network. Determine its critical path. Identify *ES, EF, LS, LF,* and slack time.

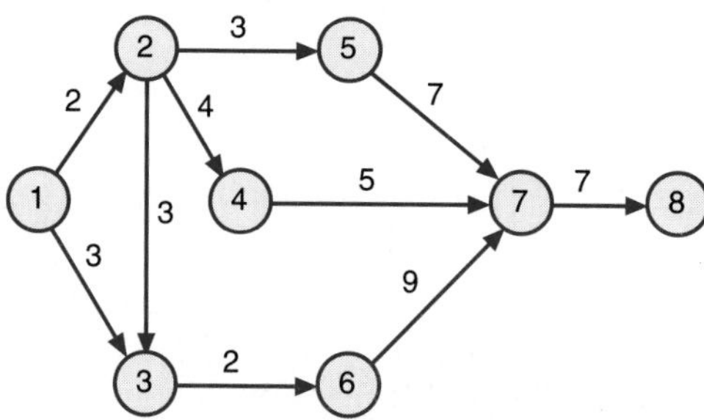

*13. Suppose that a project requires the following activities and their respective activity times:

	ACTIVITY TIME		
Activity	a	m	b
1–2	2	4	5
2–3	1	3	4
2–4	2	4	6
2–5	3	5	9
3–5	6	8	9
4–5	2	3	5
5–6	1	6	8

a. Develop a PERT network for this project.
b. What are *ES, EF, LS,* and *LF* values for each activity?
c. What is the slack time for each activity?
d. What is the critical path?

14. Suppose that a project involves the following activities and their respective activity times in days:

	ACTIVITY TIME		
Activity	a	m	b
1–2	1	4	5
2–3	2	3	4
2–4	2	4	6
3–5	6	8	10
4–5	1	3	5
5–6	1	2	3

a. Develop a PERT network for this project.
b. Determine *ES, EF, LS,* and *LF* values for each activity.
c. What is the slack time for each activity?
d. What is the critical path?
e. What is the probability of completing the project in twenty-six days?

15. Suppose that a project required the following activities and their respective activity times in days:

	ACTIVITY TIME		
Activity	a	m	b
1–2	5	6	7
2–3	4	5	8
2–4	2	4	6
3–5	6	8	10
3–6	3	6	9
4–5	1	3	5
4–7	5	7	9
5–8	1	2	3
6–8	1	2	3
7–8	2	4	6

a. Develop a PERT network for this project.
b. Determine *ES, EF, LS,* and *LF* values for each activity.
c. What is the slack time for each activity?
d. What is the critical path?
e. What is the probability of completing the project in twenty-two days?

16. Suppose that a project involves the following activities and their respective activity times in days:

	ACTIVITY TIME		
Activity	a	m	b
1–2	5	10	15
2–3	1	5	12
2–4	2	4	6
3–5	2	4	8
3–6	1	3	5
4–5	1	3	5
4–7	2	3	4
5–8	1	2	3
6–8	1	2	4
7–8	2	4	6
7–9	4	7	9
8–9	2	5	9

a. Develop a PERT network for this project.
b. What are *ES, EF, LS,* and *LF* values for each activity?
c. What is the slack time for each activity?
d. What is the critical path?
e. What is the probability of completing the project in thirty-four days? What is the probability of completing the project in forty days?

*17. Suppose that a project requires the following activities, respective normal *t* activity times in days, crash times, total normal costs, and total crash costs (activities marked with an asterisk cannot be crashed):

Activity	*Normal Activity Time* (t)	*Crash Time*	*Total Normal Cost*	*Total Crash Cost*
1–2	4	2	$ 300	$ 500
2–3	3	1	450	900
2–4	2	1	700	950
3–5	6	4	1,000	1,800
4–5	1*	1	500	500
5–6	3*	3	700	700

Perform CPM analysis using the short-cut method for finding the critical path activities and determine the following:
a. The least cost of crashing each activity for as many days as can be crashed.
b. The total cost of the project for each day crashed.
c. The total number of days that can be crashed.

18. Suppose that a project involves the activities, respective normal *t* activity times in days, crash times, total normal costs, and total crash costs listed in the table on the top of page 522.

Activity	*Normal Activity Time (t)*	*Crash Time*	*Total Normal Cost*	*Total Crash Cost*
1–2	6	4	$1,200	$2,000
2–3	5	3	2,000	3,000
2–4	6	1	2,500	5,000
2–5	2	1	300	600
3–5	3	2	1,000	1,800
4–5	3	1	500	900
5–6	6	5	700	850

Perform CPM analysis and determine the following:

a. The least cost of crashing each activity to the project completion date of eighteen days.
b. The total cost of the project for each day crashed.
c. The total maximum number of days that can be crashed for this project. Show your work by listing each day's total project cost and the activities that were crashed.

19. Suppose that a project required the following activities, respective normal t activity times in days, crash times, total normal costs, and total crash costs:

Activity	*Normal Activity Time (t)*	*Crash Time*	*Total Normal Cost*	*Total Crash Cost*
1–2	8	6	$3,200	$4,000
2–3	8	5	900	1,200
2–4	11	6	500	1,000
2–5	3	2	300	600
3–5	2	1	1,000	1,800
4–5	5	3	200	800
4–7	5	4	4,400	5,000
5–6	6	5	400	700
6–7	4	2	2,500	3,800

Perform a CPM analysis and determine the following:

a. The least cost of crashing each activity to a project completion date of thirty-two days.
b. The total cost of the project for each day crashed.
c. The maximum number of days that can be crashed for this project.

20. The probability of a project's being completed on its PERT-generated project completion date is 0.5. Suppose that we crash the project defined in Problem 19 by one day according to CPM analysis. Assume the variances for all of the nine activities in Question 19 are 1.5. What is the probable reduction from the project completion date by reducing the project by one day according to CPM? Does the reduction of probability actually take place?

CASE 10-1

A SCHEDULE OF INSUFFICIENT TIME

Tosca Furniture Company of Keene, New Hampshire was an entrepreneurial venture of five students who recently graduated from a local university. The purpose of the new company was to manufacture and market a new table and chair set called the "Sonas Set." This table and chair set consisted of one dining room table and six chairs with a black sandalwood finish and mother-of-pearl shells inlaid. The Sonas Set was a limited edition of only 500 sets and would not be produced again. The students who had engineered the product wanted to spend only the summer on the furniture manufacturing project as they were all going on to graduate school. This gave them twenty-two weeks to complete the project before school began in the fall.

The sample products were so well received by a local department store that the manager placed an order for the entire 500-unit lot. With the sale of their products ensured, the students then began estimating the time and materials it would take to complete the furniture-building project. They broke the project into fourteen different activities as listed in Exhibit 10C-1. Based on the sample table and chair sets, they estimated the time to complete each of the activities for the entire 500-set production lot. The activity time estimates ranged from optimistic (*a*) to pessimistic (*b*), with a most probable (*m*) time value thrown in for "good measure." These time estimates are presented in Exhibit 10C-1.

The department store manager was concerned that the students might give up the project before it was completed, which would waste a lot of presale advertising of the furniture sets. So the manager contractually had the students agree that for every week the furniture delivery date was exceeded it would cost the students $1,000 off the agreed price of the 500 sets. The students had agreed that delivery would take place nineteen weeks after the activities on Exhibit 10C-1 were started. The students, realizing they could be in a spot, found that by hiring extra help to complete the assemble chair activity at a cost of $800, they could reduce the expected time of this particular activity by one week. A total of

EXHIBIT 10C-1 SONAS SET FURNITURE ACTIVITIES AND TIME ESTIMATES

Description of Activity	*Activity*	*ACTIVITY TIMES (WEEKS)* a	m	b
Acquire lumber	1–2	1.5	3	6.5
Rough-cut chair legs	2–3	1	2	3
Rough-cut table legs	2–6	0.5	2	7.5
Rough-cut chair back	2–4	1	3	7.5
Rough-cut chair bottom	2–5	1	2	4
Rough-cut table top	2–7	2	2.5	4
Finish chair legs	3–8	3	4	5
Finish table legs	6–9	1	3	5
Finish chair back	4–8	4	5	6
Finish chair bottom	5–8	1	2	3
Finish table top	7–9	5	6	7
Assemble chair	8–10	4	5	6
Assemble table	9–10	2.5	3	4
Package table and chairs	10–11	3	4	5

only two weeks could be reduced or crashed for this activity using the extra help.

CASE QUESTIONS

1. Can the students expect to finish this project in the twenty-two weeks? Support your answer with computations.
2. Can the students expect to finish this project by the contracted nineteen-week deadline? Support your answer with computations.
3. Should they take advantage of the extra help to minimize their costs? If yes, why? If no, why not?

CASE 10-2

A CRITICAL PATH NOBODY WOULD FOLLOW

The Weknowitall Market Research Corporation (WMRC) is a well-known research consulting firm that has an established record of performing professional, timely, and inexpensive market analyses for companies of all sizes. WMRC was recently offered a research project opportunity by the Diddle Products Company to determine the market for a new product it is planning on introducing next year. Diddle wanted to know how customers would respond to its new product—that is, whether customers would buy it. Diddle also placed a number of special requirements on the project it hoped WMRC would perform. These special requirements included the following:

1. Diddle wanted WMRC to use more than one research method (for example, mail and telephone survey instruments) to minimize possible error in obtaining information for only one methodologic source. It felt that the investment in a new product was too great to risk possible survey error.
2. It needed the survey to be finished (a final report and market conclusions from WMRC) within 270 days from start of the project to its finish. Diddle had to commit to substantial and costly vendor contracts that could only be cancelled in the fixed period of time allowed for the research project.
3. It could not spend more than $28,500 for the entire research project. This would represent the entire fee for the research work Diddle was asking WMRC to perform.

Based on these special requirements, WMRC worked up some time and cost estimates of the eight activities required to complete the research project. The activities and their time and cost estimates are presented in Exhibit 10C-2. The cost values in Exhibit 10C-2 already have built WMRC's profit into them. Because its cost structure was competitively lower than other research companies, WMRC felt it would have to obtain the estimated cost values to obtain a fair profit on the work it was being asked to perform. The cost values in Exhibit 10C-2 were constant unitary values that the firm used to add or subtract from project estimates. If an extra day of work was required for an activity, the customer was charged the average cost value for the day. If a day's work had to be reduced because of time limitations, the extra work would have to be paid for at the same average cost per day.

WMRC management had to decide whether it wanted to accept the research project offered by Diddle. The only flexibility in the timing and cost information in Exhibit 10C-2 that WMRC had to consider was that both of the pretest activities could be reduced by seven days each because of an unusual abundance of additional research staff. The cost (and loss of profit) of these reductions in time would have to be considered in the project acceptance decision as well.

EXHIBIT 10C-2 MARKET RESEARCH PROJECT ACTIVITIES AND COSTS FOR NEW PRODUCT

Activity	*Predecessor Activity*	*Estimated Time (days)*	*Average Cost (per day)*
1–2. Select research instruments	None	10	$100
2–3. Develop mail survey instrument	1	40	87
2–4. Develop phone survey instrument	1	35	85
3–5. Pretest mail survey instrument	2	28	115
4–5. Pretest phone survey instrument	3	28	115
5–6. Run both surveys	4, 5	120	50
6–7. Summarize data from both surveys	6	15	340
7–8. Make final report on new product	7	5	500

CASE QUESTIONS

1. What are the normal costs for each activity of the market research project? What are total normal costs for this project?
2. Is CPM analysis appropriate for this type of problem? Explain.
3. Is it possible for WMRC to complete the project with its special requirements and still make a profit? Explain your answer and show your work.

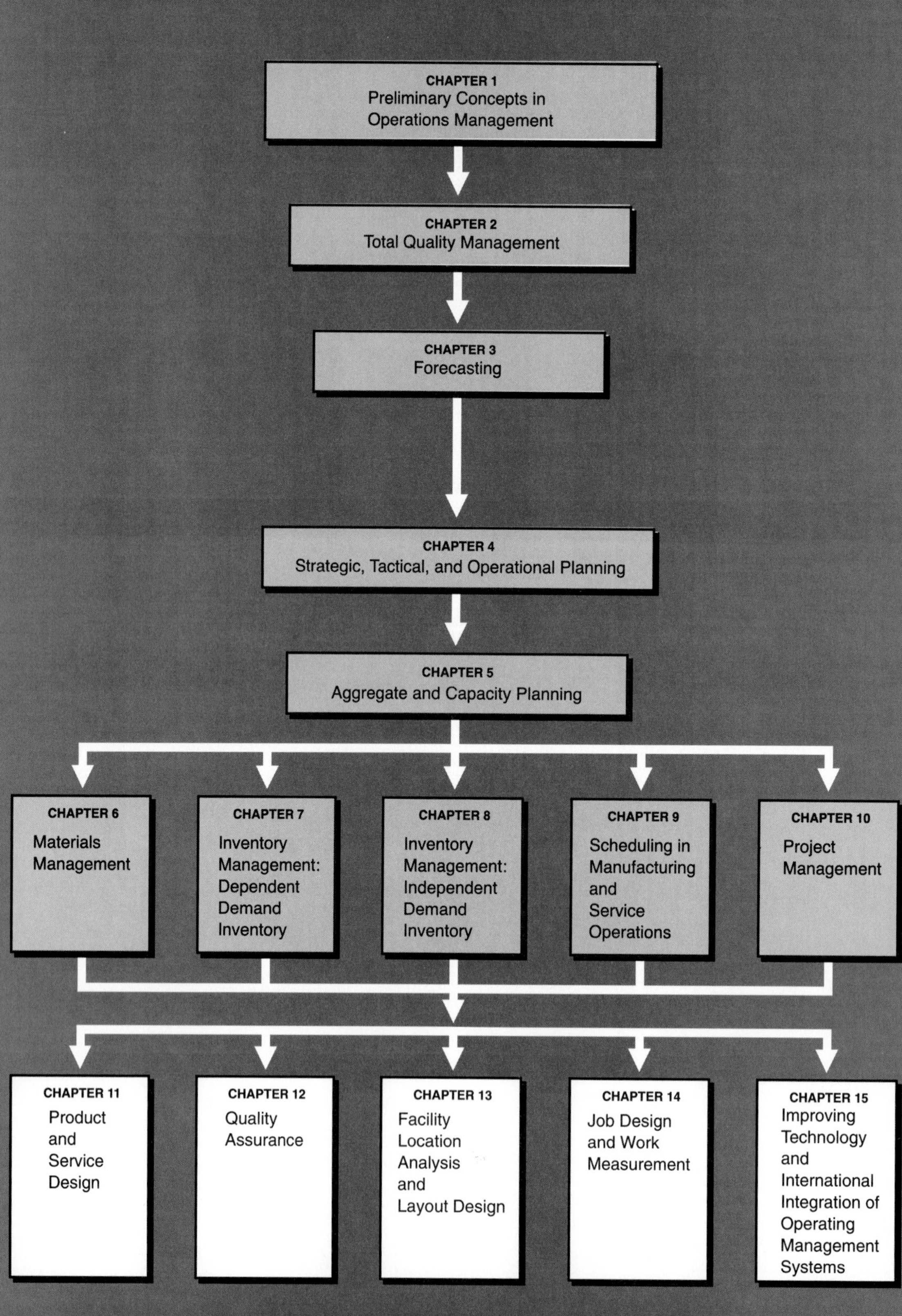
CHAPTER 1
Preliminary Concepts in
Operations Management
CHAPTER 2
Total Quality Management
CHAPTER 3
Forecasting
CHAPTER 4
Strategic, Tactical, and Operational Planning
CHAPTER 5
Aggregate and Capacity Planning
CHAPTER 6
Materials
Management
CHAPTER 7
Inventory
Management:
Dependent
Demand
Inventory
CHAPTER 8
Inventory
Management:
Independent
Demand
Inventory
CHAPTER 9
Scheduling in
Manufacturing
and
Service
Operations
CHAPTER 10
Project
Management
CHAPTER 11
Product
and
Service
Design
CHAPTER 12
Quality
Assurance
CHAPTER 13
Facility
Location
Analysis
and
Layout Design
CHAPTER 14
Job Design
and Work
Measurement
CHAPTER 15
Improving
Technology
and
International
Integration of
Operating
Management
Systems

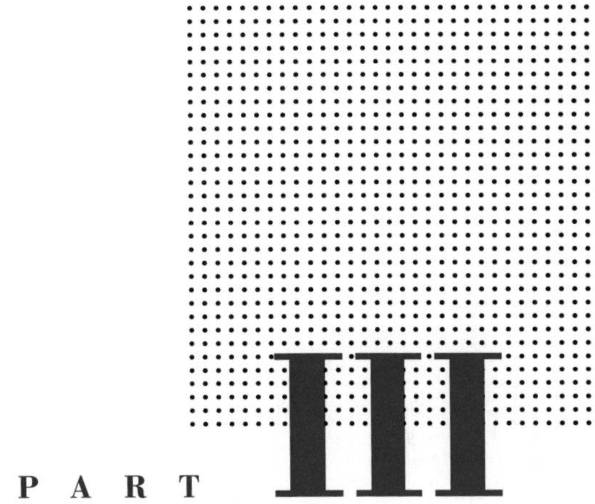

PART III

IMPROVING PRODUCTS AND SYSTEMS

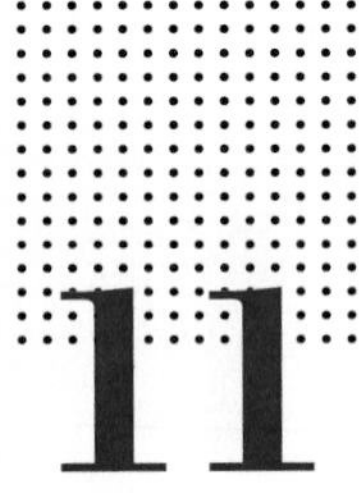

11 Product and Service Design

CHAPTER OUTLINE

CHAPTER OBJECTIVES

The material in this chapter should prepare you to do the following:

1. Explain why product and service design are necessary.
2. Understand the basics of product design and development.
3. Understand the strategic importance of product and service design.
4. Describe computer-aided design (CAD) and explain how it is used in product design.
5. Describe how expert systems are applied in product design.
6. Explain how standardization is used to reduce costs during the design process.
7. Describe group technology (GT) and how it is used in product planning.
8. Compute the reliability of a product on any given use by a customer.
9. Explain the contribution that research and development (R&D) makes to product design planning.
10. Explain how CAD and GT systems are integrated into CIM systems for improved productivity.

An organization combines human, technology, and system resources to create a product or service. This product or service should be produced to compete successfully on cost, quality, and other value-added attributes.

This chapter is about how organizations create, design, and develop new products and services. **Product and service design** involves all of the stages of development that transform a concept into a tangible manufactured product or intangible service product. Although dominated by the marketing and engineering functions, product and service design activities are highly integrated into the operations management function. Indeed, OM functions must be considered in product design to achieve effectiveness at the shop floor level of an organization.[1]

In this chapter we will examine the role of operations management in each stage of product and service design and development. We will also examine various methods used to accomplish the design and development activities during this creative process.

• • •

WHY PRODUCT AND SERVICE DESIGN ARE NECESSARY

As discussed in Chapter 4, Strategic, Tactical, and Operational Planning, each product or service goes through a product life cycle. As we can see in Figure 11-1, the product life cycle consists of the four stages of introduction, growth, maturity, and decline. The product life cycle relates a product's sales, profits, and loss over a period of time that marks its life. Eventually, the product is discontinued (or changed into a new product), which ends the life or current form of the existing product. Some product life cycles are quite short, lasting only a single season (for example, a fad), and other products last a long time. Product and service design activities, both before and during the product life cycle, affect all aspects of operations management planning. Actually, depending on the length of the product life cycle, product and service design activities have strategic, tactical, and operational planning implications.

An organization cannot conduct its strategic planning analysis (that is, an environmental situation analysis and a company situation analysis) or even establish a corporation mission statement until it has a successful product. For new organizations, selecting and developing a primary product or service usually precipitate all strategic planning efforts. As such, product and service design is necessary to define the means by which all strategic effort will be directed in new organizations.

The role of product design for organizations whose primary products and services endure over a long planning horizon (such as General Motors's automobiles and H&R Block's tax services) clearly affects strategic planning. In such established organizations, product or service design helps guide an organization's long-range (five or more years) strategic planning of investments in plant and facilities. For example, the Saturn Division **S**

[1] G. Hohner, "JIT/TQC: Integrating Product Design with Shop Floor Effectiveness," *Industrial Engineering* (September 1988), 42–47.

FIGURE 11-1 PRODUCT LIFE CYCLE, ANNUAL SALES, PROFIT, AND COST

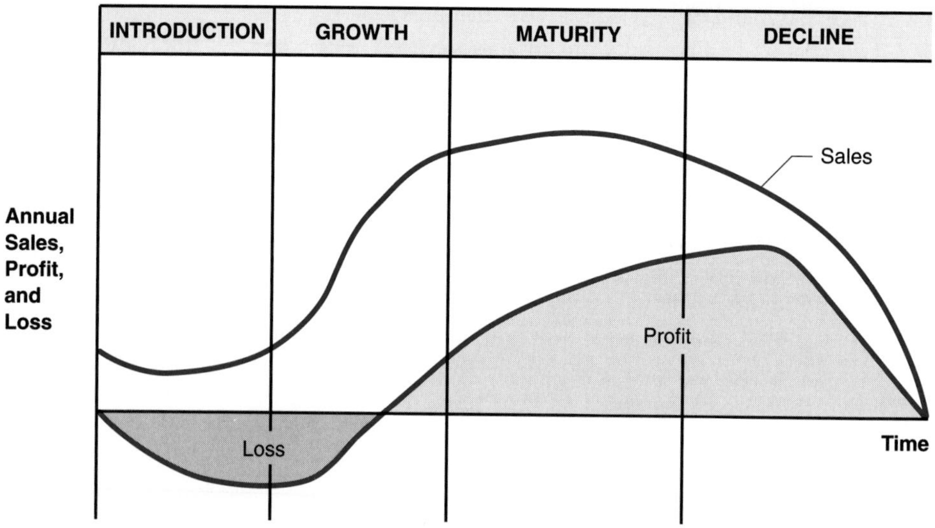

(see color photo insert) of General Motors (GM) produces automobiles that GM management believed were different enough to require their own production facility, their own separate corporate structure, and their own retail distribution system. GM management views the Saturn products and newly devised production facility as a strategy, representing more than a $1 billion investment, to meet the challenge of foreign competition in the automobile industry. The Saturn product is viewed as a strategic plan for the corporation's survival.

In the medium-range (about two years) tactical level of planning, the finance and marketing functional areas play necessary roles in the product design activities that relate to and affect the operations management area.

During the tactical stage of organization planning, the marketing area is responsible for determining and communicating customer and market requirements for products. These requirements change as the product goes through each stage of the product life cycle shown in Figure 11-1. In addition to its contribution in researching and developing new products, marketing also makes suggestions that directly alter operations management activities during the life of a product. For example, increased competition during the growth and maturity stages might necessitate cost-reducing changes in materials and production processes to remain price competitive. Marketing also helps develop and suggest new packaging methods for promotion, enhanced product deliverability, and customer protection that can only be implemented by OM personnel. For the marketing area to achieve its product and service goals, the OM area must develop tactical changes in products and processes.

During the tactical stage of organization planning, the support roles provided by finance for operations management and design activities are critically related. The OM area must secure the financial resources necessary to acquire the human, technology, and system resources to produce new products (note Figure 4-4 in Chapter 4). The finance function is responsible for planning the financial resources of an organization and therefore must ensure that sufficient financial resources exist to support the new products being developed. As presented in Figure 11-1, a product typically loses money during the initial stages of its life cycle before profit can be earned during the latter stages. Occasionally the finance area may be able to time the introduction of a product so that the expected loss period of one new product is balanced with the expected profit period from an older product. The OM area should be able to accommodate and meet these timing changes. To help the OM area have sufficient production capacity to meet these timing changes, finance staff can provide cost information on the acquisition of production equipment for new products. With the tremendous amount of investment modern automated equipment requires, the role of finance in cost justification is viewed as necessary to the success of OM.[2]

QUESTION: What is "silo management"? How is it counterproductive to product and service design? What can be done to minimize the impact of silo management in product and service design?

ANSWER: **Silo management** is a popular term used to describe the fact that most companies are vertically integrated micro-organizations.[3] That is, each functional area (marketing, engineering, finance, and so on) is a "silo" with a vice president at the top and the newest employees in each area at the bottom. Information on new product planning directives and work effort goes up and down the individual silos but is not shared with other functional areas as it is passed among departments. This can be counterproductive because input from several functional areas is often necessary to ensure a product's success. The counterproductive impact of silo management on the organization can be minimized by reorganizing a company to permit a greater sharing of information, a process called **cross-functional integration.** To implement cross-functional integration, we might use interfunctional teams (also called cross-functional teams; discussed in Chapter 2). These teams are also used as a total quality management (TQM) tactic (that is, formation of cooperative partnerships) of saving time by sharing information on work activities being performed in different functional areas. Team participants from various functional areas such as marketing and finance who work on the development of a new product along with the product design engineers are able to bring current information (and changes) back to their respective areas and avoid needless waste in planning time and costs in new product design and development.

---

[2] J. R. Meredith and M. M. Hill, "Justifying New Manufacturing Systems: A Managerial Approach," *Sloan Management Review* (Summer 1987), 49–61; and J. A. Hendricks, "Applying Cost Accounting to Factory Automation," *Management Accounting* (December 1988), 24–30.

[3] R. D. Garwood, "Trapped in the Silos?" *Production and Inventory Management,* 12, No. 2 (1992), 6.

Meeting the demand requirements placed on operations management by the marketing area and working within the financial constraints dictated by the finance area necessitate a product design sufficiently flexible to permit changes in the content of the product and the timing of the product's introduction. For tactical planning, the OM area must ensure that the product's design will permit this flexibility within the production capabilities of the OM system. Indeed, the design of the product determines the production equipment need. This makes OM product design considerations a tactical level planning activity focused on selecting and acquiring production equipment or suppliers with sufficient capacity to produce the desired products when they are required.

QUESTION: Can the integration of product design with other functional areas affect product quality?

Q

ANSWER: Yes. For most organizations, the more integrated the product design effort is within the entire organization, the better is the quality of the resulting product. For example, let's take the case of Sea Quest, a sport scuba diving equipment manufacturer.[4] In the late 1980s, consumers became increasingly interested in purchasing scuba equipment in new colors and varieties, which substantially changed the market. Sea Quest management responded to this change in market demand by redesigning its product using a modular design (we discuss modularization later in this chapter) that permitted interchangeable parts in various sizes, colors, styles, and options. This allowed customers to "customize" their scuba suits using a unique combination of colored parts. Marketing personnel were able to offer distributors (that is, Sea Quest's customers) an increased range of products without substantially increasing the current size of its inventory. It would maintain the same quantity of a scuba suit's modular parts, but increase the variety of colors so customers could create a custom suit to match their own fashion tastes. Sea Quest used cross-functional integration by having members of different departments meet to share information. At these meetings, sales staff discussed actual sales information; production staff discussed inventory, production, and capacity planning concerns; and engineering staff presented proposals for product changes and new product plans. In a single year, the results of these integrative efforts improved the quality of customer service by increasing the product's sizes and colors by 370 percent with only a 15 percent increase in distributors' inventory units. Sea Quest was also able to reduce its own total inventory by 19 percent, while still offering its customers the variety in fashion the market now demanded.

[4] G. H. French, "Linking Design, Marketing, and Shipping for Success: A Case Study in Integration," *Production and Inventory Management Journal,* 33, No. 3 (1992), 44–48.

How does product or service design help an organization implement a production schedule at the operational or shop floor level? The answer to this question is simple: The product's design determines how long the product will take in the transformation process. In other words, the product's design determines the timing of product completion or service delivery. A product design that takes production scheduling activity into consideration allows for efficiency in the overall flow and timing of product through an operation.

At the operational level of planning, product design focuses on improving the procedures and methods that increase the efficiency of operations. For example, standardizing components when the product is being designed helps improve efficiency by reducing the number of components in all of the organization's products and reducing the work effort and time needed to complete a single product. (We discuss standardization as a product design method later in this chapter.)

In summary, the role of product and service design affects the entire organization and involves strategic, tactical, and operational planning considerations. Clearly, product and service design in operations management is necessary to help improve planning activities in the OM area and the organization as a whole. In the next section we examine how design and development activities are performed.

QUESTION: What is product and service design's necessary role in an organization's total quality management (TQM) program?

ANSWER: One of product and service design's roles in TQM is related to the concept of time-based competition.[5] **Time-based competition** is the organization's basing its competitive advantage on its ability to provide a product to a customer in the least amount of time. Competitive success (and service quality) is based on the organization's ability to create, design, develop, produce, and deliver a finished product, once ordered by the customer, in the least amount of time. Although some organizations' competitive advantage is strictly time-based, all organizations are to some degree time-based. Because product and service design can involve a considerable amount of "front-end" time (that is, time before the product is finished and can be provided to the customer), efforts to reduce the months or even years it takes for product or service design and development can be critical for success in a time-based operation. Interestingly, some TQM methods (discussed in Chapter 2) can be used to support product and service design. For example, a value chain can be used to detail each step in the design and development process so that specific areas of identifiable wasted effort and time can be eliminated.

Q

[5] F. W. Hazeltine, "Zeroing in on Time-Based Competition," *APICS—The Performance Advantage*, 2, No. 11 (November 1992), 34–36.

BASICS OF DESIGN AND DEVELOPMENT

Planning the Design and Development Process

Design and development of a product or service represent a project planning activity. As we discussed in Chapter 10, project planning usually consists of a number of activities arranged in a sequence. The activities in the product design and development process are shown in Figure 11-2. To manage this process of product creation, organizations use a team management approach (discussed in Chapter 10) called product development teams. A **product development team** is responsible for a new product from the definition of its market to its evaluation as a failure or a success (stages 2 through 8 in Figure 11-2). The objective of these teams is to make the product or service a success. Product development teams include marketing, finance, and operations management personnel. The teams can also include external personnel such as new product consultants and specialists (for example, logistic specialists, speciality product consultants) as well as vendors that may be asked to provide materials and components for the new product or even the product itself (in "make versus buy" decisions).

Auxiliary planning units that support the efforts of the product planning team are often called *design for manufacturing teams, value engineering teams,* and *reliability engineering teams.* These teams are usually charged with the more narrowly focused responsibility of improving product design and specifications while the product is still in the research stage of development (stages 3 through 6). **Value engineers** use, among other things, a process called **value analysis** to reduce material costs by examining design changes that decrease the number of parts. The reduction in parts is then analyzed to decrease engineering, tooling, and direct and indirect labor costs. The expected result of value analysis is a product that will deliver the same or better value at a reduced cost.[6] Reliability engineering teams are used to enhance product consistency (a characteristic of product quality). **Reliability engineers** use a variety of analyses to study the durability of components for purposes of design improvements. (We examine some of the methods used in reliability analysis later in this chapter.) Their objective is to make certain that the product will work successfully by ensuring that each component in the product will work reliably. It is from the application of these engineering teams in design that the concept of concurrent engineering (discussed in Chapter 2) was developed.

The teams that conduct the design and development process are established after the idea of a product or service is conceived. The design and development process begins with the product idea or creation stage.

---

[6] "The Best Engineered Part Is No Part at All," *Business Week,* May 8, 1989, p. 150. For an interesting service application in the health care industry, see J. Novack, "The $550-a-Day Nursing Home," *Forbes,* January 20, 1992, pp. 41–43.

FIGURE 11-2 STAGES IN THE PRODUCT DESIGN AND DEVELOPMENT PROCESS

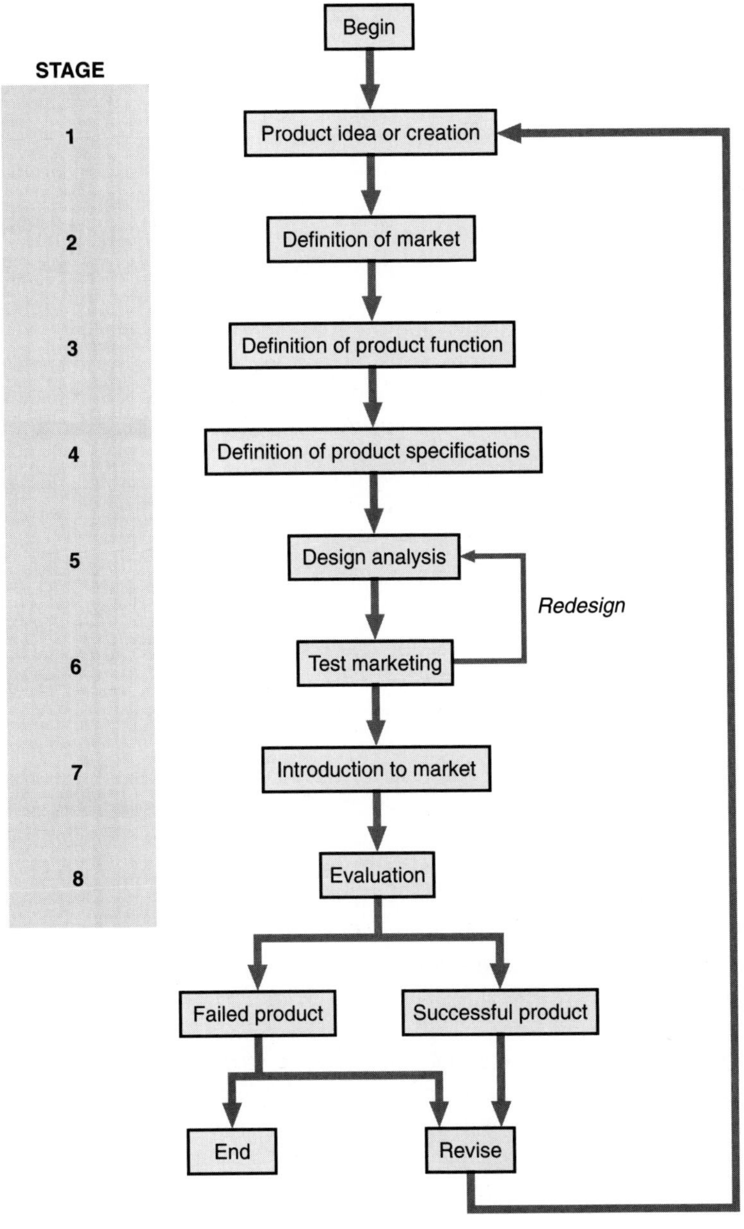

Product Design and Development

Although the stages in Figure 11-2 apply equally to products and services, we will discuss service product design later in this section. Now let's examine each of the eight stages of the product design and development process presented in Figure 11-2.

PRODUCT IDEA OR CREATION Whether creating a new product, revising an old one, or deciding to produce one similar to a competitor's, product design activities should always be conducted as part of strategic planning to continually seek new opportunities in the marketplace.[7] Factors such as sociological change (a decrease in family size can result in the need for smaller houses), economic change (an increase in disposable income can result in the need for more luxury items), technology change (improvements in technology can reduce product costs and result in increased market share), and political change (a new trade agreement can result in new opportunities in foreign countries) can all lead to the need for new products and services. Ideas for products can also come from a study of past failures or an examination of a successful product. For example, the Peterson Tool Company of Nebraska, developers of the highly successful ViceGrip pliers, has created more than one hundred different product adaptations from the same basic ViceGrip pliers product.

Product ideas come from many sources. Often, product innovation and new product ideas come from customers who buy and use a company's current products. These ideas are collected by marketing personnel, who are a primary source of information for new product ideas. Other sources include research and development (R&D) personnel who create new products, inventors who sell ideas for royalties, and engineering design consultants who are paid to develop new products.

DEFINITION OF MARKET Once the idea for the product is finalized, the next stage in the design and development process is to define the product's customers or market. If a product, regardless of its value or utility, has no market, there is little hope that the product will be successful. Marketing staff specialists and experts are responsible for identifying and quantifying the market for new products. Existing products also need their markets refocused throughout their product life cycle. Identifying the target customers and markets helps managers develop strategic, tactical, and operational plans for the product.

DEFINITION OF PRODUCT FUNCTION In this stage of the design process the product is defined in terms of what it will do and how it will work—that is, how many different functions the product should or will perform. Carried out chiefly by engineers for manufactured products, this stage involves analyzing customer requirements and converting them into a preliminary prototype model of the product. For service products, marketing staff usually perform this stage by listing characteristics of the service product

---

[7] T. Peters, "All Markets Are Now Immature," *Industry Week,* July 3, 1989, pp. 14–16; and B. Dumaine, "Design that Sells and Sells and . . . ," *Fortune,* March 11, 1991, pp. 86–88.

they plan to offer. The prototype model or listing is only used to express the functional aspects of the product or service that is to be offered. Consideration of functional design factors such as size, shape, and color may be part of the analysis at this stage.

DEFINITION OF PRODUCT SPECIFICATIONS In this stage of the design process, the prototype model or list of characteristics from stage 3 is narrowed to a more finished product or service. Performed by engineering specialists in the case of manufactured products, this stage results in detailed product specifications that define what the product is and detail how the product will be made. Engineering drawings showing dimensions, tolerances for materials, and components are made at this stage. Applications of design engineering technology, including computer-aided design (CAD), can help define the product. (We discuss CAD systems later in this chapter.) For service products this stage might be performed by marketing or a variety of other specialists (lawyers, professors, consultants). These specialists would detail specifications that define what the service is and how it should be performed or delivered.

DESIGN ANALYSIS In this stage of the design process the product or service is reexamined in terms of how it can be produced economically. Analysis from value and reliability engineers seeks to design a product the organization can produce profitably. The continued use of design engineering technology, such as CAD and computer-aided engineering (CAE) systems, is employed at this level to test the product's capabilities in reliably delivering the desired functionality to the customer. The analysis at this stage also considers the capabilities of the operations management system that constrain production. Engineers must plan a product that is within the organization's production capabilities. The output of this stage is the plan for a product that can be profitably produced and will satisfy market needs for functionality. Once the design work at this stage is complete, other production design work is required to document the production activities required to produce the product. Production documents that might be prepared at this step include an **assembly drawing** (which shows an exploded view of the product's components and where they are assembled together on a relational basis), an **assembly chart** (which shows how the product is to be assembled, from vendor materials to the finished product; this chart identifies each point where components flow into subassemblies), a **route sheet** (a listing of the operations in sequence through workcenters and throughout the entire operation), and **job instructions** (a manual or listing of each individual job task necessary to complete the product).

TEST MARKETING Principally a marketing personnel function, test marketing tries to find out if the current design of a product (from stage 5) meets the functionality requirements of the customers for whom it has been designed. Marketing opinion surveys, including mail, telephone, and actual field surveys, are conducted to determine if the newly introduced product is what the customers want. If the product does not meet the desired functionality requirement levels stated in stage 3, it is usually sent back to stage 5 for redesign. If the product meets desired expectations for a saleable product, it proceeds to the next stage.

INTRODUCTION TO MARKET Principally a marketing personnel function, this stage requires the development of promotion efforts and product strategies to expose the product to as many customers as possible. This stage is actually the first stage of the product life cycle. Because this stage might take considerable time, it is commonly used by design engineers to collect additional information from customers in the field and to make minor adjustments in materials or production processes to improve the functionality fit between the product and the user.

EVALUATION Success criteria should be established for any product. Criteria might include marketing considerations such as achieving a targeted sales level during the product's introduction to market. For operations management, success criteria focus on the product, including its reliability. The number of defective units returned for repair or warranty service executed by authorized repair service centers are two useful sources of product reliability and quality information for manufactured products. Marketing information collected from customer complaints or praise from point-of-use survey cards, letters, or telephone calls are sources of information used to evaluate the product's acceptability. Specific cut-off values for any cost-related repair activity might be set as a means of evaluating a product's success or failure. Products judged as failures might be dropped, and the product design and development efforts will end. Other products may fail for specific and identifiable reasons. During the evaluation stage, the specific and correctable reasons for product failure might be used to revise the failed product, and the product design and development effort could be initiated again. Likewise, the product life cycle of even successful products eventually dictates the need for revision. A maturing product can be revised into a new product to generate even greater profits for the firm. This revision process is performed by repeating the eight stages of the design and development process.

These eight stages provide a general outline of the design and development activities necessary to create and deliver a new product to the market. Although these stages are applicable to service products, the nature of engineering service product quality is quite complex.

Service Design and Development

S One system that has been proposed for designing quality in service systems was developed to allow organizations to identify the positioning of their product relative to some ideal quality level. The three-dimensional classification model presented in Figure 11-3 was devised as a model to assist in the design of service products.[8] The model employs three resource input items to define a service product's quality. The three resource input items are listed on the next page.

---

[8] J. Haywood-Farmer, "A Conceptual Model of Service Quality," *International Journal of Operations and Production Management,* 8, No. 6 (1988), 19–29.

FIGURE 11-3 THREE-DIMENSIONAL CLASSIFICATION MODEL

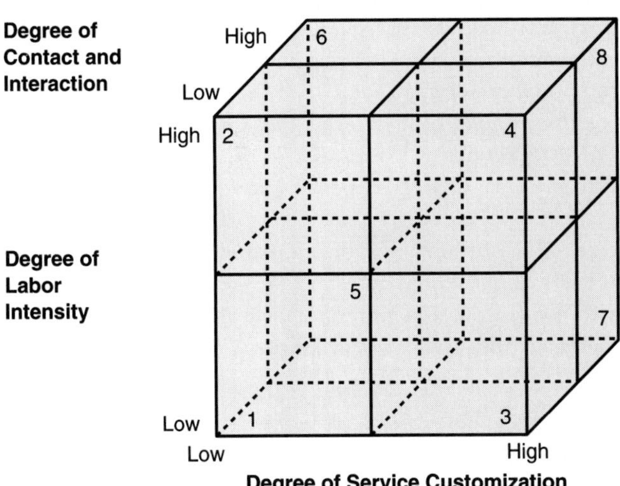

Some examples of services in each octant:

1. Utilities, transportation of goods
2. Lecture teaching, postal services
3. Stockbroking, courier services
4. Repair services, wholesaling, retailing
5. Computerized teaching, public transit
6. Fast food, live entertainment
7. Charter services, hospitals
8. Design services, advisory services, healing services

Source: International Journal of Operations and Production Management, Volume 8, No. 6 (1988), MCB University Press Ltd.

1. *Degree of contact and interaction* To what degree does the customer contact or interact with the service processes? If the customer takes an active part in the delivery of the service product (for example, customers dancing in a nightclub as a part of the entertainment service), there is a high degree of contact or interaction. If the customer takes a minor part in the delivery of the service product (for example, a student coming to class at a university where the service product is the professor's lecture), there is a low degree of contact or interaction. Design considerations must be made to ensure that the service process allows the customer to participate to the desired degree for a successful product.
2. *Degree of labor intensity* To what degree is the service product labor intensive? The degree of labor intensity has a direct relationship to product design. Products that are highly labor intensive should be designed to ensure quality service through effective training and good skills on the part of the personnel handling the product. Products with relatively low labor intensity usually require a design that focuses on timely service (that is, quality in low labor intensity products is judged on the timeliness of service delivery).
3. *Degree of service customization* To what degree is the service product customized? If a service is highly customized, it must be designed to permit a high degree of capacity flexibility to meet the diverse demand of customized products. If the service has low customization, the design should focus on providing service products in the right quantity in a timely fashion.

The three-dimensional model is used as an aid to identify sources of relevant product design information. For example, a hospital might learn more about scheduling from a limousine charter service than from a hospital that specializes in care for the elderly. The model can also be used to help conceptualize the positioning for an organization's service product relative to ideal quality service level. If an ideal positioning of an organization in one of the octants in Figure 11-3 is in the middle of the cell, an organization might observe where its service is positioned in the octant and develop design strategies around the three quality characteristics to move it toward the ideal position.

Service organizations tend to offer products that position their firm in one of the four stages of firm competitiveness as presented in Table 11-1. Depending on the product offered, most firms try to move from a beginning stage 1 (available for service), through stages 2 and 3, to stage 4 (world-class service delivery). How well a service

TABLE 11-1 FOUR STAGES OF SERVICE FIRM COMPETITIVENESS

Stage	*1. Available for Service*	*2. Journeyman*	*3. Distinctive Competence Achieved*	*4. World-Class Service Delivery*
Market	Customers patronize service firm for reasons other than performance.	Customers neither seek out nor avoid the firm.	Customers seek out the firm based on its sustained reputation for meeting customer expectations.	The company's name is synonymous with service excellence. Its service doesn't just satisfy customers, it *delights* them, and thereby expands customer expectations to levels its competitors are unable to fulfill.
Operations	Operations is reactive, at best.	Operations functions in a mediocre, uninspired fashion.	Operations continually excels, reinforced by personnel management and systems that support an intense customer focus.	Operations is a quick learner and fast innovator; it masters every step of the service delivery process and provides capabilities that are superior to competitors'.
Service quality	Is subsidiary to cost, highly variable.	Meets some customer expectations, consistent on one or two key dimensions.	Exceeds customer expectations, consistent on multiple dimensions.	Raises customer expectations and seeks challenges, improves continuously.

product competes is a function of product design factors that define the product. Service organizations must consider such factors as service quality, customers, technology, work force, and management in the design of their service products. Failure to consider any of these factors in the design of new service products can cause an entire service organization's product line to be perceived by customers as moving back to a more undesirable stage. On the other hand, careful consideration of these design factors can help service organizations gain or maintain their world-class standing.

Another reason that firms slide from world-class performance is the introduction of superior products from competitors that push the definition of "world class" to higher levels of service performance. To avoid losing ground to competitors, service organizations must undertake continuous redesign efforts. As stated in Chapter 2, world-class service products must include an element of continuous improvement to maintain their status in the highly competitive environment of the 1990s. Many firms invest

TABLE 11-1 (CONTINUED)

Stage	*1. Available for Service*	*2. Journeyman*	*3. Distinctive Competence Achieved*	*4. World-Class Service Delivery*
Back office	Counting room.	Contributes to service, plays an important role in the total service, is given attention, but is still a separate role.	Is equally valued with front office, plays integral role.	Is proactive, develops its own capabilities, and generates opportunities.
Customer	Unspecified, to be satisfied at minimum cost.	A market segment whose basic needs are understood.	A collection of individuals whose variation in needs is understood.	A source of stimulation, ideas, and opportunity.
Introduction of new technology	When necessary for survival, under duress.	When justified by cost savings.	When promises to enhance service.	Source of first-mover advantages, creating ability to do things competitors can't do.
Work force	Negative constraint.	Efficient resource, disciplined, follows procedures.	Permitted to select among alternative procedures.	Innovative, creates procedures.
First-line management	Controls workers.	Controls the process.	Listens to customers, coaches and facilitates workers.	Is listened to by top management as a source of new ideas. Mentors workers to enhance their career growth.

Source: Reprinted from "Beefing Up Operations in Service Firms" by R. B. Chase and R. H. Haynes, *Sloan Management Review,* Vol. 33, No. 1, 1991, pp. 15–26, by permission of publisher.

substantially in research and development (R&D) to maintain their competitive advantages. (We discuss R&D in the next section.)

PRODUCT AND SERVICE DESIGN METHODS

Several product and service design methods are available to support the product design and development process. In this section we will discuss the more commonly used methods including computer-aided design, expert systems, standardization, group technology, reliability analysis, and research and development.

Computer-aided Design (CAD)

CAD systems were introduced in Chapter 4 (in the Integrating Management Resources section) as a means of achieving a competitive advantage. Today, CAD systems have evolved into an essential design technology for assisting many of the stages of the product design and development process. **Computer-aided design** or **CAD** is a software system that uses geometric and mathematical functions to create an electronic drafting system with which designers can express their product ideas. CAD systems can run on simple microcomputers or on mainframe computer systems that integrate CAD with other software and production systems. Value and other engineers use CAD software in their research during product development (stages 3 through 6 in Figure 11-2). CAD can also be used in stage 1 of the product design and development process (product idea or creation) to help product design engineers take existing products and make necessary modifications to create new products. Once a product is designed on a CAD system, the software can generate drafting copies of the product so prototype modeling can begin.

One software extension of CAD is a combined CAD/CAM system. **Computer-aided manufacturing** or **CAM** is a software application of computer control to production equipment. The most widely used CAM-operated systems are numerical control (NC) machines that press, cut, and drill materials to produce high-precision parts for products. The combined CAD/CAM system works to move production from the design and development phase to the production phase, completely within the control of the computer. The CAD portion of the software generates the product design. The design and specifications from CAD are joined with work assignments stored in a CAM data base. The software then directs the CAM portion of the system to execute the necessary pressing, cutting, or drilling activities to complete the product. Although some human setup might be necessary in CAD/CAM operations, the combined system allows the organization to move from idea to finished product with minimal human intervention. Other benefits of the combined system include improved product quality (because of the reduced product variation that would be attributed to human input), a new range of production capabilities (because the computer system is only limited by the physical limitations of the NC equipment, not work rules or labor contracts), and reductions in product costs (because the combined system takes less time to design and produce).

Expert Systems

Product design work involves tasks requiring experience, creativity, and intuition on the part of a design engineer, and a number of expert systems (computer software systems that emulate human experts) that mimic these tasks have been developed to support product design activities. Although somewhat limited in application, they are becoming an important design aid. Some of the design expert systems reported in the literature include the following:

1. *AIFIX* This expert system is used to design fixtures to be machined in milling centers. The fixture is an important device used to accurately locate and constrain a workpiece on a machine so machining operations can be performed. This system can perform the design activities, given the information on the raw materials used in the manufacture of the fixture as well as the machine and tools to do the job.[9]
2. *Injection modeling cooling expert (IMCE)* This expert system is a tool for designing cooling systems for injection molding equipment. This system is capable of numerical analysis and heuristic reasoning that mimic designer cognitive processes.[10]
3. *XCON* This expert system is used to design computer configurations to meet customer requirements. This system uses heuristic reasoning to configure VAX computer equipment, peripheral equipment, and job loading equipment to meet customer requirements for computer support.[11]

Standardization

Standardization is "the process of designing and/or altering products to establish and use standard specifications for them and/or components."[12] Most products are not

[9] P. M. Ferreira and B. Kochar, "AIFIX: An Expert System Approach to Fixture Design," *Computer-Aided/Intelligent Process Planning,* PED-Vol. 19, eds. C. R. Liu, T. C. Chang, and R. Komanduri (New York: The American Society of Mechanical Engineers, 1985), pp. 73–82.

[10] H. Lee and T. H. Kwon, "Heuristic Redesign with Numerical Analysis Aids," *Computers in Engineering,* 1, eds. D. R. Riley and T. J. Cokonis (New York: The American Society of Mechanical Engineers, 1989), pp. 135–140.

[11] J. McDermott, "R1: A Rule-Based Configurer of Computer Systems," *Artificial Intelligence,* 19 (1982), 39–88.

[12] Reprinted with permission of the American Production and Inventory Control Society, Inc., *APICS Dictionary,* 7th edition, 1992.

custom made and many contain parts that share the same functions as parts of other products. Standardizing the design of parts in different products permits manufacturers to reduce the variety of parts they need to stock in inventory to cover the production of all their products. Reducing inventory permits a number of advantages including (1) reduced inventory costs (less space for less inventory), (2) reduced training costs (fewer parts mean less need for explanation about their assembly), and (3) more efficiency and lower costs in the production process (fewer setups and longer production runs).

An extension of standardization is called modularization. **Modularization** is a design activity in which groupings of parts are placed together into component "modules," like subassemblies, for use in the final assembly of a finished product. The modules can be used in the assembly of a single product to save labor time in grouping the components at the time of assembly and can be standardized to be used in more than one product as standardized components. Modular component designs have the advantage of being fairly easy to test for defects because the module can be tested "as a system" rather than testing each component that makes up the modules. The disadvantage of modular design is that if one component of a module becomes defective, the entire module (with many useful parts) will have to be replaced at greater expense than just replacing the individual defective part.

Group Technology (GT)

Group technology (GT) is an engineering and manufacturing method that is used to guide product design and plant layout toward "sameness" or "families." We will discuss GT as it relates to plant layout in Chapter 13. GT components are identified by a coding scheme in terms of materials, production tools that will be used to process them, and specifications as to the work that will be performed on the components. The numbering scheme can be as detailed as desired and use any length of numbers to make up a GT code. For example, components A and B in Figure 11-4 are cut from the same material and have two dimensions of shape that are the same. The cutting process of parts of similar shape can be grouped together into "families" to be run at the same time. The GT code number is used to identify the similar processing requirement so the grouping can take place. Product designers aware of the advantages of GT are careful to specify identical diameter holes in components as shown in Figure 11-4. Similarly, the raw materials needed for both components can be identified and grouped by the purchasing department to take advantage of possible quantity discounts.

Some of the advantages of using GT are (1) reduced raw materials and purchasing costs (because orders are bunched or grouped for several products), (2) improved job routing (because the numbering system makes routing easier to identify), (3) reduced setup time (because a variety of products that share the same production activity are run at one time), and (4) improved design efforts (because the impact of redesigning parts can be planned for many products at one time by using codes to identify similar process and product changes in other products). In general, GT reduces inventory and production costs while it increases productivity.

FIGURE 11-4 GT CODING NUMBER EXAMPLE

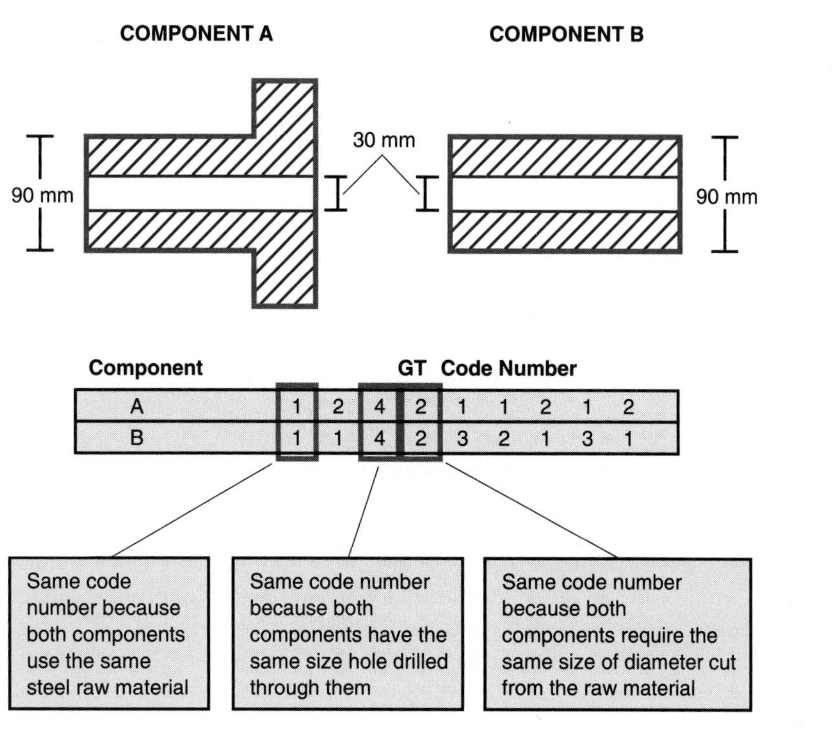

Reliability Analysis

Reliability engineering focuses on the reliability of a product as defined in stage 5 (design analysis) of the product design and development process. One type of analysis used to assess the reliability of a product is based on probability theory. Two types of probabilities can be used in assessing reliability: (1) the probability that the product will successfully function on any given use by a customer and (2) the probability that the product will successfully function over a given period of time.

1. *Reliability on a single use* The formula for determining the probability P of success (product reliability) for any given use of a product that consists of some n number of independent components or parts is

$$P(\text{product success}) = P_1(\text{success of component 1}) \times P_2(\text{success of component 2}) \times \ldots \times P_n(\text{success of component } n)$$

For example, if a product consists of three independent component parts, each with a different probability of success of 0.95, 0.98, and 0.99, its probability of product success or product reliability is

$$\begin{aligned} P(\text{product success}) &= P_1(\text{success of component 1}) \\ &\quad \times P_2(\text{success of component 2}) \\ &\quad \times P_3(\text{success of component 3}) \\ &= 0.95 \times 0.98 \times 0.99 \\ &= 0.9217 \end{aligned}$$

2. *Reliability over a given period of time* Over a period of time a product may fail for a variety of reasons. The typical failure rate of products as a function of time can be expressed as the tub-shaped curve as shown in Figure 11-5. As illustrated by the curve in Figure 11-5, many product failures occur in a relatively short period of time after a product has been put into use. The cause of these product failures (often called **infancy failures**) is usually poor product quality. Design or process problems are a part of a product's reliability problems. These problems show up quickly in the life of a product, as shown in Figure 11-5. We also expect that at the end of the curve a large number of products will wear out over time. The true average time for product failure is somewhere in the middle of this failure rate curve. We call the average product failure rate the **mean time between failures (MTBF).** An organization's objective should be to produce products that will have a large *MTBF* and therefore a

FIGURE 11-5 FAILURE RATE AS A FUNCTION OF TIME

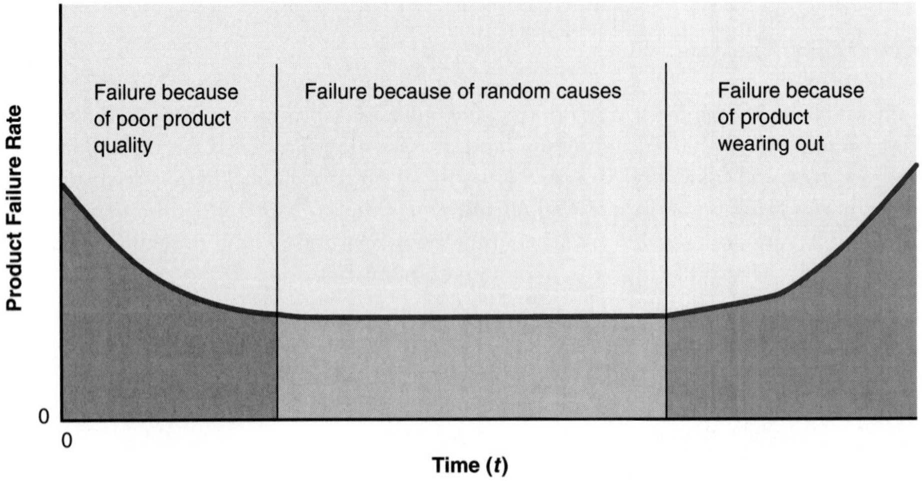

high degree of product success over time. This can be accomplished by focusing on the design and process problems that lead to early failure (first part of the curve in Figure 11-5). (We discuss process control problems in Chapter 12.)

Engineers focusing on design issues that lead to poor reliability usually begin by mathematically assessing product failure rates over a period of time. To assess the probability of success or failure over time the exponential probability distribution can be used. The area under the exponential probability distribution in Figure 11-6 represents the reliability probability. The horizontal axis of the distribution represents time. We want to compute the probability that the product will be successful at least to some t time period. The formula for the reliability probability we seek is

$$P(\text{product success before time period } t) = e^{-t/MTBF}$$

where

$$e = \text{a natural logarithm, 2.7183}$$
$$t = \text{the length of successful service before a failure}$$
$$MTBF = \text{a given mean time between failures}$$

The probability of failure is simply 1 minus the probability of success. The values for this formula can be taken from tabled values for the exponential probability distribution in Appendix G.

QUESTION: What is the probability that a light bulb will work successfully for at least 1,200 hours if its *MTBF* is 1,500 hours? What is the probability that the bulb will work at least 1,800 hours?

ANSWER: To determine the probability that the light bulb will work for 1,200 hours, we first determine the ratio of $t/MTBF$ (1,200/1,500 = 0.8). From Appendix G we find

$$P(\text{bulb successfully working for 1,200 hours}) = e^{-0.8} = 0.4493$$

The probability that the bulb will successfully work for at least 1,200 hours is 44.93 percent.

To determine the probability that the light bulb will work for 1,800 hours, we first determine the ratio of $t/MTBF$ (1,800/1,500 = 1.2). From Appendix G we find

$$P(\text{bulb successfully working for 1,800 hours}) = e^{-1.2} = 0.3012$$

The probability that the bulb will successfully work for at least 1,800 hours is 30.12 percent.

FIGURE 11-6 EXPONENTIAL PROBABILITY DISTRIBUTION AND RELIABILITY

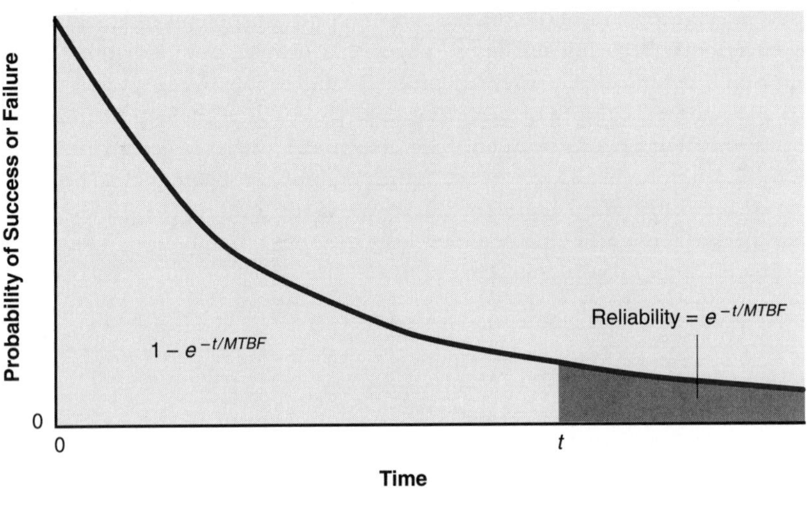

Reliability analysis points to two obvious conclusions: (1) to improve reliability, the reliability of each component must be improved, and (2) the components with the lowest individual probability of success offer the greatest opportunity and need for improvement. It is very costly to build redundant components to act as a backup system to help ensure product reliability. Instead, design efforts should be devoted to improving individual component reliability by reducing component dependence (one component that must be repeatedly used to permit other components to function) and simplifying product components through standardization to reduce the number of different components that can fail. In this way product design can help ensure product reliability and customer satisfaction.

Research and Development (R&D)

Research and development (R&D) is all of the product information collection and analysis activities that an organization performs. Because most R&D is devoted to products, it is integrated into the product design and development process. Not every organization performs R&D because of the costs involved, and other organizations hire specialists or consulting groups to perform R&D activities. R&D includes basic research, applied research, and development.

1. *Basic research* Basic research is designed to advance scientific knowledge and is not specifically designed to accomplish commercial purposes. Most university faculty are expected to conduct basic research to benefit their discipline, state, or country.

2. *Applied research* Applied research is designed to achieve commercial objectives by seeking ways to apply basic research. Business organizations that study a product's reliability under different environmental situations for purposes of enhancing product design and quality characteristics are conducting applied research.
3. *Development* Development is designed to convert applied research into commercial applications. Researching product quality might lead to new product ideas that need to be developed by further research. The purpose of developmental research is to explore the new opportunities that applied research discovers.

Although most of the greatest advances in products in the last thirty years have come from R&D, undertaking an R&D program is not without risk. Some manufacturers in today's highly competitive global environment are finding the investment in developing new technology is not work the costs. A company may spend years developing a product only to have it copied by foreign competitors who have spent little or nothing on R&D.

The United States has been the world leader in R&D activities. Recently other countries have made major advances in this area, however, especially in applied research. The United States is known for its scientific and technological breakthroughs, whereas Japan has been the most successful country in commercializing known technology through continuous innovation.

INTEGRATING MANAGEMENT RESOURCES: USING COMPUTER-AIDED DESIGN AND GROUP TECHNOLOGY TO INCREASE EFFICIENCY

CAD and GT methods of product design and devleopment are by themselves useful planning aids for improving efficiency. They are even more powerful when integrated with larger production systems.

Increasing Design Efficiency

CAD can be greatly enhanced by integrating it with a GT code or numbering system for products into a common data base. As previously discussed, a product's GT code identifies it according to the materials and processes that will be used in its construction and production processing activities (plastic, metal, shape, size, length, drilling, specifications). These production activities become a standardized work unit. In addition to GT code information, standardized setup and product processing activity times can also be assessed and stored in a GT data base. Once a product design engineer has visually created a new product using CAD, the GT data base can be referenced to call up all existing products that might have similar component parts. Visually comparing the component parts helps the designer adjust or modify the new product components to fit existing standardized components. The integrated GT data base also helps the designer envision additional functionality characteristics from the existing products that are also present in the new product.

This database system saves product designers time and improves their efficiency. The GT numbering code incorporated into a data base also saves designers time in locating part families that share similar product attributes and processing. By finding a component that is already designed and may only need a minor change to perform the desired function in a new product, the designer saves time by not reinventing a previously designed component. In this way the GT data base helps eliminate redundancy in parts design and in the number of parts, resulting in a reduction of time and costs in purchasing, planning, scheduling, and production.

Increasing Manufacturing Efficiency

Using a GT data base in design affects an entire organization. When the organization uses a computer-integrated manufacturing (CIM) system of operation, the benefits are even greater because of the shared information from the computer system on which both operate. Some of the benefits include[13]

1. *Uniformity in component part processing and execution* CIM software can easily access the GT data base and secure precise design specifications for NC machines, routing information for automated conveyance systems, and instructions to workers under the CIM control umbrella.
2. *Improved scheduling and scheduling performance* Reduction in design time and the electronic conveyance of lot-size production requirements allow more time for scheduling and thus speed up production. GT coding allows managers to more easily identify and group production effort to make lot-size scheduling changes of products that share similar production characteristics.
3. *Reduction in setup, tooling design, storage, and handling* The GT system reduces the redundancy of inventory and reduces the number of production runs for a less varied component parts inventory. As a result of the reductions, the CIM system can save the time, effort, and costs required to produce component parts inventory.
4. *Reduction in throughput time* Reduction in inventory and production runs of component parts results in time savings to complete customer jobs. There is less need to monitor component part production efforts because there are fewer component parts in the system.
5. *Less work-in-process* Fewer component parts are being produced, so there are fewer components in WIP to slow down production.

SUMMARY

In this chapter we have examined product and service design. A product design and development process was presented as a general guide in the stages of analysis necessary to create new products. A service classification model was also described as a means of considering

[13] *Modern Machine Shop: NC/CIM 1990 Guidebook,* 62, No. 9A (1990), 229.

service product quality during the design of service products. A number of product design methods were also described including computer-aided design (CAD), expert systems, standardization, group technology (GT), reliability analysis, and research and development (R&D).

Once a product is designed, a manufacturing or service organization uses some of the information from the design analysis stage to begin the design of processes and procedures to produce the newly designed product. During the design and development process, a product's quality is determined. The importance of building quality into a product is one of the most critical factors for organizational survival and success in the 1990s. For this reason, we devote the next chapter to the subject of ensuring product quality.

DISCUSSION AND REVIEW QUESTIONS

1. What is the strategic importance of product design?
2. How does product design affect tactical and operational planning?
3. What are product development teams? What do they do? Who makes up the team?
4. What is the difference between a value engineer and a reliability engineer?
5. What are the stages of the design and development process?
6. Where do product ideas come from?
7. What is the three-dimensional classification model? What can it be used for?
8. How can we build quality into a service product?
9. How does CAD help in the design of products?
10. What are standardization and modularization? How are they different?
11. What is GT? How is it used in product design?
12. Why are probability distributions used in product design?

PROBLEMS

* 1. Suppose that you have two components, A and B, that are used in a group technology (GT)–based system. The GT coding of these components is used to relate the same assembly operations (i.e., 1, 2, 3, and 4) performed on each component. The GT coding numbers for the two components are as follows:

	GT CODE NUMBER BY OPERATION			
Component	*1*	*2*	*3*	*4*
A	1	2	3	1
B	2	2	3	2

a. Which operations do these components share?
b. If it takes a simple majority of operations to permit the grouping of components into families, should these two components be grouped together?

* The solutions to the problems marked with an asterisk can be found in Appendix J.

2. Suppose that you have three components, A, B, and C, that are used in a group technology (GT)–based system. The GT coding of these components is used to relate the same assembly operations (i.e., 1, 2, 3, and 4) performed on each component. The GT coding numbers for the three components are as follows:

	GT CODE NUMBER BY OPERATION			
Component	*1*	*2*	*3*	*4*
A	1	1	3	1
B	2	1	3	1
C	1	1	3	2

   a. Which operations do these components share? Specify by operation.
   b. If it takes a simple majority of operations to permit the grouping of components into families, which components can be grouped together?

3. Suppose that you have three components, A, B, and C, that are used in a group technology (GT)–based system. The GT coding of these components is used to relate the same assembly operations (i.e., 1, 2, 3, 4, 5, 6, 7, and 8) performed on each component and to identify sameness of materials. The GT coding numbers for the three components are as follows:

	GT CODE NUMBER BY OPERATION				*GT CODE NUMBER BY MATERIAL*			
Component	*1*	*2*	*3*	*4*	*5*	*6*	*7*	*8*
A	1	1	3	1	2	2	2	1
B	2	1	3	1	2	3	1	1
C	1	1	3	2	1	2	3	1

   a. Which operations do these components share? Specify by operation.
   b. Which materials do these components share? Specify by material.
   c. If it takes a simple majority of operations and materials to permit the grouping of components into families, which components can be grouped together?

4. Suppose that you have four components, A, B, C, and D, that are used in a group technology (GT)–based system. The GT coding of these components is used to relate the same assembly operations (i.e., 1, 2, 3, 4, 5, 6, 7, and 8) performed on each component and to identify sameness of materials. The GT coding numbers for the four components are as follows:

	GT CODE NUMBER BY OPERATION				*GT CODE NUMBER BY MATERIAL*			
Component	*1*	*2*	*3*	*4*	*5*	*6*	*7*	*8*
A	1	1	3	1	2	2	2	1
B	2	1	3	1	2	3	1	1
C	1	1	3	2	1	2	3	1
D	2	1	4	1	2	3	4	1

a. Which operations do these components share? Specify by operation.
b. Which materials do these components share? Specify by material.
c. If it takes a simple majority of operations and materials to permit the grouping of components into families, which components can be grouped together?

* 5. Suppose that a product consists of three independent components that each have the same probability—0.99—of successfully working. What is the probability that the product will work successfully each time it is used?

6. Suppose that a company's product consists of four independent components. Their probabilities of successfully working are 0.93, 0.91, 0.99, and 0.98. What is the probability that the product will work successfully each time it is used?

7. Suppose that a product consists of eight independent components that have the probability of successfully working of 0.99, 0.96, 0.96, 0.99, 0.93, 0.98, 0.99, and 0.98. What is the probability that the product will work successfully each time it is used?

8. A company produces an antimissile defense system used by the military to defend strategic targets. The defense system consists of one hundred component parts whose tolerances are so precise that ninety-five of the components have a 100 percent chance of working. The probability of working for the remaining five components are 0.99, 0.99, 0.98, 0.99, and 0.97. Because the antimissile defense system can be fired only one time to intercept incoming missiles, the country leaders who are interested in purchasing the antimissile system want to know what the chances are that the antimissile system will fail to work. What is the probability of failure for this antimissile product?

* 9. Using the exponential probability distribution and an *MTBF* of 120 days, what is the probability that a product will successfully work for at least 100 days?

10. Using the exponential probability distribution and an *MTBF* of 500 hours, what is the probability that a product will successfully work for at least 600 hours? For 800 hours? Explain the difference between the two probability values.

11. Using the exponential probability distribution and given an *MTBF* of 1,000 hours, what is the probability that a product will successfully work for at least 900 hours? For 700 hours? Explain the difference between the two probability values. What is the probability it will fail in 700 hours?

12. A company manufactures a product that will either work or not. If the mean time between failure of the product is estimated to be 1,400 hours, what is the probability that it will successfully operate for at least 1,500 hours? What is the probability it will fail in 1,200 hours?

13. A CD player has an average record of successfully operating and providing listening enjoyment for more than 5,000 hours before requiring repairs or routine maintenance. A customer is planning on buying the CD player for installation in a boat that will be taking an extended cruise that will demand 4,000 hours of play before being able to obtain repairs or routine maintenance. How reliable would the CD player be for the customer? Support your answer with necessary calculations.

14. A company can purchase either of two production machines. Production machine A has an *MTBF* of 20,000 hours and is expected to have 50,000 hours of useful life. Production machine B has an *MTBF* of 24,000 hours and is expected to have 55,000 hours of useful life. Based on the reliability of each machine over its useful life, which machine should the company purchase? Show all necessary calculations.

CASE 11-1

HOW RELIABLE ARE OUR PRODUCTS?

The Shocko Corporation designs, builds, and distributes a set of five different electronic switching systems used by telephone companies to channel communications. The company has been successful for many years, over which time the five products they offer to customers have been redesigned many times. Each time Shocko has attempted to improve the *MTBF* rates as a way of improving product quality. Shocko has maintained a high level of product quality that has been recognized by Shocko's customers and reflected in its above-average product prices. The five products and their mean time between failure rates are presented in Exhibit 11C-1.

In a recent major contract negotiation session, an important telephone company complained that one of Shocko's switching products had stopped working in a relatively short period of time. The switching product, product 0402203, was routinely replaced every 25,000 hours as a preventive maintenance measure to ensure service reliability to the telephone company. The switching system broke down after only 15,000 hours of use. The telephone company reported that the product failure resulted in very costly public hearings to explain and justify the downtime. Because Shocko's products are not the least expensive on the market many customers of the telephone company questioned why Shocko's product became defective after such a short period of time. Questions of new product designs or cheapening of product quality were raised and passed on to Shocko management.

The president of Shocko knew that such comments could hurt the company's reputation and decided to institute a program to increase product quality to enhance the company's competitive position. Possible design change opportunities to improve product quality were to improve materials and production processes. The president needed to know how much of an improvement in the current product's *MTBF* would be required to provide adequate customer service. A survey of telephone company customers revealed that having an 80 percent chance of no failures at 15,000 hours of use would constitute adequate quality.

EXHIBIT 11C-1 SHOCKO CORPORATION PRODUCTS AND *MTBF*s

GT Product Code	MTBF *(hours)*
0102201	30,000
0202102	40,000
0301202	45,000
0402203	50,000
0502303	60,000

CASE QUESTIONS

1. What would the *MTBF* have to be to achieve an 80 percent chance of no failures in 15,000 hours of use for product 0102201?
2. To achieve the same 80 percent chance of no failures in 15,000 hours for product 0202102, what should be its *MTBF*?
3. For product 0301202, what would its *MTBF* have to be to achieve an 80 percent chance of no failures in 15,000 hours of use?
4. What would the *MTBF* have to be to achieve only 20 percent chance of failures in 15,000 hours of use for product 0402203?
5. To achieve only 20 percent chance of failures in 15,000 hours of use for product 0502303, what should be its *MTBF*?

CASE 11-2

WHAT IS THE DESIGN OF THE DESIGN?

The TopQuality Rug Cleaning Company is a national rug cleaning franchisor with outlets in all fifty states. TopQuality offers in-house rug cleaning service to home owners and corporations. Its franchisees' service product consists chiefly of custom rug cleaning. In addition, TopQuality franchisees' offer other rug cleaning–related special services including spot removal, deodorizing, and stain-resistant coating with chemicals. These three additional service products have been a part of their rug cleaning product line since the company was first started by its franchisor owner.

Although no new services have been added to the product line, TopQuality management made it a policy to always look for new products. Having reached the maturity level of the product life cycle, the company realized that its franchisees needed some new products to help improve declining profits. Competition from local competitors has made a major impact on profits. Indeed, franchisees were beginning to discontinue their franchise contracts with TopQuality in the highly competitive market of the 1990s and start their own private rug cleaning companies. The loss of revnues from the sale of cleaning products and franchisee royalties has become quite noticeable to TopQuality management.

The owner and president of TopQuality was a chemical engineer before starting the rug cleaning business. Recently the president developed a new chemical dye that has a unique property to bind with existing rug fibers and create a "like new" appearance. The product has the ability to make old rugs look like new. TopQuality management felt that the new dye could be incorporated as a new service. Unfortunately, nobody in the firm had any experience in designing or developing the new service product idea.

CASE QUESTIONS

1. How would you structure the design and development program for TopQuality using the product design and development process in Figure 11-2? Be specific and explain each step in your design and development program.
2. How would you suggest that the method presented in this chapter be applied to the design and development program at TopQuality? Explain which methods will apply and which will not. Explain and justify your decisions for including and excluding each method. Indicate at which stage in the program each method applies.
3. In which octant in Figure 11-3 would the new service product fall? How would the product's degree of contact, labor intensity, and customization be distributed in the octant? What does the service's positioning in the octant mean in this situation? How can we use this information for design planning purposes?

12

Quality Assurance

CHAPTER OUTLINE

CHAPTER OBJECTIVES

The material in this chapter should prepare you to do the following:

1. Describe quality assurance and explain why it is necessary.
2. Explain how total quality control (TQC) helps achieve improved product quality.
3. Describe the process of implementing a TQC program.
4. Describe how Taguchi statistical methods can be used to improve product quality.
5. Explain and apply the Pareto method of identifying quality control problems.
6. Describe process control as a quality control method.
7. Explain and apply statistical quality control (SQC) charts.
8. Explain how integrated computer-based systems can be used to achieve higher product quality.
9. Explain how acceptance sampling is used in a quality assurance program.
10. Describe quality maintenance management activities.

Japan initiated the quality revolution in the 1970s and has since received worldwide recognition for its achievements. The United States joined the quality race in the mid-1980s and has also made rapid advances. More recently, the Europeans have launched a concerted effort to improve quality. Manufacturers and service organizations in all three regions plan to continue emphasizing this "competitive variable."[1] Research is showing that European and particularly U.S. organizations have made substantial improvements in overall product quality during the last five years when compared with Japanese manufacturers.[2] But until the United States catches up in this quality revolution, there is much we can learn from the Japanese about quality in manufacturing. Quality is viewed by both U.S. and Japanese operations managers as being the most critical factor for all firms' long-range survival.[3]

QUESTION: Is there a difference in the way Japanese and U.S. operations managers manage quality?

ANSWER: Both are equally successful in implementing and using quality management methods on isolated quality control problems. Research has shown, though, that the major difference between Japanese and U.S. manufacturers' approaches to managing quality is that the Japanese have achieved a greater degree of integration of quality than their U.S. counterparts.[4] In the 1990s, U.S. operations managers are recognizing what the Japanese managers did more than a decade ago: Quality is part of an integrated approach to competitiveness that must focus on linkages among functions across the entire organization. This is a principle of total quality management, which is discussed in Chapter 2.

In Chapter 2, we used a variety of approaches to define quality, including transcendent, product-based, user-based, manufacturing-based, and value-based. Quality can also be very simply defined as "conformance to requirements."[5] In manufacturing operations, quality can be defined in terms of product characteristics including (1) consistency, (2) usability, and (3) grade.

---

[1] From J. G. Miller et al., "Factories of the Future: Executive Summary of the 1990 International Manufacturing Futures Survey" (Boston: Boston University, 1991), p. 1.

[2] J. G. Miller et al., "Factories of the Future: Executive Summary of the 1990 International Manufacturing Futures Survey" (Boston: Boston University, 1991), p. 10.

[3] D. A. Garvin, "Quality Problems, Policies, and Attitudes in the United States and Japan: An Exploratory Study," *Academy of Management Journal,* 29, No. 4 (1986), 653–673; and E. Calonius, "Smart Moves by Quality Champs," *Fortune* (December 1991), 24–28.

[4] B. B. Flynn, "Managing for Quality in the U.S. and in Japan," *Interfaces,* 22, No. 5 (1992), 69–80.

[5] Reprinted with permission of the American Production and Inventory Control Society, Inc., *APICS Dictionary,* 7th edition, 1992.

1. *Consistency* How consistent (nondeviant) is the performance of a manufactured product each time it is used? The more invariable the product's performance, the greater the perceived quality. Consistency in manufacturing is usually centered on the physical product's successfully functioning.
2. *Usability* How well can the product be used by the consumer? The easier the product is to use, the greater the perceived quality. For example, microcomputer systems that are more "user friendly" are often considered to be of higher quality than less-friendly computer systems.
3. *Grade* How is the product classified for value to the consumer? For example, meat, poultry, and other food products are graded to reflect their judged quality. The higher the grade, the higher the customer's expectation of the value of the product; the lower the grade, the lower the judged value of quality.

The definition of quality in service operations is more difficult to define because of the intangible and varied output of service systems. One researcher views the definition of service quality in terms of how much the customer values three product attributes, including (1) physical facilities, processes, and procedures; (2) people's behavior and conviviality; and (3) professional judgment.[6]

1. *Physical facilities, processes, and procedures* Value is associated with factors such as location, layout, size, decor, facility reliability, process reliability, procedure reliability, process flexibility, timeliness, speed, range of services offered, and communication of information, processes, and procedures in producing the service product.
2. *People's behavior and conviviality* Value can result from the warmth, friendliness, tact, attitude, dress, neatness, politeness, attentiveness, problem solving, complaint handling, and speed and timeliness of personnel in producing the service product.
3. *Professional judgment* Value is associated with the diagnosis, advice, guidance, honesty, confidentiality, flexibility, knowledge, and skill of the personnel in producing the service product.

It is obviously difficult to define quality in a general way, yet everyone who has had some experience as a customer knows when they have received a quality service product.

In the first half of the twentieth century, operations managers would ensure product quality by employing staff personnel called **quality control (QC)** inspectors. QC inspectors tended to be organizationally positioned as staff specialists solely under the manufacturing manager in a plant operation as presented in Figure 12-1(a). As a result, the QC inspector rarely shared product quality information with anyone but the manufacturing manager. QC inspectors used statistical techniques to establish quality standards, educate managers, and monitor ongoing quality performance in work-in-process (WIP). By using statistical sampling methods called **acceptance sampling,** QC

---

[6] J. H. Farmer, "A Conceptual Model of Service Quality," *International Journal of Operations and Production Management,* 8, No. 6 (1988), 19–29.

FIGURE 12-1 ORGANIZATIONAL POSITIONING OF QUALITY CONTROL PERSONNEL

(A) ORGANIZATIONAL CHART OF QC PERSONNEL PRIOR TO 1950

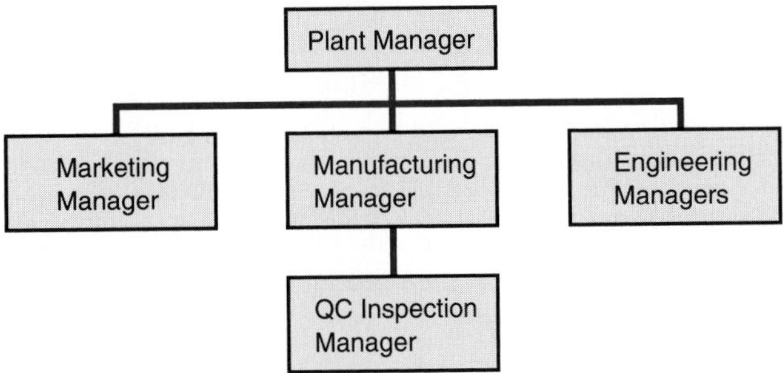

(B) ORGANIZATIONAL CHART OF QC PERSONNEL AFTER 1950

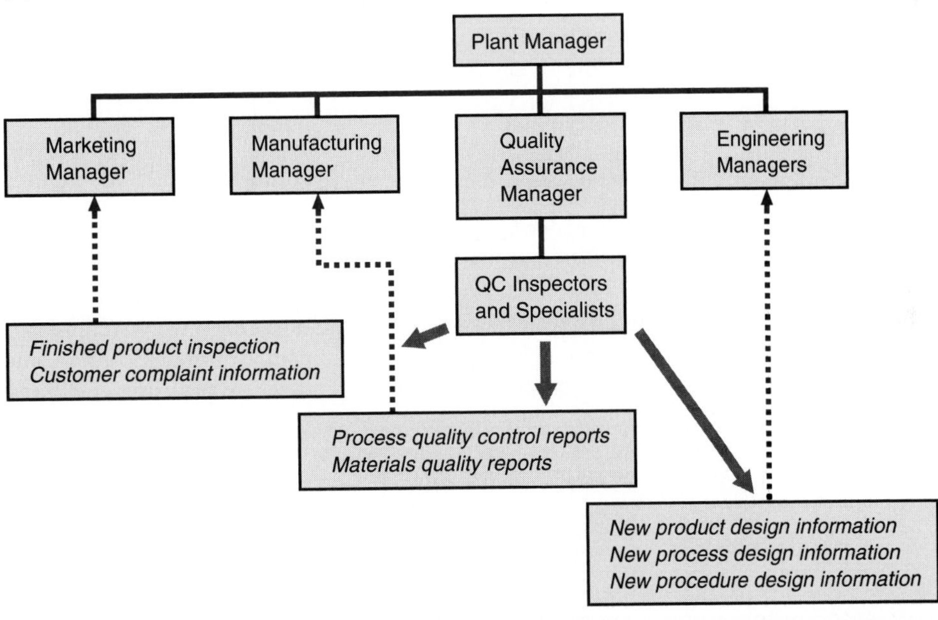

inspectors were able to randomly screen a portion of incoming and outgoing products and predict quality on the items not actually inspected. (Though less popular today, we present some acceptance sampling methods in Supplement 12-1). Monitoring and controlling WIP was performed using statistical quality control (SQC) charts in what is called process control. (We discuss process control methods later in this chapter.) These SQC charts were used to establish static quality standards that workers could achieve and maintain.

In the second half of the twentieth century, manufacturing managers still use QC inspectors, but primarily for educating workers as well as managers. As presented in Figure 12-1(b), QC inspectors tend now to be at manager-level positions within the organization and share QC information with a variety of other functional areas directly. Acceptance sampling has been chiefly replaced by 100 percent inspection, as advocated in the Japanese principles of total quality control (TQC; we discuss the TQC principles later in this chapter.) Process control methods of SQC charting are still being used, but today they are used primarily by workers and managers. The charts are now used as dynamic aids to motivate workers to achieve ever higher levels of quality rather than to maintain a static standard.

In addition to these changes in QC methods, the role of QC has broadened to include more than just ensuring the quality of the finished product. Today, QC includes every aspect of production from procurement through customer use. This broader role for QC now includes

1. Ensuring that materials, work force, equipment, processes, and procedures are secured or performed according to desired quality goals
2. Ensuring that products will permit an adequate product life span at the least cost to the producer and consumer
3. Ensuring that customers have adequate service support for a product's installation and use
4. Ensuring corrective action if warranted by market feedback

A new term now defines the broader QC management activities—**quality assurance (QA).** QA is used in this chapter to describe all quality management programs including total quality management (TQM; discussed in Chapter 2) and total quality control (TQC; discussed later in this chapter).

The purpose of this chapter is to describe how organizations perform quality assurance. In the process we will examine several currently used QA principles, methods, and technologies.

• • •

WHY QUALITY ASSURANCE IS NECESSARY

In the late 1950s, "Made in Japan" was a commonly used expression in the United States to refer to poorly made but cheap products. In the 1990s, "Made in Japan" is globally recognized as meaning fine quality in automobiles, cameras, microprocessors, and nearly all other products. Television commercials in Japan now use "Made in the U.S.A." as a slogan to describe poorly made products.

Why and how did the decline in U.S. product quality and significant improvement in product quality in Japan happen? The answer is simple: U.S. manufacturers did not make product quality a long-range strategic objective, and the Japanese did. It is important to note that the Japanese are just as interested in making a profit as U.S. firms. The Japanese, though, plan to maximize profits in the long run while most U.S. firms seek short-term profits. The long-term Japanese strategy is based on the productivity cycle discussed in Chapter 1. As we can see in Figure 12-2, improving product quality will increase a company's sales and market share, which in turn will permit the company to increase its investment in improving product quality. The cycle, if allowed to repeat, will continue until either the company controls the product's market, its product quality is perfect, or both. This makes a QA program a long-term strategic objective.

Once an organization has a large share of the market owing to the productivity cycle, profits are more easily taken without risk because there are fewer competitors. In many U.S. firms, employee reward systems are structured around short-term profit maximization. Once profits are generated, many U.S. organizations drain profits away from the system to reward the stockholders or employees rather than reinvest them to improve the quality and help the cycling strategy to continue. To remain competitive, operations management must continue to improve product quality through a QA program.

The strategic importance of quality has not gone unnoticed by national governments. For more than two decades in Japan, the annual **Deming Prize** (named after U.S. quality control expert W. Edwards Deming) has been given to manufacturing companies that have demonstrated product quality excellence. Interestingly, it was a service utility company (Florida Power & Light) that in 1989 became the first U.S. company to win the Deming Prize. In 1988, the U.S. government started its own award program for quality achievement. The **Malcolm Baldrige National Quality Award** (named after former Secretary of Commerce Malcolm Baldrige) is given annually for excellence in product quality achievement. As we discussed in Chapter 2, the winner of the Baldrige award is required as a part of acceptance to provide quality education and training to all interested parties, including competitors. In this way, the award is a proactive effort to enhance quality rather than just a postactive salute.

Improvements in quality not only help generate profits by increasing sales; improvements in quality also help decrease costs and therefore increase profits. Some of the costs of running a business that are directly related to product quality are as follows:

1. *Rework* The cost of correcting defective products to meet specifications.
2. *Scrap* The net cost of labor, materials, and overhead for defective products that cannot be reworked.
3. *Retest* The cost of reinspecting and retesting products that have undergone rework.
4. *Failure assessment time* The cost of determining the causes of product failures.
5. *Downtime* The cost of idle facilities that result from poor-quality work that must be corrected by facility alteration.
6. *Yield losses* The cost of the process that lowers total product yields. For example, a machine that overfills cans of food will lower the system's total yield of canned food.

FIGURE 12-2 THE PRODUCTIVITY CYCLE

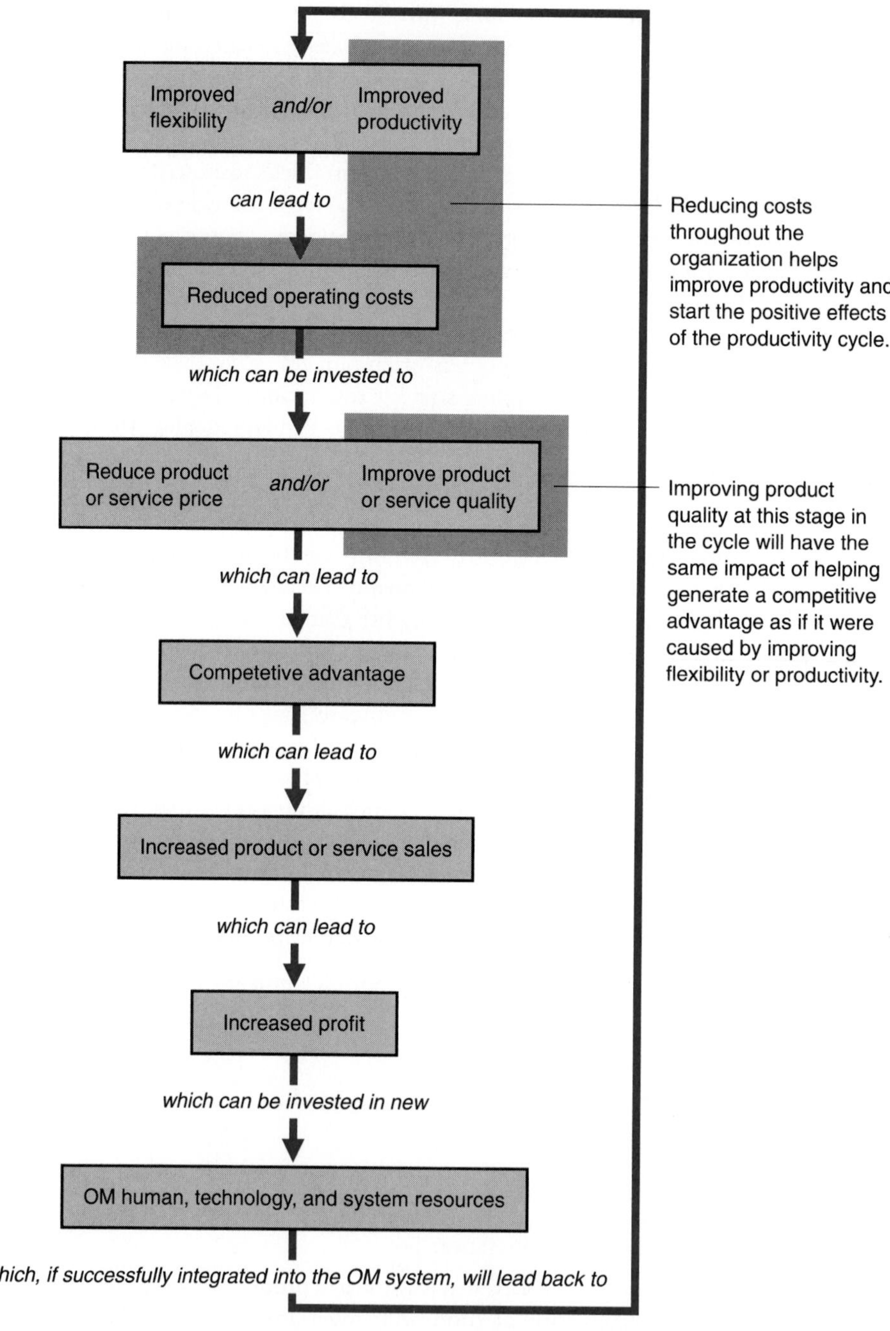

7. *Downgrading* The difference between a product's regular price and its quality discounted price. If a product's quality is lowered (such as for irregular clothes), the market will expect to pay a lower price for the product.
8. *Warranty expenses* All costs to the manufacturer that are required to service product warranties.
9. *Liability expenses* All expenses incurred as a result of product liability litigation.
10. *Returned goods* All costs for processing (such as receipt and handling) goods returned because of poor quality.

The adage of savings-investment-productivity is true when applied to the productivity cycle. Reductions in costs lead directly to competitive advantages in product pricing. QA projects that reduce costs, such as projects aimed at reducing setup times, scrap, or rework, are a necessary part of implementing a QA program. QA project objectives (that is, tactical objectives) that help management identify and implement cost savings efforts in medium-range planning horizons are a tactical means of achieving the strategic benefits of the productivity cycle. This makes a QA program a tactical means of ensuring productivity cycling and makes QA a necessary operations management activity.

To compete in the global markets of the 1990s, business organizations may have to meet some international standards of quality assurance. The **International Organization for Standardization (ISO)** is a world-wide national standards agency represented by ninety-one countries. In 1987, it published a series of global quality system standards meant to govern how businesses provide quality products and services to all their customers.[7] These standards are designed to provide businesses with a systematic approach to quality assurance. The **ISO 9000** is actually a registered certification process by which a company is certified as a deliverer of quality products. ISO 9000 certification has become so important because the European Community (EC) has adopted the certification as a part of its EC trade laws governing specific imports. ISO 9000–certified importers therefore have a competitive advantage over other importer or EC companies that do not have the certification. To become certified, a U.S. company has to bring its operation, including its suppliers, into compliance with ISO 9000 guidelines and undertake the certification process. Much like a college or school of business educational program being accredited for teaching a certain body of knowledge, the ISO 9000 certification must be overseen by accredited registrars in the United States. The United States is represented in the international ISO organization by the **American National Standards Institute (ANSI),** and its Registrar Accreditation Board (RAB) is an affiliate of the American Society for Quality Control (ASQC). (We discuss the ISO 9000 certification requirements, as they relate to implementing a quality assurance program, in the Quality Management Methods section of this chapter.)

---

[7] *ISO: 9000* (Boston: Allyn & Bacon, 1993); M. Ramsay, "ISO: The Myths and Misconceptions," *APICS—The Performance Advantage,* 2, No. 6 (1992), 55–57; and A. H. Greene, "ISO 9000: Globalizing Quality Standards," *Production and Inventory Management,* 11, No. 9 (1991), 12–15.

TOTAL QUALITY CONTROL (TQC), TOTAL QUALITY MANAGEMENT (TQM), AND QUALITY ASSURANCE (QA)

In the 1960s, a buzzword that originated from U.S. National Aeronautics and Space Administration (NASA) engineering was *zero-defects.* **Zero-defects (ZD)** referred to the desire of NASA engineers to eliminate all defects from the space equipment systems that they were developing and manufacturing. In other words, their intent was to have perfect or defect-free quality in their space systems. Unfortunately, the manufacture of space systems or any product involves more than just perfect engineering; it involves perfect performance from everyone who contributes to its production. Perfect quality involves a total commitment from everyone in an organization, from the janitor to the president of the organization.

In Japan, many organizations have adopted a total commitment to perfect quality. This Japanese quality commitment has been referred to as **total quality control (TQC).**[8] Ironically, the basic elements of TQC were introduced in Japan by U.S. quality experts such as W. Edwards Deming and J. Juran. The Japanese in the 1970s actually operationalized the ZD concept, and many Japanese organizations have achieved near perfect quality. The Japanese businesses that adopted this TQC approach did so by placing a higher strategic value on process, procedure, and product quality than on profit margin. This is not an easy step for U.S. organizations that traditionally choose short-term profit maximization as their primary strategic objective. It is, however, a necessary one if U.S. organizations hope to compete with Japanese and other foreign manufacturers who are generating superior quality products.[9]

Since about 1985, total quality management (TQM) has become another quality management movement in the United States. TQM, which is based on the principles of TQC, has been implemented in many premier U.S. organizations such as IBM, Xerox, and Motorola. Subsequently, many service and nonprofit organizations, such as universities and government agencies, have also implemented TQM. Thus, TQM has become a strategic management approach rather than a simple quality improvement program. TQC is the foundation on which TQM has built its philosophical base. To understand and implement TQM, a TQC program must be in place. Both TQM and TQC are important parts of a modern quality assurance program.

Continually seeking to improve quality, Japan is embarking on what is referred to as **zero-defects management (ZDM).**[10] ZDM is more than a zero-defects quality control system. It is a strategic management approach for the entire organization that is

---

[8] R. J. Schonberger, *Japanese Manufacturing Techniques: Nine Hidden Lessons in Simplicity* (New York: The Free Press, 1982), Chapter 3; R. J. Schonberger, *World Class Manufacturing* (New York: The Free Press, 1986), Chapter 7; M. J. Schniederjans, *Topics in Just-in-Time Management* (Boston: Allyn & Bacon, 1992), Chapter 4; and K. Ishikawa, *What Is Total Quality Control: The Japanese Way* (Englewood Cliffs, N.J.: Prentice-Hall, 1985).

[9] See R. J. Groocock, *The Chain of Quality* (New York: John Wiley & Sons, 1986).

[10] Peter F. Drucker, "Japan: New Strategies for a New Reality," *Wall Street Journal,* October 2, 1991, p. A12.

geared to improving everything continuously toward 100 percent performance. Toyota, for example, estimates that TQM can cut defects by 10 percent. Toyota believes that ZDM is now possible and not very difficult to implement. Ironically, interest in ZDM in Japan was triggered by the hugely successful Disneyland in Japan. When it opened, Disneyland ran perfectly without defects.

What some Japanese corporations are counting on is that zero-defects management will once again propel them far ahead of their overseas competitors. TQM typically requires about ten years to completely implement. By 1995, TQM will work well in U.S. organizations. By then, however, Japanese firms will have ZDM fully installed and they think they will be fifteen years ahead of their competitors. To move toward ZDM (or TQM or QA), we must understand the basics of the TQC system.

The TQC System

A TQC system has two goals: (1) to produce perfect products (zero-defect products) and (2) to make every employee quality conscious so that quality control efforts become a habit rather than a dictate of management. To accomplish these goals, several basic principles are used as guides for general operating strategy.[11] Not all of these principles are used by all organizations. They represent a set of principles that have been selectively used by many organizations, including service organizations.[12] Because these principles are usually part of a just-in-time (JIT) operation, we will present them as a combined TQC and JIT approach to quality control. The TQC principles include the following:

1. *QC is everyone's responsibility.* Each person in the organization is expected to perform quality control functions. For workers in a repetitive operation this might mean that the first workstation checks the vendor's quality and the receiving department's service, the second workstation checks the first workstation's work, the third workstation checks the second workstation's work, and so on down the work stream. This approach of one employee inspecting another's work places greater job responsibility on workers and acts to broaden the role of the worker's job. This process is commonly called **job enlargement** and is known to increase productivity and improve employees' morale. Also, genuine suggestion systems can motivate workers to offer helpful process, procedure, and product ideas on quality improvement. All employees, from the top of the organization to the bottom, must be held responsible for their operation's product quality.
2. *Ensure that everyone sees QC measures and statistics.* In the past, management would keep QC measures such as SQC charts to themselves. Yet everybody in the plant that generates a product is responsible for the product's quality.

---

[11] R. J. Schonberger, *Japanese Management Techniques: Nine Hidden Lessons in Simplicity* (New York: The Free Press, 1982), Chapter 2.

[12] See M. J. Schniederjans, *Topics in Just-in-Time Management* (Boston: Allyn & Bacon, 1992), Chapter 7.

Everyone should be made to know how good or bad the organization's product quality really is. The SQC charts are excellent graphic visual aids that once prepared can be understood with little training. The use of QC measures can, for some firms, quickly reinforce quality assurance efforts. If samples are taken and concurrently displayed, workers can see the immediate effect of increased or decreased effort to change the product's quality. Indeed, every behavioral scientists knows that the quicker the reinforcement, the more likely the desired behavior will be repeated.

3. *Ensure quality compliance.* This might entail establishing reward systems (such as bonuses or pay increases) based on product quality improvements and reprimands for poor quality performance. QC inspectors (who are traditionally staff members) are sometimes pressured by manufacturing managers (who are line members with firing and hiring authority over the QC inspector) to let rush orders pass through the organization without the necessary QC inspections. All operations managers must be motivated to think quality first and production second. Some researchers, such as R. J. Schonberger, suggest that "quality audits" be conducted by managers to ensure quality compliance in TQC programs.[13]
4. *Give greater authority for QC to employees.* In some JIT systems, workers and automated monitoring systems are actually given the authority to bring a production department or an entire plant to a halt. Other plants have lighting systems that use two lights for QC: one light signals that a minor problem has been discovered that could later cause a serious problem, and a second light signals that the line should be stopped because a serious product quality problem has been detected. The amount of QC authority that workers should be given must be dictated by the amount of QC responsibility that they are assigned by management. The basic TQC philosophy is that doing the job right the first time is not only the best way to ensure product quality but also the most economical way to meet customer demand.
5. *Poor quality should be improved by those who generate it.* The worker who creates a defect in a product or the engineer who incorrectly designs a component part should be the one to improve it. In this way, the worker will learn to do it right. Other workers will also be motivated not to make mistakes because of the embarrassing consequences of correcting their own errors.
6. *Conduct 100 percent elemental inspections.* Major appliances and automobiles are made of thousands of components (which are themselves made of different materials) that are eventually assembled into finished products. We will call these materials and components **product elements.** In automated and human inspection systems, each element is inspected before it is used in the assembly process. The prior assembly of one element is inspected before the next is incorporated into the product. Indeed, if one component is irregular, it might

[13] R. J. Schonberger, *World Class Manufacturing* (New York: The Free Press, 1986), 134–135.

keep the next component from being properly incorporated into the product. The process of inspecting the prior step in the transformation process continues until a finished product is generated. Because every product element is inspected during the inspection process, the finished product is generally defect-free and a final inspection is often not even necessary. This critical principle has led Japanese manufacturers to have some of the highest product quality ratings in the world. Elemental inspections actually build quality into the product during the transformation process.

Note the similarity of these TQC principles to Deming's "Fourteen Obligations of Top Management," shown in Table 12-1. These quality principles, like others based on Japanese management experience, are changing the way quality assurance is conducted throughout the world.

TQC Implementation Tactics

It can be difficult to tactically implement any type of new principles. Implementation begins with a training and education program to explain the value of the principles and how they can be used day-to-day. Once the basic principles are in place, management must adopt tactics that will ensure that the principles will continue to be successfully implemented. A successful TQC implementation can be drafted using one or more of the following tactics:

1. *Cut lot-sizes.* Just as when implementing a JIT inventory system, lot-sizes can be cut to identify problems quickly. In implementing TQC, we want product quality problems in lot-related production processes or products in a lot to be revealed quickly to save reworking. Quality problems in larger lots, on the other hand, will not be as quickly noticed because their size gives them a place to hide.
2. *Cut safety and buffer stock quantities.* Without the extra buffer and safety stock, product quality problems will more easily surface because they have no place to hide. The sources of nonconformity that can be identified include both vendors and the organization's own employees (who make process manufacturing errors). By identifying the problems that lead to poor product quality, the firm can improve future product quality and save considerable rework costs.
3. *Permit a production rate at less-than-full capacity.* In the beginning, we want to identify and solve product quality processing problems. To do this will take some time away from productive capacity. By scheduling production at a less-than-full capacity rate, we allow time for anticipated quality control problems to be identified and solved. The extra capacity allows the production line to be shut down, avoids overtaxing equipment (which can cause poor-quality products), and may keep management from pressuring individuals to not perform their QC functions.

TABLE 12-1 DEMING'S "FOURTEEN OBLIGATIONS OF TOP MANAGEMENT" TO QUALITY

1. Create constancy of purpose toward improvement of product and service, with the aim to stay in business and to provide jobs.
2. Adopt the new philosophy. We are in a new economic age, created by Japan. Transformation of Western-style management is necessary to halt the continued decline of industry.
3. Cease dependence on inspection to achieve quality. Eliminate the need for inspection on a mass basis by building quality into the product in the first place.
4. End the practice of awarding business on the basis of price tag. Purchasing must be combined with design of product, manufacturing, and sales to work with the chosen supplier, with the aim to minimize total cost, not merely initial cost.
5. Improve constantly and forever every activity in the company to improve quality and productivity, and thus constantly decrease costs.
6. Institute training and education on the job, including management.
7. Institute supervision. The aim of supervision should be to help people and machines and gadgets to do a better job.
8. Drive out fear, so that everyone may work effectively for the company.
9. Break down barriers between departments. People in research, design, sales, and production must work as a team to foresee problems of production and in use that may be encountered with the product or service.
10. Eliminate slogans, exhortations, and targets for the work force asking for zero defects and new levels of productivity. Such exhortations only create adversarial relationships, as the bulk of the causes of low quality and low productivity belong to the system and thus lie beyond the power of the work force.
11. Eliminate work standards that prescribe numerical quotas for the day. Substitute aids and helpful supervision.

12a. Remove the barriers that rob the hourly worker of his right to pride of workmanship. The responsibility of supervisors must be changed from sheer numbers to quality.

12b. Remove the barriers that rob people in management and in engineering of their right to pride of workmanship. This means, *inter alia,* abolishment of the annual or merit rating of management by objective, and management by the numbers.

13. Institute a vigorous program of education and retraining. New skills are required for changes in techniques, materials, and service.
14. Put everybody in the company to work in teams to accomplish the transformation.

Source: Reprinted by permission of W. Edwards Deming, "Transformation of Western Style of Management," *Interfaces,* Vol. 15, No. 3, May–June 1985. Copyright 1985 the Operations Research Society of America and the Institute of Management Sciences, 290 Westminster Street, Providence, Rhode Island 02903 USA.

4. *Revise the QC department's role from inspector to educator.* Because workers in the production system do much of the production inspection, the inspection personnel who make up QC departments have more time to spend on other TQC functions. Many can be used to educate and keep employees informed of the new approaches to quality management and to keep the organization moving

toward the QC goal of zero defects. QC personnel can also be used to help employees understand how quality is monitored and how to interpret SQC charts.

5. *Establish a daily maintenance plan for each employee.* Machine maintenance (oiling, tightening, and so on), inspecting tools (shaping and having them replaced if need be), and keeping the workstation clean should be a daily habit for each employee. This work can usually be performed during downtimes when quality problems are being corrected so the organization does not lose production time. The role of maintenance in TQC programs has become very important in automated operations management environments. Supplement 12-2 is devoted to describing the extension of TQC in maintenance (quality maintenance management or QMM).
6. *Use automated equipment where feasible.* Automated equipment for inspection is almost foolproof and can greatly improve quality. Where automation can be employed, it should be. This type of equipment, though, is expensive and is not always as cost-effective as human efforts. When human beings perform inspections, multiple human inspector teams can greatly improve quality. A two- or even three-person inspection team, each checking the same product quality characteristics, can generate almost as accurate a result as a machine.

These tactics are useful in establishing TQC systems. But it is the people in the organization that make a quality product, not the system that they operate under.[14]

QUALITY MANAGEMENT METHODS

Regardless of whether the organization implements a TQC program, TQM program, or QA program, it still involves the management of quality. In this section, we will examine a number of quality management methods used in TQC, TQM, and QA programs including ISO 9000 quality standards, quality circles, Taguchi statistical methods, cause and effective diagrams, and the Pareto method.

ISO 9000 Quality Standards

The United States and Japan are not the only countries interested in TQC. The European ISO 9000 certification program is one way that all organizations can be guided into internationally accepted standards of total quality control (as well as quality

[14] W. W. Hinze, "Quality: It's People, People, People," *Production and Inventory Management Review,* 6, No. 8 (August 1986), 24; and R. E. Stein, "Beyond Statistical Process Control," *Production and Inventory Management Journal,* 32, No. 1 (1991), 7–10.

QUESTION: Does a U.S. organization absolutely have to have ANSI/ASQC Q90 (the U.S. equivalent of ISO 9000) certification to do business in Europe or with other European Community (EC) members?

ANSWER: No. It will be increasingly difficult to do business in EC countries without it, however. For example, the ISO 9000 standards permit organizations to do business with noncertified suppliers on the condition that the noncertified supplier will become certified for future business. Even more pressure to become certified is exerted by the fact that supplier certification is a part of the buying manufacturer's certification requirements. If a certified manufacturer does too much business with noncertified suppliers, the manufacturer can lose its ISO 9000 certification. This makes quality assurance a necessary requirement for ISO certification, which in turn is an increasingly necessary requirement to do business with EC members. With other major U.S. organizations such as DuPont and the U.S. Department of Defense adopting ISO 9000 guidelines, considerable pressure for adoption by all U.S. organizations is gaining momentum.

assurance and total quality management programs).[15] As previously stated, the ISO 9000 is a series of published quality standards and terminology. In Europe, the series of standards are known as *EN 29000* and in the United States *ANSI/ASQC Q90.* The series is five sets of standards (9000, 9001, 9002, 9003, and 9004) developed for documenting quality systems and practices. The 9000 set of standards provides a roadmap that describes how an organization can achieve TQC and even provides a series of quality standard specifications as goals for a TQC program. The 9001 set of standards focuses specifically on product design and development, installation of TQC methods, and service quality standards. The 9002 set focuses on actual production processes and how quality can be documented for ISO certification. The 9003 set of standards focuses on final product inspection and testing. Finally, the 9004 set suggests what should be done within the operations management system to develop and manage quality. The 9000 and 9004 sets are general guides for setting up a quality program, and the 9001, 9002, and 9003 sets are more comprehensive in defining quality standards. These three sets of quality standards define what is to be required between buyers and sellers for purposes of quality assurance. An ISO-certified manufacturing or service company is also expected to have ISO-certified suppliers to ensure quality throughout the chain of production from supplier to customer. These five sets of quality standards are an ideal approach for any organization to implement quality control programs. It should be

[15] M. Ramsay, "ISO: The Myths and Misconceptions," *APICS—The Performance Advantage,* 2, No. 6 (1992), 55–57; and A. H. Greene, "ISO 9000: Globalizing Quality Standards," *Production and Inventory Management,* 11, No. 9 (1991), 12–15.

mentioned that although ISO 9000 certification can offer its holder a valuable competitive advantage, it is something that must be earned every day. ISO 9000 requires constantly auditing the ISO-certified company's quality control procedures and processes to ensure that the company complies with current ISO guidelines. Audits are performed by U.S. Registrar Accreditation Board (RAB) certifiers to ensure that ISO 9000 quality standards are being maintained. Companies failing to meet the ISO standards can have their certification suspended.

Quality Circles

Another method that is based entirely on people who operate the operations management system involves the use of quality circles. A **quality circle** is a small group of workers who are assembled to study ways to solve problems or help plan new production activities. A quality circle is used to solve all types of production problems, not just those concerned with product quality. The idea of a quality circle is to bring a small and interested team of employees together to study production problems. The basic idea for quality circles came from small informal groups of workers meeting to discuss mutual problems during coffee breaks and after working hours.

The formal concept of quality circles originated in Japan in the early 1960s when small groups of workers were assembled to help train other workers in QC procedures and to deal with small-scale QC problems. Toyota of Japan refers to quality circles as *small group improvement activities* (SGIAs). Not surprisingly, morale of group members is greatly improved because they participate in the group decision-making process. These company-authorized teams are given a formal agenda suggesting problem-solving tasks. Today, quality circles, sometimes called *quality teams* or *quality task forces,* are used to solve many types of problems. Their objectives include more than just improving product quality; they also improve work methods, worker morale, and motivation.

Quality circles differ from organization to organization. Generally, though, they comprise employees who actually perform the manufacturing tasks that are to be studied. The quality circles also include shop floor–level management personnel (such as supervisors) and technical specialists (such as engineers and QC inspectors). The technical specialists can include industrial engineers whose job is to improve work methods (that is, by redesigning tools or new work layouts) and conduct work studies. Quality circles are not usually given the authority to implement their problem solutions. They usually just develop a set of recommendations for management to choose from in solving a production problem.

Quality circle programs usually consist of the following steps:

1. The organization identifies production or other problems that could be solved by a quality circle.
2. The quality circle is assembled from several types of organization employees:
   a. A few workers from the problem area.
   b. One or two shop floor level supervisors from the problem area.

c. One or more technical specialists, based on their perceived background and how they can be used to solve the problem under study. For example, if we are studying a worker motivation problem, we might want to have a personnel specialist as a team member. The technical specialists can come from any engineering or technical function in the entire organization. Examples are product design engineers (specialists in material and product tolerances and specifications), process engineers (specialists in transformation processes), and methods engineers (specialists in facility layout and production procedures).

3. The quality circle is assigned a formal agenda, usually a team leader, and meeting dates, which could be daily, weekly, or monthly.
4. At each meeting, members of the group are free to comment and offer ideas on identifying problems and formulating solutions. The workers and supervisors are equal members in the group, and all are free to offer any relevant suggestion that might help deal with the problem under study. That is, the supervisor-worker relationship is temporarily suspended to permit a freer environment to offer solution suggestions. Eventually, the problem is identified and a series of possible solutions is developed. In some groups, a consensus is used to determine the most recommendable problem-solving alternative.
5. Once problem alternatives are developed, they are usually offered to management for solution choice and approval. Once the solution choice is approved, the same quality circle that came up with the solution is often asked to develop an implementation strategy.
6. Once the specific problem is dealt with, the quality circle can be disbanded until another similar problem requires its reformation.

The organization as well as the individuals that make up the quality circles benefit from this group problem-solving approach. The workers have a chance to air problems to management and technical specialists whose job it is in the group to listen. The meetings also provide a break in job routine for the workers, and in some organizations the workers are given rewards (vacations, bonuses, letters of commendation) for solving important production problems. The engineering and technical specialists benefit by obtaining information on product quality first-hand from workers who must implement their engineering ideas. The information the specialists obtain can aid them in performing their own jobs.

Management benefits in many ways from quality circles. They will generally have a more highly motivated work force because of the workers' greater job participation (that is, the added quality circle activity is a job-enlargement process). Workers accept change in work methods and physical plant layout more easily because of their participation in planning it. The ideas that are generated from the quality circles help improve product quality, which in turn reduces scrap and costs. Finally, management can use the quality circles as auxiliary problem-solving units when they do not have the time to deal with a problem.

The success of quality circles as a tactic for TQC has had mixed reviews both in the United States and in Japan.[16] Some researchers believe that quality circles have made and will continue to make notable contributions toward solving small-scale quality problems at the shop floor level and in improving worker motivation.[17]

Taguchi Statistical Methods

Focusing on eliminating all sources of production variation in the transformation process, the **Taguchi statistical methods** (named after the Japanese quality control expert Genichi Taguchi) are an ideal TQC method.[18] Taguchi's statistical approach to quality control is based on three concepts: quality robustness, quality loss function, and target specifications.

1. *Quality robustness* All processes, procedures, and products should be designed to be quality robust. Processes and procedures that are quality robust will deliver a uniform and consistent output, regardless of the type of product or variety of adverse conditions that exist in the production environment. A product is quality robust if it performs uniformly and consistently in use.
2. *Quality loss function* A quality loss function illustrates the relationships of production effort and quality. In Figure 12-3(a) a quality loss function is presented. This function is a simple quadratic formula:

   $$L = D^2 C$$

   where

   L = loss in dollars (or any measurable value)
   D = deviation from the target quality standard value
   C = the cost of deviation

   The graph in Figure 12-3(a) clearly shows that as production efforts cause deviation from a customer's quality standard, the costs to both the producer

[16] See C. S. Gray, "Total Quality Control in Japan—Less Inspection, Lower Cost," *Business Week,* July 16, 1981, pp. 23–44; J. M. Juran, "Product Quality—A Prescription for the West," *Management Review,* 70, No. 7 (July 1981), 57–61; and M. K. Hart, "Quality Control Training for Manufacturing," *Production and Inventory Management Journal,* 32, No. 3 (1991), 35–40.

[17] R. J. Schonberger, *Japanese Management Techniques: Nine Hidden Lessons in Simplicity* (New York: The Free Press, 1982), Chapter 3; and K. A. Wantuck, *Just-In-Time for America* (Milwaukee, Wis.: The Forum, Ltd., 1989), Chapter 5.

[18] R. N. Kackar, "Taguchi's Quality Philosophy: Analysis and Commentary," *Quality Progress* (December 1986), 21–29. Also see "Taguchi Methods: Special Information Package," a special publication available from the Center for Taguchi Methods in the United States, American Supplier Institute, Inc., 6 Parklane Boulevard, Suite 411, Dearborn, MI 48126.

FIGURE 12-3 TAGUCHI LOSS FUNCTION AND RELATION TO VARIATION IN DISTRIBUTION OF PRODUCTS PRODUCED

(A) QUALITY LOSS FUNCTION

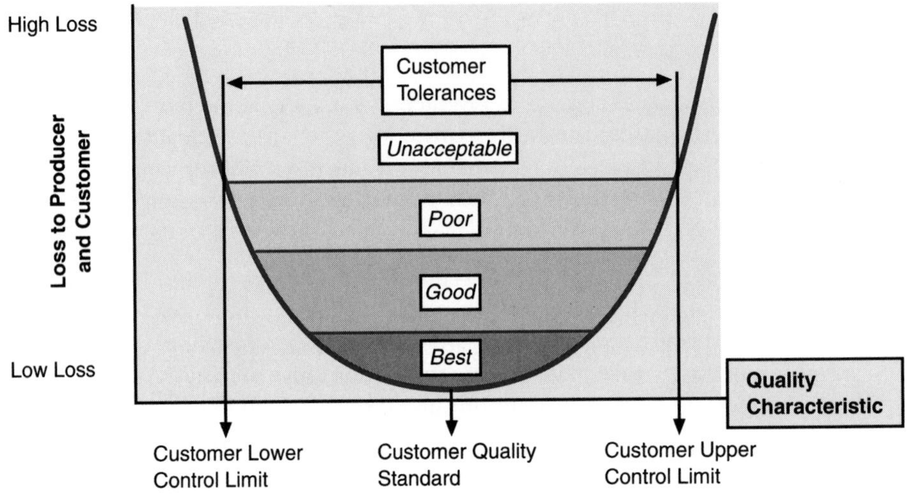

(B) DISTRIBUTION OF PRODUCTS PRODUCED

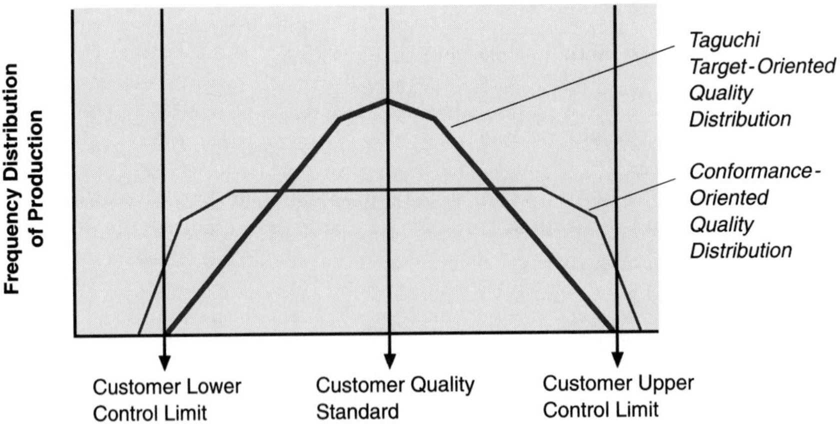

and customer increase. For example, a warranty for a piece of equipment used by a customer is more likely to be exercised if the quality of the piece is low (that is, if it deviates from the quality standard or what Taguchi calls the *production target*). The more the product deviates from the quality standard, the more likely it will break down and cost the user-customer (downtime, and so on) and the producer (warranty and guarantee costs). Equipment that most closely meets the quality standard is least costly.

3. *Target specifications* The "target of production" should always be the quality standard, not some upper and lower level of allowable variation. As we can see in Figure 12-3(b), the distribution of products produced under the traditional upper and lower quality boundary levels (characteristic of the pre-1950s use of SQC charting methods) tends to flatten out and spread evenly between the upper and lower boundary levels. This flattened distribution is usually caused by accepting products that fall into the interval of variation, rather than seeking the ideal quality standard with no variation that usually falls in the middle of the interval defined by the upper and lower boundaries. Taguchi claims that by focusing on a specific and robust target, the resulting target-oriented quality distribution of production will take on more of the bell shape portions in Figure 12-3(b). The target-oriented quality distribution is a superior quality distribution in that more of production falls closer to the desired customer quality standard.

The implementation of Taguchi methods consists of three phases: system design, parameter design, and tolerance design.

1. *System design* This phase involves investigating process, procedure, and product factors that may cause variation in the final product. These factors might include tensile strength of materials (product factor) and heating processes (process factor). These system variables that contribute variation are viewed in the Taguchi analysis as parameters that define a product's quality.
2. *Parameter design* This phase involves experimental research on the parameters that were determined in phase 1 to define a product's quality. The purpose of the research is to determine how important each parameter is in determining product quality. Considerable statistical experimental design and analysis are conducted in this phase. Also, cost information is brought into the analysis for consideration in recommending where cost-justified changes in the production process are permissible.
3. *Tolerance design* This phase involves determining product tolerances for each parameter that was found in phase 2 to be a substantial factor in generating production variation. This phase is also marked by a continual and dynamic tightening of tolerances as product variation improvements are suggested and implemented to improve quality over an extended period of time.

Cause and Effect Diagrams

A **cause and effect diagram** is a graphic aid that can be used to help managers and workers efficiently identify the causes of quality control problems. The idea of the cause and effect diagram is to allow personnel to be able to trace known symptoms or effects back to known causes. A basic cause and effect diagram (also called a "herringbone" or "fishbone" diagram) is presented in Figure 12-4. Users start by listing the problem symptoms or effects that best describe the problem they are experiencing. They then follow the arrows in the diagram back to each of the process, procedure, or product causes that are related to the symptoms. The diagram acts like a pictorial expert system to help locate the sources of problems by the observed effects.

Obviously, the list of problems has to be narrowly focused so it doesn't inundate users. These diagrams are best used in dealing with the more frequently recurring problems that personnel face every day. The diagrams can be strategically placed in locations where problems frequently are encountered.

Pareto Method

A method that helps management prioritize QC problem-solving effort is based on the Pareto principle. The **Pareto principle** suggests that management should allocate "most" of the resources to solving the "most" serious QC problems. This principle seeks to focus QC problem-solving resources on the "vital few" QC problems that occur most frequently, while leaving the "trivial many" QC problems that occur very infrequently to be dealt with later, after the more serious problems have been resolved. A simple tally of the number of times a problem is reported by workers or customers can be used to establish the priorities. Those problems receiving a greater number of tallies should be given a high priority. Their frequent recurrence reflects the potential for incurring costs to an organization, and by establishing a high priority for these

FIGURE 12-4 CAUSE AND EFFECT DIAGRAM

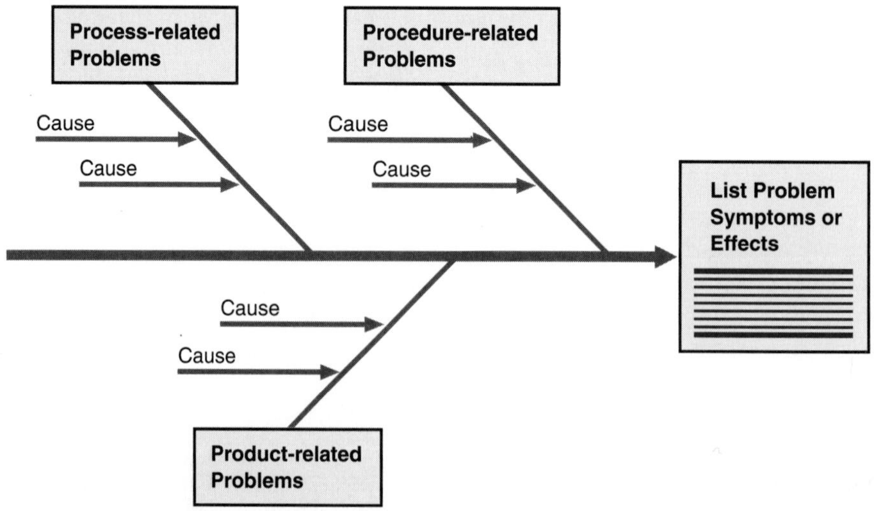

problems, available resources will be correctly channeled to aid in their resolution. Unfortunately, cost considerations are not reflected in a simple tally.

The Pareto ranking can be modified to consider the weighted cost of QC problems. For example, suppose that the daily frequency of occurrence of three QC problems (problems A, B, and C) is 5, 3, and 1, respectively. Based solely on the Pareto principle of frequency, A is ranked first, B is ranked second, and C is ranked third. Now suppose that the cost of these QC problems is fairly certain to be $100 for each occurrence of A, $200 for each occurrence of B, and $1,000 for each occurrence of C. The relatively high expense of problem C should be considered in ranking its resolution because its total cost per day is greater to the organization than all of the occurrences of either of the other two problems. To allow for the cost of the QC problems to be considered in the analysis, we must multiply the observed frequency of the problem by its assessed cost and then base the rankings on total costs. This is similar to the ABC inventory classification method discussed in Chapter 6. In this example, the total expected daily cost of problem A is $500 (5 occurrences × $100), problem B is $600 (3 occurrences × $200), and problem C is $1,000 (1 occurrence × $1,000). Based on the frequency weighed total cost for the day, the new rankings of the QC problems would be C first at $1,000, B second at $600, and A third at $500.

The TQC methods presented in this section are only a small portion of those available or being developed to aid in quality assurance programs. Some of the oldest and most essential TQC methods are the statistical quality control (SQC) charting methods used in process control.

PROCESS CONTROL

One of the ways that we can ensure product quality in WIP is by performing an inspection. During an inspection, products' characteristics are examined for variation from expected levels of quality. Some of these quality characteristics are measurable and some are not. We call measurable quality characteristics **variables.** Measurable characteristics are the weight, height, and length of a product (that is, characteristics that can be measured and converted into a continuous numbering system). Quality can also be assessed subjectively by customers for service products. Using continuous measurement scales on point-of-purchase survey cards, customers can express their opinions on the level of quality on several quality characteristics. Figure 12-5 presents two examples of such survey cards. Quality characteristics that *cannot* be measured on a continuous scale are called **attributes.** Attribute characteristics are concerned with product function (an item is defective or not defective) and appearance (an item is acceptable or not acceptable). Examples of product attributes used to gauge product quality include the proportion of system failures such as the number of light bulbs out of a lot production run that won't light on the first try and the number of flaws in the paint finish of a newly manufactured automobile.

FIGURE 12-5 EXAMPLES OF POINT-OF-PURCHASE SURVEY CARDS FOR MONITORING QUALITY IN SERVICE PRODUCTS

Thank You *for choosing **Saint Elizabeth Community Health Center** for your health care services. To help us serve you in the future, please take a few minutes to complete and return this short survey.*

Overall, how would you rate the quality of care you received at Saint Elizabeth?

Excellent	Good	Fair	Poor
4	3	2	1

Will you choose Saint Elizabeth for future health care needs?

☐ Not likely ☐ Somewhat likely ☐ Very likely

Date of Visit ____________________

Comments ____

____

____

____

____

I would like to be contacted by hospital management to discuss my care. ☐ Yes ☐ No

Name ____
(optional)

Best time to reach me is ____________ ☐ a.m. ☐ p.m. Phone ____________________

Membership Services

You have recently either utilized a service or have been in contact with the American Production and Inventory Control Society (APICS) headquarters. To ensure that a high level of service is provided to APICS members, we ask that you complete and return the following questionnaire.

How would you rate the following APICS membership service areas:

1-Poor 2-Fair 3-Good 4-Excellent
(Please circle appropriate numbers)

Telephone Service		Correspondence Service		Records Processing	
Accuracy	1 2 3 4	Accuracy	1 2 3 4	Accuracy	1 2 3 4
Courtesy	1 2 3 4	Courtesy	1 2 3 4	Courtesy	1 2 3 4
Promptness	1 2 3 4	Promptness	1 2 3 4	Promptness	1 2 3 4

(Optional)

Name: Last ____________________ First ____________________

Company: ____

Street Address: ____

City, State, ZIP: ____

Telephone: H ( ) ____________ **W ( )** ____________

***If additional comments are appropriate, please don't hesitate to forward under separate cover.**

Sources: Provided courtesy of Saint Elizabeth Community Health Center, Lincoln, Nebraska. Reprinted with permission, APICS.

In process control, we are usually monitoring the quality of products during the transformation process, hence the term **process control.** Because we often use statistics to measure quality, the term **statistical process control (SPC)** is sometimes used to refer to this monitoring process. Our objective in process control is to ensure that variation or quality in the production process, procedure, and product meets acceptable levels over a given time period. The way we monitor process quality is with product inspections. These usually involve an act of physical observation in which a QC inspector runs through a checklist of quality characteristics that must be present to meet desired specification requirements.

In modern operations management systems, many quality control inspections are performed by automated, mechanical, or electrical systems. Automated process control systems can be as simple as a scale used to weigh components or as complex as a computer-based sensory system. Advanced technology such as that used in robots and laser inspection devices has been successfully used in industry since the early 1970s.[19] Some mechanical and electrical inspection equipment is used to monitor work-in-process, and other equipment is used to monitor the equipment itself. By monitoring either the product quality or the equipment, the automated systems act to ensure that the manufacturing process is kept under control. In Japan, these mechanized QC monitors are called *bakayokes* (foolproof devices) because human beings, who can make errors, are replaced with a machine that is virtually foolproof. These devices are usually incorporated into various places throughout the OM system to monitor quality. The *bakayokes* permit a 100 percent inspection of certain product attributes or variables of the work-in-process, which helps improve quality. In the Toyota plants in Japan, most of the robots and machines are autonomous (no human control), and both the output of the machine and the machines themselves are monitored by *bakayokes* to ensure product quality.[20] Some of these monitoring machines can actually shut the system down if the process quality drops below a predesignated acceptable quality level.

Before *bakayokes* or human beings can monitor a quality, they must know what quality characteristics are important. In process control we are chiefly concerned with the quality characteristic of constancy, or the elimination of variation. Figure 12-6 shows a typical process control variation chart. Ideally, we have no or "zero" variation in our production processes from the product quality standard or target. Realistically, though, every production process introduces some variation. Even in fully automated manufacturing systems, equipment can become worn and generate a less-than-perfect-quality product. We therefore end up permitting some variation from the quality standard in the production process. If the variation exceeds some predefined limits, however, we no longer find it acceptable. This cut-off line or control limit is sometimes what determines the difference between a salable product and a defective product that must be reworked or scrapped. The major question in process control is determining what the cut-off lines or control limits should be.

---

[19] See J. Mihalasky, "Robots: Their Impact on the Quality Function," *Quality Progress* (October 1978), 12–15; and J. Mihalasky, "Laser-Based Automatic Systems," *Quality Progress* (December 1981), 26–27.

[20] Y. Monden, "What Makes the Toyota Production System Really Tick?" *Industrial Engineering* (January 1981), 36–46.

FIGURE 12-6 PROCESS CONTROL VARIATION CHART

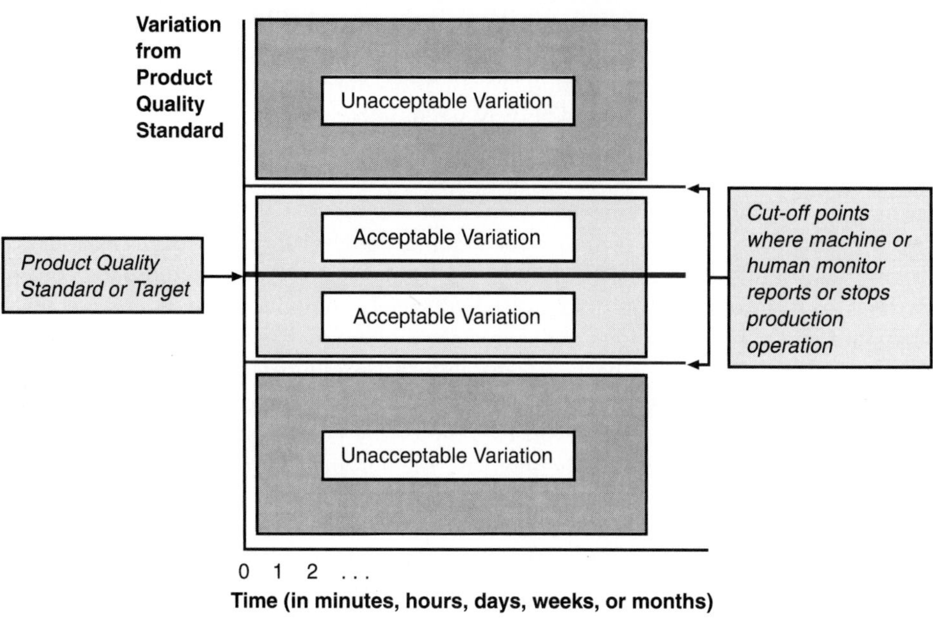

One approach to determining the control limits to monitor production process deviation is through **statistical quality control (SQC) charts.** We will examine two control charts for monitoring measurable variable quality characteristics and two control charts for monitoring attribute quality characteristics.

Control Charts for Measurable Variables

USES OF CONTROL CHARTS SQC charts are used to monitor measurable variables, based on statistical theory. We use the statistical theory to justify an interval being used about a standard or average level of quality. The interval defines the boundaries of the control limits. A sample control chart is presented in Figure 12-7. In SQC charts, the horizontal axis represents time and the vertical axis is used for the measured variation that is observed in the production process.

We also have a standard of quality (labeled *S*) that is the desired measurable variable value. Although the standard can be set as a QC target, it is usually estimated from a long-term average. The variation from the standard is used to construct the two control limits: an upper control limit (*UCL*) and a lower control limit (*LCL*). These control limits define acceptable and unacceptable deviation from the desired standard of quality. Once a standard and the control limits are established, we use them to observe changes in processing quality over a period of time into the future.

FIGURE 12-7 A STATISTICAL QUALITY CONTROL (SQC) CHART

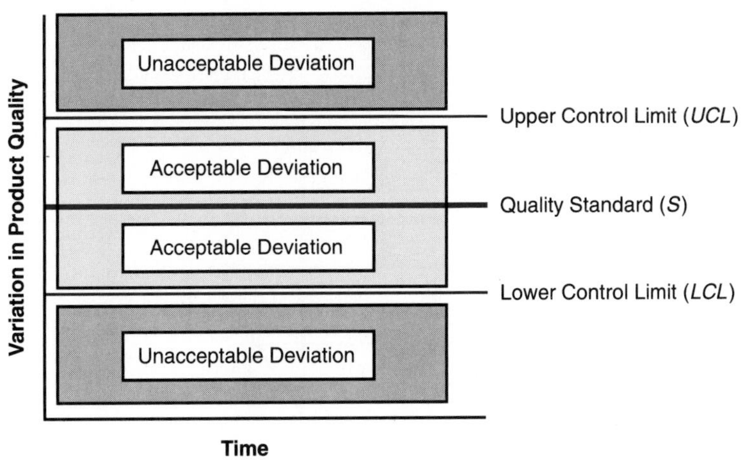

To develop the *UCL* and *LCL,* we take samples of the production process. In a repetitive operation, for example, we might establish a standard by taking very large samples or simply using product specificaitons as a QC goal. For example, when filling 12-ounce cans with food, the desired or standard amount of food to put into a can is 12 ounces. In this example the measurable variable is the weight of food in a can.

In Figure 12-8, we can see that upper and lower control limits can be based on the number of standard deviations from the standard value. (Students who have not been exposed to basic statistics should read Appendix A to better understand the material in this section.) The greater the number of standard deviations, the greater the amount of variation we are permitting within the boundaries. For example, a $\pm 3\sigma$ interval about the standard *S* should include 99.73 percent of all of the processing variation that we will observe in a production processing system. We should not allow much variation, and in fact, we try to avoid any variation in the process. Today, we use the control charts not just to monitor the variation in the production processes, but also to motivate workers to correct and eliminate sources of variation. The control limits are used as guidelines for judgment and not as a static standard of quality. Once a control chart's *UCL* and *LCL* are established, we take additional samples that measure quality from the process over a period of time to see how the variation, inherent in all production activities, is behaving.

In Figure 12-9 we have a series of control charts that do not violate their *UCLs* or *LCLs* but whose interpretations can provide management with useful information on the product quality behavior of the operating system. In Figure 12-9(a), we have a normal situation in which most of the samples taken over time fall near or on the standard line on the chart. This type of distribution of sample results is what forms the normal distribution about the standard that is depicted in Figure 12-8. In Figures 12-9(b), (c), and (d), deviation is occurring in the production processes that should be investigated by management.

FIGURE 12-8 DISTRIBUTION OF VARIATION ABOUT A QUALITY STANDARD

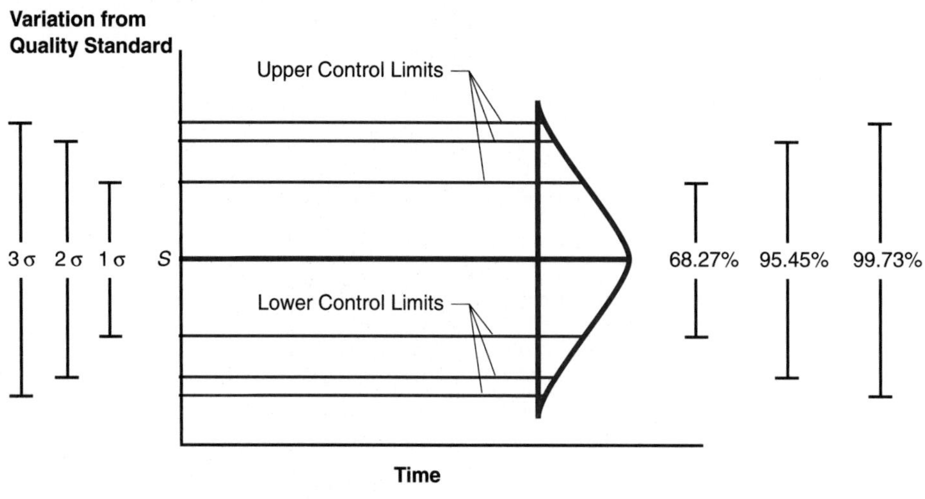

In Figure 12-9(b), we can observe that several of the samples are falling consistently against the *UCL*. The number of sample values taken to plot the points on the chart and amount of deviation for each sample should (over a period of time) be balanced on both sides of the standard line. Otherwise, the standard *S* does not apply. The type of extreme deviation in Figure 12-9(b) might indicate that the manufacturing process has changed and is generating products that are consistently above the standard or desired level of quality. This is a signal to management to investigate what is causing the above-average variation. In Figure 12-9(c), the deviation is much too erratic and might be interpreted as signaling a need for correcting the causes of variation in the operations management system or revising the control chart limits. In Figure 12-9(d), there is an obvious trend in the direction of the samples that can be interpreted as indicating that the *LCL* will be violated in the near future. Management should investigate this variation before it violates the *LCL*. In summary, Figures 12-9(b), (c), and (d) illustrate how management can use process control charts to identify a process that may be out of control even though it is producing acceptable quality products.

$\overline{X}$-CHARTS AND *R*-CHARTS As we have seen in Figure 12-9, control charts can be used as guides to help identify variation in product quality characteristics. Two commonly used variable control charts are the $\overline{x}$-chart (pronounced x-bar chart) and the *R*-chart. The $\overline{x}$-chart is used to depict, monitor, and control process dispersion about a product's quality standard. The $\overline{x}$-chart is a chart of average or mean measurable quality characteristic values. We use average values from samples to plot quality on this SQC chart. The *R*-chart measures dispersion about a desired dispersion standard. The *R*-chart of ranges are *R*s plotted to reflect the variation that exists from an average variation level

FIGURE 12-9 SAMPLE CONTROL CHARTS AND INTERPRETATIONS

(A) NORMAL BEHAVIOR: SAMPLES NEAR STANDARD

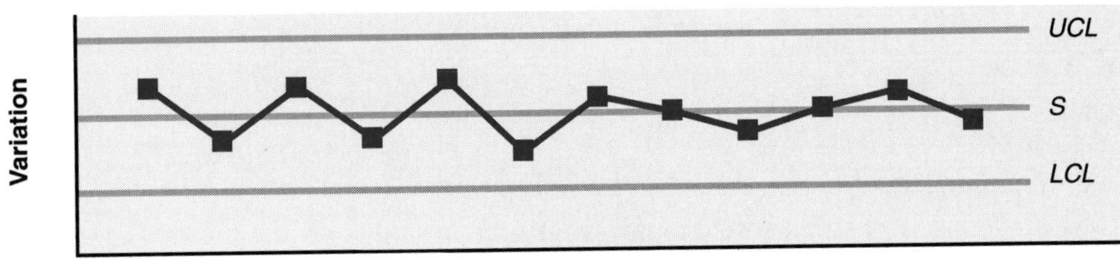

(B) ABNORMAL BEHAVIOR: SAMPLES CLOSE TO BOUNDARY

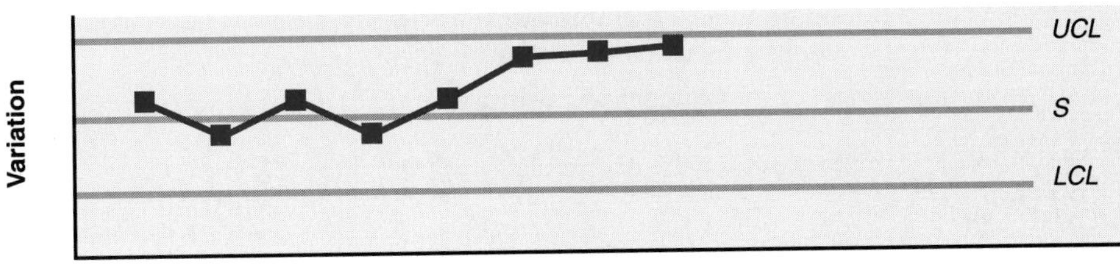

(C) ABNORMAL BEHAVIOR: SAMPLES VERY ERRATIC

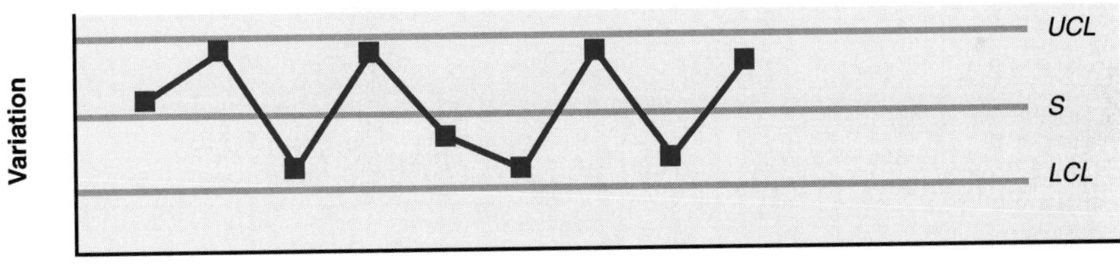

(D) ABNORMAL BEHAVIOR: SAMPLES TRENDING IN ONE DIRECTION

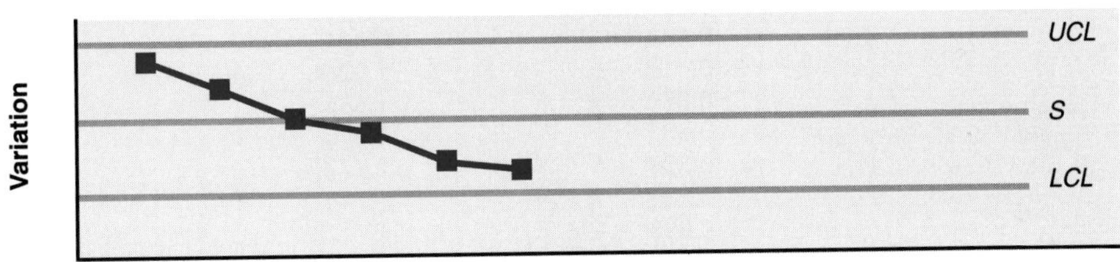

(that is, the average range) in the production process. The *LCL* and *UCL* for the $\bar{x}$-chart are computed using the following:

$$UCL = S + (A)(\bar{R})$$

$$LCL = S - (A)(\bar{R})$$

where

n = sample size

m = number of samples used to develop the control lines

R_i = range (highest − lowest) of the *i*th sample

$\bar{R} = \frac{\Sigma R_i}{m}$ = average range for all m samples

A = a tabled (found in Table 12-2) variance value to adjust the average range to reflect 3 standard deviations or a 99.73 percent confidence level

x = an observation or measurement in a sample

$\bar{x}_i = \frac{\Sigma x_i}{n}$ = sample mean for the *i*th sample

$\bar{\bar{x}} = \frac{\Sigma \bar{x}_i}{m}$ = grand mean of all samples

$S = \bar{\bar{x}}$ = quality standard

TABLE 12-2 VARIABLE CONTROL CHART FACTORS

Number of Observations in Sample of Size (n)	CONTROL CHART FACTORS FOR 3σ OR 99.73% CONFIDENCE LIMIT		
	A	B	C
2	1.880	3.267	0
3	1.023	2.574	0
4	0.729	2.282	0
5	0.577	2.114	0
6	0.483	2.004	0
7	0.419	1.924	0.076
8	0.373	1.864	0.136
9	0.337	1.816	0.184
10	0.308	1.777	0.224
11	0.285	1.744	0.256
12	0.266	1.717	0.283

Source: American Society for Testing Materials, Special Technical Publication 15-C, "Quality Control of Materials," 1951, pp. 63, 72.

Because of the computational similarity and complimentary information requirements for the $\bar{x}$- and R-charts, they are often generated together. The formulas for the UCL and LCL for the R-chart are

$$UCL = (B)(\overline{R})$$

$$LCL = (C)(\overline{R})$$

where

B = a tabled (found in Table 12-2) variance value to adjust the average range to reflect 3 standard deviations or a 99.73 percent confidence level for the UCL

C = a tabled (found in Table 12-2) variance value to adjust the average range to reflect 3 standard deviations or a 99.73 percent confidence level for the LCL

To develop $\bar{x}$- and R-charts for use in a process control system, we follow these steps:

1. *Determine the inspection sample size* n *and the number of samples to collect.* We must determine the number of averages we will use to develop the chart and the sample size for the average values. The determination of n and m used in the $\bar{x}$ and R statistics can be judgmentally based on time or on the cost to collect and perform the inspection efforts.

   As we can see in Figure 12-10, the costs of inspecting products (management time, human resource, prohibitive test costs) must be balanced with the cost of inspection error (liability costs, inaccurate information). Because these types of costs are so difficult to assess, the optimal sample size (n in Figure 12-10) determined by the total cost curve is almost impossible to determine mathematically. There are some statistical methods that can aid us in determining sample size.[21] It must be remembered that the value of n is constant for all samples.

2. *Collect the data for the SQC system derivation.* This usually involves physically inspecting products to collect the measurable data on the variable quality characteristics.

3. *Compute the UCL and LCL values.* We need to determine the level of confidence we want to have in the resulting limits. For purposes of this text, we will always use a 99.73 confidence level for all four of the control charts presented.

4. *Draw the $\bar{x}$- and R-charts.* The charts should clearly denote the S, $\overline{R}$, UCL, and LCL lines.

5. *Take new samples on the process, plot them, and interpret their meaning.* The $\bar{x}$-chart is a chart of mean values. The new data are usually converted into sample

[21] We discuss the use of a statistical sample size formula in Chapter 14.

FIGURE 12-10 COSTS OF INSPECTION AND INSPECTION SAMPLE SIZE

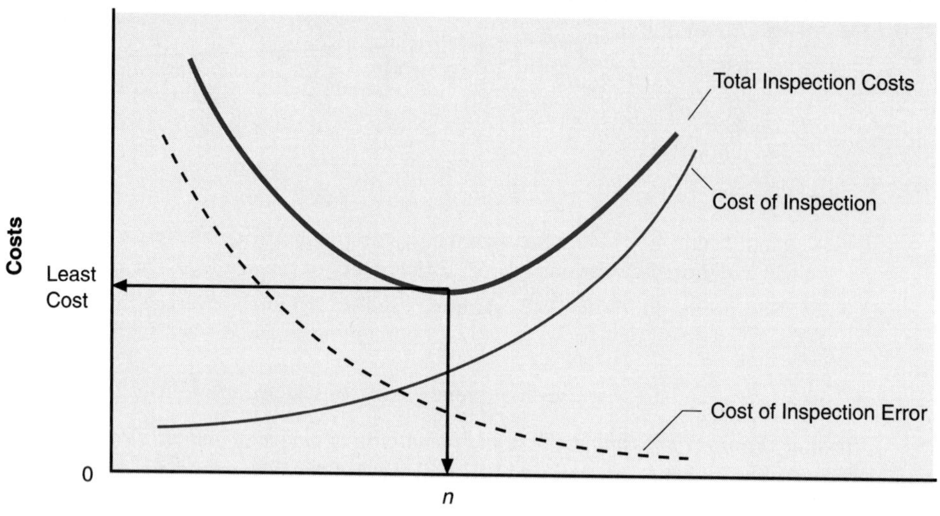

averages and then plotted. Each plot over time may provide a clue to a change in process quality. The R chart is a chart of variation. Processes with less variation generally produce higher-quality products. We continue this step until we feel the need to investigate and possibly change the process system. Once a change is made, the control charting procedure must be repeated to develop new charts.

To illustrate the $\overline{x}$- and R-chart procedure, let's look at an example problem. Suppose that we are filling 12-ounce cans with pineapple chunks. We want to develop $\overline{x}$- and R-charts to monitor our production process. The sample data for the problem are presented in Table 12-3. In this problem, we are taking four samples ($m = 4$), each consisting of an inspection that measures the weight of pineapple in each of four cans ($n = 4$). These necessary statistics are also computed in Table 12-3. As we can see, the standard S equals the 12 ounces as we expected. The UCL is calculated by using the A factor from Table 12-2. This factor adjusts the variance statistic $\overline{R}$ to 3 standard deviations from S, to give us a 99.73 percent confidence interval about the quality standard. In other words, we can expect to have 9,973 of 10,000 samples fall within the UCL and LCL or we can be 99.73 percent sure that sample observations will fall between the two control limits.

Now suppose that we plot the sample mean $\overline{x}$ and range R values from Table 12-3 between the boundaries of their control limits to see what is happening in this production system. The $\overline{x}$- and R-charts for this problem are presented in Figure 12-11. In the $\overline{x}$-chart in Figure 12-11(a), the samples fall expectedly within the boundaries but the general direction appears to indicate that the LCL may possibly be violated

TABLE 12-3 $\bar{x}$ AND R EXAMPLE PROBLEM DATA AND COMPUTATIONS

Week	X	Σ(x)	$\bar{x}$	R
1	12.0, 12.4, 12.5, 12.5	49.4	12.35	0.5
2	12.4, 12.8, 12.8, 11.4	49.4	12.35	1.4
3	11.0, 12.0, 12.6, 12.6	48.2	12.05	1.6
4	11.8, 9.8, 11.8, 11.6	45.0	11.25	2.0
			48.00	5.5

$$S = \bar{\bar{x}} = \frac{\Sigma \bar{x}}{m} = \frac{48.00}{4} = 12$$

$$\bar{R} = \frac{\Sigma R}{m} = \frac{5.5}{4} = 1.375$$

$$\begin{aligned} UCL_{\bar{x}} &= S + (A)(\bar{R}) \\ &= 12 + (0.729)(1.375) \\ &= 13.002 \end{aligned}$$

$$\begin{aligned} LCL_{\bar{x}} &= S - (A)(\bar{R}) \\ &= 12 - (0.729)(1.375) \\ &= 10.998 \end{aligned}$$

$$UCL_R = B(\bar{R}) = (2.282)(1.375) = 3.138$$

$$LCL_R = C(\bar{R}) = (0)(1.375) = 0$$

in the near future. This might mean that the food-canning process is consistently putting too little pineapple in the 12-ounce cans.

In the *R*-chart shown in Figure 12-11(b), the four samples expectedly fall within the boundaries of the control lines, but the consistent upward direction of the charted sample ranges means that the process behavior may violate the *UCL* in the future. The amount of variation observed in each sample is increasing beyond the standard levels of range statistic variation of 1.375. Larger sample sizes or the process itself could be causing the unexpected variation.

It is advisable when using the $\bar{x}$- and *R*-charts to not act hastily in making changes in the production process based only on the data used to construct the charts. New sample observations should be taken and compared with the control line values when making any necessary process change decisions.

Control Charts for Attributes

Occasionally, we do not have quality characteristics that can be measured. Attributes such as defective light bulbs or flaws in product finishes cannot be weighed or measured

FIGURE 12-11 $\overline{X}$ AND *R*-CHARTS FOR EXAMPLE PROBLEM

(A) $\bar{x}$-CHART

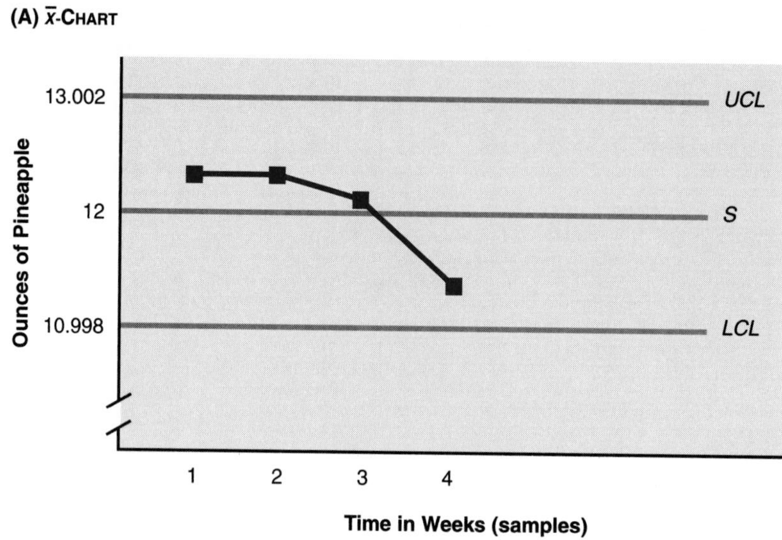

(B) *R*-CHART

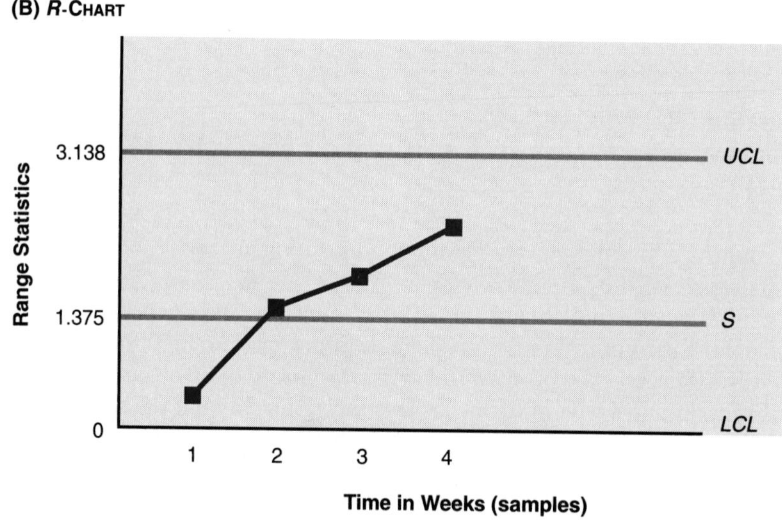

by degree. These types of inspection situations require a discrete or noncontinuous evaluation of a product. Many different control charts can be used to establish control limits for product characteristic or attribute quality. We will look at two types of statistical quality control charts. *P*-charts and *C*-charts. Because we can use the same five-step procedure for the *P*- and *C*-charts as presented for the $\bar{x}$- and *R*-charts, the procedure will not be repeated.

P-CHARTS A *P*-chart is a chart of the proportion of defective units in a sample. This type of chart can be used to monitor process control in situations in which the inspection of a lot will determine that each item is either defective or not defective. Hence, a fraction or a proportion p of the items in a lot can be classified as defective. To use a *P*-chart we must

1. Have a finite population of units or products (a lot or batch of units) in which to compute the desired fraction of defectives
2. Be able to judge the product quality as being either defective or not defective

If we sample many lots and average the proportion p or fraction of defects, we derive an average proportion defective $\overline{p}$ that can be used as a standard S. Because this fraction defective standard is an average, we can use it to calculate a standard deviation in computing control limits in much the same way as we did for the $\overline{x}$-chart. The control limits for the fraction defective attributes can be found by

$$UCL_p = S + (3)\sqrt{[\overline{p}(1 - \overline{p})]/n}$$

$$LCL_p = S - (3)\sqrt{[\overline{p}(1 - \overline{p})]/n}$$

where

n = sample size

m = number of samples taken

d_i = the number of defective items in each ith sample

$p_i = \dfrac{\Sigma d_i}{n}$ = the fraction of defective items in each ith sample

$S = \overline{p} = \dfrac{\Sigma p_i}{m}$ = the fraction of defective items for all samples

The value of $\overline{p}$ is used as the standard of quality S. The use of the control limits is much the same as the *R*-chart. Though the standard of this chart is $\overline{p}$, we desire as small an amount of fraction defectives as possible. The closer the observed process sampling results yield values near or below the *LCL*, the better the quality the process is generating. To illustrate this charting method, let's look at an example problem.

Suppose that we want to establish a *P*-chart for an electrical component we produce for a television manufacturing company. We decide to inspect a sample of 1,000 units each day for six days as data for the preparation of the control chart limits. The data collected for the study are presented in Table 12-4. The resulting six samples of 1,000 units each generated an average fraction of defective units of only 0.006. This is the average proportion defective $\overline{p}$ (or the standard S of quality) for this manufacturing process. The control limits for this problem are also presented in Table 12-4 and charted in Figure 12-12. As we can see in Figure 12-12, the second sample fraction defective actually hits the *UCL*. This is not unusual, but it should be investigated by management to see if any manufacturing process caused the excessive variation or if it is just a matter

TABLE 12-4 *P*-CHART EXAMPLE PROBLEM DATA AND COMPUTATIONS

*Sample**	*Sample Size* (n)	*Number of Defective Items* (d)	*Fraction Defective* (p)
1	1,000	8	.008
2	1,000	12	.012
3	1,000	2	.002
4	1,000	6	.006
5	1,000	4	.004
6	1,000	4	.004
			.036

$$\bar{p} = \frac{\Sigma p}{m} = \frac{.036}{6} = .006$$

$$\begin{aligned} UCL_p &= \bar{p} + 3\sqrt{\frac{\bar{p}(1-\bar{p})}{n}} \\ &= .006 + 3\sqrt{\frac{.006(1-.006)}{1{,}000}} \\ &= .006 + 3(.002) \\ &= 0.12 \end{aligned}$$

$$\begin{aligned} UCL_p &= \bar{p} - 3\sqrt{\frac{\bar{p}(1-\bar{p})}{n}} \\ &= .006 - 3\sqrt{\frac{.006(1-.006)}{1{,}000}} \\ &= .006 - 3(.002) \\ &= 0\dagger \end{aligned}$$

* Samples taken once each day.
† The LCL_p cannot be less than zero.

of sampling error. As with the $\bar{x}$- and *R*-charts, we would use this *P*-chart for future inspection of samples from the manufacturing process and not just base QC decisions on the data results that were used to construct the charts.

C-CHARTS The *C*-chart is similar to the *P*-chart in that it is used to chart attributes. With the *C*-chart, however, we do not need to know what the total number of nonconformities is. For example, if we were inspecting a paint job we might find zero flaws or some infinite number of flaws. The *C*-chart only requires that the nonconformities are countable. The control limits for the *C*-chart can be found by

$$UCL_c = \bar{c} + 3\sqrt{S}$$
$$LCL_c = \bar{c} - 3\sqrt{S}$$

FIGURE 12-12 *P*-CONTROL CHART FOR EXAMPLE PROBLEM

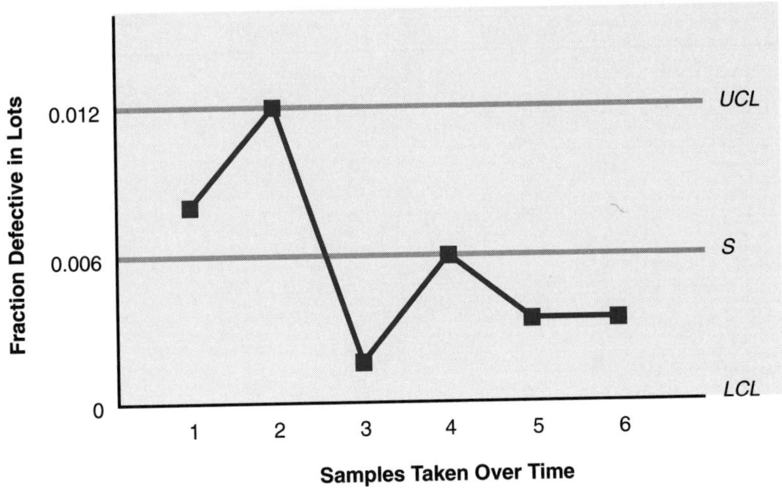

where

m = number of units inspected

$\bar{c}$ = number of flaws or defects found per unit

$$S = \bar{c} = \frac{\Sigma c}{m} = \text{average number of nonconformities per unit}$$

The value of $\bar{c}$ becomes the quality standard S for this control system. To illustrate the use of this control chart, let's look at a sample problem.

Suppose that we manufacture refrigerators and want to set up a control chart to monitor the quality of the paint job on each one. We cannot use either an $\bar{x}$- or R-chart because we cannot measure job flaws; we can only count them. We cannot use a *P*-chart because we cannot ascertain how many possible flaws can exist on a refrigerator, so a fraction defective cannot be determined. Suppose that we take a sample of one refrigerator per hour for six hours from a manufacturing process and inspect it for flaws.

The results of these inspections and the *C*-chart computations are presented in Table 12-5. Note that the LCL_c is 0. If we had subtracted 7.348 from 6 as the formula for the *LCL* indicates, we would have had an LCL_c of -1.348. Even though we might like to have a negative number of flaws, it is not possible in the real world of quality assurance. Whenever a negative *LCL* occurs, we simply use 0 as the *LCL*. The *C*-chart for this sample problem is presented in Figure 12-13. As expected, this chart is fairly normal, with most of the sample results striking around the standard line of six flaws per refrigerator.

TABLE 12-5 C-CHART EXAMPLE PROBLEM DATA AND COMPUTATIONS

Refrigerator Sample	*Defects Found in Finish*
1	6
2	3
3	9
4	6
5	9
6	3
	36

$$S = \bar{c} = \frac{36}{6} = 6$$

$$\begin{aligned} UCL_c &= \bar{c} + 3\sqrt{\bar{c}} \\ &= 6 + 3\sqrt{6} \\ &= 6 + 7.348 \\ &= 13.348 \end{aligned}$$

$$\begin{aligned} LCL_c &= \bar{c} - 3\sqrt{\bar{c}} \\ &= 6 - 3\sqrt{6} \\ &= 6 - 7.348 \\ &= 0^* \end{aligned}$$

* *LCL* cannot be less than zero.

FIGURE 12-13 C-CONTROL CHART FOR EXAMPLE PROBLEM

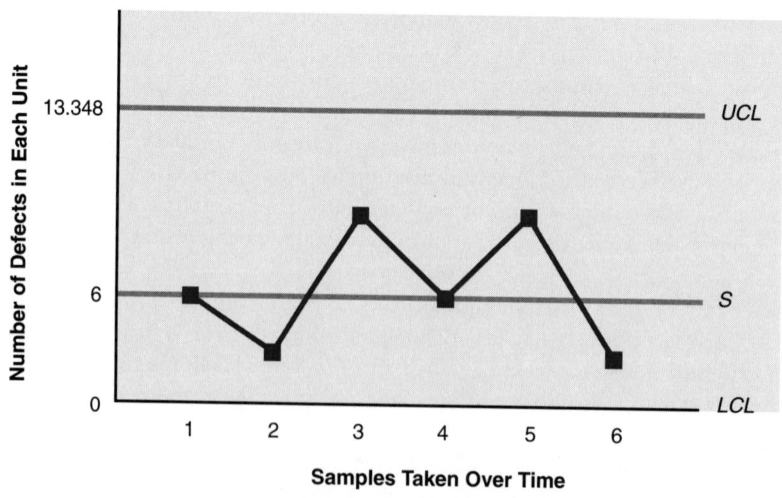

All four of the control charts presented in this section suffer from the inherent inaccuracies that exist in statistical procedures such as inaccurate data collection and sampling error. We also have to make an underlying assumption that all of the SQC chart data are normally distributed. In most cases, where samples are taken over a long period of time, this assumption usually holds. Despite the limitations, the four control charts presented in this section are commonly used in quality assurance and TQC programs to monitor, control, and motivate quality correction behavior in production processes.[22]

INTEGRATING MANAGEMENT RESOURCES: USING SQC CHARTS AND MAINTENANCE MANAGEMENT TO IMPROVE QUALITY AND PRODUCTIVITY

Achieving a modern quality assurance (QA) program requires that operations managers apply and integrate TQC principles and methods throughout their operations, including their human, technology, and system resources. TQC must be a company-wide approach seeking a goal of product perfection. A number of computer software systems have been developed in the last decade to integrate an organization's management information system with QA projects as a part of the larger QA program.

SQC Charts

The SQC charts are an important part of a TQC program when they are used to motivate improvement in product quality. Product quality will be improved when workers are able to see how their individual efforts have a direct impact on improving (or decreasing) product quality. SQC charts are used to visually communicate to workers (and coworkers) quality improvements for a plant, department, workcenter, or even a single worker. Timing is an important aspect of the motivational effect on workers. Ideally, a worker should have each unit of his or her work checked (according to TQC principles) and the quality of effort reported on an SQC chart for everybody to see (because peer pressure can also be a motivator). Over time, workers will see the revision of the *UCLs* and *LCLs* moving together. Workers will be able to see graphically that their quality efforts are making a difference as the control lines narrow and move toward the quality standard line (*S* on the SQC charts). The SQC chart will be performing as a visual reinforcing and motivating aid to encourge workers to continue their quality efforts to seek the perfection of zero variation from the quality standard line on the chart. Immediate feedback is the key to reinforcing desired product quality learning habits (one of the goals of a TQC program). SQC charts allow workers to quickly identify the "right" from "wrong" ways of doing their job as they relate to the product quality characteristics being measured. Unfortunately, the effort involved in recording each unit's quality performance measures is viewed by JIT principles as a wasteful,

---

[22] S. Tomas, "Six Sigma: Motorola's Quest for Zero Defects," *APICS—The Performance Advantage,* 1, No. 1 (1991), 36–41; and D. K. Denton, "Lessons on Competitiveness: Motorola's Approach," *Production and Inventory Management Journal,* 32, No. 3 (1991), 22–25.

nonproductive activity that adds no value to the finished product and therefore should be avoided for efficiency reasons.

To permit the SQC charts to be prepared and motivate worker quality performance on a timely basis, without the inefficiencies of workers recording the quality measurements, one software developer devised an information system to integrate all of the SQC reporting needs without the recording requirements. The Concert Corporation developed a collection of software modules that can be used to prepare, report, and statistically analyze worker product quality performance.[23] Their QE-100 module is used by workers at workcenters or anywhere on the shop floor to enter quality control measurements manually or from electronic sensors, gauges, or scales. This module then revises a variety of SQC charts, including the $\bar{x}$- and R-charts, to permit the worker to view the impact of his or her quality efforts on a unit-by-unit basis or on some predesignated sample batch. As fast as the workers complete their units and the sensor or quality measuring device takes its measures, the software generates a revised SQC chart. Their QE-1000 module (and the QE-Link) permit a quality data base to collect data from the QE-100 workcenters. From the data base managers are able to monitor overall quality and identify where problems in workcenters are being experienced for QC purposes. By integrating the SQC methodology into a computer information system, workers save productive work time (by avoiding the recording of quality measures) and receive more immediate quality performance feedback. Such timely feedback not only helps reinforce and motivate a worker to make quality a habit, but it also allows the worker to take corrective action to change work processes and procedures if necessary to avoid poor quality performance.

Maintenance Management

Many operations management researchers believe that technologically advanced and automated production environments will require the integration of quality-oriented maintenance programs into an overall production strategy that includes TQC and JIT to achieve world-class manufacturing in the 1990s.[24] (A discussion on the basics of quality maintenance management is presented in Supplement 12-2). This is a logical assumption in that poorly maintained equipment in a highly automated OM environment will reduce productivity contributions of JIT and the product quality contributions of TQC. Unfortunately, preventive maintenance (PM) programs are often expensive to manage and can reduce the cost-reduction advantages of the productivity cycle by spending profits on the program itself. To help integrate the maintenance program into a JIT environment (where workers are expected to perform some preventive or routine maintenance activities and at the same time reduce the cost of the program to make it more efficient to operate),

---

[23] "QE-100: Information Packet" (1990), Concert Corporation, 3757 Inpark Circle, Dayton, OH 45414.

[24] P. Y. Huang, L. J. Moore, and S. Shin, "World-Class Manufacturing in the 1990's: Integrating TQC, JIT, FA, and TPM with Worker Participation," *Manufacturing Review,* 4, No. 2 (June 1991), 87–95.

software developers have been devising computer-based maintenance management systems.

RMS Systems of Philadelphia, Pennsylvania developed a computer-based preventive maintenance system called TRIMAX-PM, which is a computer information system designed around a PM strategy (discussed in Supplement 12-2).[25] The computer system was successfully applied by the Westinghouse Defense Center in Baltimore, Maryland, and resulted in a $1.4 million reduction in PM efforts and a reduction in overtime of 1,000 hours a month. The computer system consists of software and uses the company's computer access terminals for JIT worker input of maintenance activities and problems. The system cut the cost of preventive maintenance by keeping track of equipment maintenance records and the PM jobs as they were being performed. Specifically, the computer system is used to

1. Generate maintenance reports that call management's attention to equipment that should be replaced rather than repaired
2. Forecast equipment failures more accurately, which permits better PM scheduling and avoids needless maintenance
3. Avoid accidentally issuing needless PM work orders for the PM staff and JIT workers
4. Generate bills immediately for interdepartmental PM charges (that is, sometimes PM charges are allocated within an organization and must be charged against each department's budget and for services performed outside the organization)
5. Improve scheduling of specialized staff and avoid needless misscheduling of inappropriate PM staff by correctly identifying specific maintenance skills needed
6. Save PM effort and reduce overtime, which is very common in PM departments

One example of performance monitoring in a system quality maintenance environment is the Production Control and Monitoring System (PCMS) of the Intersystems Management and Computer Consultant Company of Dunbarton, New Hampshire.[26] The PCMS system is used to monitor indexed machine performance. An **indexed machine** is a machine that indexes or steps through a sequence of activities. For example, one element of a machine may cut a piece of metal, another element (that is, the next step) might bend the cut piece of metal, a third element of a machine might trim the bent piece of metal, and so on. Some indexed machines run from 1,000 to 9,000 steps per hour, with as many as 100 elements working to make up the machine (that is, the system).

---

[25] *Production and Inventory Management Review, 1986 Reference Guide and Directory,* 5, No. 11 (1986), 90.

[26] *Production and Inventory Management Review, 1986 Reference Guide and Directory,* 5, No. 11 (1986), 64.

The PCMS system involves the use of quality sensors that electronically feed their readings (equipment performance measures) to a computer program that contains algorithms that determine element or equipment failure based on established criteria. The output of the computer system includes statistics that can advise management on indexed machine speeds, engineering changes, extra spare parts, new PM requirements, and operator training requirements. The PCMS system operates on both mainframe and microcomputer systems.

SUMMARY

In this chapter, we have examined the subject of quality assurance (QA). We described a number of Japanese principles and approaches used to achieve QA programs, including the TQC system, TQC implementation tactics, quality circles, Taguchi statistical methods, cause and effect diagrams, and the Pareto method. In addition, we have described the use of traditional U.S. process control methods using SQC charts for monitoring and controlling product quality. We also described some recently developed computer-based systems that are being used to integrate management sources to help support QA projects

Our treatment of QA in this chapter is meant only as a brief survey of some of the more current QC topics. We have also included substantial material on two additional topics in QA in the supplements to this chapter. Students are encouraged to read Supplement 12-1 on acceptance sampling methods and Supplement 12-2 on quality maintenance management to understand the role these methods play in a QA program.

DISCUSSION AND REVIEW QUESTIONS

1. What is quality in a manufactured product? What is quality in a service product? Explain and give examples of each.
2. Why is quality assurance (QA) necessary? How is QA different from quality control (QC)?
3. What are the objectives of a QA program?
4. What is ISO 9000?
5. What is total quality control (TQC)? How are the TQC principles supportive or similar to JIT inventory (Chapter 8) and JIT production (Chapter 9) principles?
6. How would you go about implementing a TQC program?
7. What are quality circles? How do they help support a QA program?
8. What is the quality loss function concept of the Taguchi statistical methods?
9. What is a cause and effect diagram? How is it used in QA?
10. How does the Pareto method support QA?
11. What is the difference between variables and attributes in process control?
12. What is the difference between statistical quality control (SQC) *C*- and *P*-charts?

PROBLEMS

* 1. The hospital management wants to observe, measure, and control the quality of its emergency services. Patients who have left the hospital are given a postage-paid customer comment card (like those in Figure 12-5). The scale of measurement on quality characteristics of promptness, courtesy of attending physician, and hospital cleanliness ranges from 1 (excellent service) to 10 (poor service). Which of the four SQC charts ($\bar{x}$, R, P, or C) can be used in this situation?

2. A manager of a restaurant wants to install a quality control system to monitor the quality of the food services provided by food waiters and waitresses. Restaurant customers are given a postage-paid customer comment card to survey their opinions on customer service. The scale of measurement on quality characteristics of promptness of seating, cleanliness, and courtesy of the food server ranges from 1 (excellent service) to 5 (poor service). Which of the four SQC charts ($\bar{x}$, R, P, or C) can be used in this situation?

3. A restaurant owner wants to monitor the quality of the food services provided by food waiters and waitresses. Restaurant customers are given a postage-paid customer comment card on which to write their opinions on customer service. The measurement of the quality characteristics of promptness of seating, cleanliness, and courtesy of the food server consists of a single question on each characteristic: "Was the quality of service good? Yes or no." Which of the four SQR charts ($\bar{x}$, R, P, or C) can be used in this situation?

4. A manufacturer wants to monitor the quality of the computer chip product it produces. The manufacturer's customers are given a short return-by-mail weekly survey to sample their opinions on product quality. The quality measurement is the number of chips found defective each week. Which of the four SQC charts ($\bar{x}$, R, P, or C) can be used in this situation?

* 5. Suppose that a company is experiencing three QC problems (problems A, B, and C) occurring at a rate of 14, 31, and 45 times per week, respectively. The company wants to know which of the three QC problems it should work on first if the costs per occurrence of the problems are $5, $2, and $1, respectively, based on the weighted cost Pareto method.

6. A company has been repeatedly experiencing six different and mutually exclusive QC problems—A, B, C, D, E, and F—occurring at a rate of 120, 100, 98, 64, 55, and 43 times per month, respectively. The company wants to know the order in which it should tackle the QC problems if the costs per occurrence are $1.45, $2.76, $5, $8.71, $10.92, and $14 respectively, based on the weighted cost Pareto method.

7. A company has been repeatedly experiencing eight different and mutually exclusive QC problems—A, B, C, D, E, F, G, and H—occurring at a rate of 20, 19, 17, 10, 8, 6, 5, and 3 times per week, respectively. The company attempts to determine the order in which it should tackle the QC problems if the costs per occurrence are $6, $8, $12, $13, $17, $19, $23, and $25 respectively, based on the non-weighted cost Pareto method. What is the weighted cost Pareto method ordering? Explain the difference in terms of the Pareto method logic.

---

* The solutions to problems marked with an asterisk can be found in Appendix J.

8. An organization wants to establish an SQC chart system to monitor its process manufacturing operation. The company manufactures finishing nails for hardware companies. The company decided to use an $\bar{x}$-chart and has found the grand mean ($\bar{\bar{x}}$) of its three-inch nails to be 3 inches. The R value about the standard is .450 inches based on fifty samples of ten nails each. What are the R-chart UCL_R and LCL_R values?

* 9. A candy company wants to establish an SQC chart system to monitor its packaging process. The company packages 1-pound containers of candy. Managers have decided to use an $\bar{x}$-chart and have found the grand mean ($\bar{\bar{x}}$) of its 16-ounce packages of candy to be 16 ounces. The R value about the standard is 1.25 ounces based on 120 samples, each a sample of eight containers of candy. What are the R-chart UCL_R and LCL_R values?

10. A breakfast cereal company has established an SQC chart system to monitor its packaging process. The company packages 32-ounce boxes of cereal. It has decided to use $\bar{x}$- and R-charts based on the following samples:

Sample	*Sample Data*
1	34, 35, 37, 38, 40
2	31, 29, 32, 34, 33
3	34, 33, 34, 33, 34
4	32, 32, 33, 32, 33

Each of the four samples have five weight observations of cereal boxes. What are the $\bar{x}$- and R-chart UCL and LCL values for this company's product?

11. The company in Problem 10 established its control line based on the data given in Problem 10. It then started using the SQC system by collecting the following data:

Sample	*Sample Data*
5	32, 35, 33, 34, 30
6	33, 37, 32, 34, 33
7	34, 33, 40, 33, 34
8	38, 32, 33, 40, 38

Draw a control chart based on the data in Problem 10 and enter the new data. Comment on the resulting charts based on the new data.

12. A videocassette recorder manufacturer would like to establish an SQC chart system to monitor quality in the operations management system. The VCRs are inspected by a QC inspector who tests the finished product. The tests involve playing a videotape. If the unit plays the tape, it passed the inspection; if the unit fails to play the tape, the unit fails the inspection. Four samples of 500 units each were taken and resulted in 4, 3, 6, and 7 defective units, respectively. Which SQC chart should be used and why? Determine the UCL and LCL values and plot the data. Comment on the resulting SQC chart after you plot the next four samples, which resulted in 10, 15, 25, and 35 defective units.

13. A compact disc (CD) player manufacturer has decided to use an SQC chart system to monitor quality in the operations management system. The CD players are inspected by a QC inspector who tests the finished product. The test involves playing a CD. If the unit plays the CD, it passed the inspection; if the unit fails to play the CD, the unit fails the inspection. Six samples of 1,000 units each were taken and resulted in 10, 12,

5, 7, 4, and 2 defective units, respectively. Which SQC chart should be used and why? Determine the *UCL* and *LCL* values and plot the data. Comment on the resulting SQC chart.

14. A television manufacturer attempts to established an SQC chart system to monitor quality in the operations management system. The TVs are inspected by a QC inspector who tests the finished product. The test involves checking the finish on the TV set and counting the number of flaws in the finish. Eight TV sets were sampled and resulted in 1, 3, 4, 3, 4, 3, 6, and 7 flaws per unit, respectively. Which SQC chart should be used and why? Determine the *UCL* and *LCL* values and plot the data. Comment on the resulting SQC chart.

15. A baseball card printer has established an SQC chart system to monitor quality in the operations management system. The baseball cards are inspected by a QC inspector who examines the finished product. The examination involves visually inspecting the baseball cards for physical flaws in the printing process. Six baseball cards were sampled and resulted in 2, 3, 7, 8, 10, and 9 flaws per card, respectively. Which SQC chart should be used and why? Determine the *UCL* and *LCL* values and plot the data. Comment on the resulting SQC chart.

*16. (This problem requires the contents of Supplement 12-1.) A company decides to use an acceptance sampling plan (single-sampling plan) to monitor incoming components. Under its plan, $N = 1{,}000$, $n = 30$, and $c = 2$. From the sample, 4 rejects are found. Should the lot be rejected? Why?

17. (This problem requires the contents of Supplement 12-1.) A manufacturer decides to adopt an acceptance sampling plan (single-sampling plan) to monitor quality of the incoming components. If the company uses a sampling plan in which $n = 200$ and $c = 5$, what are the OC curve values for percentage defectives of 1 through 10?

18. (This problem requires the contents of Supplement 12-1.) A firm decides to use an acceptance sampling plan (single-sampling plan) for incoming components. If the company uses a sampling plan in which $n = 300$ and $c = 6$, what are the OC curve values for percentage defectives of 1 through 9?

19. (This problem requires the contents of Supplement 12-1.) A QC inspector is using a double-sampling plan in which $N = 30{,}000$, $n_1 = 400$, $c_1 = 10$, $n_2 = 400$, and $c_2 = 5$. On the first sample of 400, the inspector found only 5 defective parts. What should the inspector do and why?

20. (This problem requires the contents of Supplement 12-1.) A QC inspector is using a double-sampling plan in which $N = 10{,}000$, $n_1 = 100$, $c_1 = 5$, $n_2 = 100$, and $c_2 = 2$. In the first sample of 100, the inspector found 15 defective parts. What should the inspector do and why?

21. (This problem requires the contents of Supplement 12-1.) A company has decided to use an acceptance sampling plan (single-sampling plan) to monitor incoming components. If the company uses a sampling plan in which $N = 10{,}000$, $n = 100$, $c = 5$, $AQL = .05$, and $LTPD = .07$, what are α, β, and *AOQL*?

22. (This problem requires the contents of Supplement 12-1.) A manufacturer decides to use an acceptance sampling plan (single-sampling plan) to monitor incoming parts. If the company uses a sampling plan in which $N = 5{,}000$, $n = 200$, $c = 4$, $AQL = .04$, and $LTPD = 0.6$, determine α, β, and *AOQL*.

23. (This problem requires the contents of Supplement 12-1.) A company decides to use an acceptance sampling plan (single-sampling plan) to monitor incoming components from a new vendor. If the company used a MIL STD 105D plan and desired an *AQL* of 0.15 percent, what would the sample size and cut-off value be? Assume that the lot-size is 250,000 units.

24. (This problem requires the contents of Supplement 12-1.) An electronics firm decides to use an acceptance sampling plan (single-sampling plan) to monitor incoming electrical components from a new vendor. If the company uses an MIL STD 105D plan and desires an *AQL* of 0.40 percent, what would the sample size and cut-off value be? Assume that the lot-size is 5,000 units.

25. (This problem requires the contents of Supplement 12-1.) A company wants to use an acceptance sampling plan (single-sampling plan) to monitor incoming components from an older vendor that has a record of providing poor-quality items. If the company uses an MIL STD 105D plan and desires an *AQL* of 0.40 percent, what would the sample size and cut-off value be? Assume that the lot-size is 150,000 units. What is the difference in the number of items sampled if this vendor is given a General Inspection Level of I?

26. (This problem requires the contents of Supplement 12-1.) A manufacturing firm decides to use an acceptance sampling plan (single-sampling plan) to monitor incoming components from an old vendor that has a record of providing poor-quality items. If the company uses an MIL STD 105D plan and desires an *AQL* of 0.65 percent, determine the sample size and cut-off value. Assume that the lot-size is 150,000 units. What is the difference in the number of items sampled if this vendor is given a General Inspection Level of I? What is the difference if the vendor is given a General Inspection Level of II?

*27. (This problem requires the contents of Supplement 12-2.) If we have a three-element (all independent of each other) system structured in a series and the elements in the system have reliability probabilities of 0.92, 0.88, and 0.98, what is the entire system's reliability coefficient?

28. (This problem requires the contents of Supplement 12-2.) Given a five-element (all independent of each other) system structured in a series and the elements in the system have reliability probabilities of 0.94, 0.98, 0.96, 0.93, and 0.98, determine the entire system's reliability coefficient.

29. (This problem requires the contents of Supplement 12-2.) A company has an SOP to invest in equipment that will return its initial cost in three or fewer years. If the initial cost of a piece of equipment is $50,000 and the yearly revenue generated by the equipment is $6,000, should the company invest in the piece of equipment?

30. (This problem requires the contents of Supplement 12-2.) A company has an SOP to invest in equipment that will return its initial cost in five or fewer years. If the initial cost of a piece of equipment is $30,000 and the expected yearly revenue generated by the equipment is $8,000, should the company invest in this equipment?

31. (This problem requires the contents of Supplement 12-2.) Suppose that a company wanted to simulate the life duration of an AGV it is planning to purchase. The life duration probability function for the piece of equipment is shown in the table at the top of the next page.

Equipment Life Duration (months)	*Probability Distribution of AGV's Life Duration*
6	.05
12	.20
18	.25
24	.20
30	.15
36	.14

The company wants to have at least six AGVs operating during a 36-month planning horizon. Using the random numbers in the last column of the random number table in Appendix F, determine the number of units that the company needs to purchase and replace to maintain at least six AGVs operating.

32. (This problem requires the contents of Supplement 12-2.) A service organization wants to simulate the life duration of a piece of office equipment it is thinking of purchasing. The life duration probability function for the piece of equipment is as follows:

Equipment Life Duration (years)	*Probability Distribution of Life Duration*
1	.10
2	.15
3	.25
4	.40
5	.05
6	.05

The company wants to have at least eight pieces of equipment operating during a six-year planning horizon. Using two-digit random numbers in the first row of the random number table in Appendix F, how many units will it have to purchase and replace to keep eight pieces of equipment operating during a six-year period?

CASE 12-1

WHERE DID OUR QUALITY GO?

The Addison Company of Tampa, Florida manufactures (on a subcontract basis) disk drive components for most of the major microcomputer companies in the United States. The primary component of the disk drive is a motor whose design and manufacture gave the Addison Company unparalleled quality recognition in the industry when it first started the operation seven years ago. The company manufactured its motor using a small assembly line or repetitive operation. Twelve workstations were located along the assembly line to assemble the motor component. The last workstation in the assembly layout tested and inspected the motor. Indeed, the only inspection performed on the motor before shipment was conducted in the last workstation. One hundred percent of the motors were inspected during the first few years of operation as a service to customers. The inspection consisted of running the motor for 30 seconds. If it ran well without problems, it was approved; if it did not run well, it was discarded for scrap.

In the first few years of operation, virtually no motors were found to be defective by either the inspection team or the company's customers. (At least none were sent back for credit during this time.) With the apparent zero-defect quality and the ever-increasing demand, the company decided that cost of 100-percent inspection was not worth the effort. Addison gradually gave up its inspection efforts, eventually abandoning inspection altogether and simply accepting the risk and cost of a percentage of defective items being sent out to customers.

In the last few years, the Addison Company started receiving return goods in significant proportions. After some preliminary investigation, it became obvious to the management that several factors were affecting quality performance in the assembly line. These factors included some of the following:

1. The part-time summer help, who replaced vacationing permanent employees on the assembly line, was not performing the work correctly.
2. Permanent employees were not as quality conscious and motivated as they were when the company was smaller and product demand was not so overwhelming.
3. The past high levels of quality and lack of inspection did not foster quality control habits.

The result was a significant decrease in product quality, and without the quality control inspections, the defective items were being sent to the customers. The completed disk drives were usually incorporated into computers by Addison customers. Many of Addison's customers used acceptance sampling procedures that would occasionally miss the defective units. Once detected by the customer's inspectors, the disk drive rework effort was very costly. Addison's customers were not impressed with the variability of quality and started cancelling long-standing orders and contracts for future business.

Addison's management immediately reinstituted some inspection of its motor component but could not afford the 100-percent inspection effort of the past. Management decided that some type of on-going quality control method would be necessary to monitor its disk drive motor production system, and that a process control chart might be the best approach to deal with monitoring requirements without having to resort to a 100-percent inspection effort. The company collected the data in Exhibit 12C-1 to use in the construction of the statistical quality control chart. The data shown in Exhibit 12C-1 represents what the Addison management believe is the current state of quality in its operation. The samples are perceived to be adequate to establish a standard of quality and a production process monitoring system. The Addison management also decided to experiment with some of the TQC principles it had observed in the literature. After install-

EXHIBIT 12C-1 INITIAL DATA FOR CHART CONSTRUCTION

Sample	*Sample Size (n)*	*Number of Motors Failing Inspection*
1	120	13
2	100	9
3	50	8
4	180	15
5	130	10
6	110	4
7	100	6
8	80	2
9	85	4
10	110	3

EXHIBIT 12C-2 POSTCHART CONSTRUCTION DATA

Sample	*Sample Size (n)*	*Number of Motors Failing Inspection*
11	100	6
12	110	4
13	75	2
14	120	5
15	150	3
16	115	3

ing some of the TQC principles, Addison management collected some additional process data to be used to see if the TQC principles had any effect on the quality performance of its motor production process. These postchart construction data are presented in Exhibit 12C-2.

CASE QUESTIONS

1. What type of statistical control chart is necessary for Addison's quality control process?
2. Draw the control chart based on the data shown in Exhibit 12C-1. What are the *UCL, S,* and *LCL* values? (Assume average sample size of 106.5 for *UCL* and *LCL* only.)
3. What TQC principles might apply or would you recommend in this type of operation? What assumptions are you making in your selection?
4. Based on the postchart data in Exhibit 12C-2, have the TQC principles had any observable effect on quality? What assumptions are you making concerning your interpretation of the charted values?

CASE 12-2

WHOSE PARETO IS IT?

The Surprise Party Company (SPC) of Charleston, South Carolina, is a small distribution business whose product is the distribution of party goods for birthdays and parties. SPC distributes party goods to individuals, small groups, and organizations that place orders over the telephone or through the mail to the Charleston distribution center.

Over a period of twenty years, SPC has established a fairly good reputation in providing goods and services to customers, but management feels that the nature of the service product requires continuous service improvements. In fact, accuracy is essential. The nature of birthdays and parties are such that they are set at a specific time and on a specific date. If the party supplies do not arrive at the right time or in the right quantity, customers get very upset. On occasion, customers who have received incorrect, mismatched, or late supplies would not only send them back for credit but promise to discourage others from ever using SPC's services. Because repeat customers and word-of-mouth advertising are the major sources of customers for SPC, disappointing a single customer could be very costly in the long-term.

SPC decides to take steps to ensure the quality of its service product. The company instituted the JIT principle of making everyone responsible for his or her own work contribution in order processing. Each administrative and factory worker who performs a task on customer orders is required to place his or her employee number on the customer order so defects in the work can be traced back to the contributor.

SPC also performs a sample inspection of one month's worth of customer orders. Every order that goes through the operation is checked by quality control inspectors for errors in administrative and factory worker contributions. A tally of the frequency of the occurrence for five types of errors observed by the inspectors is presented in Exhibit 12C-3(a). The frequency distribution of the errors in Exhibit 12C-3(b) makes it clear that both factory management and factory workers share in creating defects in product quality. Each of the errors listed in Exhibit 12C-3 leads to a variety of costs, including the loss in profit on cancelled orders (both current loss on known orders and future, expected loss on anticipated orders), idleness of workers waiting for orders bottlenecked in administrative processing, and wasted labor in duplicating and correcting other defects. Based on costing, accounting, and marketing estimates, each time that managers incorrectly file an order costs SPC $1.50, each time that factory workers incorrectly fill an order costs SPC $0.85,

EXHIBIT 12C-3 QUALITY CONTROL TALLY AND DISTRIBUTION STATISTICS

(A) QUALITY CONTROL PROBLEM AND WORKER - OBSERVED FREQUENCIES

Error	Description	Frequency
1	Total errors in filing orders	50
2	Total errors in filling orders	34
3	Total errors in order form	12
4	Total errors in shipping orders	7
5	Total errors reported by customers	3

(B) FREQUENCY DISTRIBUTION OF OBSERVED PROBLEMS

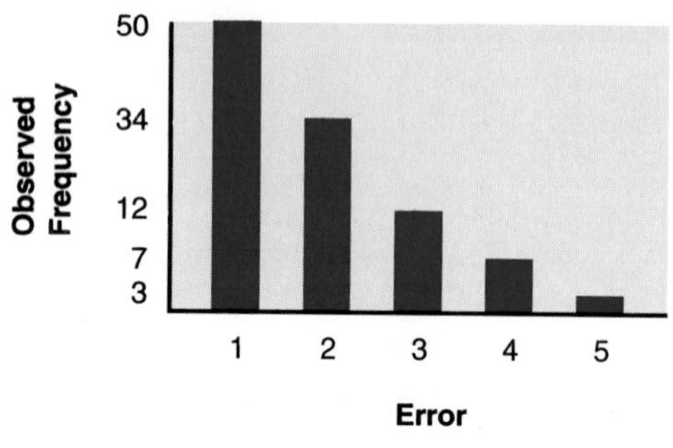

each time that sales staff incorrectly take an order (error 3) costs SPC $1.80, each time that shippers incorrectly ship an order costs SPC $4.68, and each time that quality control inspectors do not catch an order error in their final inspection that is later observed by a customer (error 5) costs SPC $15.59.

SPC management hopes to deal with all of these problems with equal effort, but finds it difficult to do so because of limited resources. This limitation has forced management to focus its efforts on dealing with only the most costly problems first.

CASE QUESTIONS

1. Using the Pareto principle on the frequency of occurrence, in what order should these problems be structured for solution effort? Which are the most trivial, and which are the most important?
2. How can SPC take the cost of these problems into consideration when dealing with their resolution?
3. What is the cost-weighted frequency ranking for these problems? Which are the most trivial, and which are the most important? What assumptions are you making when you use these values in the ranking? Explain.
4. How do these rankings help implement TQC principles in this operation? Explain.

SUPPLEMENT 12-1
Acceptance Sampling Methods

Acceptance sampling is a screening process that involves sampling items such as incoming goods, work-in-process, and finished goods. Acceptance sampling can be used in lot or batch operations in both manufacturing and service operations where time can be used to define lot or batch production (that is, a day's production). It can also be applied to service industry situations in which quality can be converted to a mathematical measurement. The objective of acceptance sampling is to screen the quality of goods that are received, produced, and sold to ensure that they are of acceptable quality. In acceptance sampling, we take samples. If a sample of goods meets quality expectations, we accept the lot. If the sampled goods do not meet quality criteria expectations, we reject the lot or rework the nonconformities.

Sampling is usually set at less than 100 percent of a lot. It is important that a sampling plan be devised to select samples from a lot that will be representative of the quality of the entire lot. Let us define a lot of goods, such as a production run of a product, by N. In a repetitive operation, N can be defined as the number of units produced in a fixed period of production time. In acceptance sampling, we must determine the fraction of N or the sample size n.

Acceptance sampling also requires a cut-off or reject value that can be used to determine if a lot is to be rejected. This cut-off number of products, which we will let be more than c (the maximum acceptable number of defective units) out of n, will cause us to reject the entire lot N because of poor quality. This requires an assumption that the sample from the lot is representative in quality of the entire lot quality. To summarize, in acceptance sampling we must do the following:

1. *Determine a sampling plan system* (that is, a procedure for taking a sample) that will help ensure that n and c will be validly used for the particular business system's application.
2. *Determine an* n that is representative of N.
3. *Determine a* c that is representative of a desired confidence we wish to have in rejecting lots that are of poor quality.

SAMPLING PLAN SYSTEMS

Several sampling plan systems can be used to validly apply a given n and c including single sampling, double sampling, and sequential sampling.

A **single-sampling plan** requires only single n and c values for the plan. In single sampling, we randomly select n items from a lot to see if the lot is of acceptable quality. Once we have determined n and c (the procedure for which will be shown soon), the single-sampling plan usually consists of the following steps:

1. *Randomly select* n *items from a lot.* We could use a random number table to select the number of n items in the lot to choose. This could be done by

assigning all N items a number according to their order in the lot and using the random numbers to locate the n numbers desired. We could also accomplish a random sample by just reaching in randomly and grabbing a unit from an open box. It is important to use a random process to select the item, otherwise a representative sample of quality may not be achieved.

2. *Inspect the* n *items and determine how many do not pass the desired quality criteria tests.* This is simply the process of adding up the number of items that do not pass the quality screening checks.
3. *Decide on sample acceptance.* If the number of items found in Step 2 is more than c, we reject the lot. If the number of items is equal to or less than c, we accept the lot. If we accept the lot, we either return the defective items to the vendor for credit or rework the items ourselves.

We can use this simple sampling plan for inspecting work-in-process as well as finished goods. In both cases, we must designate what constitutes a lot. It can be a lot-size, production run, or in the case of repetitive operations, the number of units in a day's work. This gives us an N, and with n and c values we are able to reject poor quality items before they are completed or before they leave the factory.

The single-sampling plan inspection procedure can be applied to sampling with replacement (that is, the items inspected are checked and then returned to the sample) or without replacement. An example of sampling without replacement are destructive tests in which sampled items are scrapped. Destructive tests can be very expensive, particularly if the sampling is conducted on work-in-process or finished products in which an investment in work force and materials has already been committed.

QUESTION: Suppose that we have $N = 2{,}000$, $n_1 = 40$, $c_1 = 6$, $n_2 = 40$, and $c_2 = 4$ and we find on the first sample from the lot that we have seven defective items and on the second sample only three defective items. Do we accept the lot?

ANSWER: Yes. Seven defective items is greater than the cut-off values of c_1, so the result of the first sample is inconclusive. The acceptance of the lot now rests on the defectives that will be found on the second sampling and its comparison with c_2. Because the number of defective items is less than c_2, we accept the lot.

A **double-sampling plan,** as the name implies, uses a second sampling if the results of the first sample are inconclusive. In this sampling plan, we have two *n*s: n_1 and n_2, as well as c_1 and c_2 on which they are based. In this sampling procedure, the value of c_1 must be more than c_2. This is often the case because the second sample is only taken if questionable results are found on the first sample. The criteria for the second sample should rightfully be "tougher" because of the suspect quality found in the first sample. Under this plan, we take a sample from N of n_1 and, if the defective items are less than c_1, the lot is accepted. If the number of defective items is greater than c_1, we can take a second sample of n_2 and compare it with c_2. If the number of defective items is less than c_2, the lot is accepted; if more than c_2, the lot is rejected.

Another type of sampling plan is called sequential sampling. In a **sequential-sampling plan** we again select some n number of items from a sequential delivery system such as an assembly line in a repetitive operation. For example, we might sample every ith unit (that is, every fifth or twelfth unit) from a repetitive manufacturing system. Once we have the sample n, we compare it with c to determine if the system is meeting quality expectations. This type of system is suited more to repetitive manufacturing systems than are the single and double systems, both of which favor the job and job-lot operations.

DETERMINANTS OF SAMPLE SIZE *n* AND DEFECT CUT-OFF VALUES *c*

Regardless of the sampling plan chosen, we need to determine the values of n and c. To provide these values, a number of statistically based tables of n and c values have been developed. The Military Standard 105D and the Dodge-Romig Inspection Tables are two examples of these tabled values that we discuss in this supplement. Both of these commonly used tables are based on a probability distribution of an operations management system's likelihood of generating defects. This probability distribution is called an **operating characteristic (OC) curve.** The OC curve is used to describe how well the acceptance sampling plan discriminates between good lots and bad lots. A good lot becomes a bad lot when the defective items found in the lot exceed a predefined acceptable quality level. The OC curve is a probability distribution that is a function of sample size n and the acceptance quality level c, expressed as a percentage of items in a lot of incoming goods.

If we use the TQC principle of 100 percent inspection, all incoming goods will be inspected during the production process. This type of acceptance sampling plan perfectly discriminates between acceptable good lots and unacceptable bad lots. For example, Exhibit 12S-1 presents the relationship between the probability of accepting a lot and the percent defective in a lot where $c = 2$. Between inspections by the purchasers (consumers) and the vendors (the producers), no defects are permitted. When defective items are found through inspection, they are usually returned to the vendor for credit or reworked by the consumer and charged to the vendor. As we can see in the curve in Exhibit 12S-1, lots equal to or less than the 2 percent acceptance level are rejected and lots more than c are rejected.

When less than 100 percent of a lot is sampled, it is possible that we might make an error in the lot acceptance decision because of sampling. The error might be caused by the sampling system, the size of the acceptance level c, or the sample size. Regardless of the source of the error, we are less able to discriminate between good and bad lots. Note how the curve flattens (becomes less discriminating) in Exhibit 12S-2 as the value

EXHIBIT 12S-1 PROBABILITY DISTRIBUTION WITH 100 PERCENT INSPECTION AND A 2 PERCENT c

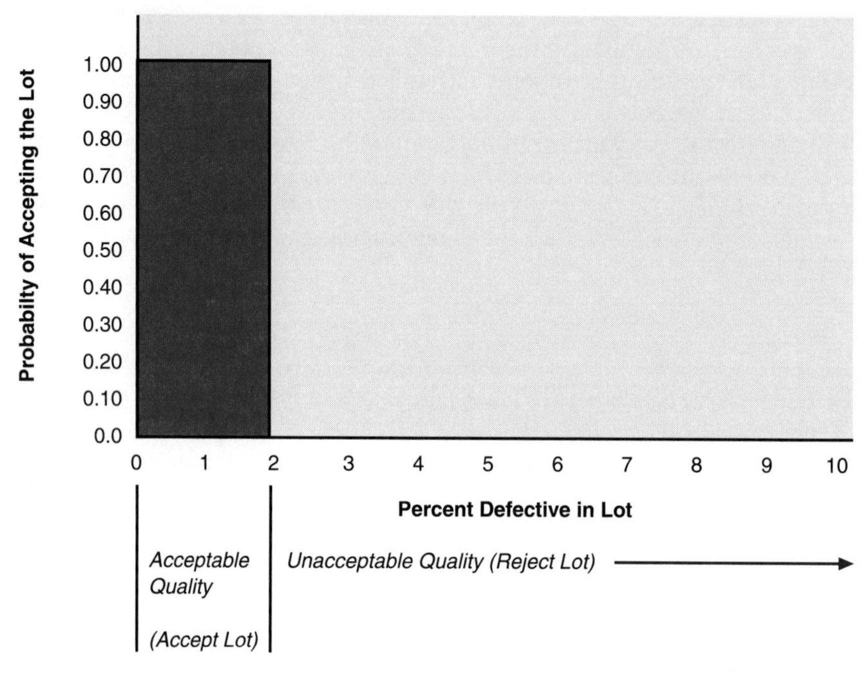

of c increases. Similarly, the curve flattens in Exhibit 12S-3 as the sample size decreases, despite the fact that the percentage of items in the lot that determines its quality stays constant at 5 percent. Indeed, these sampling results actually support the TQC notion that perfect quality ($c = 0$) and a 100 percent inspection are the best strategy for a quality assurance program.

PRODUCER'S AND CONSUMER'S RISK

A producer (the vendor) sells incoming items to a consumer (the purchaser). When acceptance sampling is used, there is risk to both parties in the decision-making process. Called the **producer's risk, type I error,** or **α** (alpha; from statistical hypothesis testing) the vendor wants to avoid the needless costs associated with rejecting a lot that is actually good. These costs include the reworking of the few items in the lot and the costs for a new lot to be shipped to the customer. The consumer wants to avoid accepting a bad lot (called the **consumer's risk, type II error,** or **β** [beta]) and incurring the negative impact on product quality and substantial rework effort that the purchaser accepted with the lot's acceptance. The summary of the outcomes of decision

EXHIBIT 12S-2 OPERATING CHARACTERISTIC CURVES FOR TWO DIFFERENT QUALITY ACCEPTANCE LEVELS ($c = 1$ AND $c = 5$) OF A GIVEN SAMPLE SIZE ($n = 100$)

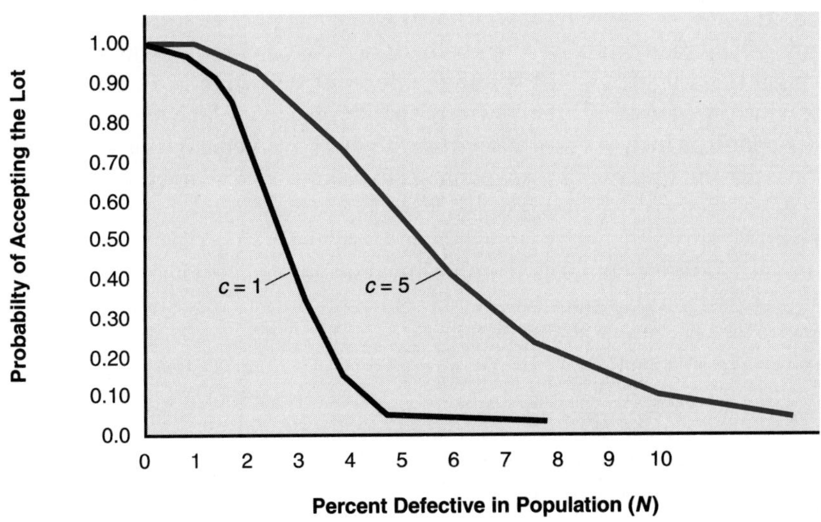

EXHIBIT 12S-3 OPERATING CHARACTERISTIC CURVES FOR TWO DIFFERENT SAMPLE SIZE LEVELS ($n = 20$ AND $n = 100$) OF A GIVEN QUALITY ACCEPTANCE PERCENTAGE (5%)

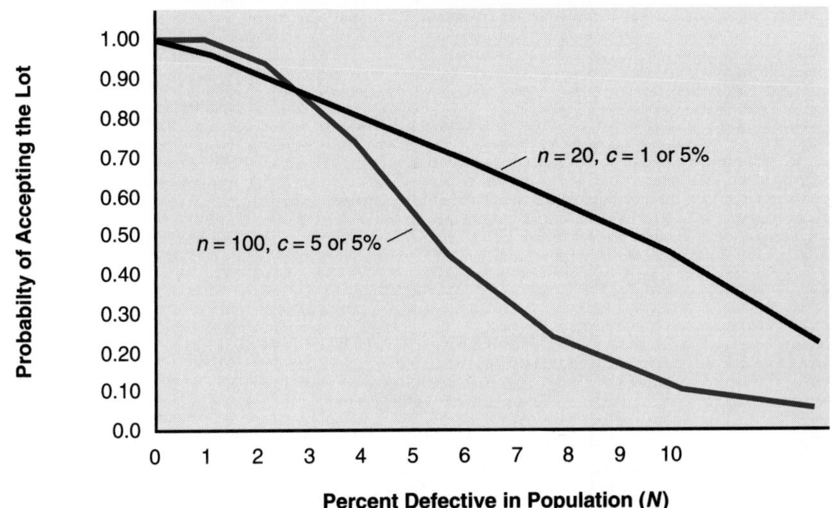

Note: The acceptance percentage on either OC curve is 5 percent because 5 of 100 is equivalent to 1 of 20 for acceptance criteria in an incoming lot of goods.

making in the risk decision environment created by sampling is presented in Exhibit 12S-4.

The α and β errors are directly related to two characteristics of the OC curve: acceptable quality level and lot tolerance percent defective. The **acceptable quality level (*AQL*)** is the quality level at which we consider a lot as being good and acceptable. If we are willing to accept a lot even with 10 defective items of 1,000, then the *AQL* is 1 percent (10/1,000). The **lot tolerance percent defective (*LTPD*)** is the quality level at which we consider that a lot is bad and if exceeded will be rejected. If we agree to reject a lot in which we find more than 50 defective items out of 1,000, then the *LTPD* is 5 percent (50/1,000). As we can see in Exhibit 12S-5, the relationship of *AQL* and *LTPD* to their corresponding α and β errors permits the risk factor's derivation for any given OC curve.

The OC curve is a cumulative probability distribution based either on the binomial or Poisson probability distribution. In a binomial probability distribution, three parameters are used to determine the probabilities: n = the number of trials, r = the number of successes out of n trials, and p = the probability of a success on any trial. In applying the binomial probability distribution to OC curves, the value of n is n and r is c. The value of p is the fraction (or percentage) defective in the lot. The binomial probability distribution for determining the probability of finding c defectives [that is, $P(c)$] in a lot is given by the function shown on the next page.

EXHIBIT 12S-4 DECISION-MAKING OUTCOMES BASED ON ACCEPTANCE SAMPLING

		DECISION BASED ON SAMPLING	
		Lot is Accepted	**Lot is Not Accepted**
ACTUAL LOT CONDITION	**A Good Lot**	Desirable impact on quality. Will maintain or improve quality of incoming goods from desired AQL.	A Type I or α error, called producer's risk. Can result in needless transportation costs in returning good quality items and unnecessary rework costs for supplier (producer).
	A Bad Lot	A Type II or β error, called consumer's risk. Can result in a loss of quality and/or necessary rework costs for purchaser (consumer).	Desirable impact on quality. Will keep quality from dropping because of poor incoming goods.

EXHIBIT 12S-5 RELATIONSHIP OF OC CURVE, *AQL*, *LTPD*, α, AND β

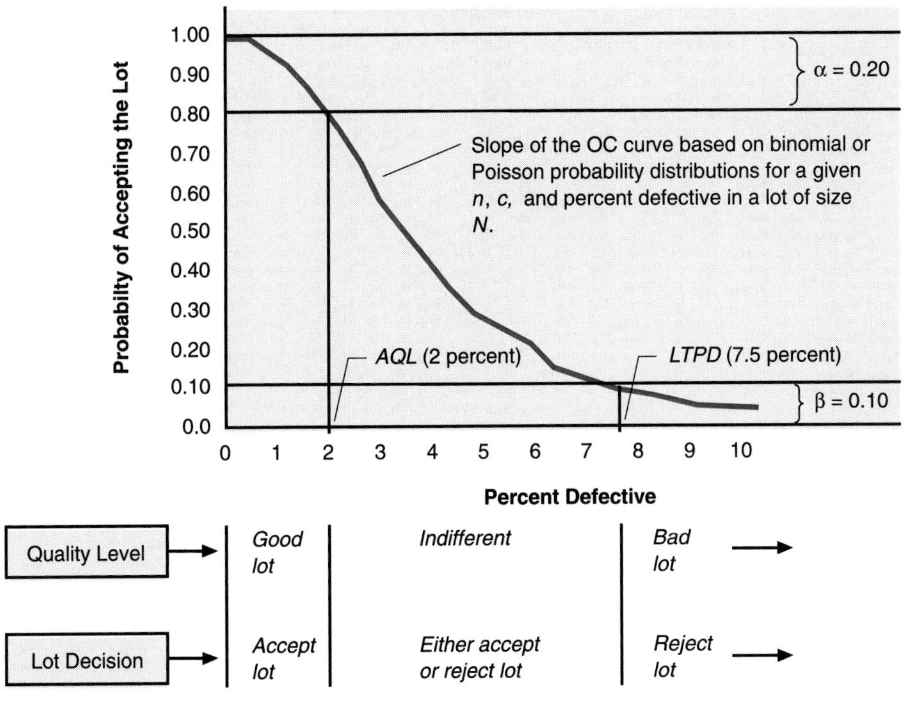

$$P(c) = \frac{n!}{c!(n - c)!}(p)^c(1 - p)^{n-c}$$

When p is less than 0.10, the Poisson probability distribution can be used to approximate the probability of finding c defectives. The Poisson probability distribution is as follows:

$$P(c) = \frac{(np)^c}{c!}(e^{-np})$$

where e = a constant value of 2.71828. To illustrate how the Poisson probability distribution can be used to develop an OC curve, let's examine the following example. Given a sample size of $n = 100$ and a quality acceptance level of $c = 3$, what is the resulting OC curve values for percent defectives of 1, 2, 3, 4, 5, 6, 7, 8, 9, and 10? To use the cumulative Poisson probability distribution in Appendix K, the value of λ (lambda) must be determined by multiplying n by the fraction (or percentage) defective, p. In Exhibit 12S-6, the values of λ are presented as well as the probability of acceptance values that make up the OC curve. The probability of acceptance values are plotted on the OC curve in Exhibit 12S-7. Once the OC curve is developed, the type I and type

EXHIBIT 12S-6 OC CURVE PROBABILITY OF ACCEPTANCE VALUES

Selected Percent Defective Values	*Mean of Poisson Distribution* (np = λ)	*Probability of Acceptance**
.01	100(0.1) = 1	.981
.02	100(.02) = 2	.857
.03	100(.03) = 3	.647
.04	100(.04) = 4	.433
.05	100(.05) = 5	.265
.06	100(.06) = 6	.151
.07	100(.07) = 7	.082
.08	100(.08) = 8	.042
.09	100(.09) = 9	.021
.10	100(.10) = 10	.010

* Values from Appendix K for given λs and $c = 3$.

II error risk values can be determined for any given *AQL* or *LTPD*. As we can see in Exhibit 12S-7 (and from the calculations in Exhibit 12S-6), the probability of a type II error is 0.265. This value is the probability of accepting a bad lot. To find the type I error of not accepting a good lot, the probability of accepting the lot is subtracted from 1 (because this is a cumulative distribution). The resulting type I error generates a probability estimate of 0.143. Its interpretation is that there is a 14.3 percent chance of rejecting a good lot with a sample plan of $N = 100$ and $c = 3$.

AVERAGE OUTGOING QUALITY (*AOQ*)

In many sampling plans, an entire lot is inspected and defective items are replaced or reworked when a lot is rejected. This approach to replacement improves the average outgoing quality in terms of percent defective. For sampling plans that use this approach, we determine the **average outgoing quality (*AOQ*)** as follows:

$$AOQ = \frac{(P_d)(P_a)(N - n)}{N}$$

where

P_d = actual or true percent defective of lot
P_a = probability of accepting the lot (from OC curve)
N = lot-size
n = sample size

EXHIBIT 12S-7 CONSTRUCTION OF OC CURVE AND ESTIMATION OF α AND β ERROR

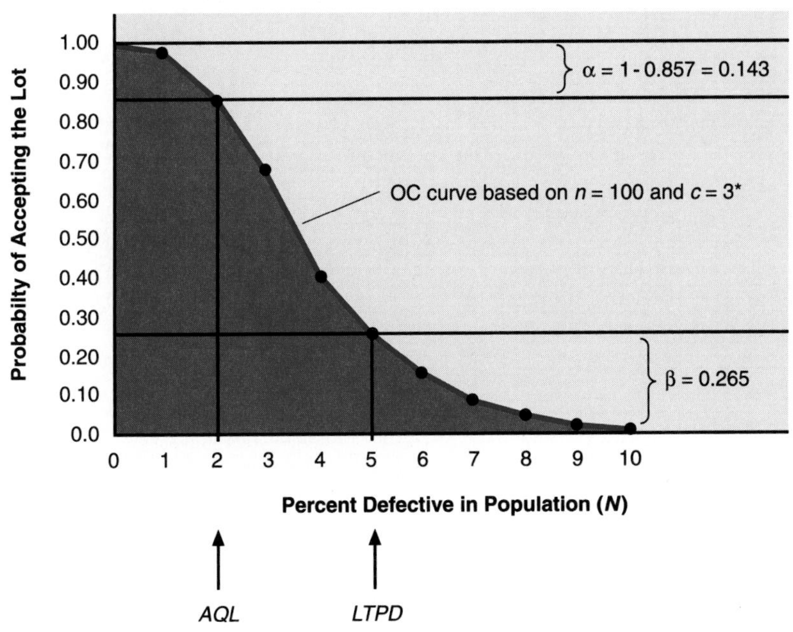

* Points on OC curve from probability of acceptance values in Exhibit 12S-6.

QUESTION: Suppose that the actual percent defective in a lot of $N = 1{,}000$ is 0.05 and the OC curve values from Exhibit 12S-6 apply for a sampling plan of $n = 100$ and $c = 3$. What is the *AOQ* for this problem?

ANSWER: Plugging the values into the formula just given, we have

$$AOQ = \frac{(0.05)(0.265)(1{,}000 - 100)}{1{,}000}$$
$$= 0.012$$

The interpretation of the *AOQ* is that the acceptance sampling plan changes the quality of the lots in percentage defective from 0.05 to 0.12. The acceptance sampling with replacement (referred to as *rectification* because it rectified the defective items in the lot) significantly increases the quality of the inspected lots.

Improvements in lot quality as reflected by the *AOQ* do have limits. The limit on quality improvement is called the average outgoing quality limit (*AOQL*). The **average**

outgoing quality limit (*AOQL*) is an expected value based on long-term performance of the sampling plan. The *AOQL* can be determined by computing *AOQ* values for selected P_d (or percent defectives) about the value of c and selecting the maximum *AOQ* value.

QUESTION: What is the *AOQL* for the sampling plan in which $N = 1{,}000$, $n = 100$, and $c = 3$?

ANSWER: The calculations of *AOQ* values for select percent defectives are presented in Exhibit 12S-8, and plotted on a graph in Exhibit 12S-9. As we can see in Exhibit 12S-9, the resulting *AOQL* is the maximum value of 0.017 or 1.7 percent. The interpretation of the *AOQL* is that 98.3 percent (1 − 0.017) of the outgoing product is of good quality when we have an incoming quality sampling plan in which $c = 3$.

Both the OC curve and the *AOQL* curve are applied in sample plan tables used in acceptance sampling. The OC curve is used in the Military Standard table and the *AOQL* curve is used in the Dodge-Romig tables.

MILITARY STANDARD 105D (ANSI/ASQC Z1.4)

Standardized or tabled sampling procedures based on the OC curve originated with the U.S. military and, in an earlier version, was used during the World War II era. The

EXHIBIT 12S-8 *AOQ* CURVE CALCULATIONS

P_d	×	P_a*	×	(N − n)/N†	=	AOQ
.01		.981		.90		.009
.02		.857		.90		.015
.03		.647		.90		.017
.04		.433		.90		.016
.05		.265		.90		.012
.06		.151		.90		.008
.07		.082		.90		.005
.08		.042		.90		.003
.09		.021		.90		.002
.10		.010		.90		.001

* Probability of acceptance values from Exhibit 12S-6.
† $(N - n)/N = (1{,}000 - 100)/1{,}000 = 0.90$.

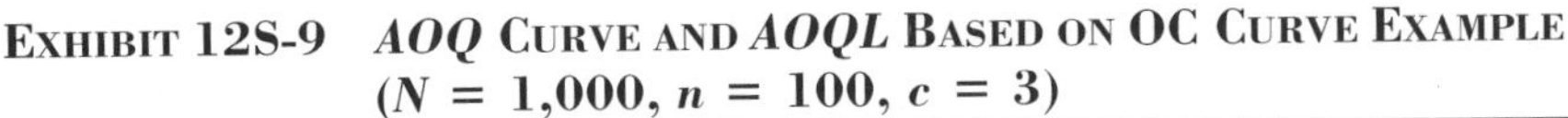

EXHIBIT 12S-9 ***AOQ* CURVE AND *AOQL* BASED ON OC CURVE EXAMPLE (N = 1,000, n = 100, c = 3)**

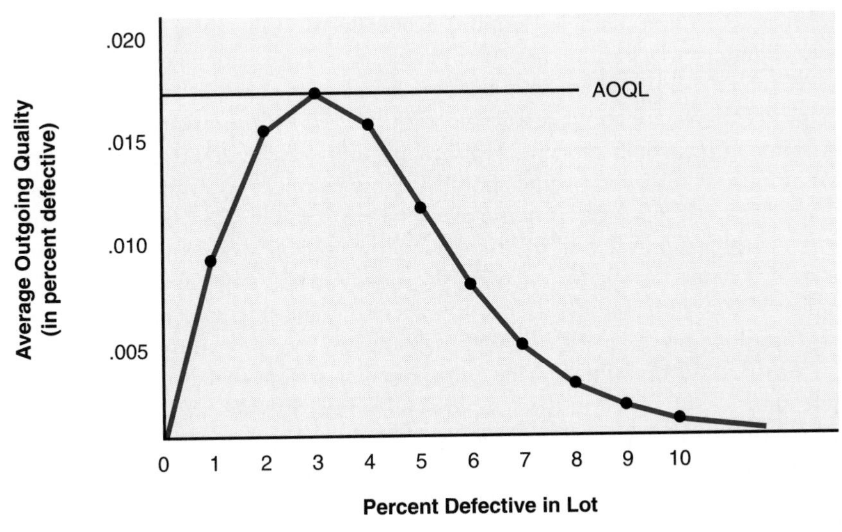

Military Standard (MIL STD) 105D sampling plan (circa 1963) is one of the most widely used acceptance sampling procedures in the world today. The civilian version of this military system is referred to as **ANSI/ASQC Z1.4.** The basic procedure and use of both sampling systems are the same.

This MIL STD 105D approach provides for three different types of sampling plans: single sampling, double sampling, and multiple sampling (an extension of double sampling). For each of these types of sampling plans modifying provisions are made for a normal inspection, tightened inspection, or reduced inspection. A **normal inspection** is used to start the inspection process and for the first-time use of new vendors. If the quality of materials from a vendor deteriorates, a **tightened inspection** approach is used with the vendor. The acceptance requirements for lots under a tightened inspection system are more stringent than under a normal inspection system. If a vendor has consistently provided high-quality materials, a **reduced inspection** system can be used. The sampling requirements and size under a reduced inspection system are less than under normal inspection (that is, a reduced inspection helps reduce the cost of the inspection).

In Exhibit 12S-10, we present the first of two MIL STD 105D tables. This table is used to relate lot-size with the type of inspection that should be performed. The Special Inspection Levels are used when very small sample sizes are desired, such as in the case of destructive tests on very expensive equipment (for example, launching a million-dollar missile to see if it will work). The most commonly used is General Inspection Level II. From Exhibit 12S-10, we can see the intersections of the inspection level columns and the lot-size rows are code letters. These letters are used in conjunction with a second MIL STD 105D table, which is presented in Exhibit 12S-11. There are separate tables for the three different types of inspection plans and separate tables for each type of sampling plan (single, double, and multiple). Exhibit 12S-11 is for a normal inspection system using a single-sampling plan. To use this table, we must have the sample code letter from Exhibit 12S-10 and a desired *AQL* value. To illustrate how we use the MIL STD 105D system to determine *n* and *c*, let's look at an example.

Suppose that we are about to receive a lot of 2,500 component parts from a new vendor. Our *AQL* is 0.65 percent. How many units of the 2,500 should we sample (what should *n* be) and what value should we use as rejection criteria (what should *c* be)? With a lot of 2,500, we first use the table in Exhibit 12S-10 to determine the sample size code letter. We will use the normal inspection level of General Inspection Level II. This results in a letter code K. We now use the table in Exhibit 12S-11 to determine the sample size *n* of 125 from the second column in the table. Following the same row until we reach an *AQL* of 0.65 percent, we can see that the cut-off value for *c* is 2. The values in the table can be interpreted as stating that if only two or fewer defective items are observed in the sample of 125, the lot is accepted. If three or more defective items are observed, the lot is rejected.

Other than some terminology and rules for taking multiple samples, the MIL STD 105D and the ANSI/ASQC Z1.4 are basically the same. All of the tables, numbers, and procedures used in the MIL STD 105D are used in the ANSI/ASQC Z1.4 sampling procedure.

EXHIBIT 12S-10 MIL STD 105D SAMPLE SIZE CODE LETTERS

Lot or Batch Size	Special Inspection Levels				General Inspection Levels		
	S-1	*S-2*	*S-3*	*S-4*	*I*	*II*	*III*
2 to 8	A	A	A	A	A	A	B
9 to 15	A	A	A	A	A	B	C
16 to 25	A	A	B	B	B	C	D
26 to 50	A	B	B	C	C	D	E
51 to 90	B	B	C	C	C	E	F
91 to 150	B	B	C	D	D	F	G
151 to 280	B	C	D	E	E	G	H
281 to 500	B	C	D	E	F	H	J
501 to 1,200	C	C	E	F	G	J	K
1,201 to 3,200	C	D	E	G	H	K	L
3,201 to 10,000	C	D	F	G	J	L	M
10,001 to 35,000	C	D	F	H	K	M	N
35,001 to 150,000	D	E	G	J	L	N	P
150,001 to 500,000	D	E	G	J	M	P	Q
500,001 and more	D	E	H	K	N	Q	R

Source: From *Military Standard Sampling Procedures and Tables for Inspection by Attributes (MIL STD 105D)* (Washington, D.C.: U.S. Government Printing Office, 1963).

EXHIBIT 12S-11 MIL STD 105D NORMAL INSPECTION—SINGLE-SAMPLING PLAN TABLE

Sample size code letter	Sample size	Acceptable Quality Levels (normal inspection)																									
		0.010	0.015	0.025	0.040	0.065	0.10	0.15	0.25	0.40	0.65	1.0	1.5	2.5	4.0	6.5	10	15	25	40	65	100	150	250	400	650	1000
		Ac Re	Ac Re	Ac Re	Ac Re	Ac Re	Ac Re	Ac Re	Ac Re	Ac Re	Ac Re	Ac Re	Ac Re	Ac Re	Ac Re	Ac Re	Ac Re	Ac Re	Ac Re	Ac Re	Ac Re	Ac Re	Ac Re	Ac Re	Ac Re	Ac Re	Ac Re
A	2	↓	↓	↓	↓	↓	↓	↓	↓	↓	↓	↓	↓	↓	↓	0 1	↓	↓	1 2	2 3	3 4	5 6	7 8	10 11	14 15	21 22	30 31
B	3	↓	↓	↓	↓	↓	↓	↓	↓	↓	↓	↓	↓	↓	0 1	↑	↓	1 2	2 3	3 4	5 6	7 8	9 10	14 15	21 22	30 31	44 45
C	5	↓	↓	↓	↓	↓	↓	↓	↓	↓	↓	↓	↓	0 1	↑	↓	1 2	2 3	3 4	5 6	7 8	10 11	14 15	21 22	30 31	44 45	↑
D	8	↓	↓	↓	↓	↓	↓	↓	↓	↓	↓	↓	0 1	↑	↓	1 2	2 3	3 4	5 6	7 8	10 11	14 15	21 22	30 31	44 45	↑	↑
E	13	↓	↓	↓	↓	↓	↓	↓	↓	↓	↓	0 1	↑	↓	1 2	2 3	3 4	5 6	7 8	10 11	14 15	21 22	30 31	44 45	↑	↑	↑
F	20	↓	↓	↓	↓	↓	↓	↓	↓	↓	0 1	↑	↓	1 2	2 3	3 4	5 6	7 8	10 11	14 15	21 22	↑	↑	↑	↑	↑	↑
G	32	↓	↓	↓	↓	↓	↓	↓	↓	0 1	↑	↓	1 2	2 3	3 4	5 6	7 8	10 11	14 15	21 22	↑	↑	↑	↑	↑	↑	↑
H	50	↓	↓	↓	↓	↓	↓	↓	0 1	↑	↓	1 2	2 3	3 4	5 6	7 8	10 11	14 15	21 22	↑	↑	↑	↑	↑	↑	↑	↑
J	80	↓	↓	↓	↓	↓	↓	0 1	↑	↓	1 2	2 3	3 4	5 6	7 8	10 11	14 15	21 22	↑	↑	↑	↑	↑	↑	↑	↑	↑
K	125	↓	↓	↓	↓	↓	0 1	↑	↓	1 2	2 3	3 4	5 6	7 8	10 11	14 15	21 22	↑	↑	↑	↑	↑	↑	↑	↑	↑	↑
L	200	↓	↓	↓	↓	0 1	↑	↓	1 2	2 3	3 4	5 6	7 8	10 11	14 15	21 22	↑	↑	↑	↑	↑	↑	↑	↑	↑	↑	↑
M	315	↓	↓	↓	0 1	↑	↓	1 2	2 3	3 4	5 6	7 8	10 11	14 15	21 22	↑	↑	↑	↑	↑	↑	↑	↑	↑	↑	↑	↑
N	500	↓	↓	0 1	↑	↓	1 2	2 3	3 4	5 6	7 8	9 10	14 15	21 22	↑	↑	↑	↑	↑	↑	↑	↑	↑	↑	↑	↑	↑
P	800	↓	0 1	↑	↓	1 2	2 3	3 4	5 6	7 8	10 11	14 15	21 22	↑	↑	↑	↑	↑	↑	↑	↑	↑	↑	↑	↑	↑	↑
Q	1250	0 1	↑	↓	1 2	2 3	3 4	5 6	7 8	10 11	14 15	21 22	↑	↑	↑	↑	↑	↑	↑	↑	↑	↑	↑	↑	↑	↑	↑
R	2000	↑	↑	1 2	2 3	3 4	5 6	7 8	10 11	14 15	21 22	↑	↑	↑	↑	↑	↑	↑	↑	↑	↑	↑	↑	↑	↑	↑	↑

↓ = Use first sampling plan below arrow. If sample size equals, or exceeds, lot or batch size, do 100 percent inspection.
↑ = Use first sampling plan above arrow.
Ac = Acceptance number.
Re = Rejection number.

Source: From *Military Standard Sampling Procedures and Tables for Inspection by Attributes (MIL STD 105D)* (Washington, D.C.: U.S. Government Printing Office, 1963).

DODGE-ROMIG SAMPLING PLAN

In the 1920s, H. F. Dodge and H. G. Romig developed some sampling inspection tables for lot inspection by attributes (or inspections that judge quality on a defective or nondefective basis). There are two types of tables: *AOQL* and *LTPD*. The *AOQL* tables are designed to minimize average total inspection subject to a specific *AOQL*. The *LTPD* tables are designed to minimize average total inspection subject to a specific *LTPD*. We refer to these tables in the plural because individual tables have been prepared for each type of sampling plan (single or double sampling) and for approaching quality from the *AOQL* producer's side or *LTPD* consumer's side minimizing risk in sampling. Because these tables are similar in appearance and use to the MIL STD 105D tables, they will not be presented.

SUPPLEMENT 12-2
Quality Maintenance Management (QMM)

The role of maintenance management for many conjures up the idea of the simple management activities required to keep equipment oiled and the floors clean. It has in the past been performed by specialists who are usually skilled mechanics or housekeeping personnel. The roles of maintenance management have and are drastically changing. The TQC approach has introduced changes that have greatly altered who performs the maintenance activities (from the specialists to the workers). Robots, automated handling systems, and advanced monitoring equipment are continually demanding an ever-increasing allocation of management time and money for maintenance. The successful use of these modern operations management approaches and technology is directly related to the successful use of a maintenance management program.

Just as the expanded role of quality control called for a new term—*quality assurance*—to reflect its new role, the increased dependence of product quality on the expanded role of maintenance management has given rise to a new term: *quality maintenance management*. **Quality maintenance management (QMM)** refers to the study and management of all maintenance activities, including the following:

1. *QMM function* This involves developing maintenance strategies for scheduling service by maintenance personnel.
2. *QMM system function* This involves developing strategies and procedures for improving the OM system's reliability (for example, minimizing a manufacturing system's downtime from maintenance problems).
3. *Asset acquisition for replacement* This involves the use of methods to plan the acquisition of equipment and facilities when old equipment needs to be replaced.

Without personnel to keep equipment running at acceptable levels of performance, variation in products or poor quality can result during their use. Unreliable production processes and manufacturing systems will generate more nonconformities or poor-quality products than reliable systems. Without the planned replacement and acquisition of new equipment and facilities, production systems can become inefficient and generate unacceptable product quality. It is for these reasons that we refer to maintenance management as quality maintenance management or QMM.

THE QMM FUNCTION

The **QMM function** is one of ensuring that the equipment, facilities, and personnel do their jobs at an acceptable level of performance. Most people are familiar with the concept of maintenance because almost everybody has maintained a bicycle or automobile and understands that equipment needs oiling, greasing, cleaning, and occasional repairs. Equipment and facilities owned by an organization also require maintenance.

In most organizations maintenance activities are usually performed by a maintenance department (a QMM department). From an organizational structure standpoint, the maintenance department provides a staff function for the organization. The manager of maintenance usually reports to the general manager of a plant. The range of skills of first-line workers in a maintenance department can be considerable. While many maintenance jobs may require little specialized training, the increased technology of modern equipment requires considerable training and skill requirements.

In the United States, the QMM function has usually been associated with corrective maintenance (CM) and preventive maintenance (PM) strategies. Under a **corrective maintenance strategy,** corrective repairs are scheduled after a machine or piece of equipment breaks down. This type of strategy seeks to minimize the size of a QMM department. This strategy is useful in operations in which the cost of equipment or facility downtime is low. Downtime costs include the cost of idle labor, overtime labor costs that are used to make up for the downtime, and the loss of sales because the machine did not produce the products in the desired time, quantity, or quality. A CM strategy is particularly useful for managing the maintenance of small-scale equipment such as a typewriter where backup equipment might be available. Many service contracts, in which equipment companies agree to provide all necessary maintenance and repairs, are structured on a CM basis.

Preventive maintenance (PM) is a strategy designed to prevent equipment and facility downtime. This is accomplished by a planned schedule of maintenance checks performed on the equipment under this program. By scheduling the routine maintenance of equipment, rather than waiting for the equipment to break down because of the lack of maintenance, the PM strategy is believed to reduced machine downtime by eliminating the major reason why machines break down: poor maintenance.

In firms that have adopted the TQC approach, much of the QMM function is performed by the individual worker, not maintenance department personnel. Some have called this PM approach to maintenance management *operator-centered PM* or *total PM.*[27] Whatever it is called, it is a QMM function in that it tries to ensure that equipment, facilities, and particularly personnel perform the necessary PM to keep the operation generating products of the highest possible quality. The Japanese approach does not eliminate maintenance departments; it changes their role by broadening their responsibilities. The maintenance personnel are still used to perform some PM activities, but only those that require specialized skills.

The routine machine maintenance is performed by the individual workers on their own machines. To ensure the quality of the workers' PM efforts, the maintenance department personnel provide education to the workers on PM and occasionally make routine maintenance audits to see that the workers are performing the PM work correctly. PM is particularly important in JIT systems because of the relationship of the entire system with each workstation and each piece of equipment and the dependency on worker participation. As we mentioned in earlier chapters, maintenance may be relegated to the expected idle times that occur when a JIT system is shut down to resolve inventory or production scheduling problems.

---

[27] R. J. Schonberger, *World Class Manufacturing* (New York: The Free Press, 1986), pp. 68–72.

During periods of high demand, worker-performed PM functions may cease so workers can return to production to meet the demand requirements. The maintenance department steps back in to perform these functions during the high-demand period. By allowing maintenance department personnel to check on the workers' ability to perform PM activities, they are in a unique position to advise supervisory personnel on work load conditions that may be disrupting worker-performed PM activities. This greater responsibility placed on maintenance department personnel not only helps management do a better job but also, through job enlargement, helps motivate the maintenance department personnel to improve their productivity.

THE QMM SYSTEM FUNCTION

The purpose of the **QMM system function** is to keep the entire operations management system operating. Where the QMM function is concerned with the individual parts of the OM system, the QMM system function is concerned with the collective interactions of the entire operation. In OM we refer to this type of collective interaction as **system reliability.** The reliability of a system can be expressed as the probability that the entire system will work correctly to create products of sufficient quality and quantity in an acceptable amount of time.

Just as we use CM and PM to improve the operation of individual pieces of equipment, we also want the entire operations management system that uses the equipment to perform all of its tasks correctly each time the system is activated. Unfortunately, not every workstation, piece of equipment, or person (that is, the **system elements** that make up the OM system) do their jobs correctly at all times. Each time one system element fails to perform correctly, the entire system becomes slightly unreliable. A system that is unreliable does not generate high-quality products and generally will not operate successfully. Our goal in the QMM system function is to make the system as reliable as possible.

Several tactics can be used to enhance system reliability. They include the following:

1. *Perform PM on the system elements.* By improving the reliability of each element in the system, we will be improving the system reliability. Consequently, we would like to improve the mean time between the element failures, if possible. The expression *mean time between failures (MTBF)* is a measure commonly used to express the reliability of an element in a system. If each element in the system has a long MTBF, the system's MTBF will be equally as long.
2. *Improve system element design.* If we can remodel or redesign an element in the system to improve its reliability, we will improve the system's reliability. For example, increasing the size of an inkwell on a printing press might reduce the frequency with which the well needs to be refilled. This redesign might possibly make the ink usage on the print more consistent (the printed copies will not have that "almost out of ink" look) and therefore will be of a higher quality.

3. *Build redundant elements into the system.* Including backup system elements into the design of the system will ensure that the entire system will not go down even if an element or two fails. The backup systems in aircraft and nuclear electric power–generating plants are redundant until they are used. When one element fails in a system with a backup system, the backup system becomes operational. The more critical the elements or the more likely they are to fail, the greater the number of redundant elements that should be built into the system to offset their possible failure.
4. *Maintain a standby system.* Maintaining an entire standby system ensures that the operation will keep on producing even if the primary operations management system fails. This tactic is an elaborate version of redundancy, and it is very costly in the sense that the entire standby system is idle until it is used. Radio and television stations sometimes maintain small standby facilities in the event their primary stations are hit by some disaster such as lightning.
5. *Improve work conditions.* Improving the work environment may improve system reliability. By reducing the work load we lessen the burden on equipment or personnel, thus preventing possible breakdowns. By improving the quality of environments with adequate heating, air conditioning, and cleaner working conditions, workers may not be as exhausted and may therefore perform their jobs more carefully. These environmental changes often result in improved product quality and more reliable output from operating personnel.

MEASURING SYSTEM RELIABILITY

System reliability is a function of two things: the probability that an element in a system will operate successfully and the type of system in which the element operates. One basic type of system is a series system or operation. In a **series operation,** the elements of the system are arranged in a series, one after another. The operation of each element in the series is independent of the others. Take, for example, a mechanized automobile plant assembly line that consists of four robots, each doing a different and unique task. Although any one of the robots can fail to do its job, the successful operation of each robot along the assembly line is independent of each other. In this type of operation, the reliability of the system of robots can be found by the product of the individual probabilities of the robots. That is,

$$R = P(1) \times P(2) \times P(3) \times P(4)$$

where

R = the reliability probability that the entire system will work correctly
$P(1)$ = the probability the first robot will work correctly
$P(2)$ = the probability that the second robot will work correctly, and so on

QUESTION: If the probability that the first robot will work correctly in the example just given is 0.98, the second 0.97, the third 0.99, and the fourth 0.94, what is the system's reliability?

ANSWER: $R = 0.98 \times 0.97 \times 0.99 \times 0.94 = 0.88$ is the system probability of the robots' doing their job correctly on any execution of their job.

EVALUATING ASSET REPLACEMENT PROPOSALS

Several methods can be used to evaluate proposals for the replacement of assets. We will discuss the use of the payback period method and simulation analysis.

The Payback Period Method

One of the simplest ways to determine if an asset is worth acquiring is with a procedure called the payback period method. A **payback period** is the period of time that it takes to retrieve the initial cost of a piece of equipment or facility. Many organizations have standard operating policies (SOPs) on the acceptable length of time to retrieve their initial cost from certain types of equipment. These SOPs are usually based on the type of equipment (for example, light or heavy machinery), expected profitability of the product the machine contributes to, and its technological life span. Some light machinery, such as a typewriter, may have an acceptable life span of five years, whereas heavier equipment, such as a printing press, might have an acceptable life span of ten or twenty years. A company that knows from experience that a printing press will last only twenty years might set a payback period for the initial cost of the equipment at ten years to ensure some profitability in the later years of the press's expected life.

A piece of equipment's payback period is determined using the following ratio:

$$\text{Payback period} = \frac{\text{Cost of the piece of equipment}}{\text{Expected revenue generated by the equipment in one year}}$$

If a piece of equipment costs \$40,000 and we expect that it will generate \$10,000 per year, its payback period is four years (\$40,000 ÷ \$10,000). If the company has an SOP that states that this type of equipment must pay its initial cost back in three years, it would not purchase the equipment.

The payback period method can only indirectly consider machine maintenance variation in cost parameters. One method that permits probabilistic variation in acquisition cost parameters is simulation analysis.

Simulation Analysis

In Chapter 8 we presented the Monte Carlo simulation technique. (Students are encouraged to review that material to understand the application in this section.) We will apply the simulation procedure here to illustrate how it can be used to evaluate an acquisition for replacement problem.

Suppose that a firm uses five automated guided vehicles (AGVs) in its manufacturing system for materials handling. The firm currently leases the AGVs at a substantial cost of $100,000 per unit per year. The firm's management wants to determine if it should replace the leased AGVs by purchasing its own. In examining this problem, the costs of both leasing and purchasing must be evaluated as well as the probabilistic behavior of the life of the AGVs. Research on the life of the AGVs was obtained from the firm based on the leased units. In Exhibit 12S-12 the life duration of an AGV is presented. As we can see, the units lasted no more than thirty-six months. Because the AGV life duration is the critical variable in the lease-purchase decision, its probabilistic behavior will be simulated using the Monte Carlo method. The random number assignment used in simulating the life duration behavior is also presented in Exhibit 12S-12.

The firm decides to use a thirty-six–month planning horizon for comparative purposes because the life of a single AGV does not exceed thirty-six months. To determine the cost of the lease option, the firm examines a contractual agreement between itself and the leasing firm. Based on the leasing cost of five units per year for three years, the total cost would be $1,500,000 (5 units × $100,000 × 3 years). The purchase decision involves several factors. First, the cost of the units are estimated (assumed) at $120,000, adjusted for forecasted price changes and tax advantages that the investment might bring. Maintenance costs are also estimated at $2,000 per six-month period of operation. To determine the total cost of purchasing the equipment and its maintenance and replacement costs, the Monte Carlo method can be used to simulate the total costs. The simulated life duration for the required AGVs is presented in Exhibit 12S-13 and Exhibit 12S-14.

EXHIBIT 12S-12 AGV UNIT LIFE DURATION PROBABILITIES AND RANDOM NUMBER ASSIGNMENT

AGV Life Duration (months)	*Probability Distribution of AGV's Life Duration*	*Accumulative Probability Distribution*	*Random Number Assignment*
6	.05	.05	00–04
12	.20	.25	05–24
18	.25	.20	25–49
24	.35	.85	50–84
30	.10	.95	85–94
36	.05	1.00	95–99
	1.00		

EXHIBIT 12S-13 SIMULATED COSTS FOR PURCHASE DECISION

Simulation Number	*Random Number**	*Resulting AGV Life Duration*	*AGV Letter Designation*	*Cost of AGV (000)*	*Maintenance Cost (000)†*	*AGV Life Duration Beyond the 36–Month Planning Horizon*
1	06	12	A	120	4	—
2	91	30	B	120	10	—
3	69	24	C	120	8	—
4	34	18	D	120	6	—
5	50	24	E	120	8	—
6	23	12	A	120	4	—
7	41	18	B	120	2	12
8	27	18	C	120	4	6
9	60	24	D	120	6	6
10	61	24	E	120	4	12
11	39	18	A	120	4	6
				1,320	60	

* Random numbers from Appendix F.
† Maintenance cost is $2,000 per 6-month period during the 36–month planning horizon; simulations 7 to 11 only include maintenance costs up to but not beyond the 36–month planning horizon.

In Exhibit 12S-13 we can see that each of the five AGVs necessary for the operation are given a letter designation of A, B, C, D, or E representing the five-unit requirement. The first five simulations (simulations 1 through 5) resulted in life duration for AGVs from twelve to thirty months. Because all five AGVs did not last the thirty-six months' planning horizon, they all require replacement during this period. To determine the life duration of the five new AGVs, five more simulations were conducted (simulations 6 to 10). For four of the five AGVs (letters B, C, D, and E), the life duration of the replacement units exceeds thirty-six months. This can easily be seen on the Gantt chart in Exhibit 12S-14. We can also see that for AGV A, the life during the replacement still falls short of the thirty-six–month planning horizon. This necessitates the simulation of still another replacement unit (simulation 11).

The total costs for the purchase of the eleven AGVs required during this planning horizon is $1,380,000 ($1,320,000 for the units and a maintenance cost of $60,000). In addition, the AGV life duration of the last five units purchased is expected to provide additional months of service as presented in Exhibit 12S-14. It would appear from this simulation that the least-cost alternative is to purchase, maintain, and replace the units rather than lease them from another company. The simulation also provides us with information on the total number of units that we can expect to purchase over the planning horizon. Such information can be used by the company's finance staff to plan financial needs during the planning horizon and possibly help negotiate a quantity discount with the AGV manufacturer.

EXHIBIT 12S-14 GANTT CHART OF SIMULATED AGV LIFE DURATION

Simulated AGV Life Duration in Years*

AGV Letter Designation	1	2	3	4
A	(1)	(6)	(11)	
B	(2)		(7)	
C	(3)		(8)	
D	(4)		(9)	
E	(5)		(10)	

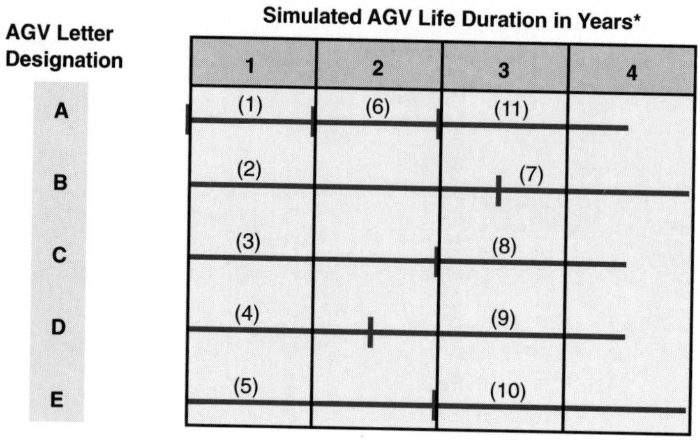

* The number in parentheses is the simulation number from Exhibit 12S-13.

CHAPTER OUTLINE

13

Facility Location Analysis and Layout Design

CHAPTER OBJECTIVES

The material in this chapter should prepare you to do the following:

1. Explain why facility location analysis and layout design are necessary.
2. Describe why and how we should use facility location analysis.
3. Analyze what factors are important in selecting a country in which to locate a new production facility.
4. Determine what factors are important in selecting a region within a country in which to locate a new production facility.
5. Explain what factors are important in selecting a site on which to place a new production facility.
6. Explain how the four facility layout designs differ from each other.
7. Describe how a cellular layout improves production flexibility.
8. Illustrate how to use the distance-minimizing layout procedure in designing a plant layout.
9. Illustrate the line balancing procedure to allocate workcenters along an assembly line.
10. Illustrate how to use the transportation method in facility location analysis.

F**acility location analysis** is a decision-making process that seeks to answer this question: Where in the world should we locate our plant or service facility? Have you ever wondered why Japanese automobile manufacturers build plants in the United States and why U.S. automobile manufacturers build plants in Canada? Why do U.S. automobile manufacturers operate most of their plants in a select few centrally located states in the United States? Why do service facilities such as gas stations tend to locate their operations on corners of street intersections and not in the middle of a block? Facility location analysis gives us the answers to these types of questions.

S

Most manufacturing and service businesses carefully plan where they will locate a plant or service facility because location can seriously affect the success of an operation. For example, suppose that a nationwide commercial trucking business wants to locate a truck terminal. Because nationwide commercial trucking businesses are so dependent on interstate highways, they must locate truck terminals along or as close to highways as possible. Every mile that a truck terminal is located away from an interstate highway represents thousands of wasted dollars in vehicle maintenance and gasoline sales for the entire operation of the terminal.

S

Facility location analysis can be viewed as an elimination process that starts with the world and reduces all possible facility locations to one specific property or site. A facility location analysis requires that hundreds of location criteria be considered; these analyses can take many hundreds of hours of planning time. Facility location analysis is one of the most important and time-consuming design activities that operations managers face. In this chapter we will discuss the process of facility location analysis and present methods used in the analysis.

Once a facility location is determined, either a new building is constructed or an old building is renovated to fit production operations requirements. Regardless of whether the building is new or old, the internal layout of the service facility or manufacturing plant must be designed. This layout design activity involves placing the floor layout (walls, hallways, doors) for the departments that will make up the facility, determining the layout of equipment used in the operation, and establishing workcenters for employee work activities. We refer to the structuring of the internal operation of a facility as **facility layout design.** Like facility location analysis, designing a layout for a building requires considering many criteria such as minimizing traveling distance and minimizing the cost of investment in the facilities that make up the operations management system. In this chapter we will discuss several approaches and methods that can be used as aids in facility layout design.

• • •

WHY FACILITY LOCATION ANALYSIS AND LAYOUT DESIGN ARE NECESSARY

S

Businesses fail for many reasons, and some of these reasons are directly related to poor location. A service facility such as a food store or fast-food restaurant must be located where high levels of traffic will bring in customers. A location on a street and particularly street corner with a high traffic level is an essential site selection criteria for successful operation of these types of businesses. For a manufacturing facility, on the other hand, customer traffic may not even be desired. Let's illustrate some of the location objective differences between a service facility and manufacturing plant with an example.

S

Suppose that a baseball bat manufacturer operates one manufacturing plant and has one retail store outlet. The manufacturing plant produces the bats that the retail store sells. The management of the company might want a location for its manufacturing plant that will help the organization achieve the following tactical objectives:

1. Minimize the transportation cost of wood shipments (for the bats) to the plant
2. Minimize the transportation cost of shipping the finished bats to the retail store
3. Obtain sufficent human resources for its operation

The management of the company might also want a location for its retail store that will help it achieve the following operational and tactical objectives:

1. Be convenient to customers
2. Be highly visible to customer traffic
3. Minimize the cost of overhead (for example, rent or cost of location) to keep prices low and ease price competition

In summary, a manufacturing plant's site location criteria are usually manufacturing-related criteria (cost of operations and access to labor), whereas a retail service facility's site location criteria are customer service–related criteria (customer convenience, traffic, and competition). This is generally true in most facility location studies. Indeed, facility location analysis is a necessary process that helps an organization achieve its tactical and operational objectives by optimizing its location decision.

Once a site is selected for a facility, a layout must be designed that will satisfy the production requirements desired of that facility. Some large, nationwide organizations, such as many petroleum retailers, have fixed layout plans for service facilities that can be used regardless of the particular location. Other organizations that use a fixed layout design include fast-food restaurants, branch bank facilities, and convenience stores. Most organizations, however, custom design their facilities around the production needs of that particular facility. Regardless of whether layout is to be fixed or custom designed, layout design will usually involve a substantial long-term investment of time and money.

S

Although modern technology and methodology (some of which, such as flexible manufacturing systems, are discussed in this chapter) permit a changeable or easily modifiable production layout system, many tactical and operational objectives of layout design must be considered in structuring a successful layout. These factors include the following:

1. *Improve labor productivity.* A layout should be convenient for workers to perform their job tasks efficiently.
2. *Minimize materials handling costs.* A layout should be designed to minimize the distance and therefore the cost of traveling or moving materials and personnel from department to department within an organization.

3. *Minimize the cost of facilities and equipment.* A layout should be structured to make use of facility space and equipment at or near full capacity. Maximizing the use of facilities and equipment minimizes the need to invest in additional facilities and equipment.
4. *Improve management supervision and communications.* A layout should be structured to make supervision or coordination of subordinates' work easy for management. Similarly, two-way communication between superiors and subordinates should be enhanced by layout and not encumbered by its design.
5. *Improve worker morale.* A layout should be structured to motivate and thus instill in workers a positive attitude about doing their tasks. Such positive motivation usually results in increased worker productivity. We discuss some approaches to improving morale in working environments in Chapter 14.
6. *Improve worker safety.* A layout should be structured to prevent workers from accidentally injuring themselves. We discuss some of the rules and consequences of worker safety in manufacturing and service facilities in Chapter 14.

In summary, the objectives of a good layout design are to improve the efficiency of the transformation process in an operations management system and to minimize the inputs of labor, equipment, and facilities by maximizing their use through an optimal interface. Layout design is a necessary management function for an efficient and effective OM system.

FACILITY LOCATION

Facility location analysis consists of three steps: selecting a country, selecting a region within a country, and selecting a site within a region. We will describe each of these steps in this section. Before we can begin a facility location analysis, however, we must justify the need for the substantial and sometimes very costly analysis. The justification of a facility location analysis is primarily related to the type of facility location problems the organization is facing. An organization may face three basic types of facility location problems: locating a site for a new facility, relocating a currently used facility, and on occasion discontinuing operations of a facility.

New facility location is justified when long-range forecast of demand exceeds current capacity capabilities. In Chapter 3, we presented several forecasting techniques used to forecast the trend of future sales and unit demand. These techniques, such as regression analysis, can be used to clearly depict the linear trend of sales over a long-range planning period.

In Figure 13-1 we can see how the linear sales trend of a company's unit demand increases over time and how the trend can be projected into the future. We can also see that at some point B in the future the company's maximum capacity will be exceeded, causing a capacity shortfall. The company has from point A in time to point B in time to decide on a course of action to make up the capacity shortfall. A company anticipating a longer-term decrease in product sales may choose not to build a new

FIGURE 13-1 IDENTIFYING A COMPANY'S PRODUCTION CAPACITY SHORTFALL

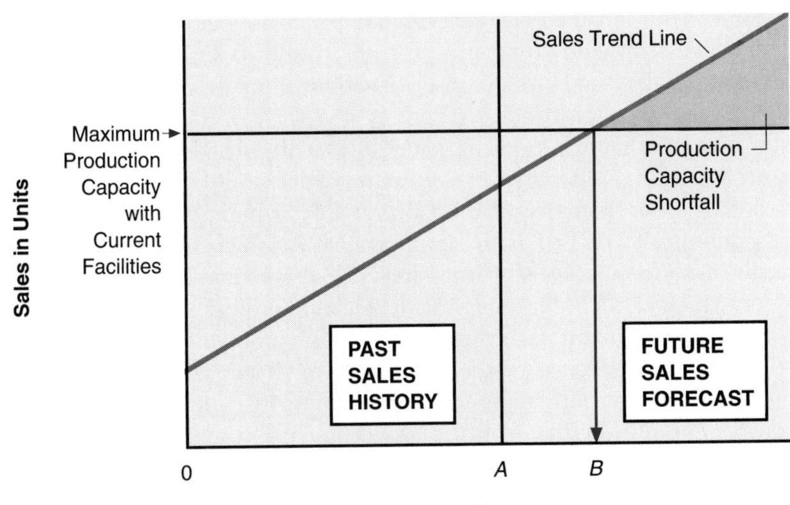

plant but instead use overtime, subcontracting, extra full-time and part-time workers, expansion of current facilities, or extra labor shifts to make up the capacity shortfall. If, on the other hand, product demand is expected to continually increase over the long term, then a more permanent new production facility is usually justified.

When a facility is relocated or discontinued, the justification for the facility location analysis usually centers around changes in the location of markets (both customers and raw material suppliers) and changes in local costs. In the early 1980s through the early 1990s, a large portion of the U.S. labor force moved from the northern and eastern areas of the country to southern and western parts of the country to seek more promising employment opportunities. As they moved, so did much of the consumer markets they represent. Subsequently, both service and manufacturing businesses followed these markets to the southern and western regions of the country. The reasons for this type of move include minimizing transportation and delivery costs for products, avoiding undesirable changes in the external environment such as a significant increase in local property taxes, and avoiding a change in zoning laws that would make profitable operations less possible.

Only after carefully considering the costs and reasons why a company might need a new facility, relocate an old one, or discontinue the operation of a current one, can management make a decision as to whether a facility location analysis should be undertaken. Who makes this type of decision? Some organizations rarely face expansion or relocation decisions and do not have specialists to handle the infrequent facility location analysis. In organizations that do not have a specialized facility location department or personnel, the chief decision makers are the top executive officers of an organization. Some organizations hire consultants to conduct facility location analyses.

Other organizations maintain facility location analysis departments that perform much of the analysis and have the responsibility for making most of the site location decisions. S These organizations include fast-food restaurants such as McDonald's and Burger King as well as retail petroleum companies that are always looking for new facilities (gas stations) to satisfy the rapid changes in the location of markets.

Major facility location problems, such as a regional headquarters for an insurance operation or a petroleum processing plant, are chiefly decided by the top executive officers because of the importance of these types of decisions for the entire organization. Indeed, facility location analysis can be a central determining factor in a corporation's strategic planning efforts. The importance of the facility location analysis of a new plant can directly affect the success of a firm's ability to compete in its industry. Burger King locates near McDonald's not just because the location is ideal but because of its strategic plan to directly compete on factors (price and unique products) other than convenience of location. When we discussed strategic planning in Chapter 4, we found that this type of planning is usually performed by top management. Even in organizations that maintain a facility location department, top management is usually involved in planning general strategies for facility location analysis but in turn leaves the tactical planning to the departmental-level specialists.

QUESTION: What is an example of how facility location analysis is used as a tactic to achieve an operations management strategy?

ANSWER: One OM strategy used to accomplish an organization strategy of world-class manufacturing is a just-in-time (JIT) program. A tactical part of implementing the OM strategy of a JIT program is to have suppliers who can dependably deliver goods "just in time" for their use (discussed in Chapter 6). A tactical approach to improving supplier dependability is having the manufacturer located geographically near the suppliers. This can be accomplished by either requiring the supplier to locate near the manufacturer (as suggested in Chapter 7), or, when the supplier is not movable (for example, a supplier of wood from a forest or ore from a mine), locating the manufacturer close to the supplier. In either case, geographical nearness will improve the dependability of supplier goods because it reduces risks of delays owing to transportation problems. The improved dependability helps the manufacturer implement JIT principles. The use of facility location analysis in this case represents a tactical means of implementing a JIT program strategy.

Country Selection

If the reasons for building a new facility or relocating an old one justify a facility location analysis, an organization usually begins by determining the country in which to locate the facility. Although many small companies may not want to locate their facilities outside of their country of origin, more and more companies are pursuing international competition opportunities. Additionally, the lower cost of operations in countries along their borders are causing companies to consider locating a facility in a foreign country. In 1990, for example, the Mexican government's wage scale for electronics manufacturing employees was $6 (average daily wages). A comparable position in the same type of operation in the United States commands an average daily wage of about $73. The cost of labor, however, may be a minor criterion among the many hundreds of criteria that can be considered in this step of the analysis.

QUESTION: After a plant is justified, does a firm have to begin its facility location analysis with the country selection step, or can it skip this or any other step?

ANSWER: If a firm has a desire to locate in a particular country, it can skip the country selection step. Indeed, a firm can skip any step where an obvious selection presents itself.

Before we begin seriously evaluating individual countries, we rule out any country that obviously does not provide a productive environment for an organization's facilities. For example, some third-world countries are so technologically underdeveloped that they are not able to provide a useful labor pool that can work on high-tech products. After eliminating obviously inappropriate countries, we can begin evaluating the remaining countries for our facility location. In general, there are three major categories of criteria used to evaluate if we should locate a facility in a particular foreign country. These three categories include

1. *Economic criteria* These include objective and subjective evaluations of the country's monetary systems, transportation systems, banking systems, rare materials (those used in the manufacturing or service company's products), industries, and communication systems. We need to make sure that the country selected can support the basic economic structure of the company's operation. If a highway system is required for shipping, we can eliminate countries where highways are not maintained or protected by the government.
2. *Social criteria* These include objective and subjective evaluations of the country's opinions about the manufacturing or service company's product, the country's or government's policies, the possible markets for the company's product within the country, the distribution of wealth and social classes in the country, and how the society feels about promotion and selling efforts required to market the product. If we find that a country does not believe that it is ethically or morally acceptable to produce or market the company's product, we can eliminate this country from further consideration.

3. *Political-legal criteria* These include objective and subjective evaluations about the stability of the country's government, its willingness to encourage the manufacturing or service company's type of business to enter the country, the government's attitude toward the type of products the company plans to manufacture, and legal restrictions or laws that may affect the operation. Most countries outside of the United States require 50 percent or more of the legal ownership of a company to be held by persons or government agencies of that country. This limits control of the foreign operation by the parent company, which may be undesirable for some organizations. If a foreign country's legal system is biased against foreign investors or is very unstable, this country should be eliminated from further analysis.

How do organizations obtain information about the economic, social, and political-legal criteria? One approach that many organizations use in amassing this type of information is to hire experts on the particular countries that are being evaluated. To obtain objective information, an organization might employ research specialists or consultants on the country it is considering. Specialists' methods usually involve researching the objective criteria using the government's secondary sources and publications. To obtain subjective information, panels of experts can be used or surveys can be conducted on the foreign country to obtain current data on attitudes and opinions.

Once the data are collected, they must be evaluated on a comparative basis. Most of the methods for this type of comparative analysis are based on tabular rankings or rating factors.[1] A procedure for using these types of evaluation systems might consist of the following steps:

1. Select the countries to be evaluated by screening those that obviously should not be considered.
2. Select the criteria that are important for the firm's successful operation in a foreign country. The three major categories of economic, social, and political-legal criteria can be broken down into hundreds of different subordinate criteria.
3. Rank each criterion for each country on a scale from 1 to 10, where 1 indicates that the country fully satisfies that criterion for the operation, and a 10 indicates that the criterion is not satisfied at all. If some criteria are more important than others, they can be weighed appropriately.
4. Sum up the ranks for all of the criteria. The country that has the smallest summed ranks represents the most desirable country in which to locate the facility.

This procedure may appear to be very simplistic, but when we consider the necessary research that is required to derive the rankings, it becomes a very involved process. One

[1] See Y. Kugel, "A Decisional Model for the Multinational Firm," *Management International Review,* 13, No. 3 (1973), 34–42; and J. J. Hoffman, G. S. Sirmans, and M. J. Schniederjans, "A Strategic Value Model for International Property Appraisal," *The Journal of Real Estate Appraisal and Economics,* 5, No. 1 (1991), 15–22.

of the more recent approaches to country selection based on these tabular approaches is to incorporate the criteria into mathematical programming models like linear and goal programming.[2]

Region Selection

Because a country can be a very large area in which to select a specific location, we usually divide a country into regions. We then evaluate each of these regions and select the one that best fits the needs of our facility. Even very small countries can be divided into regions. The determination of both the number of regions and the size of each region tends to be based on situational factors including population density, geographical terrain (rivers, mountains), language barriers, distribution of customer markets, and an alignment with a company's sales territories. A general rule used to divide a country into regions is that each region should be homogeneous, offering the same or similar set of advantages and disadvantages for location purposes. This rule does not always apply because regional divisions are often not controlled by the facility planner (such as when a country is divided into two regions by a river or difference in a spoken language). Invariably regions will differ. These differences between regions are what will be used to finally select a specific region in which to locate a facility.

Selecting a specific region can involve a considerable amount of research. Two primary criteria used to select a region are the region's potential to reduce the cost of operations (for example, reduce transportation costs) and its proximity to markets for customer convenience and to facilitate customer service. Again, an organization's overall strategic and tactical planning may affect the analysis. For example, an organization might have a strategic goal of improving customer service and a tactical strategy of establishing a complete distribution system across a country. If one of the regions of the country does not have as many distribution facilities as the others, then the importance of implementing the organization's strategic goal might heavily weigh the selection of that particular region for additional distribution facilities.

Several methods are used to aid in the region selection step of the facility location analysis. Most of the methods center around locating facilities in areas nearest to their customer markets. The transportation method, for example, can be used to determine which region will minimize an organization's transportation costs. (An application of the transportation method used in region selection is presented in Supplement 13-1.)

More frequently, forecasting methods are used to select a region. We saw in Chapter 3 that forecasting methods could be used to develop unit forecasting demand values far into the future. Regional demand also can be forecast. In most industries, sales are generated on a geographical basis. A national organization can easily call up regional sales data from its computer information systems. Just as forecasting methods are used

---

[2] J. Hoffman and M. J. Schniederjans, "An International Strategic Management Goal Programming Model for Structuring Global Decisions in the Hospitality Industry," *International Journal of Hospitality Management*, 9, No. 3 (1990), 175–190.

to generate organization-wide sales forecasts, they can also be used to develop disaggregated sales forecasts by region. Because facility investment tends to be a long-range decision, the forecasts by regions can be long-range to guide the regional selection decision.

To illustrate how we can use forecast values in region selection, let's look at an example of a region selection problem. Suppose that we have a country that has been divided into four regions—north, south, east, and west—based on a company's sales territories. As we can see in Figure 13-2(a), the current market share of an organization's total sales by region is 25 percent in each region. The company wants to relocate its manufacturing plants to regions in order to satisfy long-range forecast market shifts. Specifically, the organization wants to keep the production facilities near the markets the facilities will serve. The greater the market share of the organization's total sales a region has to satisfy, the greater the need for production facilities in that particular region.

As we can see in Figure 13-2(b), the forecast indicates that long-range market share by region will shift from the northern and eastern regions to the western and southern regions. Based on these forecasts, the organization would eliminate some of its production plants in the northern and eastern regions and relocate them to the western and southern regions. If the organization instead wanted to add a single new plant to the ones currently in operation, it would select the western region as the location of the new plant. The organization might also try to achieve a compromise and find a site that would locate the plant near the southern border of the western region to help support the obvious growth in the southern region as well. By making this compromise, we can see that the boundaries (the number and size) of the regions are not always critically important.

Site Selection

Once the region is determined, we are ready to pinpoint a specific site for the facility. A **site location** is the particular piece of property where the facility will eventually be built. A region may be a few hundred square miles or thousands of square miles. A site location for a service facility, on the other hand, may only require a few thousand square feet and for a manufacturing plant may only require a few dozen acres. To help narrow the region down to site location we can use several approaches and again, hundreds of criteria. One approach to reducing the region size is to divide the region in terms of its population density or into urban and rural areas. Most service and some manufacturing operations require location near or in heavily populated urban areas for sources of labor or access to markets; some operations, however, prefer less-populated rural areas.

One commonly used source of predefined areas of population density is the U.S. Bureau of the Census. In July 1983, the U.S. Bureau of the Census developed a classification system to define metropolitan areas. The three categories of metropolitan areas are as follows:

FIGURE 13-2 REGION SELECTION EXAMPLE PROBLEM

(A) CURRENT MARKET SHARE BY REGION OF COUNTRY

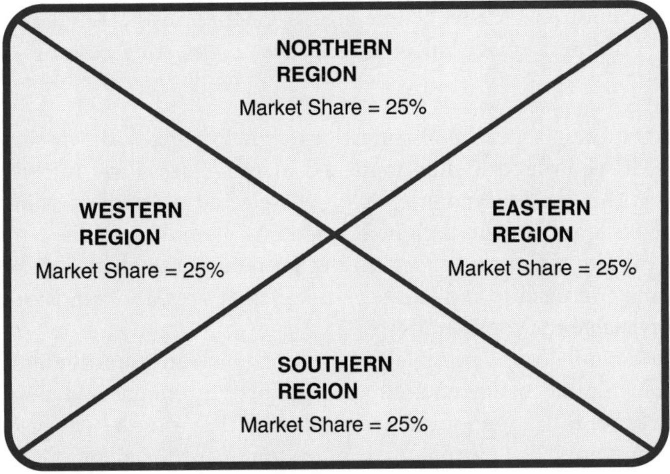

(B) LONG-RANGE FORECAST MARKET SHARE BY REGION

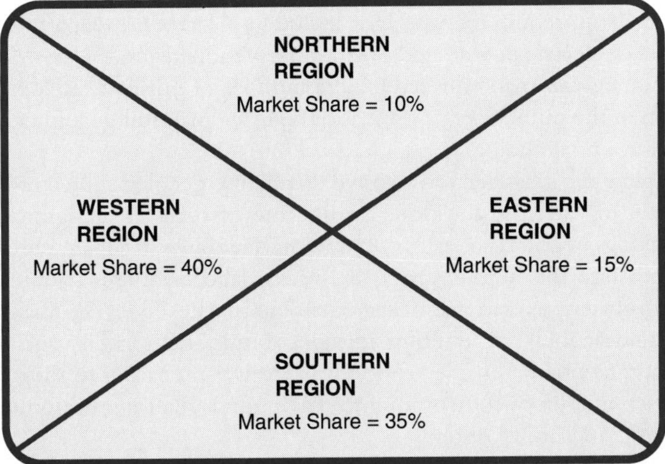

1. *Metropolitan statistical area (MSA)* is an area that is not connected to other metropolitan areas and has either a city of at least 50,000 persons or an urbanized area of 50,000 with a total population of 100,000. There are 257 MSAs in the United States, including Fargo, North Dakota and Syracuse, New York.
2. *Primary metropolitan statistical area (PMSA)* has a population of at least one million persons. The area may have clusters of people in communities tied together by

strong economic or social links. There are 78 PMSAs in the United States, including Kenosha, Wisconsin.

3. *Consolidated metropolitan statistical area (CMSA)* is made up of several overlapping and interconnected PMSAs. There are 23 CMSAs in the United States; Los Angeles, California (made up of the city and connecting counties) is one of the largest.

We can use these statistical classifications to help narrow down the region's size. For example, if we desired highly populated or urban areas, we might only consider site locations within the MSAs of the region we selected as a way to reduce site location search of the total area of the region. If we desire a rural area, we can eliminate the MSAs from the site selection process and again reduce the analysis effort. Even with this urban-rural approach to reducing the number of sites, thousands of potential sites may still be available for consideration.

To further reduce these possible site locations we can use three different types of site evaluation criteria: basic requirements, subjective criteria, and objective criteria. **Basic requirements** are site location requirements that must be satisfied to permit the operation to function. For example, a basic requirement for a barge company is dock facilities because it must be able to service, load, and manage its fleet of barges on a waterway. Only sites that permit dock access of an adequate size would be considered. A basic requirement for a gas station is access to roads to permit customers to come for service. Other basic requirements might include a nearby fire department, sources of water, sources of electric power, and operation-sanctioned zoning laws. Satisfying these basic requirements can markedly reduce the number of possible site locations. Despite this reduction in the number of possible locations, we may still be left with several from which to make a final choice.

To complete the site selection step we usually use detailed subjective and objective criteria unique to each site location. **Subjective criteria** are judgmentally obtained ratings or rankings of criteria of each site location. Examples of subjective criteria include union strength (are the unions strong or weak), labor attitudes about working with management on new operations management approaches like JIT, quality of life (is it desirable or undesirable), community attitudes about a new facility and its location (is the community favorably disposed to the firm, or is it preparing to sue), and quality of community services (does the community have good-quality transportation, communication, health, and utility systems).

Possible site locations within a small area or a single city may not be able to be differentiated by these kinds of subjective criteria because of their nearness. Yet in practice, the distance of only a few blocks can make a significant difference in what is termed the "quality of life." To obtain this type of detailed information, operations managers usually employ experts who are familiar with the cities and their social, economic, and political-legal environments to assess ratings or rankings for each of the criteria. These measures are then added together as for the country selection evaluation system, and the site with the best ratings or rankings is the one that is chosen for the facility.

If evaluating subjective criteria does not complete the site selection step, we may choose to base our decision on objective criteria. In practice, most operations managers use a combination of both subjective and objective criteria. **Objective criteria** are measurable or at least estimable criteria that pertain to the cost and availability (quantity) of inputs into the operations management system. Based on research on site location studies, the most commonly used objective criteria include the cost and availability of water, fuel, electric power, transportation facilities, labor, the land on which the site is located, construction of the facility, and state and local taxes.[3]

We can obtain objective criteria information from a number of secondary sources.[4] Most state governments also provide extensive research and site selection support to encourage new development in their states. Indeed, most states or their governors advertise the benefits of locating facilities in their states and the services the govenor's office can provide to the interested companies. The cost information can be added together for each site location to determine the least-cost site. Also, information about resources can be considered as objective constraints that may limit a facility's operation. For example, if electric power is being rationed during peak demand periods (as it is in some places in the United States during hot summer periods), then a facility may not be able to achieve capacity goals during such time periods. The cost of this underutilization of capacity can be assessed and added to the cost of that particular site location.

Several methods are used in examining the site selection step of facility location analysis. Most of these techniques examine the objective cost criteria of different sites. One cost-minimizing method used in site selection is the transportation method. (See Supplement 13-1 for an illustrative example.) The transportation method has been combined with other quantitative techniques such as goal programming to permit other types of objective and even subjective criteria to enter the decision-making process of the model.[5]

Once we have selected the site location, we have completed the multiple-step procedure of facility location analysis. Next, we must decide on the design of the facility

---

[3] Spencer et al., "AT&T's Telemarketing Site Selection System Offers Customer Support," *Interfaces,* 20, No. 1 (1990), 83–96; R. Schmenner, *Making Business Location Decisions* (Englewood Cliffs, N.J.: Prentice-Hall, 1982); K. R. Student, "Cost vs. Human Value in Plant Location," *Business Horizons,* 19 (1976), 5–14; and "Top Trends From New Plants," *Factory Manufacturing,* 3 (May 1970), 105–120.

[4] There are several industry publications that provide information such as tax benefits, labor costs, and availability of raw materials for thousands of cities across the United States. These publications include *Industrial Development* (published six times a year) and *Site Selection Handbook* (published four times a year), both from Conway Publications, Atlanta, Georgia; *Plant Location* (published annually), Simmons-Broadman Publishing, New York, New York.

[5] See S. M. Lee, G. Green, and C. Kim, "Multiple Criteria Model for the Location-Allocation Problem," *Computers and Operations Research,* 8, No. 6 (1981), 1–8; M. J. Schniederjans, N. K. Kwak, and M. C. Helmer, "An Application of Goal Programming to Resolve a Site Location Problem," *Interfaces,* 12, No. 3 (1982), 65–72; and N. K. Kwak and M. J. Schniederjans, "A Goal Programming Model as an Aid in Facility Location Analysis," *Computers and Operations Research,* 12, No. 2 (1985), 151–161.

to accomplish our facility production goals. Structuring the layout of the facility is the critical next step in designing a successful operations management facility.

FACILITY LAYOUTS

Through **facility layout design** we seek to achieve an optimal interface of the facilities, equipment, and personnel that make up the operations management system. Unfortunately the walls and equipment that make up an OM system can constrain personnel in the performance of their job tasks. By structuring the layout of a building to enhance and support production, operations managers can greatly improve the efficiency of their service or manufacturing system.

One example of this improved efficiency is illustrated by the service retailer KG Retail, a Denver-based chain of 125 apparel stores.[6] Since 1986, KG has implemented a variety of changes in its store layouts to improve efficiency. For example, KG installed laser scanning at the point of sale to read the UPC bar codes that are on every piece of its merchandise. This allows daily transactions to be sent to its vendors' electronic mailboxes. This timely transfer of inventory information achieves what the industry coins a *quick response* to changes in customer demand and inventory planning. The impact of the quick response has given KG a competitive advantage of having the lowest retail information system expenditures as a percentage of sales compared with those of other retailers. KG has also been able to cut inventory levels by 20 percent and reduce its amount of markdowns, thus saving profits. Facility layout design is an essential management function of operations management.

Although there are as many facility layout designs as there are business system layouts, we can classify the different layout designs into four types: fixed-position layouts, product layouts, process layouts, and flexible layouts.

Fixed-Position Layout

In a **fixed-position layout design** the product remains stationary and the resources used in its production are brought to the product's location. This type of layout is used in project operations such as the construction of a dam or a high-rise building. Other examples of fixed-position layouts include farming, aircraft manufacturing, highway construction, and fire fighting.

In planning fixed-position layouts care must be given to the types of resources—such as human resources—used in the production process. Human resources tend to be highly skilled or specialized and require extensive care and consideration in scheduling the use of their skills. Equipment in fixed-position layouts tends to be general purpose,

[6] B. Fox, "KG Retail Sets the Pace" *Chain Store Age Executive* (January 1991), 77–79.

such as a bulldozer or crane. One of the primary objectives of fixed-position layouts is to complete the product on schedule and at the least cost.

Product Layout

A **product layout design** is commonly used in repetitive operations. In a product layout the equipment and personnel are structured to manufacture a product or provide a service that is homogeneous and limited in style or type. Assembly lines used to manufacture automobiles, can food products, and package cigarettes are examples of systems that use product layout designs.

Product layouts tend to be capital-intensive systems, requiring a great deal of materials handling equipment such as conveyors and automated guided vehicles (AGVs). The cost of the equipment is partially offset by the specialization of human resources. Workers along assembly lines receive highly specialized training to perform a very limited number of job tasks. This permits extensive use of less costly unskilled human resources. The higher volume of production also reduces manufacturing costs and helps offset the extensive investment in equipment. The objective of a product layout is to maximize the flow of products through the operations management system by structuring the resources of the system in an orderly and efficient sequence of production stages.

Process Layout

A **process layout design** groups production resources into areas, such as departments, to process job orders. The types of job orders or products produced in a process layout are similar to those produced in a job-shop operation. A process layout is presented in Figure 13-3. As we can see, the layout is structured into departments or specialized functions. Each department permits specialization of workers and functions, which improves the efficiency of operations within that particular department. This layout also minimizes equipment requirements, particularly tools. Unlike an assembly line, in which each person on the line must have a set of tools and specialized pieces of equipment to perform his or her job tasks, the process layout only requires a few sets of tools and equipment to service the job order needs within the department.

Unfortunately, the flow of jobs or products (denoted with arrows in Figure 13-3) through a process layout is not as organized as through a product layout. Job order tracking and job scheduling are therefore more difficult management tasks in process layout operations. The ability to handle different types of job orders and manufacture different types of products is similar to a fixed-position layout. The diversity of job assignments requires very skilled personnel, but fortunately minimizes the need for their duplication in the system because the layout permits orders to back up without bottlenecking the entire system (as would occur in a product layout system). The primary objective in process layout is to improve the functional relationships of the departments

FIGURE 13-3 A PROCESS LAYOUT BY DEPARTMENT

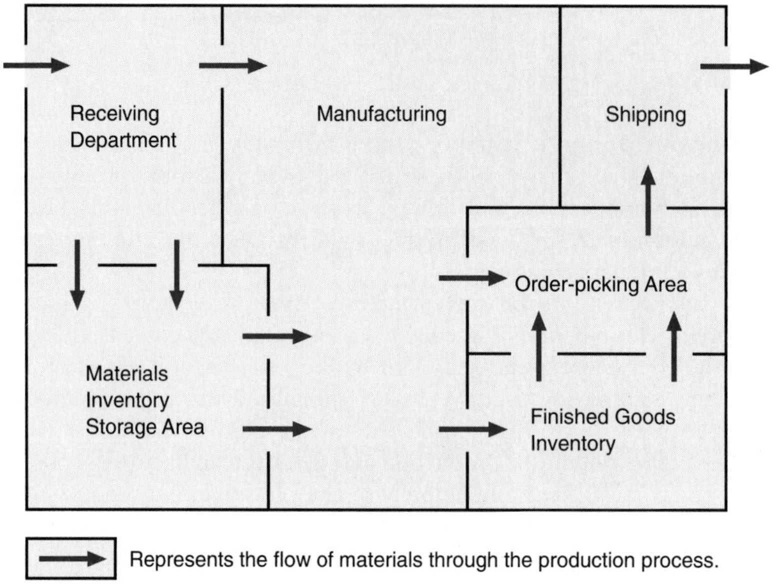

that make up the facility. We would like to position departments so that the time and cost of product flow and materials handling are minimized.

Flexible Layout

Flexible layout designs,[7] which can include and may be called **flexible manufacturing systems (FMS)**[8] and **cellular manufacturing systems,**[9] are process layouts in which the flow of the product can be altered to permit flexibility in production processing. An FMS is often characterized by a fully or partially integrated computer system that permits a rapid changeover to accommodate different products. An FMS is a hybrid version of the previously mentioned product and process layout designs.

[7] S. Babbar and A. Rai, "Computer Integrated Flexible Manufacturing: An Implementation Framework," *International Journal of Operations and Production Management,* 10, No. 1 (1990), 42–50.

[8] A. S. Carrie et al., "Introducing a Flexible Manufacturing System," *International Journal of Production Research,* 22, No. 6 (1984), 907–916; D. B. Merrifield, "FMS in USA: The New Industrial Revolution," *Managing Automation* (September 1988), 66–70; and B. Dutton, "Cat Climbs High with FMS," *Manufacturing Systems* (November 1989), 16–22.

[9] F. Choobineh, "A Framework for the Design of Cellular Manufacturing Systems," *International Journal of Production Research,* 26, No. 7 (1988), 1161–1172.

FIGURE 13-4 FLEXIBLE MANUFACTURING LAYOUT

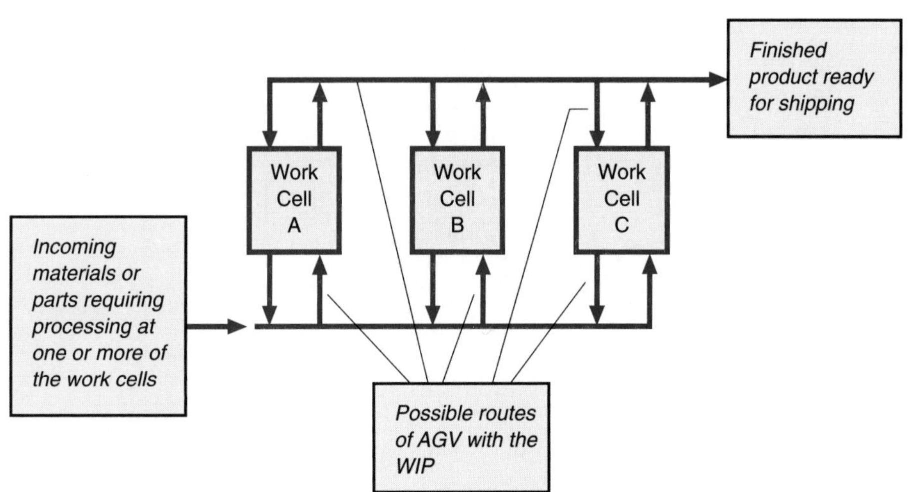

Flexible layout designs are like product layout designs in that they are often used for a variety of repetitive type products that must flow along a sequence of workcenters, like an assembly line. Flexible layout designs are also like process layout designs in that workcenter activities can be routed by using the department layout of Figure 13-3. The ideal objective of flexible layout design is to permit changes in the flow of product on a per product basis—that is, to permit easy and quick alterations in the routing of jobs (and therefore types of products) requiring diverse processing between workcenters, offices, and so on.

The FMS layout using **work cells** (or groupings of production processes, equipment, personnel, or workcenters) in Figure 13-4 typifies the basic FMS layout design. Although work cells are usually designed to produce a finished product, some products might have to move for specialized processing to more than one work cell. As we can see in Figure 13-4, the layout and routing of materials permit flexibility: WIP can travel to any work cell in any order (for example, A to B, B to A, C to A). The advances during the last few decades in materials handling automation, such as AGVs and materials handling robots (discussed in Chapter 6), permitted the development of FMS layouts.[10]

A **cellular layout design** groups production processes into work cells that are capable of producing a limited variety of finished products that share similar production characteristics. Depending on the needs of the organization, a cell might be very focused to produce only one product, or it may produce many products. A cellular layout is presented in Figure 13-5. The usual U or C shape of the cell allows the WIP to proceed in an efficient straight-line or linear manner. In Figure 13-5, the grouping of production

[10] D. Sarin, "Anatomy of FMS," *Manufacturing Systems* (November 1986), 26–30.

FIGURE 13-5 CELLULAR LAYOUT FOR CELL A, PRODUCT X

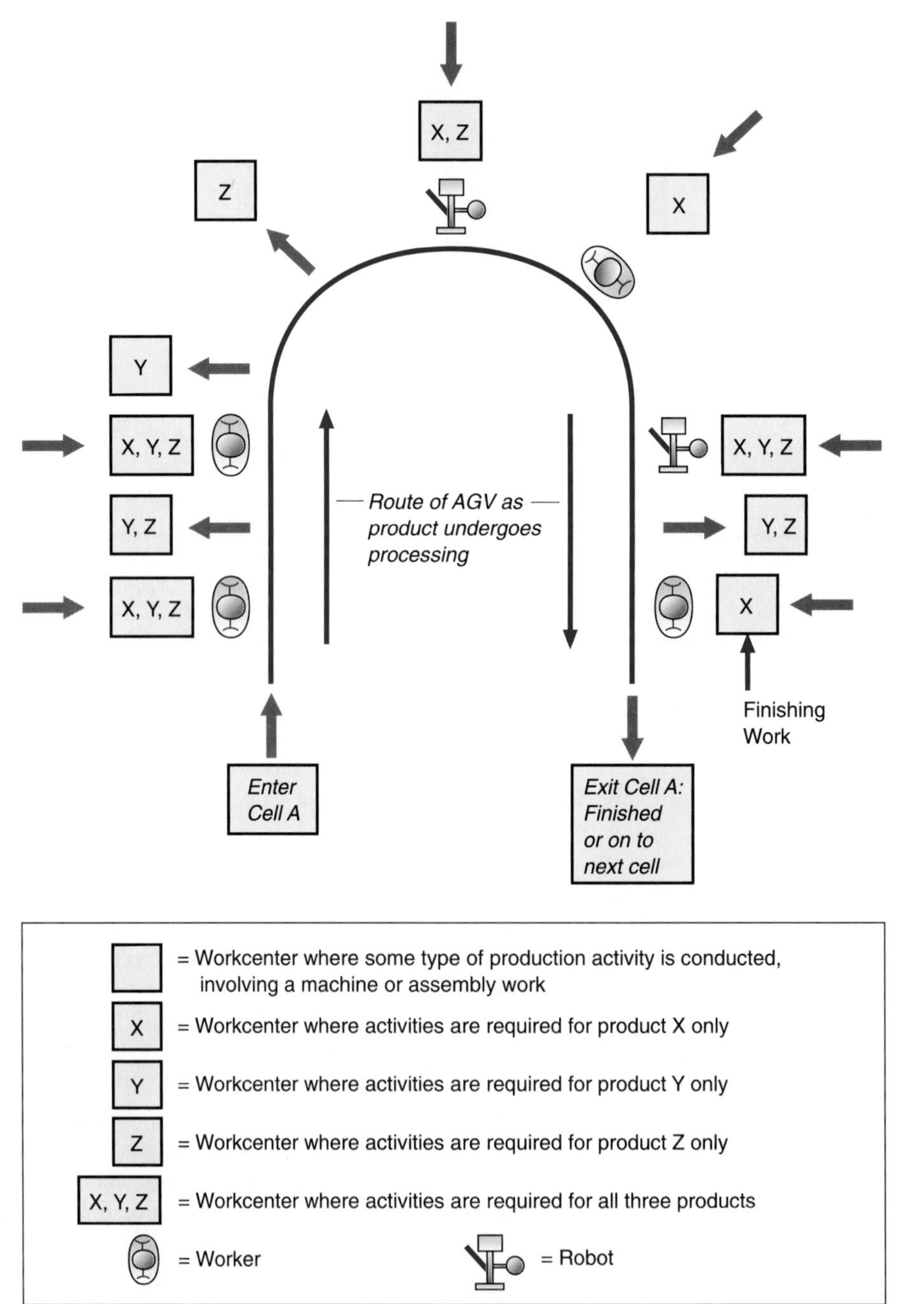

processes (some performed by human beings and some by robots) that comprise the cell are limited to the production of only three products (products X, Y, and Z). The cellular layout in Figure 13-5 is set up to run a lot of product X. The production processes used to produce product X are moved into position for the production run. When the production run for product X is complete, a run for product Y can be set up quickly by simply removing those processes that will not be required for product Y and moving the personnel, equipment, and product-processing workcenters to the cell's line that are required for product Y. The cellular layout for product Y is presented in Figure 13-6. The quick changeover from one product to another allows considerable production flexibility for this hybrid version of a product layout design. Indeed, robots or workers can easily work multiple positions in the U layout. In Figure 13-6, for example, a worker positioned on the inside of the U at one end can shift to the other end of the U to perform a second task on the same unit.

Cellular layouts are ideally supported by group technology (GT) methods (discussed in Chapter 11). The GT code number system that defines the product's various material and production processes is often used to help identify and create cells.[11]

QUESTION: Can flexible layouts be used in service operations?

ANSWER: All of the different types of layout designs in this chapter can be used for service operations, including flexible layouts. Families of similar service products can be grouped together for processing just as in manufacturing. For example, similar insurance forms can be processed by regional offices using a cellular layout. Office workers who perform all of the insurance form–processing tasks can be grouped together in a single room to complete the processing of insurance forms. The organization could simply arrange a set of tables into a U shape (like that in Figure 13-6) so that insurance forms can be passed from person to person. Each can contribute his or her individual work task to complete the processing of the forms (which represents the finished service product). If a more departmental layout of offices is used in an insurance form–processing facility, AGVs can route the forms to staff for processing. GT coding of insurance forms could also be used to route the forms to the appropriate form-processing staff or departments.

S

Cellular layout designs are also used as an implementation strategy for JIT production principles. In a JIT operation where flexibility is important, entire plants can focus on the production of a single **product family** (a group of products that share similar production requirements, inventory components, or both). A cellular focused factory is

[11] M. J. Choi and W. G. Riggs, "GT Coding and Classification for Manufacturing Cell Design," *Production and Inventory Management Journal,* 32, No. 1 (1991), 28–33.

FIGURE 13-6 CELLULAR LAYOUT FOR CELL A, PRODUCT Y

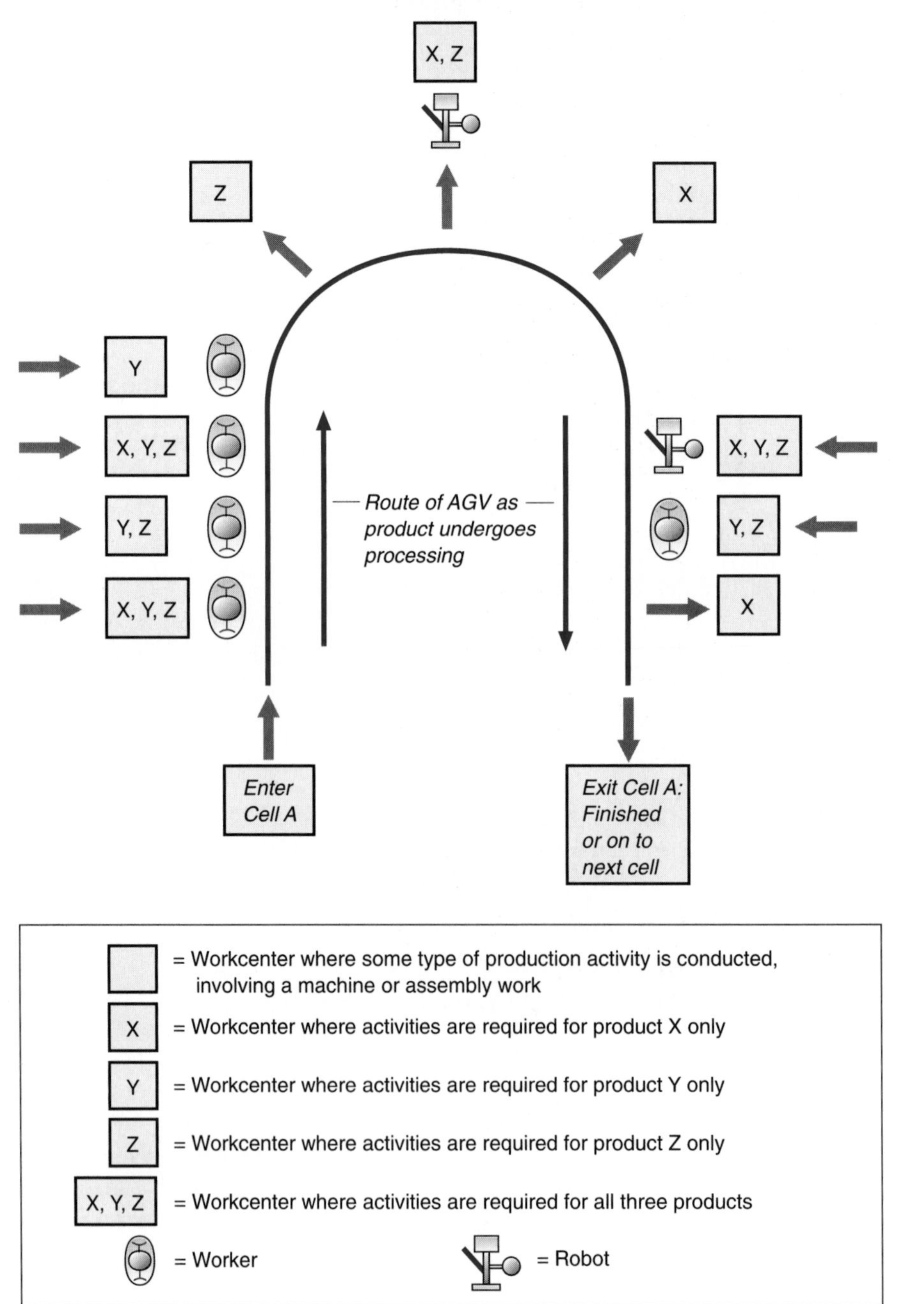

used to produce repetitive products. Two of the major objectives of JIT are usually to maximize product flow and minimize WIP lead time wastes. In large product families (many different types of products), the setup time for large lot production runs is considerable and departmental layout designs like the one in Figure 13-3 are more commonly used. In a focused JIT operation, the layout is substantially smaller (because of less inventory storage area), and less materials handling is necessary. By dedicating separate manufacturing cells to individual products, setup times are eliminated and some wasteful duplications in equipment are excluded. Also, the material and WIP chiefly flow in a linear direction through the facility, minimizing flow time. Indeed, Japanese experts actually recommend that workcenter tables, machines, and robots be equipped with casters and rollers so that they can be rolled back and forth by workers as needed.[12]

QUESTION: How can the cellular U-shaped line improve product quality?

ANSWER: Texas Instruments' Antenna Department in McKinney, Texas implemented a U-shaped line layout as a part of its effort to implement a JIT program in 1990.[13] They found that the new layout design facilitated material flow and maximized operator visibility. This helped workers see what other workers were doing, which in turn helped workers become trained for a variety of jobs. The increased visibility also helped them more easily catch errors in product assembly and more quickly communicate those errors to management for correction. The results in only two years was a 90 percent improvement in product quality.

Q

To accomplish the objectives of layout design there are many different types of layout methods available. We discuss several of these layout procedures in the next section.

FACILITY LAYOUT METHODOLOGIES

Several commonly used approaches for facility layout design include distance-minimizing layout procedure, computer software systems, line balancing procedure, and performance ratios.

[12] H. Hirano, *JIT Factory Resolution: A Pictorial Guide to Factory Design of the Future* (Cambridge, Mass.: Productivity Press, 1989), p. 121.

[13] S. Ellis and B. Conlon, "JIT Points the Way to Gains in Quality, Cost and Lead Time," *APICS—The Performance Advantage,* 2, No. 8 (1992), 16–19.

Distance Minimizing

One approach to designing a process layout for a service facility or manufacturing plant involves a series of steps that can be used to establish a departmental layout without the aid of expert judgment or computerized models. The **distance-minimizing layout procedure** allows us to structure a departmental layout that will minimize traveling distance while satisfying other layout requirements in the facility. This procedure does not guarantee an optimal layout but does provide a layout that seeks to minimize traveling time. The procedure consists of the following steps:

1. *Determine the site requirements that may limit the size or shape of departments and the structure that will contain the departments.* A facility site (real estate or a piece of property) and its location can limit the shape and arrangement of facilities that will be laid out on the site. Access to streets for loading docks, zoning limitations on building size, governmental safety regulations, and the fixed location of a building to be renovated can all limit the configuration and layout of the departments within a building.
2. *Determine space requirements and any departmental configuration requirements that might affect the size and space of the departments.* Usually the manager of a department has a fairly precise idea of how many square feet of space are required for the department's successful operation. Some departments, for example, because of their use of equipment such as an automatic storage and automatic retrieval (AS/AR) system, might require a square or rectangular configuration.
3. *Determine the expected number of trips between departments for a given planning horizon.* In most organizations, the number of trips between departments can be estimated on a daily, weekly, or even monthly planning horizon based on fixed or predetermined amount of service or manufacturing activity. For example, in a job-shop operation, the number of jobs that flow from an assembly department to a painting department can be judgmentally determined to generate the estimated number of trips between the two departments. In determining the number of trips we must realize that travel between departments may or may not be in both directions. A quality control department receiving finished units from an assembly department may send some of those units back to the assembly department if defects require reworking.
4. *Model square-feet space requirements and compute total expected trips between each department.* The square-feet space requirements can be computed by taking the square root of the square-feet space requirements for each department. We can model these squared departments using scaled-down pieces of paper proportional to the square-feet requirements of each department. The total expected trips between each department is simply the sum of all trips to and from each of the departments.
5. *Determine nearness priorities for the departmental layout.* The **nearness priorities** are a ranking used to establish which departments should be placed together. The ranking is established on the basis of the total number of expected trips

obtained in step 4. The departments that have the greatest total number of expected trips between them are given the highest priority for being assigned next to one another. We minimize traveling by keeping the distance short for those departments that must make the greatest number of trips.

6. *Using the highest-ranking priorities from step 5, make an initial allocation or layout of the square-feet departments modeled in step 4.* One of the best ways to begin this step is to determine the department with the greatest frequency of nearness priorities and position that department where it will have contact with the greatest number of other departments. The initial allocation of departments may not conform to the space and shape requirements of steps 1 and 2, but it should seek to satisfy the highest-ranking nearness priorities. The objective in using the nearness priorities is to try and satisfy the highest-level priorities first and then see if subsequent minor changes can be made to satisfy the lower-level priorities. If all combinations of departments are prioritized, it will be impossible to satisfy all nearness priorities. The initial allocation of departments usually requires some heuristic guess work and experimentation.

QUESTION: In Figure 13-7 we show six departments labeled with letters. The arrows in the figure represent where direct contacts between departments are permitted. (Note that department A is not in direct contact with department E.) Which departments have the most direct contacts with other departments?

ANSWER: Departments B and E directly contact three other departments. The remaining departments directly contact only two other departments. Departments B and E should be assigned first in the design because of their greater contact with other departments.

7. *Modify the space and shape requirements for the department layout obtained in step 6 to conform with the requirements in steps 1 and 2.* This step may also require some heuristic and creative experimentation to restructure the square-feet department layout to conform to given space and size requirements without sacrificing the highest-ranking nearness priorities. In some departments we may need to exceed desired space allocations to fit a department in a given site location or a given building structure.

To illustrate the distance-minimizing layout procedure, let's look at an example problem. Suppose that a company has purchased a site for a new manufacturing facility. Because of zoning requirements, the facility must be contained in a building 100 feet wide and 220 feet long. Also, the incoming and outgoing inventory of the plant requires separate loading docks at both ends of the building: One dock receives incoming goods and the other dock is used to ship outgoing products (step 1). The square-feet space

FIGURE 13-7 DEPARTMENTAL LAYOUT DIAGRAM

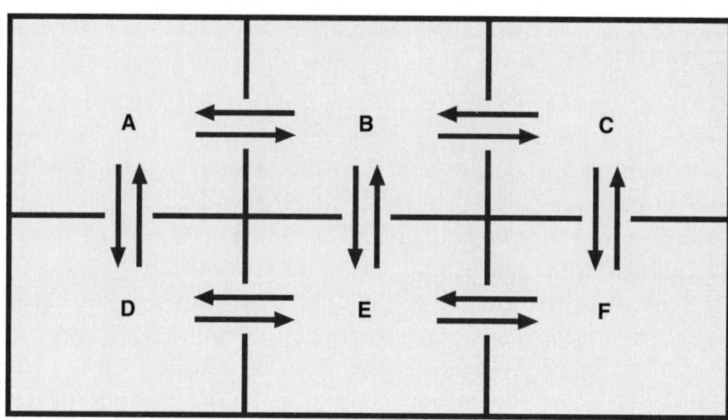

requirements for each of the six departments that will make up the manufacturing facility are presented in Figure 13-8(a) (step 2).

Based on other similar plants, the company estimated the expected number of trips between each department as presented in Figure 13-8(b). As we can see in Figure 13-8(b), the Receiving Department expects to make forty-five trips to the Machine Shop Department, and the Machine Shop Department expects to make ten trips to the Receiving Department (step 3). By taking the square root of the floor space requirements we can determine the square-feet department space requirements as presented in Figure 13-9(a) ($80 \times 80 = 6{,}400$ square feet for receiving).

We can also add the trips to and from all of the departments to determine the total expected number of trips between each department as presented in Figure 13-9(b) (step 4). As we can see in Figure 13-9(b), the total expected number of trips between the Receiving Department and the Machine Shop Department is fifty-five ($45 + 10$). The greatest total number of trips between any of the six departments is the eighty-six trips between the Machine Shop and the Assembly Departments, so these two departments should be placed next to one another to minimize distance. The nearness priorities for all fifteen combinations of the six departments are present in Table 13-1 (step 5).

In step 6 we must develop an initial allocation of the six departments. If we arbitrarily select the top five nearness priorities from Table 13-1 and determine the frequency of times each department is listed we would find the following:

Department	*Frequency*
Receiving	1
Machine shop	3
Painting	1
Assembly	2
Quality control	2
Shipping	1

FIGURE 13-8 EXAMPLE LAYOUT PROBLEM DATA

(A) FLOOR SPACE REQUIREMENTS FOR EACH DEPARTMENT

Department	Required Floor Space (sq. ft.)
Receiving	6,400
Machine Shop	8,100
Painting	1,600
Assembly	3,364
Quality Control	1,225
Shipping	784

(B) EXPECTED NUMBER OF TRIPS BETWEEN EACH DEPARTMENT

FROM \ TO	Receiving	Machine Shop	Painting	Assembly	Quality Control	Shipping
Receiving	—	45	3	6	6	0
Machine Shop	10	—	38	46	24	2
Painting	4	30	—	13	12	0
Assembly	5	40	20	—	50	4
Quality Control	3	4	11	8	—	43
Shipping	1	2	2	3	21	—

It is obvious that the Machine Shop should be positioned where it will have the greatest contact with other departments. Consistent with the first two nearness priorities, we would set the Machine Shop next to the Assembly and Painting Departments. At priorities 3 and 4 we would allocate the Assembly Department next to Quality Control, and Quality Control next to Shipping. Because Shipping must be placed on one end of the building, the Receiving Department should be placed at the other end of the building.

In Figure 13-10(a) we can see the initial layout that satisfies the nearness priorities of 1, 2, 3, 4, 5, 6, and 8 (step 6). Unfortunately, this layout's actual length exceeds the 220 feet length requirement by 36 feet (256 − 220). This requires some reconfiguration of the squared departments into rectangular forms to meet the given length zoning requirement. The reconfiguration of the departments is presented in Figure 13-10(b). The spacing of the department was accomplished by the trial-and-error method of finding two numbers (the length and width of the departments) that when multiplied together would fit the space allowed and yet be equal to or close to the required floor space stated in Figure 13-9.

FIGURE 13-9 EXAMPLE LAYOUT PROBLEM SOLUTION DATA

(A) FLOOR SPACE REQUIREMENTS FOR EACH DEPARTMENT

Department	Required Floor Space (sq. ft.)	Square Root of Required Floor Space
Receiving	6,400	80
Machine Shop	8,100	90
Painting	1,600	40
Assembly	3,364	58
Quality Control	1,225	35
Shipping	784	28

(B) TOTAL EXPECTED NUMBER OF TRIPS BETWEEN EACH DEPARTMENT

FROM \ TO	Receiving	Machine Shop	Painting	Assembly	Quality Control	Shipping
Receiving	—	55	7	11	9	1
Machine Shop		—	68	86	28	4
Painting			—	33	23	2
Assembly				—	58	7
Quality Control					—	64
Shipping						—

TABLE 13-1 PRIORITIES FOR EXAMPLE LAYOUT PROBLEM

Departments	*Total Expected Number of Trips*	*Nearness Priority*
Machine Shop near Assembly	86	1
Machine Shop near Painting	68	2
Quality Control near Shipping	64	3
Assembly near Quality Control	58	4
Receiving near Machine Shop	55	5
Painting near Assembly	33	6
Machine Shop near Quality Control	28	7
Painting near Quality Control	23	8
Receiving near Assembly	11	9
Receiving near Quality Control	9	10
Assembly near Shipping	7	11
Receiving near Painting	7	12
Machine Shop near Shipping	4	13
Painting near Shipping	2	14
Receiving near Shipping	1	15

FIGURE 13-10 DEPARTMENT ASSIGNMENT FOR EXAMPLE LAYOUT PROBLEM

(A) INITIAL ALLOCATION OF SQUARE-FEET DEPARTMENTS

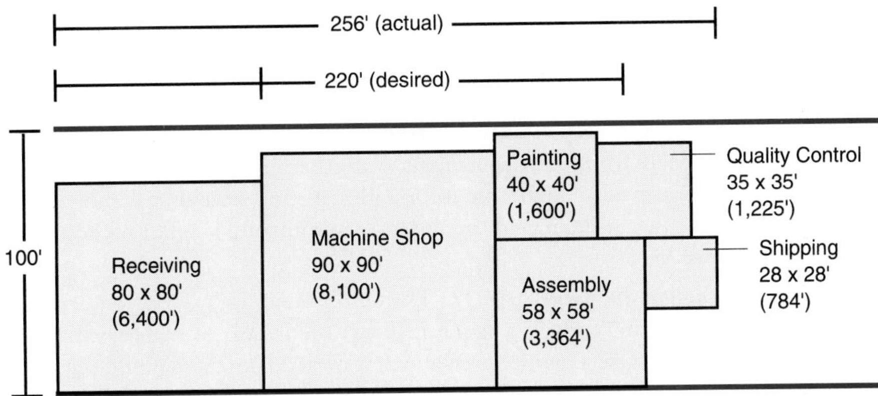

(B) FINAL ALLOCATION OF DEPARTMENTS

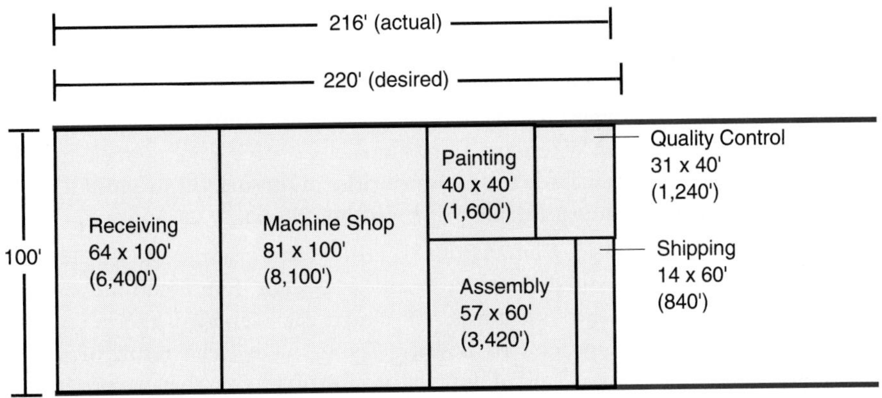

Through this trial-and-error effort of fitting the departments, we arrived at a resulting configuration that satisfied the length requirement for the building, but caused some of the departments (Assembly, Quality Control, and Shipping) to receive excess square feet of floor space. While this layout may not be optimal, it does satisfy all of the given requirements and satisfies most of the highest nearness priorities.

The distance-minimizing layout procedure is a heuristic process of developing a layout; it is not an optimization procedure. In various forms, it has been a practical approach to layout design. Several computer programs have been developed based on this method to aid in facility layout design.

Computer Software Systems

Several computer software systems or programs can be used to design process layout and product layout operations. Some of the widely used software systems include the following:

1. *Computerized Relative Allocation of Facilities (CRAFT)* This system is the most popular and widely written about of all of the layout packages to date. This program seeks to minimize distance (in feet traveled) and load costs (that is, the cost to move loads from one department to another) if such cost information is available. Unfortunately, such cost information is not usually available and for that reason is not considered in the distance-minimizing layout procedures previously discussed.
2. *Computerized Facilities Design (COFAD)* This system is an improved version of CRAFT. This program permits a more realistic calculation of materials handling costs. Unlike CRAFT, which uses a matrix of fixed points to plot distance in feet between departments, COFAD uses equations that allow the analysis of materials handling equipment. COFAD uses a CRAFT-type program to obtain an initial layout and then analyzes different layouts that might allow better use of materials handling equipment, such as a conveyor system versus mechanical vehicles for moving products.
3. *Computerized Relationship Layout Planning (CORELAP)* This system permits the recognition of high-ranked nearness priorities in layout design. CRAFT and COFAD might design a layout that absurdly puts a shipping department in the middle of the plant where it will not have access to a loading dock area. CORELAP allows us to include nearness priorities in the analysis to avoid such absurdities as well as nonquantifiable prioritization criteria.
4. *Automated Layout Design Program (ALDEP)* This system is similar to CORELAP except that it is designed to provide random designs. Even with the same input data, ALDEP may provide a different design each time it is run because it uses a randomization process to develop layout plans. The result of this randomization approach is a kind of built-in simulation process that can provide multiple, alternative layout designs. Also, this program requires that all departments be rectangular or square. This minimizes odd-shaped departments that the previous programs sometimes will generate.
5. *Plant Layout Analysis Evaluation Technique (PLANT)* This system is basically a combination of all of the other programs. Its distinctive feature is that it gives the layout designer more alternatives regarding how materials handling costs can be calculated and how nearness priorities should be recognized in the layout design.

It is interesting to note that people can perform the analysis just as well as the computer programs. Research on experienced layout planners has confirmed that human beings, using their own heuristic procedures like the distance-minimization layout procedure, can do as well as computer-aided layout programs.[14] There are also non-traditional aspects of facility planning that available computer systems are not yet able to consider.[15]

Line Balancing

In a product layout, the production rate of the operation is determined by the assignment of the work along the layout system. In an assembly line or FMS we usually designate workcenters as places for work. A single person or a group of people functioning as a team can be considered a workcenter. Each workcenter is usually assigned a specific number of tasks to perform to complete its individual workcenter production objectives. Sometimes the assignment of the work tasks at one workcenter may exceed the amount of tasks at another workcenter. If the amount of time that it takes to complete each of the workcenter's assigned tasks varies, we have an unbalanced work load assignment. When this imbalance occurs some assembly line workers will experience idle time.

The idle time at some of the workcenters is caused by production bottlenecks or line congestion forming ahead of the workcenter that requires the greatest amount of time to complete its assigned tasks. Indeed, the speed of production or the *cycle time* is determined by the production rate of the workcenter that requires the greatest amount of time on an assembly line. **Cycle time** is "the time between completion of two discrete units of production."[16] So if we have an assembly line where a finished unit is completed every 20 seconds, then we have at least one workcenter requiring 20 seconds to complete all of its tasks. This line would be producing units at a rate of 180 units per hour (3 units per minute × 60 minutes per hour).

When we have worker idle time caused by an imbalance of work task assignments, we have a problem called a *line balancing problem*. One of our objectives in designing an assembly line or product layout operation is to minimize idle time by balancing the work tasks so perfectly that there will be no idle time at any workcenter. A second objective in a line balancing problem is to minimize the number of workcenters (that is, their respective investment costs) along the assembly line. When the line balancing problem is solved we will know both the workcenter assignment of tasks and how many workcenters are required to complete the product.

When we design an assembly line operation, cellular layout, or any production layout, we need to allocate the work assignments to achieve desired production quotas or objectives. In a product layout, like an assembly line, the production rate and its

---

[14] W. Lewis and T. Block, "On the Application of Computer Aids to Plant Layout," *International Journal of Production Research,* 18, No. 1 (1980), 1–20.

[15] E. Rogers, "Ten Nontraditional Aspects of Facility Planning," *Industrial Engineering,* 24, No. 2 (1992), 18–19.

[16] Reprinted with permission of the American Production and Inventory Control Society, Inc., *APICS Dictionary,* 7th edition, 1992.

ability to achieve a production quota are determined by the cycle time. The cycle time is usually determined by a manager who sets the daily production quotas. The line balancing procedure used to design workcenter layouts consists of the following steps:

1. *Identify all of the work tasks and the amount of time that it will take to complete the desired product.* This requires listing the tasks that will be performed by all human beings, robots, and the like along the product layout. It might also require some analysis of task completion time. (We discuss the process of time study analysis in the next chapter.)
2. *Identify the order in which each task must be completed.* Just as in a PERT network, we must determine the order of tasks so that we know which task must be completed on the assembly line first, which task must be completed second, and so on. To express the immediate predecessor tasks, we can use a PERT network with nodes and arrows.
3. *Determine the cycle time or production rate of the line.* This is determined by simply dividing the production rate into the number of seconds in a minute or hour and determining the number of seconds between successive completed units coming off the assembly line. Remember, though, that the cycle time must be greater than or equal to the greatest time-consuming task assignment for all of those required in step 1.

QUESTION: Suppose that we have a production line operating at a cycle time of 30 seconds (2 units per minute × 60 minutes per hour), which is a production rate of 120 units per hour. Suppose that we have to change the work tasks along the line, and now one of the workcenters will require 45 seconds to complete its tasks before it sends the item down the line to the next workcenter. What will the new production rate for this line be?

ANSWER: Even if all of the other workcenters require only 10 seconds to complete their tasks, the one workcenter that requires 45 seconds will determine the production rate for the entire production line. The 45-second time requirement for the one workcenter becomes the cycle time for the line because it is the longest time for all of the workcenters and determines the production rate of the line. The new production rate becomes

$$\text{Production rate} = \frac{\text{Seconds in an hour}}{\text{Seconds per unit}} = \frac{3{,}600}{45} = 80 \text{ units per hour}$$

4. *Select, from those work tasks available, the one that requires the most amount of time.* This selection is limited to those tasks that have no unassigned immediate predecessors in the network.

5. *Add the task to those assigned to a workcenter.* If all of the available work tasks that can be selected will cause the total task assignment time at a single workcenter to exceed the cycle time, the workcenter is complete. Continue repeating steps 4 and 5 until all of the tasks have been assigned to as many workcenters as necessary. Note that when we have "filled up" the assignment of tasks for a workcenter, we have actually created a workcenter. If the time for the available work tasks assigned to a workcenter does not exceed the cycle time, we repeat steps 4 and 5 until we reach the cycle time or exhaust the available work tasks to be assigned.

6. *Calculate idle time statistics for comparison purposes.* One measure of a good assignment of work tasks is the minimization of idle time. If more than one assignment of work tasks is derived using the prior steps, then an idle time statistic for each of the assignments can be used to judge which assignment generates the least idle time. One idle time statistic measures the line's total idle time. The statistic is as follows:

$$I = (n)(c) - \Sigma \text{ (work task times for all workcenters)}$$

where

I = the total idle time for the entire line

n = the number of workcenters

c = the cycle time for the line

Although ideally, I should equal zero, it rarely does in real-world applications.

Idle time statistics can be used to express the degree of idle time or the percentage of idle time caused by the particular work task assignment. One ratio, designated as P, represents the percentage of idle time expected in the workcenters. The P statistic is as follows:

$$P = \frac{100(I)}{(n)(c)}$$

The lower the value of P for a given work task assignment, the more efficient and free of idle time the particular layout of workcenters will be.

The line balancing procedure does not ensure an optimal assignment. It is simply a heuristic process of establishing an assignment that will seek to minimize the number of workcenters required to achieve the desired cycle time production rate.

Let's illustrate the line-balancing procedure with an example problem. Suppose that a company would like to design an assembly line layout for a new product it plans to manufacture. Let's also assume the operations manager has identified all the work tasks (step 1) and their ordering (step 2) as presented in Figure 13-11. The operations manager wants to determine how many workcenters the company's layout will require and how the work tasks should be assigned to each workstation. The manager has determined

FIGURE 13-11 EXAMPLE LINE BALANCING PROBLEM TASKS AND NETWORK

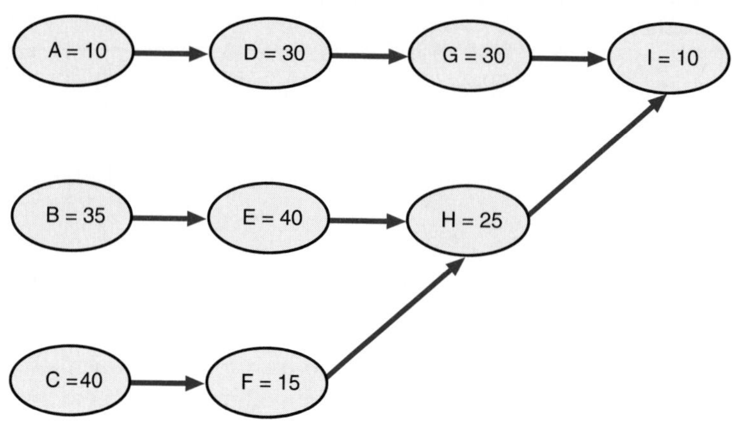

that the company must produce 90 units of the product per hour to have a profitable operation. This means that the desired cycle time (step 3) must be

$$\text{Desired cycle time} = \frac{3{,}600}{90} = 40 \text{ seconds per unit}$$

Based on this maximum time per task, the company divided the work into nine different tasks, each equal to or less than the 40-second cycle time. These work tasks (designated by letter), their times in seconds, and their order or sequence of required completion are presented in the network diagram in Figure 13-11. As we can see in the network diagram, we must complete work task A, which requires 10 seconds, before work task D becomes available for a possible assignment. Given the information in Figure 13-11, we can now use steps 4 and 5 of the line-balancing procedure to assign the work tasks to the first workcenter. Consistent with step 4, the largest available work task (out of the set of the only available work tasks of A, B, and C) is C. Because work task C takes 40 seconds, which is equal to the cycle time, we will not be able to assign any additional work tasks to this first workcenter. For the second workcenter we have a choice of work tasks A, B, and F. We choose B because it requires the most amount of time to complete. While this second workcenter's work task only requires 35 seconds (5 fewer than the cycle time of 40 seconds) we are unable to assign any of the additional work tasks (A, E, and F) without exceeding the cycle time. The work task assignments and resulting workcenters are presented in Table 13-2.

As we can see in Table 13-2, the operation will require six workcenters. The idle time statistics for this line are

$$\begin{aligned} I &= (n)(c) - \Sigma \text{ (work task times for all workcenters)} \\ &= (6)(40) - (235) \\ &= 5 \text{ seconds of idle time for the entire line} \end{aligned}$$

$$P = \frac{100(I)}{(n)(c)} = \frac{100(5)}{(6)(40)} = \frac{500}{240} = 2.08 \text{ percent of idle time}$$

We can see that only 5 seconds of idle time will occur for the entire line and the line layout design will average only 2.08 percent of the total time for all six of the workcenters.

Performance Ratios

Although the inefficiency of a poor layout can cost an operation much-needed resources and cause its failure, a layout can usually be changed and improved if necessary. To determine if a layout needs to be revised or compared with alternative layouts, layout management experts have devised a number of efficiency ratios. One such ratio is the *P* ratio (percentage of idle time) used in the last section for measuring inefficiency in work load assignments. Other ratios include the following:

$$\text{Storage space usage ratio (SSUR)} = \frac{\text{Storage space actually occupied by materials in square feet}}{\text{Total square feet storage space in facility}}$$

$$\text{Inventory turnover ratio (ITR)} = \frac{\text{Annual sales in dollars}}{\text{Average inventory}}$$

$$\text{Distance travel ratio (DTR)} = \frac{\text{Total distance in feet all orders traveled during a specific planning horizon}}{\text{Total number of orders processed during the planning horizon}}$$

TABLE 13-2 WORK TASK ASSIGNMENTS FOR EXAMPLE LINE BALANCING PROBLEM

	FIRST WORK TASK ASSIGNMENT		*SECOND WORK TASK ASSIGNMENT*		
Workcenter	*Available Work Tasks To Choose From*	*Work Task Selected*	*Available Work Tasks To Choose From*	*Work Task Selected*	*Workcenter Total Task Time (seconds)*
1	A, B, C	C	—	—	40
2	A, B, F	B	—	—	35
3	A, E, F	E	—	—	40
4	A, F	F	A, H	H	40
5	A	A	D	D	40
6	G	G	I	I	40
					235

$$\text{Damaged goods ratio (DGR)} = \frac{\text{Number of damaged loads moved during a specific planning horizon}}{\text{Total number of loads moved during the planning horizon}}$$

$$\text{Job tardiness ratio (JTR)} = \frac{\text{Number of jobs late during a specific planning horizon}}{\text{Total number of jobs processed during the planning horizon}}$$

$$\text{Order-line picking ratio (OLPR)} = \frac{\text{Number of lines (a line represents an item) on orders picked during a specific planning horizon}}{\text{Number of hours worked by all order pickers during the planning horizon}}$$

$$\text{Receiving/shipping ratio (R/SR)} = \frac{\text{Number of pounds (or pallets) shipped per day}}{\text{Number of hours worked by department personnel per day}}$$

The desirability of the values of these ratios depends on the type of organization and its layout objectives. Because layout affects virtually all of the operations management functions, it is related to activities in other management functions (such as accounting). These ratios are also commonly used in other nonlayout planning functions such as inventory management and materials management.

We can use these ratios on a comparative basis to

1. See if layout performance can be improved by making design changes and observing the results in the ratios
2. Monitor layout performance to observe shifts in ongoing operations
3. Establish performance criteria that can be used as goals to motivate improved performance

INTEGRATING MANAGEMENT RESOURCES: USING EXPERT SYSTEMS TO INCREASE CONTROL AND PRODUCTIVITY

The creation of an advanced layout methodology is not a simple task and it can actually cause problems. For example, the use of cellular layout in a highly integrated and automated manufacturing plant requires substantial cell control for unusual production problems. Without human beings available to use their experience to solve problems caused by abnormalities of production (such as defective parts stuck in the equipment), highly automated cells can be damaged and generate enormous amounts of scrap. The more that human beings are taken out of the production environments and replaced with computer-controlled systems (computer-integrated manufacturing or CIM), the more some type of expert judgment is needed in that same system for control purposes.

FIGURE 13-12 STRUCTURE OF TENG-BLACK EXPERT SYSTEM

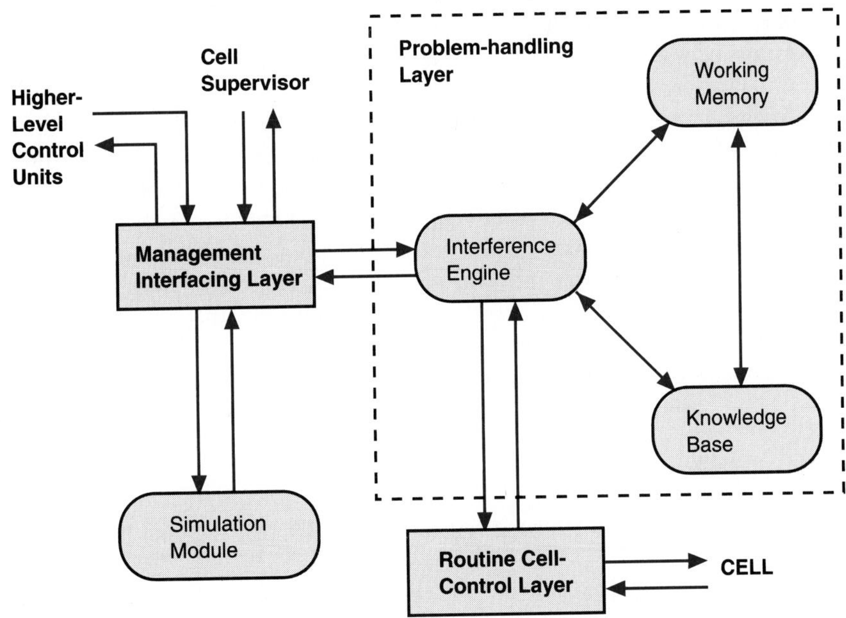

Source: Reprinted from *Computers and Industrial Engineering,* Vol. no. 17, S. H. Teng and J. T. Black, "An Expert System for Manufacturing Cell Control," pp. 18–23, copyright 1989, with permission from Pergamon Press Ltd., Headington Hill Hall, Oxford OX3 OBW, UK.

To improve control and replace the human expert input in highly automated cellular manufacturing layouts, a computer-based expert system has been suggested.[17] The idea behind all expert systems is to capture expert knowledge in a computer-based delivery system. The *Teng-Black expert system* or delivery system comprises three components: a *knowledge base* (a set of rules in this case to deal with known cellular problems), a *working memory* (a dynamic set of rules that will change the knowledge base as new problems are encountered in the cells and solved), and an *inference engine* (a set of rules that allows the system to reason, infer problems, and draw conclusions on the control of cell behavior). Electronic sensors are positioned in the cells to provide feedback on its operation against known or stated system parameters (for example, output and speed of line). The structure of the Teng-Black expert system is presented in Figure 13-12. This expert system's functions of control can be separated into three categories: (1) to control and monitor the cell operations, (2) to solve problems existing during the cell's operation, and

[17] S. Teng and J. T. Black, "An Expert System for Manufacturing Cell Control," *Computers and Industrial Engineering,* 17, Nos. 1–4 (1989), 18–23.

(3) to communicate with higher-level human controllers (the cell supervisor or plant manager). Using the knowledge base and simultation software to examine problems, the expert system provides solutions and information for the successful operation of production cells. The flow of information in the expert system is presented in Figure 13-13.

By integrating an expert system such as the Teng-Black expert system, highly automated cellular manufacturing operations can more quickly identify problems and implement computer-based solutions or call them to the attention of higher-level management. The speed of response will reduce scrap rates, reduce damage to equipment, and improve product flow by solving problems automatically. Even more, the expert system's problem-solving knowledge can grow and will avoid wasting management's time spent reinventing solutions that are contained in the expert system's data base. The result of such a system reduces waste and improves the productivity in cellular manufacturing operations.

FIGURE 13-13 FLOW OF INFORMATION IN TENG-BLACK EXPERT SYSTEM

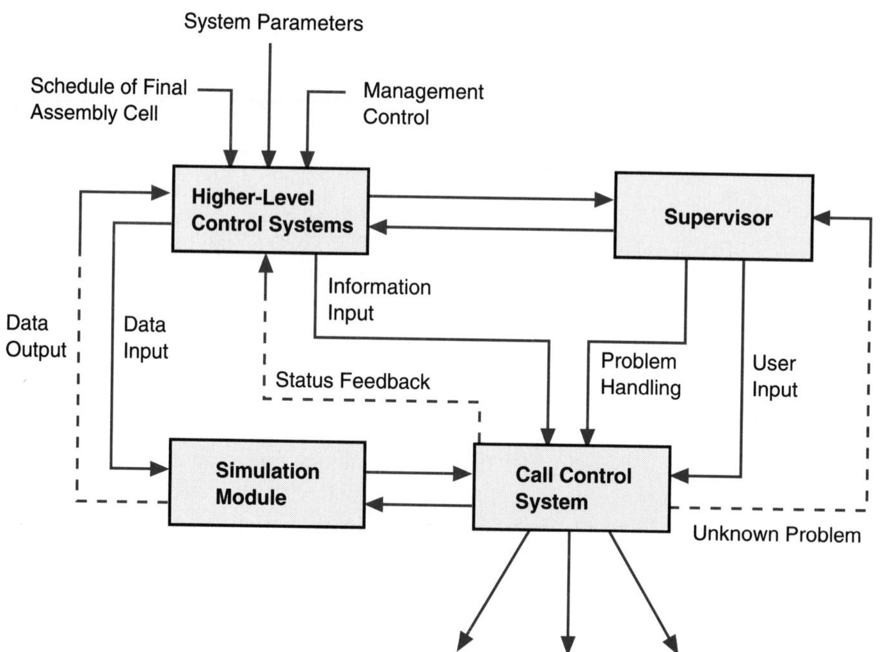

Source: Reprinted from *Computers and Industrial Engineering,* Vol. no. 17, S. H. Teng and J. T. Black, "An Expert System for Manufacturing Cell Control," pp. 18–23, copyright 1989, with permission from Pergamon Press Ltd., Headington Hill Hall, Oxford OX3 OBW, UK.

SUMMARY

In this chapter we have examined the operations management functions of facility location analysis and layout design. Facility location analysis can be used to discontinue old facilities, relocate plants, or locate sites for new plants. An organization undertaking facility location analysis first chooses a country, then a region, and finally a single site. At each step in the process numerous subjective and objective criteria are used.

We also discussed facility layout design in this chapter. There are several types of layout designs, including fixed-position layout, product layout, process layout, and flexible layouts. Each layout design has specific layout objectives. We examined the use of distance-minimizing layout procedure, line-balancing procedure, and layout design performance ratio methods as a means of accomplishing the various layout objectives.

In this chapter we concentrated on the design of facilities. A very important ingredient to consider in designing a facility is the personnel who will staff the facility. We will discuss the design of human resources and their interface with other management resources in the next chapter.

The second photo insert presents an overview of the various Au Bon Pain, Inc. food service operations. As can be seen, Au Bon Pain makes maximum use of facility location and layout design considerations to improve its serviceability and profitability.

DISCUSSION AND REVIEW QUESTIONS

1. Why are facility location analysis and layout design necessary operations management functions?
2. Briefly describe the three steps of facility location analysis. What are some of the major differences between each of these steps?
3. Why is it necessary to identify a capacity shortfall in facility location analysis?
4. How is facility location analysis tied to strategic planning?
5. What are four different types of OM layouts? Give a real-world example of each for illustration purposes. List one advantage and one disadvantage of each layout when comparing one with another.
6. What is the objective of product layout design?
7. What is a cellular layout design?
8. How is the distance-minimizing layout procedure used in layout design?
9. How are computers used in layout design? Give some examples of computer software currently used in layout design.
10. How is the line-balancing procedure used in layout design?
11. How can expert systems be used in cellular manufacturing?
12. How can the transportation method be used to evaluate more than one possible site location at a time?

PROBLEMS

1. Suppose that a company wants to relocate one of its plants from one of four regions, as shown in the following figure:

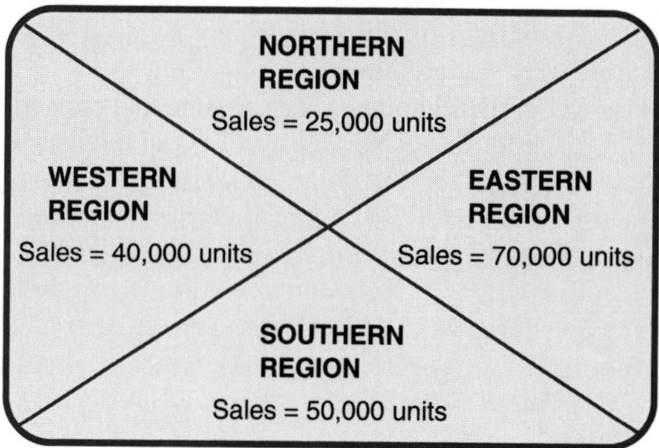

Based on long-term forecasts, the future sales by region is as follows:

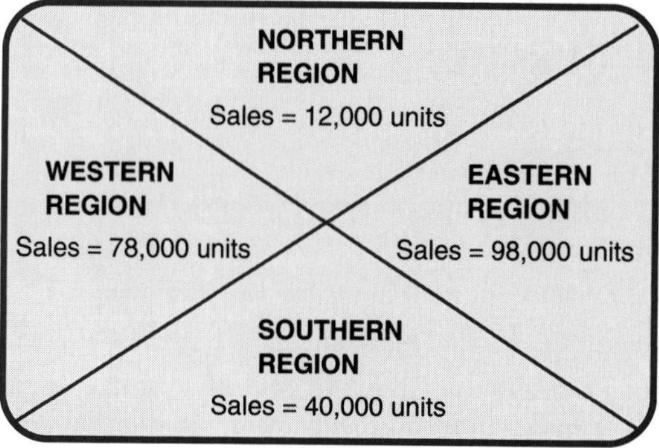

Which region would you recommend relocating a plant from? Which region would you recommend relocating a plant to? Explain and justify your answer. What are you assuming?

2. (This problem requires the contents of Supplement 13-1.) A company wants to use the transportation method to find the best plant site based on transportation cost minimization. Following is the current arrangement of its three plants (1, 2, and 3) and its markets (A, B, and C):

FROM \ TO	A	B	C	Supply
1	6	11	17	100
2	10	12	5	200
3	15	19	9	300
Demand	200	200	200	600

The company has had a unit sales forecast that shows that demand in market C will increase from 200 to 400 units. To make up this production capacity the company is going to build a new plant on either of two site locations (site X or site Y). The cost to ship one unit from site X to each of the three markets is 10, 14, and 15 dollars, respectively. The cost to ship one unit from site Y to each of the three markets is 18, 20, and 5, respectively. Which site should we recommend based on transportation cost minimization?

3. (This problem requires the contents of Supplement 13-1.) Referring to Problem 2, suppose that the demand in market C shifts from 200 to 500. The company would like a more complete analysis that would consider the addition of one new plant to the three currently in operation to make up for the capacity shortfall. The location of the new plant can be on any one of three sites: site X with costs of 8, 9, and 19; site Y with costs of 5, 20, and 14; and site Z with costs of 8, 12, and 9. Which of these three sites should be added to minimize the network transportation costs? Show your work.

4. Suppose that we have the following 3 × 3 departmental room layout for nine different departments of A, B, C, D, E, F, G, H, and I:

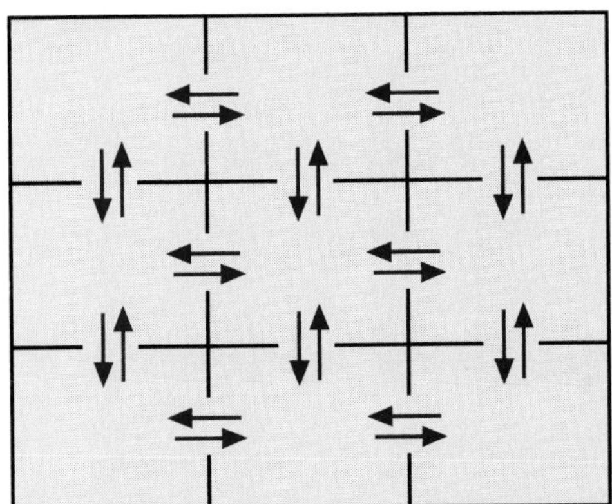

Given the following nearness priorities, what is the most desirable layout?

Departments	*Priority*
A near B	1
C near A	2
A near E	3
E near F	4
A near H	5
B near F	6
I near H	7
E near H	8
G near B	9
C near B	10

5. Suppose that we have a 2 × 3 departmental room layout for six different departments of A, B, C, D, E, and F, as shown on the top of page 666.

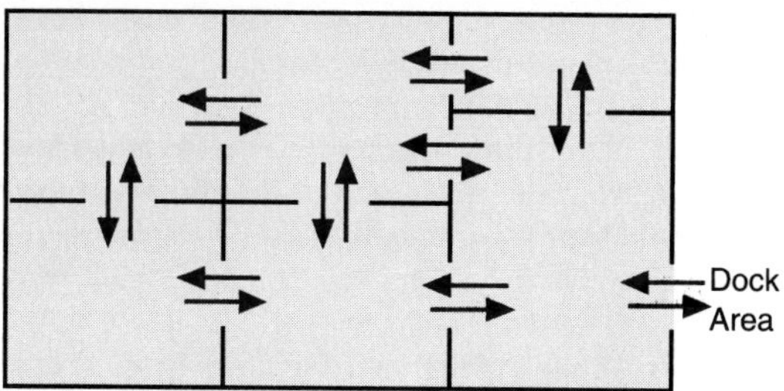

The dock area requires that department D be located next to it. Given the following nearness priorities, what is the most desirable layout?

Departments	*Priority*
D near dock area	1
C near A	2
A near D	3
B near A	4
A near F	5
B near F	6
C near F	7

* 6. Suppose that we have the following 2 × 3 departmental room layout for six different departments of A, B, C, D, E, and F.

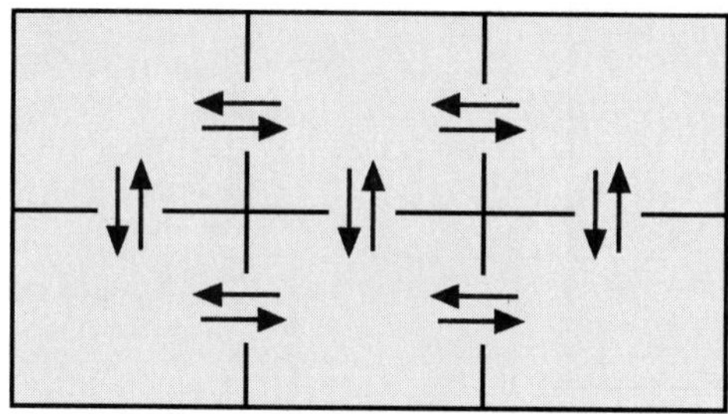

Given the following nearness priorities, what is the most desirable layout?

Departments	*Priority*
A near B	1
C near A	2
A near E	3
E near F	4
A near F	5
B near F	6

* The solutions to problems marked with an asterisk can be found in Appendix J.

7. Suppose that we have the following 3 × 3 departmental room layout for nine different departments of A, B, C, D, E, F, G, H, and I:

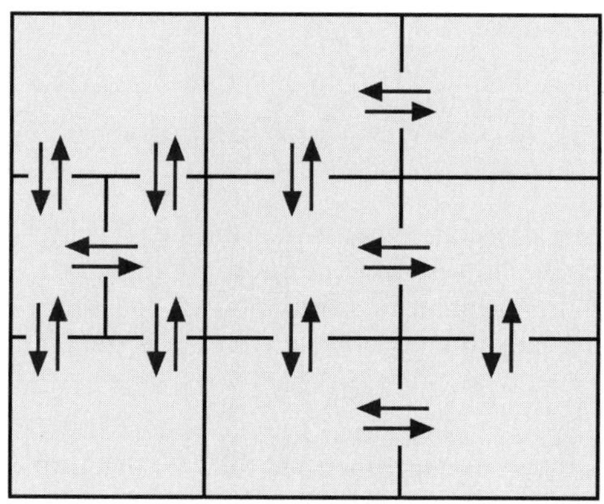

Given the following nearness priorities, what is the most desirable layout?

Departments	*Priority*
H near B	1
C near A	2
H near E	3
E near F	4
A near H	5
B near F	6
I near H	7
G near B	8
C near B	9

* 8. Given the following expected number of trips between the departments, determine their nearness priorities:

From \ To	Receiving	Machine Shop	Painting	Assembly	Quality Control	Shipping
Receiving	—	23	4	12	0	2
Machine Shop	12	—	38	27	13	0
Painting	9	45	—	13	12	0
Assembly	6	89	20	—	50	4
Quality Control	8	4	12	8	—	23
Shipping	4	2	3	3	45	—

9. Referring to Problem 8, suppose that each department required the amounts of floor space shown in the table at the top of page 668.

Department	*Required Floor Space (sq. ft.)*
Receiving	1,200
Machine Shop	1,500
Painting	1,600
Assembly	4,000
Quality Control	900
Shipping	400

Using the distance-minimizing layout procedure, determine the best facility layout design. Remember to try and satisfy the highest-level nearness priorities first. (Only place the squared departments in an arrangement to satisfy most of the priorities; do not try to convert the squared departments into rectangular forms as presented in this chapter.)

10. Given the expected number of trips between departments as follows, determine their nearness priorities:

From \ To	Receiving	Machine Shop	Painting	Assembly	Quality Control	Shipping
Receiving	—	80	58	48	14	15
Machine Shop	72	—	69	64	27	19
Painting	36	67	—	34	46	8
Assembly	37	79	20	—	78	18
Quality Control	21	37	12	9	—	52
Shipping	42	5	8	6	67	—

11. Referring to Problem 10, suppose that the departments required the following amounts of floor space:

Department	*Required Floor Space (sq. ft.)*
Receiving	5,600
Machine Shop	4,900
Painting	3,600
Assembly	8,100
Quality Control	690
Shipping	300

Using the distance-minimizing layout procedure, determine the best facility layout design, satisfying the highest-level nearness priorities first. (Only place the squared departments in an arrangement to satisfy most of the priorities; do not try to convert the squared departments into rectangular forms as presented in the chapter.)

12. Given the expected number of trips between the departments shown in the figure at the top of the next page, determine their nearness priorities.

From \ To	Receiving	Machine Shop	Painting	Assembly	Quality Control	Shipping
Receiving	—	90	58	48	14	0
Machine Shop	140	—	45	47	27	0
Painting	66	67	—	120	34	4
Assembly	37	79	20	—	110	11
Quality Control	41	37	2	9	—	25
Shipping	42	5	3	7	67	—

13. Referring to Problem 12, suppose that the departments each required the following amounts of floor space:

Department	*Required Floor Space (sq. ft.)*
Receiving	240
Machine Shop	1,200
Painting	690
Assembly	7,000
Quality Control	300
Shipping	830

Using the distance-minimizing layout procedure, determine the best facility layout design. Remember to satisfy the highest-level nearness priorities first. (Only place the squared departments in an arrangement to satisfy most of the priorities; do not try to convert the squared departments into rectangular forms as presented in the chapter.)

14. If we have eight different departments that we want to position in a process layout and each can possibly be laid out next to one another, and each has some trips to each of the other departments, how many possible nearness priorities could we determine? What if we have ten different departments?

*15. Suppose that we have a product that we want to assemble on a product layout system. The job tasks required for the completion of the product are presented with their appropriate time in seconds:

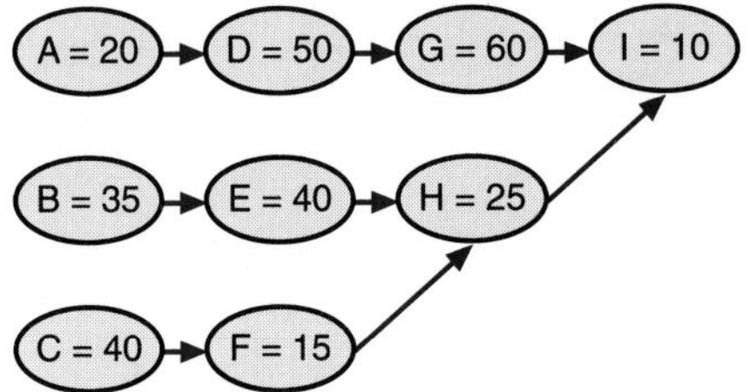

With a cycle time of 60 seconds, allocate the work tasks to the least number of workcenters possible using the line-balancing method discussed in this chapter.

16. Suppose that a firm wants to assemble a product. The job tasks required for the completion of the product, along with their appropriate time in seconds, are as follows:

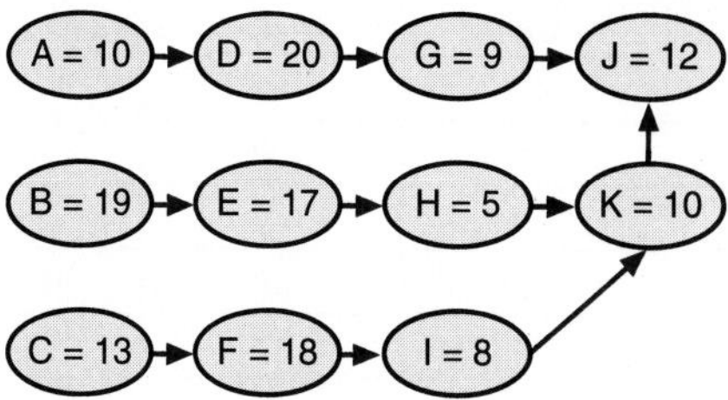

Determine the following:
a. The smallest cycle time
b. The number of workcenters required for this layout
c. I
d. P

17. Suppose that a small manufacturer plans to assemble a product. The job tasks required for the completion of the product, along with their appropriate time in seconds, are as follows:

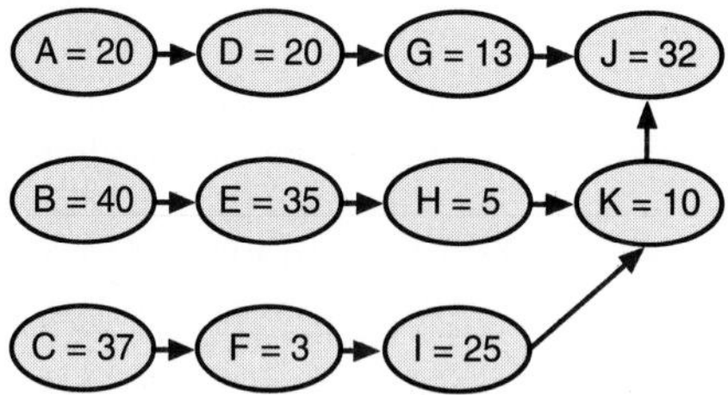

Determine the following:
a. The smallest cycle time
b. The number of workcenters required for this layout
c. I
d. P

18. A company plans to assemble a product. The job tasks required for the completion of the product, along with their appropriate time in seconds, are as follows:

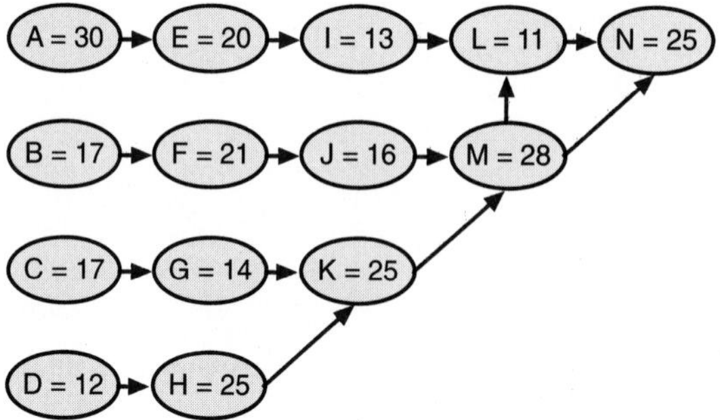

Determine the following:

a. The smallest cycle time
b. The number of workcenters required for this layout
c. *I*
d. *P*

19. Suppose that a manufacturer wants to assemble a product. The tasks required for the completion of the product, along with their appropriate time in seconds, are as follows:

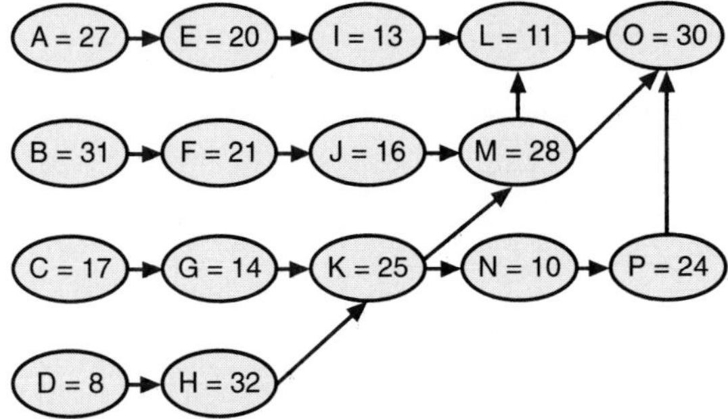

Suppose that the company wants to achieve a production rate of 72 units per hour. Determine the number of workcenters required to achieve this layout. Determine both of the line balancing procedure statistics, *I* and *P*. Explain the meaning of the layout statistics.

*20. A farm tools fabrication company started implementing an FMS layout in early 1992. Its plant at that time was fully utilizing its 22,000 total square feet of storage space. Unfortunately, the materials inventory was so packed into the plant that workers were damaging goods by moving them through the plant. For example, out of 5,000 loads moved in January 1992, 500 were damaged. Under the FMS system in January 1993, materials space required only 20,000 total square feet and only 1,000 loads out of 9,000 total loads were damaged. If a reduction in both SSUR and DGR is desired, has the move to an FMS layout been a successful strategy? Support your decision with the appropriate ratio information.

21. A manufacturer has implemented a product layout for each of the three products the manufacturer produces. In January 1993 the plant was fully utilizing its 100,000 total square feet of storage space. Unfortunately, the materials inventory was so packed into the plant that workers were damaging goods by moving them through the plant. For example, out of 10,000 loads moved in January 1993, 800 were damaged. By using the product layout in January 1994, materials space required dropped to only 90,000 total square feet, and only 1,000 loads out of 24,000 total loads were damaged. If a reduction in both SSUR and DGR is desired, has the move to a product layout been a successful strategy? Support your decision with the appropriate ratio information.

22. A manufacturer has implemented a cellular line layout such that each cell focuses on producing a specific product family of products. In January 1993 the plant was fully utilizing its 200,000 total square feet of storage space. Unfortunately, the materials inventory was so packed into the plant that workers were damaging goods by moving them through the plant. Indeed, it was estimated that the materials inventory caused the 190,000 orders processed in January 1993 to travel a total of 95 miles while being

processed. For example, out of 8,000 loads moved in January 1993, 1,000 were damaged. By using the cellular line layout in January 1994, materials space required dropped to only 120,000 total square feet, and only 4,000 loads out of 18,000 total loads were damaged. The total distance in feet the 250,000 orders traveled during January 1994 was 6 miles. If a reduction in all three ratios of SSUR, DTR, and DGR are desired, has the move to a cellular line layout been a successful strategy? Support your decision with the appropriate ratio information.

CASE 13-1

WHICH PLANT SHOULD WE SHUT DOWN?

The Gupta Tea Company of Dallas, Texas has processed and distributed food products throughout the United States for more than half a century. The company's product line consists of a variety of food products sold to retailing and wholesaling organizations. While Gupta originally started in the business selling only tea products, it has continually expanded its line of food products to meet customer demands. The company's markets are divided into five regions, each defined by its respective consolidated metropolitan statistical area (CMSA). These CMSAs include New York, St. Louis, Los Angeles, Chicago, and Miami. Gupta purchases, grows, and produces most of its own products. The tea product's raw materials are imported and processed by Gupta in four plants located in different regions of the United States. The tea products are produced and distributed to a single major warehousing facility in each of the five CMSAs for later distribution to individual stores.

In earlier years, the company had been very successful in marketing its tea products and competing with other well-known brands of tea. In the last few years, however, competition became very intense as herbal and health tea food products expanded to retail food stores. Tea product sales had definitely matured and leveled off in the last few years, despite an increase in marketing efforts to promote the tea products. Many of the production plants that processed the tea products were being underutilized. The increased costs of operations pressured the organization to increase its prices for tea products to make up the cost of underutilized capacity.

The president of Gupta Tea Company decided that something would have to be done to improve the situation. After considerable discussion with the marketing vice president and market analyst, the president decided that there was little chance that Gupta would successfully improve the demand of its tea products. The analyst presented the president with a comparison of actual sales in the current year with a forecast of yearly sales two years in the future. These forecast data are presented in Exhibit 13C-1. As we can see, the current year's hundred-box container sales in the New York CMSA is 4,500 units and its forecast demand two years hence will be only 3,350 units. This represents a decrease of 25.5 percent from sales in the current year. There appeared no choice but to reduce the tea product production capacity in the hope that it would help keep Gupta's prices competitive in the future.

Gupta's four plants are small, and all were constructed using the same fixed-design layout. Each plant has a maximum capacity of 6,000 containers of tea a year, but each is currently operating at about the 5,000-unit production level. Each of the four plants produces 5,000 units each to meet this year's sales demand of 20,000 containers. One of the four plants needed to be shut down to balance the expected forecast demand with production capacity of 15,000 containers. The president realized that it might take up to two years to officially close one of the plants because of labor and contractual agree-

EXHIBIT 13C-1 UNIT DEMAND FORECAST DATA

Sales Market	*Actual Sales This Year (containers)**	*Forecast Sales Two Years from Now (containers)*	*Percentage Decrease (%)*
New York	4,500	3,350	25.5
St. Louis	3,500	2,650	24.3
Los Angeles	2,500	1,900	24.0
Chicago	4,500	3,350	25.5
Miami	5,000	3,750	25.0
	20,000	15,000	

* A unit of tea is a one-hundred-box container that is used to protect the tea product in shipping.

ments, but one would have to be closed and the announcement for closing purposes should come as soon as possible.

From the percentage sales decrease in Exhibit 13C-1, it does not appear that any one region in the country has a significantly greater forecasted decrease than any other. This ruled out the easy decision of shutting down the plant whose region had the greatest decrease in sales. The president reasoned that the decision as to which plant should be shut down would have to come from considering (1) the costs of the individual operations and (2) the costs of the operations taken collectively as a network operation. Because of the similarity of layout, there are no individual costs of operation that differentiated the four plants. The only major cost item, when the plants are viewed as a network operation, is their transportation costs for shipping the finished product from the plants to markets. These costs are presented in Exhibit 13C-2. As we can see, the cost to ship one container of one hundred boxes of tea from manufacturing plant 1 to the New York market is $45.

CASE QUESTION

Which plant should be shut down? Show your work.

EXHIBIT 13C-2 SHIPPING COSTS

Manufacturing Plant	*SHIPPING COSTS PER CONTAINER FOR EACH MARKET LOCATION (DOLLARS/CONTAINERS)*				
	New York	*St. Louis*	*Los Angeles*	*Chicago*	*Miami*
1	45	30	10	35	42
2	5	28	51	25	41
3	37	20	56	28	5
4	32	12	38	3	28

CASE 13-2

WHO IS GOING TO LAYOUT WHOM?

The Jetson Manufacturing Company (JMC) is a major producer of an electronic sensor used in CIM control systems. The company has been very successful with this growth stage product. In fact, the line of electronic sensor products increased so rapidly in just the last few years that its current manufacturing facility could no longer support its customer demand requirements. The company has started subcontracting work as a short-range solution but wanted a more permanent solution. Because the lease on the property of JMC's current facility would expire in a few years, the management of the company felt that it was justified in building a new facility. The management decided to begin a three-year facility location analysis. At the end of the analysis it is expected to find the ideal location for the new manufacturing facility.

As an input into the site location stage of the facility location analysis, the minimum size of the land required to support the new facility must be determined. To answer this question management first estimated the minimum square footage of the building that would house its new manufacturing facility. The heads of each of the five departments that make up the current manufacturing facility were asked to estimate the square footage needed to support the future production activities of their respective departments. Based on forecast demand requirements, each department head planned the estimated square feet. Because much of the sensor manufacturing equipment was highly automated, the bulk of the facility's square-feet requirements could be fairly and accurately estimated based on size of the equipment and necessary spacing for personnel usage. The five departmental estimates are presented in Exhibit 13C-3. In addition to the square-feet requirements, the movement between the departments in terms of trips (from and to) were estimated based on current activity extrapolations to meet the increased future demand requirements. These travel estimates are presented in Exhibit 13C-4. In addition, the facility layout had to have the receiving department and the shipping department on opposite ends of the resulting structure.

A layout design consultant was hired to estimate the final structure and square-feet allocation of the new facility. The final structure should have at least the mimimum square-feet requirements of each department as shown in Exhibit 13C-3 and should

EXHIBIT 13C-3 ESTIMATED FLOOR SPACE REQUIREMENTS BY DEPARTMENT

Department	*Required Square Feet*
Receiving	5,000
Inventory	20,000
Assembly	18,000
Finishing	21,000
Shipping	5,000

EXHIBIT 13C-4 EXPECTED NUMBER OF TRIPS BETWEEN DEPARTMENTS PER DAY

From/To	*Receiving*	*Inventory*	*Assembly*	*Finishing*	*Shipping*
Receiving	—	68	96	25	2
Inventory	24	—	112	23	10
Assembly	13	56	—	101	9
Finishing	15	7	134	—	89
Shipping	4	21	11	5	—

minimize the traveling distance of the organization's personnel. Also, the building must be square-shaped to meet building design preferences of the organization's president.

CASE QUESTIONS

1. If you were the consultant in this case, what method would you use? Explain and justify your selection.
2. What are the nearness priorities for the layout of the departments in the desired facility?
3. What is the actual layout of the facility, taking the nearness priorities and other design constraints into consideration? Draw and label each department's resulting square footage.
4. What is the total square footage of the resulting facility?

SUPPLEMENT 13-1

The Transportation Method and Facility Location Analysis

In Chapter 5, we discussed the use of the transportation method in production planning and in Chapter 6 we again used it to minimize total transportation costs in planning an organization's transportation needs. The solution procedure for the transportation method is presented in Appendix I. (Students are encouraged to review this material to better understand how the transportation method is applied in this section.) The transportation method can be used in both the region selection and the site selection steps of facility location analysis, when sites are significantly distant from one another.

In either the region selection or site selection steps, the transportation method is used solely as an objective, cost-minimizing approach in the selection process. If minimizing transportation costs is the chief criterion for region or site selection, as it might be in locating a transportation terminal facility, then the transportation method can play a major role in deciding the specific region or site location. In practice, however, the results of using the transportation method are usually used in concert with other site selection criteria.

As we have seen in Chapters 5 and 6, the transportation method is an optimization procedure that seeks to determine the least-cost transportation schedule given a set of supply sources and demand destinations. The supply sources in a site selection problem are the current manufacturing plants. The demand destinations in a site selection problem are the current market locations for the products. We can use the transportation method to examine any type of site selection problem such as adding, dropping, or relocating a given plant. We can also use it to examine multiple changes of adding, dropping, or relocating several plants simultaneously.

The transportation method is used in facility location analysis to determine the least-cost network of manufacturing plants and market demand destinations. To illustrate the use of the transportation method, let's look at an example of a region-site selection problem. Suppose that a company currently operates a plant in each of three cities: Phoenix, Kansas City, and Minneapolis. The company only produces one product. The Phoenix plant manufactures 75 units of the product each day, the Kansas City plant 150 units, and the Minneapolis plant 50 units. This total production of 275 units represents the total capacity of these plants. The products are sold in three markets: 125 units each day in San Diego, 125 units in Houston, and 25 units in Atlanta. This transportation problem formulation, with its costs, supply, and demand requirements, is presented in Exhibit 13S-1, along with its solution.

Now suppose that we experience an increase in the product demand in the Atlanta market such that we may need to build a new manufacturing plant. The demand in Atlanta will shift from 25 units to 175 units, requiring a new manufacturing facility to produce 150 units (175 − 25). The company currently owns two pieces of real estate, and each is capable of housing the new plant. The site locations of the property owned by the company are in two very different regions of the country: Omaha, Nebraska (site 1) and New York, New York (site 2).

The company felt that cost minimization of transporting its finished product to the markets should be the sole criterion for site selection in this problem. How then do we consider this new region-site location problem with the transportation method? We simply make two separate transportation problems, one each for the two sites. While the transportation costs in Exhibit 13S-1 remain the same for the existing plants and markets, the addition of a new plant will alter the transportation problem. As we can see in Exhibit 13S-2, the transportation problem formulation for site 1 changes the problem formulation by adding the new costs in the Omaha row of the table. When we solve this problem using the transportation method, we end up with a total transportation cost for the network of shipments from the three existing plants along with the proposed fourth plant located in Omaha to all of the markets. As we can see in Exhibit 13S-2(b), the total transportation costs for this transportation problem is $2,250. This is not just the cost of transportation for the new plant, but the network of all plants and markets.

To continue the analysis, we drop the Omaha plant (and Omaha's transportation costs) and replace it with a plant in New York (and New York's transportation costs).

EXHIBIT 13S-1 EXAMPLE OF SITE LOCATION TRANSPORTATION PROBLEM FORMULATION AND SOLUTION: PRE-SITE LOCATION

(A) TRANSPORTATION PROBLEM FORMULATION AND SOLUTION

FROM \ TO	San Diego	Houston	Atlanta	Supply
Phoenix	6 (75)	7	9	75
Kansas City	10 (50)	4 (75)	5 (25)	150
Minneapolis	11	3 (50)	9	50
Demand	125	125	25	275

(B) TRANSPORTATION PROBLEM SCHEDULE AND TOTAL COSTS

From	To	Cost	Units	Total Costs
Phoenix	San Diego	$ 6	75	$ 450
Kansas City	San Diego	10	50	500
Kansas City	Houston	4	75	300
Kansas City	Atlanta	5	25	125
Minneapolis	Houston	3	50	150
				$1,525

EXHIBIT 13S-2 EXAMPLE OF SITE LOCATION TRANSPORTATION PROBLEM FORMULATION AND SOLUTION: SITE 1

(A) TRANSPORTATION PROBLEM FORMULATION AND SOLUTION

FROM \ TO	San Diego	Houston	Atlanta	Supply
Phoenix	6 (75)	7	9	75
Kansas City	10	4	5 (150)	150
Minneapolis	11 (25)	3	9 (25)	50
Omaha	12 (25)	2 (125)	13	150
Demand	125	125	175	275

(B) TRANSPORTATION PROBLEM SCHEDULE AND TOTAL COSTS

From	To	Cost	Units	Total Costs
Phoenix	San Diego	$ 6	75	$ 450
Kansas City	Atlanta	5	150	750
Minneapolis	San Diego	11	25	275
Minneapolis	Atlanta	9	25	225
Omaha	San Diego	12	25	300
Omaha	Houston	2	125	250
				$2,250

This transportation problem formulation and solution are presented in Exhibit 13S-3. Notice that the transportation schedule is significantly different than the one determined when the Omaha site was considered. Most importantly, the total minimized cost is different: Site 2 has a greater total cost than site 1. Based solely on the minimization of transportation costs, the company would locate a new plant at site 1 because it is less costly ($2,250 for Omaha versus $2,275 for New York).

Total minimized cost is an objective criterion on which to make a region or site selection decision. The transportation method presented here is a fairly simplistic technique that is helpful if transportation cost minimization is a major or important selection criterion.

In this sample problem, we also indirectly illustrated the use of the transportation method in the region selection step of facility location analysis. In this problem, the company had already limited the site selection decision to either Omaha or New York. It is unlikely that Omaha and New York would be grouped into the same region.

A Tour of Au Bon Pain Facilities

1. **Overview.** Au Bon Pain is a food service organization with over one hundred and fifty cafes and fast-food stands. Headquartered in Boston, the four-thousand-person operation stretches through New England and is spreading rapidly across the United States. Au Bon Pain specializes in fresh-baked French bakery items, such as baguettes, croissants, and muffins, plus sandwiches, salads, and soups.

Menu courtesy of Au Bon Pain Co., Inc.
Photo © 1992 Peter Vanderwarker.

Menu

■ Welcome to Au Bon Pain.

We're proud to offer our menu of fine foods. All of our products are made from the highest quality ingredients. And, we bake fresh throughout the day, so you can be sure that the products you purchase are absolutely fresh.

au bon pain

Coffee Roaster • Baker • Sandwich Maker • Caterer

2. **Traditional Layouts.** Where space is ample, Au Bon Pain designs a traditional straight-line deli counter layout, with separate seating for customers' convenience. This layout, which is ideal for low-traffic areas where patrons are not hurried, makes possible the preparation of customized food products.

Photos © 1992 Peter Vanderwarker.

3. **Alternative Layouts.** Where space is limited and traffic is high, Au Bon Pain uses nontraditional layouts, such as this kiosk in Boston's South Station. The additional counter space afforded by a circular layout accommodates a higher traffic flow than the straight-line deli. Because of space limitations, these food service facilities often have smaller menus. To ensure acceptable quality and service, Au Bon Pain management maintains minimum standards for menu offerings at these facilities.

4. Self-Serve Units. In very cramped spaces, Au Bon Pain installs self-serve express units, whose layout permits presence in small office buildings, where food service operations are usually prohibited.

Photo © 1992 Peter Vanderwarker.

5. Traffic Flow. In much the same way that manufacturers seek to maximize the flow of materials through production, service organizations seek to maximize customer attention and traffic flow into and through their facilities. Notice how the arrangement and color of the outdoor seating at this Au Bon Pain facility draw attention to the store in the background, inviting passersby to enter. *Photo by Jean Smith.*

6. **Technological Support.** It takes more than good products and workable layouts to make a successful business. Ron Shaich (left), and Louis Kane (right), co-chairmen of Au Bon Pain, invested in new technology. As part of their tactical planning, they installed a highly integrated computer information system to link operations at over one hundred sites. On-site NCR cash registers and integrated laptop computers help minimize managers' paperwork. Data on sales figures, weekly payroll changes, and menu items are electronically transmitted from the store sites to a central facility for use in corporate processing and planning.
Photo by Brian Smith.

7. **Strategic Improvements.** During the 1980s, Au Bon Pain was plagued by high turnover and complaints of poor service. Recognizing the strategic importance of treating employees with respect and allowing them greater authority to run their operations, management decided to place more responsibility for decision making at the store manager level. As a result, store managers like Gary Aronson became partner managers, with a $500 minimum weekly salary plus a 35 percent share of the store's profits once its goals are met. The results were a dramatic increase in per-store sales and profits, as well as higher-quality service across the board.
Photo © 1993 by Seth Resnick.

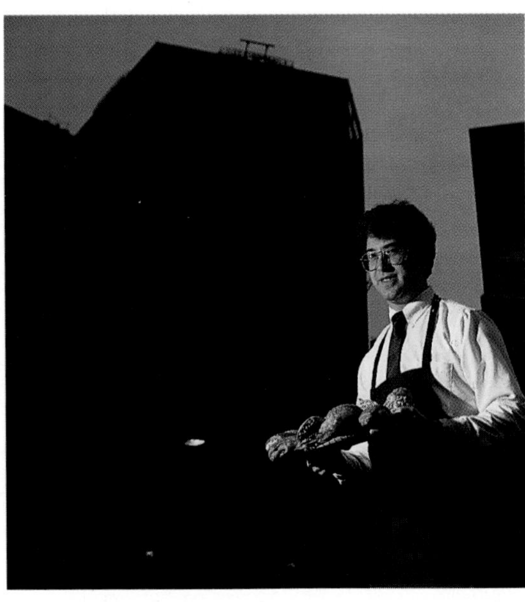

EXHIBIT 13S-3 EXAMPLE OF SITE LOCATION TRANSPORTATION PROBLEM FORMULATION AND SOLUTION: SITE 2

(A) TRANSPORTATION PROBLEM FORMULATION AND SOLUTION

FROM \ TO	San Diego	Houston	Atlanta	Supply
Phoenix	6 (75)	7	9	75
Kansas City	10 (50)	4 (75)	5 (25)	150
Minneapolis	11	3 (50)	9	50
New York	15	10	5 (150)	150
Demand	125	125	175	275

(B) TRANSPORTATION PROBLEM SCHEDULE AND TOTAL COSTS

From	To	Cost	Units	Total Costs
Phoenix	San Diego	$ 6	75	$ 450
Kansas City	San Diego	10	50	500
Kansas City	Houston	4	75	300
Kansas City	Atlanta	5	25	125
Minneapolis	Houston	3	50	150
New York	Atlanta	5	150	750
				$2,275

Because we are measuring total network transportation costs, we might have considered the costs of shipping to New York as an average estimate of the northeastern part of the United States and let Omaha transportation costs be representative of the midwestern region. The solution to this problem then would have indicated that network transportation costs could be minimized by selecting a site in the midwest region. Given this region selection decision, we then can use other facility location analyses to actually determine the specific site location within the midwest region.

14

Job Design and Work Measurement

CHAPTER OUTLINE

CHAPTER OBJECTIVES

The material in this chapter should prepare you to do the following:

1. Explain what job design is and how operations managers use it to improve operation productivity.
2. Explain why work measurement is a necessary monitoring function of management.
3. Describe how work environment factors affect worker performance.
4. Describe various monetary and nonmonetary approaches to instilling a positive work attitude.
5. Explain what anthropometric data are and how they are used in job design.
6. Describe how a micromotion analysis is conducted.
7. Explain how to conduct a time study.
8. Explain how to conduct a work sampling study.
9. Explain the use of learning curves as an aid in work measurement.
10. Describe some of the laws, acts, and government agencies that help define constraints in job design.

In the last chapter we discussed procedures for designing facility layouts, which included positioning departments, equipment, and workcenter facilities. Extending that analysis, we now turn our attention to designing the job that the worker performs. In job design the objective is to structure the worker's environment and tasks to maximize worker productivity. Human resources in operations management are not limited to blue-collar workers but also include white-collar workers. We want to design jobs so workers can perform them as efficiently and effectively as possible.

Operations managers, supervisors, industrial engineers, and quite commonly the workers themselves study and improve the work tasks that make up a worker's job. They improve job designs by changing the job's work environment, by better fitting the work task requirements with the worker's capabilities, and by redesigning the work task requirements themselves. Each of these three types of job design considerations—work environment, worker capabilities, and work tasks—will be examined in this chapter as opportunities for productivity improvement.

Once we have determined the productivity-maximizing job design, we need to make sure that workers comply with the new methods and procedures. One approach of monitoring and measuring work performance is with the use of work measurement. **Work measurement** is a collection of observational and statistical procedures that are used to measure worker job performance. The objective of work measurement is to determine a "fair day's work."

We use work measurement data to develop work standards that either define the standard amount of work a worker should perform in a given period of time or the standard amount of time a worker should be allowed in which to perform a given task. Work standards define what an organization considers a "fair day's work." Once work standards are established, they are used to measure current worker performance on a comparative basis. We will discuss work measurement concepts and methods in this chapter.

In designing new jobs, we are directly affecting people and what they do for a living. When changing people's jobs, there are a number of legal constraints that must be considered by operations managers. We will also briefly describe some of the basic laws, acts, and regulatory agencies that operations managers must consider in performing a job design or redesign.

• • •

WHY JOB DESIGN AND WORK MEASUREMENT ARE NECESSARY

In Chapter 1, we discussed the measurement of productivity as the simple ratio of output over input. In manufacturing we often measure productivity in terms of manufacturing output. In Figure 14-1 and Table 14-1, we can see that the United States's growth in manufacturing productivity as measured by output has consistently outperformed United Kingdom and European competitors. The United States, however, has consistently been outperformed by Japan since the early 1980s. As of January 1993, this relative positioning of U.S. productivity with Europe and Japan remains unchanged.

FIGURE 14-1 ANNUAL INDEXES OF MANUFACTURING PRODUCTIVITY

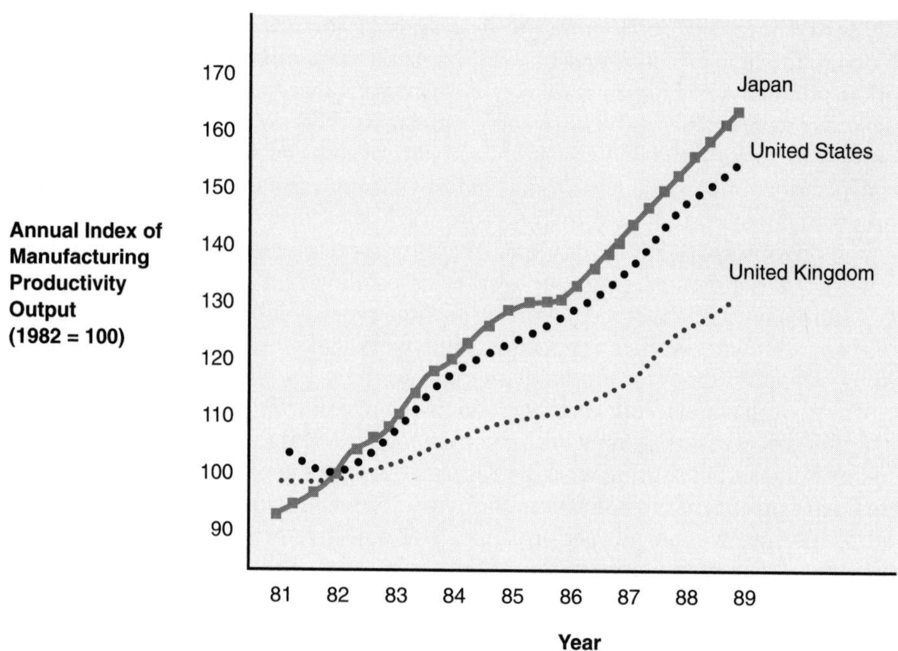

Source: Data from *National Labor Review* (August 1991), 94.

Some of the reasons for the United States's poor productivity increase can be traced to outmoded technology and lack of investment in more productive equipment. But a major contributor of a company's, and therefore a country's, productivity performance is directly traceable to the way in which workers perform their individual jobs. If we can find a new approach or philosophy for performing a worker's job that will result in the same amount of goods being produced in less time, we have improved the efficiency and productivity of the worker's job.

Sometimes, in an effort to improve worker efficiency, we create new problems that can cause inefficiencies in an operations management system. The design of assembly line manufacturing systems by Henry Ford in 1913 was viewed as the most efficient OM system of its time. But as time passed, manufacturers found that the job specialization required to operate an assembly line created other problems that actually reduced productivity. The assembly line operations of that period were designed with dangerous and unclean working environments, and the job task specialization of the repetitive operation was boring and decreased worker motivation. Researchers such as Henry Gantt (developer of the Gantt chart) quickly pointed out that worker morale played an important part in productivity. Research and industry practice have shown over the years that job design can truly be improved to enhance productivity only by a deliberate and comprehensive approach that considers work environment, worker motivation and

TABLE 14-1 ANNUAL INDEXES OF MANUFACTURING PRODUCTIVITY OUTPUT

Country	*1981*	*1982*	*1983*	*1984*	*1985*	*1986*	*1987*	*1988*	*1989*
United States	106.9	100.0	106.2	118.6	122.8	126.6	133.9	146.2	151.5
Canada	114.8	100.0	106.5	120.2	127.0	127.9	133.0	139.5	140.2
Japan	94.5	100.0	108.0	120.5	128.9	129.6	138.9	150.0	161.2
Belgium	95.8	100.0	105.0	107.2	107.9	106.8	108.9	115.6	120.8
Denmark	98.4	100.0	106.7	111.7	115.3	115.3	110.6	111.0	112.4
France	99.0	100.0	99.9	98.7	99.1	99.1	99.6	103.0	107.2
Germany	102.4	100.0	101.1	103.9	107.4	107.4	104.3	107.4	112.4
Italy	101.0	100.0	100.9	105.5	108.7	111.1	115.6	124.4	128.2
Netherlands	101.5	100.0	101.9	107.9	111.1	113.7	113.9	120.0	125.1
Norway	100.7	100.0	99.3	105.0	108.8	108.8	110.8	107.5	107.8
Sweden	99.6	100.0	105.7	113.7	115.9	116.7	119.9	122.7	124.2
United Kingdom	99.8	100.0	102.9	106.8	109.6	111.1	116.9	125.2	130.5

Source: Monthly Labor Review, Sept. 1989, p. 34.

capabilities, and the work tasks themselves. The job design function of operations management provides this necessary analysis to improve both service and manufacturing organizations' productivity.

Work measurement is a necessary extension of job design. In the past, work measurement was simply used to keep workers' performance at a standardized rate of production or at some acceptable normal level of activity. The work measurement statistics that reflected worker job performance were boundaries that defined acceptable work performance. As boundaries, they were often used in the past by workers to restrict other workers' performance. The expression *rate busters* was often used to characterize workers who, because of their unique capabilities or motivation, performed above the standard or normal level of work activity. Rate busting, or exceeding work standards, was viewed by workers as unacceptable behavior and generally caused much disruption in the organization.

Today, many of the new approaches to operations management such as JIT allow the worker some freedom to produce at above-average productivity levels. As such, work measurement, as discussed in this chapter, is used not to establish a boundary that defines a fair day's work but rather to establish a productivity goal in time or units that is meant to be exceeded. Some companies have found that the use of work measurements as a means of monitoring productivity can greatly increase an organization's overall performance. By knowing the amount of human effort required to produce a unit of goods, we can assess our labor costs precisely and use the information to accurately plan product pricing, control labor requirements usage, and schedule unit production. For these reasons, work measurement is a necessary operations management function.

The ever-increasing applications of computer-integrated manufacturing (CIM) and computer-integrated service systems (CISS) require increased use of automated equipment and often decreased or redeployed use of human resources. Indeed, highly automated plants evolve gradually, as organizations introduce automation first for simple functions (such as moving inventory with an automated guided vehicle or AGV) and then for increasingly complex and integrated functions (such as producing an entire product with automated systems). This tactical medium-range planning of the application and integration of automated equipment requires human resource job design and work measurement activities. For organizations whose operations management strategy is to move toward fully automated CIM and CISS environments, job design and work measurement are never-ending tactical planning functions. As automation gradually replaces or changes the functions of human resources, the jobs need to be redesigned to make up for activities that robots or other automated equipment cannot perform. Job design allows new job content to be identified and altered to support the requirements of new automated systems. Job design gives management a means of building a job (that is, assigning job tasks) to efficiently use the advantages of the automated equipment with the advantages of the human resource, while minimizing the disadvantages of both. Work measurement, on the other hand, is also continuously performed during the automation process. It provides management with necessary information to keep track of worker productivity during the changeover. The work measurements allow management to monitor and determine the progress of automation as it relates to improving productivity. The data from work measurement are often used to help justify the further acquisitions of automated equipment, thus allowing the OM strategic goal of a fully automated CIM or CISS. As a matter of fact, some researchers feel that job design and work measurement are a necessary part of any modern manufacturing strategy.[1]

BASICS OF JOB DESIGN

In today's operation, a great number of jobs previously performed by human beings are now being performed by equipment such as robots and AGVs. In some cases, the equipment performs jobs to minimize the risk of injury or discomfort to human beings, since this risk can be very costly to both the worker and the organization. In some cases, the equipment performs jobs because it is more productive (and therefore less costly) than human resources in actually completing the work tasks. Human beings are still necessary in situations in which new solutions are required to solve recurring problems and the ability to generalize from experience is needed. Technology is closing the gap even in this area with the introduction of artificial intelligence and expert systems (introduced in Chapter 1).

[1] R. E. Walton and G. I. Susman, "People Policies for New Machines," *Harvard Business Review* (March–April 1987), 98–106; J. R. Hettenhaus, "A Case Study on Integrating Job Redesign and CIM: International Bio Synthetics, Inc.," *CIM Review*, 5, No. 3 (1989), 13–18; and J. V. Saraph and R. J. Sebastian, "Human Resource Strategies for Effective Introduction of Advanced Manufacturing Technologies (AMT)," *Production and Inventory Management Journal*, 33, No. 1 (1992), 64–70.

There are still many jobs both in manufacturing and service industries that cannot be mechanized or automated. How do we increase the productivity of the workers performing these jobs? One way is to design or redesign these jobs to minimize workers' inputs (hours, physical effort) and maximize their outputs. We call the process of structuring jobs **job design.** The purpose of job design is to specify the job assignments, job tasks, and even the job elements of body movement that workers are expected to perform in their jobs. Specifically, in job design we want to structure the collection of job tasks that make up a worker's job in the most productive sequence possible.

For the task of job design, we borrow much of our methodology from psychology and organization behavior. The aspects of job design that deal with the psychology of workers is called the study of *human factors*. One of the most widely known job design researchers in this area of study is Frederick Herzberg.[2] His now classic research on human factors involved in a job (that is, job content) such as the work itself, work recognition, a sense of achievement, job responsibility, growth, and possible advancement were all found to be factors that could be used as motivators for improved productivity. By improving these job content factors through job design, workers would be better satisfied with their jobs and subsequently more productive. Alternatively, the job environment factors (which Herzberg called *hygiene factors*) are chief contributors to job dissatisfaction. Hygiene factors included company policy and administrative controls, work conditions, salary, and relationship with supervisor and subordinates. If dissatisfaction with these hygiene factors could be minimized by job design, the workers would be happier with their jobs and consequently more productive.

Aside from the psychological aspects of job satisfaction in job design, there are other historical bases for performing a job design.[3] They include

1. Equalizing work assignments to minimize idle time
2. Enhancing specialization of skills by grouping job tasks together and improving the efficiency of the worker in performing the grouped tasks
3. Minimizing skill requirements to reduce costs
4. Minimizing training or learning time by designing self-teaching jobs
5. Making the best use of existing equipment, plant layout facilities, and environmental conditions that might otherwise decrease productivity

JOB DESIGN CONSIDERATIONS

Job design involves considerations of the work environment, the worker's physical and psychological condition, and the work tasks themselves. Each of these types of job design considerations will be discussed in the next few sections of this chapter.

[2] F. Herzberg, "One More Time: How Do You Motivate Employees?" *Harvard Business Review* (January–February 1968), 53–62.

[3] L. E. Davis, "Job Design and Productivity," *Personnel* (March 1957), 45–65.

Work Environment

TOOLS AND EQUIPMENT Work environment considerations concern the design of the tools and equipment that workers use in their jobs and the atmosphere in which workers perform their tasks. There is no greater hindrance to productivity than a poorly designed tool that places an excessive physical burden on a worker. Tools, such as a pair of pliers, should be designed to accomplish the desired production task. They should also be designed to be easily grasped and to minimize the biomechanical stress on the hands and wrists of the human being who must grasp it. At the same time, the design should consider grasping pressure, size, weight, and ease of use in meeting the physical limitations of the user. The study of the equipment or process interface with human resources is called **ergonomics.** Performed by engineering experts, ergonomic analysis can be used to help design jobs to improve productivity, product quality, and reduce costs.[4]

Equipment and its controls should be designed to facilitate ease of use and interpretation. Wherever possible, control indicators should be structured into a pattern design. For example, research has shown that round equipment control dials should be collectively patterned so that the indicator points vertically toward a normal or acceptable performance.[5] In Figure 14-2(a) we have a series of four unpatterned control dials, each pointing to its own "normal" level of operation. To know that each dial was pointing at normal, a worker would have to be familiar with the nature of each control. In Figure 14-2(b) the same controls are all patterned to vertically point upward to their normal operating level. A worker can easily scan this arrangement of controls and quickly see if any are deviating from a vertical or normal operating level of performance.

QUESTION: Is ergonomics as applicable to service organizations as it is to manufacturing?

S

ANSWER: Yes, because human resources are involved, ergonomics is equally applicable to service and manufacturing organizations. For example, in office layout design (used in both service and manufacturing operations), ergonomics is used to set the best chair height, position and locate the word processing keyboard, and angle the computer terminal to maximize user productivity.

ATMOSPHERE The **atmosphere** in the workplace includes illumination, temperature, humidity, air pollution, noise pollution, and vibration.

[4] G. S. Vasilash, "Designing Better Places to Work," *Production,* 102, No. 2 (1990), 56–59.

[5] R. B. Sleight, "The Effect of Instrument Dial Shape on Legibility," *Journal of Applied Psychology,* 32 (1948), 170–188.

FIGURE 14-2 INDICATOR CONTROL DESIGN

(A) UNPATTERNED DESIGN OF EQUIPMENT CONTROLS

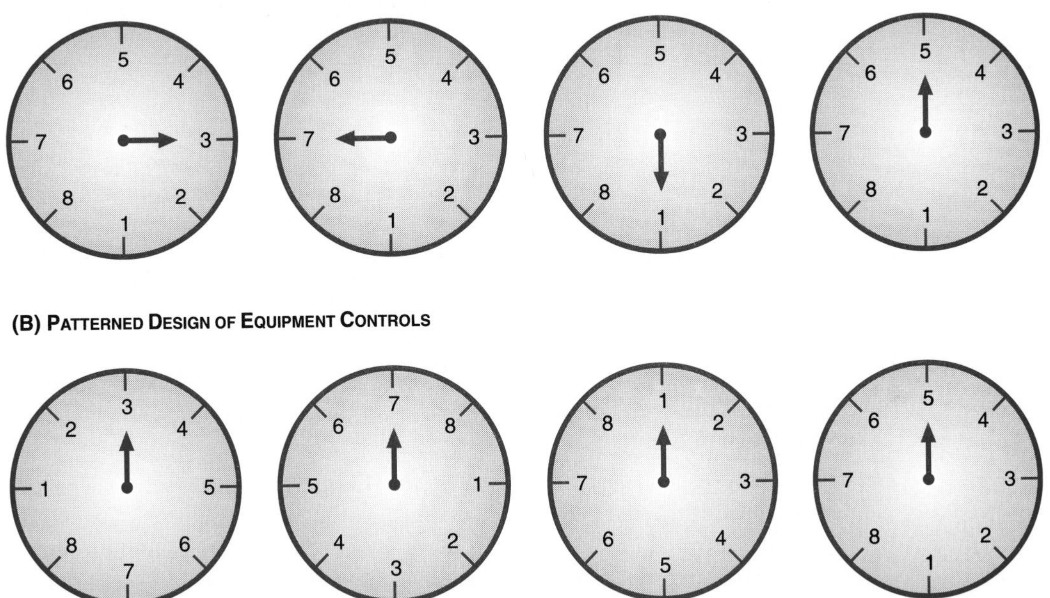

1. *Illumination.* Illumination in the work environment has become such an important factor in productivity that a society was formed to promote and foster research on the subject. The Illuminating Engineering Society (IES) has established nine categories of work task activities, based on task complexity, with accompanying recommendations of specific levels of illumination.[6]

   In general, more light is needed when speed and accuracy are required to complete job tasks. The age of employees is also a factor in lighting. Generally, workers older than 40 years of age need more light. Illumination refers not only to the quantity of light in the workplace but also the quality of light. Illumination analysis should consider such factors as luminous intensity (the light intensity in a small area or in a specific direction), reflectance (the percentage of light reflected from a surface), contrast (how much light is reflected off different-colored or angled surfaces), wavelength (electromagnetic radiation

[6] See *IES Lighting Handbook,* 6th ed. (New York: Illumination Engineering Society, 1981); IES Industrial Lighting Committee, Proposed American National Standard Practice for Industrial Lighting, *Lighting Design and Application,* 13, No. 7 (July 1983), 29–68; and IES Office Lighting Committee, Proposed American National Standard Practice for Office Lighting, *Lighting Design and Application,* 12, No. 4 (April 1982), 27–59.

that makes up electronically-generated light), and polarization (the light reflected from a surface that causes glare). Each of these quality lighting considerations has been researched, and guidelines have been recommended by the IES. Operations managers can use these illumination guidelines to determine lighting needs for individual workers in the design of their jobs.

S

The lighting analysis for the use of a single piece of equipment can be considerable. For example, the use of videodisplay units (VDUs) for word processing in an office must be carefully studied to maximize the worker's performance. Research on the use of VDUs has shown that productivity can be increased by increasing the quality of light in the office environment. The quality of light can be increased in an office by decreasing visual noise (or light that distracts the worker from using the VDU) where possible. This might involve turning off overhead lights while the VDU is used, putting blinds on windows, reducing reflective walls by using dark wall coverings, having the worker wear dark clothing, using a VDU with non-shiny keys, and reducing the VDU's screen glare with a filter or coating. The more completely illumination problems are eliminated, the more productive workers will be in the performance of their jobs.

2. *Temperature and humidity* Temperature and humidity directly affect worker performance. If the temperature in a plant or office is too high, workers tend to become fatigued quickly, require more water (that is, they take more productivity-robbing trips to the water cooler), and perform work at a slower rate. If the temperature in a plant or office is too low, the workers may spend more time trying to keep warm than doing their job. For example, workers may spend productive time making needless trips to warmer places in the plant or to the coffee machine.

   Some societies such as the American Society of Heating, Refrigeration and Air Conditioning Engineers (ASHARE) have established temperature comfort zones to aid in planning temperature control in a job design. The ASHARE basically advocates two comfort zones or temperature ranges for offices. For the winter the most productive temperature range is between 68° and 75° F or 20° or 23.9° C. For the summer the comfort range is from 73° to 79° F or 22.8° to 26.1° C. The difference in the two temperature zones is to compensate for the tendency of workers to wear heavier clothing in the winter than in the summer. Temperature ranges for industrial jobs, which take into account different work conditions such as the use of protective clothing, air velocity, and the affect on human metabolic rates, have been determined, and guidelines have been established by researchers.[7]

   Humidity in the workplace also tends to affect worker performance and can drastically amplify the negative effects of high or low temperature ranges.

[7] See E. McCullough, E. Arpin, B. Jones, S. Knoz, and F. Rohles, "Heat Transfer Characteristics of Clothing Worn in Hot Industrial Environments," *ASHARE Transactions,* 88, No. 1 (1982), pp. 36–41; and S. Knoz, *Work Design: Industrial Ergonomics* (Columbus, Ohio: Grid Publishing, 1983).

The ASHARE has developed psychrometric charts that relate humidity levels and temperature ranges. These charts are used to establish comfort zones that combine both climatic factors of temperature and humidity.[8]

3. *Air pollution* Toxic compounds in the air and physical environment not only reduce worker productivity, they can actually harm the workers. *Occupational dermatosis* is a skin disorder caused by work-related activities. In a single peak year (1972), 41 percent of the occupational illnesses reported were skin-related and they alone caused a loss of 25 percent of the working days of labor owing to illness.[9] Much of the skin disorders are caused by airborne pollutants that enter the human body through the lungs.

   To measure air pollutants and establish limits to prevent illness in work environments that cannot be pollution free, **threshold limit values** (TLVs) have been established for most toxic compounds. Because of the risk to human life that air pollution in the workplace poses for workers, guidelines for some of the most dangerous compounds are dictated by the U.S. government. The federal government's Occupational Safety and Health Administration (OSHA) established the *Federal Register* in 1974 for gases, dusts, and nonmineral dusts that define TLVs on a part-per-million (ppm) exposure rate per hour, based on an eight-hour work day. For example, exposure to benzene (a known cancer-causing agent) is limited to an average exposure of 10 ppm per hour over an eight-hour day. Information on TLVs for toxic substances not covered by government regulation is available from private sources such as the American Conference of Governmental Industrial Hygienists of Cincinnati, Ohio and publications such as the *American Industrial Hygiene Association Journal.*[10]

4. *Noise pollution and vibration* Noise and vibration can annoy workers, impair work performance, and damage workers' nervous systems. OSHA limits by law the amount of noise workers can be exposed to. The current OSHA limits for maximum daily exposure to noise are presented in Table 14-2. The dBA scale (which is a type of decimal scale) used to indicate how sound pressure corresponds to loudness. A 10 dBA increase represents a tenfold multiplication of the sound. So a 30 dBA sound level is ten times greater than a 20 dBA sound level. In general, a constant sound level below 85 dBA will not cause noticeable noise problems for workers, while a constant sound level above 115 dBA is

---

[8] See the *ASHARE Systems Handbook* (Atlanta, Ga.: American Society of Heating, Refrigeration, and Air Conditioning Engineers, 1980).

[9] See D. Birmingham, "Occupational Dematoses: Their Recognition, Control and Prevention," *The Industrial Environment* (Washington, D.C.: Superintendent of Documents, 1973), Chapter 34.

[10] For two excellent examples of the type of research support these sources can provide operations managers in planning the ventilation of toxic substances see *Industrial Ventilation: A Manual of Recommended Practice,* 17th ed. (Ann Arbor, Mich.: American Conference of Governmental Industrial Hygiene, 1982); and J. Goldfield, "Contaminant Concentration Reduction: General Ventilation vs. Local Exhaust Ventilation, *American Industrial Hygiene Association Journal,* 41, No. 11 (November 1980), 813–818.

TABLE 14-2 MAXIMUM DAILY NOISE LEVEL EXPOSURE FOR U.S. WORKERS

Sound Pressure Level (noise dBA units)	*Maximum Exposure per Day (hours)*
85	16
90	8
95	4
100	2
105	1
110	0.5
115	0.25

Source: U.S. Government, Occupational Health and Safety Administration, *Federal Register,* 48, No. 46 (March 8, 1983), 9730–9785.

not permitted in the workplace. Variable noise levels are permitted from 80 to 130 dBA if their average conforms to the hourly scale in Table 14-2.

Noise in the workplace is measured by noise meters and converted into the dBA noise scale. For example, if we had an operation that generated an average noise level of 95 dBA, we could allow our work force to operate for only four hours a day to remain in compliance with OSHA regulations. If we could reduce the noise level to just 90 dBA, we could double our production time to eight hours a day. So minimizing noise can directly improve productivity if noise pollution is a constraint in an operation.

Some of the corrective measures that managers can take to mimimize noise pollution are requiring workers to wear protective ear gear, insulating equipment with soundproof boxes, insulating the walls of plants with noise-deafening materials, and providing sound baffles that can vent noise outside of a plant. Even if sound is minimized, vibrations from equipment, tools, air conditioning units, and pumps can annoy workers and cause nervous disorders. Managers can minimize vibration by using padding on equipment and tools, shock absorbers, and other types of cushioning devices.

Despite an operations manager's best efforts to minimize detrimental factors in the environment having to do with illumination, temperature, humidity, air pollution, noise pollution, and vibration, some jobs still require fairly unhealthy work environments. For example, in manufacturing steel, workers are usually subjected to intense heat and intense cold. In some cases such jobs have been automated so human beings are not subjected to harsh environmental conditions. In situations in which automation cannot be used to control environmental conditions, management needs to concentrate its efforts on the worker rather than the environment. The Hawthorne study (mentioned in Chapter 1) revealed that if workers have a positive attitude about their work, poor environmental conditions can be overcome and high levels of productivity can be achieved or maintained.

Worker Motivation

Worker considerations in job design include worker motivation and physical capabilities of the worker. Instilling a positive attitude in a worker about his or her job involves motivation. There are two types of approaches we can use to motivate workers: a monetary approach and a nonmonetary approach.

MONETARY SYSTEMS When using a monetary approach to motivation we increase a worker's share of the organization's profits. In a capitalistic country like the United States, a worker's contribution to society is measured by the worker's accumulation of wealth. In a capitalistic society, increased effort or worker productivity is supposed to be rewarded with increased monetary rewards. These rewards can be in the form of fringe benefits, such as increases in health care benefits, retirement benefits, or free use of a company car. Other benefits such as employee discounts used to reduce the price of the organization's products for employees can be used to reward loyalty but are not always successfully applied to promote increased productivity. Department stores such as J. C. Penney and Sears, Roebuck permit employees to take discounts of 10 to 15 percent on company merchandise. The discounts show that the organization is willing to give up some of its profits as a recognition of the workers' contribution to generating those profits. S

Incentive pay systems can greatly increase productivity in that they are usually related to production and allocated on a basis of identifiable improvements in productivity. **Incentive pay** is basically extra pay for extra effort. In the mid 1980s, more than 25 percent of the manufacturing work force was paid in part under an incentive pay system.[11] Some of the more common incentive pay systems include a piece-rate system, a standard-hour wage system, a gain-sharing system, and a bonus system.

1. *Piece-rate system* This is one of the oldest incentive pay plan systems. Under this system, workers determine their pay by their production levels. In other words, workers are paid for each unit they produce. Piece-rate systems vary and are called by different names. In sales, piece-rate work is called a **commission.** For example, a real estate agent sells a house on a commission basis. The agent's pay can be entirely based on per-house sales (piece-rate system). In the transportation industry, many independent truck drivers who own and operate their own trucks in the service of a company work on a **percentage** basis. The truck driver is paid a percentage of the total transportation charge to the customer. This percentage payment system is based on a per-load or piece-rate basis.
2. *Standard-hour wage system* This system combines piece-rate work with a minimum guaranteed base wage. This type of system can ensure that workers receive

[11] E. Seiler, "Piece Rate vs. Time Rate: The Effect of Incentives on Earnings," *Review of Economics and Statistics* (August 1984), 363–376.

government minimum wage levels, yet still motivate production workers to produce at greater rates. In this kind of system we need to establish what the standard production is in units on an hourly basis to be able to determine worker compensation. The **standard production** per hour defines what the worker should normally produce. Workers who exceed the standard are paid extra for each unit produced above the standard. The amount of pay is not always as great as the standard per unit pay. That is, a worker may receive $10 for producing ten units in an hour ($1 per unit), but only receive an extra $0.50 for each unit beyond the tenth unit produced in an hour. For this system to motivate workers, the production standard must be fair and achievable.

If a production standard is so high that workers will not be able to achieve it, the system will do little to motivate worker production. On the other hand, a production standard must be high enough to ensure that the operation is profitable. A production standard then must be carefully set so it generates higher levels of worker productivity; it must be rewarding enough for workers to be motivated to achieve it. We will discuss how to establish production standards later in this chapter.

3. *Gain-sharing system* This system is an extension of a standard-hour wage system. In a gain-sharing system a minimum wage level is guaranteed and extra wages are paid for above-standard performance as in a standard-hour wage system. The extra wages are broken down into two parts: One part is directly paid to the worker and a second part is pooled to pay a larger number of support workers. Workers actually producing piece goods are supported by other workers in receiving, inventory, quality control, and materials handling. The more efficiently these support personnel perform their jobs, the more efficient the workers producing the finished products will be. It is therefore only fair that some of the extra wages that are paid out by the organization be shared by the support personnel through a wage pool. The pooled wages are often divided and paid out on a percentage basis or calculated on the basis of activity level over a period of time. For example, materials handlers may have a standard number of pallets to move in a week. If more than the standard number of pallet loads are moved in a week, then a greater portion of the pooled wages may go to the materials handlers.

4. *Bonus system* This system is an infrequent, temporary, or one-time reward given to workers whose work is designated by managers to be at a performance at above standard. In the 1930s to the 1950s, bonuses for white-collar or non-manufacturing workers were commonly used to motivate extra effort from staff and office workers. Unfortunately, unscrupulous managers did not always give bonuses to the most productive workers but instead used them to reward friendship or loyalty. Such abuses of this type of system not only destroyed worker motivation but caused the decline of their use in industry in the 1960s and 1970s. With the realization of the poor productivity performance in the United States during the 1980s (see Figure 14-1), many organizations, and even

the U.S. federal government, are again using bonus systems to reward individual worker productivity.

QUESTION: Motivating workers to participate in quality improvement is a part of all total quality management (TQM) programs. How do world-class organizations motivate workers to participate in TQM?

ANSWER: To participate in a TQM program, workers must be trained in quality conformance standards and quality principles. Training workers to overcome unique work environment situations that limit quality conformance is important to successfully implement a TQM program. Monetary rewards can be used to motivate workers to learn during training sessions. This logic was illustrated by the European-owned Glacier Vandervell Company, which operates in Iowa, using Japanese just-in-time (JIT) and TQM methods.[12] The firm instituted a skill-development program that included JIT and TQM principles, but also established an incentive pay system to reward workers for job knowledge. Using the assistance of a community college and a variety of consulting experts, Glacier Vandervell management made it easy for employees to take advantage of training opportunities. The pay system reinforced the workers' motivation to learn by increasing the value to the workers of learning. The reward and training program was credited with reducing annual rework dollars by 40 percent, reducing customer returns by 92 percent, reducing the cost of quality from 14.9 to 6.4 percent, attaining a 99.6 percent customer service level, and reducing scrap by 58 percent, all in only a few years. As a result of this significant improvement in their operations, the Glacier Vandervell Company in 1991 won the Shingo Prize for Excellence in Manufacturing. Somewhat like the Malcolm Baldrige Award (discussed in Chapter 2), the Shingo Prize is awarded annually to manufacturing companies in the United States that demonstrate excellence in manufacturing leading to quality enhancement, productivity improvement, and customer satisfaction.

NONMONETARY SYSTEMS Nonmonetary approaches to creating a positive work attitude are more intrinsic and seek to psychologically motivate workers by appealing to their self-esteem or sense of accomplishment. A manager giving a subordinate praise for a good day's work generally gives a worker a good feeling that can translate into increased productivity. Organizations have used worker recognition systems to acknowledge excellence in work performance and help build worker esteem. Many organizations use a company paper or magazine as a communication device to keep employees informed about the organization and its activities. Naming workers whose

[12] V. Adams, "An Iowa Plant's Pursuit of World-Class Manufacturing Snags the Shingo Prize," *APICS—The Performance Advantage,* 2, No. 7 (1992), 48–49.

performance is outstanding provides some organization recognition of that extra effort. It represents a form of organization praise and notoriety that may motivate other workers to achieve.

Many organizations also give nonmonetary awards to outstanding workers. For example, some companies have a "worker-of-the-week" award where the most productive worker's picture is hung where customers and workers can see it. Other companies, like Sears, Roebuck stores, give the outstanding worker a convenient parking space near the building for a week or month to reward high productivity levels. Name signing on finished products has also been used by some companies to give the worker a sense of personal accomplishment in creating a product. Other psychological approaches deal more with the way in which work tasks are assigned and organized. We will discuss these methods in the next section.

Even if we instill a positive work attitude that motivates workers to perform job tasks at above-standard performance levels, they will be unable to do their jobs if they do not have the necessary physical capabilities. The fields of *anthropometry, biomechanics,* and *ergonomics* are concerned with the study of the physical features and functions of the human body. These studies are of body weight, linear dimensions, volume (anthropometric data), range of body movements (biomechanics), and how they are related in the performance of job tasks (ergonomics).

In designing work we must be sure to either fit the person to the job or fit the job to the person. It is pointless to assign a job to someone who does not have the physical capabilities to perform the job. **Job specifications** define what is expected of the worker (for example, the ability to lift 50-pound bags) on a job and are used to specify physical requirements necessary for a job. The use of videodisplay units (VDUs) brings out many visual deficiencies of the operator's eyes. Failing to consider an operator's glasses, bifocals, or contact lenses when designing the VDU workcenter layout can greatly decrease operator productivity. Job specifications can be used to select the worker who best fits the job requirement by screening out those workers who cannot perform work tasks.

Work Tasks

Work task considerations deal with the order, number, and assignment of job tasks that comprise a worker's job. Several work task management approaches have been successfully applied over many years to improve worker productivity. These management approaches include job rotation, job enlargement, job enrichment, team work units, scheduling, micromotion analysis, and flow charting.

JOB ROTATION, ENLARGEMENT, AND ENRICHMENT In "thin jobs" (those containing few different work tasks), workers are apt to become bored and unproductive. Such jobs do not motivate people to higher levels of productivity. **Job rotation** involves the assignment of workers to different jobs. That is, one day the worker performs one type of job and the next day the worker performs an entirely different type of job. Doing different types of work provides some variety that can stimulate workers to be more productive in their jobs.

The Japanese commonly use job rotation for both blue-collar and white-collar workers.[13] Mitsubishi Electric Corporation of Japan, for example, rotates electronics experts in one department to other electronics departments where the area of application differs.[14] Unfortunately, job rotation is not a long-term solution to structuring work tasks for improved productivity. Over time, job rotation can become a process of doing different but boring and unproductive jobs.

The need for variety in a job can be dealt with by increasing the complexity of the job with different work tasks, called **job enlargement.** In a repetitive assembly operation, highly specialized work tasks might consist of only a single job task like bolting a front bumper on an automobile. Now suppose that additional tasks are added, such as putting the back bumper and trim work on the automobile. By adding the additional tasks we are enlarging the job the worker performs. We are transforming a "thin job" into a "thick job" that will provide the worker with greater variety, and hopefully, more interesting work overall.

Like job rotation, job enlargement is not a long-term solution for improving the design of jobs. Even the thickest job can become boring and lack any motivational stimulus if the worker is exposed to it for a long enough time. Redesigning a number of little boring job tasks together to make up a newly enlarged job does provide job task variety but can, in many situations, simply generate another boring job in the long run. Indeed, it is interesting to note that in a classic research study on job enlargement representing a sample of more than two hundred electronic assembly line workers, 51 percent preferred smaller or thinner jobs whereas only 12 percent preferred larger or thicker jobs.[15]

To overcome the limitations of job rotation and job enlargement, a process referred to as **job enrichment** was proposed by Frederick Herzberg and others.[16] In job enrichment we not only increase the variety of job tasks with job enlargement but also provide for the psychological growth and enrichment of the worker. We accomplish job enrichment by making the individual more accountable for his or her own work (increasing the job responsibility), removing unneeded management controls (which makes workers believe that the organization trusts them more), granting the worker sufficient authority and freedom to carry out their responsibilities, increasing the flow of information about job and organization performance to the worker, and letting the worker develop a high level of expertise by assigning specialized tasks. Job enrichment

---

[13] R. J. Schonberger, *Japanese Manufacturing Techniques* (New York: The Free Press, 1982), pp. 194–197.

[14] S. Shindo, "Conditions for Activating a Corporation," *The Oriental Economist,* Part 4 (July 1981), 38–43.

[15] M. C. Killeridge, "Do Workers Prefer Larger Jobs?" *Personnel,* 37 (1960), 26–34.

[16] See F. Herzberg, "One More Time: How Do We Motivate Employees?" *Harvard Business Review* (January–February 1968), 53–62; and W. J. Paul, K. Robertson, and F. Herzberg, "Job Enrichment Pays Off," *Harvard Business Review* (March–April 1969), 21–28.

is the forerunner of the "empowerment of personnel" tactic necessary for total quality management (discussed in Chapter 2) and is also a form of cross-training necessary for a successful just-in-time implementation. Job enrichment might alter a worker's or supervisor's job description (the listing of duties and tasks that make up the job), which can mean significantly higher levels of compensation and also increased productivity.

TEAM WORK UNITS AND SCHEDULING In a team work unit, a group of workers are assembled to work as a team. Usually each member of the team is familiar with one or more of the other workers' job tasks and can "fill in" if needed. In the early 1970s Sweden's Volvo automobile company used assembly team work units to collectively perform work on component parts for their automobiles. These teams were given the freedom to organize themselves to do the job tasks necessary, set their own assembly line speed production rates, and regulate their own coffee breaks. The production was controlled by management with quotas. Reports on this approach from the Volvo company were favorable. Results indicated that the team work units generally out-produced the traditional assembly line worker design system.[17] Unfortunately, Detroit workers did not have a favorable reaction to the team work unit approach when they were exposed to it in the mid-1970s.[18] Yet in the 1990s, Japanese quality circles and, to some degree, the teamwork atmosphere of JIT have been embraced with enthusiasm by many automobile manufacturers (such as the Saturn Division of General Motors, described in the first color-photo insert) and their workers.[19] Saturn has teams of workers follow a car down an assembly line performing a series of interrelated tasks as a team. The result is greater worker pride in the final product and better product quality.

If the work is boring and it cannot be redesigned to improve worker productivity, then the worker's exposure to the work might be changed to provide variety. Some of the currently used approaches to scheduling work include flextime, four-day work weeks, and permanent part-time jobs. **Flextime** is a scheduling system in which workers define their hours of work. Workers can come early and leave early, come late and leave late, or even leave work in the middle of the day for personal activities such as shopping or picking up children from school.

The idea of flextime came from Germany and has become a very popular approach used by many major U.S. companies including General Motors and Montgomery Ward. Allowing workers freedom to make the best use of their time for personal or family needs usually increases their satisfaction. That is, the job is not an obstacle or source of frustration in their personal lives. Having more personal time generates greater personal satisfaction and generally translates into greater productivity on the job. Of course,

---

[17] R. R. Bell and J. M. Burnham, *Managing Productivity and Change* (Cincinnati: South-Western Publishing, 1991), Chapter 12; P. J. Mullins, "Volvo's Kalmar Plant—Ten Years On," *Automotive Industries* (August 1984), 34–39; and G. Gyllanhammer, "How Volvo Adapts Work to People," *Harvard Business Review,* 55, No. 4 (July–August 1977), 102–113.

[18] "A Work Experiment: Six Americans in a Swedish Plant," Ford Foundation, 1976.

[19] "Technology Report: Saturn Corporation," *Barrons,* June 24, 1991, pp. 30–32.

trying to plan a work load schedule around a labor force on flextime can be quite challenging for an operations manager.

In a four-day work week, employees work a ten-hour day four days a week. Four-day work weeks permit a more convenient grouping of work and personal time for management planning purposes. The system also allows the worker a more extensive weekend for personal time than a five-day week.

Employees in permanent part-time jobs work for an organization on an ongoing basis, but for fewer than forty hours per week. This type of job scheduling benefits the employer in that part-timers can be used to fill in during periods of high demand and used less during periods of low demand. Part-time employees are also less costly than full-time workers because generally they are not paid overtime wages, they are given little or no company benefits such as retirement, and they are usually at the bottom of the wage scale. At the same time, permanent part-time jobs have allowed many workers to receive job training and enter new industries without having to completely give up family responsibilities.

MICROMOTION ANALYSIS AND FLOWCHARTING One approach to improving the work task arrangement of a job is called *micromotion analysis*. Originally founded on Frank and Lillian Gilbreth's work in time and motion studies, **micromotion analysis** involves dissecting basic job tasks into microelements of physical movement.[20] For example, an inventory clerk's job is made up of job assignments such as receiving inventory or storing it, each assignment is made up of job tasks or work tasks (such as filling out receiving reports, or physically checking the inventory), each job task is made up of elements (such as physically taking a pencil and writing stock numbers), and finally elements can be defined into microelements (such as the physical movement of reaching for a pencil).

In micromotion analysis physical movement activities are divided into seventeen elements called **therbligs** (*Gilbreth* spelled backwards). Therbligs include such basic microelements as grasping (closing a hand around an object), releasing (opening a hand around an object), and inspecting (comparing an object with a standard). In a micromotion analysis we dissect a job into its therbligs and determine the most productive way of performing each individual therblig element. This determination usually involves trial and error or brainstorming alternative approaches to performing each particular element of the job.

In recent years, the use of video equipment and slow-motion photography has greatly helped capture and measure workers' performance of microelements.[21] Once the performance is improved, the microelement is reassembled into the job, and productivity measurements on how well the new job design is working are made. Unfortunately, the micromotion approach is very costly in time and management effort relative to the minor productivity improvements that are possible. This approach is best

[20] See R. M. Barnes, *Motion and Time Study*, 7th ed. (New York: John Wiley & Sons, 1980).

[21] J. Bagby, "The Value of High Speed Motion Analysis," *Manufacturing Systems*, 8, No. 3 (1990), 57.

used when unnecessary movements of the worker cause fatigue, which then affects productivity or product quality. Athletes training for the Olympics have found this approach useful to identify unproductive flaws that diminish performance.

A **flow process chart** is a chart used to graphically depict all of the activities that make up a particular process. Flow process charts do not focus directly on job tasks but seek to examine how objects (such as orders, receipts, information, and product units) are processed by individuals in an organization. Flow process charts are used to itemize job activities of different workers who process objects through the organization. A flow process chart and its symbols are presented in Figure 14-3(a). The symbols are a quick way to graphically represent the five basic activities (operation, transportation, inspection, delay, and storage) that objects undergo as they pass through an operation.

In charting a process, the activities are usually listed, a symbol is assigned, and either the distance involved in transporting the object or the amount of activity time required to process the object is listed. Once all of the activities are listed, an analyst determines whether there are alternative means to reduce the distance in feet, to reduce the amount of time required to perform each activity, and possibly a way to reduce the number of activities that make up the process.

In Figure 14-3(b), a sample flow process chart is presented that shows a university's payment process for parking violation fees using a three-part form: parts A, B, and C. This chart provides only the basic requirements in time and distance for the process to be completed. These estimates usually are based on time studies of each activity. It is up to the work designer or analyst to use this information to develop a new sequence of activities that might reduce the time and distance required, and thereby increase productivity.

BASICS OF WORK MEASUREMENT

Work environment, worker, and work task considerations all play a part in worker productivity. In the process of designing a job we must be able to measure worker performance and productivity so we can determine whether management efforts in job design are improving work effort. The process of measuring work performance is called *work measurement.*

Work measurement is the field of study that tries to determine the amount of time it takes to perform a job. Once we have determined this time, it becomes a standard time in which to perform a job. **Standard time** is the length of time that a job should take or that is given as a standard to do a job. The standard time can be in time per units or units per time (units per hour). Once a standard time for a job is determined, the information is used to generate information on individual worker performance with performance measures. Performance measures, which are used to see how well workers perform relative to the standard time, are often expressed as an index in which 100 percent represents a fair day's work. A performance measure index above 100 represents above-average work performance, and an index below 100 percent

FIGURE 14-3 FLOW PROCESS CHART AND EXAMPLE

(A) A FLOW PROCESS CHART

PROCESS FLOW ACTIVITY	CHART SYMBOL	DISTANCE IN FEET	TIME IN MINUTES
	○ ⇨ □ D ▽		

Where:

○ (Operation) indicates a change in physical characteristics is taking place or an exchange of information is taking place

⇨ (Transportation) indicates object is moving or being transported

□ (Inspection) indicates some type of inspection of the object is taking place

D (Delay) indicates that an object is delayed at this point in the process flow

▽ (Storage) indicates that the object is intentionally delayed for storage purposes

(B) A FLOW PROCESS CHART EXAMPLE (PAYMENT OF PARKING VIOLATION FEES)

PROCESS FLOW ACTIVITY	CHART SYMBOL	DISTANCE IN FEET	TIME IN MINUTES
1. Receive parking violation notice at violation office from student	○ ⇨ □ ◗ ▽		1
2. Inspect for errors by officer	○ ⇨ ■ D ▽		3.5
3. Calculate fee for violation	● ⇨ □ D ▽		2.5
4. Form A to file	○ ⇨ □ D ▼		0.5
5. Form B to student	○ ➡ □ D ▽	2	
6. Form C to cashier	○ ➡ □ D ▽	21	
7. Student pays fee and surrenders form B to cashier	● ⇨ □ D ▽		4
8. Cashier matches form B with form C	● ⇨ □ D ▽		7.5
9. Cashier sends forms B and C to violation office	○ ➡ □ D ▽	21	
10. Violation office matches forms A with B and C	● ⇨ □ D ▽		6.5
11. File all forms	○ ⇨ □ D ▼		3

represents below-average performance. We can calculate a performance measure as follows:

$$\text{Performance measure} = \frac{\text{Standard time expected for job} \times 100}{\text{Actual time taken by worker for job}}$$

If the standard is in terms of units per a specific time period, we can calculate a performance measure as follows:

$$\text{Performance measure} = \frac{\text{Actual units produced during time period} \times 100}{\text{Standard units expected during time period}}$$

In the distant past, performance measures were unscrupulously used to justify firing or dismissing poor performers. This unfortunately caused workers and their unions to negatively react to their use for any purpose. Under pressure from workers, unions, and government antidiscrimination laws, the 1970s saw most organizations abandon the use of performance measures for controlling worker efforts. In the late 1980s and on into the 1990s, some innovative firms such as the Square-D Corporation (Lincoln, Nebraska plant) have been using performance measures as motivational devices rather than as primitive control devices. Workers like to know if their efforts make a difference in daily production. Performance measures can be used to gauge worker performance, and if properly managed, can act to motivate workers to higher productivity levels rather than scare them into doing extra work.

Work measurement can be used to help operations managers perform basic management functions of planning, directing, organizing, staffing, motivating, and controlling (discussed in Chapter 1). Work measurement statistics help management plan how much work can be accomplished in a given time period. Because work measurement defines standards of performance, it provides management with production rate and quota information that can be used in directing workers. Work measurement can be used to identify the most productive workers and help management better assign and

QUESTION: If a job's standard time is eight hours and a worker actually takes six hours, what is the worker's performance measure?

ANSWER: The worker's performance measure is calculated as follows:

$$\text{Performance measure} = \frac{\text{Standard time expected for job} \times 100}{\text{Actual time taken by worker for job}}$$

$$= \frac{8}{6}(100)$$

$$= 133 \text{ percent}$$

The worker's performance is 33 percent above the standard for that job.

organize workers to maximize OM system output. Because work measurement statistics can be used to determine the standard production levels, they can be used to determine staffing needs. Work measurements have been used to establish work level standards, which helps influence and motivate less-productive workers to do their fair share of the organization's work effort. Finally, work measurements are used by management to maintain and control work performance to an acceptable standard.

Who is responsible for conducting work measurement studies and determining standard times? An organization's industrial engineers (IEs) are commonly given the responsibility of determining standard time estimates. In addition, a number of professionals such as medical doctors, sociologists, psychologists, time-motion experts, quality control staff, and even statisticians can contribute to determining standard times. Finally, both workers and management may have a say in determining standard times. In practice, however, workers' input into determining standard times is usually on a contractual basis rather than a statistical estimation basis. Because standard times can determine a fair day's work, management's idea of a fair day's work may differ from that of the workers. To resolve this difference workers and management often resort to mutually agree on contractual definitions of work measurements and a fair day's work.

How are standard times and performance measures calculated? Standard time is made up of two values: normal time and standard allowances. **Normal time** is the time to perform just the labor required for the job tasks (that is, normal to those particular job tasks). Normal time is usually the average observed time to perform the labor necessary for all of the tasks that make up the job.

We add to this normal labor time the standard allowances normal for the job tasks. **Standard allowances** are defined as "the established or accepted amount by which normal time for an operation is increased within an area, plant, or industry to compensate for the usual amount of fatigue and/or personal and/or unavoidable delays."[22] Fatigue can occur when a job is boring, physically demanding, or environmentally challenging. Personal time can include trips to the restroom and time to change clothes necessary for the job. Unavoidable delays can occur when assembly lines shut down and cause idleness or when inventory shortages delay a worker's participation in production activities. All of these factors can add unproductive time to the normal time it takes to produce a product and therefore must be considered when establishing a representative standard time for production. So standard time can be expressed as follows:

Standard time = Normal time + Standard allowances

QUESTION: What is the standard time for a job task where the normal time is 4 minutes, the standard allowance for delays is 1 minute, fatigue allowance 0.5 minutes, and the standard allowance for personal time is 0.75 minutes?

(continued)

[22] Reprinted with permission of the American Production and Inventory Control Society, Inc., *APICS Dictionary,* 7th edition, 1992.

ANSWER: The standard time is as follows:

$$\begin{aligned}\text{Standard time} &= \text{Normal time} + \text{Standard allowances}\\ &= 4 + (1 + 0.5 + 0.75)\\ &= 6.25 \text{ minutes}\end{aligned}$$

In some situations, standard allowances are expressed as a percentage of standard time (called **percentage allowances**). We then use the following expression for standard time:

$$\text{Standard time} = \text{Normal time} \times \frac{100}{100 - \text{Percentage allowances}}$$

QUESTION: What is the standard time for a job task where the normal time is 4 minutes and the standard allowances are 20 percent of standard time?

ANSWER: The job task's standard time is as follows:

$$\begin{aligned}\text{Standard time} &= \text{Normal time} \times \frac{100}{100 - \text{Percentage allowances}}\\ &= 4 \times \frac{100}{100 - 20}\\ &= 5 \text{ minutes}\end{aligned}$$

Normal time can be either the average observed time from a single worker's performance of a job task or from several workers performing the same job task. (We will discuss the procedure of making time observations in the next section of this chapter.) Normal time can be expressed as

$$\text{Normal time} = \frac{\Sigma\ (\text{Observed work times})}{\text{Number of observations made}}$$

In the process of being observed some workers may not perform at a "normal" level of production. For example, they may become nervous or upset because someone is watching them closely. If a worker who is being observed is not working at a normal work pace, the time estimates observed will not be accurate. To compensate the time observations of workers who are obviously not working at a normal pace, we use a pace adjustment statistic. A **pace adjustment statistic** is a subjectively derived index used to increase or decrease the time the worker was observed as taking to complete a job.

QUESTION: Suppose that we made four timed observations of a worker performing the same job task. The four times are 3.6, 4.0, 3.7, and 4.3 minutes. If the standard allowances are 10 percent of standard time, what is the standard time for this job?

ANSWER: The job's standard time is as follows:

$$\text{Normal time} = \frac{\Sigma\ (\text{Observed work times})}{\text{Number of observations made}} = \frac{3.6 + 4.0 + 3.7 + 4.3}{4}$$

$$= 3.9 \text{ minutes}$$

$$\text{Standard time} = \text{Normal time} \times \frac{100}{100 - \text{Percentage allowances}}$$

$$= 3.9 \times \frac{100}{100 - 10}$$

$$= 4.333 \text{ minutes}$$

If a worker is performing a job task at a rate of 10 percent below our expectation (that is, taking 10 percent more time than expected), we need to decrease the observation time. A pace adjustment statistic of 0.90 (1.00 − 0.10) will reduce the observed time by 10 percent. Similarly, if a worker is performing a job task at a rate say 10 percent above our expectation (that is, taking 10 percent less time than expected), we need to increase the observation time. A pace adjustment statistic of 1.10 (1.00 + 0.10) will increase the observed time by 10 percent. Assessment of pace adjustment statistics is subjective and usually requires an expert in the field of time study and observation. We can express normal time with a pace adjustment statistic as follows:

$$\text{Normal time} = \frac{\Sigma\ (\text{Observed work times} \times \text{Pace adjustment statistic})}{\text{Number of observations made}}$$

The calculation of standard time using these simple ratios raises several questions. What procedures should we use in making the observations? How many time observations should we make? What alternative means can be used to estimate standard times if the cost of making observations is prohibitive? How do we adjust the time estimates for workers' experience? To answer these questions we turn now to work measurement methods.

QUESTION: Suppose that we observed a worker performing a job task three times. The time observations and their respective pace adjustment statistics are as follows:

Observed Time	*Pace Adjustment Statistic*	*Explanation of Pace Adjustment Statistic*
3.5	1.20	Performing 20% faster than expected
4.7	0.90	Performing 10% slower than expected
4.2	1.00	Performing at a normal pace

What is the normal time for this job task?

ANSWER: The normal time for this job task is as follows:

$$\text{Normal time} = \frac{\Sigma\ (\text{Observed work times} \times \text{Pace adjustment statistic})}{\text{Number of observations made}}$$

$$= \frac{\Sigma\ [(3.5 \times 1.20) + (4.7 \times 0.90) + (4.2 \times 1.00)]}{3}$$

$$= 4.21 \text{ minutes}$$

WORK MEASUREMENT METHODS

Several work measurement methods are used to determine standard time estimates. The work measurement methods we will discuss include time study analysis, methods-time measurement, work sampling, white-collar measures, and learning curves.

Time Study Analysis

Time study analysis is the most commonly used work measurement method in industry all over the world.[23] In **time study analysis** we try to determine normal and standard time estimates by making physical observations and using a mechanical device such as a stopwatch or videocamera. Time study analysis can be used in conjunction with micromotion analysis. By breaking down the job into its assignments, job tasks, and subsequent job elements, we reduce a complicated physical process into a small and measurable physical sequence of behavior. Small job elements do not have the timing variation that a whole job assignment or even a job task does. Once the job elements are defined, each is timed using a stopwatch or a videocamera timing instrument, which

[23] *Introduction to Work Study,* 3rd ed. (Geneva, Switzerland: International Labor Organization, 1986).

can provide both a visual record and time estimates. After several time estimates are made, they are then combined to generate an average time for each job element. The average time estimates for each job element are then reassembled into a normal time estimate for a job task, job assignment, or the whole job.

A procedure for conducting a time study analysis might consist of the following steps:

1. *Standardize the work methods.* The job or job assignments that the workers are expected to perform, the structure of the workcenter layout, the tools, and the sequence of job tasks should all be standardized and familiar to the worker. If we plan to change the job the workers will be performing or change any method the workers will be using in the performance of their jobs, then we should familiarize the worker with the change.
2. *Select the worker (or workers) for the study.* When we are measuring only a limited number of job elements, or uncomplicated job tasks that have little variation among different workers, or when we want to save observation time, we use only one worker. In studies in which the timing of the job elements varies significantly among workers, we use several workers to make the same time observations. The worker or workers selected should be representative of the "typical" worker in the company's total population of workers. The worker should possess average skills and knowledge necessary to complete the job under study.
3. *Determine the elemental structure of the job.* The sequence of job, job assignments, job tasks, and job elements must be defined for the entire job. This usually involves observing and listing of each job element as it is performed by a worker. Not all types of jobs need to be broken down. Jobs that are particularly thin and have few job assignments may not need to be elementally structured; they can be maintained as a whole for observation purposes.
4. *Determine the number of time observations to make.* To determine the number of time observations to make in a time study, we use the following sample size formula:

$$n = \left(\frac{(z)(s)}{a}\right)^2$$

where

n = the sample size of the number of time estimates

z = a confidence coefficient based on the normal probability table

s = the standard deviation of a small presample of time observations

a = the allowable inaccuracy or error in units of time

To use the z formula we must first subjectively determine the confidence we want to have in the resulting time estimate based on the sample. This is accomplished by selecting a z value from Table 14-3. (These values are based on the normal probability distribution in Appendix A, Table B, at the end of this book.)

The greater the degree of confidence, the greater the sample size. The greater the sample size, the more sure we can be that the resulting time estimate will be the true or population time estimate we seek from the sample. We next take a small presample of time observations to estimate the type of variation that exists in the population of time estimates. This presample is arbitrarily determined by management and may be as few as five time observations. The average and standard deviation values can then be computed using the following formula:

$$\overline{x} = \frac{\Sigma x}{n_p}$$

$$s = \sqrt{\frac{\Sigma (x - \overline{x})^2}{n_p - 1}}$$

where

x = a sample time value

n_p = the presample size

We next must subjectively determine an inaccuracy or error that we are willing to permit in the resulting time estimate. For example, if we do not

QUESTION: Suppose that we want to determine a sample size for a time study analysis. We take a presample and find the average time to be 4 minutes with a sample standard deviation of 1.5 minutes. If a = 1 minute and we desire a degree of confidence of 99 percent, what is the necessary sample size?

ANSWER: We determine the sample size as follows:

$$n = \left(\frac{(z)(s)}{a}\right)^2 = \left(\frac{(2.58)(1.5)}{1}\right)^2 = 14.9 \text{ or } 15 \text{ observations}$$

Because time observations are always whole units and because we need more than fourteen observations, we always round up, in this case to fifteen. If we make fifteen time observations we can be at least 99 percent confident that the resulting time estimate will be the true population time estimate and that it will not be inaccurate by more than plus or minus 1 minute.

TABLE 14-3 CONFIDENCE COEFFICIENT z VALUE

Desired Degree of Confidence in Sample Size–Generated Time Estimate (percent)	*z Value*
99	2.58
98	2.33
95	1.96
90	1.65

want a resulting time estimate based on the sample to be off by more than plus or minus 3 minutes, we would let $a = 3$.

5. *Make the desired time observations.* Using some type of timing instrument, make the number of time observations determined in step 4. We also subjectively assess any pace adjustments necessary for each time observation.
6. *Compute normal times for each job element.* Using one of the ratios presented earlier, we calculate the normal time for each job element. We then combine the job elements back into a job task, job assignments, or a whole job.
7. *Determine the standard allowances.* For some organizations, standard allowances for personal time and fatigue are defined by union contracts. For other organizations they must be estimated. A manager might limit personal time for workers to the time it takes for one trip to the bathroom or water cooler a day. Such arbitrary decisions for time allowances may not be accepted by workers and are very difficult to enforce. In subjective estimations of standard allowances, a manager may find it easier to use predetermined standard allowances. These predetermined standard allowances are found in published secondary sources of information. For example, some researchers have found that a 5 percent allowance for personal time and a fatigue allowance of 4 percent would represent an overall "fair" allowance for most job categories.[24]

   Because of the unique nature of each business operation, a predetermined allowance for fatigue may not be accurate. A common-sense approach to determining a fatigue allowance compares the first and second half of the day's production. We know from research of worker performance that workers are more productive in the first half of the day than in the second half, primarily because they become fatigued during the day. To assess a fatigue allowance we select one typical worker and measure his or her work performance on the job in both the first and second halves of the day, compute performance measures on a percentage basis, and then subtract the worker performance measure found in the second half of the day from the performance measure in the first half of

[24] B. W. Niebel, *Motion and Time Study*, 6th ed. (Homewood, Ill.: Richard D. Irwin, 1976), p. 380; and *Introduction to Work Study*, 3rd ed. (Geneva, Switzerland: International Labor Organization, 1986), pp. 265–271.

the day. The difference is the percentage allowance for fatigue. Allowances for delays normal to the job are usually calculated by observation. One method commonly used to determine a standard allowance for delays or idle time is work sampling. (We discuss work sampling later in this section.)

8. *Determine standard time.* Using the normal time determined in step 6 and the standard allowances in step 7 we can compute the standard time by using one of the ratios presented earlier.

A major problem with time study analysis is that it is based on physical observation performed by a manager or time study expert on workers doing their job tasks. Most workers do not behave normally when somebody is watching them. The abnormal behavior is caused by the psychological pressure workers feel when someone is watching them. This abnormal performance is an obvious source of bias in making physical observations because it disrupts the worker's normal work pace. The use of pace adjustment statistics can help correct the observation time estimates but the adjustment is itself so subjective that bias is almost always present in the final time estimate computations. This bias is being reduced by the use of computers in modern CIM and CISS environments. When workers log-on and log-off the jobs they are completing, the computer records the production timing information and automatically updates standard times to reflect the current worker performance.

Methods-Time Measurement

Predetermined data is time study data collected from some source prior to its application. One of the most commonly used sources of predetermined data is through a process called **methods-time measurement (MTM).** In an MTM analysis, a job is broken into microelements of physical movement (as in a micromotion analysis of job design). Then each of the physical movements is broken down into physical movement factors such as the number of degrees that an arm moves, the weight of the object that the arm must move, and the distance the arm must move. For each of these types of physical factors the MTM Association for Standards and Research has developed time-measurement units (TMUs) that equate the movement factor to a TMU (each TMU is 0.0006 minutes). For example, the movement of an arm vertically 10 degrees with a one-pound payload might equate to 100 TMUs, providing an estimate of time of 0.06 minutes (0.0006×100). These time estimates are based on a considerable amount of research on physical activity that dates back to the 1940s when this approach was first developed. Once the TMUs are assigned to the job elements, the times are then collected for all of the job elements to determine the standard time for the job.

One of the major criticisms of the MTM approach is that the amount of effort and time necessary to develop these time standards is often outweighed by the value of the information itself. Obviously, locating and identifying the appropriate TMUs for even the thinnest job can require a considerable amount of time. For highly repetitive tasks, though, the MTM approach need not require a great deal of research time. MTM is a very well-established approach that may minimize negative attitudes from workers and unions about time standard estimation.

Work Sampling

In 1934, L. H. C. Tippett introduced an approach for estimating the proportion of time a worker is actually working to the time a worker is idle. The approach is called **work sampling** and is based on random observations. Supervisors and managers usually "patrol" their operations to make sure workers are performing their assigned jobs. During the patrol a supervisor can easily perform a work sampling study. A work sampling study procedure can consist of the following steps:

1. *Determine the worker for the study.* He or she should represent most of the workers who perform the job and should be familiar with standardized work methods. The worker should not be informed that he or she has been selected for the study.
2. *Determine the number of observations to make.* Because the objective of work sampling is to obtain a proportion estimate of work time, the sample size formula is based on proportions:

$$n = \left(\frac{z}{a}\right)^2 p_s (1 - p_s)$$

   where

   n = the sample size of the number of observation samples

   z = a confidence coefficient based on the normal probability table

   a = the allowable inaccuracy or error percentage from the true population proportion that we are trying to determine with the sample

   p_s = the proportion of time that we observe the worker actually working, based on a presample of observations

   To use the formula we must first subjectively determine the confidence we want to have in the resulting time estimate based on the sample. This is accomplished by selecting a z value from Table 14-3. We next take a small presample of work observations to estimate the type of proportion variation that exists in the population. This presample may be as few as five observations and is arbitrarily determined by management. We next arbitrarily decide on a plus-or-minus allowable percentage of inaccuracy or error from the true population proportion. Once we have this information we can compute the sample size for the work sampling study.
3. *Make the work sampling observations.* This involves making the number of random observations defined in step 2 of the worker in the study. On each

QUESTION: Suppose we wanted to determine a sample size for a work sampling study. We take a presample and find that the proportion of time the worker is actually working (not idle or standing around) is 0.85. If $a = 3$ percent and we desire a degree of confidence of 95 percent, what is the necessary sample size for the work sampling study?

ANSWER: The sample size for the work sampling study is determined as follows:

$$n = \left(\frac{z}{a}\right)^2 p_s\,(1 - p_s)$$

$$= \left(\frac{1.96}{0.03}\right)^2 0.85\,(1 - 0.85)$$

$$= 544.2 \text{ or } 545 \text{ observations}$$

Because work sampling observations are always whole units and because we need more than 544 observations, we round up to 545. If we make 545 work sampling observations we can be 95 percent confident that the resulting work sampling proportion will be the true population proportion and that it will not be more than plus or minus 3 percent inaccurate or in error.

observation, the observer must determine whether the worker is working or is idle. These observations are usually recorded by the observer as tallies. Unlike time study, in which the observer must continuously observe the worker, work sampling observations can and should be made randomly at any time of the work day, week, or month. An underlying assumption of work sampling is that the resulting random sample distribution of tallied observations accurately describes the true population distribution.

4. *Convert the work sampling observations into proportions and calculate desired standard time estimates.* We convert the tallies to a proportion by dividing the number of times the worker was recorded as working by the total number of observations. One way that normal time can be computed is by using a work sampling proportion that involves a piece-work time standard as follows:

$$\text{Normal time} = \frac{\begin{bmatrix}\text{Total time of}\\ \text{the study in}\\ \text{minutes}\end{bmatrix} \times \begin{bmatrix}\text{Proportion of actual}\\ \text{work time from}\\ \text{work sampling study}\end{bmatrix} \times \begin{bmatrix}\text{Average pace}\\ \text{adjustment}\end{bmatrix}}{\text{Total number of pieces produced during study}}$$

The ratio gives the normal time in minutes that it takes to produce a unit. In the ratio, the total time of the study can be decided by management and the number of pieces of product produced during the same period must be counted.

QUESTION: A manager conducted a work sampling study during a forty-hour work week. During the study the manager made tallies of when the worker was working and when the worker was idle. Of one hundred tallies, eighty record that the worker was working. During the time of the study the worker produced 280 pieces (that is, finished products). If standard allowances for this job are 15 percent of standard time, what is the standard time in units for this job?

ANSWER: The standard time in units is determined as follows:

$$\text{Normal time} = \frac{\begin{matrix}\text{Total time of} \\ \text{the study in} \\ \text{minutes}\end{matrix} \times \begin{matrix}\text{Proportion of actual} \\ \text{work time from} \\ \text{work sampling study}\end{matrix}}{\begin{matrix}\text{Total number of pieces produced} \\ \text{during the study}\end{matrix}}$$

$$= \frac{[(40 \text{ hours})\ (60 \text{ minutes/hour})] \times (0.80)}{50}$$

$$= 38.4 \text{ minutes per piece}$$

$$\text{Standard time} = \text{normal time} \times \frac{100}{100 - \text{percentage allowance}}$$

$$= 38.4 \times \frac{100}{100 - 15}$$

$$= 45.176 \text{ minutes per piece}$$

Note: We have assumed that no pace adjustment is necessary in this example, chiefly because such subjective evaluation input is generally not required in work sampling. On the other hand, if the randomness and infrequency of the manager's observations substantially alter the worker's performance, a pace adjustment should be included as stated in the previous formula.

Work sampling does have some advantages over time study methods. They include the following:

1. A mechanical device is not required.
2. Little formal training is needed (that is, the need to make pace adjustment decisions is decreased).
3. Not much concentrated time and cost is required to perform the study.
4. The study can be temporarily stopped without affecting its results.

Work sampling does have some disadvantages over time study. They are listed at the top of page 712.

1. It is limited to fairly simple, repetitive jobs (thin jobs).
2. Observations tend to become nonrandom and thus violate the basic randomization assumption required, which can bias the tallies.
3. Time studies tend to be carried out over longer periods of time and as such the likelihood is increased that standardized methods may change, invalidating the study's results.

White-Collar Measures

White-collar personnel (managers and administrators in both manufacturing and service operations) should not be excluded from work measurement. The complexity of their work effort and the effort contributed by subordinates or peers often complicates any form of work measurement for this group of personnel. Indeed, white-collar personnel generally work in groups (in the case of administrators) or they are dependent on others (in the case of managers depending on their subordinates' performance) to accomplish their own work objectives. This dependency makes it difficult to measure managers' or administrators' individual work effort.

To overcome this difficulty in white-collar work measurement, a "menu of measurements" is suggested.[25] Rather than using a single measure of work performance (such as an index of productivity), a menu of measurements, which involves a collection of several measurements to describe the varied and complex dimensions that make up white-collar personnel work performance, is used. Some examples of suggested white-collar ratios of work measurement that could be used in all functional areas of an organization include the following:

$$\text{Supervisory ratio} = \frac{\text{Total employees}}{\text{Total supervisors}} \times 100$$

$$\text{Budgeting costs} = \frac{\text{Total department costs (\$)}}{\text{Total department budgeted costs (\$)}} \times 100$$

$$\text{Travel costs} = \frac{\text{Total travel costs (\$)}}{\text{Total cost of sales (\$)}} \times 100$$

$$\text{Cost reduction program} = \frac{\text{Total cost reduction (\$)}}{\text{Total cost of sales (\$)}} \times 100$$

$$\text{Absenteeism} = \frac{\text{Total hours absent}}{\text{Total hours scheduled}} \times 100$$

[25] D. J. Talley, *Total Quality Management: Performance and Cost Measures* (Milwaukee, Wis.: ASQC Quality Press, 1991), pp. 41–54, 90–103.

$$\text{Suggestion program} = \frac{\text{Total suggestions from subordinates}}{\text{Total number of subordinates}} \times 100$$

These ratios can be computed monthly, quarterly, or yearly. Comparisons in the ratios can then be made over time to monitor work performance changes. These ratios give only a brief sample of information sought in evaluating white-collar personnel. The ratios offered here are only a few of those that should be used to capture or assess the true work performance of white-collar personnel. Although those ratios just presented are of a general nature for managers and administrators, their application should be focused toward the functional area of the white-collar personnel. That is, when applying this approach for work measurement for a marketing manager, it is recommended that a more specific set of ratios be developed around the work activities of the marketing function such as sales generation. It is also suggested that group and team measurements be used to measure work performance in areas where team management or group effort is important (such as in total quality management programs).

Learning Curves

A worker usually learns how to do a job more efficiently as he or she repeats it. That is, workers learn how to reduce unnecessary movements and unnecessary use of tools, and they generally learn easier ways of performing their jobs. As the worker learns how to be more efficient, the amount of time it takes to perform the job is reduced.

Learning curves are mathematically devised curves that can be used to adjust work time estimates to reflect the reduction of time needed to complete a job that takes place as workers become more experienced. Learning curves are based on a logarithmic function as follows:

$$Y_n = n^r(Y_1)$$

where

Y_n = time required to produce the nth unit

Y_1 = time required to produce the first unit

n = number of unit for which time is to be estimated

$$r = \frac{\log L}{\log 2}$$

$$L = \frac{\text{time of 2nd unit}}{\text{time of 1st unit}}$$

Fortunately, tables of learning curve values exist to prevent the need to calculate logarithm values. The procedure for using learning curve statistics and their tabled values to adjust work time estimate is given in the list on the next two pages.

1. *Select a worker for the study.* The worker should not have performed the entire job before. The worker, however, should be familiar with the tools, equipment, and facilities layout. Also, the worker should be physically capable and psychologically ready (motivated) to perform the job normally for two trial completions of the job.
2. *Have the worker complete the job twice.* The jobs should be performed one after the other, preferably on the same day. The worker should be instructed not to significantly modify any of the tasks or assignments that make up the job on the second completion of the job. Otherwise, it may invalidate the study of the original job measured on the first trial. As they are completed, the job times should be recorded.
3. *Determine the learning curve to use in the study.* The learning curve is a percentage expressing how quickly a worker learns a job. The ratio of the second time to complete a job over the time for the first trial completion determines the learning curve. For example, if a worker takes 10 minutes to do a job the first time and 9 minutes to do the job a second time, the learning curve is 90 percent (9 minutes/10 minutes). Learning curve analysis then assumes that a worker reduced the labor time by 10 percent because of learning. It also means that whatever time it took to complete the first unit, the second unit would require only 90 percent of that time. From research on learning processes it was found that learning improvement follows a logarithmic function more accurately than it does a geometric function. That is, we cannot expect that a worker who has improved a job by 10 percent between the first and second completions, will improve the job by another 10 percent between the second and third completions. A logarithm function smooths the improvement and more accurately computes learning adjusted work time estimates.
4. *Determine a unit completion number that will define when complete learning will take place.* To use learning curve tables we must designate a point at which further repetitions of a job will no longer improve learning—a point of complete proficiency where the worker will not be able to reduce the time it takes to complete a job. This unit completion number tends to be fairly small for thin jobs and fairly large for thick jobs. Selection of the unit completion number is arbitrary. Obviously, learning always continues but it is logical to assume that at some number of repetitions, further learning makes an almost unnoticeable difference in the job time completion.
5. *Determine the learning curve statistic.* Three learning curves are present in Table 14-4: 70, 80, and 90 percent learning curves. To determine the learning curve statistic, we must find the value at the intersection of the learning curve (the columns in Table 14-4) found in step 2, with the row (unit completion number) found in step 4. So if we are using an 80 percent learning curve and the unit completion number is 20, we would have a learning curve statistic of 0.381. This value means that 38.1 percent of the time the job took on its first trial completion is the learning-adjusted time estimate to do the job.

TABLE 14-4 LEARNING CURVE STATISTICS

Unit Completion Number	*LEARNING CURVES*		
	70%	*80%*	*90%*
1	1.000	1.000	1.000
2	.700	.800	.900
3	.568	.702	.846
4	.490	.640	.810
5	.437	.596	.783
6	.398	.562	.762
7	.367	.534	.744
8	.343	.512	.729
9	.323	.493	.716
10	.306	.477	.705
11	.291	.462	.695
12	.278	.449	.685
13	.267	.438	.677
14	.257	.428	.670
15	.248	.418	.663
16	.240	.410	.656
17	.233	.402	.650
18	.226	.394	.644
19	.220	.388	.639
20	.214	.381	.634
30	.174	.335	.596
40	.150	.305	.571
50	.134	.284	.552
100	.094	.227	.497
1,000	.029	.108	.350

6. *Calculate the learning adjusted time estimate.* To compute the job time estimate adjusted for learning, we need only take the first job completion time from step 2 and multiply it by the learning curve statistic from step 5.

Learning curves play a major role in job time estimation and in other various decision-making operations management applications.[26] Care in their use, though, must be exercised. Their use requires several assumptions (for example, that a unit completion number must be designated) that in some situations may not permit them to generate useful information.[27]

---

[26] For a good review of learning curve applications, see Y. E. Yelle, "The Learning Curve: Historical Review and Comprehensive Survey," *Decision Sciences,* 10 (1979), 302–328.

[27] For a good review of learning curve limitation, see B. J. Finch and R. L. Luebbe, "Risk Associated with Learning Curve Estimates," *Production and Inventory Management,* 32, No. 13 (1991), 73–76.

QUESTION: Suppose that we want to adjust a job time observation for learning. We find that a team of workers takes 5 minutes to do the job the first time and 4.5 minutes the second time. If the team of workers will be fully proficient by the tenth repetition of this job, what is the learning curve adjusted time estimate for this job?

ANSWER: We use a 90 percent learning curve (4.5/5) from Table 14-4 for this problem. If the team of workers is fully proficient at ten repetitions, then the learning curve statistic is 0.705. The resulting time estimate then is 3.525 minutes (5 minutes × 0.705).

LEGAL AND REGULATORY CONSTRAINTS ON JOB DESIGN AND WORK MEASUREMENT

Although operations managers cannot always be experts on the law, they do need some idea of the more pertinent laws that govern the behavior of organizations regarding their human resources. For this reason, it is necessary to understand the government interface with and limitations on the operations management system with regard to job design limitations. It is interesting to note that many business schools have developed social responsibility and ethics courses specifically for business majors in the mid 1970s. Also, accreditation organizations, such as the American Assembly of Collegiate Schools of Business (AACSB), encourage the use of social responsibility and ethics courses in business curriculums. The role of business organizations in their community has been changing to meet the expectations of the people who make up the OM work force, the community, and the government.

In the United States, laws are expressed as legal actions or acts, and new government agencies are developed or old agencies are empowered to enforce these laws. In this section we will examine some of the more pertinent laws, acts, and regulations that guide and constrain operations. Remember that laws undergo constant change, so the specific origin of a particular piece of legislation might predate the laws, acts, and regulations briefly presented in this section.

National Labor Relations Act

In 1935 the **National Labor Relations Act** or **Wagner Act** was passed by Congress to protect workers from unfair labor practices. The law is still used as a basis for suit in circumstances where management does the following:

1. Discriminates in hiring to discourage union membership
2. Tries to run or aid a union

3. Refuses to bargain collectively
4. Interferes with employees' right to organize a union

Fair Labor Standards Act

In 1938 the **Fair Labor Standards Act** was passed to establish a minimum wage and maximum number of hours a worker can be asked to work without overtime pay. This act and its amendments in subsequent years helped establish overtime pay rates and equality of pay based on sex and child labor laws. In 1991, an employer could require employees to work at normal pay a maximum of eight hours per day and forty hours per week; overtime pay must be at least $1\frac{1}{2}$ times the rate of the worker's normal hourly pay. The minimum age at which a child can work in nonhazardous jobs is 16; the minimum age is 18 for jobs designated as hazardous by the secretary of labor. The Fair Labor Standards Act does not require extra pay on Saturdays, Sundays, holidays, or for vacation days.

Equal Pay Act

In 1963 the Fair Labor Standards Act was amended to restrict employers from paying differential wages based on sex. The purpose of the **Equal Pay Act** was to ensure that all workers (regardless of sex) who work the same job in the same office, receive the same pay. There are exceptions to the law that allow differential payment based on seniority, merit systems, piece-rate systems (that is, wages can be based on the quantity an individual produces) or differences other than sex. Under this act, a person's pay is based on job requirements and performance, not on titles or job classifications, which can be easily misused.

QUESTION: A man and a woman are both hired as file clerks to do the same job in an office with the same qualifications and job requirements. In practice, however, the man lifts heavier files than the woman. Should the man receive a higher wage?

ANSWER: No. Both were hired to do the same job with the same job qualifications and requirements. It makes no difference if the man actually does more of the heavier work. If management decided to redefine the job requirements and specify that the worker must be able to lift 50-pound files, then both employees would have the right to apply and be considered for the job. The woman might be a weightlifter and could do a better job than the man. Being fair in all operations management practices will always be productive in the long run.

Labor Management Relations Act

In 1947 the **Labor Management Relations Act,** or as it is sometimes called, the **Taft-Hartley Act,** was passed to balance the power that the Wagner Act gave labor by giving management several clearly defined rights. This act gave management the right to

1. Ask for an election to determine a bargaining agent
2. File unfair labor practices against union organizations
3. Relax the idea of a **closed shop** (that is, where a company agrees to hire only union members)

Labor Management Reporting and Disclosure Act

In 1959 the **Labor Management Reporting and Disclosure Act,** or more commonly called the **Landrum-Griffin Act,** was made a federal law to protect workers from their own union leaders. Under this law unions must

1. Provide a constitution, bill of rights, and bylaws to protect union members
2. File their organizational procedures regarding elections and organization policies with the U.S. secretary of labor
3. File their annual financial reports with the U.S. secretary of labor
4. Have their officers file a report on any possible conflicts of interest in their own personal transactions

The U.S. secretary of labor may prosecute unions for any violations of this act.

Civil Rights Act

The **Civil Rights Act of 1964** and its Title VII provisions on equal opportunity created the **Equal Employment Opportunity Commission (EEOC),** which investigates charges of discrimination against unions, employers, and employment agencies. Title VII of the act protects people against discrimination because of race, color, religion, sex, or national origin in the employment practices of recruiting, hiring, firing, promotions, and compensation. On the other hand, it is possible to hire on the basis of religion, sex, or national origin if any of these characteristics are legitimate requirements of the job. For example, an acting role may require that the person filling it be female.

The guidelines published by the EEOC change periodically, and it is highly advisable for any manager who hires employees to review the current guidelines. **Affirmative action plans (AAP)** can also affect a manager's normal hiring practices if the manager's organization is using an AAP to rectify past injustice in hiring practices. AAPs usually state hiring requirements and quotas that must be achieved by organizations to make up for past unlawful hiring practices. It is also advisable to review any state laws that may treat rest periods and pay systems differently than federal laws.

Worker's Compensation Laws

Worker's compensation refers to a worker's (or dependents', in the case of the worker's death) right to be compensated for injury or death occurring as a result of an industrial accident. It wasn't until 1948 that all of the states adopted worker's compensation laws. Worker's compensation laws vary by state, but all have the same basic objectives:

1. To reduce the delays and cost of court actions
2. To ensure a reasonable source of income for the victims of accidents or their dependents
3. To encourage employers to provide an accident-free work environment

Basically, worker's compensation laws require employers to pay for the occupational disabilities (regardless of who is at fault) of their employees. Worker's compensation systems operate in different ways. Some systems are mandatory and require organizations to take out private or state insurance policies on each employee. Other systems are voluntary and allow a company to self-insure its employees by establishing an account or reserve of funds held by the states in trust until needed. In some states, small businesses are exempt from worker's compensation laws.

Social Security Act

In 1935 the Social Security Act became a law and encouraged states, with federal tax funds, to set up their own unemployment insurance programs. **Social security** is simply a tax that employers must pay and is chiefly a matter for accounting department personnel. But part of the law called the **Unemployment Compensation Act** directly affects layoff or hiring decisions. Although each state has slightly different unemployment insurance systems, most allow workers to draw a portion of their salaries for approximately twenty-six weeks after they have been laid off by a firm or fired.

The idea of the act was to encourage employers to stabilize their work force and not hire and fire people frequently. In general, the employer pays taxes in only the first quarter of the year that the worker is employed by the firm. Once the first quarter's taxes on the new employee are paid, the unemployment compensation account is established and no additional taxes are paid into it. The employer can deduct most of these taxes paid into the account from the company's income taxes. The effect of this tax system is to encourage a company to keep the worker. If the company terminates the worker, it will have to build another unemployment compensation account out of its revenues. If the worker is temporarily laid off, money is paid out to the worker. These monies will have to be replaced when the layoff ends and the worker is brought back to work. The cost of this unemployment compensation is clearly a motivator to operations managers to minimize the need for layoffs.

Occupational Safety and Health Act

In 1971 the **Occupational Safety and Health Act (OSHA)** became law to ensure a healthy and safe work environment. The **National Institute for Occupational Safety and Health (NIOSH)** administers OSHA and has the authority to inspect any workplace, issue citations for violations of standards, and even obtain court orders to close down operations they feel are unsafe. OSHA regulations affect job design, facility layout, facility location, inventory management, scheduling, and materials handling. Under this act employers are obligated to provide a safe and healthy working environment in which employees can perform their jobs. Anything, such as facilities, equipment, and workstations, that can in any way be a source of injury or accident is under the jurisdiction of OSHA and is the responsibility of the business organization. OSHA has been particularly busy in the early 1990s handling worker claims for occupational illnesses such as **cumulative trauma disorder** (a work-stress disorder that affects the worker's nervous system over a period of time and culminates in physical disability).

OSHA has laid down specific standards for the quality of noise and air pollution (as we have seen in this chapter) as well as offered guidelines on general workplace safety. Operations managers should be aware that OSHA inspectors are free to enter and visit a plant without delay and spend a reasonable amount of time inspecting the operation. If a violation is observed, the employer is given a citation and will be given a reasonable amount of time to correct the safety violation. Even after that reasonable amount of time the government gives the employer another fifteen days to notify the Department of Labor (which is responsible for enforcing safety standards) if the company wishes to contest the citation or pay the assessed penalty for being in violation. Employers who contest the citation are given the right of a hearing before the Occupational Safety and Health Review Commission. The employer may also appeal the commission's decision in the U.S. court of appeals. Under this act employers are required to maintain accurate records of work-related deaths, injuries, and accidents. If an employer is found willfully or repeatedly violating OSHA standards, and if those violations lead to a worker's death, fines can be levied up to $100,000 and managers can be imprisoned for up to six months.

Worker Adjustment and Retraining Notification Act

Of more recent origin, the **Worker Adjustment and Retraining Notification (WARN) Act of 1988** concerns responsibilities of operations managers during plant closings.[28] The purpose of WARN is to give workers and their families time to adjust to the possibility of loss of employment so they can obtain alternative employment or new skills to compete successfully in the technologically advanced marketplace of the 1990s. WARN is not merely a minimum sixty-day notice requirement pertaining to plant closings; it is a law that imposes on employers strict compliance procedures for the notivation process. This act also makes it easier for workers to sue employers who do not comply with the notification requirements. The WARN act typifies the current attitude of the U.S. federal government in defining the socially responsible role that manufacturers should play.

When it comes to protecting the rights of workers and the people who make up the work force of an operation, the federal and state government "mean business." The laws presented in this section are but a portion of the hundreds that actually exist to guide and constrain operations management practices. Good managers know how to work within the laws to maximize their operations' outputs.

INTEGRATING MANAGEMENT RESOURCES: USING WORK MEASUREMENT TO INCREASE PRODUCTIVITY

Work measurement monitors worker performance. Work measurement provides the standard time estimates necessary to prepare worker performance measures and to monitor worker productivity. In the past, work measurement was performed by industrial engineering specialists who worked as staff personnel. The physical data collection methods used by the staff specialists were time consuming and often lagged behind the actual worker behavior by a considerable amount of time. It was common for work performance measures to be generated weekly or even monthly. This delay in work performance information did not permit timely correction of the worker or redesign of a job by management. This was particularly true in job-shop operations. Jobs that are not to be repeated should not be considered in a work measurement study. In some job-shops, though, orders are repeated infrequently; perhaps only once every month. If worker performance measurements are made only monthly, management loses timely and detailed information on worker performance for each job. This loss of information

1. Can inhibit future improvements in job design because it is not detailed enough to be useful
2. Will not be timely enough to be of any motivational value to the worker
3. Will not be timely enough to be of any correctional value to management if the worker is performing below standard time

---

[28] Part 639, Sections 639.1 to 639.10, Worker Adjustment and Retraining Notification, *Federal Register,* 54, No. 75 (1989), 16,064–16,070; and D. A. Sudbury, "The Practical Labor Lawyer: The Final Rules Under WARN—Beset with Pitfalls for the Unwary," *Employee Relations Labor Journal,* 15, No. 1 (Summer 1989), 147–156.

4. Can be misleading because it will represent a collection of job performance measures (that is, a collection of all sorts of job performance measures for all of the different jobs performed during the month)

Fortunately, modern work measurement systems operate at the speeds of computers. Many firms use integrated computer systems to monitor work performance. The InFiSy Systems Inc. of Houston, Texas has developed and applied computer software that integrates an employee performance measurement system with other software systems including product planning, job-cost manufacturing, job estimation and routing, accounts receivable, accounts payable, invoicing, payroll, and general ledger systems.[29] When this integrated system is applied, work measurement standards, including setup times, are actually placed on each job order as it is routed through each department. In this way the workers will know precisely how much time their individual work effort should take. When an order is completed by a worker in a department, the data are entered into the computer system and performance measures are calculated immediately.

This system, and others like IBM's CIM MAPICS system (introduced in Chapter 3), allows management to monitor detailed work performance almost instantaneously.[30] These systems' integration with other functions such as accounting permits detailed cost information that can be used by management to improve product pricing and control manufacturing costs (labor and materials) from expected work standards. Even the production standards themselves are improved by using a more timely computer information system. Indeed, in the application of the InFiSy System in industry it was observed that workers more readily challenged inaccurate production standards and were more willing to be of help in their revision than they were before the computer system was installed. The timeliness and detail of computerized production standards made inaccurate standards much more obvious to both workers and management. Using such systems resulted in greater accuracy in labor resource usage and reduced idleness and waste because of inaccurate estimates. A reduction in wasted labor resources improves efficiency and productivity.

SUMMARY

In this chapter we have examined the operations management functions of job design and work measurement. How job design and work measurement improve worker productivity was a central theme for this chapter. Job design centers around an analysis of work environment considerations, workers' psychological and physical considerations, and the work tasks that make up a job. We discussed wage incentive plans that can influence worker productivity. We also discussed several behavioral methods for improving job design con-

[29] "1986 Reference Guide and Directory," *Production and Inventory Management Review,* 5, No. 11 (1986), p. 102.

[30] *MAPICS/DD Information Manual* (White Plains, N.Y.: IBM, 1989).

siderations including job rotation, enlargement, and enrichment; team work units and scheduling; and micromotion analysis and flowcharting. Some of these methods are primarily designed to improve worker motivation.

In presenting work measurement, this chapter sought to answer several questions. Why should we use work measurement? Who should conduct a work measurement study? How should work measurements be calculated? What procedures should be used to make the work measurement observations? How many time observations should we take? What alternative means can we use to make work measurements? How should we adjust the time estimates for the worker's learning experience? To answer these questions several work measurement procedures and methods were presented, including time study analysis, methods-time measurement, work sampling, and learning curve analysis.

Job design and work measurement require the assistance of workers and in some cases the unions that represent them. A manager's ability to work with workers and unions is often defined by government regulation. Indeed, the operations management functions in all of the chapters we have discussed in this text are in some way regulated, defined, and dictated by government. We presented some of the major laws, acts, and agencies operations managers must work with to accomplish their job design goals.

DISCUSSION AND REVIEW QUESTIONS

1. Why are job design and work measurement necessary operations management functions?
2. What are work environment considerations and how do they affect productivity?
3. What are worker motivation considerations and how do they affect productivity?
4. How does a worker signing his or her name on a finished product help the organization accomplish its objectives?
5. What are work task considerations and how do they affect productivity?
6. What is the difference between job enlargement and job enrichment?
7. What are standard times and normal times?
8. How do we conduct a time study?
9. What is methods-time measurement and how is it used in work measurement?
10. How do we conduct a work sampling study? Is the information generated by this type of study different from a time study?
11. What are learning curves and how are they used in work measurement?
12. How does OSHA help an organization achieve its objectives?

PROBLEMS

* 1. If we want to comply with OSHA maximum noise level exposure rates for U.S. workers, and if the average sound pressure level measured in dBA units is 110, how many hours at maximum would we be allowed to operate?

---

* The solutions to the problems marked with an asterisk can be found in Appendix J.

2. A company attempts to comply with OSHA maximum noise level exposure rates for its workers. If the average sound pressure level measured in dBA units is 90, how many hours at maximum would the company be allowed to operate?
3. If the standard time to do a job is 24 hours and a worker takes 16 hours, what is the worker's performance measure? If the worker takes 30 hours, what is the performance measure?
4. If the standard time to perform a job is three units per hour and a worker produces only two units, what is the worker's performance measure? If the worker produces four units in an hour, what is the performance measure?
5. What is the standard time for a job task where the normal time is 14 minutes, the standard allowance for delays is 3 minutes, fatigue allowance is 2 minutes, and the standard allowance for personal time is 1 minute?
6. In a time study we make the following four time observations for a job task: 3.5, 4.5, 4.2, and 3.8 minutes. If the average pace adjustment statistic is 1.20 and standard allowances are 25 percent of standard time, what is the job task's standard time?
* 7. What is the standard time for a job task where the normal time is 7.5 minutes and the standard allowances are 20 percent of standard time?
8. Suppose that we made four timed observations of a worker performing the same job task. The four times observed are 6.9, 7.9, 7.1, and 8.1 minutes with an average pace adjustment statistic of 0.80. If the standard allowances are 15 percent of standard time, what is the standard time for this job?
9. Suppose that we made three observations of a worker performing a job task. The time observations and their respective pace adjustment statisics are as follows:

Observed Time	*Pace Adjustment Statistic*	*Adjustment Statistic*
2.1	1.20	Performing 20% faster than expected
3.2	0.90	Performing 10% slower than expected
2.7	1.00	Performing at a normal pace

With a standard allowance of 1.2 minutes for fatigue, what is the standard time for this job task?

*10. Suppose that we want to determine a sample size for a time study analysis. We took a presample and found that the average time was 25 minutes and the sample standard deviation was 4 minutes. If $a = 5$ minutes and we desire a degree of confidence of 99 percent, what is the necessary sample size?
11. Suppose that we want to determine a sample size for a time study analysis. We take a presample of five observations of 5.8, 5.6, 6, 6.2, and 6.3 minutes. If we do not want to be more than plus or minus 1 minute off from the population time estimate, and if we desire a degree of confidence of 95 percent, what is the necessary sample size?
12. We have been requested to determine a sample size for a work sampling study. We took a presample and found that the proportion of time the worker was actually working (not idle or standing around) was 0.95. If $a = 5$ percent and we desire a degree of confidence of 98 percent, what is the necessary sample size for the work sampling study?

13. Suppose that we want to determine a sample size for a work sampling study. We took a presample and found that the proportion of time the worker was actually working was twelve out of twenty observations. If $a = 3$ percent and we want our sample proportion to be accurate with confidence of 98 percent, what is the necessary sample size for the work sampling study?

*14. A manager conducted a work sampling study during a 40-hour work week. During the study the manager made tallies of when the worker was actually working and when the worker was idle. Of fifty-four tallies, forty-eight record that the worker was working. During the time of the study, the worker produced sixty pieces (finished products). If standard allowance for this job is 10 percent of standard time, what is the standard time in units for this job?

15. An engineer conducted a work sampling study during a 40-hour work week. During the study the engineer made tallies of when the worker was actually working and when the worker was idle. Of eighty tallies, sixty-eight recorded that the worker was working. During the time of the study, the worker produced 150 pieces. If standard allowance for this job is 5 percent of standard time, what is the standard time in units for this job?

*16. A service facility in 1992 had a total of twenty-eight employees (twenty service agents and eight supervisors). In early 1993 the service facility instituted a just-in-time (JIT) program. By the end of 1993, the service facility employed twenty-four service agents and nine supervisors.
   a. What are the 1992 and 1993 supervisory ratios?
   b. If a reduction in the supervisory ratio is desirable, has the institution of the JIT program been successful?

17. A service facility in 1992 had a total of forty employees (thirty service agents and ten supervisors). The supervisors had to travel in 1992, which cost a total of $100,000 for that year out of a total cost of sales of $2.3 million. By the end of 1993, the service facility employed twenty service agents and eight supervisors. The year-end travel expenses for the eight supervisors were $230,000 for the year end out of a total cost of sales of $3.2 million.
   a. What are the 1992 and 1993 supervisory ratios?
   b. What are the 1992 and 1993 travel costs ratios?
   c. If reductions in the supervisor and travel costs ratios are desirable, has the service operation been successful? Explain.

*18. Suppose that we want to adjust a job time observation for learning that will take place in the future. We found that a group of workers took 110 minutes to do the job the first time and 77 minutes the second time. If the group of workers will be fully proficient by the twentieth repetition of this assembly line job, what is the learning curve adjusted time estimate for this job?

19. A manager wishes to adjust a job time observation for learning that is expected to take place in the future. She found that a team of workers took 15 minutes to do the job the first time and 12 minutes the second time. If the team of workers will be fully proficient by the one hundredth repetition of this assembly line job, what is the learning curve adjusted time estimate for this job?

20. Suppose that a company wishes to adjust a job time observation for learning. A manager found that a worker took 20.5 minutes to do the job the first time and 14.35 minutes

the second time. If the worker will be fully proficient by the seventeenth repetition of this assembly line job, what is the learning curve adjusted time estimate for this job?

21. A manager conducted a work sampling study during a three-week or 120-hour period. During the study, she made tallies of when the worker was actually working and when the worker was idle. Of 140 tallies, 111 recorded that the worker was working. During the time of the study the worker produced 3,200 pieces. If standard allowances for this job are 8 percent of standard time, what is the standard time in units for this job?

22. Suppose that we made four observations of workers performing a job task. The time observations and their respective pace adjustment statistics are as follows:

Observed Time	*Pace Adjustment Statistic*
9.3	1.20
10.6	0.90
9.4	1.10
8.9	1.30

With standard allowances of 12 percent of standard time, what is the standard time for this job task?

23. Suppose that we want to determine the standard time of an assembly operation that consists of three work elements. An initial set of five observations has been collected using continuous timing (stopwatch continuously going and the completion times noted). These observations are as follows:

		OBSERVATION				
Element	*Performance Rating*	*1*	*2*	*3*	*4*	*5*
1	.87	20	64	113	157	203
2	1.40	35	81	127	172	220
3	1.00	45	92	136	183	232

We wish to determine the standard time of the operation if the allowance for personal time is 7 percent, the allowance for unavoidable delay is 6 percent, and the allowance for fatigue is 6 percent.

24. Suppose that we want to determine the standard time for an operation that consists of four work elements. An initial set of four observations has been collected:

		OBSERVATION			
Element	*Performance Rating*	*1*	*2*	*3*	*4*
1	.98	17	15	15	14
2	1.04	14	14	16	13
3	1.00	20	22	19	20
4	1.05	12	11	10	10

We wish to determine that standard time of the operation if the allowance for personal time is 5 percent, the allowance for unavoidable delay is 5 percent, and the allowance for fatigue is 6 percent.

25. Suppose that a company wishes to determine a sample size for a time study analysis. The observations have been made over a period of 320 minutes, during which the operator has produced fifty products. The allowance for personal time is 6 percent, the allowance for unavoidable delay is 5 percent, and the allowance for fatigue is 5 percent.

CASE 14-1

YOU CAN'T SQUEEZE BLOOD OUT OF A STONE

The Ashlyn Corporation of Houston, Texas manufactures oil drilling equipment. The corporation employs a total of 3,000 blue-collar workers and 1,000 white-collar workers. Until two years ago, the company was very successful in designing, manufacturing, and selling oil equipment all over the world. The company's product line was rapidly changing and new products had to be developed and produced all the time. Many of the company's products, once developed, would be produced in job-lot production runs.

Problems in manufacturing appeared in the form of late orders, missed delivery dates, and eventually canceled orders. The company responded by tightening up its human resource controls: It installed a work measurement system. To measure and determine time standards, time study methods were used over a six-month period. One of the company's most experienced manufacturing supervisors was selected to do the time studies. The supervisor's experience, though, was not in time study methods. The supervisor determined the standard times simply by making ten time observations of an entire job. The time study observations for one of the company's products, drill bit ZX, is presented in Exhibit 14C-1. The standard time estimates were just a simple average of ten time estimates; no other information was used.

The company's labor was unionized and quite willing to allow the company to measure and set up the time standards as long as they would not be used to justify dismissal of personnel for what the company might designate as below-average work performance. After only a few months, it became obvious to the workers that the time standards were totally incorrect. The time standards for some products allowed too much time for manufacturing and others did not allow enough time. Unfortunately, the supervisory-level personnel started to use the performance measures as a basis for reprimanding poor performers. The workers started filing grievances against the supervisors and everybody started disliking his or her job. Worker and supervisor morale dropped along with productivity. The most commonly used phrase found in the suggestion box during that time was "you [management] can't squeeze blood out of a stone." In other words, Ashlyn's workers felt that management was using poor production standards to squeeze extra labor out of the blue-collar workers.

The top management of the company decided that something had to be done. Consequently, an

EXHIBIT 14C-1 DRILL BIT ZX TIME STUDY PRESAMPLE OBSERVATIONS

Observation	*Time (minutes)*
1	24.5
2	25.7
3	28.9
4	26.7
5	27.0
6	25.9
7	27.2
8	28.0
9	24.5
10	25.9

industrial engineer (IE) who specialized in time study analysis was hired to correct the standard time estimates. The IE identified two basic types of products: the old standard line of products that the company continually produced year after year and the new products that were emerging each year. For the old products the IE decided to use time study observations to determine normal time estimates and then adjust them by using the industry's standard allowance estimate of 14.5 percent of standard time. For the new products, such as the new drill bit product named the "Digman," the IE decided that learning curves should be used to adjust the manufacturing time estimates. To accomplish this the IE made two time study observations and recorded each of the newly developed products' completion times. In the case of the Digman product, the first completion time was 78 minutes and the second was 62.4 minutes.

CASE QUESTIONS

1. How many time study observations should be made on drill bit ZX to be 98 percent sure of the resulting time estimate and not have more than a plus-or-minus 4 minute error in the time estimate?
2. Using the ten time estimates in Exhibit 14C-1 compute both the company's original standard time estimate and the IE's standard time estimate for drill bit ZX. Based on just this sample of observations, does it appear that labor's complaint is well founded?
3. What is the learning curve adjusted normal time for the Digman if no additional improvement in productivity will take place after the one hundredth unit is produced?
4. What would you recommend to Ashlyn's upper management to deal with the labor unrest caused by the original work measurements?

CASE 14-2

LEARNING TO ESTIMATE LABOR REQUIREMENTS

The Dara Corporation is a taxation consulting group. The company offers its clients a fairly singular consulting service. Focusing on subchapter and limited partnerships, Dara offers its clients information on how to avoid trouble during an audit by the Internal Revenue Service. Its services include general in-house counseling presentations for accounting personnel, rental of video presentations, and personal consulting (one-on-one sessions with staff lawyers or accountants.) Dara packages its educational services in a variety of ways. A team of Dara's consultants usually arrives at the client's operation and custom designs an educational package to fit its needs. While the particular service package offered clients varies according to the size of the organization and the complexity of the client's problems, the initial assessment of designing each package takes roughly the same amount of time. At least, that is what has been the case over the last ten years of its operation. During those years the average time to design a client's package (regardless of client size or problem complexity) was 16 hours, with little more than plus or minus 1 hour standard deviation.

Because of the growth in business during the early 1990s, Dara's management added an additional consulting team to handle the client load. For about a year the two teams (the "old team" consisting of experienced staffers and the "new team" consisting of newly hired staffers) operated independent of each other to service clients' needs. The new team experienced a lot of turnover and was completely replaced during its first year. As was to be expected, the inexperienced new team staffers took longer to do their design package work than the more experienced old team staffers.

The top management of Dara was concerned that the difference in package design time beween the two teams was more than just a difference in experience. Management was concerned that human factors beyond the organization's control would always keep the new team from becoming as efficient as the old team. An industrial engineering (IE) consultant was called in to advise Dara's management on its concerns. The consultant decided to run an experiment to see if the time discrepancies were really a matter of concern or just a matter of experience that would be solved over time as the new team became more stable (had less turnover) and more experienced in their jobs. As a part of the experiment, the consultant had both teams design educational packages for the same ten clients. The same packages were in fact designed by both teams, but the amount of time it took to complete the design work was different. The resulting average times for both teams are presented in Exhibit 14C-2.

EXHIBIT 14C-2 AVERAGE DESIGN TIME REQUIREMENTS PER CLIENT (IN HOURS)

Client	*Old Team Time*	*New Team Time*
1	15.8	17.2
2	16.3	19.2
3	17.0	18.3
4	14.3	19.9
5	18.9	20.4
6	16.0	21.2
7	13.9	19.2
8	16.7	17.9
9	15.1	18.5
10	16.9	19.5

CASE QUESTIONS

1. Let's assume that a 90 percent learning curve is applicable and complete learning takes place on the tenth repetition (the unit completion number). What are the ten adjusted time values for the new team? Compute the average of all ten new team client times (an overall average time for clients). Compute the average of the old team's client times. Which of the two averages is smaller? Based on the learning curve adjusted average time, what could you say about the lack of experience of the new team? Is the difference because of a lack of experience or not? Explain.
2. Let's assume that an 80 percent learning curve is applicable and complete learning takes place on the tenth repetition. What are the ten adjusted time values for the new team? Compute the average for all ten new team client times (an overall average time for clients). Compute the average of the old team's client times. Which of the two averages is smaller? Based on the learning curve adjusted average time, what could you say about the lack of experience of the new team? Is the difference because of a lack of experience? Explain.
3. What assumptions are you making in using either of the learning curve estimates in Questions 1 and 2?

15

Improving Technology and International Integration of Operations Management Systems

CHAPTER OUTLINE

CHAPTER OBJECTIVES

The material in this chapter should prepare you to do the following:

1. Explain why international integration is necessary.
2. Describe a world-class manufacturer.
3. Explain how technology affects the productivity cycle.
4. Explain how advances in telecommunications such as fiberoptics and local area networks (LANs) are changing operations management.
5. Explain how advances in decision-making technology such as artificial intelligence and expert systems are changing OM.
6. Describe how remote usage computers are changing OM.
7. Explain how electronic shopping and service systems are changing OM.
8. Describe what a manufacturing automated protocol does to help implement CIM systems.
9. Describe why the international integration of OM systems is a strategic consideration in planning manufacturing activities in the 1990s.
10. Explain how a factory or service operation can ensure its success in the future.

International competition for U.S. makers of manufactured products and service goods will be more fierce throughout the 1990s than it was in the 1980s. Despite the loss by U.S. manufacturers and service organizations of sizable portions of their domestic markets in the 1980s, they are entering the 1990s with optimism and confidence that they can regain their markets. U.S. manufacturers and service organizations have learned from their mistakes in the 1980s how to compete against foreign competition, and in the process have also learned how to compete globally with more success. U.S. firms are now going after their international competitors' markets with technologies and systems that foreign competitors used so successfully against them and with new technologies that are just now being implemented. Much of this book has been devoted to describing the technologies currently used by excellent domestic and foreign organizations to develop competitive advantages.

As a major theme of this book, we have described how organizations integrate management resources to develop competitive advantages by improving efficiency and productivity, improving management control, or producing high-quality products or services. In the examples cited in each chapter, we described how technology and technology-based systems provide the means by which integration of production resources is feasible. We also described in previous chapters how much of the need to implement new technology and production systems is caused by competition. Competition today is usually international, from countries such as Japan. Put another way, we have been suggesting through these examples that utilizing improved technology and technology-based systems is a major approach firms can use to meet and beat domestic and foreign competition.

The purpose of this chapter is to bring this book to a close by pointing new directions in the study of operations management. More specifically, we will examine how advances in technology are changing and altering the way operations management's resources are being used to accomplish production objectives. We will also examine ideas on how operations management resources (including technology), can and are being integrated internationally or globally to achieve success in markets that require world-class products and services.

• • •

WHY IMPROVING TECHNOLOGY AND INTERNATIONAL INTEGRATION OF OPERATIONS MANAGEMENT ARE NECESSARY

In the United States and other countries, a select number of companys' products dominate their markets, nationally and internationally. These companys' products define what top-level quality and customer service is in the industries in which they are marketed. The companies selling these products have achieved the greatest success in providing customers with what they want. These companies are called **world-class**

manufacturers. World-class manufacturers share a number of characteristics, some of which include[1]

1. Integrating management resources with the goal of meeting customer satisfaction
2. Continually improving product quality
3. Developing competitive advantages
4. Avoiding waste in production systems to improve productivity
5. Having excellent manufacturing capabilities (including flexibility) and always striving for improvements

In previous chapters we have described how computer-based technology can help manufacturers achieve these characteristics. Indeed, many operations management practitioners and researchers believe that incorporating advanced technologies into an integrated production system (such as a computer-integrated manufacturing [CIM] system) is necessary to achieve world-class standing.[2] Regardless of whether the operation is large or small, using some kind of improved technology is necessary to become world class.[3] Because many organizations establish a long-range strategic goal of becoming a world-class manufacturer, the use and integration of improved technology can be a necessary tactical requirement to accomplish their strategic goal.

As the cost of human resources in a country rises, manufacturers will seek human resources in foreign countries to minimize costs. The reduced costs are necessary because the international market of the 1990s requires constant cost-reduction worldwide. Said another way, a country's boundaries are no longer an acceptable excuse for high product costs when competing in an international market, and almost all markets in developed countries are considered international markets. As we can see in Figure 15-1 and Table 15-1, the hourly compensation costs in the United States, Canada, Europe, and Japan are substantially higher than in less-developed countries. Yet many new manufacturing facilities are still being built in the United States, Canada, Europe, and Japan. One of the reasons for these facility location decisions is the availability of improved technology. Improved technology (and the personnel to use it) is more available in developed countries, which can more than offset the cheaper labor rates in less-developed countries. So improved technology is necessary to save jobs in developed countries and meet ever-increasing market demand requirements for reduced product costs.

---

[1] R. R. Bell and J. M. Burnham, *Managing Productivity and Change* (Cincinnati: South-Western, 1991), p. 7.

[2] R. M. Grant et al., "Appropriate Manufacturing Technology: A Strategic Approach," *Sloan Management Review,* 33, No. 1 (1991), 43–54; R. R. Bell and J. M. Burnham, *Managing Productivity and Change* (Cincinnati: South-Western, 1991), pp. 66–116; J. Main, "Computers of the World, Unite," *Fortune,* September 24, 1990, pp. 115–119; B. Dumaine, "What the Leaders of Tomorrow See," *Fortune,* July 3, 1989, pp. 48–62; "Smart Factories: America's Turn?" *Business Week,* May 8, 1989, pp. 142–150; and E. Colonis, "Smart Moves by Quality Champs," *Fortune,* December 3, 1991, pp. 24–29.

[3] J. Wright, "World Class CIM on a Small Scale," *Manufacturing Systems* (November 1989), 42–48.

FIGURE 15-1 HOURLY COMPENSATION COSTS FOR PRODUCTION WORKERS IN MANUFACTURING*

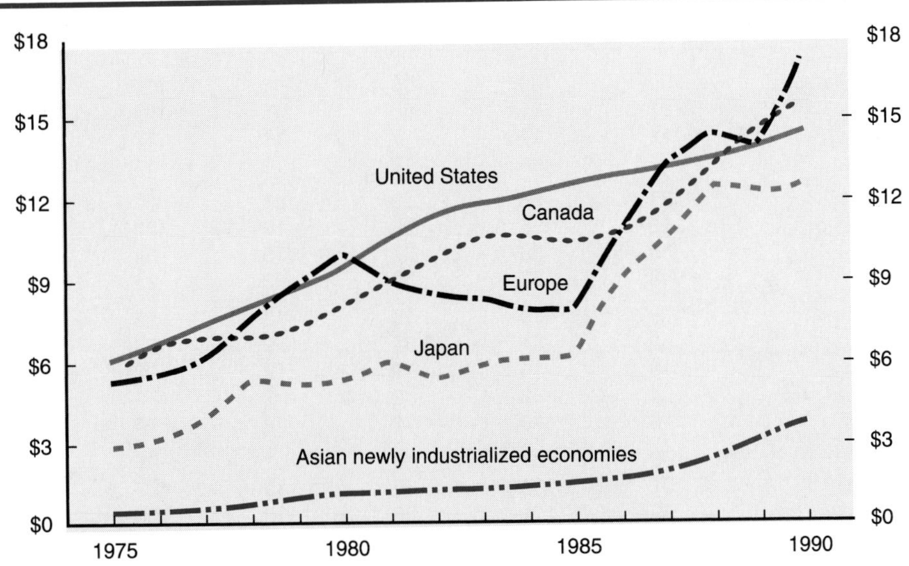

* All dollar values (vertical axis) are in U.S. dollars, adjusted for currency exchange rates.
Source: Monthly Labor Review, August 1991, page 35.

The productivity cycle (introduced in Chapter 1) has been very successfully used by Japanese automobile manufacturers to capture U.S. automobile markets. As we can see in Figure 15-2, improvements in technology can trigger the productivity cycle in a variety of places to help companies capture larger shares of markets and eventually market dominance.

In the mid 1980s, when General Motors had just started producing robots for automobile assembly operations, Japanese automobile manufacturers were acquiring improved technology such as robots at a rate five to ten times faster than U.S. manufacturers.[4] Indeed, the GM division that produced robots sold more to Japanese manufacturers than to U.S. manufacturers. Research in 1986 comparing Japanese and U.S. automobile assembly operations revealed that the Japanese automobile manufacturers were modernizing their production facilities with the latest technologically advanced equipment at a rate of 20 percent per year, while U.S. manufacturers were improving technology at a rate of less than 1 percent per year.[5] Although other Japanese innovations

[4] S. Aida, M. Hasegawa, and T. Ueda, "Technology and Corporate Culture of Industrial Robots in Japan," *Journal of Robotic Systems,* 3, No. 1 (1986), 105–131.

[5] R. W. Hall, "Empowerment: The 1990's Manufacturing Enterprise," *APICS—The Performance Advantage,* 1, No. 1 (1991), 26–29, +58.

TABLE 15-1 INDEXES OF HOURLY COMPENSATION COSTS FOR PRODUCTION WORKERS IN MANUFACTURING

Country or Area	*1975*	*1980*	*1985*	*1988*	*1989*	*1990*
United States	100	100	100	100	100	100
Canada	91	85	83	98	104	107
Brazil	14	14	9	11	12	19
Mexico	—	—	12	10	11	12
Australia	87	86	63	81	86	88
Hong Kong	12	15	13	17	20	22
Israel	35	39	31	55	54	—
Japan	48	57	50	92	88	87
Korea	6	10	10	18	25	28
New Zealand	50	54	34	59	55	56
Singapore	13	15	19	19	22	25
Sri Lanka	4	2	2	2	—	—
Taiwan	6	10	12	20	25	27
Austria	68	87	56	101	95	114
Belgium	101	133	69	112	107	127
Denmark	99	111	63	115	106	126
Finland	72	84	62	113	116	139
France	71	91	58	94	88	103
Germany	100	125	74	130	123	144
Greece	27	38	28	38	38	—
Ireland	47	60	45	70	66	77
Italy	73	81	56	93	93	110
Luxembourg	100	122	59	100	—	—
Netherlands	103	123	69	117	108	125
Norway	107	119	82	136	131	147
Portugal	25	21	12	19	20	24
Spain	41	61	37	64	64	78
Sweden	113	127	75	121	123	141
Switzerland	96	113	75	130	117	139
United Kingdom	52	76	48	76	73	84

Note: U.S. level = 100.
Source: Monthly Labor Review, August 1991, page 36.

(such as just-in-time [JIT] and total quality control [TQC] philosophies) have contributed to their productivity, technology has long been considered a major factor in their success. The comparative survey in 1986 also revealed that the rate of productivity increase in the Japanese automobile assembly lines was three times greater than that of U.S. competitors, production lead time for domestic customers in Japan averaged only twelve days versus six weeks for U.S. customers, and the average car was on the assembly line in Japan only 10.8 hours versus 24.7 hours in a U.S. operation. The long-range

FIGURE 15-2 THE PRODUCTIVITY CYCLE

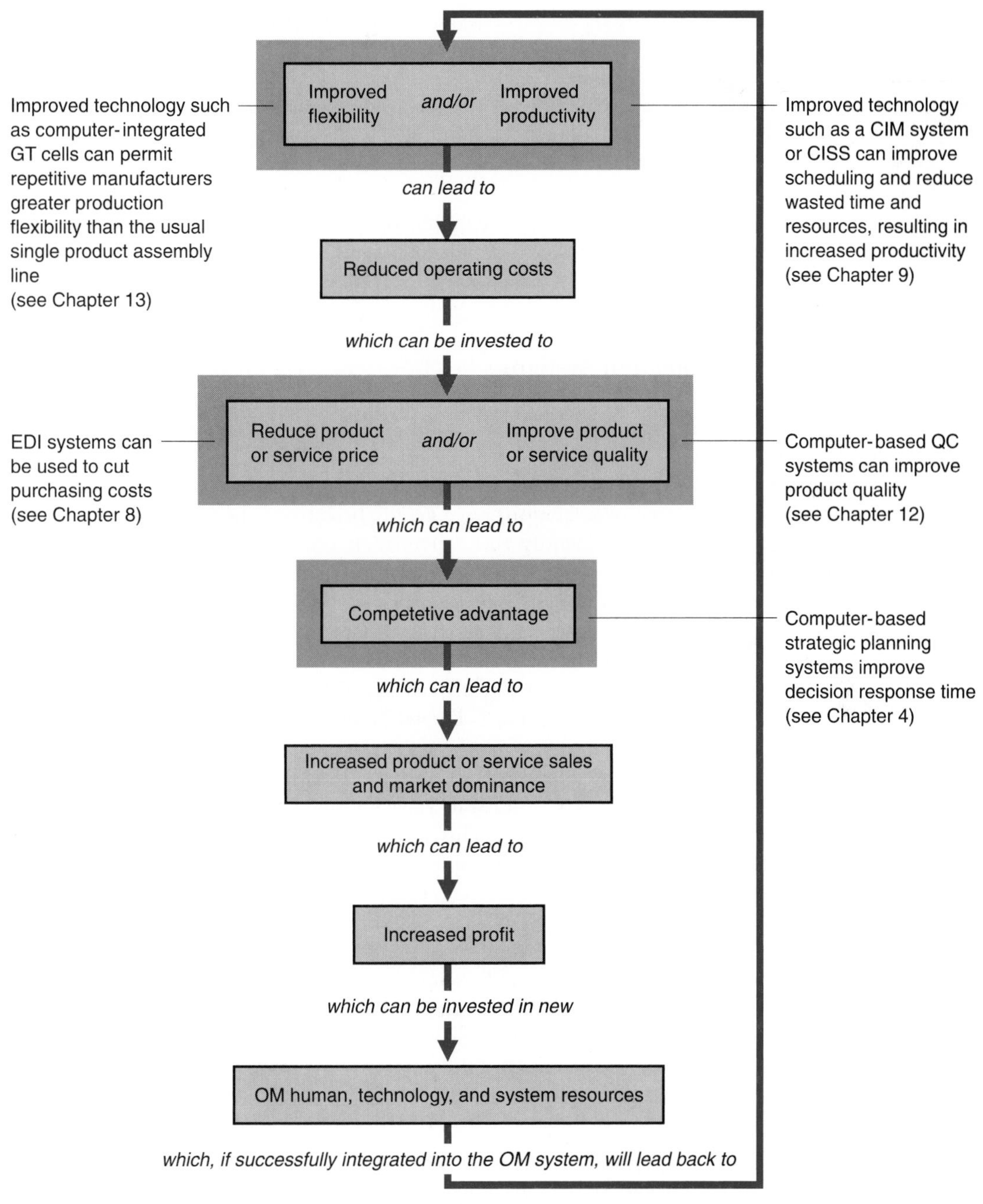

effect of these differences has resulted in more than a doubling of market share for Japanese manufacturers in the five-year period from 1986, while the U.S. automobile share has been reduced by 50 percent during the same period.

TECHNOLOGICAL ADVANCES THAT ARE CHANGING OPERATIONS MANAGEMENT

Improvements in technology are changing operations management in several major areas. These areas of technological change include telecommunication systems, decision-making technology, and computer-integrated systems.

Telecommunication Systems

Advances in telecommunication systems are allowing manufacturers to reach new markets and efficiently communicate product information to customers. Advances in **telecommunication systems** (that is, communication at a distance using cable, radio, telegraph, telephone, or television) have greatly broadened the reach of manufacturers and service operators to identify and deliver their products. Some researchers believe that telecommunication systems can themselves offer users competitive advantages by reducing production lead times.[6] Because many service products are information, telecommunication systems improvements directly affect the productivity and logistics of many service products. Some areas of improvement in telecommunications include fiber optics, satellite transmission, local area networks (LANs), the change to digital transmission, and the Information Services Digital Network (ISDN).[7]

FIBER OPTICS The development of fiber-optic transmission lines reduced installation space and effort, increased transmission capacity, and improved transmission quality (eliminated electrical interference). This technology reduces operations management communication costs and affords customers using information service products an improved level of product quality.

SATELLITE TRANSMISSION Although not useful for interactive communications (such as a person-to-person telephone call), satellite transmission is ideal for communicating large amounts of data at one time. Satellites are very flexible (they can change direction of communication to anywhere in the world), reliable, and fast (there is no waiting to use earthbound transmission cables). Operations managers are using satellites to improve

[6] P. G. W. Keen, *Competing in Time: Using Telecommunications for Competitive Advantage,* 2nd ed. (Washington, D.C.: International Center for Information Technologies, 1989).

[7] *Trends in Information Technology,* 3rd ed. (Geneva, Switzerland: Arthur Andersen Worldwide Organization, 1989), pp. 13–22.

monitoring and control functions in plants in remote geographic locations. Satellite communication systems allow managers to quickly and efficiently communicate with each plant manager, regardless of location, rather than telephone each plant, which can be time consuming.

LOCAL AREA NETWORKS (LANS) LANs are disk devices that enable computers, printers, and other peripheral computer equipment to exchange information throughout an organization (to share information within the company's network of computers) and to use information from public networks outside the corporation. Operations managers are using LANs to improve corporate-wide communication of production activity and share decision support information from outside sources. Shop floor supervisors are using LANs to efficiently monitor and control work-in-process (WIP), administrate numerical control (NC) machine activity, and communicate with workcenters on the flow of job orders.

QUESTION: How does a LAN help organizations achieve their flexibility goals in operations management?

ANSWER: LANs are highly flexible in configuration and purpose, yet cost only a fraction of traditional minicomputer systems of the 1980s.[8] Small manufacturers can afford the microcomputer-based LAN systems, permitting them the opportunity of a limited CIM system that can make them more competitive in automated product environments. Large manufacturers find that the LANs embrace a more flexible or open systems environment because they permit the introduction of state-of-the-art (and more user-friendly) software applications. This permits the large manufacturer to use newer menu-driven shortcuts in searches and editing jobs that can be performed with the LAN to support work load in other existing computer systems. Indeed, the LANs can take advantage of the latest microcomputer technology improvements of the 1990s and use them to augment existing computer and software applications.

DIGITAL TRANSMISSION The traditional analog transmission system of sending electrical waves of varying amplitude or frequency is ideal for voice communication, but is limited when it is used to send large amounts of data at one time (such as sending an electronic image of a picture). Digital transmission sends pulses of electronic information (which is the way it is stored in computers) instead of waves. When compared to analog systems, digital transmission affords users a significantly higher transmission speed, is less costly, has lower error rates, and offers flexibility to mix information of multiple types

[8] N. D. Klapper, "The New Generation: Sharing the Power of Manufacturing Information Systems," *APICS—The Performance Advantage*, 2, No. 11 (1992), 22–26.

(that is, voice and image) on the same circuit. Although only just making its appearance in plants, managers and shop floor supervisors will be able to communicate with workers by sending their image to workcenters over television monitors rather than making physical inspections. This will save time and improve efficiency.

INFORMATION SERVICES DIGITAL NETWORK (ISDN) ISDN is a combination of computer systems that will combine a variety of all communication media (public telephone systems, private data network systems, and so on). ISDN is a communication network system service that will afford users a number of communication services including call screening, voice mail, and usage reports. While not yet commonly available, this service will allow operations managers to conduct conferences electronically, saving the traveling time and inconvenience of physically transporting personnel to conduct business.

The increase in communication capacity created by improvements in technology has also helped promote the development of technologies to allow for greater use of the communication capacity. Remote or hand-held telephones are used by shop floor personnel in large plants and project operations to remain in contact for management control purposes. Facsimile (fax) machines are used to communicate written or hard copy (sometimes necessary in legal matters) to expedite the completion of products or services.

Decision-making Technology

Some of the advances in decision-making technology that are affecting operations management include artificial intelligence and expert systems and computer-integrated software engineering.

ARTIFICIAL INTELLIGENCE AND EXPERT SYSTEMS Artificial intelligence and expert systems (AI/ESs) are decision support systems that are greatly improving the efficiency of operations. They are currently being used in a variety of areas that previously required extensive use of human expert judgment. For example, they are currently used as advisors (to human decision makers) in life insurance underwriting to evaluate individual applications for insurance. By expertly taking into account factors such as health and avocations, AI/ESs are making suggestions on standard and nonstandard risk ratings and premiums. In the trucking industry, AI/ESs are being used for routing and scheduling to determine the sequence of stops a truck should make on a route for unloading purposes to provide service in a timely fashion. The U.S. Securities and Exchange Commission (SEC) uses an AI/ES that reads text from financial reports and has the capability to identify concepts such as "corporate takeover" to assist them in efficiently identifying organizations that might be violating governmental laws. Even at the shop floor level of an organization, AI/ESs are helping conserve resources. The DSSCA expert system developed by Decision Support Systems for Commercial Applications of Pittsburgh, analyzes production schedules to optimize the allocation of resources by looking for opportunities to salvage materials in the rework piles for use in filling incoming customer orders.[9]

AI/ESs allow computers to suggest and, in some cases, execute their own decisions (via CIM or computer-integrated service system [CISS] facilities) efficiently at computer speed, and with improved product consistency (improved quality). As more of the production system is controlled by AI/ESs, it is controlled less by human beings. The term **smart factories** is commonly used today to characterize these types of highly integrated and intelligent facilities.[10]

COMPUTER-INTEGRATED SOFTWARE ENGINEERING (CISE) CISE is a computer-based software system that brings a formal and consistent application of engineering science to organizations. Instead of a firm's having a separate engineering software application, CISE integrates computer-aided design (CAD; discussed in Chapter 4), computer-aided engineering (CAE; software used in the design testing of products by simulating product performance under various conditions), computer-aided process planning (CAPP; software used to improve production processes), and all other engineering software systems. Placing CISE into a management engineering information system permits users to benefit from the shared engineering efforts. The output of any one computer-aided task is made available to all other applicable task environments in the production process that might logically use the information. This reduces the wasteful effort of manually moving information from one nonintegrated engineering system to another. CISE allows engineers to be more productive, improves reliability of the production systems they engineer, and improves the quality of the production processes and products.

Computer-integrated Systems

Advances in computer-integrated systems (CIM and CISS) are greatly altering operations management. Throughout this book, we have described a number of technologies and systems that have been making a major contribution to the OM function. Additional improvements in technology and systems include remote usage computers, electronic shopping and service systems, and integrated software systems.

REMOTE USAGE COMPUTERS Lap-top computers are used by managers to perform word processing when they are away from their usual place of business. **Smart cards** are a recent European-based product that performs a limited number of computer functions, such as personnel identification, from a piece of equipment the size of a credit card.[11] The smart card contains one or more microchips and is used to interact with a

---

[9] M. Williamson, "Artificial Intelligence Takes a Stand on the Factory Floor," *Computerworld,* July 6, 1987, p. 53.

[10] "Smart Factories: America's Turn?" *Business Week,* May 8, 1989, pp. 142–150.

[11] "Smart Cards Showcased at ID Expo," *Production and Inventory Management Review with APICS News,* 11, No. 5 (1991), 37.

larger computer system for purposes of identifying the user and permitting access to restricted areas without the need for human interaction. Hand-held computers are also used to perform a variety of transactions in CIM and CISS environments. The Frito-Lay Corporation, for example, equips its salespeople (more than 10,000) with hand-held computers.[12] The salespeople can print invoices in their trucks and feed sales data to the company's mainframes to synthesize and pass on to other parts of the company.

Hand-held computers can download their information using public telephones in remote areas or by direct wire when convenient. The information is passed on to the CIM system or CISS, which in turn begins the production or distribution efforts necessary to deliver the required goods quickly and efficiently. Workers who have computers save time in their recording and paper-processing activities, which improves their productivity. Moreover, the direct input into the CIM system or CISS afforded by the remote usage computers also speeds the order processing lead time by reducing the time from when the order is taken to when it is delivered. This improves service quality to the customer and reduces the human resources needed to enter the orders.

Another set of remote usage computer systems are called **programmable controllers (PLCs)** and **cell controllers.**[13] PLCs are computer hardware and software systems that are used as communication and control links in a CIM system. They are automated controllers that operate in milliseconds, interfacing real-world operations on the plant floor. They allow workers or management an opportunity to program manufacturing functions on equipment or automated processes. PLCs are used to control the operations of individual equipment on the shop floor. When equipment is grouped into a production or work cell (Chapter 13), a cell controller is used to coordinate the PLC's activities. Cell controllers are usually responsible for coordinating multiple workcenters and their machines, or cellular unit operations that offer information- and communication-processing capability. To control groupings of cell controllers, minicomputers are usually used. An example of the integration of controllers necessary to complete a CIM enterprise is presented in Figure 15-3. PLCs and cell controllers are helpful in implementing CIM systems. PLCs enable CIM systems to have greater flexibility because workers can reprogram equipment to accommodate changes in production processing requirements. By using PLCs, plants are now able to computerize and integrate some of the more detailed work that could not be integrated or easily controlled by a central CIM system. Having the PLCs performing a localized controlling role that supports a larger CIM system, and yet having some autonomy over a limited area in a factory, has help give rise to the term *smart factory* when describing these almost fully automated operations.

ELECTRONIC SHOPPING AND SERVICE SYSTEMS Electronic shopping and service systems are part of the technology and software that permits customers to place orders for items or receive customer services from remote service facilities. These technologies

---

[12] J. Main, "Computers of the World, Unite!" *Fortune,* September 24, 1990, pp. 115–119.

[13] D. Johnson, "The Building Blocks of CIM," *Manufacturing Systems* (February 1988), 28–33.

FIGURE 15-3 INTEGRATION OF PLCs AND CELL CONTROLLERS IN CIM SYSTEMS

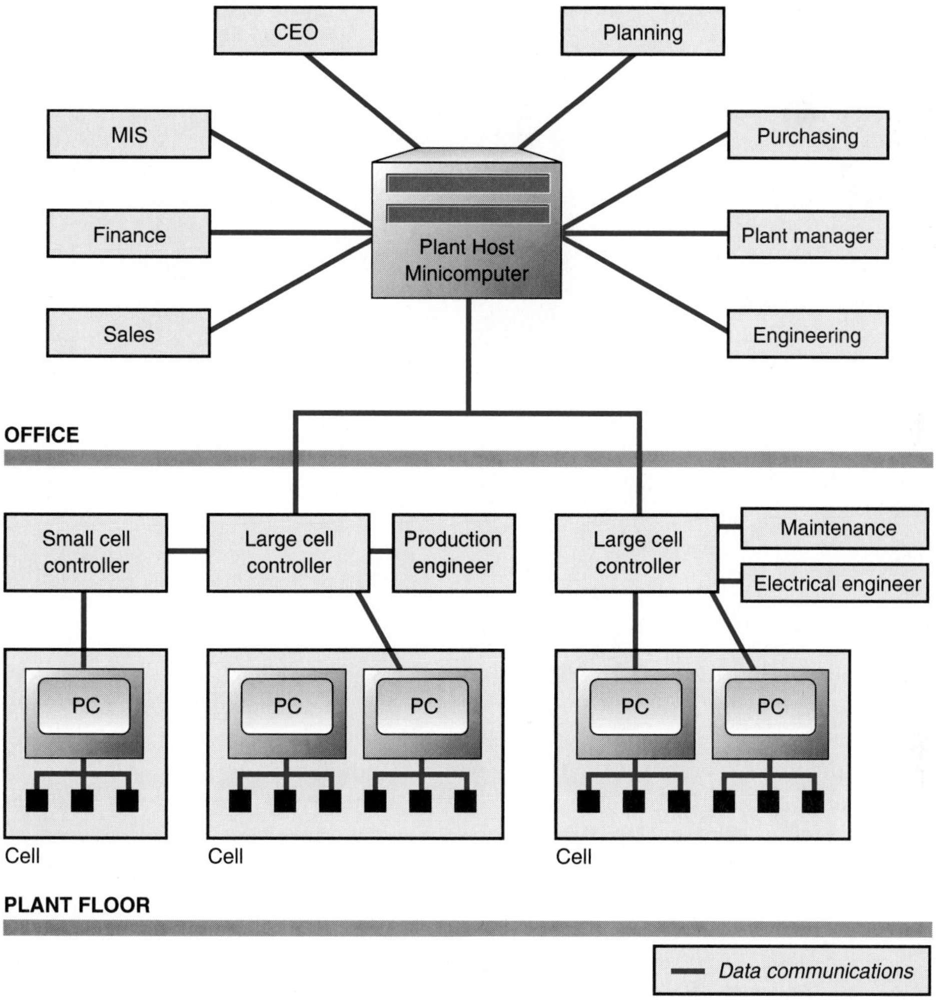

CEO
Planning
MIS
Purchasing
Finance
Plant Host Minicomputer
Plant manager
Sales
Engineering
OFFICE
Small cell controller
Large cell controller
Production engineer
Large cell controller
Maintenance
Electrical engineer
PC
PC
PC
PC
PC
Cell
Cell
Cell
PLANT FLOOR
— *Data communications*

Source: Reprinted with permission. From D. Johnson, "The Building Blocks of CIM," *Manufacturing Systems* (February 1988), 28–33.

include user-interface technology ranging from a telephone to place an order for a product seen on television to a **video kiosk** (an audiovisual display placed in a store that combines full-motion video with graphics, animation, text, and stereophonic sound to promote and sell products, and allow customers to place orders). Video kiosks usually come equipped with touch screens so customers can interact with the video monitor,

Q

QUESTION: How can PLCs or smart factories help an organization achieve its product quality goals?

ANSWER: In the 2.3 million square-foot Buick-Oldsmobile-Cadillac assembly plant in Wilmington, Delaware, PLCs help General Motors (GM) make quality automobiles.[14] Since the mid 1980s, PLCs have been used to integrate all aspects of manufacturing such that a vehicle can be assembled, painted, and tested without human beings ever touching or modifying what the customer ordered. To verify and document the quality of the vehicles that leave the plant, this GM plant uses a PLC called the assembly line diagnostic link (ALDL). It interfaces with other shop floor and plant systems during the manufacture of automobiles to ensure that quality standards are being met. The ALDL also tests the engine's electronic control module to verify its quality. This information is then shared with operators and managers for corrective action, if needed. Other PLCs in the plant perform quality control monitoring on robots, AGVs, and other automated systems to ensure that they perform in accordance with desired quality specifications. This on-line use of PLCs helps make quality information readily available and timely enough to prevent costly waste and generate a high-quality product. This plant is considered an example of how a smart factory can integrate and link almost every aspect of production activity.

S

permitting the system to close sales and accept payments.[15] Such devices can reduce retail sales staff and substantially reduce operating costs in retail operations. J. C. Penney Company has installed a video satellite network comprising twenty mainframe computers and 100,000 terminals to allow new merchandise to be displayed to buyers and store management.[16] This system not only supports the selling function but helps the company test market new styles and control buying and inventory. Because the system is integrated nationwide, it helps cut inventory costs through nationwide planning and prevents stock depletions during the heavy shopping seasons.

S

A number of other computer-based customer services are helping define new levels of customer service twenty-four hours a day. The Teachers Insurance and Annuity Association (TIAA) offers its investors an automated telephone service (ATS) to permit members to transfer their accumulated investment in retirement programs between different investment accounts.[17] By following a set of instructions over a push-button telephone, a member can shift accumulated retirement funds in any proportion between

---

[14] S. J. Hyduk, "Systems Integration Provides the Answer for Multiple System Operation," *APICS—The Performance Advantage,* 2, No. 11 (1992), 27–30.

[15] J. Kobielus, "Electronic Window Shopping," *Advance* (June 1988), 12.

[16] "Technological Advances," *Inside Lincoln Business,* Lincoln, Neb., 1991, p. 10.

[17] "The TIAA–CREF Automated Telephone Service-Information Brochure," Teachers Insurance and Annuity Association and College Retirement Equities Fund, 730 Third Avenue, New York, N.Y., 1990.

two different investment alternatives without the need for human intervention. Mobile telephone communication systems and their computer support systems are also helping link all members of an organization together at any time of day. One innovative mobile telephone service not only offers traditional telephone services but can be integrated with a company's computer systems to offer additional services including mobile message waiting and mobile information services (weather, financial news).[18]

INTEGRATED SOFTWARE SYSTEMS Large-scale CIM system and CISS software are constantly being developed. CIM-integrated software systems such as IBM's MAPICS II (introduced in Chapter 3), Arthur Andersen's MAC-PAC (introduced in Chapter 5), or the HP Manufacturing Management II (introduced in Chapter 7) are all markedly benefiting users. Some of their benefits include (1) reduced overall costs because of reduced waste; (2) more efficient use of personnel, equipment, and materials; (3) higher-quality products; (4) enhanced flexibility in production processing; and (5) greater responsiveness to the market because of an increased ability to alter product characteristics with ease. The Manufacturing Studies Board of National Research Council predicts that organizations implementing a CIM system should reduce engineering costs between 15 and 30 percent, reduce WIP by as much as 30 to 60 percent, improve the efficiency of equipment by 300 percent, and gain as much as 500 percent in engineering productivity and product quality.[19] The advances in integrated software systems are weaving the entire organization together into a single, fully integrated enterprise. As we can see in Figure 15-4, the progression toward a fully integrated CIM system requires a variety of supporting systems that become more and more dependent on integrated computer software.

One of the most important CIM system developments that is still underway is manufacturing automated protocols.[20] **Manufacturing automated protocols (MAPs)** are a set of software rules that allow computers on the shop floor to communicate with one another. They save the time that manually downloading instructions between computers that do not understand each other takes. Today's CIM systems usually use equipment that has been produced by different equipment manufacturers, all over the world, using different programming systems. MAPs provide the common language that will permit these computers to work together as needed.

CISSs are also using integrated software systems to help improve the efficiency with which service products are delivered as a means of improving product quality. The SBDS automobile analyzer system developed by Ford Motor Company for after-sale automotive repair service is an example of the type of CISS that is being developed for use in the 1990s. From 1986 to 1991, Ford spent more than $100 million to develop a computer system to be used by service repair personnel to diagnose car problems in Ford automobiles. Unlike other computer systems currently on the market, Ford's

---

[18] Ameritech *Annual Report,* 1990, 30 South Wacker Dr., Chicago, Ill.

[19] *Trends in Information Technology,* 3rd ed. (Geneva, Switzerland: Arthur Andersen Worldwide Organization, 1989), p. 70.

[20] L. M. Singer, "Closing the MAP Gap," *Manufacturing Systems* (September 1987), 42–45.

FIGURE 15-4 MANUFACTURING SYSTEM PROGRESSION TOWARD A FULLY INTEGRATED CIM

SUPPORTING SYSTEMS AND APPLICATIONS		BASIC DISCIPLINES AND CONCEPTS
CIM *Interfaces • Robotics/SMT*	**Level 6**	Integrated Manufacturing *Automated Assembly • Automated Test • Fast Response to Change • Design to Floor • Machine to Machine Input • Group Technology*
CAD/CAM/CAE *Computer-generated Routings • ECOs • BOMs • Drawings • Design Test*	**Level 5**	Flexible Manufacturing *Automated Drawings • NC Generation • Simulated Testing • Automated Routing • BOM Creation and Update • Expert Systems*
Semi-automated *Bar Code Interface • Machine Interface • Vendor Dispatch • AS/RS*	**Level 4**	Repetitive Manufacturing *Bar Coding • Single Level BOM • JIT • Alternative Cost Accounting Systems • Statistical Process Control • Floor Stocking • Participative Management • Decentralized MPS • Quality Based on Prevention • Pull System*
MRP II *CRP • Financial Interface • Simulation Software • Resource Requirements Planning • Management Report Software*	**Level 3**	High Volume Manufacturing *Capacity Requirements • Financial Planning and Simulation • What If Analysis • Modular BOM • Input/Output Control • Bottleneck Analysis • Ongoing Education • Manpower Planning • On-line Onput*
MRP I *Inventory Control • MPS • Work Order Release • Routings Update • BOM Update • MRP • Cost Roll-up • Cost Tracking • Purchase Order System • Operations Reporting*	**Level 2**	Medium Volume Manufacturing *Secured Stockroom • Bills of Material • Realistic Master Schedule • Lot Size Policies • Leadtime Definitions • Routings • Change Control • Record Accuracy • Basic Education • Priority Control • Production Costing • Procurement Policies • Measurements • Push System*
Manual Systems *Order Release • Drawings • Production Plan • Part Numbers • Order Taking • Invoicing • Mission Statement*	**Foundation**	Low Volume Manufacturing *Clip Boards • Order Launching • Expediting • Hot Stickers • Production Plan • Management • People • EOQ • Material Transfers • Shortage Sheets*

Source: Reprinted with permission. From D. W. Rasmus, "Orchestrating Change—Progressing Toward CIM," *Manufacturing Systems,* 5, No. 4 (1987), 30–32.

QUESTION: What is an example of how the growth or extension of a CIM system in an organization actually helped improve its operations? Can this give an organization a competitive advantage in the global marketplace of the 1990s?

ANSWER: General Electric's (GE) Power Generation Division, based in Schenectady, New York, teamed up its version of an IBM MAPICS system with an electronic data interchange (EDI) system (discussed in Chapter 8) to extend its CIM system into purchasing and customer service.[21] By putting these two computer-based systems together, GE brought its sprawling organization into a common network stretching from the shop floor up to the offices of its suppliers and customers. In doing so, GE found that a lot of the time-consuming and laborious procurement processes could be handled much more efficiently throughout the entire organization. The EDI system could quickly send a wide range of purchase orders, invoices, and other documents back and forth electronically to suppliers and customers, saving time and waste. The impact of the resulting changes in order transactions were shared with actual production through the integrated CIM system. According to GE, the integration of the two systems resulted in its purchasing departments being able to handle 40 percent more work without increasing staff, the elimination of fifteen temporary clerical positions and the reassignment of twelve buyers (which saved $500,000 per year), and a reduction in ordering errors (and their waste). The combination of CIM and EDI gave GE a competitive advantage that was ideal for the international market it faced in the early 1990s. By integrating the EDI system into its CIM, GE was distinct from its competitors (at the time) in allowing any customer with a personal computer to place an order from anywhere in the world. Two of GE's biggest customers were from Asia, and GE management felt that its CIM/EDI sophistication allowed it to compete successfully in the Japanese market.

system makes three times the diagnostic checks on car systems to find defects. Moreover, the system is designed to permit the temporary integration of a hand-held computer that is used on an ongoing basis to help find problems that occur infrequently during use by owners (the type of problem that service personnel never seem to be able to find when the car is in the garage for service). When the infrequent problem occurs while the owner is using the car, the owner simply presses a button on the hand-held computer to record the current status of the car's computer that is monitoring the car's systems. The hand-held computer records the status of the irregular behavior in the car's computer system. These records can be used by service personnel to recognize the problem when the hand-held computer information is downloaded into the service center's mainframe computer for a complete diagnostic analysis. It is interesting to note

[21] D. L. Echols, "Extending the Enterprise Electronically," *APICS—The Performance Advantage,* 2, No. 7 (1992), 27–31.

that as of late 1991, no car out of the thousands equipped with the SBDS has ever required a second trip to the service center for poorly implemented repairs.[22]

The advances in communications, decision making, and integrated system technologies described in this section are collectively providing the means by which organizations can reach out to markets and reach into their production processes to better match the external needs of the markets to the internal capacity capabilities of the organization. In the process of reaching out, organizations are finding themselves in international markets. The technology of the 1990s is making it easy to extend domestic operations into international operations. This extension is causing organizations to internationally integrate their operations management systems.

INTERNATIONAL INTEGRATION OF OPERATIONS MANAGEMENT SYSTEMS

The developments in telecommunication systems are helping bring about the globalization of all marketplaces. The developments in decision making technology are helping managers more quickly seize opportunities in global markets. The developments in computer-integrated software systems are helping the operations management function implement decisions and adapt quickly to meet global market product demand requirements. The globalization of markets is changing OM. The changes in OM are internationalizing OM systems, standards, and production processing.

Enhanced Computer-integrated Manufacturing Systems

The IBM MAPICS/DB computer-integrated manufacturing system has an international enhancement module used to support international transactions.[23] The purpose of the software module is to support CIM operations that do business between the United States, Europe, Japan, and Canada. The module, called MAPICS/DB International Support Enhancements, performs multiple currency support functions that automatically convert price quotations, issue purchase orders, process invoices, convert accounts payable/accounts receivable transactions, convert general ledger transactions, perform and convert financial analysis, and convert order entry transactions into the appropriate foreign currency to efficiently support user decision making regardless of the decision maker's nationality. The module also has multiple language support features that convert item descriptions, invoices, credit memos, and accounting statements into the appropriate foreign language to efficiently support communication in international operations. The module also helps organizations meet legal requirements by providing continuously

---

[22] "Ford's New Service System," Future Watch, Cable News Network Television, October 21, 1991.

[23] "MAPICS/DB Information Brochure" (White Plains, N.Y.: IBM Corporation, 1989).

upgraded value added tax calculations on invoices for the purpose of business or government records.

QUESTION: What is an example of how a CIM system has helped an operation conduct its international business transactions?

ANSWER: Sengewald, a company within the Dutch conglomerate Buhrmann-Tetterode, operates a plastic bag manufacturing plant in Marengo, Illinois.[24] This European-owned operation uses the MAC-PAC Arthur Andersen CIM system (discussed in Chapter 5). Sengewald used German and other European suppliers as a source of materials and supplies. The MAC-PAC system provided multicurrency capabilities to accurately translate and revalue supply ordering transactions made in U.S. dollars to German Deutsche marks. This made doing business with German and European suppliers easier for Sengewald management. The non-German European suppliers found it more convenient to have orders converted into Deutsche marks as they were readily used throughout Europe and their current value was easily understood.

International Quality Standards

The International Organization for Standardization (ISO) is a worldwide agency, representing ninety-one countries through each country's national standards body. The U.S. national standards body is the American National Standards Institute (ANSI). These professional organizations are trying to bring a systematic approach to quality management and assurance. They are currently establishing the ISO-9000 system (discussed in Chapter 12).[25] The ISO-9000 is an international quality assurance program that seeks a common internationally acceptable quality standard. The ISO-9000 is a series of procedures that define what is required to fulfill contractual agreements between buyers and sellers for participants in the ISO-9000 quality assurance program. The program requires that an organization's quality assurance program be certified before the organization can be registered as meeting the international standards of quality. Because European Community countries are active participants in the ISO, U.S. and Japanese organizations are highly motivated to seek ISO-9000 certification to gain access to European markets. Substantial change to tighten quality control measures in process, product, and human resources is a part of adopting this quality assurance program.

Q

---

[24] D. Iverson et al., "Software Helps Sengewald Successfully Manage Business Expansion," *APICS—The Performance Advantage,* 2, No. 2 (1992), 26–28

[25] A. H. Greene, "ISO 9000: Globalizing Quality Standards," *Production and Inventory Management,* 11, No. 9 (1991), 12–15.

Transnational Production Processing

The Europe of the 1990s brings with it an interesting look into the future of production processing in what is called a *borderless factory* of the future.[26] As country demarcations and borders are reduced in the Europe of the 1990s, international production processing in multiple countries is becoming an important strategic planning operations management issue.[27] European manufacturing organizations are establishing strategic plans and investing heavily in CIM and other automated systems to achieve maximum production flexibility objectives. The goal of the strategy is to permit manufacturing planners the production processing flexibility to shift the routing and scheduling of products to plants in any location of the Pan-European market where profit can be maximized and value added to the product. Because different countries in the Pan-European market still offer unique cost advantages to manufacturers, being able to shift the processing of products through plants in different countries will afford planners opportunities to reduce overall production costs (assuming that transportation costs do not offset the production savings). This experience of the European market may foretell the future of operations management. As more companies become multinational and locate their operations in various countries, the need for a clear OM strategy to guide the operation decisions on production processing in the international environment becomes more critical.

Large multinational firms, such as the world-class BASF Corporation, which operates chemical facilities in more than 160 countries, have the economic power and resources to achieve international production processing objectives. Yet smaller, less powerful organizations are also able to achieve international production objectives. One of the more interesting developments in production processing has come about through international joint ventures. For smaller firms to sometimes produce products necessary to enter international markets, they are forced to pool production processing resources to meet the challenge of larger competitors already entrenched in the market. For example, AT&T undertook a joint venture with Italy's Olivetti Corporation and the Netherlands' N.V. Philips Organization to manufacture and sell computer systems in Europe.[28] The joint venture brought AT&T's communications technology, Olivetti's office equipment marketing abilities, and Philips's technical superiority in semiconductor electronics together for a successful entry against other multinationals including IBM and Japan's NEC. Such joint ventures help move partners to standardize production systems, quality standards, and procedures in an effort to improve efficiency between partners to achieve their joint venture product objectives.

Whereas many technological changes have moved firms into international markets, it takes more than technology to be successful in those new markets. The internationalization of operations management systems is only one part of what is necessary to be

---

[26] J. G. Miller et al., "Factories of the Future" (Boston: Boston University, 1991).

[27] G. C. J. M. Vos, "A Production-Allocation Approach for International Manufacturing Strategy," *International Journal of Operations and Production Management,* 11, No. 3 (1991), 125–134.

[28] B. Casseres, "Joint Ventures in the Face of Global Competition," *Sloan Management Review,* 30, No. 2 (1989), 17–26.

successful in the global market of today and the future. Not every firm will go international, but all firms will be affected by those that do. To a large degree, the actions of the internationally oriented organization are defining for all types and sizes of operations what it will take to have a successful future.

THE FACTORY WITH A FUTURE

The factory of the future is the one that will have a future. Competition (both international and domestic) is a driving force to use tactics (such as improved technology) to improve product quality and service.[29] Yet many now see that automation is only one factor that will lead to a "factory with a future."[30] The factory with a future must

1. *Establish quality as a strategic goal.* Rather than just operationalizing total quality control (TQC) on the shop floor, factories (and their organizations) must set corporationwide quality goals. Quality should be defined as conformance to customer requirements rather than just conformance to product specifications. Quality should be viewed as a long-term continuous state of improvement the goal of which is perfection, as shown by total quality management (TQM) and zero-defects management (ZDM). Quality is an important part of the productivity cycle (see Figure 15-2) and a means to a competitive advantage.
2. *Improve technology and systems as a tactical means of "jump-starting" the productivity cycle.* The tactical integration of improved technology and systems can help start the productivity cycle moving to help organizations achieve their strategic profit or growth goals. Improving technology should also be used as a tactic of integration for human resource management as well.
3. *Establish a strategy that recognizes the critical role of human resources in the future.* The factory is a physical object and cannot function without people. Organizations should establish a human resource strategy that will maximize what workers do best. What workers do best is think and provide innovation and problem-solving capabilities. They also provide flexibility in operations by adjusting to change more readily than machines when market demand requires such change. Problem solving, innovation in production processing, and flexibility are all necessary requirements for achieving benefits from the productivity cycle. The human resources strategy should help workers do what they do best by including a long-term commitment to worker education and cross-training.

---

[29] G. Schwind, "Where the Automated Factory is Headed," *Material Handling Engineering* (May 1987), 52–56; and R. F. Huber, "CIM: Inevitable, but Not Easy," *Production* (April 1986), 52–57.

[30] W. Wassweiler, "The Factory with a Future," *APICS—The Performance Advantage,* 1, No. 3 (1991), 26–28; and S. L. Wallach, "Care and Feeding of the CIM System," *Managing Automation* (January 1990), 50–51.

In summary, the factory (or service organization) with a future will establish strategies and tactics to achieve customer market requirements. It will use human, technology, and system resources as a means to accomplish operations management needs for improved productivity, flexibility, and eventually a competitive advantage. This approach to OM has been the premise of this book and is the key to the success of factories that will survive into the future.

SUMMARY

In this chapter, we have examined how improvements in technology are changing operations management. A number of the more important technological advances in telecommunications, decision-making technology, and computer-integrated systems were described. The impact of technology and the globalization of OM were described as furthering the process of change that OM is currently undergoing. As an extension of the present, the characteristics of the factory with a future were also discussed. (Students are encouraged to read the article at the end of this chapter to understand how the subjects of technology and change fit together for companies seeking to achieve a world-class operation.)

It is interesting to note that in introducing the field of operations management in Chapter 1, we described OM's pre-history period as being marked by cottage operations (such as a blacksmith). In other words, OM activities were not being performed in factories, but in individuals' own homes. From our discussion in this chapter, it appears that technology is returning workers to their homes. Improved technology and technology-based systems (facsimile machines, hand-held computers, lap-top computers, microcomputers) are permitting clerical help to perform typing and filing functions from their home, stockbrokers to handle customer transactions from remote field service territories, and managers to supervise production facilities without ever needing to visit a plant, factory, or office. Operations managers will be using LANs and satellite systems to monitor worker or robot system performance from their homes. Even customers may not need to go to a service facility anymore. They can use electronic and service systems to shop at home. It appears that regardless of what area or what country workers, managers, or customers live in, they will be able to perform much of their work tasks from or near their homes using advanced communication and CIM or CISS facilities. It appears as though the field of OM is coming full circle by returning the workers to their homes to perform their work assignments. In doing so, OM is helping enhance the quality of their lives, their customers' lives, and their country's future.[31]

DISCUSSION AND REVIEW QUESTIONS

1. What characteristics do world-class manufacturers share?
2. How does technology affect the productivity cycle?
3. What are fiber optics? How are they changing operations management?
4. What is satellite transmission? How is it affecting OM?
5. What are local area networks (LANs)? What roles are they playing in OM?

---

[31] E. Faltermayer, "U.S. Companies Come Back Home," *Fortune,* December 30, 1991, pp. 106–112.

6. How will the change from analog to digital transmission communications help change OM?
7. What is an information services digital network (ISDN)? How will it affect OM?
8. How are artificial intelligence and expert systems (AI/ESs) changing OM?
9. What is computer-integrated software engineering (CISE)? How is it changing OM? What are its benefits?
10. What are remote usage computers? How are they affecting OM?
11. What are programmable controllers (PLCs)? How are they helping implement computer-integrated manufacturing (CIM)?
12. What is a video kiosk? How is it helping change OM?
13. What is a manufacturing automated protocol (MAP)? How is it used in CIM or computer-integrated service system (CISS) environments?
14. How are CIMs used to support international transactions?
15. How are quality standards becoming internationalized?
16. What is a borderless factory? How is a borderless factory related to internationalizing production processing?
17. What strategies should a factory (or a service organization) establish to ensure its future?
18. What role does automation play in organizations striving to become world-class?

ARTICLE 15-1

CIM AND WORLD CLASS PERFORMANCE—ARE THEY REALLY COMPATIBLE?

by Ray Reed

From the title of this article, one could conclude that the author has some doubt about the relationship between Computer-Integrated Manufacturing (CIM) and World Class Performance. The basis for this feeling is that I sense a popular perception that CIM means computer and automation, and that this combination is the critical path to achieving a competitive edge. This could lead to the panacea mentality which the majority of the time will lead to less than anticipated results and much frustration.

On the other hand, CIM can be a major contributing factor to World Class Performance. To better understand the potential positive relationship between these two, it is important first to understand the objectives of each.

World Class Performance in a manufacturing company means winning the competitive race. It means running faster and smarter than the competition than ever before and never letting up. The marketplace selects the winners by judging performance in categories such as flexibility, response time, total quality and value received. The road to World Class starts with a thorough understanding of your current internal environment as well as your strengths and weaknesses in the marketplace. Most often an assessment of current internal operating practices will reveal poor interdepartmental communications, a lack of integrated planning, unclear priorities in the manufacturing departments, overloaded schedules, unbalanced loads between work centers, unbalanced inventories, etc. These and other operating inefficiencies are definite constraints

---

Source: Reprinted with permission from *P&IM Review with APICS News*, April 1991 issue. Copyright 1991 TDA Publications Inc.

to World Class Performance. They are also symptoms of a lack of control over our own environment! It is unlikely that computerization alone in this environment will be able to yield any significant improvements since the root causes lie in the basic operating principles and practices. More specifically, if the annual business plan is not tied directly to sales and operation plans, with demands balanced with resources, the result will be a lack of integration between planning and execution at all levels. If management does not place a high priority on data quality (inventory records, bills of material, etc.), there will be constant mistrust of basic operating data which results in all sorts of inefficiencies. (Dual records, double-checking, second guessing, etc.) If total quality is not enthusiastically promoted and supported by management, we will continue to operate in the mode of "inspecting" quality in as opposed to quality at the source.

What all of the above is directed at is to highlight the need for a "Strategy for on the Road to Excellence," the development of which is the first step on the road to World Class Performance. A manufacturing strategy starts with an assessment of where we are now and a vision of where we want to be in 3–5 years in such key indicators as on-time delivery to customer requirements, manufacturing lead time, inventory turns, quality, new product introduction time, supplier relations, employee involvement, flexibility, et al. Figure 1 illustrates the progressive steps from assessment to World Class.

FIGURE 1

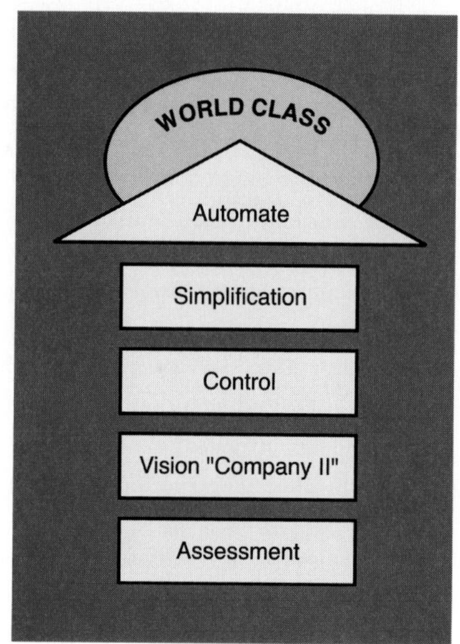

The vision step is a different kind of assessment. Here we look forward 3–5 years and say "What if?" What if our manufacturing cycle time, including procurement, was reduced by 70 percent, or more! What if our cost of quality was reduced from 20–25 percent of total sales to 2–2.5 percent of sales! What if new product introduction time was reduced from years to months, leaving the competition way behind! What if the cost of purchasing was reduced by 50 percent or more! We call the results of this vision "Company II," our new fine-tuned, highly motivated, World Class Performing Company.

The next step on the chart is control. Having assessed our strengths and weaknesses and defined our vision, we must gain control over the current environment. This step is directed at getting the basics under control, to do the routine things well, the things we always should have done. This will involve developing a process to ensure integrated planning from top to bottom, everyone "singing from the same hymn book." It involves ensuring high levels of data quality, averaging close to 100 percent consistency. It involves balancing demands and resources, ensuring valid plans and schedules. It involves systems, policies and procedures designed to support the users and the process. It involves education and training of all employees in varying degrees. It is at this stage that the Road to World Class Performance begins to yield positive results by truly building teamwork at every level of the company.

Once control has been achieved, employees at all levels in the organization can now direct their attention towards seeking a better way to perform their particular duties. This is where the simplification step begins. Now that "firefighting" has been minimized, if not eliminated, efforts can be directed at "there must be a better way." It is here that the "status quo" gets challenged. Set-up or changeover times, factory layout, restrictive job classifications, supplier relations, traditional performance measurements and cost accounting, transaction reporting, traditional rules of design engineering vs. manufacturing engineering, traditional rule of shop supervision, forecasting vs. customer partnerships, and on and on. It's called *continuous* improvement. It's called knocking down the "Berlin Walls" between departments. It's called teamwork from top to bottom! It's called, "there is no stopping us now!"

The next step on the Road to World Class is automation. In reality, automation is simplification—Phase II. In the previous phases, the "cream" has been skimmed off, yielding delicious results. Set-up/changeover times have been reduced by 50+ percent with minimal capital investment ($1,000 or less for each improvement). The cost of purchasing has been reduced by 50 percent or more by streamlining communications, paperwork, inspection, etc. In this phase, we are looking for additional significant improvements which may require capital expenditures. A key requirement for jusification now becomes, "can we afford *not* to make this investment?"

Based upon my experience, when a company reaches the automation phase, they are very close to, if not already, achieving their vision. They have achieved and are sustaining a competitive edge. The rest is called continuous improvement.

The title of this article asked the question, "Are CIM and World Class Performance really compatible?" In the author's opinion, when implemented as suggested herein, they are inseparable. It is not an "either/or" question. Nor is it a question of whether the principles and concepts of MRP II, Just-In-Time, Total Quality Control, focused factories, etc. are in conflict with one another or are collectively and individually supportive of World Class Performance. Figure 2 shows the interrelationship of these "tools" and the tremendous integrating, unifying potential.

The lines indicating MRP II, JIT, and CIM are not intended to illustrate start/stop for each. There is significant overlap and continual ongoing contribution. There is, however, a period of initial significant thrust for each as indicated on the graph. Additionally, as can be seen on the graph, total quality is the "umbrella" under which all of the principles and concepts exist.

There are marvelous tools available today to assist us on the Road to World Class. Hardware and software capabilities are incredible and getting better day-to-day. Too many companies purchase these tools looking for a panacea. The result is often less than satisfactory and of course the hardware/software supplier is blamed. The critical first step to avoid these problems is to ensure there is a well defined, and understood, strategy for excellence. Once this has been achieved, the compatibility of CIM, MRP II, JIT, TQC, etc. is unquestionable.

FIGURE 2

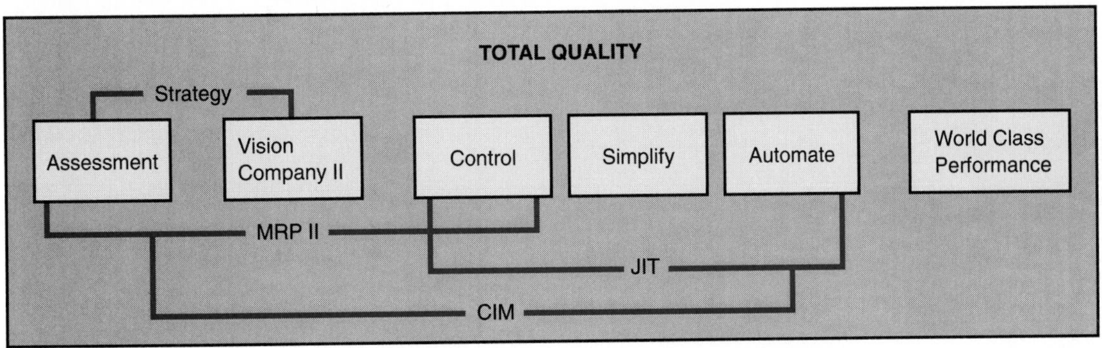

APPENDIXES

The Normal Probability Distribution

The purpose of this appendix is to provide a brief introduction to basic statistics, concentrating on the use of the normal probability distribution. This introduction is meant as a brief survey, and students are encouraged to consult additional material on the subject in basic business statistics books.[1] This appendix also contains tabled z values for areas under the normal curve. Table A should be used in determining order points (OP) and PERT probabilities. Table B should be used in sample size determination.

THE MEAN, STANDARD DEVIATION, AND AREAS UNDER THE NORMAL CURVE

The **arithmetic mean** is the sum of all of the observations in a collection of data divided by the number of observations that make up the data set. The formula used to compute the arithmetic mean is usually represented by $\overline{X}$ (pronounced *X*-bar). The value of $\overline{X}$ is found by

$$\overline{X} = \frac{\text{Sum of all values in the sample}}{\text{Number of values in the sample}} \text{ or } \frac{\Sigma X}{n}$$

where

$\overline{X}$ = the sample arithmetic mean

X = a single value in the sample

Σ = the Greek capital sigma representing the summation of the individual X values that make up the sample

n = the number of values that make up the sample (that is, the sample size)

The **standard deviation** is a measure of variation. The standard deviation is expressed in the same measure of units that is used in its construction. In other words, if we are using hourly wages in dollars to compute a standard deviation, the resulting standard deviation value is in dollars.

The formula for the standard deviation is generally represented by the small Greek sigma (σ). Although the formula for the standard deviation varies depending on the type of data, for sample data the formula for the standard deviation is

$$\text{Standard deviation} = \sigma = \sqrt{\frac{\Sigma(X - \overline{X})^2}{n}}$$

[1] See A. Webster, *Applied Statistics for Business and Economics* (Homewood, Ill.: Irwin, 1992); D. O. Oltman and J. R. Lackritz, *Statistics for Business and Economics* (Pacific Grove, Calif.: Brooks/Cole, 1991); R. D. Mason and D. A. Lind, *Statistical Techniques in Business and Economics,* 8th ed. (Homewood, Ill.: Irwin, 1993).

where

X = a value in a data collection
$\overline{X}$ = the arithmetic mean of the data collection
n = the total number of values in the sample data collection

The standard deviation has become a "standard" of statistical dispersion because of its use with the normal distribution. The normal distribution is one of the most ideal distributions to model operations management behavior. For a normal distribution of a population, the standard deviation becomes a standard unit of measure that can divide the distribution into known percentages. In Exhibit A-1 the total area under the curve can be considered 100 percent of the area. In a normal distribution it is known that the area under ± 1 standard deviaition about the mean is equal to 68.27 percent of the total area under the curve of the distribution. The area under ± 2 standard deviations is known to be 96.45 percent of the area under the curve, and ± 3 standard deviations is known to be equal to 99.73 percent of the area under the curve. We can see in Exhibit A-1 that 34.13 percent of the frequencies in the normal distribution will fall between the mean and $+1$ standard deviation.

What has made the standard deviation a very common measure of dispersion is again related to its use as a standard unit of measure for the normal curve and its

EXHIBIT A-1 AREA UNDER THE STANDARD NORMAL CURVE BY STANDARD DEVIATION

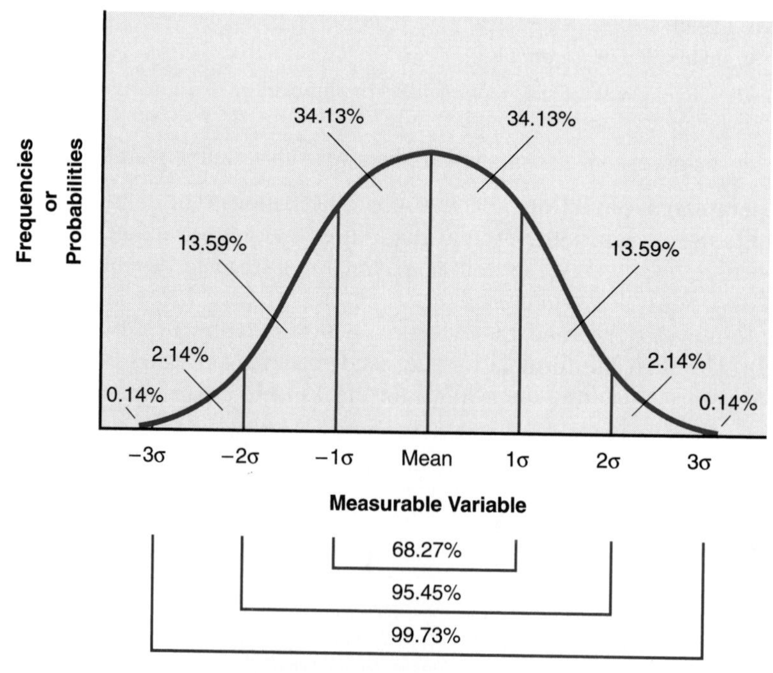

probabilistic interpretation. In Exhibit A-1 the percentages can also be viewed as probabilities. We can, for example, say that 68.27 of the time the values in a normal distribution will fall between ± 1 standard deviation. We can also say that the probability that a value in a population will fall between ± 1 standard deviation is 0.6827 or 68.27 percent. The conversion of the area under the curve to probabilities allows for an infinite number of applications in operations management situations in which the behavior of the measurable variable follows a normal distribution.

THE USE OF NORMAL PROBABILITY TABLES

In Table A, the percent areas under the standard normal curve for values to some positive z value are presented. These values are used in "one-tail" probability estimations because they represent the probabilities or area under the curve for positive values of z (that is, where the mean is zero) located in the left tail of the normal curve. Note the example in Exhibit A-2(a). The shaded region in Exhibit A-2(a) to the left of $z = +1.3$ is 0.90320 or 90.32 percent of the area under the standard normal curve. This table can be used to help estimate order point (OP) values for given levels of service and estimate the probability that a project will be completed in some desired period of time in PERT analysis.

In Table B, the percent areas under the standard normal curve are presented for values between some plus or minus z values. These values are used in "two-tail" probability estimations because they represent the probabilities or area under the curve between some $\pm z$ values. Note the example in Exhibit A-2(b). The shaded region in

EXHIBIT A-2 EXAMPLES OF AREAS UNDER THE STANDARD NORMAL CURVE

(A) TABLE "A" AREAS FOR ONE-TAIL PROBABILITY ESTIMATION FOR SOME POSITIVE NUMBER OF STANDARD DEVIATIONS Z VALUES FROM THE MEAN

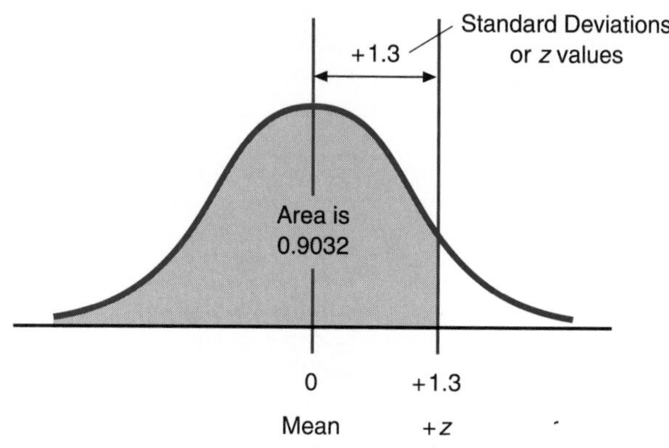

EXHIBIT A-2 (CONTINUED)

(B) TABLE "B" AREAS FOR TWO-TAIL PROBABILITY ESTIMATION FOR SOME PLUS OR MINUS NUMBER OF STANDARD DEVIATIONS OR z VALUES FROM THE MEAN

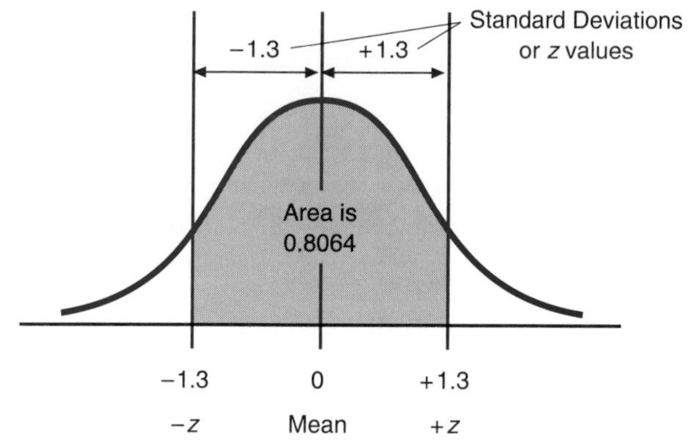

TABLE A AREAS UNDER THE STANDARD NORMAL CURVE FOR ONE-TAIL PROBABILITY ESTIMATION OR POSITIVE Z VALUES TO THE RIGHT OF THE MEAN

z	.00	.01	.02	.03	.04	.05	.06	.07	.08	.09
0.0	.50000	.50399	.50798	.51197	.51595	.51994	.52392	.52790	.53188	.53586
0.1	.53983	.54380	.54776	.55172	.55567	.55962	.56356	.56749	.57142	.57535
0.2	.57926	.58317	.58706	.59095	.59483	,59871	.60257	.60642	.61026	.61409
0.3	.61791	.62172	.62552	.62930	.63307	.63683	.64058	.64431	.64803	.65173
0.4	.65542	.65910	.66276	.66640	.67003	.67364	.67724	.68082	.68439	.68793
0.5	.69146	.69497	.69847	.70194	.70540	.70884	.71226	.71566	.71904	.72240
0.6	.72575	.72907	.73237	.73536	.73891	.74215	74537	.74857	.75175	.75490
0.7	.75804	.76115	.76424	.76730	.77035	.77337	.77637	.77935	.78230	.78524
0.8	.78814	.79103	.79389	.79673	.79955	.80234	.80511	.80785	.81057	.81327
0.9	.81594	.81859	.82121	.82381	.82639	.82894	.83147	.83398	.83646	.83891
1.0	.84134	.84375	.84614	.84849	.85083	.85314	.85543	.85769	.85993	.86214
1.1	.86433	.86650	.86864	.87076	.87286	.87493	.87698	.87900	.88100	.88298
1.2	.88493	.88686	.88877	.89065	.89251	.89435	.89617	89796	.89973	.90147
1.3	.90320	.90490	.90658	.90824	.90988	.91149	.91309	.91466	.91621	.91774
1.4	.91924	.92073	.92220	.92364	.92507	.92647	.92785	.92922	.93056	.93189
1.5	.93319	.93448	.93574	.93699	.93822	.93943	.94062	.94179	.94295	.94408
1.6	.94520	.94630	.94738	.94845	.94950	.95053	.95154	.95254	.95352	.95449
1.7	.95543	.95637	.95728	.95818	.95907	.95994	.96080	.96164	.96246	.96327
1.8	.96407	.96485	.96562	.96638	.96712	.96784	.96856	.96926	.96995	.97062
1.9	.97128	.97193	.97257	.97320	.97381	.97441	.97500	.97558	.97615	.97670

TABLE A (CONTINUED)

z	.00	.01	.02	.03	.04	.05	.06	.07	.08	.09
2.0	.97725	.97784	.97831	.97882	.97932	.97982	.98030	.98077	.98124	.98169
2.1	.98214	.98257	.98300	.98341	.98382	.98422	.98461	.98500	.98537	.98574
2.2	.98610	.98645	.98679	.98713	.98745	.98778	.98809	.98840	.98870	.98899
2.3	.98928	.98956	.98983	.99010	.99036	.99061	.99086	.99111	.99134	.99158
2.4	.99180	.99202	.99224	.99245	.99266	.99286	.99305	.99324	.99343	.99361
2.5	.99379	.99396	.99413	.99430	.99446	.99461	.99477	.99492	.99506	.99520
2.6	.99534	.99547	.99560	.99573	.99585	.99598	.99609	.99621	.99632	.99643
2.7	.99653	.99664	.99674	.99683	.99693	.99702	.99711	.99720	.99728	.99736
2.8	.99744	.99752	.99760	.99767	.99774	.99781	.99788	.99795	.99801	.99807
2.9	.99813	.99819	.99825	.99831	.99836	.99841	.99846	.99851	.99856	.99861
3.0	.99865	.99869	.99874	.99878	.99882	.99886	.99899	.99893	.99896	.99900
3.1	.99903	.99906	.99910	.99913	.99916	.99918	.99921	.99924	.99926	.99929
3.2	.99931	.99934	.99936	.99938	.99940	.99942	.99944	.99946	.99948	.99950
3.3	.99952	.99953	.99955	.99957	.99958	.99960	.99961	.99962	.99964	.99965
3.4	.99966	.99968	.99969	.99970	.99971	.99972	.99973	.99974	.99975	.99976
3.5	.99977	.99978	.99978	.99979	.99980	.99981	.99981	.99982	.99983	.99983
3.6	.99984	.99985	.99985	.99986	.99986	.99987	.99987	.99988	.99988	.99989
3.7	.99989	.99990	.99990	.99990	.99991	.99991	.99992	.99992	.99992	.99992
3.8	.99993	.99993	.99993	.99994	.99994	.99994	.99994	.99995	.99995	.99995
3.9	.99995	.99995	.99996	.99996	.99996	.99996	.99996	.99996	.99997	.99997

Exhibit A-2(b) between $z = \pm 1.3$ is 0.80640 or 80.64 percent of the area under the standard normal curve. This table can be used to help estimate sample sizes, given a desired degree of certainty in sampling accuracy.

TABLE B AREAS UNDER THE STANDARD NORMAL CURVE FOR TWO-TAIL PROBABILITY ESTIMATION OR ± z VALUES FROM THE MEAN

±z	*Area*	±z	*Area*	±z	*Area*
0.0	0.00000	1.0	0.68268	2.0	0.95450
0.1	0.07966	1.1	0.72866	2.1	0.96428
0.2	0.15852	1.28	0.79946	2.2	0.97220
0.3	0.23582	1.3	0.80640	2.3	0.97856
0.4	0.31084	1.4	0.83848	2.4	0.98360
0.5	0.38292	1.5	0.86638	2.58	0.99012
0.6	0.45150	1.645	0.90000	2.6	0.99068
0.7	0.51608	1.7	0.91086	2.7	0.99306
0.8	0.57628	1.8	0.92814	2.8	0.99488
0.9	0.63188	1.96	0.95000	2.9	0.99626
				3.0	0.99730

APPENDIX B

Instructions for In-Class Forecasting Simulation Game

The purpose of this game is to provide students with a role-playing opportunity to experience some of the problems and frustrations in forecasting, scheduling production, and inventory management.

BACKGROUND

Students will be divided into groups called "companies." Each company must have (1) a *president*, whose responsibilities will be to lead the company's decision-making efforts and provide the game proctor (usually the instructor) in a timely fashion with the company's production decision information; (2) an *accountant*, whose responsibility it will be to record the company's decisions and help calculate the costs of production and inventory; and (3) several *company officers* to help plan production decision making and inventory.

There will be several companies competing in the industry that the game is modeling. Fortunately, the companies in the industry do not compete for sales with one another. Their single product unit demand will range from 50,000 to 250,000 units weekly. Additional information on predictive variables may be provided by the game proctor to help permit forecasting of demand behavior.

Each company will make a weekly production scheduling decision and then see how well it did when the demand for that week is given. Having too much or too little inventory will result in the company's incurring costs. The goal of each company will be to minimize these costs. The companies will be evaluated on the basis of total minimized costs of operation.

INSTRUCTIONS

Each company must keep track of its decisions and costs on the Decision Sheets in Exhibit B-1. The game proctor may require a second Decision Sheet for company monitoring purposes. The decision sheet is divided into two parts: the top part lists product units and the bottom part lists costs. Each line has a purpose.

1. *Beginning inventory* We begin the game in week 1 with a beginning inventory of 120,000 units. All subsequent beginning inventories are obtained from the ending inventory (line 5) from a prior week. So if we have an ending inventory in week 1 of 130,000 units, we will have a beginning inventory in week 2 of 130,000 units.

EXHIBIT B-1 FORECASTING SIMULATION DECISION SHEETS

	WEEKS			
	1	2	3	4
1. Beginning inventory				
2. Unit production decision				
3. Available inventory				
4. Unit demand				
5. Ending inventory				
6. Inventory holding costs				
7. Excess inventory holding costs				
8. Stockout costs				
9. Production level change costs				
10. Total costs for the week				
11. Total costs for the game				

	WEEKS					
	5	6	7	8	9	10
1.						
2.						
3.						
4.						
5.						
6.						
7.						
8.						
9.						
10.						
11.						

EXHIBIT B-1 (CONTINUED)

	WEEKS				
	11	12	13	14	15
1.					
2.					
3.					
4.					
5.					
6.					
7.					
8.					
9.					
10.					
11.					

	WEEKS				
	16	17	18	19	20
1.					
2.					
3.					
4.					
5.					
6.					
7.					
8.					
9.					
10.					
11.					

2. *Unit production decision* This is the amount of unit production that your company is planning to produce during that week. Any level of unit production in 1,000-unit intervals (production runs are in 1,000-unit lots) can be established in week 1. So unit production should be in 1,000s like 50,000 or 81,000—not 50,400 or 80,600. Once established, companies can change their production levels in lots of only 1,000 units; they can change no more than 10,000 units in a single week. So if we establish a 40,000-unit production level in week 4, we can at most increase it to 50,000 in the fifth week. Also, there is a delay in the implementation of changes in unit production decisions by two full weeks. This delay is caused by the changes in labor resources (hiring or laying off personnel) necessary to implement the change in unit production. The delay works as follows: You will be planning unit production in week 4 after you receive the demand for week 1; you will be planning unit production in week 5 after you receive the demand for week 2; you will be planning unit production in week 6 after you receive the demand for week 3, and so on.

   One final factor that must be considered in making unit production decisions is a vacation period that occurs in the tenth and eleventh weeks of the game. During these two weeks, the company's manufacturing facilities are shut down, and no production is permitted. The company's distribution facilities are not shut down, however, and orders are continually processed to meet demand during the vacation period. No changes in the production levels are permitted during this vacation period. Changes in the production levels during the following periods of the twelfth and thirteenth weeks are permitted as usual.

3. *Available inventory* The available inventory is simply the summation of beginning inventory (line 1) and unit production (line 2) for the week. The unit production will be considered to be available to satisfy demand in the same week it is produced.

4. *Unit demand* Unit demand for the week will be given by the game proctor and can be any value between 50,000 and 250,000 units. The game proctor will announce the unit demand for each week.

5. *Ending inventory* Ending inventory is the difference between the available inventory and the resulting unit demand. If unit demand exceeds available inventory, you are stocked-out. You cannot have a negative ending inventory; if you are stocked-out, you should just enter a zero inventory level on the ending inventory line.

6. *Inventory holding costs* The distribution center that stores the inventory can hold a total of 150,000 units. For amounts of ending inventory equal to or less than 150,000 units, the cost rate to store 1,000 units of ending inventory per week is \$25. So, for example, if we have 100,000 units of ending inventory in a week, we would incur a \$2,500 (\$25 × 100) inventory holding cost in that particular week.

7. *Excess inventory holding costs* If ending inventory results in more than 150,000 units, in addition to ordinary holding costs outlined above, the company must

rent short-term storage facilities. The cost rate per 1,000 units of these storage facilities is $60. So, for example, if we have an ending inventory of 180,000 units (30,000 in excess of the 150,000 limit) the excess inventory holding cost would be $1,800 (30 × $60) in that particular week.

8. *Stockout costs* The cost of running out of stock includes the profit lost on each unit that could have been sold. For every 1,000 units that unit demand exceeds available inventory, the company incurs a $1,000 cost of lost profits. So if unit demand exceeds available inventory by 5,000 units, the company will incur a stockout cost of $5,000 in that particular week.
9. *Production level change cost* Each time the company changes its production level, it incurs costs (hiring, firing, training, layoff, and so on). In the game we will assume that the cost of changing the production level will be $250 per 1,000-unit change. So if we decide to increase production from one week to the next by 10,000 units (the maximum shift possible), it will cost $2,500 (10 × $250) for the production level change. If we were to decrease production by 1,000 units, then we would incur a production level change cost of $250. These costs are incurred in the week that they are implemented. Even though you will plan two weeks ahead of time, the costs are not incurred until the week they are actually made.
10. *Total costs for the week* This is simply the summation of lines 6 through 9.
11. *Total costs for the game* This is the running sum of the total costs for all the weeks.

The winner of the game will be the company with the lowest total costs for the game.

INSTRUCTIONS FOR BEGINNING THE GAME

Students will be asked to plan and make their unit production decisions for weeks 1, 2, and 3. Beginning inventory is set at 120,000 units. Once the amount of production is set for week 1, the rules for changes must be observed for all subsequent weeks. Students will be given a fixed period of planning time by the game proctor. All of the presidents for the companies must inform the game proctor as to their unit production decisions for all three weeks. Once all the companies have submitted their decisions to the game proctor, the unit demand for week 1 will be given to the companies. The costs each company incurs in week 1 should be calculated by the company accountant and shared with the rest of the company officers for planning the next period's unit production decision. The companies will then be asked to make the unit production decision for week 4. A total of 20 weeks or less will be simulated in this way.

APPENDIX C

Decision-making Methods

The purpose of this appendix is to introduce students to a few of the basic decision-making methods commonly used in operations management. Students may find the material presented here helpful in understanding the expected value methods presented throughout the textbook.

DECISION ENVIRONMENTS

In making a decision, an operations manager must consider all pertinent factors or parameters in a decision situation that may affect or be affected by the decision. One of these factors is the availability or quality of the information used to describe the decision situation. Because information is used to describe a decision situation, we classify decision environments based on the availability of such information. There are basically three types of decision environments: certainty, risk, and uncertainty.

1. *Certainty* In a decision environment of certainty, we have accurate information on all aspects of the problem and alternative solutions. The information on what will take place in the decision situation is usually complete, with clearly defined rewards or payoffs for each of the available alternatives.
2. *Risk* In a risk environment, we have imperfect information on what will take place in the decision situation. Thus, under such circumstances we usually assess probabilities of what will happen in the decision environment based on the limited available information.
3. *Uncertainty* In a situation of uncertainty, we have no information at all on the likelihood or probabilities of an outcome occurring on which to base our decision. Under such circumstances we usually use refined opinions and judgmental logic to arrive at a decision.

To illustrate these three decision environments let us examine how they would differ in an equipment purchasing decision situation. Suppose that we have to decide whether to buy a machine. Suppose that we know as a fact that if we purchase the machine, it will generate $4,000 in profit per year. If the machine is not purchased, we have no profit. This is an example of a certainty decision environment because we can base our decision on the certainty of the payoff from the machine. Now suppose that in this situation there is only a 30 percent chance of making $4,000 in profit and a 70 percent chance of losing $1,000 if we purchase the machine. This is an example of a risk decision environment because it involves some imperfect information that makes the payoff for the decision less than certain. Now suppose that the equipment purchase situation is changed and that this time there is no information at all on the profitability of the equipment. This is an example of an uncertainty decision environment because we have no information on which to base our decision.

DECISION THEORY FOR RISK DECISIONS

Decision theory refers to a collection of quantitative methods that are used to evaluate risk decision-making situations. Decision theory is used in operations management problem situations in which we are faced with a finite number of solution alternatives, each having some probability of success or failure.

A decision theory problem can be identified by certain basic elements being present.

1. *Alternative courses of action or strategies that the decision maker can choose from* These alternatives must be finite (a limited number) and mutually exclusive (the selection of one precludes the selection of any other). We can express these alternative courses of action or strategy for modeling purposes as A_i, where $i = 1$ through m alternatives.
2. *States of nature that define all possible conditions of the future decision-making environment* These states of nature must be finite and are usually outside of the control of the decision maker. We can express these states of nature as S_j, where $j = 1$ through n different states.
3. *The payoff, loss, or more commonly outcome that results when a course of action or a strategy is chosen for a specific state of nature* We can express these outcomes, whether a payoff or loss, as θ_{ij} (θ is the Greek letter theta), where $i = 1$ through m alternatives and $j = 1$ through n different states.
4. *Probabilities that are attached to the states of nature* These probabilities must be collectively exhaustive (that is, the sum of the probabilities for all of the states of nature will equal one). We can express these probabilities as p_j, where $j = 1$ through n different states.

These basic elements of decision theory are combined in Exhibit C-1 into what is commonly referred to as a **decision matrix.** We can see in Exhibit C-1 that the same probabilities are attached to each of the outcomes regardless of the alternatives chosen.

EXPECTED VALUE ANALYSIS

One of the most commonly used decision theory methods is expected value analysis.[1] **Expected value analysis** is used in a risk decision environment to determine the probabilistically weighted payoffs or losses for alternative strategies. The expected value for an alternative is the summation of the products between the outcomes for each state

[1] For excellent examples of expected value analysis, see F. Alemi and J. Agliato, "Restricting Patient's Choices of Physicians: A Decision Analytic Evaluation of Costs," *Interfaces*, 19, No. 2 (1989), 20–28; C. D. Feinstein, "Deciding Whether to Test Student Athletes for Drug Use," *Interfaces*, 20, No. 3 (1990), 80–87.

EXHIBIT C-1 A DECISION MATRIX

Alternative Actions or Strategies	*STATES OF NATURE (WITH PROBABILITIES)*		
	$S_1(p_1)$	$S_2(p_2), \ldots,$	$S_n(p_n)$
A_1	$\theta_{11}(p_1)$	$\theta_{12}(p_2), \ldots,$	$\theta_{1n}(p_n)$
A_2	$\theta_{21}(p_1)$	$\theta_{22}(p_2), \ldots,$	$\theta_{2n}(p_n)$
$\vdots$	$\vdots$	$\vdots$	$\vdots$
A_m	$\theta_{m1}(p_1)$	$\theta_{m2}(p_2), \ldots,$	$\theta_{mn}(p_n)$

of nature and their respective probabilities. The expected value computation for each alternative can be expressed as

$$\text{Expected value for alternate } 1 = \sum_{j=1}^{n} \theta_{ij}\,(p_j) \text{ (for } i = 1)$$

To use expected value analysis we calculate the expected value of each alternative and select the alternative that provides the greatest expected profit or the least expected loss. Let's illustrate the elements of decision theory and expected value analysis for an equipment purchasing problem.

An Expected Value Problem

A company must decide to purchase one of three machines: A, B, or C (alternative strategies). Each of the three machines produces the same basic product, but because of technological differences the profitability of production is dependent on market demand. Based on a market survey, customer demand for the product will be high, medium, or low (states of nature). The market survey also reveals that the likelihood of a high market demand is 40 percent, medium market demand is 25 percent, and a low market demand is 35 percent (probabilities of the states of nature). Total profit (the outcomes) in thousands of dollars (after all expenses) for each of the machines was determined in the market survey to be as follows:

	RESULTING MARKET DEMAND		
Machine	*High*	*Medium*	*Low*
A	300	150	−50
B	200	200	−10
C	400	100	−20

In this table, machine A will generate a total profit of $300,000 if the market demand is high, only $150,000 if the demand is medium, and will actually generate a loss of $50,000 if the demand is low. The decision problem is to choose the machine that will provide the most expected profit.

To determine the machine to purchase, we can calculate the expected value of the payoffs for each of the machines as follows:

$$
\begin{aligned}
\text{Expected value for machine A} &= 300(.40) + 150(.25) + (-50)(.35) \\
&= 120 + 37.5 + (-17.5) \\
&= 140 \text{ or } \$140{,}000
\end{aligned}
$$

$$
\begin{aligned}
\text{Expected value for machine B} &= 200(.40) + 200(.25) + (-10)(.35) \\
&= 80 + 50 + (-3.5) \\
&= 126.5 \text{ or } \$126{,}500
\end{aligned}
$$

$$
\begin{aligned}
\text{Expected value for machine C} &= 400(.40) + 100(.25) + (-20)(.35) \\
&= 160 + 25 + (-7) \\
&= 178 \text{ or } \$178{,}000
\end{aligned}
$$

From the results of the analysis, the machine that generates the greatest expected profit is machine C. We would therefore recommend that the company purchase machine C.

Another decision theory technique that represents an extension and a graphic aid to expected value analysis is called a decision tree. A **decision tree** is a network or graph that allows decision makers to plan and organize a sequence of decisions that are sometimes required in decision situations. Once the sequence of decisions is organized using the decision tree, expected value analysis is used to determine an expected value on which a decision choice can be made. A sequential decision tree problem is presented in Exhibit C-2.

The decision tree is made up of a network of arrows showing the direction of the sequence of decisions, boxes representing positions in the network where decisions are required, and circles or nodes that usually contain the expected values of the outcomes for each possible decision alternative. We can see in Exhibit C-2 that the same basic elements of decisions theory (outcomes, states of nature, and alternative actions) are part of the decision tree. In this decision tree only two sequential decisions are presented, but additional ones could be used to continue the figure. As the number of alternatives and states of nature increase, so do the number of decision tree branches.

In interpreting the problem in Exhibit C-2, we can see from the direction of the arrows that the first decision is dependent on outcomes for alternatives 1 and 2. The outcome for alternative 1 is dependent on the states of nature A and B. These states of nature are in turn dependent on the second decision, and so on. Decision tree problems can become very complex when two or more probabilities from states of nature must be statistically combined to calculate necessary sequential decision tree probabilities.[2]

[2] One statistical procedure used to calculate these revised probabilities is called *Bayes' theorem*. Bayes' theorem is a statistical formula that permits the calculation of the conditional probabilities used in decision trees, and is one of the most commonly used decision theory procedures. For an interesting application of Bayes' theorem in grocery store pricing, see R. J. Colantone, C. Droge, D. S. Litrack, and C. A. Benedetto, "Flanking in a Price War," *Interfaces*, 19, No. 2 (1989), 1–12. Bayes' theorem has also been extensively used in the development of AI computer software (see W. A. Gale, *Artificial Intelligence and Statistics* [Reading, Mass.: Addison-Wesley, 1986]).

EXHIBIT C-2 A DECISION TREE

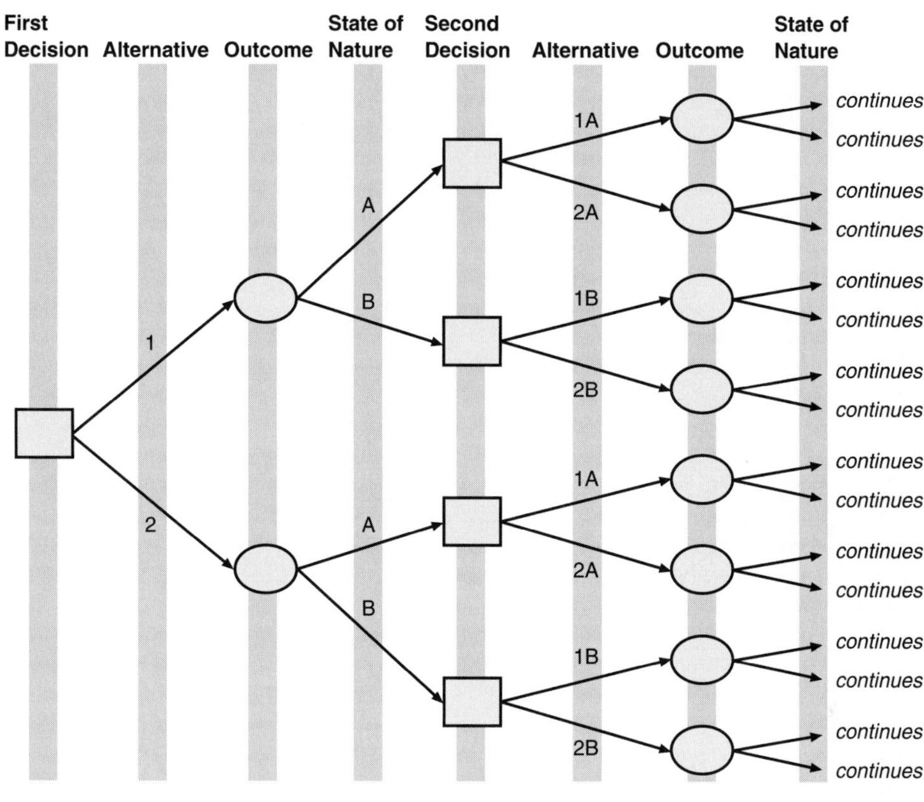

Let us illustrate the use of the decision tree in operations management planning for a facility acquisition problem.

A Decision Tree Problem

Suppose that a new company needs to decide whether to build a plant (alternative 1) or to lease a plant (alternative 2) to manufacture its products. The consumer demand for the company's products is going to be either high (state of nature 1), with an estimated probability of 0.25, or low (state of nature 2), with an estimated probability of 0.75. This problem is presented in Exhibit C-3. A second decision that is dependent on the resulting consumer demand is whether the company should plan to enlarge the facility to satisfy the type of demand it will be facing once the plant has been acquired. If the company chooses alternative 1 (build plant) and then experiences high demand, it can choose either to expand the plant it built or not to expand it.

EXHIBIT C-3 A DECISION TREE OM PROBLEM

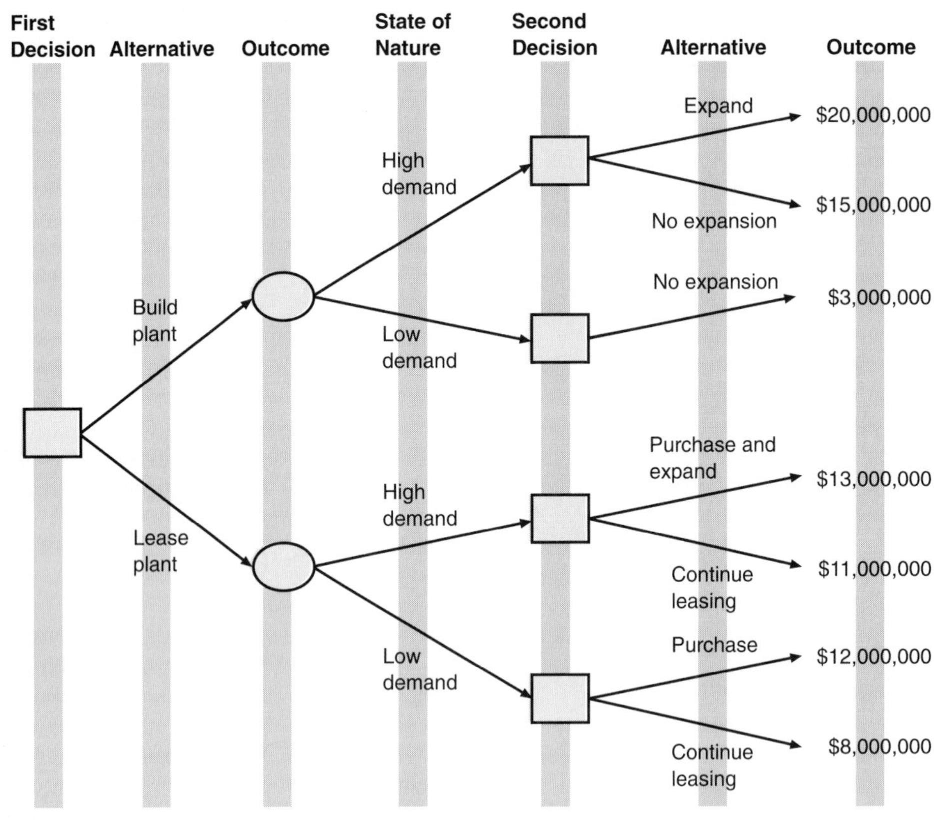

As can be seen in Exhibit C-3, if the company expands its plant it will earn an estimated $20 million in profit. If it chooses no expansion, it will only earn $15 million in profit. Should it experience low demand, it will logically choose no expansion and consequently receive only $3 million in profit. If it chooses alternative 2 (lease plant) and then experiences high demand, it can either choose to purchase and expand the plant or continue leasing the plant. As can be seen in Exhibit C-3, if the company purchases and expands, it will earn an estimated $13 million in profit. If the company chooses to continue leasing the plant, it will earn only $11 million in profit. Should it experience low demand, it might choose to purchase the plant but not expand, which will result in an estimated $12 million in profit. The company can also choose to continue leasing the plant and if it does, it will earn only $8 million in profit.

It should be obvious that the decision tree in Exhibit C-3 is a helpful graphic aid in keeping all of the alternative "branches" of this problem neatly organized. We do not have any probabilistic states of nature for the second decision, so the problem does not require any sophisticated probabilistic adjustments. We can proceed to solve the facility acquisition decision tree problem by the following steps:

1. *Starting with the second decision, determine the profit-maximizing alternative for each branch in the decision tree.* This section of the problem represents a decision situation of "certainty." In Exhibit C-4, the top branch (the high demand branch) of the decision tree permits us to choose between $20 million in profit if we expand the plant or $15 million in profit if no expansion occurs. We would choose to expand the plant to maximize our profit. Use double slash (//) marks to denote an alternative not chosen.
2. *Enter the outcome values for each branch in the decision boxes.* We can see in Exhibit C-4 that the $20 million in profit is entered in the second decision box along the high demand branch. The other outcomes ($3, $13, and $12 million) are also carried forward to the appropriate boxes.
3. *Calculate the expected value of the first decision's outcome based on the states of nature probabilities and the profit value in the second decision boxes.* This value can be calculated from the sum of the products of all of the second decision branches multiplied by the probabilities of their respective states of nature. Place the expected value of the outcomes in the nodes of each branch of the outcomes for the first decision. The expected value of the build plant alternative is $7.25 million in profit [7.25 = 20(.25) + 3(.75)] and the expected value for the lease plant alternative is $12.25 million in profit [12.25 = 13(.25) + 12(.75)].
4. *Based on the expected value outcomes for the first decision's alternatives, choose the profit-maximizing alternative from all of the branches in the decision tree.* In Exhibit C-4, we would choose the alternative lease plant to maximize our expected profit. Use double slash marks to denote that the build plant alternative is not chosen.

There are many applications of decision tree analysis in operations management. Some of the applications demonstrate how decision trees can be effective decision-making and planning aids.[3]

Expected Value Modeling Assumptions

In using expected value analysis, we are often required to make several assumptions. If we believe that the following assumptions do not apply in some decision-making

[3] See D. Cohan et al., "Using Fire in Forest Management: Decision Making Under Uncertainty," *Interfaces,* 14 (September–October 1984), 8–19; and F. W. Winter, "An Application of Computerized Decision Tree Models in Management-Union Bargaining," *Interfaces,* 15 (March–April 1985), 74–80.

EXHIBIT C-4 A DECISION TREE OM PROBLEM SOLUTION

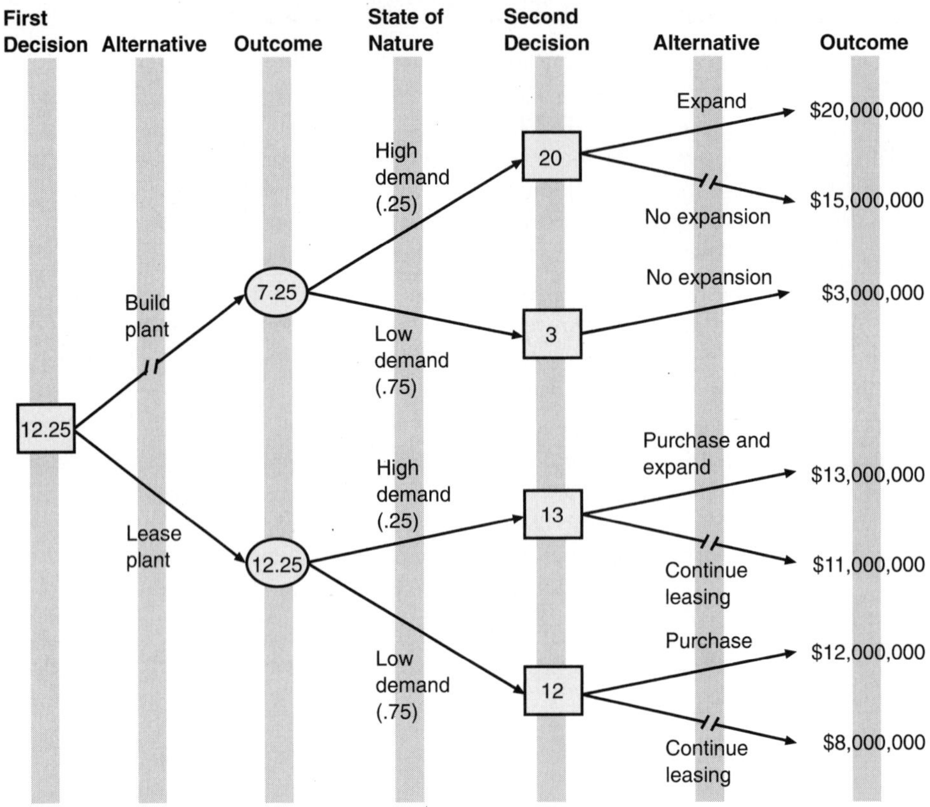

First Decision | Alternative | Outcome | State of Nature | Second Decision | Alternative | Outcome

Expand $20,000,000
20
High demand (.25)
No expansion $15,000,000
No expansion $3,000,000
Build plant
7.25
Low demand (.75)
3
12.25
Purchase and expand $13,000,000
High demand (.25)
13
Lease plant
12.25
Continue leasing $11,000,000
Purchase $12,000,000
Low demand (.75)
12
Continue leasing $8,000,000

situations, then expected value analysis should not be used to model that particular situation.

1. The error that exists in the estimation of the states of nature probabilities contributes to the inaccuracy of the resulting expected values.
2. The error that exists in the estimation of the payoffs also contributes to the inaccuracy of the resulting expected values.
3. The resulting expected value is a long-term average value that may or may not occur in any particular decision-making situation.

There are, of course, many other types of decision theory–related techniques and procedures. Some of these methods, as we have seen in chapters throughout the text, can be used to make decisions in decision environments of certainty and uncertainty.

OTHER QUANTITATIVE METHODS FOR CERTAINTY AND UNCERTAINTY DECISIONS

In a decision-making situation, when we have complete certainty on the outcomes of the alternatives, we would simply select the alternative with the highest payoff.

QUESTION: A manufacturing company has been offered three contracts to produce a special part. Because of production capacity limitations, the manufacturing company can only satisfy one of the three contracts. The company must choose from contract A, B, or C, representing $10,000, $20,000, or $25,000 in profit for the company. Which contract should the manufacturing company choose if the profit payoffs are known with certainty and the company wants to maximize profit?

ANSWER: The obvious profit-maximizing contract is C, with $25,000.

In a decision environment that is uncertain, the selection process becomes much more complex because the likelihood of the alternatives is unknown. To deal with the complexity, several decision-making strategies can be used.

Maximax strategy The **maximax strategy** is to select the alternative that, according to the payoff matrix, contains the overall maximum payoff. In other words, of the maximum payoffs for the alternative, the maximum of the maximums is chosen, hence the title "maximax."

Maximin strategy The **maximin strategy** is to select the alternative that contains the best payoff of all possible minimum payoffs. This is accomplished by first locating the minimum payoffs for each alternative, and then selecting the maximum of the minimum payoffs.

Laplace strategy The **Laplace strategy** is to select the maximum average payoff alternative. Simply compute the average payoff for each alternative, and then select the alternative with the maximum average payoff.

Minimax regret strategy In situations in which opportunity loss, or what we would "regret" losing, can be determined for alternative payoff values, we select the alternative that would minimize the maximum regret, or the **minimax regret strategy.** This is accomplished by first determining the regret payoffs, then determining the maximum regret or loss payoff for each alternative, and finally selecting the alternative with the minimum of maximum regrets.

The selection of a specific strategy for decision making in uncertain environments depends largely on the type of decision maker a person tends to be. A pessimistic person might select to minimize losses with a minimax regret or maximin strategy. An optimistic person might choose to maximize the best of all possible best outcomes with a maximax strategy. A conservative person might want to consider the average of all possible outcomes in his or her decision process with a Laplace strategy.

QUESTION: The management of a company must decide if it is going to give its workers a wage increase. If the company chooses to give its workers an increase, it will avoid a possible strike but reduce its yearly profits. If the company chooses not to give its workers a wage increase, it may have a strike but will save some of its yearly profits. The possible yearly payoff in profits is a function of the economy (the states of nature). If the company experiences a "good" economy, it will make a profit; if the company experiences a "bad" economy, it will make little or no profit. The resulting payoff matrix in millions of dollars is as follows:

	STATE OF NATURE	
Alternatives	*1. Good Economy*	*2. Bad Economy*
1. Wage increase	10	0
2. No wage increase	15	5

What is the best alternative using

a. Maximax strategy
b. Maximin strategy
c. Laplace strategy
d. Minimax regret strategy

ANSWER: (a.) According to the maximax strategy, the best payoff for alternative 1 is $10 million and for alternative 2 is $15 million. The company therefore would select alternative 2, which is the maximum of the two maximum values.

(b.) Using the maximin strategy we can see that the minimum payoff for alternative 1 is $0 and for alternative 2 is $5 million. The company therefore would select alternative 2, which is the maximum of the two minimum values.

(c.) Using the Laplace strategy, we must first compute the average payoffs for the two alternatives. The average payoff for alternative 1 is $5 million ([$10 + $0]/2), and the average payoff for alternative 2 is $10 million ([$15 + $5]/2). The company therefore would select alternative 2, which is the maximum of the two average payoff values.

(d.) Using the minimax regret strategy, we must first determine the opportunity loss or regrets. The regret values can be determined in many ways, but they are usually related to states of nature. We would regret not obtaining the best payoff under each of the two states of nature. The best payoff for state of nature 1 is $15 million and for state of nature 2 is $5 million. The actual regret values are what we lose if we do not receive the best payoff values for each state of nature.

(continued)

To determine these values you simply subtract each payoff value from the best payoff value in that column. These opportunity loss or regret values are as follows:

	STATE OF NATURE	
Alternatives	*1. Good Economy*	*2. Bad Economy*
1. Wage increase	5	5
2. No wage increase	0	0

The regret values for the good economy state of nature were found as follows: Alternative 1 has a regret value of $5 (15 − 10 = 5) and alternative 2 has a regret value of $0 (15 − 15 = 0). Now the maximum opportunity loss or regret for alternative 1 is $5 million and for alternative 2 is $0. Consistent with the minimax regret strategy, the company would choose to minimize its regrets by selecting alternative 2.

APPENDIX D

Introduction to Linear Programming and Model Formulation Procedures

The purpose of this appendix is to provide a basic introduction to linear programming concepts, modeling elements, and formulation procedures. This appendix also demonstrates the graphic solution method for linear programming and how students can use Micro Production software to obtain solutions to linear programming problems. (Students interested in the mathematically based procedures used by *Micro Production* software to generate linear programming solutions should review the material in Appendix E.)

FORMULATION PROCEDURE

One of the most commonly used management science modeling tools is linear programming.[1] **Linear programming (LP)** is a multivariable, constrained optimization technique. Linear programming models are capable of using any number of decision variables (that is, the unknowns we want to solve for) and yet permit the realistic restrictions of limited resources in the modeling process. Because operations managers may participate in the formulation of a linear programming model of an operating system, we will briefly discuss how LP models are formulated in this section. (This has also been discussed in various sections throughout the text.) The simplex solution procedure used in computer software to obtain solutions for LP models is presented in Appendix E. Operations managers use various LP solution software packages (such as *Micro Production*) available in their own organization's decision support system.

All linear programming model formulations consist of three elements: an objective function, constraints, and a set of decision variables. The **objective function** is always a linear equation that sets Z (total profit or total cost) equal to the sum of the products of x_j (the decision variables or unknowns we want to determine) and c_j (the contribution coefficient that defines the per-unit contribution to Z of each unit of x_j). The **constraints** are linear equalities or inequalities that relate b_j (the right-hand-side value usually representing total available resources or a total minimum resource value required to be satisfied) with the sum of the products of a_{ij} (the technology coefficient representing the usage of b_i per unit of x_j) and each of their respective decision variables. An LP model may have any finite number of constraints. **Decision variables** are those unknowns whose value we are trying to determine. Typically, these x_j variables must be equal to or greater than zero.

[1] For a review of some interesting applications of LP in operations management, see D. L. Rumpf et al., "Improving Efficiency in a Forest Pest Control Spray Program," *Interfaces*, 15 (September-October 1985), 1–11; R. Field, "National Forest Planning in Promoting U.S. Forest Service Acceptance of Operations Research," *Interfaces*, 14 (September–October 1984), 67–76; and T. K. Zierer et al., "Practical Applications of Linear Programming to Shell's Distribution Problems," *Interfaces*, 6 (August 1976), 13–26.

These three model elements can be seen in the generalized model presented in Exhibit D-1. There are basically two types of linear programming problems: a maximization problem (used for operations management system models in which we want to make as much profit or cash contribution as possible) and a minimization problem (used for OM system models in which we want to minimize costs or resource utilization). In the model in Exhibit D-1 we have presented a maximization problem.

The following five-step procedure is offered as a framework for modeling LP problems:

1. *Determine the type of problem.* The problem is either going to be a maximization probem or a minimization problem. If the problem situation contains only profit information, then chances are it will be a profit-maximization problem. If the problem situation contains only cost information, it is probably a cost-minimization problem. If the problem contains both cost and sales information, then it might be a maximization problem requiring the profit to be calculated from the difference between the revenue and cost information. These profit and cost values are the c_j contribution coefficients used later in the formulation.
2. *Define the decision variables.* Clearly state what each decision variable represents in the model. If a decision variable represents the number of units of product XYZ to produce next month, then define the variable in terms of units and time. The more precise the definition, the easier the rest of the formulation process will be. (**Hint:** Because we identified the c_j values in step 1, and because

EXHIBIT D-1 GENERALIZED LINEAR PROGRAMMING MODEL

$$\text{Maximize } Z = c_1 x_1 + c_2 x_2 + \dots + c_n x_n \qquad \text{Objective function}$$

$$\left.\begin{aligned} \text{subject to: } a_{11} x_1 + a_{12} x_2 + \dots + a_{1n} x_n &\le b_1 \\ a_{21} x_1 + a_{22} x_2 + \dots + a_{2n} x_n &\ge b_2 \\ &\vdots \\ a_{m1} x_1 + a_{m2} x_2 + \dots + a_{mn} x_n &= b_m \end{aligned}\right] \quad \text{Constraints}$$

$$x_1, x_2, \dots, x_n \ge 0 \qquad \text{Nonnegativity requirements}$$

where

a_{ij} = technology coefficients (given)

b_i = right-hand-side resource coefficients (given)

c_j = contribution coefficients (given)

x_j = decision variables (unknown)

Z = objective function variable (unknown)

n = number of decision variables

m = number of constraints

each c_j will be attached to each x_j variable in the objective function, we know how many x_j variables we need in the model.)

3. *State the objective function.* Express the equation summing the products of the c_j values (determined in step 1) with the x_j variables (determined in step 2) and setting it equal to the unknown value of Z.
4. *Formulate the constraints.* Express all necessary constraints as either an equation or inequality. This is one of the most difficult steps in the formulation process. One approach to obtaining the constraints is to first identify the b_i, or the right-hand-side resource coefficients. In operations management systems, the right-hand-side values in maximization problems usually represent total available resources (for example, total available hours of labor, total available parts for production). For minimization problems, the right-hand-side values usually represent total minimum usage requirements (for example, total minimum product demand, total minimum production). Once the right-hand-side values are determined, the respective a_{ij} technology coefficients can usually be more easily identified because they are directly related (that is, the per-unit usage for each x_j) to the right-hand-side value.
5. *State the nonnegative requirements.* Express the fact that all of the decision variables in the model must be greater than or equal to zero.

To illustrate the use of this LP formulation procedure and demonstrate the informational value of its output, we will look at several formulation problems. To demonstrate how LP models are used to generate constrained resource allocations in operations management, we will first formulate and then look at a graphic solution method to a production problem. We will then examine two additional problems, their formulation, and computer-based solutions. (Those interested in understanding the actual simplex algorithm used by computer software to generate a solution should review the material on the simplex solution method in Appendix E.)

FORMULATION AND GRAPHIC SOLUTION

LP models, like operations managers, seek to take maximum advantage of the limited resources they have to produce their products. LP models not only can be used to optimize unit production, but can do so using the least amount of resources. Moreover, LP solutions help provide managers with information to identify unused resources that they can reallocate to other production activities. Let's look at a simple OM problem.

Suppose that a company produces units of two products: product A and product B. The company receives $4 in profit for each unit of product A it produces and $2 in profit for each unit of product B it produces. Although the company has an unlimited market and can sell all the units of either product it produces, it has some daily resource limitations. We will label these constraints as follows:

Constraint 1: Material 1 Each unit of product A uses one unit of material 1. A maximum total of 250 units of material 1 are available for production purposes each day.

Constraint 2: Material 2 Each unit of product B uses one unit of material 2. A maximum total of 200 units of material 2 are available for production purposes each day.

Constraint 3: Labor hours Each unit of product A uses two hours of labor, and each unit of product B uses two hours of labor. A maximum total of 700 hours of labor are available for production purposes each day.

The company wants to know how many units of each product it should produce each day to make as much profit as possible.

Given this information, we can formulate an LP model of this operations management problem using the five-step formulation procedure.

Step 1: Determine the type of problem. The profit values of \$4 and \$2 are the contribution coefficients, or c_j values in the model. Because we have only been given profit information, this problem must be a profit-maximizing problem.

Step 2: Define the decison variables. The company wants to know how many units of each product it should produce each day. The definition of the decision variables are

x_1 = number of units of product A to produce per day

x_2 = number of units of product B to produce per day

Step 3: State the objective function. From step 1 we can set $c_1 = 4$ and $c_2 = 2$, and from step 2 the decision variables can be combined to form the following objective function:

$$\text{Maximize } Z = 4x_1 + 2x_2$$

Step 4: Formulate the constraints. Each of the three constraints will have a right-hand-side value, b_i, that represents in this problem a total maximum amount of a limited production resource (materials or labor). In the case of the material 1 resource, the maximum total supply that can be used for production of units of product A (x_1) is 250 units. This means that we can use a maximum of 250 units of material 1, or some lesser amount. Because only the decision variable x_1 is related to this resource, it will be the only decision variable that will appear in constraint 1. We can express constraint 1 as follows:

$$x_1 \leq 250 \text{ (material 1)}$$

In the case of the material 2 resource, the maximum total supply that can be used for production of units of product B (x_2) is 200 units. Because only the decision variable x_2 is related to this resource, it will be the only decision variable that will appear in constraint 2. We can express constraint 2 as shown at the top of page 782.

$$x_2 \le 200 \text{ (material 2)}$$

For the labor hours constraint, both product A and product B require two hours for production. With a maximum total hours for all production set at 700, we can express constraint 3 as follows:

$$2x_1 + 2x_2 \le 700 \text{ (labor hours)}$$

Step 5: State the nonnegative requirements. To complete the formulation, the nonnegative requirements stating that we can't produce negative units of either product can be expressed as

$$x_1, x_2 \ge 0$$

The complete formulation of the production company sample problem LP model is

$$\begin{aligned} \text{Maximize } Z &= 4x_1 + 2x_2 \\ \text{subject to: } \quad x_1 &\le 250 \text{ (material 1)} \\ x_2 &\le 200 \text{ (material 2)} \\ 2x_1 + 2x_2 &\le 700 \text{ (labor hours)} \\ x_1, x_2 &\ge 0 \end{aligned}$$

Once the problem is formulated as an LP model, we can use the model to generate a solution to the problem. One method that can be used to solve small, two-decision variable problems such as this one is called the graphic solution method for LP problems. The **graphic solution method** consists of four basic steps.

Step 1: Graph the LP model constraints as equalities. To graph the constraints as equalities, simply change the inequality expression to an equality and solve for the intercept values along the graph axis. It makes no difference if you let the vertical axis be x_1 or x_2, as the same solution will result either way. In the case of the first two constraints, the intercept values are the right-hand-side values, such that $x_1 = 250$ for constraint 1. The graph of this constraint is presented in Exhibit D-2(a) as a horizontal line. The graph for constraint 2 is presented in Exhibit D-2(a) as a vertical line, where $x_2 = 200$. In the case of constraint 3, we must solve for the intercept values by first plugging a zero in the constraint for one variable and then solving for the other. Let's set $x_1 = 0$. Then by substitution in constraint 3 we can find the x_2 intercept value as follows:

$$\begin{aligned} 2(0) + 2x_2 &= 700 \\ x_2 &= 350 \end{aligned}$$

Now we reverse the process by letting $x_2 = 0$ and by substitution we obtain the x_1 intercept value as follows:

$$\begin{aligned} 2x_1 + 2(0) &= 700 \\ x_1 &= 350 \end{aligned}$$

EXHIBIT D-2 GRAPHIC SOLUTION FOR SAMPLE PRODUCTION PROBLEM

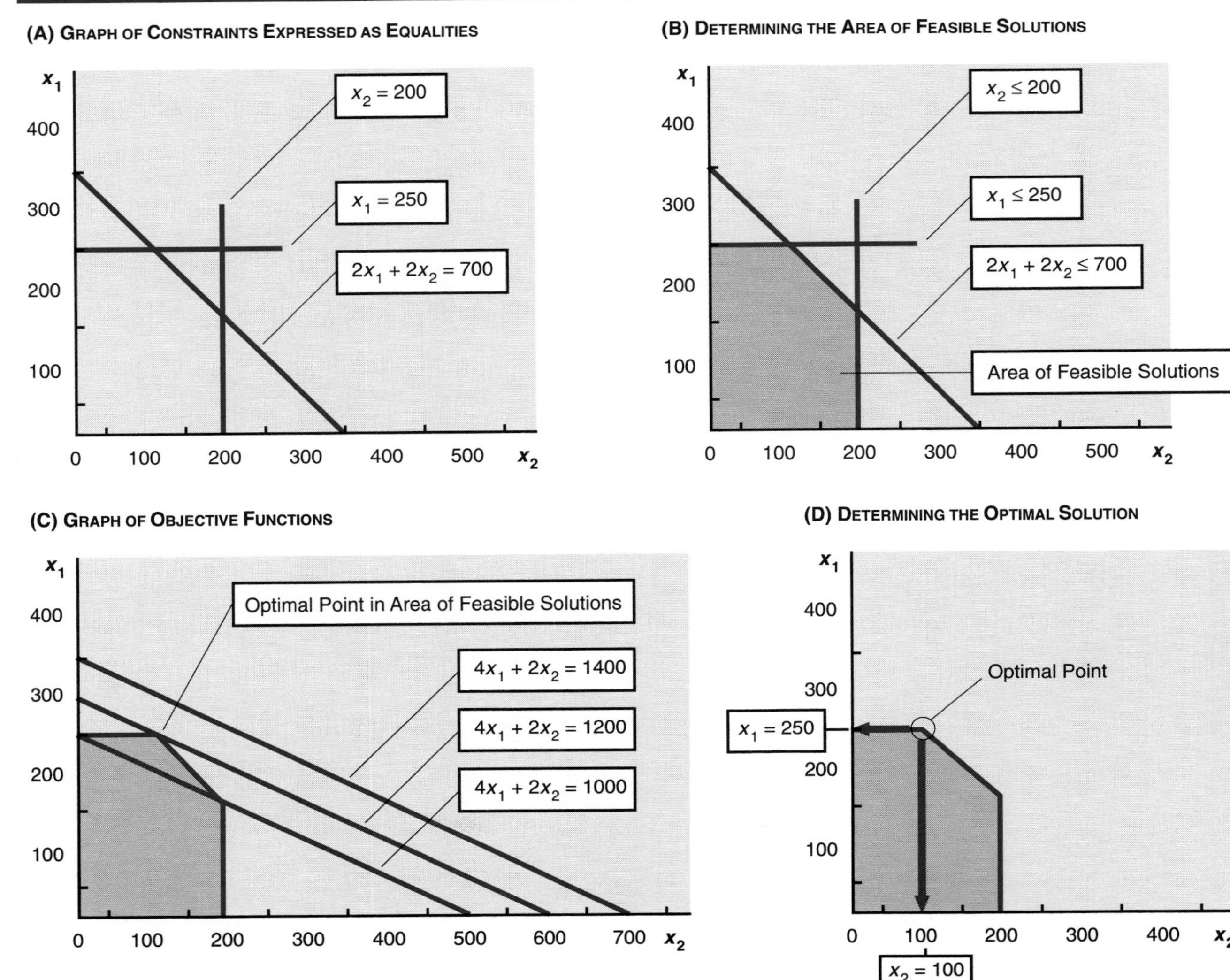

The graph of the two intercept values is plotted on the graph in Exhibit D-2(a).

Step 2: Determine the area of feasible solutions. The **area of feasible solutions** is the set of all points on the graph that will satisfy all of the constraints of the LP model at the same time. The term *feasible* is used here as a solution that satisfies all of the constraints. To find the area of feasible solutions, we must find the area on the graph that satisfies all of the constraints' inequality expressions. Consistent with the direction of the inequalities of all three constraints, this area would have to be below the horizontal line for constraint 1, to the left of the line for constraint 2, and below the line for constraint 3. The darkened area in Exhibit D-2(b) denotes the area of feasible solutions for this problem. It is from this area that the resulting optimal solution will originate.

Step 3: Determine the optimal point by graphing objective functions. The location of the optimal point in the area of feasible solutions depends on the type of problem we are solving. For a maximization problem, the optimal point(s) will occur by meeting all three of the following conditions: (1) being in the area of feasible solutions, (2) being on the slope of the objective function, and (3) being at a point furthest from the origin of the graph. (For a minimization problem, the third condition changes to the closest point to the origin.) To graph the objective function, we must determine the intercept values. Because the value of Z in the objective function is unknown, we must arbitrarily select values for Z and substitute them into the objective function to find the intercept values. For example, let's set $Z = 1{,}000$. The resulting graph of the objective function whose $Z = 1{,}000$ is presented in Exhibit D-2(c). Because the slope of the objective function is what is important, we could use a straight-edged ruler to find the optimal point in the area of feasible solutions. By moving in a parallel direction away from the origin until we reach the last point of tangency with the area of feasible solutions (that is, where $Z = 1{,}200$), the optimal point can be found. We could also use a trial-and-error method of substituting values for Z until we find the optimal point. Had we alternatively selected a large value for Z of say, 1,400, we would have graphed a line beyond the area of feasible solutions, as presented in Exhibit D-2(c). In this case, we can still find the optimal point by bringing the straight-edge from that line toward the area of feasible solutions. The result will be the same either way: We will find the optimal point in the area of feasible solutions.

Step 4: Determine the optimal solution. The optimal solution values for the decision variables are found by drawing a vertical and horizontal line from the optimal point found in step 3. As we can see in Exhibit D-2(d), the resulting optimal values for decision variables are where $x_1 = 250$ and $x_2 = 100$. Plugging these decision variable values into the objective function, the optimized profit, or Z, is \$1,200. This solution means that given the existing constraints, no other combination of values for the decision variables will generate a larger profit for the company than the \$1,200 value. The company should produce 250 units of product A and 200 units of product B.

The LP model also can provide some additional resource information. We can see by reviewing the constraints in the model that not all of the production resources need to be used to achieve the optimal \$1,200 profit level. By substituting the optimal decision variables back into the constraints, we can determine if there are any unused resources. For constraint 1, there are no unused resources because the left-hand side of the constraint equals the right-hand-side resource value:

$$\begin{aligned} x_1 &\leq 250 \\ 250 &= 250 \end{aligned}$$

For constraint 2, there are unused resources because the left-hand side of the constraint is less than the right-hand-side resource value:

$$\begin{aligned} x_2 &\leq 200 \\ 100 &< 200 \end{aligned}$$

For the material 2 resource modeled in constraint 2, we use only 100 units of the 200 units available. The difference of the 100 units used and the 200 units available is called *slack resources*. For operations managers, a **slack resource** is an unused or idle resource that could be used elsewhere to produce other products. These 100 units of unused slack resources can be reallocated by management to other production activities, making better use of these idle materials and improving productivity. For constraint 3, there are no unused resources because the left-hand side of the constraint exactly equals the right-hand-side resource value:

$$\begin{aligned} 2x_1 + 2x_2 &\leq 700 \\ 2(250) + 2(100) &= 700 \\ 700 &= 700 \end{aligned}$$

The graphic solution method for LP is a very limited solution method for two-variable LP problems, although its application here illustrates several important operations management points. The area of feasible solutions represents the fact that operations managers have a wide choice in deciding possible solutions for the use of their resources to produce their products. Guided by management science methodologies such as LP, operations managers can locate the optimal production choice that will maximize profit and minimize resource requirements.

The graphic method also can be used to understand the workings of the computer-based simplex algorithmic method. The fact that the optimal point occurred on a corner point in Exhibit D-2(d) is not an accident. The optimal point in the area of feasible solutions will either be a corner point or—in the case of multiple optimal solutions—a line segment that meets the three conditions previously stated. In either case, the simplex method algebraically moves from the origin corner point, along the area of feasible solutions, to subsequent corner points until it reaches the optimal corner point. This movement from one corner point to another corner point is called an **iteration.** The algebraic process of the simplex method is presented in Appendix E. We will use the computer-based simplex method to solve both a maximization and minimization LP modeled problem in the next section of this appendix. Before the computer can solve the problem, however, we must formulate it.

FORMULATION AND COMPUTER-BASED SOLUTION

A Maximization Problem

Suppose that a baker wants to determine how many different pies should be produced per day to make the most profit. The baker makes three different pies: cherry, peach, and pumpkin. Each cherry pie contributes \$1.50 to profit, each peach pie contributes \$1.25 to profit, and each pumpkin pie contributes \$1.00 to profit. The baker can sell all of the pies that are produced and is not constrained by anything except the following operational resources:

Constraint 1: Dough machine The dough machine the baker owns will only produce and make available a total of 1,000 ounces of dough per day. It takes five ounces of dough for a cherry pie, four ounces for a peach pie, and three ounces for a pumpkin pie.

Constraint 2: Mixing and pie preparation time The baker and staff only have a total of 80 hours of labor per day to spend on preparing the pies. It takes one-half hour for the mixing and preparation time for either a cherry or peach pie, and it takes one-fourth hour for a pumpkin pie.

Constraint 3: Display space The display space is limited to only 300 pies in the store and, because each pie takes up the same amount of display space, the maximum number of pies that can be displayed during a day is 300.

Let's formulate this decision situation as an LP model using the five-step formulation procedure.

Step 1: Determine the type of problem. We can see that this problem must be a maximization problem because (1) the baker wants to make as much profit as possible and (2) only profit information was presented in the problem. Note that the \$1.50 profit information on cherry pies is the c_1 contribution coefficient for this LP model.

Step 2: Define the decision variables. We can define these variables as follows:

x_1 = the number of cherry pies to bake per day

x_2 = the number of peach pies to bake per day

x_3 = the number of pumpkin pies to bake per day

Step 3: State the objective function. We can now state the objective function using the profit contribution coefficients found in step 1 and the decision variables defined in step 2.

$$\text{Maximize } Z = 1.50x_1 + 1.25x_2 + 1.00x_3$$

Step 4: Formulate the constraints. In this step we must structure the constraints. For this problem we can easily see that there are three constraints. The constraint for dough machine capacity is formulated by first recognizing the right-hand-side value for this constraint. In this constraint the right-hand-side value is the 1,000 ounces that represents the machine's total capacity. Because we can use 1,000 ounces of dough in a day or less, we must use a less-than or equal-to inequality to model this constraint. We then add the appropriate decision variables and technology coefficients pertaining to the use of dough to complete the constraint as follows:

$$5x_1 + 4x_2 + 3x_3 \leq 1{,}000 \text{ (dough machine capacity)}$$

The second constraint models the mixing and preparation time of the baker's staff. The right-hand-side value for this constraint represents a total available resource of 80 hours of labor. This constraint can be expressed as follows:

$$.5x_1 + .5x_2 + .25x_3 \leq 80 \text{ (mixing and preparation time)}$$

The third constraint limits the total production of all three pies to 300 because of the total display space available. Because each pie will take up the same space, the technology coefficients will all be equal to one.

$$1x_1 + 1x_2 + 1x_3 \leq 300 \text{ (display space)}$$

Step 5: State the nonnegative requirements. To complete the formulation of this problem we must state the nonnegative requirements.

$$x_1, x_2, x_3 \geq 0$$

The complete LP formulation for this pie baker's problem is as follows:

$$\text{Maximize } Z = 1.50x_1 + 1.25x_2 + 1{,}00x_3$$

$$\begin{aligned} \text{subject to:} \quad 5x_1 + 4x_2 + 3x_3 &\leq 1{,}000 \\ .5x_1 + .5x_2 + .25x_3 &\leq 80 \\ x_1 + x_2 + x_3 &\leq 300 \\ x_1, x_2, x_3 &\geq 0 \end{aligned}$$

The baker, who is functioning in this problem as an operations manager, wants to solve for the values of x_1, x_2, x_3, and Z to determine the exact number of each type of pie to produce tomorrow to maximize total profit. The computer-generated solution to this LP problem is presented in Exhibit D-3. The optimal solution values for this problem are $x_1 = 20$ cherry pies, $x_2 = 0$ peach pies, and $x_3 = 280$ pumpkin pies, which will generate a profit of $Z = \$310$. The decision variable values provided by the LP solution procedure are optimal because no other combination of values for the decision variables will generate a greater Z value.

The solution also provides the operations manager with an opportunity to identify idle resources. For example, in the dough machine capacity constraint we had a total

EXHIBIT D-3 *MICRO PRODUCTION* SOFTWARE SOLUTION OUTPUT OF BAKER'S MAXIMIZATION LP PROBLEM

```
Program: Linear Programming

Problem Title : LP Problem #1

***** Inout Data *****

Max Z = 1.50X1 + 1.25X2 + 1.00X3

Subject to

C1  5X1 + 4X2 + 3X3 <= 1000
C2  0.5X1 + 0.5X2 + 0.25X3 <= 80
C3  1X1 + 1X2 + 1X3 <= 300

*****Program Output *****

Final Optimal Solution

Z =   310.000

---------------------------------------------------
 Variable              Value          Reduced Cost
---------------------------------------------------
   X 1                20.000                 0.000
   X 2                 0.000                 0.250
   X 3               280.000                 0.000
---------------------------------------------------

---------------------------------------------------
 Constraint      Slack/Surplus        Shadow Price
---------------------------------------------------
   C 1                60.000                 0.000
   C 2                 0.000                 2.000
   C 3                 0.000                 0.500
---------------------------------------------------

***** End of Output *****
```

of 1,000 ounces available for production. Yet by substituting the optimal decision variables into the constraint we obtain the following usage information:

$$5x_1 + 4x_2 + 3x_3 \leq 1{,}000$$
$$5(20) + 4(0) + 3(280) \leq 1{,}000$$
$$940 \leq 1{,}000$$

As we can see, we do not need all 1,000 ounces, only 940. The difference of 60 ounces between the 1,000 ounces available and the 940 ounces used for optimal production are slack resources. The identification of slack resources can improve the efficiency of an operation by the better use of available resources.

QUESTION: Do we have any additional slack resources in either the mixing and preparation constraint or in the display space constraint?

ANSWER: No, there are no additional slack resources. This can be determined by either substituting the optimal decision variable values in each of the constraints and determining that the resources were totally used up or by reviewing the solution in the Slack/Surplus column of Exhibit D-3.

Another type of information useful to operations managers that the simplex method generates involves what LP modelers call the "dual problem."[2] The dual problem can give tradeoff information that operations managers can use to consider making changes in resource allocations (the LP model parameters) for specific problems. The interpretation of the Reduced Cost column in Exhibit D-3 for the maximization problem is that it provides the "relative loss" per unit of producing products that the LP model recommends not producing. Although there is no relative loss in producing cherry pies (x_1) or pumpkin pies (x_3), the 0.25 value in the Reduced Cost column in Exhibit D-3 indicates that the baker will lose $0.25 for each peach pie (x_2) produced.

This tradeoff loss would be incurred because we would have to take resources away from the production of the other pies to make the peach pies. The $0.25 is the net loss when the profit from the peach pies is substracted from the loss in profit on the other two pies. The interpretation of the Shadow Price column in Exhibit D-3 for the maximization problem provides the "marginal contribution to Z" of acquiring an additional unit of resources for production. Constraints whose right-hand-side values have shadow prices represent resources that were binding on the optimized Z. If an operations manager wants to improve the optimized value of Z, he or she should seek to alter the allocation of resources to these binding resources.

Although there is no relative contribution in acquiring additional ounces of capacity from the dough machine in constraint C1, opportunities can be added to increase profit by $2 for each hour of mixing and preparation time in constraint C2 and by $0.50 for each additional pie space. Unfortunately, the tradeoff opportunities suggested in the dual problem are limited. Only one alteration of the model can be implemented (that is, only one tradeoff can be acted on) at one time and even then the dual information may not be accurate (see footnote 2). The major value of the dual information to operations managers is that it can be used as a guide (albeit sometimes inaccurate) to identify the relative value of increasing the more binding or constraining resources in a production system. In the maximization problem, the dual shadow prices show that

[2] The "dual problem" is an advanced subject in LP modeling with a variety of limitations that can lead to misinformation unless great care is given to its interpretation. For a discussion of the dual problem see Chapter 4, S. M. Lee, L. Moore, and B. Taylor, *Management Science,* 3rd ed. (Boston: Allyn and Bacon, 1990); and David S. Rubin and H. M. Wagner, "Shadow Prices: Tips and Traps for Managers and Instructors," *Interfaces,* 20, No. 4 (1990), 150–157.

there is a profit advantage of \$2 to \$0.50 by increasing the resource of an hour of mixing and preparation time to increasing the resource of an additional pie space.

In this problem, all of the constraints were less-than or equal-to inequalities. Many problems have a mixture of the less-than or equal-to, greater-than or equal-to, and exact equality constraints in their LP formulation. These problems are called **mixed constraint problems.** Let's examine how to formulate a mixed constraint problem.

A Minimization Problem

A company produces two products: microcomputer model A and microcomputer model B. The company wants to determine how many units of each product it should manufacture next week to minimize its costs. The total cost of manufacturing a unit of model A is \$1,375, and the cost for a unit of model B is \$1,200. The company would like to meet or exceed the next week's minimum demand of 3,000 units of model A and 2,500 units of model B. Each model uses the same microchip processors but requires a different number of electronic components, referred to as "chippies." Model A requires a total of 15 chippies and model B requires only 10. The total available supply of chippies for the next week's production of microcomputers is 100,000. The company is also limited to 50,000 hours of labor from its manufacturing staff for next week. It takes 6 hours to manufacture one unit of model A and 5 hours to manufacture one unit of model B. Finally, the company has a contractual agreement with a union that the total production of model A and model B microcomputers must be equal to exactly 8,000 units for the next week.

Let's formulate this decision-making situation as an LP problem using the five-step formulation procedure.

Step 1: Determine the type of problem. We can see that only cost information, not profit information, is presented in this problem. So we are dealing with a cost-minimizing problem.

Step 2: Define the decision variables. The decision variables for this problem can be defined as follows:

x_1 = the number of units of microcomputer model A to manufacture next week

x_2 = the number of units of microcomputer model B to manufacture next week

Step 3: State the objective function. We can now state the objective function using the cost contribution coefficients found in step 1 and the decision variables defined in step 2.

$$\text{Minimize } Z = 1{,}375x_1 + 1{,}200x_2$$

Step 4: Formulate the constraints. In this step we must structure the constraints presented in the problem. To locate the constraints in this problem, try to identify the right-hand-side values first. The order with which you formulate constraints is not important, but it is important to include all of the constraints presented in a problem. The first right-hand-side value presented in the problem concerns the minimum demand of 3,000 units of model A. The constraint that will model this demand restriction is

$x_1 \geq 3{,}000$ (minimum demand for model A)

This constraint permits the number of units of model A to be greater than or equal to the minimum demand of 3,000 units. Also, it is perfectly acceptable that only one decision variable was included in the constraint. The constraint for model B is quite similar.

$x_2 \geq 2{,}500$ (minimum demand for model B)

The next constraint deals with the limitation on the use of the chippies. Because the next week's production is limited to a total of 100,000 chippies (the right-hand-side value), the constraint for this limitation is

$15x_1 + 10x_2 \leq 100{,}000$ (total supply of chippies)

The next constraint concerns the available labor hours and can be expressed as

$6x_1 + 5x_2 \leq 50{,}000$ (total supply of labor hours)

The final constraint concerns the contractual agreement restriction on total production. If total production of both model A and model B must equal 8,000 units, then the constraint for this is

$x_1 + x_2 = 8{,}000$ (total production of both models)

Step 5: State the nonnegative requirements. To complete the formulation of this problem we must state the nonnegative requirements.

$x_1, x_2 \geq 0$

The complete LP formulation for this microcomputer company's manufacturing problem is as follows:

$$\text{Minimize } Z = 1{,}375x_1 + 1{,}200x_1$$

$$\begin{aligned} \text{subject to:} \quad x_1 &\geq 3{,}000 \\ x_2 &\geq 2{,}500 \\ 15x_1 + 10x_2 &\leq 100{,}000 \\ 6x_1 + 5x_2 &\leq 50{,}000 \\ x_1 + x_2 &= 8{,}000 \\ x_1, x_2 &\geq 0 \end{aligned}$$

By solving for the optimal values of the decision variables, the microcomputer company will determine the exact number of units of both models to produce to minimize total cost, yet not violate any of the restrictions modeled as constraints. The computer-generated solution to this LP problem is presented in Exhibit D-4. The optimal solution values for this problem are $x_1 = 3{,}000$ units of model A, and $x_2 = 5{,}000$ units of model B, which will generate a total cost of $Z = \$10{,}125{,}000$. We can

EXHIBIT D-4 *MICRO PRODUCTION* SOFTWARE SOLUTION OUTPUT OF COMPUTER COMPANY'S MINIMIZATION LP PROBLEM

```
Program: Linear Programming

Problem Title : LP Problem #2

***** Input Data *****

Min Z = 1375X1 + 1200X2

Subject to

C1  1X1 >= 3000
C2  1X2 >= 2500
C3  15X1 + 10X2 <= 100000
C4  6X1 + 5X2 <= 50000
C5  1X1 + 1X2 = 8000

*****Program Output *****

Final Optimal Solution

Z =   10125000.000
```

Variable	Value	Reduced Cost
X 1	3000.000	0.000
X 2	5000.000	0.000

Constraint	Slack/Surplus	Shadow Price
C 1	0.000	-175.000
C 2	2500.000	0.000
C 3	5000.000	0.000
C 4	7000.000	0.000

```
***** End of Output *****
```

also see in the optimal solution presented in Exhibit D-2 that we had a surplus in demand of 2,500 units. We also had slack in two of the resources: 5,000 chippies not required for production and 7,000 hours of labor not required for production. These slack resources can and should be reallocated to improve the efficiency of resource utilization in the company.

For greater-than or equal-to constraints, we can have what is called surplus, like those C1 and C2 constraints seeking to constrain minimum demand in the cost-minimizing problem. The surplus in this problem represents the extra demand beyond the minimum demand levels set in C1 and C2. We can see in the Slack/Surplus column in Exhibit D-4 that there is zero surplus in C1, but 2,500 units of surplus demand beyond the minimum level of 2,500 set in C2. This information can be interpreted to mean that we must have a demand for model B of 5,000 units (2,500 + 2,500 of surplus) to minimize total costs. There is also a slack 5,000 units of chippies and 7,000 hours of slack labor resources not required to achieve the optimal cost-minimized Z value.

Although there are no values in the Reduced Cost column in Exhibit D-4, the interpretation of this column for a minimization problem is that it provides the "relative cost" of producing units of product the LP model recommended not producing. In the Shadow Price column in Exhibit D-4, we can see a value of -175 for C1. (The negative sign is because it came from a greater-than or equal-to constraint.) The interpretation of this shadow price is that there is an opportunity to increase total optimized cost by \$175 for each unit increase of minimum demand for model A, or, more importantly, for a cost-minimizing problem, we can decrease Z by \$175 for each unit of minimum demand we can decrease. For example, if we drop the current minimum demand in C1 from 3,000 units to 2,999, the resulting minimized total cost will drop \$175 from \$10,125,000 to \$10,124,825. (Students are encouraged to confirm this result by changing b_1 and rerunning the problem.)

LINEAR PROGRAMMING MODEL ASSUMPTIONS

As with many quantitative models, certain assumptions are necessary for the successful use of linear programming. If a problem facing an operations manager violates one or more of the following modeling assumptions, LP cannot be used as a decision-making technique:

1. *Linearity* The expressions used to model the constraints and the objective function must be linear.
2. *Proportionality* The values for the sum of the products of either the technology coefficients and their respective decision variables, or the contribution coefficients and their respective decision variables, must remain proportional, as the values of the decision variables change. In other words, there can be no joint interaction or synergistic change in the technology or contribution coefficients.
3. *Divisibility* We can use any fraction or whole unit of resources to generate the optimal decision variable values. The decision variable values can also be any fraction or whole number.
4. *Finiteness* The parameters and the resulting decision variables must be a finite number.
5. *Data certainty and static time period* All coefficients, a_{ij}, b_i, and c_j are assumed to be known with certainty over a static or fixed time period.

Many other management science techniques exist to model problems that do not satisfy these five assumptions of LP.[3] Many production functions, for example, are nonlinear and require nonlinear solution methods. A variety of other management science techniques are discussed in various chapters of this text.

---

[3] For a review of some of these management science techniques, see S. M. Lee, L. Moore, and B. Taylor, *Management Science,* 3rd ed. (Boston: Allyn and Bacon, 1990).

Simplex Method for Linear Programming

In several chapters of this text, the formulation process of linear programming (LP) has been applied to model operations management systems. (If you are unfamiliar with the LP formulation procedure, review the material in Appendix D.) The purpose of this appendix is to provide a brief introduction to the simplex method solution process for LP problems. The **simplex method** is a tabular or interative process that involves a series of mathematical steps. Before we can use the simplex method to solve an LP problem we must first load the LP formulation into an initial tableau form called a **simplex tableau.** Because the simplex method differs based on the type of LP problem (maximization or minimization problem), we will illustrate this solution method for both types of LP sample problems.

A MAXIMIZATION PROBLEM

Suppose that we have the following maximization problem:

Maximize $Z = 3x_1 + 2x_2$ (profit)

subject to: $3x_1 + 2x_2 \leq 18$ (hours of labor)

$x_1 \leq 4$ (units of materials)

and $x_1, x_2 \geq 0$

where x_1 is the number of units of product A to produce and x_2 is the number of units of product B to produce. Our objective is to determine the number of units of products A and B to produce that will maximize profit. To do this, we must first load the LP formulation into an initial simplex tableau.

LP Loading Procedure

The loading procedure consists of the following steps:

Step 1: Convert the constraints to equalities. For our sample problem the inequalities are converted into equalities by adding a slack variable s_i to the side of the inequality that can be less than the other side of the inequality. We can see in the first constraint that the sum of the left-hand side of the constraint can be less than 18. This constraint can be expressed as an equality as follows:

$$3x_1 + 2x_2 + s_1 = 18$$

The s_1 slack variable exists to take up any slack that would prevent the equality from holding true. If, for example, both decision variables were equal

EXHIBIT E-1 A LINEAR PROGRAMMING SIMPLEX TABLEAU CONFIGURATION

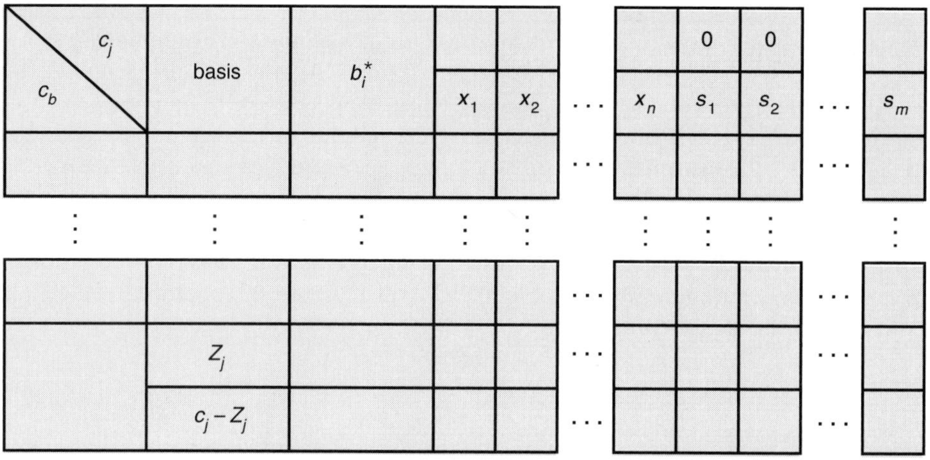

c_b \ c_j	basis	b_i^*					0	0		
			x_1	x_2	...	x_n	s_1	s_2	...	s_m
					...				...	
⋮	⋮	⋮	⋮	⋮		⋮	⋮	⋮		⋮
					...				...	
	Z_j				...				...	
	$c_j - Z_j$				...				...	

to three, then s_1 would also have to equal three to make the equation hold true. The other side constraint is similarly expressed as the equality as follows:

$$x_1 + s_2 = 4$$

Note that the slack variable in the second constraint has a different subscript because it represents the slack in a different constraint. Indeed, the two constraints really have been restructured into the following form:

$$3x_1 + 2x_2 + 1s_1 + 0s_2 = 18$$
$$x_1 + 0x_2 + 0s_1 + 1s_2 = 4$$

The zeros used as technology coefficients actually eliminate the variables they are attached to in the constraints.

Step 2: Draw the framework for the initial simplex tableau. The boxed framework used to hold the LP problem will be repeated several times with only minor changes. In Exhibit E-1 a generalized simplex tableau is presented. In Exhibit E-1 we can see several columns including c_b (the contribution coefficients for the solution basis variables), basis (the variables that make up the current solution), b_i^* (the values of the solution basis variables), x_j (columns for each of the decision variables in the model), and s_i (columns for each of the slack variables in the model). The boxes above the decision and slack variables are for their respective contribution coefficients. These values are found for the decision variables in the objective function. The slack variables are always given a value of 0 because they do not contribute anything to maximizing Z. For each constraint in the LP model, there is a separate row in the simplex tableau.

The single Z_j and the $c_j - Z_j$ rows are also part of the simplex tableau. They are always positioned under the basis column. The initial tableau framework for the sample LP maximization problem is presented in Exhibit E-2(a).

Step 3: Enter the data for the constraints into the initial simplex tableau. To enter the data for the constraints we first list the slack variables for each constraint under the basis column. We then assign the 0 contribution coefficient in the c_b column as presented in Exhibit E-2(b). We also place the right-hand-side values in the b_i^* column and place the constraint's respective technology coefficients in their appropriately labeled columns. We can see these values in Exhibit E-2(b) also.

EXHIBIT E-2 INITIAL SIMPLEX TABLEAU FOR SAMPLE MAXIMIZATION LP PROBLEM

(A) TABLEAU CONFIGURATION

c_b \ c_j	basis	b_i^*	3	2	0	0
			x_1	x_2	s_1	s_2
	Z_j					
	$c_j - Z_j$					

(B) CONSTRAINT DATA

c_b \ c_j	basis	b_i^*	3	2	0	0
			x_1	x_2	s_1	s_2
0	s_1	18	3	2	1	0
0	s_2	4	1	0	0	1
	Z_j					
	$c_j - Z_j$					

(continued on page 798)

EXHIBIT E-2 (CONTINUED)

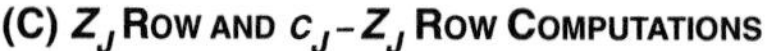

(C) Z_J ROW AND $c_J - Z_J$ ROW COMPUTATIONS

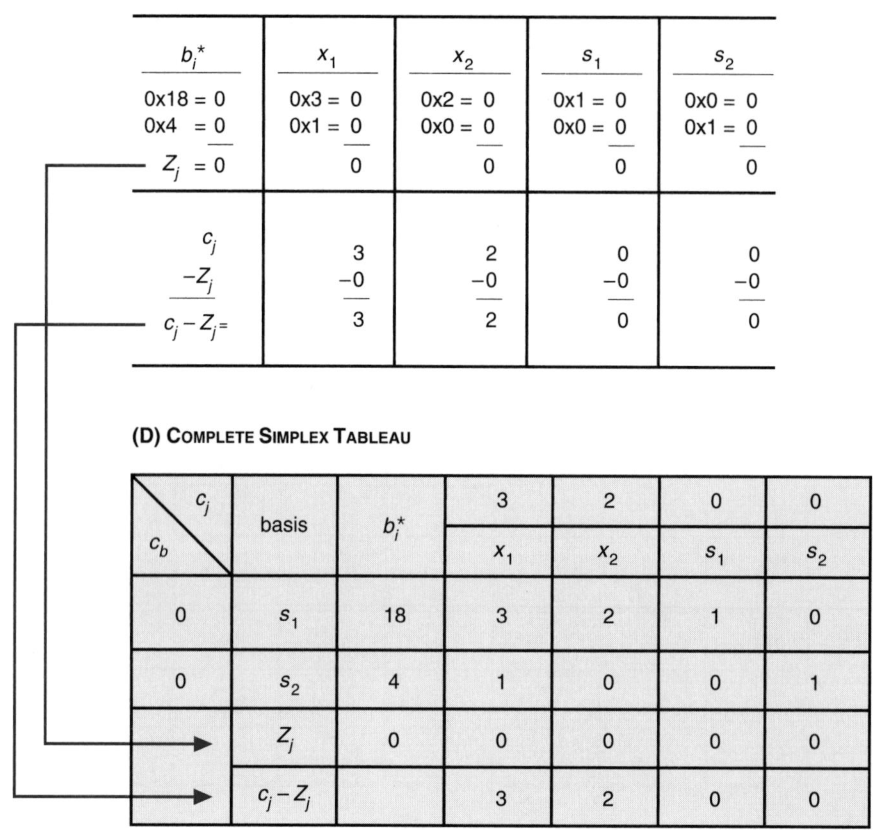

b_i^*	x_1	x_2	s_1	s_2
0x18 = 0	0x3 = 0	0x2 = 0	0x1 = 0	0x0 = 0
0x4 = 0	0x1 = 0	0x0 = 0	0x0 = 0	0x1 = 0
Z_j = 0	0	0	0	0
c_j	3	2	0	0
$-Z_j$	−0	−0	−0	−0
$c_j - Z_j$ =	3	2	0	0

(D) COMPLETE SIMPLEX TABLEAU

c_b \ c_j	basis	b_i^*	3	2	0	0
			x_1	x_2	s_1	s_2
0	s_1	18	3	2	1	0
0	s_2	4	1	0	0	1
	Z_j	0	0	0	0	0
	$c_j - Z_j$		3	2	0	0

Step 4: Calculate the values of Z_j and $c_j - Z_j$ and place them in the initial simplex tableau. The values of Z_j are calculated by using the following expression:

$$Z_j = \Sigma(c_b \times b_i^*) \text{ for } i = 1, 2, \ldots, m$$

There is one Z_j value for each of the columns starting from b_i^* and continuing to the last slack variable column. The Z_j values for the sample problem are presented in Exhibit E-2(c). The $c_j - Z_j$ values are computed for only the columns in the tableau that have a c_j value. The $c_j - Z_j$ values are simply the difference of the c_js at the top of each column and their respective Z_js. The $c_j - Z_j$ values for the sample problem are computed in Exhibit E-2(c).

As we can see in Exhibit E-2(d), the initial or first simplex tableau is now complete. We are now ready to begin using the simplex solution procedure to obtain a solution to the sample LP problem.

Simplex Solution Procedure for Maximization Problems

The simplex solution procedure consists of the following steps:

Step 1: Determine the variable to bring into the solution basis. Currently there are two variables (s_1 and s_2) in the solution basis. The **solution basis** defines, with the b_i^* column, what the current solution values are. In the initital tableau, $s_1 = 18$ and $s_2 = 4$. Because all of the variables not in the solution basis are automatically assigned a value of zero, $x_1 = 0$ and $x_2 = 0$. The variable to bring into the solution basis will be one of the variables in the columns of the simplex tableau. The choice is based on the values of the $c_j - Z_j$ row. The selection rule is as follows: The variable with the largest positive $c_j - Z_j$ value determines the variable column. We call this column the **pivot column** because it will repeatedly be used in later computations. For the sample problem, the largest positive $c_j - Z_j$ value is for the x_1 variable. We will therefore be bringing x_1 into the solution basis. To do this, we must remove one of the two variables currently in the solution basis.

Step 2: Determine the variable to remove from the solution basis. The variable to remove from the solution basis is determined by taking the positively signed technology coefficients in the pivot column and dividing them into the respective b_i^* column values. The ratio that is the smallest determines the variable (the pivot row) to remove from the solution basis. For the sample problem, the ratio for the s_1 row is 6 (18/3) and the ratio for the s_2 row is 4 (4/1). So the pivot row is s_2, and that slack variable will be removed from the solution basis to make room for the x_1 variable. We can see the pivot row (and pivot column) denoted in Exhibit E-3(a). The intersection of the pivot row and pivot column marks a tableau element referred to as the **pivot element.**

Step 3: Develop the next tableau. The simplex method is an iterative or repeating algebraic process of moving from tableau to tableau. To develop the next tableau, we start by drawing the same sized framework as was used for the first tableau. In positioning the variables we move the pivot column variable into the pivot row position as can be seen in Exhibit E-3(b). We must then compute the elements used in the second tableau. To do this, there are two required rules.

a. The elements in the new tableau that correspond to the pivot row elements in the old tableau are found by taking the ratio of each of the elements in the pivot row and the pivot element. For the sample problem, these elements are calculated in Exhibit E-3(c).

b. The elements in the new tableau that correspond to the remaining variable rows in the old tableau are found by using the following expression:

$$\text{New row value} = \text{Old row value} - \left(\begin{array}{c}\text{Corresponding} \\ \text{coefficient in} \\ \text{the old pivot} \\ \text{column}\end{array} \times \begin{array}{c}\text{New pivot} \\ \text{row value} \\ \\ \\ \end{array}\right)$$

EXHIBIT E-3 ITERATIVE SIMPLEX PROCESS APPLIED TO SAMPLE MAXIMIZATION LP PROBLEM

(A) FIRST TABLEAU FRAMEWORK WITH PIVOT ROW AND COLUMN DENOTED

Pivot Column: x_1 (↓)

c_b \ c_j	basis	b_i^*	3	2	0	0
			x_1	x_2	s_1	s_2
0	s_1	18	3	2	1	0
0 (Pivot Row →)	s_2	4	1	0	0	1
	Z_j	0	0	0	0	0
	$c_j - Z_j$		3	2	0	0

(B) SECOND TABLEAU FRAMEWORK

c_b \ c_j	basis	b_i^*	3	2	0	0
			x_1	x_2	s_1	s_2
0	s_1					
3	x_1					
	Z_j					
	$c_j - Z_j$					

For the sample problem, these elements are computed in Exhibit E-3(d). We then use the same procedure as previously discussed to calculate the Z_j and the $c_j - Z_j$ row values. These values' calculations are presented in Exhibit E-3(e).

Step 4. Interpret the solution and continue to an optimal solution. In this step we want to determine whether we have achieved an optimal solution. The optimality rule is as follows: if all of the values in the $c_j - Z_j$ row are not positive (that is, if they are zero or negative), we have an optimal solution. As we can see in Exhibit E-3(f), we do not have an optimal solution because we have a positive value in the $c_j - Z_j$ in s_2 column. This means that we should repeat

EXHIBIT E-3 (CONTINUED)

(C) x_1 ROW COMPUTATIONS

	b_i^*	x_1	x_2	s_1	s_2
x_1 →	4/1 = 4	1/1 = 1	0/1 = 0	0/1 = 0	1/1 = 1

(D) s_1 ROW COMPUTATIONS

	b_i^*	x_1	x_2	s_1	s_2
s_1 →	18−(3x4) = 6	3−(3x1) = 0	2−(3x0) = 2	1−(3x0) = 1	0−(3x1) = −3

(E) Z_J ROW AND $c_J - Z_J$ ROW COMPUTATIONS

b_i^*	x_1	x_2	s_1	s_2
0x6 = 0 3x4 = 12 Z_j = 12	0x0 = 0 3x1 = 3 3	0x2 = 0 3x0 = 0 0	0x1 = 0 3x0 = 0 0	0x−3 = 0 3x1 = 3 3
c_j $-Z_j$ $c_j - Z_j$ =	3 −3 0	2 −0 2	0 −0 0	0 −3 3

(F) COMPLETE SECOND TABLEAU

c_b \ c_j	basis	b_i^*	3	2	0	0
			x_1	x_2	s_1	s_2
0	s_1	6	0	2	1	−3
3	x_1	4	1	0	0	1
	Z_j	12	3	0	0	3
	$c_j - Z_j$		0	2	0	−3

the four steps of the simplex method to obtain the next or third tableau. These iterative steps are presented in Exhibit E-4. As we can see in Exhibit E-4(f), all of the values in the $c_j - Z_j$ row are either negative or zero. Thus, we have arrived at an optimal solution. This means that no other combinations of values exist for the basis variables that satisfy the constraints and will also increase the value of Z. What is the solution? Consistent with the solution basis in the third tableau, the solution is $x_1 = 4$, $x_2 = 3$, and $Z = 18$.

In addition to the solution of the LP problem, the simplex method also provides useful information on the contribution of resources that constrain the maximized value of Z. In Chapter 5 we described the right-hand side of a constraint typically as available resources such as hours of labor, units of materials, or square feet of inventory storage space. Operations managers can obtain information on the contribution to Z that a single unit of a resource can make when they use the simplex method to solve an LP problem.

In the LP sample problem just presented, we used two resources (hours of labor and units of materials) to produce the two products x_1 and x_2. Suppose that we now could change the problem by adding an hour of labor. How much of an increase in profit or Z can we expect for an hour's increase in labor? How much of an increase in Z can we expect for an increase in one unit of materials? What happens when we have to decrease either resource? This type of information is very valuable for planning resource changes in operations management systems. The answers to these questions can be partially obtained in the $c_j - Z_j$ row of the optimal simplex tableau.

Each constraint in an LP problem is represented with a slack variable positioned in a column in the simplex tableau. The absolute value of the $c_j - Z_j$ row element in an optimal simplex tableau reflects the marginal contribution to Z of one unit of the resource it represents. In other words,

$$\begin{pmatrix}\text{Marginal contribution}\\ \text{of a resource } b_i\end{pmatrix} = |c_j - Z_j| \text{ (for each } i\text{th slack variable)}$$

Because Z is in terms of profit dollars, the marginal contribution is also in terms of profit dollars. For the sample problem we must again turn to the optimal simplex tableau in Exhibit E-4(f). The marginal value of adding one hour of labor is \$1 (note the absolute value of the $c_j - Z_j$ row value in the s_1 column). So if we were to add an additional hour of labor to the 18 currently used (increase labor to 19 hours) in the sample problem, we can expect Z to increase from \$18 to \$19. Alternatively, if we had to decrease labor by 2 hours, we can expect Z to decrease from \$18 to \$16. In the case of the units of materials resource, the marginal value is \$0. This can be interpreted as meaning that we can increase or decrease the units of materials used to produce the products with no change in Z. Unfortunately, the values of the marginal contribution have limits or boundaries that limit how much of a change in the resource we can make before the contribution to Z changes. These boundaries can be computed using a procedure called *sensitivity analysis*. The topic of sensitivity analysis is beyond the scope of this textbook.

EXHIBIT E-4 SIMPLEX MAXIMIZATION PROCESS CONTINUED

(A) SECOND TABLEAU WITH PIVOT ROW AND COLUMN DENOTED

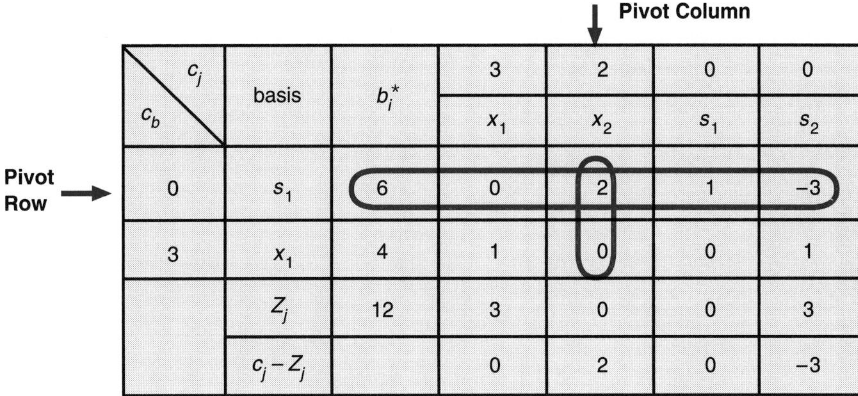

c_b \ c_j	basis	b_i^*	3	2 (Pivot Column)	0	0
			x_1	x_2	s_1	s_2
0 (Pivot Row)	s_1	6	0	2	1	−3
3	x_1	4	1	0	0	1
	Z_j	12	3	0	0	3
	$c_j - Z_j$		0	2	0	−3

(B) THIRD TABLEAU FRAMEWORK

c_b \ c_j	basis	b_i^*	3	2	0	0
			x_1	x_2	s_1	s_2
2	x_2					
3	x_1					
	Z_j					
	$c_j - Z_j$					

(continued on page 804)

A MINIMIZATION PROBLEM

Suppose that we have the following minimization problem:

$$\begin{aligned} &\text{Minimize } Z = 4x_1 + 6x_2 \\ &\text{subject to:} \quad x_1 + x_2 \geq 8 \\ &\qquad\qquad\quad 2x_1 + x_2 \geq 12 \\ &\text{and} \qquad\qquad x_1, x_2 \geq 0 \end{aligned}$$

EXHIBIT E-4 (CONTINUED)

(C) x_2 ROW COMPUTATIONS

	b_i^*	x_1	x_2	s_1	s_2
x_2 →	6/2 = 3	0/2 = 0	2/2 = 1	1/2 = 1/2	−3/2 = −3/2

(D) x_1 ROW COMPUTATIONS

	b_i^*	x_1	x_2	s_1	s_2
x_1 →	4−(0x3) = 4	1−(0x0) = 1	0−(0x1) = 0	0−(0x1/2) = 0	1−(0x−3/2) = 1

(E) Z_J ROW AND $Z_J - c_J$ ROW COMPUTATIONS

b_i^*	x_1	x_2	s_1	s_2
2x3 = 6	2x0 = 0	2x1 = 2	2x1/2 = 1	2x−3/2 = −3
3x4 = 12	3x1 = 3	3x0 = 0	3x0 = 0	3x1 = 3
Z_j = 18	3	2	1	0
c_j	3	2	0	0
$-Z_j$	−3	−2	−1	−0
$c_j - Z_j$ =	0	0	−1	0

(F) COMPLETE THIRD TABLEAU

c_b \ c_j	basis	b_i^*	3	2	0	0
			x_1	x_2	s_1	s_2
2	x_2	3	0	1	1/2	−3/2
3	x_1	4	1	0	0	1
	Z_j	18	3	2	1	0
	$c_j - Z_j$		0	0	−1	0

Our objective is to determine the values of the decision variables that will produce the minimum Z. To do this, we again must first load the LP formulation into an initial simplex tableau.

LP Loading Procedure

The loading procedure is basically the same as for the maximization problem but with a few minor differences. The procedure consists of the following steps:

Step 1: Convert the constraints to equalities. For our sample problem, the inequalities are converted into equalities by adding a slack variable s_i to the right-hand side of the inequality and adding an artificial variable A_i to the left-hand side of the inequality. The artificial variable is a necessary requirement for this type of simplex procedure. For our sample problem, the first constraint can be expressed as an equality as follows:

$$x_1 + x_2 - s_1 + A_1 = 8$$

The other constraint is similarly expressed as an equality as follows:

$$2x_1 + x_2 - s_2 + A_2 = 12$$

Note that the slack variable in the second constraint has a different subscript because it is a different variable for a different constraint. Indeed, the two constraints really have been restructured into the following form:

$$\begin{aligned} x_1 + x_2 - 1s_1 - 0s_2 + 1A_1 + 0A_2 &= 8 \\ 2x_1 + 1x_2 - 0s_1 - 1s_2 + 0A_1 + 1A_2 &= 12 \end{aligned}$$

The zeros used as technology coefficients actually eliminate the variables they are attached to in the constraints.

Artificial variables are also used in the LP loading procedure to include equality constraints. Although not illustrated in this minimization problem, the general form for including an equality constraint in a minimization problem is as follows:

$$a_{ij}\, x_j - A_i = b_i \text{ for all } i, j$$

Note that there are no slack variables necessary in this constraint because no slack is possible in an equality statement. The general form for including an equality constraint in a maximization problem is as follows:

$$a_{ij}\, x_j + A_i = b_i \text{ for all } i, j$$

Step 2: Draw the framework for the initial simplex tableau. The boxed framework used to hold the LP problem will be repeated several times with only minor changes. In addition to columns for c_b, basis, b_i^*, x_j, and s_i variables, we must also have columns for A_i or artificial variables. The boxes above the decision, slack, and artificial variables are for their respective contribution coefficients.

The values for the slack and decision variables are the same as in maximization problems. The coefficients for the artificial variables are a symbolic M, representing a very large number like one million. For each constraint in the LP model, there is a separate row in the simplex tableau. The single Z_j and the $Z_j - c_j$ rows are also part of the simplex tableau. They are always positioned under the basis column. The initial tableau framework for the sample LP minimization problem is presented in Exhibit E-5(a).

Step 3: Enter the data for the constraints into the initial simplex tableau. To enter the data for the constraints we first list the artificial variables for each constraint under the basis column. We then assign the M contribution coefficient in the c_b column as presented in Exhibit E-5(b). We then place the right-hand-side values in the b_i^* column and also place the constraints' respective technology

EXHIBIT E-5 INITIAL SIMPLEX TABLEAU FOR MINIMIZATION SAMPLE LP PROBLEM

(A) TABLEAU CONFIGURATION

c_b \ c_j	basis	b_i^*	4	6	0	0	M	M
			x_1	x_2	s_1	s_2	A_1	A_2
	Z_j							
	$Z_j - c_j$							

(B) CONSTRAINT DATA

c_b \ c_j	basis	b_i^*	4	6	0	0	M	M
			x_1	x_2	s_1	s_2	A_1	A_2
M	A_1	8	1	1	−1	0	1	0
M	A_2	12	2	1	0	−1	0	1
	Z_j							
	$Z_j - c_j$							

EXHIBIT E-5 (CONTINUED)

(C) Z_J ROW AND $Z_J - C_J$ ROW COMPUTATIONS

b_i^*	x_1	x_2	s_1	s_2	A_1	A_2
Mx8 = 8M	Mx1 = M	Mx1 = M	Mx−1 = −M	Mx0 = 0	Mx1 = M	Mx0 = 0
Mx12 = 12M	Mx2 = 2M	Mx1 = M	Mx0 = 0	Mx−1 = −M	Mx0 = 0	Mx1 = M
Z_j = 20M	3M	2M	−M	−M	M	M
Z_j	3M	2M	−M	−M	M	M
$-c_j$	−4	−6	−0	−0	−M	−M
$Z_j - c_j$	= 3M−4	2M−6	−M	−M	0	0

(D) COMPLETE SECOND TABLEAU

c_b \ c_j	basis	b_i^*	4	6	0	0	M	M
			x_1	x_2	s_1	s_2	A_1	A_2
M	A_1	8	1	1	−1	0	1	0
M	A_2	12	2	1	0	−1	0	1
	Z_j	20M	3M	2M	−M	−M	M	M
	$Z_j - c_j$		3M−4	2M−6	−M	−M	0	0

coefficients in their appropriately labeled columns. We can see these values in Exhibit E-5(b).

Step 4: Calculate the values of Z_j and $Z_j - c_j$ and place them in the initial simplex tableau. The values of Z_j are calculated by using the same type of expression as before:

$$Z_j = \Sigma\, (c_b \times b_i^*) \text{ for } i = 1, 2, \ldots, m$$

There is one Z_j value for each of the columns starting from b_i^* to the last artificial variable column. The Z_j values for the sample problem are presented in Exhibit E-5(c). The $Z_j - c_j$ values are computed for only the columns in the tableau that have a c_j value. The $Z_j - c_j$ values are simply the difference of the Z_j values at the top of each column and their respective c_j values. The $Z_j - c_j$ values for the sample problem are computed in Exhibit E-5(c).

As we can see in Exhibit E-5(d), the initial or first simplex tableau is now complete. We are ready to begin using the simplex solution procedure to obtain a solution to the sample LP problem.

Simplex Solution Procedure for Minimization Problems

The simplex solution procedure for minimization problems is the same as for maximization problems. To illustrate the steps we will apply them to the minimization problem.

Step 1: Determine the variable to bring into the solution basis. The choice is based on the values of the $Z_j - c_j$ row. The selection rule is: The variable with the largest positive $Z_j - c_j$ value determines the variable column. For the sample problem, the largest positive $Z_j - c_j$ value is for the x_1 variable. We will therefore be bringing x_1 into the solution basis.

Step 2: Determine the variable to remove from the solution basis. The variable to remove from the solution basis is again determined by taking the positively signed technology coefficients in the pivot column and dividing them into the respective b_i^* column values. The ratio that is the smallest determines the variable (pivot row) to remove from the solution basis. For the sample problem, the ratio for the A_1 row is 8 (8/1), and the ratio for the A_2 row is 6 (12/2). So the pivot row is A_2, and that artificial variable will be removed from the solution basis to make room for the x_1 variable. We can see the pivot row (and pivot column) denoted in Exhibit E-6(a). The intersection of the pivot row and pivot column marks a tableau element that is again referred to as the pivot element.

Step 3: Develop the next tableau. To develop the next tableau, we start by dropping off the column of any artificial variable that is removed from the solution basis. In positioning the variables we move the pivot column variable into the pivot row position as can be seen in Exhibit E-6(b). We must then compute the elements using the same two rules used for the maximization problem.

a. The elements in the new tableau that correspond to the pivot row elements in the old tableau are found by taking the ratio of each of the elements in the pivot row and the pivot element. For the sample problem, these elements are calculated in Exhibit E-6(c).

b. The elements in the new tableau that correspond to the remaining variable rows in the old tableau are found by using the following expression:

$$\text{New row value} = \text{Old row value} - \left(\begin{array}{ll}\text{Corresponding} \times & \text{New pivot} \\ \text{coefficient in} & \text{row value} \\ \text{the old pivot} & \\ \text{column} & \end{array}\right)$$

For the sample problem, these elements are computed in Exhibit E-6(d). We then use the same procedure as previously discussed to calculate the Z_j

EXHIBIT E-6 ITERATIVE SIMPLEX PROCESS APPLIED TO SAMPLE MINIMIZATION LP PROBLEM

(A) FIRST TABLEAU FRAMEWORK WITH PIVOT ROW AND COLUMN DENOTED

Pivot Column: x_1; Pivot Row: A_2

c_b \ c_j	basis	b_i^*	4	6	0	0	M	M
			x_1	x_2	s_1	s_2	A_1	A_2
M	A_1	8	1	1	−1	0	1	
M	A_2	12	2	1	0	−1	0	1
	Z_j	$20M$	$3M$	$2M$	$-M$	$-M$	M	M
	$Z_j - c_j$		$3M-4$	$2M-6$	$-M$	$-M$	0	0

(B) SECOND TABLEAU FRAMEWORK

c_b \ c_j	basis	b_i^*	4	6	0	0	M
			x_1	x_2	s_1	s_2	A_1
M	A_1						
4	x_1						
	Z_j						
	$Z_j - c_j$						

(*continued on page 810*)

and the $Z_j - c_j$ row values. These values' calculations are presented in Exhibit E-6(e).

Step 4: Interpret the solution and continue to an optimal solution. In this step we want to determine if we have achieved an optimal solution. The optimality rule is as follows: if all of the values in the $Z_j - c_j$ row are not positive (that is, if they are zero or negative), we have an optimal solution. As we can see in Exhibit E-6(f), we do not have an optimal solution because we have positive values in the x_2 and the s_2 columns. This means that we should repeat the four steps of the simplex method to obtain the next or third tableau. These iterative steps are presented in Exhibit E-7. As we can see in Exhibit E-7(f), all of the values in the $Z_j - c_j$ row are either negative or zero. Thus, we have arrived at

EXHIBIT E-6 (CONTINUED)

(C) x_1 ROW COMPUTATIONS

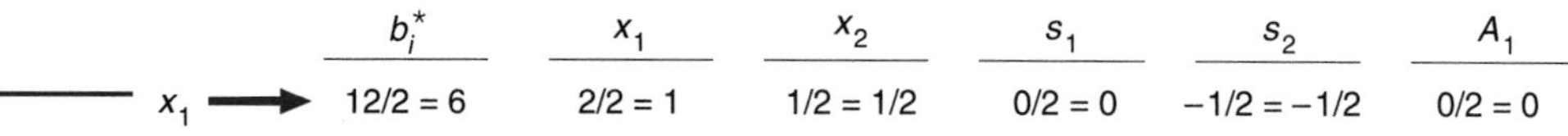

	b_i^*	x_1	x_2	s_1	s_2	A_1
x_1 →	12/2 = 6	2/2 = 1	1/2 = 1/2	0/2 = 0	−1/2 = −1/2	0/2 = 0

(D) A_1 ROW COMPUTATIONS

	b_i^*	x_1	x_2	s_1	s_2	A_1
A_1 →	8−(1x6) = 2	1−(1x1) = 0	1−(1x1/2) = 1/2	−1−(1x0) = −1	0−(1x1/2) = 1/2	1−(1x0) = 1

(E) Z_J ROW AND $Z_J - c_J$ ROW COMPUTATIONS

b_i^*	x_1	x_2	s_1	s_2	A_1
Mx2 = 2M 4x6 = 24 Z_j = 2M+24	Mx0 = 0 4x1 = 4 4	Mx1/2 = 1/2M 4x1/2 = 2 1/2M+2	Mx−1 = −M 4x0 = 0 −M	Mx1/2 = 1/2M 4x−1/2 = −2 1/2M−2	Mx1 = M 4x0 = 0 M
Z_j $-c_j$ $Z_j - c_j$ =	4 −4 0	1/2M + 2 −6 1/2M−4	−M 0 −M	1/2M−2 0 1/2M−2	M −M 0

(F) COMPLETE SECOND TABLEAU

c_b \ c_j	basis	b_i^*	4	6	0	0	M
			x_1	x_2	s_1	s_2	A_1
M	A_1	2	0	1/2	−1	1/2	1
4	x_1	6	1	1/2	0	−1/2	0
	Z_j	2M + 24	4	1/2M+2	−M	1/2M−2	M
	$Z_j - c_j$		0	1/2M−4	−M	1/2M−2	0

EXHIBIT E-7 SIMPLEX MINIMIZATION PROCESS CONTINUED

(A) SECOND TABLEAU WITH PIVOT ROW AND COLUMN DENOTED

Pivot Column: s_2 — Pivot Row: A_1

c_b \ c_j	basis	b_i^*	4	6	0	0	M
			x_1	x_2	s_1	s_2	A_1
M	A_1	2	0	1/2	−1	1/2	1
4	x_1	6	1	1/2	0	−1/2	0
	Z_j	$2M + 24$	4	$1/2M + 2$	$-M$	$1/2M - 2$	M
	$Z_j - c_j$		0	$1/2M - 4$	$-M$	$1/2M - 2$	0

(B) THIRD TABLEAU FRAMEWORK

c_b \ c_j	basis	b_i^*	4	6	0	0
			x_1	x_2	s_1	s_2
0	s_2					
4	x_1					
	Z_j					
	$Z_j - c_j$					

(continued on page 812)

an optimal solution. This means that no other combinations of values exist for our basis variables that satisfy the constraints and will also decrease the value of Z. What is the solution? Consistent with the solution basis in the third tableau, the solution is $x_1 = 8$, $x_2 = 0$, $s_2 = 4$, and $Z = 32$.

Many complications and problems can occur in the use of the simplex method in solving LP problems. The presentation here was meant only to introduce you to the basics of the simplex process. Readers are encouraged to review other books on the subject to acquaint themselves more thoroughly with the technical procedures of LP.[1]

---

[1] For a good review of linear programming, see S. M. Lee and J. P. Shim, *Micro Management Science*, 2nd ed. (Boston: Allyn and Bacon, 1990), Chapters 4 and 5.

EXHIBIT E-7 (CONTINUED)

(C) x_1 ROW COMPUTATIONS

	b_i^*	x_1	x_2	s_1	s_2
x_1 →	6−(−1/2x4) = 8	1−(−1/2x0) = 1	1/2−(−1/2x1) = 1	0−(−1/2x−2) = −1	−1/2−(−1/2x1) = 0

(D) A_1 ROW COMPUTATIONS

	b_i^*	x_1	x_2	s_1	s_2
A_1 →	2 / 1/2 = 4	0/ 1/2 = 0	1/2 / 1/2 = 1	−1/ 1/2 = −2	1/2 / 1/2 = 1

(E) Z_J ROW AND $Z_J - c_J$ ROW COMPUTATIONS

b_i^*	x_1	x_2	s_1	s_2
0x4 = 0	0x0 = 0	0x1 = 0	0x−2 = 0	0x1 = 0
4x8 = 32	4x1 = 4	4x1 = 4	4x−1 = −4	4x0 = 0
Z_j = 32	4	4	−4	0
Z_j	4	4	−4	0
$-c_j$	−4	−6	−0	−0
$Z_j - c_j$ =	0	−2	−4	0

(F) COMPLETE THIRD TABLEAU

c_b \ c_j	basis	b_i^*	4	6	0	0
			x_1	x_2	s_1	s_2
0	s_2	4	0	1	−2	1
4	x_1	8	1	1	−1	0
	Z_j	32	4	4	−4	0
	$Z_j - c_j$		0	−2	−4	0

APPENDIX F

Random Number Table

39 65 76 45 45	19 90 69 64 61	20 26 36 31 62	58 24 97 14 97	95 06 70 99 00
73 71 23 70 90	65 97 60 12 11	31 56 34 19 19	47 83 75 51 33	30 62 38 20 46
72 20 47 33 84	51 67 47 97 19	98 40 07 17 66	23 05 09 51 80	59 78 11 52 49
75 17 25 69 17	17 95 21 78 58	24 33 45 77 48	69 81 84 09 29	93 22 70 45 80
37 48 79 88 74	63 52 06 34 30	01 31 60 10 27	35 07 79 71 53	28 99 52 01 41
02 89 08 16 94	85 53 83 29 95	56 27 09 24 43	21 78 55 09 82	72 61 88 73 61
87 18 15 70 07	37 79 49 12 38	48 13 93 55 96	41 92 45 71 51	09 18 25 58 94
98 83 71 70 15	89 09 39 59 24	00 06 41 41 20	14 36 59 25 47	54 45 17 24 89
10 08 58 07 04	76 62 16 48 68	58 76 17 14 86	59 53 11 52 21	66 04 18 72 87
47 90 56 37 31	71 82 13 50 41	27 55 10 24 92	28 04 67 53 44	95 23 00 84 47
93 05 31 03 07	34 18 04 52 35	74 13 39 35 22	68 95 23 92 35	36 63 70 35 33
21 89 11 47 99	11 20 99 45 18	76 51 94 84 86	13 79 93 37 55	98 16 04 41 67
95 18 94 06 97	27 37 83 28 71	79 57 95 13 91	09 61 87 25 21	56 20 11 32 44
97 08 31 55 73	10 65 81 92 59	77 31 61 95 46	20 44 90 32 64	26 99 76 75 63
69 26 88 86 13	59 71 74 17 32	48 38 75 93 29	73 37 32 04 05	60 82 29 20 25
41 47 10 25 03	87 63 93 95 17	81 83 83 04 49	77 45 85 50 51	79 88 01 97 30
91 94 14 63 62	08 61 74 51 69	92 79 43 89 79	29 18 94 51 23	14 85 11 47 23
80 06 54 18 47	08 52 85 08 40	48 40 35 94 22	72 65 71 08 86	50 03 42 99 36
67 72 77 63 99	89 85 84 46 06	64 71 06 21 66	89 37 20 70 01	61 65 70 22 12
59 40 24 13 75	42 29 72 23 19	06 94 76 10 08	81 30 15 39 14	81 83 17 16 33
63 62 06 34 41	79 53 36 02 95	94 61 09 43 62	20 21 14 68 86	84 95 48 46 45
78 47 23 53 90	79 93 96 38 63	34 85 52 05 09	85 43 01 72 73	14 93 87 81 40
87 68 62 15 43	97 48 72 66 48	53 16 71 13 81	59 97 50 99 52	24 62 20 42 31
47 60 92 10 77	26 97 05 73 51	88 46 38 03 58	72 68 49 29 31	75 70 16 08 24
56 88 87 59 41	06 87 37 78 48	65 88 69 58 39	88 02 84 27 83	85 81 56 39 38
22 17 68 65 84	87 02 22 57 51	68 69 80 95 44	11 29 01 95 80	49 34 35 86 47
19 36 27 59 46	39 77 32 77 09	79 57 92 36 59	89 74 39 82 15	08 58 94 34 74
16 77 23 02 77	28 06 24 25 93	22 45 44 84 11	87 80 61 65 31	09 71 91 74 25
78 43 76 71 61	97 67 63 99 61	80 45 67 93 82	59 73 19 85 23	53 33 65 97 21
03 28 28 26 08	69 30 16 09 05	53 58 47 70 93	66 56 45 65 79	45 56 20 19 47
04 31 17 21 56	33 73 99 19 87	26 72 39 27 67	53 77 57 68 93	60 61 97 22 61
61 06 98 03 91	87 14 77 43 96	43 00 65 98 50	45 60 33 01 07	98 99 46 50 47
23 68 35 26 00	99 53 93 61 28	52 70 05 48 34	56 65 05 61 86	90 92 10 70 80
15 39 25 70 99	93 86 52 77 65	15 33 59 05 28	22 87 26 07 47	86 96 98 29 06
58 71 96 30 24	18 46 23 34 27	85 13 99 24 44	49 18 09 79 49	74 16 32 23 02
93 22 53 64 39	07 10 63 76 35	87 03 04 79 88	08 13 13 85 51	55 34 57 72 69
78 76 58 54 74	92 38 70 96 92	52 06 79 79 45	82 63 18 27 44	69 66 92 19 09
61 81 31 96 82	00 57 25 60 59	46 72 60 18 77	55 66 12 62 11	08 99 55 64 57
42 88 07 10 05	24 98 65 63 21	47 21 61 88 32	27 80 30 21 60	10 92 35 36 12
77 94 30 05 39	28 10 99 00 27	12 73 73 99 12	49 99 57 94 82	96 88 57 17 91

APPENDIX G

Exponential Probability Distribution

The probability values in this table are derived from *e* (or 2.7183) raised to the negative power of *x* or e^{-x} for select values of *x* from 0 to 10. When used in quality reliability estimation, the value of *x* is equal to the ratio of *t*/MTBF. Intermediate values can be obtained by using the following relationship: $e^{-(a+b)} = (e^{-a})(e^{-b})$. For example: $e^{-1.0} = 0.368$ and $e^{-0.2} = 0.819$, so $e^{-(1.0+0.2)} = e^{-1.2} = (0.368)(0.819) = 0.301$, as can also be seen in the following table.

X	e^{-x}	X	e^{-x}	X	e^{-x}	X	e^{-x}
.00	1.000	.40	.670	.80	.449	3.00	.04979
.01	.990	.41	.664	.81	.445	3.10	.04505
.02	.980	.42	.657	.82	.440	3.20	.04076
.03	.970	.43	.651	.83	.436	3.30	.03688
.04	.961	.44	.644	.84	.432	3.40	.03337
.05	.951	.45	.638	.85	.427	3.50	.03020
.06	.942	.46	.631	.86	.423	3.60	.02732
.07	.932	.47	.625	.87	.419	3.70	.02472
.08	.923	.48	.619	.88	.415	3.80	.02237
.09	.914	.49	.613	.89	.411	3.90	.02024
.10	.905	.50	.607	.90	.407	4.00	.01832
.11	.896	.51	.600	.91	.403	4.10	.01657
.12	.887	.52	.595	.92	.399	4.20	.01500
.13	.878	.53	.589	.93	.395	4.30	.01357
.14	.869	.54	.583	.94	.391	4.40	.01228
.15	.861	.55	.577	.95	.387	4.50	.01111
.16	.852	.56	.571	.96	.383	4.60	.01005
.17	.844	.57	.566	.97	.379	4.70	.00910
.18	.835	.58	.560	.98	.375	4.80	.00823
.19	.827	.59	.554	.99	.372	4.90	.00745
.20	.819	.60	.549	1.00	.368	5.00	.00674
.21	.811	.61	.543	1.10	.333	5.50	.00409
.22	.803	.62	.538	1.20	.301	6.00	.00248
.23	.795	.63	.533	1.30	.273	6.50	.00150
.24	.787	.64	.527	1.40	.247	7.00	.00091
.25	.779	.65	.522	1.50	.223	7.50	.00055
.26	.771	.66	.517	1.60	.202	8.00	.00034
.27	.763	.67	.512	1.70	.183	8.50	.00020
.28	.756	.68	.507	1.80	.165	9.00	.00012
.29	.748	.69	.502	1.90	.150	10.00	.00005
.30	.741	.70	.497	2.00	.135		
.31	.733	.71	.492	2.10	.122		
.32	.726	.72	.487	2.20	.111		
.33	.719	.73	.482	2.30	.100		
.34	.712	.74	.477	2.40	.091		
.35	.705	.75	.472	2.50	.082		
.36	.698	.76	.468	2.60	.074		
.37	.691	.77	.463	2.70	.067		
.38	.684	.78	.458	2.80	.061		
.39	.677	.79	.454	2.90	.055		

APPENDIX H

Instructions on How To Use *Micro Production* Software System

HARDWARE REQUIREMENTS FOR *MICRO PRODUCTION*

Micro Production has been developed for application on an IBM personal computer or a variety of IBM-compatible microcomputers. It will work with either a color or monochrome monitor.

Micro Production requires 640K RAM (the memory in the machine for programs and data) to run all of the programs described in this text. Other hardware requirements are: at least one disk drive and an IBM, Epson, or similar printer. If you have a printer other than those just listed or are unsure about its capabilities, test a few of the programs and see whether they print correctly. If not, utility programs are available from your printer dealer or manufacturer that will make your printer respond like an IBM or Epson printer.

INSTALLING AND STARTING *MICRO PRODUCTION*

Before you can run *Micro Production*, you must boot the computer. It is possible that your computer has already been booted, in which case you can skip the following steps. A computer that has been properly booted will display on its monitor a drive indicator, such as the following:

A>

B>

C>

C:Ø>

D:Ømpom>

If your computer has not already been booted and you are using a **floppy drive only system,** proceed according to the following steps:

1. Insert your computer's DOS disk into drive A.
2. Close the disk drive door.
3. If the computer is off, turn it on; if it is already on, press simultaneously the <Ctrl>, <Alt>, and <Del> keys.
4. If the system prompts you for date and time, enter these items.
5. You should now see an A> (or similar drive indicator) on the screen.

If your computer has not already been booted and you are using a **hard (fixed) drive system,** use the steps listed at the top of page 816.

1. Remove any disk presently in floppy drive A.
2. If the computer is off, turn it on; if it's already on do *one* of the following: (a) press the "Reboot" button on the computer; (b) press simultaneously the <Ctrl>, <Alt>, and <Del> keys; OR (c) turn off the computer, wait until all noises stop, and turn it on again.

At this point, you should have a properly booted computer with a drive indicator showing on the screen. If the indicator is not A> or A:Ø>, you will need to tell the system to change its default operating drive. You can do this by placing the *Micro Production* disk 1 into drive A, closing the drive door, and typing

A: <Enter>

<Enter> means strike the key labeled "Enter" or "Return" on your keyboard.

You can now start *Micro Production* by typing the appropriate command:

mpom <Enter>

It doesn't matter whether you use capital or lowercase letters. The light on drive A should glow, and you will shortly see the publisher's logo, followed by the *Micro Production* title screen. The main menu will appear, allowing you to choose the program you wish to use. Note that the $5\frac{1}{4}$-inch *Micro Production* disk 1 contains the program shown on the left side of the main menu, so that you need to replace it with disk 2 to execute a program on the right side of the menu. It is not necessary to replace a $3\frac{1}{2}$-inch disk.

Working Space and Data Storage

Micro Production requires working space on a disk, where it will store temporary working files to hold input, intermediate results, and output until you store the problem or exit the program. If you have no other option, you may use the *Micro Production* disk for working space and data storage, but we strongly advise against this practice. Using the program disks for data storage may damage the program's command files.

It is always safest to use *Micro Production* with the program disks in a **write-protected state.** This means that on $5\frac{1}{4}$-inch disks the notch cut into the sleeve near the upper-right corner has been covered with a write-protect tab (or strong tape), and on $3\frac{1}{2}$-inch disks the small sliding write-protect tab has been moved so that the hole through the disk is open.

To store data on the program disk, or to run the system without a data disk, you must ensure that the disk in drive A is not write-protected. It is possible that the system will exit from *Micro Production* if it cannot find working space on a non-write-protected disk.

To designate another drive as the working space and data storage disk drive, use the "Install" command, described later in these instructions. Floppy disks must be formatted before use. *Micro Production* does not have the capability to format new disks; you must use your DOS disk to accomplish this.

If your system has only one floppy drive, you may store data on a hard (fixed) drive (if your computer has one), or you may switch disks in drive A at the appropriate times, replacing the program disk with the data disk. To use the switching option, you will need to "Install" drive B as the working disk drive, even though it doesn't physically exist. Your computer's operating system will recognize the need to switch disks this way, and will inform you of the disk it requires by on-screen messages.

Hard (Fixed) Disk Program Installation

Micro Production software is not copy protected so it can be easily installed on hard disks. Please note that you should not install any programs on any hard disks that are not your own without permission of the owner. Also, copyright restrictions may apply when it is possible for multiple copies of the same disks to be used at the same time. Read the copyright notice that comes with the sofeware, or contact the publisher, if you have any questions in this regard.

Micro Production will need approximately 700K (or 700,000 bytes) of hard disk space. The exact amount of space used will depend on the technical specifications of the hard disk. Additional memory will be required for working space and data storage; this depends on the program you are using and the size of the model.

To copy *Micro Production* to a hard disk, you should first create a directory for the program files. Assuming that the hard disk you wish to use is named drive C,

1. Make C the default drive by typing

   C: <Enter>

2. Return to the root directory.

   cd Ø <Enter>

3. Make a subdirectory for *Micro Production.*

   md Ømpom <Enter>

4. Change the default to this subdirectory.

   cd Ømpom <Enter>

5. Place the *Micro Production* disk 1 in drive A, and copy the files onto the hard disk.

   copy a:*.* <Enter>

6. If you are using the 5¼-inch disks, remove disk 1 and insert disk 2 into drive A. Repeat the copy command.

   copy a:*.* <Enter>

To start *Micro Production* from the hard disk, change to the mpom subdirectory using the command given in step 4, and then type

mpom <Enter>

If you start *Micro Production* from the hard disk, you will not need to "Install" the working space/data storage disk unless you wish to specify some directory or drive other than the mpom subdirectory.

Exiting the Program

You can take out the disk whenever you want, as long as the red light is off. Then you can turn off the computer. Note that your input and output will not be stored automatically; you must use the Save command to accomplish this. Turning off the computer erases any input that has not been Saved. See the section Commands Available in *Micro Production* for details.

PROGRAM SELECTION

The *Micro Production* software package has one or two disks, depending on whether the disks are 5¼ or 3½. Every time you start the program, you will see the main menu shown in Exhibit H-1. To select the program you want to run, press the corresponding letter key shown on the menu or use the arrow keys to move the highlighter. Then select the program by striking the <Enter> key.

Command-driven Interface for Advanced Users

Micro Production 3.0 provides advanced users with a convenient interface with which to directly run a specific program at the DOS prompt, instead of selecting the program from a menu. At the DOS prompt, the user enters the program name (e.g., pom1 or pom2) with an appropriate keyword (e.g., LP for Linear Program, QUE for Queuing model). The keyword specifies the module that the user wants to run.

If you are using a floppy drive only system, place your choice of the *Micro Production* disks into drive A, close the drive door, and type

A:Ø> *pom1* (or *pom2*) *parameter*

where *parameter* is one of the following keywords:

DEC:	Decision Theory	WOM:	Work Measure
DFR:	Demand Forecasting	FIM:	Finance Models
AGP:	Aggregate Planning	LP:	Linear Programming
INV:	Inventory Models	AIP:	All Integer Programming
MRP:	MRP	Z1:	Zero One Programming
SCH:	Scheduling	GP:	Goal Programming
QUE:	Queueing Models	TRN:	Transportation
SIM:	Simulation	ASN:	Assignment
QC:	Quality Control		

EXHIBIT H-1 *MICRO PRODUCTION* MAIN MENU

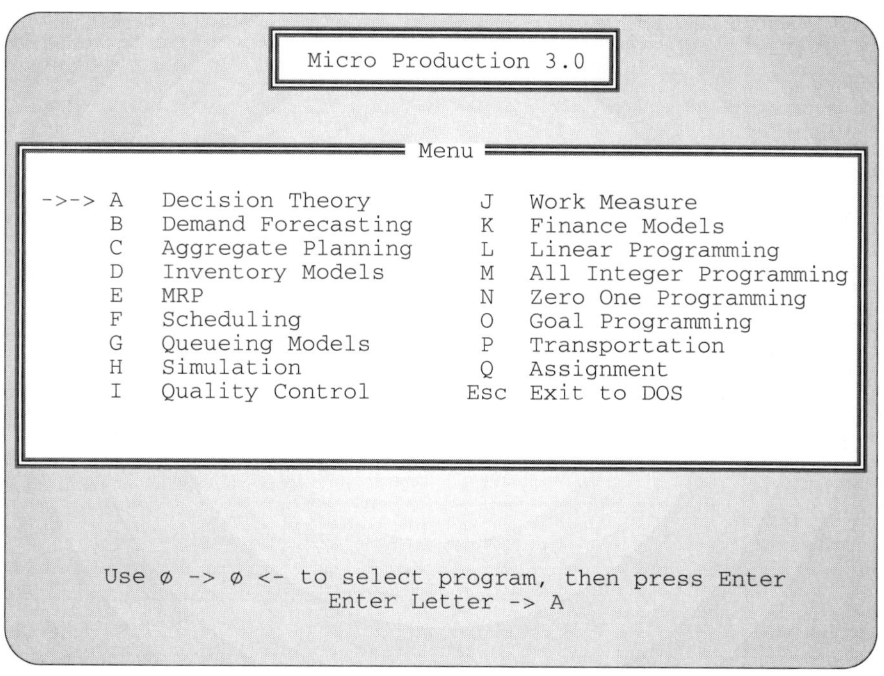

The program pom1 is accompanied with the parameters on the left-hand side of the list and pom2 with those on the right-hand side.

Note that the program name and the keyword parameter are not case-sensitive (that is, it doesn't matter if you type them in uppercase or lowercase letters), and only the first three characters are significant. Thus, pom1 LP or pom2 FOR is valid.

If you have already installed *Micro Production* on a hard disk, change the current directory to the directory where the *Micro Production* programs exist and type in pom1 or pom2.

RUNNING *MICRO PRODUCTION*

Screen Layout After Selecting a Program

Exhibit H-2 shows a typical screen layout after you select a program from the menu (in this case, linear programming). The exhibit shows the three windows listed at the top of page 820.

Upper window (the Initial Data Window)

Middle window (the Detailed Data Window)

Lower window (the Command Window)

The first two windows will be used for data entry and editing purposes. In the lower window, you can see the ten basic commands available in *Micro Production.* Other messages may appear in this window, prompting you for a filename or offering additional choices.

Help Command

You may obtain useful information through the **Help** command. This option provides the four types of information listed on the top of the next page.

EXHIBIT H-2 SCREEN LAYOUT AFTER PROGRAM SELECTION

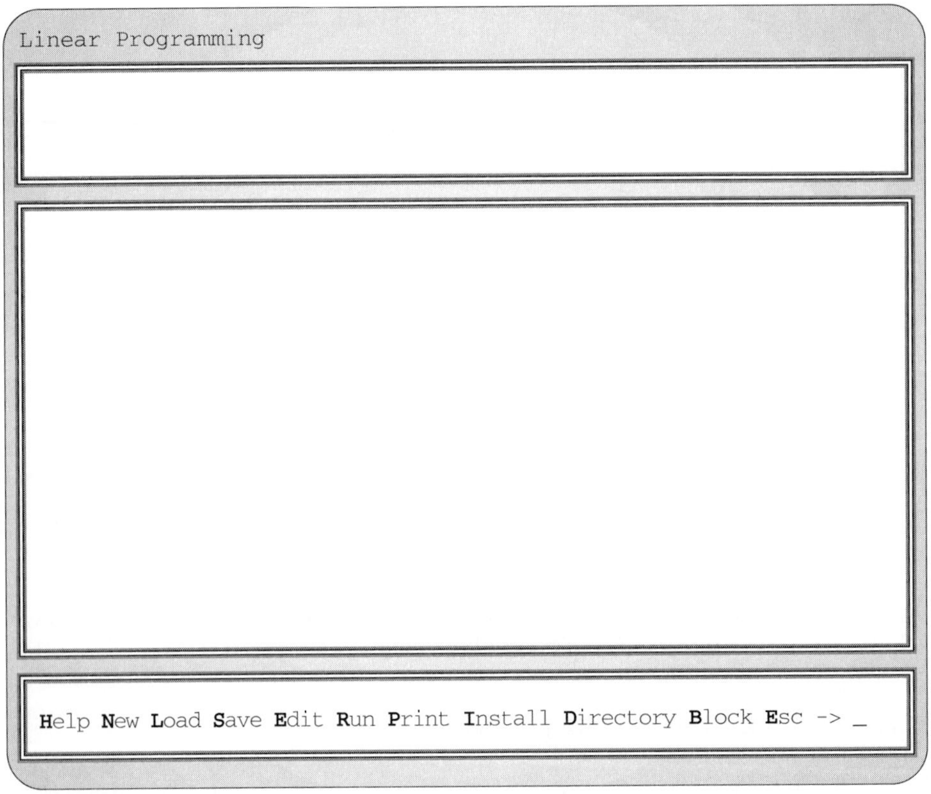

```
Linear Programming

Help New Load Save Edit Run Print Install Directory Block Esc -> _
```

1. Descriptions of the commands and keys
2. Purpose of the program you chose
3. Limitations of the system
4. Explanation of key words and how to input data

Help screen information for linear programming is as shown in Exhibit H-3.

EXHIBIT H-3 INFORMATION IN HELP SCREENS FOR LINEAR PROGRAMMING

```
Purpose
-------

Linear Programming determines the optimum allocation of scarce
resources to achieve the minimum or maximum of a single objective
criterion.

Limitations of System
---------------------

1. Maximum number of constraints         : 50
2. Maximum number of decision variables  : 50

Explanation of Key Words and How to Input Data
----------------------------------------------


<< Upper Window >>

1. Type the problem title or your comment for later reference
   purposes.
2. If the objective function for your problem is maximization,
   type 1; otherwise type 2 in the Type of Problem row.
3. If you want to include all simplex tableaux in the output and
   the number of variables and constraints are both less than or
   equal to five, type 1; type 2 for a final tableau only; type 3
   for no tableau.
4. Enter the number of constraints and decision variables in the
   problem you want to solve.


<< Middle Window >>

1. Enter the coefficient values of the decision variables in the
   objective function in row Obj.
2. Enter the coefficient values of the decision variables in each
   constraint at the intersection of the appropriate variable
   column (x1, x2, ...) and constraint row (C1, C2, ... ).
3. Enter the type of each constraint in column T.
   If the constraint is >= then enter > ;
                        <= then enter < ; or
                         = then enter =.
4. Enter the right hand side value of each constraint in column
   Rhs.
```

The *Micro Production* Editor (Data Entry/Edit)

The built-in editor provides you with a spreadsheet into which you will enter the input data for a new problem by using the **New** command, or where you will modify existing data by using the **Edit** command. *Micro Production* has two special cursors: a highlighter and a normal cursor. The highlighter is an illuminated box that indicates the current cell in Input Mode. The cursor appears as a blinking underline (_) in the cell highlighter to indicate the current location in the cell highlighter.

Upper Window (the Initial Data Window)

Type in a problem title or a comment for later reference purposes and then press the Enter key. The highlighter moves from the problem title line to the next item to be entered. In the lower window you can see the minimum and maximum values *Micro Production* can accept for each item. When you complete the initial input data entry, the labels showing the remaining required input items will appear in the middle window (the Detailed Data Window).

Each item is unique to each menu and will be discussed under the appropriate menu section. Use the movement keys to move the cell highlighter within the current worksheet. The movement keys and the actions they perform in the upper window are as follows:

Key	*Movement*
Up arrow	Moves the cursor one item up.
Down arrow	Moves the cursor one item down.
Left arrow	Moves the cursor one item left.
Right arrow	Moves the cursor one item right.

In Edit mode, you cannot change the item(s) at line 3, which are related to the spreadsheet's rows and columns. You can, however, change the number of rows or columns by using the Insert Row, Insert Column, Delete Row, and Delete Column commands.

Middle Window (the Detailed Data Window)

Use the movement keys to move the cell highlighter within the current worksheet. When you finish entering the input, hit the Esc key to move into the lower window (the Command Window). In the lower window you will see the available cursor-movement keys and insert and delete commands. The organization of these commands is individually tailored to the needs of each menu and stage. The movement keys and the actions they perform in the middle window are listed in the table at the top of the next page.

Key	*Movement*
Up arrow	Moves the cursor one cell up.
Down arrow	Moves the cursor one cell down.
Left arrow	Moves the cursor one cell left.
Right arrow	Moves the cursor one cell right.
Home	Moves to the first column.
End	Moves to the last column.
PgUp	Moves the cursor one page up.
PgDn	Moves the cursor one page down.
Esc	Moves to the Command Window after completing input.

Entering Data

To enter data, move the cell highlighter to the desired location and type a value. You signal completion of entry and record the entry into a cell by pressing the following keys according to the direction you want to move:

Up arrow key

Down arrow key

Left arrow key

Right arrow key

Enter key

It is not necessary to type in the number zero. Just leave the cell blank and *Micro Production* will assign a value of zero.

Correcting Data

If you want to edit the values, move the highlighter to the cell you want to edit, and type the correct value or strike the Del key to delete the current value of the cell. If you are in a cell, use the following movement keys to move the cursor within the highlighter. These keys and the actions they perform in the cell mode are as follows:

Key	*Description*
Backspace	Deletes character to the left of the cursor.
Del	Deletes character under cursor.
Left arrow	Moves the cursor one character left.
Right arrow	Moves the cursor one character right.

Insert and Delete Commands

You can delete and insert columns and rows in the Detailed Data (middle) window by using the function keys listed in the table at the top of page 824.

Key	*Command*	*Description*
F7	Insert row	Inserts one row below the cursor.
F8	Insert column	Inserts one column to the left of the cursor.
F9	Delete row	Deletes the row containing the cursor.
F10	Delete column	Deletes the column containing the cursor.

Commands Available in *Micro Production*

Micro Production has ten internal commands that will assist you in solving management science problems. You can issue those commands by typing the first letter of the command in either uppercase or lowercase.

```
Help New Load Save Edit Run Print Install Directory Block Esc -> _
```

HELP COMMAND The **H** command is used to get information about (1) commands and keys, (2) purpose of the program, (3) limitations of the program, (4) key words, and (5) how to enter data for the program you selected.

NEW COMMAND The **N** command is used to start a new problem. If you have a problem on the screen, *Micro Production* will ask if you wish to save the problem.

LOAD COMMAND The **L** command is used to select an existing work file from your working disk (see the Install command). The selected file is used to edit, run, print, and save. The L command will display a list of file names from which you can select by moving the cursor to an appropriate file name and pressing the Enter key.

When the data file to be loaded has been specified, the file is read from the disk, if present. If the file does not exist or if it is not consistent with the current menu, an appropriate error message will be issued. If you wish to change the loaded data, you can use the Edit command.

SAVE COMMAND The **S** command is used to save the current input data set on the working disk (which may be specified using the Install command). The S command will issue this prompt:

```
Save: Enter filename (without extension): _
```

You may respond with any legal file name: a name of one through eight characters, an optional period, and an optional file type of no more than three characters:

FILENAME.TYP

If you leave the program without saving the new input data set you created, the program requests confirmation, as shown at the top of page 825.

```
Save current data set (Y/N)? _
```

Answer Y to save; N to skip. Note: To receive a file, a disk must be formatted and must not be write-protected. (For more information on this, see Installing and Starting *Micro Production*.)

EDIT COMMAND The **E** command is used to correct any mistakes or make changes in the input. You can change all input data directly except the number of columns and rows at line 3 in the Initial Data (upper) Window. You can change these numbers by using the Insert and Delete commands, which are part of the *Micro Production* Editor and will be discussed in more detail in the Editor section.

RUN COMMAND The **R** command is used to run the program and obtain the output, provided the input data were entered correctly. If any errors are detected, *Micro Production* will position the cursor at the error point, and issue an appropriate error message in the Command (lower) Window.

PRINT COMMAND The **P** command is used to release the input and output (1) to the printer, (2) to the working disk as a text file, or (3) to both the printer and the working disk. The P command can be used only after running the program.

The P command asks you the following:

```
Printer   Disk file   Both   -> _
```

Type P for printer, D for disk file, or B for both. Note: To receive a file, a disk must be formatted and must not be write-protected. (For more information on this, see Installing and Starting *Micro Production*.)

INSTALL COMMAND The **I** command is used to change the current working disk directory. When you press I, this prompt appears:

```
Working Disk Directory:   _
```

The prompt invites you to enter a new drive and directory name, which is a letter from A through P, optionally followed by a colon and a directory name, and terminated with the Enter key. If you don't want to change the current drive and directory, just hit the Enter key.

Examples of drives and directory names are as follows:

A:

C:ØmpomØdata

Note: To be used as a working disk, a disk must be formatted and must not be write-protected. (For more information on this, see Installing and Starting *Micro Production*.)

DIRECTORY COMMAND The **D** command lists the files your working disk contains (the directory) and the amount of space used and remaining.

BLOCK COMMAND The **B** command allows you to import and export an internal or external data file.

ESCAPE COMMAND The **Esc** key is used to leave the current stage and return to the previous stage. For example, when you have completed entering input for a new problem, Esc will return from the editor to the command stage. Also, after you run a model, Esc will return from the output presentation to the command stage.

We can summarize *Micro Production's* commands as follows:

Key	*Command*	*Description*
H	Help	To get information about commands and the program.
N	New	To enter input data from the keyboard.
L	Load	To load a data set from a disk.
S	Save	To store a data set on a disk.
E	Edit	To correct the input data entered.
R	Run	To obtain solutions.
P	Print	To print input and output after running the program.
I	Install	To specify the working disk.
D	Directory	To get a working disk directory listing and information.
B	Block	To import/export data to/from a working disk.
Esc		To return to the previous stage.

We can summarize *Micro Production's* keys as follows:

Key	*Description*
Backspace	Deletes the character to the left of the cursor.
Del	Deletes the character under the cursor.
F7	Inserts one row below the cursor.
F8	Inserts one column to the left of the cursor.
F9	Deletes the row containing the cursor.
F10	Deletes the column containing the cursor.
PgUp	Moves the cursor one page up.
PgDn	Moves the cursor one page down.
Up arrow	Moves the cursor one cell (line) up.
Down arrow	Moves the cursor one cell (line) down.
Left arrow	Moves the cursor one cell (column) left. Within a cell, moves the cursor one character left.
Right arrow	Moves the cursor one cell (column) right. Within a cell, moves the cursor one character right.
Home	Moves to the first column when using New or Edit commands. Moves to the top of the file when using Run, Help, or Directory commands.
End	Moves to the last column when using New or Edit commands. Moves to the end of the file when using Run, Help, or Directory commands.

APPENDIX I

The Transportation Method

The purpose of this appendix is to acquaint you with the procedures for solving transportation problems. The solution procedures presented in this section are purposefully brief, and you are encouraged to review supplemental material referenced at the end of this appendix. Despite this appendix's brevity, the transportation method can be very tedious. Fortunately, software packages, such as the *Micro Production* system, exist to minimize the need for manual computation of transportation problems. If computers are not available, users can resort to the manual procedures presented in this appendix.

The transportation problem formulation in operations management varies to fit the nature of the problem. In all transportation problems, however, we have some amount of supply that must be allocated to satisfy given demand requirements in such a way that the resulting total transportation costs will be minimized. The basic transportation problem formulation is presented in Exhibit I-1. To use the transportation method procedure presented in this appendix, the sum of the n supply sources must equal the sum of the m demand destinations. We must also know with certainty the available s_n supply (at each supply source), the required d_m demand (at each demand destination), and the unit cost to ship a unit from each supply source to each demand destination.

To solve a transportation problem, we may have to use several procedures: an initial solution procedure, a test for degeneracy, a test for optimality, and a cell reallocation procedure. The initial solution procedure we will present is called the **least-cost method.** The purpose of the initial solution procedure is to obtain a feasible solution

EXHIBIT I-1 TRANSPORTATION PROBLEM FORMULATION

TO / FROM	Demand Destinations 1 2 . . . . *m*	Supply
Supply Sources 1, 2, ... , *n*	UNIT COST MATRIX	s_1, s_2, ... , s_n
Demand	d_1 d_2 . . . . d_m	Total

that will satisfy the supply and demand requirements of the problem. The least-cost method involves the following steps:

1. Select the least-cost cell that is open to receive an allocation and allocate as many units to that cell as possible. If the cost values are tied, select the cell that can receive the largest number of units.
2. Repeat step 1 until all of the supply has been used to satisfy all of the demand.

To illustrate the initial solution procedure, suppose that we have a transportation problem such as the one presented in Exhibit I-2. The available supply from the supply sources A, B, and C are 10, 30, and 60 units, respectively. The required demand from the demand destinations 1, 2, and 3 are 30, 40, and 30 units, respectively. Note that the sum of the supply (10 + 30 + 60) equals the sum of the demand (30 + 40 + 30). This is a necessary requirement for the use of this solution procedure. The numbers within the cost matrix are dollar values for shipping one unit from each supply source to each demand destination. For example, it costs $6 per unit to ship one unit from supply source A to demand destination 1 (called cell A-1, or the cell in row A, column 1).

The least-cost cell open in Exhibit I-2 is tied at $6 for cells A-1 and B-2. To resolve this tie we must determine to which of the two cells we can allocate the larger number of units. Cell A-1 is limited by its supply of only 10 units but cell B-2 can accept as many as 30 units because of its supply availability. So, as we can see in Exhibit I-3(a), the first allocation is 30 units to cell B-2. Having made that allocation, the cells B-1, B-2, and B-3 are all prohibited from receiving any additional units. Of the remaining cells open for an allocation, the next least cost cell is A-1. As we can see in Exhibit I-3(b), we can allocate as many as 10 units to that cell. This allocation reduces the open cells to just those in the C row. The resulting allocations to finish the initial allocation process are presented in order in Exhibit I-3(c), (d), and (e).

EXHIBIT I-2 SAMPLE TRANSPORTATION PROBLEM

TO / FROM	1	2	3	Supply
A	6	7	11	10
B	9	6	8	30
C	7	11	10	60
Demand	30	40	30	100

EXHIBIT I-3 SAMPLE TRANSPORTATION PROBLEM'S INITIAL ALLOCATION

(A) FIRST ALLOCATION

TO / FROM	1	2	3	Supply
A	6	7	11	10
B	9	6 30	8	30
C	7	11	10	60
Demand	30	40	30	100

(B) SECOND ALLOCATION

TO / FROM	1	2	3	Supply
A	6 10	7	11	10
B	9	6 30	8	30
C	7	11	10	60
Demand	30	40	30	100

(C) THIRD ALLOCATION

TO / FROM	1	2	3	Supply
A	6 10	7	11	10
B	9	6 30	8	30
C	7 20	11	10	60
Demand	30	40	30	100

(D) FOURTH ALLOCATION

TO / FROM	1	2	3	Supply
A	6 10	7	11	10
B	9	6 30	8	30
C	7 20	11	10 30	60
Demand	30	40	30	100

(E) FIFTH ALLOCATION

TO / FROM	1	2	3	Supply
A	6 10	7	11	10
B	9	6 30	8	30
C	7 20	11 10	10 30	60
Demand	30	40	30	100

Once we have an initial allocation we must check it to see if we have a degenerate solution. One precondition for using this method is that the number of allocated cells in the solution must be equal to the number of rows plus the number of columns minus one. The condition in which a transportation problem has less than (rows + columns − 1) allocations is called **degenerate.** A solution with less than this number of allocations (rows + columns − 1) cannot be evaluated for optimality. **Optimality** in transportation problems means the situation of having a solution that results in the least-cost allocation.

A degenerate solution prohibits us from testing for an optimal solution. We correct degeneracy by adding an artificial allocation in the tableau in the least-cost cell that is open. [Occasionally, this procedure will not correct degeneracy. After placing the artificial allocation, a check should be performed to determine that each empty cell has a pivotal path. A **pivotal path** is a configuration of select transportation cells that are used in cell evaluation procedures. (We discuss a cell evaluation procedure in the next paragraph.)] If an empty cell has no pivotal path, the artificial allocation should be moved to the next least-cost cell that is open. This process should be repeated until a pivotal path can be found for each empty cell. The artificial allocation is an infinitely small allocation that is just large enough to permit the optimality test to be performed but small enough not to cost anything when total transportation costs are calculated. We will illustrate later how the artificial allocation corrects degeneracy in our sample problem.

The test for optimality is conducted using a cell evaluation procedure. One of the most common cell evaluation procedures is called the *stepping-stone method.* The **stepping-stone method** obtained its name from the procedure it uses. Briefly, the procedure involves pivoting off cells that have allocations in them (called **stone cells,** hence the name *stepping stone*). The test for optimality checks to see if units can be reallocated to any of the cells that do not have an allocation (called **open cells**). The information provided by the evaluative process not only denotes when optimality in a solution has been reached, but in the case where an optimal solution has not been reached, it provides the reduction in total cost. The information provided by this method also reveals alternative optimal solutions.

Cell evaluation consists of the following four-step procedure:

1. Select any empty cell to evaluate and find the pivotal path for that cell. The pivotal path is found by starting in an empty cell and moving horizontally or vertically until an allocation (stone cell) is found. Pivoting off this allocation in a right- or left-hand turn, we must travel toward another allocation (stone cell). Continuing this process we will eventually end up in the original empty cell forming a closed path.

2. Assign a plus (+) and minus (−) sign alternately to the unit cost in each cell in the pivotal path, starting with a plus sign for the empty cell being evaluated.

3. Add up the plus- and minus-signed cost values.

4. If the result in step 3 is positive, no improvement in the solution can be made by reallocating to that cell because a positive value indicates an increase in cost

with reallocation. If the result in step 3 is zero, no cost improvement is possible but there exists an alternative solution. If the result in step 3 is negative, we can improve the solution by reallocating units to the negative evaluated cell because a negative value indicates a decrease in cost. Repeat these steps until all the empty cells are evaluated and result in positive values or zero values.

To illustrate the use of the stepping-stone method, let's look again at the sample transportation problem. In Exhibit I-4(a), the problem is again presented with the initial allocation of units. The transportation tableau has four open cells. We need to evaluate each of them so it does not matter which we begin with. Let's start with cell B-1. First we must find its pivotal path. This pivotal path will consist of a closed path that will form a square, rectangle, or adjacent squares and rectangles. Starting in cell B-1, we must travel in vertical or horizontal lines toward allocations. This gives us three choices: traveling to cell A-1, cell B-2, or cell C-1. If we go to cell A-1 we will not be able to continue toward any other allocation. In effect we would be at a dead end. If a problem is not degenerate, there will be a single pivotal path for every open cell. Now if we leave cell B-1 and travel to cell B-2, we can turn to the right or to the left. If we turn left, we will not be traveling toward an allocation so we would turn right. Stepping off of the allocation in cell C-2, we can turn right or left again. If we turn to cell C-3 we are at a dead end again, but if we turn to cell C-1, we are free to return to our original cell of B-1. This completes our pivotal path for this cell.

The specific boxes involved in the pivotal path for cell B-1 are presented to the right of the transportation tableau in Exhibit I-4(a). This pivotal path required a total of four cells to complete. By assigning the alternating + and − signs and adding the values consistent with the cell evaluation procedure steps just given, we derive the cell evaluation statistic of +7. This value can be interpreted to indicate that we should not reallocate any units to this cell. If we would allocate units to cell B-1, it would cost $7 for each unit we reallocated.

The other three open cells are evaluated in a similar fashion and are presented in Exhibit I-4(b), (c), and (d). In Exhibit I-4(d), we can see that because of the −3 for cell A-2, we do not have an optimal solution. Why? Because for every unit we can reallocate to cell A-2, we can reduce costs by $3. So we will need to perform the reallocation procedure.

The reallocation procedure involves the following four steps:

1. Select the most negative empty cell evaluation to which units can be reallocated. This improves the solution the most.
2. Retrace the pivotal path used to generate the cell evaluation, placing the alternating plus and minus signs next to the cost per unit in each cell.
3. To maintain a balance between supply and demand, select the smallest allocation on the pivotal path whose cost per unit has a minus sign by it. Subtract this amount from each of the allocations that have a minus sign by the cost per unit.
4. Add the amount subtracted in step 3 to each of the cells that have a plus sign by the cost per unit.

EXHIBIT I-4 SAMPLE TRANSPORTATION PROBLEM CELL EVALUATIONS

(A) CELL B-1 EVALUATION

TO / FROM	1	2	3	Supply
A	6 / 10	7	11	10
B	9 / +7	6 / 30	8	30
C	7 / 20	11 / 10	10 / 30	60
Demand	30	40	30	100

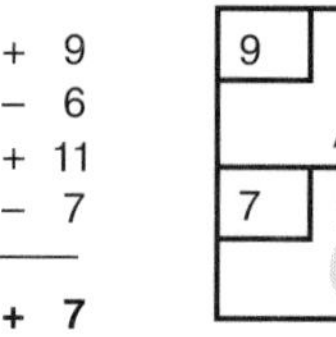

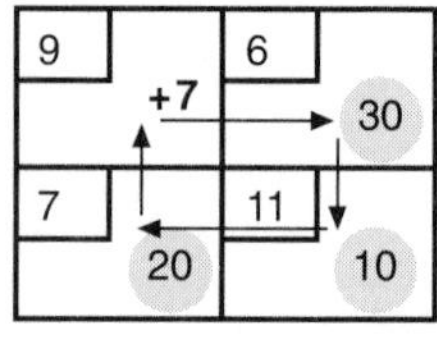

(B) CELL A-2 EVALUATION

TO / FROM	1	2	3	Supply
A	6 / 10	7 / −3	11	10
B	9 / +7	6 / 30	8	30
C	7 / 20	11 / 10	10 / 30	60
Demand	30	40	30	100

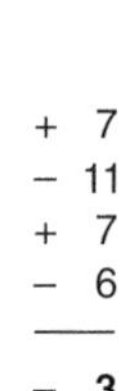

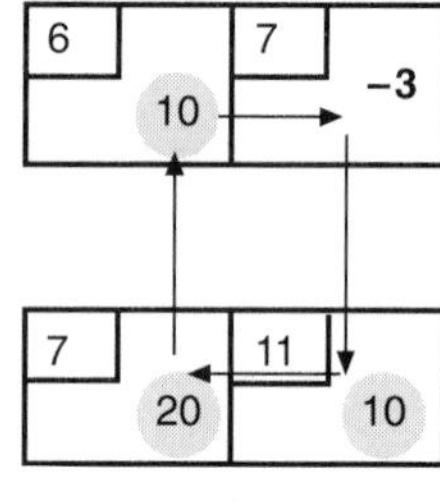

The result will be a reallocation and a new solution to the transportation problem.

To illustrate this reallocation procedure, let's look at our sample problem again. In Exhibit I-5, the reallocation process is presented. Note that the smallest allocation in the negatively signed cells is 10 units in both cell A-1 and cell C-2. When subtracted from each other, both cells are emptied and become open for a reallocation. At this point we would need to repeat the cell evaluation procedure to test for optimality. Unfortunately, we cannot perform the optimality test because the problem has become degenerate. Note we need 5 $(3 + 3 - 1)$ allocations for the optimality test and we only have four. This degeneracy prevents us from finding pivotal paths for the open cells. None of the open cells in Exhibit I-5(b) have a pivotal path. To correct the degeneracy, we need to add one artificial allocation to the four real ones. We will let a

EXHIBIT I-4 (CONTINUED)

(C) CELL A-3 EVALUATION

TO / FROM	1	2	3	Supply
A	6 / 10	7 / −3	11 / +2	10
B	9 / +7	6 / 30	8	30
C	7 / 20	11 / 10	10 / 30	60
Demand	30	40	30	100

+ 11
−10
+ 7
− 6
———
+ 2

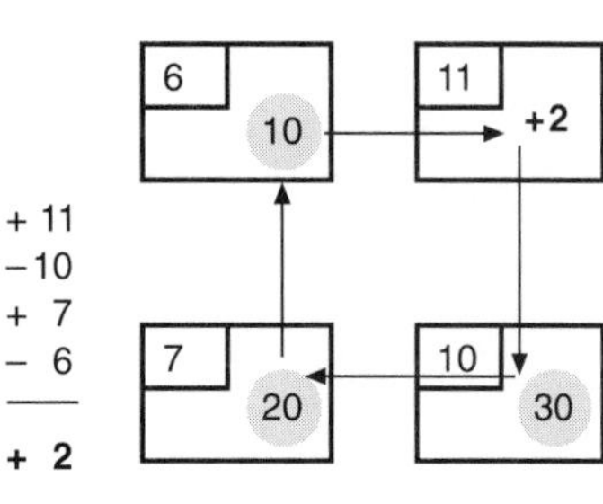

(D) CELL B-3 EVALUATION

TO / FROM	1	2	3	Supply
A	6 / 10	7 / −3	11 / +2	10
B	9 / +7	6 / 30	8 / +3	30
C	7 / 20	11 / 10	10 / 30	60
Demand	30	40	30	100

+ 8
−10
+ 11
− 6
———
+ 3

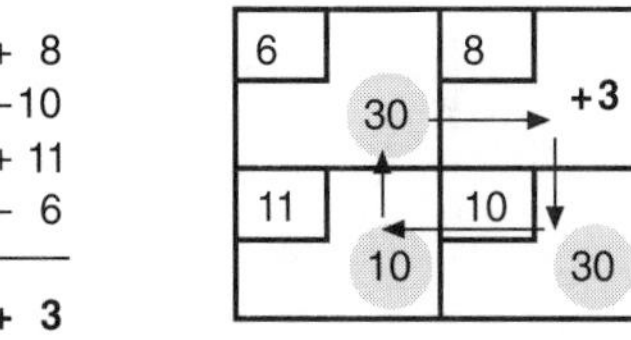

circled *a* represent the artificial allocation. Its assignment will be the least-cost open cell of A-1, as presented in Exhibit I-6(a). We are now able to find pivotal paths for the open cells and determine the cell evaluations as presented in Exhibit I-6(b). Because we do not have any negatively signed cell evaluation statistics, we have an optimal solution. It is interesting to note that the 0 in cell B-3 indicates that we have an alternative solution. We can find the alternative solution by simply reallocating units to that open cell.

To formally state the solution to the problem, we need to generate a transportation schedule. For the sample problem in this appendix, the transportation schedule is presented in Exhibit I-7. This schedule defines the shipment schedule in easy-to-understand terms and states the optimized total cost of the transportation problem. Users

EXHIBIT I-5 SAMPLE TRANSPORTATION PROBLEM REALLOCATION PROCESS

(A) INITIAL ALLOCATION REQUIRING RE-ALLOCATION

FROM \ TO	1	2	3	Supply
A	[6] 10	[7] −3	[11]	10
B	[9]	[6] 30	[8]	30
C	[7] 20	[11] 10	[10] 30	60
Demand	30	40	30	100

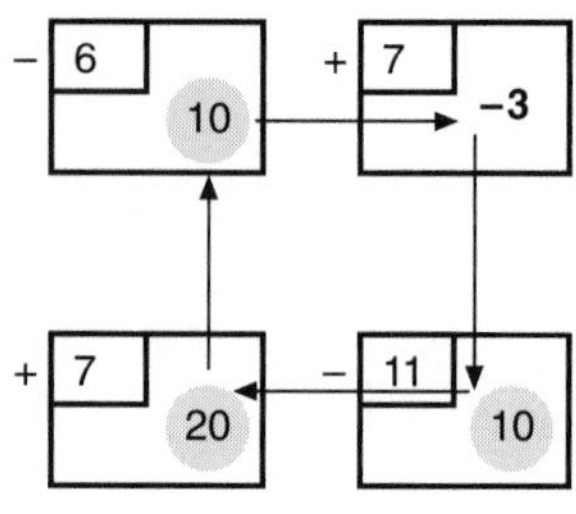

(B) REVISED TRANSPORTATION TABLEAU

FROM \ TO	1	2	3	Supply
A	[6]	[7] 10	[11]	10
B	[9]	[6] 30	[8]	30
C	[7] 30	[11]	[10] 30	60
Demand	30	40	30	100

are encouraged to review management science textbooks for more detailed transportation solution procedures.[1]

[1] For a good review of transportation method solution procedures see S. M. Lee and J. P. Shim, *Micro Management Science,* 2nd ed. (Boston: Allyn and Bacon, 1990), Chapter 7.

EXHIBIT I-6 CORRECTING DEGENERACY IN THE SAMPLE TRANSPORTATION PROBLEM

(A) ADDING THE ARTIFICIAL ALLOCATION

FROM \ TO	1	2	3	Supply
A	6 · a	7 · 10	11	10
B	9	6 · 30	8	30
C	7 · 30	11	10 · 30	60
Demand	30	40	30	100

(B) RESULTING CELL EVALUATIONS

FROM \ TO	1	2	3	Supply
A	6 · a	7 · 10	11 · **+2**	10
B	9 · **+4**	6 · 30	8 · **0**	30
C	7 · 30	11 · **+3**	10 · 30	60
Demand	30	40	30	100

EXHIBIT I-7 SAMPLE PROBLEM'S TRANSPORTATION SCHEDULE

From	*To*	*Cost Per Unit*	*Number of Units*	*Total Cost*
A	2	7	10	$ 70
B	2	6	30	180
C	1	7	30	210
C	3	10	30	300
				$760

APPENDIX J

Solutions for Selected Problems

The purpose of this appendix is to provide solutions for selected problems marked with an asterisk in each of the chapters with problems (Chapters 3 through 14). The solutions provided here are presented in brief and should not be considered as showing all necessary work to complete an answer. Also, some of the solutions have been generated using the *Micro Production* software system. Please note that the use of this software, because of rounding, may create solutions that are slightly different from solutions obtained by hand calculation.

Chapter 3

1. Three-values: 270, 288.3, 281.6, 326.3; range = 56.3.
   Five-values: 293.2, 288.8; range = 4.4.
   Variation has been reduced from 56.3 to 4.4.

2. 7th year = 311.6; no.

3. (a) 311.7; no; MAD = 64.7.

   (b) 306.7; no; MAD = 73.6.

   (c) $\alpha = 0.2$

10. (a) $Y_p = 4053.1 - 9.3X_1$

    (b) $r = 0.9996$; $r^2 = 0.9991$; 99.91 percent of the variation in haircuts is explained by the variation in average weekly earnings.

    (c) MAD = 2.7169; MSE = $[(1.119)^2 + (2.717)^2 + (1.598)^2]/3 = 3.729$; boundaries = ± 1.931.

13. The forecasting model is quite accurate and still useful.

16. 20 million units × .235 = 4.7 million units next year.

17. (a) Plot not provided; two-value smoothed values in order: 12.5, 11, 10, 10.5, 12.5, 15.5, 17.5, 18.5, 21.5, 24.5, 22.5, 15.5, 10.5, 9.5, 8.5, 9, 11, 13, 14.5, 15.5, 17, 18.5, 18.5; unsmoothed range = 17; smoothed range = 16; a reduction in ranges of 1.

    (b) Plot not provided; five-value smoothed values in order: 11.2, 11.4, 12.4, 14, 15.8, 18.4, 20.6, 21.2, 19.8, 18, 15, 11.6, 9.6, 9.8, 10.6, 11.8, 13.4, 15, 16.4, 17.2; smoothed range = 11.6; the greater the number of values taken to smooth the raw data, the greater the reduction in the resulting range statistics.

20. (a) Two-value moving averages in order: 11, 13, 15, 17, 19, 22, 27.
    (b) Four-value moving averages in order: 13, 15, 17, 19.5, 23.
    (c) Weighted averages in order: 11.4, 13.4, 15.4, 17.4, 19.8, 23.2.

23. $n = 2$; MAD $= 14.75$.
    $n = 3$; MAD $= 17.44$.
    Therefore, $n = 2$ is the best.

26. $r = 0.0444$ for Y_1; $r = 0.5743$ for Y_2; therefore, Y_2 is the better predictor.

29. Trend is increasing throughout the year. Seasonal variation is above average in first two quarters of the year and below average in last two quarters of the year.

Chapter 4

1.

	COMPANY		
Criteria	*A*	*B*	*C*
Price	4	1	2
Cost	1	4	3
Quality	5	2	1
Total	10	7	6

Company C poses the greatest threat.

Chapter 5

1. (a)

	TIME PERIODS			
	1	*2*	*3*	*4*
Forecast demand	150	240	300	200
(Beg. inv.)	0	70	50	0
Req. prod.	150	170	250	200
Type of production				
(Reg. time prod.)	220	220	220	220
(Overtime prod.)	0	0	30	0
Units for beg. inv.	70	50	0	20
Ending inv.	70	50	0	20

(b)

	TIME PERIODS				
	1	*2*	*3*	*4*	*Total*
Reg. time prod.	2,200	2,200	2,200	2,200	8,800
Overtime prod.	0	0	450	0	450
Inv. cost	210	150	0	60	420
Total cost/per.	2,410	2,350	2,650	2,260	9,670

(c)

Total cost	2,410	4,760	7,410	9,670	9,670

7. Let x_1 = number of units of product A to produce per month; x_2 = number of units of product B to produce per month; x_3 = number of units of product C to produce per month; x_4 = number of units of product D to produce per month.

Minimize $Z = 6x_1 + 8x_2 + 9x_3 + 7x_4$

subject to: $x_1 + 3x_2 + 2x_3 + x_4 \leq 2{,}400$ (max. req.)

$x_1 + 3x_2 + 2x_3 + x_4 \geq 1{,}100$ (min. req.)

$x_1 + x_2 + x_3 + x_4 \leq 1{,}350$

$x_1 + x_2 + x_3 + x_4 \geq 450$

$2x_1 + x_2 + 4x_3 + 2x_4 \leq 4{,}200$

$2x_1 + x_2 + 4x_3 + 2x_4 \geq 800$

$x_1 + x_2 + x_3 + x_4 \leq 5{,}000$ (total production)

and $x_1, x_2, x_3, x_4 \geq 0$

14. Transportation problem formulation

	Jan.	*Feb.*	*Mar.*	*End Inv.*	*Unused Cap.*	*Available Cap.*
Jan. reg. time	$2	$3	$4	$5	$0	500 units
Jan. overtime	$3	$4	$5	$6	$0	100 units
Feb. reg. time	X	$2	$3	$4	$0	250 units
Feb. overtime	X	$3	$4	$5	$0	50 units
Mar. reg. time	X	X	$2	$3	$0	150 units
Mar. overtime	X	X	$3	$4	$0	30 units
Total	300	300	200	100	180	1,080 units

21. Either the maximum output level of 134 units or the average output level of 128.8 units.

Chapter 6

1.

Item	*Annual $ Value*	*Classification*
1	1,300	A
2	1,380	B
3	1,770	B
4	700	C
5	2,400	C
	$7,550	

A's proportion = 1,300/7,550 = 17.2 percent.
B's proportion = [1,380 + 1,770]/7,550 = 41.7 percent.
C's proportion = [700 + 2,400]/7,550 = 41.1 percent.

4. Formulation of the transportation problem

	WAREHOUSE				
Plant	*1*	*2*	*3*	*4*	*Supply*
A	$12	$13	$8	$10	800 units
B	10	11	9	17	800 units
C	16	19	10	10	800 units
D	12	13	8	10	800 units
Dem.	1,000	600	500	1,100	3,200 units

Solution: Ship 200 units from plant A to warehouse 1; ship 600 units from plant A to warehouse 2; ship 800 units from plant B to warehouse 1; ship 800 units from plant C to warehouse 4; ship 500 units from plant D to warehouse 3; ship 200 units from plant D to warehouse 4. Total transportation costs: $33,200.

Chapter 7

1.

Component	*Units Required*
A	1
B	4
C	7
D	1
E	8

19. (a) All three workcenters will have the same available capacity in minutes of 1,008 (i.e., 2,400 min. × 0.6 × 0.7).

(b) Given the new part demand on this problem the setup and (run time) in minutes values are computed per week as follows:

Workcenter	*Part No.*	*1*	*2*	*3*	*4*	*5*
WC1	1	100(150)	100(150)	100(150)	100(150)	
Total		250	250	250	250	
WC2	2	60(1,162.5)	60(1,162.5)	60(1,162.5)	60(1,162.5)	
Total		1,222.5	1,222.5	1,222.5	1,222.5	
WC3	2		80(93.75)	80(93.75)	80(93.75)	80(93.75)
Total			173.75	173.75	173.75	173.75

The Total rows are the same required capacity of planned order releases as presented in Exhibit 7S-6.

(c) Assuming that there are no released orders in the operation, the answer to this question is the same as in (b).

Chapter 8

1. $Q^* = 223.607$; as long as the cost conditions in this situation hold true and the simple EOQ model fits the inventory situation of this problem, the EOQ value will best minimize costs.

4. It will decrease the EOQ. Yes, as an increase in the cost per unit raises the slope of the carrying cost function of total cost, causing the optimal EOQ to be reduced as it slides back toward the now relatively lesser costly ordering cost function. (Students are encouraged to plot the graphs of the ordering and carrying cost functions for a sample problem like those in Figure 8-5 to see the effect of the change in C.)

12. $Q^* = 3{,}000$; optimal price $= \$1.14$.

15. $Q^* \approx 3{,}184$; optimal runs per year $= 14{,}600/3{,}184 = 4.585$; days between production runs $= 365/4.585 = 79.6$.

19. $EDDLT = 10 \times 12 = 120$; $SS = 10.95$; order point $= 120 + 10.95 = 130.95$.

21. $EDDLT = 8 \times 12 = 96$; order point is found at the middle of the interval of 100 to 109, or approximately 105; $SS = 105 - 96 = 9$.

25. $EDDLT = 342.2$; std. dev. of $EDDLT = 34.93$; $z = 1.28$; order point $= 342.2 + 1.28(34.93) = 386.9$; $SS = 386.9 - 342.2 = 44.7$.

28. $EDDLT \approx 124$; $T \approx 0.088 \times 365 = 32$ days; order point $= 1{,}000 - 250 + 124 = 874$; because the order point must be recalculated each time, a new value will need to be computed for all future order points.

30. Fixed daily order of 105 to 106 units (30,000/285).

32. Rather than using the given mean value of 30, a new mean based on actual daily values can be computed at 31 units. With $z = 1.28$ and a std. dev. of 2.73, the order quantity under JIT is 34.49 $(31 + 1.28(2.73) - 0)$.

34.

Demand	*Cum. Freq.*	*Random No. Range*
60	.14	00–13
61	.32	14–31
62	.60	32–59
63	.85	60–84
64	1.00	85–99

Simulated demand (in order) = 62, 63, 63, 62, 62, 61, 64, 63, 63, 63.

Chapter 9

1. (a) A, B, C, D, E; 16 hours.
   (b) B, C, A, D, E; 16 hours.
   (c) No, the time is the same either way.

4. C, D, E, B, A (note: A can be switched with B for an alternative solution); total flow time = 28 hours.

10.

Critical Ratios	*Priority*
CR = (16 − 10)/2 = 3	2
CR = (22 − 10)/8 = 1.5	1
CR = (18 − 10)/1 = 8	3

13.

	WEEK			
	1	*2*	*3*	*4*
Cumulative input deviation	−20	−10	−10	−10
Cumulative output deviation	30	9	9	14

16. $L_s = 10/(12 - 10) = 5.$
$L_q = 10^2/[12(12 - 10)] = 4.166.$
$T_s = 1/(12 - 10) = 0.5.$
$T_q = 10/[12(12 - 10)] = 0.416.$
$P = 10/12 = 0.833.$

Chapter 10

1.

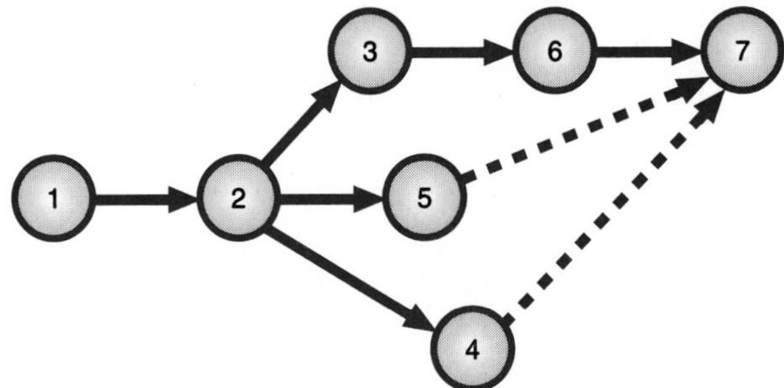

Yes, we need two dummy activities (5–7, 4–7).

5. Std. dev. = 3.193; $z = (20 - 15)/3.193 = 1.56$; tabled prob. = 0.9406.

13. (a)

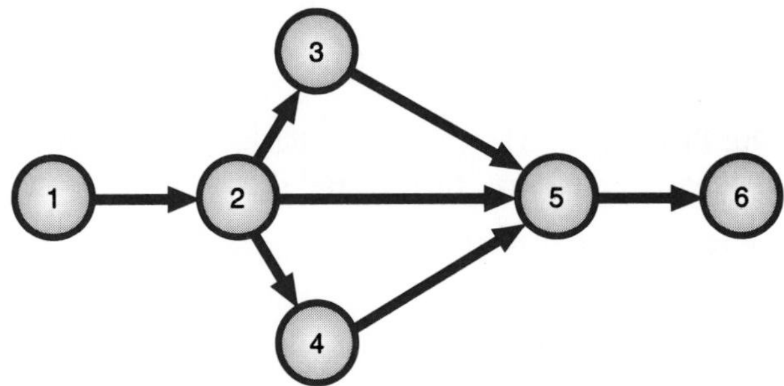

(b), (c), (d)

Act.	*ES*	*EF*	*LS*	*LF*	*Slack*
1–2	0	3.8	0	3.8	0*
2–3	3.8	6.6	3.8	6.6	0*
2–4	3.8	7.8	7.3	11.3	3.5
2–5	3.8	9.1	9.1	14.4	5.3
3–5	6.6	14.4	6.6	14.4	0*
4–5	7.8	10.9	11.3	14.4	3.5
5–6	14.4	20.0	14.4	20.0	0*

* Critical path activity.

17. (a), (b), (c)

Total Project Cost	*Activity Crashed*	*Total Time of Project*
$3,650	–	16
3,750	1–2	15
3,850	1–2	14
4,075	2–3	13
4,300	2–3	12
4,700	3–5	11
5,100	3–5	10

Chapter 11

1. (a) 2 and 3.
   (b) No.

5. $0.99^3 = 0.97$.

9. At t/MTBF = 100/120 = 0.833, the probability would fall between table values of the exponential probability distribution of 0.8 and 0.9, or between the probabilities of 0.4493 and 0.4066. See Appendix G.

Chapter 12

1. $\overline{x}$; R.

5. Problem A: 14 × 5 = 70; Problem B: 31 × 2 = 62; Problem C: 45 × 1 = 45; Problem A should be worked on first, then B, and then C.

9. $R = 1.25$; $M = 120$; $n = 8$; $UCL_R = (1.864)(1.25) = 2.33$; $LCL_R = (0.136)(1.25) = 0.17$.

16. Yes; $4 > c$.

27. $(0.92)(0.88)(0.98) = 0.793$.

Chapter 13

6. Alternative arrangements in addition to the one shown are also possible.

C	A	B
D	E	F

8.

	R	*MS*	*P*	*A*	*QA*	*S*
R	–	35	13	18	8	6
MS		–	83	116	17	2
P			–	33	24	3
A				–	58	7
QC					–	68
S						–

Departments	*Priority*
MS near A	1
MS near P	2
QC near S	3
A near QC	4
R near MS	5
P near A	6
P near QC	7
R near A	8
MS near QC	9
R near P	10
R near QC	11
A near S	12
R near S	13
P near S	14
MS near S	15

15.

Workcenter	*Assigned Job Tasks*
1	A, C
2	D
3	B, F
4	G
5	E
6	H, I

20.

	1992	*1993*
SSUR	100%	20,000/22,000 = 90%
DGR	500/5,000 = 10%	1,000/9,000 = 11%

No, because DGR went up.

Chapter 14

1. 0.5 hours per day.

7. Standard time = 7.5 × [100/(100 − 20)] = 9.375 minutes.

10. $S = 4$; $a = 5$; $z = 2.58$; $n = 4.26$ or 5 observations.

14. Normal time = (0.88)(2400 min.)/60 = 35.2 minutes/piece; standard time = 35.2 × [100/(100 − 10)] = 39.1 minutes/piece.

16. (a) Supervisory ratio 1992 = (28/8) × 100 = 350;
 Supervisory ratio 1993 = (24/9) × 100 = 266.6.

 (b) Yes.

18. 77/110 = 0.70 or 70% learning curve; tabled value at 20 repetitions = 0.214; adjusted time = 0.214 × 110 = 23.5 minutes.

Cumulative Poisson Probability Distribution

The probability values in this table are derived from the cumulative Poisson probability distribution for select values of c and λ.

	c								
λ	**0**	**1**	**2**	**3**	**4**	**5**	**6**	**7**	**8**
.02	.980	1.000							
.04	.961	.999	1.000						
.06	.942	.998	1.000						
.08	.923	.997	1.000						
.10	.905	.995	1.000						
.15	.861	.990	.999	1.000					
.20	.819	.982	.999	1.000					
.25	.779	.974	.998	1.000					
.30	.741	.963	.996	1.000					
.35	.705	.951	.994	1.000					
.40	.670	.938	.992	.999	1.000				
.45	.638	.925	.989	.999	1.000				
.50	.607	.910	.986	.998	1.000				
.55	.577	.894	.982	.998	1.000				
.60	.549	.878	.977	.997	1.000				
.65	.522	.861	.972	.996	.999	1.000			
.70	.497	.844	.966	.994	.999	1.000			
.75	.472	.827	.959	.993	.999	1.000			
.80	.449	.809	.953	.991	.999	1.000			
.85	.427	.791	.945	.989	.998	1.000			
.90	.407	.772	.937	.987	.998	1.000			
.95	.387	.754	.929	.984	.997	1.000			
1.00	.368	.736	.920	.981	.996	.999	1.000		
1.1	.333	.699	.900	.974	.995	.999	1.000		
1.2	.301	.663	.879	.966	.992	.998	1.000		
1.3	.273	.627	.857	.957	.989	.998	1.000		
1.4	.247	.592	.833	.946	.986	.997	.999	1.000	
1.5	.223	.558	.809	.934	.981	.996	.999	1.000	
1.6	.202	.525	.783	.921	.976	.994	.999	1.000	
1.7	.183	.493	.757	.907	.970	.992	.998	1.000	
1.8	.165	.463	.731	.891	.964	.990	.997	.999	1.000
1.9	.150	.434	.704	.875	.956	.987	.997	.999	1.000
2.0	.135	.406	.677	.857	.947	.983	.995	.999	1.000

(continued)

	c																				
λ	**0**	**1**	**2**	**3**	**4**	**5**	**6**	**7**	**8**	**9**	**10**	**11**	**12**	**13**	**14**	**15**	**16**	**17**	**18**	**19**	**20**
2.2	.111	.359	.623	.819	.928	.975	.993	.998	1.000												
2.4	.091	.308	.570	.779	.904	.964	.988	.997	.999	1.000											
2.6	.074	.267	.518	.736	.877	.951	.983	.995	.999	1.000											
2.8	.061	.231	.469	.692	.848	.935	.976	.992	.998	.999	1.000										
3.0	.050	.199	.423	.647	.815	.916	.966	.988	.996	.999	1.000										
3.2	.041	.171	.380	.603	.781	.895	.955	.983	.994	.998	1.000										
3.4	.033	.147	.340	.558	.744	.871	.942	.977	.992	.997	.999	1.000									
3.6	.027	.126	.303	.515	.706	.844	.927	.969	.988	.996	.999	1.000									
3.8	.022	.107	.269	.473	.668	.816	.909	.960	.984	.994	.998	.999	1.000								
4.0	.018	.092	.238	.433	.629	.785	.889	.949	.979	.992	.997	.999	1.000								
4.2	.015	.078	.210	.395	.590	.753	.867	.936	.972	.989	.996	.999	1.000								
4.4	.012	.066	.185	.359	.551	.720	.844	.921	.964	.985	.994	.998	.999	1.000							
4.6	.010	.056	.163	.326	.513	.686	.818	.905	.955	.980	.992	.997	.999	1.000							
4.8	.008	.048	.142	.294	.476	.651	.791	.887	.944	.975	.990	.996	.999	1.000							
5.0	.007	.040	.125	.265	.440	.616	.762	.867	.932	.968	.986	.995	.998	.999	1.000						
5.2	.006	.034	.109	.238	.406	.581	.732	.845	.918	.960	.982	.993	.997	.999	1.000						
5.4	.005	.029	.095	.213	.373	.546	.702	.822	.903	.951	.977	.990	.996	.999	1.000						
5.6	.004	.024	.082	.191	.342	.512	.670	.797	.886	.941	.972	.988	.995	.998	.999	1.000					
5.8	.003	.021	.072	.170	.313	.478	.638	.771	.867	.929	.965	.984	.993	.997	.999	1.000					
6.0	.002	.017	.062	.151	.285	.446	.606	.744	.847	.916	.957	.980	.991	.996	.999	.999	1.000				
6.2	.002	.015	.054	.134	.259	.414	.574	.716	.826	.902	.949	.975	.989	.995	.998	.999	1.000				
6.4	.002	.012	.046	.119	.235	.384	.542	.687	.803	.886	.939	.969	.986	.994	.997	.999	1.000				
6.6	.001	.010	.040	.105	.213	.355	.511	.658	.780	.869	.927	.963	.982	.992	.997	.999	.999	1.000			
6.8	.001	.009	.034	.093	.192	.327	.480	.628	.755	.850	.915	.955	.978	.990	.996	.998	.999	1.000			
7.0	.001	.007	.030	.082	.173	.301	.450	.599	.729	.830	.901	.947	.973	.987	.994	.998	.999	1.000			
7.2	.001	.006	.025	.072	.156	.276	.420	.569	.703	.810	.887	.937	.967	.984	.993	.997	.999	.999	1.000		
7.4	.001	.005	.022	.063	.140	.253	.392	.539	.676	.788	.871	.926	.961	.980	.991	.996	.998	.999	1.000		
7.6	.001	.004	.019	.055	.125	.231	.365	.510	.648	.765	.854	.915	.954	.976	.989	.995	.998	.999	1.000		
7.8	.000	.004	.016	.048	.112	.210	.338	.481	.620	.741	.835	.902	.945	.971	.986	.993	.997	.999	1.000		
8.0	.000	.003	.014	.042	.100	.191	.313	.453	.593	.717	.816	.888	.936	.966	.983	.992	.996	.998	.999	1.000	
8.5	.000	.002	.009	.030	.074	.150	.256	.386	.523	.653	.763	.849	.909	.949	.973	.986	.993	.997	.999	.999	1.000
9.0	.000	.001	.006	.021	.055	.116	.207	.324	.456	.587	.706	.803	.876	.926	.959	.978	.989	.995	.998	.999	1.000
9.5	.000	.001	.004	.015	.040	.089	.165	.269	.392	.522	.645	.752	.836	.898	.940	.967	.982	.991	.996	.998	.999
10.0	.000	.000	.003	.010	.029	.067	.130	.220	.333	.458	.583	.697	.792	.864	.917	.951	.973	.986	.993	.997	.998

INDEX